DICTIONARY OF
BUSINESS & LEGAL TERMS
RUSSIAN-ENGLISH/ENGLISH RUSSIAN

DICTIONARY OF BUSINESS & LEGAL TERMS
RUSSIAN-ENGLISH/ENGLISH RUSSIAN

Shane R. DeBeer

A unique and invaluable reference work for business people, lawyers, students, translators, diplomats, and anyone else dealing with business and legal terminology at the intersection of the Russian and English-speaking worlds, this dictionary contains carefully chosen entries which reflect the rapidly evolving Russian vocabulary of the recent era of economic and political transition, as well as the most intensively used (and/or misused) words and phrases of modern commerce.

With over 20,000 entries in each section, this dictionary has numerous special features, including:
- full pronunciation guide for each entry
- grammatical indications of gender, adjectives, etc.
- extensive use of sub-entries to illustrate proper usage of the terms in speech and correspondence
- extensive listing of legal and business terms of art

Shane R. DeBeer is a practicing attorney who deals extensively with transactions in or involving the nations of the former Soviet Union. He received a B.A. in Russian from the University of California at Irvine, an M.S. in Foreign Service from Georgetown University School of Foreign Service, a J.D. from the Georgetown University Law Center, and studied Russian at Leningrad State University in St. Petersburg. He is the author of numerous articles on legal and business topics and practices law in Houston, Texas.

$50.00

HIPPOCRENE BOOKS, INC.
171 Madison Avenue
New York, NY 10016

DICTIONARY OF
BUSINESS & LEGAL TERMS
RUSSIAN-ENGLISH/ENGLISH RUSSIAN

Shane R. DeBeer

HIPPOCRENE BOOKS, INC.
New York

For information, address:
HIPPOCRENE BOOKS, INC.
171 Madison Avenue
New York, NY 10016

ISBN 0-7818-0-163-X

Printed in the United States of America.

TABLE OF CONTENTS

DEDICATION AND ACKNOWLEDGEMENTS

This dictionary is dedicated to the memory of the late Professor Helen Weil, whose inspiration made it possible.

The author gratefully acknowledges the contributions of his wife, Mary Alice DeBeer and his brother, Matt DeBeer, without whose countless hours of generous assistance this dictionary would never have been completed.

INTRODUCTION

This bilingual legal and business dictionary is the product not only of a perceived demand at the intersection of the Russian and English-speaking legal and business worlds, but, indeed, of the author's own need for a compact reference of this kind.

Even before the momentous events of 1989 and 1991, many in the Soviet elite already perceived the long-term futility of the policy of autarchy and isolation which then characterized the so-called Eastern Bloc. Thus the natural effect of glasnost and perestroika was to dramatically accelerate the evolution and sheer volume of commercial and diplomatic relations between the English-speaking and Russian-speaking worlds. Since the collapse of the Soviet Union in the wake of a failed coup in 1991, and the subsequent birth (or rebirth) of fifteen independent nations in its stead, the industrialized English-speaking world has increased its commercial presence in the Russian-speaking world more than anyone could have predicted even a decade ago. And notwithstanding the ongoing political and economic upheaval in varying degrees in each of the new nations of the former Soviet Union, real commercial, diplomatic and judicial integration with the western industrialized world is advancing palpably.

Diplomatically, the discourse between the Anglo-Saxon and Eurasian communities has correspondingly broadened, resulting in new treaties governing trade, taxation, investment and law enforcement between East and West.

On the business front, the transition of the former Soviet Union has created even greater contact, as foreign trade and investment permanently alter the economic landscape. For example, by 1993 the western nations had already displaced the former Warsaw Pact (COMECON) nations as Russia's primary trading partners. Where once there was a single system which changed at a glacial pace, 15 new nation-states are now revising their legislation and regulations, and in some cases drafting their entire legal universe of normative texts anew.

Formerly, commentators described the legal system of the Soviet Union as "socialist law," as distinct from the "common law" system of the nations with a British legal inheritance, the "civil law" system of nations with other western European legal roots and the "traditional law" system found in some developing nations. In tsarist times the Russian empire followed a civil law system which was much influenced by the French civil codes and, to some degree, by the German school of civil law. The Russian empire also exhibited some diversity in its legal traditions, permitting subject nations such as the

Finns and the Baltic peoples a measure of jurisprudential autonomy. After the ascension of the Bolsheviks to power in 1917, a nominal civil law tradition (and civil code) was retained, although actual legislative and interpretive power lay firmly in the hands of the Communist Party.

The Soviet Union ultimately produced a broad array of new legal and economic terms, such as the колхоз (kolkhóz), an abbreviated form of коллективное хозяйство (kolletívnoe khoziáistvo), the term for a collective agricultural enterprise. The Soviets also added new meanings to existing words such as спекуляция (spekuliátsiia), a newly prohibited "economic crime," which expanded the meaning of speculation to selling anything at a profit. Under Gorbachev, new emphasis was placed on economic accountability, and the term хозрасчёт (khozraschiót), an abbreviated phrase meaning "cost accounting" or financial self-sufficiency, entered the everyday lexicon. To this day official Russian retains many such clipped neologisms formed from bureaucratic terminology, such as Минздрав (mínzdrav) for Министерство здравоохранения (ministérstvo zdravookhranéniia), meaning the Ministry of Health and Минфин (mínfin) for Министерство финансов (ministérstvo finánsov), meaning the Ministry of Finance. The now international word "gulag" derives from an abbreviated neologism meaning "Main Directorate of

Camps," the bureaucracy which ran the concentration camp system. There is no question that Soviet Russian was the model for George Orwell's "Newspeak," the English language of the totalitarian state in his novel <u>Nineteen-Eighty</u> <u>Four</u>. This divergent legal and lexical history illustrates the fundamental need for a comprehensive dictionary of this kind.

To some degree, Russia is rediscovering her civil law heritage (the first part of her new Civil Code became effective at the beginning of 1995), yet at the same time assimilating the business and legal expertise of the English-speaking world, and with it the terminology. The observer will find that old tsarist terms are resurrected with new connotations, foreign words are adopted directly, and calques of foreign legal terminology are moving from theoretical textbooks to newly drafted legal codes.

In fact, there is now a noticeable trend in Russian business, and to a lesser degree jurisprudence, to borrow directly from English. Some new words in this category include фьючерский рынок (f'iúcherskii rýnok), meaning "futures market" and even продакшн шеринг (prodákshn shéring) meaning "production sharing" (in the oil and gas extraction industry). This is so even where entirely adequate Russian terminology exists, such as раздел продукции (razdél prodúktsii) for "production sharing." Meanwhile, older terms which under the

Soviets were found only in textbooks, have been rehabilitated for service again. A recent example is присяжные заседатели (prisiázhnye zasedáteli), meaning "jury" which has now been reintroduced into Russian jurisprudence. (The jury system first appeared in Russia in 1864; it was begun again on an experimental basis in 1993.) And finally there are the familiar calques and other terms of international usage, such as общее право (óbshchee právo), referring to our own Anglo-Saxon "common law" and гражданское право (grazhdánskoe právo), meaning the "civil law."

While most of the former Soviet republics besides Russia have rejected the official use of Russian in favor of their indigenous languages, Russian remains the 4th most widely spoken language on Earth, with over 153 million who speak Russian as their mother tongue. Another 100 million in the fourteen other nations which formerly constituted the Soviet Union speak Russian as a second language. Undoubtedly, Russian will of necessity continue to be the *lingua franca* in this newly opened and strategically important region of the world for the foreseeable future.

Clearly, this era of political and economic reform, however fitfully it progresses, has created great opportunities as well as demanding complexities. The extent of these demanding complexities is especially remarkable in the Russian lexicon of law and business.

Of course, a bilingual dictionary can only be a snapshot, and always an incomplete snapshot, of two such dynamic business and legal lexicons as English and Russian. Moreover, the topic is broad enough that a totally exhaustive compilation in both languages would be unweildy and beyond the scope of this work. It is hoped, however, that this dictionary will be a useful tool in the hands of Anglophone and Russophone alike: the academics, attorneys, business people, charitable activists, diplomatic personnel, journalists, scientists, interested tourists and all others who are the real agents of change in the continuing evolution in East-West relations.

The author welcomes any comments, criticisms or suggestions for additional inclusions, which may be forwarded to him in care of the publisher.

Shane R. DeBeer

HOW TO USE THIS DICTIONARY

Even more than most specialized vocabularies, the language of business and law consists to an large degree of set phrases and terms of art. To that end, this dictionary is structured on the basis of primary words, followed in alphabetical order by subsidiary phrases employing the primary word. Both English and Russian (but especially English) often attach multiple meaning to the same word; as a result, many entries are followed by multiple possible definitions in the other language. In selecting the proper choice, the reader will be aided by referring to the subsidiary phrases for similar usage, as well as to context. To maximize space, the key words are represented by the tilde (~) as they appear in their subsidiary phrases.

Since Russian is a rather highly inflected language, the endings of the primary words often change to reflect different parts of speech in the subsidiary phrases. In that case, the primary word is given with a forward slash (/) included between the root and ending, to be used together with the tilde to show the changing endings in the phrases. For example, the word власть, declined in the singular prepositional and genitive cases as власти, is abbreviated with the tilde in the subsidiary phrases as follows:

Власт/ь (vlast') *f.* authority, power
 быть в своей ~/и (byt' v svoéi ~/i)
 to be within one's power
 быть вне ~/и (byt' vne ~/i) to be
 {act} ultra vires.

  Stress marks (á, é, í, ó, ú, and ý)
appear on the vowels stressed in the
transliteration of each Russian word
with more than one syllable. Similarly,
the Russian transliteration shows the
stress on the vowels for the English
entries.

  To aid in using the phrases found
herein, this dictionary supplies basic
grammatical information with every
primary entry. In the entry above, for
example, the notation "*f.*" connotes that
the preceding entry is a singular noun
of the feminine gender. (But note that
the inflected nature of Russian
generally renders such additional
information redundant in the case of
Russian definitions of English entries.)
Except where no singular exists, or
where an entry is only used in the
plural in the sense listed in this
dictionary, all nouns are provided in
the singular. A complete list of the
grammatical connotations employed in
this dictionary is provided under
Abbreviations on page viii.

  As with the other Hippocrene
Russian language dictionaries, the verbs
are generally given in the imperfective
aspect, which is normally treated as the
basic form of the simple verb. Where the

perfective of a verb is used in another sense (i.e. translated by a different verb in English) it is listed separately. Where the perfective usage is particularly common, it is noted and included in the definition of the imperfective verb in square brackets.

Another unique feature for a specialized dictionary is the transliteration/pronounciation key for every word and expression in the dictionary. For this purpose the Editors have chosen the Library of Congress transliteration system for the Russian-English pronounciation key (see *Russian to English Transliteration Table* on page ix), it being the least confusing while providing the necessary pronunciation guidance.

With respect to the English-Russian pronounciation key, this dictionary relies as much as possible on direct transliteration of the English words into the Russian alphabet on the basis of the corresponding Russian phonetic values (see *English to Russian Transliteration Table* on page x) with a few modifications as noted.

Lastly, curvilinear brackets {} are used to present additional useful information to further aid the user.

ABBREVIATIONS

abbrev.	abbreviated form now in common usage
adj.	adjective
adv.	adverb
f.	feminine singular noun
f.adj.noun	feminine adjectival noun
indecl.	indeclinable noun
m.	masculine singular noun
m.adj.noun	masculine adjectival noun
n.	neuter singular noun
n.adj.noun	neuter adjectival noun
pl.	plural noun {i.e. used only in the plural in the meaning provided}
pl.adj.noun	plural adjectival noun
v.	verb

RUSSIAN TO ENGLISH
TRANSLITERATION TABLE

<u>Russian</u> <u>Letter</u> <u>Transliteration</u>

Russian Letter	Transliteration
А, а	a
Б, б	b
В, в	v
Г, г	g
Д, д	d
Е, е	e
Ё, ё	ió
Ж, ж	zh
З, з	z
И, и	i
Й, й	i
К, к	k
Л, л	l
М, м	m
Н, н	n
О, о	o
П, п	p
Р, р	r
С, с	s
Т, т	t
У, у	u
Ф, ф	f
Х, х	kh
Ц, ц	ts
Ч, ч	ch
Ш, ш	sh
Щ, щ	shch
ъ	ʼ ʼ
Ы, ы	y
ь	ʼ
Э, э	e
Ю, ю	iu
Я, я	ia

**ENGLISH TO RUSSIAN
TRANSLITERATION TABLE**

English Transcription	Cyrillic
a as in "vat"	а, {ват}
a as in "tare"	эй, {тэйр}
a as in "father"	а, {фа́θэр}
ai as in "claim"	эй, {клэйм}
au as in "cause"	ау, {кауз}
ay as in "pay"	эй, {пэй}
b as in "base"	б, {бэйс}
c as in "case"	к, {кэйс}
c as in "cede"	с, {сид}
ch as in "check"	ч, {чэк}
ck as in "check"	к, {чэк}
d as in "deed"	д, {дид}
d as in "billed"	д, {билд}
dg as in "judge"	дж, {джадж}
e as in "net"	э, {нэт}
e as in "cede"	и, {сид}
ea as in "defeat"	и, {дифи́т}
ee as in "fee"	и, {фи}
ey as in "key"	и, {ки}
f as in "fee"	ф, {фи}
g as in "goods"	г, {гудз}
g as in "wage"	дж, {уэйдж}
h as in "hand"	х, {ханд}
i as in "fit"	и, {фит}
i as in "site"	ай, {сайт}
ia as in "trial"	айа, {тра́йал}
ie as in "pier"	и, {пир}
io as in "diode"	а́йо, {да́йод}
j as in "judge"	дж, {джадж}
k as in "key"	к, {ки}
l as in "law", "bill"	л, {ла́у, бил}

ENGLISH TO RUSSIAN
TRANSLITERATION TABLE
(continued)

m as in "money"	м,	{мо́ни}
n as in "net"	н,	{нэт}
o as in "lot"	о,	{лот}
o as in "note"	о,	{нот}
oa as in "boat"	о,	{бот}
oe as in "foe"	о,	{фо}
oi as in "void"	ой,	{войд}
oo as in "good"	у,	{гуд}
ou as in "bounce"	оу,	{боунс}
p as in "pay"	п,	{пэй}
qu as in "quit"	ку,	{куит}
qu as in "pique"	к,	{пик}
r as in "rent", "bar"	р,	{рэнт,бар}
s as in "sell", "pass"	с,	{сэл, пас}
s as in "measure"	ж,	{мэ́жюр}
s as in "as", "was"	з,	{аз, уаз}
sh as in "ship", "cash"	ш,	{шип,каш}
t as in "tare", "net"	т,	{тэйр,нэт}
th as in "the", "third"	θ,	{θи,θирд}
u as in "under"	а,	{а́ндэр}
u as in "rule"	у,	{рул}
u as in "usual"	ю,	{ю́жюал}
ua as in "usual"	ю,	{ю́жюал}
ue as in "due"	у,	{ду}
v as in "vat"	в,	{ват}
w as in "wage"	у,	{уэйдж}
wh as in "what"	у,	{уат}
wr as in "writ"	-,	{рит}
x as in "box"	кс,	{бокс}
x as in "xenophobic"	з,	{зинофо́бик}

ENGLISH TO RUSSIAN
TRANSLITERATION TABLE
(continued)

y as in "daily"	и,	{дэ́йли}
y as in "yield"	й,	{йилд}
ya as in "yard"	я,	{ярд}
z as in "zone"	з,	{зон}

DICTIONARY OF BUSINESS & LEGAL TERMS

RUSSIAN-ENGLISH

А

Абандон (abandón) *m.* abandonment

Абзац (abzáts) *m.* paragraph

Абитуриент (abituriént) *m.* undergraduate {university student}

Абонемент (abonemént) *m.* subscription, use card, certificate
   проездной ~ (proezdnói ~) train pass
   ~ библиотеки (~ bibliotéki) library card

Абонементная плата (aboneméntnaia pláta) use card fee, subscription fee

Абонент (abonént) *m.* subscriber, pass-holder

Абонировать (abonírovat') *v.* to subscribe, to obtain a pass

Абордаж (abordázh) *m.* boarding {a ship}
   взять на ~ (vziat' na ~) to take on board

Абориген (aborigén) *m.* native {person}

Аборт (abórt) *m.* abortion
   наказуемый ~ (nakazúemyi ~) criminal ~
   произвести ~ (proizvestí ~) to perform an ~
   ~ произведённый другим лицом (~ proizvediónnyi drugím litsóm) ~ performed by a third party
   ~ произведённый самой беременной (~ proizvediónnyi samói berémennoi) ~ performed by the pregnant subject, self-~

Абсентеизм (absenteízm) *m.* absenteeism

Абсолютизм (absoliutízm) *m.* absolutism
   просвещённый ~ (prosveshchiónnyi ~) enlightened ~

Авалист (avalíst) *m.* one who makes a surety, endorser

Аваль (avál') surety, endorsement
   ~ векселя (~ vékselia) surety for a bill of exchange
   дать ~ (dat' ~) to provide a surety, to endorse

Аванс (aváns) *m.* advance
   возместимый ~ (vozmestímyi ~) reimbursable ~
   гарантийный ~ (garantíinyi ~) ~ in guaranty
   денежный ~ (dénezhnyi ~) cash ~
   импортный ~ (ímportnyi ~) import ~

   перечислить ~ (perechislít' ~) to transfer an ~
   предоставить ~ (predostávit' ~) to grant an ~
   ~ в счёт платежей (~ v schiot platezhéi) ~ against payments
   ~ подлежащий возврату (~ podlezháshchii vozvrátu) ~ subject to refund
   ~ поставщикам (~ postavshchikám) ~ payment to suppliers
   ~ на расходы (~ na raskhódy) ~ on expenses
   ~ фондов (~ fóndov) ~ of funds

Авансирование (avansírovanie) *n.* advances on account
   ежемесячное ~ (ezhemésiachnoe ~) monthly ~
   денежное ~ (dénezhnoe ~) advance of funds on account

Авансировать (avansírovat') *v.* to advance

Авансодержатель (avansoderzhátel') *m.* advancee

Авантюра (avantiúra) *f.* adventure, gamble, shady business

Аварийность (avaríinost') *f.* accident rate

Авария (aváriia) *f.* accident, damage
   общая ~ (óbshchaia ~) total damage
   частная ~ (chástnaia ~) partial damage

Аверс (avérs) *m.* heads {of coin}, face {of medal, plaque}

Авиагруппа (aviagrúppa) *f.* air group

Авиадепеша (aviadepésha) *f.* air depot
   транзитная ~ (tranzítnaia ~) transit air depot

Авиакомпания (aviakompániia) *f.* aviation company

Авиалиния (avialíniia) *f.* airline

Авиамешок (aviameshók) *m.* airmail pouch

Авианакладная (aviankládnaya) *f.adj.noun* air-waybill

Авиаперевозка (aviaperevózka) *f.* air transport

Авиапосылка (aviaposýlka) *f.* air-parcel
   срочная ~ (sróchnaia ~) rush air-parcel

Авиапочта (aviapóchta) *f.* airmail

Авиапредприятие (aviapredpriiátie) *n.* aerospace enterprise

Авиапромышленность
(aviapromýshlennost') *f*. aerospace
production
Авиапуть (aviapút') *m*. airway
Авиафрахт (aviafrákht) *m*.
airfreight
Авиация (aviátsiia) *f*. aviation
   гражданская ~ (grazhdánskaia ~)
   civil ~
   коммерческая ~ (kommércheskaia
   ~) commercial ~
Авизо (avízo) *n*. aviso, notice
   инкассовое ~ (inkássovoe ~)
   notice of incoming funds
   ~ об акцепте (~ ob aktsépte)
   notice of acceptance
   ~ об открытии аккредитива (~ ob
   otkrýtii akkreditíva) notice of
   opening of a letter of credit
   ~ о платеже (~ o platezhé)
   notice of payment
Автаркия (avtárkiia) *f*. autarky
Автократия (avtokrátiia) *f*.
autocracy
Автолимитация (avtolimitátsiia) *f*.
international doctrine of
autolimitation
Автомобилестроение
(avtomobilestroénie) *n*. automobile
production
Автомобиль (avtomobíl') *m*.
automobile
   грузовой ~ (gruzovói ~) truck
Автонакладная (avtonakládnaia)
f.adj.noun road way-bill
Автономия (avtonómiia) *f*. autonomy
   административная ~
   (administratívnaia ~)
   administrative ~
   внутренняя ~ (vnútrenniaia ~)
   internal ~
   территориальная ~
   (territoriál'naia ~) territorial
   ~
   ~ воли (~ vóli) free will
Автономный (avtonómnyi) *adj*.
autonomous
Автопарк (avtopárk) automobile lot,
taxi lot
Автоперевозки (avtoperevózki) *pl*.
road carriage, road transport
Автопоезд (avtopóezd) *m*. truck
convoy
Автор (ávtor) *m*. author
   ~ изобретения (~ izobreténiia)
   inventor

   ~ открытия (~ otkrýtiia)
   discoverer
Автореферат (avtoreferát) *m*.
abstract {of document}
Авторизация (avtorizátsiia) *f*.
authorization
Авторизованный (avtorizóvannyi)
adj. authorized
Авторизовать (avtorizovát') *v*. to
authorize
Авторитет (avtoritét) *m*. authority
   высший ~ (výsshii ~) highest ~
   ~ суда (~ sudá) ~ of the court
Авторитетность (avtoritétnost') *f*.
authoritativeness, trustworthiness
Авторские (ávtorskie) *pl.adj.noun*
royalties
Авторское право (ávtorskoe právo)
n. copyright
Авторство (ávtorstvo) *n*. authorship
   совместное ~ (sovméstnoe ~)
   joint ~
   ~ на изобретение (~ na
   izobreténie) ~ of an invention
Автотранспорт (avtotránsport) *m*.
automobile transport
Автофургон (avtofurgón) *m*. van
Автохозяйство (avtokhoziáistvo) *n*.
road-transport {trucking} industry
Авуары (avuáry) *pl*. assets,
holdings
   банковские ~ (bánkovskie ~) bank
   holdings
   блокированные ~ (blokírovannye
   ~) frozen assets
   валютные ~ (valiútnye ~) foreign
   exchange assets
   иностранные ~ (inostránnye ~)
   foreign assets
   ликвидные ~ (likvídnye ~) liquid
   assets
   ~ за границей (~ za granítsei)
   assets held abroad
Агент (agént) *m*. agent
   административный ~
   (administratívnyi ~)
   administrative ~
   аккредитованный ~
   (akkreditóvannyi ~) accredited ~
   государственный ~
   (gosudárstvennyi ~) government ~
   дипломатический ~
   (diplomatícheskii ~) diplomatic
   ~
   единственный ~ (edínstvennyi ~)
   sole ~

импортный ~ (ímportnyi ~) import ~

исключительный ~ (iskliuchítel'nyi ~) exclusive ~

консигнационный ~ (konsignatsiónnyi ~) consignment ~

консульский ~ (kónsul'skii ~) consular ~

морской ~ (morskói ~) marine ~

почтовой ~ (pochtóvoi ~) postal ~

присяжный ~ (prisiázhnyi ~) sworn ~

разъездной ~ (raz"ezdnói ~) travelling salesman

тайный ~ (táinyi ~) secret ~

торговый ~ (torgóvyi ~) commercial agent, dealer

экспортный ~ (éksportnyi ~) export ~

~ для связи (~ dlia sviázi) communications ~

~ пароходных компаний (~ parokhódnykh kompánii) shipping ~

~ по закупкам (~ po zakúpkam) purchasing ~

~ фрахтователя (~ frakhtovátelia) charterer's ~

Агентирование (agentírovanie) *n.* shipping agency service

морское ~ (morskóe ~) marine ~

Агентство (agéntstvo) *n.* agency

консульское ~ (kónsul'skoe ~) consular ~

международное ~ (mezhdunaródnoe ~) international ~

монопольное ~ (monopól'noe ~) sole ~

рекламное ~ (reklámnoe ~) advertising ~

торговое ~ (torgóvoe ~) commercial ~

центральное ~ (tsentrál'noe ~) central ~

~ печати (~ pecháti) press ~

~ по продаже (~ po prodázhe) sales ~

~ для устройства браков (~ dlia ustróistva brákov) introduction agency, marriage bureau

~ с исключительными правами (~ s iskliuchítel'nymi právami) exclusive ~

~ с полным циклом услуг (~ s pólnym tsíklom uslúg) full service ~

Агентура (agentúra) agents *f.* {collect.}, secret service

Агитатор (agitátor) *m.* activist

Агитация (agitátsiia) *f.* activism

выборная ~ (výbornaia ~) election campaigning

Агитпункт (agitpúnkt) *m.* social activism center, communist party propaganda outlet

Агитпароход (agitparokhód) *m.* steamship chartered to visit ports for purposes of distribution of propaganda {hist.}

Агреман (agremán) *m.* approval

дать ~ (dat' ~) to approve

Агрессия (agréssiia) *f.* aggression

военная ~ (voénnaia ~) military ~

вооружённая ~ (vooruzhiónnaia ~) armed ~

идеологическая ~ (ideologícheskaia ~) ideological ~

косвенная ~ (kósvennaia ~) indirect ~

явная ~ (iávnaia ~) flagrant ~

Агрессор (agréssor) *m.* aggressor

Адаптация (adaptátsiia) *f.* adaptation {e.g. screenplay from novel}

Адвокат (advokát) *m.* advocate, attorney, barrister, solicitor

генеральный ~ (generál'nyi ~) attorney general

Адвокатура (advokatúra) *f.* legal profession, the Bar

Аддендум (addéndum) *m.* addendum

Административно-ссыльный (administratívno-ssýl'nyi) *m.adj.noun* administrative exile {person}

Административн/ый (administratívnyi) *adj.* administrative

~ надзор (~ nadzór) administrative oversight

~ процесс (~ protsés) administrative hearing

в ~/ом порядке (v ~/om poriádke) by administrative means

Администратор (administrátor) *m.* administrator, manager

~ имуществ (~ imúshchestv) property administrator

~ товарищества (~ továrishchestva) association manager
Администрация (administrátsiia) *f.* administration
  взимающая ~ (vzimáiushchaia ~) tax-collection ~
  военная ~ (voénnaia ~) military ~
  временная ~ (vrémennaia ~) ~ pro tempore
  гражданская ~ (grazhdánskaia ~) civil ~
  железная ~ (zheléznaia ~) railway ~
  колониальная ~ (koloniál'naia ~) colonial ~
  международная ~ (mezhdunaródnaia ~) international ~
  местная ~ (méstnaia ~) local ~
  почтовая ~ (pochtóvaia ~) postal ~
  специальная речная ~ (spetsiál'naia rechnáia ~) special riparian ~
  тюремная ~ (tiurémnaia ~) penal ~
  центральная ~ (tsentrál'naia ~) central ~
  ~ над имуществом (~ nad imúshchestvom) property ~
  ~ международного развития (~ mezhdunaródnogo razvítiia) ~ of international development
  ~ портов (~ portóv) Ports ~
Администрирование (administrírovanie) *n.* bureaucratic administration
Администрировать (administrírovat') *v.* to administer
Адрес (ádres) *m.* address
  домашний ~ (domáshnii ~) home ~
  почтовый ~ (pochtóvyi ~) postal ~
  проводительный ~ (provodítel'nyi ~) forwarding ~
  телеграфный ~ (telegráfnyi ~) telegraph ~
Адресант (adresánt) *m.* addressor, consignor
Адресат (adresát) *m.* addressee, consignee
Адхези/я (adkhéziia) *f.* adhesion
  договор ~/и (dogovór ~/i) contract of adhesion
Адъюнкт (ad"iúnkt) *adj.* adjunct
Адюльтер (adiul'tér) *m.* adulterer

Ажио (ázhio) *n.* agio
Ажиотаж (azhiotázh) *m.* agiotage {speculation}, stock-jobbing
Академия международного права (akadémiia mezhdunaródnogo práva) *f.* Academy of International Law
Аккредитация (akkreditátsiia) *f.* accreditation
Аккредитив (akkreditív) *m.* letter of credit, L/c
  автоматически возобновляемый ~ (avtomatícheski vozobnovliáemyi ~) revolving ~
  банковский ~ (bánkovskii ~) bank ~
  безотзывный ~ (bezotzývnyi ~) irrevocable ~
  бланковый ~ (blánkovyi ~) blank ~
  делимый ~ (delímyi ~) divisible ~
  документарный ~ (dokumentárnyi ~) documentary ~
  долгосрочный ~ (dolgosróchnyi ~) long term ~
  дорожный ~ (dorózhnyi ~) bill of lading
  именной ~ (imennói ~) registered ~
  компенсационный ~ (kompensatsiónnyi ~) back-to-back ~
  непереводный ~ (neperevódnyi ~) non-transferable ~
  неподтверждённый ~ (nepodtverzhdiónnyi ~) unconfirmed ~
  подтверждённый ~ (podtverzhdiónnyi ~) confirmed ~
  револьверный ~ (revol'vérnyi ~) revolving ~
  путевой ~ (putevói ~) traveler's ~
  товарный ~ (továrnyi ~) commercial ~
  циркулярный ~ (tsirkuliárnyi ~) circular ~
  чистый ~ (chístyi ~) clean ~
  экспортный ~ (éksportnyi ~) export ~
  ~ с платежом в рассрочку (~ s platezhóm v rassróchku) installment ~
  ~ с платежом в свободно конвертируемой валюте (~ s platezhóm v svobódno konvertíruemoi valiúte) ~

payable in freely convertible currency
~ сроком действия на ... (~ srókom déistviia na ...) ~ valid for ...
Аккредитование (akkreditovánie) *n.* accreditation
Аккредитованный (akkreditóvannyi) *adj.* accredited
Аккредитовать (akkreditovót') *v.* to accredit
Акр (akr) *m.* acre
Акт (akt) *m.* act, certificate, statement, statute, writ
   аварийный ~ (avaríinyi ~) general average statement
   агрессивный ~ (agressívnyi ~) act of aggression
   административный ~ (administratívnyi ~) administrative decree
   арбитражный ~ (arbitrázhnyi ~) arbitral act
   внесудебный ~ (vnesudébnyi ~) extra-judicial act
   внутригосударственный ~ (vnutrigosudárstvennyi ~) internal government act
   враждебный ~ (vrazhdébnyi ~) hostile act
   генеральный ~ (generál'nyi ~) general statement
   государственный ~ (gosudárstvennyi ~) act of state
   декларативный ~ (deklaratívnyi ~) official declaration
   дипломатический ~ (diplomatícheskii ~) diplomatic act
   договорный ~ (dogovórnyi ~) contract, contractual instrument
   доказательственный ~ (dokazátel'stvennyi ~) evidentiary act
   дополнительный ~ (dopolnítel'nyi ~) supplement, supplementary act
   заключительный ~ (zakliuchítel'nyi ~) conclusive act
   законодательный ~ (zakonodátel'nyi ~) legislative act
   индивидуальный ~ (individuál'nyi ~) individual act
   исполнительный ~ (ispolnítel'nyi ~) executive order

   коллективный ~ (kollektívnyi ~) collective act
   коммерческий ~ (kommércheskii ~) commercial act
   конститутивный ~ (konstitutívnyi ~) deed of incorporation, charter document
   конституционный ~ (konstitutsiónnyi ~) constitutional act
   консульский ~ (kónsul'skii ~) consular act
   концессионный ~ (kontsessiónnyi ~) consent decree
   медицинский ~ (meditsínskii ~) medical report
   международный ~ (mezhdunaródnyi ~) international instrument
   многосторонний ~ (mnogostorónnii ~) multilateral act
   навигационный ~ (navigatsiónnyi ~) navigational act
   недружелюбный ~ (nedruzheliúbnyi ~) unfriendly act
   незаконный ~ (nezakónnyi ~) illegal act
   нормативный ~ (normatívnyi ~) normative act, legislation
   нотариальный ~ (notariál'nyi ~) certificate of notary, notarization
   обвинительный ~ (obvinítel'nyi ~) indictment
   обязательный ~ (obiazátel'nyi ~) obligatory act
   односторонний ~ (odnostorónnii ~) unilateral act
   официальный ~ (ofitsiál'nyi ~) official act, official document
   парламентский ~ (parlaméntskii ~) act of parliament
   передаточный ~ (peredátochnyi ~) certificate of transfer, conveyance
   письменный ~ (pís'mennyi ~) written document
   подзаконный ~ (podzakónnyi ~) regulation, normative act
   правительственный ~ (pravítel'stvennyi ~) governmental decree
   правовой ~ (pravovói ~) legal act
   приемо-сдаточный ~ (priémo-sdátochnyi ~) receipt, certificate of delivery

произвольный ~ власти
(proizvól'nyi ~ vlásti)
arbitrary exercise of power
процессуальный ~
(protsessuál'nyi ~) procedural
act
публичный ~ (públíchnyi ~)
public action
рекламационный ~
(reklamatsiónnyi ~) certificate
of damage claim
руководящий ~ (rukovodiáshchii
~) directive
служебный ~ (sluzhébnyi ~)
official act, act in the line of
duty
совместный ~ (sovméstnyi ~)
jointly-authored document,
declaration
составить ~ (sostávit' ~) to
draft a document
страховой ~ (strakhovói ~)
insurance claim, claim against
insurance
судебный ~ (sudébnyi ~) court
decree
судебно-медицинский ~ (sudébno-
meditsínskii ~) court-ordered
medical report
удостоверенный ~ (udostovérennyi
~) authenticated document
учредительный ~ (uchredítel'nyi
~) founding document
факультативный ~ (fakul'tatívnyi
~) optional act
частный ~ (chástnyi ~) private
act
формальный ~ (formál'nyi ~)
formal act
юридический ~ (iuridícheskii ~)
judicial act
~ об аварии (~ ob avárii)
accident report
~ агрессии (~ agréssii) act of
aggression
~ об амнистии (~ ob amnístii)
grant of amnesty
~ аннексии (~ annéksii)
annexation
~ об арбитраже (~ ob arbitrázhe)
arbitral act
~ вандализма (~ vandalízma) act
of vandalism
~ вмешательства (~
vmeshátel'stva) act of
intervention

~ возражения (~ vozrazhéniia)
answer {in litigation}
~ о гибели (~ o gíbeli) death
certificate
~ грабежа (~ grabezhá) act of
robbery
~ гражданского состояния (~
grazhdánskogo sostoiániia) act
of a civil nature
~ о денонсации (~ o denonsátsii)
denunciation {diplomatic}
~ дипломатии (~ diplomátii) act
of diplomacy
~ испытаний (~ ispytánii) test
certification
~ о конфискации груза (~ o
konfiskátsii grúza) writ of
seizure of cargo
~ навигации (~ navigátsii)
navigation act
~ насилия (~ nasíliia) act of
violence, use of force
~ натурализации (~
naturalizátsii) act of
naturalization
~ о натурализации (~ o
naturalizátsii) decree of
naturalization
~ о национализации (~ o
natsionalizátsii) act of
nationalization {of property}
~ незаконного присвоения (~
nezakónnogo prisvoéniia)
conversion {misappropriation}
~ обследовании (~ obslédovanii)
investigation, inquest report
~ об одобрении (~ ob odobrénii)
certificate of approval
~ осмотра на месте (~ osmótra na
méste) inspection certificate
~ особого благоприятствования (~
osóbogo blagopriiatstvovániia)
most favored nation clause
~ отвода (~ otvóda) decree of
assignation
~ парламента (~ parlámenta) act
of parliament
~ о передаче правового титула (~
o peredáche pravovógo títula)
deed of conveyance
~ перенесения (~ peresséniia)
transfer
~ по пересмотру (~ po
peresmótru) official review
~ пиратства (~ pirátstva) act of
piracy

~ подтверждающий право (~ podtverzhdáiushchii právo) confirmation of right

~ о подтверждении (~ o podtverzhdénii) confirmation

~ о помиловании (~ o pomílovanii) grant of clemency

~ правительства (~ pravítel'stva) act of state

~ приёмки (~ priiómki) acceptance certificate

~ признания (~ priznániia) act of admission, official recognition

~ о принятии (~ o priniátii) act of acceptance

~ о присоединении (~ o prisoedinénii) instrument of accession, instrument of adhesion

~ о проверке (~ o provérke) certificate of inspection

~ продажи (~ prodázhi) deed of sale

~ о протесте (~ o protéste) deed of protest

~ раздела (~ razdéla) writ of partition

~ расследования (~ rasslédovaniia) preliminary investigation report

~ ратификации (~ ratifikátsii) certificate of ratification

~ регистрации брака (~ registrátsii bráka) marriage certificate

~ репрессалии (~ repressálii) act of reprisal

~ рождения (~ rozhdéniia) birth certificate

~ свидетельствования (~ svidetel'stvovániia) attest, certification {of signature, etc}

~ сдачи (~ sdáchi) certificate of remittance, receipt

~ смерти (~ smérti) death certificate

~ содержащий признание (~ soderzháshchii priznánie) written confession

~ о создании (~ o sozdánii) act of formation

~ составленный домашним порядком (~ sostávlennyi domáshnim poriádkom) privately executed contract {without witnesses or seal}

~ о суброгации (~ o subrogatsii) subrogation form

~ о судоходстве (~ o sudokhodstve) shipping act

~ сюрвейера (~ siurvéiera) surveyor's report

~ таможенного досмотра (~ tamózhennogo dosmótra) customs inspector's report

~ уведомления (~ uvedoméniia) act of notification

~ управления (~ upravléniia) administrative directive

~ об установлении ипотеки (~ ob ustanovlénii ipotéki) mortgage instrument

~ об установлении права (~ ob ustanovlénii pravá) enabling act

~ об уступке (~ ob ustúpke) deed of cession

~ экспертизы (~ ekspertízy) certificate of expert's examination

~ юрисдикции (~ iurisdíktsii) act of jurisdiction

Актив (aktív) m. asset

банковские ~/ы (bánkovskie ~/y) bank ~s

валютные ~/ы (valiútnye ~/y) hard currency ~s

замороженные ~/ы (zamorózhennye ~/y) frozen ~s

ликвидные ~/ы (likvídnye ~/y) liquid ~s

мёртвые ~/ы (miórtvye ~/y) dead ~s

неликвидные ~/ы (nelikvídnye ~/y) fixed ~s

реализуемый ~ (realizúemyi ~) realizable ~

резервные ~/ы (rezérvnye ~/y) reserve ~s

труднореализуемые ~/ы (trudnorealizúemye ~/y) slow ~s

чистый ~ (chístyi) net ~

~ баланса (~ balánsa) book ~

~/ы за границей (~ /y za granítsei) ~s held abroad

~ товарищества (~ tovaríshchestva) company ~

Актуарий (aktuárii) m. actuary

Акушерка (akushérka) f. midwife

Акцепт (aktsépt) m. acceptance {instrument at a bank, etc.},

acceptance of an offer {contract formation}
  банковский ~ (bánkovskii ~) bank acceptance
  безусловный ~ (bezuslóvnyi ~) unconditional acceptance
  бланковый ~ (blánkovyi ~) acceptance in blank
  молчаливый ~ (molchalívyi ~) silent acceptance
  ограниченный ~ (ograníchennyi ~) qualified acceptance
  положительный ~ (polozhítel'nyi ~) positive acceptance
  последующий ~ (posléduiushchii ~) subsequent acceptance
  предварительный ~ (predvarítel'nyi ~) preliminary acceptance
  «предъявить для ~/а» (pred"iávit' dlia ~/a) "present for acceptance"
  условный ~ (uslóvnyi ~) conditional acceptance
  частичный ~ (chastíchnyi ~) partial acceptance
  ~ векселя (~ vékselia) acceptance of a bill of exchange, promissory note
  ~ коммерческих документов (~ kommércheskikh dokuméntov) acceptance of commercial documents
  ~ против документов (~ prótiv dokuméntov) acceptance against documents
  ~ счёта (~ schióta) acceptance of a bill
  ~ тратты (~ trátty) acceptance of a draft
  ~ чека (~ chéka) negotiation of a check

Акцептант (aktseptánt) *m.* acceptor

Акцептовать (aktseptovát') *v.* to accept {a negotiable instrument, etc.}

Акцессия (aktséssiia) *f.* accession

Акциз (aktsíz) *m.* excise
  обложить ~/ом (oblozhít' ~/om) to levy an ~ duty
  универсальный ~ (universál'nyi ~) universal ~

Акционер (aktsionér) *m.* shareholder

Акционерное (aktsionérnoe) *adj.* shareholder
  ~ общество (~ óbshchestvo) *n.* joint-stock company, corporation

Акци/я (áktsiia) *f.* share {of stock}
  бесплатная ~ (besplátnaia ~) gratuity ~
  винкулированная ~ (vinkuliróvannaia ~) "vincular" ~, or ~ "vinculum juris" subject to surrender pursuant to agreement with the issuer
  депонированные ~/и (deponírovannye ~/i) deposited ~s
  именная ~ (imennáia ~) registered ~
  инвестиционная ~ (investitsiónnaia ~) investment ~
  многоголосная ~ (mnogogólosnaia ~) multiple voting ~
  обыкновенная ~ (obyknovénnaia ~) common ~
  плюральная ~ (pliurál'naia ~) plural voting ~
  пользовательная ~ (pol'zovátel'naia ~) "action de jouissance"; profit-sharing certificate
  предъявительские ~/и (pred"iavítel'skie ~/i) bearer ~s
  привилегированная ~ (privilegiróvannaia ~) ~ of preferred stock
  подписанная ~ (podpísannaia ~) subscription ~
  учредительские ~/и (uchredítel'skie ~) founder's ~s
  ~ покрытая деньгами (~ pokrýtaia den'gámi) ~ paid in full
  ~ на предъявителя (~ na pred"iavítelia) bearer ~

Алиби (álibi) *n.* alibi
  установить ~ (ustanovít' ~) to establish an alibi

Алименты (aliménty) *m.pl.* maintenance payments
  ~ на содержание (~ na soderzhánie) support payments, alimony

Алкоголизм (alkogolízm) *m.* alcoholism

Альпари (al'parí) *adv.* "at par"

Альтернат (al'ternát) *m.* alternate

Альфонс (al'fóns) *m.* gigolo, panderer, pimp

Альянс (al'iáns) *m.* alliance

Амбар (ambár) *m.* warehouse

Амнистировать (amnistírovat') v. to grant amnesty

Амнистия (amnístiia) f. amnesty
   общая ~ (óbshchaia ~) general amnesty

Амортизация (amortizátsiia) f. amortization, depreciation
   ежегодная ~ (ezhegódnaia ~) annual depreciation
   постепенная ~ (postepénnaia ~) gradual depreciation
   ускоренная ~ (uskórennaia ~) stepped-up depreciation

Амортизировать (amortizírovat') v. to amortize, to depreciate

Анализ (análiz) m. analysis
   ~ баланса (~ balánsa) audit of the books
   ~ доходов и расходов (~ dokhódov i raskhódov) income-expenditure analysis
   ~ конъюнктуры (~ kon"iunktúry) wholesale market analysis
   ~ рынка сбыта (~ rýnka sbytá) retail market analysis
   ~ спроса (~ sprósa) demand analysis
   ~ финансового состояния (~ finánsovogo sostoiániia) financial analysis
   ~ экономической эффективности (~ ekonomícheskoi effektívnosti) cost-effectiveness analysis

Аналог (análog) m. analog
   международные ~/и (mezhdunaródnye ~/i) international standards

Аналогичный (analogíchnyi) adj. analogous

Аналогия (analógiia) f. analogy
   проводить ~ (provodít' ~) to make an analogy

Анархизм (anarkhízm) m. anarchism

Анархист (anarkhíst) m. anarchist

Анархистский (anarkhístskii) adj. anarchistic

Анархия (anárkhiia) f. anarchy

Анатоцизм (anatotsízm) m. compound interest, double interest, usury

Ангар (angár) m. aircraft hangar

Анкета (ankéta) f. application form, blank
   ~ установленного образца (~ ustanóvlennogo obraztsá) standard application form

Анклав (ankláv) m. enclave

Аннексионист (anneksioníst) m. annexing party {nation}

Аннексировать (anneksírovat') v. to annex

Аннексия (annéksiia) f. annexation
   ~ территории (~ territórii) territorial annexation

Аннотация (annotótsiia) f. annotation

Аннотировать (annotírovat') v. to annotate

Аннулирование (annulírovanie) n. annulment
   ~ брака (~ bráka) annulment of marriage
   ~ заказа (~ zakáza) cancellation of an order
   ~ знака (~ znáka) annulment of a trademark
   ~ контракта (~ kontrákta) termination of a contract
   ~ лицензии (~ litsénzii) revocation of a license
   ~ патента (~ paténta) revocation of a patent
   ~ решения (~ reshéniia) vacation of a {judicial, administrative} decision
   ~ экзекватуры (~ ekzekvatúry) revocation of consular recognition

Аннулировать (annulírovat') v. to annul

Аннулирующий (annulíruiushchii) adj. having the power to annul or revoke

Аноним (aноním) m. anonymous {author}

Антанта (antánta) f. entente
   балканская ~ (bálkanskaia ~) Balkan entente

Антидатировать (antidatírovat') to pre-date

Анти-инфляционный (ánti-infliatsiónnyi) adj. anti-inflationary
   ~/ые меры (~ /ye méry) anti-inflationary measures

Антиконституционный (ánti-konstitutsiónnyi) adj. anti-constitutional

Антимонопольный (ánti-monopól'nyi) adj. antitrust

Антиномия (antinómiia) f. antinomy {conflict of legal authorities/propositions}

Антипарламентский (ánti-
parlaméntskii) *adj.* anti-
parliamentary
Антипартийный (ánti-partíinyi) *adj.*
anti-party
Антиправительственный (ánti-
pravítel'stvennyi) *adj.* anti-
governmental
Антисемит (ántisemít) *m.* anti-
semite
Антисемитизм (antisemitízm) *m.*
anti-semitism
Антисемитский (antisemítskii) *adj.*
anti-semitic
Антиэкономический (ánti-
ekonomícheskii) *adj.* anti-economic
Антропология (antropológiia) *f.*
anthropology
  преступная ~ (prestúpnaia ~)
criminal anthropology
Апатрид (apatríd) *m.* stateless
person
Апеллировать (apellírovat') *v.* to
appeal
Аппелянт (appeliánt) *m.* appellant
Апелляционный (appeliatsiónnyi)
adj. appellate
  ~ суд (~ sud) Court of Appeals
Апелляци/я (apelliátsiia) *f.* appeal
  подать ~/ю (podát' ~/iu) to file
an appeal
Аппарат (apparát) *m.* bureaucratic
apparatus, organs
  административный ~
  (administratívnyi ~)
  administrative apparatus
  государственный ~
  (gosudárstvennyi ~) machinery of
  state
  государственный летательный ~
  (gosudárstvennyi letátel'nyi ~)
  government aircraft
  исполнительный ~ (ispolnítel'nyi
  ~) executive organ
  коммерческий летательный ~
  (kommércheskii letátel'nyi ~)
  commercial aircraft
  летательный ~ (letátel'nyi ~)
  aircraft
  налоговой ~ (nalógovoi ~)
  taxation apparatus
  партийный ~ (partíinyi ~)
  communist party machine
  пиратский летательный ~
  (pirátskii letátel'nyi ~) pirate
  aircraft

  правительственный ~
  (pravítel'stvennyi ~) government
  apparatus
  прокурорский ~ (prokurórskii ~)
  prosecutor's {district
  attorney's} office
  следственный ~ (slédstvennyi ~)
  investigative apparatus
  судебный ~ (sudébnyi ~) judicial
  apparatus
  судейский ~ (sudéiskii ~)
  judicial staff, referees
  {sports}
  управленческий ~
  (upravléncheskii ~) directorate
  центральный ~ (tsentrál'nyi ~)
  central apparatus
  ~ суда (~ sudá) court system
  ~ управления (~ upravléniia)
  executive office
Аппаратчик (apparátchik) *m.*
"apparatchik", political
functionary {usu. communist}
Апробация (aprobátsiia) *f.*
practical approval
Арбитр (arbítr) *m.* arbitrator
  единоличный ~ (edinolíchnyi ~)
  individual arbitrator {single
  person}
  третий ~ (trétii ~) third party
  arbitrator, umpire
  ~ -председатель (~ predsedátel')
  Chairperson of Arbitration
  Tribunal
Арбитраж (arbitrázh) *m.* arbitrage,
arbitration tribunal
  биржевой ~ (birzhevói ~)
  arbitrage business
  валютный ~ (valiútnyi ~)
  currency trading
  ведомственный ~ (védomstvennyi
  ~) administrative arbitration
  вексельный ~ (véksel'nyi ~)
  note, bill of exchange arbitrage
  инструкционный ~
  (instruktsiónnyi ~) standing
  arbitral board
  коммерческий ~ (kommércheskii ~)
  commercial arbitration
  международный ~ (mezhdunaródnyi
  ~) international arbitration
  международный торговой ~
  (mezhdunaródnyi torgóvoi ~)
  international trade arbitration
  многосторонний ~ (mnogostorónnii
  ~) compound arbitration

морской ~ (morskói ~) maritime arbitration
обязательный ~ (obiazátel'nyi ~) compulsory arbitration
перманентный ~ (permanéntnyi ~) permanent arbitral institution
постоянно действующий ~ (postoiánno déistvuiushchii ~) standing arbitral institution
предоговорочный ~ (predogovórochnyi ~) pre-contract arbitration
принудительный ~ (prinudítel'nyi ~) obligatory arbitration
случайный ~ (slucháinyi ~) ad hoc arbitration
товарный ~ (továrnyi ~) commodities trading
торговой ~ (torgóvoi ~) trade arbitration
формальный ~ (formál'nyi ~) formal arbitration
факультативный ~ (fakul'tatívnyi ~) optional arbitration
~ «ад ок» (~ ad ok) ad hoc arbitration

Арбитражный (arbitrázhnyi) *adj.* arbitral

Арбитрирование (arbitrírovanie) *n.* action in arbitrage

Аргумент (argumént) *m.* argument
правовой ~ (pravovói ~) legal argument

Арена (aréna) arena, field, scene

Аренд/а (arénd/a) *f.* lease, rent
бесплатная ~ (besplátnaia ~) gratuitous lease
бессрочная ~ (bessróchnaia ~) perpetual lease
взять в ~/у (vziat' v ~/u) to lease {as lessee}
долгосрочная ~ (dolgosróchnaia ~) long-term lease
испольная ~ (ispól'naia ~) share-cropping agreement
краткосрочная ~ (kratkosróchnaia ~) short-term lease
международная ~ (mezhdunaródnaia ~) international lease
неограниченная сроком ~ (neograníchennaia srókom ~) unlimited term lease
отдать в ~/у (otdat' v ~-u) to lease {as lessor}
предоставить в ~/у (predostávit' v ~-u) to offer for lease

продовольственная ~ земли (prodovól'stvennaia ~ zemlí) tenant farming
рентная ~ (réntnaia ~) income lease {income property}
сдать в ~/у (sdat' v ~/u) to lease {as lessor}
сельскохозяйственная ~ (sel'skokhoziáistvennaia ~) agricultural lease
уступить в ~/у (ustupít' v ~-u) to give up for lease
эмфитевтическая ~ (emfitevtícheskaia ~) lease in emphyteusis {civil law lease-hold estate}
~ земли (~ zemlí) land lease
~ земли на началах эмфитевзиса (~ zemlí na nachálakh emfitevzísa) land lease on the basis of emphyteusis
~ киоска (~ kíoska) kiosk lease
~ охоты (~ okhóty) licensing of game {hunting} rights
~ площади (~ plóshchadi) lease of space
~ рыбной ловли (~ rýbnoi lóvli) license of fishing rights
~ сельскохозяйственных земель (~ sel'skokhoziáistvennykh zemél') lease of agricultural land

Арендатор (arendátor) *m.* lessee

Арендовать (arendovát') *v.* to lease {as lessor}

Арендодатель (arendodátel') *m.* lessor

Арест (arést) *m.* arrest, seizure
дисциплинарный ~ (distsiplinárnyi ~) disciplinary arrest
домашний ~ (domáshnii ~) house arrest
наложить ~ (nalozhít' ~) to place under arrest
незаконный ~ (nezakónnyi ~) false arrest
подлежать ~/у (podlezhát' ~/u) to subject to arrest
предварительный ~ (predvarítel'nyi ~) preliminary arrest
простой ~ (prostói ~) simple arrest
строгий ~ (strógii ~) strict arrest

~ движимого имущества (~
dvízhimogo imúshchestva)
attachment of movable property
~ имущества (~ imúshchestva)
attachment of property
~ на груз (~ na gruz)
confiscation of cargo
~ недвижимого имущества (~
nedvízhimogo imúshchestva)
attachment of real property
~ с содержанием на гауптвахте (~
s soderzhániem na gauptvákhte)
arrest and custody in detention
~ судна (~ súdna) maritime
seizure
Арестованный (arestóvannyi) *adj.*
detainee, suspect
Арестовать (arestovát') *v.* to
arrest
Аргументировать (argumentírovat')
v. to make an argument
Артель (artél') *m.* marketing
cooperative
сельскохозяйственная ~
(sel'skokhoziáistvennaia ~)
agricultural ~
Архивы (arkhívy) *pl.* archives
консульские ~ (kónsul'skie ~)
consular archives
Аспирант (aspiránt) *m.* graduate-
school student, candidate for
Master's degree
Аспирантура (aspirantúra) *f.* post-
graduate study, graduate students
{collect.}
Ассамблея (assambléia) *f.* assembly
европейская парламентская ~
(evropéiskaia parlaméntskaia ~)
European Parliament
Генеральная ~ Объединённых Наций
(generál'naia ~ ob"ediniónnykh
nátsii) General Assembly of the
United Nations
консультативная ~
(konsul'tatívnaia ~)
consultative assembly
федеральная ~ (federál'naia ~)
federal assembly
Ассигнован/ие ~/ия (assignovánie
~/iia) *n.pl.* 1. allocation{s} 2.
appropriation{s}
бюджетные ~ (biudzhétnye ~/iia)
budgetary appropriations
валютное ~ (valiútnoe ~)
convertible currency allocation
дополнительное ~ (dopolnítel'noe
~) supplementary allocation

сметнобюджетное ~
(smetnobiudzhétnoe ~) budgetary
allowance
специальные ~ (spetsiál'nye
~/iia) special appropriations
~ бюджета (~ biudzhéta)
allocation of the budget
~ из бюджета (~ iz biudzhéta)
appropriation from the budget
~ на капиталовложения (~ na
kapitalovlozhéniia)
appropriations for capital
expenditures
~ на просвещение (~ na
prosveshchénie) appropriations
for public education
~ на рекламу (~ na reklámu)
advertising appropriations
Ассигновать (assignovát') *v.* to
allocate, to appropriate
Ассигновк/а (assignóvka) *f.*
assignment, grant of funds
сметные ~/и (smétnye ~/i) budget
allowances
Ассимилировать (assimilírovat') *v.*
to assimilate
Ассимиляция (assimiliátsiia) *f.*
assimilation
Ассортимент (assortimént) *m.*
assortment, variety, selection
товарный ~ (továrnyi ~)
commercial range of goods
широкий ~ (shirókii ~) broad
range of goods
~ товаров (~ továrov) assortment
of goods
Ассоциация (assotsiátsiia) *f.*
association
банковская ~ (bánkovskaia ~)
bankers' ~
европейская ~ свободной торговли
(evropéiskaia ~ svobódnoi
torgóvli) European Free Trade
Association {"EFTA"}
международная ~ адвокатов
(mezhdunaródnaia ~ advokátov)
International Bar Association
международная ~ по охране прав
промышленной собственности
(mezhdunaródnaia ~ po okhráne
prav promýshlennoi
sóbstvennosti) International
Association for the Protection
of Industrial Property Rights
региональная ~ (regionál'naia ~)
regional ~
тайная ~ (táinaia ~) secret ~

торговая ~ (torgóvaia ~) trade ~
~ производителей (~
proizvodítelei) producers' ~
Атака (atáka) f. attack
Атташат (attashát) m. diplomatic
corps
Атташе (attashé) n. attache
{diplomatic}
военный ~ (voénnyi ~) military ~
коммерческий ~ (kommércheskii ~)
commercial ~
морской ~ (morskói ~) maritime ~
торговый ~ (torgóvyi ~) trade
representative
~ по вопросам культуры (~ po
voprósam kul'túry) ~ for
cultural affairs
~ по вопросам финансов (~ po
voprósam finánsov) ~ for
financial affairs
~ печати (~ pecháti) press
liaison
Аттестат (attestát) m. testimonial,
certificate
денежный ~ (dénehnyi ~)
certificate of payment
~ зрелости (~ zrélosti) school-
leaving certificate, certification of majority {age}
Аттестационн/ый (attestatsiónnyi)
adj. of Аттестация
~/ая комиссия (~ /aia komíssiia)
examination board
Аттестация (attestátsiia) f.
assessment
государственная ~
(gosudárstvennaia ~) state ~
~ продукции (~ prodúktsii)
product ~
Аудиенция (audiéntsiia) f. audience
{meeting}
публичная ~ (publíchnaia ~)
public ~
Аудитор (audítor) m. auditor,
certified public accountant
генеральный ~ (generál'nyi ~)
general auditor
Аудитория (auditóriia) f.
auditorium, audience {collective}
Аукцион (auktsión) m. auction
купить на ~/e (kupít' na ~-e) to
buy at ~
лесной ~ (lesnói ~) timber ~
международный ~ (mezhdunaródnyi
~) international ~
продать с ~/a (prodát' s ~/a) to
sell at ~

пушной ~ (pushnói ~) fur {pelt}
~
товарный ~ (továrnyi ~) ~ of
goods
Аукционист (auktsioníst) m.
auctioneer
Аукционный (auktsiónnyi) adj. of
Аукцион
~ зал (~ zal) auction-room
Аутентичность (autentíchnost') f.
authenticity
Аутентичный (autentíchnyi) adj..
authentic
Аутсайдер (autsáider) m. "outsider"
{on Board of Directors, etc.}
Афидевит (afidévit) m. affidavit
Афиша (afísha) f. placard, poster,
billboard
Аффект (affékt) m. fit of passion,
temporary insanity
Аэрограмма (aerográmma) f. airgram
Аэродром (aerodróm) m. airport
Аэропорт (aeropórt) m. airport
военный ~ (voénnyi ~) military ~
гражданский ~ (grazhdánskii ~)
civilian ~
санитарный ~ (sanitárnyi ~)
medical air station
таможенный ~ (tamózhennyi ~)
customs air station, clearing
point
~ выгрузки (~ výgruzki) ~ of
disembarkation
~ назначения (~ naznachéniia) ~
of destination
~ отправления (~ otpravléniia) ~
of origin
~ перегрузки (~ peregrúzki) air
transshipment station
~ пересадки (~ peresádki) air
transfer point
~ погрузки (~ pogrúzki) air
loading station

Б

Баз/а (báza) f. base, basis, depot
военная ~ (voénnaia ~) military
base
диверсификация экспортной ~/ы
(diversifikátsiia éksportnoi
~/y) diversification of the
export base
золотая ~ (zolotáia ~) gold
standard

контейнерная ~ (kontéinernaia ~)
container depot
материальная ~ (materiál'naia ~)
material base
на ~/е контракта (na ~/e
kontrákta) on a contractual
basis
на ~/е твёрдой цены (na ~/e
tviórdoi tsený) on a fixed price
basis
перевалочная ~ (pereválochnaia
~) transshipment terminal
плавучая ~ (plavúchaia ~) depot
ship
проектно-конструкторская ~
(proéktno-konstrúktorskaia ~)
design facility
производственная ~
(proizvódstvennaia ~) production
facility
развитие экспортной ~/ы (ravítie
éksportnoi ~/y) development of
the export base
ремонтная ~ (remontnáia ~)
repair facility
сбытовая ~ (sbytováia ~) sales
depot
складская ~ (skladskáia ~)
wholesale warehouse
создавать ~/у (sozdavát' ~/u) to
establish a base
сырьевая ~ (syr'eváia ~) raw
input (materials) source
таможенная ~ (tamózhennaia ~)
customs warehouse
торговая ~ (torgóvaia ~) supply
depot
укреплять производственную ~/у
(ukrepliát' prozvódstvennuiu
~/u) v. to expand production
facilities
финансовая ~ (finánsovaia ~)
financial base
экспортная ~ (éksportnaia ~)
export base
~ для исчисления тарифа (~ dlia
ischisléniia tarífa) tariff rate
base
~ для оказания услуг (~ dlia
okazániia uslúg) service center
~ технического обслуживания и
текущего ремонта (~
teknnícheskovo obslúzhivaniia i
tekúshchevo remónta) maintenance
depot
Базар (bazár) m. bazaar, market
Базир/овать (bazírovat') v. to base

цена ~/уется на (tséna ~/uetsia
na...) the price is based on ...
~ цену (~ tsénu) v. to base the
price
Базис (bázis) m. basis
экономический ~ (ekonómicheskii
~) economic ~
~ цены (~ tsený) price ~
Базисный (bázisnyi) adj. baseline
Бак (bak) m. tank, vat
наливать в ~ (nalivát' v ~) v.
to pour into a ~
хранить в ~ (khranít' v ~) v. to
store in a ~
Баланс (baláns) m. 1. account
balance 2. financial statement,
balance sheet
актив(ы) ~/а (aktív(y) ~/a) ~
sheet assets
активный ~ (aktívnyi ~) positive
~
активный платёжный ~ (aktívnyi
platióznnyi ~) favorable ~ of
payments
банковский ~ (bánkovskii ~) bank
financial statement
бухгалтерский ~ (bukhgálterskii
~) financial statement
бюджетный ~ (biudzhétnyi ~)
budgetary financial statement
внешнеторговый ~
(vneshnetorgóvyi ~) ~ of
(international) trade
годовой ~ (godovói ~) annual ~
дефицит платёжного ~/а (defitsít
platiózhnovo ~/a) balance of
payments deficit
дефицит торгового ~/а (defitsít
torgóvovo ~/a) trade deficit
заключительный ~
(zakliuchítel'nyi ~) summary
account ~
исправление ~/а (ispravlénie
~/a) adjustment of the ~ sheet
итоговый ~ (itógovyi ~) total ~
кредитовый ~ (kréditovyi ~)
credit ~
ликвидационный ~
(likvidatsiónnyi ~) liquidation
financial statement
межотраслевой ~ (mezhotraslevói
~) inter-sectoral ~
отрицательный ~ (otritsátel'nyi
~) negative ~
отчётный ~ (otchiótnyi ~)
financial performance report

пассивная часть ~/а (passívnaia chast' ~/a) ~ sheet liabilities
пассивный ~ (passívnyi ~) unfavorable ~
пассивный платёжный ~ (passívnyi platióznnyi ~) unfavorable ~ of payments
подробный ~ (podróbnyi ~) detailed financial statement
подводить ~ (podvodít' ~) v. to balance accounts, books, etc.
после сведения ~/а (pósle svedéniia ~/a) fig. "on balance"
предоставлять ~ (predostavliát ~) v. to produce a financial statement
расчётный ~ (raschiótnyi ~) ~ of payables and receivables
ревизия ~/а (revíziia ~/a) audit of accounts
ревизовать ~ (revizovát' ~) v. to audit accounts
сводный ~ (svódnyi ~) consolidated ~ sheet
сводить ~ (svodít' ~) v. to offset an item on a ~ sheet
сжатый ~ (szhátyi ~) condensed financial statement
статья ~/а (stat'iá ~/a) item on a ~ sheet
сумма ~/а (súmma ~/a) total listed assets
торговый ~ (torgóvyi ~) trade balance
~ движения капиталов и кредитов (~ dvizhéniia kapitálov i kredítov) capital and credit statement
~ народного хозяйства (~ naródnovo khoziáistva) national balance of accounts
~ национального дохода (~ natsionál'novo dokhóda) accounting of national income
~ текущих расчётов (~ tekúshchikh raschiótov) current account balance
~ товарной торговли (~ továrnoi torgóvli) merchandise trade balance
~ услуг и некоммерческих платежей (~ uslúg i nekommércheskikh platezhéi) invisible balance
Балансирование (balansírovanie) balancing {of accounts, etc.}

Балансировать (balansírovat') v. to balance {accounts, etc.}
Балансовый (balánsovyi) adj. balance
Бандерол/ь (banderól') f. parcel post, book-rate post
заказная ~ (zakaznáia ~) registered parcel post
почтовая ~ (pochtóvaia ~) book-rate post
простая ~ (prostáia ~) non-registered parcel post
посылать ~/ью (posylát' ~/'iu) v. to send by book-rate post
Бандит (bandít) m. bandit, gangster
~-вымогатель extortionist, racketeer
Бандитизм (banditízm) m. banditry, extortion, racketeering
Банк (bank) m. bank
авизующий ~ (avizúiushchii ~) advising, notifying ~
акцептный ~ (aktséptnyi ~) acceptance ~, merchant ~
акционерный ~ (aktsionérnyi ~) incorporated ~
ассоциированные ~/и (assotsiírovannye ~/i) associated ~/s
банкротство ~/а (bankrótstvo ~/a) ~ failure
ведущий ~ (vedúshchii ~) leading ~
взять вклад из ~/а (vziát' vklad iz ~/a) v. to make a withdrawal from a ~
вклад в ~ (vklad v ~) ~ deposit
внешнеторговый ~ (vneshnetorgóvyi ~) foreign trade ~
вносить деньги в ~ (vnosít' dén'gi v ~) v. to deposit money in a ~
государственный ~ (gosudárstvennyi ~) national ~
гарантия ~/а (garántiia ~/a) ~ guarantee
давать указания ~/у (davát' ukazániia ~/u) v. to instruct the ~
депозитный ~ (depozítnyi ~) ~ of deposit
задолженность ~/у (zadólzhennost' ~/u) ~ debt, account overdraft

закладывать товар в ~/е
(zakládyvat' továr v ~/e) v. to
pledge collateral with a ~
иметь счёт в ~/е (imét' schiót v
~/e) to have an account with a ~
инвестиционный ~
(investitsiónnyi ~) investment
~, securities dealer
иностранный ~ (inostránnyi ~)
foreign, overseas ~
ипотечный ~ (ipotéchnyi ~)
mortgage ~
клиринговый ~ (klíringovyi ~)
clearing house, clearing ~
клиенты ~/а (kliénty ~/a) ~
customers
комиссионные ~/у (kommissiónye
~/u) ~ charges
коммерческий ~ (kommércheskii ~)
commercial ~
консорциум ~/ов (konsórtsium
~/ov) ~/ing syndicate
кооперативный ~ (kooperatívnyi
~) cooperative, "co-op" ~
крупный ~ (krúpnyi ~) major ~
межгосударственный ~
(mezhgosudárstvennyi ~)
interstate ~
местный ~ (méstnyi ~) local ~
национальный ~ (natsionál'nyi)
national ~
одобренный ~ (odóbrennyi ~)
approved ~
основной ~ (osnovnói ~) primary
~
отделение ~/а (otdelénie ~/a)
branch of a ~
перевести на счёт в ~/е
(perevestí na schiot v ~/e) v.
to transfer to the account in
the ~
пересылка через ~ (peresýlka
chérez ~) remittance via ~
получать документы из ~/а
(poluchát' dokuménty iz ~/a) v.
to clear documents through the ~
помещать сумму в ~ (pomeshchát'
súmmu v ~) v. to deposit a sum
in the ~
помещать ценные бумаги в ~
(pomeshchát' tsénnyi bumági v ~)
v. to deposit securities in the
~
представитель ~/а (predstavítel'
~/a) ~ representative

проверка отчётности ~/а
(provérka otchiótnosti ~/a) ~
examination
промышленный ~ (promýshlennyi ~)
industrial
разменный ~ (razménnyi ~)
exchange ~
резервный ~ (rezérvnyi ~)
reserve ~
сберегательный ~ (sberegátel'nyi
~) savings ~
служащий ~/а (slúzhashchii ~/a)
~ clerk, ~ employee
совет ~/а (soviét ~/a) ~ Board
of Governors
счёт в ~/е (schiot v ~/e) ~
account
ссудный ~ (ssúdnyi ~) lending ~
торговый ~ (torgóvyi ~) merchant
~
уполномоченный ~
(upolnomóchennyi ~) authorized ~
управляющий ~/ом
(upravliáiushchii ~/om) ~
manager
управлять ~/ом (upravliát' ~/om)
v. to manage a ~
услуги ~/а (uslúgi ~/a) ~/ing
facilities
учётный ~ (uchiótnyi ~) discount
~
филиал ~/а (filiál ~/a)
affiliate, branch ~
центральный ~ (tsentrál'nyi ~)
central ~
частный ~ (chástnyi ~) private ~
экспортно-импортный ~
(éksportno-ímportnyi ~) export-
import ~
эмиссионный ~ (emissiónnyi ~)
issuing ~
~, выпускающий кредитные
карточки (~, vypuskáiushchii
kredítnye kártochki) ~ issuing
credit cards
~ импортёра (~ importióra)
importer's ~
~ международных расчётов (~
mezhdunaródnikh raschiótov) Bank
for International Settlements
~ по обмену валюты (~ po obménu
valiúty) foreign exchange ~
~, подтверждающий аккредитив (~,
podtverzhdáiushchii akkreditív)
confirming ~ (L/c)
~, пользующий солидной
репутацией (~, pol'zúiushchii

solídnoi reputátsiei) ~ in good
standing
~, производящий приём и оплату
документов (~, proizvodiáshchii
priióm i oplátu dokuméntov)
negotiating ~
~ третьей страны (~ trét'ei
straný) third-country ~
~ экспортёра (~ eksportióra)
exporter's ~

Банк/а (bánka) can, jar
вздувшаяся ~ (vzdúvshaiasia ~)
swollen can
герметическая ~ (germetícheskaia
~) hermetically-sealed can
запечатанная ~ (zapechátannaia
~) sealed jar
упаковывать в ~/у (upakóvyvat' v
~/u) v. to can, to preserve in a
jar

Банк-акцептант (bánk-aktseptánt) m.
merchant banker, acceptance bank

Банк-инкассатор (bánk-inkassátor)
m. collecting bank

Банкир (bankír) m. banker
рекомендация ~ (rekomendátsiia
~/a) ~'s references

Банк-корреспондент (bánk-
korrespondént) m. correspondent-
bank

Банк-кредитор (bank-kreditór) m.
creditor bank

Банкнот/а (banknóta) f. banknote,
bill
выпуск ~ (výpusk ~) issue of
bank notes
выпускать ~/ы в обращение
(vypuskát' ~/y v obrashchénie)
v. to issue banknotes into
circulation
изъятие ~ (iz"iátie ~)
withdrawal of banknotes
резервная ~ (rezérvnaia ~)
reserve banknote
фальшивая ~ (falshívaia ~)
counterfeit bill
эмиссия банкнот ~ (emíssiia ~)
issuance of banknotes
~/ы (~/y) paper money
~/ы в обращении (~/y v
obrashchénii) bills in
circulation
~ в 1 доллар (~ v odín dóllar)
one-dollar bill
~ в 1 фунт стерлингов (~ v odín
funt stérlingov) one pound note

~ достоинством ... (~
dostóinstvom ...) bill in the
denomination of ...
~/ы по купюрам (~/y po kupiúram)
banknotes by denomination

Банковский (bánkovskii) adj. bank

Банк-плательщик (bánk-
platél'shchik) m. payer's bank

Банк-ремитент (bánk-remitént) m.
remitting bank

Банкрот (bankrót) m. bankrupt,
insolvent party
объявлять ~/ом (ob"iavliát'
~/om) v. to declare oneself
bankrupt
стать ~/ом (stat' ~/om) v. to go
bankrupt

Банкротств/о (bankrótstvo) n.
bankruptcy
доводить до ~/a (dovodít' do
~/a) v. to drive into ~
объявлять ~ (ob"iavliát' ~) v.
to declare ~
~ банка (~ bánka) bank failure

Банк-учредитель (bánk-uchredítel')
m. founding bank

Банк-эмитент (bánk-emitént) m.
issuing bank

Барабан (barabán) m. drum
деревянный ~ (dereviánnyi ~)
wooden ~, cask
дощатый ~ (doshchátyi ~) board ~
железный ~ (zheléznyi ~) iron ~
картонный ~ (kartónnyi ~)
cardboard ~
фанерный ~ (fanérnyi ~) plywood
~
фибровый ~ (fibróvyi ~)
fiberboard ~

Баратри/я (barátriia) f. barratry
{maritime}
виновный в ~/и (vinóvnyi v ~/i)
barrator {maritime}

Барж/а (bárzha) f. barge
глубоководная ~ (glubokovódnaia
~) deep-sea ~
грузовая ~ (gruzováia ~) cargo ~
наливная ~ (nalivnáia ~) tanker
~
несамоходная ~ (nesamokhódnaia
~) non-propelling, "dumb" ~
обеспечивать поставку ~/и
(obespéchivat' postávku ~/i) v.
to provide for ~ shipping
океанская ~ (okeánskaia ~)
ocean-going ~

портовая ~ (portóvaia ~) utility ~
разгружать (через борт) на ~/у
(razgruzhát' chérez bort na ~/i)
v. to unload (over side) to ~
речная ~ (rechnáia ~) river ~
саморазгружающаяся ~
(samogruzháiushchaiasia ~) dump ~
самоходная ~ (samokhódnaia ~)
self-propelled ~
цена с ~/и (tsená s ~/i) price
ex ~
франко ~ (fránko ~) FOB ~
Бартерный (bárternyi) adj. barter
Барьер (bar'ér) n. barrier
дискриминационные ~/ы
(diskriminatsiónnye ~/y)
discriminatory {trade} ~/s
нетарифный (netarífnyi ~) non-
tariff {trade} ~
обходить таможенные ~/ы
(obkhodít' tamózhennye ~/y) v.
to avoid customs ~/s
протекционистские ~/ы
(protekstionístskie ~/y)
protectionist ~/s
создавать ~/ы (sozdavát' ~/y) to
erect ~/s
таможенный ~ (tamózhennyi ~)
customs ~
тарифный ~ (tarífnyi ~) tariff ~
торговый ~ (torgóvyi ~) trade ~
устранять ~/ы (ustraniát' ~/y)
v. to eliminate ~/s
Безаварийный (bezavaríinyi) adj.
trouble-free
Безвозмездно (bezvozmézdno) adv.
free, gratis
передавать ~ (peredavát' ~) v.
to transfer gratis
Безвозмездный (bezvozmézdnyi) adj.
free, uncompensated
Бездефектность (bezdeféktnost') f.
zero-defect tolerance
Бездефектный (bezdeféktnyi) adj.
fault-free
Безлицензионный (bezlitsenziónnyi)
adj. unlicensed
Безналичный (beznalíchnyi) adj.
non-cash {transaction}
Безоговорочный (bezgovórochnyi)
adj. unconditional
Безопасност/ь (bezopásnost') f.
safety, security

инструкции по технике ~/и
(instrúktsii po tékhnike ~/i)
safety instructions
меры для обеспечения ~/и (méry
dlia obespechéniia ~/i) security
measures
нарушение правил техники ~/и
(narushénie právil tékhniki ~/i)
violation of safety regulations
нормы техники ~/и (nórmy
tékhniki ~/i) safety standards
обеспечивать ~ (obespéchivat' ~)
v. to insure safety
пожарная ~ (pozhárnaia ~) fire
safety
технологическая ~
(tekhnologícheskaia ~) plant
safety
техника ~/и (tékhnikha ~/i)
safety regulations
~ мореплавания (~ moreplávaniia)
navigational safety
~ персонала (~ personála)
personnel safety
Безотзывный (bezotzývnyi) adj.
irrevocable
Безотлагательность
(bezotlagátel'nost') f. urgency
Безотлагательный (bezotlagátel'nyi)
adj. urgent
Безработница (bezrabótnitsa) f.
unemployment
Безработный (bezrabótnyi) adj.
unemployed
Безубыточный (bezubýtochnyi) adj.
without losses
Безусловный (bezuslóvnyi) adj.
unconditional
Бенефициар (benefitsiár) m.
beneficiary
наименование ~/a (naimenovánie
~/a) designation of a ~
Безконкурентный (bezkonkuréntnyi)
adj. non-competitive, without
competition
Беспатентный (bespaténtnyi) adj.
unpatented
Бесплатно (besplátno) adv. free of
charge
поставлять ~ (postavliát' ~) v.
to supply free of charge
Бесплатный (besplátnyi) adj. free,
gratuitous
Беспошлинный (bespóshlinnyi) adj.
duty-free
Бесприбыльный (bespríbyl'nyi) adj.
unprofitable, non-profit

Беспроцентный (besprotséntnyi) *adj.*
interest-free
Бессрочный (bessróchnyi) *adj.*
unlimited {period of time}
Бигамия (bigámiia) *f.* bigamy
Бизнес (bíznes) *m.* business
  большой ~ (bol'shói ~) big ~
  вялый ~ (viályi ~) slow trade,
  slack ~
  малый ~ (mályi ~) small ~
  прибыльный ~ (príbyl'nyi ~)
  profitable ~
Билет (bilét) *m.* ticket, note
  банковский ~ (bánkovskii ~) bank
  note
  вкладной ~ (vkladnói ~) deposit
  slip, certificate of deposit
  железнодорожный ~
  (zheleznodorózhnyi ~) railway
  ticket
  казначейские ~/ы (kaznachéiskie
  ~/y) treasury notes, currency
  обратный ~ (obrátnyi ~) return
  ticket
  пригласительный ~
  (priglasítel'nyi ~) invitation
  ~ на самолёте (~ na samolióte)
  airline ticket
Биотехнология (biotekhnológiia) *f.*
bio-technology
Бирж/а (bírzha) *f.* exchange, market
  валютная ~ (valiútnaia ~)
  currency exchange
  зерновая ~ (zernováia ~) grain
  market
  играть на ~/е (igrát' na ~/e) *v.*
  to play the market
  котирующийся на ~/е
  (kotíruiushchiisia na ~/e) *adj.*
  quoted on the exchange
  международная товарная ~
  (mezhdunaródnaia továrnaia ~)
  international commodities
  exchange
  на ~/е (na ~/e) on the exchange
  неофициальная ~ (neofitsiál'naia
  ~) street-market, informal
  exchange
  официальная ~ (ofitsiál'naia ~)
  recognized exchange
  специализированная ~
  (spetsializírovannaia ~)
  specialized exchange
  товарная ~ (továrnaia ~)
  commodity exchange
  фондовая ~ (fóndovaia ~) stock
  market

  фрахтовая ~ (frakhtóvaia ~)
  shipping exchange
  хлебная ~ (khlébnaia ~) grain
  exchange
  хлопковая ~ (khlópkovaia ~)
  cotton exchange
  цены при закрытии ~/и (tsény pri
  zakrýtii ~/i) closing prices
  цены при открытии ~/и (tsény pri
  otkrýtii ~/i) opening prices
  ~ лесоматериалов (~
  lesomateriálov) lumber yard
  ~ металлов (~ metállov) metals
  exchange
  ~ по шерсти (~ po shérsti) wool
  exchange
  ~ сельскохозяйственных товаров
  (~ sel'skokhoziáistvennykh
  továrov) produce market
  ~ ценных бумаг (~ tsénnikh
  bumág) securities exchange
Биржевик (birzhevík) *m.* exchange
dealer
Биржевой (birzhevói) *adj.* exchange
Бирк/а (bírka) *f.* tag, label
  багажная ~ (bagázhnaia ~)
  luggage tag
  бумажная ~ (bumázhnaia ~) paper
  tag
  металлическая ~ (metallícheskaia
  ~) metal tag
  прикреплять ~/у (prikrepliát'
  ~/u) *v.* to attach a label
  ~ с указанием цены (~ s
  ukazániem tsený) price tag
  специальная ~ (spetsial'naia ~)
  special tag
Благоприятствовани/е
(blagopriiástvovanie) *n.*
preferential treatment
  оговорка о наибольшем ~/и
  (ogovórka o naiból'shem ~/i)
  most favored nation clause
  режим наибольшего ~/я (rezhím
  naiból'shevo ~/ia) most favored
  nation (MFN) status
  тариф на основе наибольшего ~/я
  (taríf na osnóve naiból'shevo
  ~/ia) most favored nation (MFN)
  tariff treatment
  предоставлять режим наибольшего
  ~/я (predostavliát' rezhím
  naiból'shevo ~/ia) *v.* to grant
  MFN treatment
Благоприятствовать
(blagopriiátstvovat') *v.* to favor,
to be favorable

Бланк (blank) *m.* blank, form
банковский ~ (bánkovskii ~) bank
form
вексельный ~ (veksel'nyi ~)
draft form
дубликат ~/а о взносе депозита
(dublikát ~/a o vznóse depozíta)
duplicate deposit slip
заполнять ~ (zapolniát' ~) *v.* to
complete a form
образец ~/а (obrazéts ~/a)
sample form
отчётный ~ (otchiótnyi ~) report
card
печатный ~ (pechátnyi ~) printed
order form
телеграфный ~ (telegráfnyi ~)
cable blank
типографский ~ (tipográfskii ~)
printed form
фирменный ~ (fírmennyi ~)
company form
чистый ~ (chístyi ~) blank
{clean] form
~ декларации (~ deklarátsii)
declaration form
~ для вклада (~ dlia vkláda)
deposit slip
~ для письма со штампом фирмы (~
dlia pis'má so shtámpom fírmy)
letter-head
~ для регистрации покупки (~
dlia registrátsii pokúpki)
product registration form
~ для сверки депозитного счёта
(~ dlia svérki depózitnovo
schióta) reconciliation
statement (bank statement)
~ документа (~ dokuménta) form
{standard} document
~ заказа (~ zakáza) order form
~ заявки (~ zaiávki) requisition
~ заявления (~ zaiavléniia)
application
~ инкассового поручения по
документарной тратте (~
inkássovovo poruchéniia po
dokumentárnoi trátte)
documentary bill lodgement blank
~ квитанции (~ kvitántsii)
standardized receipt
~ контракта (~ kontrákta) form
{standard} contract
~ письма (~ pis'má) form letter
~ предварительной регистрации (~
predvarítel'noi registrátsii)
pre-registration form

~ телеграммы (~ telegrámmy)
cable form
~ чека (~ chéka) check form
Бланков/ый (blánkovyi) *adj.* blank
делать ~/ую надпись (délat'
~/uiu nádpis') *v.* to make a
general indorsement
~/ая надпись (~/aia nádpis')
general indorsement
Блок (blok) *m.* bloc
валютный ~ (valiútnyi ~)
currency ~
военный ~ (voénnyi ~) military ~
закрытый экономический ~
(zakrýtyi ekonomícheskii ~)
exclusive economic ~
Блокад/а (blokáda) *f.* ban,
blockade, embargo
ввести ~/у (vvestí ~/u) *v.* to
impose a blockade
кредитная ~ (kredítnaia ~)
credit block
морская ~ (morskáia ~) naval
blockade
прорыв ~/ы (prorýv ~/y) breach
of a blockade, embargo
таможенная ~ (tamózhennaia ~)
customs blockade
технологическая ~
(tekhnologícheskaia ~)
technological embargo
торговая ~ (toprgóvaia ~) trade
embargo
экономическая ~ (ekonomícheskaia
~) embargo
Блокированный (blokiróvannyi) *adj.*
blocked, frozen
Блокировать (blokírorat') *v.* to
blockade, to freeze assets, etc.
Бодмерея (bodmeréia) *f.* bottomry
Бой (boi) *m.* breakage
~ при перевалке (~ pri
pereválke) ~ during handling
~ при транспортировке (~ pri
transportiróvke) ~ in transit
Бойкот (boikót) *m.* boycott
финансовый ~ (finánsovyi ~)
financial ~
объявить ~ (ob''iavít' ~) *v.* to
impose a ~
отменить ~ (otmenít' ~) *v.* to
lift a boycott
политика ~/а (polítika ~/a) a ~
policy
экономический ~ (ekonomícheskii
~) economic ~, embargo

Бойкотировать (boikotírovat') *v.* to boycott

Большегрузный (bol'shegrúznyi) *adj.* extra-capacity (vessel, etc.)

Бона фиде (bóna fíde) *indecl.* bona fide

Бонд (bond) *m.* bond
  аварийный ~ (avaríinyi ~) general ~

Бондовой (bondovói) *adj.* bonded (in customs, etc.)

Бонитет (bonitét) *m.* bondibility, solvency

Бонификаци/я (bonifikátsiia) *f.* bonus allowance
  обратная ~ (obrátnaia ~) reimbursable ~
  экспортная ~ (éksportnaia ~) export ~
  размер ~/и (razmér ~/i) amount of ~

Бонус (bónus) *m.* cash bonus

Борт (bort) *m.* board, ship's deck
  вдоль ~/а (vdol' ~/a) alongside (ship)
  выбрасывать за ~ (vybrásyvat' za ~) *v.* to jettison over board
  за ~/ом (za ~/om) overboard
  на ~/у (na ~/u) on board
  от ~/а (ot ~/a) from alongside
  погрузить на ~ (pogruzít' na ~) *v.* to load on board
  принимать на ~ (prinimát' na ~) *v.* to accept cargo on board
  у ~/а (u ~/a) alongside
  через ~ (chérez ~) overside
  свободно на ~/у (svobódno na ~/u) free on board, FOB
  франко ~ (fránko ~) free on board, FOB
  франко ~ грузового автомобиля (fránko ~ gruzovóvo automobília) FOB truck
  франко вдоль ~/а судна (fránko vdol' ~/a súdna) FOB alongside
  франко ~ самолёта (fránko ~ samolióta) FOB air-freight, FOB airplane

Бортовой (bortovói) *adj.* deck, overside

Борьба (bor'bá) *f.* battle, campaign struggle
  конкурентная ~ (konkuréntnaia ~)
  ~ за высокое качество (~ vysókoe káchestvo) quality drive

  ~ за максимальные прибыли (~ za maksimál'nye príbyli) profit maximization drive
  ~ за рынки (~ za rýnki) competition for market share

Бот (bot) *m.* small craft (marine)
  лоцманский ~ (lotsmánskii ~) pilot craft

Бочк/а (bóchka) *f.* barrel, cask
  деревянная ~ (dereviánnaia ~) wooden barrel
  железная ~ (zheléznaia ~) steel drum
  укладывать в ~/у (ukládyvat' v ~/u) *v.* to barrel {fill}
  ~/и пустые (~/i pustýe) "barrels empty"
  ~/и текут (~/i tekút) "barrels leaking"

Брак (brak) *m.* 1. defects, rejects, spoilage 2. marriage
  производственный ~ (proizvódstvennyi ~) production reject
  допуск ~/а (dópusk ~/a) breakage rate, spoilage rate
  процент ~/а (protsént ~/a) reject rate
  обнаруживать ~ (obnarúzhivat' ~) *v.* to detect quality flaws

Бракераж (brakerázh) *m.* quality inspection, sorting

Бракованный (brakóvannyi) *adj.* defective, non-conforming (goods)

Браковать (brakovát') *v.* to reject

Браковк/а (brakóvka) *f.* rejection
  критерий ~ (kritérii ~/i) rejection criterion

Браковщик (brakovshchík) *m.* Q.C. {quality control} inspector

Братство (brátstvo) *n.* brotherhood

Брачный (bráchnyi) *adj.* conjugal, nuptial

Брезент (brezént) *m.* canvas cover, tarp[aulin]
  покрывать ~/ом (pokryvát' ~/om) *v.* to cover with a tarp

Бригада (brigáda) *f.* crew, gang, shift, team
  аварийная ~ (avaríinaia ~) emergency crew
  ремонтная ~ (remóntnaia ~) emergency crew repair team
  ~ грузчиков (~ grúzchikov) stevedore crew

~ технического обслуживания (~ tekhnícheskovo obslúzhivaniia) maintenance crew

Бригадир (brigadír) *m.* brigade leader

Брокер (bróker) *m.* broker
б856жевой ~ (birzhevói ~) stock-broker, exchange dealer
вексельный ~ (véksel'nyi ~) securities ~, bill dealer
страховой ~ (strakhovói ~) insurance ~
судовой ~ (sudovói ~) shipbroker
фрахтовый ~ (frakhtóvyi ~) freight broker
~ делькредере (~ del'krédere) *indecl.* "del credere" broker
~ по покупкам (~ po pokúpkam) commercial buyer, purchasing broker
~ по покупкам и продаже зерна (~ po pokúpkam i prodázhe zerná) grain broker
~ по фрахтованию (~ po frakhtovániiu) charter-broker
~ судовладельца (~ sudovladél'tsa) shipowner's broker
~ фондовой биржи (~ fóndovoi bírzhi) stockbroker
~ фрахтователя (~ frakhtovátelia) charterer's broker

Брокераж (brokerázh) *m.* brokerage, broker's commission

Брокерский (brókerskii) *adj.* brokerage

Бронирование (bronírovanie) *n.* booking, reservation

Бронировать (bronírovat') *v.* to book, to reserve,

Брошюра (broshiúra) *f.* brochure
рекламная (reklámnaia ~) promotional brochure

Брутто (brútto) *indecl.* gross
вес ~ (ves ~) ~ weight
масса ~ (mássa ~) ~ mass
фактический вес ~ (faktícheskii ves ~) actual ~ weight
~ баланс (~ baláns) rough balance
~ за нетто (~ za nétto) ~ for net
~ регистровый тоннаж (~ regístrovyi tonnázh) ~ register tonnage
~ тонна (~ tónna) gross ton

~ тоннаж (~ tonnázh) ~ tonnage
~ фрахт (~ frakht) ~ freight

Брутто-ставка (brútto-stávka) *f.* gross premium

Букинглист (bukinglíst) *m.* booking list

Букинг-нот (búking-nót) *m.* booking note

Букировать (bukírovat') *v.* to book {freight}

Букировк/а (bukiróvka) *f.* booking
плата за ~/у (pláta za ~/u) booking commission
~ груза (~ grúza) cargo-booking

Буклет (buklét) *m.* booklet, pamphlet
иллюстрированный ~ (illiustrírovannyi ~) illustrated pamphlet
фирменный ~ (fírmennyi ~) firm resumé

Буксир (buksír) *m.* tug-boat
портовый ~ (portóvyi ~) port tug-boat
обслуживание ~/ами (obslúzhivanie ~/ami) towing, tug service

Буксирный (buksírnyi) *adj.* towing, tuggage

Буксировать (buksírovat') *v.* to have in tow, to tug

Буксировк/а (buksiróvka) *f.* marine haulage, towing, tuggage
морская ~ (morskáia ~) marine towing, tugging
договор морской ~/и (dogovór morskói ~/i) tug contract

Бум (bum) *m.* {economic} boom
биржевой ~ (birzhevói ~) stock-market ~
инфляционный ~ (infliatsiónnyi ~) inflationary ~
спекулятивный ~ (spekuliatívnyi ~) speculative ~
~ капиталовложений (~ kapitalovlozhénii) investment ~

Бумаг/а (bumága) *f.* paper
аннулированные ~/и (annulírovannye ~/i) called bonds
водонепроницаемая ~ (vodonepronitsáemaia ~) waterproof ~
газетная ~ (gazétnaia ~) newsprint
гербовая ~ (gérbovaia ~) watermark ~, stamped ~

именные ценные ~/и (imennýe
tsénnye ~/i) registered
securities
иностранные ценные ~/и
(inostránnye tsénnye ~/i)
foreign securities
коммерческие ~/и (kommércheskie
~/i) commercial ~
легкореализуемые ценные ~/и
(legkorealizúemye tsénnye ~/i)
readily marketable securities
Бутыл/ка (butýlka) f. bottle
Бутыл/ь (butýl') f. bottle, flask
  большая, оплетённая ~
  (bol'sháia, opletiónnaia ~)
  demijohn
  упаковывать в ~/и (upakóvyvat' v
  ~/i) v. to bottle
Бухгалтер (bukhgálter) m.
accountant, bookkeeper
  главный ~ (glávnyi ~) chief
  accountant
  старший ~ (stárshii ~) senior
  bookkeeper
Бухгалтер-аналитик (bukhgálter-
analítik) m. controller
Бухгалтер-калькулятор (bukhgálter-
kal'kuliátor) m. cost accountant
Бухгалтер-контролёр (bukhgálter-
kontroliór) m. comptroller
Бухгалтер-ревизор (bukhgálter-
revizór) m. auditor
Бухгалтерский (bukhgálterskii) adj.
accounting, bookkeeping
Бухт/а (búkhta) f. bay
  выходить из ~/ы (vykhodít' iz
  ~/y) v. to clear a bay
Быстрореализуемый
(bystrorealizúemyi) adj. fast-
selling, liquid
Бьющийся (b'iúshchiisia) adj.
fragile
Бэрбоут (berbóut) m. bare-boat,
unmanned craft
  ~ чартер (~ chárter) bare-boat
  charter
Бюджет (biuzhét) m. budget
  взносы в ~ (vznósy v ~) ~
  contributions
  годовой ~ (godovói ~) annual ~
  государственный
  (gosudárstvennyi ~) state ~
  дополнительный ~ (dopolnítel'nyi
  ~) supplementary ~
  доходный ~ (dokhódnyi ~) revenue
  жёсткий ~ (zhióstkii ~) fixed-
  revenue ~

исполнение ~/a (ispolnénie ~/a)
~ implementation
местный ~ (méstnyi ~) local ~
национальный ~ (natsionál'nyi ~)
national ~
небольшой ~ (nebol'shói ~) low ~
несбалансированный ~
(nesbalansírovannyi ~)
unbalanced ~
перечислять сумму в ~
(perechisliát' súmmu v ~) v. to
transfer a figure into the ~
подготовка ~/a (podgotóvka ~/a)
~ preparation
представлять ~ на рассмотрение
(predstavliát' ~ na
rassmotrénie) v. to submit a ~
for deliberation
предусматривать в ~/e
(predusmátrivat' v ~/e) v. to
budget
проект ~/a (proékt ~/a) draft ~
размер ~/a (razmér ~/a) ~ size
расходный ~ (raskhódnyi ~) ~
expenditures
сбалансированный ~
(sbalansírovannyi ~) balanced ~
сводный ~ (svódnyi ~)
consolidated ~
сокращение ~/a (sokrashchénie
~/a) ~ cuts
сокращать ~ (sokrashchát' ~) v.
to cut the ~
составление ~/a (sostavlénie
~/a) ~ process
одобрить ~ (odobrít' ~) v. to
approve a ~
текущий ~ (tekúshchii ~) current
operating ~
увеличивать ~ (uvelíchivat' ~)
v. to increase the ~
утверждать ~ (utverzhdát' ~) v.
to pass the ~
~ капиталовложений (~
kapitalovlozhénii) capital ~
~ рекламы (~ reklámy)
advertising ~
Бюджетный (biudzhétnyi) adj.
budgetary
Бюллетень (biulletén') m. bulletin,
newsletter, report
  биржевой ~ (birzhevói ~)
  stockmarket report
  ежегодный ~ (ezhegódnyi ~)
  annual report
  ежемесячный ~ (ezhemésiachnyi ~)
  monthly newsletter

издавать ~ (izdavát' ~) v. to
publish a bulletin, newsletter
информационный ~
(informatsiónnyi ~)
informational bulletin
коммерческий ~ (kommércheskii ~)
trade bulletin
патентный ~ (paténtnyi ~) patent
~
прейскурантный ~ (preiskurántnyi
~) price bulletin
торговый ~ (torgóvyi ~) trade
report
экономический ~ (ekonomícheskii
~) economic report
~ курса валюты (~ kúrsa valiúty)
exchange-rate report
~ курса ценных бумаг на бирже (~
kúrsa tsénnykn bumág na bírzhe)
securities exchange report
Бюро (biuró) n. bureau, department,
desk
информационное ~
(informatsiónnoe ~) information
bureau
конструкторское ~
(konstrúktorskoe ~) design
department
патентное ~ (paténtnoe ~) patent
office
регистрационное ~
(registratsiónnoe ~)
registration office, registrar
рекламное ~ (reklámnoe ~)
advertising agency, department
справочное ~ (správochnoe ~)
information desk
техническое ~ (tekhnícheskoe ~)
technical department
туристическое ~ (turistícheskoe
~) travel agency
~ диспашёров (~ dispashiórov)
claims adjusters' division
~ обслуживания (~
obslúzhivaniia) service
department
~ объявлений (~ ob''iavlénii)
press-release office
~ по выдаче паспортов и виз (~
po výdache pasportóv i viz)
passport and visa office
~ по связи с общественностью (~
po sviázi s obshchéstvennost'iu)
public-relations department
~ проката (~ prokáta) rental
office

~ путешествий (~ puteshéstvii)
travel agency
~ регистрации акционерных
компаний (~ registrátsii
aktsionérnykh kompánii)
registrar of companies,
corporate registry office
~ технического надзора (~
teknícheskovo nadzóra) technical
inspection office
~ услуг (~ uslúg) service center
Бюрократия (biurokrátiia)
bureaucracy

В

Вагон (vagón) m. {railroad} car
автономный ~ (avtonómnyi ~) self
propelled ~
багажный ~ (bagázhnyi ~) baggage
~
балластный ~ (ballástnyi ~)
ballast ~
большегрузный ~ (bol'shegrúznyi
~) high capacity ~
вентилируемый крытый ~
(ventilíruemyi krýtyi ~)
ventilated box ~
грузовой ~ (gruzovói ~) box ~
железнодорожный ~
(zheleznodorózhnyi ~) railroad ~
жёсткий ~ (zhióstkii ~) "hard" ~
carriage
закрытый ~ (zakrýtyi ~) closed ~
загружать ~ (zagruzhát' ~) to
load a ~
крытый ~ (krýtyi ~) box ~
купированный ~ (kupírovannyi ~)
compartment ~
моторный ~ (mótornyi ~)
automobile ~
недогруженный ~ (nedogrúzhennyi
~) under-loaded ~
облегчённый ~ (oblegchiónnyi ~)
light ~
пассажирский ~ (passazhírskii ~)
passenger ~
поставка в ~/е (postávka v ~/e)
delivery by ~
порожний ~ (porózhnii ~) empty ~
почтовый ~ (pochtóvyi ~) postal
~
прицепной ~ (pretsepnói ~)
trailer ~
прямой сборный ~ (priamói
sbórnyi ~) consolidated ~

рефрижераторный ~
(refrizherátornyi ~)
refrigerated ~
саморазгружающий ~
(samorazgruzháiushchiisia ~)
tipping ~
сборный ~ (sbórnyi ~)
merchandise ~
спальный ~ (spál'nyi ~) sleeper
~
товарный ~ (továrnyi ~) freight
~
цена франко ~ (tsená fránko ~)
free on rail price
франко ~ (fránko ~) free on rail
~ прямого сообщения (~ priámovo
soobshchéniia) through ~
~ с боковой разгрузкой (~ s
bokovói razgrúzkoi) side dump ~
~ смешанного класса (~
sméshannovo klássa) composite ~
~/ами (~ /ami) by the ~load
Вагон-весы (vagón-vesý) m. scale
car
Вагон-лесовоз (vagón-lesovóz) m.
timber car
Вагон-мастерская (vagón-
masterskáia) m. repair car
Вагон-платформа (vagón-platfórma)
m. flatbed car
Вагон-холодильник (vagón-
kholodíl'nik) m. refrigerator car
Вагон-цистерна (vagón-tsistérna) m.
tanker car
Валовой (valovói) adj. gross
Валоризация (valorizátsiia) f.
valorization
Валют/а (valiúta) f. currency
блокированная ~ (blokírovannaia
~) blocked ~
бумажная ~ (bumázhnaia ~) paper
~
вычисление курса ~/ы
(vychislénie kúrsa ~/y)
calculation of the exchange rate
девальвированная
(deval'vírovannaia ~) devalued ~
девальвация ~/ы (deval'vátsiia
~/y) devaluation of ~
дефицит ~/ы (defitsít ~/y)
foreign exchange deficit
дефицитная ~ (defitsítnaia ~)
scarce ~
единая ~ (edínaia ~) common ~
единица ~/ы (edinítsa ~/y) unit
of ~

завышенная оценка ~/ы
(zavýshennaia otsénka ~/y) overvaluation of ~
запасы ~/ы (zapásy ~/y) ~
reserves
запрещение вывоза иностранной
~/ы (zapreshchénie vývoza
inostránnoi ~/y) ban on foreign
exchange export
зачислять ~/у на счёт
(zachisliát' ~/u na schiót) v.
to transfer ~ into an account
золотое содержание ~/ы (zolotóe
soderzhánie ~/y) gold content of
~
иностранная ~ (inostránnaia ~)
foreign ~
излишки ~/ы (izlíshki ~/y)
surplus of ~
клиринговая ~ (klíringovaia ~)
clearing ~
ключевая ~ (kliucheváia ~) key ~
колеблющаяся ~
(kolébliushchaiasia ~)
fluctuating ~
колебание курса ~/ы (kolebánie
kúrsa ~/y) ~ fluctuation
конвертируемость ~/ы
(konvertíruemost' ~/y)
convertibility of ~
конвертировать в ~/у
(konvertírovat' v ~/u) to
convert ~
"корзина" ~/ (korzína ~/) basket
of ~s
котировка иностранной ~/ы
(kotiróvka inostránnoi ~/y)
foreign exchange {rate}
крах ~/ы (krakh ~/y) collapse of
~
конвертируемая ~
(konvertíruemaia ~) convertible
~
курс иностранной ~/ы (kurs
inostránnoi ~/y) exchange rate
национальная ~ (natsionál'naia
~) national ~
неконвертируемая ~
(nekonvertíruemaia ~)
inconvertible ~
неустойчивая ~ (neustóichivaia
~) unstable ~
неустойчивость ~/ы
(neustóichivost' ~/y)
instability of ~
обесцененная ~ (obestsénennaia
~) depreciated ~

обеспечивать ~/у (obespechívat' ~/u) *v.* to back ~
обесценивать ~/у (obestsénivat' ~/u) *v.* to depreciate ~
обмен ~/ы (obmén ~/y) ~ exchange
обмен ~/ами (obmén ~/ami) ~ swap
обменивать ~/у (obménivat' ~/u) to exchange ~
обратимая ~ (obratímaia ~) convertible ~
обратимость ~/ы (obratímost' ~/y) convertibility of ~
ограничения в переводе ~/ы (ogranichéniia v perevóde ~/y) ~ exchange restrictions
операции в ~/е (operátsii v ~/e) ~ exchange transactions
операции с ~/ой (operátsii s ~/oi) exchange business {i.e. on an exchange}
отечественная ~ (otéchestvennaia ~) domestic ~
паритет ~/ы (paritét ~/y) parity of exchange
падающая ~ (pádaiushchaia ~) depreciating ~
переводить в другую ~/у (perevodít' v drugúiu ~/u) to convert into another ~
переводить ~/у на счёт (perevodít' ~/u na schiót) *v.* to transfer ~ into an account
пересчёт ~/ы по курсу (perschiót ~/y po kúrsu) conversion of ~ at the going rate
пересчёт ~/ы по паритету (pereschiót ~/y po paritétu) conversion of ~ at par value {parity}
платёж в ~/е клиринга (platiózh v ~/e klíringa) settlement in clearing ~
платёж в национальной ~/е (platiózh v natsionál'noi ~/e) settlement in national ~
по сравнению с другими ~/ами (po sravnéniiu s drugími ~/ami) against other ~s
повышать курс ~/ы (povyshát' kurs ~/y) *v.* to appreciate ~
поддельная ~ (poddél'naia ~) counterfeit ~
полноценная ~ (polnotsénnaia ~) ~ at full value
покупательная способность ~/ы (pokupátel'naia sposóbnost' ~/y) purchasing power of ~

понижение курса ~/ы (ponizhénie kúrsa ~/y) devalorization of ~
поступления ~/ы (postupléniia ~/y) foreign exchange earnings
потери на разнице курсов ~/ (potéri na ráznitse kúrsov ~/) exchange losses
распределение ~/ы (raspredelénie ~/y) allocation of foreign exchange
расчёт в иностранной ~/е (raschiót v inostránnoi ~/e) settlement in foreign ~
реализовать на ~/у (realizovát' na ~/u) *v.* to sell for {hard} ~
ревальвированная ~ (reval'vírovannaia ~) revalued ~
ревальвировать {ревалоризировать} ~/у (reval'vírovat' {revalorizírovat'} ~/u) to revalue ~
регулируемая ~ (regulíruemaia ~) controlled ~
регулировать ~/у (regulírovat' ~/u) *v.* to control ~
резервная ~ (rezérvnaia ~) reserve ~
свободная ~ (svobódnaia ~) free ~
свободно конвертируемая ~ (svobódno konvertíruemaia ~) freely convertible ~
свободно плавающая ~ (svobódno plávaiushchaia ~) freely floating ~
согласованная ~ (soglasóvannaia ~) agreed ~
стабильная ~ (stabíl'naia ~) stable ~
твёрдая ~ (tviórdaia ~) hard ~
устойчивая ~ (ustóichivaia ~) stable ~
устойчивость ~/ы (ustóichivost' ~/y) stability of ~
~, обратимая в золото (~, obratímaia v zóloto) gold-convertible ~
~, привязанная к ~/е другой страны ~ (~, priviázannaia k ~/e drugói straný) pegged ~
~, привязанная к доллару (~, priviázannaia k dóllaru) ~, pegged to the dollar
Валютно-финансовый (valiútno-finánsovyi) *adj.* monetary

Валютн/ый (valiútnyi) *adj.*
currency, monetary
  ~/ая "змея" (~/aia zméia) ~
  currency snake
Вариант (variánt) version
  серийный ~ (seríinyi ~)
  production ~
Варрант (varránt) *m.* warrant
  доковый ~ (dókovyi ~) dock ~
  складской ~ (skladskói ~)
  warehouse ~
  складской ~, выданный товарной
  пристанью (skladskói ~, výdannyi
  továrnoi prístan'iu)
  wharfinger's ~
  таможенный ~ (tamózhennyi ~)
  customs ~
  оплачивать ~ (opláchivat' ~) *v.*
  to pay ~ credit
Введение (vvedénie) *n.*
implementation, imposition
  ~ во владение (~ vo vladénie) ~
  vesting
  ~ в эксплуатацию (~ v
  ekspluatátsiiu) commissioning
  ~ закона в силу (~ zakóna v
  sílu) bringing a law into effect
  ~ импортной пошлины (~ importnói
  póshliny) imposition of import
  duties
  ~ квот (~ kvot) imposition of
  quotas
  ~ налога (~ nalóga) ~ imposition
  of a tax
  ~ поправки (~ poprávki) ~
  application of amendments
  ~ пошлины (~ póshliny)
  imposition of a duty
Ввод (vvod) *m.* commissioning
  досрочный ~ (dosróchnyi ~) ~
  ahead of schedule
  срок ~/а в действие (srok ~/a v
  déistvie) ~ period
Вводить (vvodít') *v.* to effect, to
introduce
  ~ в действие (~ v déistvie) to
  bring into effect
  ~ в строй (~ v stroi) to put
  into service
Ввоз (vvoz) *m.* importation
  беспошлинный ~ (bespóshlinnyi ~)
  duty-free ~
  дополнительный ~ (dopolnítel'nyi
  ~) additional ~
  запрет на ~ (zaprét na) import
  embargo
  запрещать ~ (zapreshchát' ~) *v.*
  to ban ~
  контингентирование ~/a
  (kontingentírovanie ~/a)
  imposition of import quotas
  облегчение ~/a (oblegchénie ~/a)
  easing of import quotas
  оформлять ~ товара в порт
  (oformliát' ~ továra v port) to
  obtain import clearance
  получать разрешение на ~
  (poluchát' razreshénie na ~) to
  obtain customs release
  порт беспошлинного ~/a и вывоза
  (port bespóshlinnogo ~/a i
  vývoza) duty free port
  превышение ~/a над вывозом
  (prevyshénie ~/a nad vývozom) ~
  import surplus
  предметы ~/a (predméty ~/a)
  import items
  разрешение на ~ в порт
  (razreshénie na ~ v port) import
  permit into port
  разрешать беспошлинный ~ товара
  (razreshát' bespóshlinnyi ~
  továra) to admit goods duty-free
  свободно для ~/a (svobódno dlia
  ~/a) free for import
  статьи ~/a (stat'í ~/a) articles
  of ~
  стоимость ~/a (stóimost' ~/a)
  valuation of imports
  таможенное свидетельство о
  временном беспошлинном ~/e
  (tamózhennoe svidétel'stvo o
  vrémennom bespóshlinnom ~/e)
  temporary customs certificate
  условно беспошлинный ~ (uslóvno
  bespóshlinnyi ~) conditional
  duty-free ~
  ~ и вывоз (~ i vývoz) imports
  and exports
Ввозить (vvozít') *v.* to import
Ввозной (vvoznói) *adj.* import
Ведомост/ь (védomost') *f.* bill,
journal, list, register, statement
  весовая ~ (vesováia ~)
  weightsheet
  вспомогательная ~
  (vspomogátel'naia ~) supporting
  schedule
  включать в платёжную ~
  (vkliuchát' v platiózhnuiu ~) *v.*
  to put on the payroll
  выписывать ~ ежедневного учёта
  времени (vypísyvat' ~ ezhednév-

novo uchióta vrémeni) *v.* to make out daily timesheets
грузовая ~ (gruzováia ~) cargo sheet
дефектная ~ (deféktnaia ~) damage report
дополнительная ~ (dopolnítel'naia ~) supporting schedule
ежедневная ~ (ezhednévnaia ~) daily timesheet
ежемесячная ~ (ezhenésiachnaia ~) monthly timesheet
инвентарная ~ (inventárnaia ~) inventory sheet
итоговая ~ (itógovaia ~) final report
калькуляционная ~ (kal'kuliatsiónnaia ~) cost sheet
комплектовочная ~ (komplektóvochnaia ~) delivery list
отчётная ~ (otchiótnaia ~) balance sheet
оплачивать платёжную ~ (oplachivát' platiózhnuiu ~) *v.* to meet payroll
передаточная ~ (peredátochnaia ~) transmission list
платёжная ~ (platiózhnaia ~) payroll
проверочная ~ (provérochnaia ~) verification list
рабочая ~ (rabóchaia ~) worksheet
рассылочная ~ (rassýlochnaia ~) mailing list
расценочная ~ (rastsénochnaia ~) price breakdown
расчётная ~ (raschiótnaia ~) paysheet
ремонтная ~ (remóntnaia ~) repair record
сводная ~ (svódnaia ~) consolidated statement
составлять ~ (sostavliát' ~) to draw up a list
согласно прилагаемой ~/и (soglásno prilagáemoi ~/i) pursuant to the enclosed statement
уточнять ~ (utochniát' ~) to verify a statement
~ бухгалтерского учёта (~ bukhgálterskogo uchióta) account bill
~ выгруженного товара (~ vygrúzhennogo továra) outturn report
~ запасных частей (~ zapasnýkh chastéi) parts list
~ запасных частей за отдельную плату (~ zapasnýkh chastéi za otdél'nuiu plátu) optional parts list
~ издержек (~ izdérzhek) cost sheet
~ материалов (~ materiálov) bill of materials
~ монтажных работ (~ montázhnykh rabót) register of construction projects
~ наличия на складе (~ nalíchiia na skláde) stock status report
~ осмотра проверок и ремонта (~ osmótra provérok i remónta) inspection test and repair report
~ работ (~ rabót) bill of work
~ учёта времени, затраченного на погрузку и выгрузку судна (~ uchióta vrémeni, zatráchennogo na pogrúzku i výgruzku sudná) time sheet {shipping}
Ведомств/о (védomstv/o) *n.* administration, department
авиационное ~ (aviatsiónnoe ~) aviation administration
железнодорожное ~ (zheleznodorózhnoe ~) railway administration
налоговое ~ (nalógovoe ~) tax administration
отраслевые ~/a (otraslevýe ~/a) branch departments
патентное ~ (paténtnoe ~) patent administration
таможенное ~ (tamózhennoe ~) customs office
Векселедатель (vékseledátel') *m.* drawer {of a bill}
Векселедержатель (vékselederzhátel') *m.* holder {of a bill}
Векселеобязанный (vékseleobiázannyi) *m.adj.noun* bill debtor
Векселеполучатель (vékselepoluchátel') *m.adj.noun* drawee {of a bill}
Векселепредъявитель (vékselepred"iavítel') *m.* bearer {of a bill}

Вексел/ь (véksel/′) *m.* bill of exchange, note

  авансовый ~ (avánsovyi ~) advance ~

  авалист по ~/ю (avalíst po ~/iu) guarantor of a ~

  аваль ~/я (avál′ ~/ia) bank guarantee of a ~

  авизовать ~ (avizovát′ ~) to advise a ~

  акцепт ~/я (aktsépt ~/ia) acceptance of a ~

  акцептованный ~ (aktseptóvannyi ~) acceptance ~

  акцептованный банком ~ (aktseptóvannyi bánkom ~) bankers acceptance

  акцептованный торговый ~ (aktseptóvannyi torgóvyi ~) trade acceptance ~

  акцептовать ~ (aktseptovát′ ~) to accept a ~

  аннулировать ~ (annulírovat′ ~) to cancel a ~

  банковский ~ (bánkovskii ~) bank bill

  безденежный ~ (bezdénezhnyi ~) accommodation bill

  беспроцентный ~ (besprotséntnyi ~) non-interest bearing note

  бланковый ~ (blánkovyi ~) bill of exhange in blank

  взыскание денег по ~/ю (vzýskanie déneg po ~/iu) collection of a bill

  внешнеторговый ~ (vneshnetorgóvyi ~) usance bill of exchange

  возвращать ~ неоплаченым (vozvrashchát′ ~ neopláchenym) to return a bill unpaid

  возвращать ~ с протестом (vozvrashchát′ ~ s protéstom) to return a bill under protest

  возобновлять ~ (vozobnovliát′ ~) to renew a bill

  временный ~ (vrémennyi ~) interim bill

  встречный ~ (vstréchnyi ~) counter bill

  выдавать ~ (vydavát′ ~) to draw a bill

  выкупать ~ (vykupát′ ~) to meet a bill

  выписывать ~ (vypísyvat′ ~) to issue a bill

  выплата по ~/ю (výplata po ~/iu) negotiation of a bill

  выставлять ~ (vystavliát′ ~) to draw out a bill of exchange

  гарантированный ~ (garantírovannyi ~) guaranteed bill of exchange

  гарант по ~/ю (garánt po ~/iu) guarantor of a bill

  гарантировать оплату ~/я {давать поручительство по ~/ю} (garantírovat′ oplátu ~/ia {davát′ poruchítel′stvo po ~/iu}) to back a bill

  гербовый сбор по ~/ю (gérbovyi sbor po ~/iu) duty stamp on a bill

  дата выпуска ~/я (dáta výpuska ~/ia) date of issue of a bill

  дебетовый ~ (debetóvyi ~) in-clearing bill

  делать на ~/е бланковую переданную надпись (délat′ na ~/e blánkovuiu peredánnuiu nádpis′) endorse a bill in blank

  депонированный ~ (deponírovannyi ~) collateral bill

  держатель ~/я (derzhátel′ ~/ia) holder of a bill

  дисконт {дисконтирование} ~/я (diskónt {diskontírovanie} ~/ia) discounting of a bill

  документированный ~ (dokumentírovannyi ~) documentary bill

  документ об опротестовании ~/я (dokumént ob oprotestovánii ~/ia) protest certificate

  долгосрочный ~ (dolgosróchnyi ~) long-term bill

  должник по ~/ю (dolzhník po ~/iu) bill debtor

  домицилировать ~ (domitsilírovat′ ~) to domicile a bill

  дубликат ~/я (dublikát ~/ia) duplicate of an exchange bill

  домицилированный ~ (domitsilírovannyi ~) domiciled bill

  дружеский ~ (drúzheskii ~) accommodation bill

  заграничный ~ (zagraníchnyi ~) foreign bill

  заложенный ~ (zalózhennyi ~) pledged bill of exchange

издержки по опротестованию ~/я
(izdérzhki po oprotestovániiu
~/ia) expenses for protesting a
bill
именной ~ (imennói ~) inscribed,
registered bill
индоссированный ~
(indossírovannyi ~) endorsed
bill
индоссировать ~ (indossírovat'
~) to endorse a bill
индоссировать ~ в пользу
(indossírovat' ~ v pól'zu) to
endorse a bill to ...
индоссант по ~/ю (indossánt po
~/iu) backer of a bill
инкассирование ~/я
(inkassírovanie ~/ia) collection
of a bill
инкассировать ~ (inkassírovat'
~) to collect a bill
иностранный ~ (inostránnyi ~)
outland bill
иск по ~/ю (isk po ~/iu) legal
action arising from a bill
казначейские ~/я (kaznachéiskie
~/ia) treasury bills
книга ~/ей (kníga ~/ei) bill
book
коммерческий ~ (kommércheskii ~)
commercial bill
копия ~/я (kópiia ~/ia) copy of
a bill
краткосрочный ~ (kratkosróchnyi
~) short-term bill
краткосрочный курс ~/я
(kratkosróchnyi kurs ~/ia)
short-term bill exchange rate
кредитор по ~/ю (kreditór po
~/iu) bill creditor
купленный ~ (kúplennyi ~)
purchased paper
курс ~/я (kurs ~/ia) bill
exchange rate
курс ~/я, указанный на обороте
(kurs ~/ia, ukázannyi na
oboróte) exchange as per
endorsement
лицо, выписывающее ~ (litsó,
vypisyváiushchee ~) drawer of a
bill
льготные дни для уплаты по ~/ю
(l'gótnye dni dlia upláty po
~/iu) grace period {days} on a
bill
местный ~ (méstnyi ~) local bill

могущий быть учтённым в банке ~
(mogúshchii byt' uchtiónnym v
bánke ~) discountable bill
надпись на ~/е (nádpis' na ~/e)
endorsement on a bill
направлять ~ для акцепта
(napravliát' ~ dlia aktsépta) to
submit a bill for acceptance
негоциировать ~ (negotsiírovat'
~) to negotiate a bill
недокументированный ~
(nedokumentírovannyi ~) clean
bill of exchange
не могущий быть переданным ~ (ne
mogúshchii byt' péredannym ~)
non-negotiable bill
не оплачивать ~ (ne opláchivat'
~) to dishonor a bill
необеспеченный ~
(neobespéchennyi ~) unsecured
bill
неоплаченный ~ (neopláchennyi ~)
outstanding bill
неоплата ~/я (neopláta ~/ia)
failure to honor a bill
обеспеченный ~ (obespéchennyi ~)
secured bill
оборотный ~ (oborótnyi ~)
negotiable bill
обратный ~ (obrátnyi ~) bill
with recourse
обратный переводной ~ (obrátnyi
perevodnói ~) return draft
обращение ~/ей (obrashchénie
~/ei) circulation of bills
обязательства по ~/ям
(obiazátel'stva po ~/iam)
liabilities on bills
оплачивать ~ (opláchivat' ~) to
honor a bill
оплачивать ~ в срок (opláchivat'
~ v srok) to meet due date on a
bill
операции с ~/ями (operátsii s
~/iámi) bill transactions
оплата ~/я (opláta ~/ia)
settlement of a bill
оплаченный ~ (opláchennyi ~)
paid bill
оплачиваемый в местной валюте ~
(oplachiváemyi v méstnoi valiúte
~) inland bill
опротестованный ~
(oprotestóvannyi ~) protested
bill

опротестовывать ~
(oprotestóvyvat' ~) to protest a
bill
ордерный ~ (órdernyi ~) order
bill
отзывать ~ (otzyvát' ~) to
withdraw a bill
отказ от акцепта ~/я (otkáz ot
aktsépta ~/ia) refusal of
acceptance of a bill
отказ от протеста ~/я (otkáz ot
protésta ~/ia) waiver of demand
on a bill
отказываться акцептовать ~
(otkázyvat'sia aktseptovát' ~)
to dishonor a bill by non-
acceptance
первоклассный ~ (pérvoklássnyi
~) first class paper
первоклассный ~, акцептованный
банком (pérvoklássnyi ~,
aktseptóvannyi bánkom) prime
banker's acceptance
переводной ~ (perevódnoi ~)
transfer note
передаваемый ~ (peredaváemyi ~)
negotiable bill
переуступать ~ (pereustupát' ~)
to negotiate a bill
передавать ~ надписью
(peredavát' ~ nádpis'iu) to
endorse a bill
передавать ~ на инкассо
(peredavát' ~ na inkásso) to
remit a bill for collection
передача ~/я (peredácha ~/ia)
transfer of a bill
переучтённый ~ (pereuchtiónnyi
~) rediscounted bill
переучёт ~/я (pereuchiót ~/ia)
rediscount of a bill
переучитывать ~ (pereuchítyvat'
~) to rediscount a bill
платить ~/ями (platít' ~/iámi)
to pay by notes
погашать ~ (pogashát' ~) to
retire a bill
погашенный ~ (pogáshennyi ~)
retired bill
покрыты ~ (pokrýtyi ~) honored
bill
подделывать ~ (poddélyvat' ~) to
forge a bill
подпись на ~/e (pódpis' na ~/e)
signature on a bill

получение денег по ~/ю
(poluchénie déneg po ~/iu)
collection on a bill
портфель ~/ей (portfél' ~/ei)
portfolio of bills
поручитель по ~/ю (poruchítel'
po ~/iu) surety on a bill
поручительство по ~/ю
(poruchítel'stvo po ~/iu) avál,
backing for a bill
поддельный ~ (poddél'nyi ~)
counterfeit bill
подложный ~ (podlózhnyi ~)
forged bill
подтоварный ~ (podtovárnyi ~)
commodity paper
получать деньги по ~/ю
(poluchát' dén'gi po ~/iu) to
collect on a bill
право выписки ~/ей (právo
výpiski ~/ei) drawing
authorization
предварительный ~
(predvarítel'nyi ~) provisional
bill
предъявительский ~
(pred"iavítel'skii ~) demand
note
предъявитель ~/я (pred"iavítel'
~/ia) bearer of a bill
предъявление ~/я (pred"iavlénie
~/ia) presentation of a bill
предъявлять ~ для оплаты
(pred"iavliát' ~ dlia opláty) to
present a bill for payment
предъявлять ~ для протеста
(pred"iavliát' ~ dlia protésta)
to present a bill for protest
предъявлять ~ к учёту
(pred"iavliát' ~ k uchiótu) to
present a bill for discount
приемлемый для переучёта ~
(priémlemyi dlia pereuchióta ~)
discountable bill
принимать ~ к учёту (prinimát' ~
k uchiótu) to discount a bill
продавать ~ (prodavát' ~) to
sell a bill
продлевать ~ (prodlevát' ~) to
extend a bill
производить акцепт ~/я
(proizvodít' aktsépt ~/ia) to
effect acceptance of a bill
производить учёт ~/я
(proizvodít' uchiót ~/ia) to
take a bill on discount

пролонгированный ~
(prolongírovannyi ~) extended
note
пролонгация ~/я (prolongátsiia
~/ia) prolongation of a bill
пролонгировать ~ (prolongírovat'
~) to prolong a bill
просроченный ~ (prosróchennyi ~)
past due bill
просрочивать ~ (prosróchivat' ~)
to have a bill expired
протестовать по поводу неоплаты
~/я (protestovát' po póvodu
neopláty ~/ia) to protest a bill
for dishonor
простой ~ (prostói ~) promissory
note
простой, краткосрочный ~
(prostói, kratkosróchnyi ~)
short-term note
простой ~, с двумя или более
подписями (prostói ~, s dvúmia
íli bólee pódpisiami) joint note
пускать ~ в обращение (puskát' ~
v obrashchénie) to negotiate a
bill
пускать в обращение с оборотом
(puskát' v obrashchénie s
oborótom) to negotiate a bill
with recourse
процентный ~ (protséntnyi ~)
interest bearing note
расходы по обратному переводу
~/я (raskhódy po obrátnomu
perevódu ~/ia) redraft charges
сдавать ~ на учёт (sdavát' ~ na
uchiót) to present a bill for
discount
срок ~/я (srok ~/ia) maturity
term of a note
срок ~/я, установленный обычаем
(srok ~/ia, ustanóvlennyi
obýchaem) usance of a bill
срок платежа по ~/ю (srok
platezhá po ~/iu) due date of a
bill
срочный по предъявлении ~
(sróchnyi po pred"iavlénii ~)
sight note
срочный ~, через ...дней после
предъявления (sróchnyi ~, chérez
... dnei pósle pred"iavléniia)
bill at ... day's sight
сумма ~/я (súmma ~/ia) amount of
a bill

сумма ~/я, обратного переводного
(súmma ~/ia, obrátnogo
perevódnogo) reexchange amount
счёт ~/ей (schiót ~/ei) bills
account
торговый ~ (torgóvyi ~) trade
paper
торговля ~/ями (torgóvlia
~/iami) note brokerage
трассированный банком на другой
банк ~ (trassírovannyi bánkom na
drugói bank ~) bank draft
трёхмесячный ~ (triókhmesiachnyi
~) three month's paper
учитывать ~ в банке (uchítyvat'
~ v bánke) to negotiate a bank
bill
учтённый ~ (uchtiónnyi ~)
discounted bill
учёт ~/я (uchiót ~/ia)
discounting of a bill
учёт ~/в банке (uchiót ~/v
bánke) bank discounting
фиктивный ~ (fiktívnyi ~)
fictitious bill
финансовый ~ (finánsovyi ~)
finance bill
форма ~/я (fórma ~/ia) form of a
bill
экземпляр ~/я (ekzempliár ~/ia)
copy of a bill
экземпляр ~/я, второй
(ekzempliár ~/ia, vtorói) second
bill of exchange
экземпляр ~/я, первый
(ekzempliár ~/ia, pérvyi) first
bill of exchange
~, акцептованный без покрытия
(~, aktseptóvannyi bez
pokrýtiia) uncovered acceptance
~, выписанный в инвалюте (~,
výpisannyi v ínvaliute) currency
bill
~, выписанный в комплекте (~,
výpisannyi v komplékte) bill
drawn in a set
~, выписанный до отправления
груза (~, výpisannyi do
otpravléniia grúza) advance bill
~, выставленный на первоклассный
банк (~, vystávlennyi na
pérvoklássnyi bank) bill drawn
on a major bank
~ для инкасирования (~ dlia
inkasírovaniia) bill for
collection

~ для сальдирования (~ dlia sal'dírovaniia) balance bill
~ к оплате (~ k opláte) note payable
~/я к получению (~/ia k poluchéniiu) notes receivable
~ на инкассо (~ na inkásso) bill for collection
~ на предъявителя (~ na pred"iavítelia) bearer note
~ на срок (~ na srok) term note
~ на срок, установленный торговым обычаем (~ na srok, ustanóvlennyi torgóvym obýchaem) bill at usance
~/я, подлежащие взысканию (~/ia, podlezháshchie vzýskaniiu) bills receiveable
~ с двумя подписями (~ s dvúmia pódpisiami) two name paper
~ с нотариальной отметкой об отказе трассата от его акцептования (~ s notariál'noi otmétkoi ob otkáze trassáta ot ego aktseptovániia) noted bill
~ собственному приказу (~ sóbstvennomu prikázu) bill to order {to oneself}
~ с оплатой по предъявлении (~ s oplátoi po pred"iavlénii) sight bill
~ с оплатой после предъявления (~ s oplátoi pósle pred"iavléniia) after sight bill
~ с передаточной надписью (~ s peredátochnoi nádpis'iu) bill endorsed over
~ чужому приказу (~ chuzhómu prikázu) bill to the order of a third party
~ просрочен (~ prosróchen) the bill is overdue
Вексельный (véksel'nyi) adj. bill
Вектор (véktor) m. vector
Величин/а (velichin/á) f. size
намеченная ~ (naméchennaia ~) target figure
натуральная ~ (naturál'naia ~) actual ~
средняя ~ (srédniaia ~) mean quantity
средней ~/ы (srédnei ~/y) middle ~
определять ~/у (opredeliát' ~/u) to ~ up
~ скидки (~ skídki) rate of markdown

Верёвк/а (verióvk/a) f. cord, rope
пеньковая ~ (pen'kóvaia ~) hemp, rope
шнуровочная ~ (shnuróvochnaia ~) packing cord
крепить ~/ой (krepít' ~/oi) to secure the lashings
связывать ~/ой (sviázyvat' ~/oi) to lash together
~ для крепления груза (~ dlia krepléniia grúza) cargo lashing
~ для подвески (~ dlia podvéski) pendant cord
~ для подъёма груза (~ dlia pod"ióma grúza) sling
Верфь (verf') f. dockyard
Верх (verkh) m. top, "this end up"
положить ~ (polozhít' ~) to put on the top
Верхний (vérkhnii) adj. upper
Вес (ves) m. weight
действительный ~ тары (deistvítel'nyi ~ táry) actual tare
допустимый ~ (dopustímyi ~) allowable ~
допуск по ~/у (dópusk po ~/u) ~ allowance
доставленный ~ (dostávlennyi ~) landed ~
единица ~/а (edinítsa ~/a) unit of ~
живой ~ (zhivói ~) live ~
заданный ~ (zádannyi ~) specified ~
заявлять ~ (zaiavliát' ~) to declare the ~
избыточный ~ (izbýtochnyi ~) excess ~
излишек ~/а (izlíshek ~/a) excess ~
коносаментный ~ (konosaméntnyi ~) bill of lading ~
контрольный ~ (kontról'nyi ~) check ~
корректировать ~ (korrektírovat' ~) to adjust the ~
легальный ~ нетто (legál'nyi ~ nétto) legal net ~
максимальный ~ (maksimál'nyi ~) maximum ~
на основе купленного ~/а (na osnóve kúplennogo ~/a) on a purchased ~ basis
на основе сухого ~/а (na osnóve sukhógo ~/a) on a dry ~ basis
насыпной ~ (nasypnói ~) bulk ~

недостающий ~ (nedostaiúshchii ~) under ~
недостача в ~/е (nedostácha v ~/e) short ~
несоответствие по ~/у (nesootvétstvie po ~/u) discrepancy in ~
нестандартный ~ (nestandártnyi ~) non-standard ~ {short weighted}
нормальный ~ (normál'nyi ~) standard ~
общий ~ (óbshchii ~) gross ~
объёмный ~ (ob"iómnyi ~) volume ~
ограничение ~/а (ogranichénie ~/a) ~ limit
определять ~ (opredeliát'~) to weigh
ориентировочный ~ (orientiróvochnyi ~) approximate ~
отгруженный ~ (otgrúzhennyi ~) shipped ~
отгрузочный ~ (otgrúzochnyi ~) ~ to be shipped
отметка о ~/е (otmétka o ~/e) indication of ~
оценочный ~ (otsénochnyi ~) estimated ~
первоначальный ~ (pervonachál'nyi ~) starting ~
полезный ~ (poléznyi ~) service load
порожный ~ (porózhnyi ~) empty tare
потеря ~/а (potéria ~/a) short ~
правила определения ~/а тары (právila opredeléniia ~/a táry) taring regulations
превышение ~/а (prevyshénie ~/a) excess ~
превосходить в ~/е (prevoskhodít' v ~/e) to overbalance
предельный ~ (predél'nyi ~) maximum ~ limit
приблизительный ~ (priblizítel'nyi ~) approximate ~
проверка ~/а (provérka ~/a) ~ checking
проверять ~ (proveriát' ~) to check the ~
продажный ~ (prodázhnyi ~) marketable ~

расчётный ~ (raschiótnyi ~) calculated ~
распределять ~ (raspredeliát' ~) to distribute the ~
сертификат ~/а (sertifikát ~/a) certificate of ~
скидка с ~/а на тару (skídka s ~/a na táru) tare allowance
собственный ~ (sóbstvennyi ~) sole ~
средний ~ (srédnii ~) average ~
стандартный ~ (standártnyi ~) standard ~
сухой ~ (sukhói ~) dry ~
счёт выгруженного ~/а (schiót vygrúzhennogo ~/a) ship's outturn tally
тарифный ~ (tarífnyi ~) tariff ~
убойный ~ (ubóinyi ~) dead ~
убыль в ~/е (ubýl' v ~/e) short delivery
увеличение ~/а (uvelichénie ~/a) increase in ~
удельный ~ (udél'nyi ~) specific ~
уменьшение в ~/е (umen'shénie v ~/e) decrease in ~
фактический ~ (faktícheskii ~) actual ~
фактический ~ брутто (faktícheskii ~ brútto) actual gross ~
фактурный ~ (faktúrnyi ~) invoice ~
фактурный ~ тары (faktúrnyi ~ táry) invoice tare
чистый ~ (chístyi ~) net ~
штемпель о ~/е (shtémpel' o ~/e) ~ stamp
эксплуатационный ~ (ekspluatatsiónnyi ~) ~ in running order
~ багажа (~ bagazhá) baggage ~
~ брутто (~ brútto) gross ~
~ брутто за нетто (~ brútto za nétto) gross ~ for net
~ груза (~ grúza) cargo ~
~ до отгрузки (~ do otgrúzki) pre-shipment ~
~ единицы одного изделия (~ edinítsy odnogó izdéliia) unit ~
~ нетто (~ nétto) net ~
~, подлежащий оплате (~, podlezháshchii opláte) chargeable ~
~ при выгрузке (~ pri výgruzke) landed ~

~ при погрузке (~ pri pogrúzke) shipped ~
~ с упаковкой (~ s upakóvkoi) packed ~
~ тары (~ táry) tare
~ тары превышающий нормальный (~ táry prevysháiushchii normál'nyi) super tare
~ тары установленный обычаем (~ táry ustanóvlennyi obýchaem) customary tare
~ товара (~ továra) weight of goods
~ упаковки (~ upakóvki) weight of packing
~ ящика (~ iáshchika) case weight
Весовой (vesovói) *adj.* weight
Весовщик (vesovshchík) *m.* weigher
официальный ~ (ofitsiál'nyi ~) official ~
присяжный ~ (prisiázhnyi ~) sworn ~
Вес/ы (ves/ý) *pl.* scales
бункерные ~ (búnkernye ~) hopper ~
десятичные ~ (desiatíchnye ~) decimal balance ~
испытательные ~ (ispytátel'nye ~) testing ~
мостовые ~ (mostovýe ~) weighbridge
точные ~ (tóchnye ~) precision ~
электронные ~ (elektrónnye ~) electronic ~
чашка ~/ов (cháshka ~/ov) ~ pan
~ для автоматической упаковки в мешки (~ dlia avtomatícheskoi upakóvki v meshkí) bagging ~
Весы-автомат (vesý-avtomát) *pl.* automatic scales
Ветеринарный (veterinárnyi) *adj.* veterinary
Вето (véto) *n.* veto
право ~ (právo ~) right of ~
налагать ~ (nalagát' ~) to ~
Вещество (veshchestvó) *n.* matter, substance
серое ~ (séroe ~) grey matter
Вещь (veshch') *f.* thing
Взаимно (vzaímno) *adv.* mutually, reciprocally
решать ~ (reshát' ~) to decide mutually
Взаимност/ь (vzaímnost/') *f.* reciprocity

договор на основе ~/и (dogovór na osnóve ~/i) reciprocal treaty
соглашение на основе ~/и (soglashénie na osnóve ~/i) reciprocal agreement
торговля на основе ~/и (torgóvlia na osnóve ~/i) reciprocal trade
Взаимный (vzaímnyi) *adj.* reciprocal
Взаимовыгодный (vzaimovýgodnyi) *adj.* mutually beneficial
Взаимодействие (vzaimodéistvie) *n.* cooperation, interaction
инвестиционное ~ (investitsiónnoe ~) investment interaction
тесное ~ (tésnoe ~) close cooperation
хозяйственное ~ (khoziáistvennoe ~) economic cooperation
~ между странами (~ mézhdu stranámi) cooperation between nations
~ спроса и предложения (~ sprósa i predlozhéniia) interaction of supply and demand
Взаимодействовать (vzaimodéistvovat') *v.* to cooperate, to interact
Взаимозаменяемость (vzaimozameniáemost') *f.* interchangeability
Взаимозаменяемый (vzaimozameniáemyi) *adj.* interchangeable
Взаимоотношения (vzaimootnoshéniia) *pl.* mutual relations
договорные ~ (dogovórnye ~) contractual relations
межгосударственные ~ (mezhgosudárstvennye ~) interstate relations
полезные ~ (poléznye ~) productive relations
торговые ~ (torgóvye ~) trade relations
юридические ~ (iuridícheskie ~) legal relations
~ сторон (~ storón) relations between the parties
Взаимопоставляемый (vzaimopostavliáemyi) *adj.* mutually provided
Взаимоприемлем/ый (vzaimopriémlem/yi) *adj.* mutually acceptable

на ~/ой основе (na ~/oi osnóve)
on a mutually acceptable basis
Взаимосогласованный
(vzaimosoglasóvannyi) *adj.* mutually
agreed
Взаймы (vzaimý) *adv.* as a loan
  брать ~ (brat' ~) to borrow
  давать ~ (davát' ~) to lend
Взвешивани/e (vzveshiváni/e) *n.*
weighing
  контрольное ~ (kontról'noe ~)
  test ~
  оборудование для ~/я
  (oborúdovanie dlia ~/ia) ~
  equipment
  плата за ~ (pláta za ~) weighage
  плата за ~ на мостовых весах
  (pláta za ~ na mostovýkh vesákh)
  weighbridge charges
  прибор для ~/я (pribór dlia
  ~/ia) ~ device
  справка о ~/и (správka o ~/i)
  weight note
  производить ~ (proizvodít' ~) to
  weigh
  производить контрольное ~
  (proizvodít' kontról'noe ~) to
  test weigh
Взвешивать (vzvéshivat') *v.* to
weigh
  в пустом виде ~ (v pustóm víde
  ~) to ~ empty
  вторично ~ (vtoríchno ~) to
  reweigh
  заново ~ (zánovo ~) ~ again
Взвинчивать (vzvínchivat') *v.* to
inflate
  ~ курсы акций (~ kúrsy áktsii) ~
  rates of shares
  ~ цены (~ tsény) ~ prices
Вздорожание (vzdorozhánie) *n.* price
increases
Вздорожать (vzdorozhát') *v.* to
increase in price
Взимание (vzimánie) *n.* levy, charge
  ~ аренды (~ aréndy) rental fee
  ~ налогов (~ nalógov) levying of
  taxes
  ~ платы (~ pláty) collection
  ~ пошлин (~ póshlin) imposting
  of duties
  ~ процентов (~ protséntov)
  collection of interest
  ~ роялти (~ róialti) charging of
  royalties
  ~ сборов (~ sbórov) imposition
  of fees

Взимать (vzimát') *v.* to levy, to
impose
Взнос (vznos) *m.* contribution,
deposit, installment
  авансовый ~ (avánsovyi ~)
  advance installment
  аварийный, страховой ~
  (avaríinyi, strakhovói ~)
  average payment
  арбитражный ~ (arbitrázhnyi ~)
  arbitration fee
  возвращённый страховой ~
  (vozvrashchiónnyi strakhovói ~)
  premium refund
  возмещаемый ~ (vozmeshcháemyi ~)
  refundable deposit
  вступительный ~ (vstupítel'nyi
  ~) admission fee
  выплачивать ~/ами (vypláchivat'
  ~/ami) to pay by installment
  годовой ~ (godovói ~) annual fee
  делать ~ (délat' ~) to make a
  contribution
  денежные и материальные ~/ы
  (dénezhnye i materiál'nye ~/y)
  monetary and material contributions
  денежные ~ (dénezhnye ~) cash
  deposits
  добровольный ~ (dobrovól'nyi ~)
  voluntary contribution
  долевой ~ (dolevói ~)
  contribution
  долевой ~ по общей аварии
  (dolevói ~ po óbshchei avárii)
  general average contribution
  дополнительный ~ (dopolnítel'nyi
  ~) additional premium
  единовременный ~ (edinovrémennyi
  ~) lumpsum contribution
  единовременный страховой ~
  (edinovrémennyi strakhovói ~)
  single premium
  ежегодный ~ (ezhegódnyi ~)
  annuity, annual installment
  ежегодный патентный ~
  (ezhegódnyi paténtnyi ~) patent
  annuity
  ежемесячный ~ (ezhemésiachnyi ~)
  monthly installment
  ежемесячными ~/ами
  (ezhemésiachnymi ~/ami) by
  monthly installments
  еженедельный ~ (ezhenedél'nyi ~)
  weekly installment

еженедельными ~/ами
(ezhenedél'nymi ~/ami) by weekly
installments
квартальный ~ (kvartál'nyi ~)
quarterly installment
минимальный ~ (minimál'nyi ~)
minimum installment
обязательный ~ (obiazátel'nyi ~)
mandatory contribution
очередной ~ (ocherednói ~) next
installment
очередной страховой ~
(ocherednói strakhovói ~)
installment premium
освобождение от уплаты ~/ов
(osvobozhdénie ot upláty ~/ov)
exemption from installment
payments
паевой ~ (paevói ~) share of
contribution
параллельный ~ (parallél'nyi ~)
counterpart contribution
паушальный ~ (paushál'nyi ~)
lumpsum payment
первоначальный ~
(pervonachál'nyi ~) initial
installment, deposit
подлежать оплате ежегодными
~/ами (podlezhát' opláte
ezhegódnymi ~/ami) to be payable
in annual installments
полугодовой ~ (polugodovói ~)
semi-annual installment
последний ~ (poslédnii ~) last
installment
последующий ~ (posléduiushchii
~) subsequent installment
предварительный ~
(predvarítel'nyi ~) payment on
account
производить ~ (proizvodít' ~) to
make a contribution
пропорциональный ~
(proportsionál'nyi ~)
proportional contribution
просроченный ~ (prosróchennyi ~)
overdue installment
прямой ~ (priamói ~) direct
payment
равные ~/ы (rávnye ~/y) equal
installments
равными ~/ами (rávnymi ~/ami) by
equal installments, in equal
installments
регистрационный ~
(registratsiónnyi ~)
registration fee

страховой ~ (strakhovói ~)
insurance premium
страховой ~ в постоянном размере
~ (strakhovói ~ v postoiánnom
razmére ~) fixed premium
средний страховой ~ (srédnii
strakhovói ~) average premium
требование гарантийного ~/а
(trébovanie garantíinogo ~/a)
margin call
уплаченный страховой ~
(upláchennyi strakhovói ~)
premium paid
уплачиваемый периодически ~
(uplachiváemyi periodícheski ~)
annuity payment
частичный ~ (chastíchnyi ~)
partial payment
членский ~ (chlénskii ~)
membership fee
~ /ы в бюджет (~ /y v biudzhét)
budget contributions
~ в...% (~ v...) deposit of ...%
~ в счёт погашения долга (~ v
schiót pogashéniia dólga)
installment against debt
~ в уставный фонд (~ v ustávnyi
fond) contribution to the
charter fund, founding
contribution
~ наличными деньгами (~
nalíchnymi den'gámi) cash
deposit
~ по общей аварии (~ po óbshchei
avárii) general average deposit
Взыскани/е (vzyskáni/e) collection,
penalty
наложение ~/я (nalozhénie ~/ia)
imposition of a fine, penalty
наложить ~ (nalozhít' ~) to
impose a fine, penalty
принудительное ~ (prinudítel'noe
~) enforced recovery
подвергнуть ~/ю (podvérgnut'
~/iu) to incur a penalty
подлежать ~/ю (podlezhát' ~/iu)
to be subject to a judgment
производить ~ (proizvodít' ~) to
recover or exact a penalty
подлежащий ~/ю (podlezháshchii
~/iu) callable
размер ~/я (razmér ~/ia) measure
of recovery
обращать ~ на (obrashchát' ~ na)
to make a claim to

обращать ~ на обеспечение
(obrashchát' ~ na obespechénie)
to enforce a security interest
~ демерреджа (~ démerredzha)
demurrage
~ денег по векселю (~ déneg po
vékseliu) collection of a bill
~ долгов (~ dolgóv) debt
collection
~ издержек (~ izdérzhek) cost
recovery
~ на имущество (~ na
imúshchestvo) claim to property
~ налогов (~ nalógov) tax
collection
~ неустойки (~ neustóiki)
recovery of damages
~ пени (~ péni) imposition of a
fine
~ пошлин (~ póshlin) imposition
of duties
~ суммы (~ súmmy) recovery of a
sum
~ убытков (~ ubýtkov) recovery
of {legal} damages
~ штрафа (~ shtráfa) collection
of a fine
Взятк/а (vziátk/a) f. bribe
брать ~/у (brat' ~/u) to take a
bribe
давать ~/у (davát' ~/u) to bribe
осудить за ~/у (osudít' za ~/u)
to convict for bribery
предлагать ~/у (predlagát' ~/u)
to offer a bribe
Вид (vid) m. kind, sort, condition
в ~/е аванса (v ~/e avánsa) by
way of an advance
в вещественном ~/е (v
veshchéstvennom ~/e) in kind
в ~/е гарантии (v ~/e garántii)
as a guarantee against
в ~/е компенсации (v ~/e
kompensátsii) as an offset
against
в натуральном ~/е (v naturál'nom
~/e) in kind
в нетоварном ~/е (v netovárnom
~/e) in an un-marketable
condition
в письменном ~/е (v pís'mennom
~/e) in writing
в разобранном ~/е (v razóbrannom
~/e) non-assembled
в товарном ~/е (v továrnom ~/e)
in marketable condition

товарный ~ (továrnyi ~)
marketable condition
~ товара (~ továra) nature of
goods
~ транспорта (~ tránsporta)
mode, means of transport
~ транспортировки (~
transportiróvki) mode of
conveyance
Виз/а (víz/a) f. visa
ввозная ~ (vvoznáia ~) import ~
вывозная ~ (vyvoznáia ~) export
~
выдача ~/ы (výdacha ~/y)
issuance of a ~
выдавать ~/у (vydavát' ~/u) to
issue a ~
въездная ~ (v"ezdnáia ~) entry ~
выездная ~ (vyezdnáia ~) exit ~
деловая ~ (delováia ~) business
~
заявление на выдачу ~/ы
{обращение за ~/ой} (zaiavlénie
na výdachu ~/y {obrashchénie za
~/oi}) ~ application
консульская ~ (kónsul'skaia ~)
consular ~
многократная ~ (mnogokrátnaia ~)
multiple entry ~
обыкновенная ~ (obyknovénnaia ~)
ordinary ~
отдел ~ (otdél ~/) ~ department
отказ в ~/е (otkáz v ~/e)
refusal of a ~
отказать в выдаче ~/ы (otkazát'
v výdache ~/y) to refuse to
grant a ~
постоянная ~ (postoiánnaia ~)
permanent ~
подтверждение ~/ы
(podtverzhdénie ~/y)
confirmation of a ~
поддерживать просьбу о
предоставлении ~/ы
(poddérzhivat' prós'bu o
predostavlénii ~/y) to support a
~ application
поддерживать ~/у (poddérzhivat'
~/u) to support a ~
получать ~/у на паспорт
(poluchát' ~/u na pásport) to
have one's passport viséd
посылать паспорт на ~/у
(posylát' pásport na ~/u) to
submit a passport for ~ stamp
продлевать ~/у (prodlevát' ~/u)
to extend a ~

проставлять ~/у в паспорте (prostavliát' ~/u v pásporte) to visé
привилегированная ~ (privilegírovannaia ~) exempt ~
продление ~/ы (prodlénie ~/y) extension of a ~
срок действия ~/ы (srok déistviia ~/y) term of a visa
транзитная ~ (tránzitnaia ~) transit ~
туристическая ~ (turistícheskaia ~) tourist ~
~ для деловой поездки (~ dlia delovói poézdki) business ~
Виза-приглашение (víza-priglashénie) f. visa-invitation
Визировать (vizírovat') v. to issue a ~
Визит (vizít) m. visit
деловой ~ (delovói ~) business ~
длительной ~ (dlítel'noi ~) extended ~
договорить о ~/е (dogovorít' о ~/e) to arrange a ~
дружеской ~ (drúzheskoi ~) a friendly ~
ежегодной ~ (ezhegódnoi ~) an annual ~
запланировать ~ (zaplanírovat' ~) to plan a ~
завершение ~/а (zavershénie ~/a) conclusion of a ~
короткий ~ (korótkii ~) short ~
наносить ~ (nanosít' ~) to pay a call
наносить ответный ~ (nanosít' otvétnyi ~) to return a ~
неудачный ~ (neudáchnyi ~) unsuccessful ~
ознакомительный ~ (oznakomítel'nyi ~) fact-finding mission
ответный ~ (otvétnyi ~) return ~
отсрочка ~/а (otsróchka ~/a) postponement of a ~
откладывать ~ (otkládyvat' ~) to put off a ~
отменять ~ (otmeniát' ~) to cancel a ~
официальный ~ (ofitsiál'nyi ~) official ~
очередной ~ (ocherednói ~) regular ~
последующий ~ (posléduiushchii ~) followup ~

подготовить программу ~/а (podgotóvit' prográmmu ~/a) to prepare an itinerary for a ~
предложенный ~ (predlózhennyi ~) proposed ~
предстоящий ~ (predstoiáshchii ~) upcoming ~
программа ~/а (prográmma ~/a) itinerary for a ~
регулярные ~/ы (reguliárnye ~/y) regular ~s
результаты ~/а (rezul'táty ~/a) the outcome of a ~
ускорять ~ (uskoriát' ~) to expedite a ~
частный ~ (chástnyi ~) private ~
цель ~/а (tsel' ~/a) the aim of a ~
~ вежливости (~ vézhlivosti) courtesy call
~ на место строительства (~ na mésto stroítel'stva) construction site ~
Виноватый (vinovátyi) adj. guilty
Виновник (vinóvnik) m. responsible party
Витрин/а (vitrín/a) f. shop window
выставочная ~ (výstavochnaia ~) display stand
оформление ~/ы (oformlénie ~/y) window dressing
экспозиция ~/у (ekspozítsiia ~/y) window display
оформлять ~/у (oformliát' ~/u) to set up a shop window
Вице-консул (vítse-kónsul) m. vice-consul
Вклад (vklad) m. contribution, deposit
владелец ~/а (vladélets ~/a) depositor
банковский ~ (bánkovskii ~) bank deposit
беспроцентный ~ (besprotséntnyi ~) non-interest bearing deposit
бессрочный ~ (bessróchnyi ~) demand deposit
благотворительный ~ (blagotvorítel'nyi ~) charitable contribution
важный ~ (vázhnyi ~) important contribution
вносить ~ (vnosít' ~) to make a deposit
возвратный ~ (vozvrátnyi ~) refundable deposit

денежный ~ (dénezhnyi ~) cash deposit
делать ~ (délat' ~) to make a contribution
добровольный ~ (dobrovól'nyi ~) voluntary contribution
долгосрочный ~ (dolgosróchnyi ~) long term deposit
долларовые ~/ы (dóllarovye ~/y) dollar denominated deposits
дополнительный ~ (dopolnítel'nyi ~) additional contribution
значительный ~ (znachítel'nyi ~) significant contribution
изъятие ~ (iz"iátie ~) withdrawal of a deposit
иметь на ~/е (imét' na ~/e) to have on deposit
квитанция банка о принятии ~/а (kvitántsiia bánka o priniátii ~/a) bank deposit receipt
краткосрочный ~ (kratkosróchnyi ~) short-term deposit
крупный ~ (krúpnyi ~) major contribution
натурально-вещественный ~ (naturál'no-véshchestvennyi ~) material contribution
остаток на ~/е (ostátok na ~/e) balance on deposit
отзывать ~ (otzyvát' ~) to recall a contribution
оценка ~/ов (otsénka ~/ov) valuation of contributions
первоначальный ~ (pervonachál'nyi ~) initial deposit
приём ~/ов (priióm ~/ov) acceptance of deposits
принимать ~ (prinimát' ~) to accept a deposit
процентный ~ (protséntnyi ~) interest bearing deposit
проценты по ~/ам (protsénty po ~/am) interest on deposits
проценты по бессрочному ~/у (protsénty po bessróchnomu ~/u) service charge on a demand deposit account
размер процента по ~ам (razmér protsénta po ~am) interest rate on deposits
сберегательный ~ (sberegátel'nyi ~) savings deposit
специальный ~ (spetsiál'nyi ~) specific deposit
срочный ~ (sróchnyi ~) fixed period deposit
ставка процента по ~/ам (stávka protsénta po ~/am) interest rate on deposit
тайна ~/ов (táina ~/ov) privacy of deposits
увеличение ~/ов (uvelichénie ~/ov) increase of deposits
~ в уставный фонд (~ v ustávnyi fond) contribution to the charter fund
~ до востребования (~ do vostrébovaniia) demand deposit
~ капитала (~ kapitála) investment of capital
~ на срок (~ na srok) fixed term deposit
~ на текущий счёт (~ na tekúshchii schiot) on call deposit
~ с длительным уведомлением (~ s dlítel'nym uvedomléniem) deposit at long notice
~ с краткосрочным уведомлением (~ s kratkosróchnym uvedomléniem) deposit at short notice
~ с уведомлением (~ s uvedomléniem) deposit at notice
Вкладной (vkladnói) adj. deposit
Вкладчик (vkládchik) m. depositor
иностранный ~ (inostránnyi ~) foreign investor
крупный ~ (krúpnyi ~) major investor
Вкладывать (vkládyvat') v. to enclose, to invest
Влагонепроницаемый (vlagonepronitsáemyi) adj. waterproof
Влагостойкий (vlagostóikii) adj. water resistant
Владел/ец (vladél/ets) m. holder, owner, proprietor
быть ~/ьцем чартер-партии (byt' ~/'tsem chárter-pártii) to hold a charter party
добросовестный ~ (dobrosóvestnyi ~) holder in good faith
единоличный ~ (edinolíchnyi ~) sole proprietor
законный ~ (zakónnyi ~) holder in due course
на риск ~/ьца (na risk ~/'tsa) at owner's risk
последующий ~ (posléduiushchii ~) subsequent holder

поручение ~/ьца патента
(poruchénie ~/'tsa paténta)
patent owner's charge
право ~/ьца (právo ~/'tsa)
owner's right
совместный ~ (sovméstnyi ~) co-
owner
частный ~ (chástnyi ~) private
owner
~ авторского права (~ ávtorskogo
práva) copyright owner
~ аккредитива (~ akkreditíva)
holder of a letter of credit
~ акций (~ áktsii) shareholder
~ банковского счёта (~
bánkovskogo schióta) account
holder
~ буксирного судна (~ buksírnogo
súdna) tug owner
~ вклада (~ vkláda) depositor
~ груза (~ grúza) cargo owner
~ долгового обязательства (~
dolgovógo obiazátel'stva)
debenture holder
~ завода (~ zavóda) factory
owner
~ именных акций (~ imenných
áktsii) registered shareholder
~ лицензии (~ litsénzii)
licensee, holder of a license
~ недвижимости (~ nedvízhimosti)
owner of real estate, tenant
~ ноу-хау (~ nóu-kháu) owner of
know-how {licensor}
~ обыкновенных акций (~
obyknovénnykh áktsii) common
shareholder
~ патента (~ paténta) patent
holder
~ патентов, продающий лицензии
на них (~ paténtov, prodaiúshch-
ii litsénzii na nikh) patent
holder and licensor
~ предприятия (~ predpriiátiia)
proprietor of an enterprise
~ регистрации товарного знака (~
registrátsii továrnogo znáka)
registered trademark holder
~ склада (~ skláda) warehouseman
~ собственности (~
sóbstvennosti) property owner
~ стенда (~ sténda) exhibition
owner
~ судна (~ súdna) ship owner
~ товара (~ továra) commodity
owner

~ товарного знака (~ továrnogo
znáka) trademark holder
~ товарной пристани (~ továrnoi
prístani) wharfinger
~ фондовых ценностей (~
fondovíkh tsénnostei) fund
holder
~ ценных бумаг (~ tsénnykh
bumág) holder of securities
Владени/е (vladéni/e) n. ownership,
proprietorship
бессрочное ~ (bessróchnoe ~)
perpetual fee ownership
введение во ~ (vvedénie vo ~)
vesting of a property interest
вводить во ~ (vvodít' vo ~) to
vest {an interest}
вступление во ~ (vstuplénie vo
~) taking possession
вступать во ~ (vstupát' vo ~) to
assume possession
долевое ~ (dolevóe ~) tenancy in
common
единоличное ~ (edinolíchnoe ~)
sole proprietorship
иностранные ~/я (inostránnye
~/ia) foreign possessions
находиться во ~/и (nakhodít'sia
vo ~/i) to be in possession
право ~/я (právo ~/ia) ownership
right
передавать во ~ (peredavát' vo
~) to give possession over to
переходить во ~ (perekhodít' vo
~) to pass into possession
получать во ~ (poluchát' vo ~)
совместное ~ (sovméstnoe ~)
joint tenancy
срок ~/я (srok ~/ia) tenure
~ акциями (~ áktsiiami)
shareholdings
~ на основе аренды (~ na osnóve
aréndy) leaseholding, tenancy
~ недвижимость (~ nedvízhimost')
tenancy, tenure of real property
Владеть (vladét') v. to own,
possess
~ совместно (~ sovméstno) to
possess jointly
Влажност/ь (vlázhnost/') f.
humidity, moisture
контроль за ~/ью (kontról' za
~/'iu) humidity control
оговорка о ~/и (ogovórka o ~/i)
moisture clause
относительная ~ (otnosítel'naia
~) relative humidity

повышенная ~ (povýshennaia ~)
excess moisture
сертификат о ~/и (sertifikát o
~/i) moisture certificate
скидка за ~ (skídka za ~)
moisture allowance
повреждать повышенной ~/ью
(povrezhdát' povýshennoi ~/'iu)
to damage by excess moisture
предохранять от ~/и
(predokhraniát' ot ~/i) to
preserve against moisture
~ воздуха (~ vózdukha) humidity
{weather}
~ древесины (~ drevesíny) timber
moisture content
Влажный (vlázhnyi) *adj.* humid,
moist
Власт/ь (vlast/') *f.* authority,
power
быть в своей ~/и (byt' v svoéi
~/i) to be within one's power
быть вне ~/и (byt' vne ~/i) to
be ultra vires
военные ~/и (voénnye ~/i)
military authorities
государственная ~
(gosudárstvennaia ~) public
authorities
гражданская ~ (grazhdánskaia ~)
civil authority
законная ~ (zakónnaia ~) lawful
authority
законодательная ~
(zakonodátel'naia ~) legislative
power
злоупотребление ~/ью
(zloupotreblénie ~/'iu) abuse of
authority
исполнительная ~
(ispolnítel'naia ~) executive
authority
иметь ~ над (imét' ~ nad) to
have power over
компетентные ~/и (kompeténtnye
~/i) competent authorities
местные ~/и (méstnye ~/i) local
authorities
монопольная ~ (monopól'naia ~)
monopoly power
муниципальные ~/и
(munitsipál'nye ~/i) municipal
authorities
органы ~/и (órgany ~/i)
authorities

органы ~/и, государственной
(órgany ~/i, gosudárstvennoi)
governmental authorities
органы ~/и, законные (órgany
~/i, zakónnye) statutory
authorities
органы ~/и, местные (órgany ~/i,
méstnye) local authorities
осуществлять ~ (osushchestvliát'
~) to exercise power
осуществлять монопольную ~ на
рынке (osushchestvliát' monopól-
'nuiu ~ na rýnke) to exercise
monopoly power in the market
в пределах предоставленной ~/и
(v predélakh predostávlennoi
~/i) within the limits of
discretionary power
официальные ~/и (ofitsiál'nye
~/i) official authorities
портовые ~/и (portovýe ~/i) port
authority
передача ~/и (peredácha ~/i)
delegation of authority
распоряжения портовых ~/ей
(rasporiazhéniia portovýkh ~/éi)
port authority regulations
соответствующие ~/и
(sootvétstvuiushchie ~/i)
appropriate authorities
судебная ~ (sudébnaia ~)
judicial authority
таможенные ~/и (tamózhennye ~/i)
customs authorities
централизованная ~
(tsentralizóvannaia ~)
centralized power
экономическая (ekonomícheskaia)
economic power
Вложени/е (vlozhéni/e) *n.*
investment, placement
капитальные ~/я (kapitál'nye
~/ia) capital investments
кредитные ~/я (kredítnye ~/ia)
provision of credits
рентабельность ~/й
(rentábel'nost' ~/i)
profitability of investments
Вместимост/ь (vmestímost/') *f.*
capacity
валовая ~ (valováia ~) gross
tonnage
грузовая ~ (gruzováia ~) cargo ~
объёмная ~ (ob"iómnaia ~) cubic
~
регистровая ~ (regístrovaia ~)
registered tonnage

чистая ~ (chístaia ~) net ~
шкала ~/и (shkalá ~/i) tonnage
scale
~ бункера (~ búnkera) bunker ~
~ вагона (~ vagóna) ~ of a
railway car
~ складских помещений (~
skladskíkh pomeshchénii)
warehousing ~
~ судна (~ súdna) ship ~
~ трюма (~ triúma) ~ of a ship's
hold
Вместительный (vmestítel'nyi) adj.
capacious
Внаём, внаймы (vnaióm, vnaimý) adv.
for lease
    брать ~ (brat' ~) to hire, to
    lease {as lessee}
    брать ~ квартиру ~ (brat' ~
    kvartíru ~) to rent an apartment
    брать ~ судно по чартеру (brat'
    ~ súdno po chúrteru) to charter
    a vessel
    сдавать ~ (sdavát' ~) to lease
    {as lessor}, to hire out
    сдавать ~ судно по чартеру
    (sdavát' ~ súdno po chárteru) to
    lease {as lessor} a vessel under
    a charter party
Внедоговорный (vnedogovórnyi) adj.
extracontractual
Внедрени/е (vnedréni/e) n.
implementation
    промышленное ~ (promýshlennoe ~)
    commercial implementation
    период ~/я (períod ~/ia) period
    for implementation
    усилия по ~/ю (usíliia po ~/iu)
    implementation efforts
    этап ~/я (etáp ~/ia)
    introduction phase
    ~ изобретения (~ izobreténiia)
    application of an invention
    ~ машин (~ mashín) introduction
    of equipment
    ~ новых видов продукции (~
    novýkh vídov prodúktsii)
    introduction of new product
    types
    ~ новой техники и технологии (~
    nóvoi tékhniki i tekhnológii)
    introduction of new technology
    ~ нормативов (~ normatívov)
    introduction of standards
    ~ прогрессивных технологий (~
    progressívnykh tekhnológii)

    introduction of progressive
    industrial processes
    ~ продукции (~ prodúktsii)
    product introduction
    ~ технологии (~ tekhnológii)
    introduction of technology
Внедрять (vnedriát') v. to
introduce
Внешнеторговый (vneshnetorgóvyi)
adj. foreign trade
Внешнеэкономический (vnéshne-
ekonomícheskii) adj. foreign
economic
Внешний (vnéshnii) adj. external,
common, foreign
Внешэкономбанк (vnéshekonómbánk)
Vneshekonom Bank {Foreign Trade
Bank of the Russian Federation}
Внутренний (vnútrennii) adj.
domestic, interior
Внутризаводской (vnutrizavódskoi)
adj. intra-factory
Внутриотраслевой (vnutriotraslevói)
adj. intra-sectoral
Вод/а (vod/á) f. water
    быть повреждённым морской ~/ой
    (byt' povrezhdiónnym morskói
    ~/ói) to be damaged by sea-~
    внутренние ~/ы (vnútrennie ~/y)
    inland waters
    высокая ~ (vysókaia ~) high tide
    запас ~/ы (zapás ~/y) water
    supply
    держаться на ~/е (derzhát'sia na
    ~/e) to keep afloat, to float
    морская ~ (morskáia ~) sea ~
    нейтральные ~/ы (neitrál'nye
    ~/y) neutral ~s
    непроницаемый для ~/ы
    (nepronitsáemyi dlia ~/ý)
    impermeable to ~
    открытая ~ (otkrýtaia ~) open ~
    охлаждаемый ~/ой (okhlazhdáemyi
    ~/ói) ~-cooled
    по ~/е (po ~/é) via ~
    повреждение ~/ой (povrezhdénie
    ~/ói) ~ damage
    пограничные ~/ы (pograníchnye
    ~/y) boundary ~s
    подмочка ~/ой (podmóchka ~/ói)
    exposure to ~
    полная ~ (pólnaia ~) deep ~
    портовые ~/ы (portovýe ~/y) port
    ~s
    прибрежные ~/ы (pribrézhnye ~/y)
    coastal ~s

проникновение морской ~/ы
(proniknovénie morskói ~/ý)
ingress of sea ~
пропитавшийся ~/ой
(propitávshiisia ~/ói) ~-logged
снабжение ~/ой (snabzhénie ~/ói)
~ supply
сточные ~/ы (stóchnye ~/y)
sewage
сточные, промышленные ~/ы
(stóchnye, promýshlennye ~/y)
industrial waste ~
территориальные ~
(territoriál'nye ~) territorial
~s
Водоизмещени/е (vodoizmeshchéni/e)
n. displacement {of a vessel}
весовое ~ (vesovóe ~) tonnage ~
стандартное ~ (standártnoe ~)
standard ~
судно ~/ем в ...тонн (súdno ~/em
v ...tonn) vessel of ... tons ~
шкала ~/я (shkalá ~/ia) ~ scale
~ при полном грузе (~ pri pólnom
grúze) full load ~
~ судна (~ súdna) ~ tonnage
Водонепроницаемый
(vodonepronitsáemyi) *adj.*
waterproof
Водоотталкивающий
(vodoottálkivaiushchii) *adj.* water
repellent
Водопроницаемый (vodopronitsáemyi)
adj. non-waterproof
Водостойкий (vodostóikii) *adj.*
water resistant
Водоупорный (vodoupórnyi) *adj.*
watertight
Возбуждать (vozbuzhdát') *v.* to
initiate
~ дело (~ délo) to initiate
proceedings
~ иск (~ isk) to prosecute a
claim
Возврат (vozvrát) *m.* call back,
redemption, refund, return
организовывать ~ (organizóvyvat'
~) to arrange for a return
подлежать ~/у (podlezhát' ~/u)
to be refundable
подлежать ~/у по первому
требованию (podlezhát' ~/u po
pérvomu trébovaniiu) to be
subject to {cash} call
подлежащий ~/у (podlezháshchii
~/u) subject to refund,
refundable

право ~/а (právo ~/a) right of
return
рекламационный ~ используемого
изделия (reklamatsiónnyi ~
ispól'zuemogo izdéliia) field
warranty return
срок ~/а денег (srok ~/a déneg)
redemption period
требование о ~/e (trébovanie o
~/e) demand for refund
требовать ~/а займа (trébovat'
~/a záima) to call in a loan
частичный ~ (chastíchnyi ~)
partial return
~ аванса (~ avánsa) return of an
advance
~ бракованного товара (~
brakóvannogo továra) return of
rejected goods
~ выплаченного вознаграждения (~
výplachennogo voznagrazhdéniia)
return of a commission
~ гарантийной суммы (~
garantíinoi súmmy) warranty
reimbursement
~ документов (~ dokuméntov)
return of documents
~ долга (~ dólga) repayment of a
debt
~ займа (~ záima) loan repayment
~ зафрахтованного судна (~
zafrakhtóvannogo súdna)
redelivery
~ из депозита (~ iz depozíta)
refund of a deposit
~ инвестированных денег (~
investírovannykh déneg) recovery
of money invested
~ к прежним ценам (~ k prézhnim
tsénam) price roll back
~ кредита (~ kredíta) repayment
of a credit
~ налога (~ nalóga) tax refund
~ налогов, взысканных по ошибке
(~ nalógov, vzýskannykh po
oshíbke) return of unduly
collected taxes
~ обеспечения (~ obespechéniia)
return of a pledge
~ переплаты (~ perepláty) rebate
of amount overpaid
~ пошлины (~ póshliny) refund of
customs duties
~ сборов (~ sbórov)
reimbursement of charges

~ страхового взноса (~
strakhovógo vznósa) return of an
insurance premium
~ уплаченной цены (~ upláchennoi
tsený) refund of purchase price
Возвратный (vozvrátnyi) *adj.*
returnable
Возвращать (vozvrashchát') *v.* to
return
Возвращени/е (vozvrashchénie) *n.*
return
Воздухонепроницаемый
(vozdukhonepronitsáemyi) *adj.*
airtight
Возмещать (vozmeshchát') *v.* to
compensate, to reimburse
Возмещени/е (vozmeshchéni/e) *n.*
compensation, recovery, reimbursement, repayment
 без обязательства ~/я ущерба
 (bez obiazátel'stva ~/ia
 ushchérba) uncompensated
 в ~ (v ~) in recompense for
 в порядке ~/я расходов по общей
 аварии (v poriádke ~/ia
 raskhódov po óbshchei avárii) in
 contribution to the general
 average
 в порядке ~/я убытков (v
 poriádke ~/ia ubýtkov) in
 compensation of damages
 выплата ~/я (výplata ~/ia)
 payment of compensation
 выплата страхового ~/я (výplata
 strakhovógo ~/ia) payment of
 insurance indemnity
 график ~/я долгов (gráfik ~/ia
 dolgóv) debt repayment schedule
 гарантировать ~ (garantírovat'
 ~) to guarantee repayment
 гарантировать ~ убытков
 (garantírovat' ~ ubýtkov) to
 guarantee against loss
 денежное ~ (dénezhnoe ~) money
 damages
 заявления о выплате страхового
 ~/я (zaiavléniia o výplate
 strakhovógo ~/ia) notice of
 claim against insurance
 заявление о ~/и убытка
 (zaiavlénie o ~/i ubýtka) notice
 of claim
 иск о ~/и (isk o ~/i) action for
 damages
 настаивать на ~/и (nastáivat' na
 ~/i) to insist on compensation

оговорка о ~/и (ogovórka o ~/i)
compensation clause, liquidated
damages clause
однократное ~ (odnokrátnoe ~)
nonrecurring compensation
определение страхового ~/я
(opredelénie strakhovógo ~/ia)
insurance loss assessment, claim
adjustment
определять сумму денежного ~/я
(opredeliát' súmmu dénezhnogo
~/ia) to assess money damages
отказ от ~/я (otkáz ot ~/ia)
abandonment of indemnity,
refusal to compensate
отказ от права на ~ (otkáz ot
práva na ~) waiver of damages
полное ~ (pólnoe ~) full
recovery
получать ~ за убытки (poluchát'
~ za ubýtki) to recover damages
получать ~ расходов (poluchát' ~
raskhódov) to receive
compensation for expenditures
подлежащий ~/ю (podlezháshchii
~/iu) liable for recovery
право на ~ (právo na ~) right to
compensation
право на ~ убытков по общей
аварии (právo na ~ ubýtkov po
óbshchei avárii) right to
compensation for general average
losses
прямое ~ затрат (priámoe ~
zatrát) direct reimbursement of
expenses
предел ~/я (predél ~/ia)
indemnity limit
предлагать ~ (predlagát' ~) to
offer compensation
предоставлять ~ (predostavliát'
~) to reimburse
работа по ~/ю убытков (rabóta po
~/iu ubýtkov) remedial work
размер ~/я убытков (razmér ~/ia
ubýtkov) measure of damages
решение суда о ~/и убытков
(reshénie sudá o ~/i ubýtkov)
award of damages
своевременность ~/я кредита
(svoevrémennost' ~/ia kredíta)
timeliness of repayment of a
credit
способ ~/я (spósob ~/ia) method
of reimbursement
страховое ~ (strakhovóe ~)
insurance indemnity

требование о ~/и убытков грузоотправителя (trébovanie o ~/i ubýtkov gruzootpravítelia) freight claim

требовать выплаты страхового ~/я (trébovat' výplaty strakhovógo ~/ia) to make an insurance claim

частичное ~ (chastíchnoe ~) partial recovery

~ ассигнований (~ assignovánii) reimbursement of expenditures

~ в натуре (~ v natúre) recovery in kind

~ долга (~ dólga) repayment of a debt

~ за задержку судна сверх срока (~ za zadérzhku súdna sverkh sróka) recovery for vessel detention

~ за поломку (~ za polómku) recovery for breakage

~ затрат (~ zatrát) reimbursement of expenses

~ капитала (~ kapitála) replacement of capital

~ кредита (~ kredíta) repayment of a credit

~ недостачи (~ nedostáchi) compensation for shortage

~ расходов (~ raskhódov) reimbursement for outlays

~ стоимости (~ stóimosti) replacement of value

~ убытков (~ ubýtkov) compensation for damages

~ ущерба (~ ushchérba) recompense

Возмужалость (vozmuzhálost') f. majority {age}, maturity

Вознагражден/е (voznagrazhdéni/e) n. bonus, commission, consideration, royalty

авторское ~ (ávtorskoe ~) author's royalty

агентское ~ (agéntskoe ~) agent's commission

в виде ~/я (v víde ~/ia) as an offset against

выплачивать ~ (vypláchivat' ~) to pay remuneration

брокерское ~ (brókerskoe ~) broker's commission

денежное ~ (dénezhnoe ~) pecuniary reward

дополнительное ~ (dopolnítel'noe ~) bonus

единовременное ~ (edinovrémennoe ~) lumpsum remuneration

иметь право на ~ (imét' právo na ~) to have the right to remuneration

исчислять ~ (ischisliát' ~) to calculate commission, fee or royalty

комиссионное ~ (komissiónnoe ~) commission

лицензионное ~ (litsenziónnoe ~) licensing fee

лицензионное, разовое ~ (litsenziónnoe, rázovoe ~) non-recurring royalty

лицензионное, текущее ~ (litsenziónnoe, tekúshchee ~) running royalty

максимальное ~ (maksimál'noe ~) maximum commission, maximum remuneration

материальное ~ (materiál'noe ~) material remuneration

месячное ~ (mésiachnoe ~) monthly rate of remuneration

минимальное ~ (minimál'noe ~) minimum commission

на базе комиссионного ~/я (na báze komissiónnogo ~/ia) on a commission basis

неизменное ~ (neizménnoe ~) fixed fee

ожидаемое ~ (ozhidáemoe ~) expected remuneration

поощрительное ~ (pooshchrítel'noe ~) incentive fee

право на {получение} ~/{я} (právo na poluchénie ~/ia) right to receive remuneration

премиальное ~ (premiál'noe ~) premium

размер ~/я (razmér ~/ia) amount of commission, remuneration

распределение ~/я за спасение (raspredelénie ~/ia za spasénie) salvage statement

с номинальным ~/ем (s nominál'nym ~/em) at a nominal fee

соответствующее ~ (sootvétstvuiushchee ~) appropriate remuneration

способ ~/я (spósob ~/ia) means of compensation

ставка ~/я (stávka ~/ia) commission rate

чистое ~ (chístoe ~) net commission
шкала комиссионного ~/я (shkála komissiónnogo ~/ia) commission scale
~ аукционисту (~ auktsionístu) lot money {auction}
~ брутто (~ brútto) gross remuneration
~ диспашеру (~ dispashéru) average adjustor fee
~ за выдачу лицензии (~ za výdachu litsénzii) consideration for licensing
~ за делькредере (~ za dél'kredére) del credere commission
~ за досрочное завершение работы (~ za dosróchnoe zavershénie rabóty) bonus for completing work ahead of schedule
~ за инкассо (~ za inkásso) collection charge
~ за консультационные услуги (~ za konsul'tatsiónnye uslúgi) consultant's fees
~ за проводку судна (~ za provódku súdna) pilotage
~ за сверхурочную работу (~ za sverkhuróchnuiu rabótu) overtime pay
~ за спасение (~ za spasénie) salvage money
~ за спасение груза (~ za spasénie grúza) salvage on cargo
~ за спасение судна (~ za spasénie súdna) salvage on ship
~ капитану с фрахта (~ kapitánu s frákhta) primage
~ натурой (~ natúroi) compensation in kind
~ подрядчику (~ podriádchiku) contractor's fee
Возобновление (vozobnovlénie) renewal, resumption
право на ~ (právo na ~) option to renew
~ аккредитива (~ akkreditíva) renewal of a letter of credit
~ аренды (~ aréndy) renewal of a lease
~ деятельности (~ déiatel'nosti) resumption of activity, resumption of operations
~ договора (~ dogovóra) renewal of an agreement

~ запасов (~ zapásov) replenishment of stocks
~ иска (~ íska) resumption of legal action
~ контракта (~ kontrákta) renewal of a contract
~ переговоров (~ peregovórov) resumption of negotiations
~ поставок (~ postávok) resumption of deliveries
~ соглашения (~ soglashéniia) renewal of an agreement
~ сотрудничества (~ sotrúdnichestva) resumption of cooperation
~ страхового полиса (~ strakhovógo pólisa) renewal of an insurance policy
Возобновля/ть (vozobnovliát') v. to renew, to resume
период, на который ~/ется соглашение (períod, na kotóryi ~/etsia soglashénie) renewal period
~ полностью (~ pólnost'iu) to fully renew
Возросший (vozrósshii) adj. increased
Войн/а (voiná) f. war
валютная ~ (valiútnaia ~) currency ~
вести ~/у (vestí ~/u) to wage ~
втянуть в ~/у (vtianút' v ~/u) to drag into ~
кредитная ~ (kredítnaia ~) credit ~
таможенная {тарифная} ~ (tamózhennaia {tarífnaia}~) tariff ~
торговая ~ (torgóvaia ~) trade ~
~ цен (~ tsen) price ~
Воплощать (voploshchát') v. to embody, to implement
Воплощаться (voploshchát'sia) v. to be embodied
Воплощение (voploshchénie) n. embodiment
Вопрос (voprós) m. matter, question
внести ясность в ~ (vnestí iásnost' v ~) to clarify the matter
деловой ~ (delovói ~) business matter
неразрешённый ~ (nerazreshiónnyi ~) unresolved issue
поднимать ~ (podnimát' ~) to raise a question

рассматриваемый
(rassmatriváemyi) issue under
consideration
рассмотрение ~/а (rassmotrénie
~/a) consideration of an issue
решение по ~/у (reshénie po ~/u)
decision on a matter
~, представляющий взаимный
интерес (~, predstavliáiushchii
vzaímnyi interés) matter of
mutual interest
Вор (vor) m. thief
~/ы в законе (~/y v zakóne)
"thieves in the law" {organized
criminal groups based in the
former USSR}
~/ы в зоне (~/y v zone) "thieves
in the zone" {organized criminal
groups in prison camps}
Воспламеняющийся
(vosplameniáiushchiiisia) adj.
inflammable
Восстанавливать (vosstanávlivat')
v. to rebuild, reconstruct,
renovate
Восстановление (vosstanovlénie) n.
rebuilding, reconstruction,
restoration
экономическое ~ (ekonomícheskoe
~) economic recovery
~ во владении (~ vo vladénii)
repossession
~ в правах (~ v pravákh)
restoration of rights
~ деталей (~ detálei)
reconditioning of parts
~ заявки (~ zaiávki) renewal of
application
~ патента, срок действия
которого истёк (~ paténta, srok
déistviia kotórogo istiók)
restoration of a lapsed patent
~ промышленности (~
promýshlennosti) reconstruction
of industry
~ торговли (~ torgóvli) business
recovery
~ уровня запасов (~ úrovnia
zapásov) replenishment of
inventories
Восток (vostók) m. east, the East
Ближний ~ (blízhnii ~) the Near
East
Дальний ~ (dál'nii ~) the Far
East
Средний ~ (srédnii ~) the Middle
East

Востребовани/е (vostrébovani/e) n.
call, claim, demand
до ~/я (do ~/ia) poste restante,
on demand
~ груза (~ grúza) claim of cargo
Временный (vrémennyi) adj. interim,
provisional, temporary
Врем/я (vrém/ia) n. period, time
в назначенное ~ (v naznáchennoe
~) at the appointed time
занимать (zanimát' ~) to take
up time
контрсталийное ~ (kontrstalíinoe
~) demurrage period
местное ~ (méstnoe ~) local time
норма ~/ени (nórma ~/eni) time
standard allowance
промежуток ~/еми (promezhútok
~/emi) interval
рабочее ~ (rabóchee ~) hours of
operation, office hours
расчётное ~ (raschiótnoe ~)
estimated time
сверхурочное ~ (sverkhuróchnoe
~) overtime
сталийное ~ (stalíinoe ~)
laydays
стояночное ~ (stoiánochnoe ~)
laydays
терять ~ (teriát' ~) to lose
time
установочное ~ (ustanóvochnoe ~)
set up time
экономия ~/ени (ekonómiia ~/eni)
time savings
экономить ~ (ekonómit' ~) to
save time
фактическое ~ (faktícheskoe ~)
effective time
~ вступления в силу (~
vstupléniia v sílu) effective
date
~ выполнения (~ vypolnéniia)
time of execution
~ действия лицензии (~ déistviia
litsénzii) licensing period
~ доставки (~ dostávki) time of
delivery
~ норма ~/ени (~ nórma ~/eni)
standard base time
~ оборота судна в порту (~
oboróta súdna v pórtu)
turnaround time {maritime}
~ отправления (~ otpravléniia)
time of departure
~ перехода к выпуску новой
продукции (~ perekhóda k výpusku

nóvoi prodúktsii) changeover time {production}
~ погрузочное (~ pogrúzochnoe) loading time
~ прибытия (~ pribýtiia) time of arrival
~ продолжительности погрузки (~ prodolzhítel'nosti pogrúzki) onloading time
~ простоя (~ prostóia) downtime, demurrage
~ стоянки судна, разрешённое (~ stoiánki súdna, razreshiónnoe) allowed laytime, laydays
~ стоянки у причала (~ stoiánki u príchala) berthing period
~ транспортировки (~ transportiróvki) transport period
~ эксплуатации (~ ekspluatátsii) operating period
Вручение (vruchénie) n. delivery, handing in
~ документов (~ dokuméntov) delivery of documents
~ нотисов (~ nótisov) presentation of notices
Вскрывать (vskryvát') v. to open, to reveal, to unseal
Вспомогательный (vspomogátel'nyi) adj. ancillary, auxiliary
Встречный (vstréchnyi) adj. counter
Вступать (vstupát') v. to enter, to join
~ в силу (~ v sílu) to take effect
~ в соглашение (~ v soglashénie) to enter into an agreement
~ в строй (~ v stroi) to come into operation, to go onstream
Вступительный (vstupítel'nyi) adj. entrance, introductory
Второстепенн/ый (vtorostepénn/yi) adj. secondary
иметь ~/ое значение (imét' ~/oe znachénie) to be of secon dary importance
Входить в действие {в силу} (vkhodít' v déistvie {v sílu}) v. to come into effect
Въезд (v"ezd) m. entrance, entry
право ~/a (právo ~/a) right of entry
разрешение на ~ (razreshénie na ~) entry permit
запрещать ~ (zapreshchát' ~) to ban entry

разрешать ~ (razreshát' ~) to permit entry
Въездной (v"ezdnói) adj. entrance
Выбор (výbor) m. assortment, choice, option
бедный ~ (bédnyi ~) poor choice
большой ~ (bol'shói ~) wide assortment
будущий ~ (búdushchii ~) future option
делать ~ (délat' ~) to make a choice
делать предварительный ~ (délat' predvarítel'nyi ~) to make a preliminary choice
иметь право ~/a (imét' právo ~/a) to have an option
иметь право ~/a товара (imét' právo ~/a továra) to have an option on goods
на ~ (na ~) at choice, by choice
не иметь ~/a (ne imét' ~/a) to not have a choice
оптимальный ~ (optimál'nyi ~) optimal choice
отсутствие ~/a (otsútstvie ~/a) absence of choice
ошибочный ~ (oshíbochnyi ~) wrong choice
по ~/у (po ~/u) at the option of ...
повторный ~ (povtórnyi ~) repeated sampling
потребительский ~ (potrebítel'skii ~) consumer choice
поставляемый по ~/у заказчика (postavliáemyi po ~/u zakázchika) available at option
право ~/a (právo ~/a) right of option
право первого ~/a (právo pervógo ~/a) right of first refusal
принцип ~/a (príntsip ~/a) principle of choice
предварительный ~ (predvarítel'nyi ~) preliminary choice
предоставлять ~ (predostavliát' ~) to leave it to ... choice
предоставлять право ~/a (predostavliát' právo ~/a) to provide options
разнообразный ~ (raznoobráznyi ~) varied selection
свободный ~ (svobódnyi ~) free choice

случайный ~ (slucháinyi ~) random choice
широкий ~ (shirókii ~) wide selection
~ агента (~ agénta) choice of an agent
~ активов (~ aktívov) choice of assets
~ альтернативы (~ al'ternatívy) choosing an alternative
~ знака (~ znáka) selection of a trademark
~ образцов (~ obraztsóv) drawing of samples, choice of samples
~ по ассортименту (~ po assortiméntu) selection from a range of goods
~ покупателя (~ pokupátelia) buyer's choice
~ по образцам (~ po obraztsám) choice from among samples
~ поставщика (~ postavshchiká) supplier's choice
~ продавца (~ prodavtsá) seller's option
~ проектного решения (~ proéktnogo reshéniia) design selection
~ решения (~ reshéniia) decision
~ товара (~ továra) range of goods
Выборочный (výborochnyi) *adj.* sample, sampling
Выбраковывать (vybrakóvyvat') *v.* to reject
Выбрасывание (vybrásyvanie) *n.* discard, rejection
~ груза за борт (~ grúza za bort) jettison of cargo
Выбрасывать (vybrásyvat') *v.* to discard, to jettison
Выбывать из строя (vybyvát' iz stróia) *v.* to fail, to break
Вывод (vývod) *m.* conclusion, removal
делать ~ (délat' ~) to come to a conclusion
ложный ~ (lózhnyi ~) false conclusion
необоснованный ~ (neobosnóvannyi ~) baseless conclusion
неправильный ~ (neprávil'nyi ~) incorrect conclusion
обоснованный ~ (obosnóvannyi ~) well-founded conclusion
окончательный ~ (okonchátel'nyi ~) final conclusion

организационный ~ (organizatsiónnyi ~) practical conclusion
поспешный ~ (pospéshnyi ~) hasty conclusion
поспешить с ~/ом (pospeshít' s ~/om) to jump to a conclusion
прийти к ~/у (priití k ~/u) to arrive at a conclusion
удовлетворительный ~ (udovletvorítel'nyi ~) satisfactory conclusion
~ из эксплуатации (~ iz ekspluatátsii) removal from service
~ /ы комиссии (~ /y komíssii) findings
~ судна лоцманов (~ súdna lotsmánov) pilotage outward
Выводить (vyvodít') *v.* to conclude, to remove
Вывоз (vývoz) *m.* exportation, removal
беспошлинный ~ (bespóshlinnyi ~) duty-free export
бросовый ~ (brósovyi ~) dumping {rejected goods}
временный ~ (vrémennyi ~) temporary export
ввоз и ~ (vvoz i ~) imports and exports
груз готов к ~/у (gruz gotóv k ~/u) cargo available for export
запрет ~/а на инвалюты (zaprét ~/a na ínvaliuty) ban on export of foreign exchange
запрет на ~ (zaprét na ~) export ban
запрещать ~ (zapreshchát' ~) to ban exports
затруднение ~/а (zatrudnénie ~/a) export barriers
место ~/а (mésto ~/a) pick-up location
объём ~/а (ob"ióm ~/a) volume of exports
ограничение ~/а (ogranichénie ~/a) export restrictions
оформлять ~ (oformliát' ~) to arrange for export permit
оформлять ~ с таможни (oformliát' ~ s tamózhni) to arrange for customs clearance
план ~/а (plan ~/a) export plan
плата за ~ (pláta za ~) pick-up fees

получать разрешение на ~ (poluchát' razreshénie na ~) to obtain an export license

превышение ~/а над ввозом (prevyshénie ~/a nad vvózom) increase in export surplus

предметы ~/а (predméty ~/a) export articles

пункт ~/а (punkt ~/a) point of exit

разрешение на ~ (razreshénie na ~) release for shipment {export}

разрешение на ~ со склада (razreshénie na ~ so skláda) dock pass {for export}

разрешение на ~ с таможенного склада (razreshénie na ~ s tamózhennogo skláda) bond note {customs}

расходы по ~/у (raskhódy po ~/u) removal expenses

сокращать ~ (sokrashchát' ~) to reduce exports

срок ~/а (srok ~/a) removal time

увеличивать ~ (uvelíchivat' ~) to increase exports

услуги по ~/у груза (uslúgi po ~/u gruza) cargo pick-up services

цена включает ~ (tséna vkliucháet ~) rates include pick-up

~ золота (~ zólota) export of gold

~ и доставка грузов (~ i dostávka grúzov) pick-up and delivery

~ капитала (~ kapitála) export of capital

~ продовольствия (~ prodovól'stviia) food exports

~ продукции сельского хозяйства (~ prodúktsii sél'skogo khoziáistva) agricultural exports

~ с пирса (~ s pírsa) pier pick-up

~ тары (~ táry) removal of empties

~ товаров (~ továrov) exportation of goods

~ товаров по бросовым ценам (~ továrov po brósovym tsénam) dumping {trade}

~ упаковки (~ upakóvki) removal of packing

~ экспонатов (~ eksponátov) removal of exhibits

Вывозить (vyvozít') v. to export, to remove

Выгадывать (vygádyvat') v. to economize, to gain

Выгод/а (výgod/a) f. advantage, benefit, profit

взаимная ~ (vzaímnaia ~) mutual advantage

для ~/ы (dlia ~/y) to the benefit

для взаимной ~/ы (dlia vzaímnoi ~/y) for mutual benefit

извлекать ~/у (izvlekát' ~/u) to derive benefit

извлекать наибольшую ~/у (izvlekát' naiból'shuiu ~/u) to derive maximum benefit

использовать с ~/ой (ispól'zovat' s ~/oi) to take advantage of

к взаимной ~/е (k vzaímnoi ~/e) to a mutual advantage

личная ~ (líchnaia ~) self-advantage, personal advantage

на основе взаимной ~/ы (na osnóve vzaímnoi ~/y) on the basis of mutual advantage

общая ~ (óbshchaia ~) general advantage

общественная ~ (obshchéstvennaia ~) social benefit

побочная ~ (pobóchnaia ~) incidental benefit

получать ~/у (poluchát' ~/u) to benefit

потенциальная ~ (potentsiál'naia ~) potential benefit

принцип равной ~/ы (príntsip rávnoi ~/y) principle of equal advantage

признавать ~/у (priznavát' ~/u) to recognize the advantage

приносить ~/у (prinosít' ~/u) to be advantageous

представлять взаимную ~/у (predstavliát' vzaímnuiu ~/u) to be of mutual advantage

равная ~ (rávnaia ~) equal advantage

ради ~/ы (rádi ~/y) for the sake of profit

с ~/ой (s ~/oi) profitably

страхование упущенной ~/ы (strakhovánie upúshchennoi ~/y) loss of profit insurance

суммарная ~ (summárnaia ~)
benefits
упущенная ~ (upúshchennaia ~)
lost opportunity
финансовая ~ (finánsovaia ~)
financial advantage
хозяйственная ~
(khoziáistvennaia ~) economic
gain
явная ~ (iávnaia ~) recognized
benefit
~/ы связанные с массовым
производством (~/y sviázannye s
mássovym proizvódstvom) gains
from economy of scale
{production}
Выгодны/й (výgodny/i) *adj*.
advantageous
быть ~/м (byt' ~/m) to be
advantageous
достаточно ~ (dostátochno ~)
reasonably beneficial
оказаться ~/м (okazát'sia ~/m)
to turn out to be advantageous,
profitable
экономически ~ (ekonomícheski ~)
economically sound
Выгружать (vygruzhát') to unload
~ из трюма (~ iz triúma) to
remove from the ship's hold
Выгрузк/а (výgruzk/a) *f*.
discharging, offloading
бесплатная ~ (besplátnaia ~)
free discharge
вынужденная ~ (výnuzhdennaia ~)
forced discharge
грейферная ~ (gréifernaia ~)
grab discharge
задерживать ~/y (zadérzhivat'
~/u) to delay offloading
место ~/и (mésto ~/i) point of
discharge
заканчивать ~/y (zakánchivat'
~/u) to complete discharge
на условиях с ~/ой на берег (na
uslóviiakh s ~/oi na bereg)
landed terms
нормы ~/и (nórmy ~/i) offloading
standards
окончание ~/и (okonchánie ~/i)
completion of discharge
опцион ~/и (optsión ~/i)
optional discharge
организовывать ~/y
(organizóvyvat' ~/u) to arrange
for offloading

отметчик при погрузке и ~/е
(otmétchik pri pogrúzke i ~/e)
tallyman
очередь на ~/y (óchered' na ~/u)
queue for unloading
платить расходы по ~/е (platít'
raskhódy po ~/e) to pay landing
charges
порядок ~/и (poriádok ~/i)
discharge procedure {shipping}
производить ~/y (proizvodít'
~/u) to effect discharge
работы по погрузке и ~/е (rabóty
po pogrúzke i ~/e) stevedoring
and handling operations
свободно от расходов по ~/е
(svobódno ot raskhódov po ~/e)
free discharge
тарифные ставки по ~/е (tarífnye
stávki po ~/e) scale of
discharge
условия погрузки и ~/и у стенки
(uslóviia pogrúzki i ~/i u
sténki) quay terms
цена с ~/ой на берег (tsená s
~/oi na béreg) landed price
фрахтователя ~ (frakhtovátelia
~) free in and out
~ из трюма за счёт фрахтователя
(~ iz triúma za schiót frakhtovátelia) free out
~ на склад (~ na sklad)
warehouse discharge
~ с судна в ж.-д. вагон (~ s
súdna v zh.-d. vagón) discharge
of ship freight to rail
Выдавать (vydavát') *v*. to give, to
grant, to offer
Выдач/а (výdach/a) *f*. delivery,
grant, issuance
дата ~/и (dáta ~/i) date of
issuance
задерживать ~/y (zadérzhivat'
~/u) to delay issuance
заявка на ~/y (zaiávka na ~/u)
application for a grant
место ~/и (mésto ~/i) place of
issuance
месяц ~/и (mésiats ~/i) month of
issuance
ордер на ~/y товара (órder na
~/u továra) delivery order
оспаривать ~/y патента
(ospárivat' ~/u paténta) contest
the issuance of a patent

отказ в ~/е патента (otkáz v ~/e paténta) rejection of a patent application
отказывать в ~/е визы (otkázyvat' v ~/e vízy) to refuse a visa application
отказывать в ~/е кредита (otkázyvat' v ~/e kredíta) to refuse credit
порядок ~/и экспортных лицензий (poriádok ~/i éksportnykh litsénzii) export licensing procedures
пошлина за ~/у патента (póshlina za ~/u paténta) patent issuance fee
правила ~/и патентов (právila ~/i paténtov) patent issuance rules
прекращение ~/и наличных денег (prekrashchénie ~/i nalíchnykh déneg) stop payment order
препятствие к ~/е патента (prepiátstvie k ~/e paténta) bar to patentability
при ~/е заказе (pri ~/e zakáze) with order
разрешение на ~/у груза (razreshénie na ~/u grúza) freight release
разрешение на ~/у товара со склада (razreshénie na ~/u továra so skláda) warehouse release
ходатайство о ~/е патента (khodatáistvo o ~/e paténta) application for grant of patent
~ аванса (~ avánsa) payment of an advance
~ авторского свидетельства (~ ávtorskogo svidétel'stva) issue of an author's certificate
~ аккредитива (~ akkreditíva) issuance of a letter of credit
~ акций (~ áktsii) issuance of stock
~ векселя (~ vékselia) issuance of a bill
~ визы (~ vízy) issuance of a visa
~ гарантии (~ garántii) issuance of a guarantee
~ груза (~ grúza) delivery of cargo
~ груза у борта судна (~ grúza u bórta súdna) delivered free alongside ship

~ денег наличными (~ déneg nalíchnymi) cash payment
~ документа (~ dokuménta) issuance of a document
~ документа о регистрации товарного знака (~ dokuménta o registrátsii továrnogo znaka) grant of trademark registration
~ документов против акцепта (~ dokuméntov prótiv aktsépta) documents against acceptance
~ заказа (~ zakáza) contract award
~ кредита (~ kredíta) issuance of a credit
~ лицензии на товар (~ litsénzii na továr) licensing of products
~ накладной (~ nakladnói) issuing an invoice
~ ноу-хау (~ nóu-kháu) provision of know-how
~ патента (~ paténta) issuance of a patent
~ против акцепта (~ prótiv aktsépta) delivery against acceptance
~ против обязательственного письма (~ prótiv obiazátel'stvennogo pis'má) delivery against a letter of commitment
~ против платежа (~ prótiv platezhá) delivery of documents against payment
~ против сохранной расписки (~ prótiv sokhránnoi raspíski) delivery against trust receipt
~ расписки (~ raspíski) issue of a receipt
~ свидетельства (~ svidétel'stva) issue of certification
~ ссуды (~ ssúdy) granting of a loan
~ субподряда (~ subpodriáda) subcontracting
~ товара (~ továra) delivery of cargo
~ транспортной накладной (~ tránsportnoi nakladnói) issuance of a waybill
Выдвигать (vydvigát') v. to advance, to promote
Выделени/е (vydeléni/e) n. allotment, assignment
извещение о ~/и товара для исполнения договора

(izveshchénie o ~/i továra dlia
ispolnéniia dogovóra) notice of
appropriation
~ ассигнований (~ assignovánii)
allocation of funds
~ денежных средств (~ dénezhnykh
sredstv) appropriation of funds
~ дополнительных средств (~
dopolnítel'nykh sredstv)
additional finance
~ площади (~ plóshchadi)
allocation of space
Выделять (vydeliát') v. to
allocate, to single out
Выдерживать (vydérzhivat') v. to
sustain, to mature
Выдержка (výderzhka) f. holding
back, holding in {as of goods from
the market in a period of glut}
Выезд (výezd) m. departure
дата ~/a (dáta ~/a) date of
departure
день ~/a (den' ~/a) day of
departure
разрешение на ~ (razreshénie na
~) exit permit
Выездной (vyezdnói) adj. exit
Вызывать (vyzyvát') v. to call for,
to provoke, to summon
Выигрывать (vyígryvat') v. to gain,
to win
~ конфликтное дело (~
konflíktnoe délo) to prevail in
a dispute
Выкладка (výkladka) f. display
открытая ~ (otkrýtaia ~) open
display
~ товара (~ továra) display of
goods
~ в магазине (~ v magazíne)
instore display
Выкуп (výkup) m. amortization,
redemption, retirement
возможность ~/a (vozmózhnost'
~/a) redeemability
досрочный ~ (dosróchnyi ~) prior
redemption
лишение права ~/a закладной
(lishénie práva ~/a zakladnói)
foreclosure
объявление о ~/e (ob"iavlénie o
~/e) redemption notice
~ акций (~ áktsii) redemption of
shares
~ документов (~ dokuméntov)
redemption of documents

~ закладной (~ zakladnói)
redemption of mortgage
~ облигаций (~ obligátsii)
retirement of bonds
Выкупать (vykupát') v. to buy out,
to redeem, to repay
Вылет (výlet) m. departure {by air}
запланированный ~
(zaplanírovannyi ~) scheduled
departure
фактический ~ (faktícheskii ~)
actual departure
Вылетать (vyletát') v. to take off
{by air}
Выписк/а (výpisk/a) f. abstract,
drawing up, excerpt, making out
заверенная ~ (zavérennaia ~)
certified account
дата ~/и счёта (dáta ~/i
schióta) issue date of an
invoice
платёж против ~/и счёта
(platiózh prótiv ~/i schióta)
payment against statement
право ~/и векселей (právo ~/i
vékselei) drawing authorization
делать ~/у из счёта (délat' ~/u
iz schióta) to make up a
statement of account
представлять ~/у из счёта
(predstavliát' ~/u iz schióta)
to render a statement
приготовить ~/у счёта
(prigotóvit' ~/u schióta) to
draw up a statement of account
~ из контракта (~ iz kontrákta)
extract from a contract
~ из протокола (~ iz protokóla)
extract from a protocol
~ из реестра (~ iz reéstra)
abstract from the registry
~ из решения (~ iz reshéniia)
extract from a decision
~ из счёта (~ iz schióta)
extract from a statement of
account
~ квитанция (~ kvitántsiia)
making out a receipt
~ о состоянии депозитов (~ o
sostoiánii depozítov) statement
of deposit
~ счёта (~ schióta) invoicing
~ счёта, представляемая банком
вкладчика (~ schióta,
predstavliáemaia bánkom
vkládchika) bank statement

~ тратты (~ trátty) issuance of a draft {note}

Выписывать (vypísyvat') *v.* to draw, to make out {draft, check}

Выплат/а (výplat/a) *f.* disbursement, payment

гарантийная ~ (garantíinaia ~) guaranteed payment

время ~/ы (vrémia ~/y) payoff time

договорённость о ~/е денег в день предъявления счёта (dogovoriónnost' o ~/e déneg v den' pred"iavléniia schióta) same day payment arrangement

денежная ~ (dénezhnaia ~) cash payment

дополнительная ~ (dopolnítel'naia ~) additional payment

дополнительная ~ наличными (dopolnítel'naia ~ nalíchnymi) cash bonus allowance

дополнительные ~/ы (dopolnítel'nye ~/y) fringe benefits

единовременная ~ (edinovrémennaia ~) lumpsum payment

заявление о ~/е страхового возмещения (zaiavlénie o ~/e strakhovógo vozmeshchéniia) insurance claim

иметь право на ~/у процентов (imét' právo na ~/u protséntov) have a right to payment of interest

квартальная ~ (kvartál'naia ~) quarterly disbursement

компенсационная ~ (kompensatsiónnaia ~) compensatory payment

обязательства по ~/е роялти (obiazátel'stva po ~/e róialti) royalty obligations

период ~/ы (períod ~/y) payout period

приказ о ~/е денег (prikáz o ~/e déneg) payout order

подлежать ~/е (podlezhát' ~/e) to mature, to be payable

премиальная ~ (premiál'naia ~) incentive payment

производить ~/у (proizvodít' ~/u) to effect payment

размер ~/ы за сверхурочную работу (razmér ~/y za

sverkhuróchnuiu rabótu) overtime rate

разрешать ~/у (razreshát' ~/u) to approve payment

требовать ~/ы страхового возмещения (trébovat' ~/y strakhovógo vozmeshchéniia) to make a claim for insurance indemnity

утверждать ~/у (utverzhdát' ~/u) to approve payment

~ вознаграждения за выслугу лет (~ voznagrazhdéniia za výslugu let) payment of seniority benefits

~ в рассрочку (~ v rassróchku) payment in installments

~ гарантийной суммы (~ garantíinoi súmmy) payment of retention money

~ дивидендов (~ dividéndov) payment of dividends

~ долга (~ dólga) liquidation of a debt

~ жалования (~ zhálovaniia) payroll payments

~ займа (~ záima) liquidation of a loan

~ за сверхурочную работу (~ za sverkhuróchnuiu rabótu) overtime payment

~ комиссионного вознаграждения (~ komissiónnogo voznagrazhdénia) commission payment

~ основной суммы займа (~ osnóvnoi súmmy záima) repayment of principle on a loan

~ по векселю (~ po vékseliu) negotiation of a bill

~ по депозиту (~ po depózitu) payment of a deposit

~ по доверенности (~ po dovérennosti) collecting payment by proxy {power of attorney}

~/ы по контракту (~/y po kontráktu) contract payments

~/ы по кредитам (~/y po kredítam) payments for credits

~/ы по патентной лицензии (~/y po paténtnoi litsénzii) patent licensing payments

~/ы по социальному обеспечению (~/y po sotsiál'nomu obespechéniiu) payment of social security benefits

~/ы по социальному страхованию
(~/y po sotsiál'nomu strakhovániiu) social insurance benefits
~ по чеку (~ po chéku)
negotiation of a check
~ прибыли (~ príbyli) payment of
profits
~ процентов (~ protséntov)
interest payment
~ процентов по долговым обяза
тельствам (~ protséntov po
dolgovým obiazátel'stvam) debt
service on bonds
~ роялти (~ róialti) payment of
royalty
~ с аккредитива (~ s
akkreditíva) payment by letter
of credit
~ страхового возмещения (~
strakhovógo vozmeshchéniia)
payment of insurance indemnity
~ страховой премии (~ strakhovói
prémii) payment of an insurance
premium
~ субсидии (~ subsídii) subsidy
payment
~ суммы (~ súmmy) payment of an
amount
~ частями (~ chastiámi) payment
by installments
Выплачивать (vypláchivat') v. to
repay
~ в рублях (~ v rubliákh) to
repay in rubles
~ ежемесячно (~ ezhemésiachno)
to pay out on a monthly basis
~ сполна {полностью} (~ spolná
{pólnost'iu}) to pay in full
Выполнени/е (vypolnéni/e) n.
execution, fulfillment,
implementation, performance
время ~/я (vrémia ~/ia) time of
execution
во время ~/я работ (vo vrémia
~/ia rabót) during the execution
of the work
высококачественное ~
(vysokokáchestvennoe ~) high
quality performance
гарантировать ~ (garantírovat'
~) to guarantee performance
гарантировать ~ монтажных работ
(garantírovat' ~ montázhnykh
rabót) to guarantee the erection
work
держать кого-л. в курсе хода ~/я
чего-л. (derzhát' kogó-l. v

kúrse khóda ~/ia chegó-l.) to
keep somebody up to date on
something
добиваться ~/я требований
(dobivát'sia ~/ia trébovanii) to
enforce demands
доброкачественное ~
(dobrokáchestvennoe ~) sound
performance
должное ~ (dólzhnoe ~) proper
execution
досрочное ~ плана (dosróchnoe ~
plána) fulfillment of a plan
ahead of schedule
завершать ~ контракта
(zavershát' ~ kontrákta) to
fulfill contractual obligations
задержка в ~/и (zadérzhka v ~/i)
delay an execution
задержаться в ~/и (zaderzhát'sia
v ~/i) to be delayed in an
execution
задерживать ~ (zadérzhivat' ~)
to delay fulfillment
метод ~/я работ (métod ~/ia
rabót) technique
мешать ~/ю программы (meshát'
~/iu prográmmy) to interfere
with the fulfillment of a
program
надзор за ~/ем (nadzór za ~/em)
work supervision
ненадлежащее ~ обязанностей
(nenadlezháshchee ~
obiázannostei) dereliction of
duty
настаивать на ~/и условий
(nastáivat' na ~/i uslóvii) to
insist on the observance of
conditions
начинать работу по ~/ю программы
(nachinát' rabótu po ~/iu
prográmmy) to start work in
accordance with the program
обеспечивать ~ (obespéchivat' ~)
to ensure performance
отказываться от ~/я
обязательства (otkázyvat'sia ot
~/ia obiazátel'stva) to waive
obligations
по ходу ~/я контракта (po khódu
~/ia kontrákta) during the
course of a contract
порядок ~/я (poriádok ~/ia)
procedure
поручать ~ плана (poruchát' ~
plána) to commit to a plan

принимать к ~/ю (prinimát' k ~/iu) to take on for fulfillment

приступать к ~/ю заказа (pristupát' k ~/iu zakáza) to proceed with an execution of an order

приступать к ~/ю программы (pristupát' k ~/iu prográmmy) to launch a program

продолжать ~ программы (prodolzhát' ~ prográmmy) to continue with a program

программа ~/я работ по контракту (prográmma ~/ia rabót po kontráktu) program of duties to be carried out pursuant to the contract

регистрировать ход ~/я (registrírovat' khod ~/ia) to record progress

своевременное ~ (svoevrémennoe ~) timely execution

своевременное ~ обязательств (svoevrémennoe ~ obiazátel'stv) timely performance {of a contract}

сотрудничать в ~/и плана (sotrúdnichat' v ~/i plána) to cooperate in the fulfillment of a plan

срок ~/я (srok ~/ia) period of execution

техническое ~ (tekhnícheskoe ~) technical execution

тщательное ~ (tshchátel'noe ~) painstaking execution

успешное ~ (uspéshnoe ~) successful execution

указания по ~/ю работ (ukazániia po ~/iu rabót) instructions for carrying out the work

ход ~/я (khod ~/ia) progress of implementation

ход ~/я заказа (khod ~/ia zakáza) position of an order

ход ~/я контракта (khod ~/ia kontrákta) progress of implementation of a contract

ход ~/я программы (khod ~/ia prográmmy) progress under a program

ход ~/я проекта (khod ~/ia proékta) progress of a project

ход ~/я работ на строительной площадке (khod ~/ia rabót na stroítel'noi ploshchádke)

progress of the construction site

ход ~/я соглашения (khod ~/ia soglashéniia) progress of the implementation of an agreement

этап ~/ia плана (etáp ~/ia plána) phase of a plan

частичное ~ (chastíchnoe ~) part performance

честное ~ (chéstnoe ~) faithful performance

эффективное ~ (effektívnoe ~) efficient implementation

~ договора (~ dogovóra) execution of a contract

~ договорных обязательств (~ dogovórnykh obiazátel'stv) fulfillment of contractual obligations

~ заказа (~ zakáza) fulfillment of an order

~ инструкций (~ instrúktsii) execution of instructions

~ контракта (~ kontrákta) implementation of a contract

~ норм выработки (~ norm výrabotki) performance up to standards

~ обязанностей (~ obiázannostei) discharge of duties

~ обязательств (~ obiazátel'stv) discharge of duties

~ обязательств по взаимным поставкам (~ obiazátel'stv po vzaímnym postávkam) meeting of mutual trade commitments

~ плана (~ plána) implementation of a plan

~ по особому заказу (~ po osobomu zakazu) execution of a special order

~ поручения (~ poruchéniia) execution of an order

~ работ (~ rabót) performance of work

~ соглашения (~ soglashéniia) implementation of an agreement

~ таможенных формальностей (~ tamózhennykh formál'nostei) attendance to customs formalities

~ указаний (~ ukazánii) execution of instructions

~ формальностей (~ formál'nostei) execution of formalities

Выполненный (výpolnennyi) *adj.*
executed, fulfilled
  ~ должным образом (~ dólzhnym
  óbrazom) duly executed
Выполнять (vypolniát') *v.* to
execute, fulfill, implement,
perform
Выпуск (výpusk) *m.* emission, issue,
output, publication
  внутренний ~ (vnútrennii ~)
  internal issue
  высококачественный ~ продукции
  (vysokokáchestvennyi ~
  prodúktsii) production of high
  quality products
  гарантировать ~ продукции
  (garantírovat' ~ prodúktsii) to
  guarantee the output
  дата ~/а (dáta ~/a) date of
  issue
  дневной ~ (dnevnói ~) daily
  output, daily publication
  еженедельный ~ (ezhenedél'nyi ~)
  weekly publication
  курс ~/а (kurs ~/a) rate of
  issue
  место ~/а (mésto ~/a) place of
  issue
  наращивать ~ продукции
  (naráshchivat' ~ prodúktsii) to
  increase manufacturing
  production
  начать ~ продукции (nachát' ~
  prodúktsii) to launch a product
  ограничивать ~ продукции
  (ograníchivat' ~ prodúktsii) to
  limit output
  осваивать ~ продукции (osváivat'
  ~ prodúktsii) to organize
  production
  план ~/а продукции (plan ~/a
  prodúktsii) output program
  планирование ~/а и сбыта
  продукции (planírovanie ~/a i
  sbýta prodúktsii) business
  planning
  планировать специальный ~
  (planírovat' spetsiál'nyi ~) to
  plan a special issue
  повторный ~ (povtórnyi ~)
  reissue
  серийный ~ (seríinyi ~) batch
  production
  согласовывать годовой ~
  продукции (soglasóvyvat' godovói
  ~ prodúktsii) to coordinate
  annual production

  сокращать ~ (sokrashchát' ~) to
  decrease output
  суточный ~ (sútochnyi ~) daily
  output
  увеличивать ~ (uvelíchivat' ~)
  to increase output
  ускорять ~ (uskoriát' ~) to
  speed up production
  разрешённое к ~/у количество
  (razreshiónnoe k ~/u
  kolíchestvo) sanction quality
  ~ акций (~ áktsii) issuance of
  shares
  ~ банкнот (~ banknót) emission
  of bank notes
  ~ в продажу (~ v prodázhu)
  release {for sale}
  ~ высококачественных товаров (~
  vysokokáchestvennykh továrov)
  production of high quality goods
  ~ денег в обращение (~ déneg v
  obrashchénie) emission of
  currency into circulation
  ~ займа (~ záima) issue of a
  loan
  ~ из печати (~ iz pecháti)
  publication release
  ~ нового продукта (~ nóvogo
  prodúkta) launching of a new
  product
  ~ облигаций (~ obligátsii) bond
  issue
  ~ продукции (~ prodúktsii)
  production
  ~ продукции на рынок (~
  prodúktsii na rýnok) commercial
  manufacturing
  ~ продукции, побочной (~
  prodúktsii, pobóchnoi) output of
  by-products
  ~ продукции, сверхплановой (~
  prodúktsii, sverkhplánovoi)
  output of production exceeding
  the target
  ~ продукции, учитываемый (~
  prodúktsii, uchítyvaemyi)
  recorded output
  ~ товара на рынок (~ továra na
  rýnok) market introduction
Выпускать (vypuskát') *v.* to emit,
to manufacture, to produce
Выравнивание (vyrávnivanie) *n.*
leveling off
Выражени/е (vyrazhéni/e) *n.*
expression
  в натуральном ~/и (v naturál'nom
  ~/i) in kind

в реальном ~/и (v reál'nom ~/i) in real terms

в стоимостном ~/и (v stóimostnom ~/i) in terms of value

в цифровом ~/и (v tsifrovóm ~/i) in figures

Выручать (vyruchát') *v.* to clear, to gain, to net

затраченное (zatráchennoe) to recover one's expenses

Выручк/а (výruchk/a) *f.* gain, proceeds, receipts

валовая ~ (valováia ~) gross earnings, gross proceeds

валовая от продажи ~ (valováia ot prodázhi ~) gross operating income

валютная ~ (valiútnaia ~) foreign exchange earnings

годовая ~ (godováia ~) annual receipts

денежная ~ (dénezhnaia ~) receipts

дневная ~ (dnevnáia ~) daily receipts

долларовая ~ (dóllarovaia ~) dollar denominated earnings

задания по валютной ~/е (zadániia po valiútnoi ~/e) currency earning targets

норма ~/и (nórma ~/i) earning rate

общая ~ (óbshchaia ~) total receipts

предполагаемая ~ (predpolagáemaia ~) estimated proceeds

перевод ~/и от продажи (perevód ~/i ot prodázhi) remittance of sale proceeds

пересчитывать ~/у в рубли (pereschítyvat' ~/u v rublí) to convert receipts to rubles

получать ~/у от продажи (poluchát' ~/u ot prodázhi) to receive the proceeds of a sale

расходовать ~/у (raskhódovat' ~/u) to expend the proceeds

сдавать ~/у от экспорта товаров (sdavát' ~/u ot éksporta továrov) to surrender export proceeds

суточная ~ (sútochnaia ~) daily receipts

торговая ~ (torgóvaia ~) trade receipts

чистая ~ (chístaia ~) net proceeds

экспортная ~ (éksportnaia ~) export earnings

~ в рублях (~ v rubliákh) returns in rubles

~ за работы, выполненные по контракту (~ za rabóty, výpolnennye po kontráktu) contract receipts

~ нетто (~ nétto) net receipts

~ от продажи {от реализации} (~ ot prodázhi {ot realizátsii}) proceeds of sales

~ от торговли (~ ot torgóvli) receipts from trade

~ от учтённого векселя (~ ot uchtiónnogo vékselia) net avails

~ от экспорта (~ ot éksporta) export proceeds

~ по договорным работам (~ po dogovórnym rabótam) proceeds from contract work

Высокодоходный (vysokodokhódnyi) *adj.* highly remunerative

Высококачественный (vysokokáchestvennyi) *adj.* high quality

Высококвалифицированный (vysokokvalifitsírovannyi) *adj.* highly qualified

Высокорентабельный (vysokorentábel'nyi) *adj.* highly profitable

Высокосортный (vysokosórtnyi) *adj.* high-grade

Высокоспециализированный (vysokospetsializírovannyi) *adj.* highly specialized

Высокотехнологический (vysokotekhnologícheskii) high technology

Выставк/а (výstavk/a) *f.* exhibition

администрация ~/и (administrátsiia ~/i) ~ administration

аренда помещения для ~/и (arénda pomeshchéniia dlia ~/i) rent of ~ site

арендовать место на ~/е (arendovát' mésto na ~/e) to lease space at an exhibition

всемирная ~ (vsemírnaia ~) World's Fair

возможность участия в ~/е (vozmózhnost' uchástiia v ~/e)

opportunity to participate in an
~
время проведения ~/и (vrémia
provedéniia ~/i) ~ period
выделять место на ~/е (vydeliát'
mésto na ~/e) to allocate a site
at an ~
выставлять экспонаты на ~/е
(vystavliát' eksponáty na ~/e)
to put exhibits on display
давать оценку ~/е (davát'
otsénku ~/e) to assess an
exhibition
демонтаж ~/и (demontázh ~/i)
dismantling of an ~
демонстрировать на ~/е
(demonstrírovat' na ~/e) to
demonstrate at an ~
директор ~/и (diréktor ~/i) ~
manager
для ~/и (dlia ~/i) for ~
purposes
ежегодная ~ (ezhegódnaia ~)
annual ~
заграничная ~ (zagraníchnaia ~)
foreign ~
закрытая ~ (zakrýtaia ~) private
~
закрывать ~/у (zakryvát' ~/u) to
close an ~
заявка на место на ~/е (zaiávka
na mésto na ~/e) application for
exhibit space
заявка на участие в ~/е (zaiávka
na uchástie v ~/e) application
to participate in an ~
крупная ~ (krúpnaia ~) major ~
место на ~/е (mésto na ~/e) ~
space
место проведения ~/и (mésto
provedéniia ~/i) ~ site
монтаж ~/и (montázh ~/i)
installation of an ~
международная ~ (mezhdunaródnaia
~) international ~
местная ~ (méstnaia ~) local ~
на время работы ~/и (na vrémia
rabóty ~/i) for the duration of
an ~
национальная ~ (natsionál'naia
~) national ~
обмен ~/ами (obmén ~/ami)
exchange of ~s
организатор ~/и (organizátor
~/i) sponsor of an ~

организовывать ~/у
(organizóvyvat' ~/u) to sponsor
an ~
осматривать ~/у (osmátrivat'
~/u) to tour an ~
осмотр ~/и (osmótr ~/i) tour of
an ~
отбор экспонатов для ~/и (otbór
eksponátov dlia ~/i) selection
of exhibits for an ~
откладывать открытие ~/и
(otkládyvat' otkrýtie ~/i) to
postpone the opening of an ~
открывать ~/у (otkryvát' ~/u) to
open an ~
отраслевая ~ (otrasleváia ~)
specialized trade ~
оформление ~/и (oformlénie ~/i)
design of an ~
оформлять ~/у (oformliát' ~/u)
to dress an ~
передвижная ~ (peredvizhnáia ~)
traveling ~
планировать ~/у (planírovat'
~/u) to plan an ~
площадь ~/и (plóshchad' ~/i) ~
grounds
помещение ~/и (pomeshchénie ~/i)
premises of an ~
посетитель ~/и (posetítel' ~/i)
~ visitor
постоянная ~ (postoiánnaia ~)
permanent ~
предстоящая ~ (predstoiáshchaia
~) upcoming ~
проводить ~/у (provodít' ~/u) to
hold an ~
программа ~/и (prográmma ~/i) ~
program
продолжительность проведения ~/и
(prodolzhítel'nost' provedéniia
~/i) ~ period
промышленная ~ (promýshlennaia
~) industrial ~
путеводитель по ~/е
(putevodítel' po ~/e) ~ guide
работа ~/и (rabóta ~/i)
operation of an ~
раздел ~/и (razdél ~/i) display
section
рекламировать товары на ~/е
(reklamírovat' továry na ~/e) to
advertise goods at an ~
речь на открытии ~/и (rech' na
otkrýtii ~/i) opening address at
an ~

рекламная ~ (reklámnaia ~)
advertising ~
сельскохозяйственная ~
(sél'skokhoziáistvennaia ~)
agricultural ~
совместная ~ (sovméstnaia ~)
joint ~
составлять график работы ~/и
(sostavliát' gráfik rabóty ~/i)
to draw up an ~ schedule
специализированная
(spetsializírovannaia ~)
specialized ~
срок проведения ~/и (srok
provedéniia ~/i) ~ period
стенд на ~/е (stend na ~/e) ~
booth
страна-участник ~/и (straná-
uchástnik ~/i) participating
nation at an ~
территория ~/и (territóriia ~/i)
~ grounds
территория ~/и под открытым
небом (territóriia ~/i pod
otkrýtym nébom) outdoor ~
grounds
техническая ~ (tekhnícheskaia ~)
technical ~
товарная ~ (továrnaia ~) goods ~
торгово-промышленная ~ (torgóvo-
promýshlennaia ~) trade and
industrial ~
торжественное открытие ~/и
(torzhéstvennoe otkrýtie ~/i)
ceremonial opening of an ~
универсальная ~ (universál'naia
~) universal ~
устроитель ~/и (ustroítel' ~/i)
~ organizer
участник ~/и (uchástnik ~/i) ~
participant
финансировать на ~/е
(finansírovat' na ~/e) to
finance an ~
франко ~/a (fránko ~/a) delivery
free to ~
церемония открытия ~/и
(tseremóniia otkrýtiia ~/i)
opening ceremony of an ~
часы работы ~/и (chasý rabóty
~/i) ~ operating hours
экспонат на ~/е (eksponát na
~/e) exhibit
экспонировать на ~/е
(eksponírovat' na ~/e) to
exhibit at a display

юбилейная ~ (iubiléinaia ~)
jubilee ~
~ в витрине (~ v vitríne) window
display
~ достижений науки и техники (~
dostizhénii naúki i tékhniki) ~
of achievements of science and
technology
~ на многосторонней основе (~ na
mnogostorónnei osnóve) multilateral ~
~ на открытом воздухе (~ na
otkrýtom vózdukhe) open air ~
~ на полках (~ na pólkakh) shelf
display
~ новинок экспорта (~ novínok
éksporta) display of new export
items
~ образцов (~ obraztsóv) sample
display
~ технических средств и
оборудования (~ tekhnícheskikh
sredstv i oborúdovaniia)
hardware ~
~ товаров широкого потребления
(~ továrov shirókogo potrebléniia) consumer goods ~
Выставка-продажа (výstavka-
prodázha) f. sales exhibit
Выставка-ярмарка (výstavka-
iármarka) f. trade fair
Выставлять (vystavliát') v. to
display, to draw up {document}
Выставочный (výstavochnyi) adj.
exhibition
Вычет (výchet) m. deduction
автоматический ~
(avtomatícheskii ~) automatic
deduction
возможность ~/a (vozmózhnost'
~/a) deductibility
до ~/a налога (do ~/a nalóga)
before tax
единый ~ (edínyi ~) block
deduction
за ~/ом (za ~/om) allowing for,
deducting
за ~/ом амортизации (za ~/om
amortizátsii) net of
depreciation
налоговый ~ (nalógovyi ~) tax
deduction
неразрешённый ~ (nerazreshiónnyi
~) unauthorized deduction
принудительный ~ (prinudítel'nyi
~) compulsory deduction

платёж без ~/ов (platiózh bez
~/ov) payment without deductions
подлежащий ~/у (podlezháshchii
~/u) deductible
прибыль за ~/ом налога (príbyl'
za ~/om nalóga) after tax profit
производить ~ (proizvodít' ~) to
deduct
цена за ~/ом скидки (tsená za
~/om skídki) price less discount
~ из зарплаты (~ iz zarpláty)
withholding {from wages}
~ процентов (~ protséntov)
rebate of interest
~ расходов (~ raskhódov)
deduction of expenses
Вычитать (vychitát') to deduct
from, to recoup
Вязкость (viázkost') viscosity,
toughness
Вялость (viálost') sluggishness
~ рынка (~ rýnka) market
stagnation
~ хозяйственной деятельности (~
khoziáistvennoi déiatel'nosti)
depressed economic activity

Г

Габарит (gabarít) *m.* dimensions
нестандартный ~ (nestandártnyi
~) over-sized
общий ~ (óbshchii ~) overall ~
соответствующий ~
(sootvétstvuiushchii ~)
corresponding ~
стандартный ~ (standártnyi ~)
standard ~
~ груза (~ grúza) total cargo
~/ы оборудования (~/y
oborúdovaniia) equipment ~
~ погрузки (~ pogrúzki)
equipment gauge
~ тары (~ táry) container size
~ ящика (~ iáshchika) case size
Гавань (gávan') *f.* harbor, haven
вольная ~ (vól'naia ~) free port
входить в ~ (vkhodít' v ~) v. to
put in at a harbor
налоговая ~ (nalógovaia ~) tax
haven
франко ~ (fránko ~) FOB. port
Газопровод (gazoprovód) *m.* gas
pipeline

прокладывать ~ (prokládyvat' ~)
v. to lay a gas pipeline
Гарант (garánt) *m.* guarantor,
sponsor, surety
совместный ~ (sovméstnyi ~)
joint surety
~ займа (~ záima) {debt}
guarantor
~ по векселю (~ po vékseliu)
guarantor of a bill
Гарантийный (garantíinyi) *adj.*
guaranteed, warranty
Гарантирование (garantírovanie) *n.*
sponsorship, support
~ цен (~ tsen) price support
program
Гарантированный (garantírovannyi)
adj. guaranteed
Гарантировать (garantírovat') v. to
guarantee, to warrant
Гарантируемый (garantírvemyi) *adj.*
guaranteed, covered by warranty
Гаранти /я (garántiia) *f.*
guarantee, warranty
аварийная ~ (avaríinaia ~)
general average bond
аннулировать ~/ю (annulírovat'
~/iu) v. to annul a guarantee
банковская ~ (bánkovskaia ~)
bank guarantee
без ущерба своих прав по ~/и
(bez ushchérba prav po ~/i)
without prejudice to rights
under warranty
безотзывная ~ (bezotzyvnaia ~)
irrevocable guarantee
безусловная ~ (bezuslóvnaia ~)
unconditional guarantee
в качестве ~/и (v káchestve ~/i)
as surety for, as guarantor
входить в ~/ю (vkhodít' v ~/iu)
v. to be covered by guarantee
вывозная ~ (vyvoznáai ~) export
guarantee
выдача ~/и (výdacha ~/i)
issuance of a guarantee
давать ~/ю (davát' ~/iu) v. to
guarantee, to make a warranty
дата окончания срока ~/и (dáta
okončániia sróka ~/i) guarantee
expiration date
действительная до ~ (~,
deistvítel'naia do...) guarantee
valid until...
добавочная ~ (dobávochnaia ~)
additional guarantee

договорные ~/и (dogovórnye ~/i) contractual guarantees

договор ~/и от убыток (dogovór ~/i ot ubýtok) indemnity agreement

долгосрочная ~ (dolgosróchnaia ~) long-term guarantee

имущественная ~ (imúhshcestvennaia ~) property guarantee

иметь ~/ю (imét' ~/iu) v. to have a guarantee

истечение срока ~/и (istechénie sróka ~/i) expiration of warrant

краткосрочная ~ (kratkosróchnaia ~) short-term warranty

личная ~ (líchnaia ~) personal security

лицо, дающее ~/ю (litsó, daiúshchee ~/iu) guarantor

надёжная ~ (nadiózhnaia) reliable guarantee

нарушение ~/и (narushénie ~/i) breach of warranty

общая ~ (óbshchala ~) general guarantee

основная ~ (osnovnáia ~) basic warranty

отзывная ~ (otzyvnáia ~) revocable guarantee

ответственность по ~/и (otvétstvennost' po ~/i) liability under the warranty

оформлять ~/ю (oformliát' ~/iu) v. to issue a guarantee

письменная ~ (pís'mennaia ~) written guarantee

по ~/и (po ~/i) under the warranty

по истечении срока ~/и (po istechénii sróka ~/i) upon expiration of the warranty

подразумеваемая ~ (podrazumeváemaia ~) implied warranty

подтверждение ~/и (podtverzhdénie ~/i) guarantee, confirmation

покрываться ~/ей (pokryvát'sia ~/ei) v. to be covered by warranty

получать ~/ю (poluchát' ~/iu) v. to obtain a guarantee

правовые ~/и (pravovýe ~/i) legal guarantees

предоставление ~/и (predostavlénie ~/i) granting of a guarantee

производственная ~ (proizvódstvennaia ~) production guarantee

продление срока ~/и (prodlénie sróka ~/i) extension of the term of the guarantee

продлевать срок ~/и (prodlevátu srok ~/i) v. to extend the term of the guarantee

пункт договора о ~/ях (punkt dogovóra o ~/iakh) guarantee clause, warranty clause

совместная ~ (sovméstnaia ~) joint surety

соответствовать условиям ~/и (sootvétstvovat' uslóviiam ~/i) v. to conform with the guarantee provisions

специальная ~ (spetsiál'naia ~) specific guarantee

срок ~/и (srok ~/i) guarantee period

ссуда под ~/ю (ssúda pod ~/iu) loan against a guarantee

страховая ~ (strakhováia ~) insurance guarantee

условная ~ (uslóvnaia ~) conditional guarantee

условия ~/и (uslóviia ~/i) guarantee terms, warranty provisions

устная ~ (ústnaia ~) oral warranty, guarantee

~ возврата платы за товар (~ vozvráta pláty za továr) money-back guarantee

~ годности товара (~ godnosti továra) warranty of fitness

~ качества (~ káchestva) quality guarantee

~ кредита (~ kredíta) credit guarantee

~ кредитоспособности (~ kreditosposóbnosti) guarantee of creditworthiness

~ оплаты (~ opláty) payment guarantee

~ основных показателей (~ osnovnýkh pokazátelei) performance guarantee

~ от убытков (~ ot ubýtkov) indemnity, guarantee against losses

~ платежа (~ platezhá) security of payment
~ пригодности для торговли (~ prigódnosti dlia torgóvli) warranty of merchantability
~ продавца (~ prodavtsá) vendor's guarantee
~ продавца о техническом обслуживании (~ prodavtsá o teknícheskom obslúzhivanii) vendor's maintenance warranty
~, распространяющая на (~, rasprostraniáiushchaia na...) guarantee applied to
~ стандартная (~ standártnaia) standard warranty
~ страховщика (~ strakhóvshchika) underwriter's guarantee
~ экспортных кредитов (~ éksportnykh kredítov) export credit guarantee
~ экспортного риска (~ éksportnovo ríska) export risk guarantee
Генеральный (generál'nyi) adj. general
Гербовый (gérbovyi) adj. stamped, watermarked
Герметический, герметичный (germetícheskii, germetíchnyi) adj. hermetically sealed
Гибел /ь (gíbel') f. loss
абсолютная (absoliútnaia ~) absolute total ~
действительная полная ~ (deistvítel'naia pólnaia ~) actual total~
конструктивная полная ~ (konstruktívnaia pólnaia ~) constructive total ~
полная ~ (pólnaia ~) total~
фактическая ~ (faktícheskaia ~) actual ~
частичная ~ (chastíchnaia ~) partial ~
~ груза (~ grúza) ~ of cargo
~ имущества (~ imúshchestva) ~ of property
~ корабля (~ korabliá) shipwreck
~ товара (~ továra) ~ of goods {spoilage or theft}
Гибкий (gíbkii) adj. flexible
Гибкость (gíbkost') f. flexibility
Глобальная (global'naia) adj. "blanket", global

Глубоководный (glubokovódnyi) adj. deep-water
Гниль (gnil') decay, spoilage
Год (god) m. year
базисный ~ (bázisnyi ~) base ~
балансовый ~ (balánsovyi~) fiscal ~
бюджетный ~ (biudzhétnyi) budget ~
договорный ~ (dogovórnyi ~) contract ~
календарный ~ (kalendárnyi ~) calendar ~
отчётный ~ (otchiótnyi ~) accounting ~
производственный ~ (proizvódstvennyi ~) production~
текущий ~ (tekúshchii ~) current ~
финансовый ~ (finánsovyi ~) fiscal, financial ~
хозяйственный ~ (khoziáistvennyi ~) production~
~ изготовления (~ izgotovléniia) ~ made
~ издания (~ izdániia) ~ published
Годны /й (gódnyi) adj. fit, valid
считать ~/м (schitát' ~/m) v. to deem fit
~ для (~ dlia...) fit for..., valid for...
~ для перевозки зерна (~ dlia perevózki zerná) fit for grain transport
Годовой (godovói) adj. annual
Голод (gólod) m. famine, lack, shortage
валютный ~ (valiútnyi ~) currency shortage
денежный ~ (dénezhnyi ~) tight money (monetary policy)
острый ~ (óstryi ~) acute shortage
Гонорар (gonorár) fee, honorarium, royalty
~ агента (~ agénta) agent's fee
договариваться об оплате ~/a (dogovarivat'sia ob opláte ~/a) v. to negotiate payment of fees
~ арбитра (~ arbítra) arbitrator's fee
~ ревизора (~ revizóra) auditor's fee
Горизонтальный (gorizontál'nyi) adj. horizontal, lateral
Горючий (goriúchii) adj. flammable

Госзаказ (goszakáz) *m.* state order
Господство (gospódstvo) *n.* command, dominance, supremacy
Государственный (gosudárstvennyi) *adj.* governmental, national, public state
Государство (gosudárstvo) *n.* country, government, state
Готовност /ь (gotóvnost') *f.* readiness
  извещение о ~/и (izveshchénie o ~/i) notice of ~
  извещение о ~/и судна к выгрузке (izveshchénie o ~/: súdna k výgruzke) notice of ~ of vessel for unloading
  сертификат о ~/и (sertifikát o ~/i) certificate of ~
  ~ к приёмке (~ k priiómke) ~ for acceptance
  ~ товара к отгрузке (~ továra k otgrúzke) ~ of goods
Грамота (grámota) *f.* certificate, official document
  верителные ~/ы (verítel'nyi ~/y) credentials
Грамотность (grámotnost') *f.* literacy
Границ /а (granítsa) *f.* border, frontier
  государственная ~ (gosudárstvennaia ~) national border
  доставка груза до ~/ы (dostávka grúza do ~/y) delivery of shipment to the border
  доставка товар до ~/ы
  перевалка груза на ~/е (pereválka grúza na ~/e) transhipment at the border
  пересекать ~/у (peresekát' ~/u) v. to cross the border
  с поставкой на ~/е (s postávkoi na ~/e) with delivery at the border
  цена франко ~ (tsená fránko ~) price FOB border
  ~ страны покупателя (~ strany pokupátelia) buyer's border
  ~ страны продавца (~ strany prodavtsá) seller's border
График (gráfik) *m.* schedule
  в соответствии с ~/ом (v sootvétstvii s ~/om)in accordance with the ~
  вне ~ (vne ~/a) off ~

  выдерживать ~ (vydérzhivat' ~) v. to operate on the ~
  выполнение ~/a (vypolnénie ~/a) meeting ~
  выполнять ~ поставок (vypolníat' ~ postá vok) v. to meet the delivery ~
  детальный ~ (detál'nyi ~) detailed ~
  контрольный ~(kontról'nyi ~) master ~
  корректировка ~/a (korrektiróvka ~/a) adjustment of ~
  линейный ~ (linéinyi ~) linear ~, time-line
  напряжённый ~ (napriazhiónnyi ~) tight ~
  нарушение ~/a (narushénie ~/a) disruption of ~
  нарушать ~ (narushát' ~) v. to break ~
  несоблюдение ~/a (nesobliudénie ~a) non-observance of ~
  окончательный ~ (okonchátel'nyi ~) final ~
  опережать ~ (operezhát ~) v. to be ahead of ~
  основной ~ (osnovnói ~) master ~
  осуществимый ~ (osushchestvímyi ~) feasible ~
  отставать от ~/a (otstavát' ot ~/a) v. to be behind ~
  пересмотренный ~ (peresmótrennyi ~) revised ~
  пересматривать ~ поставок (peresmátrivat' ~ postávok) v. to revise the delivery ~
  плотный ~ (plótnyi ~) busy ~
  предварительный ~ (predvarítel'nyi ~) preliminary ~
  предлагать ~ платежей (predlagát' ~ platezhéi) to propose a payment plan
  придерживать ~/a (pridérzhivat'sia ~/a) to adhere to ~
  производственный ~ (proizvódstvennyi ~) production ~
  работ, проектных (~ proéktnykh rabót) project ~
  работ, строительных (~ stroítel'nykh rabót) construction ~
  сводный ~ (svódnyi ~) comprehensive ~

согласовать ~ (soglasovát' ~) v. to finalize the ~
согласовывать ~ (soglasóvyvat' ~) v. to coordinate the ~
соответствие ~/у (sootvétsvie ~/a) conformance with the ~
составлять ~ (sostavliát' ~) v. to draw up a ~
составлять ежедневные временные ~/и (sostavliát' ezhednevnye vrémennye ~/i) v. to fill out daily timesheets
твёрдый ~ (tviórdi ~) firm ~
точно по ~/у (tóchno po ~/u) right on ~
устанавливать ~ работ (ustanávlivat' ~ rabót) v. to establish a production timetable
утверждать ~ (utverzhdát' ~) v. to approve a ~
~ возмещения долгов (~ vozmeshchéniia dolgóv) debt repayment ~
~ выполнения работ (~ vypolnéiia rabót) progress chart
~ выставок (~ výstavok) exhibition ~
~ отгрузок (~ otgrúzok) shipment ~
~ платежей (~ platezhéi) payment ~
~ поставок (~ postávok) delivery ~
~ проектных работ (~ proéktnykh rabót) project ~
~ работ (rabót) operating ~
~ рабочего дня (~ rabóchevodnia) daily work ~
~ строительных работ (~ stroítel'nykh rabót) construction ~
~ текущего ремонта (~ tekúshchevo remónta) maintenance ~
~ услуг (~ uslúg) ~ of services
~ хода строительства (~ khóda stroítel'stva) construction timetable

Грош (grosh) m. "grosh" {former Russian monetary unit of small value}; farthing, ha'penny

Груз (gruz) m. cargo
адресованный ~ (adresóvannyi ~) direct ~
автотранспортный (avtotránsportnyi ~) truck freight
арест на ~ (arést na ~) seizure of ~
бездокументный ~ (bezdokuméntnyi~) undocumented ~
бестарный ~ (bestárnyi ~) goods in bulk
бочковый ~ (bochkóvyi ~) goods in barrels
брать ~ (brat' ~) v. to take in
букировка ~/a (bukiróvka ~) booking of ~
бьющийся ~ (b'iúshchiisia ~) fragile ~
без ~/a (bez ~/a) empty (said of transporter)
взвешивать ~ (vzvéshivat' ~) v. to weigh ~
взрывчатый ~ (vzryvchátyi ~) explosive ~
вес ~/a (ves ~/a) weight of ~
весь ~ (ves' ~) total ~
владелец ~/a (vladélets ~) owner of the ~
возврат ~/a (vozvrát ~/a) return of ~
возвращать ~ (vozvrashchát' ~) v. to return ~
воздушный ~ (vozdúshnyi ~) air freight
востребовать ~ (vostrébovat' ~) v. to claim goods
выброшенный за борт ~ (výbroshennyi zá bort) jettisoned ~
выброшенный на берег ~ (~, výbroshennyi na béreg) stranded ~
выбрасывать ~ (vybrásyvat' ~) to jettison ~
вывоз ~/a (vývoz ~/a) ~ pick-up
вывозить ~ (vývozit' ~) v. to pick up ~
выгрузка ~/a (výgruzka ~/a) unloading of ~
выгружать ~ (vygruzhát' ~) v. to unload ~
выдача ~/a (výdacha ~/a) delivery of ~
выдавать ~ (vydavát' ~) v. to delivery ~
выдавать ~ со склада (vydavát' ~ so skláda) v. to release ~ from the warehouse
габаритный ~ (gabarítnyi ~) ~ within size range
габарит ~/a (gabarít ~/a) overall dimensions of ~

генеральный ~ (generál'nyi ~)
general ~
гибель ~/а (gíbel' ~/a) loss of
~
годный к транспортировке ~ (~,
gódnyi k transportiróvke)
transportable ~
готовый к вывозу ~ (~, gotóvyi k
vývozu) ~ available for pick-up
готовность ~/а (gotóvnost' ~/a)
readiness of ~
громоздкий ~ (gromózdkii ~)
bulky ~
дезинфекция ~/а (dezinféktsiia
~/a) disinfection of ~
декларация судового ~/а
(deklaratsia sudovóvo ~/a) ships
manifest
добавочный ~ (dobávochnoi ~)
additional ~
дозволенный ~ (dozvólennyi ~)
legal ~
досмотр ~/а (dosmótr ~/a)
inspection of ~
доставленный ~ (dostrávlennyi ~)
delivered ~
доставка ~/а (dostávka ~/a)
delivery of ~
доставлять ~ (dostavliát' ~) v.
to deliver ~
доставлять ~ к судну
(dostavliát' ~ k súdnu) v. to
deliver ~ to ship
единица ~/а (edinísa ~/a) parcel
железнодорожный ~
(zheleznodorózhnyi ~) rail
shipment
жидкий ~ (zhídkii ~) liquid ~
задержание ~/а (zaderzhánie ~/a)
detention of ~
задерживать ~ (zadérzhivat' ~)
v. to detail ~
закрепление ~/а (zakreplénie
~/a) battening of cargo
закрючивание ~/а (zakriúchivanie
~/a) hooking of ~
замена ~/а (zaména ~/a)
replacement of ~
занумеровывать ~ (zanumeróvyvat'
~) v. to number goods
запрос о местонахождении ~/а
(zaprós o mestonakhozhdénii ~/a)
~ tracer
засланный ~ (záslannyi ~)
misdirected ~
застрахованный ~
(zastrakhóvannyi ~) insured ~

засылать ~ (zasylát' ~) v. to
misdirect ~
затаривание ~/а (zatárivanie
~/a) packing
зацеплять ~ стропом (zatsepliát'
~ strópom) v. to sling ~
защищать ~ (zashchishchát' ~) v.
to safeguard ~
импортный ~ (ímportnyi ~)
imported goods
испорченный ~ (ispórchennyi ~)
spoiled ~
количество мест ~/а (kolíchestvo
mest ~/a) number of
units/parcels
коммерческий ~ (kommércheskii ~)
commercial ~
конвенциональный ~
(konventsionál'nyi ~)
conventional shipment
контейнеризованный (контейнерный)
~ (kontéinernyi ~) containerized
~
контрактный ~ (kontráktnyi ~)
contract freight
конфискация ~/а (konfiskátsiia
~/a) confiscation of ~
корабельный ~ (korábel'nyi ~)
shipload
крепление ~/а (kreplénie ~/a)
securing of ~
крепить ~ (krepít' ~) v. to
secure ~
лёгкий ~ (liógkii ~) light-
weight ~
легковоспламеняющийся ~
(legkovosplameniáiushchiisia ~)
highly-inflammable ~
маркировка ~/а (markiróvka ~/a)
marking of
мешковый ~ (meshkóvyi ~) ~ in
sacks
морской ~ (morskói ~) marine ~
навалочный ~ (naválochnyi ~)
bulk ~
на который наложен арест ~ (~,
na kotóryi nalózhen arést)
seized goods
накладная на ~ (nakladnáia na ~)
consignment note {way-bill}
накопление ~/ов в порту
(nakoplénie ~/ov v portú) ~
stockpiling
наносить ущерб ~/у (nanosít'
ushchérb ~/u) v. to cause damage
to ~

направлять ~/ы (napravliát' ~/y)
v. to route ~
невостребованный ~
(nevostrébovannyi ~) unclaimed ~
невыгруженный ~ (nevýgruzhennyi
~) short-landed ~
негабаритный ~ (negabarítnyi ~)
oversized ~
недостающий ~ (nedostaiúshchii
~) missing ~
недоставка ~/a (nedostávka ~/a)
non-delivery of ~
недостача ~/a (nedostácha ~/a)
short delivery of ~
незакреплённый ~
(nezakrepliónnyi ~) loose ~
незапечатанный ~
(nezapechátannyi ~) unsealed ~
незастрахованный ~
(nezastrakhóvannyi) un-insured ~
незатаренный ~ (nezatárennyi ~)
unsecured ~
незаявленный ~ (nezaiávlennyi ~)
undeclared ~
необъявленный ~ (neob''iávlennyi
~) ~ undeclared to customs
неправильная сдача ~/a
(neprávil'naia sdácha ~/a)
misdelivery of ~
непредъявление ~/a к перевозке
(nepred''iavlénie ~/a k
perevózke) failure to deliver
goods for shipment
обратный ~ (obrátnyi ~) return ~
обесценение ~/a (obestsenénie
~/a) depreciation of ~
оборот ~/ов (oborót ~/ov) ~
turnover
обработка ~/a (obrabótka ~/a) ~
stevedoring
обращение с ~/ом (obrashchénie s
~/om) ~ handling
объёмный ~ (ob''iómnyi ~)
voluminous ~
объём ~/a (ob''ióm ~/a) shipment
load volume
обычный ~ (obýchnyi ~)
conventional
огнеопасный ~ (ogneopásnyi ~)
flammable goods
однородный ~ (odnoródnyi ~)
uniform ~
опасный ~ (opásnyi ~) dangerous
~
опционный ~ (optsiónnyi ~)
optional ~

осматривать ~ (osmátrivat' ~) v.
to inspect ~
осуществлять перевалку ~/a
(osushchestvliát' pereválku ~/a)
v. transship ~
очистить ~/ы через таможню
(ochístit' ~/y chérez tamózhniu)
to clear goods through customs
пакетированный ~
(paketizírovanny ~) palletized ~
палубный ~ (pálubnyi ~) deck
load
первоначальный ~
(pervonachál'nyi ~) original ~
перевозить ~/ы на поддонах
(perevozít' ~/y na poddónakh) v.
to palletize goods
передача права на ~ (peredácha
práva na ~) transfer to
ownership of ~
передавать ~ (peredavát' ~) v.
to transfer
перекладывать ~/ы (perekládyvat'
~/y) v. to "rummage" goods
перемещать ~ (peremeshchát' ~)
v. to transfer ~
перечень забукированных ~/ов
(pérechen' zabukírovannykh ~/ov)
booking list
перечень ~/ов, указанных в
коносаменте (pérechen' ~/ov,
ukázannykh v konosaménte)
summary of bills of lading
плавающий ~ (plávaiushchii ~)
flotsam
повагонный ~ (povagónnyi ~)
carload
повреждённый ~ (povrezhdiónnyi
~) damaged ~
погибший ~ (pogíbshii ~) lost ~
погруженный навалом ~ (~,
pogrúzhennyi naválom) goods
loaded in bulk
погрузка ~/a (pogrúzka ~/a)
loading of ~
подвозка ~/a (podvózka ~/a)
delivery of ~
подмоченный ~ (podmóchennyi ~)
wet (water-damaged) ~
подсчёт мест ~/a (podschiót mest
~/a) tally of ~
подъём ~/a (pod''ióm ~/a)
hoisting of ~
полный ~ (pólnyi ~) complete ~
полученный ~ (polúchennyi ~)
received ~

получатель ~/а (poluchátel' ~/a)
~ consignee
получение ~/а из таможни
(poluchénie ~/a iz tamózhni)
clearance of ~ through customs
получать ~ (poluchát' ~) v. to
receive ~
попутный ~ (popútnyi ~) way
freight
порча ~/а (pórcha ~/a) damage to
~
поставленный ~ (postávlennyi ~)
delivered ~
почтовый ~ (pochtóvyi ~) ~ by
post
право на ~ (právo na ~) right to
~
право на ~, залоговое (zalógovoe
právo na ~) lien on ~
предъявление ~/а к перевозке
(pred''iavlénle ~/a k perevózke)
delivery of ~ for shipment
предохранять ~ (predokraniát' ~)
v. to safeguard ~
прибывший на судне ~ (~,
pribývshii na súdne) ~, arrived
by ship
прибытие ~/а (pribýtie ~/a)
arrival of ~
приём ~/а (priióm ~/a)
acceptance of ~
принимать ~ к перевозке
(prinimát' ~ k perevózke) v. to
accept ~ for shipping
принимать ~ на строп судна
(prinimát' ~ na strop súdna) v.
to take ~ on ship's tackle
принимать поставку ~/а
(prinimát' postávku ~/a) v. to
take delivery of ~
принятый ~ (príniatyi ~) intake
weight
проводить сепарацию ~/а
(provodít' separátsiiu ~/a) v.
to separate ~
производить транспортную
обработку ~/а (proizvodít'
tránsportnuiu obrabótku ~/a) v.
to handle ~
просроченный ~ (prosróchennyi ~)
delayed ~
разгрузка ~/а (razgrúzka ~/a)
unloading of ~
размер ~/а (razmér ~/a) ~
measurements
размещение ~/а (razmeshchénie
~/a) stowage of ~

размещение ~/а в трюме
(razmeshchénle ~/a v triúme)
trimming of the hold
разнородный ~ (raznoródnyi ~)
mixed cargo
разрешение таможни на выдачу ~/а
со склада (razreshénie tamózhni
na výdachu ~/a so skláda)
warehouseman's order
разгружать ~ (razgruzhát' ~) v.
to discharge ~
размещать ~ в трюме
(razmeshchát' ~ v triúme) v. to
trim to hold
размещать ~ на складе
(razmeshchát' ~ na skláde) v. to
warehouse ~
размещать ~ на судне
(razmeshchát' ~ na súdne) v. to
stow ~ on board ship
расписка о принятии ~/а для
отправки (raspíska o priniáti
~/a dlia otprávki) dock receipt
расположение ~/а (raspolozhénie
~/a) disposition of ~
рассортировывать ~/ы
(rassortiróvyvat' ~/y) v. to
sort out ~
раструска ~/а (rastrúska ~/a)
strewing of ~
рефрижераторный ~
(refrizherátornyi ~)
refrigerated goods
родственные ~/ы (ródstvennye
~/y) analogous goods
самовозгорание ~/а
(samovozgoránie ~/a) spontaneous
combustion of ~
с большим ~/ом (s bol'shím ~/om)
heavily-loaded
с полным ~/ом (s pólnym ~/om)
fully-loaded
сборный ~ (sbórnyi ~) general ~
свидетельство о происхождении
~/а (svidétel'stvo o
proiskhozhdénii ~/a) certificate
of origin of ~
свойства ~/а (svóistva ~/a) ~
properties
сдавать ~ в порту (sdavát' ~ v
portú) v. to deliver ~ at port
сданный на хранение ~ (~,
sdánnyi na khranénie) ~ placed
in storage
сдача ~/а на склад (sdácha ~/a
na sklad) transfer of ~ to
warehouse

сепарация ~/а (separátsiia ~/a) separation of ~

складской ~ (skladskói ~) warehoused ~

скопление ~/ов (skoplénie ~/ov) congestion of ~

скоропортящийся ~ (skoropórtiashchiisia ~) perishable ~

смешанный ~ (sméshannyi ~) mixed ~

снять ~ с судна (sniat' ~ s súdna) v. to land ~ from a ship

содержание ~/а (soderzhánie ~/a) contents of a parcel

состояние ~/а (sostoiánie ~/a) condition of ~

сохранение ~/а (sokhranénie ~/a) preservation of

сохранность ~/а (sokhránnost' ~/a) safety of ~

спасать ~ (spasát' ~) v. to salvage ~

спасение ~/а (spasénie ~/a) salvage of ~

спасённый ~ (spasiónnyi ~) salvaged ~

срочный ~ (sróchnyi ~) priority shipment

сухой ~ (sukhói ~) dry ~

сыпучий ~ (sypúchii ~) bulk-break ~

тарный ~ (tárnyi ~) packaged ~

торговый ~ (torgóvyi ~) commercial freight

транзитный ~ (tranzítnyi ~) transit ~

транспортировка ~/ов (transportiróvka ~/ov) transport of freight

трюмный ~ (triúmnyi ~) ~ held below-deck

тяжеловесный ~ (tiazhelovésnyi ~) heavyweight ~

укладка ~/а (ukládka ~/a) stowage {stevedoring} of ~

укладка ~/а на паллеты (ukládka ~/a na palléty) palletization of ~

укладывать ~ (ukládyvat' ~) v. to stow ~

укладчик ~/а (ukládchik ~/a) stower of ~

упакованный ~ (upakóvannyi ~) packaged ~

упаковка ~/а (upakóvka ~/a) packing of ~

упаковывать ~ (upakóvyvat' ~) v. to pack ~

усушка ~/а (usúshka ~/a) drying (shrinkage) of ~

утечка ~/а (utéchka ~/a) leakage of ~

утрата ~/а (utráta ~/a) loss of ~

утруска ~/а (utrúska ~/a) dissipation of ~

характер ~/а (kharákter ~/a) nature of ~

хранение ~/а (khranénie ~/a) storage of ~

хранить ~ (khranít' ~) v. to store ~

часть ~/а (chast' ~/a) portion of ~

часть ~/а, не принятая на судно (chast' ~/a, ne príniataia na súdno) short shipment

ценный ~ (tsénnyi ~) valuable ~

штабелированный ~ (shtabelírovannyi ~) stacked ~

штабелировать ~ (shtabelírovat' ~) v. to stack ~

штучный ~ (shtúchnyi ~) ~ in parcels

экспортный ~ (éksportnyi ~) outbound ~

экспедирование ~/ов (ekspidírovanie ~/ov) freight forwarding

экспедитор ~/а (ekspidítor ~/a) freight forwarder

эксперт по перевозке ~/ов (ekspért po perevózke ~/ov) freight traffic expert

ящичный ~ (iáshchichnyi ~) boxed ~

~ без порта назначения (~ bez pórta naznachéniia) optional ~

~ без упаковки (~ bez upakóvki) bulk ~

~ в кипах (~ v kípakh) baled ~

~ в коробках (~ v koróbkakh) ~ in boxes

~ в мешках (~ v meshkákh) bagged ~

~ в обрешётке (~ v obreshiótke) crated ~

~ в пакетах (~ v pakétakh) packeted ~

~ в упаковке (~ v upakóvke) packaged ~

~ затонул (~ zatonúl) the ~ has sunk

~ на паллетах (~ na pallétakh)
palletized ~
~ на плаву (~ na plavú) ~ afloat
~, не облагаемый пошлиной (~, ne
oblagáemyi póshlinoi) duty-free
~, неправильно указанный в
таможенной декларации (~,
neprávil'no ukázannyi v
tamózhennoi deklarátsii)
wrongfully declared ~
~, перевозимый автотранспортом
(~, perevozímyi avtotránsportom)
truck freight
~, перевозимые на дальние
расстояния (~, perevozímye na
da'nye rasstoiániia) long-
distance freight
~, поименованный в коносаменте
(~, poimenóvannyi v konosaménte)
~, indicated in the bill of
lading
~, принятый в хорошем состоянии
(~, príniatii v khoróshem
sostoiánii) ~ accepted in
apparent good order and
condition
~, принятый для отправки на
судно ~ (~, príniatii dlia
otprávki na súdno) ~ received
for shipment
~, принятый на склад ~ (~,
príniatii na sklad) ~ received
at warehouse
~ россыпью (~ róssyp'iu) loose ~
~ судна, терпящего бедствие (~
súdna, térpiashchego bédstvie)
distress ~
~, частично недопоставленный по
сравнению с коносаментом (~,
chastíchno nedopostávlennyi po
sravnéniiu s konosaméntom) ~
short against bill of lading
Грузить (gruzít') v. to load (with
freight)
Грузовик (gruzovík) m. truck
грузить на ~ (gruzít' na ~) v.
to load onto a ~
за перевозку на ~/e уплачено (za
perevózku n ~/e uplácheno)
shipment by ~ pre-paid
крытый ~ (krýtyi ~) closed ~
перевозить на ~/ах (perevozít'
na ~/akh) v. to ship by trucks
перегружать на ~ (peregruzhát'
na ~) v. to transfer to ~
разгружать ~ (razgruzhát' ~) v.
to unload a ~

тяжёлый ~ (tiazhiólyi ~) heavy-
duty ~
франко ~ (fránko ~) FOB truck
~ малой грузоподъёмности (~
máloi gruzopod''iómnosti) light-
duty ~
~ с прицепом (~ s pritsépom)
tractor-trailer
Грузовладелец (gruzovladélets) m.
cargo-owner
Грузовместимость (gruzovmestímost')
f. freight capacity
гарантированная ~
(garantírovannaia ~) guaranteed
~
киповая ~ (kípovaia ~) bale
capacity
максимальная ~ (maksimál'naia ~)
maximum ~
полная ~ (pólnaia ~) full ~
чистая ~ (chístaia ~) net ~
~ судна (~ súdna) freight space
~ судна для насыпного груза (~
súdna dlia nasypnógo grúza)
grain ~
Грузовой (gruzovói) adj. freight
Грузооборот (gruzooborót) m.
freight turnover
Грузоотправител/ь
(gruzootpravítel/') consignor,
shipper
декларация ~/я (deklarátsiia
~/ia) shipper's declaration
интересы ~/я (interésy ~/ia)
consignor's interests
отметка ~/я (otmétka ~/ia)
shipping mark
счёт ~/я (schiot ~/ia) shipper's
invoice
Грузоперевозка (gruzoperevózka) f.
freight traffic
Грузоподъёмник (gruzopod"iómnik) m.
load-lifter
Грузоподъёмность
(gruzopod"iómnost') f. load-lift
capacity
гарантированная ~
(garantírovannaia ~) guaranteed
deadweight capacity
полезная ~ (poléznaia ~) payload
capacity
полная грузовместимость и ~
(pólnaia gruzovmestímost' i ~)
full reach and burden
полная ~ судна (pólnaia ~ súdna)
deadweight capacity

судно ~/ю в ... тонн (súdno ~/iu
v ... tonn) ship with ... tons
burden
~ в ...тонн (~ v ...tonn) ...-
ton capacity
~ крана (~ krána) crane ~
~ подъёмного механизма (~
pod"iómnogo mekhanízma) hoisting
capacity
~ судна (~ súdna) tonnage of a
ship
Грузоподъёмный (gruzopod"iómnyi)
adj. hoisting, lifting
Грузополучател/ь
(gruzopoluchátel/') *m.* consignee
платёжеспособность ~/я
(platiózhesposóbnost' ~/ia)
solvency of a ~
склад ~/я (sklad ~/ia) ~'s
warehouse

Д

Давальческ/ий (davál'cheskii) *adj.*
"give and take"
на ~/ой основе (na ~/oi osnóve)
on a give and take basis
Давление (davlénie) *n.* pressure
выдерживать ~ (vydérzhivat') to
withstand ~
инфляционное (infliatsiónnoe ~)
inflationary ~
испытывать ~ (ispýtyvat' ~) to
be subjected to ~
оказывать ~ на (okázyvat' ~ na)
to exert ~ upon
усиливать ~ (usílivat' ~) to
increase the ~
под ~/м (pod ~/m) under ~
~ конкуренции (~ konkuréntsii) ~
of competition
~ товарных запасов (~ továrnykh
zapásov) inventory ~
~ цен (~ tsen) price ~
Давност/ь (dávnost/') *f.*
superannuation
закон об исковой ~/и (zakón ob
iskovói ~/i) statute of
limitations
исковая ~ (iskováia ~)
limitation of legal claims
приобретательная ~
(priobretátel'naia ~)
prescription, adverse possession

срок ~/и (srok ~/i) term of
limitation
Данны/е (dánny/e) *pl.* data
анализ ~/х (análiz ~/kh) ~
analysis
анкетные ~ (ankétnye ~)
biographical ~
бухгалтерские ~ (bukhgálterskie
~) bookkeeping ~
включать ~ (vkliuchát' ~) to
include ~
выборочные ~ (výborochnye ~)
sample ~
выдавать ~ (vydavát' ~) to
furnish ~
дополнительные ~ (dopolnítel'nye
~) additional ~
изучать технические ~ (izuchát'
tekhnícheskie ~) to examine
technical ~
исходные ~ (iskhódnye ~) basic ~
исчерпывающие ~
(ischérpyvaiushchie ~)
comprehensive ~
итоговые ~ (itógovye ~)
summarized ~
малодостоверные ~
(malodostovérnye ~) ill-founded
~
недостающие ~ (nedostaiúshchie
~) missing ~
необработанные ~ (neobrabótannye
~) raw ~
необходимые ~ (neobkhodímye ~)
necessary ~
неопровержимые ~
(neoproverzhímye ~) irrefutable
~
неполные ~ (nepólnye ~)
incomplete ~
неправильные ~ (neprávil'nye ~)
incorrect ~
обновлять ~ (obnovliát' ~) to
update ~
обрабатывать ~ (obrabátyvat' ~)
to process ~
оценка технических ~/х (otsénka
tekhnícheskikh ~/kh) evaluation
of technical ~
общие ~ (óbshchie ~) overall
figures
основные ~ (osnovnýe ~)
principle ~
официальные ~ (ofitsiál'nye ~)
official ~
первоначальные ~
(pervonachál'nye ~) original ~

плановые ~ (plánovye ~) initial targets
по неполным ~/м (po nepólnym ~/m) according to incomplete ~
по официальным ~/м (po ofitsiál'nym ~/m) according to official ~
по предварительным ~/м (po predvarítel'nym ~/m) according to preliminary ~
полные ~ (pólnye ~) complete ~
полученные ~ (polúchennye ~) findings
правильные ~ (právil'nye ~) correct ~
предварительные ~ (predvarítel'nye ~) preliminary ~
представление ~/х (predstavlénie ~/kh) submission of ~
приоритетные ~ (prioritétnye ~) priority ~
прогнозируемые ~ (prognozíruemye ~) predicted ~
проверять ~ (proveriát' ~) to verify ~
проектные ~ (proéktnye ~) design ~
рабочие ~ (rabóchie ~) operational ~
расположение ~/х в виде таблицы (raspolozhénie ~/kh v víde tablítsy) tabulation of ~
расчётные ~ (raschiótnye ~) rating ~
сводные ~ (svódnye ~) cumulative ~
системазированные ~ (sistemazírovannye ~) systemized ~
сметные ~ (smétnye ~) estimated ~
собирать ~ (sobirát' ~) to collect ~
справочные ~ (správochnye ~) reference ~
сравнительные ~ (sravnítel'nye ~) comparative ~
статистические ~ (statistícheskie ~) statistical ~
стоимостные ~ (stóimostnye ~) value declaration
технические ~ (tekhnícheskie ~) technical ~
фактические ~ (faktícheskie ~) fact sheet

цифровые ~ (tsifrovýe ~) numerical ~
экономический ~ (ekonomícheskii ~) economic ~
эксплуатационные ~ (ekspluatatsiónnye ~) operating ~
~ изготовления (~ izgotovléniia) manufacturing ~
~ испытаний (~ ispytánii) test results
~ о работе (~ o rabóte) operation log
~ ремонте (~ remónte) repair record
~ о ценах (~ o tsénakh) pricing ~
~ приёмно-сдаточных испытаний (~ priiómno-sdátochnykh ispytánii) acceptance test ~
Дань (dan') f. tribute {payment to conqueror}
Дат/а (dát/a) f. date
авизованная ~ аккредитива (avizóvannaia ~ akkreditíva) advice ~ of a letter of credit
изменять ~/у отгрузки (izmeniát' ~/u otgrúzki) to modify a dispatch ~
начальная ~ (nachál'naia ~) initial ~
обозначенная штемпелем ~ (oboznáchennaia shtémpelem ~) stamped ~
определять ~/у (opredeliát' ~/u) to fix a ~
определять последнюю ~/у отгрузки (opredeliát' poslédniuiu ~/u otgrúzki) to stipulate the latest shipment ~
помечать ~/ой (pomechát' ~/oi) to notate ~
последняя ~ (poslédniaia ~) latest ~
предполагаемая ~ (predpolagáemaia ~) expected ~
предполагаемая ~ прибытия (predpolagáemaia ~ pribýtiia) expected time of arrival {ETA}
предлагать другую ~/у (predlagát' drugúiu ~/u) to propose an alternative ~
приблизительная ~ (priblizítel'naia ~) approximate ~
приоритетная ~ (prioritétnaia ~) priority ~

проставлять ~/у (prostavliát'
~/u) to date
удобная ~ (udóbnaia ~)
convenient ~
указывать ~/ы отгрузки
(ukázyvat' ~/у otgrúzki) to show
shipping ~ s
установленная ~ (ustanóvlennaia
~) designated ~
~ акцепта (~ aktsépta)
acceptance ~
~ аннулирования (~
annulírovaniia) annulled ~
~ вступления в силу (~
vstupléniia v sílu) effective ~
~ вступления в силу соглашения
(~ vstupléniia v sílu soglashéniia) effective ~ of an
agreement
~ выдачи (~ výdachi) ~ of
issuance
~ выдачи патента (~ výdachi
paténta) ~ of grant of patent
~ выдачи полиса (~ výdachi
polisa) effective ~ of an insurance policy
~ выезда (~ výezda) ~ of
departure
~ выписки векселя (~ výpiski
vékselia) ~ of issue of a bill
~ выписки счёта (~ výpiski
schióta) invoice ~
~ выпуска (~ výpuska) release ~
~ выхода судна в море (~ výkhoda
súdna v móre) sailing ~
~ готовности к отгрузке ~ (~
gotóvnosti k otgrúzke ~) ~ of
ship readiness
~ заявки (~ zaiávki) application
~
~ изготовления (~ izgotovléniia)
~ of manufacture
~ испытания (~ ispytániia) test
~
~ монтажных работ (~ montázhnykh
rabót) ~ of erection {cons-
truction}
~ наступление срока (~
nastuplénie sroka) maturity ~
~ начала гарантийного периода (~
nachála garantíinogo períoda)
initial ~ of warranty period
~ начала работы (~ nachála
rabóty) ~ of commencement of
work
~ окончания срока (~ okonchániia
sróka) expiration ~

~ опубликования (~
opublikovániia) publication ~
~, от которой исчисляется срок
(~, ot kotóroi ischisliáetsia
srok) ~, from which the period
tolls
~ отгрузки (~ otgrúzki) ~ of
shipment
~ отправки (~ otprávki) dispatch
~
~ отправки корреспонденции (~
otprávki korrespondéntsii)
mailing ~
~ перехода границы (~ perekhóda
granítsy) ~ of border crossing
~ платежа (~ platezhá) payment ~
~ погрузки (~ pogrúzki) loading
~
~ подачи заявки (~ podáchi
zaiávki) filing (of application)
~
~ подписания контракта (~
podpisániia kontrákta) act ~
~ подписания протокола (~
podpisániia protokóla) protocol
~
~ поставки (~ postávki) delivery
~
~ поступления (~ postupléniia) ~
of receipt
~ почтового штемпеля (~
pochtóvogo shtémpelia) postmark
~ предложения (~ predlozhéniia)
offer ~
~ представления лицензии (~
predstavléniia litsénzii) licensing ~
~ предъявления иска (~
pred"iavléniia íska) ~ of filing
an action
~ прекращения действия контракта
(~ prekrashchéniia déistviia
kontrákta) termination ~ of a
act
~ претензии (~ preténzii) ~ of a
claim
~ прибытия (~ pribýtiia) ~ of
arrival
~ приёмки (~ priiómki) ~ of
acceptance
~ публикации (~ publikátsii)
publication ~
~ пуска в эксплуатацию (~ púska
v ekspluatátsiiu) start-up ~
~ расторжения (~ rastorzhéniia)
cancellation ~

Дата-вексель (dáta-véksel') *m.* time note, time bill
Датированный (datírovannyi) *adj.* dated
~ более поздним числом (~ bólee pózdnim chislóm) post- dated
~ задним числом (~ zádnim chislóm) ante-dated
Датировать (datírovat') *v.* to date
Датировка (datiróvka) *f.* dating {of document, etc.}
Движени/е (dvizhéni/e) *n.* traffic
воздушное ~ (vozdúshnoe ~) air ~
грузовое ~ (gruzovóe ~) freight ~
железнодорожное ~ (zheleznodorózhnoe ~) rail ~
интенсивное ~ (intensívnoe ~) heavy ~
направление ~/я цен (napravlénie ~/ia tsen) price trend
пассажирское ~ (passazhírskoe ~) passenger ~
поддерживать регулярное ~ (poddérzhivat' reguliárnoe ~) to maintain regular service
прекратить ~ (prekratít' ~) to stop ~
профсоюзное ~ (profsoiúznoe ~) labor movement
расписание ~/я поездов (raspisánie ~/ia poezdóv) train timetable
расписание ~/я судов (raspisánie ~/ia sudóv) ship timetable
товарное ~ (továrnoe ~) goods ~
транзитное ~ (tranzítnoe ~) ~ in transit
условия ~/я (uslóviia ~/ia) ~ conditions
~ вверх (~ vverkh) upward trend
~ денег (~ déneg) monetary movement
~ фондов (~ fóndov) movement of funds
~ цен (~ tsen) price movements
Двойной (dvoinói) *adj.* two-fold
Двухсторонный (dvukhstorónnyi) *adj.* bilateral
Двухпалубный (dvukhpálubnyi) *adj.* double decker
Двухцелевой (dvukhtselevói) *adj.* dual-purpose
Дебентура (debentúra) *f.* customs, debenture
Дебет (débet) *m.* debit

занесение в ~ (zanesénie v ~) debit entry
записать в ~ (zapisát' v ~) to charge a debit
записать сумму в ~ счёта (zapisát' súmmu v ~ schióta) to debit an amount to an account
~ и кредит (~ i kredít) debit and credit
~ счёта (~ schióta) debit of an account
Дебет-нот/а (débet-nót/a) *f.* debit note
отзывать ~/у (otzyvát' ~/u) to recall a ~
подробная ~ (podróbnaia ~) detailed ~
~ за услуги (~ za uslúgi) ~ for services rendered
~ на ... (~ na ...) ~ for ...
Дебетование счёта (debetovánie schióta) debit entry
Дебетовать (debetovát') *v.* to debit (as an account, etc.)
Дебитор (debitór) *m.* debtor
Девальваци/я (deval'vátsi/ia) *f.* devaluation
предстоящая ~ (predstoiáshchaia ~) impending ~
проводить ~/ю (provodít' ~/iu) to devalue
размер ~/и (razmér ~/i) extent of ~
~ валюты (~ valiúty) currency ~
Девальвированный (deval'vírovannyi) *adj.* devalued
Девальвировать (deval'vírovat') *v.* to devalue
Дегустация {бесплатная} (degustátsiia bezplátnaia) *f.* free sample tasting
Дегустировать (degustírovat') *v.* to taste
Дедвейт (dédveit) *m.* deadweight
Дееспособность (deesposóbnost') *f.* legal capacity
общая ~ (óbshchaia ~) general ~
ограниченная ~ (ograníchennaia ~) limited ~
~ сторон (~ storón) ~ of the parties
Дееспособный (deesposóbnyi) *adj.* competent
Действи/е (déistvi/e) *n.* act, effect, validity
вводить в ~ (vvodít' v ~) to bring into effect

вводить в ~ закон (vvodít' v ~ zakón) to carry a law into effect

вводить в ~ соглашение (vvodít' v ~ soglashénie) to bring an agreement into effect

возбуждать ~ против (vozbuzhdát' ~ prótiv) to bring an action against ...

вредное ~ (vrédnoe ~) ill effect

время ~/я лицензии (vrémia ~/ia litsénzii) licensing period

вступать в ~ (vstupát' v ~) to come on stream, to take effect

до начала ~/й (do nachála ~/i) prior to action

многократные ~/я (mnogokrátnye ~/ia) repeated actions

незаконное (nezakónnoe) illegal act

одностороннее ~ (odnostorónnee ~) unilateral act

оказывать ~/я (okázyvat' ~/ia) to have effect

оспоримое ~ (osporímoe ~) disputed act

официальное ~ (ofitsiál'noe ~) official action

период ~/я (períod ~/ia) service life

подверженный ~/ю (podvérzhennyi ~/iu) exposed to ...

правомерное ~ (pravomérnoe ~) lawful act

предварительные ~/я (predvarítel'nye ~/ia) preliminary acts

предельный срок ~/я (predél'nyi srok ~/ia) expiration period

предпринимать ~/я (predprinimát' ~/ia) to take action

предупреждать ~/я (preduprezhdát' ~/ia) to prevent action

прекращение ~/я (prekrashchénie ~/ia) termination

прекращение ~/я договора (prekrashchénie ~/ia dogovóra) termination of a act

прекращение ~/я лицензии (prekrashchénie ~/ia litsénzii) termination of a license

прекращение ~/я патента (prekrashchénie ~/ia paténta) termination of a patent grant

приводить в ~ (privodít' v ~) to give effect to

принудительные ~/я (prinudítel'nye ~/ia) obligatory actions, enforcement actions

продление срока ~/я (prodlénie sroka ~/ia) extension

продлевать ~ (prodlevát' ~) to extend

продлевать ~ патента (prodlevát' ~ paténta) to extend a patent

противоправные ~/я (protivoprávnye ~/ia) illegal acts

руководить ~/ями (rukovodít' ~/iami) to direct activities

санкционированное ~ (sanktsionírovannoe ~) authorized action

совместные ~/я (sovméstnye ~/ia) joint activities

срок ~/я (srok ~/ia) effective period

срок ~/я истёк (srok ~/ia istiók) term has expired

срочное ~ (sróchnoe ~) urgent action

суммарное ~ (summárnoe ~) summary action

требовать ~/й (trébovat' ~/i) to require actions

юридическое ~ (iuridícheskoe ~) juridical act

~ аккредитива (~ akkreditíva) validity of a letter of credit

~, наносящее ущерб (~, nanosiáshchee ushchérb) prejudicial action

~ обстоятельств (~ obstoiátel'stv) effective circumstances

~ патента (~ paténta) validity of a patent

Действительност/ь (deistvítel'nost/') f. validity

в ~/и (v ~/i) as a matter of fact

объективная ~ (ob"ektívnaia ~) objective reality

оспаривать ~ (ospárivat' ~) to contest the ~

признавать ~ лицензии (priznavát' ~ litsénzii) to acknowledge the ~ of a license

признавать ~ патента (priznavát' ~ paténta) to acknowledge the ~ of a patent

признавать ~ прав (priznavát' ~ prav) to acknowledge validity of rights
проверять ~ патента (proveriát' ~ paténta) to verify the validity of a patent
соответствовать ~/и (sootvétstvovat' ~/i) to correspond to the facts
~ документа (~ dokuménta) ~ of a document
~ лицензии (~ litsénzii) ~ of a license
~ патента (~ paténta) ~ of a patent
~ прав (~ prav) ~ of rights
~ предложения (~ predlozhéniia) ~ of an offer
~ товарного знака (~ továrnogo znáka) ~ of a trademark
Действительный (deistvítel'nyi) *adj.* valid
юридически ~ (iuridícheski ~) legally ~
Действовать (déistvovat') *v.* to act
Действующий (déistvuiushchii) *adj.* active, operating, valid
Деклараци/я (deklarátsi /ia) *f.* declaration
бланк ~/и (blank ~/i) ~ form
валютная ~ (valiútnaia ~) currency ~
заполнять ~/ю (zapolniát' ~/iu) to fill out a ~
налоговая ~ (nalógovaia ~) tax return
таможенная ~ (tamózhennaia ~) customs ~
тарифная ~ (tarífnaia ~) tariff ~
экспортная ~ (éksportnaia ~) export ~
~ грузоотправителя (~ gruzootpravítelia) consignor's ~
~ капитана (~ kapitána) master's ~
~ о грузах, не облагаемой пошлиной (~ o grúzakh, ne oblagáemoi póshlinoi) ~ of duty-free goods
~ о грузах, подлежащих хранению в приписных складах (~ o grúzakh, podlezháshchikh khranéniiu v pripisnýkh skládakh) warehousing ~
~ о закупке (~ o zakúpke) purchase ~

~ судового груза (~ sudovógo grúza) ship's manifest
Декларировать (deklarírovat') *v.* to declare
Делегат (delegát) *m.* delegate
избирать ~/ом (izbirát' ~/om) to elect a ~
посылать в качестве ~/а (posylát' v káchestve ~/a) to send in the capacity of a ~
~ конференции (~ konferéntsii) ~ to a conference
Делегаци/я (delegátsi/ia) *f.* delegation
большая ~ (bol'sháia ~) large ~
возглавлять ~/ю (vozglavliát' ~/iu) to head up a ~
иностранная ~ (inostránnaia ~) foreign ~
представительная ~ (predstavítel'naia ~) representative ~
правительственная ~ (pravítel'stvennaia ~) governmental ~
прибывшая для проведения переговоров ~ (pribývshaia dlia provedéniia peregovórov ~) negotiating team
принимать ~/ю (prinimát' ~/iu) to receive a ~
руководитель ~/и (rukovodítel' ~/i) head of a ~
торговая ~ (torgóvaia ~) trade ~
~ руководящих деятелей (~ rukovodiáshchikh déiatelei) high-level ~
Дел/ец (del/éts) *m.* operative
биржевой ~ (birzhevói ~) exchange operator
~ чёрного рынка (~ chiórnogo rýnka) black marketeer
Деливери-ордер (delíveri-órder) *m.* delivery order (customs)
Делимый (delímyi) *adj.* divisible
Делить (delít') *v.* to divide
Дел/о (dél/o) *n.* action, business, case, transaction
арбитражное ~ (arbitrázhnoe ~) arbitration case
банковское ~ (bánkovskoe ~) banking {business}
брокерское ~ (brókerskoe ~) brokerage
вести ~ (vestí ~) to plead a case

вести ~/а (vestí ~/a) to conduct business

вести ~/а через банк (vestí ~/a chérez bank) to transact business through a bank

внутренние ~/а (vnútrennie ~/a) domestic affairs

возобновление ~/а (vozobnovlénie ~/a) revivor

возбуждать ~ (vozbuzhdát' ~) to bring an action

выгодное ~ (výgodnoe ~) profitable business

выигрывать ~ (vyígryvat' ~) to win an action, case

делать ~ (délat' ~) to do business

заниматься рассмотрением ~ (zanimát'sia rassmotréniem ~) to look into the affair

застой в ~/ах (zastói v ~/akh) business stagnation

издательское ~ (izdátel'skoe ~) publishing business

иметь ~ с (imét' ~ s) to have business with, to deal with

исход ~/а (iskhód ~/a) outcome of a case

конфликтное ~ (konflíktnoe ~) disputed matter

ликвидировать ~ (likvidírovat' ~) to wind up a business

лоцманское ~ (lótsmanskoe ~) pilotage

маклерское ~ (máklerskoe ~) brokerage business

на ~/е (na ~/e) in practice

направлять ~ в арбитраж (napravliát' ~ v arbitrázh) to refer a case to arbitration

начать ~ (nachát' ~) to start up a business

начать ~ против (nachát' ~ prótiv) to initiate an action against

неотложное ~ (neotlózhnoe ~) urgent business

опыт в ~/ах (ópyt v ~/akh) business experience

опытный в ~/ах (ópytnyi v ~/akh) experienced in business

относящийся к ~/у (otnosiáshchiisia k ~/u) relevant (to the matter at hand)

по ~/у (po ~/u) on business {for purposes of business}

положение дел ~ (polozhénie del ~) state of affairs

посторонние ~/а (postorónnie ~/a) outside matters

правопреемник в ~/е (pravopreémnik v ~/e) successor (in a company, etc.)

прекращение ~/а (prekrashchénie ~/a) dismissal of legal action

прекращать ~ в суде (prekrashchát' ~ v sudé) to drop a case

преуспевать в ~/ах (preuspevát' v ~/ákh) to succeed in business

приводить ~/а в порядок (privodít' ~/a v poriádok) to put affairs in order

прибыльное ~ (príbyl'noe ~) profitable business

принимать ~ для решения в порядке арбитража (prinimát' ~ dlia reshéniia v poriádke arbitrázha) to accept a dispute for arbitration

принимать решение по ~/у (prinimát' reshénie po ~/u) to decide in a (disputed) matter

приобращать к ~/у (priobrashchát' k ~/u) to note in the record

приступать к ~/у (pristupát' k ~/u) to get to work

проиграть ~ (proigrát' ~) to lose a case

разбирать ~ (razbirát' ~) to hold a plea

рассматривать ~ (rassmátrivat' ~) to investigate a matter

рассмотрение ~/а о нарушении (rassmotrénie ~/a o narushénii) investigation of a violation

расширять ~ (rasshiriát' ~) to expand a business

расходы по ~/у (raskhódy po ~/u) costs {in a legal action}

сборы по ~/у (sbóry po ~/u) fees in a case

слушание ~/а (slúshanie ~/a) hearing

слушать ~ (slúshat' ~) to hear a case

создавать ~ (sozdavát' ~) to establish a business

спорное ~ (spórnoe ~) dispute

срочное ~ (sróchnoe ~) urgent matter

текущие ~/a (tekúshchie ~/a)
current affairs
торговые ~ (torgóvye ~) business
dealings
транспортное ~ (tránsportnoe ~)
transportation business
улаживать ~ (ulázhivat' ~) to
settle an affair
урегулировать ~ (uregulírovat'
~) to put matters to rights
учреждать ~ (uchrezhdát' ~) to
found a business
финансировать ~ (finansírovat'
~) to finance a business
финансовые ~ (finánsovye ~)
financial affairs
ход ~/a (khod ~/a) course of
business
экспедиторское ~ (ekspedítorskoe
~) freight forwarding business
~ большой важности (~ bol'shói
vázhnosti) a matter of great
significance
~ о явном нарушении (~ o iávnom
narushénii) a case of blatant
violation
Деловой (delovói) adj. business
Делькредере (dél'kredére) adv. del
credere
комиссионер, берущий на себя ~
(komissionér, berúshchii na
sebiá ~) ~ agent
комиссия за ~ (komíssiia za ~) ~
commission
принять на себя ~ (priniát' na
sebiá ~) to stand ~
Демерредж (démerredzh) m. demurrage
калькуляция ~/a (kal'kuliátsiia
~/a) calculation of ~
оплата ~/a (opláta ~/a) ~
payment
претензия в связи с ~/ем
(preténziia v sviázi s ~/em) ~
claim
расчёт ~/a (raschiót ~/a) ~
calculation
ставка ~/a (stávka ~/a) ~ rate
взимать ~ (vzimát' ~) to charge
~
Демзал (demzál) m. showroom
открывать ~ (otkryvát' ~) to
open a ~
Демонстрационный
(demonstratsiónnyi) adj.
demonstration
Демонстраци/я (demonstrátsi/ia) f.
demonstration

основная ~ (osnovnáia ~) basic
display
практическая ~ (praktícheskaia
~) practical ~
программа ~/и (prográmma ~/i)
program of ~s
публичная ~ (publíchnaia ~)
public ~
устраивать ~/ю (ustráivat' ~/iu)
to arrange a ~
~ изобретения (~ izobreténiia) ~
of an invention
~ образцов (~ obraztsóv) sample
display
~ полёта (~ polióta) flight ~
Демонтаж (demontázh) m. dismantling
сроки ~/a (sróki ~/a) ~ period
~ выставки (~ výstavki) ~ of an
exhibition
~ оборудования (~ oborúdovaniia)
~ of equipment
~ стендов (~ sténdov) of
(exhibition) ~ stands
~ установки (~ ustanóvki) ~ of
an installation
Демонтировать (demontírovat') v. to
dismantle
Демпинг (démping) m. dumping {trade
violation}
валютный ~ (valiútnyi ~)
currency ~
законы по борьбе с ~/ом (zakóny
po bor'bé s ~/om) anti-dumping
legislation
Демпинговый (démpingovyi) adj.
dumping (trade)
Денационализаци/я
(denatsionalizátsi/ia) f.
denationalization
проводить ~/ю (provodít' ~/iu)
to reprivatize
Денационализировать
(denatsionalizírovat') v. to
denationalize
Денежный (dénezhnyi) adj. money,
monetary
Деноминация (denominátsiia) f.
denomination
Денонсация (denonsátsiia) f.
denunciation
односторонняя (odnostorónniaia)
unilateral repudiation
~ договора (~ dogovóra)
repudiation of an agreement
Денонсировать (denonsírovat') v. to
denounce
Д/ень (d/en') m. day

в ~ (v ~) per diem
в конце ~/ня (v kontsé ~/nia) at
the end of a day
выходной ~ (vykhodnói ~) day off
календарный ~ (kalendárnyi ~)
calendar day
контрсталийные ~/ни
(kontrstalíinye ~/ni) demurrage
days
короткий ~ (korótkii ~) short
(work) day
кумулятивные ~/ни (kumuliatívnye
~/ni) cumulative days
курс ~/ня (kurs ~/nia) today's
rate of exchange
льготные ~/ни (l'gótnye ~/ni)
grace period (days)
на ~ предложения (na ~
predlozhéniia) upon date of
tender
назначать ~ (naznachát' ~) to
fix a day
неполный ~ (nepólnyi ~) part-
time
нерабочий ~ (nerabóchii ~) non-
working day
оплата за ~ (opláta za ~)
payment per diem
опоздание на ...дней (opozdánie
na ...dnei) delay of ... days
по цене ~/ня (po tsené ~/nia) at
value
погожий рабочий ~ (pogózhii
rabóchii ~) weather working day
полный ~ (pólnyi ~) full day
последовательные ~/ни
(posledovátel'nye ~/ni) consecu
tive days
праздничный ~ (prázdnichnyi ~)
holiday
приёмный ~ (priiómnyi ~) date of
acceptance
приходиться на ~ (prikhodít'sia
na ~) to fall on a day
рабочий ~ (rabóchii ~) work day
распорядок ~/ня (rasporiádok
~/nia) order of the day, routine
реверсивный ~ (reversívnyi ~)
reversible day
сбережённые ~/ни (sberezhiónnye
~/ni) days saved
со ~/ня выдачи (so ~/nia
výdachi) from the day of issue
сплошные ~/ни (sploshnýe ~/ni)
running days
сталийные ~/ни (stalíinye ~/ni)
lay days

сэкономленные ~/ни
(sekonómlennye ~/ni) days saved
через ... ~/ней после
акцептования ... (chérez ...
~/nei pósle aktseptovániia ...)
days following acceptance
через... ~/ней после
предъявления ~ ... (chérez...
~/nei pósle pred"iavléniia ~
...) days upon sight
устанавливать ~/ни отдыха ~
(ustanávlivat' ~/ni ótdykha ~)
to establish days off
~/ни демерреджа (~/ni
démerredzha) days on demurrage
~/ни диспача (~/ni díspacha)
dispatch days
~/ни на разгрузку (~/ni na
razgrúzku) permissible unloading
period
~ неплатежа (~ neplatezhá) day
of non-payment
~ открытия (~ otkrýtiia) opening
day
~ отправления (~ otpravléniia)
departure date
~ отхода судна (~ otkhóda súdna)
sailing day
~ платежа (~ platezhá) day of
payment
~/ни погрузки и разгрузки судов
(~/ni pogrúzki i razgrúzki
sudóv) lay days
~ прибытия (~ pribýtiia) day of
arrival
~ приёмки (~ priiómki) date of
acceptance
~ расчёта (~ raschióta)
settlement day
Ден/ьги (dén/'gi) pl. money
ассигновать ~ (assignovát' ~) to
allocate ~
без наличных ~/ег (bez
nalíchnykh ~/eg) out of cash
брать ~ из банка (brat' ~ iz
bánka) to make a withdrawal from
the bank
брать ~ со счёта (brat' ~ so
schióta) to withdraw from an
account
бумажные ~ (bumázhnye ~) paper ~
взнос наличными ~/ьгами (vznos
nalíchnymi ~/'gámi) cash deposit
взыскание ~/ег по векселю
(vzyskánie ~/eg po vékseliu)
collection of a bill (note)

вкладывать ~ в банк (vkládyvat′
~ v bank) to deposit ~ in a bank
вкладывать ~ из определённого
процента (vkládyvat′ ~ iz opred-
eliónnogo protsénta) to deposit
~ at a specified interest rate
вносить ~ (vnosít′ ~) to pay in
~
вносить ~ в банк (vnosít′ ~ v
bank) to place ~ in a bank
вносить ~ в депозит (vnosít′ ~ v
depozít) to place ~ on deposit
вносить ~ на счёт (vnosít′ ~ na
schiót) to place ~ on account
вносить ~ на условный счёт
(vnosít′ ~ na uslóvnyi schiót)
to place ~ in escrow
возвращать ~, взятые взаймы
(vozvrashchát′ ~, vziátye
vzaimý) to repay borrowed ~
возмещать ~ (vozmeshchát′ ~) to
refund ~
возмещать израсходованные ~
(vozmeshchát′ izraskhódovannye
~) to reimburse ~
всемирные ~ (vsemírnye ~)
universal ~
выдача ~/ег наличными (výdacha
~/eg nalíchnymi) cash payment
выпуск бумажных ~/ег (výpusk
bumázhnykh ~/eg) emission of
paper ~
выпускать ~ (vypuskát′ ~) to
issue ~
высвобождать ~ (vysvobozhdát′ ~)
to release funds
"горячие" ~ (goriáchie ~) "hot"
money
движение ~/ег (dvizhénie ~/eg)
monetary movement
держать ~ в банке (derzhát′ ~ v
bánke) to keep ~ in a bank
дешёвые ~ (deshióvye ~) cheap ~
дорогие ~ (dorogíe ~) expensive
~
доставать ~ (dostavát′ ~) to
raise ~
за неимением ~/ег (za neiméniem
~/eg) on account of lack of
funds
заём ~/ег (zaióm ~/eg) ~ loan
заменитель ~/ег (zamenítel′
~/eg) ~ substitute
занимать ~ (zanimát′ ~) to
borrow ~

занимать ~ без процентов
(zanimát′ ~ bez protséntov) to
borrow ~ at zero interest
занимать ~ до определённой суммы
(zanimát′ ~ do opredeliónnoi
súmmy) to borrow ~ up to a
specified amount
занимать ~ под закладную
(zanimát′ ~ pod zakladnúiu) to
borrow ~ under mortgage
занимать ~ под страховой
(zanimát′ ~ pod strakhovói) to
borrow ~ against an insurance
policy
запас ~/ег (zapás ~/eg) ~ supply
зарабатывать ~ (zarabátyvat′ ~)
to earn ~
изымать ~ из обращения (izymát′
~ iz obrashchéniia) to remove ~
from circulation
изъятие ~/ег из обращения
(iz"iátie ~/eg iz obrashchéniia)
withdrawal of ~ from circulation
испытывать недостаток в ~/ьгах
(ispýtyvat′ nedostátok v ~/′gá-
kh) to be short of ~
класть ~ в банк (klast′ ~ v
bank) to deposit ~ in a bank
контрсталийные ~ (kontrstalíinye
~) demurrage {payment}
копить ~ (kopít′ ~) v. to hoard
~
кредитные ~ (kredítnye ~) debt ~
мелкие ~ (mélkie ~) small change
местные ~ (méstnye ~) local
currency
менять ~ (meniát′ ~) to change ~
металлические ~ (metallícheskie
~) coins
мировые ~ (mirovýe ~) world ~
наличные ~ (nalíchnye ~) cash
наличие ~/ег (nalíchie ~/eg)
cash availability
недостаток ~/ег (nedostátok
~/eg) cash shortage
неизрасходованные ~
(neizraskhódovannye ~)
unexpended ~
необратимость бумажных ~/ег
(neobratímost′ bumázhnykh ~/eg)
inconvertibility of paper ~
непроизводительная трата ~/ег
(neproizvodítel′naia tráta ~/eg)
waste of ~
неразменные ~ (nerazménnye ~)
irredeemable ~

обесценение ~/ег (obestsenénie ~/eg) depreciation of ~
оборот наличных ~/ег (oborót nalíchnykh ~/eg) cash turnover
обращение ~/ег (obrashchénie ~/eg) circulation of ~
обращение бумажных ~/ег (obrashchénie bumázhnykh ~/eg) circulation of paper ~
остаток ~/ег (ostátok ~/eg) balance of ~
отступные ~ (otstupnýe ~) smart ~ {buy-out ~}
перевод ~/ег (perevód ~/eg) remittance of ~
переводить ~ (perevodít' ~) to remit ~
переводить ~ по почте (perevodít' ~ po póchte) to send ~ by postal money order
переводить ~ по телеграфу (perevodít' ~ po telegráfu) to wire ~
пересылать ~ (peresylát' ~) to transfer ~
пластмассовые ~ (plastmássovye ~) plastic money {credit cards}
пересылка ~/ег в форме чека (peresýlka ~eg v fórme chéka) transfer of ~ in the form of a check
подъёмные ~ (pod"iómnye ~) traveling expenses
получать ~ в банке (poluchát' ~ v bánke) to draw ~ from a bank
получать ~ в погашение (poluchát' ~ v pogashénie) to collect debts
получать ~ по векселю (poluchát' ~ po vékseliu) to collect a bill, note
получать ~ по чеку (poluchát' ~ po cheku) to cash a check
покупательная сила ~/ег (pokupátel'naia síla ~/eg) purchasing power of ~
поступления ~/ег (postupléniia ~/eg) incoming payments
призовые ~ (prizovýe ~) prize ~
предоставлять ~ (predostavliát' ~) to provide with ~
принимать ~ на вклад (prinimát' ~ na vklad) to receive ~ on deposit
разблокирование удержанных ~/ег (razblokírovanie udérzhannykh ~/eg) release of holdback ~

размен ~/ег ~- (razmén ~/eg) changing
расходование ~/ег (raskhódovanie ~/eg) expenditure of ~
расходовать ~ (raskhódovat' ~) to expend ~
реальные ~ (reál'nye ~) real ~
резервировать ~ (rezervírovat' ~) to reserve ~
сверхконтрсталийные ~ (sverkhkontrstalíinye ~) detention {of vessel beyond laydays}
символические ~ (simvolícheskie ~) token ~
снятие ~/ег со счёта (sniátie ~/eg so schióta) cash withdrawal from an account
снимать ~ со счёта (snimát' ~ so schióta) to withdraw ~ from an account
ссужать ~ под проценты (ssuzhát' ~ pod protsénty) to lend ~ at interest
суточные ~ (sútochnye ~) daily allowance (per diem)
трата ~/ег (tráta ~/eg) expense
тратить ~ (trátit' ~) v. to spend ~
требование наличных ~/ег (trébovanie nalíchnykh ~/eg) cash call
цена за наличные ~ (tsená za nalíchnye ~) cash price
фальшивые ~ (fal'shívye ~) counterfeit ~
хранить ~ в банке (khranít' ~ v bánke) to keep ~ in a bank
экономить ~ (ekonómit' ~) to save ~
эмиссия ~/ег (emíssiia ~/eg) issue of currency
~ в обращение (~ v obrashchénie) ~ in circulation
~ на покупку (~ na pokúpku) purchase ~
Депо (depó) n. depot
Депозит (depozít) m. deposit
банковский ~ (bánkovskii ~) bank ~
бланк для взноса ~/а (blank dlia vznósa ~/a) ~ slip
бессрочный ~ (bessróchnyi ~) demand ~
выплачивать деньги по ~/у (vypláchivat' dén'gi po ~/u) to pay a ~

гарантийный ~ (garantíinyi ~)
guaranteed ~
денежный ~ (dénezhnyi ~) cash ~
долларовый ~ (dóllarovyi ~)
dollar-denominated ~
застрахованный ~
(zastrakhóvannyi ~) secured ~
изъятие ~/ов (iz"iátie ~/ov)
withdrawal of ~s
иметь ~ в банке (imét' ~ v
bánke) to have a ~ at the bank
перевод денег на ~ (perevód
déneg na ~) transfer of money on
~
переводить деньги на ~
(perevodít' dén'gi na ~) to
transfer money on ~
перечислять деньги с ~/а
(perechisliát' dén'gi s ~/a) to
transfer money from ~
разблокировать ~ (razblokírovat'
~) to unblock a ~
краткосрочный ~ (kratkosróchnyi
~) short-term ~
неиспользуемый ~ (neispól'zuemyi
~) idle ~
обычный ~ (obýchnyi ~) general ~
первичный ~ (pervíchnyi ~)
primary ~
правительственный ~
(pravítel'stvennyi ~) government
~
резервный ~ (rezérvnyi ~)
reserve ~
свободно переводимые ~/ы
(svobódno perevodímye ~/y)
freely transferrable ~s
снять ~ (sniat' ~) to close out
a ~
ставка по ~/ам (stávka po ~/am)
~ rate
специальный ~ (spetsiál'nyi ~)
special ~
срочный ~ (sróchnyi ~) term ~
срочный с фиксированным сроком
(sróchnyi s fiksírovannym
srókom) fixed term ~
условный ~ (uslóvnyi ~) escrow ~
удерживать ~ (udérzhivat' ~) to
retain a ~
~ до востребования (~ do
vostrébovaniia) call ~
Депозитарий (depozitárii) m.
depositary
Депозитный (depozítnyi) adj.
deposit
Депонент (deponént) m. depositor

Депрессия (depréssiia) f.
depression
Держатель (derzhátel') m. holder
добросовестный ~ (dobrosóvestnyi
~) bona fide ~
законный ~ (zakónnyi ~) ~ in due
course
последующий ~ (posléduiushchii
~) subsequent ~
предыдущий ~ (predydúshchii ~)
previous ~
~ аккредитива (~ akkreditíva) ~
of a letter of credit
~ акций (~ áktsii) shareholder
~ векселя (~ vékselia) ~ of a
bill {note}
~ документов (~ dokuméntov) ~ of
documents
~ залога (~ zalóga) ~ of a
pledge
~ коносамента (~ konosaménta) ~
of a bill of lading
~ лицензии (~ litsénzii) ~ of a
license
~ облигаций (~ obligátsii) bond
holder
~ страхового полиса (~
strakhovógo pólisa) policy ~
~ счёта (~ schióta) account ~
~ тратты (~ trátty) ~ of a draft
{bill of exchange}
Держать (derzhát') v. to hold
Дестабилизация (destabilizátsiia)
f. destabilization
~ экономики (~ ekonómiki)
destabilization of the economy
Детализированный (detalizírovannyi)
adj. detailed
Детал/ь (detál'/') f. component,
detail, part
бракованная ~ (brakóvannaia ~)
rejected part
быстроизнашивающаяся ~
(bystroiznáshivaiushchaiasia ~)
rapidly wearing part
важная ~ (vázhnaia ~) important
part
взаимозаменяемые ~/и
(vzaimozameniáemye ~/i)
interchangeable parts
вспомогательная ~
(vspomogátel'naia ~) auxiliary
part
второстепенные ~/и
(vtorostepénnye ~/i) non-
essential parts

готовая ~ (gotóvaia ~) finished
component
заменять ~/и (zameniát' ~/i) to
replace parts
запасная ~ (zapasnáia ~) spare
part
иметь ~ на складе (imét' ~ na
skláde) to stock parts
комплектующие ~/и
(komplektúiushchie ~/i)
accessory components
недостающая ~ (nedostaiúshchaia
~) missing part
номер ~/и (nómer ~/i) part
number
основная ~ (osnovnáia ~)
principle component
отдельная ~ (otdél'naia ~)
individual part
повреждённая ~ (povrezhdiónnaia
~) damaged part
представлять ~/и (predstavliát'
~/i) to provide details
расходуемые ~/и (raskhóduemye
~/i) expendable parts
ремонтная ~ (remóntnaia ~)
repair part
сменная ~ (sménnaia ~)
replacement part
стандартная ~ (standártnaia ~)
standard part
технические ~/и (tekhnícheskie
~/i) technical details
улучшенная ~ (ulúchshennaia ~)
updated part
характерные ~/и (kharaktérnye
~/i) specific details
~ и к машине (~ i k mashíne)
machine parts
~ машины (~ mashíny) part to a
machine
~ и расценки (~ i rastsénki)
pricing details
Детально (detál'no) adv. in detail
разрабатывать ~ (razrabátyvat'
~) to elaborate
Детальный (detál'nyi) adj. detailed
Детеншен (deténshen) m. detention
{of a vessel}
Дефект (defékt) m. defect
быть ответственным за ~ (byt'
otvétstvennym za ~) to be liable
for a ~
внешний ~ (vnéshnii ~) visual ~
внутренний ~ (vnútrennii ~)
inherent ~

второстепенный ~ (vtorostepénnyi
~) minor ~
естественный ~ (estéstvennyi ~)
natural ~
заявленный ~ (zaiávlennyi ~)
stated ~
значительный ~ (znachítel'nyi ~)
serious ~
исправление ~/а (ispravlénie
~/a) correction of a ~
иметь ~/ы (imét' ~/y) to have ~s
исправлять ~ (ispravliát' ~) to
correct a ~
мелкий ~ (mélkii ~) slight ~
не иметь ~/ов (ne imét' ~/ov) to
be free of ~s
незначительный ~
(neznachítel'nyi ~)
insignificant ~
необнаруженный ~
(neobnarúzhennyi ~) undiscovered
~
несущественный ~
(nesushchéstvennyi ~) non-
existent ~
обнаруживать ~ (obnarúzhivat' ~)
to discover a ~
опасный ~ (opásnyi ~) dangerous
~
основной ~ (osnovnói ~) basic ~
описание ~/ов (opisánie ~/ov)
description of ~s
первоначальный ~
(pervonachál'nyi ~) initial ~
поверхностный ~ (povérkhnostnyi
~) surface ~
предполагаемый ~ (predpolagáemyi
~) alleged ~
причина ~/а (prichína ~/a)
reason for a ~
серьёзный ~ (ser'ióznyi ~)
serious ~
скрытый ~ (skrýtyi ~) latent ~
скрывать ~ (skryvát' ~) to
conceal a ~
случайный ~ (slucháinyi ~)
incidental ~
характер ~/а (kharákter ~/a)
nature of a ~
устранять ~ (ustraniát' ~) to
eliminate a ~
устранять ~ без ущемления прав
другой стороны (ustraniát' ~ bez
ushchemléniia prav drugói
storoný) to eliminate a ~ without prejudice to the other side

устранять ~ за счёт (ustraniát′
~ za schiót) to eliminate a ~ at
... expense
устранять ~ по соглашению сторон
(ustraniát′ ~ po soglashéniiu
storón) to eliminate a ~ by
agreement of the parties
явный ~ (iávnyi ~) obvious ~
~ в конструкции (~ v
konstrúktsii) design ~
~ завода-изготовителя (~ zavóda-
izgotovítelia) manufacturing ~
~ производства (~ proizvódstva)
production ~
~ товара (~ továra) ~ in goods
~ упаковки (~ upakóvki) packing
~
Дефектный (deféktnyi) *adj.*
defective
Дефектоскопия (defektoskopíia) *f.*
defect detection
Дефицит (defitsít) *m.* deficit,
shortage
бюджетный ~ (biudzhétnyi ~)
budget deficit
внешнеторговый ~
(vnéshnetorgóvyi ~) foreign
trade defi cit
внешний ~ (vnéshnii ~) external
deficit
вызывать ~ (vyzyvát′ ~) to cause
a deficit
долларовый ~ (dóllarovyi ~)
dollar deficit
иметь ~ (imét′ ~) to have a
deficit
исчислять ~ (ischisliát′ ~) to
calculate a deficit
кассовый ~ (kássovyi ~) cash
deficit
компенсировать ~ (kompensírovat′
~) to offset a deficit
краткосрочный ~ (kratkosróchnyi
~) short-term deficit
незначительный ~
(neznachítel′nyi ~)
insignificant defi cit
непокрытый ~ (nepokrýtyi ~)
outstanding deficit
покрывать ~ (pokryvát′ ~) to
compensate for a deficit
размер ~/a (razmér ~/a) size of
a deficit
рост ~/a (rost ~/a) growth of a
deficit
сальдировать ~ (sal′dírovat′ ~)
to balance a deficit

сбалансирование ~/a
(sbalansírovanie ~/a) balancing
of a deficit
сократить ~ (sokratít′ ~) to
reduce a deficit
существующий ~
(sushchestvúiushchii ~) existing
deficit
текущий ~ (tekúshchii ~) current
deficit
финансовый ~ (finánsovyi ~)
financial deficit
хронический ~ (khronícheskii ~)
chronic deficit
~ валюты (~ valiúty) foreign
exchange deficit
~ платёжного баланса (~
platiózhnogo balánsa) balance of
payments deficit
~ рабочей силы (~ rabóchei síly)
labor shortage
~ текущего счёта (~ tekúshchego
schióta) current account deficit
~ товаров (~ továrov) shortage
of goods
~ торгового баланса (~ torgóvogo
balánsa) trade deficit
Дефицитный (defitsítnyi) *adj.*
deficit
Дефляционный (defliatsiónnyi) *adj.*
disinflationary
Дефляция (defliátsiia) *f.*
disinflation
Деформаци/я (deformátsi/ia) *f.*
distortion
избегать ~/и (izbegát′ ~/i) to
avoid distortion
Дешёвый (deshióvyi) *adj.* cheap,
inexpensive
Деятельност/ь (déiatel′nost/′) *f.*
activity
активная ~ (aktívnaia ~)
vigorous ~
активизировать ~ (aktivizírovat′
~) to increase ~
внешнеторговая ~
(vneshnetorgóvaia ~) foreign
trade ~
внешнеэкономическая ~
(vneshneekonomícheskaia ~)
external economic ~
возобновление ~/и (vozobnovlénie
~/i) resumption of ~
возобновлять ~ (vozobnovliát′ ~)
to resume ~
деловая ~ (delováia ~) business
~

диверсификация ~/и
(diversifikátsiia ~/i)
diversification of ~
закупочная ~ (zakúpochnaia ~)
procurement ~
индивидуальная трудовая ~
(individuál'naia trudováia ~)
individual labor
коммерческая ~ (kommércheskaia
~) commercial ~
координировать ~ (koordinírovat'
~) to coordinate ~
купировать ~ (kupírovat' ~) to
supervise ~
лицензионная ~ (litsenziónnaia
~) licensed ~
место ~/и (mésto ~/i) site of ~
многообразная ~ (mnogoobráznaia
~) diversified ~s
нарушение торговой ~/и
(narushénie torgóvoi ~/i)
business disturbance
обзор хозяйственной ~/и (obzór
khoziástvennoi ~/i) business
survey
обсуждать ~ (obsuzhdát' ~) to
discuss ~
оперативная ~ (operatívnaia ~)
operating performance
основная ~ (osnovnáia ~) primary
~
относящаяся ~ (otnosiáshchaiasia
~) related ~
отчёт о ~/и агента (otchiót o
~/i agénta) agent's report
практическая ~ (praktícheskaia
~) practical ~
приостанавливать ~
(priostanávlivat' ~) to suspend
~
производственная ~
(proizvódstvennaia ~) production
~
пропагандистская ~
(propagandístskaia ~) propaganda
efforts
прошлая ~ (próshlaia ~) past ~
расширять ~ (rasshiriát' ~) to
expand ~
рационализаторская ~
(ratsionalizátorskaia ~)
rationalization efforts
рекламная ~ (reklámnaia ~)
advertising ~, promotion
род ~/и (rod ~/i) line of
business

совместная ~ (sovméstnaia ~)
joint ~
творческая ~ (tvórcheskaia ~)
creative ~
торговая ~ (torgóvaia ~) trade ~
торгово-промышленная ~ (torgóvo-
promýshlennaia ~) business ~
торгово-сбытовая ~ (torgóvo-
sbytováia ~) trade and marketing
трудовая ~ (trudováia ~) labor ~
финансовая ~ (finánsovaia ~)
financial ~
финансово-хозяйственная ~
(finánsovo-khoziástvennaia ~)
financial and economic ~
характер ~/и (kharákter ~/i)
nature of ~
хозрасчётная ~ (khozraschiótnaia
~) cost accounting
хозяйственная ~ (khoziástvennaia
~) economic ~
экономическая ~ (ekonomícheskaia
~) economic ~
экспорт и импорт результатов
творческой ~/и (éksport i ímport
rezul'tátov tvórcheskoi ~/i)
export and import of intellectual property
~ агента (~ agénta) agent's ~s
~ компании (~ kompánii) company
operations
~ лицензиара (~ litsenziára)
licensor's operations
~ лицензиата (~ litsenziáta)
licensee's operations
Диагностический (diagnostícheskii)
adj. diagnostic
Диаграмма (diagrámma) f. diagram
временная ~ (vrémennaia ~) time
chart
функциональная ~
(funktsionál'naia ~) block ~
Диверсификаци/я (diversifikátsi/ia)
f. diversification
взаимного ~ товарооборота
(vzaímnogo ~ tovarooboróta) ~ of
mutual trade
план ~/и (plan ~/i) ~ plan
программа ~/и (prográmma ~/i) ~
program
~ деятельности (~ déiatel'nosti)
~ of activity
~ продукта (~ prodúkta) ~ of a
product
~ промышленного производства (~
promýshlennogo proizvódstva) ~
of industrial production

~ торговли (~ torgóvli) ~ of trade
~ экономики (~ ekonómiki) ~ of the economy
~ экспорта (~ éksporta) ~ of exports
~ экспортных возможностей (~ éksportnykh vozmózhnostei) ~ of export capabilities
Диверсия (divérsiia) f. sabotage, subversion
Дивиденд (dividénd) m. dividend
выплата ~/ов {по ~/ам} (výplata ~/ov po ~/am) payment of ~ s
выплачивать ~ (vypláchivat' ~) to pay out a ~
годовой ~ (godovói ~) annual ~
денежный ~ (dénezhnyi ~) cash ~
квартальный ~ (kvartál'nyi ~) quarterly ~
накопленные ~/ы (nakoplennye ~/y) crude ~s
невостребованный ~ (nevostrébovannyi ~) unclaimed ~
объявленный ~ (ob"iavlennyi ~) declared ~
объявлять о выплате ~/ов (ob"iavliát' o vyplate ~/ov) to declare ~s
оплата ~/а (opláta ~/a) ~ payment
отсроченные ~/ы (otsróchennye ~/y) deferred ~s
предварительный ~ (predvarítel'nyi ~) ~ on account
размер ~/а (razmér ~/a) amount of a ~
~, выплаченный акциями (~, vypláchennyi áktsiiami) stock ~
~, выплаченный наличными (~, vypláchennyi nalíchnymi) cash ~
~ к оплате (~ k opláte) ~ payable
~/ы на вложенный капитал (~/y na vlózhennyi kapitál) ~s on investment
~ по акциям (~ po áktsiiam) ~ on shares {share earnings}
Дизажио (dizázhio) n. disagio
Дизайн (dizáin) m. design
запатентованный ~ (zapatentóvannyi ~) patented design
консультант по ~/y (konsul'tánt po ~/u) design consultant
улучшение ~/а (uluchshénie ~/a) design improvement

~ рекламного объявления (~ reklámnogo ob"iavléniia) advertising design
Дизайнер (dizáiner) m. designer
Дилер (díler) m. dealer
биржевой ~ (birzhevói ~) exchange ~
скидка ~/ам (skídka ~/am) ~ discount
~ по операциям с ценными бумагами (~ po operátsiiam s tsénnymi bumágami) securities ~
~ по продаже подержанного имущества (~ po prodázhe podérzhannogo imúshchestva) second-hand ~
~ с лицензией (~ s litsénziei) licensed ~
Димайз-чартер (dimáiz-chárter) m. demise charter
Дипломат (diplomát) m. diplomat
западный ~ (západnyi ~) western ~
иностранный ~ (inostránnyi ~) foreign ~
профессиональный ~ (professionál'nyi ~) career ~
Директив/а (direktív/a) f. directive, guidelines
административная ~ (administratívnaia ~) administrative guidelines
внешнеторговые ~/ы (vneshnetorgóvye ~/y) trade policy guidelines
следовать ~/ам (slédovat' ~/am) to follow instructions
устанавливать ~/ы (ustanávlivat' ~/y) to issue directives
Директор (diréktor) m. director, manager
генеральный ~ (generál'nyi ~) general director
генеральный ~ по сбыту (generál'nyi ~ po sbýtu) general sales manager
заместитель ~/а (zamestítel' ~/a) deputy director
заместитель генерального ~/а (zamestítel' generál'nogo ~/a) deputy general director
исполнительный ~ (ispolnítel'nyi ~) executive director
коммерческий ~ (kommércheskii ~) sales manager
совет ~/ов (sovét ~/óv) board of directors

технический ~ (tekhnícheskii ~)
technical director
финансовый ~ (finánsovyi ~)
director of finance
~ выставки (~ výstavki) exhibit
director
~ завода (~ zavóda) plant
manager
~ павильона (~ pavil'óna)
pavilion manager
~ по снабжению (~ po
snabzhéniiu) supply manager
~ предприятия (~ predpriiátiia)
director of an enterprise
Директор-администратор (diréktor-
administrátor) m. managing director
Директорат (direktorát) m.
directorate {management}
Директор-распорядитель (diréktor-
rasporiadítel') executive director
Директорский (diréktorskii) adj.
management
Дирекция (diréktsiia) f. management
генеральная ~ (generál'naia ~)
general directorate
техническая ~ (tekhnícheskaia ~)
technical management
~ ярмарки (~ iármarki) trade
fair office
Дисбаланс (disbaláns) m. imbalance
~ во внешней торговле (~ vo
vnéshnei torgóvle) foreign trade
imbalance
Дисконт (diskónt) m. discount
{fin.}
банковский ~ (bánkovskii ~) bank
~
процент ~/а (protsént ~/a)
percentage of a ~
размер ~/а (razmér ~/a) amount
of a ~
ставка ~/а (stávka ~/a) ~ rate
~ векселей (~ vékselei)
discounting of bills (notes)
Дисконтёр (diskontiór) m. discount
house
Дисконтирование (diskontírovanie)
n. discounting, negotiation
~ векселя (~ vékselia)
discounting of a bill (note)
Дисконтировать (diskontírovat')
to discount
Дисконтный (diskóntnyi) adj.
discount
Дискредитировать (diskreditírovat')
v. to discredit

Дискриминационный
(diskriminatsiónnyi) adj.
discriminatory
Дискриминаци/я (diskriminátsi/ia)
f. discrimination
кредитная ~ (kredítnaia ~)
credit ~
ликвидировать ~/ю (likvidírovat'
~/iu) to eliminate ~
торговая ~ (torgóvaia ~) trade ~
ценовая ~ (tsenováia ~) price ~
экономическая ~ (ekonomícheskaia
~) economic ~
Диспач (díspach) m. dispatch
{shipping premium}
выплата ~/а (výplata ~/a)
payment of ~
получение ~/а (poluchénie ~/a)
receipt of ~
размер ~/а (razmér ~/a) amount
of ~
свободен от ~/а (svobóden ot
~/a) free of ~
ставка ~/а (stávka ~/a) ~ rate
~ только за досрочную погрузку
(~ tól'ko za dosróchnuiu pogrúzku) ~ loading only
Диспаш/а (dispásh/a) f. average
adjustment {ins.}
аварийная ~ (avaríinaia ~)
average statement
подготовка ~ (podgotóvka ~)
preparation of average statement
проект ~/и (proékt ~/i) draft of
average statement
реестр ~/и (reéstr ~/i) register
of general average statements
составление ~/и (sostavlénie
~/i) adjustment of average
statement
оспаривать ~/у (ospárivat' ~/u)
to contest the average statement
отменять ~/у (otmeniát' ~/u) to
annul a general average
statement
регистрировать ~/у
(registrírovat' ~/u) to register
an average statement
составлять ~/у (sostavliát' ~/u)
to draw up an average statement
~ по общей аварии (~ po óbshchei
avárii) general average
adjustment
Диспашёр (dispashiór) m. average
adjustor
бюро ~/ов (avaríinyi ~ biuró
~/ov) bureau of ~s

иностранный ~ (inostránnyi ~)
foreign ~
старший ~ (stárshii ~) senior ~
Дисплей (displéi) m. display
~ ЭВМ (~ evm) computer ~
Дистрибьютер (distríb'iuter) m.
distributor
Дифференциальный
(differentsiál'nyi) adj.
differential
Дифференциация (differentsiátsiia)
f. differentiation
~ заработной платы (~ zárabotnoi
pláty) wage ~
~ цен (~ tsen) price ~
Дифференцировать
(differentsírovat') v. to
differentiate
Длина (dliná) f. length
габаритная ~ (gabarítnaia ~)
overall ~
Длительность (dlítel'nost') f.
duration
~ обработки (~ obrabótki)
processing time
~ работы (~ rabóty) running time
~ хранения (~ khranéniia) shelf
life
~ эксплуатации (~ ekspluatátsii)
working life
Длительный (dlítel'nyi) adj.
prolonged
Дн/о (dn/o) n. bottom
вверх ~/ом (vverkh ~/om) upside
down
укладка вверх ~/ом (ukládka
vverkh ~/om) upside down stacking
Добавочный (dobávochnyi) adj.
additional, extra, supplemental
Доброкачественность
(dobrokáchestvennost') f. high
quality
Доброкачественный
(dobrokáchestvennyi) adj. high
quality
Добыча (dobýcha) f. extraction,
yield
Доверенност/ь (dovérennost/') f.
power of attorney, proxy, warrant
аннулировать ~ (annulírovat' ~)
to annul a power of attorney
выдавать ~ (vydavát' ~) to grant
a power of attorney
иметь ~ (imét' ~) to have a
power of attorney

общая ~ (óbshchaia ~) general
power of attorney
отменять ~ (otmeniát' ~) to
revoke a power of attorney
оформлять ~ (oformliát' ~) to
draw up a warrant
подписывать по ~/и (podpísyvat'
po ~/i) to sign by proxy
предъявлять ~ (pred"iavliát' ~)
to present a power of attorney
по ~/и (po ~/i) by proxy
срок действия ~ (srok déistviia
~) term of a warrant
~ на имя (~ na ímia) warrant in
the name of ...
~ на получение (~ na poluchénie)
warrant for receipt
~ действительна на ...дней (~
deistvítel'na na ...dnei) power
of attorney valid for ... days
Довери/е (dovéri/e) n. confidence,
trust
взаимное ~ (vzaímnoe ~) mutual
confidence
входить в ~ (vkhodít' v ~) to
gain confidence
завоёвывать ~ (zavoióvyvat' ~)
to win confidence
злоупотребление ~/ем
(zloupotreblénie ~/em) abuse of
confidence, breach of trust
нарушение оказанного ~/я
(narushénie okázannogo ~/ia)
breach of confidence
оправдывать ~ (oprávdyvat' ~) to
justify confidence
полное ~ (pólnoe ~) complete
confidence
подрывать ~ к (podryvát' ~ k) to
shake faith in
поколебать ~ (pokolebát' ~) to
impair credibility
пользоваться ~/ем (pól'zovat'sia
~/em) to enjoy confidence
потерять ~ (poteriát' ~) to lose
trust
утрата ~/я (utráta ~/ia) loss of
confidence
Доверитель (doverítel') m.
principal, settlor
Довод (dóvod) m. argument, position
веский ~ (véskii ~) strong
argument
выдвигать ~/ы (vydvigát' ~/y) to
set forth arguments

малоубедительный ~
(maloubedítel'nyi ~) poor
argument
неопровержимый ~
(neoproverzhímyi ~) irrefutable
argument
неубедительный ~ (neubedítel'nyi
~) unconvincing argument
опровергающие ~/ы
(oprovergáiushchie ~/y) rebuttal
arguments {in litigation}
убедительный ~ (ubedítel'nyi ~)
convincing argument
Доводка (dovódka) f. operational
development
~ опытного образца (~ ópytnogo
obraztsá) engineering
development
Договариваться (dogovárivat'sia) v.
to negotiate
Договаривающий (dogovárivaiushchii)
adj. acting (parties etc.)
Договор (dogovór) m. agreement,
act, treaty
агентский ~ (agéntskii ~)
broker's act
аннулирование ~/a
(annulírovananie ~/a) annulment,
rescission of an agreement, act,
or treaty
аннулировать ~ (annulírovat' ~)
to annul, to rescind {agreement,
act, or treaty}
бессрочный ~ (bessróchnyi ~)
treaty of unlimited duration
бодмерейный ~ (bodmeréinyi ~)
bottomry bond
быть связанным ~/ом (byt'
sviázannym ~/om) to be bound by
act
внешнеэкономический ~
(vneshneekonomícheskii ~)
foreign economic agreement
возобновление ~/a о страховании
(vozobnovlénie ~/a o
strakhovánii) renewal of
insurance agreement
возобновлять ~ (vozobnovliát' ~)
to renew an (agreement, act or
treaty)
вступать в ~ (vstupát' v ~) to
enter into an agreement
выгодный только для одной
стороны ~ (výgodnyi tól'ko dlia
odnói storoný ~) "Dutch bargain"
(one-sided deal)

выполнение ~/a (vypolnénie ~/a)
performance of a agreement
выполнять ~ (vypolniát' ~) to
perform under an agreement
выходить из ~/a (vykhodít' iz
~/a) to withdraw from a treaty
денонсировать ~ (denonsírovat'
~) to denounce a treaty
гражданско-правовой ~
(grazhdánsko-pravovói ~) civil
law act
двусторонний ~ (dvustorónnii ~)
bilateral treaty
долгосрочный ~ (dolgosróchnyi ~)
long-term agreement
денонсация ~/a (denonsátsiia
~/a) denunciation of a treaty
заключённый ~ (zakliuchiónnyi ~)
concluded agreement
заключать ~ (zakliuchát' ~) to
conclude an agreement
иск из ~/a (isk iz ~/a) action
in act
коллективный ~ (kollektívnyi ~)
collective agreement
лицензионный ~ (litsenziónnyi ~)
licensing agreement
меморандум о ~/e (memorándum o
~/e) memorandum of agreement
многосторонний ~ (mnogostorónnii
~) multilateral treaty
монопольный ~ (monopól'nyi ~)
monopoly act
нарушение ~/a (narushénie ~/a)
breach of act
нарушать ~ (narushát' ~) to
breach a act
недействительный ~
(nedeistvítel'nyi ~) invalid
agreement
невыполнение ~/a (nevypolnénie
~/a) failure to perform
{agreement}
незавершённый ~ (nezavershiónnyi
~) uncompleted executory act
незаконный ~ (nezakónnyi ~)
illegal act
обязательства по ~/y
(obiazátel'stva po ~/u)
obligations under act
обусловливать ~/ом
(obuslóvlivat' ~/om) to
stipulate by agreement
односторонний ~ (odnostorónnii
~) unilateral agreement
оспоримый ~ (osporímyi ~)
voidable act

отказываться от ~/a
(otkázyvat'sia ot ~/a) to
renounce a treaty
оформлять ~ (oformliát' ~) to
draw up a act
парафировать ~ (parafírovat' ~)
to initial (agreement, treaty)
патентный ~ (paténtnyi ~) patent
agreement
по ~/y (po ~/u) by act, under
act
подписывать ~ (podpísyvat' ~) to
sign an agreement, act
предмет ~/a (predmét ~/a) object
of an agreement
прекращать действие ~/a
(prekrashchát' déistvie ~/a) to
terminate an agreement
присоединяться к ~/y
(prisoediniát'sia k ~/u) to
accede to a treaty
продление срока действия ~/a
(prodlénie sróka déistviia ~/a)
extension of the term {of
agreement, act, treaty}
продлевать ~ (prodlevát' ~) to
extend a act
проект ~/a (proékt ~/a) draft
(agreement, etc.)
пункт ~/a (punkt ~/a) clause (of
an agreement, etc.)
пункт ~/a о гарантиях (punkt ~/a
o garántiiakh) guarantee clause
пункт ~/a о монопольном праве
(punkt ~/a o monopól'nom práve)
monopoly rights clause
работа по трудовому ~/y (rabóta
po trudovómu ~/u) work on
contract basis
равноправный ~ (ravnoprávnyi ~)
equitable treaty
разовый ~ (rázovyi ~) one-time
agreement
расторжение ~/a (rastorzhénie
~/a) termination of an agreement
расторжение ~/a страхования
(rastorzhénie ~/a strakhovániia)
cancellation of an insurance
policy
расторгать ~ (rastorgát' ~) to
terminate an agreement, etc.
ратифицировать ~
(ratifitsírovat' ~) to ratify an
agreement
реализация ~ (realizátsiia ~)
performance of an agreement

соблюдать ~ (sobliudát' ~) to
observe an agreement
согласно ~/y (soglásno ~/u) as
per act
статья ~/a (stat'iá ~/a) article
of an agreement, etc.
сторона в ~/e (storoná v ~/e)
party to an agreement, etc.
сумма ~/a (súmma ~/a) amount of
an act
требования ~/a (trébovaniia ~/a)
actural requirements
трудовой ~ (trudovói ~) labor
agreement
условия ~/a (uslóviia ~/a) terms
and conditions of an agreement
устный ~ (ústnyi ~) oral
agreement
хозяйственный ~ (khoziástvennyi
~) economic treaty
штраф за невыполнение ~/a
(shtraf za nevypolnénie ~/a)
penalty for non-performance of
an act
~ гарантии от убытков (~
garántii ot ubýtkov) indemnity
act
~ консигнации (~ konsignátsii)
consignment act
~ купли-продажи (~ kúpli-
prodázhi) buy-sell act
~ мены (~ mény) barter agreement
~ морского страхования (~
morskógo strakhovániia) marine
insurance act
~ морской буксировки (~ morskói
buksiróvki) marine tug act
~ морской перевозки (~ morskói
perevózki) act of affreightment
~ на инжиниринг (~ na
inzhiníring) engineering
agreement
~ найма (~ náima) employment
agreement
~ на основе взаимности (~ na
osnóve vzaímnosti) reciprocity
agreement
~ на передачу ноу-хау (~ na
peredáchu nóu-kháu) know-how
agreement
~ на реальный товар (~ na
reál'nyi továr) spot act
~ на эксплуатацию (~ na
ekspluatátsiiu) operating
agreement
~ об аренде (~ ob arénde) rental
agreement

~ об аренде помещения (~ ob
arénde pomeshchéniia) act of
tenancy
~ об исключительном праве на
продажу (~ ob iskliuchítel'nom
práve na prodázhu) exclusive
sales act
~ обязывающий (~
obiazyváiushchii) binding act
~ о взаимопомощи (~ о
vzaímopómoshchi) mutual
assistance pact
~ односторонний (~
odnostorónnii) unilateral
agreement
~ о долгосрочной аренде (~ о
dolgosróchnoi arénde) long-term
lease
~ о найме (~ о náime) act of
employment
~ о патентах (~ о paténtakh)
patent agreement
~ о патентном сотрудничестве (~
о paténtnom sotrúdnichestve)
patent cooperation treaty
~ о передаче (~ о peredáche)
transfer agreement
~ о переуступке прав (~ о
pereustúpke prav) assignment
agreement, quitclaim agreement
~ о покупке (~ о pokúpke)
purchase agreement
~ о поручительстве (~ о
poruchítel'stve) act of
guarantee
~ о продаже в кредит (~ о
prodázhe v kredít) installment
trade agreement
~ о сдаче в аренду (~ о sdáche v
aréndu) leasing agreement
~ о сотрудничестве (~ о
sotrúdnichestve) treaty on
cooperation
~ о спасении (~ о spasénii)
salvage agreement
~ о строительстве объекта (~ о
stroítel'stve ob"ékta)
construction act
~ о товарных знаках (~ о
továrnykh znákakh) trademark
agreement
~ о торговле (~ о torgóvle)
treaty on commerce
~ о фрахтовании судна (~ о
frakhtovánii súdna) freight act

~ о фрахтовании судна без
экипажа (~ о frakhtovánii súdna
bez ekipázha) bare-boat charter
~ о фрахтовании судна,
генеральный (~ о frakhtovánii
súdna, generál'nyi) general
freight act
~ перестрахования (~
perestrakhovániia) reinsurance -
act
~ подряда (~ podriáda) turn-key
act
~ поручения (~ poruchéniia)
agency agreement
~ продажи (~ prodázhi) sales act
~ с правом продления (~ s právom
prodléniia) agreement with an
option to extend
~ с субподрядчиком (~ s
subpodriádchikom) subact
~ субфрахтования (~
subfrakhtovániia) subcharter
Договорённост/ь (dogovoriónnost/')
f. arrangement, understanding
взаимная ~ (vzaímnaia ~) mutual
understanding
достичь ~/и (dostích' ~/i) to
come to an understanding
окончательная ~ (okonchátel'naia
~) final arrangement
оформить ~ письменно (ofórmit' ~
pís'menno) to reach an
understanding in writing
по ~/и (po ~/i) by agreement
полная ~ (pólnaia ~) complete
agreement
предварительная ~
(predvarítel'naia ~) tentative
agreement
согласно нашей ~/и (soglásno
náshei ~/i) pursuant to our
understanding
устная ~ (ústnaia ~) verbal
arrangement
финансовая ~ (finánsovaia ~)
financial arrangement
частная ~ (chástnaia ~) private
understanding
~ по контракту (~ po kontráktu)
actual arrangement
Договориться (dogovorít'sia) v. to
come to an agreement
~ окончательно (~ okonchátel'no)
to finalize an agreement
Договорный (dogovórnyi) adj. actual
Догружать (dogruzhát') v. to
complete loading (of cargo)

Догрузка (dogrúzka) f. supplementary cargo

Доделка (dodélka) f. finishing touch

Дозволенный (dozvólennyi) adj. permissible

Док (dok) m. dock
  аренда ~/a (arénda ~/a) ~ rent
  вводить судно в ~ (vvodít' súdno v ~) to ~ a vessel
  вводить в ~ (vvodít' v ~) to enter a ~
  выходить из ~/a (vykhodít' iz ~/a) to depart a ~
  доставлять в ~ (dostavliát' v ~) to deliver to ~
  коммерческий ~ (kommércheskii ~) commercial ~
  крытый ~ (krýtyi ~) ~ shed
  мокрый ~ (mókryi ~) wet ~
  плавучий ~ (plavúchii ~) floating ~
  плата за стоянку в ~/e (pláta za stoiánku v ~/e) dockage fees
  портовые ~/и (portóvye ~/i) harbor ~s
  ремонтный ~ (remóntnyi ~) graving ~
  ставить судно в ~ (stávit' súdno v ~) to place a vessel in ~
  стоянка в ~/e (stoiánka v ~/e) dockage
  стоять в ~/e (stoiát' v ~/e) to lie in ~
  сухой ~ (sukhói ~) dry-dock
  франко ~ (fránko ~) free-~

Доказательств/о (dokazátel'stv/o) n. evidence, proof
  вещественное ~ (veshchéstvennoe ~) material evidence
  документальное ~ (dokumentál'noe ~) documentary evidence
  неоспоримое ~ (neosporímoe ~) irrefutable evidence
  письменное ~ (pís'mennoe ~) written evidence
  проверка ~/a (provérka ~/a) verification of evidence
  представлять ~/a (predstavliát' ~/a) to present evidence
  убедительное ~ (ubedítel'noe ~) convincing evidence
  ~ заинтересованности (~ zainteresóvannosti) proof of interest
  ~ качества (~ káchestva) proof of quality

  ~ новизны (~ novizný) proof of novelty
  ~ ущерба (~ ushchérba) proof of damages

Докер (dóker) m. docker

Доковать (dokovát') v. to dry-dock

Доковый (dókovyi) adj. dock

Документ (dokumént) m. document
  акцепт коммерческих ~/ов (aktsépt kommércheskikh ~/ov) acceptance of commercial paper
  банковский ~ (bánkovskii ~) bank ~
  бессрочный ~ (bessróchnyi ~) undated ~
  визировать ~ (vizírovat' ~) to initial a ~
  вносить в ~ (vnosít' v ~) to enter in a ~
  возврат ~/ов (vozvrát ~/ov) return of ~s
  вручение ~/ов (vruchénie ~/ov) delivery of ~s
  выдача ~/a (výdacha ~/a) release of ~s
  выдавать ~/ы (vydavát' ~/y) to issue ~s
  давать ~/ы против расписки (davát' ~/y prótiv raspíski) to deliver ~s against a trust receipt
  выдавать ссуду под залог ~/ов (vydavát' ssúdu pod zalóg ~/ov) to lend against ~s
  выкуп ~/ов (výkup ~/ov) redemption of ~s
  выписка из ~/a (výpiska iz ~/a) excerpt
  грузовые ~/ы (gruzovýe ~/y) shipping ~s
  данный ~ (dánnyi ~) present ~
  директивные ~/ы (direktívnye ~/y) directives
  договорно-правовые ~/ы (dogovórno-pravovýe ~/y) treaty and legal ~s
  достаточность ~/a (dostátochnost' ~/a) sufficiency of a ~
  заверять ~ (zaveriát' ~) to attest a ~
  залоговый ~ (zalógovyi ~) documentary pledge
  засвидетельствовать ~ (zasvidétel'stvovat' ~) to witness a ~

заявочный ~ (zaiávochnyi ~)
application ~
итоговый ~ (itógovyi ~)
concluding ~
комплект ~/ов (komplékt ~/ov)
set of ~s
копия ~/a (kópiia ~/a) copy of a
~
кредитный ~ (kredítnyi ~) credit
instrument
межведомственные ~/ы
(mezhvédomstvennye ~/y) interdepartmental ~s
на ~/е проставлен штемпель (na
~/e prostávlen shtémpel') "the
document bears the stamp"
направлять ~/ы (napravliát' ~/y)
to forward ~s
недостающий ~ (nedostaiúshchii
~) missing ~
нормативно-правовые ~/ы
(normatívno-pravovýe ~/y) legal
~s
нормативно-технические ~/ы
(normatívno-tekhnícheskie ~/y)
standard technical documentation
нормативный ~ (normatívnyi ~)
normative ~
обмен ~/ов (obmén ~/ov) exchange
of ~s
оборотный ~ (oborótnyi ~)
negotiable ~
обусловленный ~ (obuslóvlennyi
~) stipulated ~
оплата ~/ов (opláta ~/ov)
payment for ~s
оплачивать ~/ы (opláchivat' ~/y)
to honor ~s
оправдательный ~ (opravdátel'nyi
~) source ~
ордерный ~ (órdernyi ~) order
instrument
оригиналы ~/ов (originály ~/ov)
original ~s
основной ~ (osnovnói ~) primary
~
отгрузочные ~/ы (otgrúzochnye
~/y) shipping ~s
оформлять ~/ы (oformliát' ~/y)
to draw up ~s
оценочный ~ (otsénochnyi ~)
appraisal
патентный ~ (paténtnyi ~) patent
~
первичный ~ (pervíchnyi ~) basic
source ~

перевозочный ~/ы (perevózochnyi
~/y) ~s of carriage
передаваемый, денежный ~
(peredaváemyi, dénezhnyi ~)
negotiable ~
передавать ~/ы (peredavát' ~/y)
to release ~s
передавать ~/ы по индоссаменту
(peredavát' ~/y po indossaméntu)
to transfer ~s by endorsement
передавать ~/ы против акцепта
(peredavát' ~/y prótiv aktsépta)
to release ~s against acceptance
передавать ~/ы против платежа
(peredavát' ~/y prótiv platezhá)
to release ~s against payment
пересылать ~/ы (peresylát' ~/y)
to forward ~s
перечень ~/ов (pérechen' ~/ov)
list of ~s
перечислять ~/ы (perechisliát'
~/y) to list ~s
платёж против ~/ов (platiózh
prótiv ~/ov) payment against ~ s
платёж против представления ~/ов
(platiózh prótiv predstavléniia
~/ov) payment against delivery
of ~s
подготавливать ~ (podgotávlivat'
~) to prepare a ~
подделка ~/ов (poddélka ~/ov)
forgery of ~s
поддельный ~ (poddél'nyi ~)
forged ~
подлинный ~ (pódlinnyi ~)
authentic ~
подлинность ~/ов (pódlinnost'
~/ov) authenticity of ~s
подложный ~ (podlózhnyi ~)
forged ~
подписанный ~ (podpísannyi ~)
signed ~
подписывать ~ (podpísyvat' ~) to
sign a ~
подтверждающий ~
(podtverzhdáiushchii ~)
supporting ~
полнота ~/ов (polnotá ~/ov)
sufficiency of ~s
получение ~/ов на инкассо
(poluchénie ~/ov na inkásso)
receipt of ~s for collection
посылать ~ (posylát' ~) to
forward a ~
правовой ~ (pravovói ~) legal ~

предоставлять ~/ы
(predostavliát' ~/y) to furnish
~s
предъявлять ~/ы (pred"iavliát'
~/y) to submit ~s
препровождать ~/ы
(preprovozhdát' ~/y) to deliver
~s
прилагать ~/ы к (prilagát' ~/y
k) to append ~s to ...
принимать ~/ы (prinimát' ~/y) to
accept presentation of ~ s
прилагаемые ~/ы (prilagáemye
~/y) appended ~s
принятие ~/ов на инкассо
(priniátie ~/ov na inkásso)
acceptance of ~s for collection
приоритетный ~ (prioritétnyi ~)
priority ~
проверка ~/ов (provérka ~/ov)
verification of ~s
проверять ~/ы (proveriát' ~/y)
to verify ~s
проект ~/а (proékt ~/a) draft of
~s
против ~/ов (prótiv ~/ov)
against ~s
против представления ~/ов
(prótiv predstavléniia ~/ov)
against presentation of ~s
противоречить ~/ам
(protivoréchit' ~/am) to be
inconsistent with ~s
рабочий ~ (rabóchii ~) working
~s
разработка заявочного ~/а
(razrabótka zaiávochnogo ~/a)
elaboration of an application
размножать ~ (razmnozhát' ~) to
duplicate a ~
расписывать на обороте ~/а
(raspísyvat' na oboróte ~/a) to
endorse a ~
распоряжаться ~/ами
(rasporiazhát'sia ~/ami) to
dispose of ~ s
распространение ~/ов
(rasprostranénie ~/ov)
distribution of ~s
рассматривать ~ (rassmátrivat'
~) to examine a ~
расходный ~ (raskhódnyi ~)
expense report
расчётный ~/ы (raschiótnyi ~/y)
accounting ~s, accounts and
records

регистрация ~/ов (registrátsiia
~/ov) registration of ~s
регистрировать ~ (registrírovat'
~) to register ~s
руководящие ~/ы (rukovodiáshchie
~/y) guidelines
складской ~ (skladskói ~)
warehouse ~
содержание ~/а (soderzhánie ~/a)
contents of a ~
соответствие ~/ов (sootvétstvie
~/ov) conformity of ~s
соответствующий ~
(sootvétstvuiushchii ~) relevant
~
сопровождающие ~/ы
(soprovozhdáiushchie ~/y)
accompanying ~s
составлять ~ (sostavliát' ~) to
draft a ~
ссуда под платёжные ~/ы (ssúda
pod platiózhnye ~/y) loan
against payment ~s
судебный ~ (sudébnyi ~) writ
судовые ~/ы (sudovýe ~/y) ships
papers
таможенные ~/ы (tamózhennye ~/y)
customs ~s
технические ~/ы (tekhnícheskie
~/y) technical ~
товарный ~ (továrnyi ~) trade ~
товарораспорядительные ~/ы
(továrorasporiadítel'nye ~/y) ~s
of title to goods
товаросопроводительные ~/ы
(továrosoprovodítel'nye ~/y)
shipping ~s
толковать ~ (tolkovát' ~) to
interpret a ~
транспортный ~ (tránsportnyi ~)
transport ~
требовать ~ (trébovat' ~) to
require a ~
требуемый ~ (trébuemyi ~)
required ~
удостоверяющий ~
(udostoveriáiushchii ~)
cerfifying ~
удостоверять ~/ы (udostoveriát'
~/y) to attest ~s
узаконивать ~ (uzakónivat' ~) to
legalize a ~
указанный ~ (ukázannyi ~)
indicated ~
уставные ~/ы (ustávnye ~/y)
organizational ~s

учредительные ~/ы
(uchredítel'nye ~/y) constituent
~s
финансовый ~ (finánsovyi ~)
financial ~
форма ~/ов (fórma ~/ov) form of
~s
чистые погрузочные ~/ы (chístye
pogrúzochnye ~/y) clean shipping
~s
экземпляр ~/a (ekzempliár ~/a)
copy of a ~
экспортные ~/ы (éksportnye ~/y)
export documentation
юридический ~ (iuridícheskii ~)
legal ~
~ /ы для оплаты (~ /y dlia
opláty) ~s for payment
~/ы за наличный расчёт (~/y za
nalíchnyi raschiót) ~s against
payment {d/p}
~/ы на инкассо (~/y na inkásso)
~s for collection
~/ы на отгрузку (~/y na
otgrúzku) ~s for shipment
~ на отправленный товар (~ na
otprávlennyi továr) ~s covering
goods
~, подтверждающий право
собственности ~ (~,
podtverzhdáiushchii právo
sóbstvennosti ~) title deed
~ на предъявителя (~ na
pred"iavítelia) bearer ~
~/ы против акцепта (~/y prótiv
aktsépta) ~s against acceptance
(d/a)
~/ы финансовый отчётности (~/y
finánsovyi otchiótnosti)
statement of accounts
Документальный (dokumentál'nyi)
adj. documentary
Документарный (dokumentárnyi) *adj.*
documentary
Документаци/я (dokumentátsi/ia) *f.*
documentation
входная и выходная ~ (vkhodnáia
i vykhodnáia ~) in and out
documents
комплектность технической ~/и
(kompléktnost' tekhnícheskoi
~/i) completeness of technical ~
комплектовать ~/ю (komplektovát'
~/iu) to complete ~
обмен ~/ей (obmén ~/ei) exchange
of ~

объём ~/и (ob"ióm ~/i) scope of
~
окончательная ~ (okonchátel'naia
~) final ~
оформлять ~/ю (oformliát' ~/iu)
to compile ~
патентная ~ (paténtnaia ~)
patent ~
передача технической ~/и
(peredácha tekhnícheskoi ~/i)
transfer of technical ~
перепроверять ~/ю
(pereproveriát' ~/iu) to recheck
the ~
письменная ~ (pís'mennaia ~)
textual ~
платёжная ~ (platiózhnaia ~)
payment ~
полная ~ (pólnaia ~) complete ~
поступающая ~ (postupáiushchaia
~) incoming documents
правильная ~ (právil'naia ~)
correct ~
предоставлять ~/ю
(predostavliát' ~/iu) to furnish
~
проектная ~ (proéktnaia ~)
design ~
проектно-сметная ~ (proéktno-
smétnaia ~) design estimates
проектно-техническая ~
(proéktno-tekhnícheskaia ~)
technical ~
разработка проектной ~/и
(razrabótka proéktnoi ~/i)
elaboration of design ~
сметная ~ (smétnaia ~) estimate
~
страховая ~ (strakhováia ~)
insurance ~
таможенная ~ (tamózhennaia ~)
customs ~
тендерная ~ (téndernaia ~)
tender documents
техническая ~ (tekhnícheskaia ~)
technical ~
технологическая ~
(tekhnologícheskaia ~)
technological know-how
товарораспорядительная ~
(továrorasporiadítel'naia ~) ~
of title
товаросопроводительная ~
(továrosoprovodítel'naia ~)
shipping ~
транспортная ~ (tránsportnaia ~)
transport ~

учётно-регистрационная ~
(uchiótno-registratsiónnaia ~)
records
Документированный
(dokumentírovannyi) *adj.*
documentary
Документировать (dokumentírovat')
v. to document
Долг (dolg) *m.* arrears, debt,
liability
 аннулировать ~ (annulírovat' ~)
 to write off a debt
 безвозвратный ~ (bezvozvrátnyi
 ~) unrecoverable debt
 безнадёжный ~ (beznadiózhnyi ~)
 bad debt
 большой ~ (bol'shói ~) heavy
 debt
 брать в ~ (brat' v ~) to borrow
 быть в ~/у (byt' v ~/u) to be in
 debt
 взыскание ~/ов (vzyskánie ~/ov)
 debt collection
 взыскивать ~/и (vzýskivat' ~/i)
 to collect debts
 влезать в ~/и (vlezát' v ~/i) to
 incur debts
 внешний ~ (vnéshnii ~) foreign
 debt
 возврат ~/а (vozvrát ~/a)
 repayment of debt
 возмещать ~ (vozmeshchát' ~) to
 repay debt
 выплата ~/а (výplata ~/a)
 settlement of a debt
 выплачивать ~ (vypláchivat' ~)
 to settle a debt
 государственный ~
 (gosudárstvennyi ~) national
 debt
 график возмещения ~/ов (gráfik
 vozmeshchéniia ~/ov) debt
 repayment schedule
 давать в ~ (davát' v ~) to lend
 денежный ~ (dénezhnyi ~) money
 debt
 долгосрочный ~ (dolgosróchnyi ~)
 long-term debt
 замороженный ~ (zamorózhennyi ~)
 frozen debt
 зачитывать в уплату ~/а
 (zachítyvat' v uplátu ~/a) to
 account as payment of a debt
 иметь ~/и (imét' ~/i) to have
 debts
 инкассировать ~/и (inkassírovat'
 ~/i) to collect debts

 консолидированный ~
 (konsolidírovannyi ~)
 consolidated debt
 краткосрочный ~ (kratkosróchnyi
 ~) short-term debt
 ликвидация ~/ов (likvidátsiia
 ~/ov) liquidation of debts
 накопленный ~ (nakóplennyi ~)
 accrued debt
 находиться в ~/у (nakhodít'sia v
 ~/u) to find oneself in debt
 неконсолидированный ~
 (nekonsolidírovannyi ~)
 unconsolidated debt
 непогашенный ~ (nepogáshennyi ~)
 undischarged debt
 неуплаченный ~ (neupláchennyi ~)
 unpaid debt
 обеспеченный ~ (obespéchennyi ~)
 secured debt
 общий ~ (óbshchii ~) overall
 debt
 оплата ~/а (opláta ~/a)
 settlement of a debt
 оплачивать ~ (opláchivat' ~) to
 settle a debt
 освобождение от уплаты ~/а
 (osvobozhdénie ot upláty ~/a)
 remission of a debt
 остаток ~/а (ostátok ~/a)
 remainder of a debt
 отказ от уплаты ~/а (otkáz ot
 upláty ~/a) repudiation of a
 debt
 отказываться от уплаты ~/а
 (otkázyvat'sia ot upláty ~/a) to
 repudiate a debt
 отсроченный ~ (otsróchennyi ~)
 overdue debt
 переводить ~ (perevodít' ~) to
 remit a loan
 погашенный ~ (pogáshennyi ~)
 discharged debt
 погашать ~ (pogashát' ~) to
 discharge a debt
 подтверждение ~/а
 (podtverzhdénie ~/a)
 acknowledgement of a debt
 покрытие ~/а (pokrýtie ~/a) debt
 service
 покрывать ~ (pokryvát' ~) to
 service a debt
 признавать ~ (priznavát' ~) to
 acknowledge a debt
 присуждённый ~ (prisuzhdiónnyi
 ~) judgment debt

продлевать срок выплаты ~/ов
(prodlevát' srok vypláty ~/ov)
to extend the repayment period
of debts
просроченный ~ (prosróchennyi ~)
past due debt
прощать ~ (proshchát' ~) to
forgive a debt
прямой ~ (priamói ~) straight
debt
расплачиваться с ~/ами
(raspláchivat'sia s ~/ami) to
pay off debts
сомнительный ~ (somnítel'nyi ~)
doubtful debt
списывать ~ (spísyvat' ~) to
write off a debt
старый ~ (stáryi ~) old debt
сумма ~/a (súmma ~/a) amount of
a debt
текущий ~ (tekúshchii ~) current
debt
требовать уплаты ~/a (trébovat'
upláty ~/a) to demand payment of
a debt
удерживать ~ (udérzhivat' ~) to
deduct a debt
удовлетворять ~ (udovletvoriát'
~) to satisfy a debt
уплаченный ~ (upláchennyi ~) a
paid debt
уплата ~/a (upláta ~/a) payment
of a debt
уплачивать ~ (upláchivat' ~) to
pay off a debt
урегулирование ~/ов
(uregulírovanie ~/ov) settlement
of debts
условный ~ (uslóvnyi ~)
contingent liability
фундированный ~ (fundírovannyi
~) bonded debt
~/и по займам (~/i po záimam)
debt on loans
Долговечность (dolgovéchnost') f.
longevity
гарантированная ~
(garantírovannaia ~) guaranteed
~
номинальная ~ (nominál'naia ~)
rated life
расчётная ~ (raschiótnaia ~)
design ~
эксплуатационная ~
(ekspluatatsiónnaia ~) operating
~

~ при хранении (~ pri khranénii)
shelf life
Долгосрочный (dolgosróchnyi) adj.
long-term
Долево/й (dolevó/i) adj.
participation, share
~/е участие (~/e uchástie)
individual share
Должник (dolzhník) m. debtor
главный ~ (glávnyi ~) principal
~
некредитоспособный
(nekreditosposóbnyi) non-
creditworthy ~
основной (osnovnói) primary ~
несостоятельность ~/a
(nesostoiátel'nost' ~/a)
insolvency of a ~
~, нарушивший обязательство (~,
narushívshii obiazátel'stvo)
defaulting ~
~ по векселю (~ po vékseliu)
bill {note} ~
~ по закладной (~ po zakladnói)
mortgagor
~ по иску (~ po ísku) judgment ~
Должност/ь (dólzhnost/') f.
position (job), post
временная ~ (vrémennaia ~)
temporary position
вступить в ~ (vstupít' v ~) to
assume office
выдвигать на ~ (vydvigát' na ~)
to nominate to an office
занимать ~ (zanimát' ~) to
occupy a post
зачислять кого-л. на ~
(zachisliát' kogó-l. na ~) to
take somebody on in a position
понижать в ~/и (ponizhát' v ~/i)
to demote
~ штатная (~ shtátnaia) regular
appointment
Доллар (dóllar) m. dollar
банкнота в 1 ~ (banknóta v ~)
one ~ bill
заём в ~/ax ~- (zaióm v ~/akh)
denominated loan
конвертировать ~/ы в другую
валюту (konvertírovat' ~/y v
drugúiu valiútu) to convert ~s
into another currency
курс ~/a (kurs ~/a) ~ exchange
rate
нехватка ~/ов (nekhvátka ~/ov) ~
shortage

обменивать ~/ы на золото
(obménivat' ~/y na zóloto) to
exchange ~s for gold
пересчёт ~/ов в валюту платежа
(pereschiót ~/ov v valiútu
platezhá) recalculation of ~s
into currency of payment
платёж в ~/ах (platiózh v ~/akh)
payment in ~s
платить в ~/ах (platít' v ~/akh)
to pay in ~s
поступления ~/ов (postupléniia
~/ov) ~ earnings
продажа на ~/ы (prodázha na ~/y)
sale for ~s
размен ~/ов на золото (razmén
~/ov na zóloto) conversion of ~s
into gold
сумма в ~/ах (súmma v ~/akh) ~
amount
утечка ~/ов (utéchka ~/ov) ~
flow {from a country}
эквивалент в ~/ах (ekvivalént v
~/akh) ~ equivalent
Дол/я (dól/ia) f. allotment,
contribution, portion, share
    вносить ~/ю (vnosít' ~/iu) to
    contribute to
    входить в ~/ю (vkhodít' v ~/iu)
    to go by shares
    достаточная ~ (dostátochnaia ~)
    sufficient share
    значительная ~ (znachítel'naia
    ~) sizable proportion
    комиссионная ~ (komissiónnaia ~)
    share of commission
    максимальная ~ (maksimál'naia ~)
    maximum share
    малая ~ (málaia ~) small share
    минимальная ~ (minimál'naia ~)
    minimum share
    на ~/ю приходится ... % (na ~/iu
    prikhodítsia ...) a share of ...
    %
    оговорённая ~ (ogovoriónnaia ~)
    agreed share
    определять ~/ю (opredeliát'
    ~/iu) to establish share
    пропорциональная ~
    (proportsionál'naia ~) pro rata
    share
    равная ~ (rávnaia ~) equal share
    равными ~/ями (rávnymi ~/iami)
    in equal shares
    соответствующая ~
    (sootvétstvuiushchaia ~)
    respective share

~ в акционерной компании (~ v
aktsionérnoi kompánii) share of
a company
~ в капитале (~ v kapitále)
share in capital
~ в поставках (~ v postávkakh)
share of deliveries
~ в уставном фонде (~ v ustávnom
fónde) share of charter fund
~ мирового рынка (~ mirovógo
rýnka) share of the world market
~ прибыли (~ príbyli) share of
profits
~, причитающаяся по общей аварии
(~, prichitáiushchaiasia po
óbshchei avárii) share of
general average contribution
{for lost cargo, etc.}
~ услуг (~ uslúg) share of
services
~ участия (~ uchástiia)
contribution
Дом, торговый (dom, torgóvyi) m.
trading house
Доминирование (dominírovanie) n.
domination
Доминировать (dominírovat') v. to
dominate
Доминирующий (domíníruiushchii)
adj. dominant
Домицилий (domitsílii) m. domicile
    торговый ~ (torgóvyi ~)
    commercial ~
Домицилированный
(domitsilírovannyi) adj. domiciled
Домицилировать (domitsilírovat') v.
to domicile
Домогательство (domogátel'stvo) n.
importunity, solicitation
Домогаться (domogát'sia) v. to
importune, to solicit
Доплат/а (doplát/a) f. additional
payment
    без дополнительной ~/ы (bez
    dopolnítel'noi ~/y) without
    extra charge
    за особую ~/у (za osóbuiu ~/u)
    at extra cost
    письмо с ~/ой (pis'mó s ~/oi)
    collect letter
    ~ за сверхурочную работу (~ za
    sverkhuróchnuiu rabótu) overtime
    payments
Дополнени/е (dopolnéni/e) n.
addendum, addition, amendment
    в виде ~/я (v víde ~/ia) in the
    form of addendum

в ~ к письму (v ~ k pis'mú)
further to the letter
издавать ~ (izdavát' ~) to
publish a supplement
подача ~/й (podácha ~/i) filing
of amendments
подписывать ~ (podpísyvat' ~) to
sign an addendum
предлагаемое ~ (predlagáemoe ~)
proposed amendment
~ к контракту (~ k kontráktu)
amendment to a act
~ к протоколу (~ k protokólu)
amendment to a protocol
Дополнительно (dopolnítel'no) *adv.*
additionally
Дополнительный (dopolnítel'nyi)
adj. additional, supplementary
Допоставк/а (dopostávk/a) *f.*
delivery of the balance of goods
Допоставлять (dopostavliát') *v.* to
deliver the balance of the goods
Допуск (dópusk) *m.* access,
admittance, allowance
выдерживать ~/и (vydérzhivat'
~/i) to adhere to specified
tolerances
иметь ~ к (imét' ~ k) to have
access to
получить ~ к (poluchít' ~ k) to
gain access to
~ к регистрации на бирже ~ (~ k
registrátsii na bírzhe ~)
admission to "on the exchange"
~ на изготовление (~ na
izgotovlénie) manufacturing
tolerance
~ на износ (~ na iznós) wear
tolerance
~ продукции на рынок (~
prodúktsii na rýnok) product
access to the market
Допускать (dopuskát') *v.* to permit
~ к перевозке (~ k perevózke) to
permit for transport
~ овердрафт (~ overdráft) ~ to
overdraw an account
~ ошибку (~ oshíbku) to make an
error
Допустимый (dopustímyi) *adj.*
admissible, allowable, tolerable
Доработка (dorabótka) *f.*
finalization, field change orders
Дорого (dórogo) *adv.* dearly,
expensively
обходиться ~ (obkhodít'sia ~) to
turn out to be expensive

платить ~ (platít' ~) to pay
dearly
Дороговизн/а (dorogovízn/a) *f.* high
prices
надбавка на ~/у (nadbávka na
~/u) high price allowance
Дорогой (dorogói) *adj.* dear,
expensive
Дорогостоящий (dorogostoiáshchii)
adj. high-priced
Дорожать (dorozhát') *v.* to increase
in price
Дорожно-строительный (dorózhno-
stroítel'nyi) *adj.* road building
Дорожный (dorózhnyi) *adj.* road,
travel
Досматривать (dosmátrivat') *v.* to
inspect
Досмотр (dosmótr) *m.* examination,
inspection
освобождать от ~/а (osvobozhdát'
ot ~/a) to be exempt from
inspection
проводить ~ (provodít' ~) to
carry out an inspection
проводить таможенный ~
(provodít' tamózhennyi ~) to
pass through customs inspection
санитарно-карантинный ~
(sanitárno-karantínnyi ~)
quarantine and sanitary
examination
таможенный ~ (tamózhennyi ~) *m.*
customs inspection
~ багажа (~ bagazhá) inspection
of baggage
~ грузов (~ grúzov) inspection
of cargo
~ имущества (~ imúshchestva)
inspection of property
~ судна (~ súdna) examination of
a ship
Досмотровый (dosmótrovyi) *adj.*
customs
Досмотрщик (dosmótrshchik) customs
inspector
Досрочно (dosróchno) *adv.* ahead of
schedule
Досрочный (dosróchnyi) *adj.* in
advance
Доставк/а (dostávk/a) *f.*
conveyance, delivery
быстрая ~ (býstraia ~) express
delivery
досрочная ~ (dosróchnaia ~)
advance delivery

запоздавшая ~ (zapozdávshaia ~)
late delivery
задержка в ~/е (zadérzhka v ~/e)
delay in delivery
задерживать ~/у (zadérzhivat'
~/u) to delay delivery
издержки по ~/е (izdérzhki po
~/e) delivery costs
место ~/и (mésto ~/i) point of
delivery
не включая стоимость ~/и (ne
vkliucháia stóimost' ~/i) on an
ex-plant basis
немедленная ~ (nemédlennaia ~)
immediate delivery
оплата при ~/е (opláta pri ~/e)
collect on delivery (C.O.D.)
оплаченная ~ (opláchennaia ~)
paid delivery
осуществлять ~/у
(osushchestvliát' ~/u) to effect
delivery
отсрочивать ~/у (otsróchivat'
~/u) to postpone delivery
плата за ~/у (pláta za ~/u)
delivery charge
платить при ~/е (platít' pri
~/e) to pay on delivery
подлежащий ~/е (podlezháshchii
~/e) deliverable
приостанавливать ~/у
(priostanávlivat' ~/u) to
suspend delivery
производить ~/у (proizvodít'
~/u) to make delivery
с уплатой при ~/е (s uplátoi pri
~/e) payable on delivery
сохранная ~ (sokhránnaia ~) safe
delivery
средства ~/и (srédstva ~/i)
means of delivery
срок ~/и (srok ~/i) delivery
period
срочная ~ (sróchnaia ~) special
delivery
стоимость ~/и (stóimost' ~/i)
cost of delivery
цена с ~/ой (tsená s ~/oi)
delivered price
~ груза на условиях "от двери до
двери" (~ grúza na uslóviiakh ot
dvéri do dvéri) door to door
cargo delivery
~ порожняка (~ porózhniaka)
back-haul
~ франко (~ fránko) free
delivered

Доставляемый (dostavliáemyi) adj.
delivered, furnished
Доставлять (dostavliát') v. to
deliver
Достаточность (dostátochnost') f.
sufficiency
~ маркировки (~ markiróvki)
sufficiency of marking
~ упаковки (~ upakóvki)
sufficiency of packing
Достаточный (dostátochnyi) adj.
adequate, sufficient
Достигать (dostigát') v. to
achieve, to attain
Достигнутый (dostígnutyi) adj.
achieved, obtained
Достижени/е (dostizhéni/e) n.
achievement
новейшие ~/я (novéishie ~/ia)
latest achievements
отражать ~/я (otrazhát' ~/ia) to
reflect ~s
технические ~/я (tekhnícheskie
~/ia) technical ~s
уровень ~/й (úroven' ~/i) level
of ~s
экономические ~/я
(ekonomícheskie ~/ia) economic
~s
~/я науки и технологии (~/ia
naúki i tekhnológii) scienti fic
and technological ~s
Достоинство (dostóinstvo) n.
denomination {monetary unit}
Доступ (dóstup) m. access
беспрепятственный ~
(besprepiátstvennyi ~)
unobstructed ~
иметь ~ (imét' ~) to have ~
полный ~ (pólnyi ~) complete ~
свободный ~ (svobódnyi ~) free ~
~ в павилион (~ v pavilión) ~ to
the pavilion
~ к источникам сырья (~ k
istóchnikam syr'iá) ~ to natural
resources
~ к рынкам (~ k rýnkam) market ~
Доступный (dostúpnyi) adj.
accessible
Досуг (dosúg) m. leisure time
на ~/е (na ~/e) at {your}
leisure
Досье (dos'é) n. file
заявочное ~ (zaiávochnoe ~)
application ~
открытое ~ (otkrýtoe ~) open ~

составлять ~ (sostavliát' ~) to open a ~

Дотаци/я (dotátsi/ia) *f.* subsidy
бюджетная ~ (biudzhétnaia ~) budgetary ~
давать ~/ю (davát' ~/iu) to subsidize

Доход (dokhód) *m.* earnings, income, revenue, yield
бюджетные ~/ы (biudzhétnye ~/y) budget receipts
валовой ~ (valovói ~) gross income
валовой национальный ~ (valovói natsionál'nyi ~) gross national income
вменённый ~ (vmeniónnyi ~) imputed earnings
высокий ~ (vysókii ~) large income
вычет из облагаемого ~/а (výchet iz oblagáemogo ~/a) income deduction
гарантировать ~ (garantírovat' ~) to guarantee an income
годовой ~ (godovói ~) annual income, yield
государственные ~/ы (gosudárstvennye ~/y) public revenues
денежный ~ (dénezhnyi ~) cash income
дополнительный ~ (dopolnítel'nyi ~) supplementary income
ежегодный ~ (ezhegódnyi ~) annual revenue
занижение ~/ов (zanizhénie ~/ov) understatement of income
извлекать ~ (izvlekát' ~) to derive an income
источники ~/а (istóchniki ~/a) sources of income
маржинальный ~ (marzhinál'nyi ~) marginal income
налог с ~/ов акционерных компаний (nalóg s ~/ov aktsionérnykh kompánii) corporate income tax
накопленный ~ (nakóplennyi ~) accumulated income
национальный ~ (natsionál'nyi ~) national income
начисленный ~ (nachíslennyi ~) accrued income
непроизводственный ~ (neproizvódstvennyi ~) unearned income

нетрудовой ~ (netrudovói ~) unearned income
низкий ~ (nízkii ~) poor return
обеспечивать ~ (obespéchivat' ~) to ensure an income
облагаемый налогами ~ (oblagáemyi nalógami ~) taxable income
общий ~ (óbshchii ~) total gain
общая сумма ~/а (óbshchaia súmma ~/a) total income
ожидаемый ~ (ozhidáemyi ~) expected income
первичный ~ (pervíchnyi ~) primary income
получать ~ (poluchát' ~) to receive revenue
постоянный ~ (postoiánnyi ~) fixed income
предельный ~ (predél'nyi ~) marginal return
приносить ~ (prinosít' ~) to yield
приносить малый ~ (prinosít' mályi ~) to yield poorly
приносить процентный ~ (prinosít' protséntnyi ~) to yield interest
приносить хороший ~ (prinosít' khoróshii ~) to yield a good return
прирост национального ~/а (priróst natsionál'nogo ~/a) increment of national income
приток ~/ов (pritók ~/ov) inflow of earnings
процентный ~ (protséntnyi ~) interest income
размер ~/а (razmér ~/a) level of income
распределение ~/ов (raspredelénie ~/ov) distribution of income
реальный ~ (reál'nyi ~) effective yield
регулярный ~ (reguliárnyi ~) regular income
регулирование ~/ов (regulírovanie ~/ov) income adjustment
репатриация ~/ов (repatriátsiia ~/ov) repatriation of profits
репатриировать ~/ы (repatriírovat' ~/y) to repatriate profits
рентный ~ (réntnyi ~) rental income

рост ~/a (rost ~/a) growth of income
сокрытие ~/ов (sokrýtie ~/ov) concealment of income
среднегодовой ~ (srednegodovói ~) average annual income
средний ~ (srédnii ~) average income
счёт ~/ов (schiót ~/ov) revenue account
твёрдый ~ (tviórdyi ~) fixed income
текущий ~ (tekúshchii ~) current income
торговый ~ (torgóvyi ~) trade income
трудовой ~ (trudovói ~) earned income
уровень ~/a (úroven' ~/a) income level
фактический ~ (faktícheskii ~) actual income
чистый ~ (chístyi ~) net income
экспортный ~ (éksportnyi ~) export earnings
~ будущих лет (~ búdushchikh let) deferred income
~ на акцию (~ na áktsiiu) dividend yield
~ на душу населения (~ na dúshu naseléniia) per capita income
~, остающийся после уплаты налогов ~ (~, ostaiushchiisia posle upláty nalógov ~) after tax income
~ от внешней торговли (~ ot vnéshnei torgóvli) foreign trade earnings
~ от продажи (~ ot prodázhi) sales revenue
~ от капиталовложений (~ ot kapitalovlozhénii) return on investment
~ от коммерческой деятельности (~ ot kommércheskoi déiatel'nosti) trading income
~ от краткосрочных вложений (~ ot kratkosróchnykh vlozhénii) short-term interest
~ от налогов (~ ot nalógov) tax revenues
~ от невидимых статей экспорта и импорта (~ ot nevídimykh statéi éksporta i ímporta) invisible {trade} income
~ от операций (~ ot operátsii) operating income

~ от предпринимательства (~ ot predprinimátel'stva) business earnings
~ от роялти (~ ot róialti) royalty earnings
~ от фрахта (~ ot frákhta) freight revenues
~ от экспорта (~ ot éksporta) export earnings
~ предприятия (~ predpriiátiia) income of an enterprise
Доходность (dokhódnost') f. economic viability, profitability
Дочерний (dochérnii) adj. affiliated, branch, subsidiary
Дружественный (drúzhestvennyi) adj. amicable, friendly
Дубликат (dublikát) m. duplicate {copy}
Дьякон (d'iákon) m. deacon

Е

Евровалюта (evrovaliúta) f. Eurocurrency
Евровалютный (evrovaliútnyi) adj. Eurocurrency
Евродоллары (evrodóllary) pl. Eurodollars
Еврокредит (evrokredít) m. Eurocredit
Еврорынок (evrorýnok) m. Euromarket
Еврочеки (evrochéki) pl. Eurocheques
Единиц/a (ediníts/a) f. unit
валютная ~ (valiútnaia ~) currency ~
денежная ~ (dénezhnaia ~) monetary ~
денежная, основная ~ (dénezhnaia, osnovnáia ~) basic monetary ~
Европейская валютная ~ (evropéiskaia valiútnaia ~) European Currency {ECU}
международные ~/ы (mezhdunaródnye ~/y) international ~s
метрические ~/ы (metrícheskie ~/y) metric ~s
на ~/y (na ~/u) per ~
отдельная ~ (otdél'naia ~) separate ~
расчётная ~ (raschiótnaia ~) payment ~

себестоимость ~/ы продукции
(sebestóimost' ~/y prodúktsii) ~
cost
транспортная ~ (tránsportnaia ~)
transport ~
условная ~ (uslóvnaia ~)
conventional ~
цена за ~/у товара (tsená za ~/u
továra) ~ price (goods)
~ веса (~ vésa) ~ of weight
~ времени (~ vrémeni) ~ of time
~ издержек производства (~
izdérzhek proizvódstva) ~ of
production costs
~ измерения (~ izmeréniia) ~ of
measurement
~ измерения, контрактная (~
izmeréniia, kontráktnaia)
contract ~ of measurement
~ оборудования (~ oborúdovaniia)
~ of equipment
~ продукции (~ prodúktsii) ~ of
production
~ стоимости (~ stóimosti) ~ of
value
~ товара (~ továra) unit,
individual good
Единовременный (edinovrémennyi)
adj. all at once, lumpsum
Единодушие (edinodúshie) *n.*
unanimity
Единодушный (edinodúshnyi) *adj.*
unanimous
Единый (edínyi) *adj.* common,
indivisible, joint
Ежегодный (ezhegódnyi) *adj.* annual
Ежедневный (ezhednévnyi) *adj.* daily
Ежеквартальный (ezhekvartál'nyi)
adj. quarterly
Ежемесячный (ezhemésiachnyi) *adj.*
monthly

Ё

Ёмкост/ь (ióiomkost/') *f.* capacity,
tank, volume
контейнер ~/ью в ...куб.м.
(kontéiner ~/'iu v ...kub.m.)
container capacity is ... cu.m.
меры ~/и (méry ~/i) measures of
capacity
складская ~ (skládskaia ~) store
capacity
транспортная ~ (tránsportnaia ~)
transport capacity

~ для перевоза жидких грузов на
корабле (~ dlia perevóza
zhídkikh grúzov na koráble)
ship's tank
~ для хранения (~ dlia
khranéniia) storage capacity
~ рынка (~ rýnka) market volume
~ цистерны (~ tsistérny) tank
capacity

Ж

Жалоб/а (zhálob/a) *f.* appeal,
complaint
иметь ~/у на кого-л. (imét' ~/u
na kogó-líbo) to have a
complaint against somebody
иметь ~/у на что-л. (imét' ~/u
na chto-líbo) to have a
complaint about something
многочисленные ~/ы
(mnogochíslennye ~/y) numerous
complaints
неразрешённая ~
(nerazreshiónnaia ~) outstanding
complaint
несущественная ~
(nesushchéstvennaia ~)
immaterial complaint
обоснованность ~/ы
(obosnóvannost' ~/y) grounds for
an appeal
обращаться с ~/ой
(obrashchát'sia s ~/oi) to lodge
a complaint
основание для ~/ы (osnovánie
dlia ~/y) cause for complaint
отдел жалоб ~ (otdél ~/) appeals
department
письменная ~ (pís'mennaia ~)
written complaint
подавать ~/у (podavát' ~/u) to
lodge a complaint
получать ~/ы (poluchát' ~/y) to
receive complaints
рассматривать ~/у заявителя
(rassmátrivat' ~/u zaiavítelia)
to examine an applicant's
complaint
суть ~/ы (sut' ~/y) the nature
of the appeal, complaint
~ заявителя на (~ zaiavítelia
na) applicant's appeal against
Жаловаться (zhálovát'sia) *v.* to
complain, to make complaints

Железнодорожный (zheleznodorózhnyi)
adj. railroad, rail
Женитьба (zhenít'ba) *f.* marriage
{said of a man}
Жертва (zhértva) *f.* sacrifice,
victim
Жёсткий (zhióstkii) *adj.* rigid,
strict
Жёсткость (zhióstkost') *f.*
rigidity, strictness
Жестокий (zhestókii) *adj.* cruel
Жестокость (zhestókost') *f.* cruelty
Жидкий (zhídkii) *adj.* fluid, liquid
Жирант (zhiránt) *m.* endorser
Жират (zhirát) *m.* endorsee
Жиро (zhíro) *n.* endorsement
Жулик (zhúlik) *m.* cheat, swindler
Жульничать (zhúl'nichat') *v.* to
cheat, to swindle
Жульничество (zhúl'nichestvo) *n.*
scam, swindle
Журнал (zhurnál) *m.* day book,
journal, log book, magazine,
periodical
   вахтенный ~ (vákhtennyi ~) log
   book
   выписки из судового ~/a (výpiski
   iz sudovóvo ~/a) entries in the
   ship's log
   вести ~ (vestí ~) to keep a log,
   register
   заносить в ~ (zanosít' v ~) to
   log
   записывать в ~ учёта (zaísyvat'
   v ~ uchióta) to journalize
   иллюстрированный ~
   (illiustrírovannyi ~)
   illustrated magazine
   информационный ~
   (informatsiónnyi ~)
   informational magazine
   кассовый ~ (kássovyi ~) cash
   journal
   коммерческий ~ (kommércheskii ~)
   business magazine
   машинный ~ (mashínnyi ~) machine
   performance log book
   медицинский ~ (meditsínskii ~)
   medical journal
   монтажный ~ (montázhnyi ~) log
   sheet
   периодический ~ (periodícheskii
   ~) periodical
   санитарный ~ (sanitárnyi ~)
   sanitary journal

специализированный ~
(spetsializírovannyi ~)
specialized periodical
судовой ~ (sudovói ~) ship's log
технический ~ (tekhnícheskii ~)
technical journal
~ по торговле (~ po torgóvle)
trade magazine
~ регистрации приёма груза (~
registrátsii priióma grúza)
tally book
~ учёта закупок (~ uchióta
zakúpok) purchase journal
~ учёта работ (~ uchióta rabót)
operations log

З

Забастовк/а (zabastóvk/a) *f.* strike
   всеобщая ~ (vseóbshchaia ~)
   general ~
   длительная ~ (dlítel'naia ~)
   protracted ~
   кратковременная ~
   (kratkovrémennaia ~) short-term
   ~
   общенациональная ~
   (obshchenatsionál'naia ~)
   nationwide ~
   оговорка о ~/ке (ogovórka o
   ~/ke) ~ clause
   страхование от ~/ок
   (strakhovánie ot ~/ok) ~
   insurance
   объявлять ~/ку (ob"iavliát'
   ~/ku) to call a ~
   прекращать ~/ку (prekrashchát'
   ~/ku) to call off a ~
   экономическая ~ (ekonomícheskaia
   ~) economic ~
   ~ портовых рабочих (~ portovýkh
   rabóchikh) longshoremen's ~
Заблаговременно (zablagovrémenno)
adv. in advance
Заблаговременный (zablagovrémennyi)
adj. in advance
Забракованный (zabrakóvannyi) *adj.*
defective
Заведующ/ий (zavéduiushch/ii)
m.adj.noun manager
   заместитель ~/его (zamestítel'
   ~/ego) assistant ~
   ~ доком (~ dókom) dock ~
   ~ канцелярией (~ kantseláriei)
   head clerk

~ отделением (~ otdeléniem)
branch ~
~ отделом найма (~ otdélom
náima) employment ~
~ отделом рекламы (~ otdélom
reklámy) advertising department
~
~ отделом сбыта (~ otdélom
sbýta) sales ~
~ отделом статистической
информации (~ otdélom statistí-
cheskoi informátsii) statistics
~
~ отделом субподрядов (~ otdélom
subpodriádov) subcontracts
department ~
~ отделом, транспортным (~
otdélom, tránsportnym) traffic ~
~ отделом экспорта (~ otdélom
éksporta) export ~
Завершать (zavershát') v. to
complete, to finalize
Завершени/е (zavershéni/e) n.
completion
удовлетворительное ~
(udovletvorítel'noe ~)
satisfactory ~
успешное ~ (uspéshnoe ~)
successful ~
~ выполнения заказа (~
vypolnéniia zakáza) ~ of an
order
~ закупок (~ zakúpok) ~ of
purchases
~ контракта (~ kontrákta)
performance of a contract
~ курса (~ kúrsa) ~ of a course
{of study}
~ монтажа (~ montázha) ~ of
construction
~ переговоров (~ peregovórov) ~
of negotiations
~ плана (~ plána) fulfillment of
a plan
~ поставки (~ postávki) ~ of
delivery
~ работ (~ rabót) ~ of work
~ работ в установленные сроки (~
rabót v ustanóvlennye sróki) ~
of work within the contract
period
~ рейса (~ réisa) ~ of a voyage
~ шефмонтажа (~ shefmontázha) ~
of construction supervision
Заверять (zaveriát') v. to assure,
to certify

Завёртывать (zaviórtyvat') v. to
wrap
Завес (zavés) m. weighing
контрольный ~ (kontról'nyi ~)
control ~
Зависимост/ь (zavísimost/') f.
dependence
в ~/и от (v ~/i ot) subject to
взаимная ~ (vzaímnaia ~)
interdependence
личная ~ (líchnaia ~) personal ~
находиться в ~/и от
(nakhodít'sia v ~/i ot) to be
dependent upon
полная ~ (pólnaia ~) complete ~
растущая ~ (rastúshchaia ~)
increasing ~
сокращать ~ (sokrashchát' ~) to
reduce ~
финансовая ~ (finánsovaia ~)
financial ~
частичная ~ (chastíchnaia ~)
partial ~
экономическая ~ (ekonomícheskaia
~) economic dependence
Зависимый (zavísimyi) adj.
dependent
Завод (zavód) m. factory, mill
авиационный ~ (aviatsiónnyi ~)
aircraft factory
автомобильный ~ (avtomobíl'nyi
~) automobile factory
владелец ~/a (vladélets ~/a)
factory owner
вводить ~ в строй (vvodít' ~ v
stroi) to commission a plant
директор ~/a (diréktor ~/a)
plant manager
действующий ~ (déistvuiushchii
~) operating factory
закрывать ~ (zakryvát' ~) to
close down a plant
инженер ~/a (inzhenér ~/a)
factory engineer
консервный ~ (konsérvnyi ~)
cannery
крупный ~ (krúpnyi ~) major
plant
лесопильный ~ (lesopíl'nyi ~)
sawmill
литейный ~ (litéinyi ~) foundry
машиностроительный ~
(mashinostroítel'nyi ~)
engineering plant
медеплавильный ~ (medeplavíl'nyi
~) copper smelting plant

местонахождения ~/а
(mestonakhozhdéniia ~/a) plant
site
металлургический ~
(metallurgícheskii ~) iron and
steel mill
механический ~ (mekhanícheskii
~) mechanical plant
молочный ~ (molóchnyi ~) dairy
processing plant
монтаж ~/а (montázh ~/a) factory
installation
мощность ~/а (móshchnost' ~/a)
plant capacity
нефтеочистительный ~
(nefteochistítel'nyi ~) oil
refinery
нефтеперерабатывающий ~
(neftepererabátyvaiushchii ~)
petroleum processing plant
нефтехимический ~
(neftekhimícheskii ~)
petrochemical plant
обучение на ~/е (obuchénie na
~/e) on the job training
опытный ~ (ópytnyi ~) pilot
production facility
отдельные ~/ы (otdél'nye ~/y)
individual plants
планировка ~/а (planiróvka ~/a)
plant layout
площадка ~/а (ploshchádka ~/a)
plant site
посещение ~/а (poseshchénie ~/a)
factory inspection
посещать ~ (poseshchát' ~) to
visit a factory
производственные мощности ~/а
(proizvódstvennye móshchnosti
~/a) plant capacity
пуск ~/а (pusk ~/a) factory
start-up
расширять ~ (rasshiriát' ~) to
expand a factory
реконструировать ~
(rekonstruírovat' ~) to
reconstruct a factory
ремонтный ~ (remóntnyi ~)
overhaul factory
руководить ~/ом (rukovodít'
~/om) to manage a factory
с ~/а (s ~/a) ex-mill (contract
provision)
с ~/а продавца (s ~/a prodavtsá)
ex-seller's mill (contract -
provision)

смонтированный на ~/е
(smontírovannyi na ~/e) mounted
at the factory
современный ~ (soveménnyi ~)
modern factory
сооружать ~ (sooruzhát' ~) to
outfit a factory
станкостроительный ~
(stankostroítel'nyi ~) machine
tool plant
строительство ~/а (stroítel'stvo
~/a) construction of a factory
субподрядчика ~ (subpodriádchika
~) subcontractor's plant
судостроительный ~
(sudostroítel'nyi ~) shipyard
типовой ~ (tipovói ~)
representative factory
химический ~ (khimícheskii ~)
chemical plant
центральный ~ (tsentrál'nyi ~)
central factory
франко ~ (fránko ~) ex mill
франко ~ продавца (fránko ~
prodavtsá) ex seller's mill
экспериментальный ~
(eksperimentál'nyi ~)
experimental factory
эксплуатация ~/а (ekspluatátsiia
~/a) operation of a plant
~ грузовых машин (~ gruzovýkh
mashín) truck factory
~ для производства чего-л. (~
dlia proizvódstva chegó-l.)
factory for the production of
smth.
~ изготовителя (~ izgotovítelia)
manufacturer's plant
~ лицензиата (~ litsenziáta)
licensee's plant
~ начинает выпуск продукции (~
nachináet výpusk prodúktsii) the
plant goes onstream
~ работает (~ rabótaet) the
plant is operating
~ работает на полную мощность (~
rabótaet na pólnuiu móshchnost')
the plant is operating at full
capacity
~ с автоматическим управлением
(~ s avtomatícheskim
upravléniem) automated factory
~ тяжёлого машиностроения (~
tiazhiólogo mashinostroéniia)
heavy equipment factory
Завоевание (zavoevánie) n. conquest

территориальное ~
(territoriál'noe ~) territorial

~
~ Англии Норманнами (~ ánglii
normánnami) the Norman ~
{historical}
Завоеватель (zavoevátel') *m.*
conqueror
Завоевать (zavoevát') *v.* to conquer
Завоз (zavóz) *m.* carriage, delivery
Заготовитель (zagotovítel') *m.*
procurement officer
Заготовительный (zagotovítel'nyi)
adj. state procurement
Заготовка (zagotóvka) *f.* state
procurement, stockpiling
Загрузка (zagrúzka) *f.* capacity,
loading
полная ~ (pólnaia ~) full
capacity
Загрязнение (zagriaznénie) *n.*
pollution, soiling
~ окружающей среды (~
okruzháiushchei sredý) pollution
of the environment
Задание (zadánie) *n.* job, task
плановое ~ (plánovoe ~) plan
target
производственное ~
(proizvódstvennoe ~) production
target
Задаток (zadátok) *m.* deposit,
earnest money
Задержание (zaderzhánie) *n.* arrest,
detention, lien
временное ~ (vrémennoe ~)
temporary detention
законное ~ (zakónnoe ~) legal
detention
подлежать ~/ю (podlezhát' ~/iu)
to be subject to arrest,
detention
подлежащий ~/ю (podlezháshchii
~/iu) subject to arrest,
detention
~ в административном порядке (~
v administratívnom poriádke)
administrative detention
~ имущества (~ imúshchestva)
arrest of property
~ судна (~ súdna) arrest of a
vessel
~ товаров (~ továrov) detention
of goods
Задерживать (zadérzhivat') *v.* to
delay, to detain
Задержка (zadérzhka) *f.* delay

большая ~ (bol'sháia ~)
protracted delay
неоправданная ~ (neoprávdannaia
~) unjustified delay
~ в исполнении (~ v ispolnénii)
delay in performance
Задолженность (zadólzhennost') *f.*
arrears, debts, indebtedness,
liability
безнадёжная ~ (beznadiózhnaia ~)
bad debt, write-off
внешняя ~ (vnéshniaia ~) foreign
debt
государственная ~
(gosudárstvennaia ~) public debt
дебиторская ~ (debitórskaia ~)
accounts receivable
долгосрочная ~ (dolgosróchnaia
~) long-term indebtedness
ипотечная ~ (ipotéchnaia ~)
hypothecated debt, mortgage debt
ликвидная ~ (likvídnaia ~)
liquid debt
краткосрочная ~ (kratkosróchnaia
~) short-term debt
кредиторская ~ (kredítorskaia ~)
accounts payable
международная ~ (mezhdunaródnaia
~) international debt
необеспеченная ~
(neobespéchennaia ~) unsecured
debt
погасить ~ (pogásit' ~) to
extinguish debt
ссудная ~ (ssúdnaia ~) loan
indebtedness
текущая ~ (tekúshchaia ~)
current indebtedness
Заём (zaióm) *m.* borrowing, loan
банковский ~ (bánkovskii ~) bank
loan
беспроцентный ~ (besprotséntnyi
~) interest-free loan
внешний ~ (vnéshnii ~) foreign
borrowing
внутренний ~ (vnútrennii ~)
domestic borrowing
гарантированный ~
(garantírovannyi ~) guaranteed
loan
гарантировать ~ (garantírovat'
~) to guarantee a loan
государственный ~ (
gosudárstvennyi ~) public loan
денежный ~ (dénezhnyi ~) cash
loan

долгосрочный ~ (dolgosróchnyi ~)
long-term loan
заключить ~ (zakliuchít' ~) to
negotiate a loan
ипотечный ~ (ipotéchnyi ~)
mortgage loan
консолидированный ~
(konsolidírovannyi ~)
consolidated loan
краткосрочный ~ (kratkosróchnyi
~) short-term loan
льготный ~ (l'gótnyi ~) low-
interest loan
международный ~ (mezhdunaródnyi
~) international loan
облигационный ~ (obligatsiónnyi
~) funded loan
покрыть ~ (pokrýt' ~) to cover a
loan
принудительный ~ (prinudítel'nyi
~) forced loan
просроченный ~ (prosróchennyi ~)
past-due loan
процентный ~ (protséntnyi ~)
interest-bearing loan
рентный ~ (réntnyi ~) profitable
loan
частный ~ (chástnyi ~) private
loan
~ обеспеченный ипотекой (~
obespéchennyi ipotékoi) loan
secured by mortgage
~ под залог (~ pod zalóg) loan
against a pledge
Заёмщик (zaiómshchik) m. borrower,
debtor
Заимодавец (zaimodávets) m.
creditor, lender
Заимодатель (zaimodátel') m.
creditor, lender
Заимствование (zaimstvovánie)
borrowing
Заинтересованность
(zainteresóvannost') f. incentive,
interest
взаимная ~ (vzaímnaia ~) mutual
interest
личная ~ (líchnaia ~) personal
interest
Заинтересованный (zainteresóvannyi)
adj. interested
Закабалить (zakabalít') v. to
enslave
Заказ (zakáz) m. order, reservation
большой ~ (bol'shói ~) heavy
order

выполнить ~ (výpolnit' ~) to
fill an order
государственный ~
(gosudárstvennyi ~) state order
повторный ~ (povtórnyi ~) repeat
order
пробный ~ (próbnyi ~) trial
order
Заказать (zakazát') v. see
заказывать
Заказчик (zakázchik) m. buyer,
customer
Заказывать (zakázyvat') v.
[perfective: заказать] to order, to
reserve
Заклад (zaklád) m. bet, pawning,
pledge, wager
Закладная (zakladnáia) f.adj.noun
bill of sale, mortgage deed, pledge
Закладодержатель
(zakladoderzhátel') m. mortgagee
Закладчик (zakládchik) m. mortgagor
Закладывать (zakládyvat') v. to
mortgage, to pawn
Заключать (zakliuchát') v. to
conclude, to execute {e.g.
contract}, to imprison
~ в тюрьму (~ v tiur'mú) to
incarcerate
~ под стражу (~ pod strázhu) to
take into custody
~ договор (~ dogovór) to
conclude a contract
Заключение (zakliuchénie) n.
conclusion, confinement, resolution
благоприятное ~ (blagopriiátnoe
~) beneficial conclusion
неблагоприятное ~
(neblagopriiátnoe ~) unfavorable
conclusion
незаконное ~ (nezakónnoe ~)
false imprisonment
необоснованное ~ (neobosnóvannoe
~) unfounded inference
одиночное ~ (odinóchnoe ~)
solitary confinement
пожизненное ~ (pozhíznennoe ~)
life imprisonment
предварительное ~
(predvarítel'noe ~) preliminary
conclusion
тюремное ~ (tiurémnoe ~)
incarceration
~ брака (~ bráka) consummation
of a marriage
~ в тюрьме (~ v tiur'mé)
incarceration in prison

~ договора (~ dogovóra)
conclusion of a treaty, contract
~ контракта (~ kontrákta)
conclusion of a contract
~ мирного договора (~ mírnogo
dogovóra) conclusion of a peace
treaty
~ сделки (~ sdélki) conclusion
of a deal
~ соглашения (~ soglashéniia)
conclusion of an agreement
~ под стражу (~ pod strázhu)
taking into custody
~ эксперта (~ ekspérta)
conclusion of an expert
Заключённый (zakliuchiónnyi)
m.adj.noun convict, prisoner
политический ~ (politícheskii ~)
political prisoner
Закон (zakón) m. act, law, statute
антимонопольный ~
(antimonopól'nyi ~) anti-trust
statute
арбитражный ~ (arbitrázhnyi ~)
arbitration statute
банковский ~ (bánkovskii ~)
banking law
внутренний ~ (vnútrennii ~)
domestic statute
внутригосударственный ~
(vnutrigosudárstvennyi ~)
intragovernmental law
воры в ~/е (vóry v ~/e) "thieves
in the law" {organized criminal
groups based in the former USSR}
временный ~ (vrémennyi ~)
temporary law
горный ~ (górnyi ~) mining
statute
государственный ~
(gosudárstvennyi ~) government
statute
гражданский ~ (grazhdánskii ~)
civil statute
Грешема ~ (gréshema ~) Grisham's
Law
действующий ~ (déistvuiushchii
~) statute in force
дискриминационный ~
(diskriminatsiónnyi ~)
discriminatory law
дозволенный ~/ом (dozvólennyi
~/om) permitted by statute
железный ~ (zheléznyi ~) iron
law
запретительный ~ (zapretítel'nyi
~) proscriptive statute

земельный ~ (zemel'nyi ~) land
statute
избирательный ~ (izbirátel'nyi
~) electoral statute
издать ~ (izdát' ~) to publish a
statute
иммиграционный ~
(immigratsiónnyi ~) immigration
statute
колониальный ~ (koloniál'nyi ~)
colonial statute
конституционный ~
(konstitutsiónnyi ~)
constitutional law
местный ~ (méstnyi ~) local
statute
муниципальный ~ (munitsipál'nyi
~) municipal law
налоговый ~ (nalógovyi ~) tax
law
нарушить ~ (narushít' ~) to
violate a statute
национальный ~ (natsionál'nyi ~)
national law
обойти ~ (oboití ~) to evade a
law
общественный ~ (obshchéstvennyi
~) societal law
общий ~ (óbshchii ~) law of
general application
обычный ~ (obýchnyi ~) customary
law
органический ~ (organícheskii ~)
organic law
основной ~ (osnovnói ~)
fundamental statute
отдельный ~ (otdél'nyi ~)
separate act
отечественный ~ (otéchestvennyi
~) domestic statute
отменить ~ (otmenít' ~) to
repeal a statute
отменяемый ~ (otmeniáemyi ~)
repealed statute
патентный ~ (paténtnyi ~) patent
law
письменный ~ (pís'mennyi ~)
written law
применимый ~ (primenímyi ~)
applicable statute
применить ~ (primenít' ~) to
apply a statute
принять ~ (priniát' ~) to adopt
a statute
процессуальный ~
(protsessuál'nyi ~) procedural
statute

расистский ~ (rasístskii ~)
racist statute
расовый ~ (rásovyi ~) race law
специальный ~ (spetsiál'nyi ~)
special law
сухой ~ (sukhói ~) dry law
существующий ~
(sushchestvúiushchii ~) existing
law
таможенный ~ (tamózhennyi ~)
customs law
тарифный ~ (tarífnyi ~) tariff
law
территориальный ~
(territoriál'nyi ~) territorial
statute
типовой ~ (tipovói ~) model law
трудовой ~ (trudovói ~) labor
law
уголовный ~ (ugolóvnyi ~) penal
statute
федеральный ~ (federál'nyi ~)
federal law
фискальный ~ (fiskál'nyi ~)
fiscal law
формальный ~ (formál'nyi ~)
formal law
чрезвычайный ~ (chrezvycháinyi
~) emergency law
экономический ~ (ekonomícheskii
~) economic law
~ заработной платы (~
zárabotnoi pláty) minimum wage
statute
~ подлости (~ pódlosti)
"Murphy's Law" {whatever can go
wrong, will go wrong}
Законник (zakónnik) m. law-abiding
person, lawyer {colloquial}
Законно (zakónno) adv. legally
Законнорождённый
(zakonnorozhdiónnyi) adj.
legitimate {child}
Законность (zakónnost') f. legality
международная ~ (mezhdunaródnaia
~) international legality
социалистическая ~
(sotsialistícheskaia ~)
socialist legality
Законный (zakónnyi) adj. legal,
rightful
Законодатель (zakonodátel') m.
legislator
Законодательный (zakonodátel'nyi)
adj. legislative
Законодательство (zakonodátel'stvo)
n. legislation

аграрное ~ (agrárnoe ~) agrarian
~
антимонопольное ~
(antimonopól'noe ~) anti-trust ~
арбитражное ~ (arbitrázhnoe ~)
arbitration ~
банковское ~ (bánkovskoe ~)
banking ~
брачное ~ (bráchnoe ~) marital ~
бюджетное ~ (biudzhétnoe ~)
budgetary ~
валютное ~ (valiútnoe ~)
currency exchange ~
внутреннее ~ (vnútrennee ~)
internal ~
водное ~ (vódnoe ~) riparian ~
военное ~ (voénnoe ~) military ~
воздушное ~ (vozdúshnoe ~) civil
aviation ~
горное ~ (górnoe ~) mining ~
гражданское ~ (grazhdánskoe ~)
civil ~
гражданское процессуальное ~
(grazhdánskoe protsessuál'noe ~)
civil procedure ~
действующее ~ (déistvuiushchee
~) in force
жилищное ~ (zhilíshchnoe ~)
housing ~
земельное ~ (zemél'noe ~) land ~
иммиграционное ~
(immigratsiónnoe ~) immigration
~
иностранное ~ (inostránnoe ~)
foreign ~
колониальное ~ (koloniál'noe ~)
colonial ~
колхозное ~ (kolkhóznoe ~)
collective farm ~
конституционное ~
(konstitutsiónnoe ~)
constitutional ~
лесное ~ (lesnóe ~) timber ~
кредитное ~ (kredítnoe ~) credit
~
международное ~ (mezhdunaródnoe
~) international ~
местное ~ (méstnoe ~) local ~
морское ~ (morskóe ~) maritime ~
налоговое ~ (nalógovoe ~) tax ~
национальное ~ (natsionál'noe ~)
national ~
отечественное ~ (otéchestvennoe
~) domestic ~
параллельное ~ (parallél'noe ~)
parallel ~

патентное ~ (paténtnoe ~) patent ~

почтовое ~ (pochtóvoe ~) postal ~

процессуальное ~ (protsessuál'noe ~) procedural ~

расистское ~ (rasístskoe ~) racist ~

санитарное ~ (sanitárnoe ~) health ~

сельское ~ (sél'skoe ~) rural ~

семейное ~ (seméinoe ~) family ~

страховое ~ (strakhovóe ~) insurance ~

таможенное ~ (tamózhennoe ~) customs ~

торговое ~ (torgóvoe ~) commercial ~

трудовое ~ (trudovóe ~) labor ~

уголовное ~ (ugolóvnoe ~) penal ~

федеральное ~ (federál'noe ~) federal ~

финансовое ~ (finánsovoe ~) financial ~

фискальное ~ (fiskál'noe ~) fiscal ~

чрезвычайное ~ (chrezvycháinoe ~) emergency ~

экономическое ~ (ekonomícheskoe ~) economic ~

~ о квартирной плате (~ o kvartírnoi pláte) rent-control ~

~ против демпинга (~ prótiv démpinga) anti-dumping ~

Законодательствовать (zakonodátel'stvovat') v. to legislate

Закономерный (zakonomérnyi) adj. orderly, regular

Закономерность (zakonomérnost') f. legal conformity, regularity

Законоположение (zakonopolozhénie) n. statute

Законопредложение (zakonopredlozhénie) n. proposed law

Законопроект (zakonoproékt) m. draft statute

Законосовещательный (zakonosoveshchátel'nyi) adj. bill {proposed law}

Закрепить (zakrepít') v. see закреплять

Закрепление (zakreplénie) n. fastening, fixture

Закреплять (zakrepliát') v. to consolidate, to secure

Закрывать (zakryvát') v. to close, to shut down

Закрытие (zakrýtie) n. closing, closure

Закрытый (zakrýtyi) adj. closed, private

Закрыть (zakrýt') v. see закрывать

Закупать (zakupát') n. to buy, to buy up

Закупк/а (zakúpk/a) f. buying, purchasing

государственные ~/и (gosudárstvennye ~/i) state procurements

спекулятивная ~ (spekuliatívnaia ~) speculative buying

Закупщик (zakúpshchik) m. purchasing agent

Зал (zal) m. hall

~ суда (~ sudá) courtroom

Залив (zalív) m. bay, gulf

Залог (zalóg) m. deposit, hypothecation, mortgage, pledge, security

взять в ~ (vziat' v ~) to take as security

внести ~ (vnestí ~) to put up a pledge, to put up security

дать деньги под ~ (dat' dén'gi pod ~) to give money against a pledge

невыкупленный ~ (nevýkuplennyi ~) unredeemed pledge

обеспеченный ~ (obespéchennyi ~) secured pledge

одолжить под ~ (odolzhít' pod ~) to lend against security

отдать в ~ (otdát' v ~) to pledge

~ движимости (~ dvízhimosti) pledge of chattels

~ недвижимого имущества (~ nedvízhimogo imúshchestva) mortgage of real property

~ товаров в переработке (~ továrov v pererabótke) pledge of semi-finished goods

Залогов/ый (zalógov/yi) adj. mortgage, pledge

~/ое свидетельство (~/oe svidétel'stvo) mortgage-deed

Залогодатель (zalogodátel') m. depositor, mortgagor

Залогодержатель (zalogoderzhátel') m. depositee, mortgagee, pledgee

Заложить (zalozhít') v.
[imperfective: закладывать] to
mortgage, to pawn
Заложник (zalózhnik) m. hostage
Заложничество (zalozhníchestvo) n.
hostage taking
Замедление (zamedlénie) n.
deceleration, delay
Замена (zaména) f. change,
replacement, substitution
  ~ арбитра (~ arbítra)
  replacement of arbitrator
  ~ обеспечения (~ obespécheniia)
  substitution of collateral
  ~ по гарантии (~ po garántii)
  warranty replacement
Заменимый (zamenímyi) adj.
replaceable
Заменитель (zamenítel') m.
substitute
Заменять (zameniát') v.
[perfective: заменить] to replace,
to substitute
Заместитель (zamestítel') m. deputy
  ~ директора (~ diréktora) ~
  director
  ~ заместителя министра (~
  zamestítelia minístra) ~
  minister
Заместительство (zamestítel'stvo)
n. tenure of office
Заместить (zamestít') v. [see
замещать]
Заметка (zamétka) f. mark, notice
Замечание (zamechánie) n.
observation, remark, reprimand
Замещать (zameshchát') v. to
deputize, to substitute
Замещение (zameshchénie) n.
appointment, substitution
Заминка (zamínka) f. glitch
Замораживание (zamorázhivanie) n.
freeze, restraint
  ~ заработной платы (~ zárabotnoi
  pláty) wage freeze
  ~ собственности (~
  sóbstvennosti) restraint of
  property
  ~ цен (~ tsen) price freeze
Замужество (zamúzhestvo) n.
marriage {said of a woman}
Замышлять (zamyshliát') v.
[perfective: замыслить] to
contemplate, to plan
Занесение (zanesénie) n. entering
  ~ на счёт (~ na schiót) charging
  to an account

Занимать (zanimát') v. to borrow,
to hold, to occupy
Занятие (zaniátie) n. occupation,
pursuit
  временное ~ (vrémennoe ~)
  temporary pursuit
  главное ~ (glávnoe ~) primary
  occupation
  доходное ~ (dokhódnoe ~)
  remunerative pursuit
  оплачиваемое ~ (oplachiváemoe ~)
  paid occupation
Занятость (zániatost') f.
employment, work pressure
  полная ~ (pólnaia ~) full
  employment
  постоянная ~ (postoiánnaia ~)
  permanent employment
Занять (zaniát') v. see занимать
Заочно (zaóchno) adv. in one's
absence, by correspondence, by
default
Заочный (zaóchnyi) adj. by
correspondence, by default
  ~ приговор (~ prigovór) judgment
  by default
Запас (zapás) m. reserve, stock,
supply
  базовый ~ (bázovyi ~) basic
  stock
  буферный ~ (búfernyi ~) buffer
  stock
  государственный ~
  (gosudárstvennyi ~) national
  stockpile
  делать ~ (délat' ~) to stockpile
  денежный ~ (dénezhnyi ~)
  monetary reserve
  золотой ~ (zolotói ~) gold
  reserves
  металлический ~ (metallícheskii
  ~) strategic metal reserves
  мировые ~/ы (mirovýe ~/y) world
  reserves
  производственные ~/ы
  (proizvódstvennye ~/y)
  productive reserves
  ~/ы товаров (~/y továrov) stock-
  in-trade
Запатентованный (zapatentóvannyi)
adj. patented
Запатентовать (zapatentovát') v. to
patent
Запечатывать (zapechátyvat') v.
[perfective: запечатать] to seal
{with official seal}

Записать (zapisát') v. [see
записывать]
Записка (zapíska) f. note
  деловая ~ (delováia ~) deal
  memorandum
  памятная ~ (pámiatnaia ~)
  memorandum
Запись (zápis') f. deed, entry,
record
  бухгалтерская ~ (bukhgálterskaia
  ~) bookkeeping entry
  дарственная ~ (dárstvennaia ~)
  gift deed
  дебетовая ~ (debetóvaia ~) debit
  entry
  договорная ~ (dogovórnaia ~)
  contract note
  кредитовая ~ (kredítovaia ~)
  credit entry
  метрическая ~ (metrícheskaia ~)
  registration of vital statistics
  первоначальная ~
  (pervonachál'naia ~) original
  deed
  произвести ~ (proizvestí ~) to
  record an entry
  раздельная ~ (razdél'naia ~)
  partition deed
  третейская ~ (tretéiskaia ~)
  entry of arbitral judgment
  ~ акта о смерти (~ ákta o
  smérti) registry of death
  certificate
  ~ возобновления ипотеки (~
  vozobnovléniia ipotéki)
  registration of renewal of
  mortgage
  ~ ипотеки (~ ipotéki)
  registration of mortgage
  ~ привилегии (~ privilégii)
  registration of privilege
  ~ о рождении (~ o rozhdénii)
  registration of birth
Записывать (zapísyvat') v. to
devise, to register, to transfer
{e.g. property}
Заплатить (zaplatít') v. to pay
  ~ наличными (~ nalíchnymi) ~
  cash
Запломбирование (zaplombirovánie)
n. sealing
  таможенное ~ (tamózhennoe ~)
  customs seal
Запломбировать (zaplombírovat') v.
to seal
Заповедник (zapovédnik) m. park,
preserve

Заподозрить (zapodozrít') v. to
suspect of
Заполнять (zapolniát') v. to fill
out
Запрашивать (zapráshivat') v. to
inquire
Запрет (zaprét) m. ban, writ
  судебный ~ (sudébnyi ~)
  injunction
Запрещать (zapreshchát') v. to ban,
to prohibit
Запрещение (zapreshchénie) n. ban,
prohibition
  ~ атомного оружия (~ átomnogo
  orúzhiia) atomic weapons ban
  ~ ввоза (~ vvóza) import
  prohibition
  ~ вывоза (~ vývoza) export
  prohibition
Запродажа (zaprodázha) f.
preliminary {wholesale} sale
Запродажный (zaprodázhnyi) adj.
sale, selling {wholesale}
Запродать (zaprodát') v. to enter a
wholesale agreement
Запрос (zaprós) m. inquiry,
request, requirements
  официальный ~ (ofitsiál'nyi ~)
  official inquiry
Запчасть (zapchást') f. spare part
Запросить (zaprosít') v. [see
запрашивать]
Зарабатывать (zarabátyvat') v. to
earn {e.g. wages}
Заработать (zarabótat') v. [see
зарабатывать]
Заработок (zárabotok) m. earnings,
pay
  денежный ~ (dénezhnyi ~)
  monetary earnings
  минимальный ~ (minimál'nyi ~)
  minimum earnings
  недельный ~ (nedél'nyi ~) weekly
  pay
  основной ~ (osnovnói ~) basic
  pay
  сдельный ~ (sdél'nyi ~) piece
  work earnings
  случайный ~ (slucháinyi ~)
  casual earnings
  средний ~ (srédnii ~) average
  earnings
  средний часовой ~ (srédnii
  chasovói ~) average hourly pay
  фактический ~ (faktícheskii ~)
  actual earnings

часовой ~ (chasovói ~) hourly pay

Зарегистрировать (zaregistrírovat') v. to register

Зарплата (zarpláta) f. [abbrev. of заработная плата] earnings, salary, wages

гарантированная годовая ~ (garantírovannaia godováia ~) guaranteed annual wage

ежемесячная ~ (ezhemésiachnaia ~) monthly wages

задержанная ~ (zadérzhannaia ~) back pay

номинальная ~ (nominál'naia ~) nominal wages

реальная ~ (reál'naia ~) take-home pay

средняя ~ (srédniaia ~) average salary, average wages

твёрдая ~ (tviórdaia ~) fixed wage

Зарубежный (zarubézhnyi) adj. foreign

Засада (zasáda) f. ambush

Засвидетельствовать (zasvidétel'stvovat') v. to attest, to certify, to notarize

Засевать (zasevát') v. to sow

Заседание (zasedánie) n. conference, meeting, session

гражданское судебное ~ (grazhdánskoe sudébnoe ~) civil hearing

заключительное ~ (zakliuchítel'noe ~) closing session

закрытое ~ (zakrýtoe ~) closed session

закрытое ~ суда (zakrýtoe ~ suda) closed session of court

закрытое судебное ~ (zakrýtoe sudébnoe ~) closed judicial hearing

открытое ~ (otkrýtoe ~) public session

открытое судебное ~ (otkrýtoe sudébnoe ~) public hearing

официальное ~ (ofitsiál'noe ~) official meeting

очередное ~ (ocherednóe ~) regular session

пленарное ~ (plenárnoe ~) plenary session

публичное ~ (publíchnoe ~) public hearing

совместное ~ (sovméstnoe ~) joint session

судебное ~ (sudébnoe ~) hearing

уголовное судебное ~ (ugolóvnoe sudébnoe ~) session of criminal court

чрезвычайное ~ (chrezvycháinoe ~) emergency meeting

Заседатель (zasedátel') m. assessor

народный ~ (naródnyi ~) public assessor

присяжный ~ (prisiázhnyi ~) juror, juryman

Заседать (zasedát') v. to meet, to sit

Засекреченный (zasekréchennyi) adj. hush-hush, secret

Заселение (zaselénie) n. colonization, settlement

Засеять (zaséiat') v. [see засевать]

Застава (zastáva) f. barrier, town gates

пограничная ~ (pograníchnaia ~) border barrier

Застой (zastói) m. depression, recession

хозяйственный ~ (khoziástvennyi ~) economic depression

~ торговли (~ torgóvli) stagnation of trade

Застрахованный (zastrakhóvannyi) adj. insure

Застраховать (zastrakhovát') v. to indemnify, to insure

Застройка (zastróika) f. building

Застройщик (zastróishchik) m. home builder {one's own house}

Затоваривание (zatovarivánie) n. dead stock, overstock

Заточить (zatochít') v. to confine

Заточение (zatochénie) n. confinement

необоснованное ~ (neobosnóvannoe ~) false imprisonment

Затрат/а (zatrát/a) f. cost, expense, outlay

~ капитала (~ kapitála) capital expenditure

дополнительные ~/ы (dopolnítel'nye ~/y) additional expenses

капитальные ~/ы (kapitál'nye ~/y) capital costs

конкретные ~/ы (konkrétnye ~/y) concrete expenditures

косвенные ~/ы (kósvennye ~/y) indirect expenses

материальные ~/ы (materiál'nye ~/y) material expenditures

непроизводительные ~/ы (neproizvodítel'nye ~/y) non-productive expenditures

неосязаемые ~/ы (neosiazáemye ~/y) intangible expenses

начальные ~/ы (nachál'nye ~/y) initial costs

постоянные ~/ы (postoiánnye ~/y) fixed costs

производственные ~/ы (proizvódstvennye ~/y) productive costs

прямые ~/ы (priamýe ~/y) direct costs

сезонные ~/ы (sezónnye ~/y) seasonal costs

текущие ~/ы (tekúshchie ~/y) current expenses

трудовые ~/ы (trudovýe ~/y) labor expenses

фактические ~/ы (faktícheskie ~/y) actual costs

эксплуатационные ~/ы (ekspluatatsiónnye ~/y) operating costs

~/ы брутто (~/y brútto) gross expenditures

~/ы нетто (~/y nétto) net expenditures

Затребовать (zatrébovat') v. to request, to require

Затруднени/е (zatrudnéni/e) n. difficulty

бюджетное ~ (biudzhétnoe ~) budgetary ~

валютные ~/я (valiútnye ~/ia) foreign exchange difficulties

денежные ~/я (dénezhnye ~/ia) money problems

финансовые ~/я (finánsovye ~/ia) financial difficulties

Затруднительный (zatrudnítel'nyi) adj. difficult, embarrassing

Зафиксировать (zafiksírovat') v. to put on record

Зафрахтовать (zafrakhtovát') v. to charter freight

Захват (zakhvát) v. seizure, usurpation

самовольный ~ (samovol'nyi ~) self-help {repossession}

совершить ~ (sovershít' ~) to capture, to seize

~ власти (~ vlásti) seizure of power

~ корабля (~ korabliá) capture of a ship

~ рынка (~ rýnka) capture of a market

~ судна (~ súdna) seizure of a vessel

Захватчик (zakhvátchik) m. aggressor, invader

Заход (zakhód) m. call {of a vessel at port}

вынужденный ~ (vynúzhdennyi ~) distress call {of a vessel at port}

Зачесть (zachést') v. [see зачитывать]

Зачёт (zachiót) m. offset

договорный ~ (dogovórnyi ~) contractual ~

судебный ~ (sudébnyi ~) judicial ~

Зачитывать (zachítyvat') v. to account, to reckon

Защита (zashchíta) f. defense, prevention, protection

временная ~ (vrémennaia ~) temporary protection

дипломатическая ~ (diplomatícheskaia ~) diplomatic protection

законная ~ (zakónnaia ~) legal protection

консульская ~ (kónsul'skaia ~) consular protection

личная ~ (líchnaia ~) personal defense

международная ~ (mezhdunaródnaia ~) international protection

международно-правовая ~ (mezhdunaródno-pravováia ~) international legal protection

патентная ~ (paténtnaia ~) patent protection

политическая ~ (politícheskaia ~) political defense

правовая ~ (pravováia ~) legal protection

санитарная ~ (sanitárnaia ~) preservation of health

совместная ~ (sovméstnaia ~) joint defense

специальная ~ (spetsiál'naia ~) special protection

судебная ~ (sudébnaia ~) judicial protection

~ детей (~ detéi) defense of children
~ диссертации (~ dissertátsii) defense of a dissertation
~ изобретения (~ izobreténiia) protection of an invention
~ имущества (~ imúshchestva) protection of property
~ интересов (~ interésov) protection of interests
~ культурных ценностей (~ kul'túrnykh tsénnostei) preservation of cultural treasures
~ меньшинств (~ mén'shinstv) protection of minorities
~ патентного права (~ paténtnogo práva) defense of patent right
~ прав (~ prav) protection of rights
~ в суде (~ v sudé) defense in court
~ территории (~ territórii) defense of territory
Защитить (zashchitít') v. [see защищать]
Защитник (zashchítnik) m. counsel for the defense, defense attorney
общественный ~ (obshchéstvennyi ~) public defender
Защищать (zashchishchát') v. to defend, to mount a defense, to protect
Заявитель (zaiavítel') m. declarant, deponent
первоначальный ~ (pervonachál'nyi ~) original declarant
Заявлять (zaiavliát') v. [perfective: заявить] to announce, to claim, to declare
Заявка (zaiávka) f. announcement, application, declaration, tender
действительная ~ (deistvítel'naia ~) valid application
импортная ~ (ímportnaia ~) import application
кредитная ~ (kredítnaia ~) credit application
отдельная ~ (otdél'naia ~) separate application
патентная ~ (paténtnaia ~) patent claim
первичная ~ (pervíchnaia ~) parent application

первоначальная ~ (pervonachál'naia ~) original application
письменная ~ (pís'mennaia ~) written application
совместная ~ (sovméstnaia ~) joint application
Заявление (zaiavlénie) n. announcement, declaration, notice
встречное исковое ~ (vstréchnoe iskovóe ~) notice of countersuit
дипломатическое ~ (diplomatícheskoe ~) diplomatic statement
исковое ~ (iskovóe ~) notice of suit
ложное ~ (lózhnoe ~) false declaration, perjured deposition
официальное ~ (ofitsiál'noe ~) official notice
письменное ~ (pís'mennoe ~) written notification
подать ~ (podát' ~) to put in an application
предварительное ~ (predvarítel'noe ~) advance notice, preliminary statement
сделать ~ (sdélat' ~) to make a statement
совместное ~ (sovméstnoe ~) joint statement
судебное ~ о невинности (sudébnoe ~ o nevínnosti) plea of not guilty
устное ~ (ústnoe ~) oral statement
формальное ~ (formál'noe ~) formal statement
Звани/е (zváni/e) n. rank, title
военное ~ (voénnoe ~) military rank
лишить военного ~/я (lishít' voénnogo ~/ia) to demote in rank
почётное ~ (pochiótnoe ~) honorary title
юридическое ~ (iuridícheskoe ~) legal title
Звено (zvenó) n. link {of a chain, also figuratively}
Здание (zdánie) n. building, premises
административное ~ (administratívnoe ~) administrative building
жилое ~ (zhilóe ~) residential building

промышленное ~ (promýshlennoe ~)
industrial premises
Земельный (zemél'nyi) *adj.* land
Землевладелец (zemlevladélets) *m.*
land owner
Землевладение (zemlevladénie) *n.*
land ownership
Земледелие (zemledélie) *n.* farming
Землемер (zemlemér) *m.* land-
surveyor
Землепользование (zemlepól'zovanie)
n. land tenure
  единоличное ~ (edinolíchnoe ~)
  individual land tenure
Землепользователь
(zemlepol'zovátel') *m.* ground
tenant
Землеустройство (zemleustróistvo)
n. land tenure regulation
Земля (zemliá) *f.* earth, land, soil
  арендованная ~ (arendóvannaia ~)
  leased land
  возделанная ~ (vozdélannaia ~)
  cultivated land
  городская ~ (gorodskáia ~) urban
  land
  залежная ~ (zálezhnaia ~) fallow
  land
  занятая ~ (zániataia ~) occupied
  land
  казённая ~ (kaziónnaia ~) state
  lands
  пахотная ~ (pákhotnaia ~) arable
  land
  пограничная ~ (pograníchnaia ~)
  border land
Земство (zémstvo) *n.* zemstvo
{historical Russian district
council}
Злодей (zlodéi) *m.* scoundrel,
villain
Злорадство (zlorádstvo) *n.*
Schadenfreude {gloating over
others' misfortunes}
Злостный (zlóstnyi) *adj.* malicious,
willful
Злотый (zlótyi) *m.* Zloty {Polish
currency}
Злоупотребление (zloupotreblénie)
n. abuse
  ~ властью (~ vlást'iu) abusive
  authority
  ~ доверием (~ dovériem) breach
  of confidence, breach of trust
  ~ изобретением (~ izobreténiem)
  ~ of an invention

~ кредита (~ kredíta) misuse of
credit
~ правом (~ právom) ~ of a right
~ привилегиями (~ privilégiiami)
~ of privileges
~ силой (~ síloi) misuse of
force
~ служебным положением (~
sluzhébnym polozhéniem) ~ of
office
~ товарным знаком (~ továrnym
znákom) ~ of trademark
Знак (znak) *m.* mark, sign, symbol,
token
  бумажный денежный ~ (bumázhnyi
  dénezhnyi ~) paper currency
  водяной ~ (vodianói ~) watermark
  граничный ~ (graníchnyi ~)
  border sign
  денежный ~ (dénezhnyi ~) money
  зарегистрированный товарный ~
  (zaregistrírovannyi továrnyi ~)
  registered trademark
  запрещённый ~ (zapreshchiónnyi
  ~) prohibited mark
  казначейский ~ (kaznachéiskii ~)
  state logo
  общеизвестный ~
  (obshcheizvéstnyi ~) well-known
  symbol
  опознавательный ~
  (opoznavátel'nyi ~)
  identification mark
  отличительный ~ (otlichítel'nyi
  ~) distinguishing mark
  официальный ~ (ofitsiál'nyi ~)
  official sign
  официальный ~ гарантии
  (ofitsiál'nyi ~ garántii)
  official sign of guarantee
  пограничный ~ (pograníchnyi ~)
  border marker
  поддельный денежный ~
  (poddél'nyi dénezhnyi ~)
  counterfeit currency
  почётный ~ отличия (pochiótnyi ~
  otlíchiia) honorable mark of
  distinction
  почтовый ~ (pochtóvyi ~)
  postmark
  товарный ~ (továrnyi ~)
  trademark
Знак-подпись (znak-pódpis') *f.*
signature mark {e.g. x mark by
illiterate}
Значительный (znachítel'nyi) *adj.*
considerable, significant

Значок (znachók) m. badge, pin
  партийный ~ (partíinyi ~) party
  membership badge
Золовка (zolóvka) f. sister-in-law
{sister of wife's husband}
Золото (zóloto) n. gold
  высокопробное ~ (vysokopróbnoe
  ~) fine ~
  монетарное ~ (monetárnoe ~)
  monetary ~
  низкопробное ~ (nizkopróbnoe ~)
  low-grade ~
  ~ в монетах (~ v monétakh) ~ in
  coins
  ~ в самородках (~ v samoródkakh)
  ~ in nuggets
  ~ в слитках (~ v slítkakh) ~ in
  ingots
Зона (zón/a) f. area, territory,
zone
  арендованная ~ (arendóvannaia ~)
  rental space
  беспошлинная ~ (bespóshlinnaia
  ~) duty-free zone
  валютная ~ (valiútnaia ~)
  currency zone
  воздушная оборонительная
  опознавательная ~ (vozdúshnaia
  oboronítel'naia opoznavátel'naia
  ~) air defense zone
  воры в ~/е (vóry v ~/e) "thieves
  in the zone" {members of
  criminal organization in camps}
  восточная ~ (vostóchnaia ~)
  eastern territory
  демилитаризованная ~
  (demilitarizóvannaia ~)
  demilitarized zone
  долларовая ~ (dóllarovaia ~)
  dollar zone
  закрытая рыболовная ~ (zakrýtaia
  rybolóvnaia ~) closed fisheries
  zone
  запретная ~ (zaprétnaia ~)
  blockaded zone
  запретная пограничная ~
  (zaprétnaia pograníchnaia ~)
  forbidden frontier zone
  иммиграционная ~
  (immigratsiónnaia ~) immigration
  zone
  карантинизированная ~
  (karantiniziróvannaia ~)
  quarantined territory
  морская ~ (morskáia ~) maritime
  zone

  налоговая ~ (nalógovaia ~) tax
  zone
  нейтрализованная ~
  (neitralizóvannaia ~)
  neutralized zone
  нейтральная ~ (neitrál'naia ~)
  neutral territory
  оборонительная ~
  (oboronítel'naia ~) defense zone
  оккупированная ~
  (okkupírovannaia ~) occupied
  territory
  пограничная ~ (pograníchnaia ~)
  frontier zone
  пограничная таможенная ~
  (pograníchnaia tamózhennaia ~)
  frontier custom zone
  портовая ~ (portóvaia ~) port
  area
  прибрежная ~ (pribrézhnaia ~)
  coastal zone
  прибрежная морская ~
  (pribrézhnaia morskáia ~)
  coastal maritime zone
  рыболовная ~ (rybolóvnaia ~)
  fishery zone
  свободная ~ (svobódnaia ~) free
  zone
  свободная экономическая ~
  (svobódnaia ekonomícheskaia ~)
  free economic zone
  специальная морская ~
  (spetsiál'naia morskáia ~)
  special maritime zone
  спорная ~ (spórnaia ~) disputed
  territory
  стерлинговая ~ (sterlingóvaia ~)
  sterling zone
  таможенная ~ (tamózhennaia ~)
  customs zone
  ~ безопасности (~ bezopásnosti)
  security zone
  ~ надзора (~ nadzóra) supervised
  area
  ~ нейтралитета (~ neitralitéta)
  zone of neutrality
  ~ назначения (~ naznachéniia)
  designated area
  ~ свободной торговли (~
  svobódnoi torgóvli) free trade
  zone
  ~ территориальных вод (~
  territoriál'nykh vod) area of
  territorial waters
  ~ юрисдикции (~ iurisdíktsii)
  territory under jurisdiction

Зональный (zonál'nyi) *adj.*
regional, zone
Зять (ziat') *m.* brother-in-law,
son-in-law

И

Игра (igrá) *f.* gamble, game
  азартная ~ (azártnaia ~) ~ of
  chance
  ~ на бирже (~ na bírzhe) stock
  jobbing
  ~ на разнице (~ na ráznitse)
  speculating on the margin
Играть (igrát') *v.* to play, to
gamble
Игрок (igrók) *m.* gambler
Идентификация (identifikátsiia) *f.*
identification
  судебная ~ (sudébnaia ~) legal ~
Идентичность (identíchnost') *f.*
identity
Иерархи/я (ierárkhi/ia) *f.*
hierarchy
  установить ~/ю (ustanovít' ~/iu)
  to establish a ~
Иждивенец (izhdivénets) *m.*
dependent {family law}
Иждивение (izhdivénie) *n.*
maintenance
Иждивенчество (izhdivénchestvo) *n.*
dependence
Избиение (izbiénie) *n.* assault and
battery
Избиратель (izbirátel') *m.* elector,
voter
Избирательный (izbirátel'nyi) *adj.*
electoral
Избрать (izbrát') *v.* to elect
Избрание (izbránie) *n.* election
  муниципальное ~ (munitsipál'noe
  ~) municipal ~
Избранник (ízbrannik) *m.* favorite
  народа ~ (naróda ~) popularly
  favored
Избыток (izbýtok) *m.* excess,
surplus
  ~ влаги (~ vlági) excess
  moisture
  ~ капитала (~ kapitála) capital
  surplus
  ~ рабочей силы (~ rabóchei síly)
  redundancy in manpower
Избыточный (izbýtochnyi) *adj.*
excess, surplus

Извещение (izveshchénie) *n.* advice,
notice, notification
  письменное ~ (pís'mennoe ~)
  written notice
  платёжное ~ (platiózhnoe ~)
  payment advice
  почтовое ~ (pochtóvoe ~) advice
  by mail
  предварительное ~
  (predvarítel'noe ~) preliminary
  notice
  ~ об инкассо (~ ob inkásso)
  collection advice
  ~ о получении (~ o poluchénii)
  notice of receipt
  ~ о смерти (~ o smérti) death
  notice
Извинение (izvinénie) *n.* apology,
excuse, pardon
  публичное ~ (publíchnoe ~)
  public apology
Извлечение (izvlechénie) *n.* excerpt
  ~ данных (~ dánnykh) data
  excerpts
Извлечь (izvléch') *n.* to derive, to
extract
Извратить (izvratít') *v.* to
distort, to misconstrue
Извращение (izvrashchénie) *n.*
distortion, misinterpretation,
perversion
Изгнание (izgnánie) *n.* banishment,
exile
  пожизненное ~ (pozhíznennoe ~)
  life exile
Изгнанник (ízgnannik) *m.* exile
{person}
Изгнать (izgnát') *v.* to banish, to
exile
Изгородь (ízgorod') boundary, fence
Изготовитель (izgotovítel') *m.*
manufacturer
Изготовление (izgotovlénie) *n.*
preparation
  ~ монеты (~ monéty) minting of
  coins
  ~ поддельных денег (~
  poddél'nykh déneg)
  counterfeiting
Издание (izdánie) *n.* publication
  официальное ~ (ofitsiál'noe ~)
  official ~
  периодическое ~ (periodícheskoe
  ~) periodical ~
  печатное ~ (pechátnoe ~) printed
  matter

порнографическое ~
(pornografícheskoe ~)
pornographic matter
Издатель (izdátel') *m.* publisher
Издательство (izdátel'stvo) *n.*
publishing house
Издать (izdát') *v.* to publish
Изделие (izdélie) *n.* article, good,
product
   готовое ~ (gotóvoe ~) finished
good
   доброкачественное ~
(dobrokáchestvennoe ~) high-
quality product
   запатентованное ~
(zapatentóvannoe ~) patented
article
   патентованное ~ (patentóvannoe
~) patented product
   промышленное ~ (promýshlennoe ~)
manufactured product
Издержки (izdérzhki) *pl.*
disbursements, expenditures,
outlays
   военные ~ (voénnye ~) military
expenditures
   возместить ~ (vozmestít' ~) to
recoup costs
   дополнительные ~ (dopolnítel'nye
~) additional outlays
   комиссионные ~ (komissiónnye ~)
commission fees
   необходимые ~ (neobkhodímye ~)
necessary expenses
   общие ~ (óbshchie ~) total costs
   обычные ~ (obýchnye ~) usual
expenses
   переменные ~ (pereménnye ~)
variable expenses
   постоянные ~ (postoiánnye ~)
fixed costs
   путевые ~ (putevýe ~) traveling
expenses
   судебные ~ (sudébnye ~) legal
expenses
   текущие ~ (tekúshchie ~) current
costs
   транспортные ~ (tránsportnye ~)
carriage costs
   чистые ~ (chístye ~) net outlays
   ~ ведения судебного дела (~
vedéniia sudébnogo déla) court
costs
   ~ использования (~
ispól'zovaniia) user fees
   ~ обращения (~ obrashchéniia)
distribution costs

   ~ производства (~ proizvódstva)
production outlays
   ~ по хранению (~ po khranéniiu)
storage expenses
Издольщик ~ (izdól'shchik ~) *m.*
sharecropper
Издольщица ~ (izdól'shchitsa ~) *f.*
sharecropping
Излиш/ек (izlíshek) *m.* excess,
surplus
   импортные ~/ки (ímportnye ~/ki)
import surpluses
   сельскохозяйственные ~/ки
(sel'skokhoziástvennye ~/ki)
agricultural surpluses
   экспортные ~/ки (éksportnye
~/ki) export surpluses
   ~ в весе (~ v vése) excess
weight
   ~ денег в обращении (~ déneg v
obrashchénii) excess money
supply {in circulation}
   ~ доходов (~ dokhódov) excess
earnings
Изложение (izlozhénie) *n.* account
of events, description
   ~ мотивов (~ motívov) motives
{of a crime}
Измена (izména) *f.* treason
   государственная ~
(gosudárstvennaia ~) high
treason
   ~ родине (~ ródine) betrayal of
the homeland
Изменени/е (izmenéni/e) *n.*
alteration, amendment, revision
   конституционное ~
(konstitutsiónnoe ~)
constitutional amendment
   территориальное ~
(territoriál'noe ~) territoral
alteration
   ~ адреса (~ ádresa) change of
address
   ~ гражданства (~ grazhdánstva)
change of citizenship
   ~ границы (~ granítsy)
alteration of border
   ~ договора (~ dogovóra)
amendment to an agreement
   ~ закона (~ zakóna) amendment to
a law
   ~ законодательства (~
zakonodátel'stva) legislative
amendment
   ~ запасов (~ zapásov) change in
inventories

~ иска (~ íska) amendment to a suit {by plaintiff}
~ к худшему (~ k khúdshemu) a change for the worse
~ курса (~ kúrsa) change in exchange rate
~ приговора (~ prigovóra) change in amendment to sentencing
~ решения (~ reshéniia) amendment to a decision
~ ставки (~ stávki) rate change
~ статуса (~ státusa) change in status
~ стоимости (~ stóimosti) cost variation
~ судебной практики (~ sudébnoi práktiki) alteration of judicial practice
~ устава (~ ustáva) amendment to articles, amendment to charter
~ цены (~ tsený) a change in price
Изменить (izmenít') v. to alter, to amend, to modify
Изменник (izménnik) m. traitor
Измерение (izmerénie) n. measurement, testing
контрольное ~ (kontról'noe ~) test measurement
Измышление (izmyshlénie) n. fabrication
клеветническое ~ (klevetnícheskoe ~) libelous ~
Изнасилование (iznasílovanie) n. rape
Изнасиловать (iznasílovat') v. to rape
Износ (iznós) m. deterioration, wear and tear
моральный ~ (morál'nyi ~) planned obsolescence
основных фондов ~ (osnovnýkh fóndov ~) depreciation of fixed assets
Изобилие (izobílie) n. abundance
Изобретательство (izobretátel'stvo) n. inventiveness
Изобретение (izobreténie) n. discovery, invention
дополнительное ~ (dopolnítel'noe ~) additional invention
запатентованное ~ (zapatentóvannoe ~) patented invention
иностранное ~ (inostránnoe ~) foreign invention

патентоспособное ~ (patentosposóbnoe ~) patentable invention
промышленное ~ (promýshlennoe ~) industrial invention
совместное ~ (sovméstnoe ~) joint discovery, invention
~, сделанное на предприятии (~, sdélannoe na predpriiátii) in-house invention
Изобрести (izobrestí) v. to invent
Изобретатель (izobretátel') m. inventor
действительный и первый ~ (deistvítel'nyi i pérvyi ~) first and genuine ~
Изоляционизм (izoliatsionízm) m. isolationism
Изоляционист (izoliatsioníst) m. isolationist
Изоляционистический (izoliatsionistícheskii) adj. isolationist
Изоляция (izoliátsiia) f. isolation {political}, insulation {technical}
хозяйственная ~ (khoziástvennaia ~) economic isolation
Израсходовать (izraskhódovat') v. to consume, to expend
Изучение (izuchénie) n. research, study
~ возможностей выполнения (~ vozmózhnostei vypolnéniia) feasibility study
~ рынка (~ rýnka) market research
Изымать (izymát') v. to withdraw
Изъян (iz"ián) m. defect, flaw
Изъятие (iz"iátie) n. confiscation, seizure, withdrawal
налоговое ~ (nalógovoe ~) tax seizure
~ вклада (~ vkláda) withdrawal of a deposit
~ денег из обращения (~ déneg iz obrashchéniia) withdrawal of money from circulation
~ из запасов (~ iz zapásov) draw-down of inventory
~ имуществ (~ imúshchestv) confiscation of property
~ паспорта (~ pásporta) confiscation of passport
~ из юрисдикции (~ iz iurisdíktsii) removal from jurisdiction
Изъять (iz"iát') v. to withdraw

Изыскание (izyskánie) n.
investigation, research
Имение (iménie) n. estate {landed
property}
Именовать (imenovát') v. to name
Именной (imennói) adj. nominal,
registered
Иммигрант (immigrant) m. immigrant
Иммиграция (immigrátsiia) f.
immigration
   ~ капитала (~ kapitála) capital
   flight
Иммигрировать (immigrírovat') v. to
immigrate
Имидж (ímidzh) m. image
   ~ товара (~ továra) product ~
Иммунитет (immunitét) m. immunity
   абсолютный ~ (absoliútnyi ~)
   absolute ~
   дипломатический ~
   (diplomatícheskii ~) diplomatic
   ~
   личный ~ (líchnyi ~) personal ~
   консульский ~ (kónsul'skii ~)
   consular ~
   налоговый ~ (nalógovyi ~) tax ~
   парламентский ~ (parlámentskii
   ~) parliamentary ~
   судебный ~ (sudébnyi ~) legal ~
   финансовый ~ (finánsovyi ~)
   financial ~
   фискальный ~ (fiskál'nyi ~)
   fiscal ~
   функциональный ~
   (funktsionál'nyi ~) functional ~
   юрисдикционный ~
   (iurisdiktsiónnyi ~)
   jurisdictional ~
   ~ от ареста (~ ot arésta) ~ from
   arrest
   ~ от исков (~ otískov) ~ from
   suits, actions
   ~ от конфискаций (~ ot
   konfiskátsii) ~ from
   confiscation
   ~ от наложения ареста (~ ot
   nalozhéniia arésta) ~ from
   arrest
   ~ от обыска (~ ot óbyska) ~ from
   search
   ~ от реквизиций (~ ot
   rekvizítsii) ~ from
   requisitioning
   ~ суверена (~ suveréna)
   sovereign ~
Императивный (imperatívnyi) adj.
imperative

Император (imperátor) m. emperor
Империализм (imperialízm) m.
imperialism
Империалист (imperialíst) m.
imperialist
Империалистический
(imperialistícheskii) adj.
imperialist
Империя (impériia) f. empire
   колониальная ~ (koloniál'naia ~)
   colonial ~
   экономическая ~ (ekonomícheskaia
   ~) economic ~
Импорт (ímport) m. import
   косвенный ~ (kósvennyi ~)
   indirect ~
   невидимый ~ (nevídimyi ~)
   invisible ~
Импортёр (importiór) m. importer
   исключительный ~
   (iskliuchítel'nyi ~) exclusive ~
Импортировать (importírovat') v. to
import
   вновь ~ (vnov' ~) to re-import
Имуществ/о (imúshchestv/o) n.
asset, property
   арендованное ~ (arendóvannoe ~)
   leased property
   бесхозяйственно содержимое ~
   (beskhoziástvenno soderzhímoe ~)
   poorly managed property
   блокированное ~ (blokírovannoe
   ~) blocked assets
   будущее ~ (búdushchee ~) future
   interest {estate}
   государственное ~
   (gosudárstvennoe ~) state
   property
   движимое ~ (dvízhimoe ~) movable
   property {chattels}
   домашнее ~ (domáshnee ~)
   domestic property
   заложенное ~ (zalózhennoe ~)
   mortgaged property, pledged
   property
   застрахованное ~
   (zastrakhóvannoe ~) insured
   property
   коммунальные ~/a (kommunál'nye
   ~/a) communal assets
   личное ~ (líchnoe ~) personal
   property
   наличное ~ (nalíchnoe ~) liquid
   assets
   наследственное ~ (naslédstvennoe
   ~) inherited property

национализированное ~
(natsionalizírovannoe ~)
nationalized property
недвижимое ~ (nedvízhimoe ~)
real estate
неотчуждаемое ~ (neotchuzhdáemoe
~) inalienable property
обобществленное ~
(obobshchéstvlennoe ~)
collectivized property
обременённое ~ (obremenіónnoe ~)
encumbered property
общее ~ (óbshchee ~) community
property
право на ~ (právo na ~) legal
title of ownership
приобретённое ~ (priobretіónnoe
~) acquired property
публичное ~ (publíchnoe ~)
public property
раздельное ~ (razdél'noe ~)
divided property
секвестрированное ~
(sekvestrírovannoe ~)
sequestered property
сельскохозяйственное ~
(sel'skokhoziáystvennoe ~)
agricultural property
семейное ~ (seméinoe ~) family
property
собственное ~ (sóbstvennoe ~)
personal property
церковные ~/a (tserkóvnye ~/a)
church property
частное ~ (chástnoe ~) private
property
~ без наследника (~ bez
naslédnika) intestate property
~, обременённое ипотекой (~,
obremenіónnoe ipotékoi) property
encumbered by a mortgage
~ общин (~ obshchín) property of
a commune, communal property
~ отдельного лица (~ otdél'nogo
litsá) property of an individual
~ товарищества (~
továrishchestva) partnership
property
~ юридического лица (~
iuridícheskogo litsá) property
of a legal entity
Инвалид (invalíd) m. disabled
person, invalid
военный ~ (voénnyi ~) disabled
veteran
~ труда (~ trudá) disabled
worker

Инвалидность (invalídnost') f.
disability
длительная ~ (dlítel'naia ~)
long-term ~
полная ~ (pólnaia ~) full ~
постоянная ~ (postoiánnaia ~)
permanent ~
частичная ~ (chastíchnaia ~)
partial ~
Инвалюта {иностранная валюта}
(ínvaliuta) {inostránnaia valiúta}
foreign exchange {currency}
Инвентаризация (inventarizátsiia)
f. inventory, stock taking
Инвентаризировать
(inventarizírovat') v. to take
inventory
Инвентарь (inventár') m. stock
живой ~ (zhivói ~) livestock
сельскохозяйственный ~
(sel'skokhoziáystvennyi ~)
agricultural implements
торговый ~ (torgóvyi ~) stock-
in-trade
Инвестирование (investírovanie) n.
investing
Инвестировать (investírovat') v. to
invest
Инвеститор (investítor) m. investor
Инвестиции (investítsii) pl.
investments
валовые ~ (valovýe ~) gross ~
иностранные ~ (inostránnye ~)
foreign ~
портфельные ~ (portfél'nye ~)
portfolio ~
чистые ~ (chístye ~) net ~
~ за границей (~ za granítsei) ~
abroad
Индекс (índeks) m. code, index,
symbol
общий ~ (óbshchii ~) overall
index
~ бизнеса (~ bíznesa) business
index
~ денежного рынка (~ dénezhnogo
rýnka) money market index
~ зарплаты (~ zarpláty) wage
index
~ запрещённых книг (~
zapreshchіónnykh knig) banned-
book list
~ доходов населения (~ dokhódov
naseléniia) index of per capita
income
~ оптовых цен (~ optóvykh tsen)
wholesale price index

~ продукции (~ prodúktsii) production index
~ производительности (~ proizvodítel'nosti) productivity index
~ промышленного производства (~ promýshlennogo proizvódstva) industrial production index
~ розничных цен (~ róznichnykh tsen) retail price index
~ стоимости (~ stóimosti) value index
~ цен (~ tsen) price index

Индемнитет (indemnitét) *m.* indemnity

Индивидуальность (individuál'nost') *f.* individuality

Индоссамент (indossamént) *m.* endorsement
бланковый ~ (blánkovyi ~) blank ~
вексельный ~ (véksel'nyi ~) ~ of a bill {note}
именной ~ (imennói ~) special ~
инкассовый ~ (inkássovyi ~) ~ for collection
частичный ~ (chastíchnyi ~) partial ~
чековый ~ (chékovyi ~) ~ of a check
~ на предъявителя (~ na pred"iavítelia) ~ by bearer

Индоссант (indossánt) *m.* endorser, transferor

Индоссат (indossát) *m.* endorsee

Индоссировать (indossírovat') *v.* to endorse

Индустриализация (industrializátsiia) *f.* industrialization

Индустриализировать (industrializírovat') *v.* to industrialize

Индустрия (indústriia) *f.* industry
строительная ~ (stroítel'naia ~) construction ~
туристическая ~ (turistícheskaia ~) tourism ~
тяжёлая ~ (tiazhiólaia ~) heavy ~

Инициатив/а (initsiatív/a) *f.* initiative
бюджетная ~ (biudzhétnaia ~) budget ~
законодательная ~ (zakonodátel'naia ~) legislative ~

народная ~ (naródnaia ~) grass roots ~
по своей ~/е (po svoéi ~/e) on one's own ~
~ парламента (~ parlámenta) parliamentary ~

Инкассатор (inkassátor) *m.* collector
налогов ~ (nalógov ~) tax collector

Инкассация (inkassátsiia) *f.* collection

Инкассировать (inkassírovat') *v.* to cash {as a check}, to collect, to recover

Инкассо (inkásso) *n.* cashing, collection
документарное ~ (dokumentárnoe ~) documentary ~

Иностранец (inostránets) *m.* foreigner

Иностранный (inostránnyi) *adj.* foreign

Инспектор (inspéktor) *m.* inspector, surveyor
генеральный ~ (generál'nyi ~) chief inspector
налоговой ~ (nalógovoi ~) tax inspector
портовой ~ (portovói ~) surveyor of the port
страховой ~ (strakhovói ~) insurance claims inspector
таможенный ~ (tamózhennyi ~) customs inspector
фабричный ~ (fabríchnyi ~) plant surveyor

Инстанци/я (instántsi/ia) *f.* instance, level of authority
арбитражная ~ (arbitrázhnaia ~) arbitral authority
военная ~ (voénnaia ~) military authorities
вышестоящая ~ (vyshestoiáshchaia ~) recourse to superior authorities
первая ~ (pérvaia ~) first instance
последняя ~ (poslédniaia ~) final recourse
суд первой ~ (sud pérvoi ~) court of first instance
судебная ~ (sudébnaia ~) legal recourse

Институт (institút) *m.* institute, institution

банковский ~ (bánkovskii ~)
banking institution
международный ~ (mezhdunaródnyi
~) international institute
международный патентный ~
(mezhdunaródnyi paténtnyi ~)
International Patent Institute
международный ~ по унификации
частного права (mezhdunaródnyi ~
po unifikátsii chástnogo práva)
International Institute for the
Unification of Private Law
научно-исследовательский ~
(naúchno-issledovátel'skii ~)
Scientific Research Institute
научно-исследовательский ~
криминалистики (naúchno-
issledovátel'skii ~
kriminalístiki) Scientific
Research Institute for the Study
of Criminal Behavior
правовой ~ (pravovói ~) Legal
Institute
финансово-правовой ~ (finánsovo-
pravovói ~) Institute of
Financial Law
финансовый ~ (finánsovyi ~)
Financial Institute
эмиссионный ~ (emissiónnyi ~)
issuing institution
~ международного права (~
mezhdunaródnogo práva) Institute
of International Law
~ сравнительного права (~
sravnítel'nogo práva) Institute
of Comparative Law
Инструктаж (instruktázh) m.
briefing {usu. in military sense}
Инструкция (instrúktsiia) f.
directions, instructions, manual,
regulations
служебная ~ (sluzhébnaia ~)
service regulations
~ министерства (~ ministérstva)
instructions from a ministry
Интеграция (integrátsiia) f.
integration
европейская ~ (evropéiskaia ~)
European integration
политическая ~ (politícheskaia
~) political integration
экономическая ~ (ekonómicheskaia
~) economic integration
Интервенировать (intervenírovat')
v. to intervene
Интервент (intervént) m.
interventionist

Интервенционистский
(interventsionístskii) adj.
interventionist
Интервенция (intervéntsiia) f.
intervention
валютная ~ (valiútnaia ~)
currency ~
военная ~ (voénnaia ~) military
~
дипломатическая ~
(diplomatícheskaia ~) diplomatic
~
коллективная ~ (kollektívnaia ~)
collective ~
совместная ~ (sovméstnaia ~)
joint ~
экономическая ~ (ekonómicheskaia
~) economic ~
юридическая ~ (iuridícheskaia ~)
legal ~
Интерес (interés) m. interest,
interests
имущественные ~/ы
(imúshchestvennye ~/y) property
interests
жизненные ~/ы (zhíznennye ~/y)
vital interests
законный ~ (zakónnyi ~) legal
interest
защищать ~ (zashchishchát' ~) to
defend one's interest
коллективные ~/ы (kollektívnye
~/y) collective interests
общественный ~ (obshchéstvennyi
~) public interest
общие ~/ы (óbshchie ~/y) common
interest
противоречащий публичному ~/у
(protivorecháshchii publíchnomu
~/u) contrary to public interest
публичный ~ (publíchnyi ~)
public interest
финансовый ~ (finánsovyi ~)
financial interest
частный ~ (chástnyi ~) private
interest
Интернационализация ~
(internatsionalizátsiia ~) f.
internationalization
Интернационализировать ~
(internatsionalizírovat' ~) v. to
internationalize
Интернационализм
(internatsionalízm) m.
internationalism

Интернациональный
(internatsionál'nyi) adj.
internationalist
Интернированный (internírovannyi)
m.adj.noun internee
  гражданский ~ (grazhdánskii ~)
  civilian ~
  политический ~ (politícheskii ~)
  political ~
Интернировать (internírovat') v. to
intern {as in a camp}
Интернунций (internúntsii) m.
internuncio
  папский ~ (pápskii ~) papal ~
Интерпеллянт (interpelliánt) m.
interpellant
Интерпелляция (interpelliátsiia) f.
interpellation {question in
Parliament}
Интерпретация (interpretátsiia) f.
interpretation
Интрига (intríga) f. intrigue,
machinations
Инфекционный (infektsiónnyi) adj.
infectious
Инфляция (infliátsiia) f. inflation
  бюджетная ~ (biudzhétnaia ~)
  budgetary ~
  денежная ~ (dénezhnaia ~)
  monetary ~
  кредитная ~ (kredítnaia ~)
  credit ~
  неконтролируемая ~
  (nekontrolíruemaia ~)
  uncontrolled ~
Информация (informátsiia) f.
information
  патентная ~ (paténtnaia ~)
  patent ~
  секретная ~ (sekrétnaia ~)
  secret ~
Информировать (informírovat') v. to
inform
Инцидент (intsidént) m. incident
  дипломатический ~
  (diplomatícheskii ~) diplomatic
  ~
  пограничный ~ (pograníchnyi ~)
  frontier ~
Ипотека (ipotéka) f. mortgage,
pledge
  договорная ~ (dogovórnaia ~)
  mortgage agreement
  морская ~ (morskáia ~) maritime
  mortgage
  первая ~ (pérvaia ~) first
  mortgage

  привилегированная ~
  (privilegírovannaia ~)
  privileged mortgage
  обременённый ипотекой ~
  (obremeniónnyi ipotékoi ~)
  encumbered with a mortgage
  свободный от ипотек ~ (svobódnyi
  ot ipoték ~) free from
  encumbrances
  установить ~/у (ustanovít' ~/u)
  to mortgage
  ~ воздушного судна (~
  vozdúshnogo súdna) mortgage of
  an air vessel
  ~ выше по рангу (~ výshe po
  rángu) pledge, higher in
  priority
  ~ занесенная в реестр (~
  zanesénnaia v reéstr) perfected
  security interest
  ~ земельного участка (~
  zemél'nogo uchástka) mortgage of
  land
  ~ морского судна (~ morskógo
  súdna) maritime mortgage
  ~ ниже по рангу (~ nízhe po
  rángu) pledge, lower in priority
Ипотечный (ipotéchnyi) adj.
mortgage, pledge
Иск (isk) m. action, claim, suit
  вещный ~ (véshchnyi ~) action in
  rem
  возбудить ~ (vozbudít' ~) to
  bring an action, to file suit
  встречный ~ (vstréchnyi ~)
  counter-suit
  ~ о разводе ~ (~ o razvóde ~)
  suit for divorce
  вчинить ~ (vchinít' ~) to bring
  an action
  гражданский ~ (grazhdánskii ~)
  civil suit
  имущественный ~
  (imúshchestvennyi ~) claim of
  ownership
  ипотечный ~ (ipotéchnyi ~)
  foreclosure upon a mortgage
  исполнительный ~ (ispolnítel'nyi
  ~) action for an injunction
  личный ~ (líchnyi ~) personal
  action
  непрямой ~ (nepriamói ~)
  indirect claim
  основной ~ (osnovnói ~) original
  suit
  отказать в ~/е (otkazát' v ~/e)
  to dismiss a claim

отказаться от ~/а (otkazát'sia ot ~/a) to withdraw an action, to abandon a claim

отклонить ~ (otklonít' ~) to reject a claim

поссесорный ~ (possesórnyi ~) possessory action

предъявить ~ (pred"iavít' ~) to bring an action, to file suit

предъявить ~ о разводе (pred"iavít' ~ o razvóde) to file for divorce

признать ~ (priznát' ~) to acknowledge a claim, to plead nolo contendere

прямой ~ (priamói ~) direct claim

публичный ~ (publíchnyi ~) public action

регрессный ~ (regréssnyi ~) recourse action

судебный ~ (sudébnyi ~) action at law, legal action

~ к истребованию неосновательного обогащения (~ k istrébovaniiu neosnovátel'nogo obogashchéniia) claim of unjust enrichment

~ на ипотеку (~ na ipotéku) claim against a mortgage

~ об оспаривании отцовства (~ ob osparivánii ottsóvstva) paternity suit

~ об уплате заработной платы (~ ob upláte zárabotnoi pláty) claim for back wages

~ о взыскании алиментов (~ o vzyskánii aliméntov) claim for maintenance payments

~ о возмещении убытков (~ o vozmeshchénii ubýtkov) action for damages

~ о гарантии (~ o garántii) warranty action

~ о движимом имуществе (~ o dvizhímom imúshchestve) action for personalty

~ о деликтной ответственности (~ o delíktnoi otvétstvennosti) tort action

~ о нарушении патента (~ o narushénii paténta) suit for infringement of a patent

~ о наследстве (~ o naslédstve) probate action

~ о недвижимости (~ o nedvízhimosti) real property action

~ о недобросовестной конкуренции (~ o nedobrosóvestnoi konkurén-tsii) unfair competition action

~ о приведении в исполнение решения (~ o privedénii v ispolnénie reshéniia) action to enforce judgment

~ о разводе (~ o razvóde) action for divorce

~ о разделе (~ o razdéle) action for partition

~ о размежевании (~ o razmezhevánii) action to settle a boundary dispute

~ о реституции (~ o restitútsii) claim for restitution

~ в силу суброгации (~ v sílu subrogátsii) subrogated claim

Искажать (iskazhát') v. to distort, to pervert

Искажение (iskazhénie) n. distortion, perversion

Искать (iskát') v. to seek

Исключение (iskliuchénie) n. exception

~ из реестра (~ iz reéstra) striking from the register {company, etc.}

Исключительно (iskliuchítel'no) adv. exclusively

Исключительность (iskliuchítel'nost') f. exclusivity

~ решения и приговора (~ reshéniia i prigovóra) ~ of verdict and sentencing

Исключительный (iskliuchítel'nyi) adj. exclusive

Исключать (iskliuchát') v. to exclude

Исконный (iskónnyi) adj. immemorial

Ископаемое (iskopáemoe) n. mineral

Искупить (iskupít') v. to atone

Искупление (iskuplénie) n. atonement

Исполком {исполнительный комитет} (ispolkóm {ispolnítel'nyi komitét}) m. executive committee

Исполнение (ispolnénie) n. fulfillment, performance

встречное ~ (vstréchnoe ~) consideration

добровольное ~ (dobrovól'noe ~) voluntary ~

предварительное ~
(predvarítel'noe ~) preliminary
performance
принудительное ~ (prinudítel'noe
~) compulsory performance
приостановить ~ (priostanovít'
~) to delay performance
частичное ~ (chastíchnoe ~)
partial performance
~ в натуре (~ v natúre)
performance in kind
~ приговора (~ prigovóra)
imposition of sentencing
Истец (istéts) m. claimant,
complainant, plaintiff
гражданский ~ (grazhdánskii ~)
civil plaintiff
основной ~ (osnovnói ~) primary
plaintiff
первоначальный ~
(pervonachál'nyi ~) original
claimant
Истечение (istechénie) n.
expiration
~ давности (~ dávnosti)
expiration of statute of
limitations
~ давности уголовного
преследования (~ dávnosti
ugolóvnogo preslédovaniia) ~ of
statute of limitations on
criminal prosecution
~ срока (~ sróka) ~ of term
~ срока договора найма (~ sróka
dogovóra náima) ~ of lease
~ срока концессии (~ sroka
kontséssii) ~ of concession
Истечь (istéch') v. to expire
Истина (ístina) f. truth
Истолкование (istolkovánie) n.
commentary, interpretation
ограничительное ~
(ogranichítel'noe ~) limited
interpretation
Истолковывать (istolkóvyvat')
v. [perfective: истолковать] to
expound, to interpret
История (istóriia) f. history,
story
Источник (istóchnik/) m. source
верный ~ (vérnyi ~) reliable ~
самостоятельный ~ дохода
(samostoiátel'nyi ~ dokhóda)
independent ~ of income
юридические ~/и (iuridícheskie
~/i) jurisprudential ~s

~ доказательства (~
dokazátel'stva) ~ of evidence
~ дохода (~ dokhóda) ~ of income
~ кредита (~ kredíta) ~ of
credit
~ накопления (~ nakopléniia) ~
of accumulation
~ финансирования (~
finansírovaniia) ~ of financing
~ энергии (~ enérgii) ~ of
energy
Истребитель (istrebítel') m.
destroyer {ship}, fighter {jet}
Истребить (istrebít') v. [see
истреблять]
Истреблять (istrebliát') v. to
destroy, to exterminate
Истребление (istreblénie) n.
destruction
Истребование (istrébovanie) n.
demand, order
Истребовать (istrébovat') v. to
demand
~ обратно уплаченное (~ obrátno
upláchennoe) to demand one's
money back
Истязание (istiazánie) n. torture
Истязать (istiazát') v. to torture
Исход (iskhód) m. end, outcome,
resolution
~ судебного дела (~ sudébnogo
déla) outcome of a judicial
proceeding, result of a trial
Исходатайствовать
(iskhodátaistvovat') v. to obtain
by formal petition
Исцеление (istselénie) n. recovery
Исчезать (ischezát') v. to
disappear
Исчезновение (ischeznovénie) n.
disappearance
Исчезнуть (ischéznut') v. [see
исчезать]
Исчерпание (ischerpánie) n.
depletion, running out
~ товарных запасов (~ továrnykh
zapásov) inventory depletion
Исчерпывающий (ischérpyvaiushchii)
adj. exhaustive
Исчисление (ischislénie) n.
calculation
~ дохода (~ dokhóda) ~ of income
~ налога (~ nalóga) ~ of tax
~ процентов (~ protséntov) ~ of
interest
~ сроков (~ srókov) ~ of term
{time}

Исчислять (ischisliát') v. to calculate
Итерация (iterátsiia) f. iteration
Итог (itóg) m. total {sum}
   общий ~ (óbshchii ~) grand ~
Итоговый (itógovyi) adj. concluding, final

К

Кабель (kábel') m. cable
Каботаж (kabotázh) m. coasting trade
Каботажный (kabotázhnyi) adj. coastal, coasting
Кадастр (kadástr) m. land survey
Кадр/ы (kádr/y) pl. manpower, personnel, staff
   высококвалифицированные ~ (vysokokvalifitsírovannye ~) highly qualified personnel
   квалифицированные ~ (kvalifitsírovannye ~) qualified personnel
   набор ~/ов (nabór ~/ov) personnel recruitment
   научно-технические ~ (naúchnotekhnícheskie ~) scientific and technical personnel
   научные ~ (naúchnye ~) scientific personnel
   нехватка ~/ов (nekhvátka ~/ov) manpower shortage
   обеспечивать ~/ами (obespéchivat' ~/ami) to provide personnel
   обучение руководящих ~/ов (obuchénie rukovodiáshchikh ~/ov) management training
   опытные ~ (ópytnye ~) experienced staff
   отдел ~/ов (otdél ~/ov) personnel department
   подбирать ~ (podbirát' ~) to select personnel
   профессиональные ~ (professionál'nye ~) professional personnel
   руководящие ~ (rukovodiáshchie ~) management {personnel}
   сохранять ~ (sokhraniát' ~) to retain personnel
   укреплять квалифицированными ~/ами (ukrepliát' kvalifitsí-

rovannymi ~/ami) to replenish qualified personnel
   управляющий по ~/ам (upravliáiushchii po ~/am) personnel director
   учёт ~/ов (uchiót ~/ov) personnel records
Казна (kazná) f. treasury
Казначе/й (kaznaché/i) m. treasurer
   заместитель ~/я (zamestítel' ~/ia) deputy treasurer
   помощник ~/я (pomóshchnik ~/ia) assistant treasurer
   ~ корпорации (~ korporátsii) treasurer of a corporation
Казначей-бухгалтер (kaznachéi-bukhgálter) m. treasurer/bookkeeper
Казначейство (kaznachéistvo) n. treasury
Календарь (kalendár') m. calendar
Калькулировать (kal'kulírovat') v. to calculate
Калькулятор (kal'kuliátor) m. calculator
Калькуляци /я (kal'kuliátsi /ia) f. calculation, estimation
   окончательная ~ (okonchátel'naia ~) final calculation
   ~ демерреджа (~ demerredzha) demurrage calculation
   ~ расходов (~ raskhódov) calculation of expenses
   ~ себестоимости (~ sebestóimosti) calculation of prime cost
   ~ цен (~ tsen) calculation of prices
Камбист (kambíst) m. currency trader
Камера (kámera) f. chamber
   рефрижераторная ~ (refrizherátornaia ~) cold storage ~
   холодильная ~ (kholodíl'naia ~) cooling ~
   ~ хранения багажа (~ khranéniia bagazhá) cloakroom
Кампани/я (kampáni/ia) f. campaign, drive
   вести ~/ю (vestí ~/iu) to conduct a campaign
   закончить ~/ю (zakónchit' ~/iu) to conclude a campaign
   план рекламной ~/и (plan reklámnoi ~/i) add schedule
   поддерживать ~/ю (poddérzhivat' ~/iu) to support a campaign

рекламная ~ (reklámnaia ~)
advertising campaign
совместная ~ (sovméstnaia ~)
joint campaign
сорвать ~/ю (sorvát' ~/iu) to
wreck a campaign
текущая ~ (tekúshchaia ~)
ongoing campaign
телевизионная ~ (televiziónnaia
~) television campaign
торговая ~ в печати (torgóvaia ~
v pechati) trade press campaign
цель ~/и (tsel' ~/i) campaign
goal
широкая ~ (shirókaia ~) broad
campaign
~ по организации и
стимулированию сбыта (~ po
organizátsii i stimulírovaniiu
sbýta) sales promotion
~ по увеличению экспорта (~ po
uvelichéniiu éksporta) export
campaign
Канал (kanál) m. canal, channel
банковские ~/ы (bánkovskie ~/y)
banking channels
неофициальные ~/ы
(neofitsiál'nye ~/y) unofficial
channels
определять ~/ы сбыта
(opredeliát' ~/y sbyta) to
determine channels of
distribution
проходить ~ (prokhodít' ~) to
pass through a canal
сбор за проход через ~ (sbor za
prokhód chérez ~) canal toll
судоходный ~ (sudokhódnyi ~)
ship channel
торговые ~/ы (torgóvye ~/y)
trade channels
Канат (kanát) m. cable, rope
гибкий ~ (gíbkii ~) flexible
cable
грузовой ~ (gruzovói ~) load
rope
грузоподъёмный ~
(gruzopod"iómnyi ~) hoisting
cable
проволочный ~ (próvolochnyi ~)
wire rope
стальной ~ (stal'nói ~) steel
cable
Канистра (kanístra) f. canister
Кантовать (kantovát') v. to tilt
"не кантовать" (ne kantovát')
"do not tip"

Канцелинг (kántseling) m.
canceling, nullification
право ~/а (právo ~/a) right to
canceling
Канцеляри/я (kantseliári/ia) f.
office
заведующий ~/ей (zavéduiushchii
~/ei) head clerk
Канцелярский (kantseliárskii) adj.
clerical
Капитал (kapitál) m. capital
{assets, money, etc.}
авансированный (avansírovannyi
~) advanced ~
акционерный ~ (aktsionérnyi ~)
shareholder equity {in joint
stock company}
банковский ~ (bánkovskii ~) bank
~
блокированный (blokírovannyi
~) blocked ~
бегство ~/ов (bégstvo ~/ov) ~
flight
вложение ~/а (vlozhénie ~/a) ~
investment
вкладывать ~ в ... (vkládyvat' ~
v ...) to invest ~ in ...
вывоз ~/а (vývoz ~/a) export of
~
высвобождение ~/а
(vysvobozhdénie ~/a) release of
~
валовой оборотный ~ (valovói
oborótnyi ~) gross working ~
государственный ~
(gosudárstvennyi ~) state ~
движение ~/а (dvizhénie ~/a) ~
movement
действительный ~ (deistvítel'nyi
~) actual ~
денежный ~ (dénezhnyi ~)
disposable ~
долгосрочный ~ (dolgosróchnyi ~)
long-term ~
доля в ~/е (dólia v ~/e) share
in ~
добывать ~ (dobyvát' ~) to raise
~
замораживание ~/а
(zamorázhivanie ~/a) freezing of
~
затраты ~/а (zatráty ~/a) ~
expenditures
заёмный ~ (zaiómnyi ~) loan ~
запасный ~ (zapásnyi ~) reserve
~

зарегистрированный ~
(zaregistrírovannyi ~)
registered ~
избыточный ~ (izbýtochnyi ~)
surplus ~
изымать ~ (izymát' ~) to
withdraw ~
инвестированный ~
(investírovannyi ~) invested ~
иностранный ~ (inostránnyi ~)
foreign ~
используемый ~ (ispól'zuemyi ~)
employed ~
краткосрочный ~ (kratkosróchnyi
~) short-term ~
крупный ~ (krúpnyi ~) big
business
ликвидный ~ (likvídnyi ~) liquid
~
международный ~ (mezhdunaródnyi
~) international ~
мёртвый ~ (miórtvyi ~) idle ~
монополистический ~
(monopolistícheskii ~) monopoly
~
накопленный ~ (nakóplennyi ~)
accumulated ~
наличный ~ (nalíchnyi ~) cash
funds
налог на ~ (налóг na ~) tax on ~
непроизводительный ~
(neproizvodítel'nyi ~)
unproductive ~
нехватка ~/a (nekhvátka ~/a) ~
shortage
обесценение ~/a (obestsenénie
~/a) depreciation of ~
оборотный ~ (oborótnyi ~)
working ~
объявленный ~ (ob"iávlennyi ~)
stated ~
основной ~ (osnovnói ~) fixed ~
отток ~/a (ottók ~/a) ~ outflow
первоначальный ~
(pervonachál'nyi ~) initial ~
перевод ~/a за границу (perevód
~/a za granítsu) transfer of ~
abroad
переменный ~ (pereménnyi ~)
variable ~
постоянный ~ (postoiánnyi ~)
constant ~
привлечённый ~ (privlechiónnyi
~) debt ~
приток ~/a (pritók ~/a) inflow
of ~

предоставлять ~ (predostavliát'
~) to provide ~
привлекать ~ (privlekát' ~) to
attract ~
производительный ~
(proizvodítel'nyi ~) productive
~
промышленный ~ (promýshlennyi ~)
industrial ~
разблокирование ~/a
(razblokírovanie ~/a) unblocking
of ~
размещение ~/a (razmeshchénie
~/a) allocation of ~
реальный ~ (reál'nyi ~) real ~
резервный ~ (rezérvnyi ~)
reserve fund
рынок ~/a (rýnok ~/a) ~ market
свободный ~ (svobódnyi ~)
available ~
совокупный ~ (sovokúpnyi ~)
aggregate ~
спрос на ~ (spros na ~) demand
for ~
ссудный ~ (ssúdnyi ~) borrowed ~
товарный ~ (továrnyi ~)
commodity ~
торговый ~ (torgóvyi ~)
commercial ~
уставный ~ (ustávnyi ~) charter
~
фактический ~ (faktícheskii ~)
actual ~
частный ~ (chástnyi ~) private ~
Капитализированный
(kapitalizírovannyi) adj.
capitalized
Капитализм (kapitalízm) m.
capitalism
Капиталист (kapitalíst) m.
capitalist
Капиталистический
(kapitalistícheskii) adj.
capitalist
Капиталовложени/е
(kapitalovlozhéni/e) n. capital
investment
ассигнования на ~ (assignovániia
na ~) capital appropriations
бюджет ~/й (biudzhét ~/i)
capital budget
валовые ~/я (valovýe ~/ia) gross
investments
внутренние ~/я (vnútrennie ~/ia)
domestic investments

возможности для ~/й
(vozmózhnosti dlia ~/i)
opportunities for investment
государственные ~/я
(gosudárstvennye ~/ia) public
investments
заграничные ~/я (zagraníchnye
~/ia) foreign investments
крупные ~/я (krúpnye ~/ia) major
investments
малоприбыльные ~/я
(malopríbyl'nye ~/ia) low-yield
investments
надёжные ~/я (nadiózhnye ~/ia)
secure investments
первоначальные ~/я
(pervonachál'nye ~/ia) original
investments
план ~/й (plan ~/i) investment
plan
плановые ~/я (plánovye ~/ia)
planned investments
совместные ~/я (sovméstnye ~/ia)
joint capital investments
сокращать ~/я (sokrashchát'
~/ia) to curtail investments
стимулы для ~/й (stímuly dlia
~/i) investment incentives
увеличивать ~/я (uvelíchivat'
~/ia) to increase capital
investments
Капитан (kapitán) m. captain,
master
вознаграждение ~/у с фрахта
(voznagrazhdénie ~/u s frákhta)
primage
декларация ~/а (deklarátsiia
~/a) master's declaration
нотис ~/а (nótis ~/a) captain's
notice
помощник ~/а (pomóshchnik ~/a)
mate
помощник ~/а, второй
(pomóshchnik ~/a, vtorói) second
mate
помощник ~/а, старший
(pomóshchnik ~/a, stárshii)
first mate
Капитанский (kapitánskii) adj.
captains, masters
Карантин (karantín) m. quarantine
в ~/e (v ~/e) under quarantine
вводить ~ (vvodít' ~) to
introduce a quarantine
выпустить из ~/а (výpustit' iz
~/a) to release from quarantine

подвергнуть ~/у (podvérgnut'
~/u) to subject to quarantine
снятие ~/а (sniátie ~/a) lifting
of quarantine
свидетельство о снятии ~/а
(svidetél'stvo o sniátii ~/a)
quarantine certificate
Карантинный (karantínnyi) adj.
quarantine
Карательный (karátel'nyi) adj.
punitive, retaliatory
Карго (kárgo) n. cargo
Каргоплан (kargoplán) m. stowage
plan
Карго-трайлер (kárgo-tráiler) m.
cargo-trailer
Картелизация (kartelizátsiia) f.
cartelization
Картелировать (kartelírovat') v. to
cartelize
Картель (kartél') m. cartel
сбытовой ~ (sbytovói ~) sales
cartel
экспортный ~ (éksportnyi ~)
export cartel
Картельный (kartél'nyi) adj. cartel
Картотек/а (kartoték/a) f. index
card file
справиться по ~/e (správit'sia
po ~/e) to consult one's files
Карточка (kártochka) f. card
адресная ~ (ádresnaia ~) address
~
визитная ~ (vizítnaia ~) calling
~
идентификационная ~
(identifikatsiónnaia ~)
identification ~
кредитная ~ (kredítnaia ~)
credit ~
почтовая ~ (pochtóvaia ~)
postcard
регистрационная ~
(registratsiónnaia ~)
registration ~
Касс/а (káss/a) f. cashier's desk,
cash register
билетная ~ (bilétnaia ~) ticket
office
вклад в сберегательную ~/у
(vklad v sberegátel'nuiu ~/u)
savings deposit
деньги в ~/e (dén'gi v ~/e) cash
on hand
ликвидационная ~
(likvidatsiónnaia ~)
clearinghouse

остаток ~/ы (ostátok ~/y) cash
balance
проводить ревизию ~/ы (provodít'
revíziiu ~/y) to make a cash
audit
счёт ~/ы (schiót ~/y) cash
account
сберегательная ~
(sberegátel'naia ~) savings bank
страховая ~ (strakhováia ~)
social insurance office {in
Russia}
Кассаци/я (kassátsi/ia) f.
cassation
  ~ в арбитраж (~ v arbitrázh)
  appeal to arbitration
  ~ в кассационный суд (~ v
  kassatsiónnyi sud) appeal to the
  court of cassation
  ~ судебного решения (~ sudébnogo
  reshéniia) reversal of a
  judgment
Кассир (kassír) m. cashier,
paymaster, treasurer
Кассировать (kassírovat') v. to
annul, to rescind, to reverse
  ~ решение суда (~ reshénie sudá)
  to reverse a judgment
Кассовый (kássovyi) adj. cash,
cashier
Каталог (katalóg) m. catalogue
  вносить в ~ (vnosít' v ~) to
  include in a ~
  выпускать ~ (vypuskát' ~) to
  issue a ~
  выставочный ~ (výstavochnyi ~)
  exhibition ~
  детальный ~ (detál'nyi ~)
  comprehensive ~
  издатель ~/a (izdátel' ~/a)
  publisher of a ~
  иллюстрированный ~
  (illiustrírovannyi ~)
  illustrated ~
  общий ~ (óbshchii ~) general ~
  полный ~ (pólnyi ~) complete ~
  последний ~ (poslédnii ~) latest
  ~
  предоставить ~/и (predostávit'
  ~/i) to provide ~s
  раздавать ~/и (razdavát' ~/i) to
  distribute ~s
  составлять ~ (sostavliát' ~) to
  compile a ~
  типичный ~ (tipíchnyi ~) typical
  ~
  типовой ~ (tipovói ~) standard ~

фирменный ~ (fírmennyi ~)
company ~
  ~ аукциона (~ auktsióna) auction
  bill
  ~ запчастей (~ zapchastéi) parts
  ~
Катастрофа (katastrófa) f.
catastrophe
Категория (kategoriia) f. category
Кафедра (káfedra) f. faculty,
rostrum
Качественный (káchestvennyi) adj.
qualitative, quality
Качеств/о (káchestv/o) n. grade,
merit, quality, sort
  анализ ~/a продукции (análiz ~/a
  prodúktsii) product quality
  analysis
  аттестат ~/a (attestát ~/a)
  quality clearance
  базисное ~ (bázisnoe ~) base
  quality
  безупречное ~ (bezupréchnoe ~)
  unimpeachable quality
  в ~/e (v ~/e) in the capacity of
  высокое ~ (vysókoe ~) high
  quality
  высшее ~ (výsshee ~) higher
  quality
  гарантированное ~
  (garantírovannoe ~) guaranteed
  quality
  гарантировать высокое ~
  (garantírovat' vysókoe ~) to
  guarantee high quality
  гарантия ~/a (garántiia ~/a)
  quality guarantee
  деловые ~/a (delovýe ~/a)
  business qualities
  дешёвое ~ (deshióvoe ~) cheap
  quality
  допустимое ~ (dopustímoe ~)
  tolerance quality
  изменение ~/a (izmenénie ~/a)
  change in quality
  изменять ~ (izmeniát' ~) to
  change the quality
  инспекция по ~/y (inspéktsiia po
  ~/u) quality control inspection
  коммерческое ~ (kommércheskoe ~)
  commercial quality
  контролировать ~ (kontrolírovat'
  ~) to engage in quality control
  контроль ~/a (kontról' ~/a)
  quality control
  лучшее ~ (lúchshee ~) best
  quality

надлежащее ~ (nadlezháshchee ~)
appropriate quality
нарушение стандарта ~/а
(narushénie standárta ~/a)
violation of quality standards
ненадлежащее ~ (nenadlezháshchee
~) inferior quality
неудовлетворительное ~
(neudovletvorítel'noe ~)
unsatisfactory quality
низкое ~ (nízkoe ~) low quality
норма ~/а (nórma ~/a) standard
of quality
нормативное ~ (normatívnoe ~)
standard quality
обеспечивать ~ (obespéchivat' ~)
to provide quality
образец продукта для оценки ~/а
(obrazéts prodúkta dlia otsénki
~/a) sample product for quality
analysis
обусловить ~ (obuslóvit' ~) to
stipulate quality
общее ~ (óbshchee ~) overall
quality
оптимальное ~ (optimál'noe ~)
optimal quality
отличное ~ (otlíchnoe ~)
excellent quality
оценка ~/а (otsénka ~/a) quality
analysis
оценивать ~ (otsénivat' ~) to
evaluate quality
первоклассное ~ (pervoklássnoe
~) first-class quality
показатель ~/а (pokazátel' ~/a)
quality indicator
приемлемое ~ (priémlemoe ~)
acceptable quality
принимать товар по ~/у
(prinimát' továr po ~/u) to
accept goods on the basis of
quality
проверка ~/а (provérka ~/a)
quality check
самое лучшее ~ (sámoe lúchshee
~) very best quality
свидетельство о ~/е
(svidetél'stvo o ~/e) assay
certificate, quality certificate
спецификация ~/а
(spetsifikátsiia ~/a) quality
specification
среднее ~ (srédnee ~) average
quality

таблица контроля ~/а (tablítsa
kontrólia ~/a) quality control
table
техническое ~ (tekhnícheskoe ~)
technical quality
экспертиза по ~/у (ekspertíza po
~/u) expert's quality report
эксплуатационные ~/а
(ekspluatatsiónnye ~/a)
operational quality
экспортное ~ (éksportnoe ~)
export quality
~, обусловленное договором (~,
obuslóvlennoe dogovórom)
stipulated quality
Квадрат (kvadrát) m. square
Квадратный (kvadrátnyi) adj. square
Квалификационный
(kvalifikatsiónnyi) adj. qualifying
Квалификаци/я (kvalifikátsi/ia) f.
efficiency, qualification, skill
высокая профессиональная ~
(vysókaia professionál'naia ~)
high professional skill
необходимая ~ (neobkhodímaia ~)
necessary qualification
производственная ~
(proizvódstvennaia ~)
professional skill
специалист высокой ~/и
(spetsialíst vysókoi ~/i)
highly- qualified expert
повышать ~/ю (povyshát' ~/iu) to
improve skills
получать производственную ~/ю
(poluchát' proizvódstvennuiu
~/iu) to acquire professional
skill
Квалифицированный
(kvalifitsírovannyi) adj.
qualified, skilled
Квалифицировать (kvalifitsírovat')
v. to qualify
Квартал (kvartál) m. block {of a
city}, quarter
жилые ~/ы (zhilýe ~/y)
residential districts
задолжать за несколько ~/ов
(zadolzhát' za néskol'ko ~/ov)
to be several quarters past due
текущий ~ (tekúshchii ~) current
accounting quarter
Квартальный (kvartál'nyi) adj.
quarterly
Квитанци/я (kvitántsi/ia) f.
receipt

багажная ~ (bagázhnaia ~) baggage claim ticket

временная ~ (vrémennaia ~) interim ~

выдавать ~/ю (vydavát' ~/iu) to issue a ~

грузовая ~ (gruzováia ~) consignment note

грузовая воздушная ~ (gruzováia vozdúshnaia ~) air consignment note

депозитная ~ (depozítnaia ~) deposit ~

железнодорожная ~ (zheleznodorózhnaia ~) railway ~

залоговая ~ (zalógovaia ~) pawn ticket

лоцманская ~ (lótsmanskaia ~) pilot's bill

почтовая ~ (pochtóvaia ~) postal ~

представлять ~/ю (predstavliát' ~/iu) to submit a ~

складская ~ (skladskáia ~) warehouse ~

сохранная ~ (sokhránnaia ~) safe deposit ~

товаросопроводительная ~ (tovarosoprovodítel'naia ~) freight warrant

форма ~/и (fórma ~/i) ~ form

~ авиапочтового отправления (~ aviapochtóvogo otpravléniia) airmail ~

~ на почтовую посылку (~ na pochtóvuiu posýlku) parcel post ~

~ об уплате страхового взноса (~ ob upláte strakhovógo vznósa) insurance premium ~

~ о подписке (~ o podpíske) subscription ~

~ о принятии заявки (~ o priniátii zaiávki) filing ~

Квот/а (kvót/a) f. quota

введение ~/ (vvedénie ~/) introduction of ~s

иммиграционная (immigratsiónnaia ~) immigration ~

импортная ~ (ímportnaia ~) import ~

количественная ~ (kolíchestvennaia ~) quantitative ~

максимальная ~ (maksimál'naia ~) maximum ~

минимальная ~ (minimál'naia ~) minimum ~

налоговая ~ (nalógovaia ~) tax ~

общая ~ (óbshchaia ~) global ~

отмена ~/ы (otména ~/y) abolition of a ~

применять систему ~/ (primeniát' sistému ~/) to impose a system of ~s

тарифная ~ (tarífnaia ~) tariff ~

установленная ~ (ustanóvlennaia ~) established ~

экспортная ~ (éksportnaia ~) export ~

~ в Международном Валютном Фонде (~ v mezhdunaródnom valiútnom fónde) International Monetary Fund ~ {IMF quota}

~ морского фрахта (~ morskógo frákhta) sea freight ~

Квотирование (kvotírovanie) n. quota allocation

~ иностранной валюты (~ inostránnoi valiúty) ~ of foreign exchange

Киноаппаратура (kinoapparatúra) f. movie equipment

Кинозал (kinozál) m. movie theater

Кинолента (kinolénta) f. movie film

Киноматериал/ы (kinomateriál/y) pl. film clips

Кинооборудование (kinooborúdovanie) n. motion picture equipment

Кинореклама (kinoreklálma) f. trailer {motion picture}

Киноустановка (kinoustanóvka) f. movie projector

передвижная ~ (peredvizhnáia ~) portable ~

Кинофильм (kinofíl'm) m. film, movie

рекламный ~ (reklámnyi ~) advertising film

Кип/а (kíp/a) f. bale, pile, stack

быть упакованным в ~/ах (byt' upakóvannym v ~/akh) to be packed in bales

лишняя ~ (líshniaia ~) odd bale

обтягивать ~/y (obtiágivat' ~/u) to strap a bale

половина ~/ы (polovína ~/y) half a bale

~ хлопка (~ khlópka) bale of cotton

~ целлюлозы (~ tselliulózy) bale of paper pulp

~ шерсти (~ shérsti) bale of wool

Кларировать (klarírovat') *v.* to clear a vessel {through customs}

Класс (klass) *m.* class, sort
  второй ~ (vtorói ~) second class
  первый ~ (pérvyi ~) first class
  ~ судна (~ súdna) class of a vessel
  ~ товара (~ továra) class of goods

Классификация (klassifikátsiia) *f.* classification, rating
  временная ~ (vrémennaia ~) temporary classification
  официальная ~ (ofitsiál'naia ~) official classification
  таможенная ~ (tamózhennaia ~) customs classification
  ~ грузов (~ grúzov) freight classification
  ~ судов (~ sudóv) vessel rating system
  ~ услуг (~ uslúg) service classification

Классифицированный (klassifitsírovannyi) *adj.* classed

Классифицировать (klassifitsírovat') *v.* to classify

Классный (klássnyi) *adj.* class

Клевета (klevetá) *f.* calumny, slander

Клеветать (klevetát') *v.* to slander

Клеймить (kleimít') *v.* to brand, to stamp

Клеймо (kleimó) *n.* brand label, brand stamp
  заводское ~ (zavódskoe ~) manufacturer's trademark
  личное ~ (líchnoe ~) personal stamp
  опознавательное ~ (opoznavátel'noe ~) identification mark
  приёмочное ~ (priiómochnoe ~) acceptance stamp
  ставить ~ (stávit' ~) to brand, to stamp
  фабричное ~ (fabríchnoe ~) mill stamp

Клеть (klet') *f.* crate
  деревянная ~ (dereviánnaia ~) wooden ~

Клиент (kliént) *m.* client, customer
  возможные ~/ы (vozmózhnye ~/y) potential clients

крупный ~ (krúpnyi ~) major client
неисправный ~ (neisprávnyi ~) defaulting customer
основные ~/ы (osnovnýe ~/y) primary clients
солидный ~ (solídnyi ~) solid client
~ банка (~ bánka) bank customer

Клиентур/а (klientúr/a) *f.* clientele

Климат (klímat) *m.* climate
  деловой ~ (delovói ~) business ~
  жаркий ~ (zhárkii ~) hot ~
  международный ~ (mezhdunaródnyi ~) international ~
  суровый ~ (suróvyi ~) severe ~

Клип (klip) *m.* clip, video {advertisement, music}

Клиринг (klíring) *m.* clearing
  банковский ~ (bankovskii ~) bank ~
  валютный ~ (valiútnyi ~) currency ~
  двухсторонний ~ (dvukhstorónnii ~) bilateral ~
  задолженность по ~/у (zadólzhennost' po ~/u) ~ debt
  многосторонний ~ (mnogostorónnii ~) multilateral ~
  односторонний ~ (odnostorónnii ~) unilateral ~
  платёж по ~/у (platiózh po ~/u) ~ payment
  принудительный ~ (prinudítel'nyi ~) compulsory ~
  расчёты по ~/у (raschióty po ~/u) clearings
  сальдо ~/a (sal'do ~/a) ~ balance
  система ~/a (sistéma ~/a) currency clearing system
  соглашение о ~/e (soglashénie o ~/e) ~ agreement
  счёт по ~/у (schiót po ~/u) ~ account

Клиринг-банк (klíringbánk) *m.* clearing bank

Клиринговый (kliringo-vyi) *adj.* clearing

Ключ (kliuch) *m.* key
  контракт "под ~" (kontrákt pod ~) turn-key contract
  проект "под ~" (proékt pod ~) turn-key project
  ~ к шифру (~ k shífru) ~ to a code

Книг/а (kníg/a) *f.* book
адресная ~ (ádresnaia ~) address ~
банковская ~ (bánkovskaia ~) bank ~
бухгалтерская ~ (bukhgálterskaia ~) account ~, ledger
вести бухгалтерские ~/и (vestí bukhgálterskie ~/i) to keep the account ~s
вносить в ~/у (vnosít' v ~/u) to enter into the account ~
выход ~/и (výkhod ~/i) publication of a ~
грузовая ~ (gruzováia ~) cargo ~
запись в ~/е (zápis' v ~/e) ~ entry
кассовая ~ (kássovaia ~) till ~
обложка ~/и (oblózhka ~/i) jacket of a ~
перенос в бухгалтерскую ~/у (perenós v bukhgálterskuiu ~/u) carryover in the account ~
подписываться на ~/у (podpísyvat'sia na ~/u) to subscribe for a ~ {e.g. multi-volume}
приходная ~ (prikhódnaia ~) receipt ~
приходно-расходная ~ (prikhódno-raskhódnaia ~) cash receipts and payments ~
проверять бухгалтерские ~/и (proveriát' bukhgálterskie ~/i) to audit the ~s
расходная ~ (raskhódnaia ~) check register
справочная ~ (správochnaia ~) reference ~
счетоводная ~ (schetovódnaia ~) ~ of accounts
телефонная ~ (telefónnaia ~) telephone ~ {white pages}
товарная ~ (továrnaia ~) stock ~
торговая ~ (torgóvaia ~) business ~
Книжка (knízhka) *f.* booklet
расчётная банковская ~ (raschiótnaia bánkovskaia ~) bank passbook
чековая ~ (chékovaia ~) checkbook
Ковернот (kovernót) *m.* cover note, cover policy
выписывать ~ (vypísyvat' ~) to issue a cover note
Код (kod) *m.* code

международный ~ (mezhdunaródnyi ~) international ~
почтовый ~ (pochtóvyi ~) postal ~, zip ~
шифрованный ~ (shifróvannyi ~) enciphered ~
~ подрядчика (~ podriádchika) vendor ~
~ проекта (~ proékta) project ~
~ товара в каталоге (~ továra v katalóge) item number in a catalogue
Кодекс (kódeks) *m.* code {codification}
антидемпинговый ~ (antidémpingovyi ~) anti-dumping ~
гражданский ~ (grazhdánskii ~) civil ~
~ международного права (~ mezhdunaródnogo práva) ~ of international law
Кодировать (kodírovat') *v.* to codify
Колебани/е (kolebáni/e) *n.* fluctuation, variation
большие ~/я (bol'shíe ~/ia) major fluctuations
валютные ~/ (valiútnye ~/) currency fluctuations
временные ~/я (vrémennye ~/ia) temporary fluctuations
конъюнктурные ~/я (kon"iunktúrnye ~/ia) market fluctuations
кратковременные ~/я (kratkovrémennye ~/ia) short-term fluctuations
местные ~/я (méstnye ~/ia) local fluctuations
небольшие ~/я (nebol'shíe ~/ia) minor variations
нерегулярные ~/я (nereguliárnye ~/ia) irregular fluctuations
периодические ~/я (periodícheskie ~/ia) periodical fluctuations
постоянные ~/я (postoiánnye ~/ia) constant fluctuations
размах ~/и валютного курса (razmákh ~/i valiútnogo kúrsa) exchange rate fluctuation band
резкое ~ (rézkoe ~) sharp swing
с поправкой на сезонные ~/я (s poprávkoi na sezónnye ~/ia) adjusted for seasonal fluctuations

сезонные ~/я (sezónnye ~/ia)
seasonal fluctuations
устойчивые ~/я (ustóichivye
~/ia) sustained fluctuations
циклические ~/я (tsiklícheskie
~/ia) cyclical fluctuations
чрезмерные ~/я (chrezmérnye
~/ia) excessive fluctuations
~/я спроса и предложения (~/ia
sprósa i predlozhéniia) fluctuations in supply and demand
~/я стоимости (~/ia stóimosti)
fluctuations in costs
~ цен (~ tsen) variation in
prices
Колебаться (kolebát'sia) v. to
fluctuate, to vary
Колеблющийся (kolébliushchiisia)
adj. variable, fluctuating
Количественный (kolíchestvennyi)
adj. quantitative
Количеств/о (kolíchestv/o) n.
amount, number, quantity
   бесчисленное ~ (beschíslennoe ~)
   innumerable quantity
   большое ~ (bol'shóe ~) large
   quantity
   в ограниченном ~/е (v
   ograníchennom ~/e) in limited
   quantity
   выгруженное ~ (výgruzhennoe ~)
   quantity delivered
   добавочное ~ (dobávochnoe ~)
   supplementary quantity
   допустимое ~ (dopustímoe ~)
   tolerance quantity
   доставка неполного ~/а (dostávka
   nepólnogo ~/a) short delivery
   ежегодное ~ (ezhegódnoe ~)
   annual quantity
   заказное ~ (zakaznóe ~) ordered
   quantity
   значительное ~ (znachítel'noe ~)
   significant quantity
   контрактное ~ (kontráktnoe ~)
   contracted quantity
   максимальное возможное ~
   (maksimál'noe vozmózhnoe ~)
   maximum possible quantity
   малое ~ (máloe ~) small quantity
   наличное ~ (nalíchnoe ~)
   available quantity
   начальное ~ (nachál'noe ~)
   initial quantity
   недостаточное ~ (nedostátochnoe
   ~) insufficient quantity

   незначительное ~
   (neznachítel'noe ~)
   insignificant quantity
   необходимое ~ (neobkhodímoe ~)
   required quantity
   неуточнённое ~ (neutochniónnoe
   ~) unspecified quantity
   обусловленное ~ (obuslóvlennoe
   ~) stipulated quantity
   общее ~ (óbshchee ~) total
   amount, overall quantity
   ограниченное ~ (ograníchennoe ~)
   limited quantity
   ощутимое ~ (oshchutímoe ~)
   appreciable quantity
   рекордное ~ (rékordnoe ~) record
   quantity
   скидка за ~ (skídka za ~)
   quantity discount
Коллега (kolléga) f. colleague
Коллеги/я (kollégi/ia) f. board,
collegium, panel
   апелляционная ~
   (apelliatsiónnaia ~) board of
   appeals
   арбитражная ~ (arbitrázhnaia ~)
   arbitration board
   судебная ~ (sudébnaia ~)
   judicial board
   член ~/и (chlen ~/i) member of
   the collegium
Коллектив (kollektív) m. collective
{collective body}
   производственный ~
   (proizvódstvennyi ~) production
   ~ {work force}
   трудовой ~ (trudovói ~) labor ~
   {employees of an enterprise}
Коллективный (kollektívnyi) adj.
collective
Коллекци/я (kolléktsi/ia) f.
collection
   ~ образцов (~ obraztsóv) ~ of
   samples
Колонка (kolónka) f. column
Команд/а (kománd/a) f. crew, team
   аварийная ~ (avaríinaia ~)
   emergency crew
   судовая ~ (sudováia ~) ship's
   crew
   управленческая ~
   (upravléncheskaia ~) management
   team
   обучение ~/ы (obuchénie ~/y)
   training of a crew
Командировани/е (komandiróvani/e)
n. business travel

~ специалистов (~ spetsialístov)
field travel by experts
Командировать (komandírovat') *v.* to
send on a business trip
Командировк/а (komandiróvk/a) *f.*
business trip
  быть в ~/е (byt' v ~/e) to be
away on business
  длительная ~ (dlítel'naia ~)
extended ~
  зарубежная ~ (zarubézhnaia ~) ~
abroad
  краткосрочная ~ (kratkosróchnaia
~) short-term ~
  служебная ~ (sluzhébnaia ~)
official ~
Командировочные (komandiróvochnye)
pl.adj.noun traveling expenses
Комбайн (kombáin) *m.* combine-
harvester
Комбинат (kombinát) *m.* combine
{amalgamated industrial concern}
  производственные ~/ы
(proizvódstvennye ~/y)
production ~s
  промышленный ~ (promýshlennyi ~)
industrial ~
  учебный ~ (uchébnyi ~) training
center
Комбинация (kombinátsiia) *f.*
combination
  возможная ~ (vozmózhnaia ~)
possible ~
Комбинированный (kombinírovannyi)
adj. combination
Комиссар (komissár) *m.* commissar
  аварийный ~ (avaríinyi ~)
insurance surveyor
  ~/ы таможенного комитета (~/y
tamózhennogo komitéta) customs
commissioners
Комиссионер (komissionér) *m.* agent,
broker, jobber, middleman
  берущий на себя делькредере
(berúshchii na sebiá
dél'kredére) del credere agent
Комиссионны/е (komissiónny/e)
pl.adj.noun commission {fees}
  взимать ...% ~/х (vzimát' ...
~/kh) to charge ... % ~
  вычесть банковские ~ из
денежного перевода (výchest'
bánkovskie ~ iz dénezhnogo
perevóda) to deduct bank fees
from money transfer

перестраховочные ~
(perestrakhóvochnye ~) reinsurance ~
  платить ~ (platít' ~) to pay ~
  получать ~ (poluchát' ~) to
receive a ~
  процент ~/х (protsént ~/kh)
percentage rate of ~
  размер ~/х (razmér ~/kh) measure
of a ~
  ~ за продажу (~ za prodázhu)
sales ~
Комиссионный (komissiónnyi) *adj.*
commission
Комисси/я (komíssi/ia) *f.*
commission, committee
  акцептная ~ (aktséptnaia ~)
acceptance commission
  арбитражная ~ (arbitrázhnaia ~)
arbitration panel
  аттестационная ~
(attestatsiónnaia ~) certifying
committee
  банковская ~ (bánkovskaia ~)
banking committee
  брать товар на ~/ю (brat' továr
na ~/iu) to take goods on
commission
  брокерская ~ (brókerskaia ~)
brokerage fee
  бюджетная ~ (biudzhétnaia ~)
budget committee
  временная ~ (vrémennaia ~)
interim committee
  государственная ~
(gosudárstvennaia ~) state
committee
  закупочная ~ (zakúpochnaia ~)
purchasing committee
  консультативная ~
(konsul'tatívnaia ~)
consultative committee
  контрольная ~ (kontról'naia ~)
oversight committee
  координационная ~
(koordinatsiónnaia ~)
coordinating committee
  ликвидационная ~
(likvidatsiónnaia ~) liquidation
committee
  Морская Арбитражная ~ (morskáia
arbitrázhnaia ~) Maritime
Arbitration Commission
  объединённая ~ (ob"ediniónnaia
~) unified committee
  операционная ~ (operatsiónnaia
~) operating committee

отраслевая ~ (otrasleváia ~)
sectoral committee
оценочная ~ (otsénochnaia ~)
evaluating committee
плановая ~ (plánovaia ~)
planning committee
постоянная ~ (postoiánnaia ~)
standing committee
правительственная ~
(pravítel'stvennaia ~)
government commission
процентная ~ (protséntnaia ~)
percentage commission
рабочая ~ (rabóchaia ~) working
party
ревизионная ~ (reviziónnaia ~)
audit committee
смешанная ~ (sméshannaia ~)
joint committee
создавать ~/ю (sozdavát' ~/iu)
to form a committee
ставка ~/и (stávka ~/i) rate of
commission
твёрдая ~ (tviórdaia ~) fixed
commission
торговая ~ (torgóvaia ~) trade
committee
трёхсторонняя ~
(triókhstorónniaia ~) trilateral
committee
фрахтовая ~ (frakhtóvaia ~)
freight brokerage
член ~/и (chlen ~/i) member of a
committee
экономическая ~ (ekonomícheskaia
~) economic commission
экспертная ~ (ekspértnaia ~)
expert commission
~ за авизо (~ za avízo)
commission on advice
~ за аккредитив (~ za
akkreditív) commission for
letter of credit
~ за акцепт (~ za aktsépt)
commission for acceptance
Комитент (komitént) m. client,
customer, principal
Комитет (komitét) m. committee
биржевой ~ (birzhevói ~) stock
exchange ~
временный ~ (vrémennyi ~)
interim ~
исполнительный ~ (ispolnítel'nyi
~) executive ~
консультативный ~
(konsul'tatívnyi ~) advisory ~

координационный ~
(koordinatsiónnyi ~)
coordinating ~
межправительственный ~
(mezhpravítel'stvennyi ~)
intergovernmental ~
организационный ~
(organizatsiónnyi ~) organizing
~
подготовительный ~
(podgotovítel'nyi ~) preparatory
~
постоянный ~ (postoiánnyi ~)
standing ~
рабочий ~ (rabóchii ~) working ~
редакционный ~ (redaktsiónnyi ~)
drafting ~
руководящий ~ (rukovodiáshchii
~) steering ~
тендерный ~ (téndernyi ~) tender
~
управленческий ~
(upravléncheskii ~) management ~
финансовый ~ (finánsovyi ~)
financial ~
Коммерсант (kommersánt) m.
businessman, merchant
Коммерциализация
(kommertsializátsiia) f.
commercialization
Коммерци/я (kommértsi/ia) f.
commerce, trading
заниматься ~/ей (zanimát'sia
~/ei) to conduct business
Коммерческий (kommércheskii) adj.
commercial
Коммюнике (kommiuniké) n.
communiqué
совместное ~ (sovméstnoe ~)
joint ~
опубликовать ~ (opublikovát' ~)
to issue a ~
Компани/я (kompáni/ia) f. company
авиационная ~ (aviatsiónnaia ~)
airline
акционерная ~ (aktsionérnaia ~)
joint stock ~
ведущая ~ (vedúshchaia ~)
leading ~
государственная ~
(gosudárstvennaia ~) state ~
государственная ~ с ограниченной
ответственностью
(gosudárstvennaia ~ s
ograníchennoi otvétstvennost'iu)
state ~ with limited liability

дочерняя ~ (dochérniaia ~)
subsidiary ~
железнодорожная ~
(zheleznodorózhnaia ~) railway ~
заокеанская ~ (zaokeánskaia ~)
overseas ~
инвестиционная ~
(investitsiónnaia ~) investment
~
иностранная ~ (inostránnaia ~)
foreign ~
конкурентная ~ (konkuréntnaia ~)
competitive ~
контролирующая ~
(kontrolíruiushchaia ~) holding
~
крупная ~ (krúpnaia ~) major ~
крупнейшие ~/и (krupnéishie ~/i)
principal ~s
лизинговая ~ (lízingovaia ~)
leasing ~
ликвидация ~/и (likvidátsiia
~/i) liquidation of a ~
ликвидировать ~/ю (likvidírovat'
~/iu) to liquidate a ~
материнская ~ (materínskaia ~)
parent ~
международная ~ (mezhdunaródnaia
~) international ~
монополистическая ~
(monopolistícheskaia ~)
monopolistic ~
налог с доходов акционерных ~/й
(nalóg s dokhódov aktsionérnykh
~/i) corporate income tax
национализированная ~
(natsionalizírovannaia ~)
nationalized ~
нефтяная ~ (neftianáia ~) oil ~
объединённая ~ (ob"ediniónnaia
~) incorporated ~
отдельная ~ (otdél'naia ~)
separate ~
посылочная ~ (posýlochnaia ~)
mail order ~
промышленная ~ (promýshlennaia
~) industrial ~
распределительная ~
(raspredelítel'naia ~)
distribution ~
слияние ~/й (sliiánie ~/i)
merger of ~s
смешанная ~ (sméshannaia ~)
mixed ~
создавать ~/ю (sozdavát' ~/iu)
to form a ~

специализированная ~
(spetsializírovannaia ~)
specialized ~
стивидорная ~ (stividórnaia ~)
stevedoring ~
страховая ~ (strakhováia ~)
insurance ~
строительная ~ (stroítel'naia ~)
construction ~
судоходная ~ (sudokhódnaia ~)
shipping ~
торговая ~ (torgóvaia ~) trading
~
филиал ~/и (filiál ~/i)
affiliate of a ~
фиктивная ~ (fiktívnaia ~) bogus
~
финансовая ~ (finánsovaia ~)
finance ~
холдинговая ~ (khóldingovaia ~)
holding ~
частная ~ (chástnaia ~) private
~
~ с неограниченной
ответственностью (~ s
neograníchennoi
otvétstvennost'iu) unlimited
liability ~
~ с ограниченной
ответственностью (~ s
ograníchennoi otvétstvennost'iu)
limited liability ~
Компания-держатель (kompániia-
derzhátel') m. holding ~
Компания-поставщик (kompániia-
postavshchík) m. supplier {company}
Компания-проектировщик (kompániia-
proektiróvshchik) m. designing ~
Компаньон (kompan'ón) m. partner
главный ~ (glávnyi ~) managing ~
иностранный ~ (inostránnyi ~)
foreign ~
младший ~ (mládshii ~) junior ~
старший ~ (stárshii ~) senior ~
~, не принимающий активного
участия в ведении дела (~, ne
prinimáiushchii aktívnogo
uchástiia v vedénii déla) silent
~
Компенсационный (kompensatsiónnyi)
adj. buy-back, compensatory
Компенсаци/я (kompensátsi/ia) f.
compensation, recompense
в ~/ю (v ~/iu) in compensation
of
в качестве ~/и (v káchestve ~/i)
as compensation

давать ~/ю (davát' ~/iu) to give compensation
денежная ~ (dénezhnaia ~) cash refund, monetary compensation
достаточная ~ (dostátochnaia ~) adequate compensation
законная ~ (zakónnaia ~) statutory compensation
наросшая ~ (narósshaia ~) accrued indemnity
недостаточная ~ (nedostátochnaia ~) inadequate compensation
платить ~/ю (platít' ~/iu) to pay compensation
полная ~ (pólnaia ~) full compensation
причитающаяся ~ (prichitáiushchaiasia ~) compensation due
размер ~/и (razmér ~/i) measure of compensation
страховая ~ (strakhováia ~) insurance indemnity
Компенсировать (kompensírovat') v. to compensate, to indemnify, to reimburse
Компетентный (kompeténtnyi) adj. competent {in various senses}
Компетенци/я (kompeténtsi/ia) f. competence, jurisdiction
в пределах ~/и (v predélakh ~/i) within the competence of
входить в ~/ю (vkhodít' v ~/iu) to come under the jurisdiction of
выходить за пределы ~/и (vykhodít' za predély ~/i) to be outside the competence of
Комплекс (kómpleks) m. complex
агро-промышленный ~ (ágro-promýshlennyi ~) agro-industrial ~
внешнеэкономический ~ (vneshneekonomícheskii ~) foreign) economic ~
выставочный ~ (výstavochnyi ~) exhibition ~
гостиничный ~ (gostínichnyi ~) hotel ~
нефтехимический ~ (neftekhimícheskii ~) petro-chemical ~
паромный ~ (parómnyi ~) ferry ~
портовый ~ (portóvyi ~) port ~
производственный ~ (proizvódstvennyi ~) manufacturing ~

промышленный ~ (promýshlennyi ~) industrial ~
~ ноу-хау (~ nóu-kháu) know-how package
~ оборудования (~ oborúdovaniia) equipment package
~ услуг (~ uslúg) package of services
Комплексный (kómpleksnyi) adj. comprehensive, complex
Комплект (komplékt) m. set
в ~/е ... (v ~/e ...) complete with ...
двойной ~ (dvoinói ~) duplicate ~
индивидуальный ~ (individuál'nyi ~) individual ~
полный ~ (pólnyi ~) complete ~
полный ~ коносаментов (pólnyi ~ konosaméntov) complete ~ of bills of lading
поставлять в ~/е (postavliát' v ~/e) to provide as a ~
предоставлять полный ~ (predostavliát' pólnyi ~) to provide a complete ~
резервный ~ (rezérvnyi ~) stand-by ~
цена за ~ (tsená za ~) price per ~
~ документов (~ dokuméntov) ~ of documents
~ запчастей (~ zapchastéi) ~ of spare parts
~ инструментов (~ instruméntov) tool kit
~ материалов заявки (~ materiálov zaiávki) application file
~ оборудования (~ oborúdovaniia) ~ of equipment
~ образцов (~ obraztsóv) ~ of samples
~ приборов (~ pribórov) ~ of instruments
~ упаковочных листов (~ upakóvochnykh lístov) ~ of packing lists
Комплектация (komplektátsiia) f. packing list
Комплектность (kompléktnost') f. completeness
Комплектный (kompléktnyi) adj. complete
Комплектование (komplektovánie) n. completion

~ оборудования (~ oborúdovaniia)
~ of equipment
~ рабочей силой (~ rabóchei
síloi) manning, staffing
Комплектовать (komplektovát') *v.* to
complete, to make a set
Комплектовочная ведомость
(komplektóvochnaia védomost') *f.*
delivery list
Компонент (komponént) *m.* component
высококачественные ~/ы
(vysokokáchestvennye ~/y) high-
quality ~ s
отдельные ~/ы (otdél'nye ~/y)
separate ~s
специфические ~/ы
(spetsifícheskie ~/y) specific
~s
Компромисс (kompromíss) *m.*
compromise
достигать ~/а (dostigát' ~/a) to
reach a ~
пойти на ~ (poití na ~) to make
a ~
Компромиссный (kompromíssnyi) *adj.*
compromise
Компьютер (komp'iúter) *m.* computer
Конвенционный (konventsiónnyi) *adj.*
convention, conventional
Конвенци/я (konvéntsi/ia) *f.*
convention
заключать ~/ю (zakliuchát' ~/iu)
to conclude a ~
консульская ~ (kónsul'skaia ~)
consular ~
международная ~ (mezhdunaródnaia
~) international ~
подписывать ~/ю (podpísyvat'
~/iu) to sign a ~
ратифицировать ~/ю
(ratifitsírovat' ~/iu) to ratify
a ~
таможенная ~ (tamózhennaia ~)
customs ~
Конверсия (konvérsiia) *f.*
conversion
~ займа (~ záima) ~ of a loan
Конверт (konvért) *m.* cover,
envelope
в отдельном ~ (v otdél'nom ~)
under separate cover
в том же ~/e (v tom zhe ~/e)
under the same cover
вкладыш в ~/e (vkládysh v ~/e)
mailing insert

водонепроницаемый ~
(vodonepronitsáemyi ~)
waterproof cover, envelope
вскрывать ~ (vskryvát' ~) to
open an envelope
запечатанный ~ (zapechátannyi ~)
sealed envelope
запечатывать ~ (zapechátyvat' ~)
to seal an envelope
надписывать ~ (nadpísyvat' ~) to
address an envelope
~ с маркой (~ s márkoi) stamped
envelope
Конвертировать (konvertírovat') *v.*
to convert
Конвертируемость (konvertíruemost')
f. convertibility
~ валюты (~ valiúty) ~ of
currency
Конвертируемый (konvertíruemyi)
adj. convertible
свободно ~ (svobódno ~) freely ~
Конгресс (kongréss) *m.* congress
всемирный ~ (vsemírnyi ~) world
~
международный ~ (mezhdunaródnyi
~) international ~
научный ~ (naúchnyi ~)
scientific ~
проводить ~ (provodít' ~) to
hold a ~
Конечный (konéchnyi) *adj.* final,
ultimate
Конкурент (konkurént) *m.* competitor
важнейшие ~/ы (vazhnéishie ~/y)
major ~s
воспрепятствовать проникновению
~/ов (vosprepiátstvovat' pronik-
novéniiu ~/ov) to forestall the
market entry of ~s
иностранные ~/ы (inostránnye
~/y) foreign ~s
местные ~/ы (méstnye ~/y) local
~s
основной ~ (osnovnói ~) main ~
потенциальный ~
(potentsiál'nyi ~/y) potential ~
Конкурентный (konkuréntnyi) *adj.*
competitive
Конкурентоспособност/ь
(konkurentosposóbnost/') *f.*
competitiveness, competitive
position
показатель ~/и (pokazátel' ~/i)
indicator of competitiveness
повышать ~ (povyshát' ~) to
increase competitiveness

Конкурентоспособный
(konkurentosposóbnyi) *adj.*
competitive {goods, services}
Конкуренци/я (konkuréntsi/ia) *f.*
competition
   активная ~ (aktívnaia ~) active
   ~
   внутриотраслевая ~
   (vnutrioträsleváia ~)
   intrasectoral ~
   выдерживать ~/ю (vydérzhivat'
   ~/iu) to withstand ~
   глобальная ~ (globál'naia ~)
   global ~
   давление ~/и (davlénie ~/i)
   competitive pressure
   жестокая ~ (zhestókaia ~) stiff
   ~
   косвенная ~ (kósvennaia ~)
   indirect ~
   ликвидировать существующую ~/ю
   (likvidírovat' sushchestvúiu-
   shchuiu ~/iu) to eliminate
   existing ~
   межотраслевая ~ (mezhotrasleváia
   ~) intersectoral ~
   механизм ~/и (mekhanízm ~/i)
   competitive mechanism
   недобросовестная ~
   (nedobrosóvestnaia ~) unfair ~
   неограниченная ~
   (neograníchennaia ~) unlimited ~
   обострение ~/и (obostrénie ~/i)
   increase in ~
   ожесточённая ~ (ozhestochiónnaia
   ~) cutthroat ~
   оживлённая ~ (ozhivliónnaia ~)
   spirited ~
   острая ~ (óstraia ~) keen ~
   прямая ~ (priamáia ~) direct ~
   разрушительная ~
   (razrushítel'naia ~) ruinous ~
   рыночная ~ (rýnochnaia ~) market
   ~
   свободная ~ (svobódnaia ~) free
   ~
   скрытая ~ (skrýtaia ~) latent ~
   хищническая ~ (khishchnícheskaia
   ~) predatory ~
   ценовая ~ (tsenováia ~) price ~
   честная ~ (chéstnaia ~) fair ~
   чистая ~ (chístaia ~) pure ~
Конкурировать (konkurírovat') *v.* to
compete
Конкурирующий (konkuríruiushchii)
adj. competing

Конкурс (kónkurs) *m.* competition,
contest
   международный ~ (mezhdunaródnyi
   ~) international contest
   участвовать в ~/е (uchástvovat'
   v ~/e) to participate in a
   contest
Коносамент (konosamént) *m.* bill of
lading
   бортовой ~ (bortovói ~) on board
   ~
   внешний ~ (vnéshnii ~) outward ~
   в соответствии с ~/ом (v
   sootvétstvii s ~/om) under a ~
   внутренний ~ (vnútrennii ~)
   inland ~
   вручать ~ (vruchát' ~) to hand
   over a ~
   групповой ~ (gruppovói ~)
   groupage ~
   дата ~/а (dáta ~/a) date of a ~
   дата подписания ~/а (dáta
   podpisániia ~/a) signature date
   of a ~
   датированный более поздним
   числом ~ (datírovannyi bólee
   pózdnim chislóm ~) post-dated ~
   держатель ~/а (derzhátel' ~/a)
   holder of a ~
   заполненный ~ (zapólnennyi ~)
   completed ~
   именной ~ (imennói ~) straight ~
   краткий ~ (krátkii ~) short form
   ~
   линейный ~ (linéinyi ~) liner ~
   локальный ~ (lokál'nyi ~) local
   ~
   морской ~ (morskói ~) steamer ~
   необоротный ~ (neoborótnyi ~)
   non-negotiable ~
   нечистый ~ (nechístyi ~) unclean
   ~
   номер ~/а (nómer ~/a) ~ number
   ордерный ~ (órdernyi ~) order ~
   оригинальный ~ (originál'nyi ~)
   original ~
   отметка в ~/е (otmétka v ~/e)
   reservation in a ~
   по ~/у (po ~/u) against a ~
   подписывать ~ (podpísyvat' ~) to
   sign a ~
   предъявитель ~/а (pred"iavítel'
   ~/a) bearer of a ~
   проформа ~/а (profórma ~/a) pro
   forma ~
   прямой ~ (priamói ~) direct ~
   речной ~ (rechnói ~) river ~

сборный ~ (sbórnyi ~) groupage ~
сквозной ~ (skvoznói ~) through
~
складской ~ (skladskói ~)
warehouse ~
служебный ~ (sluzhébnyi ~)
service ~
транспортный ~ (tránsportnyi ~)
delivery note
условия ~/a (uslóviia ~/a) ~
terms
форма ~/a (fórma ~/a) ~ form
чистый ~ (chístyi ~) clean ~
экземпляр ~/a (ekzempliár ~/a)
copy of a ~
~, выданный на определённое лицо
(~, výdannyi na opredeliónnoe
litsó) straight ~
Консервативный (konservatívnyi)
adj. conservative
Консигнант (konsignánt) m.
consignor
Консигнатор (konsignátor) m.
consignee
Консигнационный (konsignatsiónnyi)
adj. consignment
Консигнаци/я (konsignátsi/ia) f.
consignment
    безвозвратная ~ (bezvozvrátnaia
    ~) non-returnable ~
    возвратная ~ (vozvrátnaia ~)
    returnable ~
    договор ~/и (dogovór ~/i)
    contract of ~
    срок ~/и (srok ~/i) term of ~
    условия ~/и (uslóviia ~/i) terms
    of ~
    находиться на ~/и (nakhodít'sia
    na ~/i) to be on ~
    отправлять на ~/ю (otpravliát'
    na ~/iu) to forward on ~
Консолидация (konsolidátsiia) f.
consolidation
Консолидировать (konsolidírovat')
v. to consolidate
Консорциум (konsórtsium) m.
consortium, syndicate
    банковский ~ (bánkovskii ~)
    consortium of banks
    вступать в ~ (vstupát' v ~) to
    join a consortium
    выходить из ~/a (vykhodít' iz
    ~/a) to withdraw from a consor-
    tium
    международный ~ (mezhdunaródnyi
    ~) international syndicate

Конструирование (konstruírovanie)
n. designing, engineering
Конструировать (konstruírovat') v.
to design, to engineer
Конструктивный (konstruktívnyi)
adj. constructed
Конструктор (konstrúktor) m.
designer, engineer
    ведущий ~ (vedúshchii ~) design
    project leader
    главный ~ (glávnyi ~) chief
    designer
Конструкторский (konstrúktorskii)
adj. design
Конструкци /я (konstrúktsi/ia) f.
design, construction
    анализ ~/и (análiz ~/i) design
    analysis
    выбор варианта ~/и (výbor
    variánta ~/i) design selection
    дефект в ~/и (defékt v ~/i)
    engineering defect
    изменение в ~/и (izmenénie v
    ~/i) redesign
    надёжная ~ (nadiózhnaia ~)
    reliable design
    нарушение ~/и (narushénie ~/i)
    infringement of design
    ненадёжная ~ (nenadiózhnaia ~)
    unreliable design
    неправильная ~ (neprávil'naia ~)
    faulty design
    новейшей ~/и (novéishei ~/i) of
    the latest design
    одобрение ~/и (odobrénie ~/i)
    design approval
    опорная ~ (opórnaia ~)
    supporting framework
    оптимальная ~ (optimál'naia ~)
    optimum design
    особая ~ (osóbaia ~) custom
    design
    пересмотр ~/и (peresmótr ~/i)
    design review
    применять ~/ю (primeniát' ~/iu)
    to apply a design
    проверять ~/ю (proveriát' ~/iu)
    to check a design
    современная ~ (sovreménnaia ~)
    modern design
    типовая ~ (tipováia ~) standard
    design
    уникальная ~ (unikál'naia ~)
    unique design
Консул (kónsul) m. consul
    генеральный ~ (generál'nyi ~)
    Consul-General

Консультант (konsul'tánt) *m.*
consultant
 главный ~ (glávnyi ~) chief ~
 научный ~ (naúchnyi ~)
 scientific ~
 платный ~ (plátnyi ~) paid ~
 технический ~ (tekhnícheskii ~)
 technical ~
Консультативный (konsul'tatívnyi)
adj. advisory, consultative
Консультационный
(konsul'tatsiónnyi) *adj.* consultant
Консультаци/я (konsul'tátsi/ia) *f.*
advice, consultation
 техническая ~ (tekhnícheskaia ~)
 technical consultation
 юридическая ~ (iuridícheskaia ~)
 legal clinic, legal consultation
 bureau
 ~ юриста (~ iurísta) legal
 advice
Консультироваться
(konsul'tírovat'sia) *v.* to consult
Контакт (kontákt) *m.* communication,
contact
 быть в ~/е (byt' v ~/e) to be in
 contact
 быть в постоянном ~/е (byt' v
 postoiánnom ~/e) to be in
 constant contact
 внешние ~/ы (vnéshnie ~/y)
 external communications
 внутренние ~/ы (vnútrennie ~/y)
 internal communications
 вступить в ~ (vstupít' v ~) to
 make contact
 дальнейшие ~/ы (dal'néishie ~/y)
 further contacts
 деловые ~/ы (delovýe ~/y)
 business contacts
 наладить личные ~/ы (naládit'
 líchnye ~/y) to develop personal
 contacts
 косвенные ~/ы (kósvennye ~/y)
 indirect contacts
 личные ~/ы (líchnye ~/y)
 personal contacts
 начальные ~/ы (nachál'nye ~/y)
 initial contacts
 неофициальные ~/ы
 (neofitsiál'nye ~/y) unofficial
 contacts
 непосредственные ~/ы
 (neposrédstvennye ~/y) direct
 contacts
 поддерживать ~ (poddérzhivat' ~)
 to maintain contact

 тесный ~ (tésnyi ~) close
 contact
 торговые ~/ы (torgóvye ~/y)
 trade contacts
Контанго (kontángo) *n.* contango
{futures exchange}
Контейнер (kontéiner) *m.* container
 большегрузный ~ (bol'shegrúznyi
 ~) high capacity ~
 влагонепроницаемый ~
 (vlagopronitsáemyi ~)
 moisture-proof ~
 вывозить ~ (vyvozít' ~) to pick
 up a ~
 заполнять ~ (zapolniát' ~) to
 load a ~
 грузовой ~ (gruzovói ~) cargo ~
 железнодорожный
 (zheleznodorózhnyi ~) railway ~
 крупнотоннажный ~
 (krupnotonnázhnyi ~) heavy
 tonnage ~
 неохлаждаемый ~ (neokhlazhdáemyi
 ~) unrefrigerated ~
 обработка ~/ов (obrabótka ~/ov)
 handling of ~s
 опечатанный ~ (opechátannyi ~)
 sealed ~
 охлаждаемый ~ (okhlazhdáemyi ~)
 refrigerated ~
 полногрузный ~ (polnogruznyi ~)
 fully-loaded ~
 прокат ~/ов (prokát ~/ov) ~
 leasing
 простой ~/а (prostói ~/a)
 demurrage of a ~
 пустой ~ (pustói ~) empty ~
 разгружать ~ (razgruzhát' ~) to
 unload a ~
 распаковать ~ (raspakovát' ~) to
 unpack a ~
 рефрижераторный ~
 (refrizherátornyi ~)
 refrigerated ~
 х-футовый ~ (íks-fútovyi ~) x-
 foot ~ {where x denotes footage,
 e.g. 20, 40}
 транзитный ~ (tranzítnyi ~)
 transit ~
 универсальный ~ (universál'nyi
 ~) universal ~
 усиленный ~ (usílennyi ~)
 reinforced ~
 эластичный ~ (elastíchnyi ~)
 flexitainer
Контейнеризация (konteinerizátsiia)
f. containerization

Контейнеризованный
(kontéinerizovannyi) *adj.*
containerized
Контейнерный (kontéinernyi) *adj.*
container
Контейнеровоз (konteinerovóz) *m.*
containerized vessel
Контейнер-прицеп (kontéiner-
pritsép) *m.* container trailer
Контейнер-холодильник (kontéiner-
kholodíl'nik) *m.* refrigerated
container
Контейнер-цистерна (kontéiner-
tsistérna) *f.* tank container
Контингент (kontingént) *m.*
contingent, quota
   ввозные ~/ы (vvoznýe ~/y) import
   quotas
   импортные ~/ы (ímportnye ~/y)
   import quotas
   индивидуальные ~/ы
   (individuál'nye ~/y) individual
   contingents
   отмена ~/а (otména ~/a)
   abolition of a quota
   экспортные ~/ы (éksportnye ~/y)
   export quotas
Контингентирование
(kontingentírovanie) *n.*
quantitative restrictions
Континентальный (kontinentál'nyi)
adj. continental
Контокоррент (kontokorrént) *m.*
current account {in account books}
Контокоррентный (kontokorréntnyi)
adj. current account
Контор/а (kontór/a) *f.* office
   банкирская ~ (bankírskaia ~)
   bank
   главная ~ (glávnaia ~) head ~
   грузовая ~ (gruzováia ~) freight
   ~
   директор ~/ы (diréktor ~/y) ~
   manager
   зарегистрированная ~
   (zaregistrírovannaia ~)
   registered ~
   импортная ~ (ímportnaia ~)
   import ~
   нотариальная ~ (notariál'naia ~)
   notary ~
   открыть ~/у (otkrýt' ~/u) to
   open an ~
   приёмочная ~ (priiómochnaia ~)
   reception room
   проектная ~ (proéktnaia ~)
   design ~

   разменная ~ (razménnaia ~)
   exchange ~ {currency}
   ревизионная ~ (reviziónnaia ~)
   audit ~
   страховая ~ (strakhováia ~)
   insurance ~
   фрахтовая ~ (frakhtováia ~)
   freight ~
   экспортная ~ (éksportnaia ~)
   export ~
Конторский (kontórskii) *adj.* office
Контрабанд/а (kontrabánd/a) *f.*
contraband, smuggling
   изъятие ~/ы (iz"iátie ~/y)
   seizure of contraband
   заниматься ~/ой (zanimát'sia
   ~/oi) to be engaged in smuggling
Контрабандный (kontrabándnyi) *adj.*
contraband
Контрагент (kontragént) *m.*
counterpart {party in contract}
Контракт (kontrákt) *m.* contract
   аккордный (akkórdnyi ~)
   package deal
   аннулирование ~/а
   (annulírovananie ~/a) annulment
   of a ~
   аннулировать ~ (annulírovat' ~)
   to annul a ~
   большой ~ (bol'shói ~) large ~
   будущие ~/ы (búdushchie ~/y)
   future ~s
   в исполнение ~/а (v ispolnénie
   ~/a) in performance of a ~
   в пределах ~/а (v predélakh ~/a)
   within contractual limits
   в соответствии с ~/ом (v
   sootvétstvii s ~/om) in
   accordance) with a ~
   валюта ~/а (valiúta ~/a) ~
   currency
   вводить ~ в силу (vvodít' ~ v
   sílu) to bring a ~ into effect
   взаимовыгодный ~ (vzaimovýgodnyi
   ~) mutually profitable ~
   вносить изменения в ~ (vnosít'
   izmenéniia v ~) to make
   modification to a ~
   вносить поправки в ~ (vnosít'
   poprávki v ~) to make
   corrections to a ~
   возобновлять ~ (vozobnovliát' ~)
   to renew a ~
   выгодный ~ (výgodnyi ~)
   profitable ~
   выполнение ~/а (vypolnénie ~/a)
   performance of a ~

выполнять ~ (vypolniát' ~) to
perform under a ~
гербовой сбор с ~/a (gerbovói
sbor s ~/a) stamp tax on a ~
глобальный ~ (globál'nyi ~)
global ~
дата вступления ~/a в силу (dáta
vstupléniia ~/a v sílu)
effective date of a ~
дата подписания ~/a (dáta
podpisániia ~/a) signature date
of a ~
действительный ~ (deistvítel'nyi
~) valid ~
действующий ~ (déistvuiushchii
~) operating ~
детали ~/a (detáli ~/a) details
of a ~
договорённость по ~/y
(dogovoriónnost' po ~/u)
contractual understanding
долгосрочный ~ (dolgosróchnyi ~)
long-term ~
дополнение к ~/y (dopolnénie k
~/u) appendix to a ~
ежегодные ~/ы (ezhegódnye ~/y)
annual ~s
заключать ~ (zakliuchát' ~) to
conclude a ~
заключённый ~ (zakliuchiónnyi ~)
executed ~
засекреченный ~ (zasekréchennyi
~) classified ~
изменение к ~/y (izmenénie k
~/u) modification to a ~
исключающий ~ (iskliucháiushchii
~) exclusive ~
исполнение ~/a (ispolnénie ~/a)
performance of a ~
кассировать ~ (kassírovat' ~) to
rescind a ~
краткосрочный ~ (kratkosróchnyi
~) short-term ~
на базе ~/a (na báze ~/a) on a
contractual basis
на условиях, предусмотренных в
~/e (na uslóviiakh,
predusmótrennykh v ~/e) under
the conditions contemplated in a
~
нарушать ~ (narushát' ~) to
breach a ~
нарушение ~/a (narushénie ~/a)
breach of a ~
недействительный ~
(nedeistvítel'nyi ~) void ~

невыполненный ~ (nevýpolnennyi
~) outstanding ~
образец ~/a (obrazéts ~/a) form
of a ~
обсуждать ~ (obsuzhdát' ~) to
negotiate a ~
общая стоимость ~/a (óbshchaia
stóimost' ~/a) total ~ value
общие условия ~/a (óbshchie
uslóviia ~/a) general conditions
of a ~
обязательства по ~/y
(obiazátel'stva po ~/u) ~
obligations
обязанный по ~/y (obiázannyi po
~/u) bound by ~
оговорка в ~/e (ogovórka v ~/e)
clause in a ~
оригинал ~/a (originál ~/a)
original of a ~
основной ~ (osnovnói ~) prime ~
оспоримый ~ (osporímyi ~)
voidable ~
отвечать условиям ~/a (otvechát'
uslóviiam ~/a) to conform to the
terms of a ~
открытый ~ (otkrýtyi ~) open-
ended ~
официальный ~ (ofitsiál'nyi ~)
official ~
оформленный ~ (ofórmlennyi ~)
formal ~
оформлять ~ (oformliát' ~) to
execute a ~
параграф ~/a (parágraf ~/a)
paragraph of a ~
парафировать ~ (parafírovat' ~)
to initial a ~
первоначальный ~
(pervonachál'nyi ~) original ~
переписка по ~/y (perepíska po
~/u) ~ correspondence
пересматривать ~ (peresmátrivat'
~) to revise a ~
по условиям ~/a (po uslóviiam
~/a) under the conditions of a ~
подготовить ~ (podgotóvit' ~) to
prepare a ~
подписание ~/a (podpisánie ~/a)
signing of a ~
подписывать ~ (podpísyvat' ~) to
sign a ~
подтверждать ~ (podtverzhdát' ~)
to confirm a ~
получать ~ (poluchát' ~) to be
awarded a ~

поощрительный ~
(pooshchrítel'nyi ~) incentive ~
поправка к ~/у (poprávka k ~/u)
amendment to a ~
поставка по ~/у (postávka po
~/u) contractual delivery
поставлять по ~ (postavliát' po
~) to deliver under a ~
правительственный ~
(pravítel'stvennyi ~) government
~
пределы ~/а (predély ~/a) bounds
of a ~
предлагаемый ~ (predlagáemyi ~)
proposed ~
предмет ~/а (predmét ~/a)
subject of a ~
представлять ~ на рассмотрение
(predstavliát' ~ na
rassmotrénie) to submit a ~ for
consideration
предшествующий ~
(predshéstvuiushchii ~) previous
~
прекращать действие ~/а
(prekrashchát' déistvie ~/a) to
suspend a ~
претензия по ~/у (preténziia po
~/u) claim under a ~
приемлемый ~ (priémlemyi ~)
acceptable ~
приложение к ~/у (prilozhénie k
~/u) annex to a ~
принимать ~ (prinimát' ~) to
accept a ~
проект ~/а (proékt ~/a) draft ~
противоречить ~/у
(protivoréchit' ~/u) to be in
conflict with a ~
пункт ~/а (punkt ~/a) item of a
~
рассматривать ~ (rassmátrivat'
~) to consider a ~
расторгать ~ (rastorgát' ~) to
repudiate a ~
расторгать ~ полностью
(rastorgát' ~ pólnost'iu) to
repudiate a ~ in toto
расторжение ~/а (rastorzhénie
~/a) repudiation of a ~
словесный ~ (slovésnyi ~) verbal
~
соблюдать условия ~/а
(sobliudát' uslóviia ~/a) to
observe the terms of a ~
согласно ~/у (soglásno ~/u) as
per the ~

соглашаться на ~ (soglashát'sia
na ~) to agree upon a ~
солидный ~ (solídnyi ~) solid
{substantial} ~
соответствующий ~
(sootvétstvuiushchii ~)
appropriate ~
составлять ~ (sostavliát' ~) to
draw up a ~
спор по ~/у (spor po ~/u) ~
dispute
срочный ~ (sróchnyi ~) fixed
term ~
статья ~/а (stat'iá ~/a) article
of a ~
сущность ~/а (súshchnost' ~/a)
essence of a ~
типовой ~ (tipovói ~) form ~,
standardized ~
текст ~/а (tekst ~/a) text of a
~
толкование ~/а (tolkovánie ~/a)
~ interpretation
торговый ~ (torgóvyi ~)
commercial ~
условия ~/а (uslóviia ~/a)
conditions of a ~
финансировать ~ (finansírovat'
~) to finance a ~
форма ~/а (fórma ~/a) form of a
~
фрахтовый ~ (frakhtóvyi ~)
freight ~
фьючерсный ~ (f'iúchersnyi ~)
futures ~ {commodities exchange}
цена по ~/у (tsená po ~/u) ~
price
~ купли-продажи (~ kúpli-
prodázhi) buy-sell ~
~ на обслуживание (~ na
obslúzhivanie) service ~
~ на продажу (~ na prodázhu)
sales ~
~ на реальный товар (~ na
reál'nyi továr) spot ~
{commodities exchange}
~ на строительство "под ключ" (~
na stroítel'stvo pod kliuch)
turn-key construction ~
~ на техническое обслуживание (~
na tekhnícheskoe obslúzhivanie)
technical services ~
~ на товар (~ na továr)
commodity ~
~ на фрахтования судна (~ na
frakhtovániia súdna) charter-
party ~

~ "полу-под-ключ" (~ pólu-pod-kliúch) semi-turn-key ~
~ "продакшн шеринг" (~ prodákshn shéring) production sharing ~
Контрактный (kontráktnyi) *adj.* contract
Контрактовать (kontraktovát') *v.* to contract
Контрактующий (kontraktúiushchii) *adj.* contracting {party}
Контрассигнант (kontrassignánt) *m.* countersignatory
Контрассигнация (kontrassignátsiia) *f.* countersignature
Контрассигновать (kontrassignovát') *v.* to countersign
Контрейлер (kontréiler) *m.* piggy-back trailer
Контрейлерный (kontréilernyi) *adj.* piggy-back {trailer}
Контрмера (kontrméra) *f.* counter measure
Контролёр (kontroliór) *m.* comptroller
  генеральный ~ (generál'nyi ~) general
  заводской ~ (zavódskoi ~) plant ~
  таможенный ~ (tamózhennyi ~) customs inspector
  ~ отчётности (~ otchiótnosti) auditor
Контролирование (kontrolírovanie) *n.* monitoring
  ~ процесса (~ protséssa) process ~
Контролировать (kontrolírovat') *v.* to check, to monitor
Контролируемый (kontrolíruemyi) *adj.* monitored, supervised
Контролирующий (kontrolíruiushchii) *adj.* monitoring, supervisory
Контрол/ь (kontról/') *m.* check, control, monitoring, supervision,) verification
  автоматический ~ (avtomatícheskii ~) automatic check
  административный ~ (administratívnyi ~) administrative control
  акт ~/я (akt ~/ia) certificate of inspection
  бухгалтерский ~ (bukhgálterskii ~) accounting control
  валютный ~ (valiútnyi ~) foreign exchange control

  внешний ~ (vnéshnii ~) outside control
  внутренний ~ (vnútrennii ~) internal control
  восстанавливать ~ (vosstanávlivat' ~) to re-establish control
  выборочный ~ (výborochnyi ~) random control
  государственный ~ (gosudárstvennyi ~) state control
  единообразный ~ (edinoobráznyi ~) uniform control
  жёсткий ~ (zhióstkii ~) strict control
  кредитный ~ (kredítnyi ~) credit control
  личный ~ (líchnyi ~) personal control
  метод ~/я (métod ~/ia) inspection method
  метод ~/я качества (métod ~/ia káchestva) quality control method
  народный ~ (naródnyi ~) popular control
  непосредственный ~ (neposrédstvennyi ~) direct control
  непрерывный ~ (neprerývnyi ~) uninterrupted control
  нормальный ~ (normál'nyi ~) standard control
  обеспечить ~ (obespéchit' ~) to assure control
  осуществлять ~ (osushchestvliát' ~) to exercise control
  общественный ~ (obshchéstvennyi ~) social control
  оперативный ~ (operatívnyi ~) operational control
  орган ~/я (órgan ~/ia) control authority
  отменять ~ (otmeniát' ~) to remove control
  отсутствие ~/я (otsútstvie ~/ia) lack of control
  паспортный ~ (pásportnyi ~) passport control
  периодический ~ (periodícheskii ~) periodic control
  передавать под ~ (peredavát' pod ~) to place under control
  пограничный ~ (pograníchnyi ~) border control

подробный ~ (podróbnyi ~)
detailed monitoring
полный ~ (pólnyi ~) full control
последовательный ~
(posledovátel'nyi ~) sequential
control
постоянный ~ (postoiánnyi ~)
constant supervision
правила ~/я (právila ~/ia)
control regulations
прямой ~ (priamói ~) direct
control
рабочий ~ (rabóchii ~) workers'
control
разумный ~ (razúmnyi ~)
reasonable control
регулярный ~ (reguliárnyi ~)
regular control
сохранять ~ (sokhraniát' ~) to
maintain control, to retain
control
специальный ~ (spetsiál'nyi ~)
special control
сплошной ~ (sploshnói ~) total
verification
ставить под ~ (stávit' pod ~) to
place under control
строгий ~ (strógii ~) strict
control
счётный ~ (schiótnyi ~) counting
control
таблица ~/я качества (tablítsa
~/ia káchestva) quality control
schedule
таможенный ~ (tamózhennyi ~)
customs control
текущий ~ (tekúshchii ~) current
control
технический ~ (tekhnícheskii ~)
technical control
финансовый ~ (finánsovyi ~)
financial control
эксплуатационный ~
(ekspluatatsiónnyi ~) field
inspection
экспортный ~ (éksportnyi ~)
export control
усиливать ~ (usílivat' ~) to
strengthen control
устанавливать ~ (ustanávlivat'
~) to establish control
~ качества продукции (~
káchestva prodúktsii) quality
control
~ над банковской деятельностью
(~ nad bánkovskoi
déiatel'nost'iu) banking control

~ над загрязнением окружающей
среды (~ nad zagriaznéniem
okruzháiushchei sredý)
environmental control
~ над потребительским кредитом
(~ nad potrebítel'skim kredítom)
consumer credit control
~ над ценами и заработной платой
(~ nad tsénami i zárabotnoi
plátoi) wage and price control
~ цен (~ tsen) price control
Контрольный (kontról'nyi) adj.
control
Контроффертa (kontrofférta) f.
counter offer
Контрпредложени/е
(kontrpredlozhéni/e) n. counter
proposal
Контрсталийный (kontrstalíinyi)
adj. demurrage, lay day
Контрстали/я (kontrstáli/ia) f.
demurrage, lay day
оплачивать ~/ю (opláchivat'
~/iu) to pay demurrage
Контртребование (kontrtrébovanie)
n. counter claim
выдвигать ~ (vydvigát' ~) to
advance a ~
оспаривать ~ (ospárivat' ~) to
contest a ~
отвергать ~ (otvergát' ~) to
reject a ~
предъявлять ~ (pred"iavliát' ~)
to file a ~
Конференц-зал (konferénts-zál) m.
conference hall
Конференциальный
(konferentsiál'nyi) adj. conference
Конференци/я (konferéntsi/ia) f.
conference
бюллетень ~/и (biulletén' ~/i)
journal of a ~
предварительная ~
(predvarítel'naia ~) preliminary
~
Конфиденциальност/ь
(konfidentsiál'nost/') f.
confidentiality
обеспечение ~/и (obespéchenie
~/i) guarantee of ~
соблюдать ~ (sobliudát' ~) to
keep ~
Конфиденциальны/й
(konfidentsiál'ny/i) adj.
confidential
считать ~/м (schitát' ~/m) to
consider ~

Конфискаци/я (konfiskátsi/ia) f.
forfeiture, confiscation
  акт о ~/и груза таможней (akt o
  ~/i grúza tamózhnei) seizure
  note
  подлежать ~/и (podlezhát' ~/i)
  to be subject to forfeiture
Конфискованный (konfiskóvannyi)
adj. forfeited, seized
Конфисковать (konfiskovát') v. to
confiscate
Конфликт (konflíkt) m. conflict,
dispute
  избегать ~/ов (izbegát' ~/ov) to
  avoid conflicts
  разрешение ~/a (razreshénie ~/a)
  settlement of a dispute
  трудовой ~ (trudovói ~) labor
  dispute
  ~ интересов (~ interésov)
  conflict of interests
Конфликтный (konflíktnyi) adj.
disputed
Конфликтующий (konfliktúiushchii)
adj. conflicting
Концентрация (kontsentrátsiia) f.
concentration
  допустимая ~ (dopustímaia ~)
  permitted ~
  рыночная ~ (rýnochnaia ~) market
  ~
  ~ капитала (~ kapitála) ~ of
  capital
  ~ материальных ресурсов (~
  materiál'nykh resúrsov) ~ of
  material resources
Концентрировать (kontsentrírovat')
v. to concentrate
Концепци/я (kontséptsi/ia) f.
concept
  доказанная ~ (dokázannaia ~)
  proven ~
  ~, принадлежащая фирме (~,
  prinadlezháshchaia fírme)
  proprietary ~ of a firm
Концерн (kontsérn) m. concern
  банковский ~ (bánkovskii ~)
  banking ~
  крупный ~ (krúpnyi ~) major ~
  международный ~ (mezhdunaródnyi
  ~) international ~
  многонациональный ~
  (mnogonatsionál'nyi ~)
  multinational ~
  промышленный ~ (promýshlennyi ~)
  industrial ~

Концессионер (kontsessionér) m.
concessionaire
Концессионный (kontsessiónnyi) adj.
concessionaire
Концесси/я (kontséssi/ia) f.
concession
  возобновлять ~/ю (vozobnovliát'
  ~/iu) to renew a ~
  иностранная ~ (inostránnaia ~)
  foreign ~
  получать ~/ю (poluchát' ~/iu) to
  receive a ~
  предоставлять ~/ю
  (predostavliát' ~/iu) to grant a
  ~
Конъюнктур/а (kon"iunktúr/a) f.
juncture, state of affairs, state
of the market
  благоприятная ~ (blagopriiátnaia
  ~) favorable conditions
  будущая экономическая ~
  (búdushchaia ekonomícheskaia ~)
  economic outlook
  высокая ~ (vysókaia ~) boom,
  peak in the business cycle
  вялая ~ (viálaia ~) stagnation
  in the business cycle
  деловая ~ (delováia ~) business
  conditions
  застойная ~ (zastóinaia ~)
  stagnation
  инфляционная ~ (infliatsiónnaia
  ~) inflationary conditions
  колебание ~/ы (kolebánie ~/y)
  market fluctuations
  общехозяйственная ~
  (obshchekhoziástvennaia ~)
  macroeconomic conditions
  перенапряжение ~/ы
  (perenapriazhénie ~/y) overheating of the market
  подъём ~/ы (pod"ióm ~/y)
  business recovery
  понижение ~/ы (ponizhénie ~/y)
  downturn
  прогноз ~/ы (prognóz ~/y)
  business cycle forecast
  развитие ~/ы (razvítie ~/y)
  economic trend
  спад ~/ы (spad ~/y) slump
  товарная ~ (továrnaia ~)
  commodity market conditions
  улучшение ~/ы (uluchshénie ~/y)
  improvement of the economic
  situation

ухудшение ~/ы (ukhudshénie ~/y)
deterioration of the economic
situation
~ региональных рынков (~
regionál'nykh rýnkov) conditions
of regional markets
~ рынка (~ rýnka) condition of
the market, market equilibrium
~ рынка, выгодная для покупателя
(~ rýnka, výgodnaia dlia
pokupátelia) buyer's market
~ рынка, выгодная для продавца
(~ rýnka, výgodnaia dlia prodavtsá) seller's market
Кооперант (kooperánt) *m.*
participant in a cooperative
Кооператив (kooperatív) *m.*
cooperative
потребительский ~
(potrebítel'skii ~) consumer's
cooperative
производственный ~
(proizvódstvennyi ~) production
cooperative
Кооперативный (kooperatívnyi) *adj.*
cooperative
Кооoperaци/я (kooperátsi/ia) *f.*
collaboration, cooperation
крупномасштабная ~
(krupnomasshtábnaia ~) full-
scale cooperation
международная ~ (mezhdunaródnaia
~) international cooperation
межфирменная ~ (mezhfírmennaia
~) inter-firm collaboration
плодотворная ~ (plodotvórnaia ~)
fruitful collaboration
потребительская ~
(potrebítel'skaia ~) consumer
cooperative society
экономическая ~ (ekonomícheskaia
~) economic cooperation
Кооperированный (kooperírovannyi)
adj. cooperative
Кооperировать (kooperírovat') *v.* to
cooperate
Координатор (koordinátor) *m.*
coordinator
проектный ~ (proéktnyi ~)
project ~
Координационный (koordinatsiónnyi)
adj. coordination
Координаци/я (koordinátsi/ia) *f.*
coordination
общая ~ (óbshchaia ~) overall ~
отсутствие ~/и (otsútstvie ~/i)
lack of ~

~ запродаж (~ zaprodázh) export
sales ~
Координировать (koordinírovat') *v.*
to coordinate
Копи/я (kópi/ia) *f.* copy,
counterpart, duplicate
верная ~ (vérnaia ~) true copy
выдавать ~/и (vydavát' ~/i) to
issue a duplicate
делать ~/ю (délat' ~/iu) to make
a copy
заверить ~/ю (zaverít' ~/iu) to
certify a copy
засвидетельствованная ~
(zasvidétel'stvovannaia ~)
attested copy
засвидетельствование ~/и
(zasvidétel'stvovanie ~/i)
attestation of a copy
ксероксная ~ (kséroksnaia ~)
xerox copy
легализованная ~
(legalizóvannaia ~) legalized
copy
многочисленные ~/и
(mnogochíslennye ~/i) multiple
copies
новая ~ (nóvaia ~) fresh copy
отмеченная ~ (otméchennaia ~)
red-lined copy
официальная ~ (ofitsiál'naia ~)
official copy
печатная ~ (pechátnaia ~)
printed copy
полностью оформленные ~/и
(pólnost'iu ofórmlennye ~/i)
fully executed copies
представить светописные ~/и
чертежей (predstávit'
svetopísnye ~/i chertezhéi) to
submit blueprints
прилагаемая ~ (prilagáemaia ~)
enclosed copy
приложить ~/ю (prilozhít' ~/iu)
to append a copy
светописная ~ (svetopísnaia ~)
blueprint
снимать ~/ю (snimát' ~/iu) to
take a copy
снятие ~/й (sniátie ~/i)
duplication
согласно прилагаемой ~/и
(soglásno prilagáemoi ~/i) as
per enclosed copy
точная ~ (tóchnaia ~) exact copy

фотостатическая ~
(fotostatícheskaia ~)
photostatic copy
чистовая ~ (chistováia ~) fair
copy
экземпляр ~/и (ekzempliár ~/i)
copy
~ векселя (~ vékselia) copy of a
bill, note
~ документа (~ dokumenta) copy
of a document
~ заявки (~ zaiávki) duplicate
of an application
~ квитанции (~ kvitántsii)
duplicate of a receipt
~ коносамента (~ konosaménta)
duplicate of a bill of lading
~ контракта (~ kontrákta)
counterpart of a contract
~ патента (~ paténta) copy of a
patent
~ письма (~ pis'má) copy of a
letter
~ протокола собрания (~
protokóla sobrániia) copy of
minutes of a meeting
~ счёта-фактуры (~ schióta-
faktúry) copy of an invoice
~ через копирку (~ chérez
kopirku) carbon copy
~ чертежа (~ chertezhá) print of
a drawing
Корзинка (korzínka) *f.* basket
плетённая ~ (pletiónnaia ~)
wicker ~
упаковочная ~ (upakóvochnaia ~)
crate
~ валют (~ valiút) ~ of
currencies
~ СДР (~ sdr) SDR {currencies
constituting Special Drawing
Rights}
Корм (korm) *m.* fodder
Кормовой (kormovói) *adj.* fodder
Коробейник (korobéinik) *m.* peddler
Коробк/а (koróbk/a) *f.* box, carton,
case
деревянная ~ (dereviánnaia ~)
wooden case
жестяная ~ (zhestiánaia ~) tin
box
за ~/у (za ~/u) per carton
картонная ~ (kartónnaia ~)
cardboard box
подарочная ~ (podárochnaia ~)
gift box

прочная ~ (próchnaia ~) heavy
duty box
складная ~ (skladnáia ~)
collapsible carton
стандартная ~ (standártnaia ~)
standard carton
Корпоративный (korporatívnyi) *adj.*
corporate
Корпораци/я (korporátsi/ia) *f.*
corporate body, corporation
акционерская ~ (aktsionérskaia
~) stock corporation
государственная ~
(gosudárstvennaia ~) public
corporation
дирекция ~/и (diréktsiia ~/i)
board of directors of a corporation
единоличная ~ (edinolíchnaia ~)
sole corporation
иностранная ~ (inostránnaia ~)
foreign corporation
многонациональная ~
(mnogonatsionál'naia ~)
multinational corporation
налог на ~/ю (nalóg na ~/iu)
corporate tax
налог с доходов ~/й (nalóg s
dokhódov ~/i) x corporate income
tax
печать ~/и (pechát' ~/i)
corporate seal
промышленная ~ (promýshlennaia
~) industrial corporation
секретарь ~/и (sekretár' ~/i)
corporate secretary
транснациональная ~
(transnatsionál'naia ~)
transnational corporation
устав ~/и (ustáv ~/i) charter of
a corporation {articles}
частная ~ (chástnaia ~)
privately-held corporation
Коррективы (korrektívy) *pl.*
corrective amendments
Корректировать (korrektírovat') *v.*
to adjust
~ цены (~ tsény) ~ prices
Корректировк/а (korrektiróvk/a) *f.*
adjustment, correction
статическая ~ (statícheskaia ~)
statistical adjustment
~ на сезонные колебания (~ na
sezónnye kolebániia) seasonal
adjustment
Корректировочный
(korrektiróvochnyi) *adj.* adjustment

Корректирующий (korrektirúiushchii) *adj.* correcting

Корреляционный (korreliatsiónnyi) *adj.* correlative

Корреспондент (korrespondént) *m.* correspondent
  иностранный ~ (inostránnyi ~) foreign ~
  ~ газеты (~ gazéty) newspaper ~

Корреспондентский (korrespondéntskii) *adj.* correspondent

Корреспонденци/я (korrespondéntsi/ia) *f.* correspondence
  входящая ~ (vkhodiáshchaia ~) incoming ~
  заказная ~ (zakaznáia ~) registered mail
  исходящая ~ (iskhodiáshchaia ~) outgoing ~
  коммерческая ~ (kommércheskaia ~) commercial ~
  обмен ~/ей (obmén ~/ei) exchange of ~
  почтовая ~ (pochtóvaia ~) postal ~
  предварительная ~ (predvarítel'naia ~) preliminary ~

Коррупция (korrúptsiia) *f.* corruption, venality

Котирование (kotírovanie) *n.* quoting
  ~ цен (~ tsen) ~ of prices

Котировать (kotírovat') *v.* to quote {price, rate}

Котироваться (kotírovat'sia) *v.* to be quoted {on exchange, etc.}

Котировк/а (kotiróvk/a) *f.* quotation
  биржевая ~ (birzheváia ~) exchange ~
  валютная ~ (valiútnaia ~) foreign exchange ~
  дополнительная ~ (dopolnítel'naia ~) additional ~
  начальная ~ (nachál'naia ~) starting ~
  номинальная ~ (nominál'naia ~) nominal ~
  окончательная ~ (okonchátel'naia ~) final ~
  ориентировочная ~ (orientiróvochnaia ~) specimen ~
  официальная ~ (ofitsiál'naia ~) official ~

  пересмотренная ~ (peresmótrennaia ~) revised ~
  подробная ~ (podróbnaia ~) detailed ~
  позиционная ~ (pozitsiónnaia ~) itemized ~
  предыдущая ~ (predydúshchaia ~) previous ~
  приложенная ~ (prilózhennaia ~) enclosed ~
  примерная ~ (primérnaia ~) pro forma ~
  рассмотреть ~/у (rassmotrét' ~/u) to consider a ~
  рыночная ~ (rýnochnaia ~) market ~
  твёрдая ~ (tviórdaia ~) firm ~
  ~ акций (~ áktsii) stock ~
  ~ курсов (~ kúrsov) exchange rate ~
  ~ на товары с немедленной сдачей (~ na továry s nemédlennoi sdáchei) spot market ~
  ~ при закрытии биржи (~ pri zakrýtii bírzhi) closing ~
  ~ при открытии биржа (~ pri otkrýtii bírzha) opening ~
  ~ цен (~ tsen) ~ of prices

Котировочный (kotiróvochnyi) *adj.* quoted

Коэффициент (koeffitsiént) *m.* coefficient, factor, ratio
  весовой ~ (vesovói ~) weight coefficient
  общий ~ (óbshchii ~) total rate
  расчётный ~ (raschiótnyi ~) design ratio
  ~ валовой прибыли (~ valovói príbyli) gross profit ratio
  ~ выработки (~ výrabotki) output factor
  ~ доходности (~ dokhódnosti) earnings ratio
  ~ загрузки (~ zagrúzki) coefficient of loading
  ~ затрат (~ zatrát) input coefficient
  ~ использования (~ ispól'zovaniia) utilization ratio
  ~ ликвидности (~ likvídnosti) liquidity ratio
  ~ мощности (~ móshchnosti) capacity rate
  ~ надёжности (~ nadiózhnosti) reliability index

~ окупаемости (~ okupáemosti)
return ratio
~ отдачи (~ otdáchi) output
factor
~ полезного действия (~
poléznogo déistviia) coefficient
of performance
~ потерь (~ potér') loss factor
~ продуктивности (~
produktívnosti) coefficient of
productivity
~ рентабельности (~
rentábel'nosti) net profit ratio
Краж/а (krázh/a) f. larceny, theft
~ со взломом (~ so vzlómom)
burglary {breaking and entering}
Кран (kran) m. crane
аварийный ~ (avaríinyi ~)
wrecking ~
береговой ~ (beregovói ~) shore
~
грузоподъёмный ~
(gruzopod"iómnyi ~) lifting ~
доковый ~ (dókovyi ~) dock ~
контейнерный ~ (kontéinernyi ~)
container ~
монтажный ~ (montázhnyi ~)
construction ~
палубный ~ (pálubnyi ~) deck-
mounted ~
передвижной ~ (peredvizhnói ~)
mobile ~
плавучий ~ (plavúchii ~)
floating ~
подъёмный ~ (pod"iómnyi ~)
hoisting ~
портальный ~ (portál'nyi ~)
gantry ~
Краска (kráska) f. dye, paint
антикоррозионная ~
(antikorroziónnaia ~) rust-proof
paint
быстровысыхающая ~
(bystrovysykháiushchaia ~)
quick-drying paint
водостойкая ~ (vodostóikaia ~)
waterproof paint
несмываемая ~ (nesmyváemaia ~)
indelible paint
Краткосрочный (kratkosróchnyi) adj.
short term
Крах (krakh) m. bankruptcy,
collapse
финансовый ~ (finánsovyi ~)
financial collapse
~ валюты (~ valiúty) collapse of
currency

~ кредитной системы (~ kredítnoi
sistémy) collapse of credit
system
~ фирмы (~ fírmy) bankruptcy of
a firm
~ фондовой биржи (~ fóndovoi
bírzhi) stock market crash
Кредит (kredít) m. credit, lending,
lending facility
автоматически возобновляемый ~
(avtomatícheski vozobnovliáemyi
~) revolving credit
акцептно-рамбурсный ~
(aktséptno-rámbursnyi ~)
reimbursement credit
акцептный ~ (aktséptnyi ~)
acceptance credit
беспроцентный ~ (besprotséntnyi
~) interest-free credit
бессрочный ~ (bessróchnyi ~)
unlimited {term} credit
блокированный ~ (blokírovannyi
~) blocked credit
блокировать ~/ы (blokírovat'
~/y) to block credit
в счёт ~/a (v schiót ~/a)
against credit
валюта ~/a (valiúta ~/a)
currency of credit
валютный ~ (valiútnyi ~) foreign
exchange credit
вексельный ~ (véksel'nyi ~)
paper credit
взаимный ~ (vzaímnyi ~)
reciprocal credit facilities
внешнеторговый ~
(vneshnetorgóvyi ~) foreign
trade credit
возмещение ~/a (vozmeshchénie
~/a) repayment of credit
возобновлять ~ (vozobnovliát' ~)
to renew credit
выдача ~/a (výdacha ~/a)
issuance of credit
гарантийный ~ (garantíinyi ~)
guarantee credit
гарантировать ~ (garantírovat'
~) to guarantee credit
гарантия ~/a (garántiia ~/a)
guarantee of credit
государственный ~
(gosudárstvennyi ~) government
credit
давать в ~ (davát' v ~) to lend
денежный ~ (dénezhnyi ~)
monetary credit

дешёвый ~ (deshióvyi ~) cheap credit {low interest rate}
дисконтный ~ (diskóntnyi ~) discount credit
длительный ~ (dlítel'nyi ~) extended credit
долгосрочный ~ (dolgosróchnyi ~) long term credit
за счёт ~/a (za schiót ~/a) on account of credit
закрывать ~ (zakryvát' ~) to withdraw credit
замороженный ~ (zamorózhennyi ~) frozen credit
заявка на ~ (zaiávka na ~) credit application
злоупотребление ~/ом (zloupotreblénie ~/om) abuse of credit
значительный ~ (znachítel'nyi ~) significant credit
инвестиционный ~ (investitsiónnyi ~) investment credit
иностранный ~ (inostránnyi ~) foreign credit
ипотечный ~ (ipotéchnyi ~) credit on mortgage
используемый в случае необходимости (ispol'zúemyi v slúchae neobkhodímosti) stand-by credit
источник ~/a (istóchnik ~/a) source of credit
исчерпанный ~ (ischérpannyi ~) exhausted credit
коммерческий ~ (kommércheskii ~) commercial credit
компенсационный ~ (kompensatsiónnyi ~) back-to-back credit
контокоррентный ~ (kontokorréntnyi ~) current account credit
краткосрочный ~ (kratkosróchnyi ~) short term credit
лишение ~/a (lishénie ~/a) withdrawal of credit
ломбардный ~ (lombárdnyi ~) collateral credit
льготный ~ (l'gótnyi ~) preferential credit
максимальный ~ (maksimál'nyi ~) maximum credit
маржа по ~/y (márzha po ~/u) margin of credit

межгосударственный ~ (mezhgosudárstvennyi ~) interstate credit
международный ~ (mezhdunaródnyi ~) international credit
наличный ~ (nalíchnyi ~) cash credit
начальный ~ (nachál'nyi ~) initial credit
недостаток ~/a (nedostátok ~/a) lack of credit
необеспеченный ~ (neobespéchennyi ~) unsecured credit
неограниченный ~ (neograníchennyi ~) unlimited {amount} credit
обеспеченный ~ (obespéchennyi ~) secured credit
общество взаимного ~/a (óbshchestvo vzaímnogo ~/a) credit union
объём ~/a (ob"ióm ~/a) volume of credit
ограничение ~/a (ogranichénie ~/a) credit restriction
онкольный ~ (onkól'nyi ~) on-call credit
остаток ~/a (ostátok ~/a) credit balance
отказаться от ~/a (otkazát'sia ot ~/a) to refuse credit
открытый ~ (otkrýtyi ~) open credit
плата за ~ (pláta za ~) loan charge
платежи по ~/y (platezhí po ~/u) credit payments
погашать ~ (pogashát' ~) to repay credit
погашение ~/a (pogashénie ~/a) repayment of credit
поддерживать ~/ом (poddérzhivat' ~/om) to support with credit
подтоварный ~ (podtovárnyi ~) commodity credit
покупать в ~ (pokupát' v ~) to buy on credit
покупка в ~ (pokúpka v ~) credit purchase
потребительский ~ (potrebítel'skii ~) consumer credit
превышать ~ (prevyshát' ~) to exceed credit, to overdraw an account

предельный ~ (predél'nyi ~)
marginal credit
предлагать ~ (predlagát' ~) to
offer credit
пролонгировать ~ (prolongírovat'
~) to prolong credit
просроченный ~ (prosróchennyi ~)
overdue credit
процентные ставки по ~/ам
(protséntnye stávki po ~/am)
interest rates for credit
прямой ~ (priamói ~) direct
credit
размер ~/a (razmér ~/a) extent
of credit
разовый ~ (rázovyi ~) non-
installment credit
рамбурсный ~ (rámbursnyi ~)
reimbursement credit
распределение банковских ~/ов
(raspredelénie bánkovskikh ~/ov)
allocation of bank credits
распределять ~/ы (raspredeliát'
~/y) to allocate credits
расширение ~/a (rasshirénie ~/a)
expansion of credit
резервный ~ (rezérvnyi ~)
reserve credit
риск при продаже в ~ (risk pri
prodázhe v ~) risk attendant to
credit sales
рынок ~/a (rýnok ~/a) credit
market
самоликвидирующийся ~
(samolikvidíruiushchiisia ~)
self- liquidating credit
свинговый ~ (svíngovyi ~) swing
credit
связанный ~ (sviázannyi ~) tide
credit
смешанный ~ (sméshannyi ~) mixed
credit
сокращение ~/a (sokrashchérie
~/a) credit reduction
спрос на ~ (spros na ~) credit
demand
среднесрочный ~ (srednesróchnyi
~) intermediate term credit
срок ~/a (srok ~/a) credit term
срочный ~ (sróchnyi ~) term
credit
стеснение ~/ов (stesnénie ~/ov)
credit squeeze
стоимость ~/a (stóimost' ~/a)
cost of credit
страхование ~/a (strakhovánie
~/a) credit insurance

сумма ~/a (súmma ~/a) amount of
credit
товарный ~ (továrnyi ~)
commodity credit
торговый ~ (torgóvyi ~)
mercantile credit
условия ~/a (uslóviia ~/a)
credit terms
фирменный ~ (fírmennyi ~)
company credit
экспортный ~ (éksportnyi ~)
export credit
Кредит-авизо (kredít-avízo) n.
credit advice
Кредитно-денежн/ый (kredítno-
dénezhn/yi) adj. credit and
monetary
~/ая политика (~/aia polítika)
credit and monetary policy
Кредитный (kredítnyi) adj. credit
Кредитовани/е (kreditováni/e) n.
crediting, lending
банковское ~ (bánkovskoe ~) bank
advance
валютное ~ (valiútnoe ~) foreign
exchange lending
взаимное ~ (vzaímnoe ~)
reciprocal credit arrangement
целевое ~ (tselevóe ~) targeted
lending
Кредитовать (kreditovát') v. to
extend credit
Кредитовый (kredítovyi) adj. credit
{accounting}
Кредитор (kreditór) m. creditor
главный ~ (glávnyi ~) principal
~
генеральный ~ (generál'nyi ~)
general ~
необеспеченный ~
(neobespéchennyi ~) unsecured ~
обычный ~ (obýchnyi ~) ordinary
~
привилегированный ~
(privilegírovannyi ~) preferred
~
рассчитываться с ~/ами
(rasschítyvat'sia s ~/ami) to
settle) with ~s
совокупный ~ (sovokúpnyi ~)
joint ~
частный ~ (chástnyi ~) private
lender
~ по закладной (~ po zakladnói)
mortgage ~

Кредитоспособност/ь
(kreditosposóbnost/') *f.* credit
worthiness, solvency
 гарантия ~/и (garántiia ~/i)
 guarantee of solvency
 обследование ~/и (obslédovanie
 ~/i) credit investigation
 оценка ~/и (otsénka ~/i) credit
 rating
Кредитоспособный (kreditosposóbnyi)
adj. credit-worthy, solvent
Крепить (krepít') *v.* to bind, to
brace, to fasten, to strap
 ~ болтами (~ boltámi) to bolt
 ~ верёвками (~ verióvkami) to
 lash
 ~ винтами (~ vintámi) to screw
 ~ гвоздями (~ gvozdiámi) to nail
 ~ проволокой (~ próvolokoi) to
 bind with wire
 ~ тросом (~ trósom) to bind with
 cable
Креплени/е (krepléni/e) *n.* binding,
bracing, fastening, strapping
Кривая (kriváia) *f.* curve {graphic}
 ~ предложения (~ predlozhéniia)
 supply ~
 ~ спроса (~ sprósa) demand ~
Кризис (krízis) *m.* crisis,
depression
 валютно-финансовый ~ (valiútno-
 finánsovyi ~) monetary and
 financial crisis
 валютный ~ (valiútnyi ~)
 monetary crisis
 вызывать ~ (vyzyvát' ~) to make
 critical
 денежно-кредитный ~ (dénezhno-
 kredítnyi ~) monetary and credit
 crisis
 денежный ~ (dénezhnyi ~)
 monetary crisis
 затяжной ~ (zatiazhnói ~)
 protracted crisis
 международный ~ (mezhdunaródnyi
 ~) international crisis
 мировой ~ (mirovói ~) world
 crisis
 острый ~ (óstryi ~) acute
 depression
 предотвращать ~
 (predotvrashchát' ~) to avert a
 crisis
 промышленный ~ (promýshlennyi ~)
 industrial crisis
 циклический ~ (tsiklícheskii ~)
 cyclical depression

экономический ~ (ekonomícheskii
~) economic crisis
~ платёжного баланса (~
platiózhnogo balánsa) balance of
payments crisis
Критери/й (kritéri/i) *m.* criterion
 единственный ~ (edínstvennyi ~)
 sole ~
 общий ~ (óbshchii ~) general ~
 основные ~/и (osnovnýe ~/i)
 basic criteria
 оценочный ~ (otsénochnyi ~)
 estimation ~
 соответствующие ~
 (sootvétstvuiushchie ~/i)
 applicable criteria
 экономический ~ (ekonomícheskii
 ~) economic ~
 ~ браковки (~ brakóvki)
 rejection ~
 ~/и качества (~/i káchestva)
 quality criteria
 ~/и надёжности (~/i
 nadiózhnosti) reliability
 criteria
 ~ патентоспособности (~
 patentosposóbnosti) criteria of
 patentability
Критический (kritícheskii) *adj.*
critical
Круги (krugí) *pl.* circles, quarters
 деловые ~ (delovýe ~) business
 circles
 коммерческие ~ (kommércheskie ~)
 commercial circles
 монополистические ~
 (monopolistícheskie ~) monopoly
 interests
 официальные ~ (ofitsiál'nye ~)
 official circles
 финансовые ~ (finánsovye ~)
 financial circles
 широкие ~ (shirókie ~) broad
 sections
Крупногабаритный (krupnogabarítnyi)
adj. over-sized
Крупномасштабный
(krupnomasshtábnyi) *adj.* large-
scale
Крупноформатный (krupnoformátnyi)
adj. large-format
Крупный (krúpnyi) *adj.* large,
major, principle, substantial
Крушение (krushénie) *n.* crash,
wreck
 ~ судна (~ súdna) shipwreck

потерпеть ~ (poterpét' ~) to be
wrecked
Крышка (krýshka) f. cover, lid
   металлическая ~ (metallícheskaia
   ~) metal cover
   пластмассовая ~ (plastmássovaia
   ~) plastic lid
   ~ люка (~ liúka) hatch cover
   ~ трюма (~ triúma) hatch cover
   of the hold {ship}
Крюк (kriuk) m. hook
   грузовой ~ (gruzovói ~) load ~
Ксерокс (kséroks) m. xerox
Кубатура (kubatúra) f. cubic
capacity
   общая ~ (óbshchaia ~) total
   cubic volume
Куль (kul') sack
Кумулятивный (kumuliatívnyi) adj.
cumulative
Кумуляция (kumuliátsiia) f.
accumulation
Купец (kupéts) m. merchant, trader
Купить (kupít') v. to buy, to
purchase
Купленный (kúplennyi) adj.
purchased
Купля (kúplia) f. purchase
Купл/я-продаж/а (kúpl/ia-prodázh/a)
f. purchase and sale
   договор ~/и-~/и (dogovór ~/i-~/i)
   buy-sell agreement
Купон (kupón) m. coupon, warrant
   отрывать ~ (otryvát' ~) to
   detach a coupon
   получать деньги по ~/у
   (poluchát' dén'gi po ~/u) to
   redeem a warrant
   процентный ~ (protséntnyi ~)
   interest warrant
Купчая (kúpchaia) f. bill of sale,
conveyance
Купюра (kupiúra) f. denomination
   ~ банкноты) (~ banknóty) ~ of a
   bank note
Курс (kurs) m. course, rate
   биржевой ~ (birzhevói ~) market
   share price
   благоприятный ~ (blagopriiátnyi
   ~) favorable rate of exchange
   бюллетень ~/а ценных бумаг на
   бирже (biulletén' ~/a tsénnykh
   bumág na bírzhe) stock exchange
   list
   валютный ~ (valiútnyi ~)
   currency exchange rate

взаимный ~ (vzaímnyi ~)
reciprocal rate
внутренний ~ (vnútrennii ~)
domestic rate {of exchange on
two tier system}
выкупной ~ (vykupnói ~)
redemption price
высокий ~ (vysókii ~) high rate
двойной ~ (dvoinói ~) two tier
exchange rate
денежный ~ (dénezhnyi ~)
monetary exchange rate
дополнительный ~ (dopolnítel'nyi
~) supplementary rate
единый ~ (edínyi ~) unitary rate
жёсткий ~ (zhióstkii ~) tough
policy
завершение ~/а (zaveршénie ~/a)
completion of a course
{training, university}
заканчивать ~ (zakánchivat' ~)
to complete a course
заключительный ~
(zakliuchítel'nyi ~) closing
rate
изменение ~/а (izmenénie ~/a)
change in exchange rate
колебание ~/а валюты (kolebánie
~/a valiúty) fluctuation in the
currency exchange rate
колебание ~/ов валют к рублю
(kolebánie ~/ov valiút k rubliú)
fluctuation in the exchange rate
against the ruble
колеблющийся ~
(koлébliushchiisia ~)
fluctuating exchange rate
котировка ~/ов (kotiróvka ~/ov)
quotation of exchange rates
максимальный ~ (maksimál'nyi ~)
maximum rate
меняющийся ~ (meniáiushchiisia
~) varying rate
механизм валютных ~/ов
(mekhanízm valiútnykh ~/ov)
exchange rate mechanism
минимальный ~ (minimál'nyi ~)
minimum rate
номинальный ~ (nominál'nyi ~)
nominal exchange rate
обмен по ~/у (obmén po ~/u)
trade at the going rate
обменный ~ (obménnyi ~)
conversion rate
обменивать по официальному ~/у
(obménivat' po ofitsiál'nomu

~/u) to exchange at the official
rate
обязательный ~ (obiazátel'nyi ~)
compulsory exchange rate,
required course
отклонение судна от ~/а
(otklonénie súdna ot ~/a)
deviation of a vessel from
course
отклоняться от ~/а
(otkloniát'sia ot ~/a) to
deviate from course
официальный ~ (ofitsiál'nyi ~)
official exchange rate
падение ~/а (padénie ~/a) fall
in the exchange rate
падение ~/а ценных бумаг
(padénie ~/a tsénnykh bumág)
drop in securities prices
паритетный ~ (paritétnyi ~)
exchange at par
перекрещивающиеся ~/ы
(perekréshchivaiushchiesia ~/y)
cross rates
перерасчётный ~ (pereraschiótnyi
~) rate of conversion
по ~/у ... (po ~/u ...) at the
rate of ...
по номинальному ~/у (po
nominál'nomu ~/u) at par
поддерживать ~ искусственно
(poddérzhivat' ~ iskusstvenno)
to artifically support the
exchange rate, to peg the market
полноценный ~ (polnotsénnyi ~)
full value rate
последовательный ~
(posledovátel'nyi ~) consistent
course
привязанный ~ (priviázannyi ~)
pegged rate
расчётный ~ (raschiótnyi ~)
settlement rate
рост ~/а (rost ~/a) growth of
the exchange rate
рыночный ~ (rýnochnyi ~) market
rate
свободный ~ (svobódnyi ~) free
exchange rate
сокращённый ~ (sokrashchiónnyi
~) short course {of study}
спец- ~ (spets- ~) special
course {of study}
справочный ~ (správochnyi ~)
posted rate
средний ~ (srédnii ~) mean rate
of exchange

стабилизация ~/а валюты
(stabilizátsiia ~/a valiúty)
stabilization of exchange rates
стандартный ~ (standártnyi ~)
standard rate
существующий ~
(sushchestvúiushchii ~) going
rate
урегулирование валютного ~/а
(uregulírovanie valiútnogo ~/a)
regulation of the currency
exchange rate
условный ~ (uslóvnyi ~)
conditional rate
устойчивый ~ (ustóichivyi ~)
stable exchange rate
учётный ~ (uchiótnyi ~) discount
rate
фиксированный ~ (fiksírovannyi
~) fixed rate
центральный ~ (tsentrál'nyi ~)
central bank rate of exchange
экономический ~ (ekonomícheskii
~) economic policy
эмиссионный ~ (emissiónnyi ~)
rate of issue
~ акций (~ áktsii) share price
~ выпуска (~ výpuska) rate of
issue
~ дня (~ dnia) exchange rate of
the day
~ дня фактического платежа (~
dnia faktícheskogo platezhá)
exchange rate as of the day of
actual payment
~ доллара (~ dóllara) exchange
rate of the dollar
~ корабля (~ korabliá) ship's
course
~ по сделкам "спот" (~ po
sdélkam spot) spot rate
~ почтовых переводов (~
pochtóvykh perevódov) mail
transfer rate
~ ценных бумаг (~ tsénnykh
bumág) securities rate
~ чёрного рынка (~ chiórnogo
rýnka) black market rate
Куртаж (kurtázh) *m.* courtage
{brokerage fee}
Курьер (kur'ér) *m.* courier
    дипломатический ~
    (diplomatícheskii ~) diplomatic

Кустарн/ый (kustárn/yi) *adj.*
cottage, handicraft

~/ая промышленность (~/aia promýshlennost') cottage industry

Л

Лаборатория (laboratóriia) f. laboratory
    исследовательская ~ (issledovátel'skaia ~) research ~
    совместная ~ (sovméstnaia ~) joint ~
    специально оборудованная ~ (spetsiál'no oborúdovannaia ~) specially equipped ~
Лабораторный (laboratórnyi) adj. laboratory
Лавка (lávka) f. shop, street-stand market
Лаж (lázh) m. premium
    ~ на золото (~ na zóloto) ~ on gold
Лайнер (láiner) m. airliner, oceanliner
Легализация (legalizátsiia) f. certification, legalization
    консульская ~ (kónsul'skaia ~) consular certification
Легализованный (legalizóvannyi) adj. legalized
Легальный (legál'nyi) adj. legal
Легко (legkó) adv. easily, lightly
    ~ находить сбыт (~ nakhodít' sbyt) to readily find a market
    ~ продаваться (~ prodavát'sia) to sell readily
Легковесный (legkovésnyi) adj. light {of weight}
Легковоспламеняющийся (legkovosplameniáiushchiisia) adj. highly inflammable
Легкоповреждаемый (legkopovrezhdáemyi) adj. highly fragile
Легкопортящийся (legkoportiáshchiisia) adj. highly perishable
Легкореализуемый (legkorealizúemyi) adj. marketable
Лежалый (lezhályi) adj. stale
Лент/а (lént/a) f. band, belt, ribbon
    бумажная ~ (bumázhnaia ~) paper ribbon

клейкая ~ (kléikaia ~) adhesive tape
крепить металлической ~/ой (krepít' metallícheskoi ~/oi) to fasten with a metal band
магнитная ~ (magnítnaia ~) magnetic tape
металлическая ~ (metallícheskaia ~) metal band
нейлоновая ~ (neilónovaia ~) nylon band
упаковочная ~ (upakóvochnaia ~) packing tape
Лесовоз (lesovóz) m. timber-hauling vessel
Лёгкий (liógkii) adj. light {of weight}
Либерализация (liberalizátsiia) f. liberalization
    ~ внешнеэкономических связей (~ vneshneekonomícheskikh sviázei) ~ of trade ties
    ~ импорта (~ ímporta) import ~
    ~ торговли (~ torgóvli) trade ~
    ~ экономики (~ ekonómiki) economic ~
Либор (líbor) m. LIBOR {London Inter-Bank Offering Rate}
Лизинг (lízing) m. leasing
Лизинговый (lizingóvyi) adj. leasing
Ликвидационный (likvidatsiónnyi) adj. liquidation
Ликвидаци/я (likvidátsi/ia) f. liquidation
    вынужденная ~ (výnuzhdennaia ~) forced ~
    добровольная ~ (dobrovól'naia ~) voluntary ~, winding-up
    полная ~ (pólnaia ~) complete ~
    принудительная ~ (prinudítel'naia ~) compulsory ~ {court- ordered}
    фактическая ~ (faktícheskaia ~) actual ~
    частичная ~ (chastíchnaia ~) partial ~
    ~ агентства (~ agéntstva) dissolution of an agency
    ~ долгов (~ dolgóv) settlement of debts
    ~ запасов (~ zapásov) inventory ~
    ~ компании (~ kompánii) winding up of a company
    ~ оборудования (~ oborúdovaniia) retirement of equipment

~ сделок (~ sdélok) settlement on an exchange
~ совместного предприятия (~ sovméstnogo predpriiátiia) ~ of a joint venture
~ товарищества (~ továrishchestva) dissolution of a partnership
~ убытков (~ ubýtkov) settlement of losses
~ фирмы (~ fírmy) dissolution of a firm
Ликвидированный (likvidírovannyi) adj. liquidated
Ликвидировать (likvidírovat') v. to liquidate
Ликвидност/ь (likvídnost/') f. liquidity
  избыточная ~ (izbýtochnaia ~) excess ~
  коэффициент ~/и (koeffitsiént ~/i) ~ ratio
  международная ~ (mezhdunaródnaia ~) international ~
  на базе ~/и (na báze ~/i) on a net ~ basis
  общая ~ (óbshchaia ~) overall ~
  ограниченная ~ (ograníchennaia ~) limited ~
  официальная ~ (ofitsiál'naia ~) official ~
  степень ~/и (stépen' ~/i) degree of ~
  ~ активов (~ aktívov) ~ of assets
Ликвидный (likvídnyi) adj. liquid {financial, not physical}
Ликвиды (likvídy) pl. liquid assets
  валютные ~ (valiútnye ~) liquid foreign exchange
  международные ~ (mezhdunaródnye ~) international liquid assets
Лимит (limít) m. limit, line
  валютный ~ (valiútnyi ~) foreign exchange quota
  кредитный ~ (kredítnyi ~) line of credit
  превышение кредитного ~/а (prevyshénie kredítnogo ~/a) credit overdraft
  превышать ~ (prevyshát' ~) to exceed the limit
  устанавливать ~ (ustanávlivat' ~) to fix a limit
Лимитировать (limitírovat') v. to limit

Лимитируемый (limitíruemyi) adj. limited
Лимитный (limítnyi) adj. limit
Линейный (linéinyi) adj. line, linear
Лини/я (líni/ia) f. line, service
  автобусная ~ (avtóbusnaia ~) bus line
  автоматическая ~ (avtomatícheskaia ~) automated service
  береговая ~ (beregováia ~) coastline
  быстропереналаживаемая поточная ~ (bystroperenalázhivaemaia potóchnaia ~) rapidly readjustable production line
  воздушная ~ (vozdúshnaia ~) airline
  воздушная, внутренняя ~ (vozdúshnaia, vnútrenniaia ~) domestic airline
  грузовая ~ (gruzováia ~) freightline
  грузовая судоходная ~ (gruzováia sudokhódnaia ~) overland freightline
  железнодорожная ~ (zheleznodorózhnaia ~) railway line
  контейнерная ~ (kontéinernaia ~) container line
  конференциальная ~ (konferentsiál'naia ~) conference line
  кругосветная контейнерная ~ (krugosvétnaia kontéinernaia ~) world-wide container line
  магистральная ~ (magistrál'naia ~) principal line
  малозагруженная транспортная ~ (malozagrúzhennaia transportnaia ~) low density transport service
  междугородная автобусная ~ (mezhdugoródnaia avtóbusnaia ~) inter-city busline
  нерегулярная транспортная ~ (nereguliárnaia tránsportnaia ~) unscheduled service
  опытная ~ (ópytnaia ~) experimental line
  пароходная ~ (parokhódnaia ~) steamship line
  поточная ~ (potóchnaia ~) production line
  причальная ~ (prichál'naia ~) berthage

регулярная ~ (reguliárnaia ~)
regular service
регулярная ~ воздушного
транспорта (reguliárnaia ~
vozdúshnogo tránsporta) regular
air service
смешанная ~ (sméshannaia ~)
joint line
судоходная ~ (sudokhódnaia ~)
shipping line
телефонная ~ (telefónnaia ~)
telephone line
транзитная ~ (tranzítnaia ~)
transit route
транспортная ~ (tránsportnaia ~)
transport service
транспортная ~ с челночным
движением (tránsportnaia ~ s
chelnóchnym dvizhéniem) shuttle
service
частная транспортная ~
(chástnaia tránsportnaia ~)
private transport service
экспериментальная ~
(eksperimentál'naia ~)
experimental line
~ воздушного транспорта (~
vozdúshnogo tránsporta)
scheduled air route
~ воздушного транспорта общего
пользования (~ vozdúshnogo
tránsporta óbshchego
pól'zovaniia) common air carrier
~ между портами (~ mézhdu
pórtami) shipping line
~ сборки (~ sbórki) assembly
line
~ скорых перевозок (~ skórykh
perevózok) express line
Лист (list) *m.* list, piece of
paper, sheet
вкладной ~ (vkladnói ~)
supplementary page
заглавный ~ (zaglávnyi ~) title
page
закладной ~ (zakladnói ~)
mortgage deed
исполнительный ~ (ispolnítel'nyi
~) writ of execution
калькуляционный ~
(kal'kuliatsiónnyi ~) cost sheet
обёрточный ~ (obiórtochnyi ~)
wrapper sheet
рабочий ~ (rabóchii ~) work
sheet
расчётный ~ (raschiótnyi ~)
payroll

тальманский ~ (tál'manskii ~)
tally sheet
титульный ~ (títul'nyi ~) title
page
упаковочный ~ (upakóvochnyi ~)
packing list
упаковочный в двух экземплярах
(upakóvochnyi v dvukh
ekzempliárakh) duplicate packing
list
Листов/ка (listóv/ka) *f.* handbill,
leaflet
~/ки, раздаваемые на улице
(~/ki, razdaváemye na úlitse)
handbills given out on the
street
распространение ~/ок
(rasprostranénie ~/ok)
distribution of leaflets
распространять ~/ки
(rasprostraniát' ~/ki) to
distribute leaflets
Лихтер (líkhter) *m.* lighter
{stevedore barge}
выгружать на ~ (vygruzhát' na ~)
to lighter
доставлять на ~/е (dostavliát'
na ~/e) to deliver by ~
оплачивать ~ (opláchivat' ~) to
pay lighterage
подавать ~ (podavát' ~) to place
a lighter
плата за пользование ~/ом (pláta
za pól'zovanie ~/om) lighterage
{fee}
на ~/е (na ~/e) in a ~
франко ~ (fránko ~) ex-~
Лихтерный ~ (líkhternyi ~) *adj.*
lighter
Лихтеровк/а (likhteróvk/a) *f.*
lighterage
расходы по ~/е ~ {(raskhódy po
~/e) fees}
Лихтеровоз (likhterovóz) *m.* lighter
carrier
Лицевой (litsevói) *adj.* obverse {of
a coin, etc.}, personal
Лицензиар (litsenziár) *m.* licensor
ответственность ~/а
(otvétstvennost' ~/a) ~'s
liability
право собственности ~/а (právo
sóbstvennosti ~/a) ~'s ownership
right
Лицензиат (litsenziát) *m.* licensee
будущий ~ (búdushchii ~)
prospective ~

деятельность ~/а ~′
(déiatel'nost' ~/a) s operations
обязательства ~/а
(obiazátel'stva ~/a) ~'s
obligations
персонал ~/а (personál ~/a)
licensed personnel
~ исключительной лицензии (~
iskliuchítel'noi litsénzii)
exclusive ~
~ неисключительной лицензии (~
neiskliuchítel'noi litsénzii)
non-exclusive ~
Лицензионный (litsenziónnyi) adj.
license
Лицензировани/е (litsenzírovani/e)
n. licensing
взаимное ~ (vzaímnoe ~) mutual ~
договорное ~ (dogovórnoe ~)
contractual ~
законодательство о
принудительном ~/и
(zakonodátel'stvo o prinudítel'nom ~/i) compulsory ~
legislation
зарубежное ~ (zarubézhnoe ~)
overseas ~
меры по ~/ю (méry po ~/iu) ~
arrangements
объём ~/я (ob"ióm ~/ia) scope of
~
отечественное ~ (otéchestvennoe
~) domestic ~
пакетное ~ (pakétnoe ~) package
~
перекрёстное ~ (perekrióstnoe ~)
cross ~
принудительное ~ (prinudítel'noe
~) compulsory ~
программа ~/я (prográmma ~/ia) ~
program
проект ~/я (proékt ~/ia) license
project
эффективность ~/я (effektívnost'
~/ia) effectiveness of ~
приостанавливать ~
(priostanávlivat' ~) to suspend
~
~ ноу-хау (~ nóu-kháu) ~ of
know-how
~ патента (~ paténta) ~ of a
patent
~ промышленного образца (~
promýshlennogo obraztsá) ~ of an
industrial design

~ технологической информации (~
tekhnologícheskoi informátsii) ~
of technological information
~ товарного знака (~ továrnogo
znáka) ~ of a trademark
Лицензированный (litsenzírovannyi)
adj. licensed
Лицензировать (litsenzírovat') v.
to license
Лицензи/я (litsénzi/ia) f. license
активная ~ (aktívnaia ~) active
~
аннулирование ~/и
(annulírovananie ~/i) annulment
of a ~
аннулировать ~/ю (annulírovat'
~/iu) to annul a ~
безусловная ~ (bezuslóvnaia ~)
unconditional ~
беспатентная ~ (bespaténtnaia ~)
non-patent ~
взаимная ~ (vzaímnaia ~)
reciprocal ~
владелец ~/и (vladélets ~/i)
owner of a ~
выдавать ~/ю (vydavát' ~/iu) to
grant a ~
выдача ~/и (výdacha ~/i) grant
of a ~
выпуск продукции по ~/и (výpusk
prodúktsii po ~/i) production
under ~
генеральная ~ (generál'naia ~)
general ~
глобальная ~ (globál'naia ~)
global ~
дата предоставления ~/и (dáta
predostavléniia ~/i) date of
licensing
действительная ~
(deistvítel'naia ~) valid ~
действительность ~/и
(deistvítel'nost' ~/i) validity
of a ~
действующая на определённой
территории ~ (déistvuiushchaia
na opredeliónnoi territórii ~)
geographically limited ~
держатель ~/и (derzhátel' ~/i)
holder
дилер с ~/ей (díler s ~/ei)
licensed dealer
добровольная ~ (dobrovól'naia ~)
voluntary ~
договорная ~ (dogovórnaia ~)
contractual ~

дубликат ~/и (dublikát ~/i) copy
of a ~
закупка ~/и (zakúpka ~/i)
purchase of a ~
заявка на ~/ю (zaiávka na ~/iu)
application for a ~
изготовление по ~/и
(izgotovlénie po ~/i)
manufacture under ~
иметь ~/ю (imét' ~/iu) to have a
~
импортная ~ (ímportnaia ~)
import ~
исключительная ~
(iskliuchítel'naia ~) exclusive
~
комплексная ~ (kómpleksnaia ~)
package ~
неделимая ~ (nedelímaia ~)
indivisible ~
неисключительная ~
(neiskliuchítel'naia ~) non-
exclusive ~
не подлежащая передаче ~ (ne
podlezháshchaia peredáche ~)
non-transferrable ~
обратная ~ (obrátnaia ~)
feedback ~
общая ~ (óbshchaia ~) blanket ~
объём ~/и (ob"ióm ~/i) scope of
a ~
ограниченная ~ (ograníchennaia
~) limited ~
отзывать ~/ю (otzyvát' ~/iu) to
revoke a ~
отдел ~/й (otdél ~/i) ~
department
отказ в предоставлении ~/и
(otkáz v predostavlénii ~/i)
denial of a ~
открытая общая ~ (otkrýtaia
óbshchaia ~) open general ~
пассивная ~ (passívnaia ~)
passive ~
патентная ~ (paténtnaia ~) ~
under patent
перекрёстная ~ (perekrióstnaia
~) cross ~
плата за ~/ю (pláta za ~/iu) ~
fee
по ~/и (po ~/i) under ~
полная ~ (pólnaia ~) exclusive ~
получатель ~/и (poluchátel' ~/i)
recipient of a ~
получать ~/ю (poluchát' ~/iu) to
receive a ~

предмет ~/и (predmét ~/i)
subject of a ~
предоставление ~/и
(predostavlénie ~/i) concession
of a ~
предоставлять ~/ю
(predostavliát' ~/iu) to grant a
~
предоставлять ~/ю на
производство (predostavliát'
~/iu na proizvódstvo) to license
a production process
предоставлять ~/ю на технологию
(predostavliát' ~/iu na
tekhnológiiu) to license
technology
предусматривающая уплату роялти
~ (predusmátrivaiushchaia uplátu
róialti ~) royalty-bearing ~
прекращение действия ~/и
(prekrashchénie déistviia ~/i)
termination of a ~
признавать ~/ю недействительной
(priznavát' ~/iu nedeistvítel'-
noi) to hold a ~ invalid
принудительная ~
(prinudítel'naia ~) compulsory ~
приобретать ~/ю (priobretát'
~/iu) to obtain a ~
продаваемая ~ (prodaváemaia ~)
active ~
продавать ~/ю (prodavát' ~/iu)
to sell a ~
продлевать ~/ю (prodlevát' ~/iu)
to extend a ~
продукция по ~/и (prodúktsiia po
~/i) licensed product
производить по ~/и (proizvodít'
po ~/i) to produce under ~
простая ~ (prostáia ~) simple ~
регистрация ~/и (registrátsiia
~/i) registration of a ~
ретроактивная ~ (retroaktívnaia
~) retroactive ~
рынок ~/й (rýnok ~/i) ~ market
свободная ~ (svobódnaia ~) free
~
соглашение об обмене ~/ями
(soglashénie ob obméne ~/iami)
cross-licensing agreement
срок владения ~/ей (srok
vladéniia ~/ei) tenure of a ~
срок действия ~/и (srok
déistviia ~/i) term of ~
validity
субсидируемое ~ (subsidíruemoe
~) subsidized ~

таможенная ~ (tamózhennaia ~) customs ~

торговля ~/ями (torgóvlia ~/iami) trade in ~s

экспорт ~/й (éksport ~/i) export of ~s

экспортная ~ (éksportnaia ~) export ~

юридическое ~ (iuridícheskoe ~) legal ~

~ без права передачи (~ bez práva peredáchi) ~ without right of transfer

~ без уплаты роялти (~ bez upláty róialti) royalty-free ~

~ на ввоз (~ na vvoz) import ~

~ на вывоз (~ na vývoz) export ~

~ на зарубежное патентование (~ na zarubézhnoe patentovánie) ~ for foreign patent filing

~ на изобретение (~ na izobreténie) ~ foreign invention

~ на использование (~ na ispól'zovanie) operating ~

~ на использование изобретения (~ na ispól'zovanie izobreténiia) ~ for the use of an invention

~ на ноу-хау (~ na nóu-kháu) know-how ~

~ на оборудование (~ na oborúdovanie) equipment ~

~ на патент (~ na patént) ~ for a patent

~ на перегрузку товара (~ na peregrúzku továra) transshipment ~

~ на право использования технологического процесса (~ na právo ispól'zovaniia tekhnologícheskogo protséssa) industrial process ~

~ на право производства (~ na právo proizvódstva) manufacturing ~

~ на процесс (~ na protséss) process ~

~ на сбыт (~ na sbyt) sales ~

~ на товарный знак (~ na továrnyi znak) trademark ~

~ на эксплуатацию (~ na ekspluatátsiiu) operating ~

~ на этикетку (~ na etikétku) label ~

~ с правом передачи (~ s právom peredáchi) assignable ~

~ с правом переуступки (~ s právom pereustúpki) transferrable ~

Лиц/о (lits/ó) party, person

важное ~ (vázhnoe ~) VIP {person}

доверенное ~ (dovérennoe ~) agent, fiduciary, proxy

должностное ~ (dólzhnostnoe ~) official {person}

заинтересованное ~ (zainteresóvannoe ~) interested party

застрахованное ~ (zastrakhóvannoe ~) insured {person}

назначенное ~ (naznáchennoe ~) nominee

ответственное ~ (otvétstvennoe ~) liable party

официальное ~ (ofitsiál'noe ~) official representative

подписавшее ~ (podpisavshee ~) signatory

подставное ~ (podstávnoe ~) straw man

соответствующее ~ (sootvétstvuiushchee ~) appropriate party

список ~/ (spísok ~/) roll {list of persons}

стоять перед ~/ом (stoiát' péred ~/om) to face

субсидируемое ~ (subsidíruemoe ~) grant recipient

третье ~ (trét'e ~) third party

уполномоченное ~/a (upolnomóchennoe ~/a) authorized party

физическое ~ (fizícheskoe ~) natural person {individual}

финансирующее ~ (finansíruiushchee ~) sponsor

частное ~ (chástnoe ~) private person

через третье ~ (chérez trét'e ~) via third party

юридическое ~ (iuridícheskoe ~) juridical person {legal entity}

~, в чью пользу открыт аккредитив (~, v ch'iú pól'zu otkrýt akkreditív) letter of credit beneficiary

~, в чью пользу произведён трансферт (~, v ch'iú pól'zu proizvedión transfért)

transferee, endorsee {on bill, note}
~, выставившее инкассо (~, výstavivshee inkásso) drawer {on account}
~, гарантирующее оплату векселя (~, garantíruiushchee oplátu vékselia) backer {of a bill, note}
~, имеющее право подписи (~, iméiushchee právo pódpisi) authorized signatory
~, имеющее сертификат (~, iméiushchee sertifikát) certificate holder
~, наделённое правами (~, nadeliónnoe právami) authorized person
~, передающее право на имущество (~, peredaiúshchee právo na imúshchestvo) grantor {of property}
~, переуступающее право (~, pereustupáiushchee právo) assignor
~, получающее платёж (~, poluchaiúshchee platiózh) payee
~, предлагающее цену (~, predlagáiushchee tsénu) bidder
~, предоставляющее кредит (~, predostavliáiushchee kredít) creditor
~, производящее продажи на аукционе (~, proizvodiáshchee prodázhi na auktsióne) auctioneer
~, содействующее какому-либо мероприятию (~, sodéistvuiushchee kakómu-líbo meropriiátiiu) promoter
Личност/ь (líchnost/') f. individual, personality
удостоверение ~/и (udostoverénie ~/i) personal credentials
Личный (líchnyi) adj. personal, private
Лишать (lishát') v. to deprive, to revoke
Лишени/е (lishéni/e) n. deprivation
~ кредита (~ kredíta) withdrawal of credit
~ собственности (~ sóbstvennosti) dispossession {of property}
~ экспортных привилегий (~ éksportnykh privilégii) revocation of export privileges

Локальный (lokál'nyi) adj. local
Локаут (lokáut) m. lock-out
объявить ~ (ob"iavít' ~) to declare a lock-out
Локо (lóko) n. loco
цена ~ (tsená ~) ~ price
Ломкий (lómkii) adj. brittle, fragile
"Ломкое" (lómkoe) "handle with care"
Лоро (lóro) n. loro
счёт ~ (schiót ~) ~ account
Лот (lot) m. lot
Лоток (lotók) m. pallet
Лотерея (lotoréia) f. lottery
Лоцман (lótsman) m. pilot {of a vessel}
вызывать ~/a (vyzyvát' ~/a) to apply to the ~
морской ~ (morskói ~) marine ~
направлять ~/a (napravliát' ~/a) to assign a ~
обслуживание ~/ом (obslúzhivanie ~/om) pilotage service
плавать без ~/a (plávat' bez ~/a) to sail without a ~
прибрежный ~ (pribrézhnyi ~) coasting ~
принимать ~/a (prinimát' ~/a) to take on a ~
речной ~ (rechnói ~) river ~
старший ~ (stárshii ~) senior ~
Лоцманский (lótsmanskii) adj. pilot
Лумпсум-фрахт (lúmpsum-frákht) m. lumpsum freight
Лумпсум-чартер (lúmpsum-chárter) m. lumpsum charter
Льгот/а (l'gót/a) f. benefit, exemption, immunity, privilege
добиваться ~/ (dobivát'sia ~/) to secure privileges
дополнительные ~/ы (dopolnítel'nye ~/y) fringe benefits
многочисленные ~/ы (mnogochíslennye ~/y) numerous concessions
налоговые ~/ы (nalógovye ~/y) tax exemptions
предоставление льгот по кредиту ~ (predostavlénie l'gót po kredítu ~) easing of credit
предоставлять ~/ы (predostavliát' ~/y) to grant privileges

преференциальные ~/ы
(preferentsiál'nye ~/y)
preferential advantages
таможенные ~/ы (tamózhennye ~/y)
preferential customs treatment
тарифные ~/ы (tarífnye ~/y)
preferential tariffs
транзитная ~ (tranzítnaia ~)
transit privilege
устанавливать дополнительные ~/ы
(ustanávlivat' dopolnítel'nye
~/y) to establish additional
benefits
финансовая ~ (finánsovaia ~)
cost benefit
фрахтовая ~ (frakhtóvaia ~)
freight reduction
~ на остановку в пути следования
(~ na ostanóvku v putí slédova-
niia) stop-off privilege
Льготный (l'gótnyi) *adj.* favorable,
preferential
Лэндинг (lending) *m.* landing
charges
Люк (liuk) hatch {in a vessel}
главный ~ (glávnyi ~) main ~
грузовой ~ (gruzovói ~) cargo ~
задраивать ~ (zadráivat' ~) to
batten the ~
крышка ~/a (krýshka ~/a) ~ cover
открывать ~ перед разгрузкой
(otkryvát' ~ péred razgrúzkoi)
to open the ~ for loading
разгружать ~ (razgruzhát' ~) to
unload a ~
Люковый (liúkovyi) *adj.* hatch
Лямка (liámka) *f.* strap

M

Магазин (magazín) *m.* shop, store
владелец ~ (vladélets ~) store
owner, shopkeeper
держать ~ (derzhát' ~) to keep
shop
размещение ~/ов (razmeshchénie
~/ov) store locations
розничный ~ (róznichnyi ~)
retail store
специализированный ~
(spetsializírovannyi ~)
specialty shop
универсальный ~ (universál'nyi
~) department store

фирменный ~ (fírmennyi ~) chain
store
часы торговли ~/ов (chasý
torgóvli ~/ov) store hours
~ самообслуживания (~
samoobslúzhivaniia) self-service
store
Макет (makét) *m.* mock-up, model
действующий ~ (déistvuiushchii
~) working model
технологический ~
(tekhnologícheskii ~)
engineering mock-up
~ в натуральную величину (~ v
naturál'nuiu velichinu) life-
size model
~ экспозиции (~ ekspozítsii)
floor plan layout
Маклер (mákler) *m.* broker
биржевой ~ (birzhevói ~) stock ~
вознаграждение ~/у
(voznagrazhdénie ~/u) brokerage
fees
занимающийся учётными операциями
~ (zanimáiushchiisia uchiótnymi
operátsiiami ~) discount ~
корабельный ~ (korabél'nyi ~)
ship ~
официальный биржевой ~
(ofitsiál'nyi birzhevói ~) ~
with a seat on the exchange
посредничество ~/a
(posredníchestvo ~/a) agency of
a ~
страховой ~ (strakhovói ~)
insurance ~
~ по фрахтованию судов (~ po
frakhtovániiu sudóv) shipping ~
Маклерский (máklerskii) *adj.* broker
Маклерство (máklerstvo) brokerage
Максимально (maksimál'no) *adv.* at
most
Максимальный (maksimál'nyi) *adj.*
maximum
Маловероятный (maloveroiátnyi) *adj.*
unlikely
Малодоходный (malodokhódnyi) *adj.*
marginally profitable
Малоёмкий (maloiómkii) *adj.* low
capacity
Малоопытный (maloópytnyi) *adj.*
inexperienced
Малоприбыльный (malopríbyl'nyi)
adj. marginally profitable
Малопригодный (maloprigódnyi) *adj.*
of little use

Малорентабельный (malorentábel'nyi) *adj.* insufficiently profitable
Малотоннажный (malotonnázhnyi) *adj.* of small tonnage
Малоценный (malotsénnyi) *adj.* of little value
Манифест (manifést) *m.* manifest {document}
    грузовой ~ (gruzovói ~) cargo ~
    заверенный консулом ~ (zavérennyi kónsulom ~) certified ~
    судовой ~ (sudovói ~) ship's ~ {bills of lading}
Манифестант (manifestánt) *m.* demonstrator
Марж/а (márzh/a) *f.* margin
    банковская ~ (bánkovskaia ~) bank ~
    большая ~ (bol'sháia ~) wide ~
    кредит по операциям с ~/ей (kredít po operátsiiam s ~/ei) ~ credit
    недостаточная ~ (nedostátochnaia ~) thin ~
    обычная ~ (obýchnaia ~) usual ~
    оговорка о ~/е (ogovórka o ~/e) ~ clause
    предписываемая законом ~ (predpisyváemaia zakónom ~) ~ requirement
    сделки с ~/ей (sdélki s ~/ei) ~ business
    ~ по кредиту (~ po kredítu) credit ~
Марихуана (marikhuána) *f.* marijuana
Мар/ка (már/ka) *f.* brand, model, stamp {postage}
    выбор ~/ки товара (výbor ~/ki továra) brand selection
    высшая ~ (výsshaia ~) best brand name
    высшей ~/ки (výsshei ~/ki) of the best brands
    гарантийная ~ (garantíinaia ~) guarantee stamp
    гербовая ~ (gérbovaia ~) revenue stamp
    групповая ~ (gruppováia ~) family of name brands
    заводская ~ (zavódskaia ~) manufacturer's trademark
    конверт с ~/кой (konvért s ~/koi) stamped envelope
    название ~/ки (nazvánie ~/ki) brand name

    наиболее ходкая ~ (naibólee khódkaia ~) top selling brand, make
    наклеить ~/ку (nakléit' ~/ku) to affix a stamp
    наносить ~/ку (nanosít' ~/ku) to mark
    носить фабричную ~/ку (nosít' fabríchnuiu ~/ku) to bear a trademark
    одобренная ~ (odóbrennaia ~) approved model
    отличительная ~ (otlichítel'naia ~) mark of distinction
    официально зарегистрированная ~ (ofitsiál'no zaregistrírovannaia ~) registered trademark
    снабжение товара торговой ~/кой (snabzhénie továra torgóvoi ~/koi) brand labeling
    ставить ~/ку (stávit' ~/ku) to mark
    товар высшей ~/ки (továr výsshei ~/ki) top quality goods
    товарная ~ (továrnaia ~) trademark
    условные обозначения ~/ок (uslóvnye oboznachéniia ~/ok) trademark designations
    фабричная ~ (fabríchnaia ~) manufacturer's trademark
    ~ грузового судна (~ gruzovógo súdna) model of a freighter
    ~ изделия (~ izdéliia) product brand name
    ~ производителя (~ proizvodítelia) manufacturer's brand name
    ~ товара (~ továra) brand, make, model
    ~ торгового посредника (~ torgóvogo posrédnika) private label {distributor's brand}
Маркетинг (márketing) *m.* marketing
Маркировать (markírovat') *v.* to mark
Маркировк/а (markiróvk/a) *f.* labeling, marking
    без ~/и (bez ~/i) not marked
    видимая ~ (vídimaia ~) visible marking
    внешняя ~ (vnéshniaia ~) exterior marking
    выбивать ~/у на металлической пластине (vybivát' ~/u na metallícheskoi plastíne) to emboss marking on a metal plate

выцветшая ~ (výtsvetshaia ~)
faded marking
грузовая ~ (gruzováia ~)
shipping marks
двойная ~ (dvoináia ~) duplicate
marking
достаточность ~/и
(dostátochnost' ~/i) sufficiency
of marking
запачканная ~ (zapáchkannaia ~)
stained marking
иметь ~/у (imét' ~/u) to be
marked
нанесение ~/и (nanesénie ~/i)
marking
наносить ~/у (nanosít' ~/u) to
mark
наносить ~/у водостойкой краской
(nanosít' ~/u vodostóikoi
kráskoi) to mark in water
insoluble paint
наносить ~/у выжиганием
(nanosít' ~/u vyzhigániem) to
brand
наносить ~/у краской (nanosít'
~/u kráskoi) to mark by paint
наносить ~/у несмываемой краской
(nanosít' ~/u nesmyváemoi
kráskoi) to mark in indelible
paint
наносить ~/у погодоустойчивой
краской (nanosít' ~/u
pogodoustóichivoi kráskoi) to
mark in weatherproof paint
наносить ~/у по трафарету
(nanosít' ~/u po trafarétu) to
stencil
недостаточная ~ (nedostátochnaia
~) insufficient marking
неправильная ~ (neprávil'naia ~)
incorrect marking
неясная ~ (neiásnaia ~)
indistinct marking
основная ~ (osnovnáia ~) leading
marks
отгрузочная ~ (otgrúzochnaia ~)
shipping marks
отчётливая ~ (otchiótlivaia ~)
distinct marking
патентная ~ (paténtnaia ~)
patent notice
правила ~/и (právila ~/i)
marking regulations
правильная ~ (právil'naia ~)
proper marking
специальная ~ (spetsiál'naia ~)
special marking

транспортная ~ (tránsportnaia ~)
transport marking
чёткая ~ (chiótkaia ~) clear
marking
экспортная ~ (éksportnaia ~)
export marking
~ делается на ... языке (~
délaetsia na ... iazyké) marking
in ... {language}
~ контейнера (~ kontéinera)
container marking
~ мешка (~ meshká) inscription
on a bag
~ тары (~ táry) packaging
marking
~ товара (~ továra) marking of
goods
~ товарных мест (~ továrnykh
mest) marking of packages
~ упаковки (~ upakóvki) marking
of packing container
~ цен (~ tsen) price marking
~ ящиков (~ iáshchikov) marking
of cases
Маркировщик (markiróvshchik) m.
marker {person}
Марочный (maróchnyi) adj. branded,
marked
Маршрут (marshrút) m. itinerary,
route
кратчайший ~ (kratcháishii ~)
the shortest path
магистральный ~ (magistrál'nyi
~) the arterial route
обходной ~ (obkhódnoi ~) detour
оптимальный ~ (optimál'nyi ~)
optimal route
по самому быстрому ~/у (po
sámomu býstromu ~/u) by the
fastest route
по самому дешёвому ~/у (po
sámomu deshióvomu ~/u) by the
cheapest route
протяжённый ~ (protiazhiónnyi ~)
extended route
прямой ~ (priamói ~) direct
route
обычным ~/ом (obýchnym ~/om) by
the usual route
отклонение от ~/а (otklonénie ot
~/a) deviation from the route
регулярный ~ (reguliárnyi ~)
regular route
речной ~ (rechnói ~) river route
сквозной ~ (skvoznói ~) through
route

торговый ~ (torgóvyi ~) trade route
устанавливать ~ (ustanávlivat' ~) to route
Маршрутный (marshrútnyi) *adj.* route
Масс/а (máss/a) *f.* bulk, gross, mass
в ~/e (v ~/e) in bulk
денежная ~ (dénezhnaia ~) money supply
единица ~/ы (edinítsa ~/y) unit of mass
общая ~ (óbshchaia ~) bulk mass
стандартная ~ (standártnaia ~) standard mass
товарная ~ (továrnaia ~) bulk commodities
~ брутто (~ brútto) gross mass
~ грузового места (~ gruzovógo mésta) package mass
~ нетто (~ nétto) net mass
~ прибыли (~ príbyli) mass of profit
Массовый (mássovyi) *adj.* bulk, mass
Мастер (máster) *m.* expert, foreman, craftsman
сменный ~ (sménnyi ~) shift foreman
старший ~ (stárshii ~) senior foreman
~ по текущему ремонту (~ po tekúshchemu remóntu) maintenance foreman
Мастерская (masterskáia) *f.adj.noun* workshop
ремонтная ~ (remóntnaia ~) repair station
Мастерство (masterstvó) *n.* craftsmanship, experience, skill
высокое профессиональное (vysókoe professionál'noe) great professional skill
рабочее ~ (rabóchee ~) operating skills
техническое ~ (tekhnícheskoe ~) technical skill
Масштаб (masshtáb) *m.* scale, scope
большой ~ (bol'shói ~) large scale
в ~/ах всего рынка (v ~/akh vsegó rýnka) market-wide
в большом ~/e (v bol'shóm ~/e) on a large scale
в значительном ~/e (v znachítel'nom ~/e) on a significant scale

в международном ~/e (v mezhdunaródnom ~/e) on an international scale
в меньшем ~/e (v mén'shem ~/e) on a smaller scale
в мировом ~/e (v mirovóm ~/e) on a world scale
в ограниченных ~/ах (v ogranítchennykh ~/akh) on a limited scale
в промышленных ~/ах (v promýshlennykh ~/akh) on an industrial scale
в увеличенном ~/e (v uvelíchennom ~/e) on an enlarged scale
в уменьшенном ~/e (v umén'shennom ~/e) on a reduced scale
в широком ~/e (v shirókom ~/e) on a broad scale
глобальный ~ (globál'nyi ~) a global scale
изменение ~/a (izmenénie ~/a) rescaling
крупный ~ (krúpnyi ~) major scale
модель в уменьшенном ~/e (modél' v umén'shennom ~/e) reduced scale model
нормальный ~ (normál'nyi ~) standard scale
операция производственного ~/a (operátsiia proizvódstvennogo ~/a) production scale operation
производство большого ~/a (proizvódstvo bol'shógo ~/a) volume production
расширение ~/a производственной деятельности (rasshirénie ~/a proizvódstvennoi déiatel'nosti) expansion of production operations
увеличенный ~ (uvelíchennyi ~) increased scale
уменьшенный ~ (umén'shennyi ~) reduced scale
экономически эффективный ~ (ekonomícheski effektívnyi ~) economically justified scale
~ в метрах (~ v metrákh) metric scale
~ времени (~ vrémeni) time scale
~ инфляции (~ infliátsii) magnitude of inflation
~ операций (~ operátsii) scale of operations

~ проекта (~ proékta) scope of a
project
~ работ (~ rabót) scope of work
~ участия (~ uchástiia) scope of
participation
Масштабный (masshtábnyi) *adj.* large
scale
Материал (materiál) *m.* material
аналогичный ~ (analogíchnyi ~)
analogous ~
более дешёвый ~ (bólee deshióvyi
~) cheaper ~
браковать ~/ы (brakovát' ~/y) to
reject ~
ведомость ~/ов (védomost' ~/ov)
schedule of ~s
вид упаковочного ~/а (vid
upakóvochnogo ~/a) kind of
packing ~
водонепроницаемый ~
(vodonepronitsáemyi ~)
waterproof ~
вспомогательные ~/ы
(vspomogátel'nye ~/y) auxiliary
~s
высококачественный ~
(vysokokáchestvennyi ~) high
quality ~
выставочный ~ (výstavochnyi ~)
exhibition ~
горючие ~/ы (goriúchie ~/y)
combustibles
демонстрационный ~
(demonstratsiónnyi ~)
demonstration ~
дефектный ~ (deféktnyi ~)
defective ~
дефицитный ~ (defitsítnyi ~)
scarce ~
документальный ~ (dokumentál'nyi
~) documentary ~
дополнительный ~ (dopolnítel'nyi
~) supplementary ~
закупленные ~/ы (zakúplennye
~/y) purchased ~s
затрата ~/а (zatráta ~/a) amount
of required ~
защитный ~ (zashchítnyi ~)
protective ~
заявочные ~/ы (zaiávochnye ~/y)
application ~s
иллюстрированный ~
(illiustrírovannyi ~)
illustrated ~
информационный ~
(informatsiónnyi ~)
informational ~

искусственные ~/ы (iskússtvennye
~/y) artificial ~s
использованный ~ (ispól'zovannyi
~) used ~
испытание ~/ов (ispytánie ~/ov)
testing of ~s
исходный ~ (iskhódnyi ~) source
~
классифицированный ~
(klassifitsírovannyi ~)
classified ~
коммерческий ~ (kommércheskii ~)
commercial ~
конкурентный ~ (konkuréntnyi ~)
competitive ~
конструкционные ~/ы
(konstruktsiónnye ~/y)
construction ~s
массивный ~ (massívnyi ~) bulky
~
наглядный ~ (nagliádnyi ~)
descriptive ~
наличные ~/ы (nalíchnye ~/y)
available ~s
направлять ~ (napravliát' ~) to
forward ~
недоброкачественный ~
(nedobrokáchestvennyi ~) poor
quality ~
недостаток ~/ов (nedostátok
~/ov) lack of ~s
недостающий ~ (nedostaiúshchii
~) missing ~
неиспользованный ~
(neispól'zovannyi ~) unused ~
некондиционный ~
(nekonditsiónnyi ~) substandard
~
необходимый ~ (neobkhodímyi ~)
necessary ~
непригодный ~ (neprigódnyi ~)
unfit ~
нестандартный ~ (nestandártnyi
~) nonstandard ~
низкосортный ~ (nizkosórtnyi ~)
lower grade ~
обёрточный ~ (obiórtochnyi ~)
wrapping ~
обрабатывать ~ (obrabátyvat' ~)
to process ~
описание ~/а (opisánie ~/a)
description of ~
основной ~ (osnovnói ~) basic ~
отделочный ~ (otdélochnyi ~)
finishing ~

охраняемый авторским правом
(okhraniáemyi ávtorskim právom)
copyrighted ~
первоклассный ~ (pervoklássnyi
~) first-class ~
перечень ~/ов (pérechen' ~/ov)
list of ~s
печатание ~/ов (pechátanie ~/ov)
printing of ~s
печатный ~ (pechátnyi ~) printed
~
письменный ~ (pís'mennyi ~)
written ~
подбирать ~ (podbirát' ~) to
select ~
подбор ~/а (podbór ~/a)
selection of ~
подстилочный ~ (podstílochnyi ~)
dunnage
подходящий ~ (podkhodiáshchii ~)
suitable ~
потребляемый ~/ы (potrebliáemyi
~/y) consumable ~s
представленный ~ (predstávlennyi
~) submitted ~
прилагаемый ~ (prilagáemyi ~)
enclosed ~
приобретать ~/ы (priobretát'
~/y) to procure ~
прокладочный ~ (prokládochnyi ~)
sealing ~
прочный ~ (próchnyi ~) sturdy ~
рабочий ~ (rabóchii ~) working ~
рассылка рекламных ~/ов
(rassýlka reklámnykh ~/ov)
advertising mailer
рассылка рекламных ~/ов, разовая
(rassýlka reklámnykh ~/ov,
rázovaia) one-time advertising
mailer
расход ~/а (raskhód ~/a)
consumption of ~
расходный ~ (raskhódnyi ~)
expendable ~
расходуемые ~/ы (raskhóduemye
~/y) consumable ~s
рекламный ~ (reklámnyi ~)
advertising ~
стандартный ~ (standártnyi ~)
standard ~
стоимость ~/ов (stóimost' ~/ov)
cost of ~s
стратегический ~
(strategícheskii ~) strategic ~
строительный ~ (stroítel'nyi ~)
construction ~

сырьевые ~/ы (syr'evýe ~/y) raw
~s
тарный ~ (tárnyi ~) tare ~
текстовой ~ (tekstovói ~)
textual ~
требование на ~/ы (trébovanie na
~/y) requisition of supplies
употребление ~/а (upotreblénie
~/a) ~ usage
учебный ~ (uchébnyi ~)
educational ~
художественно-оформительские ~/ы
(khudózhestvenno-oformítel'skie
~/y) display ~s
эксплуатационные ~/ы
(ekspluatatsiónnye ~/y)
operational ~s
Материалоёмкий (materialoiómkii)
adj. raw material intensive
Материалоёмкост/ь
(materialoiómkost/') f. material
input
снижать ~ производства (snizhát'
~ proizvódstva) reduction in
material input ratio
снижение ~/и (snizhénie ~/i)
reduction of material inputs
Материально-технический
(materiál'no-tekhnícheskii) adj.
material and technical
Материальный (materiál'nyi) adj.
material
Матрос (matros) m. sailor, seaman
Махиавеллевский (makhiavéllevskii)
adj. machiavellian
Махинация (makhinátsiia) f.
machination
Машин/а (mashín/a) f. automobile,
machine
аналоговая вычислительная ~
(análogovaia vychislítel'naia ~)
analog computer
арендуемые ~/ы (arendúemye ~/y)
rental machines
ассортимент ~/ (assortimént ~/)
range of machinery
бездействующая ~
(bezdéistvuiushchaia ~) idle
machine
вычислительная ~
(vychislítel'naia ~) computer
грузовая ~ (gruzováia ~) truck
грузоподъёмные ~/ы
(gruzopod"iómnye ~/y) winch
действующая ~ (déistvuiushchaia
~) working machine

176

детали ~ (detáli ~/) machine
components
длительность эксплуатации ~/ы
(dlítel'nost' ekspluatátsii ~/y)
service life of a machine
исправная ~ (isprávnaia ~) sound
machine
конструкция ~/ы (konstrúktsiia
~/y) design of a machine
металлоёмкость ~/ы
(metalloiómkost' ~/y) per unit
metal content of a machine
наблюдать за работой ~/ы
(nabliudát' za rabótoi ~/y) to
observe a machine in operation
назначить цену за ~/у
(naznáchit' tsénu za ~/u) to
quote a price on a machine
надёжность работы ~/ы
(nadiózhnost' rabóty ~/y)
reliability of a machine
норма выработки ~/ы (nórma
výrabotki ~/y) standard machine
capacity
обслуживание ~/ (obslúzhivanie
~/) machine maintenance
обслуживать ~/у (obslúzhivat'
~/u) to service a machine
отделка ~/ы (otdélka ~/y)
workmanship of a machine
паспорт ~/ы (pásport ~/y)
machine certificate
переделывать конструкцию ~/ы
(peredélyvat' konstrúktsiiu ~/y)
to redesign a machine
повреждённая ~ (povrezhdiónnaia
~) damaged machine
преимущества ~/ы
(preimúshchestva ~/y) advantages
of a machine
производительность ~/ы
(proizvodítel'nost' ~/y)
productivity of a machine
простая ~ (prostáia ~) simple
machine
простой ~/ы (prostói ~/y) idle
time of a machine
пуск ~/ы (pusk ~/y) introduction
of a machine
работа ~/ы (rabóta ~/y)
operation of a machine
рабочий режим ~/ы (rabóchii
rezhím ~/y) operating conditions
of a machine
современная ~ (sovreménnaia ~)
modern machine

срок службы ~/ы (srok slúzhby
~/y) service life of a machine
счётная ~ (schiótnaia ~)
calculator
счётно-аналитическая ~
(schiótno-analitícheskaia ~)
tabulating machine
управлять ~/ой (upravliát' ~/oi)
to operate a machine
устаревшая ~ (ustarévshaia ~)
outdated machine
цифровая вычислительная ~
(tsifróvaia vychislítel'naia ~)
digital computer
~ для расфасовки и упаковки (~
dlia rasfasóvki i upakóvki)
packing machine
Машинный (mashínnyi) adj. machine
Машиностроени/е (mashinostroéni/e)
n. mechanical engineering
завод тяжёлого ~/я (zavód
tiazhiólogo ~/ia) heavy
engineering plant
продукция ~/я (prodúktsiia ~/ia)
engineering products
сельскохозяйственное ~
(sél'skokhoziástvennoe ~)
agricultural machinery industry
точное ~ (tóchnoe ~) precision
engineering
транспортное ~ (tránsportnoe ~)
transportation engineering
тяжёлое ~ (tiazhióloe ~) heavy
engineering
химическое ~ (khimícheskoe ~)
chemical engineering
энергическое ~ (energícheskoe ~)
power plant engineering
Машиностроитель (mashinostroítel')
m. toolmaker
Машиностроительный
(mashinostroítel'nyi) adj. machine
building
Межбанковский (mezhbánkovskii) adj.
inter-bank
Межгосударственный
(mezhgosudárstvennyi) adj.
interstate
Междугородный (mezhdugoródnyi) adj.
inter-city
Международный (mezhdunaródnyi) adj.
international
Межотраслевой (mezhotraslevói) adj
inter-sectoral
Межправительственный
(mezhpravítel'stvennyi) adj. intergovernmental

Межфирменный (mezhfírmennyi) *adj.*
inter-corporation, inter-firm
Межцеховой (mezhtsekhovói) *adj.*
inter-departmental
Мелкомасштабный (melkomasshtábnyi)
adj. small-scale
Меморандум (memorándum) *m.*
memorandum
    аукционный ~ (auktsiónnyi ~)
    broker's ticket
    ~ о договоре (~ o dogovóre)
    memorandum of agreement
    ~ о намерении (~ o namerénii)
    letter of intent
    ~ о соглашении (~ o soglashénii)
    memorandum of understanding
    ~ страховой (~ strakhovói)
    insurance memorandum
Мен/а (mén/a) *f.* barter
    договор ~/ы (dogovór ~/y) ~
    agreement
Менеджер (ménedzher) *m.* manager
Менять (meniát') to alter, to
change, to exchange
Меняющийся (meniáiushchiisia) *adj.*
fluctuating, varying
Мер/а (mér/a) *f.* measure
    антиинфляционные ~/ы
    (antiinfliatsiónnye ~/y) anti-
    inflationary ~s
    безотлагательные ~/ы
    (bezotlagátel'nye ~/y) urgent ~s
    взаимоприемлемые ~/ы
    (vzaimopriémlemye ~/y) mutually
    acceptable ~s
    временные ~/ы (vrémennye ~/y)
    temporary ~s
    действенные ~/ы (déistvennye
    ~/y) effective ~s
    дискриминационные торгово-
    экономические
    (diskriminatsiónnye torgóvo-
    ekonomícheskie ~) discriminatory
    trade and economic ~s
    дополнительные ~/ы
    (dopolnítel'nye ~/y) further ~s
    достаточные ~/ы (dostátochnye
    ~/y) sufficient ~s
    единицы ~/ы (edinítsy ~/y) unit
    of ~
    законодательные ~/ы
    (zakonodátel'nye ~/y)
    legislative ~s
    защитные ~/ы (zashchítnye ~/y)
    precautions

    использовать в качестве ~/ы
    (ispól'zovat' v káchestve ~/y)
    to use as a ~
    корректировочные ~/ы
    (korrektiróvochnye ~/y)
    corrective ~s
    крайние ~/ы (kráinie ~/y)
    extreme ~s
    метрические ~/ы (metrícheskie
    ~/y) metric ~s
    надлежащие ~/ы (nadlezháshchie
    ~/y) proper ~s
    немедленные ~/ы (nemédlennye
    ~/y) immediate ~s
    неэффективные ~/ы (neeffektívnye
    ~/y) ineffective ~s
    объёма ~/ы (ob"ióma ~/y) ~s of
    volume
    ограничительные ~/ы
    (ogranichítel'nye ~/y)
    restrictive ~s {rationing}
    ответные ~/ы (otvétnye ~/y)
    counter-~s
    подготовительные ~/ы
    (podgotovítel'nye ~/y)
    preparatory ~s
    подобные ~/ы (podóbnye ~/y)
    similar ~s
    практические ~/ы (praktícheskie
    ~/y) practical ~s
    предварительные ~/ы
    (predvarítel'nye ~/y)
    preliminary ~s
    предохранительные ~/ы
    (predokhranítel'nye ~/y)
    precautionary ~s
    предупредительные ~/ы
    (predupredítel'nye ~/y)
    preventative ~s
    принимать ~/ы (prinimát' ~/y) to
    take ~s
    принудительные ~/ы
    (prinudítel'nye ~/y) compulsory
    ~s
    протекционистские ~/ы
    (protektsionístskie ~/y)
    protectionist ~s
    своевременные ~/ы (svoevrémennye
    ~/y) timely ~s
    соответствующие ~/ы
    (sootvétstvuiushchie ~/y)
    appropriate ~s
    срочные ~/ы (sróchnye ~/y)
    prompt ~s
    чрезвычайные ~/ы (chrezvycháinye
    ~/y) extraordinary ~s

экстренные ~/ы (ekstrénnye ~/y)
emergency ~s
эффективные ~/ы (effektívnye
~/y) effective ~s
~/ы безопасности (~/y
bezopásnosti) security ~s
~/ы веса (~/y vésa) ~s of
capacity
~/ы длины (~/y dliný) ~s of
length
~/ы ёмкости (~/y iómkosti) ~s of
volume
~/ы жидкости (~/y zhídkosti) ~s
of liquid
~/ы надёжности (~/y
nadiózhnosti) ~s of reliability
~/ы переходного характера (~/y
perekhódnogo kharáktera)
transitional arrangements
~/ы площади (~/y plóshchadi) ~s
of area
~/ы по исправлению (~/y po
ispravléniiu) restorative ~s
~/ы по охране труда (~/y po
okhráne trudá) ~s for labor
protection
~/ы по сдерживанию импорта (~/y
po sdérzhivaniiu ímporta) ~s for
import restraint
~/ы по сдерживанию экспорта (~/y
po sdérzhivaniiu éksporta) ~s
for export restraint
~/ы предосторожности (~/y
predostorózhnosti) safety
precautions
~ стоимости (~ stóimosti) ~ of
value
~/ы сыпучих тел (~/y sypúchikh
tel) dry ~s
~/ы точности (~/y tóchnosti) ~s
of precision
~/ы эффективности (~/y
effektívnosti) ~s of efficiency
Мерительный (merítel'nyi) adj.
measuring
Мерить (mérit') v. to measure
Мерка (mérka) f. measure {size}
Мероприяти/е (meropriiáti/e) n.
action, event, measure, step
важное ~ (vázhnoe ~) important
event
временное ~ (vrémennoe ~)
temporary arrangement
ежегодное ~ (ezhegódnoe ~)
annual event
календарь ~/й (kalendár' ~/i)
calendar of events

комплекс ~/й (kómpleks ~/i)
package of measures
осуществлять ~/я
(osushchestvliát' ~/ia) to put
measures into effect
пакет ~/й (pakét ~/i) package of
measures
план ~/й (plan ~/i) plan of
action
план ~/й по стимулированию сбыта
(plan ~/i po stimulírovaniiu
sbýta) promotion program
план рекламных ~/й (plan
reklámnykh ~/i) advertising plan
полезное ~ (poléznoe ~) useful
measure
последовательность ~/й
(posledovátel'nost' ~/i)
sequence of events
последующие ~/я (posléduiushchie
~/ia) follow-up measures
соответствующее ~
(sootvétstvuiushchee ~)
appropriate measure
~ /я по девальвации (~ /ia po
deval'vátsii) devaluation
measures
~/я по контракту (~/ia po
kontráktu) contract arrangements
~/я по спасению груза (~/ia po
spaséniiu grúza) cargo salvage
measures
~/я стимулирования сбыта (~/ia
stimulírovaniia sbýta) promotional activity
~/я экономической политики (~/ia
ekonomícheskoi polítiki)
economic policy measures
Местный (méstnyi) adj. local
Мест/о (mést/o) n. case, package,
place, seat, site, space
арендовать ~ (arendovát' ~) to
rent space
бронирование ~/a (bronírovanie
~/a) to reserve seats
в одном ~/e (v odnóm ~/e) in one
place
в указанном ~/e (v ukázannom
~/e) in the indicated place
вес грузового ~/a (ves gruzovógo
~/a) package unit weight
грузовое ~ (gruzovóe ~) cargo
space
количество ~/ (kolíchestvo ~/)
number of packages

конечное ~ назначения (konéchnoe ~ naznachéniia) final destination

"Место Подъёма Тележкой" {надпись} (mésto pod"ióma telézhkoi {nádpis'}) "lift here with forklift" {marking on crate}

на ~/e (na ~/e) on site

неудобное ~ (neudóbnoe ~) inconvenient place

номер ~/a (nómer ~/a) package number

обеспечить ~ (obespéchit' ~) to arrange shipping space

обеспечить надёжное ~/у причала (obespéchit' nadiózhnoe ~/u prichála) to assure safe berth

обслуживание на ~/e (obslúzhivanie na ~/e) field service

обучение по ~/у работы (obuchénie po ~/u rabóty) on the job training

отдельное ~ (otdél'noe ~) single package

повреждённое ~ (povrezhdiónnoe ~) damaged case

подсчёт количества ~/ груза (podschiót kolíchestva ~/ grúza) tally of cargo

подходящее ~ (podkhodiáshchee ~) appropriate place

покупка рекламного ~/a (pokúpka reklámnogo ~/a) purchase of advertising space

получить ~ на судне (poluchít' ~ na súdne) to receive cargo space

потеря ~/a груза (potéria ~/a grúza) loss of cargo

потерянное ~ (potériannoe ~) lost package

применение на ~/e работы (primenénie na ~/e rabóty) on the job application

рабочее ~ (rabóchee ~) job, position

рабочие на ~/ax (rabóchie na ~/akh) on-site workers

размеры ~/a (razméry ~/a) package dimensions

ревизия на ~/e (revíziia na ~/e) field audit

регулировка на ~/e (reguliróvka na ~/e) site adjustment

свободное ~ (svobódnoe ~) blank space

сдавать ~ в аренду (sdavát' ~ v aréndu) to rent space {as lessor}

складочное ~ (skládochnoe ~) stowage

содержание ~/a (soderzhánie ~/a) contents of a package

стоимость ~/a (stóimost' ~/a) cost of space

сухое ~ (sukhóe ~) dry place

требуемое ~ назначения (trébuemoe ~ naznachéniia) required destination

узкое ~ (úzkoe ~) narrow space

указанное ~ (ukázannoe ~) designated space {in document}

"Хранить в сухом месте" {надпись} (khranít' v sukhóm méste {nádpis'}) "keep dry" {cargo marking}

число ~/ груза (chisló ~/ grúza) number of packages

экономия ~/a (ekonómiia ~/a) savings of space

экономить ~ (ekonómit' ~) to save space

~ арбитража (~ arbitrázha) arbitration venue

~ большого размера (~ bol'shógo razméra) oversized package

~ ввоза (~ vvóza) entry location {cargo}

~ вывоза (~ vývoza) pick-up location

~ выгрузки (~ výgruzki) discharge point

~ выдачи (~ výdachi) place of issuance {documents}

~ выпуска (~ výpuska) place of issue

~ выставки, постоянной (~ výstavki, postoiánnoi) permanent exhibition site

~ деятельности (~ déiatel'nosti) place of performance

~ для выгрузки у причала (~ dlia výgruzki u prichála) discharging berth

~ для погрузки (~ dlia pogrúzki) cargo space

~ для публикации рекламы (~ dlia publikátsii reklámy) advertising space

~ для сборки и накладки оборудования (~ dlia sbórki i nakládki oborúdovaniia) fitting and assembly bay

~ для строительства (~ dlia stroítel'stva) building site

~ для установки рекламного щита или панели (~ dlia ustanóvki reklámnogo shchíta íli panéli) advertising site

~ для хранения (~ dlia khranéniia) storage space

~ для экспонатов (~ dlia eksponátov) exhibit space

~ доставки (~ dostávki) point of delivery

~ жительства (~ zhítel'stva) place of residence

~ заключения контракта (~ zakliuchéniia kontrákta) place of concluding contract

~ изготовления (~ izgotovléniia) place of fabrication

~ испытаний (~ ispytánii) test site

~ крепления верёвкой (~ krepléniia verióvkoi) lashing point

~ крепления стропов (~ krepléniia strópov) lifting point

~ монтажа (~ montázha) installation site

~ на выставке (~ na výstavke) exhibition space

~ назначения (~ naznachéniia) inland destination

~ назначения экспортного груза (~ naznachéniia éksportnogo grúza) export destination

~ на судне (~ na súdne) space on vessel

~ нахождения (~ nakhozhdéniia) business address

~ опротестования (~ oprotestovániia) place of protest

~ отгрузки (~ otgrúzki) shipping point

~ отправления (~ otpravléniia) port of shipment

~ перевалки груза (~ pereválki grúza) transhipment point

~ платежа (~ platezhá) place of payment

~ погрузки (~ pogrúzki) loading berth

~ поставки (~ postávki) place of delivery

~ пребывания (~ prebyvániia) place of residence

~ предъявления (~ pred"iavléniia) place of presentation

~ прибытия (~ pribýtiia) point of arrival

~ приёмки (~ priiómki) place of acceptance

~ причала (~ prichála) moorage

~ причала для разгрузочных работ (~ prichála dlia razgrúzochnykh rabót) discharging berth

~ происхождения (~ proiskhozhdéniia) place of origin

~ работы (~ rabóty) job site

~ разгрузки (~ razgrúzki) discharging point

~ регистрации (~ registrátsii) place of registration

~ сдачи (~ sdáchi) point of delivery

~ складирования (~ skladírovaniia) warehousing site

~ стоянки (~ stoiánki) siting place

~ установки (~ ustanóvki) installation site

Местонахождение (mestonakhozhdénie) *n.* location, site

~ завода (~ zavóda) plant site

~ средства наружной рекламы (~ srédstva narúzhnoi reklámy) outdoor advertising site

~ фирмы (~ fírmy) business address of a firm

Местоположение (mestopolozhénie) *n.* location, position

предпочтительное ~ (predpochtítel'noe ~) preferential position

~ стенда (~ sténda) location of a stand

Месторождение (mestorozhdénie) *n.* deposit {minerals, etc.}

богатое ~ (bogátoe ~) rich deposit

~ газа (~ gáza) gas field

~ нефти (~ néfti) oil field

~ полезных ископаемых (~ poléznykh iskopáemykh) mineral deposit

~ руды (~ rudý) ore deposit

~ угля (~ ugliá) coal field

Месячный (mésiachnyi) *adj.* monthly

Металлоёмкость (metalloiómkost') *f.* metal consumption

удельная ~ (udél'naia ~)
specific metal content
Металлургический
(metallurgícheskii) *adj.*
metallurgical
Металлургия (metallurgíia) *f.*
metallurgy
   чёрная ~ (chiórnaia ~) ferrous ~
   цветная ~ (tsvetnáia ~) non-
ferrous ~
Метеорологический
(meteorologícheskii) *adj.*
meteorological
Метк/а (métk/a) *f.* marker, sign,
tag
   контрольная ~ (kontról'naia ~)
checkmark
   ставить ~/y (stávit' ~/u) to
mark
Метод (métod) *m.* method, procedure
   индустриальный ~ (industriál'nyi
~) industrial method
   использовать ~ (ispól'zovat' ~)
to employ a method
   надёжный ~ (nadiózhnyi ~)
reliable method
   научный ~ (naúchnyi ~)
scientific method
   нормативные ~/ы (normatívnye
~/y) normative methods
   обобщённый ~ (obobshchiónnyi ~)
generalized method
   общий ~ (óbshchii ~) general
method
   обычный ~ (obýchnyi ~) usual
method
   одобренный ~ (odóbrennyi ~)
approved method
   определённый ~ (opredeliónnyi ~)
clear-cut procedure
   осваивать ~ (osváivat' ~) to
master a technique
   особый ~ (osóbyi ~) special
method
   пересмотреть ~ (peresmotrét' ~)
to review a procedure
   поточный ~ (potóchnyi ~)
straight flow method
   практические ~/ы (praktícheskie
~/y) practical methods
   придерживать ~/а (pridérzhivat'
~/a) to follow a method
   рационализация ~/ов работы
(ratsionalizátsiia ~/ov rabóty)
rationalization of labor
   скоростной ~ (skorostnói ~)
rapid method

   современные ~/ы сбыта,
(sovreménnye ~/y sbýta,) modern
distribution methods
   стандартный ~ (standártnyi ~)
standard method
   технологический ~
(tekhnologícheskii ~)
technological process
   традиционный ~ (traditsiónnyi ~)
traditional method
   удовлетворительный ~
(udovletvorítel'nyi ~)
satisfactory method
   экономичный ~ (ekonomíchnyi ~)
economical method
   эффективный ~ (effektívnyi ~)
effective method
   ~/ы бухгалтерского учёта (~/y
bukhgálterskogo uchióta)
accounting methods
   ~ возмещения (~ vozmeshchéniia)
mode of reimbursement
   ~/ы генной инженерии (~/y génnoi
inzhenérii) genetic engineering
methods
   ~ изготовления (~ izgotovléniia)
method of production
   ~ изготовления продукции
партиями (~ izgotovléniia
prodúktsii pártiiami) batch
method of production
   ~ испытаний (~ ispytánii)
testing technique
   ~ калькуляции (~ kal'kuliátsii)
costing method
   ~ калькуляции цен (~
kal'kuliátsii tsen) pricing
method
   ~ контроля качества продукции (~
kontrólia káchestva prodúktsii)
quality control method
   ~ косвенного импорта (~
kósvennogo ímporta) indirect
import method
   ~ косвенного экспорта (~
kósvennogo éksporta) indirect
export method
   ~/ы массового сбыта (~/y
mássovogo sbýta) mass
distribution methods
   ~/ы обучения (~/y obuchéniia)
training methods
   ~ определения качества (~
opredeléniia káchestva) quality
assessment method
   ~ отбора проб (~ otbóra prob)
sampling method

~ оценки (~ otsénki) cost method
~ печати (~ pecháti) printing method
~ планирования (~ planirovániia) method of planning
~ платежа (~ platezhá) method of payment
~ подсчёта (~ podschióta) method of calculation
~ поставки (~ postávki) method of delivery
~ проведения испытаний (~ provedéniia ispytánii) testing technique
~/ы проверки (~/y provérki) inspection methods
~/ы прогнозирования (~/y prognozírovaniia) forecasting methods
~/ы проектирования (~/y proektírovaniia) design methods
~ производства (~ proizvódstva) production methods
~ прямого импорта (~ priamógo ímporta) direct import method
~ прямого экспорта (~ priamógo éksporta) direct export method
~ работы (~ rabóty) operating method
~ распределения (~ raspredeléniia) method of distribution
~ расчёта (~ raschióta) design method
~ снижение расходов (~ snizhénie raskhódov) cost-saving method
~ сотрудничества (~ sotrúdnichestva) method of collaboration
~ сравнения (~ sravnéniia) method of comparison
~/ы строительства (~/y stroítel'stva) construction process
~/ы управления (~/y upravléniia) methods of management
~/ы финансирования (~/y finansírovaniia) credit terms
~ эксплуатации (~ ekspluatátsii) operating method
Методик/а (metódik/a) f. procedure
надлежащая ~ (nadlezháshchaia ~) proper ~
обычная ~ (obýchnaia ~) conventional ~
особая ~ (osóbaia ~) special ~

оценка ~/и (otsénka ~/i) estimation ~
пересмотренная ~ (peresmótrennaia ~) revised ~
правильная ~ (právil'naia ~) correct ~
придерживаться ~/и (pridérzhivat'sia ~/i) to adhere to a ~
принять ~/у (priniát' ~/u) to adopt a ~
рекомендуемая ~ (rekomendúemaia ~) recommended ~
стандартная ~ (standártnaia ~) standard ~
~ испытаний (~ ispytánii) testing ~
~ контроля качества (~ kontrólia káchestva) quality control ~
~ обследования (~ obslédovaniia) survey ~
~ проектирования (~ proektírovaniia) design ~
~ работы (~ rabóty) operating ~
Метраж (metrázh) m. metric area
Метрический (metrícheskii) adj. metric
Механизация (mekhanizátsiia) f. mechanization
комплексная ~ (kómpleksnaia ~) comprehensive ~
полная ~ (pólnaia ~) full ~
рациональная ~ (ratsionál'naia ~) rational ~
~ производства (~ proizvódstva) ~ of production
~ сельского хозяйства (~ sél'skogo khoziástva) ~ of agriculture
~ трудоёмких процессов (~ trudoiómkikh protséssov) ~ of labor-intensive processes
Механизированный (mekhanizírovannyi) adj. mechanized
Механизм (mekhanízm) m. device, mechanism
денежно-валютный ~ (dénezhno-valiútnyi ~) currency mechanism
организационный ~ (organizatsiónnyi ~) organizational mechanism
погрузочно-разгрузочные ~/ы (pogrúzochno-razgrúzochnye ~/y) material handling equipment
подъёмный ~ (pod"iómnyi ~) hoist
рабочий ~ (rabóchii ~) working arrangements

разгрузочный ~ (razgrúzochnyi ~) unloading mechanism
рыночный ~ (rýnochnyi ~) market mechanism
хозяйственный ~ (khoziástvennyi ~) economic mechanism
~ валютных курсов (~ valiútnykh kúrsov) exchange rate mechanism
~ валютных отчислений (~ valiútnykh otchislénii) currency allocation mechanism
~ выдачи кредита (~ výdachi kredíta) credit mechanism
~ конкуренции (~ konkuréntsii) competitive mechanism
~ перечисления денежных средств (~ perechisléniia dénezhnykh sredstv) money transfer mechanism
~ цен (~ tsen) price mechanism
Механик (mekhánik) m. mechanic, operator
главный ~ (glávnyi ~) chief mechanical engineer
~ по оборудованию (~ po oborúdovaniiu) maintenance mechanic
Механический (mekhanícheskii) adj. mechanical
Мешковин/а (meshkovín/a) f. burlap
Мешкотара (meshkotára) f. sack tare
Меш/ок (mesh/ók) m. bag, sack
груз в ~/ках (gruz v ~/kákh) cargo in bags
застроплённые ~/ки (zastropliónnye ~/kí) pre-slung bags
повреждённые ~/ки (povrezhdiónnye ~/kí) damaged bags
расфасовывать в ~/ки (rasfasóvyvat' v ~/kí) to fill sacks
складной ~ (skladnói ~) collapsible bag
Минимальный (minimál'nyi) adj. minimal, minimum
Министерство (ministérstvo) n. ministry
отраслевое ~ (otraslevóe ~) sectoral ~
~ здравоохранения (~ zdravookhranéniia) ~ of health
~ иностранных дел (~ inostránnykh del) mastery of foreign affairs

~ морского флота (~ morskógo flóta) ~ of the merchant marine
~ речного флота (~ rechnógo flóta) ~ of inland water transport
~ финансов (~ finánsov) ~ of finance
~ юстиции (~ iustítsii) ~ of justice
Министр (minístr) m. minister
заместитель ~/a (zamestítel' ~/a) deputy ~
помощник ~/a (pomóshchnik ~/a) assistant to a ~
Мир (mir) m. peace, world
деловой ~ (delovói ~) business world
торговый ~ (torgóvyi ~) trading world
Мирны/й (mírny/i) adj. peaceful
в ~/х целях (v ~/kh tséliakh) for ~ purposes
~/м путём (~/m putióm) amicably
Мировой (mirovói) adj. world, worldwide
Миссия (míssiia) f. legation, mission
торговая ~ (torgóvaia ~) trade mission
Мнимый (mnímyi) adj. feigned, sham
Многоколонный (mnogokolónnyi) adj. multilinear
Многократный (mnogokrátnyi) adj. numerous, repeated
Многолетний (mnogolétnii) adj. many years
Многообещающий (mnogoobeshcháiushchii) adj. promising
Многоотраслевой (mnogootraslevói) adj. diversified {many sectors}
Многосторонний (mnogostorónnii) adj. multilateral
Многочисленный (mnogochíslennyi) adj. frequent, numerous
Множественный (mnózhestvennyi) adj. multiple, plural
Множество (mnózhestvo) n. multitude
Мобилизация (mobilizátsiia) f. mobilization
~ наличности (~ nalíchnosti) ~ of cash
~ промышленности (~ promýshlennosti) industrial ~
~ ресурсов (~ resúrsov) ~ of resources

~ финансовых средств (~
finánsovykh sredstv) ~ of
financial resources
Мод/а (mód/a) f. fashion, style
быть в ~/e (byt' v ~/e) to be in
fashion
ввести в ~/y (vvestí v ~/u) to
set the fashion
входить в ~/y (vkhodít' v ~/u)
to become fashionable
выйти из ~/ы (výiti iz ~/y) to
go out of style
по последней ~/e (po slédnei
~/e) in the latest fashion
Модел/ь (modél/') f. make, model,
pattern
действующая ~ (déistvuiushchaia
~) working model
зарегистрированная ~
(zaregistrírovannaia ~)
registered model
защита ~/ей (zashchíta ~/ei)
protection of registered designs
испытывать ~ (ispýtyvat' ~) to
test a model
конкурирующая ~
(konkuríruiushchaia ~) competing
model
название ~/и (nazvánie ~/i)
model name
новая ~ (nóvaia ~) new model
образец ~/и (obrazéts ~/i)
sample pattern
отобранная ~ (otóbrannaia ~)
selected model
предыдущая ~ (predydúshchaia ~)
previous model
рабочая ~ (rabóchaia ~) working
model
различные ~/и (razlíchnye ~/i)
various makes and models
серийная ~ (seríinaia ~)
production model
современная ~ (sovreménnaia ~)
recent model
упрощённая ~ (uproshchiónnaia ~)
reduced model
устаревшая ~ (ustarévshaia ~)
obsolete model
финансовая ~ (finánsovaia ~)
financial model
~ в разрезе (~ v razréze) cut-
away model
~ в уменьшенном размере (~ v
umén'shennom razmére) reduced
scale model

~ экономического роста (~
ekonomícheskogo rósta) economic
growth model
Модернизация (modernizátsiia) f.
modernization
коренная ~ (korennáia ~)
fundamental modernization
~ завода (~ zavóda) plant
renovation
~ экономики (~ ekonómiki) ~ of
the economy
Модернизировать (modernizírovat')
v. to modernize
Модификаци/я (modifikátsi/ia) f.
modification
запатентованная ~
(zapatentóvannaia ~) patentable
~
Модифицированный
(modifitsírovannyi) adj. modified
Модифицировать (modifitsírovat') v.
to modify
Модный (módnyi) adj. fashionable,
high-end
Мокнуть (móknut') v. to become
soaked
Мокрый (mókryi) adj. wet
Момент (momént) m. aspect, factor,
moment
важный ~ (vázhnyi ~) important
factor
критический ~ (kritícheskii ~)
critical factor, crucial moment
~ вступления в силу (~
vstupléniia v sílu) effective
date
Монет/а (monét/a) f. coin
золотые ~/ы (zolotýe ~/y) gold
~s
размен ~/ (razmén ~/) changing
of ~s
разменные ~/ы (razménnye ~/y)
loose change
серебряная ~ (serébrianaia ~)
silver ~
~/ы крупного достоинства (~/y
krúpnogo dostóinstva) ~s of
large denominations
~/ы мелкого достоинства (~/y
mélkogo dostóinstva) ~s of small
denominations
~/ы разного достоинства (~/y
ráznogo dóstoinstva) ~s of
various denominations
Монетарный (monetárnyi) adj.
monetary
Монетный (monétnyi) adj. monetary

Монометаллизм (monometallízm) *m.* monometalism {gold, silver standard}

Монометаллический (monometallícheskii) *adj.* monometallic

Монополизация (monopolizátsiia) *f.* monopolization

Монополизировать (monopolizírovat') *v.* to monopolize

Монополи/я (monopóli/ia) *f.* monopoly

    банковская ~ (bánkovskaia ~) bank ~

    валютная ~ (valiútnaia ~) foreign exchange ~

    власть ~/й (vlast' ~/i) ~ power

    временная ~ (vrémennaia ~) temporary ~

    всеобъемлющая ~ (vseob"émliushchaia ~) all-encompassing ~

    государственная ~ (gosudárstvennaia ~) state ~

    групповая ~ (gruppováia ~) group ~

    двухсторонняя ~ (dvukhstorónniaia ~) bilateral ~

    международная ~ (mezhdunaródnaia ~) international ~

    патентная ~ (paténtnaia ~) patent ~

    полная ~ (pólnaia ~) complete ~

    промышленная ~ (promýshlennaia ~) industrial ~

    регулируемая ~ (regulíruemaia ~) regulated ~

    слияние ~/й (sliiánie ~/i) merger of ~s

    случайная ~ (slucháinaia ~) accidental ~

    торговая ~ (torgóvaia ~) commercial ~

    транснациональная ~ (transnatsionál'naia ~) multinational ~

    финансовая ~ (finánsovaia ~) financial ~

    фискальная ~ (fiskál'naia ~) fiscal ~

    частная ~ (chástnaia ~) private ~

    экспортная ~ (éksportnaia ~) export ~

Монопольный (monopól'nyi) *adj.* monopoly

Монтаж (montázh) *m.* assembly, erection, installation, mounting

    быстрый ~ (býstryi ~) rapid erection

    во время ~/а (vo vrémia ~/a) during installation

    в процессе ~/а (v protsésse ~/a) in the course of erection

    график ~/а (gráfik ~/a) construction schedule

    дата ~/а (dáta ~/a) date of assembly, erection

    до начала ~/а (do nachála ~/a) prior to installation

    завершение ~/а (zavershénie ~/a) completion of erection work

    задержка ~/а (zadérzhka ~/a) delay in installation

    инструкция по ~/у (instrúktsiia po ~/u) instructions for assembly

    исключая ~ (iskliucháia ~) exclusive of erection

    консультант по ~/у (konsul'tánt po ~/u) construction advisor

    место ~/а (mésto ~/a) installation site

    на месте ~/а (na méste ~/a) at installation site

    начало ~/а (nachálo ~/a) commencement of erection

    общие условия ~/а (óbshchie uslóviia ~/a) general conditions of erection, installation

    окончание ~/а (okonchánie ~/a) completion of erection

    персонал, занимающийся ~/ом (personál, zanimáiushchiisia ~/om) erection personnel

    полный ~ (pólnyi ~) overall erection

    правильный ~ (právil'nyi ~) proper erection

    работы по ~/у (rabóty po ~/u) erection work

    расходы по ~/у (raskhódy po ~/u) expenditures on erection

    своевременный ~ (svoevrémennyi ~) timely erection

    специалист по ~/у (spetsialíst po ~/u) erection specialist

    стоимость ~/а (stóimost' ~/a) cost of assembly, erection, installation

    ~ завода (~ zavóda) plant installation

~ оборудования (~ oborúdovaniia) equipment installation
~ стенда (~ sténda) stand construction
~ и эксплуатация (~ i ekspluatátsiia) assembly and operation
Монтажник (montázhnik) *m.* assembler, installer, mounter
Монтажный (montázhnyi) *adj.* assembly, erection
Монтёр (montiór) *m.* adjuster, repairman
   аварийный ~ (avaríinyi ~) troubleshooter
Монтировать (montírovat') *v.* to assemble, to erect, to install, to mount
Моратори/й (moratóri/i) moratorium
   вводить ~ на (vvodít' ~ na) to impose a ~
   объявить ~ (ob"iávit' ~) to declare a ~
   продление ~/я (prodlénie ~/ia) extension of a ~
   установление ~/я (ustanovlénie ~/ia) imposition of a ~
Мор/е (mór/e) *n.* sea
   бурное ~ (búrnoe ~) heavy ~
   в ~ (v ~) at ~
   внутреннее ~ (vnútrennee ~) inland ~
   выход в ~ (výkhod v ~) access to the ~
   закрытое ~ (zakrýtoe ~) closed ~
   мелководное ~ (melkovódnoe ~) shallow ~
   не иметь выхода в ~ (ne imét' výkhoda v ~) to have no access to the ~
   открытое ~ (otkrýtoe ~) open ~
   перевозимый ~/ем ~- (perevozímyi ~/em) borne
   переход ~/ем (perekhód ~/em) ~ passage
   повреждение на ~ (povrezhdénie na ~) ~ damage
   путешествие по ~/ю (puteshéstvie po ~/iu) ~ voyage
   свободное ~ (svobódnoe ~) free ~
Мореплавани/е (moreplávani/e) *n.* navigation, shipping
   безопасность ~/я (bezopásnost' ~/ia) safety of navigation
   международное торговое ~ (mezhdunaródnoe torgóvoe ~) international shipping

пригодность к ~/ю (prigódnost' k ~/iu) seaworthiness
пригодный к ~/ю (prigódnyi k ~/iu) seaworthy
торговое (torgóvoe) merchant shipping
Мореходност/ь (morekhódnost/') *f.* seaworthiness
   абсолютная ~ (absoliútnaia ~) absolute ~
   сертификат о ~/и (sertifikát o ~/i) certificate of ~
   ~ судна (~ súdna) ~ of a vessel
Мореходный (morekhódnyi) *adj.* seagoing
Морозостойкий (morozostóikii) *adj.* frost resistant
Морской (morskói) *adj.* marine, maritime
Мощност/ь (móshchnost/') *f.* capacity, output, power
   активная ~ (aktívnaia ~) active power
   большая ~ (bol'sháia ~) heavy-duty, high power
   ввод в действие новых ~/ей (vvod v déistvie nóvykh ~/ei) commissioning of new capacities
   вводить ~/и в действие (vvodít' ~/i v déistvie) to commission capаcities
   гарантированная ~ (garantírovannaia ~) guaranteed capacity
   годовая ~ (godováia ~) annual capacity, annual output
   двигателя ~ (dvígatelia ~) engine power
   действующие ~/и (déistvuiushchie ~/i) operational capacities
   длительная ~ (dlítel'naia ~) continuous capacity
   достигать проектной ~/и (dostigát' proéktnoi ~/i) to reach projected capacity
   загрузочная ~ (zagrúzochnaia ~) load capacity
   запасная ~ (zapasnáia ~) spare capacity
   избыточная ~ (izbýtochnaia ~) surplus capacity
   коэффициент ~/и (koeffitsiént ~/i) capacity rate
   максимальная ~ (maksimál'naia ~) maximum capacity
   малая ~ (málaia ~) low power

неиспользованная ~
(neispól'zovannaia ~) idle
capacity
новая ~ (nóvaia ~) fresh
capacity
номинальная ~ (nominál'naia ~)
nominal output
общая ~ (óbshchaia ~) total
capacity
полезная ~ (poléznaia ~) useful
power
полная ~ (pólnaia ~) full
capacity
потребляемая ~ (potrebliáemaia
~) power consumption
потребная ~ (potrébnaia ~)
required capacity
проектная ~ (proéktnaia ~)
design capacity
производственная ~
(proizvódstvennaia ~)
manufacturing capacity
пусковая ~ (puskováia ~)
starting power
работа на полную ~ (rabóta na
pólnuiu ~) operation at full
capacity
рабочая ~ (rabóchaia ~)
operating power
расчётная ~ (raschiótnaia ~)
rated capacity
резервная ~ (rezérvnaia ~)
reserve capacity
резерв установленной ~/и (rezérv
ustanóvlennoi ~/i) margin of
reserve capacity
средняя ~ (srédniaia ~) average
capacity
суммарная ~ (summárnaia ~)
aggregate capacity
снижение ~/ей (snizhénie ~/ei)
reduction in capacity, decline
in output
удельная ~ (udél'naia ~)
specific capacity
установленная ~ (ustanóvlennaia
~) installed capacity
фактическая ~ (faktícheskaia ~)
actual power
эксплуатационная ~
(ekspluatatsiónnaia ~) service
power
эффективная ~ (effektívnaia ~)
effective power
~ на единицу веса (~ na edinítsu
vésa) horsepower per unit of
weight

~ на производственную единицу (~
na proizvódstvennuiu edinítsu)
capacity per unit
Мощный (móshchnyi) adj. heavy-duty,
high capacity, powerful
Мультивалютный (mul'tivaliútnyi)
adj. multicurrency

Н

Набавлять (nabavliát') v. to add,
increase
Набережная (náberezhnaia)
f.adj.noun embankment, quay
    разгрузочная ~ (razgrúzochnaia
    ~) discharging quay
    франко ~ (fránko ~) free
    alongside quay {FAQ}
Наблюдение (nabliudénie) n.
observation, supervision
Набор (nabór) m. assortment,
collection, set
    полный ~ (pólnyi ~) complete set
    ~ инструментов (~ instruméntov)
    tool kit
Навалом (naválom) m. in bulk, loose
Навалочный (naválochnyi) adj. bulk,
loose {of cargo, freight}
Навигационный (navigatsiónnyi) adj.
navigating
Навигаци/я (navigátsi/ia) f.
navigation
    воздушная ~ (vozdúshnaia ~) air
    ~
    закрытый для ~/и (zakrýtyi dlia
    ~/i) closed to ~
    морская ~ (morskáia ~) marine ~
    открытый для ~/и (otkrýtyi dlia
    ~/i) open for ~
Наглость (náglost') f. impudence,
insolence
Наглый (náglyi) adj. impudent,
insolent
Нагружать (nagruzhát') v. to load
    ~ чрезмерно (~ chrezmérno) to
    overload
Нагрузк/а (nagrúzk/a) f. load
    безопасная ~ (bezopásnaia ~)
    permissible {safe} ~
    временная ~ (vrémennaia ~)
    temporary ~
    выдерживать ~/у (vydérzhivat'
    ~/u) to endure a ~
    добавочная ~ (dobávochnaia ~)
    additional ~

допускаемая ~ (dopuskáemaia ~)
permissible ~
испытание под ~/ой (ispytánie
pod ~/oi) ~ test
испытательная ~ (ispytátel'naia
~) trial ~
коммерческая ~ (kommércheskaia
~) payload
малая ~ (málaia ~) light duty
минимальная ~ (minimál'naia ~)
minimum ~
наибольшая ~ (naiból'shaia ~)
maximum ~
неполная ~ (nepólnaia ~) under ~
номинальная ~ (nominál'naia ~)
rated ~
нормативная ~ (normatívnaia ~)
prescribed ~
под ~/ой (pod ~/oi) under ~
полезная ~ (poléznaia ~) service
~
полная ~ (pólnaia ~) full ~
постоянная ~ (postoiánnaia ~)
fixed ~
пробная ~ (próbnaia ~) test ~
рабочая ~ (rabóchaia ~) work ~
расчётная ~ (raschiótnaia ~)
design ~
средняя ~ (srédniaia ~) average
~
чрезмерная ~ (chrezmérnaia ~)
over ~
Надбав/ка (nadbáv/ka) f. mark-up,
premium, surcharge
аккордная ~ (akkórdnaia ~) piece
work bonus
включать ~/ку в размере ...%
(vkliuchát' ~/ku v razmére ...)
includes a surcharge of ... %
делать ~/ку к цене (délat' ~/ku
k tsené) to add a surcharge to
the price
денежная ~ (dénezhnaia ~)
premium
дополнительная ~
(dopolnítel'naia ~) surcharge
ежегодная ~ (ezhegódnaia ~)
annual raise
платить ~/ку (platít' ~/ku) to
pay a surcharge
поощрительная ~
(pooshchrítel'naia ~) incentive
premium
премиальная ~ (premiál'naia ~)
premium
продавать с ~/кой (prodavát' s
~/koi) to sell at a premium

сезонная ~ (sezónnaia ~)
seasonal surcharge
стимулирующая ~
(stimulíruiushchaia ~)
additional incentive
цена с ~/кой (tsená s ~/koi)
price plus mark-up
шкала ~/ок и скидок (shkalá ~/ok
i skídok) escalation
~ за выслугу лет (~ za výslugu
let) seniority bonus
~ за повышенное качество (~ za
povýshennoe káchestvo) quality
bonus
~ за риск (~ za risk) risk
premium
~ за тяжеловесный груз (~ za
tiazhelovésnyi gruz) overload
premium
Надёжност/ь (nadiózhnost/') f.
dependability, reliability
анализ ~/и (análiz ~/i)
reliability analysis
изменение ~/и (izmenénie ~/i)
variations in reliability
меры ~/и (méry ~/i) measures of
reliability
обеспечение ~/и (obespéchénie
~/i) assurance of reliability
расчётная ~ (raschiótnaia ~)
design reliability
эксплуатационная ~
(ekspluatatsiónnaia ~) operating
reliability
Надёжный (nadiózhnyi) adj.
dependable, reliable
Надзор (nadzór) m. inspection,
supervision, surveillance
государственный ~
(gosudárstvennyi ~) state
supervision
осуществлять ~ (osushchestvliát'
~) to supervise
санитарный ~ (sanitárnyi ~)
sanitary inspection
строительный ~ (stroítel'nyi ~)
building inspection
технический ~ (tekhnícheskii ~)
technical inspec tion
Надлежащи/й (nadlezháshchi/i) adj.
appropriate, fitting, proper
~/м образом (~/m óbrazom) duly,
properly
Надписывать (nadpísyvat') v. to
superscribe
Надпис/ь (nádpis/') f. endorsement,
inscription

безоборотная ~ (bezoborótnaia ~)
endorsement without recourse
бланковая ~ (blánkovaia ~) blank
endorsement
делать ~ (délat' ~) to endorse
именная ~ (imennáia ~)
endorsement in full
передаточная ~ (peredátochnaia
~) endorsement
последовательные ~/и
(posledovátel'nye ~/i)
successive endorsements

Наём (naióm) *m.* employment, hire,
lease, renting
агент по найму (agént po náimu)
employment agent
договор найма (dogovór náima)
employment contract
перевозки по найму (perevózki po
náimu) hired transportation
работа по найму (rabóta po
náimu) work for hire
сдача в ~ (sdácha v ~) hiring
out
условия найма в аренду (uslóviia
náima v aréndu) lease conditions
~ персонала (~ personála) hiring
of personnel
~ рабочей силы (~ rabóchei síly)
hiring of work force

Название (nazvánie) *n.* name, title
изменить ~ (izmenít' ~) to
change the name
торговое ~ товара (torgóvoe ~
továra) trade name
~ изобретения (~ izobreténiia)
name of an invention
~ марки (~ márki) brand name
~ судна (~ súdna) ship's name

Назначать (naznachát') *v.* to
allocate, to appropriate, to
assign, to commission, to nominate

Назначени/е (naznachéni/e) *n.*
allocation, appropriation,
assignment, nomination, quotation
место ~/я (mésto ~/ia) final
destination
порт ~/я (port ~/ia) port of
entry
порт окончательного ~/я (port
okonchátel'nogo ~/ia) final port
порт первоначального ~/я (port
pervonachál'nogo ~/ia) original
port of destination
станция ~/я (stántsiia ~/ia)
station of destination

страна ~/я (straná ~/ia)
receiving country
получить ~ (poluchít' ~) to
receive an appointment
производить ~ арбитра
(proizvodít' ~ arbítra) to
nominate an arbitrator
~ документов (~ dokuméntov)
disposition of documents
~ на пост (~ na post)
appointment to a post
~ цен (~ tsen) quotation of
prices

Назначенный (naznáchennyi) *adj.*
appointed
вновь ~ (vnov' ~) newly ~

Называть (nazyvát') *v.* to entitle,
to name

Наименовани/е (naimenováni/e) *n.*
name
торговое ~ (torgóvoe ~) trade ~
условное ~ (uslóvnoe ~)
conditional ~
фирменное ~ (fírmennoe ~) ~ of a
firm
~ бенефициара (~ benefitsiára) ~
of a beneficiary
~ груза (~ grúza) description of
cargo
~ завода-изготовителя (~ zavóda-
izgotovítelia) manufacturer's ~
~ заявителя (~ zaiavítelia)
denomination of an applicant
~ изделия (~ izdéliia)
description of an article
~ изобретения (~ izobreténiia)
title of an invention
~ судна (~ súdna) ship's ~
~ товара (~ továra) description
of goods

Накапливать (nakáplivat') *v.* to
accumulate, to stockpile
~/ся (~/sia) to accrue

Накапливающийся
(nakáplivaiushchiisia) *adj.*
cumulative

Накладн/ая (nakladn/áia) *f.adj.noun*
bill of lading, way bill
авиагрузовая ~ (aviagruzováia ~)
air way bill
автодорожная ~ (avtodorózhnaia
~) truck bill of lading
грузовая ~ (gruzováia ~)
consignment note
дубликат транспортной ~/ой
(dublikát tránsportnoi ~/ói) way
bill duplicate

железнодорожная ~
(zheleznodoródzhnaia ~) railroad
way bill
копия ~/ой (kópiia ~/ói) way
bill copy
корешок ~/ой (koreshók ~/ói)
counterfoil way bill
международная ~ (mezhdunaródnaia
~) international consignment
note
оформление ~/ой (oformlénie
~/ói) drawing up of a way bill
представить ~/ую (predstávit'
~/úiu) to present a way bill
предъявлять ~/ую (pred"iavliát'
~/úiu) to submit a way bill
по ~/ой (po ~/ói) against a way
bill
речная ~ (rechnáia ~) river bill
of lading
сквозная ~ (skvoznáia ~)
transshipment bill of lading
сопроводительная ~
(soprovodítel'naia ~)
accompanying note
товаросопроводительная ~
(tovarosoprovodítel'naia ~)
consignment note
транспортная ~ (tránsportnaia ~)
way bill
Накладны/е {расходы} (nakladný/e
{raskhódy}) pl.adj.noun overhead
expenses
общезаводские ~
(obshchezavódskie ~) plant
overhead
производственные ~
(proizvódstvennye ~) production
overhead
распределение ~/х {расходов}
(raspredelénie ~/kh {raskhódov})
allocation of overhead
Накладывать (nakládyvat') v. to
apply, to impose
~ ограничения (~ ogranichéniia)
to impose restrictions
~ печать (~ pechát') v. to affix
a stamp
~ пломбу (~ plómbu) to affix a
seal
~ штраф (~ shtraf) to apply a
penalty
Наклеивать (nakléivat') to affix,
to stick {with adhesive}
Наклейк/а (nakléik/a) f. stick-on
label

бумажная ~ (bumázhnaia ~) paper
label
прикреплять ~/у (prikrepliát'
~/u) to affix a label
Накопившийся (nakopívshiisia) adj.
accrued
Накоплени/е (nakopléni/e) n.
accrual, accumulation, stockpiling
непроизводственное ~
(neproizvódstvennoe ~) non-
productive accumulation
производственное ~
(proizvódstvennoe ~) productive
accumulation
существенные ~/я
(sushchéstvennye ~/ia)
substantial accumulation
ускоренное ~ (uskórennoe ~)
accelerated accumulation
чрезмерное ~ (chrezmérnoe ~)
hoarding
~ денежных средств (~ dénezhnykh
sredstv) accumulation of funds
~ капитала (~ kapitála) capital
accumulation
~ процентов (~ protséntov)
accrual of interest
~ товарных запасов (~ továrnykh
zapásov) stockpiling
Налагать (nalagát') v. to impose,
to inflict
~ вето (~ véto) to veto
Наладк/а (naládk/a) f. adjustment,
setup
инструкции по ~/е (instrúktsii
po ~/e) adjustment instructions
период ~/и (períod ~/i)
adjustment period
проводить ~/у (provodít' ~/u) to
provide setup
руководство ~/ой (rukovódstvo
~/oi) supervision of setup
ручная ~ (ruchnáia ~) manual
setup
Налаживать (nalázhivat') v. to
adjust, to organize, to setup
Наливать (nalivát') v. to fill, to
pour
Наливом (nalívom) adv. in bulk, in
tanks
Наличи/е (nalíchi/e) n.
availability
быть в ~/и (byt' v ~/i) to be
available
при условии ~/я (pri uslóvii
~/ia) subject to availabiity

~ денег (~ déneg) availability of cash
~ документации (~ dokumentátsii) availability of documentation
~ полномочий (~ polnomóchii) authority
~ скрытого дефекта (~ skrýtogo defékta) presence of a latent defect
~ товаров (~ továrov) availability of stock

Наличност/ь (nalíchnost/') *f.* cash, cash-in-hand
денежная ~ (dénezhnaia ~) cash-in-hand
долларовая ~ (dóllarovaia ~) dollar holdings
инвалютная ~ (ínvaliutnaia ~) foreign exchange holdings
кассовая ~ (kássovaia ~) cash balance, till
мобилизация ~/и (mobilizátsiia ~/i) cash mobilization
отсутствие ~/и (otsútstvie ~/i) non-liquidity
проверять кассовую ~ (proveriát' kassovúiu ~) to check the cash balance
резервная ~ (rezérvnaia ~) reserve cash
свободная ~ (svobódnaia ~) spare cash
товарная ~ (továrnaia ~) stock-in-trade

Наличны/е (nalíchny/e) *pl.adj.noun* cash, ready money
аванс ~/ми (aváns ~/mi) cash advance
за ~ (za ~) for cash
переводить в ~ (perevodít' v ~) to convert into cash
платёж ~/ми (platiózh ~/mi) cash terms
платёж ~/ми без скидки (platiózh ~/mi bez skídki) net cash terms
платить ~/ми (platít' ~/mi) to pay cash
платить ~/ми без скидки (platít' ~/mi bez skídki) to pay net cash
подлежащий оплате ~/ми (podlezháshchii opláte ~/mi) payable in cash

Наличный (nalíchnyi) *adj.* available, present, ready

Налог (nalóg) tax
адвалорный ~ (advalórnyi ~) ad valorem ~

аккордный ~ (akkórdnyi ~) lumpsum ~
большой ~ (bol'shói ~) heavy ~
быть освобождённым от уплаты ~/ов (byt' osvobozhdiónnym ot upláty ~/ov) to be exempt from the payment of ~es
введение ~/a (vvedénie ~/a) imposition of a ~
взимать ~ (vzimát' ~) to levy a ~
возврат ~/a (vozvrát ~/a) ~ refund
выплачивать ~/и (vypláchivat' ~/i) to pay ~es
высокий ~ (vysókii ~) high ~
государственный ~ (gosudárstvennyi ~) government ~
дискриминационный ~ (diskriminatsiónnyi ~) discriminatory ~
до вычета ~/a (do výcheta ~/a) before ~ {e.g. income}
дополнительный ~ (dopolnítel'nyi ~) ~ surcharge
дорожный ~ (dorózhnyi ~) toll
доход от ~/ов (dokhód ot ~/ov) ~ revenue
единый ~ (edínyi ~) unitary ~
за вычетом ~/a (za výchetom ~/a) after ~
земельный ~ (zemél'nyi ~) land ~
косвенный ~ (kósvennyi ~) indirect ~
льготы на ~ (l'góty na ~) ~ preferences
местный ~ (méstnyi ~) local ~
натуральный ~ (naturál'nyi ~) ~ in kind
непомерный ~ (nepomérnyi ~) onerous ~
неуплата ~/a (neupláta ~/a) non-payment of a ~
неуплаченный ~ (neupláchennyi ~) delinquent ~
облагать ~/ом (oblagát' ~/om) to subject to a ~
обложение ~/ом (oblozhénie ~/om) taxation
односторонний ~ (odnostorónnii ~) one-sided ~
одноступенчатый ~ (odnostupénchatyi ~) single stage ~
освобождать от ~/ов (osvobozhdát' ot ~/ov) to exempt from ~es

освобождение от ~/ов (osvobozhdénie ot ~/ov) ~ exemption

отсрочка ~/а (otsróchka ~/a) ~ deferment

платить ~/и (platít' ~/i) to pay ~es

повышать ~/и (povyshát' ~/i) to increase ~es

подлежать обложению ~/ом (podlezhát' oblozhéniiu ~/om) to be subject to taxation

подоходный ~ (podokhódnyi ~) income ~

поимущественный ~ (poimúshchestvennyi ~) property ~

поступления от ~/ов (postupléniia ot ~/ov) proceeds from ~es

прогрессивный ~ (progressívnyi ~) progressive ~

промысловый ~ (promýslovyi ~) trade licensing ~

пропорциональный ~ (proportsionál'nyi ~) proportional ~

прямой ~ (priamói ~) direct ~

сбор ~/ов (sbor ~/ov) collection of ~es

свободный от уплаты ~/ов (svobódnyi ot upláty ~/ov) exempt from ~es

система ~/ов (sistéma ~/ov) system of taxation

скидка с ~/а (skídka s ~/a) ~ abatement

собирать ~/и (sobirát' ~/i) to collect ~

сокращение ~/ов (sokrashchénie ~/ov) reduction in ~ es

специфический ~ (spetsifícheskii ~) specific ~

ставка ~/а (stávka ~/a) ~ rate

удержание ~/ов (uderzhánie ~/ov) ~ withholding

удерживать ~/и (udérzhivat' ~/i) to withhold ~es

уклоняться от уплаты ~/ов (ukloniát'sia ot upláty ~/ov) to evade ~es

уравнительный ~ (uravnítel'nyi ~) equalization ~

федеральный ~ (federál'nyi ~) federal ~

шкала ~/ов (shkalá ~/ov) ~ schedule

~ на личное имущество (~ na líchnoe imúshchestvo) ~ on personal property

~ на зарплату (~ na zarplátu) ~ on wages

~ на импорт (~ na ímport) import ~

~ на капитал (~ na kapitál) capital ~

~ на недвижимость (~ na nedvízhimost') ~ on real property

~ на оборот (~ na oborót) turnover ~

~ с доходов акционерных компаний (~ s dokhódov aktsionérnykh kompánii) corporate income ~

~ с роялти (~ s róialti) royalty ~

Налоговый (nalógovyi) adj. tax

Налогообложени/е (nalogooblozhéni/e) n. taxation

двойное ~ (dvoinóe ~) double ~

льготное ~ (l'gótnoe ~) preferential ~

прогрессивное ~ (progressívnoe ~) progressive ~

пропорциональное ~ (proportsionál'noe ~) proportional ~

тяжёлое ~ (tiazhióloe ~) heavy ~

система ~/я (sistéma ~/ia) system of ~

Налогоплательщик (nalogoplatél'shchik) m. taxpayer

Наложение (nalozhénie) n. imposition

~ ареста на имущество (~ arésta na imúshchestvo) seizure of property, sequestration

~ ареста на товары (~ arésta na továry) seizure of goods

~ запрещения на судно и груз (~ zapreshchéniia na súdno i gruz) action in rem against vessel and cargo

~ штрафа (~ shtráfa) ~ of a fine

Намерени/е (naméréni/e) n. intention, purpose

протокол о ~/ях (protokól o ~/iakh) protocol of intent

соглашение о ~/ях (soglashénie o ~/iakh) letter of intent

Нанесение (nanesénie) n. inflicting

~ маркировки (~ markiróvki) marking

~ ущерба (~ ushchérba) prejudice

Наниматель (nanimátel') m. employer
~ судна (~ súdna) charterer
Нанимать (nanimát') v. to charter,
to employ, to hire, to rent
Наносить (nanosít') v. to cause, to
inflict, to mark
Напечатанный (napechátannyi) adj.
printed, typewritten
Наплыв (naplýv) m. inflow
~ заказов (~ zakázov) ~ of
orders
Наполнять (napolniát') v. to fill
Напоминани/е (napomináni/e) n.
reminder
многократные ~/я (mnogokrátnye
~/ia) numerous reminders
официальное ~ (ofitsiál'noe ~)
official ~
письмо с ~/ем (pis'mó s ~/em)
dunning letter
повторное ~ (povtórnoe ~) second
~
~ о платеже (~ o platezhé) ~ of
payment due
Направленный (naprávlennyi) adj.
forwarded
Направлять (napravliát') v. to
address, to forward, to route
Направляющийся
(napravliáiushchiisia) adj. bound
for
~ в порт приписки (~ v port
pripíski) homeward bound
Напрокат (naprokát) adv. for hire,
for rent
брать ~ (brat' ~) to hire
сдавать ~ (sdavát' ~) to hire
out
Напряжение (napriazhénie) n.
pressure, strain, tension
выдержать ~ (výderzhat' ~) to
withstand stress
высокое ~ (vysókoe ~) high
pressure
ослабить ~ (oslábit' ~) to
reduce tension
Напряжённост/ь (napriazhiónnost/')
f. intensity, tension
ослабление ~/и (oslablénie ~/i)
relaxation of tension
~ рынка (~ rýnka) market
pressure
Напряжённый (napriazhiónnyi) adj.
intense, tight
Нарастать (narastát') v. to accrue,
to accumulate

Наращивание (narashchivánie) n.
accumulation, build-up, increase
~ производственных мощностей (~
proizvódstvennykh móshchnostei)
increase in production capacity
~ темпа производства (~ témpa
proizvódstva) increase in the
rate of production
Наращивать (naráshchivat') v. to
build-up, to increase
Нарицательный (naritsátel'nyi) adj.
nominal
Наркоман (narkomán) m. drug addict
Наркомания (narkomániia) f. drug
addiction
Наркотик (narkótik) m. narcotic
Наросший (narósshii) adj. accrued,
accumulated
Нарочный (nárochnyi) m.adj.
courier, messenger
Нарушать (narushát') v. to breach,
to infringe, to violate
~ закон (~ zakón) to break the
law
Нарушени/е (narushéni/e) n. breach,
infringement, violation
валютные ~/я (valiútnye ~/ia)
currency violations
в ~/и инструкций (v ~/i
instrúktsii) contrary to
instructions
грубое ~ (grúboe ~) gross
infringement, gross violation
избегать ~/й (izbegát' ~/i) to
avoid violations
иск о ~/и договора (isk o ~/i
dogovóra) breach of contract
action
наложить штраф за ~ (nalozhít'
shtraf za ~) to impose a penalty
for a violation
ответственность за ~
(otvétstvennost' za ~) liability
for breach, for infringement
прекратить ~ (prekratít' ~) to
discontinue infringement
причина ~/я (prichína ~/ia)
cause of infringement
санкции за ~ (sánktsii za ~)
sanctions for violation
урегулировать ~ (uregulírovat'
~) to settle an infringement
штраф за ~ (shtraf za ~) fine
for violation
~ авторского права (~ ávtorskogo
práva) copyright infringement

~ гарантии (~ garántii) breach of warranty

~ графика (~ gráfika) breach of a schedule

~ доверия (~ dovériia) breach of confidence

~ договора (~ dogovóra) breach of contract

~ закона (~ zakóna) violation of a law

~ исключительности (~ iskliuchítel'nosti) violation of exclusivity

~ контракта (~ kontrákta) breach of contract

~ обязательства (~ obiazátel'stva) breach of an obligation

~ патента (~ paténta) infringement of a patent

~ положений договора (~ polozhénii dogovóra) breach of contract provisions

~ права (~ práva) infringement of a right

~ правил (~ právil) breaking of rules

~ правил по технике безопасности (~ právil po tékhnike bezopás-nosti) violation of safety regulations

~ равновесия (~ ravnovésiia) imbalance

~ соглашения (~ soglashéniia) breach of an agreement

~ товарного знака (~ továrnogo znáka) infringement of a trade mark

~ условий (~ uslóvii) violation of conditions

~ формальностей (~ formál'nostei) disregard of for-malities

Нарушител/ь (narushítel/') *m.* infringer, violator

преследовать ~/я (preslédovat' ~/ia) to prosecute the infringer

~ авторского права (~ ávtorskogo práva) plagiarizer, copyright pirate

~ закона (~ zakóna) law breaker

~ патентов (~ paténtov) patent infringer

Наряд (nariád) *m.* order, warrant

рабочий ~ (rabóchii ~) work card

~ на работу (~ na rabótu) work order

Наступать (nastupát') *v.* to mature {of a bill, draft}

Наступлени/е (nastupléni/e) *n.* approach, onset

Насчитывать (naschítyvat') *v.* to count, to total

Насыпать (nasypát') *v.* to fill

~ в мешки (~ v meshkí) ~ in bags

Насыпка (nasýpka) *f.* filling

Насыпной (nasypnói) *adj.* bulk

Насыпью (násyp'iu) *adv.* in bulk

перевозка груза ~ (perevózka grúza ~) bulk shipment

хранение ~ (khranénie ~) bulk storage

Насыщение (nasyshchénie) *n.* saturation

~ рынка (~ rýnka) market ~

~ спроса (~ sprósa) demand ~

Натур/а (natúr/a) *f.* in kind

возмещение в ~/е (vozmeshchénie v ~/e) compensation ~

вознаграждение ~/ой (voznagrazhdénie ~/oi) remuneration ~

оплата ~/ой (opláta ~/oi) payment ~

Натуральный (naturál'nyi) *adj.* in kind, natural

Наукоёмкий (naukoiómkii) *adj.* high technology

Научный (naúchnyi) *adj.* scientific

Наценка (natsénka) *f.* margin, mark-up

бюджетная ~ (biudzhétnaia ~) budget margin

розничная ~ (róznichnaia ~) retail mark-up

страховая ~ (strakhóvaia ~) insurance margin

торговая ~ (torgóvaia ~) trade margin

Национализация (natsionalizátsiia) *f.* nationalization

Национализировать (natsionalizírovat') *v.* to nationalize

Начал/о (nachál/o) *n.* beginning

на договорных ~/ах (na dogovórnykh ~/akh) on a con-tractual basis

на комиссионных ~/ах (na komissiónnykh ~/akh) on a commission basis

на паритетных ~/ах (na paritétnykh ~/akh) on a basis of parity

на равных ~/ах (na rávnykh ~/akh) on equal terms
Начальный (nachál'nyi) *adj.* beginning, initial
Начислени/е (nachisléni/e) *n.* calculation, charge, computation
   амортизационные ~/я (amortizatsiónnye ~/ia) depreciation charges
   общепринятые ~/я (obshchepríniatye ~/ia) generally accepted charges
   формула ~/я процентов (fórmula ~/ia protséntov) interest accrual formula
   ~ процентов (~ protséntov) calculation of interest
Начислять (nachisliát') *v.* to calculate, to charge, to compute
Неадресованный (neadresóvannyi) *adj.* unaddressed
Неактивный (neaktívnyi) *adj.* inactive
Неакцепт (neaktsépt) *m.* non-acceptance
Неакцептованный (neaktseptóvannyi) *adj.* unaccepted
Небоскрёб (neboskriób) *m.* skyscraper
Небрежность (nebrézhnost') *f.* negligence
Небрежный (nebrézhnyi) *adj.* careless, negligent
Небьющийся (neb'iúshchiisia) *adj.* unbreakable
Невзысканный (nevzýskannyi) *adj.* outstanding
Невидимый (nevídimyi) *adj.* invisible
Невиновный (nevinóvnyi) *adj.* not guilty
Невменяемый (nevmeniáemyi) *adj.* legally irresponsible {insanity, minority, etc.}
Невостребованный (nevostrébovannyi) *adj.* uncalled {pursuant to a cash call, etc.}
Невыгодный (nevýgodnyi) *adj.* disadvantageous, unprofitable
Невыкупленный (nevýkuplennyi) *adj.* unredeemed
Невыполнени/е (nevypolnéni/e) *n.* non-fulfillment, non-performance
   в случае ~/я обязательств (v slúchae ~/ia obiazátel'stv) in the event of a default

   частичное ~ (chastíchnoe ~) partial default
   штраф за ~ договора (shtraf za ~ dogovóra) penalty for ~ of a contract
   ~ договора (~ dogovóra) ~ of a contract
   ~ заказа (~ zakáza) ~ of an order
   ~ контракта (~ kontrákta) ~ of a contract
   ~ плана (~ plána) ~ of a plan {e.g. five year plan}
Невыполненный (nevýpolnennyi) *adj.* outstanding, unexecuted, unfulfilled
Невыполнимость (nevypolnímost') *f.* impossibility {of performance}
Невыполнимый (nevypolnímyi) *adj.* impracticable, impossible, infeasible
Негабарит (negabarít) *m.* oversize cargo
   ~ по высоте (~ po vysoté) over height cargo
   ~ по ширине (~ po shiriné) over width cargo
Негабаритный (negabarítnyi) *adj.* oversize
Негарантированный (negarantírovannyi) *adj.* unguaranteed
Негодность (negódnost') *f.* unfitness
Негодный (negódnyi) *adj.* unfit, unsuitable
   ~ к употреблению (~ k upotrebléniiu) unfit for intended use
Негоциант (negotsiánt) *m.* negotiator
Негоциаци/я (negotsiátsi/ia) *f.* negotiation
   производить ~/ю (proizvodít' ~/iu) to effect a ~
   ~ против документов (~ prótiv dokuméntov) ~ against documents
   ~ тратт (~ trátt) ~ of drafts
Негоциировать (negotsiírovat') *v.* to negotiate
Недвижимост/ь (nedvízhimost/') *f.* real estate
   владелец ~/и (vladélets ~/i) owner of ~
   доход с ~/и (dokhód s ~/i) rent
   закладная под ~ (zakladnáia pod ~) ~ mortgage

налог на ~ (nalóg na ~) ~ tax
рынок ~/и (rýnok ~/i) ~ market
Недвижимый (nedvizhimyi) *adj.*
immoveable
Недействительност/ь
(nedeistvítel'nost/') *f.*
invalidity, nullity
объявление о ~/и (ob"iavlénie o
~/i) notice of legal extinction
~ авторского свидетельства (~
ávtorskogo svidétel'stva)
invalidity of a certificate of
authorship
~ договора (~ dogovóra) nullity
of a contract, treaty
~ патента (~ paténta) invalidity
of a patent
~ товарного знака (~ továrnogo
znáka) invalidity of a trade
mark
Недействительны/й
(nedeistvítel'ny/i) *adj.* null and
void
признать ~/м (priznát' ~/m) to
declare ~
Неделимый (nedelímyi) *adj.*
indivisable
Недискриминационный
(nediskriminatsiónnyi) *adj.* non-
discriminatory
Недлительный (nedlítel'nyi) *adj.*
non-durable
Недоброкачественность
(nedobrokáchestvennost') *f.*
inferior quality
Недоброкачественный
(nedobrokáchestvennyi) *adj.* poor
quality
Недобросовестность
(nedobrosóvestnost') *f.* bad faith
Недобросовестный (nedobrosóvestnyi)
adj. in bad faith
Недовес (nedovés) *m.* short weight
Недогружать (nedogruzhát') *v.* to
underload
Недогруз (nedogrúz) *m.* short
shipment
~ судна (~ súdna) underloading
of a vessel
Недогрузк/а (nedogrúzk/a) *f.*
underloading
Недоимк/а (nedoímk/a) *f.* arrears
сумма ~/и (súmma ~/i) amount in
~
взыскивать ~/у (vzýskivat' ~/u)
to dun for ~

Недокументированный
(nedokumentírovannyi) *adj.* undocumented
Недооценивать (nedootsénivat') *v.*
to underestimate, to undervalue
Недооценка (nedootsénka) *f.*
underestimate, undervaluation
Недоплата (nedopláta) *f.* short
payment
Недоплачивать (nedoplachivat') *v.*
to underpay
Недополученный (nedopolúchennyi)
adj. short-received
Недопоставленный (nedopostávlennyi)
short delivered
Недоразумение (nedorazuménie) *n.*
misunderstanding
Недорогой (nedorogói) *adj.*
inexpensive
Недоставка (nedostávka) *f.* non-
delivery
Недоставленный (nedostávlennyi)
adj. undelivered
Недостат/ок (nedostát/ok) *m.*
deficiency, lack, shortage
за ~/ком ... (za ~/kom ...) for
lack of ...
исправлять ~/ки (ispravliát'
~/ki) to remedy defects
испытывать ~ (ispýtyvat' ~) to
lack for
крупные ~/ки (krúpnye ~/ki)
serious defects
мелкие ~/ки (mélkie ~/ki) minor
defects
производственные ~/ки
(proizvódstvennye ~/ki) manufacturing defects
скрытые ~/ки (skrýtye ~/ki)
latent defects
существенные ~/ки
(sushchéstvennye ~/ki) material
defects
~ вакансий (~ vakánsii) lack of
jobs
Недостаточность (nedostátochnost')
f. deficiency, inadequacy
~ снабжения (~ snabzhéniia)
supply shortage
~ спроса (~ sprósa) inadequate
demand
~ обслуживания и ремонта (~
obslúzhivaniia i remónta) inadequate maintenance and repair
Недостаточный (nedostátochnyi) *adj.*
inadequate, insufficient

Недостач/а (nedostách/a) f.
deficiency, lack, shortage
  акт о ~/е (akt o ~/e) shortage
  report
  возместить ~/у (vozmestít' ~/u)
  to compensate for shortage
  денежная ~ (dénezhnaia ~)
  monetary deficit
  заявленная ~ (zaiávlennaia ~)
  declared shortage
  крупная ~ (krúpnaia ~) major
  shortage
  ответственность за ~/у
  (otvétstvennost' za ~/u) liability for deficiency
  покрывать ~/у (pokryvát' ~/u) to
  cover a shortage
  претензия по ~/е товара
  (preténziia po ~/e továra) claim
  for shortage of goods
  фактическая ~ (faktícheskaia ~)
  actual shortage
  ~ в весе (~ v vése) shortage in
  weight
Недостающий (nedostaiúshchii) adj.
deficient, missing, short
Недоступный (nedostúpnyi) adj.
inaccessible, unobtainable
Недочёт (nedochiót) m. deficit,
shortage
Недремлющ/ий (nedrémliushch/ii)
adj. vigilant
  «Право благоприятствует ~/им»
  (právo blagopriiátstvuet ~/im)
  "the law favors the vigilant"
Незаверенный (nezavérennyi) adj.
uncertified
Незавершённый (nezavershiónnyi)
adj. incomplete, unaccomplished
Незадекларированный
(nezadeklarírovannyi) adj.
undeclared
Незаконность (nezakónnost') f.
illegality, lawlessness
Незаконный (nezakónnyi) adj.
illegal, unlawful
Незаконченный (nezakónchennyi) adj.
unfinished
Незамерзающий (nezamerzáiushchii)
adj. ice-free
Незапакованный (nezapakóvannyi)
adj. unpacked
Незапатентованный
(nezapatentóvannyi) adj. unpatented
Незапечатанный (nezapechátannyi)
adj. unsealed

Незаполненный (nezapólnennyi) adj.
not completed {line in an
application}
Незастрахованный
(nezastrakhóvannyi) adj. uninsured
Незатаренный (nezatárennyi) adj.
loose {of cargo}
Неизрасходованный
(neizraskhódovannyi) adj. unspent
Неимение (neiménie) n. absence,
lack
  за ~/м ... (za ~/m ...) for want
  of ...
Неиндоссированный
(neindossírovannyi) adj. unendorsed
Неисключительный
(neiskliuchítel'nyi) adj. non-
exclusive
Неисполнение (neispolnénie) n. non-
fulfillment, non- performance
  санкции за ~ (sánktsii za ~)
  sanctions for non-performance
Неисполненный (neispólnennyi) adj.
unexecuted
Неиспользованны/й
(neispól'zovanny/i) adj. idle,
unused
Неиспользуемый (neispól'zuemyi)
adj. idle
Неисправност/ь (neisprávnost/') f.
defect, fault, malfunction
  в ~/и (v ~/i) out of order
  избегать ~/и (izbegát' ~/i) to
  avoid damage
  нахождение ~/ей (nakhozhdénie
  ~/ei) troubleshooting
  отыскивать ~ (otýskivat' ~) to
  locate a fault
Неисправный (neisprávnyi) adj.
defective, out of order
Неисчислимый (neischislímyi) adj.
innumerable, incalculable
Нейтральный (neitrál'nyi) adj.
neutral
Некартелированный
(nekartelírovannyi) adj. non-
cartelized
Некартельный (nekartél'nyi) adj.
non-cartel
Некачественный (nekáchestvennyi)
adj. substandard
Некоммерческий (nekommércheskii)
adj. nonprofit
Некомпенсированный
(nekompensírovannyi) adj.
uncompensated

Некомплектный (nekompléktnyi) *adj.* incomplete

Неконвертируемый (nekonvertíruemyi) *adj.* inconvertible

Неконкурентност/ь (nekonkuréntnost/') *f.* non-competiveness

    оговорка о ~/и (ogovórka o ~/i) non-competition clause

Неконкурентный (nekonkuréntnyi) *adj.* non-competitive

Неконтролируемый (nekontrolíruemyi) *adj.* uncontrolled

Некорпоративный (nekorporatívnyi) *adj.* unincorporated

Некотирующийся (nekotíruiushchiisia) *adj.* unquoted

Некредитоспособный (nekreditosposóbnyi) *adj.* insolvent

Некумулятивный (nekumuliatívnyi) *adj.* non-cumulative

Нелегальный (nelegál'nyi) *adj.* illegal

Неликвидный (nelikvídnyi) *adj.* non-liquid

Неликвиды (nelikvídy) *pl.* unmarketable products

Нелимитируемый (nelimitíruemyi) *adj.* unlimited

Нелицензированный (nelitsenzírovannyi) *adj.* unlicensed

Немедленный (nemédlennyi) *adj.* immediate, prompt

Неморозостойкий (nemorozostóikii) *adj.* non-frost resistant

Ненадёжность (nenadiózhnost') *f.* insecurity, unreliability

Ненадёжный (nenadiózhnyi) *adj.* insecure, unreliable

Ненумерованный (nenumeróvannyi) *adj.* unnumbered

Необеспеченный (neobespéchennyi) *adj.* unsecured

Необлагаемый (neoblagáemyi) *adj.* non-taxable

Необработанный (neobrabótannyi) *adj.* course, crude, raw

Необратимость (neobratímost') *f.* inconvertibility

Необратимый (neobratímyi) *adj.* inconvertible, soft

Необходимост/ь (neobkhodímost/') *f.* necessity

    крайняя ~ (kráiniaia ~) paramount ~

    настоятельная ~ (nastoiátel'naia ~) pressing ~

    острая ~ (óstraia ~) exigency

    товары первой ~/и (továry pérvoi ~/i) staple commodities

Необходимый (neobkhodímyi) *adj.* essential, necessary

Необъявленный (neob"iávlennyi) *adj.* undeclared {at customs}

Необязательный (neobiazátel'nyi) *adj.* non-compulsory

Неограниченный (neograníchennyi) *adj.* unrestricted

Неоднократно (neodnokrátno) *adv.* often, repeatedly

Неоплата (neopláta) *f.* non-payment

    ~ векселя (~ vékselia) failure to honor a bill

Неоплаченны/й (neopláchenny/i) *adj.* unpaid

Неоправданный (neoprávdannyi) *adj.* unjustified

Неопротестованный (neoprotestóvannyi) *adj.* unprotested {of bill or note}

Неорганизованный (neorganizóvannyi) *adj.* unorganized

Неответственный (neotvétstvennyi) *adj.* irresponsible

Неотделимый (neotdelímyi) *adj.* inseparable

Неотложный (neotlózhnyi) *adj.* pressing, urgent

Неотправленный (neotправlennyi) *adj.* unshipped

Неотраслевой (neotraslevói) *adj.* non-sectoral

Неотъемлемый (neot"émlemyi) *adj.* inalienable, integral

Неофициальный (neofitsiál'nyi) *adj.* unofficial

Неоформленный (neofórmlennyi) *adj.* unexecuted

Неоценённый (neotseniónnyi) *adj.* unvalued

Непатентоспособный (nepatentosposóbnyi) *adj.* unpatentable

Непередаваемый (neperedaváemyi) *adj.* non-negotiable

Неплатёж (neplatiózh) *m.* default of payment

    авизо о ~/e (avízo o ~/é) advice of non-payment

    в случае ~/a (v slúchae ~/á) in case of default of payment

Неплатёжеспособност/ь
(neplatiózhesposóbnost/') f.
insolvency
    объявление о ~/и (ob"iavlénie o
    ~/i) declaration of bankruptcy
    ~ банка (~ bánka) bank failure
Неплатёжеспособны/й
(neplatiózhesposóbny/i) adj.
bankrupt, insolvent
    объявлять ~/м (ob"iavliát' ~/m)
    to declare bankruptcy
Неплательщик (neplatél'shchik) m.
defaulter
Неповреждённый (nepovrezhdiónnyi)
adj. intact, undamaged
Непогашенный (nepogáshennyi) adj.
unpaid, unsettled
Неподтверждённый
(nepodtverzhdiónnyi) adj.
unacknowledged, unconfirmed
Неподходящий (nepodkhodiáshchii)
adj. impracticable, inapplicable,
unfit
Непокрытый (nepokrýtyi) adj.
uncovered, unsecured
Неполностью (nepólnost'iu) adv.
incompletely
Неполнота (nepolnotá) f.
incompleteness, imperfection
Неполноценный (nepolnotsénnyi) adj.
defective, inferior
Неполный (nepólnyi) adj. deficient,
incomplete
Непортящийся (neportiáshchiisia)
adj. non-perishable
Непредвиденный (nepredvídennyi)
adj. contingent, unforeseen
Непредусмотренный
(nepredusmótrennyi) adj.
uncontemplated, unprovided for
Неприбыльный (nepríbyl'nyi) adj.
unprofitable, unremunerative
Непригодность (neprigódnost') f.
unfitness
Непригодный (neprigódnyi) adj.
unmerchantable, unsuitable, unfit
Неприемлемый (nepriémlemyi) adj.
inadmissible, unacceptable
Непринятӥ/е (nepriniáti/e) n. non-
acceptance
    риск ~/я (risk ~/ia) risk of ~
    ~ мер (~ mer) failure to take
    measures
    ~ товара (~ továra) ~ of goods
Непринятий (nepríniatii) adj.
unaccepted, unacceptable

Непродаваемый (nepródaváemyi) adj.
unsaleable
Непроданный (nepródannyi) adj.
unsold
Непродолжительный
(neprodolzhítel'nyi) adj. short
{period of time}
Непроизводительный
(neproizvodítel'nyi) adj. non-
productive
Непроизвольный (neproizvól'nyi)
adj. involuntary
Непрочный (nepróchnyi) adj. fragile
Нерабочий (nerabóchii) adj. non-
working
Неравенство (nerávenstvo)
inequality
Неравноправный (neravnoprávnyi)
adj. inequitable, unequal
Неравный (nerávnyi) adj. unequal
Неразгруженный (nerazgrúzhennyi)
adj. undischarged {freight}
Нерасфасованный (nerasfasóvannyi)
adj. unpre-packed
Нереализованный (nerealizóvannyi)
adj. outstanding {unsold}
Нерегулярный (nereguliárnyi) adj.
irregular
Нерентабельность (nerentábel'nost')
f. unprofitability
Нерентабельный (nerentábel'nyi)
adj. unprofitable, unremunerative
Несбалансированность
(nesbalansírovannost') f. imbalance
Несбалансированный
(nesbalansírovannyi) adj.
imbalanced
Несдача (nesdácha) v. failure to
deliver
    ~ товара (~ továra) ~ goods
Несезонный (nesezónnyi) adj. out of
season, unseasonable
Несерийный (neseríinyi) adj.
custom-built
Несмываемый (nesmyváemyi) adj.
indelible
Несоблюдение (nesobliudénie) n.
non-compliance, violation
    ~ графика (~ gráfika) non-
    observance of a schedule
    ~ порядка (~ poriádka) failure
    to follow procedure
    ~ правил (~ právil) disregard of
    rules
    ~ срока (~ sróka) failure to
    meet the term date

~ указаний (~ ukazánii)
disregard of instructions
~ условий договора (~ uslóvii
dogovóra) non-observance of the
terms of agreement
~ условий контракта (~ uslóvii
kontrákta) non-observance of the
terms of a contract
~ формальностей (~
formál'nostei) non-observance of
formalities
Несоответствие (nesootvétstvie) n.
discrepancy, disparity
Несортированный (nesortírovannyi)
adj. ungraded, unsorted
Несостоятельност/ь
(nesostoiátel'nost/') f.
bankruptcy, groundlessness,
insolvency
~ должника (~ dolzhniká)
insolvency of a debtor
Несостоятельны/й
(nesostoiátel'ny/i) adj. bankrupt,
groundless, insolvent
стать ~/м (stat' ~/m) to become
insolvent
Неспособность (nesposóbnost') f.
inability, incapacity
Несрочный (nesróchnyi) adj. non-
urgent
Нестабильность (nestabíl'nost') f.
instability
экономическая ~ (ekonomícheskaia
~) economic ~
Нестабильный (nestabíl'nyi) adj.
unstable
Нестандартный (nestandártnyi) adj.
substandard
Нести (nestí) v. [perfective of
носить] to bear, to incur
{expenses, losses}
Несудоходный (nesudokhódnyi) adj.
unnavigable
Нетаксированный (netaksírovannyi)
adj. unrated, unvalued
Нетарифный (netarífnyi) adj. non-
tariff
Неторговый (netorgóvyi) adj. non-
commercial
Нетрудоспособность
(netrudosposóbnost') f. disability,
disablement for work
временная ~ (vrémennaia ~)
temporary disability
полная ~ (pólnaia ~) total
disability

частичная ~ (chastíchnaia ~)
partial disability
Нетрудоспособный (netrudosposóbnyi)
adj. disabled, incapacitated
Нетто (nétto) n. net
брутто за ~ (brútto za ~) gross
for ~
вес ~ (ves ~) ~ weight
выручка ~ (výruchka ~) ~
proceeds
легальный вес ~ (legál'nyi ves
~) legal ~ weight
масса ~ (mássa ~) ~ mass
на основе ~ (na osnóve ~) on a ~
basis
реальный вес ~ (reál'nyi ves ~)
actual ~ weight
сумма ~ (súmma ~) ~ amount
цена ~ (tsená ~) ~ price
Нетто-баланс (nétto-baláns) m.
balanced trade
Нетто-процент (nétto-protsént) m.
pure interest
Нетто-регистровая тонна (nétto-
regístrovaia tónna) f. net
registered ton
Нетто-экспортёр товара (nétto-
eksportiór továra) m. net exporter
of a commodity
Неудобный (neudóbnyi) adj.
inconvenient
Неудобство (neudóbstvo) n.
inconvenience
Неудовлетворительный
(neudovletvorítel'nyi) adj. inadequate, unsatisfactory
Неупакованный (neupakóvannyi) adj.
unpacked
Неуплат/а (neuplát/a) f. nonpayment
ввиду ~/ы (vvídu ~/y) due to ~
в результате ~/ы (v rezul'táte
~/y) as a result of ~
в случае ~/ы (v slúchae ~/y) in
case of default of payment
~ задолженности по кредиту (~
zadólzhennosti po kredítu)
default of credit
~ налогов (~ nalógov) ~ of taxes
Неуплаченный (neupláchennyi) adj.
outstanding, unpaid
Неурегулированный
(neuregulírovannyi) adj. unsettled
Неустойк/а (neustóik/a) f. penalty
альтернативная ~
(al'ternatívnaia ~) alternative
~
большая ~ (bol'sháia ~) heavy ~

вычитать ~/у (vychitát' ~/u) to deduct liquidated damages
  договорная ~ (dogovórnaia ~) contractual ~
  исключительная ~ (iskliuchítel'naia ~) exclusive ~
Неустойчивость (neustóichivost') f. instability, variability
  ~ валютной системы (~ valiútnoi sistémy) instability of the monetary system
  ~ курса валюты (~ kúrsa valiúty) fluctuation of the exchange rate
  ~ рынков (~ rýnkov) market fluctuations
  ~ цен (~ tsen) price instability
Неустойчивы/й (neustóichivy/i) adj. changeable, unstable, variable
  быть ~/м (byt' ~/m) to fluctuate
Неустранимый (neustranímyi) adj. irremovable
Нефтевоз (neftevóz) m. oil carrier
Нефтегруз (neftegrúz) m. oil cargo
Нефтедоллары (neftedóllary) pl. petrodollars
Нефтепереработка (neftepererabótka) f. petroleum refining
Нефтепровод (nefteprovód) m. oil pipeline
  прокладывать ~ (prokládyvat' ~) to lay an ~
Нефтехранилище (neftekhranílishche) n. oil reservoir
Нехватка (nekhvátka) f. deficiency, lack, scarcity, shortage
  временная ~ (vrémennaia ~) temporary shortage
  острая ~ (óstraia ~) acute shortage
  ~ валюты (~ valiúty) lack of {foreign} exchange
  ~ денег (~ déneg) tight money
  ~ кадров (~ kádrov) personnel shortage
  ~ кредита (~ kredíta) tight credit
  ~ рабочей силы (~ rabóchei síly) manpower shortage
  ~ сырья (~ syr'iá) lack of raw materials
Неходкий (nekhódkii) adj. unmarketable, unsaleable
Нечестный (nechéstnyi) adj. dishonest
Нечет (néchet) m. odd number

Нечётный (nechiótnyi) adj. odd {numerically}
Нечистый (nechístyi) adj. impure, unclean
Неэкономичность (neekonomichnost') f. economic inefficiency
Неэкономичный (neekonomíchnyi) adj. uneconomical
Неэффективный (neeffektívnyi) adj. ineffective
Неявка (neiávka) f. failure to appear
  ~ в суд (~ v sud) default of appearance {at hearing, trial}
  ~ на работу (~ na rabótu) absenteeism {from work}
Неявный (neiávnyi) adj. implicit
Низкокачественный (nizkokáchestvennyi) adj. inferior quality
Низкосортный (nizkosórtnyi) adj. low grade
Нищета (nishchetá) f. destitution
Новация (novátsiia) f. merger {of interests}, novation
  ~ договора (~ dogovóra) novation of an agreement
Новизна (novízna) f. novelty
  патентоспособная ~ (patentosposóbnaia ~) patented ~
Новин/ка (novín/ka) f. novelty, product innovation
  выставка ~/ок (výstavka ~/ok) exhibition of novelties
  запатентовать ~/ку (zapatentovát' ~/ku) to patent an innovation
  технологические ~/ки (tekhnologícheskie ~/ki) technological innovations
  экспонирование ~/ок (eksponírovanie ~/ok) demonstrating novelties
  экспортные ~/ки (éksportnye ~/ki) exportable innovations
Новшеств/о (nóvshestv/o) n. innovation
  техническое ~ (tekhnícheskoe ~) technical ~
Номенклатур/а (nomenklatúr/a) f. assortment, classification, nomenclature
  единая ~ (edínaia ~) uniform nomenclature
  закреплённая ~ (zakrepliónnaia ~) fixed range

международная товарная ~
(mezhdunaródnaia továrnaia ~)
international commodity
classification
определять ~/у товаров
(opredeliát' ~/u továrov) to
determine the range of goods
расширение ~/ы товаров
(rasshirénie ~/y továrov)
expansion of the nomenclature of
goods
растущая ~ (rastúshchaia ~)
expanding range
товарная ~ (továrnaia ~)
classification of commodities
укрупнённая ~ (ukrupniónnaia ~)
expanded range
широкая ~ (shirókaia ~) wide
range
Номер (nómer) m. copy, issue,
number
заводской ~ (zavódskoi ~) serial
number
инвентарный ~ (inventárnyi ~)
inventory number
кодовой ~ (kodovói ~) code
number
номенклатурный ~ (nomenklatúrnyi
~) stock number
порядковый ~ (poriádkovyi ~)
ordinal number
последовательность ~/ов
(posledovátel'nost' ~/ov)
sequence of numbers
регистрационный ~
(registratsiónnyi ~)
registration number
серийный ~ (seríinyi ~) batch
number
~ аккредитива (~ akkreditíva)
letter of credit number
~ для ссылок (~ dlia ssýlok)
reference number
~ заказа (~ zakáza) order number
~ контракта (~ kontrákta)
contract number
~ партии (~ pártii) lot number
~ патента (~ paténta) patent
number
~ по порядку (~ po poriádku)
consecutive number
~ по телеграфному коду (~ po
telegráfnomu kódu) key number
~ рейса (~ réisa) flight number,
voyage number
~ телефона (~ telefóna)
telephone number

Номинал (nominál) m. face value,
par
выше ~/a (výshe ~/a) above par
ниже ~/a (nízhe ~/a) below par
по ~/у (po ~/u) at par
продавать по цене выше ~/a
(prodavát' po tsené výshe ~/a)
to sell above par
Номинальный (nominál'nyi) adj.
nominal
Норм/а (nórm/a) f. allowance, norm,
quota, standard, target
в соответствии с ~/ой (v
sootvétstvii s ~/oi) in
conformance with standard
введение ~/ (vvedénie ~/)
introduction of norms, targets
выполнять ~/у (vypolniát' ~/u)
to fulfill the quota
высокая ~ (vysókaia ~) high
target
выше ~/ы (výshe ~/y) above
standard, above target
действующие ~/ы (déistvuiushchie
~/y) present norms, present
standards
дифференцированная ~
(differentsírovannaia ~) differential quota
дневная ~ (dnevnáia ~) daily
rate
жёсткие ~/ы (zhióstkie ~/y)
tight standards
заводские ~/ы (zavódskie ~/y)
plant standards
коллизионная ~ (kolliziónnaia ~)
conflict rule
минимальные ~/ы (minimál'nye
~/y) minimum standards
нарушать ~/ы международного
права ~ (narushát' ~/y
mezhdunaródnogo práva ~) to
violate the rules of
international law
низкая ~ (nízkaia ~) low
standard
ниже ~/ы (nízhe ~/y) below
standard
новые ~/ы (nóvye ~/y) new norms
общепринятая ~
(obshchepríniataia ~) generally
accepted standard
отраслевые ~/ы (otraslevýe ~/y)
industry standards
отклонение от ~/ы (otklonénie ot
~/y) departure from accepted
standards

перевыполнять ~/у
(perevypolniát' ~/u) to
overfulfill the quota
пересматривать ~/ы
(peresmátrivat' ~/y) to revise
norms, standards
применять ~/ы (primeniát' ~/y)
to apply norms, standards
по установленной ~/е (po
ustanóvlennoi ~/e) at the
established rate
подсчитанные ~/ы (podschítannye
~/y) estimated rates
правовые ~/ы (pravovýe ~/y)
legal norms
предельная ~ (predél'naia ~)
limit
резервная ~ (rezérvnaia ~)
reserve ratio
сантехническая ~
(santekhnícheskaia ~) sanitary
standards
совпадать с ~/ами (sovpadát' s
~/ami) to fall within the
standards
соответствовать ~/ам
(sootvétstvovat' ~/am) to
conform with standards
средняя ~ (srédniaia ~) average
rate
строительные ~/ы (stroítel'nye
~/y) building code
технические ~/ы (tekhnícheskie
~/y) engineering standards
указывать ~/ы (ukázyvat' ~/y) to
prescribe norms
устанавливать ~/ы (ustanávlivat'
~/y) to establish standards
~ амортизации (~ amortizátsii)
allowable rate of depreciation
~ времени (~ vrémeni) time
standard
~/ы естественной убыли (~/y
estéstvennoi úbyli) acceptable
rate of natural loss
~/ы международного права (~/y
mezhdunaródnogo práva) rules of
international law
~ на беспошлинный ввоз (~ na
bespóshlinnyi vvoz) standards
for duty-free import
~ почасовая (~ pochasováia)
hourly rate
~ прибыли (~ príbyli) profit
rate

~/ы производительности (~/y
proizvodítel'nosti) productivity
standards
Нормализация (normalizátsiia) f.
normalization
~ международных отношений (~
mezhdunaródnykh otnoshénii) ~ of
international relations
Нормальный (normál'nyi) adj.
conventional, normal, regular
Норматив (normatív) m. norm,
specification, standard
измерительные ~/ы (izmerítel'nye
~/y) measurements
пересматривать ~/ы
(peresmátrivat' ~/y) to revise
standards
прогрессивные ~/ы (progressívnye
~/y) progressive standards
стабильность ~/ов (stabíl'nost'
~/ov) stability of norms
экономические ~/ы
(ekonomícheskie ~/y) economic
norms
~/ы рентабельности (~/y
rentábel'nosti) profitability
rates
Нормативный (normatívnyi) adj.
normative, regulatory
Нормировани/е (normírovani/e) n.
standardization
отдел ~/я (otdél ~/ia) ~
department
Нормированный (normírovannyi) adj.
normalized
Нормировать (normírovat') v. to
establish standards, to set norms
Носкость (nóskost') f. durability
Ностро (nóstro) n. nostro
{international finance}
овердрафт ~ (overdráft ~) ~
overdraft
счёт ~ (schiót ~) ~ account
Нота (nóta) f. note
Нотариально (notariál'no) adv.
notarially
засвидетельствовать ~
(zasvidétel'stvovat' ~) to
notarize
Нотариальный (notariál'nyi) adj.
notarial
Нотариус (notárius) m. notary
public
заявить протест ~/у (zaiavít'
protést ~/u) to submit a
complaint to the notary's office
Нотис (nótis) m. notice

подать ~ (podát' ~) to give ~
послать ~ (poslát' ~) to forward
a ~
предварительный ~
(predварítel'nyi ~) preliminary
~
принять ~ (priniát' ~) to accept
a ~
~ капитана (~ kapitána)
captain's ~
Нотификация (notifikátsiia) f.
notification
Ноу-хау (nóu-kháu) n. know-how
    владелец ~ (vladélets ~) owner
    of ~
    выдавать ~ (vydavát' ~) to
    furnish ~
    договор на передачу ~ (dogovór
    na peredáchu ~) ~ transfer
    agreement
    использовать ~ (ispól'zovat' ~)
    to use ~
    комплекс ~ (kómpleks ~) ~
    package
    незапатентованное ~
    (nezapatentóvannoe ~) unpatented
    ~
    неразглашённое ~
    (nerazglashiónnoe ~) undisclosed
    ~
    обмен ~ (obmén ~) exchange of ~
    общее ~ (óbshchee ~) general ~
    отказываться от ~ (otkázyvat'sia
    ot ~) to surrender ~
    охрана ~ (okhrána ~) protection
    of ~
    патентованное ~ (patentóvannoe
    ~) patented ~
    передача ~ (peredácha ~)
    transfer of ~
    предоставлять ~ (predostavliát'
    ~) to supply ~
    разглашённое ~ (razglashiónnoe
    ~) disclosed ~
    техническое ~ (tekhnícheskoe ~)
    technical ~
    ~ лицензиара (~ litsenziára)
    licensor's ~
    ~ на изготовление (~ na
    izgotovlénie) manufacturing ~
    ~ по лицензии (~ po litsénzii)
    licensed ~
Нумерация (numerátsiia) f.
numbering
    последовательная ~
    (poslédovatel'naia ~)
    consecutive ~

Нумеровать (numerovát') v. to
number

О

Обанкротившийся (obankrotívshiisia)
adj. bankrupt
Обанкротиться (obankrotít'sia) v.
to go bankrupt
Обвязывать (obviázyvat') v. to
bind, to fasten, to lash, to secure
    ~ вдоль (~ vdol') to bind
    lengthwise
    ~ вертикально (~ vertikál'no) to
    fasten vertically
    ~ горизонтально (~
    gorizontál'no) to fasten
    horizontally
    ~ поперёк (~ poperiók) to bind
    crosswise
Обгонять (obgoniát') v. to outpace,
to exceed
Обёртка (obiórtka) f. cover,
envelope, jacket
    красочная ~ (krásochnaia ~)
    colorful cover
    яркая ~ (iárkaia ~) bright
    wrapping
Обёрточный (obiórtochnyi) adj.
packing, wrapping
Обёртывать (obiórtyvat') v. to wrap
up
Обеспечени/е (obespécheni/e) n.
collateral, guarantee, maintenance,
provision
    без ~/я (bez ~/ia) unsecured
    бесперебойное (besperebóinoe)
    uninterrupted provision
    в качестве ~/я (v káchestve
    ~/ia) as collateral
    валютное ~ (valiútnoe ~)
    currency security
    вещественное ~ (veshchéstvennoe
    ~) property security
    возврат ~/я (vozvrát ~/ia)
    return of security
    двойное ~ (dvoinóe ~) collateral
    денежное ~ (dénezhnoe ~) cash
    security
    депонировать в качестве ~/я
    (deponírovat' v káchestve ~/ia)
    to deposit as security
    дополнительное ~ (dopolnítel'noe
    ~) additional collateral

достаточное ~ (dostátochnoe ~)
sufficient security
залоговое ~ (zalógovoe ~)
pledged security
замена ~/я (zaména ~/ia)
substitution of collateral
имущественное ~
(imúshchestvennoe ~) collateral
security
коммерческое ~ (kommércheskoe ~)
commercial collateral
материальное ~ (materiál'noe ~)
tangible security
патентное ~ (paténtnoe ~) patent
cover
первоклассное ~ (pervoklássnoe
~) high-grade security
под ~ (pod ~) against security
под двойное ~ (pod dvoinóe ~) on
collateral
предоставить ~ (predostávit' ~)
to provide security
служить ~/м (sluzhít' ~/m) to
serve as collateral
социальное ~ (sotsiál'noe ~)
social welfare
степень ~/я (stépen' ~/ia)
degree of cover
страховое ~ (strakhóvoe ~)
insurance coverage
требование ~/я (trébovanie ~/ia)
call on security
финансовое ~ (finánsovoe ~)
financial security
~ банкнот (~ banknót) backing of
bank notes
~ валюты (~ valiúty) backing of
currency
~ в форме банковской гарантии (~
v fórme bánkovskoi garántii)
security in the form of a bank
guarantee
~ долга (~ dólga) collateral for
a debt
~ жильём (~ zhil'ióм) provision
of housing
~ займа (~ záima) collateral for
a loan
~ иска (~ íska) security for a
claim
~ конфиденциальности (~
konfidentsiál'nosti) guarantee
of confidentiality
~ надёжности (~ nadiózhnosti)
assurance of reliability

~ с помощью закладной (~ s
pómoshch'iu zakladnói) security
by mortgage
~ товарами (~ továrami)
provision of goods
Обеспеченность (obespéchennost')
security
материальная ~ (materiál'naia ~)
material ~
~ платёжными средствами (~
platiózhnymi srédstvami)
liquidity
~ работой (~ rabótoi) job ~
Обеспеченный (obespéchennyi) adj.
secured
Обеспечивать (obespéchivat') v. to
back, to cover, to guaranty, to
provide, to secure
Обесцонени/е (obestsenéni/e) n.
devaluation, shrinkage
степень ~/я (stépen' ~/ia) rate
of devaluation
~ бумажных денег (~ bumázhnykh
déneg) devaluation of paper
money
~ валюты (~ valiúty) devaluation
of currency
~ валюты по отношению к основным
валютам (~ valiúty po
otnoshéniiu k osnovným valiútam)
depreciation of currency against
major currencies
~ доллара (~ dóllara)
depreciation of the dollar
~ золота (~ zólota) depreciation
of gold prices
~ капитала (~ kapitála)
depreciation of capital
Обесцененный (obestsénennyi) adj.
depreciated
Обесцонивать (obestsénivat') v. to
depreciate, to devalue {said of
govt. action}
~/ся (~/sia) to depreciate, to
devalue {said of currency, etc.}
Обжаловани/е (obzhálovani/e) n.
appeal
порядок ~/я (poriádok ~/ia)
order of ~
право ~/я (právo ~/ia) right of
~
предупреждение об ~/и
(preduprezhdénie ob ~/i) notice
of ~
подлежащий ~/ю (podlezháshchii
~/iu) subject to ~

~/ю не подлежит (~/iu ne podlezhít) without ~

Обжаловать (obzhálovat') *v.* to appeal, to lodge a complaint

Обзор (obzór) *m.* review, survey
бюджетный ~ (biudzhétnyi ~) budget review
делать ~ (délat' ~) to review
исчерпывающий ~ (ischérpyvaiushchii ~) exhaustive survey
периодический ~ (periodícheskii ~) periodical review
рамки ~/a (rámki ~/a) scope of survey
статистический ~ (statistícheskii ~) statistical survey
экономический ~ (ekonomícheskii ~) economic review
~ иностранных рынков (~ inostránnykh rýnkov) foreign market review
~ хозяйственной деятельности (~ khoziáistvennoi déiatel'nosti) business survey
~ цен (~ tsen) price review

Обкатк/a (obkátk/a) *f.* running-in
период ~/и (períod ~/i) running-in period
производить контрольную ~/у агрегатов (proizvodít' kontról'nuiu ~/u agregátov) to carry out a test run of units
~ агрегатов (~ agregátov) running-in of units
~ без нагрузки (~ bez nagrúzki) non-load running-in

Обкатывать (obkátyvat') *v.* to run in

Облагаемый (oblagáemyi) *adj.* dutiable, taxable

Облагать (oblagát') *v.* to assess, to impose, to levy, to tax

Обладатель (obladátel') *m.* holder, possessor
~ авторского права (~ ávtorskogo práva) copyright holder

Обладать (obladát') *m.* to hold, to possess

Област/ь (óblast/') field, "oblast" {Russian geographical and administrative subdivision}, sphere
~ деятельности (~ déiatel'nosti) sphere of activity
~ знаний (~ znánii) field of knowledge

~ применения (~ primenéniia) sphere of application
~ сотрудничества (~ sotrúdnichestva) sphere of cooperation

Облекать (oblekát') *v.* to invest with, to vest in
~ кого-то с полномочиями (~ kogó-to s polnomóchiiami) to vest someone with authority

Облигационный (obligatsiónnyi) *adj.* bonded

Облигаци/я (obligátsi/ia) *f.* bond, debenture
беспроцентная ~ (besprotséntnaia ~) passive bond
внутренняя ~ (vnútrenniaia ~) internal bond
выкуп ~/й (výkup ~/i) retirement of bonds
выкупать ~/и (vykupát' ~/i) to retire bonds
выпуск ~/й (výpusk ~/i) issue of bonds, debentures
выпускать ~/и (vypuskát' ~/i) to issue bonds, debentures
государственная ~ (gosudárstvennaia ~) government bond, savings bond
держатель ~/й (derzhátel' ~/i) bond holder, debenture holder
долгосрочная ~ (dolgosróchnaia ~) long-term bond, long-term debenture
заграничная ~ (zagraníchnaia ~) foreign bond
именная ~ (imennáia ~) registered bond, debenture
краткосрочная ~ (kratkosróchnaia ~) short-term bond, debenture
мелкая ~ (mélkaia ~) baby bond
первоклассная ~ (pervoklássnaia ~) high-grade bond
погашать ~/и (pogashát' ~/i) to redeem bonds, debentures
процентные ~/и (protséntnye ~/i) interest-bearing bonds
размещение ~/й (razmeshchénie ~/i) flotation of a bond issue
рынок ~/й (rýnok ~/i) bond market
трансферт ~/й (transfért ~/i) transfer of debentures
~ выигрышного займа (~ výigryshnogo záima) premium bond

~, выходящая в тираж (~, vykhodiáshchaia v tirázh) maturing bond
~ на предъявителя (~ na pred"iavítelia) bearer bond
~, не имеющая специального обеспечения (~, ne iméiushchaia spetsiál'nogo obespécheniia) debenture bond
~, не погашенная в срок (~, ne pogáshennaia v srok) overdue bond
~, не подлежащая погашению до наступления срока (~, ne podlezháshchaia pogashéniiu do nastupléniia sróka) irredeemable bond
~/и, подлежащие погашению (~/i, podlezháshchie pogashéniiu) maturing bonds
~, предъявленная к погашению (~, pred"iávlennaia k pogashéniiu) called bond
~ с правом досрочного погашения (~ s právom dosróchnogo pogashéniia) optionally redeemable bond
~ с правом на участие в прибылях компании (~ s právom na uchástie v príbyliakh kompánii) participation bond
~ со специальным обеспечением (~ so spetsiál'nym obespécheniem) secured bond
~ с отсроченным платежом (~ s otsróchennym platezhóm) deferred bond
Обложени/е (oblozhéni/e) n. assessment, imposition, levy, taxation
не подлежащий ~/ю (ne podlezháshchii ~/iu) non-dutiable, non-taxable
подлежащий ~/ю (podlezháshchii ~/iu) dutiable, taxable
прогрессивное ~ налогом (progressívnoe ~ nalógom) progressive taxation
таможенное ~ (tamózhennoe ~) imposition of customs duties
~ налогом (~ nalógom) taxation
~ пошлиной (~ póshlinoi) imposition of a duty
~ штрафом (~ shtráfom) penalty, imposition of a fine
Обман (obmán) m. deception, fraud

Обманны/й (obmánnyi) *adj.* deceptive, fraudulent
~/м путём (~/m putióm) by fraud
Обманщик (obmánshchik) m. cheat, con-man, fraud
Обманывать (obmányvat') v. to cheat, to deceive, to swindle
Обмен (obmén) m. conversion, exchange
банк по ~/у валюты (bank po ~/u valiúty) exchange bank
бартерный ~ (bárternyi ~) barter
безвалютный ~ (bezvaliútnyi ~) currency-free exchange
в ~ на (v ~ na) in exchange for ...
в порядке ~/а (v poriádke ~/a) by way of exchange
взаимный ~ (vzaímnyi ~) reciprocal exchange
внешнеторговый ~ (vneshnetorgóvyi ~) foreign trade exchange
возмездный ~ (vozmézdnyi ~) commercial exchange
годный для ~/а (gódnyi dlia ~/a) exchangeable
двухсторонний ~ (dvukhstorónnii ~) bilateral exchange
двухстороний торговый ~ (dvukhstorónii torgóvyi ~) bilateral trade
договор об ~/е (dogovór ob ~/e) agreement of exchange
натуральный ~ (naturál'nyi ~) exchange in kind
неэквивалентный ~ (neekvivaléntnyi ~) non-equivalent exchange
непосредственный ~ (neposrédstvennyi ~) direct barter exchange
непосредственный ~ товарами (neposrédstvennyi ~ továrami) direct commodity barter
поощрять ~ (pooshchriát' ~) to promote exchange
производить ~ (proizvodít' ~) to carry out an exchange
расширение ~/а (rasshirénie ~/a) expansion of exchange
система ~/а (sistéma ~/a) exchange system
сдавать для ~/а (sdavát' dlia ~/a) to surrender for exchange

соответствующий ~
(sootvétstvuiushchii ~)
applicable conversion
средство ~/а (srédstvo ~/a)
medium of exchange
технологический ~
(tekhnologícheskii ~)
technological exchange
торговый ~ (torgóvyi ~) trade
exchange
управление ~/ом (upravlénie
~/om) exchange control
условия ~/а (uslóviia ~/a) terms
of exchange
эквивалентный ~ (ekvivaléntnyi
~) equivalent exchange
~ акций (~ áktsii) exchange of
shares {stock}
~ валюты (~ valiúty) conversion
of currency
~ делегациями (~ delegátsiiami)
exchange of delegations
~ документов (~ dokuméntov)
renewal of documents
~ знаниями (~ znániiami)
exchange of knowledge
~ золота (~ zólota) gold
conversion
~ информацией (~ informátsiei)
exchange of information
~ мнениями (~ mnéniiami)
exchange of opinions
~ на основе взаимных расчётов (~
na osnóve vzaímnykh raschiótov)
clearinghouse exchange
~ ноу-хау (~ nóu-kháu) exchange
of know-how
~ опытом (~ ópytom) sharing of
experience
~ патентами (~ paténtami)
exchange of patents
~ по курсу ... (~ po kúrsu ...)
exchange at the rate of ...
~ по курсу, указанному на
обороте векселя (~ po kúrsu,
ukázannomu na oboróte vékselia)
exchange as per endorsement {on
bill, note}
~ по паритету (~ po paritétu)
exchange at par
~ специалистами (~
spetsialístami) exchange of
experts
~ торговыми данными (~ torgóvymi
dánnymi) exchange of trade data
~ услугами (~ uslúgami) exchange
of services

Обмениваемый (obmeniváemyi) adj.
convertible, redeemable
Обменивать (obménivat') v. to
barter, to convert, to exchange
Обменный (obménnyi) adj. exchange
Обмер (obmér) m. measurement
Обнаруживать (obnarúzhivat') v. to
detect, to uncover
не ~ (ne ~) to fail to detect
Обновление (obnovlénie) n.
modernization, renovation
коренное ~ (korennóe ~) complete
overhaul
техническое ~ (tekhnícheskoe ~)
technical modernization
~ основных производственных
фондов (~ osnovnýkh proizvódstvennykh fóndov) renewal of
fixed assets
~ производства (~ proizvódstva)
renovation of production
~ производственных мощностей (~
proizvódstvennykh móshchnostei)
renovation of productive
capacities
Обновлённый (obnovliónnyi) adj.
modernized, renovated
Обновлять (obnovliát') v. to
modernize, to renovate
Обознач/ать (oboznach/át') v. to
designate, to mark
как ~/ено на чертеже (kak ~/eno
na chertezhé) as marked on the
blueprint
Обозначени/е (oboznachéni/e) n.
notation, symbol
буквенное ~ (búkvennoe ~) letter
designation
система ~/й (sistéma ~/i) system
of notation
~ страны (~ straný) mark of
nationality
~ на схеме (~ na skhéme)
notational symbol
Обозначенный (oboznáchennyi) adj.
marked
Оборачиваемость (oboráchivaemost')
f. turnover
~ готовой продукции ~ (~ gotóvoi
prodúktsii) of finished goods
~ депозитов ~ (~ depozítov) of
deposits
~ капитала (~ kapitála) capital
~
~ незавершённого производства (~
nezavershiónnogo proizvódstva)
work-in-process ~

~ оборотных средств ~ (~
oborótnykh sredstv) of working
capital
~ основного капитала (~
osnovnógo kapitála) plant ~
~ товарных запасов ~ (~
továrnykh zapásov) of stock
{goods}
Оборот (oborót) *m.* circulation,
recourse, turnover
   без ~/a (bez ~/a) without
recourse
   без ~/a на трассанта (bez ~/a na
trassánta) without recourse to
drawer
   годовой ~ (godovói ~) annual
turnover
   денежный ~ (dénezhnyi ~) money
turnover
   дневной ~ (dnevnói ~) daily
turnover
   изымать из ~/a (izymát' iz ~/a)
to withdraw from circulation
   колебание ~/a (kolebánie ~/a)
fluctuations in turnover
   минимальный ~ (minimál'nyi ~)
minimum turnover
   на ~/e (na ~/e) on the reverse
{side of document, etc.}
   налог с ~/a (nalóg s ~/a)
turnover tax
   общий ~ (óbshchii ~) overall
turnover
   оптовый ~ (optóvyi ~) wholesale
turnover
   платёжный ~ (platiózhnyi ~)
payment transactions
   право ~/a (právo ~/a) right of
recourse
   пускать в ~ (puskát' v ~) to
release into circulation
   размер ~/a (razmér ~/a) volume
of turnover
   расписываться на ~/e документа
(raspísyvat'sia na ~/e
dokuménta) to endorse on the
reverse of a document
   регистр ~/ов (regístr ~/ov)
transaction register
   с ~/ом (s ~/om) with recourse
   скорость ~/a (skórost' ~/a) rate
of turnover
   скорость ~/a товарных запасов
(skórost' ~/a továrnykh zapásov)
rate of stock turnover {goods}
   смотри на ~/e (smotrí na ~/e)
"please see reverse"

товарный ~ (továrnyi ~)
merchandise turnover
торговый ~ (torgóvyi ~) trade
volume
   ~ акций (~ áktsii) stock
turnover {shares}
   ~ внутри страны (~ vnútri
strany) domestic turnover
   ~ грузов (~ grúzov) freight
turnover
   ~ капитала (~ kapitála) capital
turnover
   ~ наличных денег (~ nalíchnykh
déneg) cash turnover
   ~ по импорту (~ po ímportu)
import turnover
   ~ по продажам (~ po prodázham)
sales turnover
   ~ по счетам (~ po schetám)
receivables
   ~ по экспорту (~ po éksportu)
export turnover
Оборотный (oborótnyi) *adj.*
circulating, negotiable, reverse
Оборудовани/e (oborúdovani/e) *n.*
equipment, facilities, plant
   аварийное ~ (avaríinoe ~)
emergency equipment
   автоматическое ~
(avtomatícheskoe ~) automatic
equipment
   амортизация ~/я (amortizátsiia
~/ia) depreciation of equipment
   аренда ~/я (arénda ~/ia)
equipment rental
   бездействующее ~
(bezdéistvuiushchee ~) idle
equipment
   береговое портовое ~ (beregovóe
portóvoe ~) shore installations
   бывшее в эксплуатации ~ (bývshee
v ekspluatátsii ~) used
equipment
   быстроизнашивающееся ~
(bystroiznáshivaiushcheesia ~)
rapidly-wearing equipment
   ввод ~/я в эксплуатацию (vvod
~/ia v ekspluatátsiiu)
introduction of equipment {into
plant, etc.}
   ввоз ~/я (vvoz ~/ia) import of
equipment
   возврат ~/я (vozvrát ~/ia)
return of equipment
   вспомогательное ~
(vspomogátel'noe ~) accessory
equipment

встроенное ~ (vstróennoe ~)
service facilities
вывоз ~/я (vývoz ~/ia)
exportation of equipment
выпуск ~/я (výpusk ~/ia)
production of equipment
высококачественное ~
(vysokokáchestvennoe ~) high-
quality equipment
высокопроизводительное ~
(vysokoproizvodítel'noe ~)
highly productive equipment
габариты ~/я (gabaríty ~/ia)
dimensions of equipment
гаражно-ремонтное ~ (garázhno-
remóntnoe ~) auto repair
equipment
горношахтное ~ (gornoshákhtnoe
~) mining equipment
действующее ~ (déistvuiushchee
~) working equipment
демонтаж ~/я (demontázh ~/ia)
dismantling of equipment
дефектное ~ (deféktnoe ~)
defective equipment
дорожно-строительное ~
(dorózhno-stroítel'noe ~) road
building equipment
доставка ~/я (dostávka ~/ia)
delivery of equipment
единица ~/я (edinítsa ~/ia) unit
of equipment
заводское ~ (zavódskoe ~) plant
equipment
задержанное ~ (zadérzhannoe ~)
delayed equipment
заказ на ~ (zakáz na ~) order
for equipment
заказанное ~ (zakázannoe ~)
ordered equipment
замена ~/я (zaména ~/ia)
replacement of equipment
заменяемое ~ (zameniáemoe ~)
replaceable equipment
запас ~/я (zapás ~/ia) stock of
equipment
запасное ~ (zapásnoe ~) spare
equipment
износ ~/я (iznós ~/ia) wear and
tear of equipment
изношенное ~ (iznóshennoe ~)
worn out equipment
импортное ~ (ímportnoe ~)
imported equipment
испытательное ~ (ispytátel'noe
~) test equipment

капитальное ~ (kapitál'noe ~)
durable equipment
качество ~/я (káchestvo ~/ia)
quality of equipment
коммерчески эксплуатируемое ~
(kommércheski ekspluatíruemoe ~)
revenue equipment
коммерческое ~ (kommércheskoe ~)
commercial equipment
комплекс ~/я (kómpleks ~/ia)
outfit of equipment
комплектное ~ (kompléktnoe ~)
complete outfit of equipment
комплектующее ~
(komplektúiushchee ~) ancilliary
equipment
конкурентоспособное ~
(konkurentosposóbnoe ~)
competitive equipment
консервация ~/я (konservátsiia
~/ia) preservation of equipment
контейнерное ~ (kontéinernoe ~)
container equipment
конторское ~ (kontórskoe ~)
office equipment
крупногабаритное ~
(krupnogabarítnoe ~) oversized
equipment
крупное ~ специального
назначения (krúpnoe ~
spetsiál'nogo naznachéniia)
large-scale specialized
equipment
машинное ~ (mashínnoe ~)
machining equipment
металлургическое ~
(metallurgícheskoe ~)
metallurgical equipment
модифицированное ~
(modifitsírovannoe ~) modified
equipment
монтаж ~/я (montázh ~/ia)
installation of equipment
монтажное ~ (montázhnoe ~)
erection equipment
монтировать ~ (montírovat' ~) to
install equipment
наладка ~/я (naládka ~/ia)
adjustment of equipment
наличие ~/я (nalíchie ~/ia)
availability of equipment
негабаритное ~ (negabarítnoe ~)
oversized equipment
недопоставленное ~
(nedopostávlennoe ~) short-
shipped equipment, missing
equipment

недостающее ~ (nedostaiúshchee ~) missing equipment

некомплектное ~ (nekompléktnoe ~) incomplete set of equipment

нестандартное ~ (nestandártnoe ~) non-standard equipment

номенклатура ~/я (nomenklatúra ~/ia) equipment nomenclature

обеспечивать ~ (obespéchivat' ~) to secure equipment

обновить ~ цеха (obnovít' ~ tsékha) to re-equip a department

обслуживание ~/я (obslúzhivanie ~/ia) service of equipment

обслуживать ~ (obslúzhivat' ~) to service equipment

осмотр ~/я (osmótr ~/ia) inspection of equipment

основное ~ (osnovnóe ~) primary equipment

отдельное ~ (otdél'noe ~) individual units of equipment

отказаться от дефектного ~/я (otkazát'sia ot deféktnogo ~/ia) to reject defective equipment

патентованное ~ (patentóvannoe ~) patented equipment

первоклассное ~ (pervoklássnoe ~) first-class equipment

перечень ~/я (pérechen' ~/ia) equipment list

плавучее портовое ~ (plavúchee portóvoe ~) floating installations

повреждённое ~ (povrezhdiónnoe ~) damaged equipment

погрузочно-разгрузочное ~ (pogrúzochno-razgrúzochnoe ~) cargo handling equipment

подержанное ~ (podérzhannoe ~) secondary equipment

подсобное ~ (podsóbnoe ~) servicing equipment

подъёмное ~ (pod"iómnoe ~) hoisting gear

подъёмно-транспортное ~ (pod"iómno-tránsportnoe ~) hoisting and conveying gear

показ ~/я (pokáz ~/ia) demonstration of equipment

поломка ~/я (polómka ~/ia) breakdown of equipment

полуавтоматическое ~ (poluavtomatícheskoe ~) semi-automatic equipment

пользователь ~/я (pól'zovatel' ~/ia) user of equipment

портовое ~ (portóvoe ~) port facilities

поставляемое ~ (postavliáemoe ~) delivered equipment

поставщик ~/я (postavshchík ~/ia) supplier of equipment

потребитель ~/я (potrebítel' ~/ia) consumer of equipment

предъявлять ~ для осмотра (pred"iavliát' ~ dlia osmótra) to submit equipment for inspection

приёмка ~/я (priiómka ~/ia) acceptance of delivery of equipment

приобретать ~ (priobretát' ~) to obtain equipment

проверять ~ (proveriát' ~) to check equipment

програмное ~ (prográmnoe ~) software

проектировать ~ (proektírovat' ~) to design equipment

производительность ~/я (proizvodítel'nost' ~/ia) productivity of equipment

производить ~ (proizvodít' ~) to manufacture equipment

производственное ~ (proizvódstvennoe ~) manufacturing equipment

промышленное ~ (promýshlennoe ~) industrial equipment

простой ~/я (prostói ~/ia) equipment downtime

противопожарное ~ (protivopozhárnoe ~) fire fighting equipment

разборка ~/я (razbórka ~/ia) disassembly of equipment

размеры ~/я (razméry ~/ia) dimensions of equipment

разобранное ~ (razóbrannoe ~) disassembled equipment

разработка нового ~/я (razrabótka nóvogo ~/ia) development of new equipment

разрозненное ~ (razróznennoe ~) miscellaneous equipment

реализация ~/я (realizátsiia ~/ia) sale of equipment

резервное ~ (rezérvnoe ~) reserve equipment

ремонт ~/я (remónt ~/ia) repair of equipment

ремонтное ~ (remóntnoe ~) maintenance facility

реновация ~/я (renovátsiia ~/ia)
renovation of equipment
реэкспорт ~/я (reéksport ~/ia)
re-export of equipment
сборка ~/я (sbórka ~/ia)
assembly of equipment
сдаваемое в аренду ~ (sdaváemoe
v aréndu ~) rental equipment
сдавать в аренду ~ (sdavát' v
aréndu ~) to rent equipment {as
lessor}
сельскохозяйственное ~
(sel'skokhoziástvennoe ~)
agricultural equipment
серийное ~ (seríinoe ~) serial
equipment
складирование ~/я (skladírovanie
~/ia) storage of equipment
сложное ~ (slózhnoe ~) complex
equipment
современное ~ (soveménnoe ~)
modern equipment
соответствующее ~
(sootvétstvuiushchee ~)
applicable equipment, suitable
equipment
специализированное ~
(spetsializírovannoe ~)
specialized equipment
спецификация на ~
(spetsifikátsiia na ~)
specifications of equipment
спрос на ~ (spros na ~) demand
for equipment
стандартное ~ (standártnoe ~)
standard equipment
стационарное ~ (statsionárnoe ~)
fixed installations
строительное ~ (stroítel'noe ~)
construction equipment
текстильное ~ (tekstíl'noe ~)
textile machinery
техническая характеристика ~
(tekhnícheskaia kharakterístika
~) technical characteristics of
equipment
тип ~/я (tip ~/ia) type of
equipment
торговое ~ (torgóvoe ~) shop
equipment
тяжеловесное ~ (tiazhelovésnoe
~) heavy equipment {weight}
узлы ~/я (uzlý ~/ia) units of
equipment
улучшать ~ (uluchshát' ~) to
improve equipment

уникальное ~ (unikál'noe ~)
unique equipment
упаковочное ~ (upakóvochnoe ~)
packing equipment
устанавливать ~ (ustanávlivat'
~) to install equipment
установленное ~ (ustanóvlennoe
~) installed equipment
устаревшее ~ (ustarévshee ~)
obsolete equipment
уход за ~/ем (ukhód za ~/em)
maintenance of equipment
холодильное ~ (kholodíl'noe ~)
refrigeration facilities
хранение ~/я (khranénie ~/ia)
storage of equipment
цеховое ~ (tsekhovóe ~) factory
installations
шахтное ~ (shákhtnoe ~) mining
equipment
эксплуатация ~/я (ekspluatátsiia
~/ia) operation of equipment
экспонируемое ~ (eksponíruemoe
~) display equipment
электронное ~ самолёта
(elektrónnoe ~ samolióta)
avionics
электротехническое ~
(elektrotekhnícheskoe ~)
electrical equipment
энергетическое ~
(energetícheskoe ~) power plant
equipment
~ американского производства (~
amerikánskogo proizvódstva)
American-made equipment
~ аэропорта (~ aeropórta)
airport facilities
~ в действии (~ v déistvii)
working equipment
~ длительного пользования (~
dlítel'nogo pól'zovaniia)
durable equipment
~ для взвешивания (~ dlia
vzvéshivaniia) weighing
equipment
~ для выкладки и экспонирования
товара (~ dlia výkladki i
eksponírovaniia továra) display
equipment
~ для обработки пищевых
продуктов (~ dlia obrabótki
pishchevýkh prodúktov) food
processing equipment
~ для управления
производственных процессов (~
dlia upravléniia

proizvódstvennykh protséssov) process control equipment
~ на линии сборки (~ na línii sbórki) assembly line equipment
~ наукоёмкое (~ naukoiómkoe) high-tech equipment
~ новых поколений (~ nóvykh pokolénii) next generation equipment
~ отечественного производства (~ otéchestvennogo proizvódstva) domestically produced equipment
~ по контракту (~ po kontráktu) contract equipment
~ серийного производства (~ seríinogo proizvódstva) serial production equipment
~ стоимостью ... долларов ... (~ stóimost'iu ... dóllarov ...) dollars worth of equipment
~ терминала (~ terminála) terminal facilities

Оборудовать (oborúdovat') v. to equip

Обосновани/е (obosnováni/e) n. grounds, justification, substantiation
в ~ (v ~) in justification of
документальное ~ (dokumentál'noe ~) documentation
научное ~ (naúchnoe ~) scientific substantiation
представлять технико-экономическое ~ (predstavliát' tékhniko-ekonomícheskoe ~) to submit a feasibility report
расчёт технико-экономического ~/я (raschiót tékhniko-ekonomícheskogo ~/ia) feasibility study of a project
статистическое ~ (statistícheskoe ~) statistical validity
технико-экономическое ~ (tékhniko-ekonomícheskoe ~) feasibility study
техническое ~ (tekhnícheskoe ~) technical justification
экономическое ~ (ekonomícheskoe ~) economic justification
юридическое ~ (iuridícheskoe ~) legal grounds
~ претензии (~ preténzii) substantiation of a claim
~ проекта (~ proékta) expediency of a project

~ решения (~ reshéniia) grounds for a decision

Обоснованность (obosnóvannost') f. justification, soundness, validity

Обоснованный (obosnóvannyi) adj. justified, substantiated

Обосновывать (obosnóvyvat') v. to justify, to substantiate

Обособленность (obosóblennost') f. isolation

Обоюдность (oboiúdnost') f. mutuality, reciprocity

Обоюдный (oboiúdnyi) adj. mutual, reciprocal

Обработка (obrabótka) f. finishing, machining, processing
вторичная ~ (vtoríchnaia ~) secondary processing
совместная ~ земли (sovméstnaia ~ zemlí) joint cultivation of the land
~ земли (~ zemlí) cultivation of the land

Образец (obrazéts) m. exhibit, model, pattern, sample
бесплатный ~ (besplátnyi ~) free sample
промышленный ~ (promýshlennyi ~) industrial model
~ товаров (~ továrov) sample of goods

Образование (obrazovánie) n. education, formation
всеобщее ~ (vseóbshchee ~) general education
всеобщее обязательное ~ (vseóbshchee obiazátel'noe ~) compulsory general education
народное ~ (naródnoe ~) public education
светское ~ (svétskoe ~) liberal education
~ государства (~ gosudárstva) formation of a government {in parliamentary system}
~ запасов (~ zapásov) formation of stocks
~ капитала (~ kapitála) formation of capital

Образовать (obrazovát') v. to form, to make up

Образчик (obrázchik) m. pattern, specimen
~ товаров (~ továrov) sample of goods

Обратимость (obratímost') f. convertibility, exchangeability

ограниченная ~ (ograníchennaia
~) limited convertibility
свободная ~ (svobódnaia ~) free
convertibility
частичная ~ (chastíchnaia ~)
partial convertibility
~ валют (~ valiút)
convertibility of currency
Обратимый (obratímyi) *adj.*
convertible, exchangeable
ограниченно ~ (ograníchenno ~)
of limited convertibility
свободно ~ (svobódno ~) freely
convertible
Обращать (obrashchát') *v.* to pay
attention to, to realize, to turn
to
Обращени/е (obrashchéni/e) *n.*
address, appeal, approach,
circulation, handling, recourse,
treatment
банкнотное ~ (banknótnoe ~)
circulation of bank notes
бумажно-денежное ~ (bumázhno-
dénezhnoe ~) circulation of
paper money
вексельное ~ (véksel'noe ~)
circulation of bills
внутреннее ~ (vnútrennee ~)
internal circulation
выпустить в ~ (výpustit' v ~) to
issue into circulation
грубое ~ (grúboe ~) rough
handling
денежное ~ (dénezhnoe ~)
monetary circulation
дурное ~ (dúrnoe ~) mishandling
изъять из ~/я (iz"iát' iz ~/ia)
to withdraw from circulation
находить в ~/и (nakhodít'sia v
~/i) to be in circulation
параллельное ~ (parallél'noe ~)
parallel circulation
приветственное ~ (privétstvennoe
~) welcoming address
рекламное ~ (reklámnoe ~)
advertising message
товарное ~ (továrnoe ~)
circulation of commodities
~ к войне (~ k voiné) recourse
to war
~ к силе (~ k síle) recourse to
force
~ в суд (~ v sud) recourse to
the court
~ товаров (~ továrov)
circulation of goods

Обременение (obremenénie) *n.*
encumbrance
свободный от ~/й (svobódnyi ot
~/i) free from ~s
~ ипотекой (~ ipotékoi) mortgage
Обременительный (obremenítel'nyi)
adj. encumbered
Обременять (obremeniát') *v.* to
encumber
Оброк (obrók) *m.* quit-rent
Обручение (obruchénie) *n.* betrothal
Обрядност/ь (obriádnost/') *f.*
ceremony, rite
таможенные ~/и (tamózhennye ~/i)
customs formalities
Обследование (obslédovanie) *n.*
investigation
бюджетное ~ (biudzhétnoe ~)
budget ~
пробное ~ (próbnoe ~) trial run
Обследовать (obslédovat') *v.* to
investigate
Обслуживание (obslúzhivanie) *n.*
service
вежливое ~ (vézhlivoe ~) polite
service
~/я здравоохранения (~/ia
zdravookhranéniia) health
services
Обстановка (obstanóvka) *f.*
conditions, environment, situation
международная ~ (mezhdunaródnaia
~) international situation
фактическая ~ (faktícheskaia ~)
actual conditions
хозяйственная ~ (khoziástvennaia
~) economic situation
Обстоятельство (obstoiátel'stvo) *n.*
circumstances
непредвиденное ~ (nepredvídennoe
~) unforeseen ~
смягчающее ~ (smiagcháiushchee
~) extenuating ~
оправдывающее ~
(opravdyváiushchee ~) mitigating
~
случайное ~ (slucháinoe ~)
random ~
фактическое ~ (faktícheskoe ~)
factual ~
форсмажорное ~ (forsmazhórnoe ~)
conditions of force majeure
~/я дела (~/ia déla) state of
affairs
Обструкция в парламенте
(obstrúktsiia v parlámente)
obstruction in parliament

Обсуждать (obsuzhdát') v. to consider, to discuss
Обсуждение (obsuzhdénie) n. consideration, discussion
предварительное ~ (predvarítel'noe ~) preliminary discussion
~ законопроекта (~ zakonoproékta) consideration of a bill {in parliament, etc.}
~ на общем собрании (~ na óbshchem sobránii) consideration in general assembly
~ пленарном собрании (~ plenárnom sobránii) consideration in plenary assembly
Обуздание, нравственное (obuzdánie, nrávstvennoe) n. moral restraint
Обусловленность (obuslóvlennost') stipulation
взаимная ~ (vzaímnaia ~) mutual ~s
Обучение (obuchénie) n. instruction, training
бесплатное ~ (besplátnoe ~) free instruction
военное ~ (voénnoe ~) military training
всеобщее ~ (vseóbshchee ~) universal education
всеобщее обязательное ~ (vseóbshchee obiazátel'noe ~) universal compulsory education
обязательное ~ (obiazátel'noe ~) compulsory education
Обход (obkhód) m. circumvention, evasion
~ закона (~ zakóna) evasion of the law
~ налоговых законов (~ nalógovykh zakónov) tax evasion
Общегосударственный (obshchegosudárstvennyi) adj. nationwide
Общежитие (obshchezhítie) n. dormitory
Общеизвестность (obshcheizvéstnost') f. public knowledge
Общеизвестный (obshcheizvéstnyi) adj. well known
Общение (obshchénie) n. contact, intercourse, relations
межгосударственное ~ (mezhgosudárstvennoe ~) intergovernmental relations

международное ~ (mezhdunaródnoe ~) international relations
экономическое ~ (ekonomícheskoe ~) economic linkage
Общественность (obshchéstvennost') f. community, public
Общественный (obshchestvennyi) adj. public, social, voluntary
Общество (óbshchestvo) n. association, company, partnership, society
акционерное ~ (aktsionérnoe ~) joint stock company
акционерное ~ с неограниченной ответственностью (aktsionérnoe ~ s neograníchennoi otvétstvennost'iu) unlimited liability company
акционерное ~ с ограниченной ответственностью (aktsionérnoe ~ s ograníchennoi otvétstvennost'iu) limited liability company
акционерное командитное ~ (aktsionérnoe komandítnoe ~) civil law limited company {e.g. French Société Anonyme en Commandite}
бесклассовое ~ (besklássovoe ~) classless society
благотворительное ~ (blagotvorítel'noe ~) charitable organization
добровольное ~ (dobrovól'noe ~) voluntary organization
дочернее ~ (dochérnee ~) subsidiary company
контролирующее ~ (kontrolíruiushchee ~) controlling company
кооперативное ~ (kooperatívnoe ~) cooperative society
спасательное ~ (spasátel'noe ~) salvage company
охотничье ~ (okhótnich'e ~) hunting club
пароходное ~ (parokhódnoe ~) steamship company
потребительское ~ (potrebítel'skoe ~) consumer organization
смешанное ~ (sméshannoe ~) mixed joint stock company
страховое ~ (strakhóvoe ~) insurance company
тайное ~ (táinoe ~) secret society

торговое ~ (torgóvoe ~) trading company
финансовое ~ (finánsovoe ~) finance company
~ взаимопомощи (~ vzaimopómoshchi) mutual aid society
~ сравнительного права (~ sravnítel'nogo práva) comparative law society
~ в ходе ликвидации (~ v khóde likvidátsii) company in the course of liquidation
Общий (óbshchii) *adj.* aggregate, common, general, overall, total
Община (obshchína) *f.* commune, community
городская ~ (gorodskáia ~) urban community
крестьянская ~ (krest'iánskaia ~) peasant commune
религиозная ~ (religióznaia ~) religious commune
Общность (óbshchnost') *f.* community
законная ~ (zakónnaia ~) legal community
международная ~ (mezhdunaródnaia ~) international community
супружеская ~ (suprúzheskaia ~) marital community
~ владения (~ vladéniia) community of ownership
~ движимых имуществ (~ dvízhimykh imúshchestv) communal ownership of chattels
~ имущества (~ imúshchestva) communal ownership of property
~ имуществ супругов (~ imúshchestv suprúgov) community property {marital}
~ интересов (~ interésov) community of interests
Объединение (ob"edinénie) *n.* amalgamation, association, corporation, union
административное ~ (administratívnoe ~) administrative association
внешнеторговое ~ (vneshnetorgóvoe ~) foreign trade association
карательное ~ (karátel'noe ~) association of cartels
законодательное ~ (zakonodátel'noe ~) legislative association

кооперативное ~ (kooperatívnoe ~) cooperative society
монополистическое ~ (monopolistícheskoe ~) monopoly
международное ~ (mezhdunaródnoe ~) international association
межотраслевое ~ (mezhotraslevóe ~) intersectoral amalgamation
наднациональное ~ (nadnatsionál'noe ~) national association
промышленное ~ (promýshlennoe ~) industrial association
профессиональное ~ (professionál'noe ~) professional association
профсоюзное ~ (profsoiúznoe ~) trade union association
паевое ~ (paevóe ~) joint stock association
сельскохозяйственное ~ (sel'skokhoziástvennoe ~) agricultural association
синдикальное ~ (sindikál'noe ~) syndicated association
совместное ~ (sovméstnoe ~) joint association
специализированное ~ (spetsializírovannoe ~) specialized association
таможенное ~ (tamózhennoe ~) customs association
торговое ~ (torgóvoe ~) trading association
хозрасчётное ~ (khozraschiótnoe ~) self-financing enterprise
финансовое ~ (finánsovoe ~) financial institution
экспортное ~ (éksportnoe ~) export association
Объединённый (ob"ediniónnyi) *adj.* amalgamated, consolidated
Объединять (ob"ediniát') *v.* to amalgamate, to pool
Объединяться (ob"ediniát'sia) *v.* to incorporate, to unite
Объект (ob"ékt) *m.* object, project
договорный ~ (dogovórnyi ~) contractual subject
заложенный ~ (zalózhennyi ~) pledge
строительный ~ (stroítel'nyi ~) building site
~ доказательства (~ dokazátel'stva) evidentiary exhibit

~ заявки (~ zaiávki) object of application

~ международного договора (~ mezhdunaródnogo dogovóra) subject of international agreement

~ обложения (~ oblozhéniia) subject of taxation

~ преступления (~ prestupléniia) corpus delicti

Объективный (ob"ektívnyi) *adj.* fair, impartial, objective

Объём (ob"ióm) *m.* extent, scope, volume

~ валовой продукции (~ valovói prodúktsii) volume of gross output

~ внешней торговли (~ vnéshnei torgóvli) foreign trade volume

~ капитальных вложений (~ kapitál'nykh vlozhénii) volume of investment

~ оборота (~ oboróta) volume of turnover

~ потребления (~ potrebléniia) volume of demand

~ правомочий (~ pravomóchii) scope of authority

~ производства (~ proizvódstva) volume of production

~ расходов (~ raskhódov) scope of expenditures

~ рынка (~ rýnka) size of the market, volume on the exchange

~ товарооборота (~ tovaroooboróta) commodity turnover volume

~ экспорта (~ éksporta) volume of exports

Объявить (ob"iavít') *v.* [see объявлять]

Объявление (ob"iavlénie) *n.* announcement, declaration, notice

газетное ~ (gazétnoe ~) newspaper ad

настенное ~ (nasténnoe ~) wall poster

предварительное ~ (predvarítel'noe ~) preliminary announcement

~ блокады (~ blokády) proclamation of a blockade

~ войны (~ voiný) declaration of war

~ выговора права (~ výgovora práva) declaration of reservation of right

~ недееспособности в судебном порядке (~ nedeesposóbnosti v sudébnom poriádke) declaration of incapacity in a legal proceeding

~ недействительности (~ nedeistvítel'nosti) declaration of annulment

~ независимости (~ nezavísimosti) declaration of independence

~ нейтралитета (~ neitralitéta) declaration of neutrality

~ несостоятельности (~ nesostoiátel'nosti) declaration of insolvency

~ патента ничтожным (~ paténta nichtózhnym) annulment of a patent

~ приговора (~ prigovóra) pronouncement of sentence

~ смерти (~ smérti) death notice

Объявлять (ob"iavliát') *v.* to declare, to proclaim

Объяснение (ob"iasnénie) *n.* declaration, explanation

Обыкновение (obyknovénie) *n.* habit, usage

местное ~ (méstnoe ~) local custom

торговое ~ (torgóvoe ~) commercial usage

Обыск (óbysk) *m.* search

личный ~ (líchnyi ~) personal search

ордер на право ~/а (órder na právo ~/a) search warrant

производить ~ (proizvodít' ~) to conduct a search

~ на дому (~ na dómu) search of a house

~ личных вещей (~ líchnykh veshchéi) search of personal effects

Обыскивать (obýskivat') *v.* to search

Обычай (obýchai) *m.* custom, usage

банковский ~ (bánkovskii ~) banking usage

дипломатический ~ (diplomatícheskii ~) diplomatic usage

конституционный ~ (konstitutsiónnyi ~) constitutional usage

международно-правовой ~
(mezhdunaródno-pravovói ~)
international law usage
международный ~ (mezhdunaródnyi
~) international usage
местный ~ (méstnyi ~) local
custom
морской ~ (morskói ~) maritime
usage
правовой ~ (pravovói ~) legal
custom
торговый ~ (torgóvyi ~)
commercial usage
Обязанност/ь (obiázannost/') f.
duty, liability, obligation
абсолютная ~ (absoliútnaia ~)
absolute duty
алиментная ~ (aliméntnaia ~)
maintenance obligation {e.g.
alimony}
военная ~ (voénnaia ~) military
duty
исполнить ~ (ispolnít' ~) to
fulfill, to perform a duty
основная ~ (osnovnáia ~) primary
responsibility
повседневные ~/и (povsednévnye
~/i) every-day duties
правовая ~ (pravováia ~) legal
duty
принять ~ на себя (priniát' ~ na
sebiá) to undertake an
obligation
профессиональная ~
(professionál'naia ~)
professional responsibility
служебная ~ (sluzhébnaia ~)
official duty
уставная ~ (ustávnaia ~) charter
obligations
юридическая ~ (iuridícheskaia ~)
legal obligation
~ брать лоцмана (~ brat'
lótsmana) duty to take on
pilotage
Обязательный (obiazátel'nyi) adj.
binding, compulsory, obligatory
Обязательств/о (obiazátel'stv/o) n.
commitment, engagement, liability,
obligation
алиментное ~ (aliméntnoe ~)
maintenance obligation {e.g.
alimony}
безусловное ~ (bezuslóvnoe ~)
unconditional promise {e.g. in
contract}

бессрочное ~ (bessróchnoe ~)
sight liability
будущее ~ (búdushchee ~) future
liability
взаимные ~/a (vzaímnye ~/a)
mutual obligations
встречные ~/a (vstréchnye ~/a)
consideration {in contract}
гарантийное ~ (garantíinoe ~)
warranty obligation
гражданское ~ (grazhdánskoe ~)
civic responsibility
денежное ~ (dénezhnoe ~)
pecuniary obligation
денежные ~/a (dénezhnye ~/a)
monetary commitments
договорное ~ (dogovórnoe ~)
contractual obligation
долговое ~ (dolgovóe ~)
promissory note
долгосрочное ~ (dolgosróchnoe ~)
long-term obligation
заёмное ~ (zaiómnoe ~)
acknowledgement of debt
законное ~ (zakónnoe ~)
statutory obligation
ипотечное ~ (ipotéchnoe ~)
mortgage obligation
казначейские ~/a (kaznachéiskie
~/a) treasury bonds
краткосрочное ~ (kratkosróchnoe
~) short-term obligation
международное правовое ~
(mezhdunaródnoe pravovóe ~)
international legal obligations
международные ~/a
(mezhdunaródnye ~/a)
international obligations
многостороннее ~ (mnogostorónnee
~) multilateral obligation
моральное ~ (morál'noe ~) moral
duty
налоговое ~ (nalógovoe ~) tax
liability
непокрытые ~/a (nepokrýtye ~/a)
outstanding liabilities
открытые ~/a (otkrýtye ~/a)
uncovered liabilities
отсроченные ~/a (otsróchennye
~/a) deferred liabilities
освободить от ~/a (osvobodít' ot
~/a) to release from an
obligation
первоочередное ~
(pervoocherednóe ~) prior
commitment

первоначальное ~
(pervonachál'noe ~) original
commitment
правовое ~ (pravovóe ~) legal
obligation
придаточное ~ (pridátochnoe ~)
supplementary obligation
прямое ~ (priamóe ~) direct
obligation
срочные ~/a (sróchnye ~/a)
accrued liabilities
совместное ~ (sovméstnoe ~)
joint liability
финансовое ~ (finánsovoe ~)
financial obligation
условное ~ (uslóvnoe ~)
contingent liability
~ возмещения убытка (~
vozmeshchéniia ubýtka)
obligation to compensate loss
~ по гарантии (~ po garántii)
obligation under warranty
~ по депозиту (~ po depozítu)
deposit liability
~ казначейства (~ kaznachéistva)
treasury bond
~ не конкурировать (~ ne
konkurírovat') covenant not to
compete
~ на предъявителя (~ na
pred"iavítelia) bearer
obligation {bearer paper}
Обязывать (obiázyvat') v. to bind,
to commit, to oblige
Обязываться (obiázyvat'sia) v. to
be bound
~ договором (~ dogovórom) to be
contractually bound
Овердрафт (overdráft) m. overdraft
Овладения (ovladéniia) n.
domination
~ рынка (~ rýnka) market ~
Оглавление (oglavlénie) n. table of
contents
Огласить (oglasít') v. [see
оглашать]
Огласка (ogláska) f. publicity
Оглашать (oglashát') v. to
announce, to divulge, to proclaim
Оглашени/е (oglashéni/e) n.
publication
не подлежит ~/ю (ne podlezhít
~/iu) not for publication
~ о предстоящем браке (~ o
predstoiáshchem bráke) marriage
announcement

~ решения суда (~ reshéniia
sudá) publication of a court
decision
Оговорить (ogovorít') v. to
stipulate
Оговор (ogovór) m. slander
Оговор/ка (ogovór/ka) f. clause,
proviso, reservation, stipulation
с ~/кой (s ~/koi) with
reservation
без ~/ок (bez ~/ok) without
reservation
арбитражная ~ (arbitrázhnaia ~)
arbitration clause
валютная ~ (valiútnaia ~)
exchange clause
золотая ~ (zolotáia ~) gold
clause
дополнительная ~
(dopolnítel'naia ~) superimposed
clause
курсовая ~ (kursováia ~)
exchange rate clause
монопольная ~ (monopól'naia ~)
monopoly clause
общая ~ (óbshchaia ~) general
reservation
письменная ~ (pís'mennaia ~)
written provision
специальная ~ (spetsiál'naia ~)
special provision
существенная ~ (sushchéstvennaia
~) material provision {of a
contract}
территориальная ~
(territoriál'naia ~) territory
clause
транзитная ~ (tranzítnaia ~)
transit clause
факультативная ~
(fakul'tatívnaia ~) optional
clause
~ о взаимности (~ o vzaímnosti)
reciprocity clause
~ к договору (~ k dogovóru)
proviso
~ о компетенции (~ o
kompeténtsii) sanity clause
~ о наибольшем
благоприятствовании (~ o
naiból'shem
blagopriiatstvovánii) most
favored nation clause
~ об обязательном арбитраже (~
ob obiazátel'nom arbitrázhe)
compulsory arbitration clause

~ об обмене акций (~ ob obméne áktsii) conversion provision

~ при ратификации (~ pri ratifikátsii) reservation upon ratification {e.g. convention}

~ о праве удержания (~ o práve uderzhániia) lien clause

~ о пролонгации (~ o prolongátsii) continuation clause

~ о форс-мажоре (~ o forsmazhóre) force majeure clause

~ язона (~ iázona) Jacob's clause

Огородить (ogorodít') *v.* to enclose, to fence

Огосударствление (ogosudarstvlénie) *n.* nationalization {e.g. of foreign property}

Ограбить (ográbit') *v.* to rob

Ограбление (ograblénie) *n.* burglary, robbery

Ограждение (ograzhdénie) *n.* barrier, protection

~ прав (~ prav) protection of rights

поставить ~ (postávit' ~) to install guard rails

Ограничение (ograničénie) *n.* limitation, restriction

качественное ~ (káchestvennoe ~) qualitative restriction

количественное ~ (kolíchestvennoe ~) quantitative restriction

таможенное ~ (tamózhennoe ~) customs restriction

территориальное ~ (territoriál'noe ~) territorial limitation

~ вооружений (~ vooruzhénii) arms limitation

~ движения (~ dvizhéniia) traffic restriction

~ дееспособности (~ deesposóbnosti) restriction of legal capacity

~ импорта (~ ímporta) import restraint

~ конкуренции (~ konkuréntsii) restraint of competition

~ лицензии (~ litsénzii) license restriction

~ личной свободы (~ líchnoi svobódy) restraint of personal liberty

~ обмена денег (~ obména déneg) monetary exchange restrictions

~ ответственности (~ otvétstvennosti) limitation of liability

~ по эмиграции (~ po emigrátsii) restrictions on emigration

~ прав в выборах (~ prav v výborakh) limitation of suffrage

~ права (~ práva) restriction of rights

~ реэкспорта (~ reéksporta) restriction of re-export

~ свободы (~ svobódy) restraint of liberty

~ скорости (~ skórosti) speed limit

~ суверенитета (~ suverenitéta) limitation of sovereignty

~ экспорта (~ éksporta) restraint of exports

~ юрисдикции (~ iurisdíktsii) limitation of jurisdiction

Ограниченный (ograníchennyi) *adj.* limited, qualified, restricted

Ограничивать (ograníchivat') *v.* to limit, to restrict

Ограничивающий (ogranichiváiushchii) *adj.* limiting {tending to limit}

Ограничительный (ogranichítel'nyi) *adj.* limiting {tending to limit}

Одарённый (odariónnyi) *adj.* gifted, talented

Одаряемый (odariáemyi) *adj.* donated, given as a gift

Однократный (odnokrátnyi) *adj.* single {one time only}

Односторонний (odnostorónnii) *adj.* unilateral

Однотомник (odnotómnik) *m.* single-volume edition

Одобрение (odobrénie) *n.* approval

единодушное ~ (edinodúshnoe ~) unanimous ~

предварительное ~ (predvarítel'noe ~) preliminary ~

~ закона ~ (~ zakóna) of a law, statute

~ правительства ~ (~ pravítel'stva) of a government

~ протокола ~ (~ protokóla) of a letter of intent, ~ of minutes of a meeting

~ сметы ~ (~ sméty) of an estimate

Одобрять (odobriát') *v.* to approve

Одалживать (odálzhivat') *v.* [perfective: одолжить] to lend

Одурманивающий (odurmaniváiushchii) *adj.* intoxicating, stupefying {as of a narcotic}

Оживление (ozhivlénie) *v.* rally {e.g. stock market}, recovery {e.g. economic}
    экономическое ~ (ekonomícheskoe ~) economic recovery
    ~ конъюнктуры (~ kon"iunktúry) recovery of the business cycle

Оздоровление (ozdorovlénie) *n.* improvement, normalization, recovery
    ~ экономии (~ ekonómii) economic recovery

Оказание (okazánie) *n.* provision, rendering
    ~ услуг (~ uslúg) provision of services

Оккупант (okkupánt) *m.* invader, occupying force

Оккупация (okkupátsiia) *f.* occupation {military}

Оккупировать (okkupírovat') *v.* to occupy {militarily}

Оклад (oklád) *m.* salary scale, tax assessment
    должностной ~ (dólzhnostnoi ~) salary
    месячный ~ (mésiachnyi ~) monthly salary
    основной ~ (osnovnói ~) basic pay
    почасовой ~ (pochasovói ~) hourly wage
    фактический ~ (faktícheskii ~) actual pay

Окладчик (okládchik) *m.* salaried worker

Окончание (okonchánie) *n.* completion, termination
    ~ испытаний (~ ispytánii) completion of testing
    ~ операционного года (~ operatsiónnogo góda) completion of operational year
    ~ срока гарантии (~ sróka garántii) expiration of warranty
    ~ трудовой жизни (~ trudovói zhízni) end of working life {e.g. equipment}
    ~ форс-мажорной ситуации (~ forsmazhórnoi situátsii) termination of a force majeure situation

Окончательный (okonchátel'nyi) *adj.* final

Окрик (ókrik) *m.* hail, shout

Округ (ókrug) *m.* district, okrug {territorial division of the Russian Federation}
    административный ~ (administratívnyi ~) administrative district
    военный ~ (voénnyi ~) military command district
    избирательный ~ (izbirátel'nyi ~) electoral district
    судебный ~ (sudébnyi ~) judicial district
    ~ апелляционной палаты (~ apelliatsiónnoi paláty) appellate district

Окружной (okruzhnói) *adj.* district
    ~ суд (~ sud) circuit court

Олигархия (oligárkhiia) *f.* oligarchy

Омоложение (omolozhénie) *n.* rejuvenation
    демографическое ~ (demografícheskoe ~) demographic ~
    ~ населения ~ (~ naseléniia) of the population

Онколь (onkól') call account, demand account

Онкольный (onkól'nyi) *adj.* on-call {e.g. accounts}

Опасность (opásnost') *f.* danger
    общественная ~ (obshchéstvennaia ~) social ~
    ~ в предприятиях ~ (~ v predpriiátiiakh) in the workplace

Опек/а (opék/a) *f.* guardianship, trusteeship
    административная ~ (administratívnaia ~) administrative trusteeship
    законная ~ (zakónnaia ~) statutory trusteeship
    международная ~ (mezhdunaródnaia ~) International Trusteeship
    находиться под ~/ой (nakhodít'sia pod ~/oi) to be under trusteeship
    под ~/ой (pod ~/oi) under surveillance

Опекаемый (opekáemyi) *m.adj.noun* ward {person under guardianship}

Опекун (opekún) *m.* guardian, trustee

    законный ~ (zakónnyi ~) statutory trustee

    ~ назначенный в завещании (~ naznáchennyi v zaveshchánii) executor of a will

Опекунство (opekúnstvo) *n.* guardianship

Операция (operátsiia) *f.* operation, transaction

    арбитражная ~ (arbitrázhnaia ~) arbitrage

    банковская ~ (bánkovskaia ~) banking transaction

    биржевая ~ (birzheváia ~) exchange transaction {e.g. stock exchange}

    валютная ~ (valiútnaia ~) exchange transaction {currency}

    военные ~/и (voénnye ~/i) military operations

    деловая ~ (delováia ~) business transaction

    денежные ~/и (dénezhnye ~/i) monetary transactions

    инкассовая ~ (inkássovaia ~) collection of a payment

    кассовая ~ (kássovaia ~) cash payment

    клиринговая ~ (klíringovaia ~) clearinghouse transaction

    комиссионная ~ (komissiónnaia ~) consignment transaction

    коммерческая ~ (kommércheskaia ~) commercial operation

    кредитная ~ (kredítnaia ~) lending operation

    межбанковская ~ (mezhbánkovskaia ~) inter-bank transaction

    рентабельная ~ (rentábel'naia ~) profitable transaction

    спекулятивная ~ (spekuliatívnaia ~) speculative transaction

    ссудная ~ (ssúdnaia ~) loan operation

    страховая ~ (strakhóvaia ~) insurance operation

    торговая ~ (torgóvaia ~) trade operation

    учётная ~ (uchiótnaia ~) discount transaction

    учётно-ссудная ~ (uchiótno-ssúdnaia ~) discount lending transaction

    финансовая ~ (finánsovaia ~) financial transaction

    экспортно-импортная ~ (éksportno-ímportnaia ~) export/import operation

    эмиссионная ~ (emissiónnaia ~) issuing transaction

    ~ на срок (~ na srok) forward operation, future transaction

    ~ на чёрном рынке (~ na chiórnom rýnke) transaction on the black market

    ~ «под ключ» (~ pod kliuch) turnkey operation

    ~ по закупке (~ po zakúpke) purchasing operation

    ~ хеджирования (~ khedzhírovaniia) hedging operation

Опечатать (opechátat') *v.* to seal up

Опечатка (opechátka) *f.* erratum, misprint {e.g. book, inventory list}

Опечаток (opechatok) *m.* impression, imprint

    ~ пальца (~ pál'tsa) fingerprint

Описание (opisánie) *n.* account, description

    патентное ~ (paténtnoe ~) patent description

    ~ дефектов (~ deféktov) description of defects

    ~ изобретения (~ izobreténiia) description of invention

    ~ имуществ (~ imúshchestv) description of chattels

    ~ недвижимых имуществ (~ nedvízhimykh imúshchestv) description of real property

    ~ предмета найма (~ predméta náima) description of the subject of a lease

    ~ растрат (~ rastrát) description of expenditures

Описать (opisát') *v.* to describe, to inventory

    ~ имущество (~ imúshchestvo) to distrain property

Опись (ópis') *f.* distraint, inventory, list, schedule

    инвентарная ~ (inventárnaia ~) inventory list

    составить ~ (sostávit' ~) to inventory

    ~ движимых имуществ (~ dvízhimykh imúshchestv) distraint of chattels

~ недвижимого имущества (~ nedvízhimogo imúshchestva) distraint of real property
~ наследства (~ naslédstva) distraint of inheritance

Оплата (opláta) *f.* payment, remuneration
аккредитивная ~ (akkreditívnaia ~) payment by letter of credit
высокая ~ (vysókaia ~) high pay
гарантированная ~ (garantírovannaia ~) guaranteed pay
денежная ~ (dénezhnaia ~) cash payment
дополнительная ~ (dopolnítel'naia ~) additional payment
досрочная ~ (dosróchnaia ~) prepayment, payment ahead of schedule
ежемесячная ~ (ezhemésiachnaia ~) monthly payment
натуральная ~ (naturál'naia ~) payment in kind
немедленная ~ (nemédlennaia ~) prompt payment
повременная ~ труда (povrémennaia ~ trudá) time wages
подённая ~ труда (podiónnaia ~ trudá) day wages
понедельная ~ (ponedél'naia ~) weekly wages
поощрительная ~ (pooshchrítel'naia ~) incentive pay
почасовая ~ (pochasováia ~) hourly wages
премиальная ~ (premiál'naia ~) bonus payment
равная ~ труда (rávnaia ~ trudá) equal pay
сдельная ~ (sdél'naia ~) piece-work pay

Оплачивать (opláchivat') *v.* to defray, to pay, to settle
Оплаченный (opláchennyi) *adj.* paid
Оплачиваемый (oplachiváemyi) *adj.* payable
Опломбирование (oplombírovanie) *n.* affixing of a {company} seal
Опломбировать (oplombírovat') *v.* to affix a seal
Оповещать (opoveshchát') *v.* to inform, to notify

Оповещение (opoveshchénie) *n.* notification
Опоздание (opozdánie) *n.* delay, tardiness
неоправданное ~ (neoprávdannoe ~) unexcused delay
Опознание (opoznánie) *n.* identification
ложное ~ (lózhnoe ~) false identification
Опознать (opoznát') *v.* to identify
Ополчение (opolchénie) *n.* militia
народное ~ (naródnoe ~) national guard
Оппозиционный (oppozitsiónnyi) *adj.* opposition
Оппозиция (oppozítsiia) *f.* opposition {usu. political}
Оппонент (opponént) *m.* opponent
Оппортунизм (opportunízm) *m.* opportunism
Оппортунист (opportuníst) *m.* opportunist
Оппортунистический (opportunistícheskii) *adj.* opportunistic
Оправдание (opravdánie) *n.* acquittal, excuse
Оправдать (opravdát') *v.* to acquit, to excuse, to warrant
Опрашивать (opráshivat') *v.* to cross-examine, to interrogate
Определение (opredelénie) *n.* decision, definition, determination
временное ~ (vrémennoe ~) interim decision
кассационное ~ (kassatsiónnoe ~) decision of the court of cassation {in Civil Law countries}
судебное ~ (sudébnoe ~) judicial decision
~ границы (~ granítsy) determination of a border
~ компетенций (~ kompeténtsii) determination of legal competency
~ правонарушения (~ pravonarushéniia) determination of violation
Определённый (opredeliónnyi) *adj.* definite, fixed
Определять (opredeliát') *v.* to appoint, to determine, to fix
Опробовать (opróbovat') *v.* to take something on trial

Опровергать (oprovergát') *v.*
[perfective: опровергнуть] to
disprove, to refute
Опровержение (oproverzhénie) *n.*
denial, refutation
Опровержимый (oproverzhímyi) *adj.*
refuted
Опрос (oprós) *m.* examination {cross
or direct}, interrogation
Опросный (oprósnyi) *adj.*
examination, interrogation
   ~ лист (~ list) interrogatory
Опротестование (oprotestovánie) *n.*
protest, protestation
   кассационное ~ (kassatsiónnoe ~)
   appeal to the Court of Cassation
   ~ векселя (~ vékselia) protest
   of a bill
Опротестовать (oprotestovát') *v.* to
appeal, to dishonor, to protest
Оптация (optátsiia) *f.* option {e.g.
of dual citizenship}
Оптировать (optírovat') *v.* to opt
for {e.g. citizenship}
Оптовик (optóvik) *m.* wholesaler
Оптовый (optóvyi) *adj.* wholesale
Опубликование (opublikovánie) *n.*
promulgation, publication
   официальное ~ (ofitsiál'noe ~)
   official publication
   ~ закона (~ zakóna) promulgation
   of a law
   ~ решения (~ reshéniia)
   publication of a decision
Оптом (óptom) *adv.* in gross, by
wholesale
Опцион (optsión) *m.* call, option,
put
Опыт (ópyt) *m.* experiment,
experience, know-how
   производственный ~
   (proizvódstvennyi ~) operational
   know-how
Оратор (orátor) *m.* orator
Орган (órgan) *m.* agency, authority,
organ {of government, etc.}
   автономный ~ (avtonómnyi ~)
   autonomous organ
   административный ~
   (administratívnyi ~)
   administrative authority,
   administrative body
   верховный ~ (verkhóvnyi ~)
   supreme authority
   вспомогательный ~
   (vspomogátel'nyi ~) auxiliary
   body

высший ~ (výsshii ~) higher
authority
вышестоящий ~ (vyshestoiáshchii
~) superior authority
государственный ~
(gosudárstvennyi ~) government
agency
директивный ~ (direktívnyi ~)
policy-making authority
жилищный ~ (zhilíshchnyi ~)
housing authority
законодательный ~
(zakonodátel'nyi ~) legislative
body
закупочный ~ (zakúpochnyi ~)
purchasing organ
исполнительный ~ (ispolnítel'nyi
~) executive agency
коллективный ~ (kollektívnyi ~)
collective body
компетентный ~ (kompeténtnyi ~)
competent authority
конституционный ~
(konstitutsiónnyi ~)
constitutional authority
консультативный ~
(konsul'tatívnyi ~) consultative
body
контрольный ~ (kontról'nyi ~)
oversight agency
международный ~ (mezhdunaródnyi
~) international agency
межпарламентский ~
(mezhparlámentskii ~) inter-
parliamentary body
межправительственный ~
(mezhpravítel'stvennyi ~) intergovernmental body
налоговый ~ (nalógovyi ~) tax
authority
нотариальный ~ (notariál'nyi ~)
notarial authority {civil law}
ответственный ~ (otvétstvennyi
~) responsible authority
официальный ~ печати
(ofitsiál'nyi ~ pecháti)
official press agency
парламентский ~ (parlámentskii
~) parliamentary body
плановой ~ (plánovoi ~) planning
authority {under communism}
правоохранительный ~
(pravookhranítel'nyi ~) law
enforcement agency
постоянный арбитражный ~
(postoiánnyi arbitrázhnyi ~)
permanent arbitral body

правительственный ~
(pravítel'stvennyi ~) government
agency
представительный ~
(predstavítel'nyi ~)
representative body
прокурорский ~ (prokurórskii ~)
prosecutorial authority,
prosecutor's office
профсоюзный ~ (profsoiúznyi ~)
labor union
распорядительный ~
(rasporiadítel'nyi ~) efficient
agency
руководящий ~ (rukovodiáshchii
~) supervisory authority
совещательный ~
(soveshchátel'nyi ~)
deliberative body
соответствующий ~
(sootvétstvuiushchii ~)
appropriate authority
судебно-следственный ~ (sudébno-
slédstvennyi ~) judicial
investigative body
судебный ~ (sudébnyi ~) judicial
body
таможенный ~ (tamózhennyi ~)
customs authority
третейский ~ (tretéiskii ~)
arbitral authority
финансовый ~ (finánsovyi ~)
fiscal authority
ценорегулирующий ~
(tsenoregulíruiushchii ~) price
regulating authority
~ валютного контроля (~
valiútnogo kontrólia) currency
control authority
~ дознания (~ doznániia) board
of inquest
~ контроля над ценами (~
kontrólia nad tsénami) price
control board
~ милиции (~ milítsii) militia
{police}
~ расследования (~
rasslédovaniia) investigative
agency
~ санитарного надзора (~
sanitárnogo nadzóra) sanitary
oversight agency
~ социального обеспечения (~
sotsiál'nogo obespécheniia)
social welfare authority
~ управления (~ upravléniia)
managerial body

Организация (organizátsiia) f.
organization
автономная ~ (avtonómnaia ~)
autonomous ~
административная ~
(administratívnaia ~)
administrative ~
арбитражная ~ (arbitrázhnaia ~)
arbitral ~
внешнеторговая ~
(vneshnetorgóvaia ~) foreign
trade ~
Всемирная ~ Здравоохранения
(vsemírnaia ~ zdravookhranéniia)
World Health Organization {WHO}
инспекционная ~ (inspektsiónnaia
~) inspection ~
кооперативная ~ (kooperatívnaia
~) cooperative ~
корпоративная ~ (korporatívnaia
~) corporate body
кредитная ~ (kredítnaia ~)
credit institution
массовая ~ (mássovaia ~) mass ~
некоммерческая ~
(nekommércheskaia ~) nonprofit ~
официальная ~ (ofitsiál'naia ~)
official ~
партийная ~ (partíinaia ~) party
organization {esp. communist}
подрывная ~ (podrývnaia ~)
subversive ~
подрядная ~ (podriádnaia ~)
contractors
постоянная ~ (postoiánnaia ~)
permanent ~
правовая ~ (pravováia ~) legal ~
преступная ~ (prestúpnaia ~)
criminal ~
продовольственная и
сельскохозяйственная ~
объединённых наций {ФАО}
(prodovól'stvennaia i
sel'skokhoziástvennaia ~
ob"ediniónnykh nátsii {fao})
Food and Agricultural
Organization of the United
Nations {FAO}
промышленная ~ (promýshlennaia
~) industrial ~
профессиональная ~
(professionál'naia ~)
professional ~
профсоюзная ~ (profsoiúznaia ~)
labor ~
региональная ~ (regionál'naia ~)
regional ~

страховая ~ (strakhóvaia ~)
insurance agency
судебная ~ (sudébnaia ~)
judicial ~
торговая ~ (torgóvaia ~) trade ~
финансовая ~ (finánsovaia ~)
financial ~
хозрасчётная ~ (khozraschiótnaia
~) self-financing ~
хозяйственная ~ (khoziástvennaia
~) economic ~
частная ~ (chástnaia ~) private
agency
экономическая ~ (ekonomícheskaia
~) economic ~
~ Американских Государств {ОАГ}
(~ amerikánskikh gosudárstv
{oag}) Organization of American
States {OAS}
~ Африканского Единства (~
afrikánskogo edínstva)
Organization of African Unity
{OAU}
~ по вопросам образования и
культуры {ЮНЕСКО} (~ po voprósam
obrazóvaniia i kul'túry
{iunésko}) UNESCO
~ договора юго-восточной Азии
{СЕАТО} (~ dogovóra
iugovostóchnoi ázii {seato})
Southeast Asian Treaty
Organization {SEATO}
~ международной гражданской
авиации (~ mezhdunaródnoi
grazhdánskoi aviátsii)
International Civil Aviation
Organization
~ объединённых наций {ООН} (~
ob"ediniónnykh nátsii {oon})
United Nations Organization {UN}
~ северо-атлантического договора
(~ sévero-atlantícheskogo
dogovóra) North Atlantic Treaty
Organization {NATO}
~ экономического сотрудничества
и развития (~ ekonomícheskogo
sotrúdnichestva i razvítiia)
Organization of Economic
Cooperation and Development
{OECD}
Организм (organízm) m. human body,
organism
Орда (ordá) f. horde
Золотая ~ (zolotáia ~) Golden
Horde
Орден (órden) m. order {award,
group}

Иезуитский ~ (iezuítskii ~)
Order of Jesus {Jesuits}
Мальтийский ~ (mal'tíiskii ~)
Order of Malta
религиозный ~ (religióznyi ~)
religious order
~ Ленина (~ lénina) Order of
Lenin {Soviet Award}
Ордер (órder) m. order, warrant,
writ
кассовый ~ (kássovyi ~) cash
order
обменный ~ (obménnyi ~) payment
order
приходный ~ (prikhódnyi ~)
receipt voucher
расходный ~ (raskhódnyi ~)
expenditure voucher
~ на обыск (~ na óbysk) search
warrant
~ на покупку (~ na pokúpku)
coupon
~ на расквартирование (~ na
raskvartírovanie) order of
eviction
Ординарец (ordinárets) m. batman,
orderly
Оригинал (originál) m. original
Ориентация (orientátsiia) f.
orientation
Ориентировать (orientírovat') v. to
orient
Орудие (orúdie) n. instrument,
ordnance, tool
кредитное ~ (kredítnoe ~) credit
instrument
~ платежа (~ platezhá)
instrument of payment
Оружие (orúzhie) n. arms, weapons
запрещённое ~ (zapreshchiónnoe
~) banned weaponry
Осада (osáda) f. siege
Осведомление (osvedomlénie) n.
notification
Осведомлять (osvedomliát') v. to
inform
~/ся по первоисточникам (~/sia
po pervoistóchnikam) to be
informed from first-hand sources
Освещение (osveshchénie) n.
illumination, lighting
Освобождать (osvobozhdát') v.
[perfective: освободить] to
emancipate, to exempt, to free, to
release
~ на волю (~ na vóliu) to set at
liberty

~ от обязанности (~ ot obiázannosti) to release from an obligation

Освобождение (osvobozhdénie) n. discharge, dismissal, emancipation, exemption, liberation, release
досрочное ~ (dosróchnoe ~) early release
полное ~ от наказания (pólnoe ~ ot nakazániia) complete immunity from punishment
частичное ~ от наказания (chastíchnoe ~ ot nakazániia) partial immunity from punishment
частичное ~ от уплаты налога (chastíchnoe ~ ot upláty nalóga) partial exemption from payment of tax
~ от пошлин (~ ot póshlin) exemption from duties

Освобождённый (osvobozhdiónnyi) adj. exempt
~ от военной службы ~ (~ ot voénnoi slúzhby) from military service
~ полностью (~ pólnost'iu) totally ~

Освоение (osvoénie) n. mastery {of a process, etc.}

Оседлост/ь (osédlost/') f. settlement, settled lifestyle
Черта ~/и (chertá ~/i) Pale of Settlement {historical}

Осквернение (oskvernénie) n. defilement

Оскорбитель (oskorbítel') m. offender

Оскорбительный (oskorbítel'nyi) adj. abusive, insulting

Оскорбить (oskorbít') v. [see оскорблять]

Оскорбление (oskorblénie) n. assault, insult, offense
тяжкое ~ (tiázhkoe ~) serious offense
~ действием (~ déistviem) assault and battery
~ словом (~ slóvom) contumely

Оскорблённый (oskorbliónnyi) adj. insulted, offended
~/ая невинность (~/aia nevínnost') outraged innocence

Оскорблять (oskorbliát') v. to insult, to offend

Осматривать (osmátrivat') v. to examine, to inspect

Осмотр (osmótr) m. check, examination, inspection
санитарный ~ (sanitárnyi ~) health inspection
судебный ~ (sudébnyi ~) judicial examination
таможенный ~ (tamózhennyi ~) customs inspection
~ вещественных доказательств (~ veshchéstvennykh dokazátel'stv) examination of substantive evidence
~ места происшествия, ~ на месте (~ mésta proisshéstviia, ~ na méste) examination in situ
~ товаров (~ továrov) inspection of goods

Осмотреть (osmotrét') v. [see осматривать]

Оснащение (osnashchénie) n. equipping, outfitting
~ судна (~ súdna) rigging of a vessel

Основа (osnóva) f. base, bases, basis, foundation
взаимовыгодная (vzaimovýgodnaia ~) a mutually profitable basis
компенсационная ~ (kompensatsiónnaia ~) compensatory basis
правовая ~ (pravováia ~) legal foundation

Основани/е (osnováni/e) n. foundation, grounds, reason
без всяких ~/й (bez vsiákikh ~/i) without any grounds
законное ~ (zakónnoe ~) statutory ground
мнимое ~ (mnímoe ~) false pretense
прочное ~ (próchnoe ~) solid basis
юридическое ~ (iuridícheskoe ~) legal grounds

Основатель (osnovátel') m. founder

Основывать (osnóvyvat') v. to found

Основоположник (osnovopolózhnik) m. initiator

Оспаривание (ospárivanie) contention, contest
~ отцовства (~ ottsóvstva) contest of paternity
~ права (~ práva) contest of right

Оспаривать (ospárivat') v. to contest, to dispute

Оставить (ostávit') v. [see
оставлять]
Оставление (ostavlénie) n.
abandonment
  злостное ~ ребёнка (zlóstnoe ~
  rebiónka) malicious abandonment
  of child
  злостное ~ семьи (zlóstnoe ~
  sem'í) malicious abandonment of
  family
  ~ за собой узуфрукта (~ za sobói
  uzufrúkta) abandonment of
  usufruct
  ~ обременённого ипотекой
  имущества (~ obremeniónnogo
  ipotékoi imúshchestva)
  abandonment of encumbered
  property
  ~ одного из супругов другим (~
  odnogó iz suprúgov drugím)
  abandonment by one spouse of the
  other
  ~ погибающего корабля (~
  pogibáiushchego korabliá)
  abandonment of ship
  ~ решения в силе (~ reshéniia v
  síle) leaving a decision in
  force
Оставлять (ostavliát') v. to
reserve
  ~ за собой право (~ za sobói
  právo) to reserve the right
Остановка в порту (ostanóvka v
portú) v. call at port
Остаток (ostátok) m. balance,
remainder, residual
  компенсационный ~
  (kompensatsiónnyi ~)
  compensatory balance
  кредитовый ~ (kredítovyi ~)
  credit balance
  наличный ~ (nalíchnyi ~) in-
  house balance
  ~ долга (~ dólga) balance of a
  debt
  ~ запасов (~ zapásov) remainder
  of stock
  ~ суммы (~ súmmy) remainder of a
  sum
  ~ счёта (~ schióta) account
  balance
Осуждать (osuzhdát') v. to condemn,
to convict, to sentence
Осуждение (osuzhdénie) n.
conviction, sentence
  заочное ~ (zaóchnoe ~)
  conviction by default

условное ~ (uslóvnoe ~)
suspended sentence
  ~ уголовным судом (~ ugolóvnym
  sudóm) conviction by the
  criminal court
Осуждённый (osuzhdiónnyi) m. adj.
convict, convicted
Осуществить (osushchestvít') v.
[see осуществлять]
Осуществление (osushchestvlénie) n.
accomplishment, implementation,
realization
  немедленное ~ (nemédlennoe ~)
  prompt implementation
  промышленное ~ изобретения
  (promýshlennoe ~ izobreténiia)
  industrial application of an
  invention
Осуществлять (osushchestvliát') v.
to accomplish, to implement, to
realize
Отбирать (otbirát') v. [perfective:
отобрать] to collect, to seize, to
take away
Отбывание (otbyvánie) n. serving
time {e.g. a prison sentence}
  ~ ссылки (~ ssýlki) state of
  exile
Отвергать (otvergát') v. to
overturn, to reject
Отвести (otvestí) v. to challenge,
to reject {e.g. a juror}
Ответ (otvét) m. answer, reply
Ответственност/ь (otvétstvennost/')
f. liability, responsibility
  административная ~
  (administratívnaia ~)
  administrative responsibility
  взаимная ~ (vzaímnaia ~) joint
  liability
  внедоговорная ~ (vnedogovórnaia
  ~) non-contractual liability
  гарантийная ~ (garantíinaia ~)
  liability under warranty
  гражданская ~ (grazhdánskaia ~)
  civil liability
  деликтная ~ (delíktnaia ~) tort
  liability
  договорная ~ (dogovórnaia ~)
  contractual liability
  долговая ~ (dolgováia ~)
  liability for debts
  дополнительная ~
  (dopolnítel'naia ~) additional
  responsibility

имущественная ~
(imúshchestvennaia ~) property
accountability
индивидуальная ~
(individuál'naia ~) individual
responsibility, solo liability
исключить ~ (iskliuchít' ~) to
exclude liability
коллективная ~ (kollektívnaia ~)
collective liability
личная ~ (líchnaia ~) personal
responsibility
максимальная ~ (maksimál'naia ~)
maximum liability
материальная ~ (materiál'naia ~)
material liability
моральная ~ (morál'naia ~) moral
responsibility
налоговая ~ (nalógovaia ~) tax
liability
нести ~ (nestí ~) to incur
liability
неограниченная ~
(neograníchennaia ~) unlimited
liability
непосредственная ~
(neposrédstvennaia ~) direct
responsibility
ограниченная ~ (ograníchennaia
~) limited liability
основная ~ (osnovnáia ~) primary
liability
персональная ~ (personál'naia ~)
personal responsibility
повышенная ~ (povýshennaia ~)
increased liability
подлежать судебной ~/и
(podlezhát' sudébnoi ~/i) to be
subject to judicial liability
полная ~ (pólnaia ~) full
responsibility
профессиональная ~
(professionál'naia ~)
professional responsibility
служебная ~ (sluzhébnaia ~)
official responsibility
совместная ~ (sovméstnaia ~)
joint responsibility
солидарная ~ (solidárnaia ~)
joint liability
судебная ~ (sudébnaia ~)
judicial liability
уголовная ~ (ugolóvnaia ~)
criminal liability
условная ~ (uslóvnaia ~)
contingent liability

Ответственный (otvétstvennyi) adj.
liable, responsible
Ответчик (otvétchik) m. respondent
{in judicial proceeding}
Отвечать (otvechát') v. to answer,
to reply
Отвод (otvód) m. challenge,
rejection
    ~ арбитра (~ arbítra) to
    challenge an arbitrator
Отводить (otvodít') v. to
challenge, to reject {e.g.
arbitrator}
Отгружать (otgruzhát') v. to ship
Отгрузка (otgrúzka) f. shipment
Отдача (otdácha) f. letting,
payment, reimbursement
    ~ в залог (~ v zalóg) pledging
    ~ в наём (~ v naióm) letting for
    rent
    ~ под опеку (~ pod opéku)
    mortgaging
Отдел (otdél) m. department,
division, section
    жилищный ~ (zhilíshchnyi ~)
    housing department
    консульский ~ (kónsul'skii ~)
    consular section
    финансовый ~ (finánsovyi ~)
    financial department
    ~ Виз и Регистрации {ОВИР} (~
    viz i registrátsii {ovír})
    Department of Visas and
    Registration
Отделение (otdelénie) n. branch,
office, outlet
    местное ~ (méstnoe ~) local
    branch
    почтовое ~ (pochtóvoe ~) post
    office
    торговое ~ (torgóvoe ~) sales
    office
Отец (otéts) m. father
    приёмный ~ (priiómnyi ~)
    adoptive ~
    родной ~ (rodnói ~) birth ~
Отечественный (otéchestvennyi) adj.
domestic, patriotic
Отечество (otéchestvo) n.
fatherland, homeland
Отзыв (ótzyv) m. criticism,
reference, withdrawal
    дать хороший ~ (dat' khoróshii
    ~) to give a good recommendation
    ~ на заочное решение (~ na
    zaóchnoe reshénie) entering of a
    default judgment

~ кредита (~ kredíta) withdrawal of credit
Отзыв (otzýv) *m.* recall of diplomatic personnel
Отзывать (otzyvát') *v.* to take aside, to recall {a representative}
Отзывной (otzyvnói) *adj.* revocable
Отказ (otkáz) *m.* abandonment, denial, refusal, renunciation
молчаливый ~ (molchalívyi ~) implicit rejection
общий ~ (óbshchii ~) total rejection
прямой ~ (priamói ~) direct refusal
публичный ~ (publíchnyi ~) public rejection
~ в выдаче патента (~ v výdache paténta) rejection of a patent application
~ в иске (~ v íske) dismissal of action, suit
~ от выполнения (~ ot vypolnéniia) refusal to perform
~ от дачи показаний (~ ot dáchi pokazánii) refusal to give evidence
~ от долгов (~ ot dolgóv) repudiation of debts
~ от имущества (~ ot imúshchestva) abandonment of property
~ от иска (~ ot íska) abandonment of action, suit
~ от наследства (~ ot naslédstva) repudiation of inheritance
~ от прав (~ ot prav) waiver of rights
~ от права обжалования (~ ot práva obzhálovaniia) waiver of right to appeal
~ платить (~ platít') refusal to pay
Отказать (otkazát') *v.* to decline, to refuse, to renounce, to repudiate
~ в иске (~ v íske) to abandon an action, suit
Откладывать (otkládyvat') *v.* to continue, to postpone, to suspend
Отклонение (otklonénie) *n.* denial, deviation, discrepancy, inadequacy
~ в качестве (~ v káchestve) defect in quality
~ заявки (~ zaiávki) rejection of application

~ от паритета (~ ot paritéta) deviation from parity
~ предложения (~ predlozhéniia) rejection of an offer
~ ходатайства (~ khodátaistva) rejection of a petition
~ цен (~ tsen) deviation of prices
Отклонять (otkloniát') *v.* to decline, to deny, to refuse, to reject
Открытие (otkrýtie) *n.* discovery, opening
~ аккредитива (~ akkreditíva) opening of a letter of credit
~ конференции (~ konferéntsii) opening of a conference
~ кредита (~ kredíta) opening of a line of credit
~ магазина (~ magazína) opening of a store
~ новых рынков (~ nóvykh rýnkov) penetration of new markets
~ переговоров (~ peregovórov) initiation of negotiations
~ рынка (~ rýnka) opening of a market
~ счёта (~ schióta) opening of an account
Открыто (otkrýto) *adv.* openly
Отлагательство (otlagátel'stvo) *n.* delay, procrastination
Отличие (otlíchie) *n.* distinction
Отложение дела (otlozhénie déla) *n.* continuance of a case
Отложить (otlozhít') *v.* [see откладывать]
Отлучка (otlúchka) absence
самовольная ~ (samovól'naia ~) absence without leave {AWOL}
Отмена (otména) *f.* abolition, abrogation, cancellation, repeal
~ дарения (~ daréniia) revocation of a gift
~ доверенности (~ dovérennosti) revocation of power of attorney
~ завещания (~ zaveshchániia) revocation of a will
~ закона (~ zakóna) repeal of a law
~ иммунитета (~ immunitéta) revocation of immunity
~ мандата (~ mandáta) repeal of a mandate
~ налога (~ nalóga) roll-back of a tax

~ приговора (~ prigovóra) overturn of a sentence
~ решения (~ reshéniia) reversal of a sentence
Отменять (otmeniát') v. to disaffirm
Отметить (otmetít') v. [see отмечать]
Отметка (otmétka) f. clause, mark, notation, reservation, tally
контрольная ~ (kontról'naia ~) checkmark
~ в коносаменте (~ v konosaménte) reservation in bill of lading
Отмечать (otmechát') v. to mark, to note
Относительность (otnosítel'nost') f. relativity
Относительный (otnosítel'nyi) adj. relative
Отношени/е (otnoshéni/e) n. attitude, relation, relationship
договорное ~ (dogovórnoe ~) contractual relation
правовое ~ (pravovóe ~) legal relation
валютные ~/я (valiútnye ~/ia) currency relations
внешнеторговые ~/я (vneshnetorgóvye ~/ia) foreign trade relations
деловые ~/я (delovýe ~/ia) business relations
длительные ~/я (dlítel'nye ~/ia) long-term relations
дипломатические ~/я (diplomatícheskie ~/ia) diplomatic relations
добрососедские ~/я (dobrososédskie ~/ia) good neighborly relations
имущественные ~/я (imúshchestvennye ~/ia) property relations
консульские ~/я (kónsul'skie ~/ia) consular relations
международные ~/я (mezhdunaródnye ~/ia) international relations
мирные ~/я (mírnye ~/ia) peaceful relations
родственные ~/я (ródstvennye ~/ia) family relations
финансовые ~/я (finánsovye ~/ia) financial relations

хозрасчётные ~/я (khozraschiótnye ~/ia) self-supporting relations
членские ~/я (chlénskie ~/ia) member relations
экономические~ (ekonomícheskie~) economic relations
Отобрать (otobrát') v. [see отбирать]
Отождествлять (otozhdestvliát') v. to identify
Отозвать (otozvát') v. [see отзывать]
Отомстить (otomstít') v. to avenge
Отослать (otoslát') v. to dispatch, to remit
Отпечаток (otpechátok) m. impress, imprint {variant}
~ пальца (~ pál'tsa) fingerprint
Отпор (otpór) m. rebuff, repulse
дать ~ (dat' ~) to repulse
Отправитель (otpravítel') m. consignor, forwarder, shipper
Отправить (otprávit') v. [see отправлять]
Отправка (otprávka) f. dispatch, forwarding, shipment
Отправление (otpravlénie) n. departure, mailing, sailing
заказное ~ (zakaznóe ~) registered mail
международное почтовое ~ (mezhdunaródnoe pochtóvoe ~) international post
почтовое ~ (pochtóvoe ~) mailing
Отправлять (otpravliát') v. to dispatch, to ship
Отпуск (ótpusk) m. distribution, furlough, leave
дополнительный ~ (dopolnítel'nyi ~) additional leave
дородовой ~ (dorodovói ~) pre-maternity leave
ежегодный ~ (ezhegódnyi ~) annual leave
оплачиваемый ~ (oplachiváemyi ~) paid vacation
послеродовой ~ (poslerodovói ~) post-maternity leave
~ по беременности и родам (~ po berémennosti i rodám) maternity leave
~ по болезни (~ po bolézni) sick leave
Отпускать (otpuskát') v. to release
~ на волю (~ na vóliu) to release from confinement

Отпускник (otpuskník) *m.* worker on leave, soldier on furlough

Отпустить (otpustít') *v.* [see отпускать]

Отработка (otrabótka) *f.* working off {e.g. of a debt}

Отравление (otravlénie) *n.* poisoning

Отравлять (otravliát') *v.* to poison

Отрасль (ótrasl') *f.* branch, sector
    производственная ~ (proizvódstvennaia ~) branch of industry
    ~ деятельности (~ déiatel'nosti) sphere of activity
    ~ права (~ práva) field of law
    ~ предприятия (~ predpriiátiia) branch of an enterprise
    ~ производства (~ proizvódstva) sphere of production
    ~ промышленности (~ promýshlennosti) sphere of industry
    ~ сельского хозяйства (~ sél'skogo khoziástva) branch of agriculture

Отрекаться (otrekát'sia) *v.* to abdicate, to renounce
    ~ от престола (~ ot prestóla) to abdicate the throne

Отречение (otrechénie) *n.* abdication, renunciation
    ~ от должности (~ ot dólzhnosti) resignation of a post
    ~ от данного права (~ ot dánnogo práva) renunciation of a given right
    ~ от престола (~ ot prestóla) abdication of the throne

Отречься (otréch'sia) *v.* [see отрекаться]

Отрицание (otritsánie) *n.* denial

Отрицать (otritsát') *v.* to deny, to disclaim
    ~ виновность (~ vinóvnost') to plead not guilty

Отрыв (otrýv) *m.* disengagement

Отрывок (otrývok) *m.* excerpt, passage

Отряд (otriád) *m.* detachment
    передовой ~ (peredovói ~) vanguard

Отсроченный (otsróchennyi) *adj.* deferred, postponed

Отсрочивать (otsróchivat') *v.* to defer, to postpone

Отсрочка (otsróchka) *f.* delay, extension, postponement

Отставк/а (otstávk/a) *f.* discharge, dismissal, resignation
    выйти в ~/у (výiti v ~/u) to resign, to retire
    подать в ~/у (podát' v ~/u) to submit one's resignation
    уволить в ~/у (uvólit' v ~/u) to dismiss

Отставной (otstavnói) *adj.* retired

Отсталость (otstálost') *f.* backwardness

Отстранение (otstranénie) *n.* discharge, dismissal
    ~ от должности (~ ot dólzhnosti) dismissal from a post
    ~ от работы (~ ot rabóty) discharge from work

Отстранять (otstraniát') *v.* to discharge, to dismiss

Отступать (otstupát') *v.* to depart from, to deviate from

Отступление (otstuplénie) *n.* departure, deviation
    ~ от правил (~ ot právil) deviation from the rules

Отступные (otstupnýe) *pl.adj.noun* "smart-money" {compensation for recision of contract}

Отсутствие (otsútstvie) *n.* absence, lack
    преднамеренное ~ (prednamérennoe ~) premeditated absence
    ~ вины (~ viný) absence of guilt
    ~ кворума (~ kvóruma) lack of quorum
    ~ ответственности (~ otvétstvennosti) absence of liability
    ~ доказательства (~ dokazátel'stva) lack of evidence
    ~ правомочий (~ pravomóchii) lack of authority
    ~ согласия (~ soglásiia) lack of agreement
    ~ судимости (~ sudímosti) lack of previous convictions

Отсутствовать (otsútstvovat') *v.* to be absent, to be lacking

Отсутствующий (otsútstvuiushchii) *adj.* missing

Отсылать (otsylát') *v.* to refer to, to return

Оттиск (óttisk) *m.* impress, print, stamp

~ печати (~ pecháti) impress of a seal {of a company}

Отход (otkhód) *m.* departure, sailing

Отцеубийство (ottseubíistvo) *n.* parricide {crime}

Отцеубийца (ottseubíitsa) *m.* parricide {person}

Отцовство (ottsóvstvo) *n.* paternity
внебрачное ~ (vnebráchnoe ~) paternity out of wedlock
законное ~ (zakónnoe ~) legitimate paternity
незаконное ~ (nezakónnoe ~) illegitimate paternity

Отчёт (otchiót) *m.* account

Отчим (ótchim) *m.* stepfather

Отчисление (otchislénie) *n.* allocation, deduction, fee
амортизационное ~ (amortizatsiónnoe ~) amortized deduction, amortization
~ в бюджет (~ v biudzhét) budget allocation
~ от прибыли (~ ot príbyli) deduction from profits

Отчитываться (otchítyvat'sia) *v.* to give an account of

Отчуждаемый (otchuzhdáemyi) *adj.* alienable

Отчуждать (otchuzhdát') *v.* to alienate

Отчуждение (otchuzhdénie) *n.* alienation
безвозмездное ~ (bezvozmézdnoe ~) uncompensated alienation
возмездное ~ (vozmézdnoe ~) compensated alienation
недобросовестное ~ (nedobrosóvestnoe ~) bad faith alienation
принудительное ~ (prinudítel'noe ~) condemnation

Отягчающ/ий (otiagcháiushch/ii) *adj.* aggravating
~/ие обстоятельства (~/ie obstoiátel'stva) aggravating circumstances

Отягчать (otiagchát') *v.* to aggravate

Оферент (oferént) *m.* offeror

Оферта (oférta) *f.* offer

Офертант (ofertánt) *m.* offeree

Офицер (ofitsér) *m.* officer
~ полиции (~ polítsii) police ~

Официально (ofitsiál'no) *adv.* officially

Официальный (ofitsiál'nyi) *adj.* official

Официоз (ofitsióz) *m.* semi-official organ {of the press}

Официозный (ofitsióznyi) *adj.* semi-official

Оформление (oformlénie) *n.* execution, issuance, legalization, registration
правильное ~ договора (právil'noe ~ dogovóra) proper drafting of an agreement
правовое ~ (pravovóe ~) legalization, legal registration
~ договора (~ dogovóra) drafting of an agreement
~ заказа (~ zakáza) drawing up of an order
~ патента (~ paténta) execution of a patent
~ чертежей (~ chertezhéi) preparation of drawings

Оформленный (ofórmlennyi) *adj.* executed, formal

Оформлять (oformliát') *v.* to legalize, to register, to draft {e.g. a document}

Охота (okhóta) *f.* hunting
незаконная ~ (nezakónnaia ~) poaching

Охрана (okhrána) *f.* guarding, protection
береговая ~ (beregováia ~) coast guard
двойная ~ (dvoináia ~) double protection
пограничная ~ (pograníchnaia ~) border guard
патентная ~ (paténtnaia ~) patent protection
правовая ~ (pravováia ~) legal protection
~ авторского права (~ ávtorskogo práva) copyright protection
~ границы (~ granítsy) protection of the border
~ детей (~ detéi) protection of children
~ здоровья (~ zdoróv'ia) preservation of health
~ патента (~ paténta) patent protection
~ прав (~ prav) protection of rights
~ прав на изобретения (~ prav na izobreténiia) protection of rights to an invention

~ прав несовершеннолетних (~ prav nesovershennolétnikh) protection of the rights of minors

~ промышленных рисунков и моделей (~ promýshlennykh risúnkov i modélei) protection of industrial drawings and models

~ промышленной собственности (~ promýshlennoi sóbstvennosti) protection of industrial property

~ товарных знаков и торговых марок (~ továrnykh znákov i torgóvykh márok) protection of trademarks

Охранение (okhranénie) *n.* safeguarding

сторожевое ~ (storozhevóe ~) outposts

Оценивать (otsénivat') *v.* to appraise, to estimate, to evaluate

Оценка (otsénka) *f.* appraisal, estimate, evaluation

выборочная ~ (výborochnaia ~) sample estimate

годовая ~ (godováia ~) annual estimate

завышенная ~ (zavýshennaia ~) overvaluation

заниженная ~ (zanízhennaia ~) low estimate

инвентарная ~ (inventárnaia ~) inventory evaluation

приблизительная ~ (priblizítel'naia ~) approximate estimate

совместная ~ (sovméstnaia ~) joint assessment

статистическая ~ (statistícheskaia ~) statistical estimate

судебная ~ (sudébnaia ~) judicial assessment

таможенная ~ (tamózhennaia ~) customs evaluation

~ данных (~ dánnykh) data assessment

~ кредитоспособности (~ kreditosposóbnosti) credit rating

~ доказательств (~ dokazátel'stv) evaluation of evidence

~ налога (~ nalóga) tax assessment

~ риска (~ ríska) estimation of risk

Оценщик (otsénshchik) *m.* appraiser

Очаг (ochág) *m.* center, hearth

домашний ~ (domáshnii ~) hearth and home

Очевидец (ochevídets) *m.* eye witness

Очередность (ócherednost') *f.* sequence, succession

Очередь (óchered') *f.* queue, turn

первая ~ (pérvaia ~) first priority

Очистк/а (ochístka) *f.* purge

произвести ~/у (proizvestí) to carry out a ~

~ недвижимости от ипотеки (~ nedvízhimosti ot ipotéki) release of real property from mortgage

Ошибка (oshíbka) *f.* error, mistake

канцелярская ~ (kantseliárskaia ~) clerical error

навигационная ~ (navigatsiónnaia ~) navigational error

правовая ~ (pravováia ~) legal error

судебная ~ (sudébnaia ~) judicial error

фактическая ~ (faktícheskaia ~) factual error

юридическая ~ (iuridícheskaia ~) jurisprudential error

Ошибочный (oshíbochnyi) *adj.* mistaken

Оштрафованный (oshtrafóvannyi) *adj.* fined, penalized

Оштрафовать (oshtrafovát') *v.* to fine, to penalize

П

Падение (padénie) *n.* decline, drop, fall

~ курса валюты (~ kúrsa valiúty) drop in the exchange rate of currency

~ покупательной силы (~ pokupátel'noi síly) decline in spending power

~ рождаемости (~ rozhdáemosti) decline in birth rate

~ цен (~ tsen) drop in prices

Паёк (paiók) *m.* ration

Пай (pai) *m.* share

кооперативный ~ (kooperatívnyi ~) cooperative ~
учредительный ~ (uchredítel'nyi ~) founding ~
~ акционерного общества (~ aktsionérnogo óbshchestva) ~ of a joint stock company
~ товарищества (~ továrishchestva) ~ of a partnership

Пайщик (páishchik) *m.* stockholder

Пакет (pakét) *m.* block, parcel, packet
контрольный ~ (kontról'nyi ~) controlling block
в отдельном ~/е (v otdél'nom ~/e) under separate cover
~ акций (~ áktsii) block of shares

Пакт (pakt) *m.* pact
агрессивный ~ (agressívnyi ~) aggressive ~
балканский ~ (balkánskii ~) Balkan ~
военный ~ (voénnyi ~) military ~
международный ~ (mezhdunaródnyi ~) international ~
организационный ~ (organizatsiónnyi ~) organizational ~
рейнский ~ (réinskii ~) Rhine ~
северо-атлантический ~ (sévero-atlantícheskii ~) North Atlantic ~
трёхсторонний ~ (triókhstorónnii ~) Trilateral ~
федеральный ~ (federál'nyi ~) federal ~
четырёхсторонний ~ (chetyriókhstorónnii ~) Quadrilateral ~
~ о безопасности (~ o bezopásnosti) security ~
~ о взаимной помощи (~ o vzaímnoi pómoshchi) mutual aid ~
~ лиги наций (~ lígi nátsii) ~ of League of Nations
~ мира (~ míra) Peace ~
~ о нейтралитете (~ o neitralitéte) neutrality ~
~ о совместной обороне (~ o sovméstnoi oboróne) mutual defense ~

Палата (paláta) *f.* chamber, house
апелляционная ~ (apelliatsiónnaia ~) Court of Appeals
арбитражная ~ (arbitrázhnaia ~) Arbitration Court
верхняя ~ (vérkhniaia ~) upper chamber
законодательная ~ (zakonodátel'naia ~) legislative chamber
конституционная ~ (konstitutsiónnaia ~) constitutional chamber
международная торговая ~ (mezhdunaródnaia torgóvaia ~) International Chamber of Commerce
нижняя ~ (nízhniaia ~) lower chamber
постоянная ~ международ ного правосудия (postoiánnaia ~ mezhdunaródnogo právosudiia) Permanent Court of International Justice
промышленная и торговая ~ (promýshlennaia i torgóvaia ~) Chamber of Commerce and Industry
профсоюзная ~ (profsoiúznaia ~) union hall
расчётная ~ (raschiótnaia ~) clearing house
судебная ~ (sudébnaia ~) judicial chamber
торговая ~ (torgóvaia ~) Chamber of Commerce
торгово-промышленная ~ (torgóvo-promýshlennaia ~) Chamber of Commerce and Industry
~ по гражданским делам (~ po grahdánskim delám) civil court
~ депутатов (~ deputátov) House of Deputies
~ лордов (~ lórdov) House of Lords
~ по судебным делам (~ po sudébnym delám) judicial court

Палач (palách) *m.* hangman

Памятник (pámiatnik) *m.* monument
исторический ~ (istorícheskii ~) historical ~
~ старины (~ stariný) ~ of Antiquity

Панамериканизм (panamerikanízm) *m.* Panamericanism

Панамериканский (panamerikánskii) *adj.* panamerican

Парафирование (parafirovánie) *n.* initialing
~ договора (~ dogovóra) ~ of an agreement

Парафировать (parafírovat') v. to
initial
Пари (parí) adv. par {in the phrase
аль пари = at par}
Паритет (paritét) m. parity
    валютный ~ (valiútnyi ~)
    exchange rate ~
    золотой ~ (zolotói ~) gold ~
    монетный ~ (monétnyi ~) mint ~
    официальный ~ (ofitsiál'nyi ~)
    official ~
    по ~/у (po ~/u) at par
    ~ с долларом (~ s dóllarom)
    dollar ~
Паритетный (paritétnyi) adj. parity
Парк (park) m. park
    автомобильный ~ (avtomobíl'nyi
    ~) automobile lot
Парламент (parláment) m. Parliament
    европейский ~ (evropéiskii ~)
    European ~
    распустить ~ (raspustít' ~) to
    dissolve ~
Парламентарий (parlamentárii) m.
parliamentarian
Парламентаризм (parlamentarízm) m.
parliamentarianism
Парламентёр (parlamentiór) m. peace
envoy
Парламентский (parlámentskii) adj.
parliamentary
Пароль (paról') countersign,
password
Пароход (parokhód) m. steamship
    грузовой ~ (gruzovói ~) cargo
    steamer
    пассажирский ~ (passazhírskii ~)
    passenger ~
    почтовый ~ (pochtóvyi ~) mail
    ship
Пароходство (parokhódstvo) n.
steamship line
Партактив (partaktív) m. party
activist
Партбилет (partbilét) m. party
membership card
Партизан (partizán) m. partisan
Партийность (partíinost') f. party
boosterism {i.e. Communist}
Партикуляризм (partikuliarízm) m.
particularism
Партия (pártiia) f. consignment,
lot, party
    большевистская ~
    (bol'shevístskaia ~) Bolshevik
    Party

демократическая ~
(demokratícheskaia ~) Democratic
Party
единая ~ (edínaia ~) unified
party
исключить из ~/и (iskliuchít' iz
~/i) to exclude from the party
коалиционная ~ (koalitsiónnaia
~) coalition party
коммунистическая ~
(kommunistícheskaia ~) Communist
Party
консервативная ~
(konservatívnaia ~) Conservative
Party
крестьянская ~ (krest'iánskaia
~) Peasant Party {rural party}
лейбористская ~ (leiborístskaia
~) Labor Party
либеральная ~ (liberál'naia ~)
Liberal Party
либерально-демократическая ~
(liberál'no-demokratícheskaia ~)
Liberal-Democratic Party
народная ~ (naródnaia ~)
People's Party
объединённая социалистическая ~
(ob"ediniónnaia sotsialístíche-
skaia ~) Unified Socialist Party
оппозиционная ~ (oppozitsiónnaia
~) Opposition Party
политическая ~ (politícheskaia
~) political party
правящая ~ (praviáshchaia ~)
ruling party
прогрессивная ~ (progressívnaia
~) progressive party
рабочая ~ (rabóchaia ~) Worker's
Party
радикальная ~ (radikál'naia ~)
Radical Party
радикально-демократическая ~
(radikál'no-demokratícheskaia ~)
Radical Democratic Party
революционная ~
(revoliutsiónnaia ~)
Revolutionary Party
социал-демократическая ~
(sotsiál-demokratícheskaia ~)
Social Democratic Party
социалистическая ~
(sotsialistícheskaia ~)
Socialist Party
христианско-демократическая ~
(khristiánsko-demokratícheskaia
~) Christian Democrat Party

Парткабинет (partkabinét) *m.* party reading room, propaganda center
Партком (partkóm) *m.* party committee *[abbrev.]*
Партконференция (partkonferéntsiia) *f.* party conference *[abbrev.]*
Партнёр (partniór) *m.* associate, partner {see also компаньон}
Парторг (partórg) *m.* party organizer *[abbrev.]*
Парторганизация (partorganizátsiia) *f.* party organization *[abbrev.]*
Партсъезд (parts"ézd) *m.* party congress
Паспорт (pásport) *m.* passport
    выдать ~ (výdat' ~) to issue a ~
    государственный ~ (gosudárstvennyi ~) government ~
    действительный ~ (deistvítel'nyi ~) valid ~
    дипломатический ~ (diplomatícheskii ~) diplomatic ~
    заграничный ~ (zagraníchnyi ~) foreign travel ~ {under Soviet regime}
    иностранный ~ (inostránnyi ~) foreign ~
    нансеновский ~ (nánsenovskii ~) Nansen ~
Пассажир (passazhír) *m.* passenger
Пассажирооборот (passazhirooborót) *m.* passenger turnover
Пассив (passív) *m.* liabilities
    общая сумма ~/a (óbshchaia súmma ~/a) gross liabilities
    статья ~/a (stat'iá ~/a) liability {entry in accounts}
Пастбище (pástbishche) *n.* pasture
    общее ~ (óbshchee ~) common ~
Пасынок (pásynok) *m.* stepchild
Патент (patént) *m.* patent
    возобновляемый ~ (vozobnovliáemyi ~) reinstated ~
    выданный ~ (výdannyi ~) issued ~
    дополнительный ~ (dopolnítel'nyi ~) additional ~
    иностранный ~ (inostránnyi ~) foreign ~
    исключительный ~ (iskliuchítel'nyi ~) exclusive ~
    консульский ~ (kónsul'skii ~) consular ~
    международный ~ (mezhdunaródnyi ~) international ~
    отечественный ~ (otéchestvennyi ~) domestic ~

    отчудить ~ (otchudít' ~) to assign a ~
    признать ~ недействительным (priznát' ~ nedeistvítel'nym) to invalidate a ~
    промышленный ~ (promýshlennyi ~) industrial ~
    судовой ~ (sudovói ~) ship ~
    ~ на изобретение (~ na izobreténie) ~ foreign invention
    ~ на право самостоятельно заниматься ремеслом (~ na právo samostoiátel'no zanimát'sia remeslóm) artisan's ~
    ~ признанный недействительным (~ príznannyi nedeistvítel'nym) invalidated ~
Патентование (patentovánie) *n.* patenting
    заграничное ~ (zagraníchnoe ~) foreign ~
Патентованный (patentóvannyi) *adj.* patented
Патентовать (patentovát') *v.* to patent
Патентовладелец (patentovladélets) *m.* patent holder
Патентообладатель (patentoobladátel') *m.* patent holder
Патентоспособность (patentosposóbnost') *f.* patentability
Патентоспособный (patentosposóbnyi) *adj.* patentable
Патронаж (patronázh) *m.* home health care
Пацифизм (patsifízm) *m.* pacificism
Пачка (páchka) *f.* package, parcel
Пенитенциарный (penitentsiárnyi) penitentiary
Пенсионер (pensionér) *m.* pensioner
    ~ - инвалид войны (~ invalíd voiný) disabled veteran pensioner
    ~ по инвалидности (~ po invalídnosti) disabled pensioner
    ~ по старости (~ po stárosti) old age pensioner
Пенси/я (pénsi/ia) *f.* pension
    военная ~ (voénnaia ~) military ~
    выдать ~/ю (výdat' ~/iu) to issue a ~
    государственная ~ (gosudárstvennaia ~) state ~
    гражданская ~ (grahdánskaia ~) civil ~

пожизненная ~ (pozhíznennaia ~)
lifetime ~
пожизненная ~ по инвалидности
(pozhíznennaia ~ po
invalidnosti) lifetime ~ for
disability
уйти на ~/ю (uití na ~/iu) to
retire on ~
~ вдовам (~ vdovám) widow's ~
~ за выслугу лет (~ za výslugu
let) service ~
~ по нетрудоспособности (~ po
netrudosposóbnosti) disabled
worker ~
~ при выходе в отставку (~ pri
výkhode v otstávku) retirement ~
Пеня (pénia) penalty
~ натурой (~ natúroi) ~ in kind
Первенство (pérvenstvo) n. first
place
Первоочерёдность
(pervoocheriódnost') f. precedence,
priority
~ поставки (~ postávki)
precedence of delivery
Перебаллотировка (pereballotiróvka)
f. reballotting
Перебежчик (perebézhchik) m.
deserter
Перевалка (perevalka) f. transfer,
transshipping
Перевес (perevés) m. overweight,
surplus
~ экономический (~
ekonomícheskii) economic ~
~ сил (~ sil) excessive force
Перевести (perevestí) [perfective
of переводить] to transfer, to
translate
Перевод (perevód) m. transfer,
translation
банковский ~ (bánkovskii ~) bank
transfer
денежный ~ (dénezhnyi ~) money
transfer
денежный почтовый ~ (dénezhnyi
pochtóvyi ~) postal money order
международный ~ (mezhdunaródnyi
~) international transfer
письменный ~ (pís'mennyi ~)
written translation
принудительный ~ (prinudítel'nyi
~) compulsory transfer
сберегательный ~ (sberegátel'nyi
~) savings transfer
телеграфный ~ (telegráfnyi ~)
wire transfer

~ за границу (~ za granítsu)
foreign remittance
~ на другую работу (~ na drugúiu
rabótu) assignment transfer
{work}
~ иностранной валюты (~
inostránnoi valiúty) transfer of
foreign exchange
~ капитала (~ kapitála) transfer
of capital
~ капиталов за границу (~
kapitálóv za granítsu) transfer
of capital abroad
~ на низшую должность (~ na
nízshuiu dólzhnost') demotion
~ полиса (~ pólisa) assignment
of policy {insurance}
~ судна под другой флаг (~ súdna
pod drugói flag) reflagging of a
vessel
~ фондов (~ fóndov) transfer of
funds
~ через банк (~ chérez bank)
transfer through a bank
Переводить (perevodít') v. to
transfer, to translate
Переводоотправитель
(perevodootpravítel') m. transferor
Переводополучатель
(perevodopoluchátel') m. transferee
Переводчик (perevódchik) m.
translator
судебный ~ (sudébnyi ~) court ~
Перевозить (perevozít') v. to haul,
to transport
~ железнодорожным транспортом (~
zheleznodorózhnym tránsportom)
to ship by rail
~ по воде (~ po vodé) to ship by
water
Перевозка (perevózka) f. carriage,
shipment
автомобильная ~ (avtomobíl'naia
~) carriage by truck
безвозмездная ~ (bezvozmézdnaia
~) free transportation
водная ~ (vodnáia ~) water-borne
shipment
военная ~ (voénnaia ~) military
transport
воздушная ~ (vozdúshnaia ~) air
transport
воздушная ~ груза (vozdúshnaia ~
grúza) air transport of freight
воздушная ~ пассажиров
(vozdúshnaia ~ passazhírov) air
transport of passengers

воздушная ~ почты (vozdúshnaia ~ póchty) airmail transport
грузовая ~ (gruzováia ~) freight hauling
железнодорожная ~ (zheleznodorózhnaia ~) rail transport
каботажная ~ (kabotázhnaia ~) coasting-trade transport
коммерческая ~ (kommércheskaia ~) commercial transport
международная ~ (mezhdunaródnaia ~) international transport
международная воздушная ~ (mezhdunaródnaia vozdúshnaia ~) international air transport
морская ~ (morskáia ~) marine transport
пассажирская ~ (passazhírskaia ~) passenger transport
почтовая ~ (pochtóvaia ~) mail transport
прямая ~ (priamáia ~) direct transport
речная ~ (rechnáia ~) river transport
смешанная ~ (sméshannaia ~) mixed transport
шоссейная ~ (shosséinaia ~) highway transport
~ военнопленных (~ voennoplénnykh) transport of P.O.W.s
~ на барже (~ na bárzhe) transport by barge
~ на грузовиках (~ na gruzovikákh) transport by trucks
~ на палубе (~ na pálube) transport on deck
~ пассажиров (~ passazhírov) passenger transport
~ в прямом железнодорожно-дорожно-автомобильном сообщении (~ v priamóm zheleznodorózhno-dorózhno-avtomobíl'nom soobshchénii) transportation in direct railroad-truck link
Перевозчик (perevózchik) m. carrier
генеральный ~ (generál'nyi ~) common carrier
Перевооружить (perevooruzhít') v. to re-arm, to retool
Переворот (perevorót) m. revolution
государственный ~ (gosudárstvennyi ~) coup d'état
дворцовый ~ (dvortsóvyi ~) palace revolt

политический ~ (politícheskii ~) political revolution
промышленный ~ (promýshlennyi ~) industrial revolution
Перевоспитание (perevospitánie) n. reeducation
Перевыборы (perevýbory) pl. reelection
Перевыполнение (perevypolnénie) n. over-fulfillment
~ бюджета (~ biudzhéta) budget overrun
Перевыполнять (perevýpolniát') v. to over-fulfill [perfective: перевыполнить]
Переговор/ы (peregovór/y) m.pl. discussions, negotiations, talks
вести ~ (vestí ~) to conduct negotiations
двухсторонние ~ (dvukhstorónnie ~) bilateral negotiations
дипломатические ~ (diplomatícheskie ~) diplomatic negotiations
дружественные ~ (drúzhestvennye ~) amicable discussions
коллективные ~ (kollektívnye ~) collective negotiations
коммерческие ~ (kommércheskie ~) commercial negotiations
межправительственные ~ (mezhpravítel'stvennye ~) intergovernmental negotiations
многосторонние ~ (mnogostorónnie ~) multilateral negotiations
непосредственные ~ (neposredstvennye ~) direct negotiations
мирные ~ (mírnye ~) peace talks
плодотворные ~ (plodotvórnye ~) fruitful discussions
предварительные ~ (predvarítel'nye ~) preliminary discussions
предварительные ~ о мире (predvarítel'nye ~ o mire) preliminary negotiations for peace
секретные ~ (sekrétnye ~) secret talks
торговые ~ (torgóvye ~) trade negotiations
финансовые ~ (finánsovye ~) financial negotiations
экономические ~ (ekonómícheskie ~) economic talks

~ о мире (~ o míre) negotiations for peace
~ о перемирии (~ o peremírii) armistice talks

Перегружать (peregruzhát') *v.* to reload, to turn over {cargo}, to overload

Перегрузка (peregrúzka) *f.* overloading, transshipment

Перегруппировать (peregruppírovat') *v.* to regroup

Перегруппировка (peregruppiróvka) *f.* regrouping

Передавать (peredavát') *v.* to transfer
~ дело в суд (~ délo v sud) to take a matter to court

Передача (peredácha) *f.* assignation, assignment, broadcast, conveyance, transfer
безвозмездная ~ (bezvozmézdnaia ~) gratuitous assignment
безоговорочная ~ (bezogovórochnaia ~) unconditional assignment
без права ~/и (bez práva ~/i) non-negotiable, non-transferrable
возмездная ~ (vozmézdnaia ~) compensated assignment
~ авторских прав (~ ávtorskikh prav) assignment of copyright
~ на арбитраж (~ na arbitrázh) submission to arbitration
~ в аренду (~ v aréndu) assignment of lease
~ голоса (~ gólosa) proxy {vote}
~ дела (~ déla) assignment of a case
~ дела на новое судебное рассмотрение (~ déla na nóvoe sudébnoe rassmotrénie) assignment of a matter for judicial reconsideration
~ дела в суд (~ déla v sud) submission of a matter to a court
~ договора (~ dogovóra) assignment of a contract
~ лого (~ lógo) assignment of a logo
~ изобретения (~ izobreténiia) transfer of an invention
~ имуществ (~ imúshchestv) transfer of property
~ лицензии (~ litsénzii) transfer of a license

~ между живыми (~ mézhdu zhivými) inter-vivos transfer
~ по наследству (~ po naslédstvu) conveyance by inheritance
~ патента (~ paténta) assignment of a patent
~ подсудимого на поруки (~ podsudímogo na porúki) release of defendant on bail
~ полиса (~ pólisa) assignment of a policy
~ полномочий (~ polnomóchii) delegation of authority
~ портфеля (~ portfélia) transfer of a portfolio
~ поставок (~ postávok) assignment of deliveries
~ прав (~ prav) assignment of rights
~ прав на торговое предприятие (~ prav na torgóvoe predpriiátie) transfer of right in a trading enterprise
~ по принуждению (~ po prinuzhdéniiu) compulsory transfer
~ путём завещания (~ putióm zaveshchániia) testamentary transfer
~ в секвестр (~ v sekvéstr) sequestration
~ собственности (~ sóbstvennosti) assignment of property
~ суверенитета (~ suverenitéta) transfer of sovereignty
~ территории (~ territórii) transfer of territory
~ чека (~ chéka) negotiation of a check
~ юрисдикции (~ iurisdíktsii) change of venue

Передвигать (peredvigát') *v.* to shift

Передвижение (peredvizhénie) *n.* conveyance
воздушное ~ (vozdúshnoe ~) air conveyance
свободное ~ (svobódnoe ~) free movement
~ войск (~ vóisk) troop movements
~ капиталов (~ kapitalóv) capital movements
~ кредита (~ kredíta) credit movements

Передвижной (peredvizhnói) *adj.*
mobile, traveling
Передел (peredél) *m.*
redistribution, repartition
Переделка (peredélka) *f.* alteration
Передоверить (peredovérit') *v.*
[perfective of передоверять] to
transfer power of attorney
Передовик производства (peredovík
proizvódstva) *m.* exemplary
production worker {Communist
terminology}
Передоверять (peredoveriát') to
transfer power of attorney
Переезд границы (pereézd granítsy)
m. crossing the border
Переживать (perezhivát') *v.* to
endure, to worry
Перезаклад (perezaklád) *m.*
reencumbrance
Перезаключение договора
(perezakliuchénie dogovóra) *n.*
renewal of a contract
Переизбирать (pereizbirát') *v.* to
reelect
Переизбрание (pereizbránie) *n.*
reelection
Переименование (pereimenovánie) *n.*
renaming
Перейти в наступление (pereití v
nastuplénie) *v.* to go on the
offensive
Переквалификация
(perekvalifikátsiia) *f.*
requalification
Перелёт (pereliót) *m.* flight
Перелом (perelom) *m.* crisis,
turning point
Переложение бремени доказания
(perelozhénie brémeni dokazániia)
shifting of the burden of proof
Перемена (pereména) *f.* change
  ~ адреса (~ ádresa) change of
  address
  ~ гражданства (~ grazhdánstva)
  change of citizenship
  ~ занятия (~ zaniátiia) change
  of occupation
  ~ места жительства (~ mésta
  zhítel'stva) change of residence
  ~ подданства (~ póddanstva)
  change of nationality
  ~ режима (~ rezhíma) change of
  regime
  ~ суверенитета (~ suverenitéta)
  change of sovereignty

Переменять (peremeniát') *v.* to
change, to shift
Перемещать (peremeshchát') *v.* to
handle, to move, to transport
Перемещение (peremeshchénie) *n.*
handling, moving, transport
Перемирие (peremírie) *n.* armistice
  короткое ~ (korótkoe ~) short
  armistice
  местное ~ (méstnoe ~) local
  armistice
  общее ~ (óbshchee ~) general
  armistice
Перенаселение (perenaselénie) *n.*
overpopulation
  аграрное ~ (agrárnoe ~) agrarian
  ~
Перенасыщение (perenasyshchénie) *n.*
glut
Переносить (perenosít') *v.* to carry
forward, to postpone, to transfer
Перенос (perenós) *m.* carryover,
postponement
  сальдо с ~/a (sál'do s ~/a)
  balance brought forward
Переотправка (pereotprávka) *f.*
reforwarding {freight}
Переоценивать (pereotsénivat') *v.*
to overestimate, to overvalue
Переоценка (pereotsénka) *f.*
overvaluation, revaluation
Перепечатка (perepechátka) *f.*
reprint
Переписка (perepíska) *f.*
correspondence
  ведущий ~/y (vedúshchii ~/u)
  corresponding {party}
  коммерческая ~ (kommércheskaia
  ~) commercial ~
  официальная ~ (ofitsiál'naia ~)
  official ~
Перепись (pérepis') *f.* census,
inventory
  производить ~ (proizvodít' ~) to
  take inventory
  промышленная ~ (promýshlennaia
  ~) industrial inventory
  сельскохозяйственная ~
  (sel'skokhoziáistvennaia ~)
  agricultural inventory
  специальная ~ (spetsiál'naia ~)
  special census
  статистическая
  (statistícheskaia) statistical
  inventory
  частичная ~ (chastíchnaia ~)
  partial inventory

~ населения (~ naseléniia)
census of the population
Переплавить (pereplávit') v. to
float, to raft
Переплатить (pereplatít') v. to
overpay
Переподготовка (perepodgotóvka) f.
refresher course
Перепоручить (pereporuchít') v. to
turn over
 ~ дело (~ délo) to transfer a
 case
Перепродавец (pereprodávets) m.
reseller
Перепродавать (pereprodavát') v. to
resell
Перепродажа (pereprodázha) f.
resale
Перепроизводство (pereproizvódstvo)
n. overproduction
 ~ товара (~ továra)
 overproduction of commodities
Переработка (pererabótka) f.
overtime work, processing, revision
Перераспределение
(pereraspredelénie) n.
redistribution
 ~ доходов (~ dokhódov)
 redistribution of income
 ~ территории (~ territórii)
 redistribution of territory
Перерасход (pereraskhód) m. cost
overrun
Перерасчёт (pereraschiót) m.
conversion, recalculation
Перерыв (pererýv) m. break,
interruption, pause
 ~ заседания (~ zasedániia)
 production downtime
 ~ прений (~ prénii) interval in
 the proceedings
 ~ в работе (~ v rabóte)
 interruption of work
 ~ срока (~ sróka) break in the
 period
 ~ течения давности (~ techéniia
 dávnosti) interruption in
 prescription period, in the
 period of the running of the
 statute of limitations
Переселенец (pereselénets) m.
migrant, settler
Переселение (pereselénie) n.
resettlement
 внутреннее ~ (vnútrennee ~)
 internal ~

принудительное ~ (prinudítel'noe
~) compulsory ~
Переселяться (pereseliát'sia) v. to
resettle
Пересечение границы (peresechénie
granítsy) n. intersection of the
border
Пересылать (peresylát') v. to
forward, to send
Пересмотр (peresmótr) m.
reexamination, review
 ~ договора (~ dogovóra) revision
 of a contract
 ~ приговора (~ prigovóra)
 reconsideration of a sentence
 ~ конституции (~ konstitútsii)
 revision of a constitution
 ~ решения (~ reshéniia)
 reconsideration of a decision
 ~ по существу (~ po sushchestvú)
 substantive review
Перестановка (perestanóvka) f.
rearrangement, shifting
Перестрахование (perestrakhovánie)
n.reinsurance
 добровольное ~ (dobrovól'noe ~)
 voluntary ~
 личное ~ (líchnoe ~) personal ~
 морское ~ (morskóe ~) marine ~
Перестраховать (perestrakhovát') v.
to reinsure
Перестраховщик (perestrakhóvshchik)
m. reinsurer
Перестрелка (perestrélka) f.
exchange of gunfire
Перестройка (perestróika) f.
readjustment, reconstruction,
reorganization, "perestroika"
Пересчёт (pereschiót) m.
recalculation
 ~ валют (~ valiút) ~ of foreign
 exchange
 ~ в золоте (~ v zólote) ~ into
 gold
Пересылка (peresýlka) f.
remittance, transfer
 бесплатная ~ (besplátnaia ~)
 free dispatch
 обратная ~ (obrátnaia ~) return
 dispatch
Перетарка (peretárka) f.
repackaging
Переуступать (pereustupát') v. to
assign, to cede
Переуступка (pereustúpka) f.
assignment, cession

~ прав (~ prav) cession of rights

Переучёт (pereuchiót) *m.* rediscount
~ векселя (~ vékselia) rediscount of a bill

Переход (perekhód) *m.* crossing, transition
   незаконный ~ границы (nezakónnyi ~ granítsy) illegal border crossing
   ~ границы (~ granítsy) border crossing
   ~ имущества (~ imúshchestva) transfer of property
   ~ имущества по наследству (~ imúshchestva po naslédstvu) transfer of property by inheritance
   ~ между живыми (~ mézhdu zhivými) inter-vivos transfer
   ~ наследства к государству (~ naslédstva k gosudárstvu) escheatment
   ~ по наследству (~ po naslédstvu) transfer by inheritance
   ~ прав (~ prav) transfer of rights
   ~ риска (~ ríska) shifting of risk
   ~ на сторону врага (~ na stóronu vragá) defection to the enemy
   ~ суверенитета (~ suverenitéta) transfer of sovereignty

Переходный (perekhódnyi) *adj.* transitional

Перечень (pérechen') *m.* catalog, enumeration, list
   исчерпывающий ~ (ischérpyvaiushchii ~) exhaustive list
   контрольный ~ (kontról'nyi ~) checklist
   ~ вопросов (~ voprósov) list of questions
   ~ заявленных претензий (~ zaiávlennykh preténzii) enumeration of claims
   ~ налогов и сборов (~ nalógov i sbórov) specification of taxes and fees

Перечисление (perechislénie) *n.* enumeration, remittance
   банковское ~ сумм со счёта на счёт (bánkovskoe ~ summ so schióta na schiót) bank transfer of sums from one account to another
   почтовое ~ (pochtóvoe ~) postal transfer
   ~ сумм (~ summ) transfer of sums
   ~ на счёт (~ na schiót) transfer to an account

Перечислять (perechisliát') *v.* to remit, to transfer

Перила отделяющие судей от публики (períla otdeliáiushchie sudéi ot públiki) *f.* courtroom bannister

Период (períod) *m.* period {time}
   бюджетный ~ (biudzhétnyi ~) budget ~
   календарный ~ (kalendárnyi ~) calendar ~
   льготный ~ (l'gótnyi ~) grace ~
   отчётный ~ (otchiótnyi ~) reporting ~
   переходный ~ (perekhódnyi ~) transition ~

Периодичность (periodíchnost') *f.* periodical basis
   помесячная ~ (pomésiachnaia ~) monthly ~
   ~ поставок (~ postávok) ~ of deliveries

Перлюстировать (perliustírovat') *v.* to review correspondence

Персона нон грата (persóna non gráta) *f.* persona non grata

Персонал (personál) *m.* personnel, staff
   административный ~ (administratívnyi ~) administrative personnel
   военный ~ (voénnyi ~) military personnel
   вспомогательный ~ (vspomogátel'nyi ~) support personnel
   вспомогательный судебный ~ (vspomogátel'nyi sudébnyi ~) auxiliary court personnel
   гражданский ~ (grahdánskii ~) civil service {personnel}
   дипломатический ~ (diplomatícheskii ~) diplomatic personnel
   обслуживающий домашний ~ (obslúzhivaiushchii domáshnii ~) domestic staff
   исполнительный ~ (ispolnítel'nyi ~) executive personnel
   канцелярский ~ (kantseliarskii ~) clerical staff

консульский ~ (kónsul'skii ~) consular personnel

подсобный ~ (podsóbnyi ~) ancillary personnel

полувоенный ~ (poluvoénnyi ~) paramilitary personnel

производственный ~ (proizvódstvennyi ~) production personnel

служебный ~ (sluzhébnyi ~) office staff

специальный ~ (spetsiál'nyi ~) special staff

средний руководящий ~ (srédnii rukovodiáshchii ~) middle management

управленческий ~ (upravléncheskii ~) management personnel

штатный ~ (shtátnyi ~) regular staff

Перспектив/а (perspektív/a) f. outlook, perspective, prospect

рыночные ~/ы (rýnochnye ~/y) market prospects

экономические ~/ы (ekonomícheskie ~/y) economic prospects

~ развития экономики (~ razvítiia ekonómiki) outlook for economic development

~ рынка (~ rýnka) market outlook

Перспективный (perspektívnyi) adj. prospective

Петиционер (petitsionér) m. petitioner

Петиция (petítsiia) f. petition

Пехота (pekhóta) f. marines {military force}

Пехотинец (pekhotínets) m. marine {soldier in the marines}

Печат/ь (pechát'/') f. printing, the press, seal, stamp

агенство ~/и (agénstvo ~/i) press agency

гербовая ~ (gérbovaia ~) official stamp

государственная ~ (gosudárstvennaia ~) state-owned press

национальная ~ (natsionál'naia ~) national press

официальная ~ (ofitsiál'naia ~) official press

поставить ~ (postávit' ~) to affix a seal to, to stamp

скреплять ~/ью (skrepliát' ~/'iu) to stamp with a seal

~ таможни (~ tamózhni) customs stamp

Пик (pik) m. peak

час ~ (chas ~) rush hour

Пилот (pilót) m. pilot

Пилотаж (pilotázh) m. pilotage

Пилотировать (pilotírovat') v. to pilot

Пирамида (piramída) f. ponzi investment, pyramid, pyramid scheme

Пират (pirát) m. pirate {in various senses}

Пиратство (pirátstvo) n. piracy

Письм/о (pis'm/ó) n. letter

аккредитивное ~ (akkreditívnoe ~) ~ of credit

анонимное ~ (anonímnoe ~) anonymous ~

гарантийное ~ (garantíinoe ~) guarantee bond

кассовое ~ (kássovoe ~) cash ~

заказное ~ (zakaznóe ~) registered ~

заказное ~ с обратной распиской (zakaznóe ~ s obrátnoi raspískoi) registered ~ with return notification

обменные ~/а (obménnye ~/a) ~s of exchange

служебное ~ (sluzhébnoe ~) official ~

сопроводительное ~ (soprovodítel'noe ~) cover ~

срочное ~ (sróchnoe ~) express ~

угрожающее ~ (ugrozháiushchee ~) threatening ~

ценное ~ (tsénnoe ~) registered ~ with declared value

циркулярное ~ министра (tsirkuliárnoe ~ minístra) ministry circular

~ о назначении консула (~ o naznachénii kónsula) ~ of consular credentials

~ с требованием уплаты долга (~ s trébovaniem upláty dólga) dunning ~

Питомец (pitómets) m. foster-child, pupil, ward

~ нации (~ nátsii) ward of the state

Плавание (plávanie) n. navigation, shipping, voyage

первое ~ (pérvoe ~) maiden voyage

внутреннее ~ (vnútrennee ~)
inland navigation
каботажное ~ (kabotázhnoe ~)
coastal navigation
океанское ~ (okeánskoe ~) ocean
shipping
Плавать (plávat') v. to float, to
sail
Плагиат (plagiát) m. plagiarism
Плагиатор (plagiátor) m. plagiarist
Плакат (plakát) m. placard, poster
План (plan) m. plan
бюджетный ~ (biudzhétnyi ~)
budgeted ~
генеральный ~ (generál'nyi ~)
master ~
долгосрочный ~ (dolgosróchnyi ~)
long-term ~
встречный ~ (vstréchnyi ~)
counter ~
перспективный ~ (perspektívnyi
~) forward ~
производственный ~
(proizvódstvennyi ~) production
~
пятилетний ~ (piatilétnii ~)
five-year ~
семилетний ~ (semilétnii ~)
seven-year ~
финансовый ~ (finánsovyi ~)
financial ~
экономический ~ (ekonomícheskii
~) economic ~
~ закупок (~ zakúpok)
procurement ~
~ индустриализации (~
industrializátsii) ~ of
industrialization
~ кадастра (~ kadástra) land
survey ~
~ капиталовложений (~
kapitalovlozhénii) investment ~
~ модернизации (~ modernizátsii)
~ of modernization
Планирование (planírovanie) n.
planning
бюджетное ~ (biudzhétnoe ~)
budget ~
централизованное ~
(tsentralizóvannoe ~)
centralized ~
экономическое ~ (ekonomícheskoe
~) economic ~
Планируемый (planíruemyi) adj.
planned, projected
Плановый (plánovyi) adj. planned,
routine

Плата (pláta) f. pay, payment,
remuneration
аккордная ~ (akkórdnaia ~)
lumpsum payment
арендная ~ (aréndnaia ~) rental
payment
базовая ~ (bázovaia ~) base pay
денежная ~ (dénezhnaia ~) cash
payment
дополнительная ~
(dopolnítel'naia ~) additional
charge
заработная ~ (zárabotnaia ~)
wage
квартирная ~ (kvartírnaia ~)
apartment rent
минимальная ~ (minimál'naia ~)
minimal payment
номинальная ~ (nominál'naia ~)
nominal payment
почасовая ~ (pochasováia ~)
hourly pay
реальная ~ (reál'naia ~) take-
home pay
справедливая ~ (spravedlívaia ~)
fair wage
средняя ~ (sredniaia ~) average
pay
средняя почасовая ~ (sredniaia
pochasováia ~) average hourly
wage
~ натурой (~ natúroi) payment in
kind
Платёж (platiózh) m. payment,
settlement
авансовый ~ (avánsovyi ~)
advance payment
алиментный ~ (aliméntnyi ~)
support payment
арендный ~ (aréndnyi ~) rental
payment
годовой ~ (godovói ~) annual
payment
денежный ~ (dénezhnyi ~) money
payment
дополнительный ~ (dopolnítel'nyi
~) additional payment
досрочный ~ (dosróchnyi ~) on-
time payment
единовременный ~ (edinovrémennyi
~) lumpsum payment
ежемесячный ~ (ezhemésiachnyi ~)
monthly payment
квартальный ~ (kvartál'nyi ~)
quarterly payment
международный ~ (mezhdunaródnyi
~) international remittance

наложенный ~ (nalózhennyi ~)
cash on delivery, C.O.D.
неторговый ~ (netorgóvyi ~) non-
commercial payment
отсроченный ~ (otsróchennyi ~)
deferred payment
отсрочить ~ (otsrochít' ~) to
defer payment
перестраховочный ~
(perestrakhóvochnyi ~)
reinsurance premium
периодический ~ (periodícheskii
~) periodic payment
предварительный ~
(predvarítel'nyi ~) preliminary
payment
просроченный ~ (prosróchennyi ~)
past-due payment
рассроченный ~ (rassróchennyi ~)
lapsed payment
совершить ~ (sovershít' ~) to
affect payment
срочный ~ (sróchnyi ~) timely
payment
страховой ~ (strakhovói ~)
insurance premium
частичный ~ (chastíchnyi ~)
partial payment
~ в бюджет (~ v biudzhét)
payment into the budget
~ в инвалюте (~ v ínvaliute)
payment in foreign exchange
~ за наличный расчёт (~ za
nalíchnyi raschiót) payment in
cash
~ за прокат фильмов (~ za prokát
fíl'mov) video rental, payment
for screening
~ превышающий действительную
сумму долга (~ prevysháiushchii
deistvítel'nuiu súmmu dólga)
payment exceeding the amount of
the debt
~ с суброгацией (~ s
subrogátsiei) payment under
subrogation
~ чеком (~ chékom) payment by
check
Платежеспособность
(platezhesposóbnost') f. solvency
Платежеспособный
(platezhesposóbnyi) adj. solvent
Плательщик (platél'shchik) m. payer
неаккуратный ~ (neakurátnyi ~)
slow payer
Платить (platít') v. to pay

~ наличными (~ nalíchnymi) ~ in
cash
~ по сдельно (~ po sdél'no) ~ on
a piece-work basis
Платформа (platfórma) f. platform
избирательная ~ (izbirátel'naia
~) campaign ~
Плебисцит (plebistsít) m.
plebiscite
Племянник (plemiánnik) m. nephew
Племянница (plemiánnitsa) f.
niece
Плен (plen) m. captivity
взять в ~ (vziat' v ~) to take
prisoner
военный ~ (voénnyi ~) captivity
of prisoners of war
гражданский ~ (grahdánskii ~)
civil incarceration
Пленный (plénnyi) adj. captive,
[also used as m.adj.noun]
Пленум (plénum) m. plenary session,
plenum
~ верховного суда (~ verkhóvnogo
sudá) plenary session of the
Supreme Court
~ всех палат (~ vsekh palát)
plenary session of all chambers
Плодоносный (plodonósnyi) adj.
fruitful
Плод (plod) m. fruit, usufruct
запретный ~ (zaprétnyi ~)
forbidden fruit
Пломба (plómba) f. official seal
сорванная ~ (sórvannaia ~)
broken seal
таможенная ~ (tamózhennaia ~)
customs seal
~ отправителя (~ otpravítelia)
seal of the consignor
Плотность населения (plótnost'
naseléniia) f. population density
Площадь (plóshchad') f. area,
space, square
жилая ~ (zhiláia ~) residential
floor space
застроенная ~ (zastróennaia ~)
built-up area
рабочая ~ (rabóchaia ~) working
space
торговая ~ (torgóvaia ~) sales
floor space
Плюральный вотум (pliurál'nyi
vótum) m. plural vote
Побег (pobég) m. escape
Победа (pobéda) f. victory

~ на выборах (~ na výborakh)
election victory
Поборы (pobóry) extortion
Побочный (pobóchnyi) adj.
collateral
Побуждение (pobuzhdénie) n. motive
Поведение (povedénie) n. conduct
   недостойное ~ (nedostóinoe ~)
   unbecoming ~
   хорошее ~ (khoróshee ~) good ~
Повелеть (povelét') v. to command
Поверенный (povérennyi) m.adj.noun
agent, attorney, chargé d'affaires,
solicitor
   временный ~ в делах (vrémennyi ~
   v delákh) chargé d'affaires pro
   tempore
   патентный ~ (paténtnyi ~) patent
   agent
   судебный ~ (sudébnyi ~) attorney
   at law
   ~ в делах (~ v delákh) chargé
   d'affaires
Повестка (povéstka) f. notification
   судебная ~ (sudébnaia ~) summons
   предварительная ~ дня
   (predvarítel'naia ~ dnia)
   preliminary agenda
   ~ о вызове в суд (~ o výzove v
   sud) subpoena, writ
   ~ дня (~ dnia) agenda
Повешение (poveshénie) n. hanging
Повешенный (povéshennyi) adj.
hanged {person hanged}
Повинност/ь (povínnost/') f. duty,
obligation
   военно-квартирная ~ (voénno-
   kvartírnaia ~) billeting
   воинская ~ (voínskaia ~)
   military conscription
   денежная ~ (dénezhnaia ~)
   monetary obligation
   личная ~ (líchnaia ~) personal
   obligation
   натуральная ~ (naturál'naia ~)
   natural duty
   освобождённый от ~/ей
   (osvobozhdiónnyi ot ~/ei)
   exempted from duty
Повинный (povínnyi) adj. guilty
Повод (póvod) m. cause, grounds
   без ~/a (bez ~/a) without cause
   решающий ~ к разводу
   (resháiushchii ~ k razvódu)
   grounds for divorce
   ~ к войне (~ k voiné) causus
   belli

Повреждать (povrezhdát') v. to
harm, to injure
Повреждение (povrezhdénie) n.
breakage, damage, prejudice
   незначительное ~
   (neznachítel'noe ~)
   insignificant damage
   телесное ~ (telésnoe ~) bodily
   harm
   тяжкое телесное ~ (tiázhkoe
   telésnoe ~) serious bodily harm
   физическое ~ (fizícheskoe ~)
   physical injury
   частичное ~ (chastíchnoe ~)
   partial damage
   ~ водой (~ vodói) water damage
   ~ имущества (~ imúshchestva)
   property damage
   ~ личного имущества (~ líchnogo
   imúshchestva) damage to personal
   property
   ~ от пожара (~ ot pozhára)
   damage from fire
   ~ сельскохозяйственных культур
   (~ sel'skokhoziáistvennykh
   kul'túr) damage to crops
Повстанец (povstánets) m. insurgent
Повстанческий (povstáncheskii) adj.
insurgent
Повторение (povtorénie) n.
repetition
Повышать (povyshát') v. to
increase, to raise
Повышение (povyshénie) n. boost,
improvement, increase, mark-up,
raise
   играть на ~ (igrát' na ~) to
   speculate on price increases
   инфляционное ~ (infliatsiónnoe
   ~) inflationary increase
   искуственное ~ (iskústvennoe ~)
   artificial increase
   искуственное ~ курса
   (iskústvennoe ~ kúrsa)
   artificial increase in the
   exchange rate
   незаконное ~ цен (nezakónnoe ~
   tsen) illegal price inflation
   ~ доходов (~ dokhódov) increase
   in incomes
   ~ заработной платы (~ zárabotnoi
   pláty) raise in wages
   ~ курса (~ kúrsa) increase in
   the exchange rate
   ~ покупательной силы (~
   pokupátel'noi síly) increase in
   buying power

~ пошлин (~ póshlin) increase in duties
~ производительности (~ proizvodítel'nosti) increase in productivity
~ размера пенсии (~ razméra pénsii) pension increase
~ ранга (~ ránga) promotion in rank
~ рентабельности (~ rentábel'nosti) increase in profitability
~ риска (~ ríska) increase in risk
~ спроса (~ sprósa) increase in demand
~ ставки (~ stávki) rate increase
~ таможенных пошлин (~ tamózhennykh póshlin) increase in customs duty
~ тарифа (~ tarífa) increase in tariff
~ цен (~ tsen) price increase
Погашать (pogashát') v. to liquidate, to pay down
Погашение (pogashénie) n. discharge, redemption, repayment, settling
досрочное ~ долга (dosróchnoe ~ dólga) prepayment of a debt
недостаточное ~ (nedostátochnoe ~) insufficient settlement
равномерное ~ (ravnomérnoe ~) equitable settlement
~ задолженности (~ zadólzhennosti) debt repayment
~ записи (~ zápisi) extinguishment of a deed
~ кредита (~ kredíta) repayment on credit
~ облигации (~ obligátsii) redemption of a bond
~ обязательств (~ obiazátel'stv) repayment of obligations
~ ссуды (~ ssúdy) repayment of a loan
Поголовье скота (pogolóv'e skotá) n. head of livestock {number}
Погоня (pogónia) pursuit
Пограничник (pograníchnik) m. border guard
Пограничный (pograníchnyi) adj. border
Погребать (pogrebát') v. to bury
Погром (pogróm) m. pogrom

Погромщик (pogrómshchik) m. organizer of a pogrom
Погружать (pogruzhát') v. to load, to submerge
Погрузка (pogrúzka) f. shipment
Подавление (podavlénie) n. repression
Подарок (podárok) m. gift
Податель (podátel') m. bearer, filer
~ декларации (~ deklarátsii) declarant
~ жалобы (~ zháloby) complainant
Подать (podát') assessment
Подача (podácha) f. filing, presentment, submission
~ жалобы (~ zháloby) filing of a complaint
~ заявки (~ zaiávki) filing of an application
~ заявки на патент (~ zaiávki na patént) filing of a patent application
~ искового заявления (~ iskovógo zaiavléniia) filing of an action
~ кассационной жалобы (~ kassatsiónnoi zháloby) submission of a cassation
Подведомственный (podvédomstvennyi) adj. within the jurisdiction
Подвергаться аресту (podvergát'sia aréstu) v. to be subject to arrest
Подготовка (podgotóvka) f. preparation, training
~ бюджета (~ biudzhéta) budget preparation
~ кадров (~ kádrov) management training, personnel training
Подгруппа (podgrúppa) f. subgroup
Подданный (póddannyi) adj. national [also used as m.adj.noun]
иностранный ~ (inostránnyi ~) foreign national
Подданство (póddanstvo) n. nationality
преобретать ~ (preobretát' ~) to obtain citizenship
Подделка (poddélka) f. counterfeit, forgery
~ денежных знаков (~ dénezhnykh znákov) counterfeiting of currency
~ документов (~ dokuméntov) forging of documents
~ избирательного документа (~ izbirátel'nogo dokuménta) electoral fraud

~ монеты (~ monéty) counterfeiting of coins
~ товарного знака (~ továrnogo znáka) forgery of a trademark
Поддельный (poddél'nyi) adj. forged
Подделыватель (poddélyvatel') m. counterfeiter, forger
Подделывать (poddélyvat') v. to counterfeit, to forge
Поддержание (podderzhánie) n. maintenance
~ мира (~ míra) ~ of peace
~ порядка (~ poriádka) ~ of order
~ публичного порядка (~ publíchnogo poriádka) maintenance of public order
~ цен (~ tsen) ~ of price levels
Поддержка (poddérzhka) f. seconding, support
дипломатическая ~ (diplomatícheskaia ~) diplomatic support
финансовая ~ (finánsovaia ~) financial support
Поджигатель (podzhigátel') m. arsonist, incendiary
Поджигать (podzhigát') v. to commit arson
Подзащитный (podzashchítnyi) adj. client {of a lawyer}
Подкидывание ребёнка (podkídyvanie rebiónka) n. abandonment of a child
Подкомитет (pódkomitét) m. subcommittee
Подкуп (pódkup) m. graft
~ должностного лица (~ dólzhnostnogo litsá) bribery of an official
Подкупать (podkupát') v. to bribe
Подкупной (podkupnói) adj. bribed
Подлежащий (podlezháshchii) adj. subject to
Подлиник (pódlinik) m. original {of a document}
~ решения (~ reshéniia) original copy of a decision
Подлиность (pódlinost') f. authenticity
установить ~ (ustanovít' ~) to establish ~
Подлинный (pódlinnyi) adj. authentic
Подлог (podlóg) m. forgery
Подмастерье (podmastér'e) apprentice

Подмен ребёнка (podmén rebiónka) m. switching children {at the hospital, etc.}
Поднадзорный (podnazórnyi) adj. under surveillance
Подношение (podnoshénie) n. present, tribute
Поднятие флага (podniátie flága) n. flagging, raising of the flag
Подозревать (podozrevát') v. to suspect
Подозрение (podozrénie) n. suspicion
возбуждающий ~ (vozbuzhdáiushchii ~) inciting suspicion
Подопечный (podopéchnyi) adj. under wardship
Подотдел (podotdél) m. subdivision
Подотчётность (podotchiótnost') f. accountability
Подотчётный (podotchiótnyi) adj. accountable
Подписание (podpisánie) n. signing
«открыто для подписания» (otkrýto dlia podpisániia) "open for signing" {of a convention, etc.}
~ договора (~ dogovóra) signing of a contract
Подписк/а (podpísk/a) f. bond, subscription
покрывать ~/ой (pokryvát' ~/oi) to cover a subscription
непосредственная ~ у издателя (neposrédstvennaia ~ u izdátelia) direct subscription from the publisher
публичная ~ (publíchnaia ~) public subscription
~ на акции (~ na áktsii) subscription for shares
~ по почте (~ po póchte) mail subscription
~ на ценные бумаги (~ na tsénnye bumági) subscription for securities
Подписчик (podpíschik) m. subscriber
~ на акции (~ na áktsii) subscriber to shares
~ на облигации (~ na obligátsii) bond subscriber
Подпись (pódpis') f. signature
вторая ~ (vtoráia ~) second ~
заверенная ~ (zavérennaia ~) attested ~

личная ~ (líchnaia ~) personal ~
удостоверять ~ (udostoveriát' ~)
to authenticate a ~
собственноручная ~
(sóbstvennoruchnaia ~) one's own
~
Подписывать (podpísyvat') v. to
sign
Подполье (podpól'e) underground
Подпольный (podpól'nyi) adj.
underground
Подражание (podrazhánie) n.
imitation
Подразделение (podrazdelénie) n.
division, subdivision
территориальное ~
(territoriál'noe ~) territorial
subdivision
Подразумеваемый (podrazumeváemyi)
adj. implied
Подрыв (podrýv) m. injury,
undermining
~ дисциплины (~ distsiplíny)
undermining of discipline
~ кредитной системы (~ kredítnoi
sistémy) undermining the credit
system
~ экономики (~ ekonómiki)
undermining the economy
Подрядить (podriádit') v. to hire
for contracting work
Подрядчик (podriádchik) m.
contractor
Подследственный (podslédstvennyi)
adj. under investigation
Подсобный (podsóbnyi) adj.
ancillary
Подстрекатель (podstrekátel') m.
instigator
Подстрекательство
(podstrekátel'stvo) n. instigation
~ к войне (~ k voiné)
instigation to war
~ к порочной деятельности (~ k
poróchnoi déiatel'nosti)
entrapment
~ к преступлению (~ k
prestupléniiu) criminal
entrapment
Подстрекать (podstrekát') v. to
instigate
Подсудимый (podsudímyi) adj.
accused [also used as m.adj.noun]
Подсудность (podsúdnost') f.
jurisdiction

альтернативная ~
(al'ternatívnaia ~) alternative
~
гражданская ~ (grahdánskaia ~)
civil ~
исключительная ~
(iskliuchítel'naia ~) exclusive
~
общая ~ (óbshchaia ~) general ~
обязательная ~ (obiazátel'naia
~) mandatory ~
предметная ~ (predmétnaia ~)
subject matter ~
территориальная ~
(territoriál'naia ~) territorial
~
уголовная ~ (ugolóvnaia ~)
criminal ~
~ дела (~ déla) ~ over a case
~ по предмету (~ po predmetu) ~
over subject matter
Подсудный (podsúdnyi) adj. within
the jurisdiction of
Подсчёт (podschiót) m. calculation,
count
неправильный ~ голосов
(neprávil'nyi ~ golosóv)
improper vote count
~ голосов (~ golosóv) vote count
Подтверждать (podtverzhdát') v. to
affirm, to acknowledge, to attest,
to authenticate
Подтверждение (podtverzhdénie) m.
affirmation, confirmation
аккредитивное ~ (akkreditívnoe
~) confirmation of a letter of
credit
подразумеваемое ~
(podrazumeváemoe ~) implied
acknowledgement
прямое ~ (priamóe ~) direct
acknowledgement
~ заказа (~ zakáza) confirmation
of an order
~ подлинности (~ pódlinnosti)
attestation of authenticity
Подчинение (podchinénie) n.
subordination
юридическое ~ (iuridícheskoe ~)
legal subordination
~ юрисдикции (~ iurisdíktsii)
subject to the jurisdiction
Подчинённость (podchiniónnost') f.
subordination
Подчинённый (podchiniónnyi) adj.
subordinate

Подчиниться (podchinít'sia) v. to be subordinate to
Подчинять (podchiniát') v. to subordinate
Подъём (pod"ióm) m. improvement, lift, recovery, upswing
промышленный ~ (promýshlennyi ~) industrial recovery
циклический ~ (tsiklícheskii ~) cyclical recovery
экономический ~ (ekonómícheskii ~) economic upswing
~ конъюнктуры (~ kon'iunktúry) economic boom
~ производительности (~ proizvodítel'nosti) upswing in productivity
~ производства (~ proizvódstva) upswing in production
~ цен выше стоимости (~ tsen výshe stóimosti) increase of prices over cost
Подъёмные (pod"iómnye) pl.adj. derrick, jenny, lifting
Поезд (póezd) m. train
санитарный ~ (sanitárnyi ~) hospital train
Поездка (poézdka) f. journey, trip
служебная ~ (sluzhébnaia ~) business trip
Пожертвование (pozhertvovánie) n. donation
собирать ~ (sobirát' ~) to collect ~s
Пожизненн/ый (pozhíznenn/yi) adj. lifetime
~/ая рента (~/aia rénta) lifetime annuity
~/ое заключение (~/oe zakliuchénie) life imprisonment
Поземельный (pozemél'nyi) adj. land
~ налог (~ nalóg) land tax
Позиция (pozítsiia) f. position
ключевая ~ (kliuchevája ~) key ~
конкурентная ~ (konkuréntnaia ~) competitive ~
монопольная ~ (monopól'naia ~) monopoly
привилегированная ~ (privilegiróvannaia ~) privileged ~
~ на рынке (~ na rýnke) market ~
Поиск (poísk) m. search
автоматизированный ~ (avtomatizírovannyi ~) computer ~

Показание (pokazánie) n. evidence, indication, testimony
дать ~ (dat' ~) to give evidence
ложное ~ (lózhnoe ~) false evidence, misleading indicator
медицинское ~ (meditsínskoe ~) medical evidence
письменное ~ (pís'mennoe ~) written evidence
свидетельское ~ по судебным делам (svidétel'skoe ~ po sudébnym delám) evidence of witnesses
устное ~ (ústnoe ~) oral evidence
~ обвиняемого (~ obviniáemogo) testimony of the defendant
~ свидетелей (~ svidételei) testimony of witnesses
Показатель (pokazátel') m. indicator
производственный ~ (proizvódstvennyi ~) industrial indicator
качественный ~ (káchestvennyi ~) quality index
количественный ~ (kolíchestvennyi ~) quantitative index
моментный ~ (moméntnyi ~) momentary indicator
общий стоимостный ~ (óbshchii stóimostnyi ~) overall cost parameter
окончательный ~ (okonchátel'nyi ~) final indicator
основной ~ (osnovnói ~) index base point
пересмотренный ~ (peresmótrennyi ~) revised index
предварительный ~ (predvarítel'nyi ~) preliminary indicator
производственный ~ (proizvódstvennyi ~) industrial index
средневзвешенный ~ (srednevzvéshennyi ~) weighted average index
средний годовой ~ (srédnii godovói ~) average annual index
стоимостный ~ (stóimostnyi ~) cost parameter
финансовый ~ (finánsovyi ~) financial indicator
экономический ~ (ekonómícheskii ~) economic indicator

~ валовой продукции (~ valovói prodúktsii) index of gross production
~ качества (~ káchestva) quality index
~ плотности населения (~ plótnosti naseléniia) index of population density
~ производительности (~ proizvodítel'nosti) productivity figures
~ производительности труда (~ proizvodítel'nosti trudá) labor productivity figures
~ промышленной деятельности (~ promýshlennoi déiatel'nosti) indicator of industrial activity
~ рентабельности (~ rentábel'nosti) index of profitability
~ стоимости (~ stóimosti) parameter of cost
~ эффективности (~ effektívnosti) indicator of efficiency
Покидать (pokidát') v. to abandon, to forsake
Покончить жизнь самоубийством (pokónchit' zhizn' samoubíistvom) to commit suicide
Покорение (pokorénie) n. subjugation
Покорять (pokoriát') v. to subjugate
Покровитель (pokrovítel') m. patron
Покровительствовать (pokrovítel'stvovát') v. to patronize, to protect
Покрытие (pokrýtie) n. covering, defrayment, wrapping
~ дефицита (~ defitsíta) meeting a deficit
~ затрат (~ zatrát) covering of expenditures
~ издержек (~ izdérzhek) covering of expenses
~ расходов (~ raskhódov) defrayal of expenses
~ рисков (~ rískov) coverage of risks
~ убытков (~ ubýtkov) compensation for losses
Покупатель (pokupátel') m. purchaser
непосредственный ~ (neposrédstvennyi ~) direct purchaser

Покупка (pokúpka) f. purchase
дополнительная ~ (dopolnítel'naia ~) additional ~
преимущественная ~ (preimúshchestvennaia ~) advantageous ~
спекулятивная ~ (spekuliatívnaia ~) speculative ~
~ на бирже (~ na bírzhe) purchase on the exchange
~ в кредит (~ v kredít) purchase on credit
~ за наличный расчёт (~ za nalíchnyi raschiót) purchase for cash
Покупной (pokupnói) adj. purchase
Покушаться (pokushát'sia) v. to encroach
~ на права (~ na pravá) ~ upon rights
Покушение (pokushénie) n. attempt {to commit crime}
~ на жизнь (~ na zhizn') ~ on a life, attempted murder
~ на побег (~ na pobég) attempted escape
~ на преступление (~ na prestuplénie) attempted crime
Полезность (poléznost') f. use, utility
предельная ~ (predél'naia ~) marginal use
Полемизировать (polemizírovat') v. to polemicize
Полемика (polémika) f. polemics
Полемист (polemíst) m. polemicist
Полёт (poliót) m. flight
беспосадочный ~ (besposádochnyi ~) nonstop ~
международный ~ (mezhdunaródnyi ~) international ~
транзитный ~ (tranzítnyi ~) transit ~
Полигамия (poligámiia) f. polygamy
Полис (pólis) m. policy
групповой ~ (gruppovói ~) group ~
открытый ~ (otkrýtyi ~) open cover ~
страховой ~ (strakhovói ~) insurance ~
~ на предъявителя (~ na pred''iavítelia) ~ on bearer
Политбюро (politbiuró) indecl. Politburo {Soviet}
Политик (polítik) m. politician

Политика (polítika) *f.* policy,
politics
  аграрная ~ (agrárnaia ~)
agrarian policy
  валютная ~ (valiútnaia ~)
international monetary policy
  внешнеторговая ~
(vneshnetorgóvaia ~) trade
policy
  внешняя ~ (vnéshniaia ~) foreign
policy
  внутренняя ~ (vnútrenniaia ~)
domestic policy
  девизная ~ (devíznaia ~) foreign
exchange policy
  демографическая ~
(demografícheskaia ~)
demographic policy
  денежная ~ (dénezhnaia ~)
monetary policy
  дефляционная ~ (defliatsiónnaia
~) deflationary policy
  дисконтная ~ (diskóntnaia ~)
discount policy
  дискриминационная ~
(diskriminatsiónnaia ~)
discriminatory policy
  единая сельскохозяйственная ~
(edínaia sel'skokhoziáistvennaia
~) unified agricultural policy
  земельная ~ (zemél'naia ~) land
policy
  иммиграционная ~
(immigratsiónnaia ~) immigration
policy
  инвестиционная ~
(investitsiónnaia ~) investment
policy
  кредитная ~ (kredítnaia ~)
credit policy
  мировая ~ (mirováia ~) worldwide
policy
  налоговая ~ (nalógovaia ~) tax
policy
  нейтралистская ~
(neitralístskaia ~) policy of
neutrality
  общая ~ (óbshchaia ~) general
policy
  правительственная ~
(pravítel'stvennaia ~)
government policy
  протекционистская ~
(protektsionístskaia ~) protectionist policy

  противоциклическая ~
(protivotsiklícheskaia ~) anti-
cyclical policy
  расистская ~ (rasístskaia ~)
racist policy
  социальная ~ (sotsiál'naia ~)
social policy
  таможенная ~ (tamózhennaia ~)
customs policy
  таможенно-тарифная ~
(tamózhenno-tarífnaia ~) cus-
toms/tariff policy
  тарифная ~ (tarífnaia ~) tariff
policy
  торговая ~ (torgóvaia ~) trade
policy
  финансовая ~ (finánsovaia ~)
financial policy
  экономическая ~ (ekonomícheskaia
~) economic policy
  экспанционистская ~
(ekspantsionístskaia ~) expansionist policy
  ядерная (iádernaia) nuclear
policy
  ~ аннексий (~ annéksii) policy
of annexation
  ~ дискриминации (~
diskriminátsii) policy of discrimination
  ~ добрососедских отношений (~
dobrososédskikh otnoshénii)
policy of good neighborly
relations
  ~ заработной платы (~ zárabotnoi
pláty) wage policy
  ~ интервенции (~ intervéntsii)
policy of intervention
  ~ капитальных вложений (~
kapitál'nykh vlozhénii) policy
of capital investments
  ~ невмешательства (~
nevmeshátel'stva) non-interference policy
  ~ неприсоединения к блокам (~
neprisoedinéniia k blókam) non-
alignment policy
  ~ в области занятости (~ v
óblasti zaniátosti) employment
policy
  ~ в области энергетики (~ v
óblasti energétiki) energy
policy
  ~ с позиции силы (~ s pozítsii
síly) policy from position of
strength

~ полной занятости (~ pólnoi zaniátosti) policy of full employment
~ расизма (~ rasízma) policy of racism
~ сокращения кредита (~ sokrashchéniia kredíta) tight credit policy
Политический (politícheskii) adj. political
Политэкономия (politekonómiia) f. political economy
Политэмигрант (politemigránt) m. political emigrant
Полицейский (politséiskii) adj. police [also used as m.adj.noun]
Полиция (polítsiia) f. police
    военная ~ (voénnaia ~) military ~
    городская ~ (gorodskáia ~) metropolitan ~
    государственная ~ (gosudárstvennaia ~) government ~
    железнодорожная ~ (zheleznodorózhnaia ~) railroad ~
    криминальная ~ (kriminál'naia ~) criminal investigation unit
    местная ~ (méstnaia ~) local ~
    морская ~ (morskáia ~) maritime ~
    сыскная ~ (sysknáia ~) criminal investigation department
    тайная ~ (táinaia ~) secret
Поличн/ое (políchn/oe) adj. red-handed {in expression}
    поймать с ~/ым (poimát' s ~/ym) to catch red-handed
Полновластие (polnovlástie) n. sovereignty
Полномочный (polnomóchnyi) adj. plenipotentiary
    ~ представитель (~ predstavítel') ~ ambassador
Полномочи/е (polnomóchi/e) n. authority, commission, proxy, warrant
    взаимное ~ (vzaímnoe ~) mutual authority
    делегированное ~ (delegiróvannoe ~) delegated authority
    дискреционное ~ (diskretsiónnoe ~) discretionary authority
    законодательное ~ (zakonodátel'noe ~) legislative authority

исполнительное ~ (ispolnítel'noe ~) executive authority
конституционное ~ (konstitutsiónnoe ~) constitutional authority
облекать кого-то с ~/ями (oblekát' kogó-to s ~/iami) to vest someone with authority
письменное ~ (pís'mennoe ~) written authority
письменное ~ на представительство (pís'mennoe ~ na predstavítel'stvo) written authority for representation
подразумеваемое ~ (podrazumeváemoe ~) implicit authority
президентское ~ (prezidéntskoe ~) presidential authority
специальное ~ (spetsiál'noe ~) special warrant
федеральное ~ (federál'noe ~) federal authority
особые ~/я (osóbye ~/ia) special powers
чрезвычайные ~/я (chrezvycháinye ~/ia) emergency powers
Полноправный (polnoprávnyi) adj. competent, having full rights
Полнота (polnotá) f. fullness, plentitude
    ~ власти (~ vlásti) absolute power
    ~ документов (~ dokuméntov) sufficiency of documents
Половничество (polovníchestvo) n. sharecropping
Положени/е (polozhéni/e) n. condition, provision, status
    валютное ~ (valiútnoe ~) foreign exchange position
    военное ~ (voénnoe ~) martial law
    денежное ~ (dénezhnoe ~) monetary position
    договорное ~ (dogovórnoe ~) contract provision
    доминирующее ~ (dominíruiushchee ~) dominating position
    дополнительное ~ (dopolnítel'noe ~) additional provision
    законодательное ~ (zakonodátel'noe ~) legislative provision
    имущественное ~ (imúshchestvennoe ~) material situation

исключительное ~
(iskliuchítel'noe ~) exceptional
position
конституционное ~
(konstitutsiónnoe ~)
constitutional provision
личное ~ (líchnoe ~) personal
situation
мирное ~ (mírnoe ~) peaceful
situation
нелегальное ~ (nelegál'noe ~)
illegal condition
неловкое ~ (nelóvkoe ~) awkward
situation
общее экономическое ~ (óbshchee
ekonomícheskoe ~) general
economic situation
общие ~/я (óbshchie ~/ia)
overall provisions
основное ~ права (osnovnóe ~
práva) basic provision of the
law
правовое ~ (pravovóe ~) legal
standing
правовое ~ иностранцев (pravovóe
~ inostrántsev) legal standing
of foreigners
преимущественное ~
(preimúshchestvennoe ~)
privileged status
принципиальные ~/я
(printsipiál'nye ~/ia)
principles
семейное ~ (seméinoe ~) marital
status
фактическое ~ (faktícheskoe ~)
actual situation
финансовое ~ (finánsovoe ~)
financial status
чрезвычайное ~ (chrezvycháinoe
~) state of emergency
экономическое ~ (ekonomícheskoe
~) economic situation
юридическое ~ (iuridícheskoe ~)
legal status
~ о выборах (~ o výborakh)
regulation of elections
~ закона (~ zakóna) statute
~ контракта (~ kontrákta)
provision of a contract
~ в отношении занятости (~ v
otnoshénii zaniátosti)
employment regulations
~ на рынке (~ na rýnke)
condition of the market

~ о социальном обеспечении (~ o
sotsiál'nom obespéchenii)
statute on social welfare
Полоса (polosá) f. band, belt,
phase, zone
запретная ~ (zaprétnaia ~)
forbidden zone
запретная пограничная ~
(zaprétnaia pograníchnaia ~)
forbidden border zone
морская ~ (morskáia ~) maritime
zone
Полпред (polpréd) m.
plenipotentiary ambassador [abbrev.
form of полномочный представитель]
Полувоенный (poluvoénnyi) adj.
paramilitary
Полугосударственный
(polugosudárstvennyi) adj. quasi-
state
Полуколониальный (polukoloniál'nyi)
adj. semi-colonial
Полуофициальный (poluofitsiál'nyi)
adj. semi-official
Полуфабрикаты (polufabrikáty) pl.
semi-processed goods
Получатель (poluchátel') m.
consignee, recipient
~ чека (~ chéka) payee on a
check
Получени/e (poluchéni/e) n.
acquisition, collection, receipt
расписаться в ~/и (raspisát'sia
v ~/i) to sign a receipt
~ взятки (~ vziátki) acceptance
of a bribe
~ груза (~ grúza) acceptance of
cargo
~ письма (~ pis'má) receipt of a
letter
~ показания (~ pokazániia)
introduction of testimony
~ присяги (~ prisiági) taking of
an oath
Получать (poluchát') v. to acquire,
to receive
Польза (pól'za) f. benefit, use
общественная ~ (obshchéstvennaia
~) social benefit
Пользование (pól'zovanie) n.
enjoyment, use
Пользоваться (pól'zovat'sia) v. to
enjoy, to use
Полюбовно (poliubóvno) adv.
amicably
Помеха (pomékha) f. hindrance,
obstacle

Помещать (pomeshchát') v. to
accommodate, to lodge, to invest
Помещение (pomeshchénie) n.
accommodation, location
   вспомогательное жилое ~
   (vspomogátel'noe zhilóe ~)
   ancillary housing
   жилое ~ (zhilóe ~) housing
   консульское ~ (kónsul'skoe ~)
   consular residence
   меблированное ~ (mebliróvannoe
   ~) furnished housing
   основное жилое ~ (osnovnóe
   zhilóe ~) basic housing
   складное ~ (skládnoe ~)
   warehouse space
   частное ~ (chástnoe ~) private
   housing
   ~ без мебели (~ bez mébeli)
   unfurnished housing
Помиловани/е (pomílovani/e) n.
pardon
   просьба о ~/и (prós'ba o ~/i)
   appeal for a pardon
Помиловать (pomílovat') v. to
pardon
Помолвка (pomólvka) f. betrothal
Помощник (pomóshchnik) m. assistant
   ~ бухгалтера (~ bukhgáltera) ~
   to the bookkeeper
   ~ генерального секретаря (~
   generál'nogo sekretariá) ~ to
   the general secretary
   ~ государственного секретаря (~
   gosudárstvennogo sekretariá) ~
   to the state secretary
   ~ мэра (~ méra) ~ to the mayor
   ~ прокурора (~ prokuróra) ~ to
   the prosecutor
Помощь (pómoshch') f. aid, help
   административная ~
   (administratívnaia ~)
   administrative assistance
   безвозмездная ~ (bezvozmézdnaia
   ~) gratuitous help
   бесплатная медицинская ~
   (besplátnaia meditsínskaia ~)
   free medical care
   бесплатная правовая ~
   (besplátnaia pravováia ~) free
   legal aid
   взаимная ~ (vzaímnaia ~) mutual
   assistance
   внешняя ~ (vnéshniaia ~) foreign
   aid
   военная ~ (voénnaia ~) military
   assistance

   государственная ~
   (gosudárstvennaia ~) government
   aid
   дополнительная ~
   (dopolnítel'naia ~) additional
   assistance
   медицинская ~ (meditsínskaia ~)
   medical care
   общественная ~ (obshchéstvennaia
   ~) social assistance
   правовая ~ (pravováia ~) legal
   aid
   правовая ~ по семейным делам
   (pravováia ~ po seméinym delám)
   family legal aid
   продовольственная ~
   (prodovól'stvennaia ~) food
   assistance
   скорая ~ (skóraia ~) first aid
   техническая ~ (tekhnícheskaia ~)
   technical assistance
   условная ~ (uslóvnaia ~)
   conditional aid
   финансовая ~ (finánsovaia ~)
   financial aid
   экономическая ~ (ekonomícheskaia
   ~) economic aid
   юридическая ~ (iuridícheskaia ~)
   legal assistance
   ~ по безработице (~ po
   bezrabótitse) unemployment
   assistance
   ~ престарелым (~ prestarélym)
   assistance to the aged
   ~ слаборазвитым странам (~
   slaborázvitym stránam) aid to
   underdeveloped countries
   ~ старикам (~ starikám) aid to
   the elderly
Понижать (ponizhát') v. to
decrease, to lower
Понижение (ponizhénie) n. decline,
fall, lowering, sinking
   играть на ~ (igrát' na ~) to
   speculate on a decrease
   ~ в должности (~ v dólzhnosti)
   demotion
   ~ зарплаты (~ zarpláty) pay cut
   ~ курса (~ kúrsa) fall in the
   exchange rate
   ~ пошлин (~ póshlin) lowering of
   duties
   ~ спроса (~ sprósa) fall in
   demand
   ~ ссудного процента (~ ssúdnogo
   protsénta) fall in the interest
   rate on a loan

Понятие (poniátie) n. understanding
   юридическое ~ (iuridícheskoe ~)
   legal concept
Понятой (poniatói) m. official
witness
Поощрение (pooshchrénie) n.
encouragement, promotion
   ~ экспорта (~ éksporta) export
   promotion
Попечение о детях (popechénie o
detiákh) n. custody of children
Попечитель (popechítel') m.
guardian, trustee
   ~ над наследством (~ nad
   naslédstvom) executor of an
   inheritance
Попечительство (popechitel'stvo) n.
guardianship, trusteeship
Поправка (poprávka) f. amendment,
correction, modification
   законодательная ~
   (zakonodátel'naia ~) legislative
   amendment
   ~ к закону (~ k zakónu)
   amendment to a law
   ~ в конституцию (~ v
   konstitútsiiu) amendment to a
   constitution
   ~ к уставу (~ k ustávu)
   amendment to a charter
Попрошайничать (poprosháinichat')
v. to panhandle
Попрошайничество
(poprosháinichestvo) n. panhandling
Попустительство (popustítel'stvo)
n. connivance, permissiveness
Попытка (popýtka) f. attempt
   ~ побега (~ pobéga) attempted
   escape
   ~ правонарушения (~
   pravonarushéniia) attempted
   violation
Поработить (porabotít') v. to
enslave, to enthrall
Порабощение (poraboshchénie) n.
enslavement, enthrallment
Поражение (porazhénie) n. defeat,
disenfranchisement
   ~ гражданских прав (~
   grahdánskikh prav)
   disenfranchisement of civil
   rights
   ~ в правах (~ v pravákh)
   disenfranchisement
Поранить (poránit') v. to injure,
to wound

Порицание (poritsánie) n. censure,
reprimand
   общественное ~ (obshchéstvennoe
   ~) public censure
Порицать (poritsát') v. to censure
Порок (porók) m. defect, flaw, vice
Порочный (poróchnyi) adj. vicious,
wanton
   ~ круг (~ krug) vicious circle
Порт (port) m. port
   блокированный ~ (blokiróvannyi
   ~) blockaded port
   военный ~ (voénnyi ~) naval port
   воздушный ~ (vozdúshnyi ~)
   airport
   коммерческий ~ (kommércheskii ~)
   commercial port
   морской ~ (morskói ~) seaport
   нейтральный ~ (neitrál'nyi ~)
   neutral port
   открытый ~ (otkrýtyi ~) open
   port
   попутный ~ (popútnyi ~)
   intermediate port
   речной ~ (rechnói ~) river port
   рыбный ~ (rýbnyi ~) fishing port
   свободный ~ (svobódnyi ~) free
   port
   таможенный ~ (tamózhennyi ~)
   customs port
   торговый ~ (torgóvyi ~) trading
   port
   ~ выгрузки (~ výgruzki) port of
   discharge
   ~ захода (~ zakhóda) port of
   call
   ~ назначения (~ naznachéniia)
   port of destination
   ~ отправления (~ otpravléniia)
   port of departure
   ~ погрузки (~ pogrúzki) loading
   port
   ~ прибытия (~ pribýtiia) port of
   arrival
   ~ приписки (~ pripíski) port of
   registry, home port
   ~ регистрации (~ registrátsii)
   port of registry
   ~ - убежище (~ ubézhishche) port
   of refuge
Портить (pórtit') v. to damage, to
spoil
Портфель (portfél') m. portfolio
   банковский ~ (bánkovskii ~) bank
   ~
   вексельный ~ (véksel'nyi ~) ~ of
   bills

деловой ~ (delovói ~) business ~
министерский ~ (ministérskii ~)
ministerial ~
страховой ~ (strakhovói ~)
insurance ~
~ акций (~ áktsii) ~ of stock
~ ценных бумаг (~ tsénnykh
bumág) ~ of securities
Порубка (porúbka) f. woodcutting
безбилетная ~ (bezbilétnaia ~)
unlicensed ~
незаконная ~ (nezakónnaia ~)
illegal ~
Порука (porúk/a) f. bail, guarantee
брать на ~/и (brat' na ~/i) to
put up bail for
отпустить на ~/и (otpustít' na
~/i) to release on bail
круговая ~ (krugováia ~)
collective guarantee
Поручать (poruchát') v. to charge,
to commission, to entrust, to
instruct
Поручение (poruchénie) n.
commission, errand, instruction,
order
банковское ~ (bánkovskoe ~)
banker's instructions
импортное ~ (ímportnoe ~) import
assignment
денежное ~ (dénezhnoe ~) money
order
дипломатическое ~
(diplomatícheskoe ~) diplomatic
instructions
комиссионное ~ (komissiónnoe ~)
commission
переводное ~ (perevódnoe ~)
transfer order
платёжное ~ (platiózhnoe ~)
payment order
почтовое ~ (pochtóvoe ~) postal
order
специальное ~ (spetsiál'noe ~)
special assignment
Поручитель (poruchítel') m.
guarantor, surety, warrantor
в качестве ~/я (v káchestve
~/ia) as surety
вексельный ~ (véksel'nyi ~)
surety on a bill
главный ~ (glávnyi ~) primary
guarantor
совместный ~ (sovméstnyi ~)
joint surety
~ по долгам (~ po dolgám)
guarantor for debts

Поручительство (poruchítel'stvo) n.
guarantee, surety, warranty
вексельное ~ (véksel'noe ~)
surety for a bill
имущественное ~
(imúshchestvennoe ~) security
кредитное ~ (kredítnoe ~) credit
guaranty
личное ~ (líchnoe ~) personal
security
совместное ~ (sovméstnoe ~)
joint surety
Поручиться за ... (poruchít'sia za
...) v. to stand as security for
...
Порча (pórcha) f. damage, spoiling,
wear and tear
~ имущества (~ imúshchestva)
destruction of property
~ товара (~ továra) damage to
goods
Поряд/ок (poriád/ok) m.
arrangement, method, order,
procedure
административный ~
(administratívnyi ~)
administrative procedure
алфавитный ~ (alfavítnyi ~)
alphabetical order
арбитражный ~ (arbitrázhnyi ~)
arbitral procedure
в обязательном ~/ке (v
obiazátel'nom ~/ke) without fail
в полном ~/ке и должной форме (v
pólnom ~/ke i dólzhnoi fórme) in
good order and proper form
в соответствии с ~/ком (v
sootvétstvii s ~/kom) in
accordance with the procedure
в судебном ~/ке (v sudébnom
~/ke) by legal means
в установленном ~/ке (v
ustanóvlennom ~/ke) in the
established manner, in
accordance with the established
procedure
внесудебный ~ (vnesudébnyi ~)
extrajudicial procedure
дипломатический ~
(diplomatícheskii ~) diplomatic
procedure, diplomacy
заведённый ~ (zavediónnyi ~)
routine
законный ~ (zakónnyi ~) legal
procedure

законодательный ~ (zakonodátel'nyi ~) legislative order

конституционный ~ (konstitutsiónnyi ~) constitutional procedure

международный юридический ~ (mezhdunaródnyi iuridícheskii ~) international legal procedure

новый международный экономический ~ (nóvyi mezhdunaródnyi ekonomícheskii ~) new international economic order

нормативный ~ (normatívnyi ~) normative procedure

нотариальный ~ (notariál'nyi ~) notarial procedure

обратный ~ (obrátnyi ~) reverse order

общественный ~ (obshchéstvennyi ~) social order

обычный ~ (obýchnyi ~) regular practice

правовой ~ (pravovói ~) legal order

преследовать в судебном ~/ке (preslédovat' v sudébnom ~/ke) to prosecute

призвать к ~/ку (prizvát' k ~/ku) to call to order

принудительным ~/ком (prinudítel'nym ~/kom) compulsorily

противоречащий публичному ~/ку (protivorecháshchii publíchnomu ~/ku) violating public order

публичный ~ (publíchnyi ~) public order

специальный ~ (spetsiál'nyi ~) special procedure

строгий ~ (strógii ~) strict order

уголовный ~ (ugolóvnyi ~) criminal procedure

упрощённый ~ (uproshchiónnyi ~) simplified procedure

установленный ~ (ustanóvlennyi ~) established procedure

экономический ~ (ekonomícheskii ~) economic order

явочным ~/ком (iávochnym ~/kom) without prior arrangement

юридический ~ (iuridícheskii ~) legal order

~ арбитража (~ arbitrázha) arbitration procedure

~ аттестации (~ attestátsii) attestation procedure

~ выборов (~ výborov) election procedure

~ выдачи патентов (~ výdachi paténtov) patent issuance procedure

~ голосования (~ golosóvaniia) voting procedure

~ дня (~ dnia) agenda

~ обжалования (~ obzhálovaniia) order of appeal

~ очерёдности (~ ocheriódnosti) priority list

~ платежей (~ platezhéi) payment procedure

~ предпочтения (~ predpochténiia) order of preference

~ предъявления претензии (~ pred"iavléniia preténzii) procedure for making a claim

~ примирения (~ primiréniia) reconciliation procedure

~ приоритета (~ prioritéta) order of priority

~ разрешения споров (~ razreshéniia spórov) dispute resolution procedure

~ распределения (~ raspredeléniia) order of distribution

~ ратификации (~ ratifikátsii) ratification procedure

~ старшинства (~ starshinstvá) order of seniority

~ уплаты (~ upláty) order of payment

~ эксплуатации (~ ekspluatátsii) operating procedure

Посадка (posádka) *f.* embarkation, landing

вынужденная ~ (výnuzhdennaia ~) forced landing

непредвиденная ~ (nepredvídennaia ~) unforeseen landing

~ на мель (~ na mel') running aground

Поселение (poselénie) *n.* deportation, settlement

городское ~ (gorodskóe ~) urban settlement

~ в новое помещение (~ v nóvoe pomeshchénie) resettlement

Посёлок (posiólok) *m.* housing estate {public housing}

Посещать (poseshchát') v. to
attend, to visit
Посещение (poseshchénie) m. visit
Посещаемость (poseshcháemost') f.
attendance
  ~ учебных заведений (~ uchébnykh
  zavedénii) matriculation at
  university level
Посланец (poslánets) m. messenger
Послание (poslánie) n. epistle,
message
  ~ папы (~ pápy) Papal Encyclical
Посланник (poslánnik) m. envoy
  дипломатический ~
  (diplomatícheskii ~) diplomatic
  ~
  чрезвычайный ~ (chrezvycháinyi
  ~) special ~
  чрезвычайный и полномочный ~
  (chrezvycháinyi i polnomóchnyi
  ~) extraordinary and minister
  plenipotentiary
Послать (poslát') v. to send
  ~ обратно (~ obrátno) to send
  back
Последовательность
(poslédovatel'nost') f. rotation,
succession
Последовательный (poslédovatel'nyi)
adj. consecutive, gradual,
successive
Последстви/е (poslédstvi/e) n.
consequence, outcome
  законное ~ (zakónnoe ~) legal
  outcome
  правовые ~/я (pravovýe ~/ia)
  legal implications
Пособие (posóbie) n. assistance,
benefit, relief
  временное ~ (vrémennoe ~)
  temporary assistance
  денежное ~ (dénezhnoe ~)
  monetary assistance
  единовременное ~ (edinovrémennoe
  ~) one-time assistance
  пожизненное ~ (pozhíznennoe ~)
  lifetime assistance
  предварительное ~
  (predvarítel'noe ~) preliminary
  assistance
  семейное ~ (seméinoe ~) family
  assistance
  ~ по безработице (~ po
  bezrabótitse) unemployment
  benefit
  ~ по болезни (~ po bolézni) sick
  pay

  ~ по временной
  нетрудоспособности (~ po
  vrémennoi netrudosposóbnosti)
  temporary disability benefit
  ~ по беременности и родам (~ po
  berémennosti i ródam) maternity
  benefit
  ~ многодетным матерям (~
  mnogodétnym materiám) large
  family allowance
  ~ по нетрудоспособности (~ po
  netrudosposóbnosti) disability
  benefit
  ~ одиноким матерям (~ odinókim
  materiám) aid to single mothers
  ~ при переезде (~ pri pereézde)
  relocation assistance
  ~ по переквалификации (~ po
  perekvalifikátsii) retraining
  benefit
Пособник (posóbnik) m. abettor
Пособничество (posobníchestvo) n.
aiding and abetting
Посол (posól) m. ambassador
  полномочный ~ (polnomóchnyi ~)
  plenipotentiary ~
  постоянный ~ (postoiánnyi ~)
  permanent ~
  чрезвычайный ~ (chrezvycháinyi
  ~) extraordinary ~
  чрезвычайный и полномочный ~
  (chrezvycháinyi i polnomóchnyi
  ~) extraordinary and
  plenipotentiary ~
Посольство (posól'stvo) n. embassy
Посредник (posrédnik) m. agent,
dealer, middleman
  вексельный ~ (véksel'nyi ~) bill
  broker
  уполномоченный ~
  (upolnomóchennyi ~) authorized
  dealer
  финансовый ~ (finánsovyi ~)
  financial intermediary
Посредничать (posrédnichat') to act
as an agent, to mediate
Посредничество (posrédnichestvo)
agency, mediation
Посредство (posrédstvo) agency,
mediation
Пост (post) post
  вакантный ~ (vakántnyi ~) vacant
  ~
  государственный ~
  (gosudárstvennyi ~) government ~

дипломатический ~
(diplomatícheskii ~) diplomatic
~
директорский ~ (diréktorskii ~)
director's ~
консульский ~ (kónsul'skii ~)
consular ~
пограничный ~ (pogranichnyi ~)
border ~
руководящий ~ (rukovodiáshchii
~) leading position
таможенный ~ (tamózhennyi ~)
customs ~
Постав/ка (postáv/ka) f. delivery,
shipment, supply
бесплатная ~ (besplátnaia ~)
delivery free of charge
быстрая ~ (býstraia ~) speedy
delivery
внутренняя ~ (vnútrenniaia ~)
internal delivery
договорные ~/ки (dogovórnye
~/ki) contracted deliveries
ленд-лизовская ~ (lend-
lízovskaia ~) lend lease
delivery
комплектная ~ (kompléktnaia ~)
complete delivery, package
delivery
неполная ~ (nepólnaia ~) short
delivery
новые ~/ки (nóvye ~/ki) fresh
deliveries
пробная ~ (próbnaia ~) trial
delivery
разовая ~ (rázovaia ~) single
shipment
удовлетворительная ~
(udovletvorítel'naia ~)
satisfactory delivery
ускоренная ~ (uskórennaia ~)
expedited delivery
~ по частичным партиям (~ po
chastíchnym pártiiam) delivery
in partial consignments
~ на экспорт (~ na éksport)
delivery for export
Поставлять (postavliát') v. to
supply
Поставщик (postavshchík) m.
supplier
главный ~ (glávnyi ~) principal
~
оптовый ~ (optóvyi ~) wholesale
~

Постановление (postanovlénie) n.
decision, decree, enactment,
resolution
административное ~
(administratívnoe ~)
administrative decree
военное ~ (voénnoe ~) military
regulation
военно-воздушное ~ (voénno-
vozdúshnoe ~) air force
regulation
военно-морское ~ (voénno-morskóe
~) naval regulation
законодательное ~
(zakonodátel'noe ~) legislative
resolution
законное ~ (zakónnoe ~) legal
enactment
запретительное ~ (zapretítel'noe
~) prohibition
исполнительное ~ (ispolnítel'noe
~) executive decree
конституционное ~
(konstitutsiónnoe ~)
constitutional resolution
мотивированное ~ (motivírovannoe
~) motivated resolution
общее ~ (óbshchee ~) general
resolution
обязательное ~ (obiazátel'noe ~)
compulsory regulation
основное ~ (osnovnóe ~) basic
regulation
политическое ~ (politícheskoe ~)
political resolution
процедурное ~ (protsedúrnoe ~)
procedural regulation
специальное ~ (spetsiál'noe ~)
special resolution
судебное ~ (sudébnoe ~) court
ruling
таможенное ~ (tamózhennoe ~)
customs regulation, ruling
тарифное ~ (tarífnoe ~) tariff
regulation, ruling
уставное ~ (ustávnoe ~) charter
resolution
финансовое ~ (finánsovoe ~)
financial regulation
экономическое (ekonomícheskoe)
economic regulation
~ об амнистии (~ ob amnístii)
decree of amnesty
~ правительства (~
pravítel'stva) government act
~ приговора (~ prigovóra)
sentencing

~ реквизиции (~ rekvizítsii)
requisition
~ суда (~ sudá) decision of the
court
Постановлять (postanovliát') *v.* to
decree, to enact, to resolve
Постой (postói) *m.* billeting,
quartering
военный ~ (voénnyi ~) military
billeting
Пострадавший (postradávshii)
m.adj.noun victim {of crime, etc.}
Постройка (postróika) *f.* building,
building site
Поступлени/е (postupléni/e) *n.*
arrival, earnings, inflow, revenue
безденежные ~/я (bezdénezhnye
~/ia) non-cash receipts
бюджетные ~/я (biudzhétnye
~/ia) budget receipts
валовые ~/я (valovýe ~/ia) gross
returns
валютные ~/я (valiútnye ~/ia)
foreign exchange earnings
денежные ~/я (dénezhnye ~/ia)
incoming receivables
кассовые ~/я (kássovye ~/ia)
cash receipts
лицензионные ~/я (litsenziónnye
~/ia) licensing earnings
наличные ~/я (nalíchnye ~/ia)
encashment
налоговые ~/я (nalógovye ~/ia)
tax revenues
текущие ~/я (tekúshchie ~/ia)
operating receipts
~ жалобы (~ zháloby) receipt of
a complaint
~ заказов (~ zakázov) incoming
orders
~ заявок (~ zaiávok) inflow of
applications
~ иностранной валюты (~
inostránnoi valiúty) earnings of
foreign currency
Посылка (posýlka) *f.* consignment,
dispatch, parcel
авиапочтовая ~ (aviapochtóvaia
~) airmail parcel
безвозмездная ~ (bezvozmézdnaia
~) forwarding free of charge
громоздкая ~ (gromózdkaia ~)
unwieldy package
почтовая ~ (pochtóvaia ~) postal
parcel
почтовая ~ с объявленной
ценностью (pochtóvaia ~ s

ob"iávlennoi tsénnost'iu) postal
parcel with declared value
срочная ~ (sróchnaia ~) express
parcel
ценная ~ (tsénnaia ~)
consignment of valuables
хрупкая ~ (khrúpkaia ~) fragile
parcel
Посягательство (posiagátel'stvo) *n.*
encroachment, infringement
преступное ~ (prestúpnoe ~)
criminal infringement
~ на жизнь ... (~ na zhizn' ...)
an attempt on the life of ...
~ на моральное развитие
малолетних (...~ na morál'noe
razvítie malolétnikh) corruption
of minors
~ на права (~ na pravá)
encroachment upon rights
~ на свободу (~ na svobódu)
false imprisonment, infringement
of liberty
~ на собственность (~ na
sóbstvennost') infringement of
property
~ на суверенитет (~ na
suverenitét) encroachment on
sovereignty
Посягать (posiagát') *v.* to
encroach, to infringe
Потенциал (potentsiál) *m.* potential
военный ~ (voénnyi ~) military
potential
промышленный ~ (promýshlennyi ~)
industrial potential
экономический ~ (ekonomícheskii
~) economic potential
~ производства (~ proizvódstva)
potential production
Потенция (poténtsiia) *f.*
potentiality
экономическая ~ (ekonomícheskaia
~) economic ~
Потерпевший (poterpévshii) *m. adj.*
survivor, victim
~ вреда (~ vredá) victim of harm
Потер/я (potér/ia) *f.* loss, waste
возместимые ~/и (vozmestímye
~/i) recoverable losses
незначительные ~/и
(neznachítel'nye ~/i)
insignificant losses
~ гражданства (~ grazhdánstva)
loss of citizenship
~ права (~ pravá) loss of right

~ причиненная стихийными бедствиями (~ prichinénnaia stikhíinymi bédstviiami) casualty losses

~ суверенитета (~ suverenitéta) loss of sovereignty

~ трудоспособности (~ trudosposóbnosti) disability

Потерять (poteriát') v. [perfective of терять] to lose

Поток (potók) m. flow, line, stream

денежные ~/и (dénezhnye ~/i) monetary flows

кредитные ~/и (kredítnye ~/i) credit flows

~ наличности (~ nalíchnosti) cash flow

Потомок (potómok) m. descendant, progeny

Потомственный (potómstvennyi) adj. hereditary

Потомство (potómstvo) n. descendants, posterity

Потрава (potráva) f. crop damage {by livestock, etc.}

Потребитель (potrebítel') m. consumer, user

внутренний ~ (vnútrennii ~) domestic consumer

конечный ~ (konéchnyi ~) end user

крупный ~ (krúpnyi ~) bulk purchaser

мелкий ~ (mélkii ~) small customer

оптовый ~ (optóvyi ~) wholesale consumer

предельный ~ (predél'nyi ~) marginal user

розничный ~ (róznichnyi ~) retail consumer

Потребление (potreblénie) n. consumption, demand, use

внутреннее ~ (vnútrennee ~) domestic consumption

государственное ~ (gosudárstvennoe ~) government consumption

домашнее ~ (domáshnee ~) household consumption

конечное ~ (konéchnoe ~) final consumption

индивидуальное ~ (individuál'noe ~) individual consumption

личное ~ (líchnoe ~) personal consumption

массовое ~ (mássovoe ~) mass consumption

общее ~ (óbshchee ~) total consumption

производственное ~ (proizvódstvennoe ~) productive consumption

среднее ~ (srédnee ~) average consumption

частное ~ (chástnoe ~) private consumption

~ на душу населения (~ na dúshu naseléniia) per capita consumption

Потреблять (potrebliát') v. to consume, to use

Потребност/ь (potrébnost/') f. demand, need, requirement

будущие ~/и (búdushchie ~/i) future needs

внутренние ~/и (vnútrennie ~/i) domestic demand

разовая ~ (rázovaia ~) one-time requirement

~/и в площади (~/i v plóshchadi) space requirements

~/и рынка (~/i rýnka) market requirements

Похищать (pokhishchát') v. to abduct, to hijack, to kidnap, to steal

Похищение (pokhishchénie) n. abduction, hijacking, kidnapping, theft

~ государственного имущества (~ gosudárstvennogo imúshchestva) theft of government property

~ ребёнка (~ rebiónka) kidnapping

Поход (pokhód) m. cruise, march

Почва (póchva) f. soil

Почётный (pochiótnyi) adj. honorary, honorable

Почин (pochín) m. initiative, first sale of the day

по своему почину (po svoemú ~/u) on one's own initiative

Почт/а (pócht/a) f. mail, post office

воздушная ~ (vozdúshnaia ~) airmail

дипломатическая ~ (diplomatícheskaia ~) diplomatic pouch

заказная ~ (zakaznáia ~) registered mail

обычная ~ (obýchnaia ~) surface mail
отправить по ~/е (otprávit' po ~/e) to mail
простая ~ (prostáia ~) unregistered mail
Почтовый (pochtóvyi) *adj.* mail, postal
Пошлина (póshlina) *f.* duty, toll
адвалорная ~ (advalórnaia ~) ad valorem duty
антидемпинговая ~ (antidémpingovaia ~) anti-dumping duty
валютная ~ (valiútnaia ~) currency defense duty
ввозная ~ (vvoznáia ~) import duty
ввозная таможенная ~ (vvoznáia tamózhennaia ~) import customs duty
взимаемая ~ (vzimáemaia ~) levied duty
внешнеторговая ~ (vneshnetorgóvaia ~) foreign trade duty
внутренняя таможенная ~ (vnútrenniaia tamózhennaia ~) internal customs duty
возобновительная ~ (vozobnovítel'naia ~) renewal fee
временная ~ (vrémennaia ~) temporary duty
вывозная ~ (vyvoznáia ~) customs export duty
вывозная таможенная ~ (vyvoznáia tamózhennaia ~) export customs duty
гербовая ~ (gérbovaia ~) stamp tax
дифференциальная ~ (differentsiál'naia ~) differential duty
договорные ~/ы (dogovórnye ~/y) conventional tariff
дополнительная ~ (dopolnítel'naia ~) additional duty
дорожная ~ (dorózhnaia ~) road toll
ежегодная ~ (ezhegódnaia ~) annual duty
запретительная ~ (zapretítel'naia ~) prohibitive duty

импортная ~ (ímportnaia ~) import duty
импортная таможенная ~ (ímportnaia tamózhennaia ~) import customs duty
ипотечная ~ (ipotéchnaia ~) hypothecation duty
компенсационная ~ (kompensatsiónnaia ~) compensatory duty
максимальная ~ (maksimál'naia ~) maximum duty
минимальная ~ (minimál'naia ~) minimum duty
муниципальная ~ (munitsipál'naia ~) municipal duty
патентная ~ (paténtnaia ~) patent fee
покровительственная ~ (pokrovítel'stvennaia ~) protective duty
прогрессивная ~ (progressívnaia ~) progressive duty
протекционистская ~ (protektsionístskaia ~) protectionist duty
регистрационная ~ (registratsiónnaia ~) registration fee
смешанная ~ (sméshannaia ~) compound duty
специфическая ~ (spetsifícheskaia ~) specific duty
судебные ~/ы (sudébnye ~/y) legal costs and expenses
таможенная ~ (tamózhennaia ~) customs duty
транзитная ~ (tranzítnaia ~) transit duty
транзитная таможенная ~ (tranzítnaia tamózhennaia ~) transit customs duty
фискальная ~ (fiskál'naia ~) revenue duty
штрафная ~ (shtrafnáia ~) fine, penalty duty
экспортная ~ (éksportnaia ~) export duty
экспортная таможенная ~ (éksportnaia tamózhennaia ~) export customs duty
~ на наследование (~ na naslédovanie) inheritance tax
~ на наследственное имущество (~ na naslédstvennoe imúshchestvo) estate tax

~ на переход имущества (~ na perekhód imúshchestva) conveyance fees

~ на право охоты (~ na právo okhóty) hunting license fee

~ на удостоверение акта (~ na udostoverénie ákta) certification fee

Пощада (poshcháda) *f.* mercy

Появление (poiavlénie) *n.* appearance

~ в пьяном виде (~ v p'iánom víde) public intoxication

Пояс (póias) *m.* band, belt, zone
морской ~ (morskói ~) maritime zone

Пояснительный (poiasnítel'nyi) *adj.* explanatory

Поясной (poiasnói) *adj.* zonal

Правая (právaia) *adj.* right
крайняя (kráiniaia) *adj.* extreme right

Правил/о (právil/o) *n.* custom, law, regulation, rule
административное ~ (administratívnoe ~) administrative rule

валютное ~ (valiútnoe ~) foreign exchange regulation

внутренние ~/a (vnútrennie ~/a) domestic rules

жёсткое ~ (zhióstkoe ~) firm rule

иммиграционные ~/a (immigratsiónnye ~/a) immigration regulation

карантинное ~ (karantínnoe ~) quarantine regulation

международное почтовое ~ (mezhdunaródnoe pochtóvoe ~) international postal regulation

международные ~/a (mezhdunaródnye ~/a) international customs

международные санитарные ~/a (mezhdunaródnye sanitárnye ~/a) international sanitary standards

навигационные ~/a (navigatsiónnye ~/a) navigational rules

налоговые ~/a (nalógovye ~/a) tax rulings

общие ~/a (óbshchie ~/a) general terms and conditions

основное ~ (osnovnóe ~) ground rule

портовые ~/a (portóvye ~/a) port authority regulations

почтовые ~/a (pochtóvye ~/a) postal regulations

противопожарные ~/a (protivopozhárnye ~/a) fire safety rules

процессуальное ~ (protsessuál'noe ~) procedural rule

рыночные ~/a (rýnochnye ~/a) market regulations

санитарные ~/a (sanitárnye ~/a) sanitary standards

специальное ~ (spetsiál'noe ~) special rule

судебное ~ (sudébnoe ~) rule of court procedure

таможенное ~ (tamózhennoe ~) customs rule

финансовое ~ (finánsovoe ~) financial regulation

фискальные ~/a (fiskál'nye ~/a) fiscal rules

~/a безопасности (~/a bezopásnosti) safety regulations

~/a внутреннего распорядка (~/a vnútrennego rasporiádka) house rules, internal regulations {of a particular establishment}

~/a голосования (~/a golosovániia) voting regulations

~/a конкуренции (~/a konkuréntsii) rules of competition

~/a международных полётов (~/a mezhdunaródnykh poliótov) international flight regulations

~ о личном составе (~ o líchnom sostáve) regulation of personnel

~ о подведомственности (~ o podvédomstvennosti) jurisdiction rule

~ о подсудности (~ o podsúdnosti) rule of cognizance, jurisdiction

~ о приоритете (~ o prioritéte) regulation of priority

~/a о работе (~/a o rabóte) work rules

~ о финансах (~ o finánsakh) regulation of finances

~ оплаты (~ opláty) payment rule

~ относящееся к существу (~ otnosiáshcheesia k sushchestvú) substantive rule

~/а охоты (~/а okhóty) hunting regulations
~ перевозки (~ perevózki) regulation of transportation
~/а передвижения в воздухе (~/а peredvizhéniia v vózdukhe) air traffic regulations
~/а проживания иностранцев (~/а prozhivániia inostrántsev) regulations for resident foreigners
~ публичного порядка (~ publíchnogo poriádka) rule of public order
~/а рыбной ловли (~/а rybnói lóvli) fishing regulations
~/а судоходства (~/а sudokhódstva) shipping regulations
~ техники безопасности (~ tékhniki bezopásnosti) safety equipment regulation
~ эксплуатации (~ ekspluatátsii) operating regulation
Правильно (právil'no) *adv.* correctly, properly, regularly
Правильность (právil'nost') *f.* accuracy, correctness, propriety, regularity
Правильный (právil'nyi) *adj.* accurate, correct, proper, regular
Правительственный (pravítel'stvennyi) *adj.* governmental
Правительство (pravítel'stvo) *n.* administration {e.g. as U.S. presidential administration}, government
  враждебное ~ (vrazhdébnoe ~) hostile government
  временное ~ (vrémennoe ~) interim government
  демократическое ~ (demokratícheskoe ~) democratic government
  диктаторское ~ (diktátorskoe ~) dictatorial government
  законное ~ (zakónnoe ~) legal government
  коалиционное ~ (koalitsiónnoe ~) coalition government
  конституционное ~ (konstitutsiónnoe ~) constitutional government
  лейбористское ~ (leiborístskoe ~) labor government

  либеральное ~ (liberál'noe ~) liberal government
  марионеточное ~ (marionétochnoe ~) puppet government
  неподписавшееся ~ (nepodpisávsheesia ~) nonsignatory government
  парламентское ~ (parlámentskoe ~) parliamentary government
  переходное ~ (perekhódnoe ~) transitional government
  подписавшееся ~ (podpisávsheesia ~) signatory government
  провинциальное ~ (provintsiál'noe ~) provincial government
  революционное ~ (revoliutsiónnoe ~) revolutionary government
  свергнуть ~ (svergnút' ~) to overthrow the government
  составить ~ (sostávit' ~) to constitute a government
  стабильное ~ (stabil'noe ~) stable government
  тоталитарное ~ (totalitárnoe ~) totalitarian government
  сформировать ~ (sformírovat' ~) to form a government
  фактическое ~ (faktícheskoe ~) actual government
  федеральное ~ (federál'noe ~) federal government
  ~-депозитарий (~ depozitárii) depositary government {to a convention}
  ~ де-факто (~ dé-fákto) de facto government
  ~ де-юре (~ dé-iúre) de jure government
  ~ в изгнании (~ v izgnánii) government in exile
  ~ национального единства (~ natsionál'nogo edínstva) government of national unity
  ~ общественного спасения (~ obshchéstvennogo spaséniia) government of social salvation
Правление (pravlénie) *n.* directorate, management
  центральное ~ (tsentrál'noe ~) central management
Прав/о (práv/o) *n.* law {in various senses}, right
  абсолютное ~ (absoliútnoe ~) absolute right
  автономное ~ (avtonómnoe ~) autonomous right

авторское ~ (ávtorskoe ~)
copyright
административное ~
(administratívnoe ~)
administrative law
арбитражное ~ (arbitrázhnoe ~)
law of arbitration
бессрочное ~ (bessróchnoe ~)
unlimited right
бестелесное ~ (bestelésnoe ~)
incorporeal right
благоприобретенное ~
(blagopriobreténnoe ~) acquired
right
божественное ~ (bozhéstvennoe ~)
divine right
брачное ~ (bráchnoe ~) conjugal
right
вексельное ~ (véksel'noe ~) law
of bills of exchange
вечное ~ (véchnoe ~) eternal
right
вещное ~ (véshchnoe ~) law of
estates
внутригосударственное ~
(vnutrigosudárstvennoe ~)
intergovernmental law
военное ~ (voénnoe ~) military
law
военное уголовное ~ (voénnoe
ugolóvnoe ~) military criminal
law
всеобщее избирательное ~
(vseóbshchee izbirátel'noe ~)
universal suffrage
горное ~ (górnoe ~) law of
subterranean resources
государственное ~
(gosudárstvennoe ~) public law
гражданские ~/a (grahdánskie
~/á) civil rights
гражданские и политические ~/a
(grahdánskie i politícheskie
~/á) civil and political rights
гражданское ~ (grahdánskoe ~)
civil law
гражданское процессуальное ~
(grahdánskoe protsessuál'noe ~)
law of civil procedure
действующее ~ (déistvuiushchee
~) law in force
дипломатическое ~
(diplomatícheskoe ~) diplomatic
right
договорное ~ (dogovórnoe ~) law
of contracts

доказательственное ~
(dokazátel'stvennoe ~) law of
evidence
естественное ~ (estéstvennoe ~)
natural law
законное ~ (zakónnoe ~) legal
right
законные ~/a (zakónnye ~/á)
legal rights
залоговое ~ (zalógovoe ~) lien
избирательное ~ (izbirátel'noe
~) suffrage
избирательное ~ женщин
(izbirátel'noe ~ zhénshchin)
women's suffrage
изобретательское ~
(izobretátel'skoe ~) inventor's
right
имеющий ~ (iméiushchii ~) having
a right
иметь ~ (imét' ~) to have a
right
имущественное ~
(imúshchestvennoe ~) property
right, law of property
имущественные ~/a
(imúshchestvennye ~/á) property
rights
имущественные авторские ~/a
(imúshchestvennye ávtorskie ~/á)
proprietary copyrights
исключительное ~
(iskliuchítel'noe ~) exclusive
right
исключительное ~ на издание
(iskliuchítel'noe ~ na izdánie)
exclusive publication right
исключительное ~ продажи
(iskliuchítel'noe ~ prodázhi)
exclusive right to sell
исключительное ~ производства
(iskliuchítel'noe ~
proizvódstva) exclusive right to
manufacture
исключительное ~ на эксплуатацию
(iskliuchítel'noe ~ na ekspluatátsiiu) exclusive right to
operate
исключительные ~/a
(iskliuchítel'nye ~/á) exclusive
rights
каноническое ~ (kanonícheskoe ~)
Canon law
карательное ~ (karátel'noe ~)
penal law

кодифицированное ~
(kodifitsírovannoe ~) codified
law
коллективное ~ (kollektívnoe ~)
collective right
коммерческое ~ (kommércheskoe ~)
commercial law
конституционное ~
(konstitutsiónnoe ~)
constitutional law
космическое ~ (kosmícheskoe ~)
the law of outer space
культурные ~/a (kul'túrnye ~/á)
cultural rights
материальное ~ (materiál'noe ~)
material right
межгосударственное ~
(mezhgosudárstvennoe ~)
intergovernmental right
международное ~ (mezhdunaródnoe
~) international law
международное административное ~
(mezhdunaródnoe administratívnoe
~) international administrative
law
международное гражданское ~
(mezhdunaródnoe grahdánskoe ~)
international civil law
международное космическое ~
(mezhdunaródnoe kosmícheskoe ~)
international law of outer space
международное морское ~
(mezhdunaródnoe morskóe ~)
international admiralty law
международное обычное ~
(mezhdunaródnoe obýchnoe ~)
international customary law
международное позитивное ~
(mezhdunaródnoe pozitívnoe ~)
international positive law
международное публичное ~
(mezhdunaródnoe publíchnoe ~)
international public law
международное торговое ~
(mezhdunaródnoe torgóvoe ~)
international trade law
международное уголовное ~
(mezhdunaródnoe ugolóvnoe ~)
international criminal law
международное частное ~
(mezhdunaródnoe chástnoe ~)
international private law
местное ~ (méstnoe ~) local law
монопольное ~ (monopól'noe ~)
monopoly right

монопольное эмиссионное ~
(monopól'noe emissiónnoe ~)
monopoly right to issue
морское ~ (morskóe ~) admiralty
law
мусульманское ~ (musul'mánskoe
~) Islamic law
наднациональное ~
(nadnatsionál'noe ~)
supranational law
налоговое ~ (nalógovoe ~) tax
law
национальное ~ (natsionál'noe ~)
national law
недвижимое имущественное ~
(nedvízhimoe imúshchestvennoe ~)
law of real property
неотъемлемое ~ (neot"émlemoe ~)
inalienable right
неотчуждаемое ~ (neotchuzhdáemoe
~) inalienable right
неписаное ~ (nepísanoe ~)
unwritten law
обладать ~/м (obladát' ~/m) to
have the right
общее ~ (óbshchee ~) common law
обычное ~ (obýchnoe ~) customary
law
обязательственное ~
(obiazátel'stvennoe ~) law of
obligations
опекунское ~ (opekúnskoe ~) law
of guardianship
основное ~ (osnovnóe ~)
fundamental right
основные ~/a обязанности граждан
(osnovnýe ~/á obiázannosti
grázhdan) basic rights and
obligations of citizens
осуществлять суверенные ~/a
(osushchestvliát' suverénnye
~/á) to affect sovereign rights
отказаться от своих ~
(otkazát'sia ot svoíkh ~) to
waive one's rights
отстаивать свои ~/a (otstáivat'
svoí ~/á) to insist on one's
rights
патентное ~ (paténtnoe ~) patent
right
патентное ~ на изобретение
(paténtnoe ~ na izobreténie)
inventor's patent
писанное ~ (písannoe ~) written
law
по ~/y (po ~/u) by rights

позитивное ~ (pozitívnoe ~)
positive law
политические ~/a (politícheskie
~/á) politial rights
положительное ~ (polozhítel'noe
~) affirmative right
получивший ~/a гражданства
(poluchívshii ~/á grazhdánstva)
receiving citizenship rights
преимущественное ~
(preimúshchestvennoe ~)
preferential right
применимое ~ (primenímoe ~)
applicable law
приобретенное ~ (priobreténnoe
~) acquired right
противоречащее ~
(protivorecháshchee ~)
contradictory right
процессуальное ~
(protsessuál'noe ~) procedural
law
прямое избирательное ~ (priamóe
izbirátel'noe ~) direct suffrage
публичное ~ (publíchnoe ~)
public law
римское ~ (rímskoe ~) Roman law
родительские ~/a (rodítel'skie
~/á) parental rights
рыболовное ~ (rybolóvnoe ~)
fishing right
семейное ~ (seméinoe ~) family
law
советское ~ (sovétskoe ~) Soviet
law
сравнительное ~ (sravnítel'noe
~) comparative law
территориальное ~
(territoriál'noe ~) territorial
right
торговое ~ (torgóvoe ~) trade
law
трудовое ~ (trudovóe ~) labor
law
уголовное ~ (ugolóvnoe ~)
criminal law
условное ~ (uslóvnoe ~)
conditional right
уставное ~ (ustávnoe ~) charter
right
ущемить ~ (ushchemít' ~) to
encroach on a right
формальное ~ (formál'noe ~)
formal law
цензовое избирательное ~
(tsénzovoe izbirátel'noe ~)
qualified voting right

церковное ~ (tserkóvnoe ~)
ecclesiastical law
частное ~ (chástnoe ~) private
law
частное морское ~ (chástnoe
morskóe ~) private admiralty law
человеческие ~/a (chelovécheskie
~/á) human rights
юридические ~/a (iuridícheskie
~/á) juridical rights
~ быть выслушанным в суде (~
byt' výslushannym v sudé) right
to be heard in court
~ быть избранным (~ byt'
ízbrannym) right to be elected
~ водителя (~ vodítelia)
driver's license
~ выкупа (~ výkupa) right of
redemption
~ выпаса скота (~ výpasa skotá)
grazing right
~ голоса (~ gólosa) right to
vote
~ гражданства (~ grazhdánstva)
right of citizenship
~ денонсации (~ denonsátsii)
prescriptive right
~ доступа (~ dóstupa) right of
access
~ завещать (~ zaveshchát') right
to devise by will
~/a и интересы (~/á i interésy)
rights and interests
~/a из патента (~/á iz paténta)
patent rights
~ кассационного опротестования
(~ kassatsiónnogo
oprotestovániia) right of appeal
~ на вето (~ na veto) véto right
~ на возмещение (~ na
vozmeshchénie) right to
compensation
~ на возмещение вреда (~ na
vozmeshchénie vredá) right to
compensation of harm
~ на возмещение убытков (~ na
vozmeshchénie ubýtkov) right to
compensation of losses
~ на возражение (~ na
vozrazhénie) right to object
~ на вывешивание флага (~ na
vyveshivánie flága) flagging
right
~ на въезд (~ na v"ezd) right of
entry
~ на дивиденд (~ na dividénd)
right to dividend

~ на забастовку (~ na zabastóvku) right to strike
~ на расторжение договора (~ na rastorzhénie dogovóra) right of rescission of contract
~ на реституцию (~ na restitútsiiu) right to restitution
~ на самооборону (~ na samooborónu) right of self-defense
~ на самоопределение (~ na samoopredelénie) right of self-determination
~ на судебную защиту (~ na sudébnuiu zashchítu) right to an attorney
~ пастбища (~ pástbishcha) pasturage right
~/а перешедшие по наследству (~/á pereshédshie po naslédstvu) rights passing by inheritance
~ расторжения (~ rastorzhéniia) right of rescission
~ старшинства (~ starshinstvá) right of seniority
~ стоянки на якоре (~ stoiánki na iákore) anchorage right
~/а человека (~/á chelovéka) rights of man
Правовед (pravovéd) m. jurist
Правоведение (pravovédenie) n. science of law
  сравнительное ~ (sravnítel'noe ~) study of comparative law
Правовым средством (pravovým srédstvom) adv. by legal means
Правовой (pravovói) adj. lawful, legal
Правомерный (pravomérnyi) adj. fair, just
Правомочие (pravomóchie) n. competence {legal, e.g. to contract}
Правомочный (pravomóchnyi) adj. competent
Правонарушение (pravonarushénie) n. infringement, offense
  гражданское ~ (grahdánskoe ~) civil offense
  международное ~ (mezhdunaródnoe ~) international infringement
  совершить ~ (sovershít' ~) to commit an offense
  ~ на несовершеннолетних (~ na nesovershennolétnikh) offense against minors

Правонарушитель (pravonarushítel') m. offender
  невменяемый ~ (nevmeniáemyi ~) mentally incompetent offender
  несовершеннолетний ~ (nesovershennolétnii ~) juvenile offender
Правоотношения (pravootnoshéniia) pl. legal relations
Правопорядок (pravoporiádok) m. law and order
  внутригосударственный ~ (vnutrigosudárstvennyi ~) intergovernmental ~
  международный ~ (mezhdunaródnyi ~) international ~
Правопреемник (pravopreémnik) m. assignee
Правопреемство (pravopreémstvo) n. assignment
  общее ~ (óbshchee ~) general ~
Правопритязание (pravopritiazánie) n. legal claim
Правоспособность (pravosposóbnost') f. legal capacity
  административная ~ (administratívnaia ~) administrative standing
  договорная ~ (dogovórnaia ~) contractual standing
  ~ иностранцев (~ inostrántsev) ~ of foreigners
  ~ искать и отвечать на суде (~ iskát' i otvechát' na sudé) standing to prosecute and defend in court
  ~ искать на суде (~ iskát' na sudé) standing to sue
Правосудие (pravosúdie) n. justice
  международное ~ (mezhdunaródnoe ~) international ~
  отправлять ~ (otpravliát' ~) to administer the law
  уголовное ~ (ugolóvnoe ~) criminal ~
  ~ по уголовным делам (~ po ugolóvnym delám) administration of criminal justice
Практика (práktika) f. practice
  адвокатская ~ (advokátskaia ~) of law
  административная ~ (administratívnaia ~) administrative ~
  арбитражная ~ (arbitrázhnaia ~) arbitration ~

банковская ~ (bánkovskaia ~)
banking ~
дипломатическая ~
(diplomatícheskaia ~) diplomatic
~
дискриминационная ~
(diskriminatsiónnaia ~)
discriminatory ~
законодательная ~
(zakonodátel'naia ~) legislative
~
запрещённая ~ (zapreshchiónnaia
~) prohibited ~
коммерческая ~ (kommércheskaia
~) commercial ~
консульская ~ (kónsul'skaia ~)
consular ~
международная ~ (mezhdunaródnaia
~) international ~
международная судебная ~
(mezhdunaródnaia sudébnaia ~)
international legal ~
нотариальная ~ (notariál'naia ~)
notarial ~
торговая ~ (torgóvaia ~) trade ~
юридическая ~ (iuridícheskaia ~)
jurisprudencial ~
~ адвокатуры (~ advokatúry) ~ of
law
Преамбула (preámbula) f. preamble
Пребывание (prebyvánie) n.
residence, stay
постоянное ~ (postoiánnoe ~)
permanent residence
Превентивный (preventívnyi) adj.
preventive
Превышать (prevyshát') v. to exceed
Превышение (prevyshénie) n.
exceeding, excess
~ банковского кредита (~
bánkovskogo kredíta) overdraft
of bank credit
~ бюджета (~ biudzhéta)
exceeding the budget
~ власти (~ vlásti) exceeding
one's authority
~ платёжного баланса (~
platiózhnogo balánsa) exceeding
the balance of payments
~ полномочий (~ polnomóchii)
exceeding one's commission
~ пределов необходимой обороны
(~ predélov neobkhodímoi
oboróny) exceeding limits of
necessary defense
~ пределов самозащиты (~
predélov samozashchíty)

exceeding the limits of self-
defense
~ предложения (~ predlozhéniia)
exceeding the offer
~ спроса (~ sprósa) exceeding
demand
Предание суду (predánie sudú) n.
bringing to court
Предатель (predátel') m. traitor
Предательство (predátel'stvo) n.
betrayal, treachery
Предварительный (predvarítel'nyi)
adj. preliminary
Предвосхищение (predvoskhishchénie)
n. anticipation
Предел (predél) m. limit, margin
высший ~ наказания (výsshii ~
nakazániia) most severe
punishment
максимальный ~ (maksimál'nyi ~)
maximum limit
минимальный ~ (minimál'nyi ~)
minimal limit
нижний ~ (nízhnii ~) lower limit
низший ~ наказания (nízshii ~
nakazániia) most lenient
punishment
территориальный ~
(territoriál'nyi ~) territorial
limit
~ веса (~ vésa) weight limit
~ кредита (~ kredíta) credit
limit
~ ответственности (~
otvétstvennosti) limit of
liability
~ правомочия (~ pravomóchiia)
limit of competence
~ территориальных вод (~
territoriál'nykh vod) limit of
territorial waters
~ территории (~ territórii)
territorial limit
Предельный (predél'nyi) adj. limit
Предлагать (predlagát') v. to
offer, to propose, to suggest
Предложение (predlozhénie) n. bid,
offer, proposal, quote, suggestion
комплексное ~ (kómpleksnoe ~)
package proposal
компромиссное ~ (kompromíssnoe
~) compromise proposal
конкретное ~ (konkrétnoe ~)
concrete proposal
отклонить ~ (otklonít' ~) to
reject an offer

реальное ~ (reál'noe ~)
practical proposition
самое выгодное ~ (sámoe výgodnoe
~) highest bid
совокупное ~ (sovokúpnoe ~)
aggregate offer
условное ~ (uslóvnoe ~)
conditional offer
~ вступить в договор (~ vstupít'
v dogovór) offer to contract
~ конкуренции (~ konkuréntsii)
tender for competitive bids
~ кредита (~ kredíta) offer of
credit
~ на рынке (~ na rýnke) supply
on the market
~ товаров (~ továrov) supply of
goods
~ труда (~ trudá) supply of
labor
Предмет (predmét) m. article,
commodity, item, subject matter
законный ~ (zakónnyi ~) legal
subject
запатентованный ~
(zapatentóvannyi ~) patented
subject
контрабандный ~ (kontrabándnyi
~) contraband item
реквизированный ~
(rekvizíróvannyi ~)
requisitioned item
хрупкий ~ (khrúpkii ~) fragile
item
экспонируемый ~ (eksponíruemyi
~) exhibited item
~ договора (~ dogovóra) subject
matter of a contract
~ ипотеки (~ ipotéki)
hypothecated subject matter
~ иска (~ íska) cause of action
~ контрабанды (~ kontrabandy)
item of contraband
~/ы обычной домашней обстановки
и обихода (~/y obýchnoi do-
máshnei obstanóvki i obikhóda)
housewares
~ патента (~ paténta) subject of
a patent
~/ы первой необходимости (~/y
pérvoi neobkhodímosti) basic
necessities
~/ы потребления (~/y
potrebléniia) items of
consumption
~ разногласия (~ raznoglásiia)
point of contention

~ роскоши (~ róskoshi) luxury
item
~ спора (~ spóra) subject matter
of a dispute
~ экспорта (~ éksporta) article
of export
Предназначать (prednaznachát') v.
to designate, to earmark
Предназначение (prednaznachénie) n.
earmarking
Преднамеренно (prednamérenno) adv.
deliberately
Преднамеренность (prednamérennost')
f. premeditation
Преднамеренный (prednamérennyi)
adj. premeditated
Пред/ок (préd/ok) m. ancestor
~/ки (~/ki) ancestors,
forefathers
Предопределять (predopredeliát') v.
to predetermine
Предоставление (predostavlénie) n.
allocation, granting
~ гражданства (~ grazhdánstva)
granting of citizenship
~ жилой площади (~ zhilói
plóshchadi) provision of housing
~ займа (~ záima) granting a
loan
~ концессии (~ kontséssii)
granting a concession
~ кредита (~ kredíta) providing
a credit
~ кредита под залог (~ kredíta
pod zalóg) providing a credit
under pledge
~ кредита под залог ценных бумаг
(~ kredíta pod zalóg tsénnykh
bumág) providing a credit under
pledge of securities
~ лицензии (~ litsénzii)
granting a license
~ независимости (~
nezavísimosti) granting
independence
~ ноу-хау (~ nóu-kháu) providing
know-how
~ овердрафта (~ overdráfta)
providing overdraft facilities
~ приоритета (~ prioritéta)
granting priority
~ скидки (~ skídki) granting a
discount
~ убежища (~ ubézhishcha)
granting of asylum
~ услуг (~ uslúg) provision of
services

Предоставлять (predostavliát') v. to grant
   безвозмездно ~ (bezvozmézdno ~) to provide at no cost
Предостерегать (predosteregát') v. to precaution against, to warn against
Предостережение (predosterezhénie) n. precaution
Предотвратить (predotvratít') v. to avert, to prevent
Предотвращение (predotvrashchénie) n. prevention
   ~ внезапного нападения (~ vnezápnogo napadéniia) prevention of surprise attack
   ~ конфликтов (~ konflíktov) prevention of conflicts
   ~ несчастных случаев (~ neschástnykh slúchaev) prevention of accidents
   ~ преступлений (~ prestuplénii) prevention of crime
Предписание (predpisánie) n. injunction, order
   нормативное ~ (normatívnoe ~) normative instruction
   прямое ~ (priamóe ~) direct order
   ~ суда (~ sudá) court order
Предписывать (predpísyvat') v. to enjoin, to order
Предполагать (predpolagát') v. to contemplate, to intend
Предположение (predpolozhénie) n. intention, presumption
   абсолютное законное ~ (absoliútnoe zakónnoe ~) absolute legal presumption
   законодательное ~ (zakonodátel'noe ~) legislative intent
   законное ~ (zakónnoe ~) legal presumption
   законное ~ вины (zakónnoe ~ viný) legal presumption of guilt
Предпосылка (predposýlka) f. prerequisite
   юридическая ~ (iuridícheskaia ~) juridical prerequisite
Предпочитать (predpochitát') v. to prefer
Предпочтение (predpochténie) n. preference
Предпочтительный (predpochtítel'nyi) adj. preferable

Предприниматель (predprinimátel') m. entrepreneur
   сельскохозяйственный ~ (sel'skokhoziáistvennyi ~) agricultural ~
   частный ~ (chástnyi ~) private ~
Предпринимательство (predprinimátel'stvo) n. business enterprise
   свободное ~ (svobódnoe ~) free enterprise
   частное ~ (chástnoe ~) private enterprise
Предприятие (predpriiátie) n. enterprise
   воздушно-транспортное ~ (vozdúshno-tránsportnoe ~) air transport ~
   горное ~ (górnoe ~) mining ~
   государственное ~ (gosudárstvennoe ~) state ~
   дочернее ~ (dochérnee ~) branch ~
   единоличное ~ (edinolíchnoe ~) sole proprietorship
   коммерческое ~ (kommércheskoe ~) commercial ~
   конкурирующее ~ (konkuríruiushchee ~) competing ~
   концессионное ~ (kontsessiónnoe ~) concessionaire
   кооперативное ~ (kooperatívnoe ~) cooperative ~
   кустарническое ~ (kustárnicheskoe ~) cottage ~
   национализированное ~ (natsionalizírovannoe ~) nationalized ~
   национальное ~ (natsionál'noe ~) national ~
   нерентабельное ~ (nerentábel'noe ~) unprofitable ~
   оптовое ~ (optóvoe ~) wholesaler ~
   подсобное ~ (podsóbnoe ~) subsidiary ~
   промышленное ~ (promýshlennoe ~) industrial ~
   розничное ~ (róznichnoe ~) retail ~
   сельскохозяйственное ~ (sel'skokhoziáistvennoe ~) agricultural ~
   смешанное ~ (sméshannoe ~) mixed ~
   совместное ~ (sovméstnoe ~) joint venture

среднее ~ (srédnee ~) medium-sized ~
строительное ~ (stroítel'noe ~) construction ~
судоходное ~ (sudokhódnoe ~) shipping ~
торговое ~ (torgóvoe ~) trading ~
торгово-промышленное ~ (torgóvo-promýshlennoe ~) trading and manufacturing ~
транспортное ~ (tránsportnoe ~) transport ~
убыточное ~ (ubýtochnoe ~) unprofitable ~
хозрасчётное ~ (khozraschiótnoe ~) self-supporting ~
частное ~ (chástnoe ~) private ~
~ -покупатель (~ pokupátel') buyer
~ -поставщик (~ postavshchík) supplier

Предрешать (predreshát') v. to predetermine

Председатель (predsedátel') m. chairman, chairperson
временный ~ (vrémennyi ~) ~ pro tem
постоянный ~ (postoiánnyi ~) permanent ~
почётный ~ (pochiótnyi ~) honorable ~

Председательство (predsedátel'stvo) n. chairmanship, presidency

Председательствовать (predsedátel'stvovat') v. to chair

Председательствующий (predsedátel'stvuiushchii) adj. chairman, chairperson [also used as m.adj.noun]

Представитель (predstavítel') m. representative
аккредитованный ~ (akkreditóvannyi ~) accredited ~
генеральный ~ (generál'nyi ~) general agent
дипломатический ~ (diplomatícheskii ~) diplomatic ~
договорный ~ (dogovórnyi ~) contractual ~
законный ~ (zakónnyi ~) legal ~
исключительный ~ (iskliuchítel'nyi ~) exclusive ~
консульский ~ (kónsul'skii ~) consular ~

народный ~ (naródnyi ~) people's ~
полномочный ~ {полпред} (polnomóchnyi ~ {polpréd}) ambassador plenipotentiary
постоянный ~ (postoiánnyi ~) permanent ~
специальный ~ (spetsiál'nyi ~) special ~
торговый ~ (torgóvyi ~) trade ~
юридический ~ (iuridícheskii ~) juridical ~

Представительный (predstavítel'nyi) adj. representative

Представительство (predstavítel'stvo) n. representation, representative office
временное ~ (vrémennoe ~) temporary representation
дипломатическое ~ (diplomatícheskoe ~) diplomatic representation
договорное ~ (dogovórnoe ~) contractual representation
заграничное ~ (zagraníchnoe ~) foreign representation
законное ~ (zakónnoe ~) legal representation
исключительное ~ (iskliuchítel'noe ~) exclusive representation
консульское ~ (kónsul'skoe ~) consular representation
международное ~ (mezhdunaródnoe ~) international representation
постоянное ~ (postoiánnoe ~) permanent representation
постоянное дипломатическое ~ (postoiánnoe diplomatícheskoe ~) permanent diplomatic representation
пропорциональное ~ (proportsionál'noe ~) proportional representation

Представлени/е (predstavléni/e) n. presentation, submission, surrender
оплачиваемый по ~/ю (oplachiváemyi po ~/iu) payable upon presentation
~ доказательств (~ dokazátel'stv) production of proof
~ документов (~ dokuméntov) production of documents

Представленный (predstávlennyi) adj. presented, produced, submitted

Представлять (predstavliát') v. to submit, to present

Предупредительный (predupredítel'nyi) adj. preventative

Предупреждать (preduprezhdát') v. to caution, to warn

Предупреждени/е (preduprezhdéni/e) n. warning
    получить выговор с ~/ем (poluchít' výgovor s ~/em) to be let off with a warning

Предшественник (predshéstvennik) m. predecessor
    ~ по праву (~ po pravu) predecessor in title

Предъявитель (pred"iavítel') m. bearer
    на ~/я (na ~/ia) to bearer
    ~ векселя (~ vékselia) bearer of a bill
    ~ чека (~ chéka) payee of a check

Предъявление (pred"iavlénie) n. presentation, submission, sight
    оплачиваемый по ~/ю (oplachiváemyi po ~/iu) payable on sight
    ~ встречного иска (~ vstréchnogo íska) filing of a counter suit
    ~ для акцепта (~ dlia aktsépta) presentation for acceptance
    ~ на инкассо (~ na inkásso) presentation for payment
    ~ иска (~ íska) filing of a suit
    ~ обвинения (~ obvinéniia) bringing of an indictment
    ~ требования (~ trébovaniia) submission of a demand
    ~ чека (~ chéka) presentation of a check

Преемник (preémnik) m. successor
    законный ~ (zakónnyi ~) legal ~

Преемственность (preémstvennost') f. succession
    ~ сервитута (~ servitúta) continuity of a servitude

Преемство (preémstvo) n. succession

Президент (prezidént) m. president
    почётный ~ (pochiótnyi ~) honorable ~
    ~ правительства (~ pravítel'stva) ~ of the government
    ~ республики (~ respúbliki) ~ of the republic

Президиум (prezídium) m. presidium

почётный ~ (pochiótnyi ~) honorable ~

Презумпци/я (prezúmptsi/ia) f. presumption
    доказательственная ~ (dokazátel'stvennaia ~) evidentiary ~
    законная ~ (zakónnaia ~) legal ~
    неопровержимая ~ (neoproverzhímaia ~) irrefutable ~
    опровержимая ~ (oproverzhimaia ~) rebuttable ~
    установить ~/ю (ustanovít' ~/iu) to establish a ~

Презюмировать (preziumírovat') v. to presume

Преимущество (preimúshchestvo) n. advantage, preference, privilege
    правовое ~ (pravovóe ~) legal preference

Прейскурант (preiskuránt) m. price list

Прекращение (prekrashchénie) n. cessation, stoppage, termination
    временное ~ (vrémennoe ~) suspension
    ~ аренды (~ aréndy) withholding of rent
    ~ давности (~ dávnosti) extinguishment of a prescriptive easement
    ~ действия (~ déistviia) discontinuance of activity
    ~ дела (~ déla) dismissal of a case
    ~ доверенности (~ dovérennosti) termination of a power of attorney
    ~ договора (~ dogovóra) termination of a contract
    ~ патента (~ paténta) lapse of a patent
    ~ поручения (~ poruchéniia) termination of a commission

Прелюбодейный (preliubodéinyi) adj. adulterous

Прелюбодеяние (preliubodéianie) n. adultery

Премиальные (premiál'nye) adj. bonus [also used as pl.adj.noun]

Премия (prémiia) f. bonus, bounty, premium
    вывозная ~ (vyvoznáia ~) export bounty

единовременная ~
(edinovrémennaia ~) lumpsum
bonus
ежегодная ~ (ezhegódnaia ~)
annual bonus
импортная ~ (ímportnaia ~)
import bonus
минимальная ~ (minimál'naia ~)
minimum premium
новогодняя ~ (novogódniaia ~)
New Year's bonus
поощрительная ~
(pooshchrítel'naia ~) incentive
bonus
предварительная ~
(predvarítel'naia ~) call
premium
чистая ~ (chístaia ~) net bonus
эмиссионная ~ (emissiónnaia ~)
share premium
~ за качество (~ za káchestvo)
bonus for quality
~ за риск (~ za risk) risk
premium
Премьер-министр (prem'ér-minístr)
m. prime minister
Пренебрежение (prenebrezhénie) *n.*
negligence, negligent behavior
~ своими обязанностями (~ svoími
obiázannostiami) dereliction of
duty
Прения (préniia) *f.* proceedings,
speech
парламентские ~ (parlámentskie
~) parliamentary debate
судебные ~ (sudébnye ~)
pleadings
Преобладание (preobladánie) *n.*
predominance
Преобладающий (preobladáiushchii)
adj. predominant
Преобразование (preobrazovánie) *n.*
reform, reorganization
аграрное ~ (agrárnoe ~) agrarian
reform
земельное ~ (zemél'noe ~) land
reform
экономическое ~ (ekonomícheskoe
~) economic reform
~ общества (~ óbshchestva)
reorganization of society
Преобразователь (preobrazovátel')
m. reformer
Преобразовывать (preobrazóvyvat')
v. to reform, to reorganize
Препровождать (preprovozhdát') *v.*
to dispatch

Препятствие (prepiátstvie) *n.*
hindrance, impediment, obstacle
запретительное ~ (zapretítel'noe
~) forbidding obstacle
Препятствовать (prepiátstvovat') *v.*
to hinder, to impede
Прерогатива (prerogatíva) *f.*
prerogative
Преследование (preslédovanie) *n.*
proceeding, prosecution
административное ~
(administratívnoe ~)
administrative proceeding
возбудить уголовное ~ (vozbudít'
ugolóvnoe ~) to file criminal
charges
дисциплинарное ~
(distsiplinárnoe ~) disciplinary
proceeding
судебное ~ (sudébnoe ~)
prosecution
уголовное ~ (ugolóvnoe ~)
criminal prosecution
Преследовать (preslédovat') *v.* to
prosecute
Пресловутый (preslovútyi) *adj.*
notorious
Пресса (préssa) *f.* the press
{media}
Пресс-атташе (préss-attashé) *n.*
press attaché
Пресс-конференция (préss-
konferéntsiia) *f.* press conference
Пресс-референт (préss-referént) *m.*
press center
Престол (prestól) *m.* throne
вступить на ~ (vstupít' na ~) to
mount the throne
отречься от ~/а (otréch'sia ot
~/a) to abdicate the throne
свергнуть с ~/а (svérgnut' s
~/a) to dethrone
Престол святейший (préstol
sviatéishii) *m.* heavenly throne
Престолонаследие (prestolonaslédie)
n. succession to the throne
Престолонаследник
(prestolonaslédnik) *m.* heir to the
throne
Преступлени/е (prestuplénie) *n.*
crime, felony offense
военное ~ (voénnoe ~) war crime
государственное ~
(gosudárstvennoe ~) treason
малозначительное ~
(maloznachítel'noe ~)
insignificant crime

материальное ~ (materiál'noe ~)
material offense
первое ~ (pérvoe ~) first
offense
повторное ~ (povtórnoe ~)
repeated offense
половое ~ (polovóe ~) sexual
offense
продолжаемое ~ (prodolzháemoe ~)
continuing offense
состав ~/я (sostáv ~/ia) corpus
delecti
тяжкое ~ (tiázhkoe ~) serious
offense
уголовное ~ (ugolóvnoe ~)
criminal offense
~ небрежности (~ nebrézhnosti)
crime of negligence
~ против избирательной системы
(~ prótiv izbirátel'noi sistémy)
electoral offense
~ против имущества (~ prótiv
imúshchestva) crime against
property
~ против личной свободы (~
prótiv líchnoi svobódy) crime
against personal freedom
~ против личной собственности (~
prótiv líchnoi sóbstvennosti)
crime against personal property
~ против общественной
нравственности (~ prótiv
obshchéstvennoi nrávstvennosti)
offense against public morals
~ по службе (~ po slúzhbe)
malfeasance
~ совершённое в состоянии
опьянения (~ sovershiónnoe v
sostoiánii op'ianéniia) offense
committed in a state of
intoxication
~ характеризующееся применением
насилия (~ kharakterizúiu-
shcheesia primenéniem nasíliia)
offense characterized by the use
of violence
Преступник (prestúpnik) m. criminal
военный ~ (voénnyi ~) war ~
профессиональный ~
(professionál'nyi ~) career ~
уголовный ~ (ugolóvnyi ~) felon
Преступность (prestupnost') f.
criminality
детская ~ (détskaia ~) juvenile
delinquency

профессиональная ~
(professionál'naia ~) career
criminality
Преступный (prestúpnyi) adj.
criminal
Пресыщенность рынка
(presýshchennost' rýnka) f. glut of
the market
Претензи/я (preténzi/ia) f. claim
встречная ~ (vstréchnaia ~)
counter claim
денежная ~ (dénezhnaia ~)
monetary claim
исковая ~ (ískovaia ~) lawsuit
предъявить ~/ю (pred"iávit'
~/iu) to sue, to file suit
финансовая ~ (finánsovaia ~)
financial claim
~ на возмещение убытков (~ na
vozmeshchénie ubýtkov) suit for
compensation of damages
Префект (prefékt) m. prefect
Префектура (prefektúra) f.
prefecture
Преференциальный
(preferéntsiál'nyi) adj.
preferential
Преференци/я (preferentsi/ia) f.
preferential treatment
взаимные ~/и (vzaímnye ~/i)
mutual preferences
имперские ~/и (impérskie ~/i)
imperial preferences
односторонняя ~ (odnostorónniaia
~) unilateral preference
таможенные ~/и (tamózhennye ~/i)
customs preferences
Прецедент (pretsedént) m. precedent
судебный ~ (sudébnyi ~) legal
{case} precedent
Прибавка к заработной плате
(pribávka k zárabotnoi pláte) f.
raise in pay
Прибыль (príbyl') f. profit
балансовая ~ (balánsovaia ~)
balance sheet profit
валовая ~ (valováia ~) gross
profit
вероятная ~ (veroiátnaia ~)
anticipated ~
монопольная ~ (monopól'naia ~)
monopoly ~
непредвидимая ~ (nepredvídimaia
~) unexpected ~
нераспределённая ~
(neraspredeliónnaia ~)
undistributed ~

облагаемая ~ (oblagáemaia ~) taxable ~

предпринимательская ~ (predprinimátel'skaia ~) entrepreneurial ~

распределённая ~ (raspredeliónnaia ~) distributed ~

распределяемая ~ (raspredeliáemaia ~) distributable ~

реализованная ~ (realizóvannaia ~) realized ~

реализовать ~ (realizovát' ~) to realize ~

ростовщическая ~ (rostovshchícheskaia ~) usurious ~

случайная ~ (slucháinaia ~) windfall ~

спекулятивная ~ (spekuliatívnaia ~) speculative ~

торговая ~ (torgóvaia ~) trade ~

фактическая ~ (faktícheskaia ~) actual ~

фиктивная ~ (fiktívnaia ~) false ~

чистая ~ (chístaia ~) net ~

Прибыльность (príbyl'nost') f. profitability

Прибыльный (príbyl'nyi) adj. profitable

Привилегия (privilégiia) f. benefit, priority, privilege

дипломатическая ~ (diplomatícheskaia ~) diplomatic privilege

консульская ~ (kónsul'skaia ~) consular privilege

королевская ~ (korolévskaia ~) royal privilege

Привлечение (privlechénie) n. application, attraction, utilization

~ к гражданской ответственности (~ k grahdánskoi otvétstvennosti) subjection to civil liability

~ к дисциплинарной ответственности (~ k distsiplinárnoi otvétstvennosti) subjection to disciplinary action

~ к ответственности (~ k otvétstvennosti) subjection to liability

~ покупателей (~ pokupátelei) attraction of buyers

~ сбережений (~ sberezhénii) attraction of savings

~ средств (~ sredstv) attraction of resources

Привлекать (privlekát') v. [perfective: привлечь] to attact, to draw, to recruit

~ к судебной ответственности (~ k sudébnoi otvétstvennosti) to make {legally} answerable

~ к суду (~ k sudú) to bring to trial

~ к участию в деле (~ k uchástiiu v déle) to call to account

~ к уголовной ответственности (~ k ugolóvnoi otvétstvennosti) to institute criminal proceedings

Привод (privód) m. subpoena, taking into custody

Привычка (privýchka) f. custom, practice

правовая ~ (pravováia ~) legal custom

Приглашение (priglashénie) m. invitation, offer

~ на работу (~ na rabótu) offer of employment

Приговор (prigovór) m. sentence, verdict

вынести ~ (výnesti ~) to pass sentence

заочный ~ (zaóchnyi ~) judgment by default

неправосудный ~ (nepravosúdnyi ~) unjust verdict

общественный ~ (obshchéstvennyi ~) public verdict

оправдательный ~ (opravdátel'nyi ~) acquittal

оставлять ~ (ostavliát' ~) to confirm a sentence

отменять ~ (otmeniát' ~) to reverse a sentence

отменять ~ в апелляционной инстанции (otmeniát' ~ v appeliatsiónnoi instántsii) to reverse a sentence on appeal

приводить ~ в исполнение (privodít' ~ v ispolnénie) to carry out a sentence

смертный ~ (smértnyi ~) death sentence

судебный ~ (sudébnyi ~) judgment of the court

уголовный ~ (ugolóvnyi ~)
criminal sentence
условный ~ (uslóvnyi ~)
suspended sentence
Приговорить (prigovorít') v. to
condemn, to sentence
Пригодность к работе (prigódnost' k
rabóte) f. applicability, fitness,
suitability
Пригород (prígorod) m. suburb
Придани/е (pridáni/e) n. imparting
для ~/я законной силы (dlia ~/ia
zakónnoi síly) for the
enforcement of
Приданое (pridánoe) n. dowry,
trousseau
Придаток (pridátok) m. adjunct,
appendage
Приём (priióm) m. employment,
receipt, reception
~ в гражданство (~ v
grazhdánstvo) granting of
citizenship
~ в ООН (~ v oon) acceptance
into the U.N.
~ в члены (~ v chlény)
admittance to membership
~ на работу (~ na rabótu) hiring
{individual to a job}
~ на хранение (~ na khranénie)
acceptance for safe deposit
Приёмка (priiómka) f. acceptance
Приемлемость (priémlemost') f.
acceptability, admissibility
Приёмлемый (priémlemyi) adj.
acceptable, admissible
Приёмщик (priiómshchik) m.
inspector {of goods, etc.}
Приёмыш (priiómysh) m. adopted
child
Приз (priz) m. prize
Призвание (prizvánie) n. calling,
vocation
~ к порядку (~ k poriádku)
calling to order
Признавать (priznavát') v. to
admit, to plead, to recognize
не ~ виновным (ne ~ vinóvnym) to
find not guilty
~ действительным (~
deistvítel'nym) to validate
~ недействительным (~
nedeistvítel'nym) to nullify
~ себя не виновным (~ sebiá ne
vinóvnym) to plead not guilty
Признак (príznak) m. feature,
identification, sign

идентификационный ~
(identifikatsiónnyi ~)
identifying feature
Признание (priznánie) n.
acknowledgment, admission,
recognition
взаимное ~ (vzaímnoe ~) mutual
acknowledgment
внесудебное ~ (vnesudébnoe ~)
extralegal admission
дипломатическое ~
(diplomatícheskoe ~) diplomatic
recognition
добровольное ~ (dobrovól'noe ~)
voluntary admission
квалификационное ~
(kvalifikatsiónnoe ~) qualified
admission
коллективное ~ (kollektívnoe ~)
collective recognition
международное ~ (mezhdunaródnoe
~) international recognition
международное правовое ~
(mezhdunaródnoe pravovóe ~)
international legal recognition
одностороннее ~ (odnostorónnee
~) unilateral recognition
посмертное ~ (posmértnoe ~)
death-bed acknowledgment
правовое ~ (pravovóe ~) legal
recognition
предварительное ~
(predvarítel'noe ~) preliminary
recognition
судебное ~ (sudébnoe ~)
recognition by the court
~ аннексии (~ annéksii)
acknowledgment of annexation
~ брака недействительным (~
bráka nedeistvítel'nym)
annulment of a marriage
~ виновности (~ vinóvnosti)
admission of guilt
~ внебрачного ребёнка (~
vnebráchnogo rebiónka)
acknowledgment of illegitimate
child
~ границы (~ granítsy)
recognition of border
~ де-факто (~ dé-fákto) de facto
recognition
~ де-юре (~ dé-iúre) de jure
recognition
~ долга (~ dólga) acknowledgment
of a debt

~ законных прав (~ zakónnykh prav) recognition of lawful rights
~ материнства (~ materínstva) acknowledgment of maternity
~ на авторство (~ na ávtorstvo) recognition of authorship
~ недействительности (~ nedeistvítel'nosti) nullification
~ недействительности регистрации (~ nedeistvítel'nosti registrátsii) nullification of registration
~ независимости (~ nezavísimosti) acknowledgment of independence, recognition of independence
~ ответственности (~ otvétstvennosti) admission of liability
~ отцовства (~ ottsóvstva) acknowledgment of paternity
~ подписи (~ pódpisi) acknowledgment of signature
~ суверенитета (~ suverenitéta) recognition of sovereignty
~ судебных решений (~ sudébnykh reshénii) recognition of legal precedents
~ с оговоркой (~ s ogovórkoi) acknowledgment with reserve

Призыв (prizýv) m. appeal, call, conscription
~ в армию (~ v ármiiu) conscription into the army

Приказ (prikáz) m. order
по его приказу (po egó prikázu) on his ~
издать ~ о конфискации (izdát' ~ o konfiskátsii) to issue an ~ to confiscate
исполнительный ~ (ispolnítel'nyi ~) executive ~
письменный ~ (pís'mennyi ~) written ~
судебный ~ (sudébnyi ~) writ
~ по войскам (~ po voiskám) ~ of the day
~ суда (~ súda) ~ of the court

Приказание (prikazánie) n. command, injunction
Приказчик (prikázchik) m. bailiff
Приказывать (prikázyvat') v. to command, to enjoin, to order
Прикрепление (prikreplénie) n. attachment, registration

Прилив капитала (prilív kapitála) m. inflow of capital
Приложение (prilozhénie) n. annex, appendix, enclosure
~ визы (~ vízy) annex to a visa
~ к договору (~ k dogovóru) annex to a contract
~ печати (~ pecháti) affixing of a seal
~ к протоколу (~ k protokólu) annex of minutes of a meeting

Примат (primát) m. primacy
~ внутреннего права (~ vnútrennego práva) primacy of domestic law
~ международного права (~ mezhdunaródnogo práva) primacy of international law

Применение (primenénie) n. application, employment, use
законное ~ (zakónnoe ~) legal application
коммерческое ~ (kommércheskoe ~) commercial application
конечное ~ (konéchnoe ~) end use
незаконное ~ товарного знака (nezakónnoe ~ továrnogo znáka) illegal use of trademark
противоправное ~ (protivoprávnoe ~) illegal use
территориальное ~ (territoriál'noe ~) territorial application
~ законодательства (~ zakonodátel'stva) application of legislation
~ изобретения (~ izobreténiia) application of an invention
~ рабочей силы (~ rabóchei síly) employment of the work force
~ санкции (~ sánktsii) application of sanctions
~ силы (~ síly) use of force
~ смертной казни (~ smértnoi kázni) employment of the death penalty
~ товарного знака (~ továrnogo znáka) employment of trademark

Применимость (primenímost') f. applicability
~ исковой давности (~ ískovoi dávnosti) applicability of the statute of limitations

Применимый (primenímyi) adj. applicable, suitable
Применять (primeniát') v. to apply, to employ

Примета (priméta) *f.* mark, sign, token
  дурная ~ (dúrnaia ~) bad omen
  хорошая ~ (khoróshaia ~) good omen
Примиренец (primirénets) *m.* compromiser {usu. pejorative}
Примирение (primirénie) *n.* reconciliation
Примиримый (primirimyi) *adj.* reconcilable
Примирительный (primirítel'nyi) *adj.* conciliatory
Примирять (primiriát') *v.* to reconcile
Принадлежность (prinadlézhnost') *f.* accessory, belonging
  национальная ~ (natsionál'naia ~) nationality
Принимать (prinimát') *v.* to accept, to adopt
  ~ присягу (~ prisiágu) to take an oath
Приносить (prinosít') *v.* to bear, to bring, to yield
Принудительный (prinudítel'nyi) *adj.* coercive, compulsory
Принуждать (prinuzhdát') *v.* to coerce, to compel
Принуждени/е (prinuzhdéni/e) *n.* coercion, compulsion
  административное ~ (administratívnoe ~) administrative compulsion
  государственное ~ (gosudárstvennoe ~) governmental compulsion
  индивидуальное ~ (individuál'noe ~) individual coercion
  коллективное ~ (kollektívnoe ~) collective coercion
  моральное ~ (morál'noe ~) moral coercion
  по ~/ю (po ~/iu) under duress
  прямое ~ (priamóe ~) direct coercion
  психическое ~ (psikhícheskoe ~) psychological coercion
  физическое ~ (fizícheskoe ~) physical coercion
  экономическое ~ (ekonomícheskoe ~) economic coercion
Принцип (príntsip) *m.* principle
  конституционный ~ (konstitutsiónnyi ~) constitutional ~

  национально-территориальный ~ (natsionál'no-territoriál'nyi ~) national-territorial ~
  общепризнанные ~/ы (obshchepríznannye ~/y) generally recognized ~s
  общие ~/ы права (óbshchie ~/y práva) general ~s of law
  основной ~ (osnovnói ~) basic ~
  территориальный ~ (territoriál'nyi ~) territorial ~
  ~ взаимности (~ vzaímnosti) ~ of mutuality
Принятие (priniátie) *n.* acceptance, adoption
  безоговорочное ~ (bezogovórochnoe ~) unconditional acceptance
  ~ векселя (~ vékselia) acceptance of a bill
  ~ в гражданство (~ v grazhdánstvo) naturalization
  ~ закона (~ zakóna) adoption of a law
  ~ регламента (~ reglaménta) promulgation of a regulation
  ~ риска (~ ríska) acceptance of risk
  ~ под условием (~ pod uslóviem) acceptance under condition
  ~ на хранение товарным складом (~ na khranénie továrnym skládom) warehouse acceptance
  ~ чека (~ chéka) acceptance of a check
Приобретательн/ый (priobretátel'nyi) *adj.* adverse, prescriptive
  ~/ая давность (~/aia dávnost') adverse possession, prescription, prescriptive easement
Приобретать (priobretát') *v.* to acquire, to obtain, to procure
Приобретение (priobreténie) *n.* acquisition, procurement
  безвозмездное ~ (bezvozmézdnoe ~) unpaid acquisition
  возмездное ~ (vozmézdnoe ~) paid acquisition
  добросовестное ~ (dobrosóvestnoe ~) good faith acquisition
  мнимое ~ (mnímoe ~) sham acquisition

первоначальное ~
(pervonachál'noe ~) original
acquisition
преимущественное ~
(preimúshchestvennoe ~)
advantageous acquisition
совместное ~ (sovméstnoe ~)
joint acquisition
территориальное ~
(territoriál'noe ~) territorial
acquisition
~ гражданства (~ grazhdánstva)
acquisition of citizenship
~ гражданства по браку (~
grazhdánstva po bráku)
acquisition of citizenship by
marriage
~ гражданства по усыновлению (~
grazhdánstva po usynovléniiu)
acquisition of citizenship by
parentage
~ по давности (~ po dávnosti)
acquisition by prescription
~ имущества (~ imúshchestva)
acquisition of property
~ права (~ práva) acquisition of
right
~ права собственности (~ práva
sóbstvennosti) acquisition of
right of property
~ супружеской общности (~
suprúzheskoi óbshchnosti)
acquisition of community
property {by marriage}
Приоритет (prioritét) m. priority
авторский ~ (ávtorskii ~) ~ of
authorship
высокий ~ (vysókii ~) high ~
государственный ~
(gosudárstvennyi ~) governmental
~
конвенционный ~ (konventsiónnyi
~) convention ~
льготный ~ (l'gótnyi ~)
preferential ~
претендовать на ~ (pretendovát'
na ~) to claim ~
частичный ~ (chastíchnyi ~)
partial ~
~ на изобретение (~ na
izobreténie) ~ of an invention
~ подачи заявки (~ podáchi
zaiávki) ~ of filing
Приостановить (priostanovít') v. to
halt, to suspend

~ исполнение приговора (~
ispolnénie prigovóra) to suspend
a sentence
Приостановка (priostanóvka) f.
halt, suspension
~ военных действий (~ voénnykh
déistvii) suspension of military
activities
~ платежей (~ platezhéi)
suspension of payments
~ работы (~ rabóty) work
stoppage
Припасы (pripásy) pl. stores,
supplies
военные ~ (voénnye ~) munitions
контрабандные съестные ~
(kontrabándnye s"éstnye ~)
smuggled food stocks
Приплод (priplód) m. increase,
issue {livestock}
Приравнивать (prirávnivat') v. to
equate
Приращение (prirashchénie) n.
increase, increment
~ наследственной доли (~
naslédstvennoi dóli) increase in
share of inheritance
Природа (priróda) f. character,
nature
нормативная ~ (normatívnaia ~)
normative character
правовая ~ (pravováia ~) legal
character
юридическая ~ (iuridícheskaia ~)
jurisprudential character
Прирост (priróst) m. gain, growth,
increase
Присваивать (prisváivat') v. to
appropriate, to award, to confer,
to misappropriate
Присвоение (prisvoénie) n.
appropriation, awarding
незаконное ~ (nezakónnoe ~)
misappropriation
~ авторства (~ ávtorstva)
conferment of authorship
~ найденного имущества (~
náidennogo imúshchestva)
appropriation of found property
~ патента (~ paténta) awarding
of a patent
~ чужих денежных средств (~
chuzhíkh dénezhnykh sredstv)
embezzlement
Присвоить (prisvoít') v. [see
присваивать]

Прислуга (prislúga) *f.* crew, maid, servant

Присоединени/е (prisoedinénie) *n.* addition, adhesion, annexation
обязательное ~ (obiazátel'noe ~) adhesion, compulsory annexation
открыто для ~/я (otkrýto dlia ~/ia) open for association
~ к иску (~ k ísku) joinder to a suit
~ конвенции (~ konvéntsii) accession to a convention
~ территории (~ territórii) annexation of territory

Присоединять (prisoediniát') *v.* to add, to annex, to join

Присоединяться (prisoediniát'sia) *v.* o associate with, to join

Приспособление (prisposoblénie) *n.* accommodation, adaptation, contrivance
экономическое ~ (ekonomícheskoe ~) economic adaptation
~ цен (~ tsen) price accommodation

Пристав (prístav) *m.* police-officer {historical}
судебный ~ (sudébnyi ~) bailiff

Пристань (prístan') berth, quay, wharf

Пристрасти/е (pristrásti/e) *n.* partiality, predilection
допрос с ~/ем (doprós s ~/em) interrogation under torture

Пристрастный (pristrástnyi) *adj.* biased, partial

Пристройка (pristróika) *f.* annex, extension

Присуждать (prisuzhdát') *v.* to award a judgment

Присуждение (prisuzhdénie) *n.* award, judgment
~ к возмещению (~ k vozmeshchéniiu) award of damages
~ к смерти (~ k smérti) death sentence
~ к уплате денежной суммы (~ k upláte dénezhnoi súmmy) money judgment

Присяг/а (prisiág/a) *f.* oath
ложная ~ (lózhnaia ~) perjury
под ~/ой (pod ~/oi) under oath
показание под ~/ой (pokazánie pod ~/oi) sworn testimony
привести к ~/е (privestí k ~/e) to administer an oath

принести ~/у (prinestí ~/u) to take an oath
судебная ~ (sudébnaia ~) judicial oath
~ на верность (~ na vérnost') oath of loyalty

Присягать (prisiagát') *v.* to take an oath, to swear

Присяжн/ый (prisiázhn/yi) *adj.* sworn
~ заседатель (~ zasedátel') juror, juryman
~ поверенный (~ povérennyi) barrister

Притеснять (pritesniát') *v.* to oppress

Приток (pritók) *m.* flow, inflow
~ капиталов (~ kapitálov) capital inflow

Притон (pritón) *m.* den, haunt
воровской ~ (vorovskói ~) den of thieves
игорный ~ (igórnyi ~) gambling den

Притязание (pritiazánie) *n.* ambition, claim
дополнительное ~ (dopolnítel'noe ~) supplementary claim
законное ~ (zakónnoe ~) statutory claim
территориальное ~ (territoriál'noe ~) territorial ambitions
~ собственности (~ sóbstvennosti) claim of ownership

Притязать (pritiazát') *v.* to lay a claim to

Прифронтовой (prifrontovói) *adj.* front line

Приход (prikhód) *m.* advent, proceeds, receipts
~ к власти (~ k vlásti) ascension to power
~ иностранной валюты (~ inostránnoi valiúty) foreign exchange receipts

Причал (prichál) *m.* berth, quay, wharf
контейнерный ~ (kontéinernyi ~) container berth

Причина (prichína) *f.* cause, reason
уважительная ~ (uvazhítel'naia ~) good cause

Причинность (prichínnost') *f.* causality

Причитаться (prichitát'sia) *v.* to
be due from, to be owing
Проба (próba) *f.* sample, standard,
trial run
Пробег (probég) *m.* run
 порожний ~ (porózhnii ~) empty
 run
Проблема (probléma) *f.* issue,
problem, question
 правовая ~ (pravováia ~) legal
 issue
Пробный (próbnyi) *adj.*
experimental, trial
Пробовать (próbovat') *v.* to
attempt, to test, to try
Провалить (provalít') *v.* to fail
{transitive}, to reject
Проведение (provedénie) *n.*
conducting, execution
 ~ анализа (~ análiza) carrying
 out an analysis
 ~ следствия (~ slédstviia)
 carrying out investigation
Проверка (provérka) *f.* checkup,
examination, verification
 административная ~
 (administratívnaia ~)
 administrative examination
 выездная ~ (vyezdnáia ~) field
 examination
 окончательная ~ (okonchátel'naia
 ~) final inspection
 плановая ~ (plánovaia ~) routine
 checkup
Проверять (proveriát') *v.* to audit,
to examine, to verify
Провиант (proviánt) *m.* provisions,
victuals
 ~ на судне (~ na súdne)
 provisions on a vessel
Провиниться (provinít'sia) *v.* to
commit an offense
Провинность (provínnost') *f.* fault,
offense
Провинция (províntsiia) *f.*
province, {the provinces}
Провожать (provozhát') *v.* to carry
out, to conduct, to pursue
Проводка (provódka) *f.* entry,
pilotage
 дебетовая ~ (debetóvaia ~) debit
 entry {bookkeeping}
 кредитовая ~ (kredítovaia ~)
 credit entry {bookkeeping}
 лоцманская ~ (lótsmanskaia ~)
 pilotage {service, not fee}

Провоз (provóz) *m.* carriage,
conveyance, transportation
 бесплатный ~ (besplátnyi ~) free
 carriage
 обратный ~ (obrátnyi ~) return
 trip
 речной ~ (rechnói ~) river
 transport
Провозглашать (provozglashát') *v.*
to advance, to proclaim
Провозглашение (provozglashénie) *n.*
declaration, proclamation
 ~ брака (~ bráka) marriage
 announcement
 ~ независимости (~
 nezavísimosti) declaration of
 independence
 ~ состояния войны (~ sostoiániia
 voiný) declaration of war
 ~ суверенитета (~ suverenitéta)
 declaration of sovereignty
Провозоспособность
(provozosposóbnost') *f.* carrying
capacity {railroad}
Провокатор (provokátor) *m.* agent
provocateur, instigator
Провокация (provokátsiia) *f.*
provocation
 военная ~ (voénnaia ~) military
 provocation
Прогноз на ближайшее будущее
(prognóz na blizháishee búdushchee)
m. forecast, projection
Проголосовать (progolosovát') *v.* to
vote
Программа (prográmma) *f.* program,
schedule
 выполнимая ~ (vypolnímaia ~)
 feasible program
 правительственная ~
 (pravítel'stvennaia ~)
 government program
 производственная ~
 (proizvódstvennaia ~)
 manufacturing program
 экономическая ~ (ekonomícheskaia
 ~) economic program
 ~ инвестиций (~ investítsii)
 investment program
 ~ капиталовложений (~
 kapitalovlozhénii) capital
 investment program
 ~ поставки (~ postávki) schedule
 of deliveries
 ~ экспансии (~ ekspánsii)
 expansion program
Прогресс (progréss) *m.* progress

социальный ~ (sotsiál'nyi ~) social progress

Прогрессивный (progressívnyi) *adj.* progressive

Прогрессия обложения (progréssiia oblozhéniia) *f.* progressive taxation

Прогул (progúl) *m.* absenteeism, truancy

Продавец (prodavéts) *m.* salesman, vendor

Продаж/а (prodázha) *f.* distribution, marketing, sales, selling

    аукционная ~ (auktsiónnaia ~) sale at auction

    вступить в ~/у (vstupít' v ~/u) to go on sale

    вторичная ~ (vtoríchnaia ~) secondary selling

    вынужденная ~ (výnuzhdennaia ~) distress selling

    дисконтная ~ (diskóntnaia ~) discount sale

    исключительная ~ (iskliuchítel'naia ~) exclusive sale

    комиссионная ~ (komissiónnaia ~) sale by commission

    кооперативная ~ (kooperatívnaia ~) co-op sale

    массовая ~ (mássovaia ~) bulk sale

    оптовая ~ (optóvaia ~) wholesale trade

    отложенная ~ (otlózhennaia ~) delayed sale

    полуоптовая ~ (poluoptóvaia ~) semi-wholesale

    посредническая ~ (posrédnicheskaia ~) intermediate sale

    принудительная ~ с публичных торгов (prinudítel'naia ~ s publíchnykh torgóv) forced sale

    публичная ~ (publíchnaia ~) direct sale

    розничная ~ (róznichnaia ~) retail sale

    спекулятивная ~ (spekuliatívnaia ~) speculative sale

    тайная ~ (táinaia ~) secret sale

    условная ~ (uslóvnaia ~) conditional sale

    фиктивная ~ (fiktívnaia ~) sham sale

    уличная ~ (úlichnaia ~) street sale

    ~ движимых имуществ (~ dvízhimykh imúshchestv) sale of chattels

    ~ в кредит (~ v kredít) credit sale

    ~ лицензии (~ litsénzii) sale of a license

Продажность (prodázhnost') *f.* venality

Продажн/ый (prodázhnyi) *adj.* mercenary, for sale, venal

    ~/ая душа (~/aia dúsha) mercenary

    ~/ая женщина (~/aia zhénshchina) streetwalker

Продвигать (prodvigát') *v.* to advance, to promote

Продвижение (prodvizhénie) *n.* progress, promotion

    ~ по службе (~ po slúzhbe) promotion {in employment}

Проделка (prodélka) *f.* prank, trick

    мошенническая ~ (moshénnicheskaia ~) fraud, swindle

Продлевать (prodlevát') *v.* to extend, to prolong, to renew

Продление (prodlénie) *n.* extension, prolongation, renewal

    автоматическое ~ (avtomatícheskoe ~) automatic extension

    молчаливое ~ (molchalívoe ~) tacit extension

    ~ срока (~ sróka) extension of time limit

    ~ срока давности (~ sróka dávnosti) extension of the statute of limitations

    ~ срока действия (~ sróka déistviia) extension of validity

Продналог (prodnalóg) *m.* tax in kind

Продовольствие (prodovól'stvie) *n.* foodstuffs, rations

Продолжение (prodolzhénie) *n.* continuation

Продолжительность (prodolzhítel'nost') *f.* duration, length

    максимальная ~ рабочего времени (maksimál'naia ~ rabóchego vrémeni) maximum daily working hours

~ гарантийного срока (~ garantíinogo sróka) continuation of the warranty period
Продразвёрстка (prodrazviórstka) *f.* requisitioning of produce
Продукт (prodúkt) *m.* commodity, product
  аграрный ~ (agrárnyi ~) agrarian commodity
  валовой ~ (valovói ~) gross product
  валовой национальный ~ (valovói natsionál'nyi ~) gross national product
  валовой внутренний ~ (valovói vnútrennii ~) gross domestic product
  высококачественный ~ (vysokokáchestvennyi ~) high-quality product
  готовый ~ (gotóvyi ~) finished product
  импортный ~ (ímportnyi ~) imported product
  конечный ~ (konéchnyi ~) final product
  конкурирующий ~ (konkuríruiushchii ~) competing product
  кормовые ~/ы (kormovýe ~/y) fodder products
  основной ~ (osnovnói ~) staple
  побочный ~ (pobóchnyi ~) by-product
  промышленный ~ (promýshlennyi ~) industrial product
  сельскохозяйственный ~ (sél'skokhoziáistvennyi ~) agricultural product
Продуктивность (produktívnost') *f.* efficiency, productivity
  ~ сельского хозяйства (~ sel'skogo khoziáistva) agricultural productivity
Продукция (prodúktsiia) *f.* output, production
  валовая ~ (valováia ~) gross output
  готовая ~ (gotóvaia ~) finished production
  дефицитная ~ (defitsítnaia ~) deficit production
  импортная ~ (ímportnaia ~) imported production
  местная ~ (méstnaia ~) local production

  промышленная ~ (promýshlennaia ~) industrial output
  сельскохозяйственная ~ (sel'skokhoziáistvennaia ~) agricultural output
  товарная ~ (továrnaia ~) output of commodities
  чистая ~ (chístaia ~) net output
  экспортная ~ (éksportnaia ~) export output
Проезд (proézd) *m.* journey, passage, thoroughfare
Проект (proékt) *m.* design, draft, plan, project, projection
  крупномасштабный (krupnomasshtábnyi ~) major project
  первоначальный ~ (pervonachál'nyi ~) original plan
  правительственный ~ (pravítel'stvennyi ~) government scheme
  предварительный ~ (predvarítel'nyi ~) preliminary design
  типовой ~ (tipovói ~) model project
  финансовый ~ (finánsovyi ~) financial plan
  ~ бюджета (~ biudzhéta) draft budget
  ~ договора (~ dogovóra) draft treaty
  ~ закона (~ zakóna) draft of a law
  ~ резолюции (~ rezoliútsii) draft resolution
Проектирование (proektírovanie) *n.* designing, engineering
Проживать (prozhivát') *v.* to live, to reside
Прозвище (prózvishche) *n.* nickname, sobriquet
Проиграть (proigrát') *v.* to lose
Проигрыш (próigrysh) *m.* loss {judgment, debt}
Произведени/е (proizvedéni/e) *n.* production, {creative} work
  анонимное ~ (anonímnoe ~) anonymous work
  неизданное ~ (neizdánnoe ~) unpublished work
  оригинальное ~ (originál'noe ~) original work
  подделанное ~ (poddélannoe ~) plagiarized work

посмертное ~ (posmértnoe ~)
posthumous work
~ выпущенное анонимно (~
vypúshchennoe anonímno)
anonymously released work
~ выпущенное под псевдонимом (~
vypúshchennoe pod psevdonímom)
work released under pseudonym
литературные и художественные
~/я (literatúrnye i
khudózhestvennye ~/ia) literary
and artistic works
Производитель (proizvodítel') m.
maker, manufacturer, producer
сельскохозяйственный ~
(sel'skokhoziáistvennyi ~)
agricultural producer
Производительность
(proizvodítel'nost') f. operating
efficiency, productivity
высшая ~ (výsshaia ~) higher
productivity
промышленная ~ (promýshlennaia
~) industrial productivity
~ труда (~ trudá) productivity
of labor
Производительный (proizvodítel'nyi)
adj. efficient, productive
Производить (proizvodít') v. to
make, to manufacture, to produce
Производство (proizvódstvo) n.
proceedings, manufacturing, production
административное ~
(administratívnoe ~)
administrative proceedings
апелляционное ~ (apelliatsiónnoe
~) appellate proceedings
арбитражное ~ (arbitrázhnoe ~)
arbitration proceedings
бесспорное ~ (besspornoe ~) non-
adversarial proceedings
военное ~ (voénnoe ~) court
martial proceedings
внутреннее ~ (vnútrennee ~)
domestic production
гражданское ~ (grahdánskoe ~)
civil proceedings
кустарное ~ (kustárnoe ~)
cottage industry production
массовое ~ (mássovoe ~) mass
production
мировое ~ (mirovóe ~) world
production
национальное ~ (natsionál'noe ~)
national production

начать ~ по делу (nachát' ~ po
délu) to institute proceedings
незавершённое ~ (nezavershiónnoe
~) semi-finished goods,
unfinished production
поточное ~ (potóchnoe ~)
assembly line production
промышленное ~ (promýshlennoe ~)
industrial production
сезонное ~ (sezónnoe ~) seasonal
production
сельскохозяйственное ~
(sel'skokhoziáistvennoe ~)
agricultural production
серийное ~ (seríinoe ~) batch
production
следственное ~ (slédstvennoe ~)
investigatory proceedings
сокращённое ~ (sokrashchiónnoe
~) curtailed production
спорное ~ (spórnoe ~)
adversarial proceedings
судебное ~ (sudébnoe ~) judicial
proceeding
суммарное ~ (summárnoe ~)
summary proceedings
товарное ~ (továrnoe ~)
commodity production
устное ~ (ústnoe ~) oral
proceedings
Произвол (proizvól) m.
arbitrariness
административный ~
(administratívnyi ~)
administrative caprice
Произвольно (proizvól'no) adv.
arbitrarily
Произвольный (proizvól'nyi) adj.
arbitrary
Происки (próiski) pl. intrigues,
machinations
Происходить (proiskhodít') v. to go
on, to occur
Происхождени/е (proiskhozhdéni/e)
n. descent, extraction, origin,
parentage, provenance
место ~/я (mésto ~/ia) place of
origin
свидетельство о ~/и
(svidétel'stvo o ~/i)
certificate of origin
семейное ~ (seméinoe ~) family
background
~ изделия (~ izdéliia) origin of
a product

~ от кровосмешения (~ ot krovosmeshéniia) product of miscegenation

Происшествие (proisshéstvie) n. accident, event, incident
    аварийное ~ (avaríinoe ~) accident, casualty

Прокат (prokát) m. hire, rent

Прокатный (prokátnyi) adj. hired, rented

Прокладка (prokládka) f. lining, packing

Прокуратура (prokuratúra) f. office of the prosecutor {e.g. as district attorney}
    городская ~ (gorodskáia ~) office of the municipal prosecutor

Прокурор (prokurór) m. prosecutor, public prosecutor
    генеральный ~ (generál'nyi ~) general prosecutor {attorney general}

Пролетариат (proletariát) m. proletariat
    промышленный ~ (promýshlennyi ~) industrial proletariat
    сельский ~ (sél'skii ~) rural proletariat

Пролетаризация (proletarizátsiia) f. proletarianization

Пролетарий (proletárii) m. proletarian

Пролетарский (proletárskii) adj. proletarian

Пролив (prolív) m. sound, strait {geographical feature}

Пролонгация (prolongátsiia) f. extension {of contract, etc.}

Пролонгировать (prolongírovat') v. to extend {contract, etc.}

Промедление (promedlénie) n. delay

Промедлить (promedlít') v. to delay, to procrastinate

Промежуток (promezhútok) m. interim, interval

Промежуточный (promezhútochnyi) adj. intermediate, interim

Промфинплан (promfinplán) m. industrial and financial plan [abbrev.]

Промысел (prómysel) m. business, trade, works
    горный ~ (górnyi ~) mining
    кустарный ~ (kustárnyi ~) cottage industry

нефтяной ~ (neftianói ~) petroleum industry

отхожий ~ (otkhózhii ~) seasonal work

прибрежный рыбный ~ (pribrézhnyi rýbnyi ~) coastal fisheries

Промышленник (promýshlennik) m. industrialist

Промышленность (promýshlennost') f. industry
    авиационная ~ (aviatsiónnaia ~) aircraft ~
    автомобильная ~ (avtomobíl'naia ~) automobile ~
    атомная ~ (átomnaia ~) atomic ~
    военная ~ (voénnaia ~) munitions ~
    газовая ~ (gázovaia ~) natural gas ~
    горная ~ (górnaia ~) mining ~
    горнодобывающая ~ (gornodobyváiushchaia ~) mining extraction ~
    государственная ~ (gosudárstvennaia ~) state-owned ~
    деревообрабатывающая ~ (derevoobrabátyvaiushchaia ~) wood products ~
    добывающая ~ (dobyváiushchaia ~) extractive ~
    золото-добывающая ~ (zóloto-dobyváiushchaia ~) gold mining ~
    кинематографическая ~ (kinematografícheskaia ~) motion picture ~
    кооперативная ~ (kooperatívnaia ~) cooperative ~
    крупная ~ (krúpnaia ~) major ~
    кустарная ~ (kustárnaia ~) cottage ~
    легкая ~ (légkaia ~) light ~
    лесная ~ (lesnáia ~) timber ~
    машиностроительная ~ (mashinostroítel'naia ~) machine building ~
    местная ~ (méstnaia ~) local ~
    металлообрабатывающая ~ (metalloobrabátyvaiushchaia ~) metal processing ~
    металлургическая ~ (metallurgícheskaia ~) metallurgical ~
    молочная ~ (molóchnaia ~) dairy ~

национализированная ~
(natsionalizírovannaia ~)
nationalized ~
нефтяная ~ (neftianáia ~)
petroleum ~
оборонная ~ (oborónnaia ~)
defense ~
обрабатывающая ~
(obrabátyvaiushchaia ~)
processing ~
обувная ~ (óbuvnaia ~) footwear
~
петрохимическая ~
(petrokhimícheskaia ~) petro-
chemical ~
пищевая ~ (pishcheváia ~) food
processing ~
пластмассовая ~ (plastmássovaia
~) plastic ~
строительная ~ (stroítel'naia ~)
construction ~
судостроительная ~
(sudostroítel'naia ~)
shipbuilding ~
текстильная ~ (tekstil'naia ~)
textile ~
тяжёлая ~ (tiazhiólaia ~) heavy
~
фармацевтическая ~
(farmatsevtícheskaia ~)
pharmaceutical ~
химическая ~ (khimícheskaia ~)
chemical ~
частная ~ (chástnaia ~) private
~
экспортная ~ (éksportnaia ~)
export ~
электронная ~ (elektrónnaia ~)
electronic ~
энергетическая ~
(energetícheskaia ~) power ~
ядерная ~ (iádernaia ~) nuclear
energy ~
Проникновение (proniknovénie) n.
penetration
экономическое ~ (ekonomícheskoe
~) economic ~
Пропаганда (propagánda) f.
propaganda
Пропагандист (propagandíst) m.
propagandist
Прописать (propisát') v. to
prescribe, to register
Прописка (propíska) f. propiska
{residence permit}
Пропуск (própusk) m. blank, pass,
permit

беспошлинный ~ (bespóshlinnyi ~)
duty-free entry
постоянный ~ (postoiánnyi ~)
permanent pass
Пропустить (propustít') v. to
admit, to permit
Просвещение (prosveshchénie) n.
education, enlightenment
народное ~ (naródnoe ~) public
education
Проситель (prosítel') m. applicant,
petitioner
Просить (prosít') v. to apply, to
ask, to intercede
Проспект (prospékt) m. prospectus
Просрочка (prosróchka) f. arrears,
delay, term overrun
Проститутка (prostitútka) f.
prostitute
зарегистрированная ~
(zaregistrírovannaia ~)
registered ~
Проституция (prostitútsiia) f.
prostitution
Простой (prostói) m. deadtime,
demurrage, adj. simple
Пространство (prostránstvo) n.
expanse, space
воздушное ~ (vozdúshnoe ~) air
space
запретное воздушное ~ (zaprétnoe
vozdúshnoe ~) forbidden air
space
Проступок (prostúpok) m.
misdemeanor
антиобщественный ~
(antiobshchéstvennyi ~) anti-
social misdemeanor
~ против общественного порядка
(~ prótiv obshchéstvennogo
poriádka) disturbing the peace
{misdemeanor against social
order}
Просьб/а (prós'b/a) f. request
неформальная ~ (neformál'naia ~)
informal ~
письменная ~ (pís'mennaia ~)
written ~
почтительная ~ (pochtítel'naia
~) official ~
предварительная ~
(predvarítel'naia ~) preliminary
~
удовлетворить ~/y (udovletvorít'
~/u) to grant a ~

Протежировать (protezhírovat') v.
to do official favors, to pull
strings for
Протекторат (protektorát) m.
protectorate
  колониальный ~ (koloniál'nyi ~)
  colonial protectorate
  международный ~ (mezhdunaródnyi
  ~) international protectorate
Протекционизм (protektsioنízm) m.
protectionism
Протекционист (protektsioníst) m.
protectionist
Протест (protést) m. notice of
dishonor, objection, protest
  коллективный ~ (kollektívnyi ~)
  collective protest
  морской ~ об авариях (morskói ~
  ob aváriiakh) ship's protest
  ~ векселя (~ vékselia) notice of
  dishonor of a bill, note
  ~ прокурора (~ prokuróra)
  objection by the prosecution
Противник (protívnik) m. adversary,
opponent
  ~ в споре (~ v spóre) opponent
  in a dispute
Противовес (protivovés) m. counter-
balance
Противодействие (protivodéistvie)
n. counteraction, opposition
Противозаконность
(protivozakónnost') f. illegality
Противозаконный (protivozakónnyi)
adj. illegal
Противопоставить (protivopostávit')
v. to set off against
Противопоставление
(protivopostavlénie) n. setting off
against
Противоправный (protivoprávnyi)
adj. illegal
Противоречиво (protivorechívo) n.
contradictorily
Противоречивость
(protivorechívost') f.
contradiction
Противоречивый (protivorechívyi)
adj. conflicting, contradictory,
discrepant
Противоречие (protivoréchie) n.
contradiction
  ~ в законах (~ v zakónakh)
  statutory ~
Противоречить (protivoréchit') v.
to contradict

Протокол (protokól) m. minutes {of
a meeting, etc.}, protocol, record,
report, statement
  административный ~
  (administratívnyi ~)
  administrative record
  временный ~ (vrémennyi ~)
  temporary protocol
  дополнительный ~ (dopolnítel'nyi
  ~) supplementary protocol
  итоговый ~ (itógovyi ~) final
  protocol
  морской ~ (morskói ~) ship's
  protocol
  составить ~ (sostávit' ~) to
  draw up a report
  ~ о внесении изменений (~ o
  vnesénii izménénii) protocol of
  change order
  ~ допроса (~ doprósa)
  examination record
  ~ заседания (~ zasedániia)
  minutes of proceedings
  ~ собрания (~ sobrániia) minutes
  of a meeting
  ~ соглашения (~ soglashéniia)
  protocol of agreement
  ~ судебного заседания (~
  sudébnogo zasedániia) record of
  a judicial hearing
Протоколировать (protokolírovat')
v. to protocol, to record
Протокольный (protokól'nyi) adj.
protocol
Прототип (prototíp) m. prototype
Профбилет (profbilét) m. union card
Професси/я (proféssiia) f.
profession
  по ~/и (po ~/i) by profession
Профилактика (profiláktika) f.
routine maintenance
Профилактический
(profilaktícheskii) adj.
preventative
Профилакторий (profilaktórii) m.
dispensary
Проформа (profórma) f. proforma
Профсоюз (profsoiúz) m. labor union
Профсоюзный (profsoiúznyi) adj.
labor union
Проход (prokhód) m. passage, way
  мирный ~ (mírnyi ~) peaceful
  passage
  право на ~ (právo na ~) right-
  of-way
Процедура (protsedúra) f. procedure

административная ~
(administratívnaia ~) formality
конституционная ~
(konstitutsiónnaia ~)
constitutional procedure
парламентская ~ (parlámentskaia
~) parliamentary procedure
предварительная ~
(predvarítel'naia ~) preliminary
procedure
специальная ~ (spetsiál'naia ~)
special procedure
судебная ~ (sudébnaia ~)
judicial procedure
~ выборов (~ výborov) electoral
procedure
~ обжалования (~ obzhalovániia)
appellate procedure
Процент (protsént) *m.* interest,
percentage, per cent
банковский ~ (bánkovskii ~) bank
interest
комиссионный ~ (komissiónnyi ~)
commission
договорные ~/ы (dogovórnye ~/y)
contractual interest
ипотечные ~/ы (ipotéchnye ~/y)
mortgage interest
наросшие ~/ы (narósshie ~/y)
accumulating interest
простые ~/ы (prostýe ~/y) simple
interest
ростовщические ~/ы
(rostovshchícheskie ~/y)
usurious interest
сложные ~/ы (slózhnye ~/y)
compound interest
текущие ~/ы (tekúshchie ~/y)
current interest
узаконенные ~/ы (uzakónennye
~/y) permissible interest
Процесс (protséss) *m.* hearing,
proceedings, process, trial
арбитражный ~ (arbitrázhnyi ~)
arbitral proceedings
бракоразводный ~ (brakorazvódnyi
~) divorce proceedings
бюджетный ~ (biudzhétnyi ~)
budget process
гражданский ~ (grahdánskii ~)
civil proceedings
законодательный ~
(zakonodátel'nyi ~) legislative
proceedings
запатентованный ~
(zapatentóvannyi ~) patented
process

инквизиционный ~
(inkvizitsiónnyi ~) inquisition
международный ~ (mezhdunaródnyi
~) international proceedings
открытый ~ (otkrýtyi ~) open
hearing
производственный ~
(proizvódstvennyi ~)
manufacturing process
судебный ~ (sudébnyi ~) legal
proceedings
уголовный ~ (ugolóvnyi ~)
criminal proceedings
~ при закрытых дверях (~ pri
zakrýtykh dveriákh) proceedings
behind closed doors
Процессуальный (protsessuál'nyi)
adj. procedural
Прошение (proshénie) *n.* application
Прощение (proshchénie) *n.*
forgiveness, pardon
закономерное ~ (zakonomérnoe ~)
legal pardon
~ долга (~ dólga) forgiveness of
a debt
Псевдоним (psevdoním) *m.* pseudonym
Публикация (publikátsiia) *f.*
publication
отраслевая ~ (otrasleváia ~)
trade publication
разрешённая ~ (razreshiónnaia ~)
press release
Публиковать (publikovát') *v.* to
publish
Публицист (publitsíst) *m.*
commentator, publicist
Публично (publíchno) *adv.* openly,
publicly
Публичность (publíchnost') *f.*
publicity
Публичн/ый (publíchnyi) *adj.* public
~ дом (~ dom) brothel
~/ое право (~/oe právo) public
law
Пункт (punkt) *m.* article, clause,
item, point
входной ~ (vkhodnói ~) point of
entry
выходной ~ (vykhodnói ~) point
of exit
командный ~ (komándnyi ~)
command point
конечный ~ морского пути
(konéchnyi ~ morskógo putí)
final destination
пограничный ~ (pograníchnyi ~)
border post

спорный ~ (spórnyi ~)
controversial issue
таможенный ~ (tamózhennyi ~)
customs post
~ договора (~ dogovóra) item,
provision of a contract, treaty
~ иска (~ íska) count {of a
complaint, indictment}
~ назначения (~ naznachéniia)
destination
Путёвка (putióvka) f.
authorization, pass, vacancy {in
resort, tourist group}
льготная ~ (l'gótnaia ~)
preferential authorization
Путём (putióm) adv. by means of
Путешествие (puteshéstvie) journey,
travels, voyage
международное ~ (mezhdunaródnoe
~) international travel
Путч (putch) m. putsch
Путь (put') m. course, path, road,
track, way
внутренний водный ~ (vnútrennii
vódnyi ~) inland water course
водный ~ (vódnyi ~) water course
дипломатический
(diplomatícheskii ~) diplomatic
means
конституционный ~
(konstitutsiónnyi ~)
constitutional path
морской ~ (morskói ~) sea route
наземный ~ (nazémnyi ~) land
route
судоходный ~ (sudokhódnyi ~)
overland route
Пытать (pytát') v. to attempt
Пытка (pýtka) f. attempt
Пятилетка (piatilétka) f. five-year
plan

Р

Раб (rab) m. slave
Рабовладелец (rabovladélets) m.
slaveholder
Рабовладельческий
(rabovladél'cheskii) adj.
slaveholder, slaveholding
Работ/а (rabóta) f. operation, work
аккордная ~ (akkórdnaia ~) piece
work
временная ~ (vrémennaia ~)
temporary job

дополнительная ~
(dopolnítel'naia ~) additional
job
завершённая ~ (zavershiónnaia ~)
completed work
канцелярская ~ (kantseliárskaia
~) clerical work
ночная ~ (nochnáia ~) night work
обычная ~ (obýchnaia ~) routine
operation
подготовительная ~
(podgotovítel'naia ~)
preparatory work
постоянная ~ (postoiánnaia ~)
regular work
поточная ~ (potóchnaia ~)
assembly line work
проверочная ~ (provérochnaia ~)
testing work
сверхурочная ~ (sverkhuróchnaia
~) overtime work
сдельная ~ (sdél'naia ~) piece
work
сезонная ~ (sezónnaia ~)
seasonal work
сменная ~ (sménnaia ~) shift
work
спасательные ~/ы (spasátel'nye
~/y) salvage operations
срочная ~ (sróchnaia ~) rush job
трудоёмкая ~ (trudoiómkaia ~)
labor-intensive work
Работать (rabótat') v. to operate,
to work
~ по найму (~ po náimu) to work
for hire, for wages
Работник (rabótnik) m. employee,
office worker
временный ~ (vrémennyi ~)
temporary worker
домашний ~ (domáshnii ~)
domestic worker
компетентный ~ (kompeténtnyi ~)
skilled worker
Работодатель (rabotodátel') m.
employer
Работоспособный (rabotosposóbnyi)
adj. able-bodied
Рабочий (rabóchii) m.adj.noun
worker, worker's
временный ~ (vrémennyi ~) casual
laborer
вспомогательный ~
(vspomogátel'nyi ~) auxiliary
laborer
заводской ~ (zavodskói ~)
factory worker

квалифицированный ~
(kvalifitsírovannyi ~) skilled
worker
наёмный ~ (naiómnyi ~) hired
laborer
неквалифицированный ~
(nekvalifitsírovannyi ~)
unskilled laborer
подённый ~ (podiónnyi ~) day
laborer
промышленный ~ (promýshlennyi ~)
industrial worker
сезонный ~ (sezónnyi ~) seasonal
laborer
сельскохозяйственный ~
(sel'skokhoziáistvennyi ~)
agricultural worker, farmhand
фабричный ~ (fabríchnyi ~)
millhand
~ от станка (~ ot stanká) bench
worker

Рабство (rábstvo) n. slavery

Равенство (rávenstvo) n. equality,
parity
~ перед законом (~ péred
zakónom) equality before the law
~ прав (~ prav) n. equal rights

Равновесие (ravnovésie) n. balance,
equilibrium
демографическое ~
(demografícheskoe ~) demographic
equilibrium
денежное ~ (dénezhnoe ~)
monetary equilibrium
~ бюджета (~ biudzhéta) balanced
budget

Равноправие (ravnoprávie) equal
rights
~ в экономических отношениях (~
v ekonomícheskikh otnoshéniiakh)
equality in economic relations

Равный (rávnyi) adj. equal

Радикал (radikál) m. radical

Радикализм (radikalízm) m.
radicalism

Радикальный (radikál'nyi) adj.
radical

Радиореклама (radioreklámа) f.
radio advertising

Разбазаривание (razbazárivanie) n.
squandering

Разбивка (razbívka) f. breakdown
{of figures, etc.}

Разбазарить (razbazárit') v. to
squander

Разбирательство (razbirátel'stvo)
n. examination, investigation

арбитражное ~ (arbitrázhnoe ~)
arbitral proceedings
закрытое судебное ~ (zakrýtoe
sudébnoe ~) closed court
proceedings
открытое ~ (otkrýtoe ~) public
proceedings
судебное ~ (sudébnoe ~) legal
proceedings
третейское ~ (tretéiskoe ~)
arbitration examination

Разблокирование (razblokírovanie)
n. release {e.g. of a blocked
account}

Разблокировать (razblokírovat') v.
to release {e.g. a blocked account}

Разбой (razbói) m. brigandage,
robbery
морской ~ (morskói ~) piracy

Разбойник (razbóinik) m. pirate,
robber

Разбойничий (razbóinichii) adj.
robber, piratical
~ притон (~ pritón) den of
thieves

Разбор дела (razbór déla) m.
hearing {court}

Развал (razvál) m. breakdown,
disintegration

Разведать (razvedát') v. [see
разведывать]

Разведка (razvédka) f.
intelligence, prospecting,
reconnaissance

Разведчик (razvédchik) m.
intelligence officer

Разведывать (razvédyvat') v. to
ascertain, to prospect, to reconnoitre

Развёрстка (razviórstka) f.
allotment, apportionment
продовольственная ~
(prodovól'stvennaia ~) food
ration

Развестись (razvestís') v. [see
разводиться]

Развитие (razvítie) n. development
бурное ~ (búrnoe ~) rapid ~
естественное ~ (estéstvennoe ~)
natural ~
коммерческое ~ (kommércheskoe ~)
commercial ~
мирное ~ (mírnoe ~) peaceful ~
экономическое ~ (ekonomícheskoe
~) economic ~

Развод (razvód) m. divorce

~ по взаимному согласию ~ (~ po vzaímnomu soglásiiu) by mutual consent

Разводиться (razvodít'sia) *v.* to get divorced

Разграбление (razgrablénie) *n.* pillage, plunder

Разглашать (razglashát') *v.* [perfective: разгласить] to divulge

Разглашение (razglashénie) *n.* unauthorized disclosure

Разговор (razgovór) *m.* conversation

Разграбление (razgrablénie) *n.* pillage and plunder

Разграничение (razgranichénie) *n.* demarcation

    правовое ~ (pravovóe ~) legal differentiation

    территориальное ~ (territoriál'noe ~) territorial demarcation

Разграничивать (razgraníchivat') *v.* to demarcate, to distinguish

Разгром (razgróm) *m.* defeat, devastation

Разгромить (razgromít') *v.* to devastate, to destroy

Разгружать (razgruzhát') *v.* to discharge, to offload

Разгрузка (razgrúzka) *f.* discharging, offloading

Раздел (razdél) *m.* division, section

    вступительный ~ (vstupítel'nyi ~) introduction {of a book, etc.}

    добровольный ~ (dobrovól'nyi ~) volunteer division

    натуральный ~ (naturál'nyi ~) partition in kind

    судебный ~ (sudébnyi ~) judicial division

    финансовый ~ (finánsovyi ~) financial section

    ~ в бесспорном порядке (~ v besspórnom poriádke) uncontested partition

    ~ имущества (~ imúshchestva) partition of property

Разделение (razdelénie) *n.* division, sharing

    ~ властей (~ vlastéi) separation of powers

    ~ труда (~ trudá) division of labor

Разделимый (razdelímyi) *adj.* divisible

Раздельный (razdél'nyi) *adj.* separate

Разжигание (razzhigánie) *n.* kindling

    ~ войны (~ voiný) brewing of a war

Различи/е (razlíchi/e) *n.* difference, distinction, inequality

    основные ~/я (osnovnýe ~/ia) fundamental differences

    ~ мнений (~ mnénii) difference of opinions

Различать (razlichát') *v.* to discern, to distinguish

Разлука (razlúka) *f.* separation {e.g. of spouses}

    пробная ~ (próbnaia ~) trial separation

Размежевание (razmezhevánie) *n.* demarcation

    национально-государственное ~ (natsionál'no-gosudárstvennoe ~) demarcation of national boundaries

Размежевать (razmezhevát') *v.* to delimit, to demarcate

Размен (razmén) *m.* exchange

    ~ денег (~ déneg) exchange of money

Разменивать (razménivat') *v.* [see разменять]

Разменн/ый (razménn/yi) *adj.* change

    ~/ая монета (~/aia monéta) small change

Разменять (razmeniát') *v.* to exchange

Размер (razmér) *m.* amount, dimensions, extent, measurement, size

    гарантированный минимальный ~ заработной платы (garantírovannyi minimál'nyi ~ zárabotnoi pláty) guaranteed minimum wage

    громадный ~ (gromádnyi ~) vast extent

    максимальный ~ (maksimál'nyi ~) maximum size, upper limit

    максимальный ~ страховой суммы (maksimál'nyi ~ strakhovói súmmy) maximum amount insurable

    минимальный ~ (minimál'nyi ~) minimum size, lower limit

    минимальный ~ заработной платы (minimál'nyi ~ zárabotnoi pláty) minimum wage

номинальный ~ (nominál'nyi ~)
nominal size
общий ~ (óbshchii ~) total
measurements
общий ~ доходов (óbshchii ~
dokhódov) gross income
повышенный ~ (povýshennyi ~)
increased size
ростовщический ~
(rostovshchícheskii ~) usurious
amount
стандартный ~ (standártnyi ~)
standard dimensions
физические ~/ы (fizícheskie ~/y)
physical dimensions
~ амортизации (~ amortizátsii)
amount of depreciation, size of
depreciation
~ ассигнований (~ assignovánii)
funding level
~ взноса (~ vznósa) amount of
deposit
~ дохода (~ dokhóda) level of
income
~ иска (~ íska) extent of a
claim
~ кредита (~ kredíta) extent of
credit
~ обеспечения претензии (~
obespécheniia preténzii) extent
of security for a claim
~ операции (~ operátsii) extent
of operations
~ пенсии (~ pénsii) size of
pension
~ персонала (~ personála) size
of staff
~ премии (~ prémii) rate of
option, rate of premium
~ преференциальных скидок (~
preferentsiál'nykh skídok)
preferential discount rate
~ прибыли (~ príbyli) profit
margin
~ расходов (~ raskhódov) volume
of expenses
~ страховки (~ strakhóvki)
extent of insurance coverage
~ фрахта (~ frákhta) rate of
freight
~ ущерба (~ ushchérba) extent of
loss
~ штрафа (~ shtráfa) size of
penalty
Размещать (razmeshchát') v.
[perfective: разместить] to

allocate, to arrange, to float, to
place, to stow, to trim
Размещение (razmeshchénie) n.
arrangement, disposition,
deployment, floating
~ акции (~ áktsii) placing of
shares
~ государственного долга (~
gosudárstvennogo dólga) placing
of government debt
~ займа (~ záima) floating of a
loan
~ заказов (~ zakázov) placing of
orders
Размораживать (razmorázhivat') v.
to unfreeze {e.g. assets}
Разнарядка (raznariádka) f.
distribution list
Разница (ráznitsa) f. difference,
discrepancy, gap, margin, spread
~ в валютах (~ v valiútakh)
exchange rate spread
~ в курсах (~ v kúrsakh)
difference in rates
~ в ценах (~ v tsenákh) price
differential
Разнобой (raznobói) m.
disagreement, lack of coordination
Разновидность (raznovídnost') f.
variety, diversity
Разногласие (raznoglásie) n.
difference, disagreement,
discrepancy
Разнос (raznós) m. delivery,
distribution
Разносчик (raznóschik) m. peddler
Разойтись (razoitís') v. to
divorce, to be sold out
Разорвать (razorvát') v. to break
off, to tear apart
~ дипломатические сношения (~
diplomatícheskie snoshéniia) to
sever diplomatic relations
Разоружать (razoruzhát') v. to
dismantle
Разоружение (razoruzhénie) n.
disarmament
Разрабатывать (razrabátyvat') v. to
cultivate, to elaborate, to work
{in a mine}
Разработка (razrabótka) f.
cultivation, mine working
горная ~ (górnaia ~) mining
Разработать (razrabótat') v. [see
разрабатывать]

Разрешать (razreshát') *v.* to allow, to approve, to authorize, to permit, to settle

Разрешение (razreshénie) *n.* authorization, license, permission, settlement, solution

    валютное ~ (valiútnoe ~) foreign exchange permit

    временное ~ (vrémennoe ~) temporary permit

    исключительное ~ (iskliuchítel'noe ~) exclusive authorization

    карантинное ~ (karantínoe ~) quarantine certificate

    письменное ~ (pís'mennoe ~) written permission

    постоянное ~ (postoiánnoe ~) standing permission

    предварительное ~ (predvarítel'noe ~) preliminary permission

    разовое ~ (rázovoe ~) single entry permit

    судебное ~ (sudébnoe ~) judicial settlement

    чрезвычайное ~ (chrezvycháinoe ~) extraordinary authorization

    экспортное ~ (éksportnoe ~) export permit

    ~ на ввоз (~ na vvoz) import approval

    ~ на полёт над (~ na poliót nad) overflight permission

    ~ на право охоты (~ na právo okhóty) hunting license

    ~ на право работы (~ na právo rabóty) work permit

    ~ на разведку месторождений (~ na razvédku mestorozhdénii) prospecting permit

    ~ на свидание с заключённым (~ na svidánie s zakliuchiónnym) visiting permission {with prisoner}

    ~ спора (~ spóra) settlement of a dispute

Разрешить (razreshít') *v.* [see разрешать]

Разруха (razrúkha) *f.* ruin

    экономическая ~ (ekonomícheskaia ~) economic collapse

Разрыв (razrýv) *m.* break, gap, rupture, severance

    инфляционный ~ (infliatsiónnyi ~) inflationary gap

    ~ дипломатических сношений (~ diplomatícheskikh snoshénii) severance of diplomatic relations

    ~ переговоров (~ peregovórov) breaking off of negotiations

    ~ экономических связей (~ ekonomícheskikh sviazéi) severance of economic ties

    ликвидировать ~ (likvidírovat' ~) to bridge the gap

Разряд (razriád) *m.* bracket, category, rank, sort

    второго ~/a (vtorógo ~/a) second rate

    первого /a (pérvogo /a) first rate

    тарифный ~ (tarífnyi ~) wage category

    третьего ~/a (trét'ego ~/a) third rate

Разукрупнять (razukrupniát') *v.* to devolve into smaller units

Разъединение (raz"edinénie) *n.* breaking, partition, separation

    ~ имуществ (~ imúshchestv) partitioning of properties

Разъединить (raz"edinít') *v.* to break, to separate

Разъездн/ой (raz"ezdn/ói) *adj.* traveling

    ~/ые деньги (~/ýe dén'gi) traveling expenses

Разъяснение (raz"iasnénie) *n.* explanation, interpretation

    ~ верховного суда (~ verkhóvnogo sudá) interpretation of the Supreme Court

Райисполком (raiispolkóm) *m.* regional executive committee *[abbrev.]*

Район (raión) *m.* area, region, raion {administrative division of Russian Federation}

    автономный ~ (avtonómnyi ~) autonomous region

    валютный ~ (valiútnyi ~) currency zone

    городской ~ (gorodskói ~) urban district

    запретный ~ (zaprétnyi ~) forbidden zone

    консульский ~ (kónsul'skii ~) consular district

    пограничный ~ (pogranίchnyi ~) border zone

промышленный ~ (promýshlennyi ~) industrial district

рыболовный ~ (rybolóvnyi ~) fishing zone

таможенный ~ (tamózhennyi ~) custom zone

Рамбурс (rámburs) *m.* reimbursement

Рана (rána) *f.* wound

Ранг (rang) *m.* class rank

служебный ~ (sluzhébnyi ~) civil service rank

Ранение (ranénie) *n.* injury

Ранить (ranít') *v.* to injure, to wound

Рантье (rant'é) *m.* rentier

пожизненный ~ (pozhíznennyi ~) life ~

Расизм (rasízm) *m.* racism

Расист (rasíst) *m.* racist

Расистский (rasístskii) *adj.* racist

Раскаяние (raskaiánie) *n.* repentance

чистосердечное ~ (chistosérdechnoe ~) heartfelt ~

Расквартирование (raskvartirovánie) *n.* billeting {e.g. of soldiers}

Расквартировать (raskvartírovat') *v.* to billet

Раскол (raskól) *m.* schism, split

Раскольник (raskól'nik) *m.* dissenter, schismatic

Раскольнический (raskól'nicheskii) *adj.* dissenting, schismatic

Раскрепостить (raskrepostít') *v.* to emancipate {serfs}

Раскрепощение (raskreposhchénie) *n.* emancipation

Распад (raspád) *m.* collapse, disintegration

~ государства (~ gosudárstva) fall of a government

Расписание (raspisánie) *n.* schedule, time table

доходное ~ (dokhódnoe ~) income schedule

тарифное ~ (tarífnoe ~) rate scale

штатное ~ (shtátnoe ~) personnel schedule

Расписаться (raspisát'sia) *v.* to sign for

~ в получении заказного письма (~ v poluchénii zakaznógo pis'má) to sign for a registered letter

Расписк/а (raspísk/a) *f.* certificate, receipt, warrant

выдать ~/у (výdat' ~/u) to issue a receipt

долговая ~ (dolgováia ~) promissory note

ломбардная ~ (lombárdnaia ~) pawn ticket

официальная ~ (ofitsiál'naia ~) official receipt

сохранная ~ (sokhránnaia ~) bailee receipt

Расплачиваться (raspláchivat'sia) *v.* [perfective: расплатиться] to settle accounts

Расположение (raspolozhénie) *n.* arrangement, disposition, location

Распорядитель (rasporiadítel') *m.* manager, master of ceremonies

~ кредитов (~ kredítov) credit manager

Распорядительный (rasporiadítel'nyi) *adj.* capable, efficient

Распорядиться (rasporiadít'sia) *v.* to manage, to see to

Распорядок (rasporiádok) *m.* order, routine

внутренний ~ (vnútrennii ~) routine

~ дня (~ dnia) order of the day

Распоряжаться (rasporiazhát'sia) *v.* to command, to dispose of, to order

свободно ~ (svobódno ~) to freely dispose of

Распоряжение (rasporiazhénie) *n.* direction, disposition, decree, instruction, regulation

административное ~ (administratívnoe ~) administrative regulation

завещательное ~ (zaveshchátel'noe ~) testamentary disposition

законное ~ (zakónnoe ~) legal enactment

постоянное ~ банку (postoiánnoe ~ bánku) standing order to the bank

правительственное ~ (pravítel'stvennoe ~) governmental instruction

предварительное ~ (predvarítel'noe ~) preliminary regulation

~ об авизовании (~ ob avizovánii) instruction to advise

~ о доставке (~ o dostávke) instruction to deliver
~ о наложении ареста (~ o nalozhénii arésta) writ of arrest

Расправа (raspráva) f. punishment, rough justice
короткая ~ (korótkaia ~) short shrift
кровавая ~ (krovávaia ~) massacre

Распределение (raspredelénie) n. apportionment, distribution
оптовое ~ (optóvoe ~) wholesale distributorship
пропорциональное ~ (proportsionál'noe ~) proportional allotment
~ акций (~ áktsii) allotment of shares
~ валютный рисков (~ valiútnyi rískov) sharing of currency risks
~ выгод (~ výgod) profit sharing
~ дивидендов (~ dividéndov) apportionment of dividends
~ доходов (~ dokhódov) distribution of income
~ запасов (~ zapásov) distribution of inventory
~ затрат (~ zatrát) cost sharing
~ капиталовложений (~ kapitalovlozhénii) breakdown of capital investment
~ общей аварии (~ óbshchei avárii) general average adjustment
~ наследства (~ naslédstva) distribution of inheritance
~ в натуре (~ v natúre) distribution in kind
~ расходов (~ raskhódov) allocation of expenses
~ рисков (~ rískov) sharing of risks
~ труда (~ trudá) division of labor
~ убытков (~ ubýtkov) sharing of losses

Распределитель (raspredelítel') m. distributor
закрытый ~ (zakrýtyi ~) members only retail establishment

Распределить (raspredelít') v. to allocate, to distribute
~ по паям (~ po paiám) to allocate by shares

Распродажа (rasprodázha) f. sale, sell-out
срочная ~ (sróchnaia ~) fire sale, panic sale
~ земельных участков (~ zemél'nykh uchástkov) sale of plots of land
~ по пониженным ценам (~ po ponízhennym tsenám) sale at discount prices

Распространение (rasprostranénie) n. distribution, merchandising
территориальное ~ (territoriál'noe ~) territorial distribution

Распространять (rasprostraniát') v. to circulate, to distribute, to spread

Распустить (raspustít') v. to disband, to dismiss, to spoil
~ парламент (~ parláment) to dissolve parliament

Расследование (rasslédovanie) n. inquiry
предварительное ~ (predvarítel'noe ~) preliminary inquiry
предварительное ~ по существу (predvarítel'noe ~ po sushchestvú) preliminary substantive inquiry
произвести ~ (proizvestí ~) to hold an inquiry
~ доказательства (~ dokazátel'stva) evidentiary hearing

Расследовать (rasslédovat') v. to hold an inquiry, to investigate

Рассматривать (rassmátrivat') v. to consider, to examine

Рассмотрение (rassmotrénie) n. consideration, examination, scrutiny
предварительное ~ (predvarítel'noe ~) preliminary examination
судебное ~ (sudébnoe ~) judicial consideration
~ бюджета (~ biudzhéta) scrutiny of the budget
~ дела (~ déla) consideration of a case
~ дела по существу (~ déla po sushchestvú) substantive consideration of a case
~ жалобы (~ zháloby) to consider a complaint

~ заявки (~ zaiávki) consideration of an application
Рассмотреть (rassmotrét') v. [see рассматривать]
Рассрочка (rassróchka) f. installment plan
платить в рассрочку (platít' v rassróchku) to pay by installment
~ исполнения (~ ispolnéniia) extension of deadline
Расстановка сил (rasstanóvka síl) f. placement of forces
Расстаться (rasstát'sia) v. to exit, to leave, to part
Расстрел (rasstrél) m. execution {by firing squad}
Расстрелять (rasstreliát') v. to execute by firing squad, to fire at close range, to exhaust ammunition
Рассылка (rassýlka) f. delivery, distribution
Рассыльный (rassýl'nyi) adj. delivery, delivery boy
Расторгать (rastorgát') v. [perfective: расторгнуть] to abrogate, annul, rescind
~ договор (~ dogovór) to rescind a contract
Расторжение (rastorzhénie) n. abrogation, annulment, cancellation, dissolution
~ брака (~ bráka) annulment of a marriage
~ договора (~ dogovóra) rescission of a contract
~ договора займа (~ dogovóra záima) cancellation of a lease
~ по суду (~ po súdu) judicial dissolution
Расточать (rastochát') v. to squander, to waste
~ похвалы (~ pokhvály) to lavish praise upon
Расточитель (rastochítel') m. spendthrift
Расточительство (rastochítel'stvo) n. squandering, waste
Расточительный (rastochítel'nyi) adj. spendthrift
Растрата (rastráta) f. wasteful spending, squandering
~ казённых денег (~ kaziónnykh déneg) official embezzlement
Растратить (rastrátit') v. to embezzle, to squander, to waste

Растратчик (rastrátchik) m. embezzler
Расформирование (rasformirovánie) n. breakup {e.g. of company}, disbandment
Расхититель (raskhitítel') m. plunderer
Расхищать (raskhishchát') v. [perfective: расхитить] to misappropriate, to plunder
Расхищение (raskhishchénie) n. misappropriation, plundering
Расход (raskhód) m. expense, expenditure, outlay
адвокатские ~/ы (advokátskie ~/y) attorney fees
административные ~/ы (administratívnye ~/y) administrative expenses
амортизационные ~/ы (amortizatsiónnye ~/y) amortized expenditures, depreciated expenditures
бюджетные ~/ы (biudzhétnye ~/y) budgeted expenditures
внебюджетные ~/ы (vnebiudzhétnye ~/y) extra budgetary expenditures
военные ~/ы (voénnye ~/y) military expenditures
государственные ~/ы (gosudárstvennye ~/y) public expenditures
дисбурсментские ~/ы (disbursméntskie ~/y) disbursements
добавочные ~/ы (dobávochnye ~/y) supplementary costs
долларовые ~/ы (dóllarovye ~/y) dollar denominated expenditures
дорожные ~/ы (dorózhnye ~/y) traveling expenses
канцелярские ~/ы (kantseliárskie ~/y) clerical expenses, office expenses
косвенные ~/ы (kósvennye ~/y) indirect expenses
материальные ~/ы (materiál'nye ~/y) material expenditures
накладные ~/ы (nakladnýe ~/y) overhead
неизменные ~/ы (neizménnye ~/y) fixed expenses
необходимый ~ (neobkhodímyi ~) necessary expense

непредвиденные ~/ы (nepredvídennye ~/y) unforeseen expenditures

непроизводственные ~/ы (neproizvódstvénnye ~/y) non-productive expenditures

общие ~/ы (óbshchie ~/y) total outlays

обыкновенные ~/ы (obyknovénnye ~/y) ordinary expenses

обязательный ~ (obiazátel'nyi ~) obligatory expense

побочный ~ (pobóchnyi ~) incidental expense

покрыть ~/ы (pokrýt' ~/y) to cover expenses

портовые ~/ы (portóvye ~/y) court costs

постоянные ~/ы (postoiánnye ~/y) fixed charges

почтовые ~/ы (pochtóvye ~/y) postage costs

представительские ~/ы (predstavítel'skie ~/y) representation costs

разовой ~ (rázovoi ~) non-recurrent expenditure

складские ~/ы (skladskíe ~/y) storage costs

социальные ~/ы (sotsiál'nye ~/y) social expenditures

страховые ~/ы (strakhovýe ~/y) insurance charges

судебные ~/ы (sudébnye ~/y) court costs

таможенные ~/ы (tamózhennye ~/y) customs charges

текущие ~/ы (tekúshchie ~/y) current expenditures

транспортные ~/ы (tránsportnye ~/y) transportation costs

фактические ~/ы (faktícheskie ~/y) actual expenditures

частные ~/ы (chástnye ~/y) private expenditures

чрезвычайные ~/ы (chrezvycháinye ~/y) extraordinary expenditures

экспедиторские ~/ы (ekspedítorskie ~/y) freight forwarding costs

эксплуатационные ~/ы (ekspluatátsiónnye ~/y) operating costs

экспортные ~/ы (éksportnye ~/y) export costs

~ иностранной валюты (~ inostránnoi valiúty) foreign exchange expenditure

Расходование (raskhódovanie) *n.* expenditure

~ капиталовложения (~ kapitalovlozhéniia) capital expenditure

Расходовать (raskhódovat') *v.* to consume, to expend

Расхождение (raskhozhdénie) *n.* divergence

~ в законодательстве (~ v zakonodátel'stve) statutory divergence

~ во мнениях (~ vo mnéniiakh) difference of opinions

Расцвечивание флагами (rastsvéchivanie flágami) dressing of vessels {admiralty}

Расценка (rastsénka) *f.* valuation, wage rate

единичная ~ (ediníchnaia ~) unit price

прогрессивная ~ (progressívnaia ~) progressive pricing

приемлемая ~ (priémlemaia ~) acceptable pricing

сдельная ~ (sdél'naia ~) piece rate

Расчёт (raschiót) *m.* quotation, payment transaction, settlement

безналичный ~ (beznalíchnyi ~) non-cash transaction, clearing account

валютный ~ (valiútnyi ~) currency settlement

за наличный ~ (za nalíchnyi ~) payment by cash

клиринговый ~ (klíringovyi ~) clearinghouse settlement

межбанковский ~ (mezhbánkovskii ~) interbank settlement

международный ~ (mezhdunaródnyi ~) international settlement

наличный ~ (nalíchnyi ~) cash payment

окончательный ~ (okonchátel'nyi ~) final payment, final settlement

почтовый ~ (pochtóvyi ~) postal payment

приблизительный ~ (priblizítel'nyi ~) approximate calculation

сводный ~ (svódnyi ~) summary calculation

сводный годовой ~ (svódnyi godovói ~) annual summary calculation

финансовый ~ (finánsovyi ~) financial payment

хозяйственный ~ (khoziáistvennyi ~) cost counting, profit and loss

Расчленение (raschlenénie) n. deployment {military}, dismemberment

Расчленять (raschleniát') v. to deploy {military}, to dismember

Расширение (rasshirénie) n. expansion, extension

быстрое ~ (býstroe ~) rapid expansion

~ кредита (~ kredíta) expansion of credit

~ прав (~ prav) expansion of rights

~ предприятия (~ predpriiátiia) expansion of an enterprise

~ производства (~ proizvódstva) expansion of production

~ рынка (~ rýnka) market development

~ спроса (~ sprósa) expansion of demand

~ экспорта (~ éksporta) expansion of exports

Расширять (rasshiriát') v. to broaden, to expand, to extend

Расшифровка (rasshifróvka) f. deciphering, decoding

Ратификаци/я (ratifikátsi/ia) f. ratification

подлежит ~/и (podlezhít ~/i) subject to ~

Ратифицированный (ratifitsírovannyi) adj. ratified

Ратифицировать (ratifitsírovat') v. to ratify, to validate

Ратуша (rátusha) f. town hall {usu. in Belarus, Poland, etc.}

Рацион (ratsión) m. ration {e.g. food}

Рационализация (ratsionalizátsiia) f. rationalization

~ труда (~ trudá) rationalization of labor

Рационализировать (ratsionalizírovat') v. to improve, to rationalize

Рациональный (ratsionál'nyi) adj. efficient, rational

Реабилитация (reabilitátsiia) f. rehabilitation

Реабилитировать (reabilitírovat') v. to rehabilitate

Реакционер (reaktsionér) m. reactionary

Реакционный (reaktsiónnyi) adj. reactionary

Реакция (reáktsiia) f. reaction, entrenched faction

Реализация (realizátsiia) f. implementation, sale

~ заложенного имущества (~ zalózhennogo imúshchestva) fore-closure sale

~ товара (~ továra) sale of goods

~ ценных бумаг (~ tsénnykh bumág) conversion of securities

Реализовывать (realizóvyvat') v. to implement, to sell

Реализованный (realizóvannyi) adj. realized, sold

Ребёнок (rebiónok) m. child, infant

внебрачный ~ (vnebráchnyi ~) child born out of wedlock

законный ~ (zakónnyi ~) legitimate child

кровный ~ (króvnyi ~) birth child {as opposed to adopted child}

покинутый ~ (pokínutyi ~) abandoned child

незаконный ~ (nezakónnyi ~) illegitimate child

приёмный ~ (priiómnyi ~) adopted child

признанный ~ (príznannyi ~) acknowledged child

признанный незаконный ~ (príznannyi nezakónnyi ~) acknowledged illegitimate child

родной ~ (rodnói ~) one's own child {birth child}

узаконенный ~ (uzakónennyi ~) legitimized child

узаконить внебрачного ребёнка (uzakónit' vnebráchnogo rebiónka) to legitimize a child born out of wedlock

Ревалоризация (revalorizátsiia) f. revalorization

~ валюты (~ valiúty) revalorization of currency

Ревальвация (reval'vátsiia) f. revaluation

Реверс (révers) *m.* reverse {e.g. of a coin}

Ревизионизм (revizionízm) *m.* revisionism

Ревизионист (revizioníst) *m.* revisionist

Ревизионистский (revízionístskii) *adj.* revisionist

Ревизия (revíziia) *f.* audit, revision
    бухгалтерская ~ (bukhgálterskaia ~) audit of the books
    финансовая ~ (finánsovaia ~) financial audit

Ревизор (revizór) *m.* auditor, comptroller

Революционер (revoliutsionér) *m.* revolutionary

Революционный (revoliutsiónnyi) *adj.* revolutionary

Революция (revoliútsiia) *f.* revolution
    аграрная ~ (agrárnaia ~) agrarian rebellion
    буржуазная ~ (burzhuáznaia ~) bourgeouise revolution
    демографическая ~ (demografícheskaia ~) demographic revolution
    октябрьская ~ (oktiábr'skaia ~) October revolution
    промышленная ~ (promýshlennaia ~) Industrial revolution

Регент (régent) *m.* regent

Регентство (régentstvo) *n.* regency

Регистр (regístr) *m.* account book, journal, register
    гражданский ~ (grahdánskii ~) civil register
    учётный ~ (uchiótnyi ~) account book
    ~ акционерных компаний (~ aktsionérnykh kompánii) register of companies

Регистратор (registrátor) *m.* recorder, registrar

Регистратура (registratúra) *f.* registry

Регистраци/я (registrátsi/ia) *f.* registration
    земельная ~ (zemél'naia ~) land ~
    международная ~ (mezhdunaródnaia ~) international ~
    нотариальная ~ (notariál'naia ~) notarial ~
    обязательная ~ (obiazátel'naia ~) compulsory ~
    официальная ~ (ofitsiál'naia ~) official ~
    правовая ~ судна (pravováia ~ súdna) legal ~ of a vessel
    предварительная ~ (predvarítel'naia ~) pre-~
    признать ~/ю недействительной (priznát' ~/iu nedeistvítel'noi) to nullify ~
    торговая ~ (torgóvaia ~) trade ~
    уголовная ~ (ugolóvnaia ~) ~ of criminal offenders

Регистрировать (registrírovat') *v.* to register

Регламент (regláment) *m.* regulations, standing orders
    административный ~ (administratívnyi ~) administrative regulations
    внутренний ~ (vnútrennii ~) internal rules
    дополнительный ~ (dopolnítel'nyi ~) additional orders
    заводской ~ (zavdskói ~) plant rules
    исполнительный ~ (ispolnítel'nyi ~) executive orders
    консульский ~ (kónsul'skii ~) consular orders
    санитарный ~ (sanitárnyi ~) health regulations
    служебный ~ (sluzhébnyi ~) official regulations

Регламентный (reglaméntnyi) *adj.* regulation, routine

Регламентация (reglámentátsiia) *f.* regulation

Регламентировать (reglamentírovat') *v.* to regulate

Регресс (regréss) *m.* recourse
    право ~/a (právo ~/a) right of recourse
    с ~/ом (s ~/om) with recourse

Регулирование (regulírovanie) *n.* adjustment, control, management, regulation
    бюджетное ~ (biudzhétnoe ~) budget control
    валютное ~ (valiútnoe ~) currency exchange control
    государственное ~ (gosudárstvennoe ~) public regulation

гражданско-правовое ~
(grahdánsko-pravovóe ~) civil
law regulation
денежное ~ (dénezhnoe ~)
monetary control
коммерческое ~ (kommércheskoe ~)
commercial regulation
кредитное ~ (kredítnoe ~) credit
control
налоговое ~ (nalógovoe ~) fiscal
regulation
правовое ~ (pravovóe ~) legal
regulation
экономическое ~ (ekonómícheskoe
~) economic regulation
юридическое ~ (iuridícheskoe ~)
jurisprudencial regulation
~ автодвижения (~
avtodvizhéniia) traffic
regulation
~ валюты (~ valiúty) control of
exchange
~ квартирной платы (~ kvartírnoi
pláty) rent control
~ нормы процента (~ nórmy
protsénta) interest rate
adjustments
~ радиосношения (~
radiosnoshéniia) regulation of
the air waves {radio}
~ рыболовства (~ rybolóvstva)
commercial fishing control
~ рынка (~ rýnka) market
regulation
~ цен (~ tsen) price controls
Регулировать (regulírovat') v. to
control, to regulate
Регулярно (reguliárno) adv.
regularly
Регулярный (reguliárnyi) adj.
periodic, regular
Редактировать (redáktírovat') v. to
edit
Редактор (redáktor) m. editor
главный ~ (glávnyi ~) editor-in-
chief
Редакция (redáktsiia) f. editing,
editorial staff
Редисконт (rediskónt) m. rediscount
Реестр (reéstr) m. list, register,
role, table
государственный ~ гражданских
воздушных судов (gosudárstvennyi
~ grahdánskikh vozdúshnykh
súdov) state registry of civil
aircraft

основной ~ (osnovnói ~)
principle register
патентный ~ (paténtnyi ~) patent
register
публичный ~ (publíchnyi ~)
public record
торговый ~ (torgóvyi ~) trade
register
~ арестов и запрещений (~
aréstov i zapreshchénii) police
blotter
~ авторских прав (~ ávtorskikh
prav) copyright register
~ наименований фирм (~
naimenovánii firm) business
names register
Режим (rezhím) m. conditions,
regime, treatment
благоприятный ~ (blagopriiátnyi
~) favorable treatment
валютный ~ (valiútnyi ~)
currency control regime
дискриминационный ~
(diskriminatsiónnyi ~)
discriminatory {trade} regime
иммиграционный ~
(immigratsiónnyi ~) immigration
control
лицензионный ~ (litsenziónnyi ~)
licensing regime
льготный ~ (l'gótnyi ~)
preferential treatment
национальный ~ (natsionál'nyi ~)
national treatment
налоговый ~ (nalógovyi ~) tax
regime, tax treatment
переходный ~ (perekhódnyi ~)
transitional regime
пограничный ~ (pograníchnyi ~)
border control
политический ~ (politícheskii ~)
political regime
правовой ~ (pravovói ~) legal
regime
санитарный ~ (sanitárnyi ~)
health controls
таможенный ~ (tamózhennyi ~)
customs regime
тоталитарный ~ (totalitárnyi ~)
totalitarian regime
фашистский ~ (fashístskii ~)
fascist regime
фискальный ~ (fiskál'nyi ~)
fiscal control
~ наиболее благоприятствуемой
нации (~ naibólee blagopriiát-

stvuemoi nátsii) most favored
nation treatment

Резерв (rezérv) *m.* fund, provision,
reserves, stock
  кассовый ~ (kássovyi ~) cash
reserve
  ликвидный ~ (likvídnyi ~) liquid
funds
  валютные ~/ы (valiútnye ~/y)
currency reserves
  денежные ~/ы (dénezhnye ~/y)
monetary reserves
  золотые ~/ы (zolotýe ~/y) gold
reserves
  материальные ~/ы (materiál'nye
~/y) material reserves
  общий ~ (óbshchii ~) general
reserve
  производственные ~/ы
(proizvódstvennye ~/y)
productive reserves
  свободный ~ (svobódnyi ~) free
reserve
  скрытые ~/ы (skrýtye ~/y) hidden
reserves
  текущие ~/ы (tekúshchie ~/y)
current reserves
  финансовый ~ (finánsovyi ~)
financial reserve
  ~ на погашение задолженности (~
na pogashénie zadólzhennosti)
sinking fund

Резидент (rezidént) *m.* resident
{also: in-country intelligence
officer}

Резиденция (rezidéntsiia) *f.*
residence
  временная ~ (vrémennaia ~)
temporary residence

Резолюция (rezoliútsiia) *f.*
resolution
  окончательная ~ (okonchátel'naia
~) final resolution
  подтвердительная ~
(podtverdítel'naia ~) confirming
resolution
  совместная ~ (sovméstnaia ~)
joint resolution
  ~ доверия (~ dovériia)
resolution of confidence
  ~ недоверия (~ nedovériia)
resolution of no confidence

Результат (rezul'tát) *m.* effect,
outcome, result
  желательный ~ (zhelátel'nyi ~)
desired effect

  конечный ~ (konéchnyi ~) end
result
  ~/ы выборов (~/y výborov)
results of elections

Реимпорт (reímport) *m.* reimport

Реимпортировать (reimportírovat')
v. to reimport

Реинвестиция (reinvestítsiia) *f.*
reinvestment

Рейс (reis) *m.* trip, voyage
  круговой ~ (krugovói ~) round
trip
  очередной ~ (ocherednói ~)
regular voyage
  ~, в один конец (~, v odin
konets) one-way trip

Реквизировать (rekvizírovat') *v.* to
requisition

Реквизиты (rekvizíty) *pl.*
requisites

Реквизиция (rekvizítsiia) *f.*
requisition

Реклама (rekláma) *f.* advertisement,
promotion

Рекламация (reklamátsiia) *f.* return
of goods {e.g. damaged}

Рекомендация (rekomendátsiia) *f.*
recommendation

Реконверсия (rekonvérsiia) *f.*
reconversion

Реконструкция (rekonstrúktsiia) *f.*
reconstruction

Рекрутировать (rekrutírovat') *v.* to
recruit

Религия (relígiia) *f.* religion
  государственная ~
(gosudárstvennaia ~) state ~

Ремесленник (reméslennik) *m.*
artisan, craftsman

Ремесленный (reméslennyi) *adj.*
craft, trade {also pejorative
stereotype}

Ремесленничество
(reméslennichestvo) *n.*
craftsmanship, workmanship

Ремилитаризация (remilitarizátsiia)
f. remilitarization

Ремитент (remitént) *m.* remitter

Ремитирование (remitírovanie) *n.*
remittance

Ремонт (remónt) *m.* repair, upkeep
  восстановительный ~
(vosstanovítel'nyi ~) overhaul
  мелкий ~ (mélkii ~) minor repair
  текущий ~ (tekúshchii ~) regular
maintenance

Рент/а (rént/a) rent

абсолютная ~ (absoliútnaia ~) absolute rent

временная ~ (vrémennaia ~) temporary annuity

выплачивать ~/у (vypláchivat' ~/u) to pay an annuity

государственная ~ (gosudárstvennaia ~) government annuity

денежная ~ (dénezhnaia ~) money rent

дифференциальная ~ (differentsiál'naia ~) differential rent

добавочная ~ (dobávochnaia ~) supplemental rent

земельная ~ (zemél'naia ~) ground lease

капитализированная ~ (kapitalizírovannaia ~) capitalized rent

монопольная ~ (monopól'naia ~) monopoly rent

натуральная ~ (naturál'naia ~) rent in kind

пожизненная ~ (pozhíznennaia ~) lifetime annuity

срочная ~ (sróchnaia ~) terminable annuity

чистая ~ (chístaia ~) pure rent

Рентабельност/ь (rentábel'nost/') *f.* profitability

коэффициент ~/и (koeffitsiént ~/i) net profit ratio

Рентабельный (rentábel'nyi) *adj.* profitable

Реорганизация (reorganizátsiia) *f.* reorganization

~ правительства ~ (~ pravítel'stva) of the government

Реорганизовать (reorganizovát') *v.* to reorganize

Репарация (reparátsiia) *f.* reparation

Репатриант (repatriánt) *m.* repatriate

Репатриация (repatriátsiia) *f.* repatriation

~ капитала (~ kapitála) repatriation of capital

Репатриировать (repatriírovat') *v.* to repatriate

Реплика (réplika) *f.* rejoinder, retort

Репорт (repórt) *m.* carry-over, contango

Репрессалии (repressálii) *n.* retaliation, reprisals, sanctions

применять ~ (primeniát' ~) to retaliate

Репрессия (représsiia) *f.* punitive measure

дисциплинарная ~ (distsiplinárnaia ~) disciplinary measure

Реприватизация (reprivatizátsiia) *f.* reprivatization

Реприватизировать (reprivatizírovat') *v.* to reprivatize

Репутация (reputátsiia) *f.* reputation, standing

коммерческая ~ (kommércheskaia ~) commercial standing

Республика (respúblika) *f.* republic

автономная ~ (avtonómnaia ~) autonomous republic

народная (naródnaia) People's Republic

объединённая арабская ~ (ob"ediniónnaia arábskaia ~) United Arab Republic

президентская ~ (prezidéntskaia ~) Presidential Republic

унитарная ~ (unitárnaia ~) Unitary Republic

федеративная ~ (federatívnaia ~) Federal Republic

Федеративная ~ Германии {ФРГ} (federatívnaia ~ germánii {frg}) Federal Republic of Germany {FRG}

Республиканец (respublikánets) *m.* republican {of various Republican parties}

Республиканский (respublikánskii) *adj.* republican {historically also of Soviet republics}

Реставрация (restavrátsiia) *f.* restoration

Реставрировать (restavrírovat') *v.* to restore

Реституция (restitútsiia) *f.* restitution

~ в натуре (~ v natúre) restitution in kind

Рестрикция (restríktsiia) *f.* limitation, restriction

кредитная ~ (kredítnaia ~) credit squeeze

Ресурсы (resúrsy) *pl.* resources

денежные ~ (dénezhnye ~) monetary ~

истощимые ~ (istoshchímye ~)
exhaustible ~
кредитные ~ (kredítnye ~) credit
~
материальные ~ (materiál'nye ~)
material ~
природные ~ (priródnye ~)
natural ~
производственные ~
(proizvódstvennye ~) productive
~
финансовые ~ (finánsovye ~)
financial ~
экономические ~ (ekonomícheskie
~) economic ~
Реторсия (retórsiia) f. retorsion
Рефакция (refáktsiia) f. loss
allowance, volume discount
Референдум (referéndum) m.
referendum
обязательный ~ (obiazátel'nyi ~)
mandatory referendum
факультативный ~ (fakul'tatívnyi
~) optional referendum
Референт (referént) m. advisor,
expert, reviewer
Реформа (refórma) f. reform
аграрная ~ (agrárnaia ~)
agrarian ~
административная ~
(administratívnaia ~)
administrative ~
банковская ~ (bánkovskaia ~)
bank ~
валютная ~ (valiútnaia ~)
currency ~
земельная ~ (zemél'naia ~) land
~
избирательная ~ (izbirátel'naia
~) electoral ~
кредитная ~ (kredítnaia ~)
credit ~
налоговая ~ (nalógovaia ~) tax ~
парламентская ~ (parlámentskaia
~) parliamentary ~
социальная ~ (sotsiál'naia ~)
social ~
судебная ~ (sudébnaia ~)
judicial ~
финансовая ~ (finánsovaia ~)
financial ~
Реформизм (reformízm) m. reformism
Реформист (reformíst) m. reformist
Реформистский (reformístskii) adj.
reformer, reformist
Рецензент (retsenzént) m. reviewer
Рецензия (retsénziia) f. review

Рецидив (retsidív) m. repeated
offense
Рецидивист (retsidivíst) m.
recidivist
Речь (rech') f. speech
защитительная ~
(zashchitítel'naia ~) argument
for the defense {at trial}
тронная ~ (trónnaia ~) royal
speech
~ прокурора (~ prokuróra)
argument by the prosecution {at
trial}
Решать (reshát') v. to decide, to
resolve, to settle
Решение (reshénie) n. decision,
settlement, solution
административное ~
(administratívnoe ~)
administrative decision
аннулировать ~ (annulírovat' ~)
to annul a decision
арбитражное ~ (arbitrázhnoe ~)
arbitral award
возможное ~ (vozmózhnoe ~)
possible solution
вынести ~ (výnesti ~) to carry
out a decision
гражданско-правовое ~
(grahdánsko-pravovóe ~) civil
law decision
декларативное ~ (deklaratívnoe
~) declaratory decision
единогласное ~ (edinoglásnoe ~)
unanimous decision
заочное ~ (zaóchnoe ~) decision
by default
иностранное ~ (inostránnoe ~)
foreign decision
иностранное арбитражное ~
(inostránnoe arbitrázhnoe ~)
foreign arbitral decision
компромиссное ~ (kompromíssnoe
~) compromise settlement
мирное ~ (mírnoe ~) amicable
settlement
мотивированное ~ (motivírovannoe
~) motivated settlement
мотивировать ~ (motivírovat' ~)
to motivate a settlement
национальное арбитражное ~
(natsionál'noe arbitrázhnoe ~)
national arbitral settlement
неотменяемое ~ (neotmeniáemoe ~)
irrevocable decision
обоснованное ~ (obosnóvannoe ~)
justified decision

общее ~ (óbshchee ~) general settlement

обязательное ~ (obiazátel'noe ~) compulsory decision

окончательное ~ (okonchátel'noe ~) final decision

окончательное судебное ~ (okonchátel'noe sudébnoe ~) final judicial decision

оставить ~ в силе (ostávit' ~ v síle) to leave a decision in force

отменить судебное ~ (otmenít' sudébnoe ~) to overturn a judicial decision

первоначальное ~ (pervonachál'noe ~) original decision

подтвердить ~ (podtverdít' ~) to affirm a decision

предварительное ~ (predvarítel'noe ~) preliminary decision

предварительное судебное ~ (predvarítel'noe sudébnoe ~) preliminary judicial decision

принципиальное ~ (printsipiál'noe ~) principal decision

противоречивое ~ (protivorechívoe ~) contradictory decision

сенатское ~ (senátskoe ~) senate decision

судебное ~ (sudébnoe ~) judicial decision

третейское ~ (tretéiskoe ~) decision by arbitration

уголовное ~ (ugolóvnoe ~) criminal conviction

~ апелляционного суда (~ apelliatsiónnogo sudá) appellate decision

~ вынесенное судом последней инстанции (~ vynesénnoe sudóm poslédnei instántsii) decision by a court of final instance

Решить (reshít') v. [see решать]

Реэкспорт (reéksport) m. reexport

Реэкспортировать (reeksportírovat') v. to reexport

Риал (riál) m. Rial {Middle Eastern currency}

Риск (risk) m. hazard, peril, risk

валютный ~ (valiútnyi ~) currency risk

военный ~ (voénnyi ~) risk of war

застрахованный ~ (zastrakhóvannyi ~) insured risk

коммерческий ~ (kommércheskii ~) commercial risk

морской ~ (morskói ~) maritime risk

нестрахуемый ~ (nestrakhúemyi ~) uninsurable risk

особый ~ (osóbyi ~) special risk

принятый ~ (príniatyi ~) accepted risk

профессиональный ~ (professionál'nyi ~) professional risk

страховой ~ (strakhovói ~) insurance risk

условный ~ (uslóvnyi ~) conditional risk

~ потери (~ potéri) risk of loss

Рисковый (rískovyi) adj. risk, risky

Рисун/ок (risún/ok) m. drawing {picture}

промышленные ~/ки (promýshlennye ~/ki) industrial drawings

Ровня (róvniá) equal, match

Род (rod) m. family, genre, kind, origin, type

Родина (ródina) f. homeland

Родител/ь (rodítel/') m. parent

кровные ~/и (króvnye ~/i) birth parents

приёмные ~/и (priiómnye ~/i) adoptive parents

Родной (rodnói) adj. native

Родственник (ródstvennik) m. relative

кровный ~ (króvnyi ~) blood ~

Родство (ródstvo) n. kinship, relationship

внебрачное ~ (vnebráchnoe ~) illegitimate kinship

законное ~ (zakónnoe ~) legal relationship

кровное ~ (króvnoe ~) blood relationship

Рождаемость (rozhdáemost') f. birth-rate, fertility

Рождение (rozhdénie) n. birth

внебрачное ~ (vnebráchnoe ~) birth out of wedlock

законное ~ (zakónnoe ~) legitimate birth

незаконное ~ (nezakónnoe ~) illegitimate birth

Розница (róznitsa) f. retail
продать в ~/у (prodát' v ~/u) to
sell at retail
в ~/у (v ~/u) at retail
Розничный (róznichnyi) adj. retail
Рознь (rozn') f. difference,
dissension
Розыск (rózysk) m. inquiry, search
уголовный ~ (ugolóvnyi ~)
criminal investigation
Роспись (róspis') f. inventory,
list
бюджетная ~ (biudzhétnaia ~)
budget schedule
~ доходов (~ dokhódov) schedule
of earnings
~ расходов (~ raskhódov)
schedule of expenses
Роспуск (róspusk) m. dismissal,
dissolution
~ парламента (~ parlámenta)
dissolution of parliament
~ собрания (~ sobrániia) breakup
of a meeting
Рост (rost) m. expansion, growth,
increase, rise
бурный ~ численности населения
(búrnyi ~ chíslennosti naseléniia) explosive population
growth
значительный ~ (znachítel'nyi ~)
significant growth
~ занятости (~ zaniatosti)
growth in employment
~ заработной платы (~ zárabotnoi
pláty) wage increase
~ населения (~ naseléniia)
population growth
~ покупательной способности (~
pokupátel'noi sposóbnosti)
increase in purchasing power
~ потребительского спроса (~
potrebítel'skogo sprósa)
increase in consumer demand
~ производительности (~
proizvodítel'nosti) increase in
productivity
~ производительности труда (~
proizvodítel'nosti trudá)
increase in labor productivity
~ производства (~ proizvódstva)
increase in production
~ спроса (~ sprósa) increase in
demand
~ суммы оборота (~ súmmy
oborota) increase in turnover
~ цен (~ tsen) upsurge in prices

Ростовщик (rostovshchík) m. usurer
Ростовщический (rostovshchícheskii)
adj. usurious
Ростовщичество (rostovshchíchestvo)
n. usury
Росчерк (róscherk) m. flourish
одним ~/ом пера (odním ~/om
perá) with a single stroke of
the pen
Роялти (róialti) n. royalty
ступенчатое ~ (stupénchatoe ~)
graduated scale ~
Рублёвый (rublióvyi) adj. ruble
Рубль (rubl') m. Ruble (Russian
currency)
Рук/а (rúk/a) f. hand
рабочие ~/и (rabóchie ~/i) hands
{figuratively, workers}
Руководитель (rukovodítel') m.
chief, manager, leader
~ предприятия (~ predpriiátiia)
chief of an enterprise
Руководить (rukovodít') v. to be in
charge, to manage, to supervise
Руководство (rukovódstvo) n.
guidance, leadership, management
высшее ~ (výsshee ~) top
management
квалифицированное ~
(kvalifitsírovannoe ~) competent
management
~ завода (~ zavóda) plant
management
~ фирмы (~ fírmy) company
management
Руководящий (rukovodiáshchii) adj.
administrative, leading, managing
Русло (rúslo) n. channel, course
Рупия (rúpiia) f. Rupee {currency
of certain Asian nations}
Ручательство (ruchátel'stvo) n.
guaranty, surety, warranty
~ за доброкачественность (~ za
dobrokáchestvennost') guaranty
of quality
Ручаться (ruchát'sia) v. to
guarantee, to stand security, to
stand del credere, to warrant
Рыболовство (rybolóvstvo) n.
fishing, fishing industry
береговое ~ (beregovóe ~)
coastal fishing trade
Рын/ок (rýnok) m. market
акцептный ~ (aktséptnyi ~)
acceptance ~
биржевой ~ (birzhevói ~) stock

валютный ~ (valiútnyi ~) currency ~
вексельный ~ (véksel'nyi ~) bill {note} ~
внешний ~ (vnéshnii ~) external ~
внутренний ~ (vnútrennii ~) domestic ~
выпустить на ~ (vypustít' na ~) to introduce into the ~
вялый ~ (viályi ~) stagnant ~
денежный ~ (dénezhnyi ~) money ~
заграничный ~ (zagraníchnyi ~) foreign ~
замкнутый ~ (zamknútyi ~) closed ~
зарубежный ~ (zarubézhnyi ~) overseas ~
защищённый ~ (zashchishchiónnyi ~) protected ~
импортный ~ (ímportnyi ~) import ~
иностранный ~ (inostránnyi ~) foreign ~
интегрированный ~ (integrírovannyi ~) integrated ~
капиталистический ~ (kapitalistícheskii ~) capitalist ~
конкурирующий ~ (konkuríruiushchii ~) competitive ~
контролируемый ~ (kontrolíruemyi ~) controlled ~
котируемый на ~/ке (kotíruemyi na ~/ke) listed on the exchange
международный ~ (mezhdunaródnyi ~) international ~
международный валютный ~ (mezhdunaródnyi valiútnyi ~) international currency ~
местный ~ (méstnyi ~) local ~
мировой ~ (mirovói ~) global ~
национальный ~ (natsionál'nyi ~) national ~
неофициальный ~ (neofitsiál'nyi ~) unofficial ~
общий ~ (óbshchii ~) common ~
оживлённый ~ (ozhivliónnyi ~) broad ~
организованный ~ (organizóvannyi ~) organized ~
открытый ~ (otkrýtyi ~) open ~
официальный ~ (ofitsiál'nyi ~) official ~
переполнить ~ (perepólnit' ~) to glut the ~

полулегальный ~ (polulegál'nyi ~) gray ~
пересыщенный ~ (peresýshchennyi ~) glutted ~
преференциальный ~ (preferentsiál'nyi ~) preferential ~
региональный ~ (regionál'nyi ~) regional ~
регулируемый ~ (regulíruemyi ~) regulated ~
свободный ~ (svobódnyi ~) free ~
свободный валютный ~ (svobódnyi valiútnyi ~) free currency ~
сельскохозяйственный ~ (sel'skokhoziáistvennyi ~) agricultural ~
товарный ~ (továrnyi ~) commodities ~
традиционный ~ (traditsiónnyi ~) traditional ~
учётный ~ (uchiótnyi ~) discount ~
фрахтовый ~ (frákhtovyi ~) tonnage ~
чёрный ~ (chiórnyi ~) black ~
экспортный ~ (éksportnyi ~) export ~
~ вооружений (~ vooruzhénii) arms ~
~ капитала (~ kapitála) capital ~
~ рабочей силы (~ rabóchei síly) labor ~
~ ссудных капиталов (~ ssúdnykh kapitálov) capital lending ~
~ ценных бумаг (~ tsénnykh bumág) securities ~
Рыночный (rýnochnyi) *adj.* market
Рычаг (rychág) *m.* lever, linchpin
экономический ~ (ekonomícheskii ~) lever of economic control
~ управления (~ upravléniia) control lever

С

Саботаж (sabotázh) *m.* sabotage
Саботажник (sabotázhnik) *m.* saboteur
Саботировать (sabotírovat') *v.* to sabotage
Салазк/и (salázk/i) *pl.* skids
Сальдо (sál'do) *n.* balance

дебетовое ~ (debetóvoe ~)
balance due, debit balance
кредитовое ~ (kredítovoe ~)
credit balance
нулевое ~ (nulevóe ~) zero
balance
отрицательное ~ (otritsátel'noe
~) negative balance
положительное ~ (polozhítel'noe
~) positive balance
~ счёта (~ schióta) balance of
an account
~ текущего счёта (~ tekúshchego
schióta) current account balance
Самоволие (samovólie) n.
licentiousness
Самогон (samogón) m. moonshine
{illegal spirits}
Самогонщик (samogónshchik) m.
moonshiner {maker of illegal
spirits}
Самодержавие (samoderzhávie) n.
autocracy
Самодержавно (samoderzhávno) adv.
autocratically
Самодержавный (samoderzhávnyi) adj.
autocratic
Самодержец (samodérzhets) m.
autocrat
Самозащита (samozashchíta) f. self-
defense {e.g. martial arts}
Самолёт (samoliót) m. aircraft,
airplane
гражданский ~ (grahdánskii ~)
civil aircraft
Самолётостроение
(samoliótostroénie) n. aircraft
construction
Самонадеянность (samonadéiannost')
f. arrogance, conceit
преступная ~ (prestúpnaia ~)
criminal conceit
Самооборона (samooboróna) f. self-
defense {as defense to charge of
assault, murder}
законная ~ (zakónnaia ~) legal
self-defense
Самоопределение (samoopredelénie)
n. self-determination
Самоотвод (samootvód) m. withdrawal
of candidacy, refusal to accept
nomination
заявить о ~/e (zaiavít' o ~/e)
to declare withdrawal from
candidacy
Самопомощь (samopómoshch') f.
mutual aid, self-help

Самостоятельность
(samostoiátel'nost') f.
independence
законодательная ~
(zakonodátel'naia ~) legislative
independence
хозяйственная ~
(khoziáistvennaia ~) economic
independence
юридическая ~ (iuridícheskaia ~)
legal independence
Самостоятельный (samostoiátel'nyi)
adj. independent
Самосуд (samosúd) m. mob justice,
lynching party
Самоубийство (samoubiístvo) n.
suicide
Самоубийца (samoubiítsa) m. suicide
{person committing}
Самоуправление (samoupravlénie) n.
self-government, self-management
рабочее ~ (rabóchee ~) workers'
self-management
Самоуправный (samouprávnyi) adj.
arbitrary
Самофинансирование
(samofinánsirovanie) n. self-
financing
Санкционировать (sánktsionírovat')
v. to sanction
Санкци/я (sanktsi/ia) f. sanction
административная ~
(administratívnaia ~)
administrative ~
военная ~ (voénnaia ~) military
~
гражданская ~ (grahdánskaia ~)
civil ~
дипломатическая ~
(diplomatícheskaia ~) diplomatic
~
договорная ~ (dogovórnaia ~)
contractual ~
коллективная ~ (kollektívnaia ~)
collective ~
кредитная ~ (kredítnaia ~)
credit ~
моральная ~ (morál'naia ~) moral
~
налоговая ~ (nalógovaia ~) tax
penalty
парламентская ~ (parlámentskaia
~) parliamentary ~
применить ~/ю (primenít' ~/iu)
to apply a ~
репрессивная ~ (repressívnaia ~)
oppressive ~

торговая ~ (torgóvaia ~) trade ~
уголовная ~ (ugolóvnaia ~)
criminal ~
финансовая ~ (finánsovaia ~)
financial ~
фискальная ~ (fiskál'naia ~)
fiscal ~
штрафная ~ (shtrafnáia ~)
penalty ~
экономическая ~ (ekonomícheskaia
~) economic ~
~ закона (~ zakóna) ~ of the law
Сановник (sanóvnik) m. dignitary
Сбалансировать (sbalansírovat') v.
to balance {e.g. accounts}
Сберегательный (sberegátel'nyi)
adj. savings
~/ая книжка (~/aia knízhka)
savings account pass book
Сбережение (sberezhénie) n.
economizing, savings
валовое ~ (valovóe ~) gross
savings
вынужденное ~ (výnuzhdennoe ~)
forced economies
денежное ~ (dénezhnoe ~) money
saving
личные ~/я (líchnye ~/ia)
personal savings
чистые ~/я (chístye ~/ia) net
savings
Сберегать (sberegát') v. to
protect, to save
Сберкасса (sberkássa) f. savings
bank
Сберкнижка (sberknízhka) f. savings
account pass book [abbreviated
form]
Сближение (sblizhénie) n.
rapprochement
Сбор (sbor) m. assembly,
collection, dues, duty
акцизный ~ (aktsíznyi ~) excise
duty
арбитражный ~ (arbitrázhnyi ~)
arbitration fee
балластный ~ (ballástnyi ~)
ballast dues
ввозной ~ (vvoznói ~) import tax
весовой ~ (vesovói ~) weighing
fee
гербовый ~ (gérbovyi ~) stamp
duty
годовой ~ (godovói ~) annual fee
грузовой ~ (gruzovói ~) cargo
dues

дополнительный ~ (dopolnítel'nyi
~) surcharge
дорожный ~ (dorózhnyi ~) road
toll
импортный ~ (ímportnyi ~) import
dues
инспекционный ~ (inspektsiónnyi
~) inspection fee
ипотечный ~ (ipotéchnyi ~)
mortgage fee
железнодорожный ~
(zheleznodorózhnyi ~) railway
toll
комиссионный ~ (komissiónnyi ~)
commission
консульский ~ (kónsul'skii ~)
consular fee
корабельный ~ (korabél'nyi ~)
ship's dues
лихтерный ~ (líkhternyi ~)
lighterage
лицензионный ~ (litsenziónnyi ~)
license fee
лоцманский ~ (lótsmanskii ~)
pilotage {dues}
маячный ~ (maiáchnyi ~)
lighthouse dues
местный ~ (méstnyi ~) local
charge
минимальный ~ (minimál'nyi ~)
minimal fee
навигационный ~ (navigatsiónnyi
~) navigation dues
налоговый ~ (nalógovyi ~) tax
levy
наследственный ~ (naslédstvennyi
~) inheritance tax
патентный ~ (paténtnyi ~) patent
fee
поземельный ~ (pozemél'nyi ~)
land tax
портовые ~/ы (portóvye ~/y)
harbor dues
почтовый ~ (pochtóvyi ~) postal
charge
пошлинный ~ (póshlinnyi ~) duty
пристанский ~ (prístanskii ~)
berthage
профессиональный ~
(professionál'nyi ~)
professional fee
разовый ~ (rázovyi ~) one-time
fee
регистрационный ~
(registratsiónnyi ~)
registration fee

санитарный ~ (sanitárnyi ~)
health fee, sanitation fee
складской ~ (skladskói ~)
warehouse fee
страховой ~ (strakhovói ~)
insurance fee
таможенный ~ (tamózhennyi ~)
customs duty
тоннажный ~ (tonnázhnyi ~)
tonnage dues
установленный ~ (ustanóvlennyi
~) established fee
экспедиционный ~
(ekspeditsiónnyi ~) freight
forwarding charge
якорный ~ (iákornyi ~) anchorage
~ с перехода имуществ по
наследству (~ s perekhóda
imúshchestv po naslédstvu)
inheritance transfer tax
Сборище (sbórishche) n. assemblage,
gang, mob
Сборник (sbórnik) m. collection {of
written materials}
Сборщик (sbórshchik) m. collector
~ налогов (~ nalógov) tax
collector
~ пошлин (~ póshlin) collector
of duties
Сбыт (sbyt) m. sale
контрабандный ~ (kontrabándnyi
~) sale of contraband
массовый ~ (mássovyi ~) bulk
sales
оптовый ~ (optóvyi ~)
wholesaling
прямой ~ (priamói ~) direct
sales
Сбытовой (sbytovói) adj. marketing,
sales
Сбыть (sbyt') v. to market, to sell
Свадьба (svád'ba) f. wedding
Свалка (sválka) f. dust-up, scuffle
Сведение (svédenie) n. information,
knowledge
дополнительное ~ (dopolnítel'noe
~) additional information
надёжное ~ (nadiózhnoe ~)
reliable information
Свёкор (sviókor) m. father-in-law
{father of husband}
Свекровь (svékrov') f. mother-in-
law {mother of husband}
Свергнуть (svérgnut') v. to
dethrone, to overthrow
Свержение (sverzhénie) n.
dethronement, overthrow

~ правительства (~
pravítel'stva) overthrow of the
government
~ режима (~ rezhíma) overthrow
of the regime
~ с престола (~ s prestóla)
dethronement
Сверка (svérka) f. tally
Сверхнациональный
(sverkhnatsionál'nyi) adj.
supranational
Сверхприбыль (sverkhpríbyl') f.
excess profit
Сверхсрочный (sverkhsróchnyi) adj.
additional service {e.g. serving
beyond contract, conscription}
Сверхурочный (sverkhuróchnyi) adj.
overtime
Светский (svétskii) adj. temporal,
worldly
Свидетель (svidétel') m. witness
обвиняемый ~ (obviniáemyi ~)
accused witness
~ защиты (~ zashchíty) witness
for the defense
~ обвинения (~ obvinéniia)
witness for the prosecution
~ очевидец (~ ochevídets) eye
witness
Свидетельство (svidétel'stvo) n.
certificate, evidence, testimony
авторское ~ (ávtorskoe ~)
certificate of authorship
брачное ~ (bráchnoe ~) marriage
certificate
вкладное ~ (vkladnóe ~) deposit
receipt
врачебное ~ о смерти (vrachébnoe
~ o smérti) medical death
certificate
долговое ~ (dolgovóe ~)
certificate of indebtedness
закладочное ~ (zakládochnoe ~)
pawn ticket
залоговое ~ (zalógovoe ~) letter
of hypothecation, mortgage
certificate
карантинное ~ (karantínnoe ~)
quarantine certificate
лоцманское ~ (lótsmanskoe ~)
certificate of pilotage
медицинское ~ (meditsínskoe ~)
medical certificate
меритльное ~ (merítel'noe ~)
tonnage slip {of a vessel}
метрическое ~ (metrícheskoe ~)
birth certificate

нотариальное ~ (notariál'noe ~)
notarial certificate
предварительное ~
(predvarítel'noe ~) preliminary
testimony
складочное ~ (skládochnoe ~)
warehouse certificate
таможенное ~ (tamózhennoe ~)
customs certificate
Свидетельствовать
(svidétel'stvovat') v. to give
evidence, to testify
Свита (svíta) f. retinue
Свобода (svobóda) f. freedom,
liberty
личная ~ (líchnaia ~) personal
liberty
основная ~ (osnovnáia ~) basic
freedom
поднадзорная ~ (podnadzórnaia ~)
at liberty, under surveillance
профсоюзная ~ (profsoiúznaia ~)
trade union freedom
религиозная ~ (religióznaia ~)
religious freedom
~ движения (~ dvizhéniia)
freedom of movement
~ движения капиталов (~
dvizhéniia kapitálov) freedom of
capital movement
~ движения рабочей силы (~
dvizhéniia rabóchei síly)
freedom of movement of labor
~ действия (~ déistviia) freedom
of action
~ религии (~ relígii) freedom of
religion
~ слова (~ slóva) freedom of
speech
~ собраний (~ sobránii) freedom
of assembly
~ совести (~ sóvesti) freedom of
conscience
Свободно-конвертируемый (svobódno-
konvertíruemyi) adj. freely
convertible
Свободный (svobódnyi) adj. free
Свод (svod) m. code, collection
~ законов (~ zakónov) code of
laws
Сводка (svódka) f. summary
Сводник (svódnik) m. panderer,
pimp, procurer
Сводничество (svodníchestvo) n.
pandering, pimping, procuring
Своевременно (svoevrémenno) adv. in
due course

Своевременный (svoevrémennyi) adj.
prompt, timely
Свойственник (svóistvennik) m. in-
law {relation by marriage}
Свойство (svóistvo) n. affinity,
in-law relationship
Свояк (svoiák) m. brother-in-law
{husband of wife's sister}
Свояченица (svoiáchenitsa) f.
sister-in-law {wife's sister}
Связать (sviazát') v. [see
связывать]
Связист (sviazíst) m.
telecommunications worker
Связной (sviaznói) m.adj.noun
messenger
Связь (sviaz') f. communication,
connection, link, relation, tie
брачная ~ (bráchnaia ~) marital
relation
казуальная ~ (kazuál'naia ~)
causal link
правовая ~ (pravováia ~) legal
relationship
Связывать (sviázyvat') v. to bind,
to be bound, to be connected {by
phone}, to involve
Священнослужитель
(sviashchennosluzhítel') m.
clergyman
Сговор (sgovór) m. deal, plot
карательный ~ (karátel'nyi ~)
cartel arrangement
Сдавать (sdavát') v.[perfective:
сдать] to deliver, to give, to
surrender
~ в наём (~ v naióm) to let
~ поднаём (~ podnaióm) to sublet
Сдача (sdácha) f. delivery, hiring
out, leasing
будущая ~ (búdushchaia ~)
forward delivery
запоздалая ~ (zapozdálaia ~)
late delivery
неполная ~ (nepólnaia ~) short
delivery
частичная ~ (chastíchnaia ~)
partial delivery
юридическая ~ (iuridícheskaia ~)
legal delivery
~ в наём (~ v naióm) letting
~ в поднаём (~ v podnaióm)
subletting
~-приёмка (~priiómka) acceptance
of goods
~ на хранение (~ na khranénie)
delivery for storage

Сдел/ка (sdél/ka) *f.* bargain, deal, transaction
    банковская ~ (bánkovskaia ~) bank transaction
    бартерная ~ (bárternaia ~) barter deal
    биржевая ~ (birzheváia ~) {stock} exchange transaction
    биржевая ~ на срок (birzheváia ~ na srok) forward transaction {on the exchange}
    внешнеторговая ~ (vneshnetorgóvaia ~) foreign trade transaction
    выгодная ~ (výgodnaia ~) good bargain
    двухсторонняя ~ (dvukhstorónniaia ~) bilateral transaction
    заключить ~/ку (zakliuchít' ~/ku) to conclude a deal
    кассовая ~ (kássovaia ~) cash transaction, spot market transaction
    коммерческая ~ (kommércheskaia ~) business deal
    компенсационная ~ (kompensatsiónnaia ~) buy-back transaction
    комплексная ~ (kómpleksnaia ~) package deal
    кредитная ~ (kredítnaia ~) credit transaction
    международная ~ купли-продажи (mezhdunaródnaia ~ kúpli-prodázhi) international buy-sell transaction
    меновая ~ (menováia ~) barter-exchange transaction
    наличная ~ (nalíchnaia ~) cash deal
    недобросовестная ~ (nedobrosóvestnaia ~) bad faith transaction
    оптовая ~ (optóvaia ~) wholesale deal
    посредническая ~ (posrédnicheskaia ~) middleman transaction
    прибыльная ~ (príbyl'naia ~) profitable transaction
    разовая ~ (rázovaia ~) single transaction
    реэкспортная ~ (reéksportnaia ~) re-export deal
    спекулятивная ~ (spekuliatívnaia ~) speculative transaction
    срочная ~ (sróchnaia ~) futures transaction
    срочная ~ с иностранными валютами (sróchnaia ~ s inostránnymi valiútami) forward currency transaction
    товарообменная ~ (tovaroobménnaia ~) commodity swapping transaction
    торговая ~ (torgóvaia ~) trade deal
    тайная ~ (táinaia ~) secret deal
    убыточная ~ (ubýtochnaia ~) money-losing transaction
    учётная ~ (uchiótnaia ~) discount transaction
    фиктивная ~ (fiktívnaia ~) fictitious transaction, sham deal
    финансовая ~ (finánsovaia ~) financial transaction
    хеджевая ~ (khédzhevaia ~) hedge transaction
    честная ~ (chéstnaia ~) fair deal
    ~ купли-продажи (~ kúpli-prodázhi) buy-sell transaction
Сдельщик (sdél'shchik) *m.* pieceworker
Сдельщина (sdél'shchina) *f.* piecework
Себестоимость (sebestóimost') *f.* base cost, prime cost
    фабрично-заводская ~ (fabríchno-zavódskaia ~) manufacturing prime cost
Сезон (sezón) *m.* season
    мёртвый ~ (miórtvyi ~) off season
Сейф (seif) *m.* safe {storage of valuables}
Секвестр (sekvéstr) *m.* sequestration
    наложить ~ (nalozhít' ~) to embargo, to sequestrate
    судебный ~ (sudébnyi ~) judicial sequestration
Секрет (sekrét) *m.* secret
    промышленный ~ (promýshlennyi ~) trade ~
    профессиональный ~ (professionál'nyi ~) professional ~
Секретариат (sekretariát) *m.* secretariat
    генеральный ~ (generál'nyi ~) general ~

Секретарь (sekretár') *m.* secretary
  административный ~ (administratívnyi ~) administrative ~
  генеральный ~ (generál'nyi ~) general ~
  государственный ~ (gosudárstvennyi ~) state ~
  исполнительный (ispolnítel'nyi) executive ~
  парламентский ~ (parlámentskii ~) parliamentary ~
  первый ~ (pérvyi ~) first ~
  постоянный ~ (postoiánnyi ~) permanent ~
  старший ~ (stárshii ~) senior ~
  ~ казначейства (~ kaznachéistva) of the treasury
  ~ мирового судьи ~ (~ mirovógo súd'i) of the world court
Сектор (séktor) *m.* sector
  государственный ~ (gosudárstvennyi ~) state ~
  ключевой ~ (kliuchevói ~) key ~
  национализированный ~ (natsionalizírovannyi ~) nationalized ~
  производственный ~ (proizvódstvennyi ~) productive ~
  промышленный ~ (promýshlennyi ~) industrial ~
  сельскохозяйственный ~ (sel'skokhoziáistvennyi ~) agricultural ~
  частный ~ (chástnyi ~) private ~
  экономический ~ (ekonomícheskii ~) economic ~
Секуляризация (sekuliarizátsiia) *f.* secularization
Секуляризировать (sekuliarizírovat') *v.* to secularize
Секция (séktsiia) *f.* section
  административная ~ (administratívnaia ~) administrative ~
  юридическая ~ (iuridícheskaia ~) legal ~
Селение (selénie) *n.* settlement
Сельскохозяйственный (sel'skokhoziáistvennyi) *adj.* agricultural
Семейство (seméistvo) *n.* family
Семья (sem'iá) *f.* family
  законная ~ (zakónnaia ~) legal ~

  многодетная ~ (mnogodétnaia ~) large ~ {many children}
  приёмная ~ (priiómnaia ~) adopted ~
  родная ~ (rodnáia ~) birth ~
Сенат (senát) *m.* senate
Сенатор (senátor) *m.* senator
Сенатский (senátskii) *adj.* senate
Сепаратизм (separatízm) *m.* separatism
Сепаратист (separatíst) *m.* separatist
Сепаратистский (separatístskii) *adj.* separatist
Сервитут (servitút) *m.* servitude
Серебро (serebró) *n.* silver
  ~ в монете (~ v monéte) silver in a coin
Середняк (seredniák) *m.* average person, peasant of modest earnings
Сертификат (sertifikát) *m.* certificate
  валютный ~ (valiútnyi ~) currency ~
  вкладной ~ (vkladnói ~) ~ of deposit
  залоговый ~ (zalógovyi ~) ~ of pledge, mortgage ~
  медицинский ~ (meditsínskii ~) medical ~
  платёжный ~ (platiózhnyi ~) ~ of payment
  экспортный ~ (éksportnyi ~) export ~
  ~ о мореходности (~ o morekhódnosti) ~ of seaworthiness
  ~ о происхождении (~ o proiskhozhdénii) ~ of origin
Сессия (séssiia) *f.* session, term
  бюджетная ~ (biudzhétnaia ~) budgetary session
  внеочередная ~ (vneocherednáia ~) extraordinary session
  годовая ~ (godováia ~) annual term
  очередная ~ (ocherednáia ~) regular session
  чрезвычайная ~ (chrezvycháinaia ~) emergency session
  ~ парламента (~ parlámenta) session of parliament
Сестра (sestrá) *f.* sister
  внебрачная ~ (vnebráchnaia ~) illegitimate ~
  двоюродная ~ (dvoiúrodnaia ~) cousin {female}

Сетка (sétka) *f.* scale
  тарифная ~ (tarífnaia ~) tariff
  ~
  тарифная ~ заработной платы
  (tarífnaia ~ zárabotnoi pláty)
  wage rate ~
  тарифная ~ цен (tarífnaia ~
  tsen) price schedule
Сеть (set') *f.* network
  дилерская ~ (dílerskaia ~)
  dealership ~
  железнодорожная ~
  (zheleznodoróznaia ~) railway ~
  распределительная ~
  (raspredelítel'naia ~)
  distribution ~
  торговая ~ (torgóvaia ~)
  commercial ~, sales outlets
  ~ связи (~ sviázi)
  communications ~
  ~ торговли (~ torgóvli) ~ of
  trade relations
Сжатие рынка (szhátie rýnka) *n.*
market pressure
Сжигать (szhigát') *v.* to compress
Сигнал бедствия (signál bédstviia)
m. distress signal
Сил/а (síl/a) *f.* force, power,
strength, validity
  войти в ~/у (voití v ~/u) to
  come into force
  вооружённые ~/ы (vooruzhiónnye
  ~/y) armed forces
  законная ~ (zakónnaia ~) legal
  force
  исполнительная ~
  (ispolnítel'naia ~) executive
  power
  квалифицированная рабочая ~
  (kvalifitsírovannaia rabóchaia
  ~) qualified work force
  международные ~/ы
  (mezhdunaródnye ~/y)
  international force
  непреодолимая ~ (nepreodolímaia
  ~) force majeure
  обратная ~ (obrátnaia ~)
  retroactive effect
  с обратной ~/ой (s obrátnoi
  ~/oi) with retroactive effect
  обязательная ~ (obiazátel'naia
  ~) compulsory force
  оккупационные ~/ы
  (okkupatsiónnye ~/y) occupying
  forces
  оставаться в ~/е (ostavát'sia v
  ~/e) to remain in force

относительная ~ (otnosítel'naia
~) relative force
покупательная ~ (pokupátel'naia
~) purchasing power
полицейские ~/ы (politséiskie
~/y) police force{s}
полная ~ (pólnaia ~) full
capacity
производительные ~/ы
(proizvodítel'nye ~/y)
productive forces
рабочая ~ (rabóchaia ~) labor
force
сельскохозяйственная рабочая ~
(sel'skokhoziáistvennaia
rabóchaia ~) agricultural labor
force
~ закона (~ zakóna) force of law
~ судебного решения (~ sudébnogo
reshéniia) force of a judicial
decision
Симулянт (simuliánt) *m.* malingerer
Симуляция (simuliátsiia) *f.*
malingering, simulation
Синдикализм (sindikalízm) *m.*
syndicalism
Синдикалист (sindikalíst) *m.*
syndicalist
Синдикалистский (sindikalístskii)
adj. syndicalist
Синдикат (sindikát) *m.* syndicate
  промышленный ~ (promýshlennyi ~)
  industrial ~
  рабочий ~ (rabóchii ~) labor ~
  ~ предпринимателей ~ (~
  predprinimátelei) of
  entrepreneurs
Синдицировать (sinditsírovat') *v.*
to syndicate
Сирота (sirota) *f.* orphan
  казанская ~ (kazánskaia ~)
  loser, sad sack {colloquial}
Сиротство (sirótstvo) orphanhood
Система (sistéma) *f.* system
  банковская ~ (bánkovskaia ~)
  banking ~
  бюджетная ~ (biudzhétnaia ~)
  budget ~
  валютная ~ (valiútnaia ~)
  currency ~
  двухпалатная ~ (dvukhpalátnaia
  ~) bicameral ~
  двухпартийная (dvukhpartíinaia
  ~) two-party ~
  денежная ~ (dénezhnaia ~)
  monetary ~

избирательная ~ (izbirátel'naia ~) electoral ~
конституционная ~ (konstitutsiónnaia ~) constitutional ~
кредитная ~ (kredítnaia ~) credit ~
метрическая ~ (metrícheskaia ~) metric ~
многосторонняя ~ платежей (mnogostorónniaia ~ platezhéi) multilateral ~ of payments
налоговая ~ (nalógovaia ~) tax ~
однопалатная ~ (odnopalátnaia ~) unicameral ~
парламентарная (parlamentárnaia ~) parliamentary ~
паспортная ~ (pásportnaia ~) passport ~
пенитенциарная (penitentsiárnaia ~) penal ~
правовая ~ (pravováia ~) legal ~
преференциальная (preferentsiál'naia ~) preferential ~
пропорциональная ~ выборов (proportsionál'naia ~ výborov) proportional ~ of voting
пропорциональная избирательная ~ (proportsionál'naia izbirátel'naia ~) proportional electoral ~
судебная ~ (sudébnaia ~) judicial ~
финансовая ~ (finánsovaia ~) financial ~
экономическая ~ (ekonomícheskaia ~) economic ~
Ситуация (situátsiia) f. situation
Скамья подсудимых (skam'iá podsudímykh) the dock {courtroom seats for accused}
Скидка (skídka) f. discount
валютная ~ (valiútnaia ~) foreign exchange premium {trade gain through foreign exchange}
дилерская ~ (dílerskaia ~) dealer ~
коммерческая ~ (kommércheskaia ~) commercial ~
максимальная ~ (maksimál'naia ~) maximum ~
обычная ~ (obýchnaia ~) customary ~
сезонная ~ (sezónnaia ~) seasonal ~

~ за количество (~ za kolíchestvo) quantity ~
~ на бой (~ na boi) breakage ~
Склад (sklad) m. depot, storehouse, warehouse
бондовый ~ (bóndovyi ~) bonded warehouse
лесной ~ (lesnói ~) timber yard
таможенный ~ (tamózhennyi ~) customs store
товарный ~ (továrnyi ~) station warehouse
частный ~ (chástnyi ~) private warehouse
Складирование (skladírovanie) n. storage, warehousing
Складированный (skladírovannyi) adj. stored
Скользящий (skol'ziáshchii) adj. sliding, sliding scale
Скорость (skórost') f. speed
грузовая ~ (gruzováia ~) loaded ~
малая ~ (málaia ~) slow ~
~ оборота (~ oboróta) rate of turnover
~ полёта (~ polióta) air speed
Скот (skot) m. livestock
Скрепить подписью (skrepít' pódpis'iu) v. to authenticate, to countersign
Скрепа (skrépa) f. counter-signature
Скрепка (skrépka) f. paperclip
Скрепление (skreplénie) n. authentication, countersigning
Скрытие (skrýtie) n. concealment
Скрывать (skryvát') v. to conceal, to hide
Скрытый (skrýtyi) adj. concealed, latent
Скупать (skupát') v. to buy up, to buy all of {corner the market}
Скупка (skúpka) f. buying up, cornering the market
Скупой (skupói) adj. cheap, miserly
Скупщик (skúpshchik) m. one who corners the market
~ краденого (~ krádenogo) fence {of stolen goods}
Слаборазвитый (slaborázvityi) adj. underdeveloped {nation}
Слабоумный (slaboúmnyi) adj. feebleminded
Следователь (slédovatel') m. investigator

судебный ~ (sudébnyi ~) judicial investigator
Следовать (slédovat') *v.* to comply, to follow
Следствие (slédstvie) *n.* consequence, investigation
предварительное ~ (predvarítel'noe ~) preliminary investigation
прекратить ~ (prekratít' ~) to call off an investigation
производить ~ (proizvodít' ~) to carry out an investigation
судебное ~ (sudébnoe ~) inquest
устное ~ (ústnoe ~) oral inquest
Слежка (slézhka) *f.* shadowing {closely following someone}
Слёт (sliót) *m.* gathering, rally
Слит/ок (slít/ok) *m.* ingot
золота в ~/ках (zólota v ~/kakh) gold ~s
Сливать (slivát') *v.* to amalgamate
Сливаться (slivát'sia) *v.* to merge
Слияние (sliiánie) *n.* amalgamation, merger
~ капитала (~ kapitála) amalgamation of capital
~ отдельных землепользований (~ otdél'nykh zemlepól'zovanii) merger of separate uses in land
~ предприятий (~ predpriiátii) merger of enterprises
Словесный (slovésnyi) *adj.* oral, verbal
Слово (slóvo) *n.* word
дать свое ~ (dat' svóe ~) to give one's ~
заключительное ~ (zakliuchítel'noe ~) a ~ in conclusion
освободить под честное ~ (osvobodít' pod chéstnoe ~) to release on one's own recognizance
честное ~ (chéstnoe ~) on one's ~
~ чести ~ (~ chesti) of honor
Сложение (slozhénie) *n.* composition, {physical} constitution
Сложный (slózhnyi) *adj.* complex, complicated, multiple
Слуга (slugá) *f.* servant
Служащий (slúzhashchii) *m.adj.noun* clerk, employee
банковский ~ (bánkovskii ~) bank employee

государственный ~ (gosudárstvennyi ~) civil servant
канцелярский ~ (kantseliárskii ~) clerical worker
квалифицированный ~ (kvalifitsírovannyi ~) qualified employee
муниципальный ~ (munitsipál'nyi ~) municipal worker
почтовый ~ (pochtóvyi ~) postal worker
торговый ~ (torgóvyi ~) sales clerk
Служб/а (slúzhb/a) *f.* department, service
авиапочтовая ~ (aviapochtóvaia ~) airmail service
внешняя ~ (vnéshniaia ~) overseas service
внутренняя ~ (vnútrenniaia ~) domestic service
военная ~ (voénnaia ~) military service
годный к военной ~/e (gódnyi k voénnoi ~/e) fit for military service
не пригодный к военной ~/e (ne prigódnyi k voénnoi ~/e) unfit for military service
вспомогательная ~ (vspomogátel'naia ~) auxiliary services
государственная ~ (gosudárstvennaia ~) civil service
дипломатическая ~ (diplomatícheskaia ~) diplomatic corps
добровольная ~ (dobrovól'naia ~) voluntary service
заграничная ~ (zagraníchnaia ~) service abroad
иммиграционная ~ (immigratsiónnaia ~) immigration service
коммунальные ~/ы (kommunál'nye ~/y) communal services
консульская ~ (kónsul'skaia ~) consular corps
лоцманская ~ (lótsmanskaia ~) pilotage service
публичная ~ (publíchnaia ~) public service
публичные ~/ы (publíchnye ~/y) public services

разведочная ~ (razvédochnaia ~)
intelligence service
санитарная ~ (sanitárnaia ~)
health services, sanitary
services
социальная ~ (sotsiál'naia ~)
social service
судебная ~ (sudébnaia ~)
judicial service
юридическая ~ (iuridícheskaia ~)
legal service
Служебный (sluzhébnyi) *adj.*
business, official
Служить (sluzhít') *v.* to serve
Слухач (slukhách) *m.* monitor
Случай (slúchai) *m.* accident, case,
chance, event, opportunity
благоприятный ~ (blagopriiátnyi
~) opportunity
непредвиденный ~ (nepredvídennyi
~) unforeseen situation
непреодолимый ~ (nepreodolímyi
~) unavoidable situation,
situation of force majeure
несчастный ~ (neschástnyi ~)
accident
Случайный (slucháinyi) *adj.*
accidental, casual, fortuitous,
incidental
~/ое убийство (~/oe ubíistvo)
homicide by misadventure
Слушание (slúshanie) *n.* hearing
~ дела (~ déla) hearing on a
case
Смежный (smézhnyi) *adj.* adjacent,
contiguous
Смена (aména) *f.* changing,
replacement, shift
дневная ~ (dnevnaia ~) day shift
ночная ~ (nochnáia ~) night
shift
~ владельца (~ vladél'tsa)
change of owner
~ кабинета (~ kabinéta) change
of cabinet
~ правительства (~
pravítel'stva) change of
government
~ режима (~ rezhíma) change of
regime
Сменить (smenít') *v.* [see сменять]
Сменяемость (smeniáemost') *f.*
interchangeability
Сменяемый (smeniáemyi) *adj.*
interchangeable
Сменять (smeniát') *v.* to change, to
replace

Смертность (smértnost') *f.*
mortality
детская ~ (détskaia ~) infant ~
Смерть (smert') *f.* death
Сместить (smestít') *v.* [see
смещать]
Смет/а (smét/a) *f.* estimate,
statement
бюджетная ~ (biudzhétnaia ~)
budgetary estimate
годовая ~ (godováia ~) annual
statement
годовая бюджетная ~ (godováia
biudzhétnaia ~) annual budgetary
statement
дополнительная бюджетная ~
(dopolnítel'naia biudzhétnaia ~)
additional budgetary estimate
одобрить ~/у (odobrít' ~/u) to
approve an estimate
предварительная ~
(predvarítel'naia ~) preliminary
estimate
приблизительная ~
(priblizítel'naia ~) approximate
estimate
расходная ~ (raskhódnaia ~)
estimate of expenditures
~ доходов (~ dokhódov) estimate
of income
~ затрат (~ zatrát) estimate of
outlays
~ расходов (~ raskhódov)
estimate of expenses
Смешанный (sméshannyi) *adj.* joint,
mixed
Смешать (smeshát') *v.* [see
смешивать]
Смешение (smeshénie) *n.* confusion,
mixture
Смешивать (sméshivat') *v.* to blend,
to confuse, to mix
Смещать (smeshchát') *v.* to
displace, to remove
Смещение (smeshchénie) *n.*
dismissal, displacement, removal
~ на низшую должность (~ na
nízshuiu dólzhnost') demotion to
a lower position
Смягчающий (smiagcháiushchii) *adj.*
mitigating
Смягчение (smiagchénie) *n.*
mitigation
Смятение (smiaténie) *n.* commotion,
confusion, disarray
Снабдить (snabdít') *v.* [see
снабжать]

Снабжать (snabzhát') v. to furnish, to supply
Снабжение (snabzhénie) n. provision, supply
  ~ рынка (~ rýnka) supply on the market
Снаряжение (snariazhénie) n. equipment, outfit
Снижение (snizhénie) n. cut, decline, decrease, reduction
  ~ в воинском звании (~ v voínskom zvánii) reduction in rank {military}
  ~ зарплаты (~ zarpláty) cut in wages
  ~ затрат (~ zatrát) reduction in outlays
  ~ курса (~ kúrsa) drop in exchange rate
  ~ налогов (~ nalógov) reduction of taxes
  ~ пошлин (~ póshlin) reduction of duties
  ~ себестоимости (~ sebestóimosti) decline in the prime cost
  ~ стоимости (~ stóimosti) decline in cost
  ~ таможенных барьеров (~ tamózhennykh bar'érov) lowering of customs barriers
  ~ тарифа (~ tarífa) reduction of tariff
  ~ цен (~ tsen) decline in prices
Снимать (snimát') v. to gather, to harvest, to remove, to take, to withdraw
Снисходительность (sniskhodítel'nost') f. condescension, indulgence, tolerance
Сноха (snokhá) f. daughter-in-law {of father}
Сношени/е (snoshéni/e) n. dealings, intercourse, relations, sexual intercourse
  внешние ~/я (vnéshnie ~/ia) foreign relations
  дипломатические ~/я (diplomatícheskie ~/ia) diplomatic relations
  международные ~/я (mezhdunaródnye ~/ia) international relations
  пограничные ~/я (pograníchnye ~/ia) border relations

  почтовые ~/я (pochtóvye ~/ia) postal relations
  торговые ~/я (torgóvye ~/ia) trade relations
Снятие (sniátie) n. gathering, lifting, removal, taking
  судебное ~ запрета (sudébnoe ~ zapréta) judicial removal of an injunction
  ~ блокады (~ blokády) removal of a blockade
  ~ записи ипотеки (~ zápisi ipotéki) removal of a mortgage
  ~ иммунитета (~ immunitéta) lifting of immunity
  ~ ограничений (~ ogranichénii) dropping of restrictions
  ~ показаний (~ pokazánii) recantation of testimony
Снять (sniat') v. [see СНИМАТЬ]
Соавтор (soávtor) m. co-author
Соавторство (soávtorstvo) n. co-authorship
Собирать (sobirát') v. to convene, to gather, to poll, to prepare
Соблазнитель (soblaznítel') m. seducer
Соблазнить (soblaznít') v. to seduce
Соблюдение (sobliudénie) n. conformity, compliance, observance
  ~ права (~ práva) observance of a right
  ~ условия (~ uslóviia) conformity with a condition
  ~ формальностей ~ (formál'nostei) observance of formalities
Собрание (sobránie) n. assembly, collection, gathering, meeting
  внеочередное ~ (vneocherednóe ~) extraordinary assembly, extraordinary meeting
  ежегодное ~ (ezhegódnoe ~) annual assembly
  законодательное ~ (zakonodátel'noe ~) legislative assembly
  избирательное ~ (izbirátel'noe ~) electoral assembly
  народное ~ (naródnoe ~) people's assembly
  национальное ~ (natsionál'noe ~) national assembly
  общее ~ (óbshchee ~) general meeting

общественное ~ (obshchéstvennoe
~) public assembly
обыкновенное ~ (obyknovénnoe ~)
customary gathering
очередное ~ (ocherednóe ~)
regular assembly
пленарное ~ (plenárnoe ~)
plenary assembly
представительное ~
(predstavítel'noe ~)
representative assembly
совещательное ~
(soveshchátel'noe ~) advisory
assembly
учредительное ~ (uchredítel'noe
~) constituent assembly
{historical}
учредительское ~
(uchredítel'skoe ~) founder's
meeting {e.g. of joint stock
company}
федеральное ~ (federál'noe ~)
federal assembly
чрезвычайное ~ (chrezvycháinoe
~) emergency meeting
чрезвычайное общее ~
(chrezvycháinoe óbshchee ~)
emergency general meeting
~ акционеров (~ aktsionérov)
shareholders' meeting
Собрать (sobrát') v. [see собирать]
Собственник (sóbstvennik) m. owner,
proprietor
Собственность (sóbstvennost') f.
ownership, possession, property
авторская ~ (ávtorskaia ~)
copyright property
арендованная земельная ~
(arendóvannaia zemél'naia ~)
leasehold property
безраздельная ~ (bezrazdél'naia
~) undivided property
государственная ~
(gosudárstvennaia ~) state
ownership, state-owned property
движимая ~ (dvízhimaia ~)
chattels
земельная ~ (zemél'naia ~)
landed property
индивидуальная ~
(individuál'naia ~) individual
ownership
интеллектуальная ~
(intellektuál'naia ~)
intellectual property

исключительная ~
(iskliuchítel'naia ~) exclusive
ownership, exclusive property
коммерческая ~ (kommércheskaia
~) commercial ownership
кооперативная ~ (kooperatívnaia
~) cooperative property
кооперативная земельная ~
(kooperatívnaia zemél'naia ~)
cooperative landed property
литературная ~ (literatúrnaia ~)
literary property
литературная и художественная ~
(literatúrnaia i
khudózhestvennaia ~) literary
and artistic property
личная ~ (líchnaia ~) personal
property
народная ~ (naródnaia ~) public
property
недвижимая ~ (nedvízhimaia ~)
real property
нейтральная ~ (neitrál'naia ~)
mutual ownership
общая ~ (óbshchaia ~) common
property
общая ~ супругов (óbshchaia ~
suprúgov) community property
общественная ~ (obshchéstvennaia
~) common ownership
приобрести в ~ (priobrestí v ~)
to acquire property
промышленная ~ (promýshlennaia
~) industrial property
реальная ~ (reál'naia ~)
tangible property
совместная ~ (sovméstnaia ~)
joint ownership
супружеская ~ (suprúzheskaia ~)
community property
частная ~ (chástnaia ~) private
property
Собственный (sóbstvennyi) adj. own,
personal
Совершение (sovershénie) n.
accomplishment, fulfillment,
perpetration
~ преступления (~ prestupléniia)
perpetration of a crime
~ сделки (~ sdélki)
accomplishment of a deal
Совершеннолетие (sovershennolétie)
n. majority {age of adulthood}
брачное ~ (bráchnoe ~) marital
majority

общегражданское ~
(obshchegrahdánskoe ~) general
civil majority
юридическое ~ (iuridícheskoe ~)
legal majority
Совершеннолетний
(sovershennolétnii) *adj.* adult {of
majority age}
Совершать (sovershát') *v.* to
accomplish, to carry out, to
commit, to perpetrate
Совет (sovét) *m.* advice, board,
council, Soviet {historical}
  административный ~
  (administratívnyi ~)
  administrative council
  большой ~ (bol'shói ~) grand
  council
  верховный ~ (verkhóvnyi ~)
  Supreme Soviet {historical}
  военный ~ (voénnyi ~) military
  council
  городской ~ (gorodskói ~) city
  council
  государственный ~
  (gosudárstvennyi ~) state
  council
  европейский ~ (evropéiskii ~)
  European council
  исполнительный ~ (ispolnítel'nyi
  ~) executive council
  консультативный ~
  (konsul'tatívnyi ~) consultative
  council
  краевой ~ (kraevói ~) krai
  council
  муниципальный ~ (munitsipál'nyi
  ~) municipal council
  наблюдательный ~
  (nabliudátel'nyi ~) supervisory
  council
  народный ~ (naródnyi ~) people's
  council, Soviet
  национальный ~ (natsionál'nyi ~)
  national council
  опекунский ~ (opekúnskii ~)
  board of guardians
  парламентский ~ (parlámentskii
  ~) parliamentary council
  постоянный ~ (postoiánnyi ~)
  permanent council
  рабочий ~ (rabóchii ~) workers'
  council
  революционный ~ (revoliutsiónnyi
  ~) revolutionary council
  регентский ~ (régentskii ~)
  council of regents

  санитарный ~ (sanitárnyi ~)
  sanitary council, board of
  sanitation
  семейный ~ (seméinyi ~) family
  council
  социальный ~ (sotsiál'nyi ~)
  social council
  федеральный ~ (federál'nyi ~)
  federal board
  ~ безопасности ~ (bezopásnosti)
  security council
  ~ министров (~ minístrov)
  council of ministers
  ~ министров иностранных дел (~
  minístrov inostránnykh del)
  council of ministers of foreign
  affairs
  ~ народных комиссаров (~
  naródnykh komissárov) [*abbrev.*
  as совнарком] (sovnarkóm)
  council of people's commissars,
  Sovnarkom {historical
  predecessor to council of
  ministers}
  ~ обороны (~ oboróny) defense
  council
Советник (sovétnik) *m.* advisor,
councillor
  военный ~ (voénnyi ~) military
  advisor
  генеральный ~ (generál'nyi ~)
  general advisor
  городской ~ (gorodskói ~) city
  councillor
  государственный ~
  (gosudárstvennyi ~) state
  councillor
  муниципальный ~ (munitsipál'nyi
  ~) municipal councillor
  технический ~ (tekhnícheskii ~)
  technical advisor
  торговый ~ (torgóvyi ~) trade
  advisor
  финансовый ~ (finánsovyi ~)
  financial advisor
  экономический ~ (ekonomícheskii
  ~) economic advisor
  юридический ~ (iuridícheskii ~)
  legal advisor
Советский (sovétskii) *adj.* Soviet
Совещание (soveshchánie) *n.*
conference, council, meeting
  предварительное ~
  (predvarítel'noe ~) preliminary
  conference
  предвыборное ~ (predvýbornoe ~)
  pre-election conference

закрытое ~ (zakrýtoe ~) closed meeting
инструктивное ~ (instruktívnoe ~) briefing
~ глав государств (~ glav gosudárstv) conference of heads of state
~ глав правительств Семерки (~ glav pravítel'stv semerki) conference of the G-7
~ министров (~ minístrov) ministerial conference
Совещательный (soveshchátel'nyi) *adj.* consultative, deliberative
Совещаться (soveshchát'sia) *v.* to consult, to deliberate
Совладелец (sovladélets) *m.* co-owner, partner
Совладение (sovladénie) *n.* co-ownership
Совместимость (sovmestímost') *f.* compatibility
Совместимый (sovmestímyi) *adj.* compatible
Совместительство (sovmestítel'stvo) *n.* pluralism of officership {e.g. same person holding more than one office}
Совместить (sovmestít') *v.* [see совмещать]
Совместный (sovméstnyi) *adj.* combined, joint
~/ое предприятие (~/oe predpriiátie) joint venture
Совмещать (sovmeshchát') *v.* to combine
Совокупность (sovokúpnost') *f.* aggregate, totality
Совоюющий (sovoiúiushchii) *adj.* co-belligerent
Совратитель (sovratítel') *m.* corrupter, perverter
Совратить (sovratít') *v.* to corrupt, to pervert
Совхоз (sovkhóz) *m.* state farm
Согласие (soglásie) *n.* agreement, consent
взаимное ~ (vzaímnoe ~) mutual consent
добровольное ~ (dobrovól'noe ~) voluntary consent
молчаливое ~ (molchalívoe ~) tacit consent
обоюдное ~ (oboiúdnoe ~) reciprocal consent
общее ~ (óbshchee ~) common consent

предварительное ~ (predvarítel'noe ~) preliminary agreement
письменное ~ (pís'mennoe ~) written consent
прямое ~ (priamóe ~) direct consent
словесное ~ (slovésnoe ~) verbal consent
устное ~ (ústnoe ~) oral consent
Согласиться (soglasít'sia) *v.* [see соглашаться]
Согласование (soglasovánie) *n.* agreements, concordance
предварительное ~ (predvarítel'noe ~) preliminary coordination
~ текста договора (~ téksta dogovóra) concordance of the text of an agreement
Согласовать (soglasovát') *m.* to come to an agreement, to coordinate
Соглашатель (soglashátel') *m.* appeaser
Соглашательский (soglashátel'skii) *adj.* appeasement, appeasing
Соглашаться (soglashát'sia) *v.* to agree to, to consent to
Соглашение (soglashénie) *n.* agreement, arrangement, contract, understanding
административное ~ (administratívnoe ~) administrative agreement
арбитражное ~ (arbitrázhnoe ~) arbitration agreement
бартерное ~ (bárternoe ~) barter agreement
валютное ~ (valiútnoe ~) monetary agreement
взаимное ~ (vzaímnoe ~) reciprocal arrangement
военное ~ (voénnoe ~) military agreement
вспомогательное ~ (vspomogátel'noe ~) auxiliary agreement
генеральное ~ (generál'noe ~) general agreement
двухстороннее ~ (dvukhstorónnee ~) bilateral agreement
джентльменское ~ (dzhentl'ménskoe ~) gentlemen's agreement
договорное ~ (dogovórnoe ~) contractual agreement

долгосрочное ~ (dolgosróchnoe ~)
long-term agreement
долгосрочное торговое ~
(dolgosróchnoe torgóvoe ~) long-
term trade agreement
дополнительное ~ (dopolnítel'noe
~) supplementary agreement
исполнительное ~ (ispolnítel'noe
~) executive agreement
картельное ~ (kartél'noe ~)
cartel agreement
клиринговое ~ (klíringovoe ~)
clearing arrangement
комплексное ~ (kómpleksnoe ~)
package agreement
концессионное ~ (kontsessiónnoe
~) concessionary agreement
кредитное ~ (kredítnoe ~) credit
agreement
лицензионное ~ (litsenziónnoe ~)
licensing agreement
межбанковское ~ (mezhbánkovskoe
~) interbank agreement
межгосударственное ~
(mezhgosudárstvennoe ~)
intergovernmental agreement
межведомственное ~
(mezhvédomstvennoe ~)
interdepartmental agreement
международное ~ (mezhdunaródnoe
~) international agreement
местное ~ (méstnoe ~) local
agreement
мировое ~ (mirovóe ~) global
agreement
многостороннее ~ (mnogostorónnee
~) multilateral agreement
молчаливое ~ (molchalívoe ~)
tacit agreement
налоговое ~ (nalógovoe ~) tax
agreement
общее ~ (óbshchee ~) general
agreement
основное ~ (osnovnóe ~) basic
agreement
патентное ~ (paténtnoe ~) patent
agreement
платёжное ~ (platiózhnoe ~)
payment agreement
подразумеваемое ~
(podrazumeváemoe ~) implicit
agreement
предварительное
(predvarítel'noe) provisional
agreement

преференциальное ~
(preferentsiál'noe ~)
preferential agreement
промышленное ~ (promýshlennoe ~)
industrial agreement
прямое ~ (priamóe ~) direct
agreement
рабочее ~ (rabóchee ~) working
agreement
региональное ~ (regionál'noe ~)
regional agreement
секретное ~ (sekrétnoe ~) secret
agreement
словесное ~ (slovésnoe ~) verbal
agreement
соответствующее ~
(sootvétstvuiushchee ~)
appropriate agreement
специальное ~ (spetsiál'noe ~)
special agreement
судебное ~ (sudébnoe ~) judicial
agreement
таможенное ~ (tamózhennoe ~)
customs convention
типовое ~ (tipovóe ~) standard
agreement
торговое ~ (torgóvoe ~) trade
agreement
устное ~ (ústnoe ~) oral
agreement
финансовое ~ (finánsovoe ~)
financial agreement
формальное ~ (formál'noe ~)
formal agreement
частичное ~ (chastíchnoe ~)
partial agreement
частное ~ (chástnoe ~) private
understanding
экономическое ~ (ekonomícheskoe
~) economic agreement
~ об аренде (~ ob arénde) rental
agreement
~ об атомном сотрудничестве (~
ob átomnom sotrúdnichestve)
agreement on atomic cooperation
Согражданин (sograzhdanín) m.
fellow citizen
Содействие (sodéistvie) n.
assistance, cooperation, help
взаимное ~ (vzaímnoe ~) mutual
assistance
техническое ~ (tekhnícheskoe ~)
technical assistance
финансовое ~ (finánsovoe ~)
financial aid
~ в развитии (~ v razvítii)
development assistance

Содействовать (sodéistvovat') v. to assist, to contribute to, to help

Содержание (soderzhánie) n. allowance, contents, maintenance, upkeep
    золотое ~ (zolotóe ~) gold content
    металлическое ~ монеты (metallícheskoe ~ monéty) metal content of a coin
    техническое ~ (tekhnícheskoe ~) maintenance {of equipment}
    ~ влаги (~ vlági) moisture content
    ~ примесей (~ prímesei) content of impurities {precious metals, etc.}

Содерживать (sodérzhivat') v. [perfective: содержать] to keep, to maintain, to support

Содокладчик (sodokládchik) m. presenter of supplementary report

Содружество (sodrúzhestvo) n. commonwealth
    британское ~ наций (británskoe ~ nátsii) the British Commonwealth of Nations
    ~ Независимых Государств {СНГ} (~ nezavísimykh gosudárstv sng) {Commonwealth of Independent States} {CIS}

Соединение (soedinénie) n. conjunction, joining

Соединённ/ый (soediniónn/yi) adj. united
    ~/ое Королевство (~/oe korolévstvo) United Kingdom
    ~/ые Штаты Америки (~/ye shtáty amériki) United States of America

Сожительница (sozhítel'nitsa) f. mistress

Сожительство (sozhítel'stvo) n. coexistence, cohabitation
    внебрачное ~ (vnebráchnoe ~) extramarital cohabitation
    мирное ~ (mírnoe ~) peaceful coexistence

Сожительствовать (sozhítel'stvovat') v. to cohabit, to coexist

Созвать (sozvát') v. [see созывать]

Создание (sozdánie) n. creation, development
    ~ запасов (~ zapásov) accumulation of stocks

    ~ резервов (~ rezérvov) creation of reserves

Создавать (sozdavát') v. [perfective: создать] to create, to found, to originate

Созидатель (sozidátel') m. creator

Сознаваться (soznavát'sia) v. [perfective: сознаться] to plead guilty

Созывать (sozyvát') v. to convene, to convoke, to call

Созыв (sozýv) m. convocation
    ~ избирателей (~ izbirátelei) summoning of the electors
    ~ собрания (~ sobrániia) calling of a meeting

Соискание (soiskánie) n. competition

Сокращать (sokrashchát') v. [perfective: сократить] to abbreviate, to curtail, to reduce

Сокращение (sokrashchénie) n. contraction, cut, decline, reduction
    ~ ассигнований (~ assignovánii) reduction of allocations
    ~ бумажных денег в обращении (~ bumázhnykh déneg v obrashchénii) contraction of paper money in circulation
    ~ вооружений (~ vooruzhénii) arms reduction
    ~ дефицита (~ defitsíta) reduction of a deficit
    ~ доходов (~ dokhódov) reduction in revenue
    ~ импорта (~ ímporta) decline in imports
    ~ кредита (~ kredíta) contraction of credit
    ~ налога (~ nalóga) tax cut
    ~ пошлины (~ póshliny) cut in duties
    ~ производства (~ proizvódstva) decrease in production
    ~ расходов (~ raskhódov) cut in expenses
    ~ спроса (~ sprósa) drop in demand
    ~ таможенных барьеров (~ tamózhennykh bar'érov) reduction of customs barriers
    ~ таможенного тарифа (~ tamózhennogo tarífa) reduction of customs tariff
    ~ штатов (~ shtátov) contraction of staff

Сокровище (sokróvishche) *n.*
treasure
Сокрытие (sokrýtie) *n.* concealment
  ~ краденого (~ krádenogo)
  receiving of stolen goods
  ~ прибыли (~ príbyli)
  concealment of profits
Солидарно (solidárno) *adv.*
collectively, jointly
Солидарность (solidárnost') *f.*
joint liability, solidarity,
Solidarity {Polish political
movement}
Солидарный (solidárnyi) solidary
{civil law obligation}
Соло-вексель (sólo-véksel') *m.*
single-name note
Соль (sol') *m.* Sol {Peruvian
currency}
Сомнение (somnénie) *n.* doubt,
uncertainty
Сомнительный (somnítel'nyi) *adj.*
doubtful, dubious
Сонаследник (sonaslédnik) co-heir
Сонаследовать (sonaslédovat') *v.* to
inherit jointly
Сообвиняемый (soobviniáemyi)
m.adj.noun co-defendant {in
criminal proceedings}
Сообщать (soobshchát') *v.* to
announce, to communicate, to
inform, to report
Сообщение (soobshchénie) *n.*
communication, information,
message, traffic
  воздушное ~ (vozdúshnoe ~) air
  traffic
  железнодорожное ~
  (zheleznodorózhnoe ~) railway
  service
  местное ~ (méstnoe ~) short-haul
  traffic
  морское ~ (morskóe ~) overseas
  traffic
  официальное ~ (ofitsiál'noe ~)
  official report
  пароходное ~ (parokhódnoe ~)
  shipping traffic
  речное ~ (rechnóe ~) weather
  traffic
  сухопутное ~ (sukhopútnoe ~)
  overland traffic
  транспортное ~ (tránsportnoe ~)
  transportation
  удобное ~ (udóbnoe ~) convenient
  transportation

  шифрованное ~ (shifróvannoe ~)
  encoded message
  экстренное ~ (ékstrennoe ~) news
  flash
Сообщество (soóbshchestvo)
*n.*community
  атлантическое ~ (atlantícheskoe
  ~) Atlantic ~
  Европейское Экономическое ~
  (evropéiskoe ekonomícheskoe ~)
  European Economic ~
  международное ~ (mezhdunaródnoe
  ~) international ~
  специализированное ~
  (spetsializírovannoe ~)
  specialized ~
  ~ наций (~ nátsii) ~ of nations
Сообщить (soobshchít') *v.* [see
сообщать]
Соопекун (soopekún) *m.* co-guardian,
co-trustee
Сооружение (sooruzhénie) *n.*
building, defense installation,
structure
Сооснователь (soosnovátel') *m.* co-
founder
Соответстви/е (sootvétstvi/e) *n.*
accordance, conformity, correspondence
  в ~/и с Вашей просьбой (v ~/i s
  váshei prós'boi) in accordance
  with your request
  в ~/и с законодательством (v ~/i
  s zakonodátel'stvom) in
  accordance with legislation
  полное ~ (pólnoe ~) full
  conformance
Соответствовать (sootvétstvovat')
v. to accord, to conform
Соответствующий
(sootvétstvuiushchii) *adj.*
appropriate, relative, respective,
suitable
Соотечественник (sootéchestvennik)
m. compatriot
Соотношение (sootnoshénie) *n.*
correlation, parity, ratio
  ~ валют (~ valiút) parity of
  currencies
  ~ спроса и предложения (~ sprós
  i predlozhéniia) ratio of suppl
  and demand
  ~ цен (~ tsen) parity of prices
Соперник (sopérnik) *m.* rival
Соперничество (sopérnichestvo) *n.*
rivalry

Сопоставимость (sopostavímost') *f.* comparability

Сопоставимый (sopostavímyi) *adj.* comparable

Сопоставление (sopostavlénie) *n.* comparison
  ~ цен (~ tsen) comparison of prices

Сопротивление (soprotivlénie) *n.* confrontation, resistance
  пассивное ~ (passívnoe ~) passive resistance

Сопротивляться (soprotivliát'sia) *v.* to oppose, to resist

Сопряжённый (sopriazhiónnyi) *adj.* attended by, entailing

Соревнование (sorevnovánie) *n.* competition
  предвыборное ~ (predvýbornoe ~) electoral campaign competition

Сорт (sort) *m.* class, grade, kind, sort

Сортамент (sortáment) *m.* assortment, range of products

Сортировать (sortírovat') *v.* to assort, to classify, to grade, to size

Сортировка (sortiróvka) *f.* assorting, classifying, grading, sizing

Сослать (soslát') *v.* [perfective: ссылать] to banish, to exile

Сословие (soslóvie) *n.* estate, professional association

Сособственник (sosóbstvennik) *m.* co-proprietor

Сособственность (sosóbstvennost') *f.* co-ownership

Сосредоточение (sosredotóchenie) *n.* concentration
  ~ сил (~ sil) concentration of forces

Состав (sostáv) *m.* composition, constitution, corpus, makeup, staff
  административный ~ (administratívnyi ~) administrative personnel
  включать в ~ (vkliuchát' v ~) to incorporate, to make part of
  дипломатический ~ (diplomatícheskii ~) diplomatic personnel
  личный ~ (líchnyi ~) personnel
  общий ~ (óbshchii ~) total composition
  основной ~ (osnovnói ~) key staff

подвижной ~ (podvizhnói ~) rolling stock

руководящий ~ (rukovodiáshchii ~) managerial personnel

узкий ~ комитета (úzkii ~ komitéta) narrow composition of a committee

узкий ~ совета (úzkii ~ sovéta) narrow composition of a council

~ населения (~ naseléniia) composition of population

~ правления (~ pravléniia) composition of management

~ преступления (~ prestupléniia) corpus delicti

Составитель (sostavítel') *m.* author, compiler
  ~ протокола (~ protokóla) secretary of a meeting {compiler of minutes}

Составление (sostavlénie) *n.* drafting {of a document}, working out
  ~ акта (~ ákta) drafting of a deed, document
  ~ баланса (~ balánsa) drawing up of a balance sheet
  ~ бюджета (~ biudzhéta) drafting of a budget
  ~ завещания (~ zaveshchániia) drafting of a will
  ~ описи (~ ópisi) drafting of a distraint

Состояние (sostoiánie) *n.* condition, position, state, status
  гражданское ~ (grahdánskoe ~) civil status
  мореходное ~ (morekhódnoe ~) seaworthiness
  правовое ~ (pravovóe ~) legal status
  судоходное ~ (sudokhódnoe ~) working order
  финансовое ~ (fínánsovoe ~) doubtful condition
  экономическое ~ (ekonomícheskoe ~) operating condition

Сосуществование (sosushchestvovánie) *n.* coexistence
  мирное ~ (mírnoe ~) peaceful coexistence

Сотрудник (sotrúdnik) *m.* employee, worker

Сотрудничество (sotrúdnichestvo) *n.* collaboration, cooperation, working relationship

валютное ~ (valiútnoe ~)
exchange rate coordination
внешнеэкономическое ~
(vneshneekonomícheskoe ~)
foreign economic cooperation
комплексное ~ (kómpleksnoe ~)
integrated cooperation
международное ~ (mezhdunaródnoe
~) international cooperation
правовое ~ (pravovóe ~) legal
cooperation
финансовое ~ (finánsovoe ~)
financial cooperation
экономическое ~ (ekonomícheskoe
~) economic cooperation
~ в судебной области (~ v
sudébnoi óblasti) cooperation in
the judicial sphere
Соучастие (souchástie) n.
complicity, participation
Соучастник (souchástnik) m.
accomplice, participant
~ преступления (~ prestupléniia)
accessory to a crime
Сохранение (sokhranénie) n.
conservation, custody, preservation
Сохранить (sokhranít') v. [see
сохранять]
Сохранность (sokhránnost') f.
intact state, safety
Сохранять (sokhraniát') v. to keep,
to keep in custody, to preserve
Социализация (sotsializátsiia) f.
socialization
Социализм (sotsialízm) m. socialism
государственный ~
(gosudárstvennyi ~) state
socialism
Социалист (sotsialíst) m. socialist
{person}
Социалистический
(sotsialistícheskii) adj. socialist
Сочетание (sochetánie) n.
combination
Союз (soiúz) m. union
административный ~
(administratívnyi ~)
administrative ~
атлантический ~ (atlantícheskii
~) Atlantic ~
брачный ~ (bráchnyi ~) marital ~
валютный ~ (valiútnyi ~)
currency ~
коммунистический ~ молодёжи
{комсомол} (kommunistícheskii ~
molodiózhi {kómsomol}) Communist
Youth League {Komsomol}

межпарламентский ~
(mezhparlámentskii ~)
interparliamentary ~
монетный ~ (monétnyi ~) monetary
~
профессиональный ~ {профсоюз}
(professionál'nyi ~ {profsoiuz})
labor ~
Советский ~ (sovétskii ~) Soviet
Union {historical}
таможенный ~ (tamózhennyi ~)
customs ~
~ предпринимателей ~ (~
predprinimátelei) of
industrialists
~ Советских Социалистических
Республик {СССР} ~ (~ sovetskikh
sotsialistícheskikh respublik
{es-es-es-ér}) of Soviet
Socialist Republics {USSR}
{historical}
Союзник (soiúznik) m. ally
привилегированный ~
(privilegiróvannyi ~) privileged
~
Спад (spad) m. decline, downturn,
recession, stagnation
~ конъюнктуры (~ kon"iunktúry)
decline in the business cycle
Спасение (spasénie) n. salvage
~ на море (~ na móre) maritime
salvage
Спекулировать (spekulírovat') v. to
gamble, to speculate
~ на повышение (~ na povyshénie)
to speculate on an upturn
~ на понижение (~ na ponizhénie)
to speculate on a downturn
Спекулянт (spekuliánt) m. jobber,
speculator
биржевой ~ (birzhevói ~) jobber
Спекулятивный (spekuliatívnyi) adj.
speculative
Спекуляция (spekuliátsiia) f.
speculation
биржевая ~ (birzheváia ~) stock
jobbing
валютная ~ (valiútnaia ~)
currency speculation
денежная ~ (dénezhnaia ~)
monetary speculation
неудачная ~ (neudáchnaia ~)
unsuccessful speculation
товарная ~ (továrnaia ~)
commodity speculation
удачная ~ (udáchnaia ~)
successful speculation

Специализация (spetsializátsiia) f. specialization

~ производства (~ proizvódstva) specialization of product line

Специалист (spetsialíst) m. expert, specialist

Специальный (spetsiál'nyi) adj. special, specific

Спецификация (spetsifikátsiia) f. specification

Списание (spisánie) n. withdrawal, writing off

~ долгов (~ dolgóv) writing off of debts

~ со счёта (~ so schióta) writing off an account, withdrawal from an account

Список (spísok) m. bill, list, sheet

именной ~ (imennói ~) nominal roll

контрольный ~ (kontról'nyi ~) checklist

партийный ~ (partíinyi ~) party membership roll

персональный ~ (personál'nyi ~) personnel list

послужной ~ (posluzhnói ~) service record

справочный ~ (správochnyi ~) reference list

чёрный ~ (chiórnyi ~) black list

экспортный ~ (éksportnyi ~) export list

~ адресатов (~ adresátov) mailing list

~ избирателей (~ izbirátelei) electoral roll

~ кандидатов (~ kandidátov) slate of candidates

~ населения (~ naseléniia) waiting list

~ пассажиров (~ passazhírov) passenger manifest

~ присяжных заседателей (~ prisiázhnykh zasedátelei) jury list

~ присутствующих (~ prisútstvuiushchikh) list of attendees

~ товаров (~ továrov) tally list

~ требований (~ trébovanii) list of demands

Сплав (splav) m. floating timber

Сплочённость (splochiónnost') f. cohesion, unity

Спокойствие (spokóistvie) n. calm, order, tranquility

общественное ~ (obshchéstvennoe ~) public order

Спор (spor) m. argument, controversy, dispute

административный ~ (administratívnyi ~) administrative dispute

валютный ~ (valiútnyi ~) monetary dispute

гражданско-правовой ~ (grahdánsko-pravovói ~) civil law dispute

жилищный ~ (zhilíshchnyi ~) housing dispute

земельный ~ (zemél'nyi ~) land dispute

имущественный ~ (imúshchestvennyi ~) property dispute

коммерческий ~ (kommércheskii ~) commercial dispute

конституционный ~ (konstitutsiónnyi ~) constitutional controversy

межгосударственный ~ (mezhgosudárstvennyi ~) interstate dispute

международный ~ (mezhdunaródnyi ~) international dispute

пограничный ~ (pograníchnyi ~) border dispute

правовой ~ (pravovói ~) legal controversy

разрешить ~ (razreshít' ~) to resolve a dispute

таможенный ~ (tamózhennyi ~) customs dispute

территориальный ~ (territoriál'nyi ~) territorial dispute

торговый ~ (torgóvyi ~) trade dispute

трудовой ~ (trudovói ~) labor dispute

Спорный (spórnyi) adj. controversial, disputed

Способ (spósob) m. manner, means, method, mode, way

единственный ~ (edínstvennyi ~) only way

запатентованный ~ (zapatentóvannyi ~) patented method

обычный ~ (obýchnyi ~) usual method

~ изготовления (~ izgotovléniia) production technique
~ обработки (~ obrabótki) method of processing
~ оплаты (~ opláty) means of payment
~ оплаты натурой (~ opláty natúroi) means of payment in kind
~ перевозки (~ perevózki) mode of conveyance
~ платежа (~ platezhá) manner of payment
~ применения (~ primenéniia) mode of application

Способность (sposóbnost') f. ability, capability, capacity
конкурентная ~ (konkuréntnaia ~) competitive ability
платёжная ~ (platióżhnaia ~) payment ability
покупательная ~ (pokupátel'naia ~) purchasing power
потребительская ~ (potrebítel'skaia ~) traffic capacity
реальная покупательная ~ (reál'naia pokupátel'naia ~) actual purchasing power
юридическая ~ (iuridícheskaia ~) legal capacity
~ вступать в договор (~ vstupát' v dogovór) capacity to enter into an agreement
~ дать показание (~ dat' pokazánie) capacity to testify
~ завещать (~ zaveshchát') capacity to devise {property by will}
~ к труду (~ k trudú) capacity for labor

Способный (sposóbnyi) adj. able, capable, gifted

Справедливость (spravedlívost') f. equity, fairness, justice
социальная ~ (sotsiál'naia ~) social justice

Справедливый (spravedlívyi) adj. equitable, fair, just

Справка (správka) f. certificate, information, reference
служебная ~ (sluzhébnaia ~) service information
таможенная ~ (tamózhennaia ~) tariff schedule
~ с места работы (~ s mésta rabóty) work reference

Справочник (správochnik) m. guidebook, reference book

Справочный (správochnyi) adj. guide, informational, reference

Спровоцировать (sprovotsírovat') v. to provoke

Спрос (spros) m. demand
внешний ~ (vnéshnii ~) external ~
внутренний ~ (vnútrennii ~) domestic ~
вялый ~ (viályi ~) sluggish ~
жёсткий ~ (zhióstkii ~) inelastic ~
живой ~ (zhivói ~) brisk ~
общий ~ (óbshchii ~) overall ~
оживлённый ~ (ozhivliónnyi ~) active ~
платёжеспособный ~ (platióżhesposóbnyi ~) solvent ~
постоянный ~ (postoiánnyi ~) persistent ~
потребительский ~ (potrebítel'skii ~) consumer ~
растущий ~ (rastúshchii ~) increasing ~
срочный ~ (sróchnyi ~) immediate ~
эластичный ~ (elastíchnyi ~) elastic ~
эффективный ~ (effektívnyi ~) effective ~
~ и предложение (~ i predlozhénie) supply and ~ {literally: ~ and supply}
~ займы (~ zaimý) loan ~
~ на кредит ~ (~ na kredít) for credit

Сравнение (sravnénie) n. comparison

Средств/о (srédstv/o) n. asset, facility, means, medium
блокированные ~/a (blokírovannye ~/a) blocked assets
бюджетные ~/a (biudzhétnye ~/a) budgetary funds
валютные ~/a (valiútnye ~/a) foreign exchange funds
государственные ~/a (gosudárstvennye ~/a) public funds
денежные ~/a (dénezhnye ~/a) monetary resources
дипломатические ~/a (diplomatícheskie ~/a) diplomatic means
заёмные ~/a (zaiómnye ~/a) borrowed funds

замороженные ~/a (zamorózhennye
~/a) frozen funds
имущественные ~/a
(imúshchestvennye ~/a) property
мирные ~/a (mírnye ~/a) peaceful
means
наличные ~/a (nalíchnye ~/a)
cash resources
ликвидные ~/a (likvídnye ~/a)
liquid resources
оборотные ~/a (oborótnye ~/a)
working capital
основные ~/a (osnovnýe ~/a)
fixed assets
обычные ~/a (obýchnye ~/a)
conventional means
перевалочные ~/a (pereválochnye
~/a) handling facilities {cargo}
плавучее портовое ~ (plavúchee
portóvoe ~) harbor craft
резервные ~/a (rezérvnye ~/a)
standby funds
свободные денежные ~/a
(svobódnye dénezhnye ~/a)
available resources
собственные ~/a (sóbstvennye
~/a) internal funds
современные ~/a (sovreménnye
~/a) modern means
финансовые ~/a (finánsovye ~/a)
financial resources
частные денежные ~/a (chástnye
dénezhnye ~/a) private monetary
resources
~ защиты (~ zashchíty) means of
defense
~ на непредвиденные расходы (~
na nepredvídennye raskhódy)
contingency funds
~ производства (~ proizvódstva)
means of production
Срок (srok) *m.* date, duration,
maturity, term, time
возможный ~ (vozmózhnyi ~)
possible date
гарантируемый ~ (garantíruemyi
~) warranty period
договорный ~ (dogovórnyi ~)
contractual period
испытательный ~ (ispytátel'nyi
~) test period
конечный ~ (konéchnyi ~)
expiration date
крайний ~ (kráinii ~) deadline
кредитный ~ (kredítnyi ~) credit
period

льготный ~ (l'gótnyi ~) grace
period
назначенный ~ (naznáchennyi ~)
designated term
начальный ~ (nachál'nyi ~)
initial term
неопределённый ~
(neopredeliónnyi ~) indefinite
term
определённый ~ (opredeliónnyi ~)
definite term
сокращённый ~ давности
(sokrashchiónnyi ~ dávnosti)
abbreviated statute of
limitations
справедливый ~ (spravedlívyi ~)
reasonable period of time
условленный ~ (uslóvlennyi ~)
contingent period
установленный ~ (ustanóvlennyi
~) established period
юридический ~ (iuridícheskii ~)
legal period
~ амортизации (~ amortizátsii)
term of amortization,
depreciation period
~ аренды (~ aréndy) term of
lease
~ векселя (~ vékselia) maturity
of bill
~ давности (~ dávnosti) term of
prescription
~ действия (~ déistviia) period
of effect, period of validity
~ договора (~ dogovóra) term of
contract
~ доставки (~ dostávki) date of
delivery
~ заявления (~ zaiavléniia) date
of application
~ исполнения (~ ispolnéniia)
date of performance
Срочност/ь (sróchnost/') *f.*
promptness, urgency
порядок ~/и (poriádok ~/i)
priority {of payment, etc.}
Срочный (sróchnyi) *adj.* due,
immediate, prompt, urgent
Срыв (sryv) *m.* disruption
~ переговоров (~ peregovórov)
breakdown of negotiations
~ работы (~ rabóty) work
stoppage
Ссуда (ssúda) *f.* accommodation,
advance, loan
банковская ~ (bánkovskaia ~)
bank loan

беспроцентная ~ (besprotséntnaia ~) interest-free loan
возвратная ~ (vozvrátnaia ~) demand loan
выкупная ~ (vykupnáia ~) redeemable loan
денежная ~ (dénezhnaia ~) money loan
долгосрочная ~ (dolgosróchnaia ~) long-term loan
коммерческая ~ (kommércheskaia ~) commercial loan
краткосрочная ~ (kratkosróchnaia ~) short-term loan
льготная ~ (l'gótnaia ~) easy loan, loan on easy terms
потребительская (potrebítel'skaia) consumer loan
промышленная ~ (promýshlennaia ~) industrial loan
просроченная ~ (prosróchennaia ~) bad loan
сельскохозяйственная ~ (sel'skokhoziáistvennaia ~) agricultural loan
срочная ~ (sróchnaia ~) fixed date loan
~ денег (~ déneg) loan of money
~ под залог (~ pod zalóg) loan against security
~ под залог ценных бумаг (~ pod zalóg tsénnykh bumág) loan against securities
~ под залог товаров (~ pod zalóg továrov) loan against commodities
Ссудить (ssudít') v. [see ссужать]
Ссудный (ssúdnyi) adj. lending, loan
Ссужать (ssuzhát') v. to advance, to lend
Ссылка (ssýlka) f. banishment, exile, reference
административная ~ (administratívnaia ~) administrative exile
Ссыльнопоселенец (ssyl'noposelénets) m. convict settler {exile who settles distant territory}
Ссыльный (ssýl'nyi) m.adj.noun exile
политический ~ (politícheskii ~) political exile
Стабилизация (stabilizátsiia) f. stabilization

экономическая ~ (ekonomícheskaia ~) economic ~
~ валютных курсов ~ (~ valiútnykh kúrsov) of exchange rates
~ цен ~ (~ tsen) of prices
Стабилизированный (stabilizírovannyi) adj. stabilized
Стабилизировать (stabilizírovat') v. to stabilize
Стабилизирующий (stabilizíruiushchii) adj. stabilizing
~/ee влияние (~/ee vliiánie) stabilizing influence
Стабильность (stabíl'nost') f. stability
~ занятости ~ (~ zániatosti) of employment
~ кадров ~ (~ kádrov) of personnel
~ курса ~ (~ kúrsa) of exchange rate
~ рынка (~ rýnka) market ~
~ цен (~ tsen) price ~
Ставка (stávka) f. rate
аккордная ~ (akkórdnaia ~) flat ~
базисная ~ (bázisnaia ~) prime ~
двойная ~ (dvoináia ~) dual ~
действующая ~ (déistvuiushchaia ~) going ~
дневная ~ (dnevnáia ~) per diem ~
единая ~ (edínaia ~) uniform ~
комиссионная ~ (komissiónnaia ~) commission ~
льготная ~ (l'gótnaia ~) preferential ~
минимальная ~ (minimál'naia ~) minimum ~
налоговая ~ (nalógovaia ~) tax ~
открытая ~ (otkrýtaia ~) open ~
очная ~ (óchnaia ~) confrontation {of witness, etc.}
плавающая ~ (plávaiushchaia ~) floating ~
повышенная ~ (povýshennaia ~) increased ~
почтовая ~ (pochtóvaia ~) postal ~
предельная ~ (predél'naia ~) marginal ~
премиальная ~ (premiál'naia ~) premium ~

преференциальная ~
(preferentsiál'naia ~)
preferential ~
прогрессивная ~ (progressívnaia
~) progressive ~
процентная ~ (protséntnaia ~)
interest ~
регрессивная ~ (regressívnaia ~)
regressive ~
средняя годовая ~ (sredniaia
godováia ~) average annual ~
средняя ~ (sredniaia ~) average
~
твердая ~ (tvérdaia ~) fixed ~
учётная ~ (uchiótnaia ~)
discount ~
фрахтовая ~ (frákhtovaia ~)
freight ~

Ставленник (stávlennik) *m.* protégé

Стади/я (stádi/ia) *f.* phase, stage
в начальной ~/и (v nachál'noi
~/i) initially
конечная ~ (konéchnaia ~) final
stage
процессуальная ~
(protsessuál'naia ~) procedural
phase
~ предварительного следствия (~
predvarítel'nogo sledstviia)
preliminary investigation phase
~ производства (~ proizvódstva)
production phase

Стаж (stazh) *m.* length of service,
service record
военный ~ (voénnyi ~) military
service
испытательный ~ (ispytátel'nyi
~) probationary period
~ работы (~ rabóty) record of
service

Стажёр (stazhiór) *m.* intern,
probationer

Стажировка (stazhiróvka) *f.*
internship, training

Сталинизм (stalinízm) *m.* Stalinism

Стандарт (standárt) *m.* standard
бумажный ~ (bumázhnyi ~) paper ~
государственный ~
(gosudárstvennyi ~) state ~
золотой ~ (zolotói ~) gold ~
золото-монетный ~ (zóloto-
monetnyi ~) gold coin ~
золото-слитковый ~ (zóloto-
slítkovyi ~) gold bullion ~
монетный ~ (monétnyi ~) monetary
~

~ качества ~ (~ káchestva) of
quality

Стандартизация (standartizátsiia)
f. standardization

Стандартизировать
(standartizírovat') *v.* to
standardize

Станция (stántsiia) *f.* station
автозаправочная ~
(avtozaprávochnaia ~) gas ~
железнодорожная ~
(zheleznodorózhnaia ~) railway ~
пограничная ~ (pograníchnaia ~)
border ~
промежуточная ~
(promezhútochnaia ~) way ~
санитарная ~ (sanitárnaia ~)
sanitary-health ~
таможенная ~ (tamózhennaia ~)
customs ~
узловая ~ (uzlóvaia ~) railway
junction
центральная ~ (tsentrál'naia ~)
central ~

Старение (starénie) *n.* aging,
deterioration
естественное ~ (estéstvennoe ~)
natural aging
~ населения (~ naseléniia) aging
of the population

Староста (stárosta) *f.* elder,
senior {of a group}

Старший (stárshii) *adj.* senior
~ по званию (~ po zvániiu)
higher-ranking

Старшина (starshiná) *f.* senior
representative
~ присяжных заседателей (~
prisiázhnykh zasedátelei)
foreman of the jury

Старшинств/о (starshinstv/ó) *n.*
seniority
по ~/у (po ~/ú) by seniority

Статистика (statístika) *f.*
statistic, statistics
демографическая ~
(demografícheskaia ~)
demographic statistics
сельскохозяйственная ~
(sel'skokhoziáistvennaia ~)
agricultural statistics
судебная ~ (sudébnaia ~)
judicial statistics
таможенная ~ (tamózhennaia ~)
customs statistics
транспортная ~ (tránsportnaia ~)
transportation statistics

~ внешнеторгового оборота (~ vneshnetorgóvogo oboróta) foreign trade turnover statistics
~ заработной платы (~ zárabotnoi pláty) wage figures
~ населения (~ naseléniia) census figures
~ преступности (~ prestúpnosti) crime statistics
~ промышленности (~ promýshlennosti) industrial figures
~ рождаемости (~ rozhdáemosti) birth rate
~ смертности (~ smértnosti) mortality rate
~ торговли (~ torgóvli) trade figures
Статус (státus) *m.* status
дипломатический ~ (diplomatícheskii ~) diplomatic ~
колониальный ~ (koloniál'nyi ~) colonial ~
консультативный ~ (konsul'tatívnyi ~) consultative ~
культурный ~ (kul'túrnyi ~) cultural ~
международный ~ (mezhdunaródnyi ~) international ~
политический ~ (politícheskii ~) political ~
правовой ~ (pravovói ~) legal ~
привилегированный ~ (privilegiróvannyi ~) privileged ~
социальный ~ (sotsiál'nyi ~) social ~
Статус-кво (státus-kvó) *m.* status quo
территориальный ~ (territoriál'nyi ~) territorial ~
Статья (stat'iá) *f.* article, clause, item, paragraph
газетная ~ (gazétnaia ~) newspaper article
доходная ~ (dokhódnaia ~) item of income
ликвидная ~ актива (likvídnaia ~ aktíva) liquid asset
типовая ~ (tipováia ~) model article
~ актива (~ aktíva) asset {on balance sheet}

~ баланса (~ balánsa) balance sheet item
~ пассива (~ passíva) liability {on balance sheet}
~ экспорта (~ éksporta) item of export
Стачечник (stáchechnik) *m.* striker
Стачка (stáchka) *f.* strike
дикая ~ (díkaia ~) wildcat ~
политическая ~ (politícheskaia ~) political ~
Стена (stená) *f.* wall
общая ~ (óbshchaia ~) common ~
разграничивающая ~ (razgranichiváiushchaia ~) border ~
Степень (stépen') *f.* degree, extent
докторская ~ (dóktorskaia ~) doctoral degree
учёная ~ (uchiónaia ~) academic degree
~ виновности (~ vinóvnosti) degree of guilt
Стивидор (stividór) *m.* stevedore
Стипендия (stipéndiia) *f.* grant, stipend
государственная ~ (gosudárstvennaia ~) government grant, government stipend
Стимул (stímul) *m.* incentive, stimulus
Стоимость (stóimost') *f.* cost, value
арендная ~ (aréndnaia ~) rental value
балансовая ~ (balánsovaia ~) book cost
валовая ~ (valováia ~) gross value
весовая ~ (vesováia ~) cost of weight
внутренняя ~ (vnútrenniaia ~) domestic value
действительная ~ (deistvítel'naia ~) actual cost
денежная ~ (dénezhnaia ~) cash value
единичная ~ (edeníchnaia ~) unit value
запродажная ~ (zaprodázhnaia ~) sale value
заявленная ~ (zaiávlennaia ~) declared value
капитализированная ~ (kapitalízírovannaia ~) capitalized value

коммерческая ~ (kommércheskaia ~) commercial value

конечная ~ (konéchnaia ~) final cost

ликвидационная ~ (likvidatsiónnaia ~) liquidation value, salvage cost

курсовая ~ (kúrsovaia ~) market value

меновая ~ (menováia ~) barter value, exchange value

наёмная ~ (naiómnaia ~) higher value

нарицательная ~ (naritsátel'naia ~) nominal value

общая ~ (óbshchaia ~) aggregate value

объективная ~ (ob"ektívnaia ~) objective value

объявленная ~ (ob"iávlennaia ~) declared value

оценочная ~ (otsénochnaia ~) assessed value

первоначальная ~ (pervonachál'naia ~) original cost

покупная ~ (pokupnáia ~) purchase value

полагаемая ~ (polagáemaia ~) probable cost

полная ~ (pólnaia ~) full cost

потребительная ~ (potrebítel'naia ~) use value

прибавочная ~ (pribávochnaia ~) surplus value

продажная ~ (prodázhnaia ~) sales value

реальная ~ (reál'naia ~) actual value

рыночная ~ (rýnochnaia ~) market value

сметная ~ (smétnaia ~) estimated cost

средняя ~ (srédniaia ~) average cost

субъективная ~ (sub"ektívnaia ~) subjective value

условная ~ (uslóvnaia ~) conditional cost

фактическая ~ (faktícheskaia ~) actual cost

чистая ~ (chístaia ~) net cost

Стол (stol) *m.* table

круглый ~ (krúglyi ~) roundtable

Столб (stolb) *m.* pole, post

пограничный ~ (pograníchnyi ~) border post {marker}

Столица (stolítsa) *f.* capital city

Столкновение (stolknovénie) *n.* clash, conflict, collision

военное ~ (voénnoe ~) military conflict

пограничное ~ (pograníchnoe ~) border clash

случайное ~ (slucháinoe ~) accidental collision

~ интересов (~ interésov) clash of interests

Сторож (stórozh) *m.* watchman

ночной ~ (nochnói ~) night watchman

Сторона (storoná) *f.* party, side

виновная ~ (vinóvnaia ~) guilty party

возражающая ~ (vozrazháiushchaia ~) opposing party

заинтересованная ~ (zainteresóvannaia ~) interested party

лицевая ~ (litseváia ~) obverse side {coin}

невиновная ~ (nevinóvnaia ~) innocent party

оборотная ~ (oborótnaia ~) reverse side {coin}

ответственная ~ (otvétstvennaia ~) liable party

отсутствующая ~ (otsútstvuiushchaia ~) absent party

подписавшаяся ~ (podpisávshaiasia ~) signatory

потерпевшая ~ (poterpévshaia ~) injured party

противная ~ (protívnaia ~) adverse party

спорящая ~ (sporiáshchaia ~) disputant, disputing party

третья ~ (trét'ia ~) third party

~ в споре (~ v spóre) contestant

~ в суде (~ v sudé) party to the proceedings

Сторонник (storónnik) *m.* adherent, supporter

~ мира (~ míra) peace activist

~ нейтралитета (~ neitralitéta) adherent of neutrality

~ свободной торговли (~ svobódnoi torgóvli) adherent of free trade

Стоянка (stoiánka) *f.* mooring, parking space, taxi stand

~ запрещена (~ zapreshchená) mooring prohibited

~ в порту (~ v portú) moorage
Стоять (stoiát') v. to moor, to
stand, to stay
Страна (straná) f. country {nation}
аграрная ~ (agrárnaia ~)
agrarian ~
воюющая ~ (voiúiushchaia ~)
belligerent ~
враждебная ~ (vrazhdébnaia ~)
enemy ~
импортирующая ~
(importíruiushchaia ~) importing
~
индустриализованная ~
(industrializóvannaia ~)
industrialized ~
морская ~ (morskáia ~) maritime
~
нейтральная ~ (neitrál'naia ~)
neutral ~
оккупированная ~
(okkupírovannaia ~) occupied ~
отдалённая ~ (otdaliónnaia ~)
distant ~
побеждённая ~ (pobezhdiónnaia ~)
conquered ~
развивающая ~ (razviváiushchaia
~) developing ~
сельскохозяйственная ~
(sel'skokhoziáistvennaia ~)
agricultural ~
слаборазвитая ~ (slaborázvitaia
~) underdeveloped ~
соседняя ~ (sosédniaia ~)
neighboring ~
суверенная ~ (suvérennaia ~)
sovereign ~
транзитная ~ (tránzitnaia ~)
transit ~
третья ~ (trét'ia ~) third ~
экспортирующая ~
(eksportíruiushchaia ~)
exporting ~
Страх (strakh) m. fear, risk
на свой ~ и риск (na svoi ~ i
risk) at one's own risk
Страхование (strakhovánie) n.
insurance
взаимное ~ (vzaímnoe ~) mutual ~
воздушное ~ (vozdúshnoe ~)
aviation ~
государственное ~ {ГОССТРАХ}
(gosudárstvennoe ~ {gosstrakh})
state ~ {Gosstrakh, Russian
State Insurance Company}
групповое ~ (gruppovóe ~) group
~

дополнительное ~ (dopolnítel'noe
~) supplementary ~
имущественное ~
(imúshchestvennoe ~) property ~
личное ~ (líchnoe ~) personal ~
морское ~ (morskóe ~) maritime ~
обязательное ~ (obiazátel'noe ~)
mandatory ~
пожизненное ~ (pozhíznennoe ~)
life ~
совместное ~ (sovméstnoe ~)
joint ~
частное ~ (chástnoe ~) private ~
~ от аварий (~ ot avárii)
casualty ~
~ валютных рисков (~ valiútnykh
rískov) exchange risk ~
Страхователь (strakhovátel') m.
insurant {insured party}
Страховать (strakhovát') v. to
insure
Страховка (strakhóvka) f. insurance
coverage
Страховщик (strakhóvshchik) m.
insurer, underwriter
морской ~ (morskói ~) marine
underwriter
Страхуемый (strakhúemyi) adj.
insurable
Стрелок (strelók) m. rifleman, shot
Строение (stroénie) n. building,
composition, structure
жилое ~ (zhilóe ~) residential
building
хозяйственное ~ (khoziáistvennoe
~) business structure
Строй (stroi) m. order, regime,
social order, system
аграрный ~ (agrárnyi ~) agrarian
order
государственный ~
(gosudárstvennyi ~) governmental
regime
политический ~ (politícheskii ~)
political system
экономический ~ (ekonomícheskii
~) economic order
Стройбанк (stróibank) m.
construction bank
Строительство (stroítel'stvo) n.
building, construction, project
гражданское ~ (grahdánskoe ~)
civil engineering
промышленное ~ (promýshlennoe ~)
industrial engineering
Структура (struktúra) f. structure

административная ~
(administratívnaia ~)
administrative arrangements
коммерческая ~ (kommércheskaia
~) commercial ~
правовая ~ (pravováia ~) legal ~
производственная ~
(proizvódstvennaia ~) system of
production
финансовая ~ (finánsovaia ~)
financial ~
экономическая ~ (ekonomícheskaia
~) economic ~
юридическая ~ ~ (iuridícheskaia
~) of the legal system
Стряпчий (striápchii) m.adj.noun
scrivener
Стукач (stukách) m. informer,
stool-pigeon
Ступень (stupén') grade, level,
phase, rung
~ развития (~ razvítiia) phase
of development
Стык (styk) m. crossroads, junction
Стычка (stýchka) f. skirmish
Стяжатель (stiazhátel') m. money-
grubber
Субаренда (subarénda) f. sublease
Субарендатор (subarendátor) m. sub-
tenant
Субвенция (subvéntsiia) f.
subvention
~ от государства (~ ot
gosudárstva) state subsidy,
state subvention
~ при вывозе (~ pri vývoze)
export subsidy, export
subvention
Сублицензия (sublitsénziia) f.
sublicense
Субподряд (subpodriád) m.
subcontract
Субподрядчик (subpodriádchik) m.
subcontractor
Суброгация (subrogátsiia) f.
subrogation
оговорка ~/и (ogovórka ~/i)
subrogation clause
Субсидирование (subsidírovanie) n.
subsidizing
Субсидировать (subsidírovat') v. to
subsidize
Субсиди/я (subsídi/ia) f. subsidy
безвозмездная ~ (bezvozmézdnaia
~) grant
военная ~ (voénnaia ~) military
subsidy

государственная ~
(gosudárstvennaia ~) state
subsidy
косвенная ~ (kósvennaia ~)
indirect subsidy
предоставить ~/ю (predostávit'
~/iu) to provide a subsidy
прямая ~ (priamáia ~) direct
subsidy
федеральная ~ (federál'naia ~)
federal subsidy
экономическая ~ (ekonomícheskaia
~) economic subsidy
Субститут (substitút) m.
substitution
Субъект (sub"ékt) m. subject
договорный ~ (dogovórnyi ~)
contractual ~
~ гражданского права (~
grahdánskogo práva) civil law ~
Суверен (suverén) m. sovereign
Суверенитет (suverenitét)
sovereignty
внешний ~ ~ (vnéshnii ~) in
foreign affairs
внутренний ~ (vnútrennii ~)
domestic ~
военный ~ (voénnyi ~) military ~
ограниченный ~ (ograníchennyi ~)
limited ~
полный ~ (pólnyi ~) full ~
правовой ~ (pravovói ~) legal ~
территориальный ~
(territoriál'nyi ~) territorial
~
Суд (sud) m. court, court of law,
hearing, trial, tribunal
административный ~
(administratívnyi ~)
administrative court
апелляционный ~ (apelliatsiónnyi
~) court of appeals
арбитражный ~ (arbitrázhnyi ~)
arbitral court
быстрый ~ (býstryi ~) speedy
trial
верховный ~ (verkhóvnyi ~)
Supreme Court
верховный ~ автономной
республики (verkhóvnyi ~
avtonómnoi respubliki) Supreme
Court of an autonomous republic
военный ~ (voénnyi ~) court
martial
вызвать в ~ (výzvat' v ~) to
summons, to subpoena

вызов в ~ (výzov v ~) summons, subpoena
высший ~ (výsshii ~) upper court
вышестоящий ~ (vyshestoiáshchii ~) superior court
городской ~ (gorodskói ~) municipal court
гражданский ~ (grahdánskii ~) civil court
детский ~ (détskii ~) juvenile court
духовный ~ (dukhóvnyi ~) ecclesiastical court
изъять из ~/a (iz"iát' iz ~/a) to drop a suit
искать в ~ (iskát' v ~) to sue
кассационный ~ (kassatsiónnyi ~) court of cassation
коммерческий ~ (kommércheskii ~) commercial court
компетентный ~ (kompeténtnyi ~) competent court
конституционный ~ (konstitutsiónnyi ~) constitutional court
консульский ~ (kónsul'skii ~) consular tribunal
краевой ~ (kraevói ~) krai court
международный ~ (mezhdunaródnyi ~) international court
международный арбитражный ~ (mezhdunaródnyi arbitrázhnyi ~) international arbitration court
местный ~ (méstnyi ~) local court
мировой ~ (mirovói ~) world court
морской ~ (morskói ~) maritime court
народный ~ (naródnyi ~) people's court
нижестоящий ~ (nizhestoiáshchii ~) inferior court
областной ~ (oblastnói ~) oblast court, regional court
обратиться в ~ (obratít'sia v ~) to apply to court
общий ~ (óbshchii ~) law court
окружной ~ (okruzhnói ~) okrug court
подать в ~ (podát' v ~) to bring an action
патентный ~ (paténtnyi ~) patent court
привлечь к ~/y (privléch' k ~/u) to bring an action against

районный ~ (raiónnyi ~) raion court, regional court
революционный ~ (revoliutsiónnyi ~) revolutionary court
специальный ~ (spetsiál'nyi ~) special court
третейский ~ (tretéiskii ~) arbitration tribunal
уголовный ~ (ugolóvnyi ~) criminal court
федеральный ~ (federál'nyi ~) federal court
федеральный конституционный ~ (federál'nyi konstitutsiónnyi ~) federal constitutional court
явиться в ~ (iavít'sia v ~) to make an appearance in court
~ Божий (~ bózhii) trial by combat
~ второй инстанции (~ vtorói instántsii) court of second instance
~ высшей инстанции (~ výsshei instántsii) court of higher instance
~ обычного права (~ obýchnogo práva) court of customary law
~ первой инстанции (~ pérvoi instántsii) court of first instance
~ присяжных (~ prisiázhnykh) jury trial
Судебномедицинский (sudébnomeditsinskii) adj. forensic
Судебный (sudébnyi) adj. legal, judicial
Судимость (sudímost') f. conviction, convictions
   снять ~ (sniat' ~) to expunge a conviction
Судить (sudít') v. to judge, to try
   ~ при закрытых дверях (~ pri zakrýtykh dveriákh) to try behind closed doors
Судиться (sudít'sia) v. to be in litigation with
Судно (súdno) n. craft, vessel
   арестовать ~ (arestovát' ~) to arrest a vessel
   буксирное ~ (buksírnoe ~) tugboat
   военно-морское ~ (voénno-morskóe ~) naval vessel
   госпитальное ~ (gospitál'noe ~) hospital vessel

государственное ~
(gosudárstvennoe ~) government
vessel

гражданское воздушное ~
(grahdánskoe vozdúshnoe ~) civil
aircraft

грузовое ~ (gruzovóe ~) cargo
vessel, freighter

зарегистрированное ~
(zaregistrírovannoe ~)
registered vessel

каботажное ~ (kabotázhnoe ~)
coasting vessel

контейнерное ~ (kontéinernoe ~)
container vessel

морское ~ (morskóe ~) seagoing
vessel

моторное ~ (motórnoe ~)
motorboat

насыпное ~ (nasypnóe ~) bulk
carrier

неповреждённое ~
(nepovrezhdiónnoe ~) sound
vessel

нефтеналивное ~ (neftenalivnóe
~) oil tanker

однотипное ~ (odnotípnoe ~)
sister ship

пассажирское ~ (passazhírskoe ~)
passenger liner

пиратское ~ (pirátskoe ~) pirate
vessel

портовое ~ (portóvoe ~) harbor
vessel

почтовое ~ (pochtóvoe ~) mail
boat

прибывающее ~ (pribyváiushchee
~) incoming vessel

речное ~ (rechnóe ~) riverboat

спасательное ~ (spasátel'noe ~)
salvage vessel

сухогрузное ~ (sukhogrúznoe ~)
dry cargo ship

таможенное ~ (tamózhennoe ~)
Coast Guard vessel

торговое ~ (torgóvoe ~) merchant
vessel

трамповое ~ (trámpovoe ~) cargo
tramp vessel

Судоверфь (sudovérf') shipyard

Судовладелец (sudovladélets) *m.*
ship owner

Судоговорение (sudogovorénie) *n.*
pleadings

Судопроизводство (sudoproizvódstvo)
n. legal proceedings

административное ~
(administratívnoe ~)
administrative proceedings

гражданское ~ (grahdánskoe ~)
civil proceedings

уголовное ~ (ugolóvnoe ~)
criminal proceedings

устное ~ (ústnoe ~) oral
proceedings

Судостроение (sudostroénie) *n.*
shipbuilding

Судостроительный (sudostroítel'nyi)
adj. shipbuilding

Судоходный (sudokhódnyi) *adj.*
navigable

Судоходство (sudokhódstvo) *n.*
navigation, shipping

внутреннее ~ (vnútrennee ~)
internal shipping

каботажное ~ (kabotázhnoe ~)
coastal shipping

международное ~ (mezhdunaródnoe
~) international shipping

морское ~ (morskóe ~) ocean
shipping

речное ~ (rechnóe ~) inland
shipping

трамповое ~ (trámpovoe ~) tramp
shipping

торговое ~ (torgóvoe ~) merchant
shipping

Судья (sud'iá) *m.* judge

верховный ~ (verkhóvnyi ~)
justice

кантональный ~ (kantonál'nyi ~)
Canton Magistrate

компетентный ~ (kompeténtnyi ~)
competent ~

местный ~ (méstnyi ~) local ~

мировой ~ (mirovói ~) justice of
the peace

полицейский ~ (politséiskii ~)
police magistrate

третейский ~ (tretéiskii ~)
arbitral referee

федеральный ~ (federál'nyi ~)
federal judge

Суеверие (suevérie) *n.* superstition

Суждение (suzhdénie) *n.* judgment,
opinion

Сумасшедший (sumasshédshii) *adj.*
insane

Сумасшествие (sumasshéstvie) *n.*
insanity

Сумма (súmma) *f.* sum

амортизационная ~
(amortizatsiónnaia ~) amortized
~
авансовая ~ (avánsovaia ~)
advance ~
большая ~ (bol'sháia ~) large ~
валовая ~ (valováia ~) gross ~
выкупная ~ (vykupnáia ~)
redemption ~
выплачиваемая ~ (vyplachiváemaia
~) amount paid
вырученная ~ (výruchennaia ~)
proceeds
гарантийная ~ (garantíinaia ~)
guaranteed ~
денежная ~ (dénezhnaia ~)
monetary ~
залоговая ~ (zalógovaia ~)
pledged ~
исковая ~ ~ (ískovaia ~) claimed
капитальная ~ долга
(kapitál'naia ~ dólga) principal
~
крупная ~ (krúpnaia ~)
substantial ~
лицензионная ~ (litsenziónnaia
~) licensing ~
максимальная ~ (maksimál'naia ~)
maximum ~
минимальная ~ (minimál'naia ~)
minimum ~
ничтожная ~ (nichtózhnaia ~)
trivial ~
номинальная ~ (nominál'naia ~)
nominal ~
общая ~ (óbshchaia ~) aggregate
~
отступная ~ ~ (otstupnáia ~) of
indemnity
паевая ~ (paeváia ~) share ~
паушальная ~ (paushál'naia ~)
lumpsum amount
спорная ~ ~ (spórnaia ~) in
controversy
страховая ~ (strakhóvaia ~)
insured ~
твёрдая ~ (tviórdaia ~) firm
figure
чистая ~ (chístaia ~) net ~
Суперарбитр (superarbítr) m. umpire
{arbitration}
Супруг (suprúg) m. spouse {husband}
разведённый ~ (razvediónnyi ~)
divorced ~
Супруга (suprúga) f. spouse {wife}
разведённая ~ (razvediónnaia ~)
divorced ~

Супружество (suprúzhestvo) n.
marriage, married life
Суррогат (surrogát) m. substitute
денежный ~ (dénezhnyi ~)
monetary substitute
Суточный (sútochnyi) m.adj.noun per
diem allowance
Суть (sut') central part, essential
part
~ дела (~ déla) the crux of the
matter
Существо (sushchestvó) n. essence,
substance
Сущность (súshchnost') f. essence,
real significance
Сфера (sféra) f. realm, sphere
~ влияния (~ vliiániia) sphere
of influence
~ интересов (~ interésov) sphere
of interests
Схема (skhéma) f. chart, diagram,
plan, schematic
Сходный (skhódnyi) adj. fair,
reasonable
Счёт (schiót) m. account, bill,
invoice
авансовый ~ (avánsovyi ~)
deposit account
банковский ~ (bánkovskii ~) bank
account
беспроцентный ~ (besprosséntnyi
~) non-interest bearing account
блокированный ~ (blokírovannyi
~) blocked account
блокировать ~ (blokírovat' ~) to
block an account
бухгалтерский ~ (bukhgálterskii
~) accounting records
бюджетный ~ (biudzhétnyi ~)
budget account
валютный ~ (valiútnyi ~) foreign
exchange account
внести в ~ (vnestí v ~) to
deposit into an account
внешний ~ (vnéshnii ~) external
account
внутренний ~ (vnútrennii ~)
domestic account
временный ~ (vrémennyi ~) time
deposit
государственный ~
(gosudárstvennyi ~) governmental
account
двухсторонний ~ (dvukhstorónnii
~) bilateral account
деблокировать ~ (deblokírovat'
~) to unblock an account

депозитный ~ (depozítnyi ~) deposit account

закрыть ~ (zakrýt' ~) to close an account

инвестиционный ~ (investitsiónnyi ~) investment account

иностранный ~ (inostránnyi ~) foreign account

капитальный ~ (kapitál'nyi ~) capital account

клиринговый ~ (klíringovyi ~) clearing account

конвертируемый ~ (konvertíruemyi ~) convertible account

консолидированный ~ (konsolidírovannyi ~) consolidated account

корреспондентский ~ (korrespondéntskii ~) correspondent account

лицевой ~ (litsevói ~) personal account

общий ~ (óbshchii ~) joint account

особый ~ (osóbyi ~) special account

отдельный ~ (otdél'nyi ~) separate account

открыть ~ (otkrýt' ~) to open an account

отрицательный ~ (otritsátel'nyi ~) negative balance

переводный ~ (perevódnyi ~) transferrable account

почтовый ~ (pochtóvyi ~) postal account

расчётный ~ (raschiótnyi ~) settlement account

регистрированный ~ (registrírovannyi ~) registered account

резервный ~ (rezérvnyi ~) reserve account

сводный ~ (svódnyi ~) closing account

ссудный ~ (ssúdnyi ~) loan account

текущий ~ (tekúshchii ~) current account

текущий банковский ~ (tekúshchii bánkovskii ~) checking account

Счётчик (schiótchik) m. bank teller
~ голосов (~ golosóv) vote counter

Счетовод (schetovód) m. ledger clerk

Счетоводство (schetovódstvo) n. accounting

Счёт-фактура (schiót-fáktura) f. commercial invoice

Съезд (s"ezd) m. conference, congress

внеочередной ~ (vneocherednói ~) extraordinary congress

национальный ~ (natsionál'nyi ~) national conference

учредительный ~ (uchredítel'nyi ~) constituent congress

~ компартии (~ kompártii) Congress of the Communist Party

Съёмщик (s"iómshchik) m. lessee, tenant

основной ~ (osnovnói ~) primary lessee

Сын (syn) m. son

приёмный ~ (priiómnyi ~) adopted ~

Сырьё (syr'ió) n. raw material

Сэкономить (sekonómit') v. to economize, to save

Сюзеренитет (siuzerenitét) m. suzerainty

Т

Табель (tábel') m. schedule, table, timesheet

текущий ~ (tekúshchii ~) monthly timesheet {especially for factory workers}

Таблиц/а (tablíts/a) f. schedule, table

вносить в ~/у (vnosít' v ~/u) to tabulate

детализированная ~ (detalizírovannaia ~) individual table

курсовая ~ (kúrsovaia ~) stock exchange rate list

налоговая ~ (nalógovaia ~) tax table

однотипная ~ (odnotípnaia ~) single tabulation table

разработочная ~ (razrabótochnaia ~) spread sheet

расчётная ~ (raschiótnaia ~) computational table

сводная ~ (svódnaia ~) summary table

сокращённая ~ (sokrashchiónnaia ~) abridged table

составлять ~/у (sostavliát' ~/u)
to compile a table
справочная ~ (správochnaia ~)
reference table
сравнительная ~ (sravnítel'naia
~) comparative table
~ тарифных ставок (~ tarífnykh
stávok) tariff rate table
Тайм-чартер (táim-chárter) m. time
charter {of a vessel}
Тайна (táina) f. privacy, secret
коммерческая ~ (kommércheskaia
~) commercial secret
~ вкладов (~ vkládov)
confidentiality of deposits
Такс/а (táks/a) f. government-fixed
rate
плата по ~/е (pláta po ~/e)
fixed-rate payments {by
government}
Талон (talón) m. coupon, pass
абонементный ~ (aboneméntnyi ~)
coupon
отрывать ~/ы (otryvát' ~/y) to
detach a coupon
отрывной ~ (otryvnói ~)
detachable coupon
посадочный ~ (posádochnyi ~)
boarding pass
Тальман (tál'man) m. tallyman
береговой ~ (beregovói ~) shore
checker
Тальманский (tál'manskii) adj.
tally
Таможенник (tamózhennik) m. customs
agent
Таможенный (tamózhennyi) adj.
customs
Таможн/я (tamózhn/ia) customs
акт о конфискации груза ~/ей
(akt o konfiskátsii grúza ~/ei)
seizure note
декларация ~/и (deklarátsiia
~/i) ~ declaration
квитанция ~/и об уплате пошлины
(kvitántsiia ~/i ob upláte
póshliny) ~ receipt
печать ~/и (pechát' ~/i) ~ seal
предъявлять разрешение ~/и
(pred"iavliát' razreshénie ~/i)
to present a ~ permit
провозить через ~/ю (provozít'
chérez ~/iu) to bring through ~
проходить через ~/ю (prokhodít'
chérez ~/iu) to clear ~
сотрудник ~/и (sotrúdnik ~/i) ~
officer

товары, пломбированные ~/ей
(továry, plombiróvannye ~/ei)
goods under ~ seal
Танкер (tánker) m. tanker
загружать ~ (zagruzhát' ~) to
load a ~
крупнотоннажный ~
(krupnotonnázhnyi ~) major ~
нефтяной ~ (neftianói ~) oil ~
Танкер-бункеровщик (tánker-
bunkeróvshchik) m. bunkering tanker
Танкер-заправщик (tánker-
zaprávshchik) m. refueling tanker
Танкер-рудовоз (tanker-rudovóz) m.
ore bulk carrier
Тар/а (tára) f. container, tare
арктическая ~ (arktícheskaia ~)
arctic container
вес ~/ы (ves ~/y) tare weight
возвратная ~ (vozvrátnaia ~)
reusable container
габариты ~/ы (gabaríty ~/y)
container dimensions
грузить без ~/ы (gruzít' bez
~/y) to load in bulk
действительный вес ~/ы
(deistvítel'nyi ves ~/y) actual
tare weight
делать скидку на ~/у (délat'
skídku na ~/u) to tare
дефекты ~/ы (defékty ~/y)
defects in tare
закрытая ~ (zakrýtaia ~) closed
container
инвентарная ~ (inventárnaia ~)
returnable container
индивидуальная ~
(individuál'naia ~) unit pack
картонная ~ (kartónnaia ~)
cardboard container
крупногабаритная ~
(krupnogabarítnaia ~) large
dimensioned container
маркированная ~ (markiróvannaia
~) marked container
многооборотная ~
(mnogooborótnaia ~) reusable
tare
открытая ~ (otkrýtaia ~) open
container
повреждённая ~ (povrezhdiónnaia
~) damaged tare
полимерная ~ (polimérnaia ~)
polymer container
полиэтиленовая ~
(polietilénovaia ~) polyethylene
container

порожняя ~ (porózhniaia ~) empty container

пригодная ~ (prigódnaia ~) suitable container

прочная ~ (próchnaia ~) strong container

разовая ~ (rázovaia ~) disposable container

решётчатая ~ (reshiótchataia ~) crate

фактурный вес ~/ы (faktúrnyi ves ~/y) invoice tare

хранение ~/ы на складе (khranénie ~/y na skláde) warehousing of tare

Тариф (taríf) *m.* tariff, tariff table

автономный ~ (avtonómnyi ~) autonomous tariff

агентский ~ (agéntskii ~) agency tariff

багажный ~ (bagázhnyi ~) baggage rate

базисный ~ (bázisnyi ~) base rate

в соответствии с железнодорожным ~/ом (v sootvétstvii s zhelez- nodorózhnym ~/om) in accordance with railway tariff

высокий ~ (vysókii ~) high tariff

гибкий ~ (gíbkii ~) flexible tariff rate

государственный ~ (gosudárstvennyi ~) government tariff

грузовой ~ (gruzovói ~) freight rate

групповой ~ (gruppovói ~) group rate

действующий ~ (déistvuiushchii ~) current rate

дискриминационный ~ (diskriminatsiónnyi ~) discriminatory tariff

дифференциальный ~ (differentsiál'nyi ~) sliding scale tariff

единый ~ (edínyi ~) blanket tariff

железнодорожный ~ (zheleznodorózhnyi ~) railway tariff

жёсткий ~ (zhióstkii ~) basic tariff

запретительный ~ (zapretítel'nyi ~) prohibitive tariff

зональный ~ (zonál'nyi ~) zone tariff

изменять ~ (izmeniát' ~) to adjust a tariff

импортный ~ (ímportnyi ~) import tariff

карательный ~ (karátel'nyi ~) retaliatory tariff

классный ~ (klássnyi ~) class rate

комбинированный ~ (kombinírovannyi ~) combined rate

конвенционный ~ (konventsiónnyi ~) convention tariff

конференциальный ~ (konferentsiál'nyi ~) conference tariff

линейный ~ (linéinyi ~) liner rates

льготный ~ (l'gótnyi ~) preferential tariff

максимальный ~ (maksimál'nyi ~) maximum tariff

международный ~ (mezhdunaródnyi ~) international rate

местный ~ (méstnyi ~) local tariff

минимальный ~ (minimál'nyi ~) minimum tariff

морской ~ (morskói ~) marine transport rate

начальный ~ (nachál'nyi ~) basing rate

низкий ~ (nízkii ~) load tariff

общий ~ (óbshchii ~) general tariff

одноразовый ~ (odnorázovyi ~) one-time rate

основной ~ (osnovnói ~) standard rate

особый ~ (osóbyi ~) special tariff

повышение ~/ов (povyshénie ~/ov) increase in tariffs

поднимать ~ (podnimát' ~) to increase a tariff

покровительственный ~ (pokrovítel'stvennyi ~) protective tariff

почтовый ~ (pochtóvyi ~) postal tariff

прейскурант ~/ов (preiskuránt ~/ov) rate schedule

применять ~ к (primeniát' ~ k) to apply a tariff

промежуточный ~ (promezhútochnyi
~) bridge rate
пропорциональный ~
(proportsionál'nyi ~)
proportional rate
простой ~ (prostói ~) straight
line tariff
протекционистский ~
(protektsionístskii ~)
protectionist tariff
расхождение между ~/ами
(raskhozhdénie mézhdu ~/ami)
discrepancy between tariff rates
рекламный ~ (reklámnyi ~)
advertising rate
система множественных ~/ов
(sistéma mnózhestvennykh ~/ov)
multiple tariff system
сквозной ~ (skvoznói ~) through
rate
сложный ~ (slózhnyi ~)
multilinear tariff
снижение ~/ов (snizhénie ~/ov)
reduction in tariffs
ставки ~/ов (stávki ~/ov) tariff
rates
таможенный ~ (tamózhennyi ~)
customs schedule
таможенный ~ иностранного
государства (tamózhennyi ~
inostránnogo gosudárstva)
customs schedule of a foreign
government
тарный ~ (tárnyi ~) tariff for
tare carriage
транзитный ~ (tranzítnyi ~)
transit tariff
транспортный ~ (tránsportnyi ~)
traffic rate
унифицированный ~
(unifitsírovannyi ~) unified
tariff
экспортный ~ (éksportnyi ~)
export tariff
~ аккордных ставок (~ akkórdnykh
stávok) flat rate tariff
Тарификация (tarifikátsiia) *f.*
tariff rating
Тарифицировать (tarifitsírovat') *v.*
to rate, to set a tariff upon
Тарифный (tarífnyi) *adj.* tariff
Текст (tekst) *m.* text
вставка в ~ (vstávka v ~)
insertion
дополнение к ~/у (dopolnénie k
~/u) supplement to a ~

исправление ~/a (ispravlénie
~/a) alteration of a ~
исправленный ~ (isprávlennyi ~)
altered ~
одобрять ~ (odobriát' ~) to
approve a ~
первоначальный ~
(pervonachál'nyi ~) original ~
печатать ~ (pechátat' ~) to
print a ~
подлинный ~ (pódlinnyi ~)
authentic ~
полный ~ (pólnyi ~) full ~
рекламный ~ (reklámnyi ~)
advertising copy
согласованный ~ (soglasóvannyi
~) agreed ~
~ контракта (~ kontrákta) ~ of a
contract
~ телекса (~ téleksa) ~ of a
telex
Текущий (tekúshchii) *adj.* current,
routine
Телеграмм/а (telegrámm/a) *f.* cable,
telegram
бланк ~/ы (blank ~/y) telegram
form
вызывать ~/ой (vyzyvát' ~/oi) to
wire for, to cable for
высылать ~/у (vysylát' ~/u) to
send a cable, telegram
обычная ая ~ (obýchnaia aia ~)
ordinary telegram
отправка ~/ы (otprávka ~/y)
dispatch of a cable
служебная ~ (sluzhébnaia ~)
official cable {regulatory
instructions}
срочная ~ (sróchnaia ~) urgent
cable
уведомлять ~/ой (uvedomliát'
~/oi) to notify by cable,
telegram
шифрованная ~ (shifróvannaia ~)
encoded telegram
Телеграмма-молния (telegrámma-
mólniia) *f.* express telegram
Телеграф (telegráf) *m.* telegraph
Телеграфировать (telegrafírovat')
v. to telegraph, to wire
Телеграфный (telegráfnyi) *adj.*
telegraphic
Телекс (téleks) *m.* telex
направлять ~ (napravliát' ~)
send a telex
ответ на ~ (otvét na ~) reply to
a telex

подтверждать ~ (podtverzhdát' ~)
to confirm a telex
служебный ~ (sluzhébnyi ~)
official telex
срочный ~ (sróchnyi ~) urgent
telex
Телексный (téleksnyi) *adj.* telex
Телетайп (teletáip) *m.* teletype
Телетайпный (teletáipnyi) *adj.*
teletype
Телефакс (telefáks) *m.* facsimile,
fax
Телефон (telefón) *m.* telephone
запрос по ~/у (zaprós po ~/u) ~
inquiry
звонить по ~/у с оплатой
абонентом (zvonít' po ~/u s
oplátoi abonéntom) to call
collect
номер ~/а (nómer ~/a) ~ number
по ~/у (po ~/u) by ~
уведомление по ~/у (sviazát'sia
po ~/u uvedomlénie po ~/u)
notice by ~
Телефонный (telefónnyi) *adj.*
telephone
Телефонограмма (telefonográmma) *f.*
telephone message
Темп (temp) *m.* pace, rate, speed,
tempo
в ускоренном ~/е (v uskórennom
~/e) at a rapid pace
замедление ~/ов развития
(zamedlénie ~/ov razvítiia)
slowing the rates of development
замедление ~/ов роста
(zamedlénie ~/ov rósta) slowing
the rates of growth
замедлять ~ (zamedliát' ~) to
slow the pace
ускорять ~ (uskoriát' ~) to pick
up the pace
~ инфляции (~ infliátsii) the
rate of inflation
~ работы (~ rabóty) pace of work
~ развития (~ razvítiia) pace of
development
~ роста (~ rósta) pace of growth
Тенденци/я (tendéntsi/ia) *f.*
tendency, trend
анализ ~/й (análiz ~/i) trend
analysis
анализ ~/й рынка (análiz ~/i
rýnka) market trend analysis
долговременная ~
(dolgovrémennaia ~) long term
trend

кратковременная ~
(kratkovrémennaia ~) short-term
trend
общая ~ (óbshchaia ~) general
trend
определённая ~ (opredeliónnaia
~) definitive trend
основная ~ (osnovnáia ~) basic
tendency
повышательная ~ (povyshátel'naia
~) upward trend
понижательная ~ (ponizhátel'naia
~) downward trend
преобладающая ~
(preobladáiushchaia ~)
prevailing tendency
протекционистские ~/и
(protektsionístskie ~/i)
protectionist tendencies
проявлять ~/ю (proiavliát' ~/iu)
to exhibit a tendency
рыночная ~ (rýnochnaia ~) market
trend
~ цен (~ tsen) price trend
Тендер (ténder) *m.* bid, tender
законный ~ (zakónnyi ~) legal
tender
изолированные ~/ы (izolírovannye
~/y) isolated tenders
международные ~/ы
(mezhdunaródnye ~/y)
international tenders
объявленный ~ (ob"iávlennyi ~)
invited bid
полный ~ (pólnyi ~) full bid,
tender
направлять ~ (napravliát' ~) to
forward a tender
номер ~/а (nómer ~/a) tender
number
период подачи ~/ов (períod
podáchi ~/ov) bidding period
условия ~/а (uslóviia ~/a)
tender conditions
Теплоход (teplokhód) *m.* motorized
vessel
наливной ~ (nalivnói ~)
motorized tanker
Термин (términ) *m.* term
научные ~/ы (naúchnye ~/y)
scientific terms
торговые ~/ы (torgóvye ~/y)
terms of art {for a specific
trade}
Терминал (terminál) *m.* terminal
контейнерный ~ (kontéinernyi ~)
container ~

морской ~ (morskói ~) marine ~
~ для грузовых судов (~ dlia
gruzovýkh sudóv) freight liner ~
Терминология (terminológiia) f.
terminology
научная ~ (naúchnaia ~)
scientific ~
юридическая ~ (iuridícheskaia ~)
legal ~
Территориальный (territoriál'nyi)
adj. territorial
Территория (territóriia) f. area,
territory
исключительная ~
(iskliuchítel'naia ~) exclusive
territory
лицензированная ~
(litsenzírovannaia ~) licensed
territory
сбытовая ~ (sbytováia ~) sales
territory
складская ~ (skladskáia ~)
storage area
согласованная ~ (soglasóvannaia
~) agreed territory
таможенная ~ (tamózhennaia ~)
customs territory
Терция (tértsiia) f. third bill of
exchange
Тест (test) m. test
выдерживать ~ (vydérzhivat' ~)
to stand the ~
подвергать ~/у (podvergát' ~/u)
to put to the ~
проводить ~ (provodít' ~) to ~
Техник (tékhnik) m. mechanic,
technician
Техник/а (tékhnik/a) f.
engineering, equipment, machinery,
technology
достижения ~/и (dostizhéniia
~/i) technological achievements
заводские правила ~/и
безопасности (zavódskie právila
~/i bezopásnosti) plant safety
rules
инструкция по ~/е безопасности
(instrúktsiia po ~/e
bezopásnosti) safety
instructions
область ~/и (óblast' ~/i) field
of technology
особо точная ~ (osóbo tóchnaia
~) high precision equipment
оценка ~/и (otsénka ~/i)
technology assessment

передовая ~ (peredováia ~)
advanced technology
превосходство в ~/е
(prevoskhódstvo v ~/e) technical
excellence
сложная ~ (slózhnaia ~)
sophisticated equipment
соблюдать правила ~/и
безопасности (sobliudát' právila
~/i bezopásnosti) to observe
safety rules
~ безопасности (~ bezopásnosti)
safety rules
~ новых поколений (~ nóvykh
pokolénii) next generation
technology
~ связи (~ sviázi)
communications technology
Технико-экономический (tékhniko-
ekonomícheskii) adj. technical and
economic
Технически (tekhnícheski) adv.
technically
~ возможный (~ vozmózhnyi) ~
feasible
~ оптимальное решение (~
optimál'noe reshénie) ~ optimal
solution
~ правильный (~ právil'nyi) ~
correct
~ приемлемый (~ priémlemyi) ~
acceptable
Технический (tekhnícheskii) adj.
technical
Технолог (tekhnólog) m. process
engineer
Технологический (tekhnologícheskii)
adj. technological
Технологи/я (tekhnológi/ia) f.
technology
базовая ~ (bázovaia ~) basic ~
безотходная ~ (bezotkhódnaia ~)
low waste ~
владеть ~/ей (vladét' ~/ei) to
master ~
внедрение новой ~/и (vnedrénie
nóvoi ~/i) introduction of new ~
делать ~/ю доступной (délat'
~/iu dostúpnoi) to make ~
accessible
капиталоёмкая ~ (kapitaloiómkaia
~) capital intensive ~
комплексная ~ (kómpleksnaia ~)
package ~
монополия на ~/ю (monopóliia na
~/iu) monopoly on ~

наукоёмкая ~ (naukoiómkaia ~)
high ~
недавно разработанная ~ (nedávno
razrabótannaia ~) recently
developed ~
новая ~ (nóvaia ~) new ~
обновлять ~/ю (obnovliát' ~/iu)
to update ~
общая ~ (óbshchaia ~) general ~
одобрять ~/ю (odobriát' ~/iu) to
approve ~
оценивать ~/ю (otsénivat' ~/iu)
to evaluate ~
передача ~/и (peredácha ~/i) ~
transfer
передовая ~ (peredováia ~)
advanced ~
подходящая ~ (podkhodiáshchaia
~) suitable ~
привлекать современную ~/ю
(privlekát' soveménnuiu ~/iu)
to apply modern ~
приобретать ~/ю (priobretát'
~/iu) to obtain ~
превосходная ~ (prevoskhódnaia
~) superior ~
применение ~/и (primenénie ~/i)
application of ~
развивать ~/ю (razvivát' ~/iu)
to develop ~
ресурсосберегающая ~
(resursosberegáiushchaia ~)
resource- conserving ~
трудоёмкая ~ (trudoiómkaia ~)
labor-intensive ~
трудосберегающая ~
(trudosberegáiushchaia ~) labor-
saving ~
утечка ~/и (utéchka ~/i) leak of
~
характеристика ~/и
(kharakterístika ~/i)
performance of ~
экспорт ~/и (éksport ~/i) export
of ~
энергосберегающая ~
(energosberegáiushchaia ~)
energy-saving ~

Техобслуживани/е
(tekhobslúzhivani/e) m. technical
maintenance
базы ~/я (bázy ~/ia) ~ station
станция ~/я (stántsiia ~/ia)
service station

Типовой (tipovói) adj. model,
standard

Тираж (tirázh) m. circulation, run

большой ~ (bol'shói ~) large
circulation
выйти в ~ (výiti v ~) to be
drawn {as of lots}
договорный ~ (dogovórnyi ~)
franchise circulation
массовый ~ (mássovyi ~) mass
circulation
предполагаемый ~ (predpolagáemyi
~) projected circulation
~ печатных изданий (~ pechátnykh
izdánii) press run

Титул (títul) m. title {of
ownership}
законный ~ (zakónnyi ~) good ~
оспоримый ~ (osporímyi ~)
voidable ~
правовой ~ (pravovói ~) legal ~
передача правового ~/а
(peredácha pravovógo ~/a)
conveyance of legal ~
справка о ~/е (správka o ~/e)
abstract of ~
показать законный ~ (pokazát'
zakónnyi ~) to show good ~
~ на движимое имущество (~ na
dvízhimoe imúshchestvo) ~ to
chattels
~ на недвижимое имущество (~ na
nedvízhimoe imúshchestvo) ~ to
real property

Титульный (títul'nyi) adj. title

Товар (továr) m. article,
commodity, goods, merchandise,
wares
апробировать ~ (aprobírovat' ~)
to take goods on a trial basis
арест на ~/ы (arést na ~/y)
seizure of goods
ассортимент ~/а (assortimént
~/a) assortment of goods
аукционный ~ (auktsiónnyi ~)
auction goods
бакалейные ~/ы (bakaléinye ~/y)
groceries
беспошлинные ~/ы (bespóshlinnye
~/y) non-dutiable commodities
бестарный ~ (bestárnyi ~) loose
goods
биржа сельскохозяйственных ~/ов
(bírzha sel'skokhoziástvennykh
~/ov) agricultural commodities
market
биржевые ~/ы (birzhevýe ~/y)
market commodities

большое разнообразие ~/ов
(bol'shóe raznoobrázie ~/ov)
great diversity of goods
бондовый ~ (bóndovyi ~) bonded
goods
браковать ~ (brakovát' ~) to
reject goods
браковка ~/a (brakóvka ~/a)
rejection of goods
быстро продающийся ~ (býstro
prodaiúshchiisia ~) fast selling
goods
быстро реализуемый ~ (býstro
realizúemyi ~) highly marketable
goods
бытовые ~/ы (bytovýe ~/y)
household appliances
взаимозаменяемые ~/ы
(vzaimozameniáemye ~/y)
substitutable goods
вид ~/a (vid ~/a) kind, nature
of goods
владелец ~/a (vladélets ~/a)
owner of goods
внедрять ~/ы на рынок (vnedriát'
~/y na rýnok) to introduce goods
to market
второсортные ~/ы (vtorosórtnye
~/y) second rate goods
второстепенные ~/ы
(vtorostepénnye ~/y) non-
essentials
выбрасывать ~/ы на рынок
(vybrásyvat' ~/y na rýnok) to
dump goods on the market
выгодно демонстрировать ~
(výgodno demonstrírovat' ~) to
profitably demonstrate wares
выгружать ~ (vygruzhát' ~) to
unload goods
выгружать ~ на причал
(vygruzhát' ~ na prichál) to
unload goods on the dock
выкладка ~/ов (výkladka ~/ov)
display of goods
выкладка ~/ов в витрине
(výkladka ~/ov v vitríne)
display of goods in a store
window
выкупать заложенный ~ (vykupát'
zalózhennyi ~) to redeem pledged
goods
выписка ~/ов (výpiska ~/ov)
ordering of goods
галантерейные ~/ы (galanteréinye
~/y) haberdashery goods

громоздкие ~/ы (gromózdkie ~/y)
bulky goods
группировка ~/ов (gruppiróvka
~/ov) grouping of products
данный ~ (dánnyi ~) subject
goods
декларировать ~ (deklarírovat'
~) to declare goods {to customs
etc.}
держать ~ на складе (derzhát' ~
na skláde) to keep goods in a
warehouse
дефектный ~ (deféktnyi ~)
defective goods
дефицитный ~ (defitsítnyi ~)
critical goods, scarce
commodities
доброкачественный ~
(dobrokáchestvennyi ~) high
quality goods
доставка ~/a (dostávka ~/a)
delivery of goods
доставлять ~ на условиях СИФ
(dostavliát' ~ na uslóviiakh
sif) to deliver goods CIF
доставлять ~ на условиях ФОБ
(dostavliát' ~ na uslóviiakh
fob) to deliver goods FOB
единица ~/a (edinítsa ~/a) unit
of commodity
животноводческие ~/ы
(zhivotnovódcheskie ~/y)
livestock goods
жидкий ~ (zhídkii ~) liquid
goods
жизненный цикл ~/a (zhíznennyi
tsikl ~/a) life cycle of goods
забирать ~ (zabirát' ~) to
collect goods
забракованный ~ (zabrakóvannyi
~) rejected goods
заграничные ~/ы (zagraníchnye
~/y) foreign-made products
задержанный ~ (zadérzhannyi ~)
delayed goods
заказ на ~ (zakáz na ~) order
for goods
заказной ~ (zakaznói ~) ordered
goods
закладная на ~ (zakladnáia na ~)
pledge on goods
закладывать ~ (zakládyvat' ~) to
pledge goods
закладывать ~ в банке
(zakládyvat' ~ v bánke) to
pledge goods to the bank

закупка ~/а (zakúpka ~/a)
purchase of goods
залежалый ~ (zalezhályi ~) stale
goods
заложенный ~ (zalózhennyi ~)
pledged goods
заменённые ~/ы (zameniónnye ~/y)
replacements
заменять дефектный ~ (zameniát'
deféktnyi ~) to replace
defective goods
замороженный ~ (zamorózhennyi ~)
refrigerated goods
застрахованные ~/ы
(zastrakhóvannye ~/y) insured
goods
защита ~/а (zashchíta ~/a)
protection of goods
заявлять о повреждении ~/а
(zaiavliát' o povrezhdénii ~/a)
to report damage to goods
извещение о готовности ~/а к
осмотру (izveshchénie o
gotóvnosti ~/a k osmótru)
readiness advice {of goods for
inspection}
излишки ~/а (izlíshki ~/a)
surplus goods
имидж ~/а (ímidzh ~/a) product
image
импорт ~/ов (ímport ~/ov) import
of goods
импортировать ~ (importírovat'
~) to import goods
импортные ~/ы (ímportnye ~/y)
import goods
инвестиционный ~
(investitsiónnyi ~) investment
goods
испорченный ~ (ispórchennyi ~)
spoiled goods
испытывать ~ (ispýtyvat' ~) to
test goods
кампания по продвижению ~/а на
рынок (kampániia po prodvizhé-
niiu ~/a na rýnok) marketing
campaign
категория ~/ов (kategóriia ~/ov)
category of commodities
качество ~/а (káchestvo ~/a)
quality of goods
количество ~/а (kolíchestvo ~/a)
quantity of goods
конкурентоспособные ~/ы
(konkurentosposóbnye ~/y)
competitive goods

консигнационный ~
(konsignatsiónnyi ~) consignment
goods
контрабандный ~ (kontrabándnyi
~) contraband, smuggled goods
косметические ~/ы
(kosmetícheskie ~/y) cosmetics
котировка ~/а с немедленной
сдачей и оплатой (kotiróvka ~/a
s nemédlennoi sdáchei i oplátoi)
quotation on the commodities
spot market
лесобумажные ~/ы (lesobumázhnye
~/y) timber and paper goods
любые ~/ы (liubýe ~/y) goods of
every sort and kind
малоценный ~ (malotsénnyi ~) low
cost goods
марка ~/а (márka ~/a) product
brand
массовые ~/ы (mássovye ~/y) bulk
commodities
модные ~/ы (módnye ~/y)
fashionable products
наукоёмкие ~/ы (naukoiómkie ~/y)
high technology products
небьющиеся ~/ы (neb'iúshchiesia
~/y) unbreakable products
невыгодный ~ (nevýgodnyi ~)
unmerchantable goods
недоброкачественный ~
(nedobrokáchestvennyi ~) poor
quality goods
недопоставленный ~
(nedopostávlennyi ~) short-
delivered goods
недостаточный запас ~/ов
(nedostátochnyi zapás ~/ov)
insufficient stock of goods
незаказанный ~ (nezakázannyi ~)
unordered goods
незатаренный ~ (nezatárennyi ~)
unpacked goods {especially for
shipment}
неистребованный ~
(neistrébovannyi ~) unclaimed
goods
неконкурентоспособные ~/ы
(nekonkurentosposóbnye ~/y) non-
competitive goods
неопасный ~ (neopásnyi ~) non-
hazardous goods
неповреждённый ~
(nepovrezhdiónnyi ~) undamaged
goods
непроданный ~ (nepródannyi ~)
unsold goods

непродовольственные ~/ы
(neprodovól'stvennye ~/y) non-
comestibles {non-food} goods
нетрадиционные ~/ы
(netraditsiónnye ~/y) non-
traditional goods
неходовой ~ (nekhodovói ~)
unsalable goods
низкосортный ~ (nizkosórtnyi ~)
low quality goods
новые ~/ы (nóvye ~/y) new
products
номенклатура ~/ов (nomenklatúra
~/ov) bill of goods
обеспечивать ~/ами
(obespéchivat' ~/ami) to provide
goods
обмен ~/ов (obmén ~/ov) barter
of commodities
обмениваться ~/ами
(obménivat'sia ~/ami) to barter
commodities
образец ~/a (obrazéts ~/a)
sample good
обращение ~/a (obrashchénie ~/a)
commodities circulation
общая стоимость ~/a (óbshchaia
stóimost' ~/a) total cost of
goods
огнеопасный ~ (ogneopásnyi ~)
flammable goods
опасный ~ (opásnyi ~) hazardous
goods
описание ~/a (opisánie ~/a)
description of goods
освоение новых ~/ов для экспорта
(osvoénie nóvykh ~/ov dlia
éksporta) development of new
export products
основные ~/ы (osnovnýe ~/y)
staple commodities
остродефицитные ~/ы
(ostrodefitsítnye ~/y) goods in
{very} short supply
отборный ~ (otbórnyi ~) selected
goods
отгружать ~ (otgruzhát' ~) to
unload goods
отказ от ~/a (otkáz ot ~/a)
rejection of goods
отказываться от ~/a
(otkázyvat'sia ot ~/a) to reject
goods
оценивать ~ (otsénivat' ~) to
value goods
партия ~/a (pártiia ~/a) batch
of goods

патентованные ~/ы (patentóvannye
~/y) patented goods
перечень ~/ов (pérechen' ~/ov)
tally sheet
перечисленные ниже ~/ы
(perechíslennye nízhe ~/y) goods
listed hereinbelow
перспективный ~ (perspektívnyi
~) promising product
первоклассные ~/ы (pervoklássnye
~/y) first class goods
перевалка ~/a (pereválka ~/a)
transshipment of goods
повреждённый ~ (povrezhdiónnyi
~) damaged goods
порок в ~/e (porók v ~/e) defect
in goods
поставщик ~/ов (postavshchík
~/ov) supplier of goods
поступающий ~ (postupáiushchii
~) incoming goods
посылать ~ (posylát' ~) to send
goods
посылать ~ на консигнацию
(posylát' ~ na konsignátsiiu) to
send goods on consignment
посылать ~ на одобрение
(posylát' ~ na odobrénie) to
send goods on approval
потребительские ~/ы
(potrebítel'skie ~/y) consumer
goods
потребительские ~/ы длительного
пользования (potrebítel'skie ~/y
dlítel'nogo pól'zovaniia)
consumer durables
приемлемый ~ (priémlemyi ~)
acceptable goods
приёмка ~/a (priiómka ~/a)
acceptance of goods
проданный ~ (pródannyi ~) sold
goods
продвижение ~/a на рынок
(prodvizhénie ~/a na rýnok)
sales promotion
продовольственные ~/ы
(prodovól'stvennye ~/y)
foodstuffs
происхождение ~/a
(proiskhozhdénie ~/a) origin of
goods
промышленные ~/ы (promýshlennye
~/y) industrial products
пропуск ~/a через таможню
(própusk ~/a chérez tamózhniu)
clearance of goods through
customs

просроченный ~ (prosróchennyi ~)
past due goods
пушной ~ (pushnói ~) fur
products
расфасованный ~ (rasfasóvannyi
~) pre-packaged goods
расфасовка пищевых ~/ов
(rasfasóvka pishchevýkh ~/ov)
pre-packaging of food products
реализация ~/а (realizátsiia
~/a) sale of goods
реализованный ~ (realizóvannyi
~) sold {realized} goods
реализовывать ~ (realizóvyvat'
~) to sell {realize} goods
реализуемый ~ (realizúemyi ~)
merchantable goods
реальный ~ (reál'nyi ~) physical
commodity
редкий ~ (rédkii ~) rare
commodity
рекламировать ~ (reklamírovat'
~) to advertise products
рекламируемый ~ (reklamíruemyi
~) advertised products
реэкспортные ~/ы (reéksportnye
~/y) re-exported goods
розничные ~/ы (róznichnye ~/y)
retail goods
рынок ~/ов (rýnok ~/ov)
commodities market
рынок сырьевых ~/ов (rýnok
syr'evýkh ~/ov) market for raw
materials
сбыт ~/ов (sbyt ~/ov) sale of
goods
сдача ~/а (sdácha ~/a) delivery
of goods
сделка на наличный ~ (sdélka na
nalíchnyi ~) spot market
transaction
сельскохозяйственные ~/ы
(sel'skokhoziáistvennye ~/y)
agricultural commodities
складированный ~ (skladírovannyi
~) warehoused goods
складировать ~ (skladírovat' ~)
to warehouse goods
следить за движением ~/а
(sledít' za dvizhéniem ~/a) to
trace goods
сложный ~ (slózhnyi ~)
sophisticated goods
собственник ~/а (sóbstvennik
~/a) proprietor of goods

собственность на ~
(sóbstvennost' na ~) ownership
of goods
спасённый ~ (spasiónnyi ~)
salvage goods
спецификация ~/а
(spetsifikátsiia ~/a)
specification of goods
список ~/ов (spísok ~/ov) index
of goods
список ~/ов, не облагаемых
пошлиной (spísok ~/ov, ne
oblagáemykh póshlinoi) index of
non-dutiable goods
спортивные ~/ы (sportívnye ~/y)
sporting goods
спрос на ~/ы массового
потребления (spros na ~/y
mássovogo potrebléniia) consumer
demand
стандартизованный ~
(standartizóvannyi ~)
standardized goods
стандартная партия ~/а
(standártnaia pártiia ~/a)
standard batch of goods
стоимость ~/а (stóimost' ~/a)
cost of goods
стоимость ~/а на внутреннем
рынке (stóimost' ~/a na
vnútrennem rýnke) cost of goods
on the domestic market
стоимость ~/а на условиях СИФ
(stóimost' ~/a na uslóviiakh
sif) cost of goods delivered CIF
стоимость ~/а на условиях ФОБ
(stóimost' ~/a na uslóviiakh
fob) cost of goods delivered FOB
стратегические ~/ы
(strategícheskie ~/y) strategic
goods
страховать ~ (strakhovát' ~) to
insure goods
сухой ~ (sukhói ~) dry goods
сходные ~/ы (skhódnye ~/y)
similar goods
сырьевой ~ (syr'evói ~) raw
materials
текстильные ~/ы (tekstíl'nye
~/y) textiles
тип ~/а (tip ~/a) type of goods
торговать ~/ом (torgovát' ~/om)
to deal in commodities
торговля "стратегическими" ~/ами
по спискам КОКОМ (torgóvlia
strategícheskimi ~/ami po
spískam kókom) trade in

strategic commodities on the
COCOM list
торговое название ~/a (torgóvoe
nazvánie ~/a) trade name of a
product
труднореализуемый ~
(trudnorealizúemyi ~) slow
selling goods
трудоёмкий ~ (trudoiómkii ~)
labor-intensive goods
трюмный ~ (triúmnyi ~) under
deck cargo
упакованные ~/ы (upakóvannye
~/y) packaged goods
уценённый ~ (utséniónnyi ~)
marked down goods
уценка ~/a (utsenka ~/a) price
reduction of goods
фактурная стоимость ~/a
(faktúrnaia stóimost' ~/a)
invoice cost of a product
фармацевтические ~/ы
(farmatsevtícheskie ~/y)
pharmaceutical products
фасованный ~ (fasóvannyi ~) pre-
packed goods
фирменный ~ (fírmennyi ~) brand
name goods
характер ~/a (kharákter ~/a)
nature of goods
химические ~/ы (khimícheskie
~/y) chemical products
хлопчатобумажные ~/ы
(khlopchatobumázhnye ~/y) cotton
products
ходкий ~ (khódkii ~) popular
goods
хозяйственные ~ (khoziáistvennye
~) household goods
экспортный ~ (éksportnyi ~)
export goods
~ в тюках (~ v tiukákh) baled
goods
~ в упаковке (~ v upakóvke)
wrapped goods
Товариществ/о (továrishchestv/o) n.
partnership
вступать в ~ (vstupát' v ~) to
enter into a ~
выходить из ~/a (vykhodit' iz
~/a) to withdraw from a ~
коммандитное ~ (kommandítnoe ~)
~ en commandité {civil law form
of limited partnership}
кооперативное ~ (kooperatívnoe
~) cooperative society
полное ~ (pólnoe ~) general ~

~ с ограниченной
ответственностью (~ s
ograníchennoi otvétstvennost'iu)
limited {liability} ~
Товарный (továrnyi) adj. commodity,
goods, trade
Товаровед (tovarovéd) m.
commodities expert
Товарообмен (tovaroobmén) m.
barter, commodities exchange
Товарообменный (tovaroobménnyi)
adj. barter, exchangeable
Товарооборот (tovarooborót) m.
commodity turnover
валовой ~ (valovói ~) gross ~
Товароотправитель
(tovarootpravítel') m. shipper {of
goods}
Товарополучатель
(tovaropoluchátel') m. consignee
{of goods}
Товаропроизводитель
(tovaroproizvodítel') m. commodity
producer
Товарораспорядительный документ
(tovarorasporiadítel'nyi dokumént)
m. document of title {to shipped
commodities}
Тоннаж (tonnázh) m. tonnage
бездействующий ~
(bezdéistvuiushchii ~) idle ~
буксировать ~ (buksírovat' ~) to
book ~
валовой ~ (valovói ~) gross ~
грузовой ~ (gruzovói ~) cargo ~
дополнительный ~ (dopolnítel'nyi
~) additional shipping
facilities
зафрахтованный ~
(zafrakhtóvannyi ~) chartered ~
значительный ~ (znachítel'nyi ~)
significant ~
компенсированный ~
(kompensírovannyi ~) compensated
~
линейный ~ (linéinyi ~) liner ~
максимальный ~ (maksimál'nyi ~)
maximum ~
морской ~ (morskói ~) maritime ~
наливной ~ (nalivnói ~) tanker ~
обусловленный ~ (obuslóvlennyi
~) stipulated ~
общий ~ (óbshchii ~) total ~
речной ~ (rechnói ~) inland ~
спрос на ~ (spros na ~) ~ demand
трамповый ~ (trámpovyi ~) tramp
~

Топливо (tóplivo) *n.* fuel
бункерное ~ (búnkernoe ~) bunker oil
жидкое ~ (zhídkoe ~) liquid ~
заправка ~/м (zaprávka ~/m) bunkering
твёрдое ~ (tviórdoe ~) solid ~

Торг/и (torg/í) *pl.* auction, bid, tenders
выигрывать ~ (vyígryvat' ~) to win tenders
закрытые ~ (zakrýtye ~) closed bidding
извещение о ~/ах (izveshchénie o ~/ákh) notice of tenders
международные ~ (mezhdunaródnye ~) international tenders
объявление ~/ов (ob"iavlénie ~/óv) invitation of tenders
открытые ~ (otkrýtye ~) open bidding
публичные ~ (publíchnye ~) public auction sale

Торговать (torgovát') *v.* to deal in, to trade

Торговаться (torgovát'sia) *v.* to bargain

Торгов/ец (torgóv/ets) *m.* dealer, merchant, vendor
биржевой ~ (birzhevói ~) exchange dealer
индивидуальный ~ (individuál'nyi ~) independent trader
мелкий ~ (mélkii ~) small trader
оптовый ~ (optóvyi ~) wholesale trader
разъездной ~ (raz"ezdnói ~) traveling salesman
розничный ~ (róznichnyi ~) retail tradesman
рыночный ~ (rýnochnyi ~) market trader

Торговец-импортёр (torgóvets-importiór) *m.* dealer-importer

Торговл/я (torgóvl/ia) *f.* commerce, marketing, trade, traffic
бартерная ~ (bárternaia ~) barter trade
беспошлинная ~ (bespóshlinnaia ~) duty-free trade
биржевая ~ (birzheváia ~) exchange trading
бойкая ~ (bóikaia ~) bull market
вести ~/ю (vestí ~/iu) to do business, to trade
"видимая" ~ (vídimaia ~) visible trade

внешняя ~ (vnéshniaia ~) foreign trade
внутрення ~ (vnútrennia ~) domestic trade
встречная ~ (vstréchnaia ~) counter trade
выгодная ~ (výgodnaia ~) profitable business
выручка от ~/и (výruchka ot ~/i) receipts from trade
вялая ~ (viálaia ~) stagnant trade
годовая ~ (godováia ~) annual trade
государственная ~ (gosudárstvennaia ~) state trading
двусторонняя ~ (dvustorónniaia ~) bilateral trade
диверсификация ~/и (diversifikátsiia ~/i) diversification of trade
дипломатическая ~ (diplomatícheskaia ~) diplomatic trade
дисбаланс ~/и (disbaláns ~/i) trade imbalance
договор о ~/е (dogovór o ~/e) commerce treaty
законная ~ (zakónnaia ~) lawful trade
заниматься ~/ей (zanimát'sia ~/ei) to be in business
застой в ~/е (zastói v ~/e) stagnation in trade
значительная ~ (znachítel'naia ~) significant trade
каботажная ~ (kabotázhnaia ~) coasting trade
контрабандная ~ (kontrabándnaia ~) illicit trade
косвенная транзитная ~ (kósvennaia tranzítnaia ~) indirect transit trade
либерализация ~/и (liberalizátsiia ~/i) trade liberalization
лицензионная ~ (litsenziónnaia ~) licensed trade
межгосударственная ~ (mezhgosudárstvennaia ~) interstate trade
межрегиональная ~ (mezhregionál'naia ~) interregional trade
меновая ~ (menováia ~) bartering

мировая ~ (mirováia ~) world trade
многосторонняя (mnogostorónniaia) multilateral trade
морская ~ (morskáia ~) maritime commerce
национальная ~ (natsionál'naia ~) national trade
"невидимая" ~ (nevídimaia ~) invisible trade
незаконная ~ (nezakónnaia ~) unlawful trade
объём ~/и (ob"ióm ~/i) volume of trade
ограничение ~/и (ogranichénie ~/i) trade restriction
оживление ~и (ozhivlénie ~i) trade recovery
оживлённая ~ (ozhivliónnaia ~) brisk trade
оптовая ~ (optóvaia ~) wholesale trade
отрасль ~/и (ótrasl' ~/i) field of trade
перспективы ~/и (perspektívy ~/i) trade prospects
политика расширения ~/и (polítika rasshiréniia ~/i) trade expansion policy
помехи в ~/е (pomékhi v ~/e) trading obstacles
поощрять ~/ю (pooshchriát' ~/iu) to encourage trade
посредническая ~ (posrédnicheskaia ~) intermediary trade
посылочная ~ (posýlochnaia ~) mail order business
препятствовать развитию ~/и (prepiátstvovat' razvítiiu ~/i) to impede the development of trade
преференциальная ~ (preferentsiál'naia ~) preferential trade
прямая транзитная ~ (priamáia tranzítnaia ~) direct transit trade
развёртывание ~/и (razviórtyvanie ~/i) expansion of trade
региональная ~ (regionál'naia ~) regional trade
розничная ~ (róznichnaia ~) retail trade

свободная ~ (svobódnaia ~) free trade
сезонная ~ (sezónnaia ~) seasonal trade
частная ~ (chástnaia ~) private trade
экспортная ~ (éksportnaia ~) export trade
~ за наличные (~ za nalíchnye) cash trade
~ металлами (~ metállami) metals trading
Торговый (torgóvyi) *adj.* commercial, mercantile, trade
Торгпред (torgpréd) *m.* trade representative
Торгпредство (torgprédstvo) *n.* trade mission
Точно (tóchno) *adv.* accurately, correctly, exactly, precisely
~ по графику (~ po gráfiku) right on schedule
~ идентифицировать (~ identifitsírovat') to identify precisely
~ определять (~ opredeliát') to determine precisely
~ по размеру (~ po razméru) exactly to measurement
~ указанный (~ ukázannyi) expressly indicated
Точност/ь (tóchnost/') *f.* accuracy, correctness, exactness, precision, punctuality
абсолютная ~ (absoliútnaia ~) absolute precision
анализ ~/и (análiz ~/i) precision analysis
в ~/и (v ~/i) precisely
возможная ~ (vozmózhnaia ~) possible accuracy
максимальная ~ (maksimál'naia ~) maximum accuracy
необходимая ~ (neobkhodímaia ~) required accuracy
оценка ~/и (otsénka ~/i) estimate of precision
Традиция (tradítsiia) *f.* tradition
Трамп (tramp) *m.* tramp steamer
Трамповый (trámpovyi) *adj.* tramp {of vessel, not person}
Транзит (tranzít) *m.* traffic, transit
виза для ~/а (víza dlia ~/a) transit visa
обратный ~ (obrátnyi ~) back haul

~/ом (~/om) in transit
Транзитный (tranzítnyi) adj.
through, transit
Трансакция (transáktsiia) f.
transaction
    банковская ~ (bánkovskaia ~)
    bank ~
    биржевая ~ (birzheváia ~)
    exchange ~
    валютная ~ (valiútnaia ~)
    currency exchange ~
    финансовая ~ (finánsovaia ~)
    financial ~
Трансатлантический
(transatlantícheskii) adj. trans-
Atlantic
Трансконтинентальный
(transkontinentál'nyi) adj.
transcontinental
Транспорт (tránsport) m.
conveyance, means of conveyance,
transport
    авиационный ~ (aviatsiónnyi ~)
    air transport
    автомобильный ~ (avtomobíl'nyi
    ~) automobile transport
    вид ~/a (vid ~/a) mode of
    transport
    внутренний ~ (vnútrennii ~)
    inland transport
    внутренний водный ~ (vnútrennii
    vódnyi ~) inland water transport
    водный ~ (vódnyi ~) water
    transport
    воздушный ~ (vozdúshnyi ~) air
    transport
    городской ~ (gorodskói ~) urban
    transport
    гражданский ~ (grahdánskii ~)
    civil transport
    грузовой ~ (gruzovói ~) freight
    transport
    дорожный ~ (dorózhnyi ~) road
    transport
    железнодорожный ~
    (zheleznodorózhnyi ~) rail
    transport
    морской ~ (morskói ~) marine
    transport
    общественный ~ (obshchéstvennyi
    ~) public transport
    пассажирский ~ (passazhírskii ~)
    passenger transport
    речной ~ (rechnói ~) river
    transport
    система ~/a (sístema ~/a)
    transportation system

Транспортирование
(transportírovanie) n. carriage,
transporting
Транспортировать (transportírovat')
v. to carry, to haul, to ship, to
transport
Транспортировк/а (transportiróvk/a)
f. carriage, haulage, transport
    контейнерная ~ (kontéinernaia ~)
    container shipping
    морская ~ (morskáia ~) seagoing
    shipping
    обеспечивать ~/ой (obespéchivat'
    ~/oi) to provide shipping
Транспортно-экспедиторский
(tránsportno-ekspedítorskii) adj.
forwarding
Транспортный (tránsportnyi) adj.
transportation
Трансферт (transfért) m. deed of
transfer, transfer
    банковский ~ (bánkovskii ~) bank
    transfer
    кредитный ~ (kredítnyi ~) credit
    transfer
    получатель по ~/у (poluchátel'
    po ~/u) transferee
Трансфертный (transfértnyi) adj.
transfer
Трасса (trássa) f. direction, route
    воздушная ~ (vozdúshnaia ~) air
    route
Трассант (trassánt) m. drawer,
maker of a bill
Трассат (trassát) m. drawee
Трассировать (trassírovat') v. to
draw a bill of exchange
    ~ на ... долларов (~ na ...
    dóllarov) to draw for ...
    dollars
Трата (tráta) f. expenditure,
spending
    непроизводительная ~
    (neproizvodítel'naia ~) wasteful
    expenditure
Тратить (trátit') v. to expend, to
spend
    ~ напрасно (~ naprásno) to waste
Тратт/а (trátt/a) f. acceptance,
bill of exchange, draft
    аванс против документарной ~/ы
    (aváns prótiv dokumentárnoi ~/y)
    advance against a documentary
    draft
    авансовая ~ (avánsovaia ~)
    advance bill of exchange

акцепт ~/ы (aktsépt ~/y)
acceptance of a draft
акцептованная ~ (aktseptóvannaia
~) acceptance draft
банковская ~ (bánkovskaia ~)
banker's draft
внутренняя ~ (vnútrenniaia ~)
inland bill of exchange
возвращать ~/у с протестом
(vozvrashchát' ~/u s protéstom)
to return a bill of exchange
under protest
возобновлять ~/у (vozobnovliát'
~/u) to renew a bill
встречная ~ (vstréchnaia ~)
redraft
выписка ~/ы (výpiska ~/y)
drawing of a draft
действительная ~
(deistvítel'naia ~) valid draft
держатель ~/ы (derzhátel' ~/y)
holder of a bill of exchange
документированная ~
(dokumentírovannaia ~)
documentary draft, secured bill
of exchange
долгосрочная ~ (dolgosróchnaia
~) long term draft
домицилированная ~
(domitsilírovannaia ~) domiciled
bill of exchange
инкассировать ~/у (inkassírovat'
~/u) to collect a bill, draft
инкассо ~/ы (inkásso ~/y)
collection against a bill, draft
иностранная ~ (inostránnaia ~)
foreign bill
коммерческая ~ (kommércheskaia
~) commercial draft
краткосрочная ~ (kratkosróchnaia
~) short term bill
неакцептованная ~
(neaktseptóvannaia ~) unaccepted
draft
недокументированная ~
(nedokumentírovannaia ~) clean
draft
неоплаченная ~ (neopláchennaia
~) outstanding bill of exchange
переуступать ~/у (pereustupát'
~/u) to negotiate a bill, draft
переучитывать ~/у
(pereuchítyvat' ~/u) to
rediscount a bill, draft
платить ~/ой (platít' ~/oi) to
pay through a bill, draft

плательщик по ~/е (platél'shchik
po ~/e) drawee of a draft
платёж ~/ами (platiózh ~/ami)
payment by drawing
платёж против ~/ (platiózh
prótiv ~/) payment against
drafts
представлять ~/у (predstavliát'
~/u) to present a bill, draft
представлять ~/у для акцепта
(predstavliát' ~/u dlia
aktsépta) to present a bill for
acceptance
предъявительская ~/а
(pred"iavítel'skaia ~/a) site
draft
рамбурсная ~ (rámbursnaia ~)
reimbursement draft
срок ~/ы (srok ~/y) tenor of a
bill, draft
срок платежа по ~/е (srok
platezhá po ~/e) maturity of a
draft
срочная ~ (sróchnaia ~) time
draft
ставка по учёту ~/ы (stávka po
uchiótu ~/y) discount rate
сумма ~/ы (súmma ~/y) amount of
a draft
торговая ~ (torgóvaia ~)
commercial paper
Требовани/е (trébovani/e) n.
application, claim, demand,
request, requirement
встречное ~ (vstréchnoe ~)
counter claim
выдвигать ~/я (vydvigát' ~/ia)
to make demands
выполнение ~/й (vypolnénie ~/i)
fulfillment of requirements
денежное ~ (dénezhnoe ~)
monetary claim
дополнительное ~ (dopolnítel'noe
~) supplementary claim
заявлять ~ (zaiavliát' ~) to
present a demand
иметь особые ~/я (imét' osóbye
~/ia) to have specific
requirements
исковое ~ (ískovoe ~) action at
law
квалификационные ~/я
(kvalifikatsiónnye ~/ia) job
specifications
количественные ~/я
(kolíchestvennye ~/ia)
quantitative requirements

нарушение ~/й (narushénie ~/i)
violation of requirements
настаивать на ~/ях (nastáivat'
na ~/iakh) to press claims
настойчивое ~ (nastóichivoe ~)
insistent demand
настоятельное ~ (nastoiátel'noe
~) urgent request
обоснование претензионного ~/я
(obosnovánie pretenziónnogo
~/ia) grounds for a claim
обоснованное ~ (obosnóvannoe ~)
reasonable demand
общие ~/я (óbshchie ~/ia)
general requirements
общие эксплуатационные ~/я
(óbshchie ekspluatatsiónnye
~/ia) general operating
requirements
обычное ~ (obýchnoe ~) common
requirement
обязательное ~ (obiazátel'noe ~)
mandatory requirement
окончательное ~ (okonchátel'noe
~) end requirement
платёжное ~ (platiózhnoe ~)
payment request
преимущественное ~
(preimúshchestvennoe ~)
preferential claim
претензионное ~ (pretenziónnoe
~) claim
признавать ~/я (priznavát' ~/ia)
to acknowledge a claim
регрессное ~ (regréssnoe ~)
recourse
санитарно-гигиенические ~/я
(sanitárno-gigienícheskie ~/ia)
sanitary hygiene standards
специальное ~ (spetsiál'noe ~)
specific requirement
справедливое ~ (spravedlívoe ~)
just demand
срочное ~ (sróchnoe ~) urgent
demand
строгое ~ (strógoe ~) strict
requirement
технические ~/я (tekhnícheskie
~/ia) technical requirements
точные ~/я (tóchnye ~/ia) exact
requirements
эксплуатационные ~/я
(ekspluatatsiónnye ~/ia)
operating requirements
~/я истца (~/ia isttsá)
plaintiff's demands

Требовать (trébovat') v. to claim,
to demand, to require
Трест (trest) m. "trust" {group of
enterprises under centralized
management}
Трещина (tréshchina) f. crack,
crevice
Тримминг (trímming) m. trimming {of
a vessel}
Тропический (tropícheskii) adj.
tropical
Трос (tros) m. cable, rope
проволочный ~ (próvolochnyi ~)
wire rope
стальной ~ (stal'nói ~) steel
cable
Трубопровод (truboprovód) m.
pipeline
Труд (trud) m. labor
внутризаводское разделение ~/a
(vnutrizavódskoe razdelénie ~/á)
in-factory division of ~
высококвалифицированный ~
(vysokokvalifitsírovannyi ~)
highly skilled ~
квалифицированный ~
(kvalifitsírovannyi ~) skilled ~
непроизводительный ~
(neproizvodítel'nyi ~) non-
productive ~
нормирование ~/a (normirovánie
~/a) setting of ~ quotas
оплата ~/a (opláta ~/a)
remuneration of ~
охрана ~/a (okhrána ~/a) worker
safety
продуктивный ~ (produktívnyi ~)
productive ~
производительность ~/a
(proizvodítel'nost' ~/a)
productivity of ~
производительный ~
(proizvodítel'nyi ~) efficient ~
разделение ~/a (razdelénie ~/a)
division of ~
ручной ~ (ruchnói ~) manual ~
условия ~/a (uslóviia ~/a)
working conditions
Труднодоступный (trudnodostúpnyi)
adj. laborious
Труднореализуемый
(trudnorealizúemyi) adj. poor
selling
Трудност/ь (trúdnost/') f.
difficulty, problem, trouble
большие ~/и (bol'shíe ~/i) major
difficulties

ввиду ~/ей (vvidú ~/ei) in view of difficulties
встречаться с ~/ями (vstrechát'sia s ~/iami) to meet with difficulties
выдерживать ~/и (vydérzhivat' ~/i) to withstand trouble
вызывать ~/и (vyzyvát' ~/i) to cause problems
выносить ~/и (vynosít' ~/i) to bear trouble
значительные ~/и (znachítel'nye ~/i) significant difficulties
испытывать ~/и (ispýtyvat' ~/i) to experience difficulties
небольшие ~/и (nebol'shíe ~/i) minor difficulties
непредвиденные ~/и (nepredvídennye ~/i) unforeseen difficulties
огромные ~/и (ogrómnye ~/i) enormous difficulties
платёжные ~/и (platiózhnye ~/i) payment problems
постоянные ~/и (postoiánnye ~/i) persistent difficulties
преодолевать ~/и (preodolevát' ~/i) to overcome difficulties
преувеличивать ~/и (preuvelíchivat' ~/i) to exaggerate difficulties
серьёзные ~/и (ser'ióznye ~/i) serious problems
создавать ~/и (sozdavát' ~/i) to create problems
технические ~/и (tekhnícheskie ~/i) technical difficulties
указывать на ~/и (ukázyvat' na ~/i) to indicate difficulties
финансовые ~/и (finánsovye ~/i) financial difficulties
экономические ~/и (ekonomícheskie ~/i) economic difficulties
эксплуатационные ~/и (ekspluatatsiónnye ~/i) operational difficulties
Трудный (trúdnyi) adj. difficult, hard
Трудоёмкий (trudoiómkii) adj. labor intensive
Трудоёмкость (trudoiómkost') f. labor content
Трудоспособность (trudosposóbnost') f. work capacity
Трудоспособный (trudosposóbnyi) adj. able-bodied

Трюм (trium) m. hold {of a vessel}
вместимость ~/a (vmestímost' ~/a) capacity of the ~
вместительный ~ (vmestítel'nyi ~) ample ~
главный ~ (glávnyi ~) main ~
задний ~ (zádnii ~) aft ~
Трюмный (triúmnyi) adj. hold {of a vessel}
Туризм (turízm) m. tourism
иностранный ~ (inostránnyi ~) foreign ~
международный (mezhdunaródnyi ~) international ~
развитие ~/a (razvítie ~/a) development of ~
Туристический (turistícheskii) adj. tourist
Тщательно (tshchátel'no) adv. carefully, thoroughly
~ исследовать (~ islédovat') to thoroughly investigate
~ осматривать (~ osmátrivat') to carefully inspect
~ проверять (~ proveriát') to carefully examine
~ разрабатывать (~ razrabátyvat') to elaborate
~ рассматривать (~ rassmátrivat') to scrutinize
Тщательный (tshchátel'nyi) adj. careful, thorough
Тюк (tiuk) m. bale, bundle
Тяжеловес (tiazhelovés) m. extra weight cargo
Тяжеловесный (tiazhelovésnyi) adj. heavy weight
Тяжёлый (tiazhiólyi) adj. difficult, heavy

У

Убежище (ubézhishche) n. asylum, sanctuary
налоговое ~ (nalógovoe ~) tax haven
Убыль (úbyl') f. loss
естественная ~ (estéstvennaia ~) natural ~
нормальная ~ и нормальный износ (normál'naia ~ i normál'nyi iznós) normal wear and tear
~ веса во время морской перевозки (~ vésa vo vrémia

morskói perevózki) ~ of weight
during ocean shipment
Убыт/ок (ubýt/ok) *m.* damages, loss,
waste
аварийные ~/ки (avaríinye ~/ki)
average losses
анализ ~/ков (análiz ~/kov) loss
analysis
большие ~/ки (bol'shíe ~/ki)
heavy losses
взыскание ~/ков (vzyskánie
~/kov) recovery of damages
взыскать ~/ки (vzyskát' ~/ki) to
recover damages
включать ~/ки или ущерб
(vkliuchát' ~/ki íli ushchérb)
to include loss or damage
возбуждать иск об ~/ках
(vozbuzhdát' isk ob ~/kakh) to
bring an action for damages
возмещаемый ~ (vozmeshcháemyi ~)
loss to be compensated
возмещать ~/ки (vozmeshchát'
~/ki) to compensate for losses
возмещать ~/ки истцу
(vozmeshchát' ~/ki isttsú) to
pay judgment damages
возмещение ~/ков (vozmeshchénie
~/kov) compensation
возмещение будущих ~/ков
(vozmeshchénie búdushchikh
~/kov) anticipatory damages
возмещение ожидаемых ~/ков
(vozmeshchénie ozhidáemykh
~/kov) prospective damages
возмещение ~/ков, причинённых
неприятием товара (vozmeshchénie
~/kov, prichiniónnykh
nepriiátiem továra) damages for
non-acceptance
возмещённый ~ (vozmeshchiónnyi
~) compensated loss
возможные ~/ки (vozmózhnye ~/ki)
eventual losses
в порядке возмещения ~/ков (v
poriádke vozmeshchéniia ~/kov)
by way of damages
гарантировать от ~/ков
(garantírovat' ot ~/kov) to
indemnify
гарантия от ~/ков (garántiia ot
~/kov) guarantee against losses
денежный ~ (dénezhnyi ~)
monetary loss
единичные ~/ки (ediníchnye ~/ki)
single losses

заявление об ~/ках (zaiavlénie
ob ~/kakh) damage claim
значительные ~/ки (znachítel'nye
~/ki) significant losses
избавлять кого-л. от
ответственности за ~/ки
(izbavliát' kogó-l. ot
otvétstvennosti za ~/ki) to hold
someone harmless for damages
избежать ~/ков (izbezhát' ~/kov)
to avoid losses
иск об ~/ках (isk ob ~/kakh)
action for damages
компенсация з (kompensátsiia z)
а ~/ки compensation for damages
компенсировать ~/ки
(kompensírovat' ~/ki) to
compensate damages
косвенные ~/ки (kósvennye ~/ki)
indirect damages
крупные ~/ки (krúpnye ~/ki)
major losses
материальный ~ (materiál'nyi ~)
property loss
нести ~ (nestí ~) to suffer
damage
нести ~/ки (nestí ~/ki) to incur
losses
нести значительные ~/ки (nestí
znachítel'nye ~/ki) to incur
significant losses
общая сумма ~/ков (óbshchaia
súmma ~/kov) total losses
оплата ~/ков (opláta ~/kov)
payment of damages
определение ~/ков (opredelénie
~/kov) determination of damages
определять сумму ~/ков
(opredeliát' súmmu ~/kov) to
determine the amount of damages
ответственность за ~/ки
(otvétstvennost' za ~/ki)
liability for damages
отказ от права на возмещение
~/ков (otkáz ot práva na vozmeshchénie ~/kov) waiver of right
to damages
оценённые ~/ки (otseniónnye
~/ki) estimated losses
оценивать ~/ки по общей аварии
(otsénivat' ~/ki po óbshchei
avárii) to adjust general
average losses
оценка ~/ков (otsenka ~/kov)
assessment of damages

паушальная сумма ~/ков
(paushál'naia súmma ~/kov)
lumpsum damages
"перевозчик не отвечает за ~/ки"
(perevózchik ne otvecháet za
~/ki) "carrier not liable for
damages"
платить заранее оценённые и
согласованные ~/ки (platít'
zaránee otseniónnye i
soglasóvannye ~/ki) to pay
liquidated damages
повлечь ~/ки (povléch' ~/ki) to
entail losses
показывать ~/ки (pokázyvat'
~/ki) to show losses
покрывать ~/ки (pokryvát' ~/ki)
to cover losses
получать возмещение ~/ков
(poluchát' vozmeshchénie ~/kov)
to recover damages
право на взыскание ~/ков (právo
na vzyskánie ~/kov) right to
recover damages
предельные ~/ки (predél'nye
~/ki) marginal damages
предотвращать ~/ки
(predotvrashchát' ~/ki) to avert
losses
предполагаемый ~ (predpolagáemyi
~) anticipated loss
приносить ~/ки (prinosít' ~/ki)
to sustain losses
присуждать ~/ки (prisuzhdát'
~/ki) to award damages
причины возникновения ~/ков
(prichíny vozniknovéniia ~/kov)
causes of damages
причинять ~/ки (prichiniát'
~/ki) to inflict harm, to cause
damages
продавать с ~/ком (prodavát' s
~/kom) to sell at a loss
проценты по погашению ~/ков
(protsénty po pogashéniiu ~/kov)
interest on losses
работать с ~/ком (rabótat' s
~/kom) to operate at a loss
размер ~/ков (razmér ~/kov)
measure of damages
реальные ~/ки (reál'nye ~/ki)
actual losses
решение о возмещении ~/ков
(reshénie o vozmeshchénii ~/kov)
award of damages
сводный счёт прибылей и ~/ков
(svódnyi schiót príbylei i

~/kov) consolidated profit and
loss statement
случайный ~ (slucháinyi ~)
accidental loss
согласованные и заранее
оценённые ~/ки (soglasóvannye i
zaránee otseniónnye ~/ki)
liquidated damages
сокращать ~/ки до минимума
(sokrashchát' ~/ki do mínimuma)
to minimize loss
стоимость ~/ков, возникших в
производстве (stóimost' ~/kov,
vozníkshikh v proizvódstve)
production loss value
страховой ~ (strakhovói ~)
indemnified loss
сумма ~/ков (súmma ~/kov) amount
of damages
счёт прибылей и ~/ков (schiót
príbylei i ~/kov) profit and
loss statement
считать кого-л. ответственным за
~/ки (schitát' kogó-l.
otvétstvennym za ~/ki) to hold
someone liable for damages
терпеть ~/ки (terpét' ~/ki) to
sustain losses
требовать возмещения ~/ков
(trébovat' vozmeshchéniia ~/kov)
to demand compensation for
losses
уменьшение ~/ков (umen'shénie
~/kov) reduction in damages
уточнять ~/ки (utochniát' ~/ki)
to adjust losses
фактические ~/ки (faktícheskie
~/ki) actual losses
финансовый ~ (finánsovyi ~)
financial loss
частичный ~ (chastíchnyi ~)
partial loss
чистый ~ (chístyi ~) net loss
чрезмерные ~/ки (chrezmérnye
~/ki) excessive losses
~/ки от общей аварии (~/ki ot
óbshchei avárii) general average
losses
~/ки от частной аварии (~/ki ot
chástnoi avárii) particular
average losses
~/ки по займам (~/ki po zaimam)
loss on loans
~/ки, понесённые в связи с ...
(~/ki, ponesiónnye v sviázi s
...) losses suffered in
connection with ...

~ при разгрузке (~ pri razgrúzke) loss during discharge

~ при реализации спасённого имущества (~ pri realizátsii spasiónnogo imúshchestva) salvage loss

~, причинённый поломкой (~, prichiniónnyi polómkoi) breakage loss

~/ки при эксплуатации (~/ki pri ekspluatátsii) operating losses

Уведомлени/е (uvedomléni/e) *n.* advice, notice, notification

банковское ~ (bánkovskoe ~) bank notification

заблаговременное ~ (zablagovrémennoe ~) advance notice

надлежащее ~ (nadlezháshchee ~) due notice

официальное ~ (ofitsiál'noe ~) official notification

письменное ~ (pís'mennoe ~) written notification

по ~/и (po ~/i) upon notification

получать ~ (poluchát' ~) to receive notice

посредством письменного ~/я (posrédstvom pís'mennogo ~/ia) by written notice

посылать ~ (posylát' ~) to send notification

посылать ~ заблаговременно (posylát' ~ zablagovrémenno) to provide advance warning

предварительное ~ (predvarítel'noe ~) preliminary notice

представлять письменное ~ (predstavliát' pís'mennoe ~) to provide written notification

предписанное законом ~ (predpísannoe zakónom ~) statutory notice

при ~/и (pri ~/i) under advice

при условии немедленного ~/я (pri uslóvii nemédlennogo ~/ia) subject to timely notice

регистрировать ~ (registrírovat' ~) to file a notice

с заблаговременным ~/ем (s zablagovrémennym ~/em) within a reasonable period from notification

своевременное ~ (svoevrémennoe ~) timely notice

срочное ~ (sróchnoe ~) immediate notice

считайте это письмо официальным ~/ем ... (schitáite eto pis'mó ofitsiál'nym ~/em ...) consider this letter to be official notification ...

~ за одну неделю (~ za odnú nedéliu) one week's notice

~ о готовности (~ o gotóvnosti) advice of readiness

~ о дебетовании (~ o debetovánii) debit advice

~ о денежном переводе (~ o dénezhnom perevóde) remittance advice

~ о кредитовании (~ o kreditovánii) credit advice

~ о платеже (~ o platezhé) advice of payment

~ о погрузке (~ o pogrúzke) loading notification

~ о предъявлении претензии (~ o pred"iavlénii preténzii) notice of claim

~ о прибытии (~ o pribýtii) notice of arrival

~ о прибытии на железнодорожную станцию (~ o pribýtii na zheleznodorózhnuiu stántsiiu) railway advice

~ об аккредитиве (~ ob akkreditíve) notification of a letter of credit

~ об аукционе (~ ob auktsióne) auction notice

~ об иске (~ ob íske) notice of legal action

~ об истечении срока (~ ob istechénii sróka) notice of expiration

~ об отгрузке (~ ob otgrúzke) shipping advice

~ об отмене (~ ob otméne) cancellation notice

~ об отправке (~ ob otprávke) forwarding advice

~ по почте (~ po póchte) notice by mail

~ по телеграфу (~ po telegráfu) notice by cable

~ по телексу (~ po téleksu) notice by telex

~ по телефону (~ po telefónu) telephonic notification

Уведомлять (uvedomliát') *v.* to advise, inform, notify

официально ~ (ofitsiál'no ~) to give formal notice
предварительно ~ (predvarítel'no ~) to give prior notice
Увеличени/е (uvelichéni/e) *n.* expansion, increase
вероятное ~ (veroiátnoe ~) probable increase
допустимое ~ (dopustímoe ~) permitted increase
значительное ~ (znachítel'noe ~) significant increase
общее ~ (óbshchee ~) overall increase
общее ~ в процентном выражении (óbshchee ~ v protséntnom vyrazhénii) overall percentage increase
ограниченное ~ (ograníchennoe ~) limited increase
планировать ~ (planírovat' ~) to project an increase
подлежать ~/ю (podlezhát' ~/iu) to be subject to escalation
покрыть ~ цены (pokrýt' ~ tsený) to absorb a price increase
разовое ~ (rázovoe ~) one-time increase
резкое ~ (rézkoe ~) sharp increase
содействовать ~/ю продажи (sodéistvovat' ~/iu prodázhi) to promote sales
способствовать ~/ю производительности (sposóbstvovat' ~/iu proizvodítel'nosti) to facilitate higher productivity
~ вкладов (~ vkládov) increase of deposits
~ выставочной площади (~ výstavochnoi plóshchadi) expansion of exhibit space
~ до ... (~ do ...) increase to ...
~ доходов (~ dokhódov) increase in income
~ зарплаты (~ zarpláty) raise {in pay}
~ импорта (~ ímporta) increase in imports
~ капиталовложений (~ kapitalovlozhénii) increase in capital investments
~ квоты (~ kvóty) extension of a quota

~ надбавки к цене (~ nadbávki k tsené) increased bid {auction}
~ налогов (~ nalógov) increase in taxes
~ объёма торговли (~ ob"ióma torgóvli) increase in trade volume
~ поставок (~ postávok) increase in deliveries
~ поступлений валюты (~ postuplénii valiúty) increase in convertible currency receipts
~ производительности (~ proizvodítel'nosti) increase in productivity
~ производительности оборудования (~ proizvodítel'nosti oborúdovaniia) increase in equipment productivity
~ производительности труда (~ proizvodítel'nosti trudá) increase in labor productivity
~ производства (~ proizvódstva) expansion of output
~ процентов (~ protséntov) interest rate increase
~ сбыта (~ sbýta) increase in sales
~ численного состава (~ chíslennogo sostáva) increase in manpower
Увеличивать (uvelíchivat') *v.* to increase
Увольнение (uvol'nénie) *n.* dismissal, firing {from a job}
Увольнять (uvol'niát') *v.* to dismiss, to fire {from a job}
Углевоз (uglevóz) *m.* coal ship
Уголовное дело (ugolóvnoe délo) *n.* criminal case
возбуждать ~ (vozbuzhdát' ~) to press criminal charges against
Удержани/е (uderzháni/e) *n.* deduction, detention, withholding
до ~/я налогов (do ~/ia nalógov) pre-tax
после ~/я налогов (pósle ~/ia nalógov) after-tax
право ~/я (právo ~/ia) lien
прогрессивное ~ (progressívnoe ~) progressive deduction
производить ~ (proizvodít' ~) to deduct
пропорционально ~ (proportsionál'no ~) proportional deduction

~ из платежей (~ iz platezhéi) withholding from payments
~ налогов (~ nalógov) tax withholding
~ суммы (~ súmmy) deduction of an amount
~ франшизы (~ franshízy) deduction of franchise
Удерживать (udérzhivat') v. to deduct, to retain
Удешевление (udeshevlénie) n. drop in price
Удешевлять (udeshevliát') v. to make cheaper
Удлинять (udliniát') v. to extend, to prolong
Удобный (udóbnyi) adj. comfortable, convenient
Удовлетворени/е (udovletvoréni/e) n. consideration, satisfaction
в ~ (v ~) in satisfaction
в полное и окончательное ~ (v pólnoe i okonchátel'noe ~) in full and final satisfaction
встречное ~ (vstréchnoe ~) consideration {contractual}
встречное благоприятное ~ (vstréchnoe blagopriiátnoe ~) favorable consideration
встречное будущее ~ (vstréchnoe búdushchee ~) executory consideration
встречное действительное ~ (vstréchnoe deistvítel'noe ~) valid consideration
встречное денежное ~ (vstréchnoe dénezhnoe ~) monetary consideration
встречное достаточное ~ (vstréchnoe dostátochnoe ~) sufficient consideration
встречное надлежащее ~ (vstréchnoe nadlezháshchee ~) valuable consideration
встречное недостаточное ~ (vstréchnoe nedostátochnoe ~) insufficient consideration
встречное предшествовавшее ~ (vstréchnoe predshestvovávshee ~) past consideration
дать ~ (dat' ~) to give satisfaction
делать к чьему-л. ~/ю (délat' k ch'ému-l. ~/iu) to perform to someone's satisfaction
к взаимному ~/ю (k vzaímnomu ~/iu) to mutual satisfaction

к полному ~/ю (k pólnomu ~/iu) to complete satisfaction
к ~/и всех сторон (k ~/i vsekh storón) to the satisfaction of all concerned
находить ~ (nakhodít' ~) to meet with satisfaction
отказываться от ~/я (otkázyvat'sia ot ~/ia) to refuse to settle
получить полное ~ (poluchít' pólnoe ~) to be fully satisfied
частичное ~ (chastíchnoe ~) partial settlement
~ иска (~ íska) judgment for the plaintiff
~ кредитора (~ kredítora) satisfaction of a creditor
~ потребностей (~ potrébnostei) satisfaction of requirements
~ претензии (~ preténzii) satisfaction of a claim
~ просьбы (~ prós'by) satisfaction of a request
~ спроса (~ sprósa) meeting demand {economic}
~ требований (~ trébovanii) satisfaction of demands
Удовлетворительный (udovletvorítel'nyi) adj. satisfactory
Удорожание (udorozhánie) n. rise in price
~ экспорта (~ éksporta) rise in export prices
Удостоверени/е (udostoveréni/e) n. attestation, authentication, certificate
выдача ~/я (výdacha ~/ia) certification
выдавать ~ (vydavát' ~) to certify
надлежащее ~ личности (nadlezháshchee ~ líchnosti) proper credentials
по письменному ~/ю (po pís'mennomu ~/iu) certified in writing
представить ~ личности (predstávit' ~ líchnosti) to present credentials
с целью ~/я личности (s tsél'iu ~/ia líchnosti) for purposes of identification
санитарное ~ (sanitárnoe ~) bill of health

~ таможни на возврат таможенной пошлины (~ tamózhni na vozvrat tamózhennoi póshliny) customs debenture
~ для специалистов (~ dlia spetsialístov) professional credentials
~ личности (~ líchnosti) identification card
~ подписи (~ pódpisi) attestation of signature
Удостоверять (udostoveriát') v. to attest, to authenticate, to certify
Указ (ukáz) m. decree
Указани/е (ukazáni/e) n. indication, instructions
в ожидании дальнейших ~/й (v ozhidánii dal'néishikh ~/i) pending further instructions
в соответствии с ~/ями (v sootvétstvii s ~/iami) in accordance with instructions
в упаковке и с маркировкой согласно ~/ям (v upakóvke i s markiróvkoi soglásno ~/iam) packed and marked as per instructions
выполнять ~/я (vypolniát' ~/ia) to comply with instructions
давать ~/я (davát' ~/ia) to give instructions
давать ~/я банку (davát' ~/ia bánku) to instruct the bank
давать письменные ~/я (davát' pís'mennye ~/ia) to give written instructions
делать по ~/ю (délat' po ~/iu) to perform per instructions
директивные ~/я (direktívnye ~/ia) directives
дополнительные ~/я (dopolnítel'nye ~/ia) further instructions
заблаговременное ~ (zablagovrémennoe ~) forward direction
на основании ~/й (na osnovánii ~/i) under the instructions of ...
независимо от ~/й (nezavísimo ot ~/i) notwithstanding instructions
неправильные ~/я (neprávil'nye ~/ia) improper directions
несоблюдение ~/й (nesobliudénie ~/i) non-observance of instructions

общие ~/я (óbshchie ~/ia) general instructions
ожидать ~/й (ozhidát' ~/i) to await further instructions
передавать ~/я (peredavát' ~/ia) to transmit instructions
письменное ~ (pís'mennoe ~) written instructions
по ~/ю (po ~/iu) by order of ...
подробные ~/я (podróbnye ~/ia) detailed instructions
правильные ~/я (právil'nye ~/ia) proper directions
при отсутствии иных ~/й (pri otsútstvii inýkh ~/i) unless otherwise specified
противоположные ~/я (protivopolózhnye ~/ia) contrary instructions
руководящие ~/я (rukovodiáshchie ~/ia) guidelines
с ~/ем (s ~/em) with the indication
следовать ~/ям (slédovat' ~/iam) to follow instructions
согласно ~/ю (soglásno ~/iu) as per instructions
счёт-фактура с ~/ем позиций (schiót-faktúra s ~/em pozítsii) itemized invoice
технические ~/я (tekhnícheskie ~/ia) technical instructions
устные ~/я (ústnye ~/ia) oral instructions
~/я заявителя (~/ia zaiavítelia) applicant's instructions
~ количества (~ kolíchestva) indication of quantity
~/я о порядке сборки (~/ia o poriádke sbórki) assembly instructions
~/я относительно маркировки (~/ia otnosítel'no markiróvki) marking instructions
~/я по выполнению работы (~/ia po vypolnéniiu rabóty) work instructions
~ потребностей (~ potrébnostei) indication of requirements
~/я по эксплуатации (~/ia po ekspluatátsii) operating instructions
~ происхождения (~ proiskhozhdéniia) indication of origin
~ срока (~ sróka) time indication

~ стоимости (~ stóimosti)
indication of the value
Указател/ь (ukazátel/') *m.*
handbook, index
  алфавитный ~ (alfavítnyi ~)
  alphabetical index
  заносить в ~ (zanosít' v ~) to
  index
  патентный ~ (paténtnyi ~) patent
  index
  предметный ~ (predmétnyi ~)
  index of a book
  сводный ~ (svódnyi ~)
  consolidated index
  систематический ~
  (sistematícheskii ~) classified
  index
  снабжать ~/ем (snabzhát' ~/em)
  to compile an index
  ~ заявителей (~ zaiavítelei)
  index of applicants
  ~ заявок (~ zaiávok) index of
  applications
  ~ классов (~ klássov)
  classification manual
  ~ лицензий (~ litsénzii) index
  of licenses
  ~ методов (~ métodov) manual of
  methods
  ~ товарных знаков (~ továrnykh
  znákov) index of trademarks
  ~ цен (~ tsen) price index
Указывать (ukázyvat') *v.* to
indicate, to specify
  как указано ниже (kak ukázano
  nízhe) as indicated hereinbelow
Укладк/а (ukládk/a) *f.* stacking,
stowing, trimming
  завершить ~/у (zavershít' ~/u)
  to complete stowing
  многоярусная ~ ящиков
  (mnogoiárusnaia ~ iáshchikov)
  multi-level stowing
  небрежная ~ (nebrézhnaia ~)
  negligent stowage
  обеспечивать ~/у (obespéchivat'
  ~/u) to stow
  операция по ~/е (operátsiia po
  ~/e) stevedoring operation
  плотная ~ (plótnaia ~) tight
  stow
  расходы по ~/е (raskhódy po ~/e)
  stowage {fees}
  свободная ~ (svobódnaia ~) loose
  stow
  требования по ~/е (trébovaniia
  po ~/e) stowage requirements

~ вверх дном (~ vverkh dnom)
upside down stacking
~ внизу (~ vnizú) bottom stow
~ в рефрижераторном помещении (~
v refrizherátornom pomeshchénii)
refrigerated stowage
~ в ящики (~ v iáshchiki)
stowage in crates
~ груза на паллеты (~ grúza na
palléty) palletization of cargo
~ пиломатериалов на прокладки (~
pilomateriálov na prokladki)
stacking
~ сверху (~ svérkhu) top stow
Укладывать (ukládyvat') *v.* to
stack, to stow
Укомплектовывать (ukomplektóvyvat')
v. to complete
~ личным составом (~ líchnym
sostávom) to furnish personnel
Укрупнение (ukrupnénie) *n.*
amalgamation
Укрупнять (ukrupniát') *v.* to
amalgamate
Улучшать (uluchshát') *v.* to improve
Улучшени/е (uluchshéni/e) *n.*
advance, improvement
  быстрые ~/я (býstrye ~/ia) rapid
  improvements
  добиваться ~/я (dobivát'sia
  ~/ia) to seek improvements
  иметь тенденцию к ~/ю (imét'
  tendéntsiiu k ~/iu) to tend to
  improve
  патентоспособные ~/я
  (patentosposóbnye ~/ia)
  patentable improvements
  потенциальное ~ (potentsiál'noe
  ~) potential improvement
  приводить к ~/ю (privodít' k
  ~/iu) to bring about an improvement
  ~ графика (~ gráfika)
  improvement of schedule
  ~ деловой активности (~ delovói
  aktívnosti) improvement of
  business
  ~ деловой конъюнктуры (~ delovói
  kon"iunktúry) improvement of
  business conditions
  ~ качества (~ káchestva) quality
  improvement
  ~ конструкции (~ konstrúktsii)
  design improvement
  ~ технического уровня продукции
  (~ tekhnícheskogo úrovnia

prodúktsii) increase in the
technical level of production
~ условий труда (~ uslóvii
trudá) improvement of working
conditions
Уменьшать (umen'shát') *v.* to
decrease, to reduce
 ~ в ... раз (~ v ... raz) to
reduce by ... times
 ~ вчетверо (~ vchétvero) to
reduce by a quarter
 ~ до (~ do) to decrease to
 ~ на (~ na) to decrease by
Уменьшени/е (umen'shéni/e) *n.*
decrease, reduction
 ~ акционерного капитала (~
aktsionérnogo kapitála)
reduction of share capital
 ~ арендной платы (~ aréndnoi
pláty) decrease in rent
 ~ в весе (~ v vése) decrease in
weight
 ~ размера арбитражного сбора (~
razméra arbitrázhnogo sbóra)
decrease in arbitration fee
 ~ расходов (~ raskhódov)
reduction in expenses
 ~ стоимости (~ stóimosti)
depreciation
 ~ цен (~ tsen) decrease in
prices
Умеренный (umérennyi) *adj.*
moderate, reasonable
Универсальный (universál'nyi) *adj.*
universal
Уникальный (unikál'nyi) *adj.* unique
Унификация (unifikátsiia) *f.*
unification
 ~ документов (~ dokuméntov)
unification of documents
Упакованный (upakóvannyi) *adj.*
covered, packed, sealed, wrapped
Упаковк/а (upakóvk/a) *f.* container,
packaging, wrapping
 аэрозольная ~ (aerozól'naia ~)
aerosol container
 без ~/и (bez ~/i) uncovered,
exposed
 безвозвратная ~ (bezvozvrátnaia
~) nonreturnable packing
 брезентовая ~ (brezéntovaia ~)
tarp covering
 в ~/е (v ~/e) covered
 в ~/е и с маркировкой согласно
указаниям (v ~/e i s markiróvkoi
soglásno ukazániiam) packed and
marked as specified

вакуумная ~ (vákuumnaia ~)
vacuum packed
вес ~/и (ves ~/i) tare weight
вес ~/и, указанный в счёте (ves
~/i, ukázannyi v schióte)
invoice tare weight
вид ~/и (vid ~/i) kind of
packing
вкладыш в ~/у (vkládysh v ~/u)
insert in a package
включать ~/у (vkliuchát' ~/u) to
include packing
внутренняя ~ (vnútrenniaia ~)
inner wrapping
в окончательной ~/е (v
okonchátel'noi ~/e) in final
packaged form
в отдельной ~/е (v otdél'noi
~/e) under separate cover
в процессе ~/и (v protsésse ~/i)
in the process of packaging
во время ~/и (vo vrémia ~/i)
during packing
водонепроницаемая ~
(vodonepronitsáemaia ~)
waterproof packaging
воздухонепроницаемая ~
(vozdukhonepronitsáemaia ~)
airtight packaging
вывоз ~/и (vývoz ~/i) removal of
packing
герметичная ~ (germetíchnaia ~)
hermetically sealed packing
годная ~ (gódnaia ~) suitable
packing
громоздкая ~ (gromózdkaia ~)
oversized packing
деревянная ~ (dereviánnaia ~)
wooden packing
дефектная ~ (deféktnaia ~)
defective packing
доброкачественная ~
(dobrokáchestvennaia ~) good
quality packing
достаточная ~ (dostátochnaia ~)
adequate packing
жёсткая ~ (zhióstkaia ~) sturdy
packaging
за ~/у будет начислена отдельная
плата (za ~/u búdet nachíslena
otdél'naia pláta) packing will
be charged extra
завершать ~ (zavershát' ~) to
complete packing
заводская ~ (zavódskaia ~)
factory packaging

защитная ~ (zashchítnaia ~) protective packaging
импортная ~ (ímportnaia ~) import packing
картонная ~ (kartónnaia ~) cardboard container
контейнерная ~ (kontéinernaia ~) container packing
контракт на ~/у товара (kontrákt na ~/u továra) packing contract
лента, используемая при ~/е (lénta, ispól'zuemaia pri ~/e) packing tape
метод ~/и (métod ~/i) packaging technique
многоразовая ~ (mnogorázovaia ~) returnable packaging
морская ~ (morskáia ~) maritime packing
мягкая ~ (miágkaia ~) soft packing
надлежащая ~ (nadlezháshchaia ~) proper packaging
наружная ~ (narúzhnaia ~) external packaging
начинать ~/у (nachinát' ~/u) to commence packaging
небрежная ~ (nebrézhnaia ~) negligent packing
негабаритная ~ (negabarítnaia ~) oversized packing
недоброкачественная ~ (nedobrokáchestvennaia ~) poor quality packing
недостаточная ~ (nedostátochnaia ~) insufficient packing
ненужная ~ (nenúzhnaia ~) unnecessary packing
неповреждённая ~ (nepovrezhdiónnaia ~) undamaged packing
неподходящая ~ (nepodkhodiáshchaia ~) unsuitable packing
непригодная ~ (neprigódnaia ~) unfit packing
несоответствующая ~ (nesootvétstvuiushchaia ~) inappropriate packaging
нестандартная ~ (nestandártnaia ~) non-standard packing
неудовлетворительная ~ (neudovletvorítel'naia ~) unsatisfactory packing
новый вид ~/и (nóvyi vid ~/i) new type of packaging

обеспечивать должную ~/у (obespéchivat' dólzhnuiu ~/u) to secure the necessary packaging
обеспечивать своевременную ~/у (obespéchivat' svoevrémennuiu ~/u) to secure timely packing
оборудование для ~/и (oborúdovanie dlia ~/i) packing equipment
образец ~/и (obrazéts ~/i) sample packing
общая ~ (óbshchaia ~) total packaging
обыкновенная ~ (obyknovénnaia ~) ordinary packaging
обычная экспортная ~ (obýchnaia éksportnaia ~) standard export packing
определять достаточность ~/и (opredeliát' dostátochnost' ~/i) to determine the sufficiency of packing
осуществлять ~/у (osushchestvliát' ~/u) to pack
отгружать товар в ~/е (otgruzhát' továr v ~/e) to ship packed goods
парусиновая ~ (parusínovaia ~) canvas packing
перевозить без ~/и (perevozít' bez ~/i) to ship uncovered
плата за экспортную ~/у (pláta za éksportnuiu ~/u) export packing charge
платить за ~/у (platít' za ~/u) to pay for packing
плотная ~ (plótnaia ~) tight packing
плохая ~ (plokháia ~) bad packaging
повреждённая ~ (povrezhdiónnaia ~) damaged packaging
погрузка без ~/и (pogrúzka bez ~/i) shipment in bulk
подарочная ~ (podárochnaia ~) gift wrapping
"подмоченная ~ " (podmóchennaia ~) "packing wet" {marking on cargo}
подходящая ~ (podkhodiáshchaia ~) suitable packing
посылать в ~/е (posylát' v ~/e) to send in packing
правила ~/и (právila ~/i) packing instructions
правильность ~/и (právil'nost' ~/i) adequacy of packing

приступать к ~/е (pristupát' k ~/e) to proceed with packing
проверять ~/у (proveriát' ~/u) to examine packaging
производить ~/у (proizvodít' ~/u) to handle packing
прочная ~ (próchnaia ~) strong packing
прочность ~/и (próchnost' ~/i) strength of packaging
размеры ~/и (razméry ~/i) package dimensions
размеры в ~/е (razméry v ~/e) packed measurements
разорванная ~ (razórvannaia ~) torn packing
расходы по ~/е (raskhódy po ~/e) packing expenses
расходы по ~/е в ящики (raskhódy po ~/e v iáshchiki) crate costs
рекомендации по ~/е (rekomendátsii po ~/e) packaging recommendations
своевременная ~ (svoevrémennaia ~) timely packaging
соответствующая ~ (sootvétstvuiushchaia ~) appropriate packaging
специальная ~ (spetsiál'naia ~) special packaging
способ ~/и (spósob ~/i) packaging method
средства ~/и (srédstva ~/i) packing facilities
стандарты ~/и (standárty ~/i) packing standards
стандартная ~ (standártnaia ~) standard packaging
стоимость ~/и (stóimost' ~/i) cost of packing
стоимость ~/и в ящики (stóimost' ~/i v iáshchiki) cost of crating
тара для ~/и (tára dlia ~/i) packing container
товар, продающийся в ~/е (továr, prodaiúshchiisia v ~/e) prepackaged goods
транспортная ~ (tránsportnaia ~) freight packing
требования к ~/е (trébovaniia k ~/e) packaging requirements
тропическая ~ (tropícheskaia ~) packaging for tropical conditions
удовлетворительная ~ (udovletvorítel'naia ~) satisfactory packing

услуги по ~/е (uslúgi po ~/e) packing services
услуги по ~/е товара на экспорт (uslúgi po ~/e továra na éksport) export packing services
фабричная ~ (fabríchnaia ~) factory packaging
целая ~ (tsélaia ~) intact packaging
целесообразная ~ (tselesoobráznaia ~) feasible packaging
цена без ~/и (tsená bez ~/i) packing not included {in cost}
цена, включая ~/у (tsená, vkliucháia ~/u) price includes packaging
экспортная ~ (éksportnaia ~) export packaging
эффективная ~ (effektívnaia ~) effective packaging
~ без повреждений (~ bez povrezhdénii) undamaged packaging
~ без ящиков (~ bez iáshchikov) uncrated packaging
~ вакуумная (~ vákuumnaia) vacuum-packed
~ в коробки (~ v koróbki) packaging in cartons
~ в мешки (~ v meshkí) packing in bags
~ в обрешётке (~ v obreshiótke) frame packaging
~ в полиэтиленовую плёнку (~ v polietilénovuiu pliónku) polyethylene wrapping
~ в ящики (~ v iáshchiki) crating
~ за счёт покупателя (~ za schiót pokupátelia) packing extra
~ по контракту (~ po kontráktu) packing per contract
~ по себестоимости за счёт покупателя (~ po sebestóimosti za schiót pokupátelia) packing extra at cost
~ поставщика (~ postavshchiká) supplier's packaging
~, предназначенная для воздушной транспортировки (~, prednaznáchennaia dlia vozdúshnoi transportiróvki) airfreight packaging
~, пригодная для (~, prigódnaia dlia) packing suitable for ...

~, пригодная для морской
перевозки (...~, prigódnaia dlia
morskói perevózki) seaworthy
packaging
~ с верёвочными ручками (~ s
verióvochnymi rúchkami)
packaging with rope handles
~ с инструкциями (~ s
instrúktsiiami) packaging with
instructions included
Упаковочный (upakóvochnyi) adj.
packing
Упаковывать (upakóvyvat') v. to
handle, to pack, to wrap
~ вручную (~ vruchnúiu) to hand
pack
~ должным образом (~ dólzhnym
óbrazom) to pack in the proper
manner
~ машинным способом (~ mashínnym
spósobom) to machine pack
~ прочно (~ próchno) to pack
securely
Уплат/а (uplát/a) f. payment,
repayment, settlement
    авансировать деньги на ~/у
    (avansírovat' dén'gi na ~/u) to
    advance money in payment
    дополнительная ~ фрахта
    (dopolnítel'naia ~ frákhta)
    extra freight charge
    досрочная ~ (dosróchnaia ~)
    early settlement
    ежемесячная ~ (ezhemésiachnaia
    ~) monthly payment
    квитанция за ~/у премии
    (kvitántsiia za ~/u prémii)
    receipt for premium
    квитанция таможни об ~/е пошлины
    (kvitántsiia tamózhni ob ~/e
    póshliny) customs clearance bill
    напоминать об ~/е долга
    (napominát' ob ~/e dólga) to dun
    настаивать на немедленной ~/е
    (nastáivat' na nemédlennoi ~/e)
    to insist on immediate payment
    немедленная ~ (nemédlennaia ~)
    immediate payment
    обеспечение ~/ы (obespéchenie
    ~/y) security for payment
    окончательная ~ долга
    (okonchátel'naia ~ dólga) final
    repayment of a debt
    освобождать от ~/ы (osvobozhdát'
    ot ~/y) to exempt from payment

    отказываться от ~/ы
    (otkázyvat'sia ot ~/y) to refuse
    payment
    отметка об ~/е фрахта (otmétka
    ob ~/e frákhta) "freight
    prepaid" stamp
    полная ~ (pólnaia ~) payment in
    full
    полная ~ долга (pólnaia ~ dólga)
    complete discharge of debt
    полная ~ фрахта (pólnaia ~
    frákhta) payment of full freight
    процент к ~/е (protsént k ~/e)
    outstanding interest
    расписка об ~/е долга (raspíska
    ob ~/e dólga) acquittance
    расходы по ~/е процентов
    (raskhódy po ~/e protséntov)
    interest charges
    резерв по ~/е подоходного налога
    (rezérv po ~/e podokhódnogo
    nalóga) reserve for income tax
    своевременная ~ (svoevrémennaia
    ~) prompt payment
    скидка за досрочную ~/у по
    векселю (skídka za dosróchnuiu
    ~/u po vékseliu) time discount
    (on bill, note)
    срок ~/ы процентов (srok ~/y
    protséntov) interest date
    требование ~/ы (trébovanie ~/y)
    demand for payment
    требование ~/ы взноса за акции
    (trébovanie ~/y vznósa za
    áktsii) cash call on shares
    требование ~/ы возмещения за
    спасение (trébovanie ~/y vozme-
    shchéniia za spasénie) salvage
    claim
    требование ~/ы мёртвого фрахта
    (trébovanie ~/y miórtvogo
    frákhta) dead freight claim
    требование ~/ы разницы
    (trébovanie ~/y ráznitsy) margin
    call
    уклонение от ~/ы налогов
    (uklonénie ot ~/y nalógov) tax
    evasion
    цена при ~/е наличными (tsená
    pri ~/e nalíchnymi) cash price
    частичная ~ (chastíchnaia ~)
    partial payment
    чек в ~/у (chek v ~/u) check in
    payment
    ~ арбитражного сбора (~
    arbitrázhnogo sbóra) payment of
    the arbitration fee

~ вознаграждения (~ voznagrazhdéniia) payment of compensation, remuneration
~ в рассрочку (~ v rassróchku) installment {payment}
~ денежного возмещения (~ dénezhnogo vozmeshchéniia) payment of monetary damages
~ долга (~ dólga) payment of debt
~ займа (~ záima) redemption of a loan
~ золотом (~ zólotom) payment in gold
~ капитала и процентов (~ kapitála i protséntov) payment of principal and interest
~ комиссии (~ komíssii) payment of a commission
~ комиссии за услуги (~ komíssii za uslúgi) payment of a service commission
~ наличными (~ nalíchnymi) payment in cash
~ налогов (~ nalógov) payment of taxes
~ натурой (~ natúroi) payment in kind
~ первоначального взноса (~ pervonachál'nogo vznósa) payment of initial deposit
~ пошлины (~ póshliny) payment of duty
~ при поставке (~ pri postávke) payment on delivery
~ процентов (~ protséntov) interest payment
~ процентов по вкладу (~ protséntov po vkládu) payment of interest on deposit
~ процентов по займу (~ protséntov po záimu) interest payment on a loan
~ раньше сроков (~ rán'she srókov) pre-payment
~ сбора (~ sbóra) payment of a fee
~ страховых взносов (~ strakhovýkh vznósov) payment of insurance premiums
~ суммы (~ súmmy) payment of an amount
~ фрахта (~ frákhta) freight payment
Управленческий (upravléncheskii) adj. administrative, management

Управляющ/ий (upravliáiushch/ii) m.adj.noun managing director, manager
главный ~ (glávnyi ~) general manager
помощник ~/его (pomóshchnik ~/ego) assistant manager
~ группой (~ grúppoi) group manager
~ заводом (~ zavódom) plant manager
~ недвижимостью (~ nedvízhimost'iu) property manager
~ отделом кредитования (~ otdélom kreditovániia) credit manager
~ отделом маркетинга (~ otdélom márketinga) head of the marketing department
~ отделом развития торговли (~ otdélom razvítiia torgóvli) manager of business development
~ отделом сбыта (~ otdélom sbýta) manager of sales department
~ по импорту (~ po ímportu) import manager
~ по кадрам (~ po kádram) personnel manager
~ по экспорту (~ po éksportu) export manager
~ производством (~ proizvódstvom) production manager
~ складом (~ skládom) warehouseman
Уравнивание (urávnivanie) n. equalization
~ условий (~ uslóvii) leveling of conditions
Уравнивать (urávnivat') v. to equalize
Урегулирование (uregulírovanie) n. adjustment, settlement
вести переговоры об ~/и (vestí peregovóry ob ~/i) to negotiate a settlement
достигать мирного ~/я (dostigát' mírnogo ~/ia) to achieve an amicable settlement
дружественное ~ (drúzhestvennoe ~) amicable settlement
компромиссное ~ (kompromíssnoe ~) compromise settlement

мирное ~ претензии (mírnoe ~ preténzii) amicable settlement of a claim

окончательное ~ (okonchátel'noe ~) final settlement

переговоры по ~/ю (peregovóry po ~/iu) settlement negotiations

судебное ~ (sudébnoe ~) judicial settlement

частичное ~ (chastíchnoe ~) partial settlement

~ долгов (~ dolgóv) settlement of debts

~ претензии (~ preténzii) settlement of a claim

~ расчётов (~ raschiótov) clearance of accounts

~ спора (~ spóra) dispute resolution

~ цен (~ tsen) price adjustment

Урегулированный (uregulírovannyi) adj. adjusted, settled

Урегулировать (uregulírovat') v. to adjust, to settle

~ путём переговоров (~ putióm peregovórov) to settle by means of negotiation

Уров/ень (úrov/en') m. degree, level, standard

быть на ~/не мировых стандартов (byt' na ~/ne mirovýkh standár-tov) to be on the level of world standards

восстановление ~/ня запасов (vosstanovlénie ~/nia zapásov) restocking of inventories

высший ~ (výsshii ~) peak level

гарантировать высокий ~ обслуживания (garantírovat' vysókii ~ obslúzhivaniia) to guarantee a high level of service

льготный ~ (l'gótnyi ~) preferential level

минимальный ~ (minimál'nyi ~) minimum level

на высоком ~/не (na vysókom ~/ne) at a high level

на должном ~/не (na dólzhnom ~/ne) at the required level

на любом ~/не (na liubóm ~/ne) at any level

на ~/не министров (na ~/ne minístrov) at the ministerial level

на ~/не мировых стандартов (na ~/ne mirovýkh standártov) at the level of world standards

на одном ~/не (na odnóm ~/ne) at the same level

наивысший мировой ~ (naivýsshii mirovói ~) top world standard

научно-технический ~ (naúchno-tekhnícheskii ~) scientific and technological level

первоклассный ~ (pervoklássnyi ~) first-class

переговоры на высшем ~/не (peregovóry na výsshem ~/ne) high level negotiations

повышение ~/ня жизни (povyshénie ~/nia zhízni) increase in the standard of living

профессиональный ~ (professionál'nyi ~) professional level

рост ~/ня жизни (rost ~/nia zhizni) growth in the standard of living

рост ~/ня заработной платы (rost ~/nia zárabotnoi pláty) growth in wage levels

стоять на ~/не ... (stoiát' na ~/ne ...) to be at the level of ...

средний ~ (srédnii ~) average level

технический ~ (tekhnícheskii ~) level of engineering

установленный ~ риска (ustanóvlennyi ~ ríska) assigned risk

устойчивый ~ (ustóichivyi ~) stable level

~ арендной платы (~ aréndnoi pláty) level of rental payment

~ деловой активности (~ delovói aktívnosti) level of business activity

~ достижений (~ dostizhénii) level of achievements

~ дохода (~ dokhóda) income level

~ жизни (~ zhízni) standard of living

~ запродаж (~ zaprodázh) sales level

~ зарплаты (~ zarpláty) wage level

~ комплектности (~ kompléktnosti) stage of prefabrication

372

~ лучших мировых образцов (~
lúchshikh mirovýkh obraztsóv)
level of best world standards
~ образования и опыта (~
obrazovániia i ópyta) level of
education and experience
~ обслуживания (~
obslúzhivaniia) degree of
service
~ оформления (~ oformléniia)
standard of design
~ патентоспособности (~
patentosposóbnosti) standard of
patentability
~ проектирования (~
proektírovaniia) design standard
~ производства (~ proizvódstva)
level of production
~ процента на денежном рынке (~
protsénta na dénezhnom rýnke)
market interest rate
~ развития (~ razvítiia) degree
of development
~ рентабельности (~
rentábel'nosti) level of
profitability
~ риска (~ ríska) degree of risk
~ сбыта (~ sbýta) level of sales
~ ставок (~ stávok) level of
rates
~ цен (~ tsen) level of prices
~ экономического развития (~
ekonomícheskogo razvítiia) level
of economic development
~ экономической активности (~
ekonomícheskoi aktívnosti) level
of economic activity
~ экспертизы (~ ekspertízy)
standard of examination

Урожа/й (urozhá/i) *m.* crop, yield
валовой ~ (valovói ~) gross
yield
продавать ~ на корню (prodavát'
~ na kórniu) to sell a standing
crop
рекордный ~ (rékordnyi ~) record
crop
средний ~ (srédnii ~) average
yield
размер ~/я (razmér ~/ia) size of
the harvest
расходы, связанные с уборкой ~/я
(raskhódy, sviázannye s ubórkoi
~/ia) harvesting expenses
убирать ~ (ubirát' ~) to harvest
уборка ~/я (ubórka ~/ia)
harvesting

Услови/е (uslóvi/e) *n.* condition,
proviso, term
аварийные ~/я (avaríinye ~/ia)
emergency conditions
анализ ~/й окружающей среды
(análiz ~/i okruzháiushchei
sredý) environmental analysis
аналогичные ~/я (analogíchnye
~/ia) similar terms
аренда на ~/и исчисления платы в
процентном отношении (arénda na
~/i ischisléniia pláty v
protséntnom otnoshénii) lease on
percentage of sales basis
атмосферные ~/я (atmosférnye
~/ia) atmospheric conditions
базисные ~/я поставки (bázisnye
~/ia postávki) basic terms of
delivery
благоприятные ~/я
(blagopriiátnye ~/ia) favorable
terms
быть ограниченным ~/ем (byt'
ograníchennym ~/em) to be
subject to a condition
быть связанным ~/ями (byt'
sviázannym ~/iami) to be bound
by conditions
в ~/ях (v ~/iakh) under
conditions
в зависимости от ~/й (v
zavísimosti ot ~/i) subject to
the terms and conditions
в производственных ~/ях (v
proizvódstvennykh ~/iakh) under
conditions of production
в рабочих ~/ях (v rabóchikh
~/iakh) under working conditions
в реальных ~/ях (v reál'nykh
~/iakh) under actual conditions
в соответствии с ~/ями (v
sootvétstvii s ~/iami) in
accordance with the provisions
во влажных ~/ях (vo vlázhnykh
~/iakh) in humid conditions
вероятные ~/я (veroiátnye ~/ia)
probable provisions
взаимовыгодные ~/я
(vzaimovýgodnye ~/ia) mutually
profitable terms
взаимоприемлемые ~/я
(vzaimopriémlemye ~/ia) mutually
agreeable conditions
включать ~/я (vkliuchát' ~/ia)
to include conditions

включать ~/я дополнительно
(vkliuchát' ~/ia dopolnítel'no)
to include additional conditions
включать в ~/я аккредитива
(vkliuchát' v ~/ia akkreditíva)
to incorporate terms in the
letter of credit
вносить поправки к ~/ям
аккредитива (vnosít' poprávki k
~/iam akkreditíva) to amend a
letter of credit
возможные ~/я (vozmózhnye ~/ia)
possible conditions
вредные ~/я работы (vrédnye ~/ia
rabóty) unhealthy working
conditions
временные технические ~/я
(vrémennye tekhnícheskie ~/ia)
temporary specifications
выгодные ~/я (výgodnye ~/ia)
profitable terms
выдвигать ~/я (vydvigát' ~/ia)
to set out terms and conditions
вызывать изменения ~/й
соглашения (vyzyvát' izmenéniia
~/i soglashéniia) to entail
amendment of the terms and
conditions
выполнять ~/я (vypolniát' ~/ia)
to meet the terms
выполнять ~/я контракта
(vypolniát' ~/ia kontrákta) to
fulfill the terms and conditions
of a contract
выполнять ~/я кредита
(vypolniát' ~/ia kredíta) to
honor the terms of credit
выполнять ~/я платежа
(vypolniát' ~/ia platezhá) to
honor the payment terms
выставлять ~/я (vystavliát'
~/ia) to present conditions
выходить за пределы ~/й
контракта (vykhodít' za predély
~/i kontrákta) to fall outside
the terms of the contract
действовать в рамках ~/й
контракта (déistvovat' v rámkakh
~/i kontrákta) to act within the
terms and conditions of a
contract
действовать в соответствии с
~/ями контракта (déistvovat' v
sootvétstvii s ~/iami kontrákta)
to act in accordance with the
terms and conditions of a
contract

договариваться об ~/ях
(dogovárivat'sia ob ~/iakh) to
negotiate terms
договориться о приемлемых ~/ях
(dogovorít'sia o priémlemykh
~/iakh) to agree to acceptable
terms
дополнительное ~ (dopolnítel'noe
~) additional condition
другие ~/я (drugíe ~/ia) other
conditions
единые ~/я (edínye ~/ia) uniform
terms
если ~/я аккредитива не
предписывают иного (ésli ~/ia
akkreditíva ne predpísyvaiut
inógo) unless otherwise provided
by the terms of the letter of
credit
если эти ~/я всё ещё будут
существовать ... (ésli eti ~/ia
vsió eshchió búdut
sushchestvovát') if present
conditions continue ...
жёсткие технические ~/я
(zhióstkie tekhnícheskie ~/ia)
stringent technical conditions
жилищные ~/я (zhilíshchnye ~/ia)
housing conditions
заём с определёнными ~/ями
(zaióm s opredeliónnymi ~/iami)
loan with certain conditions
записанные ~/я (zapísannye ~/ia)
written provisions
изучать ~/я (izuchát' ~/ia) to
study the terms
изучать технические ~/я
(izuchát' tekhnícheskie ~/ia) to
examine technical specifications
изучать экономические ~/я
(izuchát' ekonomícheskie ~/ia)
to study economic conditions
иные ~/я платежа (inýe ~/ia
platezhá) alternative terms of
payment
климатические ~/я
(klimatícheskie ~/ia) climactic
conditions
коммерческие ~/я (kommércheskie
~/ia) commercial terms
критические ~/я (kritícheskie
~/ia) critical conditions
линейные ~/я (linéinye ~/ia)
berth terms
льготные ~/я (l'gótnye ~/ia)
preferential terms

местные ~/я (méstnye ~/ia) local conditions

метеорологические ~/я (meteorologícheskie ~/ia) meteorological conditions

на ~/ях ... (na ~/iakh ...) subject to conditions of ...

на ~/ях аренды (na ~/iakh aréndy) on a rental basis

на ~/ях банковского кредита (na ~/iakh bánkovskogo kredíta) under bank credit

на ~/ях взаимности (na ~/iakh vzaímnosti) on a reciprocal basis

на ~/ях генерального подряда (na ~/iakh generál'nogo podriáda) on general contract terms

на ~/ях консигнации (na ~/iakh konsignátsii) on a consignment basis

на ~/ях кредита (na ~/iakh kredíta) on credit terms

на ~/ях "под ключ" (na ~/iakh pod kliuch) on a turn-key basis

на ~/ях, предусмотренных в контракте (na ~/iakh, predusmótrennykh v kontrákte) under the terms stipulated in the contract

на взаимосогласованных ~/ях (na vzaimosoglasóvannykh ~/iakh) under the mutually agreed terms

на выгодных ~/ях (na výgodnykh ~/iakh) on profitable terms

на льготных ~/ях (na l'gótnykh ~/iakh) on preferential terms

на любых ~/ях (na liubýkh ~/iakh) under any conditions

на обычных ~/ях (na obýchnykh ~/iakh) on usual terms

на основании ~/й (na osnovánii ~/i) under the conditions

на прочих равных ~/ях (na próchikh rávnykh ~/iakh) on other similar terms

на следующих ~/ях (na sléduiushchikh ~/iakh) on the following conditions

назначать ~/я (naznachát' ~/ia) to quote terms

наилучшие ~/я (nailúchshie ~/ia) best conditions

намечать ~/я (namechát' ~/ia) to outline terms and conditions

напечатанные ~/я (napechátannye ~/ia) printed provisions

нарушать ~/я (narushát' ~/ia) to violate terms, conditions

нарушать ~/я контракта (narushát' ~/ia kontrákta) to violate the terms of a contract

нарушение ~/й (narushénie ~/i) violation of conditions

неблагоприятные ~/я (neblagopriiátnye ~/ia) unfavorable conditions

неблагоприятные погодные ~/я (neblagopriiátnye pogódnye ~/ia) unfavorable weather conditions

невыполнение ~/й (nevypolnénie ~/i) non-fulfillment of conditions

ненормальные ~/я (nenormál'nye ~/ia) abnormal conditions

неподходящие ~/я (nepodkhodiáshchie ~/ia) inappropriate conditions

непременное ~ (nepreménnoe ~) indispensible condition

неприемлемые ~/я (nepriémlemye ~/ia) unacceptable terms, conditions

неравноправные ~/я (neravnoprávnye ~/ia) inequitable terms

ни при каких ~/ях (ni pri kakíkh ~/iakh) under no conditions whatsoever

нормальные ~/я (normál'nye ~/ia) normal conditions

нормальные ~/я работы (normál'nye ~/ia rabóty) normal working conditions

несоблюдение ~/й (nesobliudénie ~/i) non-observance of terms, conditions

облегчать ~/я (oblegchát' ~/ia) to ease conditions

обременительные ~/я (obremenítel'nye ~/ia) exacting conditions

обсуждать ~/я (obsuzhdát' ~/ia) to discuss terms and conditions

обучать специалистов в заводских ~/ях (obuchát' spetsialístov v zavódskikh ~/iakh) in-plant training

обусловливать ~/я (obuslóvlivat ~/ia) to stipulate conditions

общепринятые ~/я (obshchepríniatye ~/ia) prevailing conditions

общие ~/я (óbshchie ~/ia) general terms and conditions
общие ~/я контракта (óbshchie ~/ia kontrákta) general terms and conditions of the contract
обычные ~/я (obýchnye ~/ia) usual terms
обычные ~/я платежа (obýchnye ~/ia platezhá) usual terms of payment
обязательные ~/я (obiazátel'nye ~/ia) obligatory conditions
обязательные ~/я договора (obiazátel'nye ~/ia dogovóra) obligatory conditions of a contract
основные ~/я договора (osnovnýe ~/ia dogovóra) fundamental provisions of a contract
основные ~/я страхования (osnovnýe ~/ia strakhovániia) basic insurance conditions
определять ~/я (opredeliát' ~/ia) to define terms
отвергать ~/я контракта (otvergát' ~/ia kontrákta) to reject the terms and conditions of a contract
отвечать ~/ям (otvechát' ~/iam) to meet conditions
отказываться от ~/й (otkázyvat'sia ot ~/i) to waive provisions
отсроченные ~/я платежа (otsróchennye ~/ia platezhá) deferred terms of payment
отступать от ~/й контракта (otstupát' ot ~/i kontrákta) to deviate from contractual provisions
первоначальные ~/я контракта (pervonachál'nye ~/ia kontrákta) original terms of a contract
пересматривать ~/я (peresmátrivat' ~/ia) to revise terms and conditions
платить на ~/ях кредита (platít' na ~/iakh kredíta) to pay on credit terms
плохие ~/я работы (plokhíe ~/ia rabóty) poor working conditions
по ~/ям контракта (po ~/iam kontrákta) under the terms and conditions of a contract
по ~/ям статей (po ~/iam statéi) under the provisions of clauses

подробные ~/я (podróbnye ~/ia) detailed terms
подходящие ~/я (podkhodiáshchie ~/ia) appropriate conditions
покупать с ~/ем предварительного осмотра и одобрения (pokupát' s ~/em predvarítel'nogo osmótra i odobréniia) to buy subject to inspection and approval
пользоваться ~/ями гарантии (pól'zovat'sia ~/iami garántii) to enjoy warranty provisions
последующие ~/я (posléduiushchie ~/ia) subsequent conditions
поставка на ~/ях ФОБ (postávka na ~/iakh fob) delivery FOB
практические ~/я (praktícheskie ~/ia) practical conditions
предварительное ~ (predvarítel'noe ~) precondition
предложенные ~/я (predlózhennye ~/ia) proposed terms
предоставлять ~/я (predostavliát' ~/ia) to grant terms and conditions
предоставлять ~/я гарантии (predostavliát' ~/ia garántii) to offer warranty provisions
предоставлять необходимые ~/я (predostavliát' neobkhodímye ~/ia) to furnish necessary facilities
предоставлять самые благоприятные ~/я (predostavliát' sámye blagopriiátnye ~/ia) to offer the most favorable terms
предусматривать ~/я (predusmátrivat' ~/ia) to stipulate terms and conditions
предусмотренные ~/я (predusmótrennye ~/ia) contemplated terms and conditions
преимущественные ~/я (preimúshchestvennye ~/ia) advantageous terms
преобладающие ~/я (preobladáiushchie ~/ia) prevailing conditions
при ~/и (pri ~/i) on condition
при ~/и изменений (pri ~/i izmenénii) subject to alterations

при ~/и наличия (pri ~/i nalíchiia) subject to availability

при ~/и немедленного уведомления (pri ~/i nemédlennogo uvedom-léniia) subject to prompt notice

при ~/и одобрения (pri ~/i odobréniia) subject to approval

при ~/и окончания (pri ~/i okonchániia) subject to termination

при ~/и правильной поставки (pri ~/i právil'noi postávki) subject to proper delivery

при ~/и, что {если} (pri ~/i, chto ésli) on condition that, provided that ...

при одном ~/и (pri odnóm ~/i) upon the sole condition

при определённых ~/ях (pri opredeliónnykh ~/iakh) under certain conditions

при соблюдении следующих ~/й (pri sobliudénii sléduiushchikh ~/i) subject to observance of the following conditions

привлекательные ~/я (privlekátel'nye ~/ia) attractive terms

придерживаться ~/й (pridérzhivat'sia ~/i) to maintain terms

приемлемые ~/я (priémlemye ~/ia) acceptable terms

принимать ~/я (prinimát' ~/ia) to accept conditions

приспосабливать к местным ~/ям (prisposáblivat' k méstnym ~/iam) to adapt to local conditions

причальные ~/я (prichál'nye ~/ia) berth terms

проектные ~/я (proéktnye ~/ia) design conditions

производственные ~/я (proizvódstvennye ~/ia) production conditions

пройти испытания в лабораторных ~/ях (proití ispytániia v laboratórnykh ~/iakh) to be laboratory tested

противоречить ~/ям спецификации (protivoréchit' ~/iam spetsifikátsii) to be contrary to specifications

рабочие технические ~/я (rabóchie tekhnícheskie ~/ia) performance specifications

равноправные ~/я (ravnoprávnye ~/ia) competitive conditions

равные ~/я (rávnye ~/ia) equal terms

рассматривать ~/я (rassmátrivat' ~/ia) to review terms and conditions

реальные ~/я (reál'nye ~/ia) actual conditions

с аналогичными ~/ями (s analogíchnymi ~/iami) under similar terms

соблюдать ~/я (sobliudát' ~/ia) to comply with terms and conditions

согласно ~/ям (soglásno ~/iam) as per conditions

согласованные ~/я (soglasóvannye ~/ia) agreed terms and conditions

создавать ~/я (sozdavát' ~/ia) to provide conditions

создавать ~/я для работы (sozdavát' ~/ia dlia rabóty) to provide working conditions

соответствовать ~/ям (sootvétstvovat' ~/iam) to be in accordance with conditions

сотрудничество на подрядных ~/ях (sotrúdnichestvo na podriádnykh ~/iakh) contractual cooperation

социально-бытовые ~/я (sotsiál'no-bytovýe ~/ia) social conditions

специальные ~/я (spetsiál'nye ~/ia) special conditions

специальные ~/я платежа (spetsiál'nye ~/ia platezhá) special terms of payment

ставить ~/ем (stávit' ~/em) to stipulate

ставить ~/я (stávit' ~/ia) to impose conditions

стандартные ~/я (standártnye ~/ia) standard provisions

столкнуться с ~/ем (stolknút'sia s ~/em) to encounter conditions

строгие ~/я (strógie ~/ia) strict conditions

технические ~/я (tekhnícheskie ~/ia) technical conditions

технические ~/я для обеспечения безопасности (tekhnícheskie ~/ia

dlia obespécheniia bezopásnosti)
safety specifications
технические ~/я договора
(tekhnícheskie ~/ia dogovóra)
contract specifications
технические ~/я контракта
(tekhnícheskie ~/ia kontrákta)
contract specifications
технические ~/я
производственного процесса
(tekhnícheskie ~/ia
proizvódstvennogo protséssa)
process specifications
технологические ~/я
(tekhnologícheskie ~/ia)
technological conditions
типовые ~/я (tipovýe ~/ia) model
conditions
торговать на ~/ях консигнации
(torgovát' na ~/iakh
konsignátsii) to trade on a
consignment basis
удовлетворять ~/ям
(udovletvoriát' ~/iam) to
satisfy conditions
улучшать ~/я (uluchshát' ~/ia)
to improve conditions
установленные ~/я (ustanóvlennye
~/ia) established conditions
финансовые ~/я (finánsovye ~/ia)
financial conditions
формулировать ~/я контракта
(formulírovat' ~/ia kontrákta)
to phrase the terms and
conditions of a contract
хранить товар в подходящих ~/ях
(khranít' továr v podkhodiá-
shchikh ~/iakh) to store goods
under proper conditions
цена при ~/и оплаты наличными
(tsená pri ~/i opláty
nalíchnymi) cash price
частные ~/я (chástnye ~/ia)
particular conditions
экономические ~/я
(ekonomícheskie ~/ia) economic
conditions
эксплуатационные ~/я
(ekspluatatsiónnye ~/ia)
operating conditions
~/я аварийного бонда (~/ia
avaríinogo bónda) terms of an
average bond
~/я аккредитива (~/ia
akkreditíva) terms of a letter
of credit

~/я аннулирования (~/ia
annulírovaniia) terms of
annulment
~/я аренды (~/ia aréndy) lease
terms
~/я аукциона (~/ia auktsióna)
terms and conditions of an
auction
~ гарантии (~ garántii) warranty
provisions
~/я движения (~/ia dvizhéniia)
traffic conditions
~/я, действующие автоматически
(~/ia, déistvuiushchie avtomatícheski) automatic conditions
~/я, действующие в настоящее
время (~/ia, déistvuiushchie v
nastoiáshchee vrémia) present
conditions
~/я договора (~/ia dogovóra)
terms and conditions of a
contract, treaty
~/я долгового обязательства
(~/ia dolgovógo obiazátel'stva)
terms of debenture
~/я заказа (~/ia zakáza) order
specifications
~/я инкассо (~/ia inkásso)
collection terms
~/я испытаний (~/ia ispytánii)
test conditions
~/я коммерческой сделки (~/ia
kommércheskoi sdélki) terms of a
commercial transaction
~/я коносамента (~/ia
konosaménta) terms of a bill of
lading
~/я консигнации (~/ia
konsignátsii) terms and
conditions of consignment
~/я контракта (~/ia kontrákta)
provisions of a contract
~/я кредита (~/ia kredíta)
credit terms
~/я купли-продажи (~/ia kúpli-
prodázhi) terms and conditions
of a buy-sell contract
~/я лицензионного договора (~/ia
litsenziónnogo dogovóra) terms
and conditions of a licensing
agreement
~/я мены (~/ia mény) barter
terms
~/я монтажа (~/ia montázha)
conditions for construction

~/я обслуживания (~/ia obslúzhivaniia) service conditions

~/я о переуступке (~/ia o pereustúpke) assignment clause

~/я о продлении срока (~/ia o prodlénii sroka) extension clause

~/я о производстве платежа векселем {траттой} (~/ia o proizvódstve platezhá vékselem tráttoi) draft terms

~/я о размере и порядке уплаты фрахта (~/ia o razmére i poriádke upláty frákhta) freight clause

~/я "от всех рисков" (~/ia ot vsekh rískov) "against all risks" condition

~/я отгрузки (~/ia otgrúzki) shipment terms

~/я перевозки (~/ia perevózki) transport clause

~/я платежа (~/ia platezhá) payment terms

~/я платежа за импорт товара (~/ia platezhá za ímport továra) import payment terms

~/я поездки (~/ia poézdki) travel conditions

~/я покупки (~/ia pokúpki) purchase terms

~/я полиса (~/ia pólisa) policy provisions

~/я поставки (~/ia postávki) delivery terms

~/я предложения (~/ia predlozhéniia) terms and conditions of a bid, offer, tender

~/я предоставления финансовых услуг (~/ia predostavléniia finánsovykh uslúg) terms and conditions of a financing package

~/я приёмки (~/ia priiómki) terms of acceptance

~/я продажи (~/ia prodázhi) sales terms

~/я продажи с аукциона (~/ia prodázhi s auktsióna) auction sale conditions

~/я продления чартера (~/ia prodléniia chártera) continuation clause {charter}

~/я работы (~/ia rabóty) conditions of work

~/я расчёта (~/ia raschióta) settlement terms

~/я рынка (~/ia rýnka) market conditions

~/я сдачи в аренду (~/ia sdáchi v aréndu) lease conditions

~/я сделки (~/ia sdélki) terms of a deal

~/я сотрудничества (~/ia sotrúdnichestva) terms of cooperation

~/я торговли (~/ia torgóvli) terms of trade

~/я транспортировки (~/ia transportiróvki) terms of conveyance

~/я труда (~/ia trudá) labor conditions

~/я финансирования (~/ia finansírovaniia) terms of financing

~/я фрахта (~/ia frákhta) terms of freight

~/я хозяйствования (~/ia khoziáistvovaniia) conditions of economic management

~/я хранения (~/ia khranéniia) storage conditions

~/я чартера (~/ia chártera) charter-party terms

Условность (uslóvnost') f. reserve

Условный (uslóvnyi) adj. conditional

Услуг/a (uslúg/a) f. service

ассортимент ~/ (assortimént ~/) range of ~s

аудиторские ~/и (audítorskie ~/i) auditing ~s

банковские ~/и (bánkovskie ~/i) banking ~s

бесплатные ~/и (besplátnye ~/i) free ~s

бюро ~/ (biuró ~/) ~ center

взаимные ~/и (vzaímnye ~/i) reciprocal ~s

внешнеторговые ~/и (vneshnetorgóvye ~/i) foreign trade ~s

воспользоваться ~/ами ... (vospól'zovat'sia ~/ami ...) to employ the ~s of ...

договор о предоставлении ~/ (dogovór o predostavlénii ~/) ~ agreement

дополнительные ~/и (dopolnítel'nye ~/i) additional ~s

дружеская ~ (drúzheskaia ~)
friendly ~
импорт ~/ (ímport ~/) import of
~s
инженерно-строительные ~/и
(inzhenérno-stroítel'nye ~/i)
construction engineering ~s
инжиниринговые ~/и
(inzhiníringovye ~/i)
engineering ~s
к Вашим ~/ам (k váshim ~/am) at
your ~
комиссия за ~/и (komíssiia za
~/i) commission for ~
коммерческие ~/и (kommércheskie
~/i) commercial ~s
комплекс ~/ (kómpleks ~/)
package of ~s
комплексные ~/и (kómpleksnye
~/i) comprehensive ~
конкурентные ~/и (konkuréntnye
~/i) competitíve ~
конструкторские ~/и
(konstrúktorskie ~/i) design ~s
консультационные ~/и
(konsul'tatsiónnye ~/i)
consulting ~s
маркетинговые ~/и (márketingovye
~/i) marketing ~s
максимальный объём ~/
(maksimál'nyi ob"ióm ~/) maximum
volume of ~s
минимальные ~/и (minimál'nye
~/i) minimum facilities
"невидимые" ~/и (nevídimye ~/i)
invisible ~
объём ~/ (ob"ióm ~/) scope of ~s
оказание ~/ (okazánie ~/)
rendering of ~s
операции по торговле ~/ами
(operátsii po torgóvle ~/ami) ~
business
оплата ~/ (opláta ~/) payment
for ~s
пакет ~/ (pakét ~/) package of
~s
пакет ~/, предоставляемых по
лицензии (pakét ~/,
predostavliáemykh po litsénzii)
licensing package
плата за таможенные ~/и (pláta
za tamózhennye ~/i) customs fee
плата за экспедиторские ~/и
(pláta za ekspedítorskie ~/i)
freight forwarding charge
платные ~/и (plátnye ~/i) paid
~s

полнота ~/ (polnotá ~/)
thoroughness of ~s
полный цикл ~/ (pólnyi tsikl ~/)
full-~
пользоваться ~/ами
(pól'zovat'sia ~/ami) to utilize
~s
портовые ~/и (portóvye ~/i)
harbor ~s
посреднические ~/и
(posrédnicheskie ~/i)
intermediary ~s
потребление ~/ (potreblénie ~/)
use of ~s
предлагать пакет ~/ (predlagát'
pakét ~/) to bid a ~ package
прибегать к ~/ам (pribegát' k
~/am) to require ~s
производственно-технические ~/и
(proizvódstvenno-tekhnícheskie
~/i) industrial ~s
профессиональные ~/и
(professionál'nye ~/i)
professional ~s
рынок ~/ (rýnok ~/) market for
~s
стоимость ~/ (stóimost' ~/) cost
of ~s
сфера ~/ (sféra ~/) ~s sector
технические ~/и (tekhnícheskie
~/i) technical ~s
технологические ~/и
(tekhnologícheskie ~/i)
technological ~s
торговля ~/ами (torgóvlia ~/ami)
trade of ~s
транспортные ~/и (tránsportnye
~/i) transportation ~s
туристические ~/и
(turistícheskie ~/i) tourist ~s
управленческие ~/и
(upravléncheskie ~/i) management
~s
финансовые ~/и (finánsovye ~/i)
financial ~s
характер ~/ (kharákter ~/)
nature of ~s
экспертные ~/и (ekspértnye ~/i)
expert ~s
экспорт ~/ (éksport ~/) export
of ~s
~/и агента (~/i agénta) agent's
~s
~/и агентства (~/i agéntstva)
agency ~s
~/и персонала (~/i personála)
personnel ~s

~/и по обучению (~/i po obuchéniiu) training ~s
~/и по организации продажи (~/i po organizátsii prodázhi) pre-sales ~s
~/и по перевозке (~/i po perevózke) transportation ~s
~/и по поддержанию (~/i po podderzhániiu) support ~s
~/и по страхованию (~/i po strakhovániiu) insurance ~s
~/и по уборке (~/i po ubórke) cleaning ~s
~/и по фрахтованию (~/i po frakhtovániiu) chartering ~s

Усовершенствовани/е (usovershenstvováni/e) n. improvement, perfection
внедрять ~ (vnedriát' ~) to incorporate improvements
возможное ~ (vozmózhnoe ~) potential improvement
запатентованное ~ (zapatentóvannoe ~) patented improvement
многочисленные ~/я (mnogochíslennye ~/ia) numerous improvements
новое ~ (nóvoe ~) new development
патент на ~ (patént na ~) patent on an improvement
показывать ~ (pokázyvat' ~) to demonstrate an improvemen
разработать ~ (razrabótat' ~) to develop an improvement
патентоспособное ~ (patentosposóbnoe ~) patentable improvement
сделать ~ (sdélat' ~) to make an improvement
техническое ~ (tekhnícheskoe ~) technical improvement
технологическое ~ (tekhnologícheskoe ~) technological improvement
~/я контейнерной службы (~/ia kontéinernoi slúzhby) improvement of containerization

Устав (ustáv) m. articles, by-laws, charter
~ акционерного общества (~ aktsionérnogo óbshchestva) charter of a joint stock company
~ корпорации (~ korporátsii) articles of incorporation

~ совместного предприятия (~ sovméstnogo predpriiátiia) charter of a joint venture

Установк/а (ustanóvk/a) f. guidelines, installation, set-up
~/и (~/i) guidelines

Устойчивость (ustóichivost') f. soundness, stability
~ курса валюты (~ kúrsa valiúty) exchange rate stability
~ цен (~ tsen) price stability

Устроитель (ustroítel') m. organizer, promoter
иностранный ~ (inostránnyi ~) foreign promoter
~ ярмарки (~ iármarki) fair promoter

Уступ/ка (ustúp/ka) f. concession, discount, rebate
взаимные ~/ки (vzaímnye ~/ki) mutual concessions
вынужденная ~ (výnuzhdennaia ~) forced concession
делать ~/ки (délat' ~/ki) to make concessions
добиваться ~/ок (dobivát'sia ~/ok) to seek concessions
максимальная ~ (maksimál'naia ~) maximum concession
налоговые ~/ки (nalógovye ~/ki) tax concessions
нетарифные ~/ки (netarífnye ~/ki) non-tariff concessions
специальные ~/ки (spetsiál'nye ~/ki) special concessions
тарифные ~/ки (tarífnye ~/ki) tariff concessions
~/ки в цене (~/ki v tsené) discount
~/ки патента (~/ki paténta) cession of a patent

Участи/е (uchásti/e) m. participation
возобновлять заявку на ~ (vozobnovliát' zaiávku na ~) to renew an application
выйти из ~/я в работе над проектом (vyití iz ~/ia v rabót nad proéktom) to withdraw from project
давать заявку на ~ (davát' zaiávku na ~) to apply for participation
договорённость об ~/и (dogovoriónnost' ob ~/i) partnership arrangement

доля ~/я (dólia ~/ia) interest, share {of ownership, etc.}
доля ~/я в акционерном капитале (dólia ~/ia v aktsionérnom kapitále) share of capital contribution
заявка на ~ (zaiávka na ~) application for participation
коллективное ~ (kollektívnoe ~) collective participation
крупное ~ (krúpnoe ~) large-scale participation
масштаб ~/я (masshtáb ~/ia) scale of participation
назначать людей для ~/я (naznachát' liudéi dlia ~/ia) to designate people to participate
непосредственное ~ (neposrédstvennoe ~) direct participation
облигации на ~ в прибылях компании (obligátsii na ~ v príbyliakh kompánii) participating bond
обосновать ~ (obosnovát' ~) to justify participation
отказ экспонента от ~/я (otkáz eksponénta ot ~/ia) withdrawal of an exhibitor
отказаться от ~/я (otkazát'sia ot ~/ia) to withdraw
официальное ~ на правительственном уровне (ofitsiál'noe ~ na pravítel'stvennom úrovne) official governmental participation
оформление ~/я в выставке (oformlénie ~/ia v výstavke) registration of exhibitors
подтверждать ~ (podtverzhdát' ~) to confirm participation
поочерёдное ~ (poocheriódnoe ~) alternating participation
предлагать ~ (predlagát' ~) to offer a share in
принимать ~ (prinimát' ~) to participate
принимать ~ в торгах (prinimát' ~ v torgákh) to bid
принимать активное ~ (prinimát' aktívnoe ~) to actively participate
разрешение на ~ (razreshénie na ~) admission
расходы по ~/ю (raskhódy po ~/iu) participation expenses

с ~/ем иностранных фирм (s ~/em inostránnykh firm) with the participation of foreign firms
совместное ~ (sovméstnoe ~) joint participation
финансовое ~ (finánsovoe ~) financial participation

Участник/ (uchástnik) m. participant, partner, party
основной ~ (osnovnói ~) major participant
общее число ~/ов (óbshchee chisló ~/ov) total participation
постоянный ~ (postoiánnyi ~) permanent exhibitor
потенциальный ~ (potentsiál'nyi ~) potential participant
предполагаемые ~/и (predpolagáemye ~/i) prospective participants
равноправные ~/и (ravnoprávnye ~/i) equal parties
регистрация ~/ов (registrátsiia ~/ov) registration of participants
список ~/ов (spísok ~/ov) listed participants
~ аукциона (~ auktsióna) bidder {at auction}
~ в совместных предприятиях (~ v sovméstnykh predpriiátiiakh) party to a joint venture
~ выставки (~ výstavki) exhibitioner
~ договора (~ dogovóra) party to an agreement, contracting party
~ переговоров (~ peregovórov) negotiating party
~/и соглашения (~/i soglashéniia) parties to an agreement
~ торгов, предложивший наивысшую цену (~ torgóv, predlozhívshii naivýsshuiu tsénu) highest bidder
~ ярмарки (~ iármarki) exhibitor at a fair

Учёт (uchiót) m. accounting, discount, registration
бланк ~/а экспортных операций (blank ~/a éksportnykh operátsii) export note
бухгалтерский ~ (bukhgálterskii ~) accounting books
быть пригодным к ~/у (byt' prigódnym k ~/u) to be discountable

382

ведение ~/а (vedénie ~/a) record
keeping
вести ~ (vestí ~) to keep
records
взять на ~ (vziat' na ~) to
register
для ~/а в бюджете (dlia ~/a v
biudzhéte) for budgetary
purposes
денежный ~ (dénezhnyi ~) money
accounting
методы бухгалтерского ~/а
(métody bukhgálterskogo ~/a)
accounting practices
оперативный ~ (operatívnyi ~)
routine accounting
период ~/а (períod ~/a) discount
period {bill, note}
повышение ставки банковского ~/а
(povyshénie stávki bánkovskogo
~/a) increase in the bank rate
предъявлять вексель или тратту к
~/у (pred"iavliát' véksel' íli
tráttu k ~/u) to present a bill
for discount
принимать к ~/у (prinimát' k
~/u) to take on discount
проводить ~ (provodít' ~) to
take stock of
проектировать с ~/ом требований
... (proektírovat' s ~/om
trébovanii ...) to design to the
requirements of ...
производственный ~
(proizvódstvennyi ~) performance
record
расходы по ~/у (raskhódy po ~/u)
discount charges
с ~/ом риска (s ~/om ríska)
allowing for risk
с ~/ом сезонных колебаний (s
~/om sezónnykh kolebánii) seasonally adjusted
с ~/ом этой возможности (s ~/om
étoi vozmózhnosti) with this
possibility in mind ...
снимать с ~/а (snimát' s ~/a) to
write off {accounts}
становиться на ~ (stanovít'sia
na ~) to be registered
статистический ~
(statistícheskii ~) statistical
accounting
табель ~/а отработанных часов
(tábel' ~/a otrabótannykh
chasóv) time sheet

тарифная ставка с ~/ом скидок
(tarífnaia stávka s ~/om skídok)
net rate {tariff}
~ векселей (~ vékselei) discount
of bills, notes
~ денежных поступлений (~
dénezhnykh postuplénii) entry of
payments received
~ производственных затрат (~
proizvódstvennykh zatrát) cost
accounting
~ кадров (~ kádrov) personnel
records
~ количества отработанных часов
(~ kolíchestva otrabótannykh
chasóv) total operating hours
~ работы (~ rabóty) work records
~ спроса (~ sprósa) demand
records
~ тратт (~ tratt) discount of
drafts
Учётный (uchiótnyi) adj. discount,
registration
Учитывать (uchítyvat') v. to
account for, to discount, to tally
Учредитель (uchredítel') m. founder
Учреждать (uchrezhdát') v. to
establish, to found
Учреждени/е (uchrezhdéni/e) n.
establishment, foundation,
institution
административное ~
(administratívnoe ~)
administrative office
государственное ~
(gosudárstvennoe ~) government
institution
закупочное ~ (zakúpochnoe ~)
purchasing agency
здание ~/я (zdánie ~/ia) office
premises
компетентное ~ (kompeténtnoe ~)
competent authorities
кредитное ~ (kredítnoe ~)
lending institution
кредитно-финансовое ~ (kredítno-
finánsovoe ~) credit and
financial institution
научное ~ (naúchnoe ~)
scientific institution
научно-исследовательское ~
(naúchno-isslédovatel''skoe ~)
research establishment
правительственные ~/я
(pravítel'stvennye ~/ia)
governmental office

правовые ~/я (pravovýe ~/ia)
legal institutions
расходы по ~/ю акционерного
общества (raskhódy po ~/iu
aktsionérnogo óbshchestva)
promotion expenses {of joint
stock company}
страховое ~ (strakhovóe ~)
insurance company
финансовое ~ (finánsovoe ~)
financial institution
часы работы ~/я (chasý rabóty
~/ia) office hours
~ по продаже (~ po prodázhe)
sales office
~, содействующее продаже товара
(~, sodéistvuiushchee prodázhe
továra) sales promotion agency
Ущерб (ushchérb) m. damage, loss,
prejudice {in legal proceedings}
без ~/а (bez ~/a) without
prejudice
без ~/а для контракта (bez ~/a
dlia kontrákta) without
prejudice to the contract
без ~/а для договора страхования
(bez ~/a dlia dogovóra strakhovániia) without prejudice to the
insurance policy
без ~/а прав ... (bez ~/a prav
...) without detriment to the
rights of ...
без ~/а прав покупателя (bez ~/a
prav pokupátelia) without
prejudice to the purchaser's
rights
большой ~ (bol'shói ~) great
damage
будет нанесён огромный ~, если
... (búdet nanesión ogrómnyi ~,
ésli ...) it will be extremely
detrimental, if ...
быть ответственным за ~ (byt'
otvétstvennym za ~) to be liable
for damage
возмещать ~ (vozmeshchát' ~) to
indemnify for damage
возмещение ~/а (vozmeshchénie
~/a) compensation for damages
возможный ~ (vozmózhnyi ~)
possible damage
в случае ~/а (v slúchae ~/a) in
case of damage
дальнейший ~ (dal'néishii ~)
further damage
действовать в ~ (déistvovat' v
~) to work against

денежный ~ (dénezhnyi ~)
monetary damage, loss
застраховать кого-л. от ~/а
имуществу (zastrakhovát' kogó-l.
ot ~/a imúshchestvu) to
indemnify someone against
property damage
заявить об ~/е (zaiavít' ob ~/e)
to report damage
заявление об /е (zaiavlénie ob
/e) damage report
значительный ~ (znachítel'nyi ~)
significant damage, significant
loss
компенсация за ~ (kompensátsiia
za ~) compensation for damages
компенсировать ~ (kompensírovat'
~) to compensate damages
косвенный ~ (kósvennyi ~)
indirect damage
крупный ~ (krúpnyi ~) major
damage
материальный ~ (materiál'nyi ~)
material damage
минимальный ~ (minimál'nyi ~)
minimal loss
нанесённый ~ (nanesiónnyi ~)
actual damage caused
наносить ~ (nanosít' ~) to
inflict a loss, to inflict
damage
наносить ~ интересам (nanosít' ~
interésam) to harm the interests
наносить ~ правам (nanosít' ~
pravám) to prejudice the rights
наносящий ~ (nanosiáshchii ~)
prejudicial
незначительный ~
(neznachítel'nyi ~)
insignificant damage, loss
непоправимый ~ (nepopravimyi ~)
irreparable harm
обязательство возместить ~
(obiazátel'stvo vozmestít' ~)
obligation to compensate for
damage
освидетельствование ~/а
(osvidétel'stvovanie ~/a) damage
survey
ответственность за ~
(otvétstvennost' za ~) liability
оценивать размер ~/а (otsénivat'
razmér ~/a) to assess the damage
оценка ~/а (otsénka ~/a) damage
assessment
понести ~ (ponestí ~) to suffer
damage, loss

предотвращать ~
(predotvrashchát' ~) to prevent
damage
причина ~/a (prichína ~/a) cause
of damage
работа по возмещению ~/a (rabóta
po vozmeshchéniiu ~/a) remedial
work
размер ~/a (razmér ~/a) extent
of damage
уровень ~/a (úroven' ~/a) level
of damage
характер ~/a (kharákter ~/a)
nature of the damage
частичный ~ (chastíchnyi ~)
partial damage
~ в виде упущенной выгоды (~ v
víde upúshchennoi výgody) loss
of profit
~ вследствие неисполнения
обязательств (~ vslédstvie
neispolnéniia obiazátel'stv)
loss due to non-fulfillment of
obligations
~, вызванный ... (~, výzvannyi
...) damage caused by ...
~, нанесённый водой (~,
nanesiónnyi vodói) water damage
~ от выбрасывания груза за борт
(~ ot vybrasyvániia grúza za
bort) loss by reason of jettison
~ от пожара (~ ot pozhára) fire
damage
~ от шторма (~ ot shtórma) storm
damage
~ собственности (~
sóbstvennosti) property damage

Ф

Фабрик/а (fábrik/a) f. factory,
plant
бумажная ~ (bumázhnaia ~) paper
mill
директор ~/и (diréktor ~/i)
plant manager
консервная ~ (konsérvnaia ~)
cannery
обогатительная ~
(obogatítel'naia ~) dressing
mill
опытная ~ (ópytnaia ~) pilot
plant
прядильная ~ (priadíl'naia ~)
spinning mill

текстильная ~ (tekstíl'naia ~)
textile mill
хлопкопрядильная ~
(khlopkopriadíl'naia ~) cotton
spinning mill
ткацкая ~ (tkátskaia ~) weaving
mill
управлять ~/ой (upravliát' ~/oi)
to manage a factory
шелкопрядильная ~
(shelkopriadíl'naia ~) silk mil
Фабричный (fabríchnyi) adj.
factory, plant
Факсимиле (faksímile) indecl.
facsimile {of signature}
Факт (fakt) m. fact
веский ~ (véskii ~) grave ~
в соответствии с ~/ами (v
sootvétstvii s ~/ami) in
accordance with the ~s
вышеупомянутый
(vysheupomiánutyi ~) the above
выявить ~/ы (výiavit' ~/y) to
elicit ~s
достоверный ~ (dostovérnyi ~)
established ~
искажать ~/ы (iskazhát' ~/y) to
distort the ~s
исходный ~ (iskhódnyi ~) datum
малодостоверный
(malodostovérnyi ~) ill-grounde
~
неопровержимый ~
(neoproverzhímyi ~) irrefutable
~
общеизвестный ~
(obshcheizvéstnyi ~) a matter o
common knowledge
основанный на ~/ax (osnóvannyi
na ~/akh) well-founded
остаётся ~/ом (ostaiótsia ~/om)
the ~ remains
отдельный ~ (otdél'nyi ~)
separate ~
поставить перед ~/ом (postávit
péred ~/om) to confront with a
fait accompli
соответствующий ~
(sootvétstvuiushchii ~) releva
~
сталкиваться с реальными ~/ами
(stálkivat'sia s reál'nymi
~/ami) to face ~s
стоять перед ~/ом (stoiát' pér
~/om) to be faced with the ~
установленный ~ (ustanóvlennyi
~) established ~

~, имеющий отношение к данному вопросу (~, iméiushchii otnoshénie k dánnomu voprósu) the ~, pertaining to this matter
~/ы говорят о том, что (~/y govóriat o tom, chto) the ~s shows that

Фактор (fáktor) *m.* factor {agent}, development
благоприятный ~ (blagopriiátnyi ~) favorable development
важный ~ (vázhnyi ~) important factor
внешний ~ (vnéshnii ~) external factor
второстепенный ~ (vtorostepénnyi ~) secondary factor
вышеназванный ~ (vyshenázvannyi ~) the above factor
новый ~ (nóvyi ~) new development
основной ~ (osnovnói ~) the principal factor
побудительный ~ (pobudítel'nyi ~) incentive
постоянно действующий ~ (postoiánno déistvuiushchii ~) permanent factor
решающий ~ (resháiushchii ~) decisive factor
случайный ~ (slucháinyi ~) chance development
человеческий ~ (chelovécheskii ~) human factor
учитываемый ~ (uchityváemyi ~) accountable factor
экономический ~ (ekonomícheskii ~) economic factor
~ времени (~ vrémeni) time factor
~ долговременного действия (~ dolgovrémennogo déistviia) long-term factor ·
~ кратковременного действия (~ kratkovrémennogo déistviia) short-term factor
~ сбыта (~ sbýta) market factor
~ стоимости (~ stóimosti) cost factor

Факторинг (faktóring) *m.* factoring

Фактур/а (faktúr/a) *f.* invoice
включать в ~/у (vkliuchát' v ~/u) to include in an ~
выписывать ~/у (vypísyvat' ~/u) to issue an ~
дата ~/ы (dáta ~/y) d ~ date

заверенная ~ (zavérennaia ~) certified ~
коммерческая ~ (kommércheskaia ~) commercial ~
консульская ~ (kónsul'skaia ~) consular ~
копия ~/ы (kópiia ~/y) ~ copy
окончательная ~ (okonchátel'naia ~) final ~
оригинал ~/ы (originál ~/y) original of the ~
ориентировочная ~ (orientiróvochnaia ~) pro forma ~
переделывать ~/у (peredélyvat' ~/u) to fraudulently alter an ~
предварительная ~ (predvarítel'naia ~) preliminary ~
прилагать копию ~/ы (prilagát' kópiiu ~/y) to append a copy of an ~
примерная ~ (primérnaia ~) specimen ~
сумма ~/ы (súmma ~/y) ~ amount
уменьшать сумму ~/ы (umen'shát' súmmu ~/y) to reduce the ~ amount
~ на (~ na) ~ for ...

Фактура-лицензия (faktúra-litsénziia) *f.* invoice-license

Фактура-спецификация (faktúra-spetsifikátsiia) *f.* invoice specification

Фактурирование (fakturírovanie) *n.* invoicing
~ по завышенным ценам (po zavýshennym tsenám) over-invoicing

Фактурный (faktúrnyi) *adj.* invoiced

Фасовать (fasovát') *v.* to pre-pack

Фасовк/а (fasóvk/a) *f.* pre-packing
отдел ~/и и упаковки (otdél ~/i i upakóvki) packaging department

Федеральный (federál'nyi) *adj.* federal

Федеративный (federatívnyi) *adj.* federated

Фиксация (fiksátsiia) *f.* fixation
цен (tsen) price fixing

Фиксированный (fiksírovannyi) *adj.* fixed

Фиксировать (fiksírovat') *v.* to fix

Фиктивный (fiktívnyi) *adj.* bogus, false

Филиал (filiál) *m.* affiliate, branch

руководитель ~/а (rukovodítel'
~/a) branch manager
~ банка (~ bánka) branch bank
~ компании (~ kompánii) branch
office
~ предприятия (~ predpriiátiia)
affiliated enterprise
Финансировани/е (finansírovanie) *n.*
financing
банковское ~ (bánkovskoe ~) bank
~
безвозвратное ~ (bezvozvrátnoe
~) irrevocable ~
бюджетное ~ (biudzhétnoe ~)
budgetary ~
взаимное ~ (vzaímnoe ~) back-to-
back ~
внешнее ~ (vnéshnee ~) foreign ~
внутреннее ~ (vnútrennee ~)
domestic ~
вторичное ~ (vtoríchnoe ~)
secondary ~
гарантировать ~ (garantírovat'
~) to guarantee ~
государственное ~
(gosudárstvennoe ~) public ~
договориться о ~/и
(dogovorít'sia o ~/i) to arrange
for ~
долгосрочное ~ (dolgosróchnoe ~)
long-term ~
долевое ~ (dolevóe ~)
participation in ~
дополнительное ~ (dopolnítel'noe
~) supplementary ~
источники ~/я (istóchniki ~/ia)
sources of ~
компания по ~/ю продаж в
рассрочку (kompániia po ~/iu
prodázh v rassróchku) sales
finance company
компенсационное ~
(kompensatsiónnoe ~)
compensatory ~
краткосрочное ~ (kratkosróchnoe
~) short-term ~
кредитное ~ (kredítnoe ~) credit
~
международное ~ (mezhdunaródnoe
~) international ~
обеспечивать ~/е контракта
(obespéchivat' ~/e kontrákta) to
provide ~ for a contract
объём ~/я (ob"ióm ~/ia) amount
of ~
план ~я (plan ~ia) plan of ~

прекратить ~ (prekratít' ~) to
cut off funding
разрешение на ~ (razreshénie na
~) financial authorization
смешанное ~ (sméshannoe ~) mixed
~
совместное ~ (sovméstnoe ~) co-
sponsored ~
среднесрочное ~ (srednesróchnoe
~) medium-term ~
условия ~/я (uslóviia ~/ia)
terms of ~
фонды ~/я (fóndy ~/ia) ~ funds
формы и методы ~/я (fórmy i
métody ~/ia) forms and methods
of ~
~ ассигнований (~ assignovánii)
~ of appropriations
~ импорта (~ ímporta) import ~
~ с помощью выпуска акций (~ s
pómoshch'iu výpuska áktsii)
equity {stock} ~
~ торговли (~ torgóvli) trade ~
~ экспорта (~ éksporta) export ~
Финансировать (finansírovat') *v.* t
finance
Финансирующий (finansíruiushchii)
adj. financing
Финансист (finansíst) *m.* financier
Финансово-кредитный (finánsovo-
kredítnyi) *adj.* finance and credit
Финансово-хозяйственный (finánsovo-
khoziáistvennyi) *adj.* finance and
economic
Финансовый (finánsovyi) *adj.*
financial
Финанс/ы (fináns/y) *pl.* finances
государственные ~
(gosudárstvennye ~) public
finance
Министерство ~/ов (ministérstvo
~/ov) Ministry of Finance
{Russian Federation}
Министр ~/ов (minístr ~/ov)
Minister of Finance
отдел ~/ов и отчётности (otdél
~/ov i otchiótnosti) finance-
and-accounts department
Фирм/а (fírm/a) *f.* company, firm,
house
агентская ~ (agéntskaia ~)
brokerage house
арендная ~ (aréndnaia ~) leasing
company
брокерская (brókerskaia)
brokerage firm

ведущая ~ (vedúshchaia ~)
leading firm
венчурная ~ (vénchurnaia ~)
venture capital firm
внешнеторговая ~
(vneshnetorgóvaia ~) foreign
trade company
возбуждать иск против ~/ы
(vozbuzhdát' isk prótiv ~/y) to
file suit against a company
генеральный директор ~/ы
(generál'nyi diréktor ~/y)
general director of a company
глава ~/ы (gláva ~/y) head of a
company, senior partner of a
firm
государственная ~
(gosudárstvennaia ~) state-owned
company
деятельность ~/ы (déiatel'nost'
~/y) operations of a company
дочерняя ~ (dochérniaia ~)
subsidiary company
железнодорожная транспортная ~
(zheleznodorózhnaia
tránsportnaia ~) rail carrier
импортная ~ (ímportnaia ~)
import merchants
инженерно-консультационная ~
(inzhenérno-konsul'tatsiónnaia
~) engineering consulting firm
инжиниринговая ~
(inzhiníringovaia ~) engineering
firm
иностранная ~ (inostránnaia ~)
foreign company
капитал ~/ы (kapitál ~/y)
capital of a firm
капиталистическая ~
(kapitalistícheskaia ~)
capitalist firm
конкурирующие ~/ы
(konkuríruiushchie ~/y) rival
firms
кооперативная ~ (kooperatívnaia
~) cooperative company
крупная ~ (krúpnaia ~) major
firm
лизинговая ~ (lízingovaia ~)
leasing company
ликвидация ~/ы (likvidátsiia
~/y) liquidation of a ~
маркетинговая ~ (márketingovaia
~) marketing firm
мелкая ~ (mélkaia ~) small
business

местная ~ (méstnaia ~) local
company
местонахождение ~/ы
(mestonakhozhdénie ~/y) business
address of a company
название ~/ы (nazvánie ~/y)
company name
национальная ~ (natsionál'naia
~) national company
начинающая ~ (nachináiushchaia
~) entrant firm
обанкротившаяся ~
(obankrotívshaiasia ~) bankrupt
company
оптовая ~ (optóvaia ~) wholesale
merchant
основывать ~/у (osnóvyvat' ~/u)
to found a ~
отдел ~/ы (otdél ~/y) division
of a firm
отделение ~/ы (otdelénie ~/y)
branch business
отраслевая производственная ~
(otrasleváia proizvódstvennaia
~) industrial sector firm
патентная ~ (paténtnaia ~)
patent agency, law firm with a
patent practice
переименовывать ~/у
(pereimenovyvát' ~/u) to change
the name of a company
платежеспособная ~
(platezhesposóbnaia ~) solvent
company
подрядная ~ (podriádnaia ~)
contractor
посредническая ~
(posrédnicheskaia ~) business
brokering firm
посылочная ~ (posýlochnaia ~)
mail order house
представитель ~/ы (predstavítel'
~/y) representative of a firm
представлять ~/у (predstavliát'
~/u) to represent a firm
президент ~/ы (prezidént ~/y)
president of a firm
производственная ~
(proizvódstvennaia ~)
manufacturing company
промышленная ~ (promýshlennaia
~) industrial company
размещать заказ у ~/ы
(razmeshchát' zakáz u ~/y) to
place an order with a company

регистрировать ~/у
(registrírovat' ~/u) to register
a company, firm
репутация ~/ы (reputátsiia ~/y)
reputation of a company
розничная ~ (róznichnaia ~)
retail firm
руководить ~/ой (rukovodít'
~/oi) to direct a business
сбытовая ~ (sbytováia ~) direct
marketing company
смешанная торговая ~
(sméshannaia torgóvaia ~) mixed
trading company
совладелец ~/ы (sovladélets ~/y)
co-owner of a firm
совместные ~/ы (sovméstnye ~/y)
joint firms
солидная ~ (solídnaia ~) solid
firm
сотрудничать с ~/ой
(sotrúdnichat' s ~/oi) to do
business with a firm
специализированная
(spetsializírovannaia ~)
specialized firm
средняя ~ (srédniaia ~) medium-
sized firm
статус ~/ы (státus ~/y) status
of a firm
стивидорная ~ (stividórnaia ~)
stevedoring company
страховая ~ (strakhováia ~)
insurance company
строительная ~ (stroítel'naia ~)
civil engineering company
структура ~/ы (struktúra ~/y)
structure of a company
субподрядная ~ (subpodriádnaia
~) subcontractor
судовладельческая ~
(sudovladél'cheskaia ~) ship
owners
судоходная ~ (sudokhódnaia ~)
shipping firm
торговая ~ (torgóvaia ~) trading
house
транспортная ~ (tránsportnaia ~)
transport company
транспортно-экспедиционная
(tránsportno-ekspeditsiónnaia ~)
freight forwarding company
турагентская ~ (turagéntskaia ~)
tour company
туристическая ~ (turistícheskaia
~) travel agency

универсальная ~ (universál'naia
~) universal company
упаковочная ~ (upakóvochnaia ~)
packing house
филиал ~/ы (filiál ~/y) branch
office of a company
финансовая ~ (finánsovaia ~)
financial firm
частная ~ (chástnaia ~) private
company
штемпель ~/ы (shtémpel' ~/y)
business stamp
экспортная ~ (éksportnaia ~)
export merchants
~ с хорошей репутацией (~ s
khóroshei reputátsiei) ~ with a
good reputation
Фирма-арендодатель (fírma-
arendodátel') m. company-lessor
Фирма-изготовитель (fírma-
izgotovítel') m. manufacturer
Фирма-исполнитель (fírma-
ispolnítel') m. contractor
Фирма-подрядчик (fírma-podriádchik)
m. engineering contractor
Фирма-покупатель (fírma-pokupátel')
m. purchasing company
Фирма-поставщик (fírma-
postavshchík) m. supplier
Фирма-производитель (fírma-
proizvodítel') m. producer
Фирма-участница (fírma-uchástnitsa
f. participating firm
~ договора (~ dogovóra)
contracting firm
Фирменный (fírmennyi) adj. brand-
name, firm
Флот (flot) m. fleet
воздушный ~ (vozdúshnyi ~) air ~
морской ~ (morskói ~) marine ~
наливной ~ (nalivnói ~) tanker ~
нефтеналивной танкерный ~
(neftenalivnói tánkernyi ~) oil
tanker ~
океанский ~ (okeánskii ~) ocean
going ~
прикольный ~ (prikól'nyi ~)
inactive ~
речной ~ (rechnói ~) inland
water ~
рыболовный ~ (rybolóvnyi ~)
fishing ~
сухогрузный ~ (sukhogrúznyi ~)
dry cargo ~
танкерный ~ (tánkernyi ~) tanke
~

торговый ~ (torgóvyi ~) merchant marine ~

Флотский (flótskii) *adj.* fleet, naval

Фон (fon) *m.* background

Фонд (fond) *m.* asset, fund, reserve, stocks

автоматически возобновляемый ~ (avtomatícheski vozobnovliáemyi ~) revolving fund

амортизационный ~ (amortizatsiónnyi ~) amortization fund

базовый ~ (bázovyi ~) basic fund

банковские ~/ы (bánkovskie ~/y) bank's funds

валютный ~ (valiútnyi ~) monetary reserve

вклад в уставный ~ (vklad v ustávnyi ~) contribution to charter capital

выкупной ~ (vykupnói ~) sinking fund

денежный ~ (dénezhnyi ~) cash fund

доля в уставном ~/e (dólia v ustávnom ~/e) share of the charter fund

дополнительные ~/ы (dopolnítel'nye ~/y) supplementary funds

замороженные ~/ы (zamorózhennye ~/y) frozen capital

инвестировать ~/ы (investírovat' ~/y) to invest funds

инвестиционные ~/ы (investitsiónnye ~/y) investment funds

иностранные ~/ы (inostránnye ~/y) foreign funds

компенсационный ~ (kompensatsiónnyi ~) indemnification fund

консолидированный ~ (konsolidírovannyi ~) consolidated fund

кредитные ~/ы (kredítnye ~/y) credit resources

ликвидные ~/ы (likvídnye ~/y) liquid funds

неделимые ~/ы (nedelímye ~/y) indivisible funds

обновление производственных ~/ов (obnovlénie proizvódstvennykh ~/ov) rehabilitation of production assets

оборотные ~/ы (oborótnye ~/y) working assets

образование ~/ов (obrazovánie ~/ov) asset formation

общий ~ (óbshchii ~) pool {of funds}

общественные ~/ы (obshchéstvennye ~/y) public funds

объединённый долларовый ~ (ob"ediniónnyi dóllarovyi ~) dollar pool

основные ~/ы (osnovnýe ~/y) fixed funds

отчисления в валютный ~ (otchisléniia v valiútnyi ~) allocations to the monetary reserve

патентный ~ (paténtnyi ~) patent holdings

пенсионный ~ (pensiónnyi ~) pension fund

переходящие ~/ы (perekhodiáshchie ~/y) carry-over assets

правительственные ~/ы (pravítel'stvennye ~/y) government funds

привлекать ~/ы (privlekát' ~/y) to raise funds

резервный ~ (rezérvnyi ~) reserve fund

создавать ~/ы (sozdavát' ~/y) to set aside funds

страховой ~ (strakhovói ~) insurance fund

уставный ~ (ustávnyi ~) charter capital

формирование ~/ов (formirovánie ~/ov) formation of funds

чрезвычайный ~ (chrezvycháinyi ~) contingency fund

~ валютных отчислений (~ valiútnykh otchislénii) currency reserves

~ капитальных вложений (~ kapitál'nykh vlozhénii) capital investment fund

~ материального поощрения (~ materiál'nogo pooshchréniia) incentive fund

~ накопления (~ nakopléniia) cumulation fund

~ погашения (~ pogashéniia) redemption fund

~ помощи (~ pómoshchi) relief fund

~ потребления (~ potребléniia) consumption fund
~ премирования (~ premiroványiia) bonus fund
~ развития производства (~ razvítiia proizvódstva) expansion fund
~ экономического стимулирования (~ ekonomícheskogo stimulírovaniia) economic stimulus fund
Фондирование (fondirovánie) n. state funding
Фондовый (fóndovyi) adj. share, stock
Фондоотдач/а (fondootdách/a) f. capital investment yield
увеличивать ~/у (uvelíchivat' ~/u) to increase returns on capital investment
Форм/а (fórm/a) f. form, method
организационные ~/ы (organizatsiónnye ~/y) organizational forms
печатная ~ (pechátnaia ~) printed form
различительная ~ (razlichítel'naia ~) distinct configuration {as of a logo}
~ документов (~ dokuméntov) form of documents
~ квитанции (~ kvitántsii) receipt form
~ коносамента (~ konosaménta) form of bill of lading
~ контракта (~ kontrákta) standard form contract
~ платежа (~ platezhá) method of payment
~ расписки (~ raspíski) receipt form
~ расчёта (~ raschióta) method of payment
Фрахт (frakht) m. freight
аванс ~/а (aváns ~/a) ~ advance
аккордный ~ (akkórdnyi ~) lumpsum ~
базисный ~ (bázisnyi ~) base ~
взыскание ~/а (vzyskánie ~/a) collection of ~
двойной ~ (dvoinói ~) double ~
дистанционный ~ (distantsiónnyi ~) distance ~
доходы от ~/а (dokhódy ot ~/a) ~ revenues
комиссия с ~/а (komíssiia s ~/a) ~ commission
мёртвый ~ (miórtvyi ~) dead ~

морской ~ (morskói ~) ocean-going ~
надбавка к ~/у (nadbávka k ~/u) surcharge on ~
налог на ~ (nalóg na ~) ~ tax
обратный ~ (obrátnyi ~) return ~
обусловленный ~ (obuslóvlennyi ~) agreed ~
оплата ~/а (opláta ~/a) collection of ~
плата за ~ по чартеру (pláta za ~ po chárteru) charter hire
повышать ~ (povyshát' ~) to increase ~
получить ~ (poluchít' ~) to receive ~
поступления от ~/а (postupléniia ot ~/a) ~ earnings
прибавка к ~/у (pribávka k ~/u) primage
размер ~/а (razmér ~/a) amount of ~
расчёт ~/а (raschiót ~/a) calculation of ~
речной ~ (rechnói ~) inland (river) ~
сквозной ~ (skvoznói ~) through ~
скидка с ~/а (skídka s ~/a) ~ rebate
ставки ~/а (stávki ~/a) shipping rates
трамповый ~ (trámpovyi ~) tramp ~
уплатить ~ (uplatít' ~) to pay ~
условия ~/а (uslóviia ~/a) terms of ~
экспортный ~ (éksportnyi ~) outbound ~
~ "ад валорем" (~ ad valórem) ad valorem ~
~ в оба конца (~ v óba kontsá) ~ both ways
~ в один конец (~ v odín konéts) outgoing ~
~ за транзитный провоз грузов (~ za tranzítnyi provóz grúzov) in-transit ~
~ и плата за простой судна (~ i pláta za prostói súdna) ~ and demurrage
~, исчисляемый со стоимости груза (~, ischisliáemyi so stóimosti grúza) ~ ad valorem
~ оплачен до (~ opláchen do) ~ paid to ...

~ оплачивается предварительно (~ opláchivaetsia predvarítel'no) ~ is prepayable
~ по чартеру (~ po chárteru) charter ~
~, уплачиваемый в месте назначения (~, uplachiváemyi v méste naznachéniia) ~ payable at destination
~, уплачиваемый в порту выгрузки (~, uplachiváemyi v portú výgruzki) ~ forward

Фрахтовани/е (frakhtováni/e) n. affreightment, chartering
договор о ~/и судна (dogovór o ~/i súdna) freight contract
договор о ~/и судна на время (dogovór o ~/i súdna na vrémia) time charter
письмо, подтверждающее ~ (pis'mó, podtverzhdáiushchee ~) fixing letter
производить ~ судов (proizvodít' ~ sudóv) to perform vessel chartering
рейсовое ~ (réisovoe ~) voyage chartering
стоимость ~/я (stóimost' ~/ia) freightage
~ в тайм-чартер (~ v táim-chárter) time chartering
~ на круговой рейс (~ na krugovói reis) round trip chartering
~ на последовательные рейсы (~ na poslédovatel'nye réisy) consecutive voyage charter
~ судна без экипажа (~ súdna bez ekipázha) bare-boat charter
~ судна необходимого тоннажа (~ súdna neobkhodímogo tonnázha) chartering at necessary tonnage
~ тоннажа (~ tonnázha) freight booking

Фрахтовател/ь (frakhtovátel/') m. affreighter, charterer
агент ~/я (agént ~/ia) charterer's agent
брокер ~/я (bróker ~/ia) charterer's broker
оговорка о прекращении ответственности ~/я (ogovórka o prekrashchénii otvétstvennosti ~/ia) cessation clause
ответственность ~/я по тайм-чартеру (otvétstvennost' ~/ia po

táim-chárteru) time-charter's liability
по выбору ~/ей (po výboru ~/ei) at charterer's option
пошлины подлежат оплате ~/ем (póshliny podlezhát opláte ~/em) charterer pays duties
согласно распоряжению ~/ей (soglásno rasporiazhéniiu ~/ei) as ordered by the charterers

Фрахтовать (frakhtovát') v. to affreight, to charter
Фрахтовщик (frakhtovshchik) m. carrier (freight)
Фрахтовый (frakhtóvyi) adj. charter, freight
Фри-аут (frí-áut) adv. free out and free discharge
Фри-ин (fri-in) free in
~ со штивкой (~ so shtívkoi) free in and stowed
~ с размещением (~ s razmeshchéniem) free in and trimmed

Функционировать (funktsionírovat') v. to function
Фунт (funt) m. pound
в ~/ах стерлингов (v ~/akh stérlingov) in ~s sterling
девальвация ~/a стерлингов (deval'vátsiia ~/a stérlingov) devaluation of the ~ sterling
египетский ~ (egípetskii ~) Egyptian ~
заём в ~/ах стерлингов (zaióm v ~/akh stérlingov) loan denominated in ~s sterling
кредит в ~/ах стерлингов (kredít v ~/akh stérlingov) credit denominated in ~s sterling
курс в ~/ах стерлингов (kurs v ~/akh stérlingov) sterling rate
обменивать ~/ы на доллары (obménivat' ~/y na dóllary) to exchange ~s for dollars
паритет ~/a стерлингов (paritét ~/a stérlingov) parity of the ~ sterling
платёж в ~/ах стерлингов (platiózh v ~/akh stérlingov) payment in ~s sterling
разменять ~/ы (razmeniát' ~/y) to change a ~ note
спрос на ~/ы стерлингов (spros na ~/y stérlingov) demand for ~s sterling

счёт в ~/ах стерлингов (schiót v ~/akh stérlingov) account denominated in ~s sterling
тратта с платежом в ~/ах стерлингов (trátta s platezhóm v ~/akh stérlingov) sterling draft bill
~ стерлингов (~ stérlingov) ~ sterling

Фьючерский (f'iúcherskii) *adj.* futures
~ рынок (~ rýnok) ~ market

Х

Хайринг (kháiring) *m.* hiring
Халатность (khalátnost') *f.* carelessness, slipshod work
Халатный (khalátnyi) *adj.* careless, part-time, slipshod
Халтура (khaltúra) *f.* part-time job, slipshod work
Халтурить (khaltúrit') *v.* to moonlight, to work in a slipshod manner
Характеристика (kharakterístika) *f.* characteristics, personnel report
качественная ~ (káchestvennaia ~) qualitative characteristics
подробная ~ (podróbnaia ~) detailed characteristics
техническая ~ (tekhnícheskaia ~) technical characteristics
эксплуатационная ~ (ekspluatatsiónnaia ~) operational characteristics
Хеджирование (khedzhirovánie) *n.* hedging
~ покупкой (~ pokúpkoi) buying hedge
~ продажей (~ prodázhei) selling hedge
Хищени/е (khishchéni/e) *n.* embezzlement, pilferage, plunder
страховать товар против ~/я (strakhovát' továr prótiv ~/ia) to insure goods against pilferage
Ходатайств/о (khodátaistv/o) *n.* application, petition, request
обращаться с ~/ом (obrashchát'sia s ~/om) to petition
отказывать в ~/е (otkázyvat' v ~/e) to deny an application

подавать ~ (podavát' ~) to make a petition
принимать ~ (prinimát' ~) to receive a petition
удовлетворять ~ (udovletvoriát' ~) to grant a petition
~ об аннулировании (~ ob annulírovanii) application for cancellation
~ об отсрочке (~ ob otsróchke) petition for postponement
~ о возмещении убытков (~ o vozmeshchénii ubýtkov) application for compensation
~ о выдаче патента (~ o výdache paténta) patent application
~ о пересмотре решения (~ o peresmótre reshéniia) petition for review
~ о проведении экспертизы (~ o provedénii ekspertízy) request for examination
~ о регистрации (~ o registrátsii) application for registration
Ходк/ий (khódk/ii) *adj.* saleable
~/ая продукция (~/aia prodúktsiia) salable products
Хозрасчёт (khozraschiót) *m.* cost accounting, self-sufficiency
быть на ~/е (byt' na ~/e) to operate on a cost accounting basis
внутрисистемный ~ (vnutrisistémnyi ~) intra-system cost accounting
переводить ~ (perevodít' ~) to transfer to cost accounting
переход предприятия на ~ (perekhód predpriiátiia na ~) transition of enterprise to self-sufficiency
переходить на полный ~ (perekhodít' na pólnyi ~) to transition to complete self-sufficiency
полный ~ (pólnyi ~) full-scale cost accounting
работа на базе ~/a (rabóta na báze ~/a) work on a cost accounting basis
система ~/a (sistéma ~/a) economic accounting system
Хозрасчётный (khozraschiótnyi) *adj.* cost accounting, self-sustaining
Хозяин (khoziáin) *m.* boss, master of the household, owner, proprietor

Хозяйка (khoziáika) f. boss, mistress of the household, landlady, proprietress

Хозяйственный (khoziáistvennyi) adj. economic

Хозяйств/о (khoziáistv/o) n. economy, farm, industry

ведение сельского ~/a (vedénie sél'skogo ~/a) farming

внедрение в народное ~ (vnedrénie v naródnoe ~) application to the national economy

всемирное ~ (vsemírnoe ~) global economy

городское ~ (gorodskóe ~) urban economy

зерновое ~ (zernovóe ~) grain economy

лесное ~ (lesnóe ~) forestry

мировое ~ (mirovóe ~) world economy

многоотраслевое ~ (mnogootraslevóe ~) multiple production farm

народное ~ (naródnoe ~) national economy

натуральное ~ (naturál'noe ~) natural economy

опытное ~ (ópytnoe ~) experimental farm

плановое ~ (plánovoe ~) planned economy

развитие народного ~/a (razvítie naródnogo ~/a) national economic development

рентабельное ~ (rentábel'noe ~) profitable economy

рыбное ~ (rýbnoe ~) fish industry

рыночное ~ (rýnochnoe ~) market economy

сельское ~ (sél'skoe ~) agriculture

складское ~ (skládskoe ~) storage facilities

структура ~/a (struktúra ~/a) structure of the economy

транспортное ~ (tránsportnoe ~) transport facilities

Хозяйствовани/е (khoziáistvovani/e) n. economic management

методы ~/я (métody ~/ia) methods of ~

Холст (kholst) m. canvas

упаковочный ~ (upakóvochnyi ~) packing ~

Хранение (khranénie) n. storage

временное ~ (vrémennoe ~) temporary ~

длительное {долгосрочное} ~ (dlítel'noe {dolgosróchnoe} ~) long-term ~

договор ~/я (dogovór ~/ia) ~ agreement

закрытое ~ (zakrýtoe ~) indoor ~

качество ~/я (káchestvo ~/ia) ~ quality

кратковременное ~ (kratkovrémennoe ~) short-term ~

место для ~/я (mésto dlia ~/ia) ~ space

на ~/и у перевозчика (na ~/i u perevózchika) in carrier's custody

небрежное ~ (nebrézhnoe ~) negligent ~

неправильное ~ (neprávil'noe ~) improper ~

несоответствующее ~ (nesootvétstvuiushchee ~) inadequate ~

нормальное ~ (normál'noe ~) normal ~

обеспечивать ~ (obespéchivat' ~) to provide ~

ограниченное ~ (ograníchennoe ~) limited ~

открытое ~ {под открытым небом} (otkrýtoe ~ {pod otkrýtym nébom}) outside ~

операция ~/я (operátsiia ~/ia) ~ operations

правила ~/я (právila ~/ia) ~ regulations

принимать на ~ (prinimát' na ~) to accept for ~

проверка ~/я (provérka ~/ia) ~ inspection

расходы по ~/ю (raskhódy po ~/iu) ~ expenses

резервное ~ (rezérvnoe ~) standby ~

сдавать на ~ (sdavát' na ~) to turn in for ~

система ~/я (sistéma ~/ia) ~ system

складское ~ (skladskóe ~) warehousing

соответствующее ~ (sootvétstvuiushchee ~) adequate ~

способ ~/я (spósob ~/ia) mode of ~

срок ~/я (srok ~/ia) period of ~
сто́имость ~/я (stóimost' ~/ia)
cost of ~
температу́ра ~/я (temperatúra
~/ia) ~ temperature
усло́вия ~/я (uslóviia ~/ia) ~
conditions
~ в мешка́х (~ v meshkákh) ~ in
bags
~ в холоди́льнике (~ v
kholodíl'nike) cold ~
~ гото́вой проду́кции (~ gotovói
prodúktsii) shelf ~
~ гру́за (~ grúza) ~ of cargo
~ гру́зов на при́стани (~ grúzov
na prístani) wharfage
~ дел (~ del) document ~
~ запчасте́й (~ zapchastéi) ~ of
spare parts
~ нава́лом (~ naválom) bulk ~
~ на тамо́женном скла́де (~ na
tamózhennom skláde) ~ at a
customs warehouse
~ проду́кции (~ prodúktsii) ~ of
goods
~ проду́кции ма́лыми па́ртиями (~
prodúktsii málymi pártiiami)
small-lot ~
~ ремо́нтного фо́нда (~ remóntnogo
fónda) pending-repair ~
~ с перехо́дящим оста́тком (~ s
perekhodiáshchim ostátkom)
carryover ~
~ та́ры на скла́де (~ táry na
skláde) warehousing of tare
~ това́ров на ~/e (~ továrov na
~/e) ~ of goods at a warehouse
~ у термина́ла (~ u terminála)
terminal ~
Храни́лище (khranílishche) n.
depository, depot, reservoir,
storage
Ху́тор (khútor) m. farm {private}

Ц

Царь (tsar') m. tsar
Цари́зм (tsarízm) m. tsarism
Цвет (tsvet) m. color
в ~/e (v ~/e) in ~
измене́ние ~/a (izmenénie ~/a)
discoloration
основно́й ~ (osnovnói ~) primary
~

отклоне́ние (расхожде́ние) в ~/e
(otklonénie raskhozhdénie v ~/e)
deviation in ~
Целево́й (tselevói) adj. purposeful
Целесообра́зность
(tselesoobráznost') f.
advisability, expediency
экономи́ческая и технологи́ческая
~ (ekonomícheskaia i tekhnologícheskaia ~) economic and
technological expediency
Це́лостность (tsélostnost') f.
integrity
Цен/а́ (tsen/á) f. price
ба́зисная ~ (bázisnaia ~) base ~
без нарица́тельной ~/ы (bez
naritsátel'noi ~/y) no par value
биржева́я ~ (birzheváia ~)
exchange ~
бро́совая ~ (brósovaia ~) dumping
~
валова́я ~ (valováia ~) gross ~
валова́я ~ на мирово́м ры́нке
(valováia ~ na mirovóm rýnke)
world gross ~
веду́щая ~ (vedúshchaia ~)
guideline ~
взду́тые ~/ы (vzdútye ~/ý)
inflated ~/s
взима́ть ~/у (vzimát' ~/ú) to
charge a ~
включа́ть в ~/у това́ра
(vkliuchát' v ~/u továra) to
include in the ~ of a good
внешнеторго́вые ~/ы
(vneshnetorgóvye ~/ý) external
~s
внутрифи́рменные ~/ы
(vnutrifírmennye ~/ý) transfer
~s
возмеща́ть ~/у (vozmeshchát' ~/ú
to recover a ~
возро́сшие ~/ы (vozrósshie ~/ý)
increased ~s
война́ ~/ (voiná ~/) ~ war
вы́годная ~ (výgodnaia ~)
profitable ~
вы́купная ~ (vykupnáia ~)
redemption ~
выпускна́я ~ (vypusknáia ~) issu
~
выруча́ть ~/у (vyruchát' ~/u) to
realize a ~
высо́кая ~ (vysókaia ~) high ~
вы́сшая ~ (výsshaia ~) highest ~
вы́чет из ~/ы (výchet iz ~/ý)
deduction from a ~

вышеуказанная ~ (vysheukázannaia ~) above-mentioned ~
вычитать из ~/ы (vychitát' iz ~/ý) to deduct from a ~
гарантированная ~ (garantírovannaia ~) guaranteed ~
гибкая ~ (gíbkaia ~) flexible ~
глобальная ~ (globál'naia ~) global ~
государственные ~/ы (gosudárstvennye ~/y) government-set ~s
данные о ~/ах (dánnye o ~/ákh) pricing data
движение ~/ (dvizhénie ~/) ~ behavior
двойная ~ (dvoináia ~) dual ~
действительная ~ (deistvítel'naia ~) real ~
демпинговая ~ (démpingovaia ~) dumping ~
диктовать ~/ы (diktovát' ~/y) to dictate ~s
дилерская ~ (dílerskaia ~) dealer ~
дифференциация ~/ (differentsiátsiia ~/) ~ differentiation
добиться более высокой ~/ы (dobít'sia bólee vysókoi ~/ý) to obtain a lower ~
добиться снижения ~/ы (dobít'sia snizhéniia ~/ý) to obtain a discount
договариваться о ~/е (dogovárivat'sia o ~/é) to negotiate a ~
договориться о ~/е (dogovorít'sia o ~/é) to come to an agreement on a ~
договорённость о ~/е (dogovoriónnost' o ~/é) agreement on a ~
договорная ~ (dogovórnaia ~) contract ~
дополнительная ~ (dopolnítel'naia ~) additional ~
доступная ~ (dostúpnaia ~) moderate ~
дутая ~ (dútaia ~) "fancy" ~ {pejorative}
единая ~ (edínaia ~) uniform ~
ежеквартальный пересмотр ~/ (ezhekvartál'nyi peresmótr ~/) quarterly ~ review

желаемая ~ (zheláemaia ~) desired ~
зависеть от ~/ы (zavíset' ot ~/ý) to depend on a ~
завышать ~/у (zavyshát' ~/u) to overcharge
завышенная ~ (zavýshennaia ~) overcharge
закупочная ~ (zakúpochnaia ~) purchase ~
замораживание ~ (zamorázhivanie ~) ~ freeze
замораживать ~/ы (zamorázhivat' ~/y) to freeze ~s
занижать ~/у (zanizhát' ~/u) to lower a ~
заниженная ~ (zanízhennaia ~) undercharged ~
запрашиваемая ~ (zapráshivaemaia ~) asking ~
запродажная ~ (zaprodázhnaia ~) selling ~
зональная ~ (zonál'naia ~) zone ~
зональное установление ~/ (zonál'noe ustanovlénie ~/) zonal pricing
изменение ~/ы (izmenénie ~/y) ~ adjustment
импортная ~ (ímportnaia ~) import ~
индекс ~/ (índeks ~/) ~ index
информация о ~/ах (informátsiia o ~/ákh) ~ information
итоговая ~ (itógovaia ~) aggregate ~
калькулировать ~/у (kal'kulírovat' ~/u) to calculate a ~
калькуляция ~/ (kal'kuliátsiia ~/) ~ calculation
категория ~/ (kategóriia ~/) ~ category
колебания ~/ (kolebániia ~/) ~ fluctuations
колебания ~/ на рынке (kolebániia ~/ na rýnke) market fluctuations
колеблющаяся ~ (kolébliushchaiasia ~) fluctuating ~
конкретная ~ (konkrétnaia ~) concrete (solid) ~
конкуренция по ~/ам (konkuréntsiia po ~/am) ~ competition

конкурирующая ~
(konkuríruiushchaia ~)
competitive ~
контроль над ~/ами (kontról' nad
~/ámi) ~ control
контрактная ~ (kontráktnaia ~)
contract ~
конъюнктурная ~ (kon"iunktúrnaia
~) equilibrium ~s
корректировать ~/ы
(korrektírovat' ~/y) to correct
~s
котировальная ~ (kotirovál'naia
~) quoted ~
котировать ~/у (kotírovat' ~/u)
to quote a ~
крайняя ~ (kráiniaia ~) outside
~
купить по ~/е, ниже предложенной
(kupít' po ~/é, nízhe
predlózhennoi) to buy at less
than asking price
лимит / (limít ~/) ~ ceiling
лучшая ~ (lúchshaia ~) best ~
льготная ~ (l'gótnaia ~)
preferential ~
максимальная ~ (maksimál'naia ~)
maximum ~
маркировка ~/ (markiróvka ~/) ~
marking
масштаб ~/ (masshtáb ~/)
standard of ~s
международная ~ (mezhdunaródnaia
~) international ~
местная ~ (méstnaia ~) local ~
метод калькуляции ~/ (métod
kal'kuliátsii ~/) method of
calculation of ~s
механизм ~/ (mekhanízm ~/) ~
mechanism
минимальная ~ (minimál'naia ~)
minimum ~
монопольная ~ (monopól'naia ~)
monopoly ~
набавлять ~/у (nabavliát' ~/u)
to bid up a ~ {at auction}
надбавка к ~/е (nadbávka k ~/é)
mark-up
назначать ~/у (naznachát' ~/u)
to set a ~
назначать более низкую ~/у
(naznachát' bólee nízkuiu ~/u)
to set a lower ~
назначать завышенную ~/у
(naznachát' zavýshennuiu ~/u) to
overcharge

назначать низкую ~/у (naznachát'
nízkuiu ~/u) to set a low ~
назначать твёрдую ~/у
(naznachát' tviórduiu ~/u) to
give a firm ~
назначение ~/ нетто (naznachénie
~/ nétto) net pricing
назначение ~/ с надбавкой
(naznachénie ~/ s nadbávkoi)
cost plus pricing
назначенная ~ (naznáchennaia ~)
set ~
наилучшая ~ (nailúchshaia ~)
better ~
наилучшая возможная ~
(nailúchshaia vozmózhnaia ~)
best possible ~
накидка на ~/у (nakídka na ~/u)
addition to the ~
нарицательная ~ (naritsátel'naia
~) nominal ~
начальная ~ (nachál'naia ~)
starting ~
невысокая ~ (nevysókaia ~)
moderate ~
негибкая ~ (negíbkaia ~)
inflexible ~
недоступные ~/ы (nedostúpnye
~/y) prohibitive ~s
неизменная ~ (neizménnaia ~)
constant ~
неконтролируемые ~/ы
(nekontrolíruemye ~/y)
uncontrollable ~ s
непомерная ~ (nepomérnaia ~)
ramp pricing
нереальные ~/ы (nereál'nye ~/ý)
unrealistic ~s
несоответствие в ~/ах
(nesootvétstvie v ~/ákh)
maladjustment of ~s
неустойчивость ~/
(neustóichivost' ~/) instability
of ~s
неустойчивые (нестабильные) ~/ы
(neustóichivye {nestabíl'nye}
~/ý) unstable ~s
низкая ~ (nízkaia ~) low ~
новые ~/ы (nóvye ~/ý) new ~s
ножницы ~/ (nózhnitsy ~/) ~
discrepancy {~ scissors}
номинальная ~ (nominál'naia ~)
nominal ~
нормальная ~ (normál'naia ~)
normal ~
нормативы ~/ (normatívy ~/) ~
norms

обзор ~/ (obzór ~/) ~ review

обозначенная ~ (oboznáchennaia ~) marked ~

обоснованная ~ (obosnóvannaia ~) reasonable ~

обосновывать ~/ы (obosnóvyvat' ~/ý) to justify ~s

обсуждаемые ~/ы (obsuzhdáemye ~/ý) ~s under consideration

обусловленная ~ (obuslóvlennaia ~) stipulated ~

общая (óbshchaia) total ~

общедоступные ~/ы (obshchedostúpnye ~/ý) affordable ~s

обычная ~ (obýchnaia ~) conventional ~

ограничение ~/ (ogranichénie ~/) restriction of ~s

одинаковая ~ (odinákovaia ~) identical ~

ожидаемые ~/ы (ozhidáemye ~/ý) anticipated ~s

оказывать влияние на ~/ы (okázyvat' vliiánie na ~/ý) to exert influence on ~s

окончательная ~ (okonchátel'naia ~) final ~

окончательно договориться о ~/е (okonchátel'no dogovorít'sia o ~/é) to finalize a ~

округление ~/ (okruglénie ~/) rounding off of ~s

определение ~/ы (opredelénie ~/ý) determination of a ~

определять ~/у (opredeliát' ~/u) to determine a ~

оптовая ~ (optóvaia ~) wholesale ~

опубликовывать ~/ы (opublikóvyvat' ~/ý) to publish ~s

ориентировочная ~ (orientiróvochnaia ~) approximated ~

основывать ~/у на (osnóvyvat' ~/u na) to base a ~ on ...

особая ~ (osóbaia ~) extra ~

отдельная ~ (otdél'naia ~) individual ~

отклонения ~/ от стоимости (otklonéniia ~/ ot stóimosti) deviation of ~s from value

относительная ~ (otnosítel'naia ~) relative ~

отправная ~ (otpravnáia ~) reserve ~

официальная ~ (ofitsiál'naia ~) official ~

официально объявленная ~ (ofitsiál'no ob"iávlennaia ~) officially posted ~

оценка ~/ы (otsénka ~/ý) ~ evaluation

ошибка в ~/е (oshíbka v ~/é) error in a ~

падать в ~/е (pádat' v ~/é) to sink in ~

падать резко в ~/е (pádat' rézko v ~/é) to sink sharply in ~

паритетная ~ (paritétnaia ~) parity ~

паушальная ~ (paushál'naia ~) lumpsum ~

первоначальные ~/ы (pervonachál'nye ~/ý) original ~s

переговоры по ~/ам (peregovóry po ~/ám) ~ negotiations

переменные ~/ы (pereménnye ~/ý) cost-related ~s

пересматривать ~/ы (peresmátrivat' ~/ý) to review ~s

пересматривать ~/ы в сторону повышения (peresmátrivat' ~/ý v stóronu povyshéniia) to revise ~s upwards

пересматривать ~/ы в сторону понижения (peresmátrivat' ~/ý v stóronu ponizhéniia) to revise ~s downwards

пересмотр ~/ (peresmótr ~/) ~ renegotiation

пересчитывать ~/ы (pereschítyvat' ~/ý) to recalculate ~s

плановая ~ (plánovaia ~) target ~

платёж по согласованным ~/ам (platiózh po soglasóvannym ~/ám) payment of mutually agreed ~s

платить ~/у (platít' ~/u) to pay the ~

по ~/е (po ~/é) at the ~ of

по ~/е дня (po ~/é dnia) at value

по возросшей ~/е (po vozrósshei ~/é) at an increased ~

по конкретной ~/е (po konkrétnoi ~/é) at a concrete ~

по любой ~/е (po liubói ~/é) at any ~

по максимальной ~/е (po
maksimál'noi ~/é) at a maximum ~
по минимальной ~/е (po
minimál'noi ~/é) at a minimum ~
по нарицательной ~/е (po
naritsátel'noi ~/é) at par
по рыночной ~/е (po rýnochnoi
~/é) at the market ~
по сниженной ~/е (po snízhennoi
~/é) at a reduced ~
по согласованной ~/е (po
soglasóvannoi ~/é) at the agreed
~
по указанной ~/е (po ukázannoi
~/é) at the indicated ~
повышать ~/у (povyshát' ~/u) to
increase the ~
поддержание ~/ (podderzhánie ~/)
~ supports
поддерживать ~/ы (poddérzhivat'
~/ý) to support ~s
поддерживать рыночные ~/ы на
одном уровне (poddérzhivat'
rýnochnye ~/ý na odnóm úrovne)
to peg the market
поднимать ~/у (podnimát' ~/u) to
raise the ~
подписная ~ (podpisnáia ~)
subscription ~
подробная ~ (podróbnaia ~)
detailed ~s
подтверждать ~/у (podtverzhdát'
~/u) to confirm a ~
подтверждение ~/ы
(podtverzhdénie ~/ý)
confirmation of a ~
подтверждённые ~/ы
(podtverzhdiónnye ~/ý) confirmed
~s
подходящая ~ (podkhodiáshchaia
~) fair ~
позиционная ~ (pozitsiónnaia ~)
itemized ~
показывать ~/у каждой позиции в
отдельности (pokázyvat' ~/u
kázhdoi pozítsii v otdél'nosti)
to itemize ~s
покрывать увеличение ~/ы
(pokryvát' uvelichénie ~/ý) to
cover a ~ increase
покупать по ~/е (pokupát' po
~/é) to buy at the ~ of ...
покупать по ~/е ниже
нарицательной (pokupát' po ~/é
nízhe naritsátel'noi) to buy at
below par

покупная ~ (pokupnáia ~)
purchase ~
полная ~ (pólnaia ~) full ~
получать ~/у (poluchát' ~/u) to
get a ~
полученная ~ (polúchennaia ~)
received ~
поправка в ~/е (poprávka v ~/é)
~ adjustment
поправка на изменение ~/ы
(poprávka na izmenénie ~/ý) ~
level adjustment
поставлять товар по ~/ам
(postavliát' továr po ~/ám) to
supply goods at ... ~s
постоянная ~ (postoiánnaia ~)
fixed ~
посчитать отдельную ~/у
(poschitát' otdél'nuiu ~/u) to
charge an extra ~
поштучная ~ (poshtúchnaia ~) ~
per item
правильная ~ (právil'naia ~)
correct ~
превышать ~/у (prevyshát' ~/u)
to exceed a ~
предварительная ~
(predvarítel'naia ~) preliminary
~
предварительная итоговая ~
(predvarítel'naia itógovaia ~)
estimated total ~
предельная ~ (predél'naia ~)
limit ~
предлагаемая ~ (predlagáemaia ~)
offering ~
предлагать ~/у (predlagát' ~/u)
to make a bid
предложение ~/ы (predlozhénie
~/ý) bid, offer
предложение по самой низкой ~/е
(predlozhénie po sámoi nízkoi
~/é) lowest bid
предоставлять особую ~/у
(predostavliát' osóbuiu ~/u) to
grant a special ~
представлять бюджетные ~/ы
(predstavliát' biudzhétnye ~/ý)
to present a budget
прейскурант базисных ~/
(preiskuránt bázisnykh ~/) base
~ schedule
прейскурант с ~/ами СИФ
(preiskuránt s ~/ámi sif) CIF ~-
list

прейскурант с ~/ами ФОБ
(preiskuránt s ~/ámi fob) FOB ~-
list
прейскурантная ~
(preiskurántnaia ~) standard
list ~
преобладающая ~
(preobladáiushchaia ~)
prevailing ~
препятствовать падению ~/
(prepiátstvovat' padéniiu ~/) to
prevent a decline in ~s
приблизительная ~
(priblizítel'naia ~) approximate
~
привлекательная ~
(privlekátel'naia ~) attractive
~
приемлемые ~/ы (priémlemye ~/ý)
acceptable ~s
применять ~/у к (primeniát' ~/u
k) to apply ~s to ...
принимать ~/у (prinimát' ~/u) to
accept a ~
проверять ~/ы (proveriát' ~/ý)
to verify ~s
продавать выше номинальной ~/ы
(prodavát' výshe nominál'noi
~/ý) to sell over par
продавать ниже номинальной ~/ы
(prodavát' nízhe nominál'noi
~/ý) to sell below par
продавать по ~/е (prodavát' po
~/é) to sell at a ~ of ...
продажная ~ (prodázhnaia ~)
sales ~
производить расчёт по ~/е
(proizvodít' raschiót po ~/é) to
effect payment at a ~ of ...
просить ~/у (prosít' ~/u) to ask
a ~
публикуемая ~ (publikúemaia ~)
published ~
пункт об изменении ~/ (punkt ob
izменénii ~/) ~ variation clause
разбивать ~/у (razbivát' ~/u) to
break down a ~
разница в ~/ax (razbívka ~/ po
kolíchestvu i sórtam ráznitsa v
~/ákh) difference in ~s
разумная ~ (razúmnaia ~)
reasonable ~
рассчитывать ~/ы (rasschítyvat'
~/ý) to calculate ~s
растущие ~/ы (rastúshchie ~/ý)
escalating ~s

расхождения ~/ (raskhozhdéniia
~/) ~ disbursion, divergence
расчёт ~/ (raschiót ~/) ~
computation
расчётная ~ (raschiótnaia ~)
settlement ~
реализационная ~
(realizatsiónnaia ~) realizable
~
реализовать ~/у (realizovát'
~/u) to realize a ~
регулировать ~/ы (regulírovat'
~/ý) to regulate ~s
регулирование ~/ (regulírovanie
~/) ~ regulation
регулируемые ~/ы (regulíruemye
~/ý) regulated ~s
резервируемая ~ (rezervíruemaia
~) reserve ~
рекомендуемые ~/ы (rekomendúemye
~/ý) recommended ~s
розничная ~ (róznichnaia ~)
retail ~
рост ~/ (rost ~/) growth of ~s
рыночная ~ (rýnochnaia ~) market
~
самая высокая ~ (sámaia vysókaia
~) highest ~
самая низкая ~ (sámaia nízkaia
~) lowest ~
сбалансированная ~
(sbalansírovannaia ~)
equilibrium ~
сбивать ~/ы (sbivát' ~/ý) to
undercut ~
сегодняшняя ~ (segódniashniaia
~) today's ~
сезонные ~/ы (sezónnye ~/ý)
seasonal ~s
скользящие ~/ы (skol'ziáshchie
~/ý) sliding-scale ~s
скорректированная ~
(skorrektírovannaia ~) corrected
~
скидка с ~/ы (skídka s ~/ý)
discount ~
скольжение ~/ (skol'zhénie ~/) ~
escalation
снижать ~/ы (snizhát' ~/ý) to
lower ~s
снижающиеся ~/ы
(snizháiushchiesia ~/ý) falling
~s
сниженная ~ (snízhennaia ~)
reduced ~

совместный пересмотр ~/
(sovméstnyi peresmótr ~/) ~
renegotiation
согласиться на ~/у (soglasít'sia
na ~/u) to agree to a ~
согласованная ~ (soglasóvannaia
~) agreed ~
согласовать ~/ы (soglasovát'
~/ý) to agree on ~s
создать конкуренцию по ~/ам
(sozdát' konkuréntsiiu po ~/ám)
to effect ~ competition
соответствующая ~
(sootvétstvuiushchaia ~)
corresponding ~
соотношение цен (sootnoshénie
~/) parity of ~s
сопоставимые ~/ы (sopostavímye
~/ý) comparable ~s
сопоставление цен (sopostavlénie
~/) comparison of ~s
сохранять ~/ы (sokhraniát' ~/ý)
to maintain ~s
спираль ~/ (spirál' ~/) ~ spiral
справочная ~ (správochnaia ~)
posted ~
сравнивать ~/ы (srávnivat' ~/ý)
to compare ~s
средняя ~ (srédniaia ~) average
~
средняя рыночная ~ (srédniaia
rýnochnaia ~) average market ~
стабилизация ~/ (stabilizátsiia
~/) ~ stabilization
стабилизировать ~/ы
(stabilizírovat' ~/ý) to
stabilize ~s
стабильная ~ (stabíl'naia ~)
stable ~
стабильность ~/ (stabíl'nost'
~/) stability of ~s
стандартная ~ (standártnaia ~)
standard ~
структура ~/ (struktúra ~/) ~
structure
существующие ~/ы
(sushchestvúiushchie ~/ý)
prevailing ~s
сходная ~ (skhódnaia ~) fair ~
тарифная ~ (tarífnaia ~) tariff
~
твёрдая ~ (tviórdaia ~) firm ~
текущая ~ (tekúshchaia ~)
current ~
тенденция ~/ (tendéntsiia ~/) ~
trend

тенденция рыночных ~/
(tendéntsiia rýnochnykh ~/)
market ~ trend
типичная ~ (tipíchnaia ~)
typical ~
торговаться о ~/е (torgovát'sia
o ~/é) to bargain
торговая ~ (torgóvaia ~) trade ~
точная ~ (tóchnaia ~) exact ~
увеличивать ~/ы (uvelíchivat'
~/ý) to increase ~s
увеличивать ~/у в 2 раза
(uvelíchivat' ~/u v dva ráza) to
double the ~
увеличивать ~/у в 3 раза
(uvelíchivat' ~/u v tri ráza) to
triple the ~
увеличивать ~/у на ... %
(uvelíchivat' ~/u na ...) to
increase the ~ by ... %
удержание из ~/ы (uderzhánie iz
~/ý) deduction from the ~
удерживать ~/у (udérzhivat' ~/u)
to sustain a ~
удерживать из ~/ы (udérzhivat'
iz ~/ý) to deduct from a ~
удовлетворительные ~/ы
(udovletvorítel'nye ~/ý)
satisfactory ~ s
указанная ~ (ukázannaia ~)
indicated ~
указатель ~/ (ukazátel' ~/) ~
index
указывать ~/у (ukázyvat' ~/u) to
indicate a ~
уменьшать ~/у (umen'shát' ~/u)
to reduce a ~
умеренная ~ (umérennaia ~)
moderate ~
упорядочить ~/ы (uporiádochit'
~/ý) to rationalize ~s
урегулировать ~/у (uregulírovat'
~/u) to settle a ~
уровень ~/ (úroven' ~/) ~ level
условленная ~ (uslóvlennaia ~)
stipulated ~
условная ~ (uslóvnaia ~)
conditional ~
устанавливать ~/у (ustanávlivat'
~/u) to establish a ~
установление ~/ (ustanovlénie
~/) establishment of ~s
установленная ~ (ustanóvlennaia
~) established ~
устойчивая ~ (ustóichivaia ~)
steady ~

401

устойчивость ~/ (ustóichivost'
~/) ~ stability
уступать в ~/e (ustupát' v ~/é)
to give a discount
уступка в ~/e (ustúpka v ~/é)
discount
уточнять ~/y (utochniát' ~/u) to
specify a ~
фабричная ~ (fabríchnaia ~)
factory ~
фактическая ~ (faktícheskaia ~)
actual ~
фактурная ~ (faktúrnaia ~)
invoice ~
фактурная ~ за единицу товара
(faktúrnaia ~ za edinítsu
továra) invoice unit ~
фиксация ~/ (fiksátsiia ~/) ~
fixing
фиксированная ~ (fiksírovannaia
~) fixed ~
фиксировать ~/y (fiksírovat'
~/u) to fix a ~
формула ~/ы (fórmula ~/ý) ~
formula
формула пересмотра ~/ (fórmula
peresmótra ~/) ~ revision
formula
штучная ~ (shtúchnaia ~) piece ~
эквивалентная ~ (ekvivaléntnaia
~) equivalent ~
экономить на ~/ах (ekonómit' na
~/ákh) to economize on ~s
экономия на ~/ах (ekonómiia na
~/ákh) ~ savings
экспортная ~ (éksportnaia ~)
export ~
эскалация ~/ (eskalátsiia ~/)
escalation of ~s
этикетка с ~/ой (etikétka s
~/ói) ~ tag
~ без включения пошлины (~ bez
vkliuchéniia póshliny) inbond ~
~ без обязательства (~ bez
obiazátel'stva) ~ without
obligation
~ без упаковки (~ bez upakóvki)
~ excluding packing
~ в валюте (~ v valiúte) ~ in
convertible currency
~/ы включают ВАТ (~/ý
vkliucháiut vat) ~ including VAT
~, включающая пошлину (~,
vkliucháiushchaia póshlinu)
duty- paid ~
~, включающая расходы по
доставке (~, vkliucháiushchaia

raskhódy po dostávke) delivered
~
~, включающая фрахт и пошлину
(~, vkliucháiushchaia frakht i
póshlinu) ~ including freight
and duty
~ внутреннего рынка (~
vnútrennego rýnka) domestic
market ~
~, выгодная для покупателей (~,
výgodnaia dlia pokupátelei)
buyers' ~
~, выгодная для продавцов (~,
výgodnaia dlia prodavtsóv)
sellers' ~
~ выше номинала (~ výshe
nominála) premium ~
~ действительна до (~
deistvítel'na do) ~ valid until
~ для оптовых покупателей (~
dlia optóvykh pokupátelei)
wholesale ~
~ дня (~ dnia) present-day ~
~ до повышения (~ do
povyshéniia) pre-increase ~
~ за весовую единицу (~ za
vesovúiu edinítsu) ~ per weight
unit
~ завода-изготовителя (~ zavóda-
izgotovítelia) manufacturer's ~
~ за вычетом скидки (~ za
výchetom skídki) ~ less discount
~ за единицу товара (~ za
edinítsu továra) ~ per unit
~ за комплект (~ za komplékt) ~
per set
~ за метрическую тонну (~ za
metrícheskuiu tónnu) ~ per
metric ton
~ за наличные (~ za nalíchnye)
cash ~
~ за фунт (~ za funt) ~ per
pound
~ за штуку (~ za shtúku) ~ per
piece
~ КАФ (~ kaf) ~ C&F
~ локо (~ lóko) loco ~
~ местного рынка (~ méstnogo
rýnka) local market ~
~ мирового рынка (~ mirovógo
rýnka) world market ~
~/ы могут быть аннулированы или
изменены без предупреждения (~/ý
mógut byt' annulírovany íli
izméneny bez preduprezhdéniia)
~s may be annulled or changed
without warning

~ на день отгрузки (~ na den'
otgrúzki) ~ on day of shipment
~ на мировом рынке (~ na mirovóm
rýnke) ~ on the world market
~/ы на потребительские товары
(~/ý na potrebítel'skie továry)
consumer ~s
~ на рекламу (~ na reklámu)
advertising charge
~ на сельскохозяйственные
продукты (~ na
sel'skokhoziástvennye prodúkty)
produce ~s
~ на товар (~ na továr)
commodity ~
~ на импортные товары (~ na
ímportnye továry) import ~s
~ на сырьевые товары (~ na
syr'evye továry) raw material ~s
~/ы не включают ВАТ (~/ý ne
vkliucháiut vat) ~ does not
include VAT
~ нетто (~ nétto) net ~
~/ы остаются без изменений (~/ý
ostaiútsia bez izmenénii) ~s
remain unchanged
~/ы остаются неустойчивыми (~/ý
ostaiútsia neustóichivymi) ~s
remain unsettled
~/ы остаются устойчивыми (~/ý
ostaiútsia ustóichivymi) ~s
remain stable
~, относимая за счёт покупателя
(~, otnosímaia za schiót pokupátelia) ~ chargeable to the buyer
~/ы падают (~/ý pádaiut) ~ s are
falling
~ по валютному курсу (~ po
valiútnomu kúrsu) ~ at the
current exchange rate
~/ы повысились (~/ý povýsilis')
~s are up
~/ы повысились на ... % (~/ý
povýsilis' na) ~s are up ... %
~ подлежит изменению (~
podlezhít izmenéniiu) ~ is
subject to change
~/ы подлежат изменению без
предупреждения (~/ý podlezhát
izmenéniiu bez preduprezhdéniia)
~s are subject to change without
warning
~/ы подлежат изменению в любое
время (~/ý podlezhát izmenéniiu
v liubóe vrémia) ~s are subject
to change at any time

~/ы подлежат подтверждению (~/ý
podlezhát podtverzhdéniiu) ~s
subject to confirmation
~ по кассовым сделкам (~ po
kássovym sdélkam) spot ~
~ по контракту (~ po kontráktu)
contract ~
~ покупателя (~ pokupátelia)
buyer's ~
~/ы понизились (~/ý ponízilis')
~s have dropped
~ по прейскуранту (~ po
preiskurántu) list ~
~ по себестоимости (~ po
sebestóimosti) prime cost
~ по срочным сделкам (~ po
sróchnym sdélkam) terminal ~s
~ поставки (~ postávki) supply ~
~ по тарифу (~ po tarífu) tariff
~
~, предлагаемая изготовителем
(~, predlagáemaia izgotovítelem)
manufacturer's suggested ~
~ предложения (~ predlozhéniia)
~ of an offer
~, предложенная на торгах (~,
predlózhennaia na torgákh)
tender ~
~, предоставляемая конечному
потребителю (~,
predostavliáemaia konéchnomu
potrebíteliu) end-user ~
~ предыдущей сделки (~
predydúshchei sdélki) ~ of the
previous transaction
~ при закрытии биржи (~ pri
zakrýtii bírzhi) closing ~
~ при открытии биржи (~ pri
otkrýtii bírzhi) opening ~
~ при перепродаже (~ pri
pereprodázhe) resale ~
~ при продаже с торгов (~ pri
prodázhe s torgóv) tender ~
~ при уплате наличными (~ pri
upláte nalíchnymi) cash ~
~ при условии немедленной оплаты
наличными (~ pri uslóvii
nemédlennoi opláty nalíchnymi)
spot ~
~/ы применимы к (~/ý primenímy
k) ~s apply to ...
~ производителя (~
proizvodítelia) producer's ~
~ производства (~ proizvódstva)
cost ~
~ с баржи (~ s bárzhi) ~ ex-
barge

~ свободного рынка (~ svobódnogo rýnka) free market ~
~ с выгрузкой на берег (~ s výgruzkoi na béreg) landed ~
~ с доставкой (~ s dostávkoi) delivered ~
~ с надбавкой (~ s nadbávkoi) ~ plus mark-up
~ с немедленной сдачей (~ s nemédlennoi sdáchei) spot market ~
~ со всеми надбавками (~ so vsémi nadbávkami) blanket ~
~ со скидкой (~ so skídkoi) discount ~
~ со склада (~ so skláda) ~ ex-warehouse
~ спасательных работ (~ spasátel'nykh rabót) salvage ~
~ с поправкой на фрахтовые ставки (~ s poprávkoi na frakhtóvye stávki) ~s adjusted for shipping rates
~ с приплатой (~ s priplátoi) cost plus ~
~ спроса (~ sprósa) demand ~
~ с разбивкой по позициям (~ s razbívkoi po pozítsiiam) breakdown ~s
~ с судна (~ s súdna) ~ ex-ship
~ тары (~ táry) packing ~
~ товара (~ továra) commodity ~
~, требуемая продавцом (~, trébuemaia prodavtsóm) seller's asking ~
~, указанная в предложении (~, ukázannaia v predlozhénii) ~ quoted in an offer
~ фактической сделки (~ faktícheskoi sdélki) actual transaction ~
~ ФАС (~ fas) ~ FAS
~ ФАС порт отгрузки, указанный продавцом (~ fas port otgrúzki, ukázannyi prodavtsóm) ~ FAS port of shipment designated by seller
~ ФОБ (~ fob) ~ FOB
~ ФОБ без фабричной упаковки (~ fob bez fabríchnoi upakóvki) ~ FOB factory unboxed
~ ФОБ со штивкой (~ fob so shtívkoi) ~ FOB stowed
~ ФОР (~ for) ~ FOR
~ ФОТ (~ fot) ~ FOT
~ франко-баржа (~ fránko-bárzha) ~ ex-barge

~ франко-вагон (~ fránko-vagón) ~ FOR
~ франко вдоль борта (~ fránko vdol' bórta) ~ FAS
~ франко граница (~ fránko granítsa) ~ free at border
~ франко-завод (~ fránko-zavód) ~ ex factory
~ франко-пристань (~ fránko-prístan') ~ ex quay
~ франко-склад (~ fránko-sklád) ~ ex warehouse
~ франко-судно (~ fránko-súdno) ~ ex ship
~ фрахта (~ frákhta) ~ of freight
~, указанная в счёте-фактуре (~, ukázannaia v schióte-faktúre) ~, indicated in the invoice
Ценз (tsenz) m. qualification
возрастной ~ (vozrastnói ~) age ~
имущественный ~ (imúshchestvennyi ~) property ~
налоговый ~ (nalógovyi ~) tax ~
образовательный ~ (obrazovátel'nyi ~) educational ~
Ценник (tsénnik) m. price list
Ценност/ь (tsénnost/') f. value
валютные ~/и (valiútnye ~/i) securities
депонировать ~/и в банке (deponírovat' ~/i v bánke) to deposit valuables in a bank
единица ~/и (edinítsa ~/i) unit of ~
заложенные ~/и (zalózhennye ~/i) mortgaged valuables
иметь большую ~ (imét' bol'shúiu ~) to have great ~
иметь малую ~ (imét' máluiu ~) to have little ~
материальная ~ (materiál'naia ~) material ~
не иметь никакой ~/и (ne imét' nikakói ~/i) to have no ~
не имеющий ~/и (ne iméiushchii ~/i) valueless
не представлять никакой ~/и (ne predstavliát' nikakói ~/i) to have no ~
переоценка ~/тей (pereotsénka ~/tei) reappraisal of ~s
реальная ~ (reál'naia ~) real ~
Ценный (tsénnyi) adj. valuable

Ценообразовани/е
(tsenoobrazováni/e) *n.* price
formation
    конкурентное ~ (konkuréntnoe ~)
    competitive pricing
    методика ~/я (metódika ~/ia)
    methods of price formation
    практика ~/я (práktika ~/ia)
    pricing practice
    принципы ~/я (príntsipy ~/ia)
    principles of price formation
Центр (tsentr) *m.* center
    быть в ~/е внимания (byt' v ~/e
    vnimániia) to be in the ~ of
    attention
    в ~/е (v ~/e) in the ~
    вычислительный ~
    (vychislítel'nyi ~) computer ~
    деловой ~ (delovói ~) business ~
    информационно-вычислительный ~
    (informatsiónno-vychislítel'nyi
    ~) data processing ~
    информационный ~
    (informatsiónnyi ~) information
    ~
    коммерческий ~ (kommércheskii ~)
    commercial ~
    координационный ~
    (koordinatsiónnyi ~)
    coordination ~
    культурный ~ (kul'túrnyi ~)
    cultural ~
    место в ~/е (mésto v ~/e)
    central location
    научно-исследовательский ~
    (naúchno-isslédovatel'skii ~)
    research ~
    научно-технический ~ (naúchno-
    tekhnícheskii ~) scientific and
    technical ~
    промышленный ~ (promýshlennyi ~)
    industrial ~
    технический ~ (tekhnícheskii ~)
    technical ~
    технологический ~
    (tekhnologícheskii ~)
    technological ~
    торговый ~ (torgóvyi ~) shopping
    ~
    финансовый ~ (finánsovyi ~)
    financial ~
    ~ международной торговли (~
    mezhdunaródnoi torgóvli) world
    trade ~
    ~ обучения (~ obuchéniia)
    training ~

    ~ по профессиональной подготовке
    (~ po professionál'noi
    podgotóvke) professional
    training ~
    ~ распределения (~
    raspredeléniia) distribution ~
Централизованный
(tsentralizóvannyi) *adj.*
centralized
Центральный (tsentrál'nyi) *adj.*
central
Цепной (tsepnói) *adj.* chain
Цессия (tséssiia) *f.* cession,
transfer
Цикл (tsikl) *m.* cycle
    жизненный ~ товара (zhíznennyi ~
    továra) product life ~
Циркуляр (tsirkuliár) *m.* circular
Циркулярный (tsirkuliárnyi) *adj.*
circular
Циркуляция (tsirkuliátsiia) *f.*
circulation
    ~ денег (~ déneg) ~ of money
Цистерн/а (tsistérn/a) *f.* cistern,
tank
    в ~/ах (v ~/akh) in tanks
    железнодорожная ~
    (zheleznodorózhnaia ~) tank car
    ёмкость ~/ы (iómkost' ~/y) tank
    capacity
    перевозить в ~/ах (perevozít' v
    ~/akh) to transport by tank cars
    франко-цистерна (fránko-~) ex-
    tank
    хранить в ~/е (khranít' v ~/e)
    to store in a tank
Цифр/а (tsífr/a) *f.* figure, number,
numeral
    в круглых ~/ах (v krúglykh
    ~/akh) in round figures
    валовые ~/ы (valovýe ~/y) gross
    figures
    вычеркнуть ~/у (výcherknut' ~/u)
    to delete a number
    вышеуказанные ~/ы
    (vysheukázannye ~/y) above-
    mentioned figures
    дать точную ~/у (dat' tóchnuiu
    ~/u) to give an exact figure
    действительная ~
    (deistvítel'naia ~) actual
    figure
    конечная ~ (konéchnaia ~) final
    number
    контрольные ~/ы (kontról'nye
    ~/y) target numbers

круглые ~/ы (krúglye ~/y) round numbers

малодостоверные ~/ы (malodostovérnye ~/y) ill-founded figures

малоубедительные ~/ы (maloubedítel'nye ~/y) unconvincing figures

намеченная ~ (naméchennaia ~) target figure

плановая ~ (plánovaia ~) financial target

предварительная ~ (predvarítel'naia ~) preliminary figure

представлять ~/ы (predstavliát' ~/y) to submit figures

представлять ~/ы в виде таблицы (predstavliát' ~/y v víde tablítsy) to tabulate

приблизительная ~ (priblizítel'naia ~) approximate number

сравнительные ~/ы (sravnítel'nye ~/y) comparable numbers

сумма ~/ами (súmma ~/ami) amount in figures

установить фактическую ~/y (ustanovít' faktícheskuiu ~/u) to establish the actual figure

~/ами (~/ami) in figures

~ переноса (~ perenósa) carryover digit

~/ы с поправкой на сезонные колебания (~/y s poprávkoi na sezónnye kolebániia) adjusted figures

Цифров/ой (tsifrov/ói) adj. digital, numerical

~/ая вычислительная машина (~/áia vychislítel'naia mashína) digital computer

Ч

Чартер (chárter) m. charter

аннулирование ~/a (annulírovanie ~/a) cancellation of a ~

аннулировать ~ (annulírovat' ~) to cancel a ~

банковский ~ (bánkovskii ~) bank ~

брать судно в ~ (brat' súdno v ~) to ~ a vessel

владеть ~/ом (vladét' ~/om) to hold a ~

генеральный ~ (generál'nyi ~) general ~

долгосрочный ~ (dolgosróchnyi ~) long-term ~

зерновой ~ (zernovói ~) grain ~

лесной ~ (lesnói ~) timber ~

линейный ~ (linéinyi ~) berth ~

морской ~ (morskói ~) marine ~

ответственность по ~/y (otvétstvennost' po ~/u) liability on a ~

открытый ~ (otkrýtyi ~) open ~

портовой ~ (portóvoi ~) port ~

подписывать ~ (podpísyvat' ~) to sign a ~

причальный ~ (prichál'nyi ~) berthing ~

проформа ~/a (profórma ~/a) pro forma ~

расторгать ~ (rastorgát' ~) to cancel a ~

рейсовой ~ (réisovoi ~) single voyage ~

речной ~ (rechnói ~) river ~

сдавать судно в наём по ~/y (sdavát' súdno v naióm po ~/u) to ~ a vessel

специальный ~ (spetsiál'nyi ~) special ~

сухогрузный ~ (sukhogrúznyi ~) dry cargo ~

типовой ~ (tipovói ~) standard ~

условия ~/a (uslóviia ~/a) terms and conditions of a ~

угольный ~ (úgol'nyi ~) coal ~

хлебный ~ (khlébnyi ~) grain ~

фрахт по ~/y (frakht po ~/u) freight

чистый ~ (chístyi ~) clean ~

широкий ~ (shirókii ~) broad ~

~ бэрбоут (~ bérbout) bare-boat ~

~ лумпсум (~ lúmpsum) lumpsum ~

~ на срок (~ na srok) time ~

~ с посуточной оплатой (~ s posútochnoi oplátoi) daily hire

~ фрахтование судна без экипажа (~ frakhtovánie súdna bez ekipázha) bare-boat ~

~ фрахтования судна на рейс в оба конца (~ frakhtovániia súdna na reis v óba kontsá) round trip ~

Чартер-партия (chárter-pártiia) f. charter party

Час (chas) m. hour
вне рабочих ~/ов банка (vne rabóchikh ~/óv bánka) after banking hours
накопившиеся ~/ы (nakopívshiesia ~/ý) cumulative ~s
наработанные ~/ы (narabótannye ~/ý) ~s worked
нерабочие ~/ы (nerabóchie ~/ý) non-working ~s
присутственные ~/ы (prisútstvennye ~/ý) office ~s
проработанные ~/ы (prorabótannye ~/ý) worked ~s
рабочие ~/ы банка (rabóchie ~/ý bánka) working ~s of the bank
сверхурочные ~/ы (sverkhuróchnye ~/ý) overtime ~s
свободные ~/ы (svobódnye ~/ý) off ~s
служебные ~/ы (sluzhébnye ~/ý) office ~s
фактически проработанные ~/ы (faktícheski prorabótannye ~/ý) actual ~s worked
~/ы простоя (~/y prostóia) idle ~s

Частично (chastíchno) adv. partially
выполнять обязательства ~ (vypolniát' obiazátel'stva ~) to ~ perform obligations
изменять ~ (izmeniát' ~) to ~ modify
списывать ~ со счёта (spísyvat' ~ so schióta) to write down (as a debt)
удовлетворять ~ (udovletvoriát' ~) to ~ satisfy
~ занятые служащие (~ zaniátye slúzhashchie) part-time employees
~ оплаченные акции (~ opláchennye áktsii) ~ paid shares
~ отгруженная партия товара (~ otgrúzhennaia pártiia továra) part load consignment
~ принадлежащий (~ prinadlezháshchii) ~ owned by

Частичный (chastíchnyi) adj. partial

Частновладельческий (chastnovladél'cheskii) adj. privately-owned

Частный (chástnyi) adj. private

Част/ь (chast'/') f. allotment, installment, part, portion
большая ~ (bol'sháia ~) the greater part
быстроизнашивающиеся ~/и (bystroiznashiváiushchiesia ~/i) rapidly wearing parts
важная ~ (vázhnaia ~) important part
выплачивать ~/ями (vypláchivat' ~/iámi) to pay by installments
дефектные ~/и (deféktnye ~/i) defective parts
запасные ~/и (zapásnye ~/i) spare parts
значительная ~ (znachítel'naia ~) substantial part
меньшая ~ (mén'shaia ~) the lesser part
небольшая ~ прибыли (nebol'sháia ~ príbyli) small proportion of profits
недоплаченная ~ акционерного капитала (nedopláchennaia ~ aktsionérnogo kapitála) unpaid capital
неотъемлемая ~ (neot"émlemaia ~ integral part
основная ~ (osnovnáia ~) principal part
платёж ~/ями (platiózh ~/iámi) payment by installments
по ~/ям (po ~/iám) in parts
поставка по ~/ям (postávka po ~/iám) delivery in lots
пропорциональная ~ фрахта (proportsionál'naia ~ frákhta) pro rata freight
разбирать на ~/и (razbirát' na ~/i) to take apart
сдача по ~/ям (sdácha po ~/iám) delivery in installments
сменная ~ (sménnaia ~) replacement part
составная ~ (sostavnáia ~) component
~ переводного аккредитива (~ perevódnogo akkreditíva) fraction of a transferrable letter of credit
~ прибыли (~ príbyli) share of profits
~ рынка (~ rýnka) market share

Чек (chek) m. check
аллонж к ~/у (allónzh k ~/u) allonge on a check

банковский ~ (bánkovskii ~) cashier's ~

бланковый ~ (blánkovyi ~) blank ~

бланк ~/а (blank ~/a) ~ form

валютный ~ (valiútnyi ~) currency ~

возвратный ~ (vozvrátnyi ~) redemption ~

возвращённый ~ (vozvrashchiónnyi ~) returned {"bounced"} ~

выдавать ~ (vydavát' ~) to make out a ~

выписывать ~ в пользу (vypísyvat' ~ v pól'zu) to make out a ~ in favor of

выписывать ~ сверх остатка на текущем счету (vypísyvat' ~ sverkh ostátka na tekúshchem schetú) to overdraw an account

выплата по ~/у (výplata po ~/u) negotiation of a ~

выплачивать по ~/у (vypláchivat' po ~/u) to negotiate a ~

выставлять ~ (vystavliát' ~) to make out a ~

датированный более поздним числом ~ (datírovannyi bólee pózdnim chislóm ~) postdated ~

дорожный ~ (dorózhnyi ~) traveler's ~

зачёт ~/ов (zachiót ~/ov) clearance of ~s

единый ~ на производство нескольких платежей (edínyi ~ na proizvódstvo néskol'kikh platezhéi) single multi-payment ~

именной ~ (imennói ~) check payable to ...

индоссамент на ~/е (indossamént na ~/e) endorsement on a ~

иностранный ~ (inostránnyi ~) foreign ~

кроссированный ~ (krossírovannyi ~) crossed ~

корешок ~/а (koreshók ~/a) ~ counterfoil

курс ~/ов ~ (kurs ~/ov) ~ rate

недействительный ~ (nedeistvítel'nyi ~) cancelled ~

незаполненный ~ (nezapólnennyi ~) blank ~

некроссированный ~ (nekrossírovannyi ~) open ~

неоплаченный ~ (neopláchennyi ~) outstanding ~

непередаваемый ~ (neperedaváemyi ~) non-negotiable ~

непокрытый ~ (nepokrýtyi ~) NSF (insufficient funds) ~

не принятый к оплате банком ~ (ne príniatyi k opláte bánkom ~) dishonored ~

номер ~/а (nómer ~/a) ~ number

обменивать ~/и (obménivat' ~/i) to exchange ~s

обращение ~/ов (obrashchénie ~/ov) currency ~s

оплата ~/а (opláta ~/a) settlement of a ~

оплата ~/ом (opláta ~/om) payment by ~

оплаченный ~ (opláchennyi ~) paid ~

опротестованный ~ (oprotestóvannyi ~) protested ~

ордерный ~ (órdernyi ~) order ~

отказ в оплате ~/а (otkáz v opláte ~/a) refusal to pay a ~

отказываться от уплаты ~/а (otkázyvat'sia ot upláty ~/a) to refuse to honor a ~

открытый ~ (otkrýtyi ~) open ~

отменять ~ (otmeniát' ~) to cancel a ~

переделанный ~ (peredélannyi ~) altered ~

передавать ~ (peredavát' ~) to negotiate a ~

перевод ~/ом (perevód ~/om) transfer by ~

передаточная надпись на ~/е (peredátochnaia nádpis' na ~/e) ~ endorsement

передача ~/а (peredácha ~/a) negotiation of a ~

пересылать ~ (peresylát' ~) to remit a ~

пересылать деньги ~/ом (peresylát' dén'gi ~/om) to remit money by ~

платёж ~/ом (platiózh ~/om) payment by ~

платить ~/ом (platít' ~/om) to pay by ~

погашать ~ (pogashát' ~) to pay on a ~

погашенный ~ (pogáshennyi ~) cancelled ~

подделывать ~ (poddélyvat' ~) to forge a ~

поддельный ~ (poddél'nyi ~) forged ~

подделка ~/a (poddélka ~/a) forgery of a ~

подтверждённый банком ~ (podtverzhdiónnyi bánkom ~) confirmed ~

получать деньги по ~/у (poluchát' dén'gi po ~/u) to cash a ~

подписывать ~ (podpísyvat' ~) to sign a ~

посылать ~ в банк (posylát' ~ v bank) to forward a ~ to the bank

предъявительский ~ (pred"iavítel'skii ~) bearer ~

представлять (предъявлять) ~ к оплате (predstavliát' {pred"iavliát'} ~ k opláte) to present a ~ for payment

прекратить платёж по ~/у (prekratít' platiózh po ~/u) to stop payment on a ~

просроченный ~ (prosróchennyi ~) stale ~

разменивать ~ (razménivat' ~) to negotiate a ~

расчётный ~ (raschiótnyi ~) clearinghouse ~

туристский ~ (turístskii ~) traveler's ~

трассировать ~ на банк (trassírovat' ~ na bank) to draw a ~ against the bank

удостоверенный ~ (udostovérennyi ~) certified ~

уплачивать ~/ом (upláchivat' ~/om) to pay by ~

уплачивать по ~/у (upláchivat' po ~/u) to honor a ~

фиктивный ~ (fiktívnyi ~) bad ~

~ без права передачи (~ bez práva peredáchi) non-negotiable ~

~, выданный отдельным лицом (~, výdannyi otdél'nym litsóm) personal ~

~, выписанный банком на другой банк (~, výpisannyi bánkom na drugói bank) banker's ~

~, выписанный на банк (~, výpisannyi na bank) ~ drawn on a bank

~, выписанный на предъявителя (~, výpisannyi na pred"iavítel-ia) ~ payable to bearer

~, выписанный в оплату по нескольким сделкам (~, výpisannyi v oplátu po

néskol'kim sdélkam) multiple payment ~

~ в погашение (~ v pogashénie) ~ in settlement

~ в счёт суммы (~ v schiót súmmy) ~ on account

~ на предъявителя (~ na pred"iavítelia) ~ made out to bearer

~ на сумму (~ na súmmu) ~ in the amount of ...

~ по клиринговым расчётам (~ po klíringovym raschiótam) clearinghouse ~

~, по которому приостановлен платёж (~, po kotóromu priostanóvlen platiózh) stopped {payment} ~

Чековый (chékovyi) *adj.* check

Чекодатель (chekodátel') *m.* drawer of a check

Чекодержатель (chekoderzhátel') *m.* holder of a check

Человекодень (chelovekodén') *m.* man-day

Человек-месяц (chelovék-mésiats) *m* man-month

Человек-неделя (chelovék-nedélia) man-week

Человеко-час (chelovéko-chas) *m.* man-hour

Честный (chéstnyi) *adj.* honest

Чехол (chekhól) *m.* covering

брезентовый ~ (brezéntovyi ~) tarpaulin

внешний ~ (vnéshnii ~) external ~

плёночный ~ (pliónochnyi ~) plastic ~

полиэтиленовый ~ (polietilénovy ~) polyethylene sheeting

Численность (chíslennost') *f.* quantity

общая ~ (óbshchaia ~) total number

фактическая ~ (faktícheskaia ~) actual number

штатная ~ (shtátnaia ~) regular staffing

Числ/о (chisl/ó) *n.* date, number, quantity

без ~/a (bez ~/á) without a dat

выводить среднее ~ (vyvodít' srédnee ~) to find the average

датировать более поздним ~/ом (datírovat' bólee pózdnim ~/óm to affix a later date датировать более ранним ~/ом (datírovat' bólee ránnim ~/óm) to affix an earlier date

датировать задним ~/ом (datírovat' zádnim ~/óm) to back date

дробное ~ (dróbnoe ~) fractional number

максимальное ~ (maksimál'noe ~) maximum number

минимальное ~ (minimál'noe ~) minimal number

нечётное ~ (nechiótnoe ~) odd number

общее ~ (óbshchee ~) total quantity

округлённое ~ (okrugliónnoe ~) round figure

помечать ~/ом (pomechát' ~/óm) to date (as a document)

помеченный более поздним ~/ом (poméchennyi bólee pózdnim ~/óm) adj. post-dated

порядковое ~ (poriádkovoe ~) ordinal number

постоянное ~ (postoiánnoe ~) fixed number

превосходить ~/ом (prevoskhodít' ~/óm) to outnumber

рекордное ~ (rékordnoe ~) record number

среднее ~ (srédnee ~) average

чётное ~ (chiótnoe ~) even number

~ мест (~ mest) number of cases (freight)

Чистый (chístyi) adj. clean, net, pure

Член (chlen) m. member
вступать в ~/ы (vstupát' v ~/y) to join (organization, etc.)
полноправный ~ (polnoprávnyi ~) full-fledged ~
постоянный ~ (postoiánnyi ~) permanent ~
~ без права голоса (~ bez práva gólosa) non-voting ~
~ коллегии (~ kollégii) collegium ~
~ конгресса (~ kongréssa) ~ of congress
~ парламента (~ parlámenta) ~ of parliament
~ правления (~ pravléniia) board ~
~ экипажа (~ ekipázha) crew ~

Членский (chlénskii) adj. member, membership

Членство (chlénstvo) n. membership

Чрезвычайный (chrezvycháinyi) adj. emergency, extraordinary

Чрезмерный (chrezmérnyi) adj. excessive, exorbitant

Ш

Шаблон (shablón) m. template

Шаблонность (shablónnost') f. banality, unoriginality

Шаблонный (shablónnyi) adj. banal, routine, unoriginal

Шаг (shag) m. pace, stage, step

Шахта (shákhta) f. mine

Шахтёр (shakhtiór) m. miner

Швартоваться (shvartovát'sia) v. to moor

Швартовк/а (shvartóvk/a) f. mooring
место ~/и (mésto ~/i) berthing place

Шефмонтаж (shefmontázh) m. contract supervision
график проведения ~/a (gráfik provedéniia ~/a) construction schedule
компетентный ~ (kompeténtnyi ~) competent ~
обеспечивать ~ (obespéchivat' ~) to provide ~
осуществлять ~ (osushchestvliát' ~) to supervise a construction contract
полный ~ (pólnyi ~) complete ~
проведение ~/a (provedénie ~/a) performance of ~

Шефмонтёр (shefmontiór) m. construction supervisor
старший ~ (stárshii ~) senior ~
пользоваться услугами ~/a (pól'zovat'sia uslúgami ~/a) to employ the services of a ~

Шефперсонал (shefpersonál) m. supervisory personnel
соответствующий ~ (sootvétstvuiushchii ~) appropriate ~
~ продавца (~ prodavtsá) seller's ~

Шипчандлер (shípchándler) m. ship chandler

Ширина (shiriná) f. width

Шифр (shifr) m. cipher, code

ключ к ~/у (kliuch k ~/u) key to a code
~ единицы оборудования (~ edinítsy oborúdovaniia) machine code
~ ом (~ om) in cipher
Шифрованный (shifróvannyi) adj. encoded
Шифровка (shifróvka) f. encoding
Шкала (shkalá) f. escalation, scale
внутренняя ~ (vnútrenniaia ~) internal scale
грузовая ~ (gruzováia ~) deadweight scale
официальная ~ (ofitsiál'naia ~) official scale
скользящая ~ (skol'ziáshchaia ~) sliding scale
~ вместимости (~ vmestímosti) tonnage scale
~ водоизмещения (~ vodoizmeshchéniia) displacement scale
~ выгрузки (~ výgruzki) discharge scale
~ заработной платы (~ zárabotnoi pláty) wage scale
~ комиссионного вознаграждения (~ komissiónnogo voznagrazhdén-iia) commission scale
~ надбавок и скидок (~ nadbávok i skídok) escalation
~ оплаты (~ opláty) pay scale
~ расходов (~ raskhódov) scale of charges
~ сборов (~ sbórov) scale of fees
~ скидок (~ skídok) scale of discounts
Шоу (shóu) program, show
рекламное ~ (reklámnoe ~) n. advertising program, infomercial
Шпагат (shpagát) m. twine
увязочный ~ (uviázochnyi ~) binder ~
Штабелировать (shtabelírovat') v. to stack (as cargo)
Штабел/ь (shtábel/') stack
укладывать в ~/я (ukládyvat' v ~/ia) to stack up
Штамп (shtamp) m. stamp
гарантийный ~ (garantíinyi ~) guarantee ~
заверять ~/ом (zaveriát' ~/om) to certify by ~
ставить ~ (stávit' ~) to affix a ~

Штамповать (shtampovát') v. to stamp
Штат (shtat) m. personnel, staff
быть в ~/е (byt' v ~/e) to be on the staff
высококвалифицированный ~ (vysokokvalifitsírovannyi ~) highly qualified staff
зачислять в ~ (zachisliát' v ~) to add to a staff
набор ~/а (nabór ~/a) recruitment
основной ~ (osnovnói ~) basic staff
постоянный ~ (postoiánnyi ~) permanent staff
производственный ~ (proizvódstvennyi ~) production personnel
раздутый ~ (razdútyi ~) staff overage
сокращать ~ (sokrashchát' ~) to reduce personnel
~ технических сотрудников (~ tekhnícheskikh sotrúdnikov) technical personnel
Штатный (shtátnyi) adj. staff
Штемпелевать (shtempelevát') v. to impress
Штемпел/ь (shtémpel/') m. impress, seal, stamp
дата ~/я пограничной станции (dáta ~/ia pograníchnoi stántsii) date stamp by border station
дата почтового ~/я (dáta pochtóvogo ~/ia) postmark date
контрольный ~ (kontról'nyi ~) control stamp
почтовый ~ (pochtóvyi ~) postmark
проставлять ~ (prostavliát' ~) to stamp, to seal
~ банка (~ bánka) bank stamp
~ о весе (~ o vése) weight stamp
~ переводчика (~ perevódchika) translator's seal (on official translation)
Штивк/а (shtívk/a) f. stowage
небрежная ~ (nebrézhnaia ~) negligent ~
неправильная ~ (neprávil'naia ~) improper ~
свидетельство о ~/е (svidétel'stvo o ~/e) ~ certificate

специальная ~ (spetsiál'naia ~)
special ~
стоимость ~/и (stóimost' ~/i) ~
cost
производить ~/y (proizvodít'
~/u) to stow
цена ФОБ со ~/ой (tsená fob so
~/oi) price FOB with ~
ФОБ включая ~/y (fob vkliucháia
~/u) FOB stowed
фри ин со ~/ой (fri in so ~/oi)
free in and stowed
Шторм (shtorm) *m.* storm
сильный ~ (síl'nyi ~) strong ~
Штраф (shtraf) *m.* fine, penalty,
surcharge
взыскивать ~ (vzýskivat' ~) to
enforce a penalty
денежный ~ (dénezhnyi ~) money
fine
договорный ~ (dogovórnyi ~)
contractual penalty
исчислять ~ со стоимости
(ischisliát' ~ so stóimosti) to
calculate a penalty on the cost
of ...
налагать ~ (nalagát' ~) to
impose a penalty
начислять ~ (nachisliát' ~) to
calculate a penalty
наложение ~/a (nalozhénie ~/a)
imposition of a penalty,
surcharge
обычный ~ (obýchnyi ~)
conventional penalty
освобождение от уплаты ~/a
(osvobozhdénie ot upláty ~/a)
penalty relief
отказываться от оплаты ~/a
(otkázyvat'sia ot opláty ~/a) to
renounce a penalty
платить ~ (platít' ~) to pay a
fine
подвергать ~/y (podvergát' ~/u)
to impose a fine
подвергаться ~/y (podvergát'sia
~/u) to incur a fine
подлежащий ~/y (podlezháshchii
~/u) subject to penalty
признавать ~ (priznavát' ~) to
accept a fine
применять пункт о ~/ax
(primeniát' punkt o ~/akh) to
apply the penalty clause
пункт о ~/ax (punkt o ~/akh)
penalty clause

размер ~/a (razmér ~/a) size of
penalty
сумма ~/a (súmma ~/a) amount of
penalty
таможенный ~ (tamózhennyi ~)
customs penalty
~ за задержку (~ za zadérzhku)
penalty for delay
~ за задержку поставки (~ za
zadérzhku postávki) penalty for
late delivery
~ за задержку разгрузки (~ za
zadérzhku razgrúzki) detention
charges
~ за просрочку платежа (~ za
prosróchku platezhá) penalty for
late payment
~ за просрочку поставки (~ za
prosróchku postávki) penalty for
late delivery
~ за простой (~ za prostói)
demurrage penalty
Штрафной (shtrafnói) *adj.* penal
Штрафовать (shtrafovát') *v.* to
fine, to penalize
Штука (shtúka) *f.* item, piece, unit
Штурман (shtúrman) *m.* navigation
officer
Штучный (shtúchnyi) *adj.* piece

Щ

Щадить (shchadít') *v.* to spare
{show mercy}
не ~ сил (ne ~ sil) to spare no
effort
Щедрость (shchédrost') *f.*
generosity
Щедрый (shchédryi) *adj.* generous
Щит (shchit) *m.* display, shield
рекламный ~ (reklámnyi ~)
billboard
Щекотлив/ый (shchekotlív/yi) *adj.*
delicate, awkward
~/ая тема (~/aia téma) delicate
topic
~/ое дело (~/oe délo) delicate
matter
Щепетильный (shchepetíl'nyi) *adj.*
punctilious, scrupulous

Э

Экземпляр (ekzempliár) *m.* copy,
specimen
в двух ~/ах (v dvukh ~/akh) in
duplicate
в пяти ~/ах (v piatí ~/akh) in
five copies
в трёх ~/ах (v triokh ~/akh) in
triplicate
в четырёх ~/ах (v chetyriókh
~/akh) in four copies
второй ~ (vtorói ~) second copy
выставлять трату в трёх ~/ах
(vystavliát' trátu v triokh
~/akh) to issue a bill in
triplicate
действительный ~ (deistvítel'nyi
~) negotiable copy
единственный ~ (edínstvennyi ~)
single copy
единственный ~ траты
(edínstvennyi ~ tráty) single
bill
количество ~/ов (kolíchestvo
~/ov) number of copies
комплект ~/ов (komplékt ~/ov)
set of copies
контрольный ~ (kontról'nyi ~)
control copy
недействительный ~
(nedeistvítel'nyi ~) non-
negotiable copy
основной ~ (osnovnói ~) primary
copy
отмеченный ~ (otméchennyi ~)
marked copy
оформленный ~ (ofórmlennyi ~)
executed copy
первый ~ (pérvyi ~) first copy
последний ~ (poslédnii ~) last
copy
приложить документы в трёх ~/ах
(prilozhít' dokuménty v triokh
~/akh) to enclose documents in
triplicate
рекламный ~ (reklámnyi ~)
complimentary copy
сигнальный ~ (signál'nyi ~)
advance copy
судовой ~ коносамента (sudovói ~
konosaménta) copy of a shipped
bill of lading
тождественный ~ (tozhdéstvennyi
~) identical copy

уникальный ~ (unikál'nyi ~)
unique copy
~ векселя (~ vékselia) copy of a
bill (note)
~ документа (~ dokuménta) copy
of a document
~ коносамента (~ konosaménta)
copy of a bill of lading
Экипаж (ekipázh) *m.* crew
Экономик/а (ekonómik/a) *f.*
economics, economy
внутренняя ~ (vnútrenniaia ~)
domestic economy
государственный сектор ~/и
(gosudárstvennyi séktor ~/i)
state-owned sector
диверсификация ~/и
(diversifikátsiia ~/i)
diversification of the economy
застойная ~ (zastóinaia ~)
stagnant economy
конкурирующие ~/и
(konkuríruiushchie ~/i)
competitive economies
контролируемая ~
(kontrolíruemaia ~) directed
economy
мировая ~ (mirováia ~) global
economy
многоотраслевая ~
(mnogootrasleváia ~) diversified
economy
национальная ~ (natsional'náia
~) national economy
неустойчивая ~ (neustóichivaia
~) unstable economy
оживление ~/и (ozhivlénie ~/i)
revival of the economy
оживлять ~/у (ozhivliát' ~/u) to
revive the economy
оздоровление ~/и (ozdorovlénie
~/i) recovery of the economy
отрасли ~/и (ótrasli ~/i)
branches of the economy
отсталая ~ (otstálaia ~)
backwards economy
перестраивать ~/у (perestráivat'
~/u) to restructure the economy
перестройка ~/и (perestróika
~/i) restructuring of the
economy
плановая ~ (plánovaia ~) planned
economy
предпринимательская ~
(predprinimátel'skaia ~)
entrepreneurial economy

промышленная ~ (promýshlennaia ~) industrial economy

процветающая ~ (protsvetáiushchaia ~) thriving economy

развивающаяся ~ (razviváiushchaiasia ~) expanding economy

развитая ~ (razvítaia ~) developed economy

развитие ~/и (razvítie ~/i) economic development

рыночная ~ (rýnochnaia ~) market economy

самообеспеченная ~ (samoobespéchennaia ~) self-sufficient economy

состояние ~/и (sostoiánie ~/i) state of the economy

страны с рыночной ~/ой (strány s rýnochnoi ~/oi) market economies

товарная ~ (továrnaia ~) commodity-based economy

устойчивая ~ (ustóichivaia ~) stable economy

укрепление ~/и (ukreplénie ~/i) strengthening of the economy

централизованно-планируемая ~ (tsentralizóvanno-planíruemaia ~) centrally planned economy

частный сектор ~/и (chástnyi séktor ~/i) private sector

Экономист (ekonomíst) *m.* economist

главный ~ (glávnyi ~) head ~

промышленный ~ (promýshlennyi ~) industrial ~

старший ~ (stárshii ~) senior ~

Экономить (ekonómit') *v.* to economize

~ на {чём-либо} (~ na {chióm-libo}) ~ on {something}

Экономический (ekonomícheskii) *adj.* economic

Экономично (ekonomíchno) *adv.* economically

Экономичност/ь (ekonomíchnost/') *f.* economic efficiency

определение ~/и (opredelénie ~/i) determination of profitability

повышение ~/и (povyshénie ~/i) improvement of ~

Экономичный (ekonomíchnyi) *adj.* economical, cost-saving

Экономи/я (ekonómi/ia) *f.* economy, economic rationalization, savings

валютная ~ (valiútnaia ~) foreign exchange savings

годовая ~ (godováia ~) annual savings

гарантировать ~/ю (garantírovat' ~/iu) to insure economic measures

добиться ~/и средств (dobít'sia ~/i sredstv) to achieve savings

значительная ~ (znachítel'naia ~) significant saving

максимальная ~ (maksimál'naia ~) maximum saving

меры ~/и (méry ~/i) economizing measures

незапланированная ~ (nezaplanírovannaia ~) unintended economies

~ обусловленная специализацией (~ obuslóvlennaia spetsializátsiei) economy of specialization

осуществлять ~/ю (osushchestvliát' ~/iu) to economize

оценка ~/и (otsénka ~/i) estimate of economization

получить ~/ю на (poluchít' ~/iu na) to achieve savings on ...

режим ~/и (rezhím ~/i) cost cutting drive

строгая ~ (strógaia ~) rigid economy

~ в расходах (~ v raskhódakh) cutback of expenditures

~ в результате сокращения объёма запасов (~ v rezul'táte sokrashchéniiaia ob"ióma zapásov) economic rationalization of inventories

~ времени (~ vrémeni) time savings

~ материала (~ materiála) economizing on material

~ места (~ mésta) space savings

~ на издержках (~ na izdérzhkakh) cost savings

~ на торговых издержках (~ na torgóvykh izdérzhkakh) savings on sales costs

~ на ценах (~ na tsénakh) price savings

~ от разделения труда (~ ot razdeléniia trudá) economizing through division of labor

~ финансовых ресурсов (~
finánsovykh resúrsov) saving of
financial resources
Экономный (ekonómnyi) *adj.*
economical, thrifty
Экспансия (ekspánsiia) *f.* expansion
внешнеторговая ~
(vneshnetorgóvaia ~) foreign
trade ~
кредитная ~ (kredítnaia ~)
credit ~
экономическая ~ (ekonomícheskaia
~) economic ~
Экспедитор (ekspedítor) *m.* freight
forwarder
выступать в качестве ~/a
(vystupát' v káchestve ~/a) to
act in the capacity of ~
быть назначенным ~/ом (byt'
naznáchennym ~/om) to be
designated as ~
генеральный ~ (generál'nyi ~)
general ~
поручение ~/y (poruchénie ~/u)
order to the ~
расписка ~/a (raspíska ~/a) ~'s
certificate of receipt
~ по сборным отправкам (~ po
sbórnym otprávkam) groupage
operator
Экспедиторский (ekspedítorskii)
adj. forwarding
Эксперт (ekspért) *m.* consultant,
expert, specialist
возражения ~/a (vozrazhéniia
~/a) examiner's objections
главный ~ (glávnyi ~) examiner-
in-chief
группа ~/ов (grúppa ~/ov) panel
of experts
заключение ~/a (zakliuchénie
~/a) expert's report
комиссия ~/ов (komíssiia ~/ov)
commission of experts
коммерческий ~ (kommércheskii ~)
commercial expert
консультироваться с ~/ом
(konsul'tírovat'sia s ~/om) to
consult a specialist
назначать ~/a (naznachát' ~/a)
to appoint an expert
показания ~/a (pokazániia ~/a)
expert's findings
помощник ~/a (pomóshchnik ~/a)
assistant examiner
постоянный ~ (postoiánnyi ~)
resident expert

посылать ~/ов (posylát' ~/ov) to
send experts
технический ~ (tekhnícheskii ~)
technical expert
торговый ~ (torgóvyi ~) trade
expert
транспортный ~ (tránsportnyi ~)
transportation expert
~, владеющий несколькими языками
(~, vladéiushchii néskol'kimi
iazykámi) multilingual expert
~ патентного ведомства (~
paténtnogo védomstva) patent
examiner
~ по оценке {недвижимости} (~ po
otsénke nedvízhimosti) assessor
{real estate}
~ по перевозкам грузов (~ po
perevózkam grúzov) traffic
expert {freight}
~ по промышленным образцам (~ po
promýshlennym obraztsám) design
expert
~ по товарным знакам (~ po
továrnym znákam) trademark
examiner
~ по экономическим вопросам (~
po ekonomícheskim voprósam)
economic expert
Экспертиз/а (ekspertíz/a) *f.*
examination, findings
акт ~/ы (akt ~/y) examiners'
statement
возобновлять ~/y (vozobnovliát'
~/u) to resume examination
государственная ~
(gosudárstvennaia ~) state
examination
группа ~/ы (grúppa ~/y)
examining panel
заключительная ~
(zakliuchítel'naia ~) final
examination
заключение ~/ы (zakliuchénie
~/y) expert findings
затребовать ~/y (zatrébovat'
~/u) to request an expert
examination
контрольная ~ (kontról'naia ~)
control examination
назначать ~/y (naznachát' ~/u)
to schedule an examination
независимая ~ (nezavísimaia ~)
independent examination
нуждаться в технической ~/e
(nuzhdát'sia v tekhnícheskoi

~/e) to require technical expertise

объективная ~ (ob"ektívnaia ~) objective examination

окончательная ~ (okonchátel'naia ~) final examination

отдел ~/ы (otdél ~/y) examination department

отсроченная ~ (otsróchennaia ~) postponed examination

патентная ~ (paténtnaia ~) patent examination

повторная ~ (povtórnaia ~) follow-up examination

подвергать ~/e (podvergát' ~/e) to examine

приостанавливать ~/y (priostanávlivat' ~/u) to withhold an examination

прекращать ~/y (prekrashchát' ~/u) to stop an examination

предварительная ~ (predvarítel'naia ~) preliminary examination

пункт решения ~/ы (punkt reshéniia ~/y) expert examination clause

результаты ~/ы (rezul'táty ~/y) examination results

решение ~/ы (reshénie ~/y) expert's decision

специальная ~ (spetsiál'naia ~) special examination

срочная ~ (sróchnaia ~) urgent examination

техническая ~ (tekhnícheskaia ~) technical examination

тщательная ~ (tshchátel'naia ~) painstaking examination

формальная ~ (formál'naia ~) formal examination

~ заявки (~ zaiávki) examination of an application

~ на осуществимость (~ na osushchestvímost') feasibility study

~ на патентоспособность (~ na patentosposóbnost') patentability examination

Экспертный (ekspértnyi) adj. expert

Эксплуатация (ekspluatátsiia) f. maintenance, operation, running, service, utilization

бесперебойная ~ (besperebónaia ~) trouble-free operation

ввод в ~/ю (vvod v ~/iu) putting into operation

вводить в ~/ю (vvodít' v ~/iu) to bring into operation

время ~/и (vrémia ~/i) operating period

вступать в ~/ю (vstupát' v ~/iu) to go into operation

выводить из ~/и (vyvodít' iz ~/i) to take out of service

вывод из ~/и (vývod iz ~/i) retirement from operation

в условиях ~/и (v uslóviiakh ~/i) under operating conditions

гарантийная ~ (garantíinaia ~) guaranteed operation

годный к ~/и (gódnyi k ~/i) serviceable

готовый к ~/и (gotóvyi k ~/i) ready for use

дата пуска в ~/ю (dáta púska v ~/iu) start-up date

метод ~/и (métod ~/i) method of operation

находиться в ~/и (nakhódit'sia v ~/i) to be in service

надёжный в ~/и (nadiózhnyi v ~/i) reliable operation

ненадёжный в ~/и (nenadiózhnyi v ~/i) unreliable operation

непригодный к дальнейшей ~/и (neprigódnyi k dal'néishei ~/i) unfit for further operation

неправильная ~ (neprávil'naia ~) misuse

нормальная ~ (normál'naia ~) normal operation

опыт ~/и (ópyt ~/i) service experience

отчёт об ~/и (otchiót ob ~/i) operations report

промышленная ~ (promýshlennaia ~) commercial operation

предназначенный для ~/и (prednaznáchennyi dlia ~/i) designed for operation

период ~/и (períod ~/i) period of operation

правила ~/и (právila ~/i) service regulations

право на ~/ю (právo na ~/iu) operating right

программа ввода в ~/ю (prográmma vvóda v ~/iu) start-up program

процесс ~/и (protséss ~/i) operating process

пуск завода в ~/ю (pusk zavóda v ~/iu) factory start-up

пускать в ~/ю назначенный срок
(puskát' v ~/iu naznáchennyi
srok) to meet start-up date
руководство по ~/и (rukovódstvo
po ~/i) operating manual
сдать в ~/ю (sdat' v ~/iu) to
put into operation
техника ~/и (tékhnika ~/i)
operating techniques
техника ~/и и монтажа
оборудования (tékhnika ~/i i
montázha oborúdovaniia) plant
engineering
условия ~/и (uslóviia ~/i)
operating conditions
~ завода (~ zavóda) factory
maintenance
~ международной линии (~
mezhdunaródnoi línii)
international operation
Эксплуатировать (ekspluatírovat')
v. to exploit, to operate, to run
Экспозици/я (ekspozítsi/ia) f.
exposition
графическая ~ (grafícheskaia ~)
graphic ~
коллективная ~ (kollektívnaia ~)
collective exhibit
национальная ~ (natsionál'naia
~) national ~
организовать ~/ю (organizovát'
~/iu) to organize an ~
осматривать ~/ю (osmátrivat'
~/iu) to review a ~
подготовка ~/и (podgotóvka ~/i)
preparation of an ~
раздел ~/и (razdél ~/i) section
of an ~
совместная ~ (sovméstnaia ~)
joint ~
традиционная ~ (traditsiónnaia
~) traditional ~
устраивать ~/ю (ustráivat' ~/iu)
to hold an ~
~ витрины (~ vitríny) window
display
Экспонат (eksponát) m. exhibit,
sample
ассортимент ~/ов (assortimént
~/ov) range of exhibits
выставочный ~ (výstavochnyi ~)
display unit
выставлять ~/ы (vystavliát' ~/y)
to put samples on display
главный ~ (glávnyi ~) major
exhibit

демонстрировать ~/ы
(demonstrírovat' ~/y) to show
samples
действующий ~ (déistvuiushchii
~) working exhibit
демонстрация ~/ов
(demonstrátsiia ~/ov)
demonstration of exhibits
конкурентоспособный ~
(konkurentosposóbnyi ~)
competitive exhibit
отбор ~/ов (otbór ~/ov)
selection of exhibits
отбирать ~ (otbirát' ~) to
remove a sample
подбор ~/ов (podbór ~/ov)
selection of samples
подготовка ~/ов (podgotóvka
~/ov) preparation of exhibits
открытый показ ~/ов (otkrýtyi
pokáz ~/ov) open display of
exhibits
продажа ~/ов со стенда (prodázha
~/ov so stenda) "off-the-floor"
sale
представлять ~/ы (predstavliát'
~/y) to present exhibits
размещать ~/ы (razmeshchát' ~/y)
to arrange exhibits
расположение ~/ов (raspolozhénie
~/ov) layout of exhibits
рекомендуемый ~ (rekomendúemyi
~) recommended exhibit
Экспонент (eksponént) m. exhibitor
~, выставляющий в первый раз (~,
vystavliáiushchii v pérvyi raz)
first-time ~
главный ~ (glávnyi ~) major ~
заграничный ~ (zagraníchnyi ~)
foreign ~
зарубежный ~ (zarubézhnyi ~)
overseas ~
индивидуальный ~ (individuál'nyi
~) individual ~
коллективный ~ (kollektívnyi ~)
collective ~
основной ~ (osnovnói ~) main ~
отечественный ~ (otéchestvennyi
~) domestic ~
постоянный ~ (postoiánnyi ~)
permanent ~
Экспонирование (eksponírovanie) n.
demonstrating, exhibiting
Экспонируемый (eksponíruemyi) adj.
on display
Экспорт (éksport) m. export,
exportation, exports

беспошлинный ~ (bespóshlinnyi ~) duty-free exportation

бросовой ~ (brosovói ~) dumping {trade}

быть упакованным для ~/a (byt' upakóvannym dlia ~/a) to be packed for export

возможность ~/a (vozmózhnost' ~/a) export opportunity

вопросы ~/a (voprósy ~/a) export matters

диверсификация ~/a (diversifikátsiia ~/a) diversification of exports

доля ~/a (dólia ~/a) share of exports

заниматься ~/ом (zanimát'sia ~/om) to be in the business of exporting

запрет на ~ (zaprét na ~) ban on exports

заявка ~ (zaiávka ~) export application

значительный ~ (znachítel'nyi ~) significant export

иметь в наличии для ~/a (imét' v nalíchii dlia ~/a) to be available for export

качество ~/a (káchestvo ~/a) quality of exports

контроль за ~/ом (kontról' za ~/om) export control

кредитование ~/a (kreditovánie ~/a) export credits

косвенный ~ (kósvennyi ~) indirect exports

малоприбыльный ~ (malopríbyl'nyi ~) marginally profitable exports

наращивать ~ (naráshchivat' ~) to increase exports

невидимый ~ (nevídimyi ~) invisible exports

неоплаченный ~ (neopláchennyi ~) unpaid exports

несельскохозяйственный ~ (nesel'skokhoziáistvennyi ~) non- agricultural exports

оборот по ~/y (oborót po ~/u) export turnover

общий ~ (óbshchii ~) total exports

объём ~/a (ob"ióm ~/a) export volume

ограничение ~/a (ogranichénie ~/a) export restrictions

ограничивать ~ (ograníchivat' ~) to restrict exports

падение ~/a (padénie ~/a) decline in exports

поступление от ~/a (postuplénie ot ~/a) proceeds from exports

прямой ~ (priamói ~) direct exports

превышение ~/a над импортом (prevyshénie ~/a nad ímportom) export surplus

предметы ~/a (predméty ~/a) articles of export

продажа на ~ (prodázha na ~) export sale

производство на ~ (proizvódstvo na ~) production for export

развитие ~/a (razvítie ~/a) development of exports

растущий ~ (rastúshchii ~) increasing exports

расширять ~ (rasshiriát' ~) to expand exports

рационализация ~/a (ratsionalizátsiia ~/a) rationalization of export

сделка на ~ (sdélka na ~) export transaction

содействие ~/y (sodéistvie ~/u) export promotion

сокращать ~ (sokrashchát' ~) to reduce exports

спрос на ~ (spros na ~) demand for exports

статьи ~/a (stat'í ~/a) items of export

стимулирование ~/a (stimulírovanie ~/a) export stimulation

стоимость ~/a (stóimost' ~/a) value of exports

страна ~/a (straná ~/a) country of exportation

структура ~/a (struktúra ~/a) composition of exports

товары традиционного ~/a (továry traditsiónnogo ~/a) traditional export goods

технический ~ (tekhnícheskii ~) technical exportation

традиционный ~ (traditsiónnyi ~) traditional exports

увеличивать объём ~/a (uvelíchivat' ob"iom ~/a) to increase the volume of exports

удорожание ~/a (udorozhánie ~/a) increase in export prices

ужесточение ~/a (uzhestochénie ~/a) restriction of exports

финансирование ~/a
(finansírovanie ~/a) financing
of exports
финансировать ~ (finansírovat'
~) to finance exports
эмбарго на ~ (embárgo na ~)
embargo on exports
  ~ машин и оборудования (~ mashín
i oborúdovaniia) exportation of
machinery and equipment
  ~ наукоёмкой продукции (~
naukoiómkoi prodúktsii) high
technology exports
  ~ научно-технических результатов
(~ naúchno-tekhnícheskikh
rezul'tátov) export of R&D
intensive products
  ~ по всему миру (~ po vsemú
míru) world-wide exports
  ~ продовольствия (~
prodovól'stviia) export of
foodstuffs
  ~ продукции сельского хозяйства
(~ prodúktsii sél'skogo
khoziáistva) export of
agricultural goods
  ~ результатов творческой
деятельности (~ rezul'tátov
tvórcheskoi déiatel'nosti)
exports of intellectual property
  ~ технологии (~ tekhnológii)
export of technology
  ~ товаров и услуг (~ továrov i
uslúg) export of goods and
services
  ~ услуг (~ uslúg) export of
services
Экспортёр (eksportiór) m. exporter
  единственный ~ (edínstvennyi ~)
sole ~
  исключительный ~
(iskliuchítel'nyi ~) exclusive ~
  ~ продовольственных товаров (~
prodovól'stvennykh továrov) ~ of
foodstuffs
  ~ промышленных товаров (~
promýshlennykh továrov) ~ of
industrial goods
  ~ сырьевых товаров (~ syr'evýkh
továrov) ~ of raw materials
Экспортировать (eksportírovat') v.
to export
Экспортно-импортный (éksportno-
ímportnyi) adj. export-import
Экспортный (éksportnyi) adj. export
Экспресс-служба (ekspréss-slúzhba)
f. express service

Экстенсивный (ekstensívnyi) adj.
extensive
Экстренный (ékstrennyi) adj. urgent
Эмбарго (embárgo) n. embargo
  наложить ~ (nalozhít' ~) to
impose an ~
  политика ~ (polítika ~) ~ policy
  снимать ~ (snimát' ~) to lift an
~
  ~ на экспорт ~ (~ na éksport) ~
on exports
Эмиссионный (emissiónnyi) adj.
issuing
Эмиссия (emíssiia) f. emission,
issue (bonds, currency, etc.)
  ~ банкнот (~ banknót) issue of
bank notes
  ~ денег (~ déneg) emission of
currency
  ~ ценных бумаг (~ tsénnykh
bumág) issue of securities
Энергоёмкость (energoiómkost') f.
energy consumption
Эскалация (eskalátsiia) f.
escalation
  подлежать ~/и (podlezhát' ~/i)
to be subject to escalation
  формула ~/и цен (fórmula ~/i
tsen) price escalation formula
  ~ цен (~ tsen) price escalation
Этикет/ка (etikét/ka) f. label, tag
  бумажная ~ (bumázhnaia ~) paper
label
  без ~/ок (bez ~/ok) without
labels
  наклеивать ~/ку (nakléivat'
~/ku) to attach a label
  подробная ~ (podróbnaia ~)
detailed label
  прикреплять ~/ку (prikrepliát'
~/ku) to apply a label
  описательная ~ (opisátel'naia ~)
descriptive label
  подробная ~ (podróbnaia ~)
detailed label
  прилагаемая ~ (prilagáemaia ~)
enclosed label
  с ~/ками (s ~/kami) with labels
  ~ багажа (~ bagazhá) luggage tag
  ~ груза (~ grúza) cargo label
  ~ "красная" (~ krásnaia) "red"
label {denotes dangerous cargo}
  ~ места (~ mésta) package label
  ~ на задней части упаковки (~ na
zádnei chásti upakóvki) back
label

~ с артикулом (~ s artíkulom) coded label

~ с ценой (~ s tsenói) price tag

~, содержащая рецепт для приготовления продуктов (~, soderzháshchaia retsépt dlia prigotovléniia prodúktov) recipe label

Эффект (effékt) *m.* effect, result

давать экономический ~ (davát' ekonomícheskii ~) to be economically effective

обеспечивать экономический ~ (obespéchivat' ekonomícheskii ~) to yield an economic effect

общий ~ (óbshchii ~) cumulative effect

побочный ~ (pobóchnyi ~) spillover effect

положительный ~ (polozhítel'nyi ~) positive effect

технический ~ (tekhnícheskii ~) technical effect

экономический ~ (ekonomícheskii ~) economic effect

~ искажения цены (~ iskazhéniia tsený) price distorting effect

Эффективност/ь (effektívnost/') *f.* efficiency

высокая ~ (vysókaia ~) high ~

коммерческая ~ (kommércheskaia ~) commercial ~

коэффициент ~/и (koeffitsiént ~/i) effectiveness ratio

общая ~ (óbshchaia ~) overall effectiveness

оптимальная ~ (optimál'naia ~) optimum ~

определять ~ (opredeliát' ~) to determine ~

повышение ~/и (povyshénie ~/i) an increase in ~

расчёт экономической ~/и (raschiót ekonomícheskoi ~/i) calculation of economic ~

снижение ~/и (snizhénie ~/i) decline in ~

уровень ~/и (úroven' ~/i) level of ~

экономическая ~ (ekonomícheskaia ~) economic ~

эксплуатационная ~ (ekspluatatsiónnaia ~) operating ~

~ изобретения (~ izobreténiia) ~ of an invention

~ информации (~ informátsii) ~ of information

~ капиталовложения (~ kapitalovlozhéniia) investment ~

~ лицензирования (~ litsenzírovaniia) ~ of licensing

~ модификации (~ modifikátsii) ~ of modification

~ патентования (~ patentovániia) ~ of patenting

~ производства (~ proizvódstva) ~ of production

~ рекламы (~ reklámy) advertising ~

~ экспорта (éksporta) ~ of exports

Эффективный (effektívnyi) *adj.* effective, efficient

Ю

Юридически (iuridícheski) *adv.* juridically, legally

Юридическ/ий (iuridícheskii) *adj.* juridical, legal

с ~/ой точки зрения (s ~/oi tóchki zréniia) from a legal standpoint

~/ая консультация (~/aia konsul'tátsiia) legal advice department, legal clinic

~/ие науки (~/ie naúki) jurisprudence, legal sciences

~/ое лицо (~/oe litsó) juridical person {legal entity}

~ факультет (~ fakul'tét) law department {law school}

Юрисдикци/я (iurisdíktsiia) *f.* jurisdiction

государственная ~ (gosudárstvennaia ~) state ~

гражданская ~ (grazhdánskaia ~) civil ~

иностранная ~ (inostránnaia ~) foreign ~

исключительная ~ (iskliuchítel'naia ~) exclusive ~

консульская ~ (kónsul'skaia ~) consular ~

консультативная ~ (konsul'tatívnaia ~) advisory ~

национальная ~ (natsionál'naia ~) national ~

общая ~ (óbshchaia ~) general ~

подпадать под ~/ю (popadát' pod ~/iu) to fall within the ~
Юрисконсульт (iuriskónsul't) m. legal advisor, in-house counsel
внешний ~ (vnéshnii ~) outside counsel
генеральный ~ по патентам (generál'nyi ~ po paténtam) general patent counsellor
Юриспруденция (iurisprudéntsiia) f. jurisprudence
Юрист (iuríst) m. lawyer
консультация ~/a (konsul'tátsiia ~/a) legal advice
Юстици/я (iustítsiia) f. justice
Министерство ~/и (ministérstvo ~/i) Ministry of Justice
Юрфак (iúrfák) m. [see юридический факультет]

Я

Явиться (iavít'sia) v. to appear, to report {show up}
~ в суд (~ v sud) to appear before the court
~ на службу (~ na slúzhbu) to report for duty
~ с повинной (~ s povínnoi) to give oneself up, to turn oneself in {to the authorities}
Явка (iávka) f. appearance, attendance, rendezvous
~ в суд (~ v sud) court appearance
Явление (iavlénie) n. occurence, phenomenon
Явный (iávnyi) adj. open, overt, patent
Явочный (iávochnyi) adj. attendance
~ пункт (~ punkt) call-up point {for military conscription}
~ участок (~ uchástok) recruiting office
Явствовать (iávstvovat') v. to be clear {in meaning}
Язык (iazýk) m. language, tongue
Языковой (iazykovói) adj. language
~ барьер (~ bar'ér) ~ barrier
Якобы (iákoby) adv. allegedly
Якорн/ый (iákornyi) adj. anchor
~/ая стоянка (~/aia stoiánka) anchorage
Ярлык (iarlýk) m. label, tag

бумажный ~ (bumázhnyi ~) paper tag
инвентарный ~ (inventárnyi ~) inventory tag
металлический ~ (mettalícheskii ~) tin plate
наклеивать ~ (nakléivat' ~) to attach a tag
отрывной ~ (otryvnói ~) tear-away tag
пластмассовый ~ (plastmássovyi ~) plastic tag
товарный ~ (továrnyi ~) goods tear-away tag
~ с указанием цены (~ s ukazániem tsený) price tag
Ярмарк/а (iármarka) f. fair
администрация ~/и (administrátsiia ~/i) ~ administration
весенняя ~ (vesénniaia ~) sprin ~
всемирная ~ (vsemírnaia ~) world's ~
дни работы ~/и, отведённые для бизнесменов (dni rabóty ~/i, otvediónnye dlia biznesménov) trade days
заявка на участие в ~/e (zaiávk na uchástie v ~/e) application to participate in a ~
ежегодная ~ (ezhegódnaia ~) annual ~
коммерческий центр ~/и (kommércheskii tsentr ~/i) commercial center of a ~
на ~/e (na ~/e) at a ~
международная ~ (mezhdunaródnai ~) international ~
общий план ~/и (óbshchii plan ~/i) general plan of a ~
оптовая ~ (optóvaia ~) wholesal ~
организаторы ~/и (organizátory ~/i) organizers of a ~
осмотр ~/и (osmótr ~/i) tour of a ~
открывать ~/y (otkryvát' ~/u) t open a ~
осенняя ~ (osénniaia ~) autumn ~
отраслевая ~ (otraslevária ~) specialized trade ~
план участия в ~/ах (plan uchástiia v ~/akh) plan of participation in ~s
площадь ~/и (plóshchad' ~/i) area of a ~

принимать участие в ~/е (prinimát' uchástie v ~/e) to participate in a ~
предстоящая ~ (predstoiáshchaia ~) upcoming ~
проводить ~/у (provodít' ~/u) to hold a ~
пропуск на ~/у (própusk na ~/u) entrance pass to a ~
раздел ~/и (razdél ~/i) section of a ~
региональная ~ (regionál'naia ~) regional ~
специализированная ~ (spetsializírovannaia ~) specialized ~
специалист по ~/ам (spetsialíst po ~/am) trade fair expert
территория ~/и ~ (territóriia ~/i) ~ grounds
техническая ~ (tekhnícheskaia ~) technical ~
торговая ~ (torgóvaia ~) trade ~
традиционная ~ (traditsiónnaia ~) traditional ~
устраивать ~/у (ustráivat' ~/u) to arrange a ~
участники ~/и (uchástniki ~/i) participants in a ~
экспозиция ~/и (ekspozítsiia ~/i) exposition of a ~
юбилейная ~ (iubiléinaia ~) jubilee ~
~ образцов (~ obraztsóv) sample ~

Ярмарка-выставка (iármarka-výstavka) *f.* trade show
Ярмарочный (iármarochnyi) *adj.* fair
Ящик (iáshchik) *m.* box, case
вес ~/а (ves ~/a) weight of a case
водонепроницаемый ~ (vodonepronitsáemyi ~) watertight case
вскрывать ~/и (vskryvát' ~/i) to open boxes
габариты ~/а (gabaríty ~/a) case dimensions
деревянный ~ (dereviánnyi ~) wooden box
забивать ~ (zabivát' ~) to nail down a case
карточный ~ (kártochnyi ~) cardboard box
комплект из нескольких ~/ов (komplékt iz néskol'kikh ~/ov) set of cases

крышка ~/а (krýshka ~/a) box top
маркировать ~ (markírovat' ~) to mark a case
металлический ~ (metallícheskii ~) metal box
многооборотный ~ (mnogooborótnyi ~) multi-use case
негабаритный ~ (negabarítnyi ~) oversized case
непрочный ~ (nepróchnyi ~) weak case
повреждённый ~ (povrezhdiónnyi ~) damaged case
почтовый ~ (pochtóvyi ~) post office box
прочный ~ (próchnyi ~) strongbox
перевозить в ~/ах (perevozít' v ~/akh) to carry in cases
разборно-складной ~ (razbórno-skladnói ~) fold-down box
разборный ~ (razbórnyi ~) collapsible case
размер ~/а (razmér ~/a) case size
решётчатый ~ (reshiótchatyi ~) skeleton case, crate
содержимое ~/а (soderzhímoe ~/a) contents of a case
сортировать ~/и (sortírovat' ~/i) to sort cases
складной ~ (skladnói ~) folding case
стальной ~ (stal'nói ~) steel box
стандартный ~ (standártnyi ~) standard box
тёсовый ~ (tiósovyi ~) timber case
товар в ~/ах (továr v ~/akh) cased goods
упаковочный ~ (upakóvochnyi ~) packing case
фанерный ~ (fanérnyi ~) plywood box
щитовой ~ (shchitovói ~) panel case
экспортный ~ (éksportnyi ~) export case
~ для морской перевозки (~ dlia morskói perevózki) overseas trunk
~ одноразового пользования (~ odnorázovogo pól'zovaniiaia) disposable case
~ со съёмной крышкой (~ so s"iómnoi krýshkoi) box with hinged lid

~ имеет пятна от морской воды (~
iméet piátna ot morskói vodý)
the case is stained by seawater
~ имеет следы течи (~ iméet
sledý téchi) the case shows
signs of leakage
~/и повреждены (~/i povrezhdený)
the cases are damaged
Ящик-лоток (iáshchik-lotók) *m.*
pallet
Ящичный (iáshchichnyi) *adj.* box,
case

DICTIONARY OF
BUSINESS & LEGAL TERMS

ENGLISH-RUSSIAN

A

bandon, to ~ (аба́ндон, ту ~)
окидать
  to ~ an action (ту ~ ан акшн)
отказать в иске
  to ~ a suit (ту ~ а сут)
отказать в иске
bandonment (аба́ндонмэнт) абандон,
ставление, отказ
  malicious ~ of child (мали́шэс ~
оф чайлд) злостное оставление
ребёнка
  malicious ~ of family (мали́шэс ~
оф фа́мили) злостное оставление
семьи
  ~ by one spouse of the other (~
бай уа́н спо́ус оф θи о́θэр)
оставление одного из супругов
другим
  ~ of action (~ оф акшн) отказ от
иска
  ~ of a child (~ оф а чайлд)
подкидывание ребёнка
  ~ of encumbered property (~ оф
энка́мбэрд про́пэрти) оставление
обремененного ипотекой имущества
  ~ of indemnity (~ оф индэ́мнити)
отказ от возмещения
  ~ of property (~ оф про́пэрти)
отказ от имущества
  ~ of ship (~ оф шип) оставление
погибающего корабля
  ~ of suit (~ оф сут) отказ от
иска
  ~ of usufruct (~ оф ю́суфрукт)
оставление за собой узуфрукта
breviate, to ~ (аббри́виэйт, ту ~)
кращать
breviation (аббривиэ́йшн)
кращение
dicate, to ~ (а́бдикэйт, ту ~)
рекаться [perfective: отречься]
  to ~ the throne (ту ~ θи θрон)
отрекаться от престола
dication (абдикэ́йшн) отречение
  ~ of the throne (~ оф θи θрон)
отречение от престола
duct, to ~ (абда́кт, ту ~)
хищать
duction (абдакшн) похищение
etting, aiding and ~ (абэ́ттинг,
динг энд ~) пособничество
ettor (абэ́ттор) пособник
ility (аби́лити) способность
  competitive ~ (компэ́титив ~)
конкурентная способность

payment ~ (пэ́ймэнт ~) платёжная
способность
Able (эйбл) способный
Able-bodied (э́йбл-бо́дид)
работоспособный, трудоспособный
Abolition (аболи́шн) отмена
Abortion (або́ршн) аборт
  criminal ~ (кри́минал ~)
наказуемый аборт
  self-~ (сэлф-~) аборт
произведённый самой беременной
  to perform an ~ (ту пэрфо́рм ан
~) произвести аборт
  ~ performed by the subject (~
пэрфо́рмд бай θи са́бджэкт) аборт
произведённый самой беременной
  ~ performed by a third party (~
пэрфо́рмд бай а θирд па́рти) аборт
произведённый другим лицом
Abrogate, to ~ (а́брогэйт, ту ~)
расторгать [perfective:
расторгнуть]
Abrogation (аброгэ́йшн) отмена,
расторжение
Absence (а́бсэнс) неимение, отлучка,
отсутствие
  in one's ~ (ин уа́нз ~) заочно
  premeditated ~ (примэ́дитэйтэд ~)
преднамеренное отсутствие
  ~ of guilt (~ оф гилт)
отсутствие вины
  ~ of liability (~ оф лайаби́лити)
отсутствие ответственности
  ~ without leave {AWOL} (~ уиθо́ут
лив {э́йуол}) самовольная отлучка
Absent (а́бсэнт) отсутствующий
  to be ~ (ту би ~) отсутствовать
  ~ without leave {AWOL} (~ уиθо́ут
лив {эй-уол}) в самовольной
отлучке
Absenteeism (абсэнти́изм)
абсентеизм, неявка на работу,
прогул
Absolutism (абсолю́тизм) абсолютизм
  enlightened ~ (энла́йтэнд ~)
просвещённый абсолютизм
Abstract (а́бстракт) автореферат {of
document}, выписка
  ~ from the registry (~ фром θи
рэ́джистри) выписка из реестра
Abundance (аба́нданс) изобилие
Abuse (абю́с) злоупотребление
  ~ of authority (~ оф аθо́рити)
злоупотребление властью
  ~ of an invention (~ оф ан
инвэ́ншн) злоупотребление
изобретением

~ **of office** (~ оф óффис) злоупотребление служебным положением

~ **of privileges** (~ оф прíвэлэджэз) злоупотребление привилегиями

~ **of a right** (~ оф а райт) злоупотребление правом

~ **of trademark** (~ оф трэ́йдмарк) злоупотребление товарным знаком

Abusive (абю́сив) оскорбительный

Academy (ака́дэми) академия

~ **of International Law** (~ оф интэрна́шэнал лау) международного права

Accept, to ~ (аксэ́пт, ту ~) акцептовать, принимать {a negotiable instrument, etc.}

Acceptability (аксэптабíлити) приемлемость

Acceptable (аксэ́птабл) приемлемый

Acceptance (аксэ́птанс) акцепт {instrument, contract formation}, приёмка, принятие, тратта

act of ~ (акт оф ~) акт о принятии

bank ~ (банк ~) банковский акцепт

conditional ~ (кондíшнал ~) условный акцепт

notice of ~ (нóтис оф ~) авизо об акцепте

partial ~ (паршл ~) частичный акцепт

positive ~ (пóзитив ~) положительный акцепт

preliminary ~ (прилíминэри ~) предварительный акцепт

"present for ~**"** (прэзэ́нт фор ~) «предъявить для акцепта

qualified ~ (куа́лифайд ~) ограниченный акцепт

silent ~ (са́йлэнт ~) молчаливый акцепт

subsequent ~ (са́бсикуэнт ~) последующий акцепт

unconditional ~ (анкондíшнал ~) безоговорочное принятие, безусловный акцепт

uncovered ~ (анкóвэрд ~) вексель, акцептованный без покрытия

warehouse ~ (уэ́рхаус ~) принятие на хранение товарным складом

~ **against documents** (~ агэ́нст дóкюмэнтс) акцепт против документов

~ **certificate** (~ сэртíфикэт) акт приёмки

~ **for safe deposit** (~ фор сэйф дипóзит) приём на хранение

~ **in blank** (~ ин бланк) бланковый акцепт

~ **into the U.N.** (~ íнту θи ю-эн) приём в ООН

~ **of a bill** (~ оф а билл) акцепт счёта

~ **of a bill of exchange** (~ оф а билл оф эксчэ́йндж) акцепт векселя

~ **of a bribe** (~ оф а брайб) получение взятки

~ **of cargo** (~ оф ка́рго) получение груза

~ **of a check** (~ оф а чэк) принятие чека

~ **of commercial documents** (~ оф коммэ́ршл дóкюмэнтс) акцепт коммерческих документов

~ **of a draft** (~ оф а драфт) акцепт тратты

~ **of goods** (~ оф гудз) сдача-приёмка

~ **of risk** (~ оф риск) принятие риска

~ **under condition** (~ а́ндэр кондíшн) принятие под условием

Acceptor (аксэ́птор) акцептант

Access (а́ксэс) допуск, доступ

complete ~ (комплíт ~) полный доступ

free ~ (фри ~) свободный доступ

market ~ (ма́ркэт ~) доступ к рынкам

product ~ **to the market** (прóдукт ~ ту θи ма́ркэт) допуск продукции на рынок

to gain ~ **to** (ту гэйн ~ ту) получить допуск к

to have ~ **to** (ту хэв ~ ту) иметь допуск к

unobstructed ~ (анобстра́ктэд ~) беспрепятственный доступ

~ **to natural resources** (~ ту на́чюрал рисóрсэз) доступ к источникам сырья

~ **to the pavilion** (~ ту θи павíльон) доступ в павильон

Accessible (аксэ́ссибл) доступный

Accession (аксэ́шн) акцессия

instrument of ~ (íнструмэнт оф ~) акт о присоединении

~ **to a convention** (~ ту а конвэ́ншн) присоединение конвенции
Accessory (аксэ́ссори) принадлежность, соучастник
~ **to a crime** (~ ту а крайм) соучастник преступления
Accident (а́ксидэнт) аварийное происшествие, авария, несчастный случай
~ **rate** (~ рэйт) аварийность
Accidental (аксидэ́нтал) случайный
Accommodate, to ~ (акко́модэйт, ту ~) помещать, приспособлять
Accommodation (аккомодэ́йшн) помещение, приспособление, ссуда {loan}
price ~ (прайс ~) приспособление цен
Accomplice (акко́мплис) соучастник
Accomplish, to ~ (акко́мплиш, ту ~) осуществлять [perfective: осуществить], совершать
Accomplishment (акко́мплишмэнт) достижение, осуществление, совершение
~ **of a deal** (~ оф а дил) совершение сделки
Accord (акко́рд) согласие
to ~ (ту ~) соответствовать
Accordance (акко́рданс) соответствие
in ~ **with legislation** (ин ~ уиθ лэджислэ́йшн) в соответствии с законодательством
in ~ **with your request** (ин ~ уиθ ёр рикуэ́ст) в соответствии с Вашей просьбой
Account (акко́унт) описание, отчёт, счёт
bank ~ (банк ~) банковский счёт
bilateral ~ (байла́тэрал ~) двухсторонний счёт
blocked ~ (блокд ~) блокированный счёт
budget ~ (ба́джэт ~) бюджетный счёт
call ~ (калл ~) онколь
capital ~ (ка́питал ~) капитальный счёт
checking ~ (чэ́ккинг ~) текущий банковский счёт
clearing ~ (кли́ринг ~) безналичный расчёт, клиринговый счёт
closing ~ (кло́синг ~) сводный счёт

consolidated ~ (консо́лидэйтэд ~) консолидированный счёт
convertible ~ (конвэ́ртибл ~) конвертируемый счёт
correspondent ~ (коррэспо́ндэнт ~) корреспондентский счёт
current ~ (ку́ррэнт ~) текущий счёт
demand ~ (дима́нд ~) онколь
deposit ~ (дипо́зит ~) авансовый счёт, депозитный счёт
domestic ~ (домэ́стик ~) внутренний счёт
external ~ (экстэ́рнал ~) внешний счёт
foreign ~ (фо́рэн ~) иностранный счёт
foreign exchange ~ (фо́рэн эксчэ́йндж ~) валютный счёт
governmental ~ (говэрнмэ́нтал ~) государственный счёт
investment ~ (инвэ́стмэнт ~) инвестиционный счёт
joint ~ (джойнт ~) общий счёт
loan ~ (лон ~) ссудный счёт
non-interest bearing ~ (нон-и́нтэрэст бэ́ринг ~) беспроцентный счёт
personal ~ (пэ́рсонал ~) лицевой счёт
postal ~ (по́стал ~) почтовый счёт
registered ~ (рэ́джистэрд ~) регистрированный счёт
reserve ~ (рисэ́рв ~) резервный счёт
separate ~ (сэ́парат ~) отдельный счёт
settlement ~ (сэ́тлмэнт ~) расчётный счёт
special ~ (спэшл ~) особый счёт
to ~ (ту ~) зачитывать [perfective: зачесть]
to ~ **for** (ту ~ фор) учитывать
to call to ~ (ту калл ту ~) привлекать к участию в деле
to overdraw an ~ (ту овэрдра́у ан ~) превышать кредит
to block an ~ (ту блок ан ~) блокировать счёт
to close an ~ (ту клоз ан ~) закрыть счёт
to deposit into an ~ (ту дипо́зит и́нту ан ~) внести в счёт
to give an ~ **of** (ту гив ан ~ оф) отчитываться

to **open an** ~ (ту о́пэн ан ~)
открыть счёт
to **unblock an** ~ (ту анбло́к ан ~)
деблокировать счёт
transferrable ~ (трансфэ́рабл ~)
переводный счёт
~ **of events** (~ оф ивэ́нтс)
изложение
Accountability (аккоунтаби́лити)
подотчётность
property ~ (про́пэрти ~)
имущественная ответственность
Accountable (акко́унтабл)
подотчётный
Accountant (акко́унтант) бухгалтер
certified public ~ (сэ́ртифайд
па́блик ~) аудитор
chief ~ (чиф ~) главный
бухгалтер
cost ~ (кост ~)
бухгалтер-калькулятор
Accounting (акко́унтинг)
бухгалтерский {adj.}, счетоводство,
учёт
cost ~ (кост ~) учёт
производственных затрат,
хозрасчёт, хозрасчётная
деятельность, хозрасчётный
{adj.}
economic ~ **system** (эконо́мик ~
си́стэм) система хозрасчёта
full-scale cost ~ (фул-скэйл
кост ~) полный хозрасчёт
intra-system cost ~ (и́нтра-
си́стэм кост ~) внутрисистемный
хозрасчёт
money ~ (мо́ни ~) денежный учёт
profit and loss ~ (про́фит энд
лос ~) хозяйственный расчёт
routine ~ (рути́н ~) оперативный
учёт
statistical ~ (стати́стикал ~)
статистический учёт
to **operate on a cost** ~ **basis** (ту
о́пэрэйт он а кост ~ бэ́йсис) быть
на хозрасчёте
to **transfer to cost** ~ (ту
тра́нсфэр ту кост ~) переводить
хозрасчёт
work on a cost ~ **basis** (уо́рк он
а кост ~ бэ́йсис) работа на базе
хозрасчёта
~ **of national income** (~ оф
на́шэнал и́нком) баланс
национального дохода
~ **practices** (~ пра́ктисэз) методы
бухгалтерского учёта

~ **records** (~ рэ́кордз)
бухгалтерский счёт
Accredit, to ~ (аккрэ́дит, ту ~)
аккредитовать
Accreditation (аккрэдитэ́йшн)
аккредитация, аккредитование
Accredited (аккрэ́дитэд)
аккредитованный
Accrual (аккру́ал) накопление
interest ~ **formula** (и́нтэрэст ~
фо́рмюла) формула начисления
процентов
~ **of interest** (~ оф и́нтэрэст)
накопление процентов
Accrue, to ~ (аккру́, ту ~)
накапливаться, нарастать
Accrued (аккру́д) накопившийся,
наросший
Accumulate, to ~ (акки́мюлэйт, ту ~)
накапливать, нарастать
Accumulated (акки́мюлэйтэд) наросший
Accumulation (аккюмюлэ́йшн)
кумуляция, накопление, наращивание
accelerated ~ (аксэ́лэрэйтэд ~)
ускоренное накопление
capital ~ (ка́питал ~) накопление
капитала
non-productive ~ (нон-
прода́ктив~) непроизводственное
накопление
productive ~ (прода́ктив ~)
производственное накопление
substantial ~ (сабста́ншл ~)
существенные накопления
~ **of funds** (~ оф фандз)
накопление денежных средств
~ **of stocks** (~ оф стокс)
создание запасов
Accuracy (а́ккюрэси) правильность,
точность
maximum ~ (ма́ксимум ~)
максимальная точность
possible ~ (по́ссибл ~) возможная
точность
required ~ (рикуа́йрд ~)
необходимая точность
Accurate (а́ккюрат) правильный
Accurately (а́ккюратли) точно
Accused (аккю́зд) подсудимый
Achieve, to ~ (ачи́в, ту ~)
достигать
Achieved (ачи́вд) достигнутый
Achievement (ачи́вмэнт) достижение
economic ~**s** (эконо́мик ~с)
экономические достижения
latest ~**s** (лэ́йтэст ~с) новейшие
достижения

level of ~s (лэ́вэл оф ~с)
уровень достижений
scientific and technological ~s
(сайэнти́фик энд тэкноло́джикал
~с) достижения науки и
технологии
technical ~s (тэ́кникал ~с)
технические достижения
to reflect ~s (ту рифлэ́кт ~с)
отражать достижения
Acknowledge, to ~ (акно́лэдж, ту ~)
подтверждать, признать
Acknowledgment (акно́лэджмэнт)
признание
death-bed ~ (дэ́θ-бэд ~)
посмертное признание
direct ~ (дирэ́кт ~) прямое
подтверждение
implied ~ (импла́йд ~)
подразумеваемое подтверждение
mutual ~ (мю́чуал ~) взаимное
признание
~ of annexation (~ оф
аннэксэ́йшн) признание аннексии
~ of a debt (~ оф а дэт)
признание долга
~ of illegitimate child (~ оф
иллэджи́тэмат чайлд) признание
внебрачного ребёнка
~ of independence (~ оф
индэпэ́ндэнс) признание
независимости
~ of maternity (~ оф матэ́рнити)
признание материнства
~ of paternity (~ оф патэ́рнити)
признание отцовства
~ of signature (~ оф си́гначэр)
признание подписи
~ with reserve (~ уиθ рисэ́рв)
признание с оговоркой
Acquire, to ~ (акуа́йр, ту ~)
получать, приобретать [perfective:
приобрести]
Acquisition (аккуизи́шн) получение,
приобретение
advantageous ~ (адвантэ́йджэс ~)
преимущественное приобретение
good faith ~ (гуд фэйθ ~)
добросовестное приобретение
joint ~ (джойнт ~) совместное
приобретение
original ~ (ори́джинал ~)
первоначальное приобретение
paid ~ (пэйд ~) возмездное
приобретение
sham ~ (шам ~) мнимое
приобретение

territorial ~ (тэррито́риал ~)
территориальное приобретение
unpaid ~ (анпэ́йд ~)
безвозмездное приобретение
~ by prescription (~ бай
прэскри́пшн) приобретение по
давности
~ of citizenship by marriage (~
оф си́тизэншип бай мэ́ррэдж)
приобретение гражданства по
браку
~ of citizenship by parentage (~
оф си́тизэншип бай па́рэнтэдж)
приобретение гражданства по
усыновлению
~ of citizenship (~ оф
си́тизэншип) приобретение
гражданства
~ of community property {by
marriage} (~ оф камми́нити
про́пэрти {бай мэ́ррэдж})
приобретение супружеской
общности
~ of property (~ оф про́пэрти)
приобретение имущества
~ of right (~ оф райт)
приобретение права
~ of right of property (~ оф
райт оф про́пэрти) приобретение
права собственности
Acquit, to ~ (аккуи́т, ту ~)
оправдать
Acquittal (аккуи́ттал) оправдание,
оправдательный приговор
Acquittance (аккуи́ттанс) расписка
об уплате долга
Acre (эйкр) акр
Act (акт) акт, действие, договор,
закон
action in ~ (акшн ин ~) иск из
договора
arbitral ~ (а́рбитрал ~) акт об
арбитраже, арбитражный акт
as per ~ (аз пэр ~) согласно
договору
breach of ~ (брич оф ~)
нарушение договора
broker's ~ (бро́кэрз ~) агентский
договор
buy-sell ~ (бай-сэл ~) договор
купли-продажи
by ~ (бай ~) по договору
civil law ~ (си́вил лау ~)
гражданско-правовой договор
collective ~ (колле́ктив ~)
коллективный акт

commercial ~ (коммэ́ршл ~) коммерческий акт

conclusive ~ (конклю́сив ~) заключительный акт

consignment ~ (конса́йнмэнт ~) договор консигнации

constitutional ~ (конститу́шнал ~) конституционный акт

consular ~ (ко́нсюлар ~) консульский акт

diplomatic ~ (диплома́тик ~) дипломатический акт

disputed ~ (диспю́тэд ~) оспоримое действие

enabling ~ (энэ́йблинг ~) акт об установлении права

evidentiary ~ (эвидэ́ншиэри ~) доказательственный акт

extra-judicial ~ (э́кстра-джюди́шл ~) внесудебный акт

formal ~ (фо́рмал ~) формальный акт

freight ~ (фрэйт ~) договор о фрахтовании судна

general freight ~ (джэ́нэрал фрэйт ~) генеральный договор о фрахтовании судна

government ~ (го́вэрнмэнт ~) постановление правительства

hostile ~ (хо́стайл ~) враждебный акт

illegal ~ (илли́гал ~) незаконный акт, незаконный договор

illegal ~s (илли́гал ~с) противоправные действия

indemnity ~ (индэ́мнити ~) договор гарантии от убытков

individual ~ (индиви́дюал ~) индивидуальный акт

internal government ~ (интэ́рнал го́вэрнмэнт ~) внутригосударственный акт

judicial ~ (джюди́шл ~) юридический акт

juridical ~ (джюри́дикал ~) юридическое действие

lawful ~ (ла́уфул ~) правомерное действие

legal ~ (ли́гал ~) правовой акт

legislative ~ (лэ́джислэйтив ~) законодательный акт

marine insurance ~ (мари́н иншю́ранс ~) договор морского страхования

marine tug ~ (мари́н тауг ~) договор морской буксировки

monopoly ~ (моно́поли ~) монопольный договор

multilateral ~ (мултила́тэрал ~) многосторонний акт

navigation ~ (навигэ́йшн ~) акт навигации, навигационный акт

normative ~ (но́рматив ~) нормативный акт, подзаконный акт

obligations under ~ (облигэ́йшнз а́ндэр ~) обязательства по договору

obligatory ~ (обли́гатори ~) обязательный акт

official ~ (оффи́шл ~) официальный акт, служебный акт

optional ~ (о́пшнал ~) факультативный акт

penalty for non-performance of an ~ (пэ́налти фор нон-пэрфо́рманс оф ан ~) штраф за невыполнение договор

performance of a ~ (пэрфо́рманс оф а ~) выполнение договор

preliminary ~s (прили́минэри ~с) предварительные действия

private ~ (пра́йват ~) частный акт

procedural ~ (проси́дюрал ~) процессуальный акт

separate ~ (сэ́парат ~) отдельный закон

shipping ~ (ши́ппинг ~) акт о судоходстве

supplementary ~ (сапплэмэ́нтари ~) дополнительный акт

to ~ (ту ~) действовать

to be bound by ~ (ту би бо́унд бай ~) быть связанным договором

to breach a ~ (ту брич а ~) нарушать договор

to draw up a ~ (ту дра́у ап а ~) оформлять договор

to extend an ~ (ту экстэ́нд ан ~) продлевать договор

to perform under a ~ (ту пэрфо́рм а́ндэр а ~) выполнять договор

to sign an ~ (ту сайн ан ~) подписывать договор

uncompleted executory ~ (анкомпли́тэд экзэ́кютори ~) незавершённый договор

under ~ (а́ндэр ~) по договору

unfriendly ~ (анфрэ́ндли ~) недружелюбный акт

unilateral ~ (юнила́тэрал ~) односторонний акт, одностороннее действие

voidable ~ (во́йдабл ~) оспоримый договор
~ in the line of duty (~ ин θи лайн оф дю́ти) служебный акт
~ of affreightment (~ оф аффрэ́йтмэнт) договор морской перевозки
~ of a civil nature (~ оф а си́вил нэ́йчэр) акт гражданского состояния
~ of employment (~ оф эмпло́ймэнт) договор о найме
~ of guarantee (~ оф гяранти́) договор о поручительстве
~ of jurisdiction (~ оф джюрисди́кшн) акт юрисдикции
~ of parliament (~ оф па́рламэнт) акт парламента, парламентский акт
~ of state (~ оф стэйт) акт правительства, государственный акт
~ of tenancy (~ оф тэ́нанси) договор об аренде помещения
Acting (а́ктинг) договаривающий {parties etc.}
Action (акшн) дело, иск, мероприятие
authorized ~ (а́уθорайзд ~) санкционированное действие
dismissal of legal ~ (дисми́ссал оф ли́гал ~) прекращение дела
enforcement ~s (энфо́рсмэнт ~с) принудительные действия
legal ~ (ли́гал ~) судебный иск
obligatory ~s (обли́гатори ~с) принудительные действия
official ~ (оффи́шл ~) официальное действие
personal ~ (пэ́рсонал ~) личный иск
plan of ~ (план оф ~) план мероприятий
possessory ~ (позэ́ссори ~) поссесорный иск
prejudicial ~ (прэджюди́шл ~) действие наносящее ущерб
prior to ~ (пра́йор ту ~) до начала действий
probate ~ (про́бэйт ~) иск о наследстве
public ~ (па́блик ~) публичный акт, публичный иск
real property ~ (ри́ал про́пэрти ~) иск о недвижимости
recourse ~ (ри́корс ~) регрессный иск

repeated ~s (рипи́тэд ~с) многократное действие
summary ~ (са́ммари ~) суммарное действие
to bring an ~ (ту бринг ан ~) возбуждать дело, возбудить иск, вчинить иск, подать в суд, предъявить иск
to bring an ~ against (ту бринг ан ~ агэ́нст) возбуждать действие против, привлечь к суду
to initiate an ~ against (ту ини́шиэйт ан ~ агэ́нст) начать дело против
to prevent ~ (ту привэ́нт ~) предупреждать действия
to require ~s (ту рикуа́йр ~с) требовать действий
to take ~ (ту тэйк ~) предпринимать действия
to win an ~ (ту уин ан ~) выигрывать дело
to withdraw an ~ (ту уиθдра́у ан ~) отказаться от иска
tort ~ (торт ~) иск о деликтной ответственности
unfair competition ~ (анфэ́йр компэти́шн ~) иск о недобросовестной конкуренции
urgent ~ (у́рджэнт ~) срочное действие
warranty ~ (уа́рранти ~) иск о гарантии
~ at law (~ ат лау) исковое требование, судебный иск
~ for damages (~ фор да́мэджэз) иск о возмещении убытков
~ for divorce (~ фор диво́рс) иск о разводе
~ for an injunction (~ фор ан инджю́нкшн) исполнительный иск
~ for partition (~ фор парти́шн) иск о разделе
~ for personalty (~ фор пэ́рсоналти) иск о движимом имуществе
~ in rem (~ ин рэм) вещный иск
~ to enforce judgment (~ ту энфо́рс джа́джмэнт) иск о приведении в исполнение решения
~ to settle a boundary dispute (~ ту сэтл а бо́ундари диспю́т) иск о размежевании
Active (а́ктив) действующий
Activism (а́ктивисм) агитация
Activist (а́ктивист) агитатор
party ~ (па́рти ~) партактив

peace ~ (пис ~) сторонник мира
Activity (активити) деятельность
    advertising ~ (адвэртайзинг ~)
рекламная деятельность
    agent's ~ (эйджэнтс ~)
деятельность агента
    business ~ (бизнэс ~) деловая
деятельность, торгово-
промышленная деятельность
    commercial ~ (коммэршл ~)
коммерческая деятельность
    creative ~ (криэйтив ~)
творческая деятельность
    diversification of ~
(дивэрсификэйшн оф ~)
диверсификация деятельности
    diversified ~ (дивэрсифайд ~)
многообразная деятельность
    economic ~ (экономик ~)
хозяйственная деятельность,
экономическая деятельность
    external economic ~ (экстэрнал
экономик ~) внешнеэкономическая
деятельность
    financial ~ (файнаншл ~)
финансовая деятельность
    financial and economic ~
(файнаншл энд экономик ~)
финансово-хозяйственная
деятельность
    foreign trade ~ (форэн трэйд ~)
внешнеторговая деятельность
    joint ~s (джойнт ~с) совместные
действия, совместная
деятельность
    labor ~ (лэйбор ~) трудовая
деятельность
    licensed ~ (лайсэнсд ~)
лицензионная деятельность
    nature of ~ (нэйчэр оф ~)
характер деятельности
    past ~ (паст ~) прошлая
деятельность
    practical ~ (практикал ~)
практическая деятельность
    primary ~ (праймари ~) основная
деятельность
    procurement ~ (прокюрмэнт ~)
закупочная деятельность
    production ~ (продакшн ~)
производственная деятельность
    promotional ~ (промошнал ~)
мероприятия стимулирования сбыта
    related ~ (рилэйтэд ~)
относящаяся деятельность
    resumption of ~ (ризумпшн оф ~)
возобновление деятельности

    site of ~ (сайт оф ~) место
деятельности
    to coordinate ~ (ту координэйт
~) координировать деятельность
    to direct ~s (ту дирэкт ~с)
руководить действиями
    to discuss ~ (ту дискас ~)
обсуждать деятельность
    to expand ~ (ту экспанд ~)
расширять деятельность
    to increase ~ (ту инкрис ~)
активизировать деятельность
    to resume ~ (ту ризум ~)
возобновлять деятельность
    to supervise ~ (ту супэрвайз ~)
купировать деятельность
    to suspend ~ (ту саспэнд ~)
приостанавливать деятельность
    trade ~ (трэйд ~) торговая
деятельность
    vigorous ~ (вигорос ~) активная
деятельность
Actual (акчуал) договорный
Actuary (акчуари) актуарий
Ad (ад) реклама
    newspaper ~ (ньюзпэйпэр ~)
газетное объявление
Adaptation (адаптэйшн) адаптация
{e.g. screenplay from novel},
приспособление
    economic ~ (экономик ~)
экономическое приспособление
Add, to ~ (ад, ту ~) набавлять,
присоединять
Addendum (аддэндам) аддендум,
дополнение
    in the form of ~ (ин θи форм оф
~) в виде дополнения
Addition (аддишн) дополнение,
присоединение
Additional (аддишнал) добавочный,
дополнительный
    ~ finance (~ файнанс) выделение
дополнительных средств
    ~ service (~ сэрвис)
сверхсрочный
    ~ payment (~ пэймэнт) доплата
Additionally (аддишналли)
дополнительно
Address (аддрэс) адрес, обращение
    business ~ (бизнэс ~) место
нахождения
    business ~ of a firm (бизнэс ~
оф а фирм) местонахождение фирмы
    forwarding ~ (форуардинг ~)
проводительный адрес
    home ~ (хом ~) домашний адрес

postal ~ (постал ~) почтовый адрес
telegraph ~ (тэлэграф ~) телеграфный адрес
to ~ (ту ~) направлять
welcoming ~ (уэлкоминг ~) приветственное обращение
Addressee (аддрэси́) адресат
Addressor (аддрэсо́р) адресант
Adequate (а́дэкуэт) достаточный
Adherent (адхэ́рэнт) сторонник
   ~ of free trade (~ оф фри трэйд) сторонник свободной торговли
   ~ of neutrality (~ оф нутра́лити) сторонник нейтралитета
Adhesion (адхи́жн) адхезия, обязательное присоединение
   contract of ~ (ко́нтракт оф ~) договор адхезии
   instrument of ~ (и́нструмэнт оф ~) акт о присоединении
Adjacent (аджэ́йсэнт) смежный
Adjunct (а́джюнкт) адъюнкт, придаток
Adjust, to ~ (аджа́ст, ту ~) корректировать, налаживать, урегулировать
   to ~ prices (ту ~ пра́йсэз) корректировать цены
Adjusted (аджа́стэд) урегулированный
   seasonally ~ (си́зоналли ~) с учётом сезонных колебаний
Adjuster (аджа́стэр) диспашёр, монтёр
   bureau of average ~s (бю́ро оф а́вэрэдж ~c) бюро диспашёров
   foreign average ~ (фо́рэн а́вэрэдж ~) иностранный диспашёр
   senior average ~ (си́ниор а́вэрэдж ~) старший диспашёр
Adjustment (аджа́стмэнт) корректировка, корректировочный {adj.}, наладка, регулирование, урегулирование
   claim ~ (клэйм ~) определение страхового возмещения
   general average ~ (джэ́нэрал а́вэрэдж ~) распределение общей аварии
   interest rate ~s (и́нтэрэст рэйт ~c) регулирование нормы процента
   price ~ (прайс ~) урегулирование цен
   seasonal ~ (си́зонал ~) корректировка на сезонные колебания
   statistical ~ (стати́стикал ~) статистическая корректировка

   ~ instructions (~ инстра́кшнс) инструкции по наладке
   ~ period (~ пи́риод) период наладки
Administration (администрэ́йшн) администрация, ведомство, правительство {e.g. as of a U.S. president}
   aviation ~ (эйвиэ́йшн ~) авиационное ведомство
   bureaucratic ~ (бюрокра́тик ~) администрирование
   central ~ (сэ́нтрал ~) центральная администрация
   civil ~ (си́вил ~) гражданская администрация
   colonial ~ (коло́ниал ~) колониальная администрация
   international ~ (интэрна́шэнал ~) международная администрация
   local ~ (ло́кал ~) местная администрация
   military ~ (ми́литари ~) военная администрация
   patent ~ (па́тэнт ~) патентное ведомство
   penal ~ (пи́нал ~) тюремная администрация
   ports ~ (портс ~) администрация портов
   postal ~ (по́стал ~) почтовая администрация
   property ~ (про́пэрти ~) администрация над имуществом
   railway ~ (рэ́йлуэй ~) железнодорожное ведомство
   special riparian ~ (спэшл райпэ́йриан ~) специальная речная администрация
   tax ~ (такс ~) налоговое ведомство
   tax-collection ~ (такс-колле́кшн ~) взимающая администрация
   ~ of international development (~ оф интэрна́шэнал дивэ́лопмэнт) администрация международного развития
   ~ pro tempore (~ про тэмпо́рэ) временная администрация
Administrative (адми́нистрэйтив) административный, руководящий, управленческий
   by ~ means (бай ~ минз) в административном порядке
Administrator (адми́нистрэйтор) администратор

property ~ (про́пэрти ~)
администратор имуществ
Admissibility (адмисиби́лити)
приемлемость
Admissible (адми́ссибл) допустимый,
приемлемый
Admission (адми́шн) признание,
разрешение на участие
    act of ~ (акт оф ~) акт
признания
    extralegal ~ (экстрали́гал ~)
внесудебное признание
    qualified ~ (куа́лифайд ~)
квалификационное признание
    voluntary ~ (во́лунтэри ~)
добровольное признание
    ~ **of guilt** (~ оф гилт) признание
виновности
    ~ **of liability** (~ оф лайаби́лити)
признание ответственности
    ~ **to "on the exchange"** (~ ту "он
θи эксчэ́йндж") допуск к
регистрации на бирже
Admit, to ~ (адми́т, ту ~)
признавать, пропустить
Admittance (адми́танс) допуск
    ~ **to membership** (~ ту мэ́мбэршип)
приём в члены
Adopt, to ~ (адо́пт, ту ~) принимать
Adopted (адо́птэд) заимствованный,
приёмный
    ~ **child** (~ чайлд) приёмыш
Adoption (адо́пшн) принятие,
удочерение {daughter}, усыновление
{son}
    ~ **of a child** (~ оф а чайлд)
удочерение {daughter},
усыновление {son}
    ~ **of a law** (~ оф а лау) принятие
закона
Adult (ада́лт) взрослый,
совершеннолетний
Adulterer (ада́лтэрэр) адюльтер
Adulterous (ада́лтэрос)
прелюбодейный
Adultery (ада́лтэри) прелюбодеяние
Advance (адва́нс) аванс, авансовые
{adj.}, ссуда, улучшение
    bank ~ (банк ~) банковское
кредитование
    cash ~ (каш ~) денежный аванс
    import ~ (и́мпорт ~) импортный
аванс
    in ~ (ин ~) досрочный {adj.},
заблаговременно {adv.},
заблаговременный {adj.}

monthly ~s **on account** (мо́нθли ~с
он акко́унт) ежемесячное
авансирование
reimbursable ~ (риэмбу́рсабл ~)
возместимый аванс
to ~ (ту ~) авансировать,
выдвигать, провозглашать,
продвигать, ссужать [**perfective:**
ссудить]
to grant an ~ (ту грант ан ~)
предоставить аванс
to transfer an ~ (ту тра́нсфэр ан
~) перечислить аванс
~ **against payments** (~ агэ́нст
пэ́ймэнтс) аванс в счёт платежи
~ **in guarantee** (~ ин гяранти́)
гарантийный аванс
~ **of funds** (~ оф фандз) аванс
фондов
~ **of funds on account** (~ оф
фандз он акко́унт) денежное
авансирование
~s **on account** (~с он акко́унт)
авансирование
~ **on expenses** (~ он экспэ́нсэз)
аванс на расходы
~ **payment to suppliers** (~
пэ́ймэнт ту сапла́йэрс) аванс
поставщикам
~ **subject to refund** (~ са́бджэкт
ту ри́фунд) аванс подлежащий
возврату
Advancee (адванси́) авансодержатель
Advantage (адва́нтэдж) выгода,
преимущество
    equal ~ (и́куал ~) равная выгода
    financial ~ (файна́ншл ~)
финансовая выгода
    general ~ (джэ́нэрал ~) общая
выгода
    on the basis of mutual ~ (он θи
бэ́йсис оф мю́чуал ~) на основе
взаимной выгоды
    personal ~ (пэ́рсонал ~) личная
выгода
    preferential ~s (прэфэрэ́ншл ~с)
преференциальные льготы
    principle of equal ~ (при́нсипл
оф и́куал ~) принцип равной
выгоды
    self-~ (сэлф-~) личная выгода
    to a mutual ~ (ту а мю́чуал ~) к
взаимной выгоде
    to be of mutual ~ (ту би оф
мю́чуал ~) представлять взаимную
выгоду

to **recognize the** ~ (ту рэ́когнайз θи ~) признавать выгоду
to **take** ~ **of** (ту тэйк ~ оф) использовать с выгодой
Advantageous (адвантэ́йджэс) выгодный
to **be** ~ (ту би ~) быть выгодным, приносить выгоду
to **turn out to be** ~ (ту турн о́ут ту би ~) оказаться выгодным
Advent (а́двэнт) приход
Adventure (адвэ́нчур) авантюра
Adversary (а́двэрсари) противник
Advertisement (адвэрта́йзмэнт) реклама
Advice (адва́йс) извещение, консультация, совет, уведомление
collection ~ (коллэ́кшн ~) извещение об инкассо
credit ~ (крэ́дит ~) уведомление о кредитовании
debit ~ (дэ́бит ~) уведомление о дебетовании
forwarding ~ (фо́руардинг ~) уведомление об отправке
legal ~ (ли́гал ~) консультация юриста
payment ~ (пэ́ймэнт ~) платёжное извещение
railway ~ (рэ́йлуэй ~) уведомление о прибытии на железнодорожную станцию
remittance ~ (римми́ттанс ~) уведомление о денежном переводе
shipping ~ (ши́ппинг ~) уведомление об отгрузке
under ~ (а́ндэр ~) при уведомлении
~ **by mail** (~ бай мэйл) почтовое извещение
~ **of payment** (~ оф пэ́ймэнт) уведомление о платеже
~ **of readiness** (~ оф рэ́динэсс) уведомление о готовности
Advisability (адвайзаби́лити) целесообразность
Advise, to ~ (адва́йз, ту ~) уведомлять
Advisor (адва́йзор) референт, советник
economic ~ (эконо́мик ~) экономический советник
financial ~ (файна́ншл ~) финансовый советник
general ~ (джэ́нэрал ~) генеральный советник

legal ~ (ли́гал ~) юридический советник
military ~ (ми́литари ~) военный советник
technical ~ (тэ́кникал ~) технический советник
trade ~ (трэйд ~) торговый советник
Advisory (адва́йзори) консультативный
Advocate (а́двокат) адвокат
Affair (аффэ́йр) дело
current ~**s** (ку́ррэнт ~с) текущие дела
domestic ~**s** (домэ́стик ~с) внутренние дела
financial ~**s** (файна́ншл ~с) финансовые дела
state of ~**s** (стэйт оф ~с) обстоятельства дела, положение дел
to **look into the** ~ (ту лук и́нту θи ~) заниматься рассмотрением дело
to **put** ~**s in order** (ту пут ~с ин о́рдэр) приводить дела в порядок
to **settle an** ~ (ту сэтл ан ~) улаживать дело
Affidavit (аффидэ́йвит) афидевит
Affiliate (аффи́лиат) филиал
Affiliated (аффи́лиэйтэд) дочерний
~ **enterprise** (~ э́нтэрпрайз) филиал предприятия
Affinity (аффи́нити) свойство, склонность
Affirm, to ~ (аффи́рм, ту ~) подтверждать
Affirmation (аффирмэ́йшн) подтверждение
Affix, to ~ (аффи́кс, ту ~) наклеивать
to ~ **a seal** (ту ~ а сил) накладывать пломбу, опломбировать
to ~ **a stamp** (ту ~ а стамп) накладывать печать
Affixing (аффи́ксинг) опломбирование, приложение
~ **of a** {company} **seal** (~ оф а {ко́мпани} сил) приложение фирменной печати
Affreight, to ~ (аффрэ́йт, ту ~) фрахтовать
Affreighter (аффрэ́йтэр) фрахтователь
Affreightment (аффрэ́йтмэнт) фрахтование

After-tax (а́фтэр-такс) после удержания налогов
  ~ profit (~ про́фит) прибыль за вычетом налога
Against (агэ́нст) против
  to work ~ (ту уо́рк ~) действовать в ущерб
Agency (э́йджэнси) агентство, орган, посредничество, посредство
  advertising ~ (а́двэртайзинг ~) рекламное агентство, рекламное бюро
  central ~ (сэ́нтрал ~) центральное агентство
  commercial ~ (коммэ́ршл ~) торговое агентство
  consular ~ (ко́нсюлар ~) консульское агентство
  efficient ~ (эффи́шэнт ~) распорядительный орган
  exclusive ~ (эксклю́сив ~) агентство с исключительными правами
  executive ~ (экзэ́кютив ~) исполнительный орган
  full service ~ (фул сэ́рвис ~) агентство с полным циклом услуг
  government ~ (го́вэрнмэнт ~) государственный орган, правительственный орган
  insurance ~ (иншю́ранс ~) страховая организация
  international ~ (интэрна́шэнал ~) международное агентство, международный орган
  introduction ~ (интрода́кшн ~) агентство для устройства браков
  investigative ~ (инвэ́стигэйтив ~) орган расследования
  law enforcement ~ (лау энфо́рсмэнт ~) правоохранительный орган
  marine shipping ~ service (мари́н ши́ппинг ~ сэ́рвис) морское агентирование
  official press ~ (оффи́шл прэс ~) официальный орган печати
  oversight ~ (о́вэрсайт ~) контрольный орган
  patent ~ (па́тэнт ~) патентная фирма
  press ~ (прэс ~) агентство печати
  private ~ (пра́йват ~) частная организация
  purchasing ~ (пу́рчасинг ~) закупочное учреждение

  sales ~ (сэйлз ~) агентство по продаже
  sanitary oversight ~ (са́нитари о́вэрсайт ~) орган санитарного надзора
  shipping ~ service (ши́ппинг ~ сэ́рвис) агентирование
  sole ~ (сол ~) монопольное агентство
  travel ~ (тра́вэл ~) бюро путешествий, туристическое бюро, туристическая фирма
Agenda (аджэ́нда) повестка дня, порядок дня
  preliminary ~ (прили́минэри ~) предварительная повестка дня
Agent (э́йджэнт) агент, доверенное лицо, комиссионер, поверенный, посредник **~s** агентура {collective}
  accredited ~ (аккрэ́дитэд ~) аккредитованный агент
  administrative ~ (адми́нистрэйтив ~) административный агент
  charterer's ~ (ча́ртэрэрэз ~) агент фрахтователя
  commercial ~ (коммэ́ршл ~) торговый агент
  communications ~ (коммюника́йшнс ~) агент для связи
  consignment ~ (конса́йнмэнт ~) консигнационный агент
  consular ~ (ко́нсюлар ~) консульский агент
  del credere ~ (дэл крэдэ́рэ ~) комиссионер, берущий на себя делькредере
  diplomatic ~ (диплома́тик ~) дипломатический агент
  exclusive ~ (эксклю́сив ~) исключительный агент
  export ~ (э́кспорт ~) экспортный агент
  general ~ (джэ́нэрал ~) генеральный представитель
  government ~ (го́вэрнмэнт ~) государственный агент
  import ~ (и́мпорт ~) импортный агент
  marine ~ (мари́н ~) морской агент
  postal ~ (по́стал ~) почтовой агент
  purchasing ~ (пу́рчасинг ~) агент по закупкам
  secret ~ (си́крэт ~) тайный агент
  shipping ~ (ши́ппинг ~) агент пароходных компаний

sole ~ (сол ~) единственный агент

sworn ~ (суóрн ~) присяжный агент

to act as an ~ (ту акт ас ан ~) посредничать

~'s report (~'с рипóрт) отчёт о деятельности агента

Aggravate, to ~ (áггравэйт, ту ~) отягчать

Aggravating (áггравэйтинг) отягчающий

~ circumstances (~ сúркамстансэз) отягчающие обстоятельства

Aggregate (áггрэгат) общий {adj.}, совокупность, совокупный {adj.}

Aggression (аггрэ́шн) агрессия

act of ~ (акт оф ~) агрессивный акт, акт агрессии

armed ~ (áрмэд ~) вооруженная агрессия

flagrant ~ (флэ́йгрант ~) явная агрессия

ideological ~ (айдиолóджикал ~) идеологическая агрессия

indirect ~ (индайрэ́кт ~) косвенная агрессия

military ~ (мúлитари ~) военная агрессия

Aggressor (аггрэ́ссор) агрессор, захватчик

Aging (э́йджинг) старение

natural ~ (нáчюрал ~) естественное старение

~ of the population (~ оф θи попюлэ́йшн) старение населения

Agio (áжио) ажио

Agiotage (ажиотáж) ажиотаж {speculation}

Agree, to ~ to (агрú, ту ~ ту) соглашаться [perfective: согласиться]

Agreement (агрúмэнт) договор, согласие, соглашение **~s** согласование

administrative ~ (адмúнистрэйтив ~) административное соглашение

agency ~ (э́йджэнси ~) договор поручения

appropriate ~ (аппрóприат ~) соответствующее соглашение

arbitration ~ (арбитрэ́йшн ~) арбитражное соглашение

article of an ~ (áртикл оф ан ~) статья договора

assignment ~ (ассáйнмэнт ~) договор о переуступке прав

auxiliary ~ (ауксúлиэри ~) вспомогательное соглашение

barter ~ (бáртэр ~) бартерное соглашение, договор мены

basic ~ (бэ́йсик ~) основное соглашение

bilateral ~ (байлáтэрал ~) двухстороннее соглашение

binding ~ (бáйндинг ~) договор обязывающий

by ~ (бай ~) по договорённости

cartel ~ (картэ́л ~) картельное соглашение

clause of an ~ (клауз оф ан ~) пункт договора

collective ~ (коллэ́ктив ~) коллективный договор

complete ~ (комплúт ~) полная договорённость

concessionary ~ (консэ́шнэри ~) концессионное соглашение

concluded ~ (конклю́дэд ~) заключённый договор

construction ~ (констрýкшн ~) договор о строительстве объекта

contractual ~ (контрáкчуал ~) договорное соглашение

credit ~ (крэ́дит ~) кредитное соглашение

cross-licensing ~ (крос-лáйсэнсинг ~) соглашение об обмене лицензиями

direct ~ (дирэ́кт ~) прямое соглашение

draft ~ (драфт ~) проект договора

economic ~ (эконóмик ~) экономическое соглашение

employment ~ (эмплóймэнт ~) договор найма

engineering ~ (инджэнúринг ~) договор на инжиниринг

exclusive sales ~ (эксклю́сив сэйлз ~) договор об исключительном праве на продажу

executive ~ (экзэ́кютив ~) исполнительное соглашение

financial ~ (файнáншл ~) финансовое соглашение

foreign economic ~ (фóрэн эконóмик ~) внешнеэкономический договор

formal ~ (фóрмал ~) формальное соглашение

general ~ (джэ́нэрал ~) генеральное соглашение, общее соглашение

gentlemen's ~ (джэ́нтлмэнз ~) джентльменское соглашение

global ~ (гло́бал ~) мировое соглашение

implicit ~ (импли́сит ~) подразумеваемое соглашение

indemnity ~ (индэ́мнити ~) договор гарантии от убыток

industrial ~ (инду́стриал ~) промышленное соглашение

installment trade ~ (инста́ллмэнт трэйд ~) договор о продаже в кредит

interbank ~ (интэрба́нк ~) межбанковское соглашение

interdepartmental ~ (интэрдэпартмэ́нтал ~) межведомственное соглашение

intergovernmental ~ (интэрговэрнмэ́нтал ~) межгосударственное соглашение

international ~ (интэрна́шэнал ~) международное соглашение

invalid ~ (инва́лид ~) недействительный договор

judicial ~ (джюди́шл ~) судебное соглашение

know-how ~ (но́у-ха́у ~) договор на передачу ноу-хау

labor ~ (лэ́йбор ~) трудовой договор

leasing ~ (ли́синг ~) договор о сдаче в аренду

licensing ~ (ла́йсэнсинг ~) лицензионный договор, лицензионное соглашение

local ~ (ло́кал ~) местное соглашение

long-term ~ (лонг-тэрм ~) долгосрочный договор , долгосрочное соглашение

long-term trade ~ (лонг-тэрм трэйд ~) долгосрочное торговое соглашение

memorandum of ~ (мэмора́ндум оф ~) меморандум о договоре

military ~ (ми́литари ~) военное соглашение

monetary ~ (мо́нэтари ~) валютное соглашение

mortgage ~ (мо́ргэдж ~) договорная ипотека

multilateral ~ (мултила́тэрал ~) многостороннее соглашение

object of an ~ (о́бджэкт оф ан ~) предмет договора

one-time ~ (уа́н-тайм ~) разовый договор

operating ~ (о́пэрэйтинг ~) договор на эксплуатацию

oral ~ (о́рал ~) устный договор, устное соглашение

package ~ (па́кэдж ~) комплексное соглашение

partial ~ (паршл ~) частичное соглашение

party to an ~ (па́рти ту ан ~) сторона в договоре

patent ~ (па́тэнт ~) договор о патентах, патентный договор, патентное соглашение

payment ~ (пэ́ймэнт ~) платёжное соглашение

performance of an ~ (пэрфо́рманс оф ан ~) реализация договора

preferential ~ (прэфэрэ́ншл ~) преференциальное соглашение

preliminary ~ (прили́минэри ~) предварительное согласие

provisional ~ (прови́жнал ~) предварительное

purchase ~ (пу́рчас ~) договор о покупке

quitclaim ~ (куи́тклэйм ~) договор о переуступке прав

reciprocity ~ (рэсипро́сити ~) договор на основе взаимности

regional ~ (ри́джонал ~) региональное соглашение

reinsurance ~ (рэиншю́ранс ~) договор перестрахования

renewal of insurance ~ (ринью́ал оф иншю́ранс ~) возобновление договора о страховании

rental ~ (рэ́нтал ~) договор об аренде, соглашение об аренде

rescission of an ~ (риси́жн оф ан ~) аннулирование договора

sales ~ (сэйлз ~) договор продажи

salvage ~ (са́лвэдж ~) договор о спасении

secret ~ (си́крэт ~) секретное соглашение

sharecropping ~ (шэ́йркроппинг ~) испольная аренда

special ~ (спэшл ~) специальное соглашение

standard ~ (ста́ндард ~) типовое соглашение

supplementary ~ (сапплэмэ́нтари
~) дополнительное соглашение
tacit ~ (та́сит ~) молчаливое
соглашение
tax ~ (такс ~) налоговое
соглашение
tentative ~ (тэ́нтатив ~)
предварительная договорённость
termination of an ~ (тэрминэ́йшн
оф ан ~) расторжение договора
terms and conditions of an ~
(тэрмз энд конди́шнс оф ан ~)
условия договор
to come to an ~ (ту ком ту ан ~)
договориться
to conclude an ~ (ту конклю́д ан
~) заключать договор
to enter into an ~ (ту э́нтэр
и́нту ан ~) вступать в договор
to finalize an ~ (ту фа́йналайз
ан ~) договориться окончательно
to observe an ~ (ту обзэ́рв ан ~)
соблюдать договор
to ratify an ~ (ту ра́тифай ан ~)
ратифицировать договор
to renew an ~, act or treaty (ту
риню́ ан ~, акт ор три́ти)
возобновлять договор
to sign an ~ (ту сайн ан ~)
подписывать договор
to stipulate by ~ (ту сти́пюлэйт
бай ~) обусловливать договором
to terminate an ~ (ту тэ́рминэйт
ан ~) прекращать действие
договора, расторгать договор
to come to an ~ (ту ком ту ан ~)
согласовать
trade ~ (трэйд ~) торговое
соглашение
trademark ~ (трэ́йдмарк ~)
договор о товарных знаках
transfer ~ (тра́нсфэр ~) договор
о передаче
turn-key ~ (турн-ки ~) договор
подряда «под ключ»
unilateral ~ (юнила́тэрал ~)
односторонний договор
verbal ~ (вэ́рбал ~) словесное
соглашение
working ~ (уо́ркинг ~) рабочее
соглашение
~ on atomic cooperation (~ он
ато́мик коопэрэ́йшн) соглашение об
атомном сотрудничестве
~ with an option to extend (~
уиθ ан опшн ту экстэ́нд) договор
с правом продления

Agricultural (агрику́лчурал)
сельскохозяйственный
Agriculture (а́грикулчур) сельское
хозяйство
Ahead (ахэ́д) вперёд, впереди
~ of schedule (~ оф скэ́джюл)
досрочно
Aid (эйд) помощь
conditional ~ (конди́шнал ~)
условная помощь
economic ~ (эконо́мик ~)
экономическая помощь
family legal ~ (фа́мили ли́гал ~)
правовая помощь по семейным
делам
financial ~ (файна́ншл ~)
финансовая помощь, финансовое
содействие
first ~ (фэрст ~) скорая помощь
foreign ~ (фо́рэн ~) внешняя
помощь
free legal ~ (фри ли́гал ~)
бесплатная правовая помощь
government ~ (го́вэрнмэнт ~)
государственная помощь
legal ~ (ли́гал ~) правовая
помощь
mutual ~ (мю́чуал ~) самопомощь
~ to single mothers (~ ту сингл
мо́θэрс) пособие одиноким матерям
~ to the elderly (~ ту θи
э́лдэрли) помощь старикам
~ to underdeveloped countries (~
ту андэрдивэ́лопд ку́нтриз) помощь
слаборазвитым странам
Aiding (э́йдинг) оказание помощи
~ and abetting (~ энд абэ́ттинг)
пособничество
Air (эйр) воздух, воздушный {adj.}
customs ~ station (ка́стомз ~
стэ́йшн) таможенный аэродром
rush ~ parcel (раш ~ па́рсэл)
срочная авиапосылка
medical ~ station (мэ́дикал ~
стэ́йшн) санитарный аэродром
transit ~ depot (тра́нзит ~ ди́по)
транзитная авиадепеша
~ depot (~ ди́по) авиадепеша
~ freight (~ фрэйт) авиафрахт
~ group (~ груп) авиагруппа
~ parcel (~ па́рсэл) авиапосылка
~ transport (~ тра́нспорт)
авиаперевозка
Aircraft (э́йркрафт) летательный
аппарат, самолёт

civil ~ (си́вил ~) гражданское воздушное судно, гражданский самолёт
commercial ~ (комме́ршл ~) коммерческий летательный аппарат
government ~ (го́вэрнмэнт ~) государственный летательный аппарат
pirate ~ (па́йрат ~) пиратский летательный аппарат
~ construction (~ констру́кшн) самолётостроение
Airgram (э́йрграм) аэрограмма
Airline (э́йрлайн) авиалиния, авиационная компания, воздушная линия
domestic ~ (доме́стик ~) внутренняя воздушная линия
Airliner (э́йрлайнэр) лайнер
Airmail (э́йрмэйл) авиапочта, воздушная почта
~ pouch (~ по́уч) авиамешок
Airplane (э́йрплэйн) самолёт
civilian ~ (сиви́лян ~) гражданский аэродром
military ~ (ми́литари ~) военный аэродром
Airport (э́йрпорт) аэродром, аэропорт, воздушный порт
Airtight (э́йртайт) воздухонепроницаемый
Airway (э́йруэй) авиапуть
Alcoholic (алкохо́лик) алкогольный {*adj.*}, алкоголик {person}
~ drink (~ дринк) спиртная напитка
Alcoholism (а́лкохолисм) алкоголизм
Alibi (а́либай) алиби
Alienable (э́йлиэнабл) отчуждаемый
Alienate, to ~ (э́йлиэнэйт, ту ~) отчуждать
Alienation (эйлиэнэ́йшн) отчуждение
bad faith ~ (бад фэйθ ~) недобросовестное отчуждение
compensated ~ (ко́мпэнсэйтэд ~) возмездное отчуждение
uncompensated ~ (анко́мпэнсэйтэд ~) безвозмездное отчуждение
Alimony (а́лимони) алименты на содержание
Allegedly (алле́джэдли) якобы
Alliance (алла́йанс) альянс
Allocate, to ~ (а́локэйт, ту ~) ассигновать, выделять, назначать, размещать, распределить
to ~ by shares (ту ~ бай шэйрс) распределить по паям

Allocation (алокэ́йшн) назначение, отчисление, предоставление **~s** ассигнования
budget ~ (ба́джэт ~) отчисление в бюджет
convertible currency ~ (конве́ртибл ку́ррэнси ~) валютное ассигнование
supplementary ~ (сапплэме́нтари ~) дополнительное ассигнование
~ of the budget (~ оф θи ба́джэт) ассигнование бюджета
~ of expenses (~ оф экспе́нсэз) распределение расходов
~ of funds (~ оф фандз) выделение ассигнований
~ of space (~ оф спэйс) выделение площади
Allonge (алло́нж) аллонж
Allotment (алло́тмэнт) выделение, доля, развёрстка, часть
proportional ~ (пропо́ршнал ~) пропорциональное распределение
~ of shares (~ оф шэйрс) распределение акций
Allow, to ~ (алло́у, ту ~) разрешать [perfective: разрешить]
Allowable (алло́уабл) допустимый
Allowance (алло́уанс) допуск, норма, содержание
budget ~s (ба́джэт ~с) сметные ассигновки
budgetary ~ (ба́джэтари ~) сметнобюджетное ассигнование
daily ~ {per diem} (дэ́йли ~ {пэр ди́эм}) суточные деньги
large family ~ (лардж фа́мили ~) пособие многодетным матерям
loss ~ (лос ~) рефакция
Allowing for (алло́уинг фор) за вычетом
~ risk (~ риск) с учётом риска
Ally (а́ллай) союзник
Alongside (алонгса́йд) вдоль борта {ship}, у борта {ship}
Alter, to ~ (а́лтэр, ту ~) изменить, менять
Alteration (алтэрэ́йшн) изменение, переделка
territorial ~ (тэррито́риал ~) территориальное изменение
~ of border (~ оф бо́рдэр) изменение границы
~ of judicial practice (~ оф джуди́шл пра́ктис) изменение судебной практики
Alternate (а́лтэрнат) альтернат

Amalgamate, to ~ (амáлгамэйт, ту ~)
объединять, сливать, укрупнять
Amalgamated (амáлгамэйтд)
объединённый
Amalgamation (амалгамэ́йшн)
объединение, слияние, укрупнение
    intersectoral ~ (интэрсэктóрал
~) межотраслевое объединение
    ~ of capital (~ оф кáпитал)
слияние капитала
Ambassador (амбáссадор) посол
    extraordinary ~ (экстраóрдинари
~) чрезвычайный посол
    extraordinary and
    plenipotentiary ~
(экстраóрдинари энд
плэнипотэ́ншиари ~) чрезвычайный
и полномочный посол
    permanent ~ (пэ́рманэнт ~)
постоянный посол
    ~ plenipotentiary (~
плэнипотэ́ншиари) полномочный
представитель {полпред}
Ambition (амби́шн) притязание
    territorial ~s (тэрритóриал ~с)
территориальное притязание
Ambush (áмбуш) засада
Amend, to ~ (амэ́нд, ту ~) изменить
    to ~ a letter of credit (ту ~ а
лэ́ттэр оф крэ́дит) вносить
поправки к условиям аккредитива
Amendment (амэ́ндмэнт) дополнение,
изменение, поправка
    constitutional ~ (конститу́шнал
~) конституционное изменение
    filing of ~s (фáйлинг оф ~с)
подача дополнений
    legislative ~ (лэ́джислэйтив ~)
законодательная поправка,
изменение законодательства
    proposed ~ (пропóзд ~)
предлагаемое дополнение
    to sign an ~ (ту сайн ан ~)
подписывать дополнение
    ~ to a act (~ ту ан акт)
дополнение к контракту
    ~ to an agreement (~ ту ан
агри́мэнт) изменение договора
    ~ to articles (~ ту áртиклс)
изменение устава
    ~ to a charter (~ ту а чáртэр)
изменение устава, поправка к
уставу
    ~ to a constitution (~ ту а
конститу́шн) поправка в
конституцию

    ~ to a decision (~ ту а дисѝжн)
изменение решения
    ~ to a law (~ ту а лау)
изменение закона, поправка к
закону
    ~ to a protocol (~ ту а
прóтокол) дополнение к протоколу
    ~ to a suit {by plaintiff} (~ ту
а сут {бай плэ́йнтиф}) изменение
иска
Amicable (áмикабл) дружественный
Amicably (áмикабли) мирным путём,
полюбовно
Ammunition (аммюни́шн) боеприпасы
    to exhaust ~ (ту экзáуст ~)
расстрелять
Amnesty (áмнэсти) амнистия
    general ~ (джэ́нэрал ~) общая
амнистия
    grant of ~ (грант оф ~) акт об
амнистии
    to grant ~ (ту грант ~)
амнистировать
Amortization (амортизэ́йшн)
амортизация, амортизационное
отчисление, выкуп
Amortize, to ~ (áмортайз, ту ~)
амортизировать
Amount (амóунт) количество, размер
    lumpsum ~ (лáмпсум ~) паушальная
сумма
    maximum ~ insurable (мáксимум ~
иншу́рабл) максимальный размер
страховой суммы
    total ~ (тóтал ~) общее
количество
    usurious ~ (юсу́риос ~)
ростовщический размер
    ~ of damages (~ оф дáмэджэз)
сумма возмещения убытков
    ~ of deposit (~ оф дипóзит)
размер взноса
    ~ of depreciation (~ оф
диприши э́йшн) размер амортизации
    ~ paid (~ пэйд) выплачиваемая
сумма
Analog (áналог) аналог
Analogous (анáлогос) аналогичный
Analogy (анáлоджи) аналогия
    to make an ~ (ту мэйк ан ~)
проводить аналогию
Analysis (анáлисис) анализ
    cost-effectiveness ~ (кост-
эффéктивнэс ~) анализ
экономической эффективности
    demand ~ (димáнд ~) анализ
спроса

financial ~ (файна́ншл ~) анализ
финансового состояния
income-expenditure ~ (и́нком-
экспэ́ндичэр ~) анализ доходов и
расходов
retail market ~ (ри́тэйл ма́ркэт
~) анализ рынка сбыта
wholesale market ~ (хо́лсэйл
ма́ркэт ~) анализ конъюнктуры
Anarchism (а́наркизм) анархизм
Anarchist (а́наркист) анархист
Anarchistic (анарки́стик)
анархистский
Anarchy (а́нарки) анархия
Ancestor (а́нсэстор) предок ~s
предки
Anchor (а́нкор) якорный
Anchorage (а́нкорэдж) якорная
стоянка
~ fee (~ фи) якорный сбор
Ancillary (а́нсиллари)
вспомогательный, подсобный
~ housing (~ хо́узинг)
вспомогательное жилое помещение
Annex (а́ннэкс) приложение,
пристройка
to ~ (ту ~) аннексировать,
присоединять
~ of minutes of a meeting (~ оф
ми́нутс оф а ми́тинг) приложение к
протоколу
~ to a contract (~ ту а
ко́нтракт) приложение к договору
~ to a visa (~ ту а ви́са)
приложение визы
Annexation (аннэксэ́йшн) акт
аннексии, аннексия, присоединение
compulsory ~ (компу́лсори ~)
обязательное присоединение
territorial ~ (тэррито́риал ~)
аннексия территории
~ of territory (~ оф тэ́рритори)
присоединение территории
Annexing party {nation} (а́ннэксинг
па́рти {нэ́йшн}) аннексионист
Annotate, to ~ (а́ннотэйт, ту ~)
аннотировать
Annotation (аннотэ́йшн) аннотация
Announce, to ~ (анно́унс, ту ~)
заявлять [perfective: заявить],
оглашать [perfective: огласить],
сообщать [perfective: сообщить]
Announcement (анно́унсмэнт) заявка,
заявление, объявление
marriage ~ (мэ́ррэдж ~) оглашение
о предстоящем браке,
провозглашение брака

preliminary ~ (прили́минэри ~)
предварительное объявление
Annual (а́ннюал) годовой, ежегодный
Annuity (анню́ити) ежегодный взнос
government ~ (го́вэрнмэнт ~)
государственная рента
lifetime ~ (ла́йфтайм ~)
пожизненная рента
patent ~ (па́тэнт ~) ежегодный
патентный взнос
temporary ~ (тэ́мпорари ~)
временная рента
terminable ~ (тэ́рминабл ~)
срочная рента
to pay an ~ (ту пэй ан ~)
выплачивать ренту
Annul, to ~ (анну́л, ту ~)
аннулировать, кассировать,
расторгать [perfective:
расторгнуть]
empowered to ~ (эмпо́уэрд ту ~)
аннулирующий
Annulment (анну́лмэнт)
аннулирование, расторжение
~ of a marriage (~ оф а мэ́ррэдж)
признание брака
недействительным, расторжение
брака
~ of a patent (~ оф а па́тэнт)
объявление патента ничтожным
Anonymous (ано́нимос) аноним
{author}
Answer (а́нсэр) акт возражения {in
litigation}, ответ
to ~ (ту ~) отвечать
Answerable (а́нсэрабл) ответственный
to make {legally} ~ (ту мэйк
{ли́галли} ~) привлекать к
судебной ответственности
Anthropology (ан θ ропо́лоджи)
антропология
criminal ~ (кри́минал ~)
преступная антропология
Anthropometric (ан θ ропомэ́трик)
антропометрический
Anthropometry (ан θ ропо́мэтри)
антропометрия
Anti-constitutional (а́нти-
конститу́шнал) антиконституционный
Anti-dumping (а́нти-да́мпинг)
антидемпинговый
~ legislation (~ лэджислэ́йшн)
законы по борьбе с демпингом
Anti-economic (а́нти-эконо́мик)
антиэкономический
Anti-governmental (а́нти-
говэрнмэ́нтал) антиправительственный

Anti-inflationary (áнти-
инфлэ́йшнари) анти-инфляционный
   ~ measures (~ мэ́жюрз) антиинфляционные меры
Anti-parliamentary (áнти-
парламэ́нтари) антипарламентский
Anti-party (áнти-пáрти)
антипартийный
Anti-semite (áнти-сэ́майт) антисемит
Anti-semitic (áнти-сэми́тик)
антисемитский
Anti-semitism (áнти-сэ́митизм)
антисемитизм
Anticipation (антисипэ́йшн)
предвосхищение
Antinomy (антино́ми) антиномия
Antitrust (антитрáст)
антимонопольный
Apart (апáрт) в стороне
   to take ~ (ту тэйк ~) разбирать
на части
Apology (апо́лоджи) извинение
   public ~ (пáблик ~) публичное
извинение
Apparatchik (аппарáтчик) аппаратчик
Apparatus (аппарáтус) аппарат
   administrative ~ (адми́нистрэйтив
~) административный аппарат
   bureaucratic ~ (бюрокрáтик ~)
аппарат
   central ~ (сэ́нтрал ~)
центральный аппарат
   government ~ (го́вэрнмэнт ~)
правительственный аппарат
   investigative ~ (инвэ́стигэйтив
~) следственный аппарат
   judicial ~ (джюди́шл ~) судебный
аппарат
   taxation ~ (таксэ́йшн ~)
налоговой аппарат
Appeal (аппи́л) апелляция, жалоба,
обжалование, обращение, призыв
   applicant's ~ against
(áппликантс ~ агэ́нст) жалоба
заявителя на
   Court of ~ (ко́урт оф ~)
апелляционный суд
   grounds for an ~ (гро́ундз фор ан
~) обоснованность жалобы
   nature of the ~ (нэ́йчэр оф θи ~)
суть жалобы
   notice of ~ (но́тис оф ~)
предупреждение об обжаловании
   order of ~ (о́рдэр оф ~) порядок
обжалования
   right of ~ (райт оф ~) право
обжалования

   subject to ~ (сáбджэкт ту ~)
подлежащий обжалованию
   to ~ (ту ~) апеллировать,
обжаловать, опротестовать
   to file an ~ (ту файл ан ~)
подать апелляцию
   without ~ (уиθо́ут ~) обжалованию
не подлежит
   ~s department (~с дипáртмэнт)
отдел жалоб
   ~ to arbitration (~ ту
арбитрэ́йшн) кассация в арбитраж
   ~ to the court of Cassation (~
ту θи ко́урт оф кассэ́йшн)
кассация в кассационный суд,
кассационное опротестование
Appear, to ~ (аппи́р, ту ~) явиться
   to ~ before the court (ту ~
бифо́р θи ко́урт) явиться в суд
Appearance (аппи́ранс) появление,
явка
   court ~ (ко́урт ~) явка в суд
Appeasement (аппи́змэнт)
соглашательский {adj.},
умиротворение
Appeaser (аппи́зэр) соглашатель
Appeasing (аппи́зинг)
соглашательский
Appellant (аппэ́ллант) аппелянт
Appellate (аппэ́лат) аппеляционный
Appendage (аппэ́ндадж) придаток
Appendix (аппэ́ндикс) приложение
Appliance (апплáйанс) хозяйственный
товар
   household ~ (хо́усхолд ~) бытовые
товары
Applicability (аппликаби́лити)
применимость, пригодность к работе
   ~ of the statute of limitations
(~ оф θи стáтют оф лимитэ́йшнс)
применимость исковой давности
Applicable (аппли́кабл) применимый
Applicant (áппликант) проситель
Application (аппликэ́йшн) бланк
заявления, заявка, привлечение,
применение, прошение, требование,
ходатайство
   commercial ~ (комме́ршл ~)
коммерческое применение
   credit ~ (крэ́дит ~) кредитная
заявка
   economic ~ (эконо́мик ~)
внедрение в народное хозяйство
   elaboration of an ~ (илаборэ́йшн
оф ан ~) разработка заявочного
документа

import ~ (и́мпорт ~) импортная
заявка
industrial ~ of an invention
(инду́стриал ~ оф ан инвэ́ншн)
промышленное осуществление
изобретения
joint ~ (джойнт ~) совместная
заявка
legal ~ (ли́гал ~) законное
применение
object of ~ (о́бджэкт оф ~)
объект заявки
on the job ~ (он θи джоб ~)
применение на месте работы
original ~ (ори́джинал ~)
первоначальная заявка
parent ~ (па́рэнт ~) первичная
заявка
patent ~ (па́тэнт ~) ходатайство
о выдаче патента
separate ~ (сэ́парат ~) отдельная
заявка
territorial ~ (тэррито́риал ~)
территориальное применение
to deny an ~ (ту дина́й ан ~)
отказывать в ходатайстве
to put in an ~ (ту пут ин ан ~)
подать заявление
to renew an ~ (ту риню́ ан ~)
возобновлять заявку на участие
valid ~ (ва́лид ~) действительная
заявка
written ~ (ри́ттэн ~) письменная
заявка
~ for cancellation (~ фор
кансэллэ́йшн) ходатайство об
аннулировании
~ for compensation (~ фор
компэнсэ́йшн) ходатайство о
возмещении убытков
~ for registration (~ фор
рэджистрэ́йшн) ходатайство о
регистрации
~ of amendments (~ оф
амэ́ндмэнтс) введение поправки
~ of an invention (~ оф ан
инвэ́ншн) внедрение изобретения
применение изобретения
~ of legislation (~ оф
лэджислэ́йшн) применение
законодательства
~ of sanctions (~ оф санкшнс)
применение санкции
Apply, to ~ (аппла́й, ту ~)
накладывать, применять, просить
to ~ a penalty (ту ~ а пэ́налти)
накладывать штраф

Appoint, to ~ (аппо́йнт, ту ~)
определять
Appointed (аппо́йнтэд) назначенный
newly ~ (ню́ли ~) вновь
назначенный
Appointment (аппо́йнтмэнт) замещение
regular ~ (рэ́гюлар ~) должность
штатная
to receive an ~ (ту риси́в ан ~)
получить назначение
~ to a post (~ ту а пост)
назначение на пост
Apportionment (аппо́ршнмэнт)
развёрстка, распределение
~ of dividends (~ оф ди́видэндс)
распределение дивидендов
Appraisal (аппрэ́йзал) оценка,
оценочный документ
Appraise, to ~ (аппрэ́йз, ту ~)
оценивать
Appraiser (аппрэ́йзэр) оценщик
Apprentice (аппрэ́нтис) подмастерье
Approach (аппро́ч) наступление,
обращение
Appropriate (аппро́приат)
надлежащий, соответствующий
to ~ (ту ~) ассигновать,
назначать, присваивать
[perfective: присвоить]
Appropriation (аппроприэ́йшн)
назначение, присвоение, ~s
ассигнования
budgetary ~s (ба́джэтари ~с)
бюджетные ассигнования
special ~s (спэшл ~с)
специальные ассигнования
~s for capital expenditures (~с
фор ка́питал экспэ́ндичюрз)
ассигнование на капиталовложения
~s for public education (~с фор
па́блик эдюкэ́йшн) ассигнование на
просвещение
~ from the budget (~ фром θи
ба́джэт) ассигнование из бюджета
~ of found property (~ оф фо́унд
про́пэрти) присвоение найденного
имущества
~ of funds (~ оф фандз)
выделение денежных средств
Approval (аппро́вал) агреман,
одобрение
certificate of ~ (сэрти́фикэт оф
~) акт об одобрении
import ~ (и́мпорт ~) разрешение
на ввоз
practical ~ (пра́ктикал ~)
апробация

preliminary ~ (прилѝминэри ~) предварительное одобрение
unanimous ~ (юнàнимос ~) единодушное одобрение
~ of an estimate (~ оф ан ѐстимат) одобрение сметы
~ of a government (~ оф а гòвэрнмэнт) одобрение правительства
~ of a law (~ оф а лау) одобрение закона
~ of a letter of intent (~ оф а лѐттэр оф интѐнт) одобрение протокола
~ of minutes of a meeting (~ оф мѝнутс оф а мѝтинг) одобрение протокола
~ of a statute (~ оф а стàтют) одобрение закона
Approve, to ~ (аппрòв, ту ~) дать агреман, одобрять, разрешать [perfective: разрешить]
Arbitrage (àрбитраж) арбитраж, арбитражная операция
action in ~ (акшн ин ~) арбитрирование
ad hoc ~ (ад хок ~) арбитраж «ад ок»
bill of exchange ~ (билл оф эксчѐйндж ~) вексельный арбитраж
note ~ (нот ~) вексельный арбитраж
Arbitral (àрбитрал) арбитражный
Arbitrarily (арбитрàрили) произвольно
Arbitrariness (арбитрàринэс) произвол
Arbitrary (àрбитрари) произвольный, самоуправный
Arbitration (арбитрѐйшн) арбитраж
ad hoc ~ (ад хок ~) случайный
administrative ~ (адмѝнистрэйтив ~) ведомственный арбитраж
chairperson of ~ tribunal (чѐйрпэрсон оф ~ трибю̀нал) арбитр-председатель
commercial ~ (коммѐршл ~) коммерческий арбитраж
compound ~ (кòмпоунд ~) многосторонний арбитраж
compulsory ~ (компу̀лсори ~) обязательный арбитраж
formal ~ (фòрмал ~) формальный арбитраж
international ~ (интэрнàшэнал ~) международный арбитраж

international trade ~ (интэрнàшэнал трэйд ~) международный торговой арбитраж
maritime ~ (мàритайм ~) морской арбитраж
obligatory ~ (облѝгатори ~) принудительный арбитраж
optional ~ (òпшнал ~) факультативный арбитраж
pre-contract ~ (при-кòнтракт ~) предоговорочный арбитраж
trade ~ (трэйд ~) торговой арбитраж
Arbitrator (àрбитрэйтор) арбитр
individual ~ (индивѝдюал ~) единоличный арбитр
third party ~ (θирд пàрти ~) третий арбитр
Archives (àркайвз) архивы
consular ~ (кòнсюлар ~) консульские архивы
Area (ѐйриа) зона, площадь, район, территория
built-up ~ (билт-ап ~) застроенная площадь
designated ~ (дѐзигнэйтэд ~) зона назначения
port ~ (порт ~) портовая зона
storage ~ (стòрэдж ~) складская территория
supervised ~ (су̀пэрвайзд ~) зона надзора
~ of territorial waters (~ оф тэрритòриал уàтэрс) зона территориальных вод
Argument (àргюмэнт) аргумент, довод, спор
convincing ~ (конвѝнсинг ~) убедительный довод
irrefutable ~ (иррифю̀табл ~) неопровержимый довод
legal ~ (лѝгал ~) правовой аргумент
poor ~ (пур ~) малоубедительный довод
rebuttal ~s (рибàттал ~с) опровергающие доводы
strong ~ (стронг ~) веский довод
to make an ~ (ту мэйк ан ~) аргументировать
to set forth ~s (ту сэт форθ ~с) выдвигать доводы
unconvincing ~ (анконвѝнсинг ~) неубедительный довод
~ by the prosecution (~ бай θи просэкю̀шн) речь прокурора

~ for the defense (~ фор θи дифэнс) защитительная речь

Armistice (áрмистис) перемирие

general ~ (джэнэрал ~) общее перемирие

local ~ (лóкал ~) местное перемирие

short ~ (шорт ~) короткое перемирие

Arms (армз) оружие

Arrange, to ~ (аррэ́йндж, ту ~) размещать

Arrangement (аррэ́йнджмэнт) договорённость, порядок, размещение, расположение, соглашение

actual ~ (áкчуал ~) договорённость по контракту

administrative ~**s** (адми́нистрэйтив ~с) административная структура

cartel ~ (картэ́л ~) карательный сговор

clearing ~ (кли́ринг ~) клиринговое соглашение

contract ~**s** (кóнтракт ~с) мероприятия по контракту

final ~ (фáйнал ~) окончательная договорённость

financial ~ (файнáншл ~) финансовая договорённость

reciprocal ~ (риси́прокал ~) взаимное соглашение

temporary ~ (тэ́мпорари ~) временное мероприятие

transitional ~**s** (транзи́шнал ~с) меры переходного характера

verbal ~ (вэ́рбал ~) устная договорённость

without prior ~ (уиθóут прáйор ~) явочным порядком

working ~**s** (уóркинг ~с) рабочий механизм

Arrears (арри́рз) долг, задолженность, недоимка, просрочка

amount in ~ (амóунт ин ~) сумма недоимки

Arrest (аррэ́ст) арест, задержание

disciplinary ~ (ди́сиплинари ~) дисциплинарный арест

false ~ (фалс ~) незаконный арест

house ~ (хаус ~) домашний арест

preliminary ~ (прили́минэри ~) предварительный арест

simple ~ (симпл ~) простой арест

strict ~ (стрикт ~) строгий арест

subject to ~ (сáбджэкт ту ~) подлежащий задержанию

to ~ (ту ~) арестовать

to be subject to ~ (ту би сáбджэкт ту ~) подлежать задержанию

to place under ~ (ту плэйс áндэр ~) наложить арест

to subject to ~ (ту сáбджэкт ту ~) подлежать аресту

~ **and custody in detention** (~ энд кáстоди ин дитэ́ншн) арест с содержанием на гауптвахте

~ **of property** (~ оф прóпэрти) задержание имущества

~ **of a vessel** (~ оф а вэ́ссэл) задержание судна

Arrival (аррáйвал) поступление

Arrogance (э́рроганс) самонадеянность

Arson (áрсон) поджог

to commit ~ (ту комми́т ~) поджигать

Arsonist (áрсонист) поджигатель

Article (áртикл) изделие, предмет, пункт, статья, товар

model ~ (мóдэл ~) типовая статья

newspaper ~ (ньюзпэйпэр ~) газетная статья

patented ~ (пáтэнтэд ~) запатентованное изделие

~ **of export** (~ оф э́кспорт) предмет экспорта

~ **s of incorporation** (~ с оф инкорпорэ́йшн) устав корпорации

Artisan (áртизан) ремесленник

Ascension (асэ́ншн) восхождение

~ **to power** (~ ту пóуэр) приход к власти

Ascertain, to ~ (асэртэ́йн, ту ~) разведывать [**perfective:** разведать]

Ask, to ~ (аск, ту ~) просить

Aspect (áспэкт) момент

Assault (ассáлт) оскорбление

~ **and battery** (~ энд бáттэри) избиение, оскорбление действием

Assay (áссэй) испытание

~ **certificate** (~ сэрти́фикэт) свидетельство о качестве

Assemblage (ассэ́мбладж) сборище

Assemble, to ~ (ассэ́мбл, ту ~) монтировать

Assembler (ассэ́мблэр) монтажник

Assembly (ассэ́мбли) ассамблея {people}, монтаж {machinery}, монтажный {adj.}, сбор, собрание
  advisory ~ (адва́йзори ~) совещательное собрание
  annual ~ (а́ннюал ~) ежегодное собрание
  Constituent ~ (консти́тюэнт ~) учредительное собрание
  consultative ~ (ко́нсултэ́йтив ~) консультативная ассамблея
  cost of ~ (кост оф ~) стоимость монтажа
  date of ~ (дэйт оф ~) дата монтажа
  electoral ~ (элэ́кторал ~) избирательное собрание
  extraordinary ~ (экстрао́рдинари ~) внеочередное собрание
  Federal ~ (фэ́дэрал ~) федеральная ассамблея
  General ~ **of the United Nations** (джэ́нэрал ~ оф θи юна́йтэд нэ́йшнз) генеральная ассамблея Объединенных Наций
  instructions for ~ (инстра́кшнз фор ~) инструкция по монтажу
  legislative ~ (лэ́джислэйтив ~) законодательное собрание
  national ~ (на́шэнал ~) национальное собрание
  people's ~ (пиплз ~) народное собрание
  plenary ~ (плэ́нари ~) пленарное собрание
  public ~ (па́блик ~) общественное собрание
  regular ~ (рэ́гюлар ~) очередное собрание
  representative ~ (рэпрэзэ́нтатив ~) представительное собрание
  ~ **and operation** (~ энд опэрэ́йшн) монтаж и эксплуатация
Assess, to ~ (ассэ́сс, ту ~) облагать
Assessment (ассэ́ссмэнт) аттестация, обложение, подать
  data ~ (да́та ~) оценка данных
  insurance loss ~ (иншю́ранс лос ~) определение страхового возмещения
  joint ~ (джойнт ~) совместная оценка
  judicial ~ (джюди́шл ~) судебная оценка
  product ~ (про́дукт ~) аттестация продукции

  state ~ (стэйт ~) государственная аттестация
  tax ~ (такс ~) оклад, оценка налога
Assessor (ассэ́ссор) асессор, заседатель, эксперт по оценке {недвижимости}
  public ~ (па́блик ~) народный заседатель
Asset (а́ссэт) актив, имущество, средство, фонд ~s авуары
  bank ~s (банк ~с) банковские активы
  blocked ~s (блокд ~с) блокированное имущество, блокированные средства
  book ~ (бук ~) актив баланса
  carryover ~s (кэ́рриовэр ~с) переходящие фонды
  communal ~s (комму́нал ~с) коммунальные имущества
  company ~ (ко́мпани ~) актив товарищества
  dead ~s (дэд ~с) мертвые активы
  fixed ~s (фиксд ~с) неликвидные активы, основные средства
  foreign ~s (фо́рэн ~с) иностранные авуары
  foreign exchange ~s (фо́рэн эксчэ́йндж ~с) валютные авуары
  frozen ~s (фро́зэн ~с) блокированные авуары, замороженные активы
  hard currency ~s (хард ку́ррэнси ~с) валютные активы
  liquid ~ (ли́куид ~) ликвидная статья актива
  liquid ~s (ли́куид ~с) наличное имущество, ликвидные авуары, ликвидные активы, ликвиды
  net ~ (нэт ~) чистый актив
  realizable ~ (ри́алайзабл ~) реализуемый актив
  rehabilitation of production ~s (рихабилитэ́йшн оф прода́кшн ~с) обновление производственных фондов
  renewal of fixed ~s (риню́ал оф фиксд ~с) обновление основных производственных фондов
  reserve ~s (рисэ́рв ~с) резервные активы
  slow ~s (слоу ~с) труднореализуемые активы
  to freeze ~s (ту фриз ~с) блокировать

total listed ~s (тóтал лúстэд
~с) сумма баланса
working ~s (уóркинг ~с)
оборотные фонды
~ formation (~ формэ́йшн)
образование фондов
~s held abroad (~с хэлд абрóд)
авуары за границей
~ on balance sheet (~ он бáланс
шит) статья актива
Assign, to ~ (ассáйн, ту ~)
назначать, переуступать
Assignation (ассигнэ́йшн) передача
decree of ~ (дикрú оф ~) акт
отвода
Assignee (ассинú) правопреемник
general ~ (джэ́нэрал ~) общее
правопреемство
Assignment (ассáйнмэнт) ассигновка,
выделение, назначение, передача,
переуступка, правопреемство
compensated ~ (кóмпэнсэйтэд ~)
возмездная передача
gratuitous ~ (гратýитос ~)
безвозмездная передача
import ~ (úмпорт ~) импортное
поручение
special ~ (спэшл ~) специальное
поручение
unconditional ~ (анкондúшнал ~)
безоговорочная передача
~ of a case (~ оф а кэйс)
передача дела
~ of a contract (~ оф а
кóнтракт) передача договора
~ of copyright (~ оф кóпирайт)
передача авторских прав
~ of deliveries (~ оф дэлúвэриз)
передача поставок
~ of lease (~ оф лис) передача в
аренду
~ of a logo (~ оф а лóго)
передача лого
~ of a matter for judicial
reconsideration (~ оф а мáттэр
фор джюдúшл риконсидэрэ́йшн)
передача дела на новое судебное
рассмотрение
~ of a patent (~ оф а пáтэнт)
передача патента
~ of a policy (~ оф а пóлиси)
передача полиса
~ of property (~ оф прóпэрти)
передача собственности
~ of rights (~ оф райтс)
передача прав

Assignor (ассинóр) лицо,
переуступающее право
Assimilate, to ~ (ассúмилэйт, ту ~)
ассимилировать
Assimilation (ассимилэ́йшн)
ассимиляция
Assist, to ~ (ассúст, ту ~)
содействовать
Assistance (ассúстанс) пособие,
содействие
additional ~ (аддúшнал ~)
дополнительная помощь
administrative ~ (адмúнистрэйтив
~) административная помощь
development ~ (дивэ́лопмэнт ~)
содействие в развитии
family ~ (фáмили ~) семейное
пособие
food ~ (фуд ~) продовольственная
помощь
legal ~ (лúгал ~) юридическая
помощь
lifetime ~ (лáйфтайм ~)
пожизненное пособие
military ~ (мúлитари ~) военная
помощь
monetary ~ (мóнэтари ~) денежное
пособие
mutual ~ (мю́чуал ~) взаимная
помощь, взаимное содействие
one-time ~ (уáн-тайм ~)
единовременное пособие
preliminary ~ (прилúминэри ~)
предварительное пособие
relocation ~ (рилокэ́йшн ~)
пособие при переезде
social ~ (сошл ~) общественная
помощь
technical ~ (тэ́кникал ~)
техническая помощь, техническое
содействие
temporary ~ (тэ́мпорари ~)
временное пособие
unemployment ~ (анэмплóймэнт ~)
помощь по безработице
~ to senior citizens (~ ту
сúниор сúтизэнз) помощь
престарелым
Assistant (ассúстант) помощник
~ to the bookkeeper (~ ту θи
бýккипэр) помощник бухгалтера
~ to the general secretary (~ т
θи джэ́нэрал сэ́крэтари) помощник
генерального секретаря
~ to the mayor (~ ту θи мэ́йор)
помощник мэра

~ to the prosecutor (~ ту θи прóсэкютэр) помощник прокурора
~ to the secretary of state (~ ту θи сэ́крэтари оф стэйт) помощник государственного секретаря
Associate (ассóсиэт) партнёр, сотрудник
to ~ with (ту ~ уиθ) присоединяться
Association (ассосиэ́йшн) ассоциация, общество, объединение
administrative ~ (адми́нистрэйтив ~) административное объединение
agricultural ~ (агрику́лчурал ~) сельскохозяйственное объединение
bankers' ~ (бáнкэрз ~) банковская ассоциация
customs ~ (кáстомз ~) таможенное объединение
export ~ (э́кспорт ~) экспортное объединение
foreign trade ~ (фóрэн трэйд ~) внешнеторговое объединение)
industrial ~ (инду́стриал ~) промышленное объединение
international ~ (интэрнáшэнал ~) международное объединение
joint ~ (джойнт ~) совместное объединение
joint stock ~ (джойнт сток ~) паевое объединение
legislative ~ (лэ́джислэйтив ~) законодательное объединение
national ~ (нáшэнал ~) наднациональное объединение
open for ~ (óпэн фор ~) открыто для присоединения
producers' ~ (продю́сэрз ~) ассоциация производителей
professional ~ (профэ́шнал ~) профессиональное объединение
regional ~ (ри́джонал ~) региональная ассоциация
secret ~ (си́крэт ~) тайная ассоциация
specialized ~ (спэ́шлайзд ~) специализированное объединение
syndicated ~ (сы́ндикэйтэд ~) синдикальное объединение
trade ~ (трэйд ~) торговая ассоциация
trade union ~ (трэйд ю́нион ~) профсоюзное объединение
trading ~ (трэ́йдинг ~) торговое объединение

European Free Trade ~ {EFTA} (юропи́ан фри трэйд ~ {э́фта}) европейская ассоциация свободной торговли
International ~ for the Protection of Industrial Property Rights (интэрнáшэнал ~ фор θи протэ́кшн оф инду́стриал прóпэрти райтс) международная ассоциация по охране прав промышленной собственности
International Bar ~ (интэрнáшэнал бар ~) международная ассоциация адвокатов
Assort, to ~ (ассóрт, ту ~) сортировать
Assorting (ассóртинг) сортировка
Assortment (ассóртмэнт) ассортимент, выбор, набор, номенклатура, сортамент
wide ~ (уайд ~) большой выбор
~ of goods (~ оф гудз) ассортимент товаров
Assurance (ашу́ранс) заверение, обеспечение
~ of reliability (~ оф рилайаби́лити) обеспечение надёжности
Assure, to ~ (ашу́р, ту ~) заверять
Asylum (асáйлум) убежище
Atone, to ~ (атóн, ту ~) искупить
Atonement (атóнмэнт) искупление
Attaché (атташэ́) атташе {diplomatic}
commercial ~ (коммэ́ршл ~) коммерческий атташе
maritime ~ (мáритайм ~) морской атташе
military ~ (ми́литари ~) военный атташе
press ~ (прэс ~) пресс-атташе
~ for cultural affairs (~ фор ку́лчурал аффэ́йрс) атташе по вопросам культуры
~ for financial affairs (~ фор файнáншл аффэ́йрс) атташе по вопросам финансов
Attachment (аттáчмэнт) арест, прикрепление
~ of movable property (~ оф мóвабл прóпэрти) арест движимого имущества
~ of property (~ оф прóпэрти) арест имущества

~ of real property (~ оф ри́ал про́пэрти) арест недвижимого имущества
Attack (атта́к) атака, нападение
Attain, to ~ (атта́йн, ту ~) достигать
Attempt (аттэ́мпт) покушение {assault}, попытка, пытка
  to ~ (ту ~) пробовать, пытать
  ~ on a life (~ он а лайф) покушение на жизнь, посягательство на жизнь
Attempted (аттэ́мптэд) неудавшийся
  ~ crime (~ крайм) покушение на преступление
  ~ escape (~ эскэ́йп) покушение на побег, попытка побега
  ~ murder (~ му́рдэр) покушение на жизнь
  ~ violation (~ вайолэ́йшн) попытка правонарушения
Attend, to ~ (аттэ́нд, ту ~) посещать
Attendance (аттэ́нданс) посещаемость, явка, явочный {adj.}
  ~ to customs formalities (~ ту ка́стомз фо́рмалитиз) выполнение таможенных формальностей
Attended by (аттэ́ндэд бай) сопряжённый
Attention (аттэ́ншн) внимание
  to pay ~ to (ту пэй ~ ту) обращать
Attest (аттэ́ст) акт свидетельствования
  to ~ (ту ~) засвидетельствовать, подтверждать, удостоверять
Attestation (аттэстэ́йшн) подтверждение, удостоверение
  ~ of authenticity (~ оф ауθэнти́сити) подтверждение подлинности
  ~ of signature (~ оф си́гначэр) удостоверение подписи
Attitude (а́ттитуд) отношение
Attorney (атто́рни) адвокат, поверенный
  ~ at law (~ ат лау) судебный поверенный
Attract, to ~ (аттра́кт, ту ~) привлекать [perfective: привлечь]
Attraction (аттра́кшн) привлечение
  ~ of buyers (~ оф ба́йэрз) привлечение покупателей
  ~ of resources (~ оф рисо́рсэз) привлечение средств

~ of savings (~ оф сэ́йвингс) привлечение сбережений
Auction (аукшн) аукцион, торги
  fur {pelt} ~ (фур {пэлт} ~) пушной аукцион
  international ~ (интэрна́шэнал ~) международный аукцион
  public ~ sale (па́блик ~ сэйл) публичные торги
  timber ~ (ти́мбэр ~) лесной аукцион
  to buy at ~ (ту бай ат ~) купить на аукционе
  to sell at ~ (ту сэл ат ~) продать с аукциона
  ~ of goods (~ оф гудз) товарный аукцион
  ~ room (~ рум) аукционный зал
Auctioneer (аукшни́р) аукционист, лицо, производящее продажи на аукционе
Audience (а́удиэнс) аудиенция {meeting}, аудитория {collective}
  public ~ (па́блик ~) публичная аудиенция
Audit (а́удит) ревизия
  financial ~ (файна́ншл ~) финансовая ревизия
  to ~ (ту ~) проверять
  to ~ accounts (ту ~ акко́унтс) ревизовать баланс
  ~ of accounts (~ оф акко́унтс) ревизия баланса
  ~ of the books (~ оф θи букс) анализ баланса, бухгалтерская ревизия
Auditor (а́удитор) аудитор, бухгалтер-ревизор, контролёр отчётности, ревизор
  general ~ (джэ́нэрал ~) генеральный аудитор
Auditorium (аудито́риум) аудитория
Autarky (а́утарки) автаркия
Authentic (ауθэ́нтик) аутентичный, подлинный
Authenticate, to ~ (ауθэнтикэ́йт, ту ~) подтверждать, скрепить подписью, удостоверять
Authentication (ауθэнтикэ́йшн) скрепление, удостоверение
Authenticity (ауθэнти́сити) аутентичность, подлиность
  to establish ~ (ту эста́блиш ~) установить подлиность
Author (а́уθор) автор, составитель
Authoritativeness (ауθоритэ́йтивнэс) авторитетность

to dun for ~ (ту дан фор ~) взыскивать недоимку

Authority (аθо́рити) авторитет, власть, орган, полномочие **~s** органы власти

abuse of ~ (абю́с оф ~) злоупотребление властью

administrative ~ (адми́нистрэйтив ~) административный орган

appropriate ~s (аппро́приат ~с) соответствующие власти, соответствующий орган

arbitral ~ (а́рбитрал ~) арбитражная инстанция, третейский орган

civil ~ (си́вил ~) гражданская власть

competent ~s (ко́мпэтэнт ~с) компетентные власти, компетентный орган, компетентное учреждение

constitutional ~ (конститу́шнал ~) конституционный орган, конституционное полномочие

currency control ~ (ку́ррэнси контро́л ~) орган валютного контроля

customs ~s (ка́стомз ~с) таможенные власти, таможенный орган

delegated ~ (дэ́лэгэйтэд ~) делегированное полномочие

delegation of ~ (дэлэгэ́йшн оф ~) передача власти

discretionary ~ (дискрэ́шнари ~) дискреционное полномочие

executive ~ (экзэ́кютив ~) исполнительная власть, исполнительное полномочие

federal ~ (фэ́дэрал ~) федеральное полномочие

governmental ~s (говэрнмэ́нтал ~с) органы государственной власти

fiscal ~ (фи́скал ~) финансовый орган

higher ~ (ха́йэр ~) высший орган

highest ~ (ха́йэст ~) высший авторитет

housing ~ (хо́узинг ~) жилищный орган

implicit ~ (импли́сит ~) подразумеваемое полномочие

judicial ~ (джюди́шл ~) судебная власть

lawful ~ (ла́уфул ~) законная власть

legislative ~ (лэ́джислэйтив ~) законодательное полномочие

level of ~ (лэ́вэл оф ~) инстанция

local ~s (ло́кал ~с) местные власти

military ~s (ми́литари ~с) военная инстанция, военные власти

municipal ~s (мюни́сипал ~с) муниципальные власти

mutual ~ (мю́чуал ~) взаимное полномочие

notarial ~ {civil law} (нотэ́йриал ~ {си́вил лау}) нотариальный орган

official ~s (оффи́шл ~с) официальные власти

planning ~ {under communism} (пла́ннинг ~ {а́ндэр ко́ммюнизм}) плановой орган

policy-making ~ (по́лиси-мэ́йкинг ~) директивный орган

port ~ (порт ~) портовые власти

port ~ regulations (порт ~ рэгюлэ́йшнс) распоряжения портовых властей

presidential ~ (прэзидэ́ншл ~) президентское полномочие

price regulating ~ (прайс рэ́гюлэйтинг ~) ценорегулирующий орган

public ~s (па́блик ~с) государственная власть

prosecutorial ~ (про́сэкютэриал ~) прокурорский орган

recourse to superior ~s (ри́корс ту супи́риор ~с) вышестоящая инстанция

responsible ~ (риспо́нсибл ~) ответственный орган

scope of ~ (скоп оф ~) объём правомочий

social welfare ~ (сошл уэ́лфэйр ~) орган социального обеспечения

statutory ~s (ста́тютори ~с) законные органы власти

superior ~ (супи́риор ~) вышестоящий орган

supervisory ~ (супэрва́йзори ~) руководящий орган

supreme ~ (супри́м ~) верховный орган

tax ~ (такс ~) налоговый орган

to vest someone with ~ (ту вэст со́муон уиθ ауθо́рити ~) облекать кого-то полномочиями

written ~ (ри́ттэн ~) письменное
полномочие
written ~ for representation
(ри́ттэн ~ фор рэприсэнтэ́йшн)
письменное полномочие на
представительство
~ of the court (~ оф θи ко́урт)
авторитет суда
Authorization (ауθоризэ́йшн)
авторизация, путёвка, разрешение
drawing ~ (дра́уинг ~) право
выписки векселей
exclusive ~ (эксклю́сив ~)
исключительное разрешение
extraordinary ~ (экстрао́рдинари
~) чрезвычайное разрешение
preferential ~ (прэфэрэ́ншл ~)
льготная путёвка
Authorize, to ~ (а́уθорайз, ту ~)
авторизовать, разрешать
[perfective: разрешить]
Authorized (а́уθорайзд)
авторизованный
Authorship (а́уθоршип) авторство
joint ~ (джойнт ~) совместное
авторство
~ of an invention (~ оф ан
инвэ́ншн) авторство на
изобретение
Autocracy (ауто́краси) автократия,
самодержавие
Autocrat (а́утократ) самодержец
Autocratic (аутокра́тик)
самодержавный
Autocratically (аутокра́тикалли)
самодержавно
Autolimitation (аутолимитэ́йшн)
автолимитация {doctrine}
Automobile (аутомоби́л) автомобиль,
машина
~ lot (~ лот) автопарк
Autonomous (ауто́номос) автономный
Autonomy (ауто́номи) автономия
administrative ~ (адми́нистрэйтив
~) административная автономия
internal ~ (интэ́рнал ~)
внутренняя автономия
territorial ~ (тэррито́риал ~)
территориальная автономия
Auxiliary (аукзи́лиэри)
вспомогательный
Availability (авайлаби́лити) наличие
subject to ~ (са́бджэкт ту ~) при
условии наличия
~ of cash (~ оф каш) наличие
денег

~ of documentation (~ оф
докюмэнтэ́йшн) наличие
документации
~ of stock (~ оф сток) наличие
товаров
Available (ава́йлабл) наличный
to be ~ (ту би ~) быть в наличии
Aval (ава́л) поручительство по
векселю
Avenge, to ~ (авэ́ндж, ту ~)
отомстить
Average (а́вэрэдж) среднее число
adjustment of ~ statement
(аджа́стмэнт оф ~ стэ́йтмэнт)
составление диспаши
draft of ~ statement (драфт оф ~
стэ́йтмэнт) проект диспаши
general ~ adjustment (джэ́нэрал ~
аджа́стмэнт) диспаша по общей
аварии
preparation of ~ statement
(прэпарэ́йшн оф ~ стэ́йтмэнт)
подготовка диспаша
register of general ~ statements
(рэ́джистэр оф джэ́нэрал ~
стэ́йтмэнтс) реестр диспаши
to annul a general ~ statement
(ту анну́л а джэ́нэрал ~
стэ́йтмэнт) отменять диспашу
to contest the ~ statement (ту
контэ́ст θи ~ стэ́йтмэнт)
оспаривать диспашу
to draw up an ~ statement (ту
дра́у ап ан ~ стэ́йтмэнт)
составлять диспашу
to find the ~ (ту файнд θи ~)
выводить среднее число
to register an ~ statement (ту
рэ́джистэр ан ~ стэ́йтмэнт)
регистрировать диспашу
~ adjustment (~ аджа́стмэнт)
диспаша {insurance}
~ adjustor (~ аджа́стор) диспашёр
~ statement (~ стэ́йтмэнт)
аварийная диспаша
Avert, to ~ (авэ́рт, ту ~)
предотвратить
Aviation (эйвиэ́йшн) авиация
civil ~ (си́вил ~) гражданская
авиация
commercial ~ (комме́ршл ~)
коммерческая авиация
Avionics (эйвио́никс) электронное
оборудование самолёта
Aviso (ави́со) авизо
Award (ауа́рд) награда, присуждение

arbitral ~ (а́рбитрал ~)
арбитражное решение
to ~ (ту ~) присваивать
[**perfective:** присвоить]
to ~ a judgment (ту ~ а
джа́джмэнт) присуждать
~ of damages (~ оф да́мэджэз)
присуждение к возмещению
Awarding (ауа́рдинг) присвоение
~ of a patent (~ оф а па́тэнт)
присвоение патента
Awkward (а́куард) щекотливый
~ subject (~ са́бджэкт)
щекотливая тема

B

Back (бак) назад, спина
to ~ (ту ~) обеспечивать
Back-haul (бак-хаул) доставка
порожняка
Backer (ба́кэр) лицо, гарантирующее
оплату векселя {of a bill, note}
Background (ба́кгро́унд)
происхождение {heritage}, фон
{scene}
family ~ (фа́мили ~) семейное
происхождение
Backwardness (ба́куарднэс)
отсталость
Badge (бадж) значок
party membership ~ (па́рти
мэ́мбэршип ~) партийный значок
Bag (баг) мешок
cargo in ~s (ка́рго ин ~с) груз в
мешках
collapsible ~ (колла́псибл ~)
складной мешок
damaged ~s (да́маджд ~с)
повреждённые мешки
pre-slung ~s (при-слунг ~с)
застроплённые мешки
Bail (бэйл) порука
to put up ~ for (ту пут ап ~
фор) брать на поруки
to release on ~ (ту рили́с он ~)
отпустить на поруки
Bailiff (бэ́йлиф) приказчик,
судебный пристав
Balance (ба́ланс) баланс, балансовый
{adj.}, остаток, равновесие, сальдо
account ~ (акко́унт ~) баланс,
остаток счёта

adjustment of the ~ sheet
(аджа́стмэнт оф θи ~ шит)
исправление баланса
compensatory ~ (компэ́нсатори ~)
компенсационный остаток
consolidated ~ sheet
(консо́лидэйтэд ~ шит) сводный
баланс
credit ~ (крэ́дит ~) кредитовый
остатокб кредитовое сальдо
current account ~ (ку́ррэнт
акко́унт ~) баланс текущих
расчётов, сальдо текущего счета
debit ~ (дэ́бит ~) дебетовое
сальдо
decimal ~ (дэ́симал ~) десятичные
весы
delivery of the ~ of goods
(дэли́вэри оф θи ~ оф гудз)
допоставка
favorable trade ~ (фэ́йворабл
трэйд ~) активный торговый
баланс
in-house ~ (ин-хаус ~) наличный
остаток
intersectoral ~ sheet
(интэрсэкто́рал ~ шит)
межотраслевой баланс
invisible ~ (инви́зибл ~) баланс
услуг и некоммерческих платежей
merchandise trade ~ (мэ́рчандайс
трэйд ~) баланс товарной
торговли
national ~ of accounts (на́шэнал
~ оф акко́унтс) баланс народного
хозяйства
negative ~ (нэ́гатив ~)
отрицательное сальдо,
отрицательный счёт
on ~ (он ~) после сведения
баланса, в итоге
positive ~ (по́зитив ~)
положительное сальдо
rough ~ (руф ~) брутто баланс
to ~ (ту ~) балансировать,
сбалансировать
to ~ accounts (ту ~ акко́унтс)
подводить баланс
to ~ books (ту ~ букс) подводить
баланс
to deliver the ~ of the goods
(ту дэли́вэр θи ~ оф θи гудз)
допоставлять
trade ~ (трэйд ~) торговый
баланс
unfavorable ~ (анфэ́йворабл ~)
пассивный баланс

unfavorable ~ of payments
(анфэ́йворабл ~ оф пэ́ймэнтс)
пассивный платёжный баланс
unfavorable trade ~ (анфэ́йворабл
трэйд ~) пассивный торговый
баланс
zero ~ (зи́ро ~) нулевое сальдо
~ due (~ ду) дебетовое сальдо
~ of an account (~ оф ан
акко́унт) сальдо счёта
~ of a debt (~ оф а дэт) остаток
долга
~ of international trade (~ оф
интэрна́шэнал трэйд)
внешнеторговый баланс
~ of payments deficit (~ оф
пэ́ймэнтс дэ́фисит) дефицит
платёжного баланса
Balance Sheet (ба́ланс шит) баланс,
заключительный баланс
annual ~ (а́ннюал ~) годовой
баланс
credit ~ (крэ́дит ~) кредитовый
баланс
debit ~ (дэ́бит ~) дебетовый
баланс
favorable ~ (фэ́йворабл ~)
благоприятный баланс
favorable ~ of payments
(фэ́йворабл ~ оф пэ́ймэнтс)
активный платёжный баланс
item on a ~ (а́йтэм он а ~)
статья баланса
material ~ (мати́риал ~)
материальный баланс
negative ~ (нэ́гатив ~)
отрицательный баланс
positive ~ (по́зитив ~) активный
баланс
preliminary ~ (прили́минэри ~)
предварительный баланс
preparation of the ~ (прэпарэ́йшн
оф θи ~) составление баланса
to offset an item on a ~ (ту
о́фсэт ан а́йтэм он а ~) сводить
баланс
to prepare a ~ (ту припэ́йр а ~)
составлять баланс
total ~ (то́тал ~) итоговый
баланс
~ assets (~ а́ссэтс) активы
баланса
~ liabilities (~ лайаби́литиз)
пассивная часть баланса
~ of payables and receivables (~
оф пэ́йаблс энд риси́ваблс)
расчётный баланс

Balanced (ба́лансд)
сбалансированный, уравновешенный
~ budget (~ ба́джэт) равновесие
бюджета
~ trade (~ трэйд) нетто-баланс
Balancing (ба́лансинг)
балансирование {of accounts, etc.}
Bale (бэйл) кипа, тюк
half a ~ (хаф а ~) половина кипы
odd ~ (од ~) лишняя кипа
to be packed in ~s (ту би пакд
ин ~с) быть упакованным в кипах
to strap a ~ (ту страп а ~)
обтягивать кипу
~ of cotton (~ оф ко́ттон) кипа
хлопка
~ of paper pulp (~ оф пэ́йпэр
пулп) кипа целлюлозы
~ of wool (~ оф уу́л) кипа шерсти
Ban (бан) блокада, запрет,
запрещение
atomic weapons ~ (ато́мик уэ́понз
~) запрещение атомного оружия
to ~ (ту ~) запрещать
Banal (бана́л) пошлый, шаблонный
Banality (бана́лити) пошлость,
шаблонность
Band (банд) лента, полоса, пояс
metal ~ (мэ́тал ~) металлическая
лента
nylon ~ (на́йлон ~) нейлоновая
лента
to fasten with a metal ~ (ту
фа́ссэн уиθ а мэ́тал ~) крепить
металлической лентой
Bandit (ба́ндит) бандит
Banish, to ~ (ба́ниш, ту ~) изгнать,
сослать
Banishment (ба́нишмэнт) изгнание,
ссылка
Bank (банк) банк, банковский
{adj.}, банкирская контора
"co-op" ~ (ко-оп ~)
кооперативный банк
acceptance ~ (аксэ́птанс ~)
акцептный банк, банк-акцептант
advice of the ~ (адва́йс оф θи ~)
извещение банка
advising ~ (адва́йзинг ~)
авизующий банк
affiliate ~ (аффи́лиат ~) филиал
банка
approved ~ (аппро́вд ~)
одобренный банк
associated ~s (ассо́сиятэд ~с)
ассоциированные банки

authorized ~ (áуθорайзд ~) уполномоченный банк

branch ~ (бранч ~) филиал банка

branch of a ~ (бранч оф а ~) отделение банка

central ~ (сэ́нтрал ~) центральный банк

circulating ~ (си́ркюлэйтинг ~) банк-эмитент

clearing ~ (кли́ринг ~) клиринговый банк

collecting ~ (коллэ́ктинг ~) банк-инкассатор

commercial ~ (коммэ́ршл ~) коммерческий банк

confirming ~ (конфи́рминг ~) банк, подтверждающий аккредитив

cooperative ~ (коо́пэратив ~) кооперативный банк

correspondent-~ (коррэспо́ндэнт-~) банк-корреспондент

credit ~ (крэ́дит ~) ссудный банк

creditor ~ (крэ́дитор ~) банк-кредитор

discount ~ (ди́скоунт ~) учётный банк

exchange ~ (эксчэ́йндж ~) разменный банк

export-import ~ (э́кспорт-и́мпорт ~) экспортно-импортный банк

exporter's ~ (э́кспортэрз ~) банк экспортёра

first-class ~ (фэрст-класс ~) первоклассный банк

foreign ~ (фо́рэн ~) иностранный банк

foreign exchange ~ (фо́рэн эксчэ́йндж ~) банк по обмену валюты

foreign trade ~ (фо́рэн трэйд ~) внешнеторговый банк

founding ~ (фо́ундинг ~) банк-учредитель

importer's ~ (и́мпортэрз ~) банк импортёра

incorporated ~ (инкорпорэ́йтэд ~) акционерный банк

industrial ~ (инду́стриал ~) промышленный банк

interstate ~ (и́нтэрстэйт ~) межгосударственный банк

investment ~ (инвэ́стмэнт ~) инвестиционный банк

issuing ~ (и́шюинг ~) эмиссионный банк

leading ~ (ли́динг ~) ведущий банк

local ~ (ло́кал ~) местный банк

major ~ (мэ́йджор ~) крупный банк

merchant ~ (мэ́рчант ~) акцептный банк, торговый банк

merger of ~s (мэ́рджэр оф ~с) слияние банков

mortgage ~ (мо́ргэдж ~) ипотечный банк

national ~ (на́шэнал ~) государственный банк, национальный банк

negotiating ~ (нэго́шиэйтинг ~) банк, производящий приём и оплату документов

notice of the ~ (но́тис оф θи ~) извещение банка

notifying ~ (но́тифайинг ~) авизующий банк

originating ~ (ори́джинэйтинг ~) банк, выдающий аккредитив

overseas ~ (овэрси́з ~) иностранный банк

payer's ~ (пэ́йэрз ~) банк-плательщик

primary ~ (пра́ймари ~) основной банк

private ~ (пра́йват ~) частный банк

remittance via ~ (рими́ттанс ви́а ~) пересылка через банк

remitting ~ (рими́ттинг ~) банк-ремитент

reserve ~ (рисэ́рв ~) резервный банк

savings ~ (сэ́йвингс ~) сберегательный банк, сберегательная касса

secondary ~ (сэ́кондари ~) второстепенный банк

third-country ~ (θирд-ку́нтри ~) банк третьей страны

to authorize a ~ (ту а́уθорайз а ~) уполномочивать банк

to clear documents through the ~ (ту клир до́кюмэнтс θру θи ~) получать документы из банка

to deposit a sum in the ~ (ту дипо́зит а сум ин θи ~) помещать сумму в банк

to deposit money in a ~ (ту дипо́зит мо́ни ин а ~) класть деньги в банк, вносить деньги в банк

to deposit securities in the ~ (ту дипо́зит сэкю́ритиз ин θи ~) помещать ценные бумаги в банк

to have an account with a ~ (ту хэв ан аккóунт уиθ а ~) иметь счёт в банке
to instruct the ~ (ту инстрýкт θи ~) давать указания банку
to keep money in a ~ account (ту кип мóни ин а ~ аккóунт) держать деньги в банке
to make a withdrawal from a ~ (ту мэйк а уиθдрáуал фром а ~) взять вклад из банка
to manage a ~ (ту мáнадж а ~) управлять банком
to open a letter of credit with a ~ (ту óпэн а лэ́ттэр оф крэ́дит уиθ а ~) открывать аккредитив в банке
to open an account at the ~ (ту óпэн ан аккóунт ат θи ~) открывать счёт в банке
to pay via ~ (ту пэй вúа ~) платить через банк
to pledge collateral with a ~ (ту плэдж коллáтэрал уиθ а ~) закладывать товар в банке
to present documents through the ~ (ту прэзэ́нт дóкюмэнтс θру θи ~) представлять документы через банк
to transfer to the account in the ~ (ту трáнсфэр ту θи аккóунт ин θи ~) перевести на счёт в банке
under ~ credit (áндэр ~ крэ́дит) на условиях банковского кредита
~ account (~ аккóунт) счёт в банке
~ board of governors (~ борд оф гóвэрнорс) совет банка
~ certificate (~ сэртúфикэт) сертификат банка
~ charges (~ чáрджэз) комиссионные банку
~ clerk (~ клэрк) служащий банка
~ customers (~ кáстомэрс) клиенты банка
~ debt (~ дэт) задолженность банку
~ deposit (~ дипóзит) вклад в банк
~ discounting (~ дúскоунтинг) учёт вексель векселя в банке
~ employee (~ эмплóйй) служащий банка
~ examination (~ экзаминэ́йшн) проверка отчётности банка

~ failure (~ фэ́йлюр) банкротство банка
~ for international settlements (~ фор интэрнáшэнал сэ́тлмэнтс) банк международных расчётов
~ guarantee (~ гярантú) гарантия банка
~ in good standing (~ ин гуд стáндинг) банк, пользующий солидной репутацией
~ issuing credit cards (~ úшюинг крэ́дит кардс) банк, выпускающий кредитные карточки
~'s liquid assets (~'с лúкуид áссэтс) ликвидный фонд банка
~ manager (~ мáнаджэр) управляющий банком
~ of deposit (~ оф дипóзит) депозитный банк
~ receipt (~ рисúт) квитанция банка
~ representative (~ рэпрэзэ́нтатив) представитель банка
~ statement (~ стэ́йтмэнт) выписка счёта, представляемая банком вкладчика
~ transactions (~ трансáкшнс) операции банка
Banker (бáнкэр) банкир
first-class ~ (фэрст-класс ~) первоклассный банкир
merchant ~ (мэ́рчант ~) банк-акцептант
~'s acceptance (~'с аксэ́птанс) акцептованный банком вексель
~'s references (~'с рэ́фэрэнсэз) рекомендация банкир
Banking (бáнкинг) банковское дело {business}
  ~ facilities (~ фасúлитиз) услуги банка
Banknote (бáнкнот) банкнота
reserve ~ (рисэ́рв ~) резервная банкнота
issuance of ~ (úшюанс оф ~) эмиссия банкнот банкнота
issue of ~ (úшю оф ~) выпуск банкнота
support of ~ (суппóрт оф ~) обеспечение банком банкнота
to issue ~ into circulation (ту úшю úнту сиркюлэ́йшн) выпускать банкноты в обращение
withdrawal of ~ (уиθдрáуал оф ~) изъятие банкнота

~ **by denomination** (~ бай диноминэ́йшн) банкноты по купюрам
Bankrupt (ба́нкрупт) банкрот, неплатёжеспособный {adj.}, несостоятельный {adj.}, обанкротившийся {adj.}
  to declare oneself ~ (ту диклэ́йр уа́нсэлф ~) объявлять банкротом
  to go ~ (ту го ~) стать банкротом, обанкротиться
Bankruptcy (ба́нкрупси) банкротство, крах, несостоятельность
  declaration of ~ (дэкларэ́йшн оф ~) объявление о неплатёжеспособности
  to declare ~ (ту диклэ́йр ~) объявлять банкротство, объявлять неплатёжеспособным
  to drive into ~ (ту драйв и́нту ~) доводить до банкротства
  ~ **of a firm** (~ оф а фирм) крах фирмы
Bannister (ба́ннистэр) перила
  courtroom ~ (ко́уртрум ~) перила отделяющие судей от публики
Bar (бар) адвокатура, запрет, препятствие
  the ~ (θи ~) адвокатура {legal profession}
  ~ **to patentability** (~ ту па́тэнтаби́лити) препятствие к выдаче патента
Bare-boat (бэйр-бот) бэрбоут
  ~ **charter** (~ ча́ртэр) бэрбоут чартер
Bargain (ба́ргэн) сделка
  "Dutch ~" {one-sided deal} (дутч ~ {уа́н-са́йдэд дил}) договор, выгодный только для одной стороны
  good ~ (гуд ~) выгодная сделка
  to ~ (ту ~) торговаться о цене
Barge (бардж) баржа
  cargo ~ (ка́рго ~) грузовая баржа
  deep-sea ~ (дип-си ~) глубоководная баржа
  "dumb" ~ (думб ~) несамоходная баржа
  dump ~ (думп ~) саморазгружающаяся баржа
  fob ~ (эф-о-би ~) франко баржа
  non-propelling ~ (нон-пропэ́ллинг ~) несамоходная баржа
  ocean-going ~ (ошн-го́инг ~) океанская баржа

  price ex ~ (прайс экс ~) цена с баржи
  river ~ (ри́вэр ~) речная баржа
  self-propelled ~ (сэлф-пропэ́лд ~) самоходная баржа
  tanker ~ (та́нкэр ~) наливная баржа
  to deliver by ~ (ту дэли́вэр бай ~) доставлять на барже
  to provide for ~ **shipping** (ту прова́йд фор ~ ши́ппинг) обеспечивать поставку баржи
  to unload {over side} **to** ~ (ту анло́д {о́вэр сайд} ту ~) разгружать на баржу
  utility ~ (юти́лити ~) портовая баржа
Barrator (ба́рратор) виновный в баратрии
Barratry (ба́рратри) баратрия {maritime}
Barrel (ба́ррэл) бочка
  ~**s empty** (~с э́мпти) бочки пустые
  ~**s leaking** (~с ли́кинг) бочки текут
  to ~ (ту ~) укладывать в бочку
  wooden ~ (уу́дэн ~) деревянная бочка
Barrier (ба́рриэр) барьер, застава, ограждение
  border ~ (бо́рдэр ~) пограничная застава
  customs ~ (ка́стомз ~) таможенный барьер
  discriminatory trade ~**s** (дискри́минатори трэйд ~с) дискриминационные барьеры
  language ~ (ла́нгуадж ~) языковой барьер
  non-tariff trade ~ (нон-та́риф трэйд ~) нетарифный барьер
  protectionist ~**s** (протэ́кшнист ~с) протекционистские барьеры
  to avoid customs ~**s** (ту аво́йд ка́стомз ~с) обходить таможенные барьеры
  to eliminate ~**s** (ту или́минэйт ~с) устранять барьеры
  to erect ~**s** (ту ирэ́кт ~с) создавать барьеры
  tariff ~ (та́риф ~) тарифный барьер
  trade ~ (трэйд ~) торговый барьер
Barrister (ба́рристэр) адвокат, присяжный поверенный

Barter (бáртэр) бартерный обмен,
бартерный {adj.}, мена,
товарообмен, товарообменный {adj.}
    direct commodity ~ (дирэ́кт
коммóдити ~) непосредственный
обмен товарами
    to ~ (ту ~) обменивать
    ~ **agreement** (~ агрúмэнт) договор
мены
Bartering (бáртэринг) меновая
торговля
Base (бэйс) база, основа
    development of the export ~
(дивэ́лопмэнт оф θи э́кспорт ~)
развитие экспортной базы
    diversification of the export ~
(дивэрсификэ́йшн оф θи э́кспорт ~)
диверсификация экспортной базы
    export ~ (э́кспорт ~) экспортная
база
    financial ~ (файнáншл ~)
финансовая база
    material ~ (матúриал ~)
материальная база
    material and technical ~
(матúриал энд тэ́кникал ~)
материально-техническая база
    military ~ (мúлитари ~) военная
база
    research ~ (рúсэрч ~)
опытно-экспериментальная база
    tariff rate ~ (тáриф рэ́йт ~)
база для исчисления тарифа
    to ~ (ту ~) базировать
    to ~ **the price** (ту ~ θи прайс)
базировать цену
    to establish a ~ (ту эстáблиш а
~) создавать базу
    ~ **cost** (~ кост) себестоимость
Based (бэйсд) основанный
    the price is ~ **on ...** (θи прайс
из ~ он ...) цена базируется на
Baseline (бэ́йслайн) базисный
Basis (бэ́йсис) база, базис, основа
    compensatory ~ (компэ́нсатори ~)
компенсационная основа
    delivery ~ (дэлúвэри ~) базис
поставки
    economic ~ (экономúк ~)
экономический базис
    lease on percentage of sales ~
(лис он пэрсэ́нтадж оф сэйлз ~)
аренда на условии исчисления
платы в процентном отношении
    mutually profitable ~ (мю́чуалли
прóфитабл ~) взаимовыгодная
основа

    on a contractual ~ (он а
контрáкчуал ~) на базе контракта
    on a fixed price ~ (он а фиксд
прайс ~) на базе твёрдой цены
    on a commission ~ (он а коммúшн
~) на комиссионных началах
    on a consignment ~ (он а
консáйнмэнт ~) на условиях
консигнации
    on a contractual ~ (он а
контрáкчуал ~) на договорных
началах
    on a reciprocal ~ (он а
рисúпрокал ~) на условиях
взаимности
    on a rental ~ (он а рэ́нтал ~) на
условиях аренды
    on a turn-key ~ (он а турн-ки ~)
на условиях "под ключ"
    periodical ~ (пэриóдикал ~)
периодичность
    price ~ (прайс ~) базис цены
    solid ~ (сóлид ~) прочное
основание
    to trade on a consignment ~ (ту
трэйд он а консáйнмэнт ~)
торговать на условиях
консигнации
Basket (бáскэт) корзинка
    SDR ~ (эс-ди-ар ~) корзинка СДР
{Special Drawing Rights
currencies}
    wicker ~ (уúккэр ~) плетёная
корзинка
    ~ **of currencies** (~ оф кýррэнсиз)
корзинка валют
Batman (бáтман) ординарец
Battery (бáттэри) побои
    assault and ~ (ассáлт энд ~)
оскорбление действием
Battle (бáтл) борьба
Bay (бэй) бухта, залив
    fitting and assembly ~ (фúттинг
энд ассэ́мбли ~) место для сборки
и накладки оборудования
    to clear a ~ (ту клир а ~)
выходить из бухты
Bazaar (базáр) восточный базар
Bear (бэйр) медведь
    to ~ (ту ~) нести [**imperfective:**
носить], приносить
Bearer (бэ́йрэр)
векселепредъявитель, податель,
предъявитель
    to ~ (ту ~) на предъявителя
    ~ **of a bill** (~ оф а билл)
предъявитель векселя

Before (бифóр) раньше
   ~ tax (~ такс) до вычета налога
Beginning (бигúннинг) начало,
начальный {*adj.*}
Belonging (билóнгинг)
принадлежность
Belt (бэлт) лента, полоса, пояс
Beneficial (бэнэфúшл)
бенефициарный, выгодный, полезный
   mutually ~ (мю́чуалли ~)
   взаимовыгодный
Beneficiary (бэнэфúшиари)
бенефициар
   designation of a ~ (дэсигнэ́йшн
   оф а ~) наименование бенефициара
   letter of credit ~ (лэ́ттэр оф
   крэ́дит ~) лицо, в чью пользу
   открыт аккредитив
Benefit (бэнэфит) выгода, льгота,
польза, пособие, привилегия
   cost ~ (кост ~) финансовая
   льгота
   disability ~ (дисабúлити ~)
   пособие по нетрудоспособности
   for mutual ~ (фор мю́чуал ~) для
   взаимной выгоды
   incidental ~ (инсидэ́нтал ~)
   побочная выгода
   maternity ~ (матэ́рнити ~)
   пособие по беременности и родам
   potential ~ (потэ́ншл ~)
   потенциальная выгода
   retraining ~ (ритрэ́йнинг ~)
   пособие по переквалификации
   social ~ (сошл ~) общественная
   выгода, общественная польза
   temporary disability ~
   (тэ́мпорари дисабúлити ~) пособие
   по временной нетрудоспособности
   to ~ (ту ~) получать выгоду
   to derive ~ (ту дирáйв ~)
   извлекать выгоду
   to derive maximum ~ (ту дирáйв
   мáксимум ~) извлекать наибольшую
   выгоду
   to the ~ (ту θи ~) для выгоды
   unemployment ~ (анэмплóймэнт ~)
   пособие по безработице
   fringe ~s (фриндж ~с)
   дополнительные льготы
   to establish additional ~s (ту
   эстáблиш аддúшнал ~с)
   устанавливать дополнительные
   льготы
   ~ payment (~ пэ́ймэнт) пособие
   ~s (~с) суммарная выгода
Berth (бэрθ) пристань, причал

   container ~ (контэ́йнэр ~)
   контейнерный причал
   discharging ~ (дисчáрджинг ~)
   место для выгрузки у причала,
   место причала для разгрузочных
   работ
   loading ~ (лóдинг ~) место
   погрузки
   to assure safe ~ (ту ашýр сэйф
   ~) обеспечить надёжное месту
   причала
Berthage (бэ́рθадж) пристанский
сбор, причальная линия
Bet (бэт) заклад
Betrayal (битрэ́йял) предательство
   ~ of the homeland (~ оф θи
   хóмланд) измена родине
Betrothal (бэтрóθал) помолвка,
обручение
Biased (бáйасд) пристрастный
Bid (бид) предложение, предложение
цены, тендер, торги
   full ~ (фул ~) полный тендер
   highest ~ (хáйэст ~) самое
   выгодное предложение
   invited ~ (инвáйтэд ~)
   объявленный тендер
   lowest ~ (лóуэст ~) предложение
   по самой низкой цене
   to ~ (ту ~) принимать участие в
   торгах
   to make a ~ (ту мэйк а ~)
   предлагать цену
Bidder (бúддэр) лицо, предлагающее
цену, участник аукциона {at
auction}
   highest ~ (хáйэст ~) участник
   торгов, предложивший наивысшую
   цену
Bidding (бúддинг) торги
   closed ~ (клозд ~) закрытые
   торги
   open ~ (óпэн ~) открытые торги
   ~ period (~ пúриод) период
   подачи тендеров
Bigamy (бúгами) бигамия
Bilateral (байлáтэрал)
двухсторонний
Bill (билл) банкнота, ведомость,
вексель, вексельный {*adj.*},
законопроект, список, счёт
   accommodation ~ (аккомодэ́йшн ~)
   безденежный вексель, дружеский
   вексель
   account ~ (аккóунт ~) ведомость
   бухгалтерского учёта

advance ~ (адва́нс ~) вексель, выписанный до отправления груза
advance ~ of exchange (адва́нс ~ оф эксчэ́йндж) авансовая тратта
after sight ~ (а́фтэр сайт ~) вексель с оплатой после предъявления
amount of a ~ (амо́унт оф а ~) сумма векселя
auction ~ (аукшн ~) каталог аукциона
backer of a ~ (ба́кэр оф а ~) индоссант по векселю
backing for a ~ (ба́кинг фор а ~) поручительство по векселю
balance ~ (ба́ланс ~) вексель для сальдирования
bank ~ (банк ~) банковский вексель
bearer of a ~ (бэ́йрэр оф а ~) предъявитель векселя
collateral ~ (колла́тэрал ~) депонированный вексель
collection of a ~ (колле́кшн оф а ~) взыскание денег по векселю, инкассирование векселя
collection against a ~ (колле́кшн аге́нст а ~) инкассо тратты
commercial ~ (комме́ршл ~) коммерческий вексель
copy of a ~ (ко́пи оф а ~) копия векселя, экземпляр векселя
counter ~ (ко́унтэр ~) встречный вексель
counterfeit ~ (ко́унтэрфит ~) поддельный вексель, фальшивая банкнота
credit ~ (крэ́дит ~) вексель, выписанный против открытого аккредитива
currency ~ (ку́ррэнси ~) вексель, выписанный в инвалюте
currency of a ~ (ку́ррэнси оф а ~) валюта векселя
date of issue of a ~ (дэйт оф и́шю оф а ~) дата выпуска векселя
discountable ~ (диско́унтабл ~) могущий быть учтенным в банке вексель, приемлемый для переучёта вексель
discounted ~ (ди́скоунтэд ~) учтённый вексель
discounting of a ~ (ди́скоунтинг оф а ~) дисконт векселя, учёт векселя
documentary ~ (докюмэ́нтари ~) документированный вексель

domiciled ~ (до́мисайлд ~) домицилированный вексель
domiciled ~ of exchange (до́мисайлд ~ оф эксчэ́йндж) домицилированная тратта
drawer of a ~ (дра́уэр оф а ~) лицо, выписывающее вексель
due date of a ~ (ду дэйт оф а ~) срок платежа по векселю
duplicate of an exchange ~ (ду́пликат оф ан эксчэ́йндж ~) дубликат векселя
endorsed ~ (эндо́рсд ~) индоссированный вексель
endorsement on a ~ (эндо́рсмэнт он а ~) надпись на векселе
failure to honor a ~ (фэ́йлюр ту хо́нор а ~) неоплата векселя
fictitious ~ (фикти́шос ~) фиктивный вексель
finance ~ (файна́нс ~) финансовый вексель
foreign ~ (фо́рэн ~) заграничный вексель, иностранная тратта
forged ~ (форджд ~) подложный вексель
form of a ~ (форм оф а ~) форма векселя
grace period on a ~ (грэйс пи́риод он а ~) льготные дни для уплаты по векселю {days}
guaranteed ~ of exchange (гяранти́д ~ оф эксчэ́йндж) гарантированный вексель
guarantor of a ~ (гяранто́р оф а ~) гарант по векселю
holder of a ~ (хо́лдэр оф а ~) держатель векселя
holder of a ~ of exchange (хо́лдэр оф а ~ оф эксчэ́йндж) держатель тратты
honored ~ (о́норд ~) погашенный {покрытый} вексель
in-clearing ~ (ин-кли́ринг ~) дебетовый вексель
inland ~ (и́нланд ~) оплачиваемый в местной валюте вексель
inland ~ of exchange (и́нланд ~ оф эксчэ́йндж) внутренняя тратта
inscribed ~ (инскра́йбд ~) именной вексель
interim ~ (и́нтэрим ~) временный вексель
issue of a ~ (и́шю оф а ~) выдача векселя

legal action arising from a ~ (лйгал акшн арáйзинг фром а ~) иск по векселю

local ~ (лóкал ~) местный вексель

long-term ~ (лонг-тэрм ~) долгосрочный вексель

negotiable ~ (нэгóшабл ~) оборотный вексель, передаваемый вексель

negotiation of a ~ (нэгошиэ́йшн оф а ~) выплата по векселю

non-negotiable ~ (нон-нэгóшабл ~) не могущий быть переданным вексель

noted ~ (нóтэд ~) вексель с нотариальной отметкой об отказе трассата от его акцептования

one-dollar ~ (уáн-дóллар ~) банкнота в 1 доллар

order ~ (óрдэр ~) ордерный вексель

outland ~ (óутланд ~) иностранный вексель

outstanding ~ (оутстáндинг ~) неоплаченный вексель

outstanding ~ of exchange (оутстáндинг ~ оф эксчэ́йндж) неоплаченная тратта

paid ~ (пэйд ~) оплаченный вексель

past due ~ (паст ду ~) просроченный вексель

payment ~ (пэ́ймэнт ~) подлежащий оплате вексель

pilot's ~ (пáйлотс ~) лоцманская квитанция

presentation of a ~ (прэзэнтэ́йшн оф а ~) предъявление векселя

prolongation of a ~ (пролонгэ́йшн оф а ~) пролонгация векселя

protest of a ~ (прóтэст оф а ~) протест векселя

protest of a ~ for non-acceptance (прóтэст оф а ~ фор нон-аксэ́птанс) протест векселя из-за неакцепта, протест векселя из-за неплатежа

protestation of a ~ (протэстэ́йшн оф а ~) опротестование векселя

protested ~ (протэ́стэд ~) опротестованный вексель

provisional ~ (провúжнал ~) предварительный вексель

rediscount of a ~ (ридúскоунт оф а ~) переучёт векселя

rediscounted ~ (ридúскоунтэд ~) переучтённый вексель

refusal of acceptance of a ~ (рифю́зал оф аксэ́птанс оф а ~) отказ от акцепта векселя

retired ~ (ритáйрэд ~) погашенный вексель

secured ~ (сэкю́рд ~) обеспеченный вексель

secured ~ of exchange (сэкю́рд ~ оф эксчэ́йндж) документированная тратта

settlement of a ~ (сэ́тлмэнт оф а ~) оплата векселя, платёж по векселю, погашение векселя

short-term ~ (шорт-тэрм ~) краткосрочный вексель, краткосрочная тратта

short-term commercial ~ (шорт-тэрм коммэ́ршл ~) краткосрочный коммерческий вексель

sight ~ (сайт ~) вексель с оплатой по предъявлении

signature on a ~ (сúгначэр он а ~) подпись на векселе

single ~ (сингл ~) вексель, выставленный в одном экземпляре, единственный экземпляр траты

stamp duty on a ~ (стамп дю́ти он а ~) гербовый сбор по векселю

surety on a ~ (шю́рэти он а ~) поручитель по векселю

tenor of a ~ (тэ́нор оф а ~) срок тратты

to back a ~ (ту бак а ~) гарантировать оплату векселя

to collect a ~ (ту коллэ́кт а ~) инкассировать вексель, инкассировать тратту, получать деньги по векселю

to discount a ~ (ту дúскоунт а ~) покупать вексель, принимать вексель к учёту

to dishonor a ~ (ту дисóнор а ~) не оплачивать вексель

to dishonor a ~ by non-acceptance (ту дисóнор а ~ бай нон-аксэ́птанс) отказываться акцептовать вексель

to domicile a ~ (ту дóмисайл а ~) домицилировать вексель

to draw a ~ (ту дрáу а ~) выдавать вексель

to draw out a ~ of exchange (ту дрáу óут а ~ оф эксчэ́йндж) выставлять вексель to **effect acceptance of a ~** (ту иффэ́кт аксэ́птанс оф а ~) производить акцент векселя

to **endorse a ~** (ту эндо́рс а ~) индоссировать вексель, передавать вексель надписью, переводить вексель

to **endorse a ~ to ...** (ту эндо́рс а ~ ту ...) индоссировать вексель в пользу

to **extend a ~** (ту экстэ́нд а ~) продлевать вексель

to **forge a ~** (ту фордж а ~) подделывать вексель

to **guarantee a ~** (ту гяранти́ а ~) давать поручительство по векселю

to **have a ~ discounted** (ту хэв а ~ ди́скоунтэд) учитывать вексель

to **have a ~ expired** (ту хэв а ~ экспа́йрд) просрочивать вексель

to **honor a ~** (ту о́нор а ~) оплачивать вексель

to **issue a ~** (ту и́шю а ~) выписывать вексель

to **issue a short-term ~** (ту и́шю а шорт-тэрм ~) выписывать краткосрочный вексель

to **issue a long-term ~** (ту и́шю а лонг-тэрм ~) выписывать долгосрочный вексель

to **make a ~ out to order** (ту мэйк а ~ о́ут ту о́рдэр) выписывать вексель приказу

to **make a ~ payable to order** (ту мэйк а ~ пэ́йабл ту о́рдэр) выписывать ордерный вексель

to **meet a ~** (ту мит а ~) выкупать вексель

to **meet due date on a ~** (ту мит ду дэйт он а ~) оплачивать вексель в срок

to **negotiate a ~** (ту нэго́шиэйт а ~) негоциировать вексель, передавать {переуступать} вексель, переуступать тратту, пускать вексель в обращение

to **negotiate a ~ with recourse** (ту нэго́шиэйт а ~ уиθ ри́корс) пускать в обращение с оборотом

to **negotiate a bank ~** (ту нэго́шиэйт а банк ~) учитывать вексель в банке

to **note a ~** (ту нот а ~) делать на векселе нотариальную отметку об отказе трассата

to **pay through a ~** (ту пэй θру а ~) платить траттой

to **present a ~** (ту прэзэ́нт а ~) представлять тратту

to **present a ~ for acceptance** (ту прэзэ́нт а ~ фор аксэ́птанс) представлять тратту для акцепта

to **present a ~ for discount** (ту прэзэ́нт а ~ фор ди́скоунт) сдавать вексель на учёт, предъявлять вексель к учёту

to **present a ~ for payment** (ту прэзэ́нт а ~ фор пэ́ймэнт) предъявлять вексель для оплаты

to **present a ~ for protest** (ту прэзэ́нт а ~ фор про́тэст) предъявлять вексель для протеста

to **prolong a ~** (ту проло́нг а ~) пролонгировать вексель

to **protest a ~** (ту про́тэст а ~) опротестовывать вексель

to **protest a ~ for dishonor** (ту про́тэст а ~ фор дисо́нор) протестовать по поводу неоплаты векселя

to **re-draw a ~** (ту ри-дра́у а ~) выписывать обратный переводной вексель

to **rediscount a ~** (ту риди́скоунт а ~) переучитывать вексель, переучитывать тратту

to **remit a ~ for collection** (ту ри́мит а ~ фор коллэ́кшн) передавать вексель на инкассо

to **renew a ~** (ту риню́ а ~) возобновлять вексель, возобновлять тратту

to **retire a ~** (ту рита́йр а ~) погашать вексель

to **return a ~ of exchange under protest** (ту риту́рн а ~ оф эксчэ́йндж а́ндэр про́тэст) возвращать тратту с протестом

to **return a ~ under protest** (ту риту́рн а ~ а́ндэр про́тэст) возвращать вексель с протестом

to **return a ~ unpaid** (ту риту́р а ~ анпэ́йд) возвращать вексель неоплаченым

to **sell a ~** (ту сэл а ~) продавать вексель

to **submit a ~ for acceptance** (субми́т а ~ фор аксэ́птанс) направлять вексель для акцепта

to **take a ~ on discount** (ту тэ́ а ~ он ди́скоунт) производить учёт векселя

to withdraw a ~ (ту уиθдра́у а ~) отзывать вексель

transfer of a ~ (тра́нсфэр оф а ~) передача {переуступка} векселя

uncovered ~ (анко́вэрд ~) непокрытый вексель

unsecured ~ (ансэкю́рд ~) необеспеченный вексель

usance ~ of exchange (ю́санс ~ оф эксчэ́йндж) внешнеторговый вексель

usance of a ~ (ю́санс оф а ~) срок векселя, установленный обычаем

waiver of demand on a ~ (уэ́йвэр оф дима́нд он а ~) отказ от протеста векселя

~ after date (~ а́фтэр дэйт) вексель со сроком платежа, исчисляемым со дня выдачи

~ at ... day's sight (~ ат ... дэйз сайт) срочный вексель, через ... дней после предъявления

~ at usance (~ ат ю́санс) вексель на срок, установленный торговым обычаем

~ book (~ бук) книга векселей

~ creditor (~ крэ́дитор) кредитор по векселю

~ debtor (~ дэ́тор) должник по векселю

~ drawn in a set (~ дра́ун ин а сэт) вексель, выписанный в комплекте

~ drawn on a major bank (~ дра́ун он а мэ́йджор банк) вексель, выставленный на первоклассный банк

~ drawn on non-existent party (~ дра́ун он нон-экзи́стэнт па́рти) вексель, выписанный на несуществующее лицо

~ endorsed over (~ эндо́рсд о́вэр) вексель с передаточной надписью

~ for collection (~ фор коллэ́кшн) вексель на инкассо, вексель для инкасирования

~s in circulation (~с ин сиркюлэ́йшн) банкноты в обращении

~ in the denomination of ... (~ ин θи диноминэ́йшн оф ...) банкнота достоинством ...

~ not yet matured (~ нот ёт мачу́рд) непросроченный вексель

~ to order (~ ту о́рдэр) вексель собственному приказу {to oneself}

~ to the order of a third party (~ ту θи о́рдэр оф а θирд па́рти) вексель чужому приказу

~ transactions (~ транса́кшнс) операции с векселями

~ with recourse (~ уиθ ри́корс) обратный вексель

~ of health (~ оф хэлθ) санитарное удостоверение

~ of materials (~ оф мати́риалс) ведомость материалов

~ of sale (~ оф сэйл) закладная, купчая

~ of work (~ оф уо́рк) ведомость работ

Bill of Exchange (билл оф эксчэ́йндж) вексель, тратта

acceptance of a ~ (аксэ́птанс оф а ~) акцепт векселя

acceptance ~ (аксэ́птанс ~) акцептованный вексель

advance ~ (адва́нс ~) авансовый вексель

bank guarantee of a ~ (банк гяранти́ оф а ~) аваль векселя

circulation of ~s (сиркюлэ́йшн оф ~с) обращение векселей

clean ~ (клин ~) недокументированный вексель

expenses for protesting a ~ (экспэ́нсэз фор про́тэстинг а ~) издержки по опротестованию векселя

first ~ (фэрст ~) первый экземпляр векселя

guarantor of a ~ (гяранто́р оф а ~) авалист по векселю

liabilities on ~s (лайаби́литиз он ~с) обязательства по векселям

pledged ~ (плэджд ~) заложенный вексель

portfolio of ~s (портфо́лио оф ~с) портфель векселей

returned ~s (риту́рнд ~с) возвращённый векселя

second ~ (сэ́конд ~) второй экземпляр векселя

sterling ~ (стэ́рлинг ~) вексель, выписанный в фунтах стерлингов

to accept a ~ (ту аксэ́пт а ~) акцептовать вексель

to advise a ~ (ту адва́йз а ~) авизовать вексель

to cancel a ~ (ту кáнсэл а ~)
аннулировать вексель
treasury ~s (трэ́жюри ~с)
казначейские векселя
the ~ is overdue (θи ~ из
овэрдý) вексель просрочен
~s in blank (~с ин бланк)
бланковый вексель
~s receivable (~с рисúвабл)
векселя, подлежащие взысканию
Bill of Lading (билл оф лэ́йдинг)
дорожный аккредитив, коносамент,
накладная
~ form (~ форм) форма
коносамента
~ number (~ нýмбэр) номер
коносамента
~ terms (~ тэрмз) условия
коносамента
against a ~ (агэ́нст а ~) по
коносаменту
bearer of a ~ (бэ́йрэр оф а ~)
предъявитель коносамента
clean ~ (клин ~) чистый
коносамент
completed ~ (комплúтэд ~)
заполненный коносамент
copy of a ~ (кóпи оф а ~)
экземпляр коносамента
date of a ~ (дэйт оф а ~) дата
коносамента
direct ~ (дирэ́кт ~) прямой
коносамент
groupage ~ (грýпадж ~) сборный
коносамент, групповой коносамент
holder of a ~ (хóлдэр оф а ~)
держатель коносамента
inland ~ (úнланд ~) внутренний
коносамент
liner ~ (лáйнэр ~) линейный
коносамент
local ~ (лóкал ~) локальный
коносамент
non-negotiable ~ (нон-нэгóшабл
~) необоротный коносамент
on board ~ (он борд ~) бортовой
коносамент
order ~ (óрдэр ~) ордерный
коносамент
original ~ (орúджинал ~)
оригинальный коносамент
outward ~ (óутуард ~) внешний
коносамент
post-dated ~ (пост-дэ́йтэд ~)
датированный более поздним
числом коносамент

pro forma ~ (про фóрма ~)
проформа коносамента
reservation in a ~ (рэзэрвэ́йшн
ин а ~) отметка в коносаменте
river ~ (рúвэр ~) речная
накладная, речной коносамент
service ~ (сэ́рвис ~) служебный
коносамент
short form ~ (шорт форм ~)
краткий коносамент
signature date of a ~ (сúгначэр
дэйт оф а ~) дата подписания
коносамента
steamer ~ (стúмэр ~) морской
коносамент
straight ~ (стрэ́йт ~) именной
коносамент, коносамент, выданны[
на определённое лицо
summary of ~ (сáммари оф ~)
перечень грузов, указанных в
коносаменте
through ~ (θру ~) сквозной
коносамент
to hand over a ~ (ту ханд óвэр
~) вручать коносамент
to sign a ~ (ту сайн а ~)
подписывать коносамент
transshipment ~ (трансшúпмэнт
сквозная накладная
truck ~ (трак ~) автодорожная
накладная
unclean ~ (анклúн ~) нечистый
коносамент
under a ~ (áндэр а ~) в
соответствии с коносаментом
warehouse ~ (уэ́рхаус ~)
складской коносамент
Billboard (бúлборд) афиша,
рекламный щит
Billet, to ~ (бúллэт, ту ~)
расквартировать
Billeting (бúллэтинг) военно-
квартирная повинность, постой,
расквартирование
military ~ (мúлитари ~) военны[
постой
Bind (бáйнд) скука {situation}
to ~ (ту ~) обязывать, крепить
связывать [perfective: связать]
to ~ crosswise (ту ~ крóсуайз)
обвязывать поперёк
to ~ lengthwise (ту ~ лэ́нгθуай
обвязывать вдоль
to ~ with wire (ту ~ уиθ уáйр)
крепить проволокой
to ~ with cable (ту ~ уиθ кэ́й[
крепить тросом

Binding (ба́йндинг) крепление,
обязательный {adj.}
Bio-technology (байо-тэкно́лоджи)
биотехнология
Birth (бир𝜃) рождение
    illegitimate ~ (иллэджи́тэмат ~)
незаконное рождение
    legitimate ~ (лэджи́тэмат ~)
законное рождение
    ~ out of wedlock (~ о́ут оф
уэ́длок) внебрачное рождение
    ~-rate (~-рэйт) рождаемость
Blank (бланк) бланк, бланковый
{adj.}, пропуск
    application ~ (апплике́йшн ~)
анкета
    cable ~ (кэйбл ~) телеграфный
бланк
    documentary bill lodgement ~
(докюмэ́нтари билл ло́джмэнт ~)
бланк инкассового поручения по
документарной тратте
Blanket (бла́нкэт) глобальный {adj.}
Blend (блэнд) смесь, сочетание
    to ~ (ту ~) смешивать
[perfective: смешать]
Bloc (блок) блок
    ~ currency ~ (~ ку́ррэнси ~)
валютный блок
    ~ exclusive economic ~ (~
эксклю́сив эконо́мик ~) закрытый
экономический блок
    ~ military ~ (~ ми́литари ~)
военный блок
Block (блок) квартал {of a city},
пакет
    controlling ~ (контро́ллинг ~)
контрольный пакет
    credit ~ (крэ́дит ~) кредитная
блокада
    ~ of shares (~ оф шэйрс) пакет
акций
Blockade (блоке́йд) блокада
    breach of a ~ (брич оф а ~)
прорыв блокады
    customs ~ (ка́стомз ~) таможенная
блокада
    naval ~ (нэ́йвал ~) морская
блокада
    to ~ (ту ~) блокировать
    to impose a ~ (ту импо́с а ~)
ввести блокаду
Blocked (блокд) блокированный
Blotter (бло́ттэр) бювар
    police ~ (поли́с ~) реестр
арестов и запрещений

Blueprint (блу́принт) светописная
копия
    to submit ~s (ту субми́т ~с)
представить светописные копии
чертежей
Board (борд) борт, коллегия, совет
    arbitration ~ (арбитрэ́йшн ~)
арбитражная коллегия
    examination ~ (экзамине́йшн ~)
аттестационная комиссия
    federal ~ (фэ́дэрал ~)
федеральный совет
    free on ~, {f.o.b.} (фри он ~,
{эф-о-би}) франко борт
    judicial ~ (джюди́шл ~) судебная
коллегия
    on ~ (он ~) на борту
    price control ~ (прайс контро́л
~) орган контроля над ценами
    standing arbitral ~ (ста́ндинг
а́рбитрал ~) инструкционный
арбитраж
    to accept cargo on ~ (ту аксэ́пт
ка́рго он ~) принимать на борт
    to load on ~ (ту лод он ~)
погрузить на борт
    to take on ~ (ту тэйк он ~)
взять на абордаж
    ~ of appeals (~ оф аппи́лс)
апелляционная коллегия
    ~ of guardians (~ оф га́рдианс)
опекунский совет
    ~ of sanitation (~ оф санитэ́йшн)
санитарный совет
Boarding (бординг) абордаж {a ship}
Boat (бот) лодка, судно
    mail ~ (мэйл ~) почтовое судно
Body (бо́ди) орган, тело
    administrative ~ (адми́нистрэйтив
~) административный орган
    auxiliary ~ (аукзи́лиэри ~)
вспомогательный орган
    collective ~ (колле́ктив ~)
коллективный орган
    consultative ~ (ко́нсултэ́йтив ~)
консультативный орган
    corporate ~ (ко́рпорат ~)
корпоративная организация,
корпорация
    deliberative ~ (дили́бэратив ~)
совещательный орган
    human ~ (хю́ман ~) организм
    intergovernmental ~
(интэрговэрнмэ́нтал ~)
межправительственный орган

inter-parliamentary ~ (интэр-парламэнтари ~) межпарламентский орган

judicial ~ (джюдишл ~) судебный орган

judicial investigative ~ (джюдишл инвэстигэйтив ~) судебно-следственный орган

legislative ~ (лэджислэйтив ~) законодательный орган

managerial ~ (мáнаджриал ~) орган управления

parliamentary ~ (парламэнтари ~) парламентский орган

permanent arbitral ~ (пэрманэнт áрбитрал ~) постоянный арбитражный орган

representative ~ (рэпрэзэнтатив ~) представительный орган

Bogus (бóгус) фиктивный

Bolt (болт) болт

to ~ (ту ~) крепить болтами

Bona fide (бóна фáйдэ) бона фиде

Bond (бонд) бонд, облигация, подписка

baby ~ (бэйби ~) мелкая облигация

bearer ~ (бэйрэр ~) облигация на предъявителя

bottomry ~ (бóттомри ~) бодмерейный договор

called ~ (калд ~) облигация, предъявленная к погашению

called ~s (калд ~с) аннулированные бумаги

debenture ~ (дибэнчур ~) облигация, не имеющая специального обеспечения

deferred ~ (дифэрд ~) облигация с отсроченным платежом

flotation of a ~ issue (флотэйшн оф а ~ ишю) размещение облигаций

foreign ~ (фóрэн ~) заграничная облигация

general ~ (джэнэрал ~) аварийный бонд

general average ~ (джэнэрал áвэрэдж ~) аварийная гарантия

government ~ (гóвэрнмэнт ~) государственная облигация

guarantee ~ (гяранти ~) гарантийное письмо

high-grade ~ (хай-грэйд ~) первоклассная облигация

internal ~ (интэрнал ~) внутренняя облигация

interest-bearing ~s (интэрэст-бэринг ~с) процентные облигации

irredeemable ~ (иррэдимабл ~) облигация, не подлежащая погашению до наступления срока

issue of ~s (ишю оф ~с) выпуск облигаций

long-term ~ (лонг-тэрм ~) долгосрочная облигация

maturing ~ (мачуринг ~) облигация, выходящая в тираж

maturing ~s (мачуринг ~с) облигации, подлежащие погашению

optionally redeemable ~ (óпшналли ридимабл ~) облигация с правом досрочного погашения

overdue ~ (овэрдý ~) облигация, не погашенная в срок

participation ~ (партисипэйшн ~) облигация с правом на участие в прибылях компании

passive ~ (пáссив ~) беспроцентная облигация

premium ~ (прúмиум ~) облигация выигрышного займа

registered ~ (рэджистэрд ~) именная облигация

retirement of ~s (ритáйрмэнт оф ~с) выкуп облигаций

savings ~ (сэйвингс ~) государственная облигация

secured ~ (сэкюрд ~) облигация со специальным обеспечением

short ~ (шорт ~) краткосрочная облигация

to issue ~s (ту ишю ~с) выпускать облигации

to redeem ~s (ту ридим ~с) погашать облигации

to retire ~s (ту ритáйр ~с) выкупать облигации

treasury ~ (трэжюри ~) обязательство казначейства

treasury ~s (трэжюри ~с) казначейские обязательства

~ issue (~ ишю) выпуск облигаций

~ market (~ мáркэт) рынок облигаций

~ note {customs} (~ нот {кáстомз}) разрешение на вывоз таможенного склада

Bondability (бондабúлити) бонитет

Bonded (бóндэд) бондовой {customs} облигационный

Bonus (бóнус) вознаграждение, дополнительное вознаграждение, премиальные, премия

annual ~ (áннюал ~) ежегодная
премия
cash ~ (каш ~) бонус
import ~ (úмпорт ~) импортная
премия
incentive ~ (инсэнтив ~)
поощрительная премия
lumpsum ~ (лáмпсум ~)
единовременная премия
net ~ (нэт ~) чистая премия
New Year's ~ (нью йúрз ~)
новогодняя премия
piece work ~ (пис уóрк ~)
аккордная надбавка
quality ~ (куáлити ~) надбавка
за повышенное качество
seniority ~ (синёрити ~)
надбавка за выслугу лет
~ for completing work ahead of
schedule (~ фор комплúтинг уóрк
ахэд оф скэджюл) вознаграждение
за досрочное завершение работы
~ for quality (~ фор куáлити)
премия за качество
Bonus Allowance (бóнус аллóуанс)
бонификация
amount of ~ (амóунт оф ~) размер
бонификации
export ~ (эکспорт ~) экспортная
бонификация
reimbursable ~ (риэмбýрсабл ~)
обратная бонификация
Book (бук) книга, регистр
account ~ (аккóунт ~)
бухгалтерская книга, регистр,
учётный регистр
accounting ~s (аккóунтинг ~с)
бухгалтерский учёт
address ~ (аддрэс ~) адресная
книга
bank ~ (банк ~) банковская книга
business ~ (бúзнэс ~) торговая
книга
cargo ~ (кáрго ~) грузовая книга
carryover in the account ~
(кэрриовэр ин θи аккóунт ~)
перенос в бухгалтерскую книгу
cash receipts and payments ~
(каш рисúтс энд пэймэнтс ~)
приходно-расходная книга
day ~ (дэй ~) журнал
jacket of a ~ (джáкэт оф а ~)
обложка книги
log ~ (лог ~) вахтенный журнал,
журнал

machine performance log ~ (машúн
пэрфóрманс лог ~) машинный
журнал
publication of a ~ (пáбликэйшн
оф а ~) выход книги
receipt ~ (рисúт ~) приходная
книга
reference ~ (рэфэрэнс ~)
справочная книга
stock ~ (сток ~) товарная книга
tally ~ (тáлли ~) журнал
регистрации приёма груза
telephone ~ (тэлэфон ~)
телефонная книга {white pages}
till ~ (тил ~) кассовая книга
to ~ (ту ~) бронировать,
букировать {freight}
to audit the ~s (ту áудит θи ~с)
проверять бухгалтерские книги
to enter into the account ~ (ту
энтэр úнту θи аккóунт ~) вносить
в книгу
to keep the account ~s (ту кип
θи аккóунт ~с) вести
бухгалтерские книги
to subscribe for a ~ (ту
субскрáйб фор а ~) подписываться
на книгу {e.g. multi-volume}
~ entry (~ энтри) запись в книге
~ of accounts (~ оф аккóунтс)
счетоводная книга
Booking (бýкинг) бронирование,
букировка
cargo-~ (кáрго-~) букировка
груза
freight ~ (фрэйт ~) фрахтование
тоннажа
~ commission (~ коммúшн) плата
за букировку
~ list (~ лист) букинглист,
перечень забукированных грузов
~ note (~ нот) букинг-нот
Bookkeeper (бýккипэр) бухгалтер
senior ~ (сúниор ~) старший
бухгалтер
Bookkeeping (бýккипинг)
бухгалтерский
Booklet (бýклэт) буклет, книжка
Boom (бум) бум
economic ~ (экономик ~) подъём
коньюнктуры
inflationary ~ (инфлэйшнари ~)
инфляционный бум
investment ~ (инвэстмэнт ~) бум
капиталовложений
speculative ~ (спэкюлатив ~)
спекулятивный бум

stock-market ~ (сток-ма́ркэт ~)
биржевой бум
Boost (буст) повышение
Border (бо́рдэр) граница,
пограничный {adj.}
 buyer's ~ (ба́йэрз ~) граница
 страны покупателя
 delivery of shipment to the ~
 (дэли́вэри оф ши́пмэнт ту θи ~)
 доставка груза до границы
 national ~ (на́шэнал ~)
 государственная граница
 price FOB ~ (прайс эф-о-би ~)
 цена франко граница
 seller's ~ (сэ́ллэрз ~) граница
 страны продавца
 to cross the ~ (ту крос θи ~)
 пересекать границу
 transhipment at the ~
 (транши́пмэнт ат θи ~) перевалка
 груза на границе
 with delivery at the ~ (уиθ
 дэли́вэри ат θи ~) с поставкой на
 границе
Borrow, to ~ (бо́рро, ту ~) брать
взаймы, брать в долг
Borrower (бо́рроуэр) заёмщик
Borrowing (бо́рроуинг) заём,
заимствование
 domestic ~ (доме́стик ~)
 внутренний заём
 foreign ~ (фо́рэн ~) внешний заём
Boss (бос) начальник, хозяин
{male}, хозяйка {female}
Bottle (ботл) бутылка, бутыль
 to ~ (ту ~) упаковывать в бутыли
Bottom (бо́ттом) дно
Bottomry (бо́ттомри) бодмерея
Bound (бо́унд) направляющийся
{headed for}, обязанный {obligated}
 homeward ~ (хо́муард ~)
 направляющийся в порт приписки
 to be ~ (ту би ~) обязываться,
 связывать [perfective: связать]
 to be contractually ~ (ту би
 контра́кчуалли ~) обязываться
 договором
 ~ for (~ фор) направляющийся
Boundary (бо́ундари) изгородь
Bounty (бо́унти) премия
 export ~ (э́кспорт ~) вывозная
 премия
Box (бокс) коробка, ящик, ящичный
{adj.}
 cardboard ~ (ка́рдборд ~)
 картонная коробка, карточный
 ящик

 fold-down ~ (фолд-до́ун ~)
 разборно-складной ящик
 gift ~ (гифт ~) подарочная
 коробка
 heavy duty ~ (хэ́ви дю́ти ~)
 прочная коробка
 metal ~ (мэ́тал ~) металлический
 ящик
 plywood ~ (пла́йуу́д ~) фанерный
 ящик
 post office ~ (пост о́ффис ~)
 почтовый ящик
 standard ~ (ста́ндард ~)
 стандартный ящик
 steel ~ (стил ~) стальной ящик
 to open ~es (ту о́пэн ~эз)
 вскрывать ящики
 tin ~ (тин ~) жестяная коробка
 wooden ~ (уу́дэн ~) деревянный
 ящик
 ~ top (~ топ) крышка ящика
 ~ with hinged lid (~ уиθ хинжд
 лид) ящик со съёмной крышкой
Boycott (бо́йкот) бойкот
 economic ~ (эконо́мик ~)
 экономический бойкот
 financial ~ (файна́ншл ~)
 финансовый бойкот
 to ~ (ту ~) бойкотировать
 to impose a ~ (ту импо́з а ~)
 объявить бойкот
 to lift a ~ (ту лифт а ~)
 отменить бойкот
Brace (брэйс) крепление, подпорка,
связь
 to ~ (ту ~) крепить
Bracing (брэ́йсинг) крепление
Bracket (бра́кэт) разряд
Branch (бранч) дочерний {adj.},
отделение, отрасль, филиал
 local ~ (ло́кал ~) местное
 отделение
 ~ of agriculture (~ оф
 а́грикулчур) отрасль сельского
 хозяйства
 ~ of an enterprise (~ оф ан
 э́нтэрпрайз) отрасль предприятия
 ~ of industry (~ оф и́ндустри)
 производственная отрасль
 ~ bank (~ банк) филиал банка
 ~ manager (~ ма́наджэр)
 руководитель филиала
 ~ office (~ о́ффис) филиал
 компании
Brand (бранд) марка, марка товара
 best ~ name (бэст ~ нэйм) высшая
 марка

family of name ~s (фа́мили оф нэйм ~с) групповая марка
manufacturer's ~ name (манюфа́кчурэрз ~ нэйм) марка производителя
of the best ~s (оф θи бэст ~с) высшей марки
product ~ name (про́дукт ~ нэйм) марка изделия
to ~ (ту ~) клеймить, наносить маркировку выжиганием {cattle}, ставить клеймо
top selling ~ (топ сэ́ллинг ~) наиболее ходкая марка
~ name (~ нэйм) название марки, фирменный
~ selection (~ сэлэ́кшн) выбор марки товара
Branded (бра́ндэд) марочный
Breach (брич) нарушение
to ~ (ту ~) нарушать
~ of an agreement (~ оф ан агри́мэнт) нарушение соглашения
~ of confidence (~ оф ко́нфидэнс) злоупотребление доверием, нарушение доверия
~ of contract (~ оф ко́нтракт) нарушение договора, нарушение контракта
~ of contract action (~ оф ко́нтракт акшн) иск о нарушении договора
~ of contract provisions (~ оф ко́нтракт прови́жнз) нарушение положений договора
~ of an obligation (~ оф ан облигэ́йшн) нарушение обязательства
~ of a schedule (~ оф а скэ́джюл) нарушение графика
~ of trust (~ оф траст) злоупотребление доверием
~ of warranty (~ оф уа́рранти) нарушение гарантии
Break (брэйк) перерыв, разрыв
to ~ (ту ~) выбывать из строя, разъединить
to ~ the law (ту ~ θи лау) нарушать закон
to ~ off (ту ~ офф) разорвать
~ in the period (~ ин θи пи́риод) перерыв срока
Breakage (брэ́йкадж) бой, повреждение
~ during handling (~ ду́ринг ха́ндлинг) бой при перевалке

~ in transit (~ ин тра́нзит) бой при транспортировке
~ rate (~ рэйт) допуск брака
Breakdown (брэ́йкдоун) разбивка, развал
price ~ (прайс ~) расценочная ведомость
~ of capital investment (~ оф ка́питал инвэ́стмэнт) распределение капиталовложений
~ of negotiations (~ оф нэгоши́эйшнс) срыв переговоров
Breaking (брэ́йкинг) разъединение
~ of rules (~ оф рулз) нарушение правил
~ off of negotiations (~ офф оф нэгоши́эйшнс) разрыв переговоров
Breakup (брэ́йкап) расформирование {e.g. company}
~ of a meeting (~ оф а ми́тинг) роспуск собрания
Bribe (брайб) взятка
to ~ (ту ~) давать взятку, подкупать
to offer a ~ (ту о́ффэр а ~) предлагать взятку
to take a ~ (ту тэйк а ~) брать взятку
Bribed (брайбд) подкупной
Bribery (бра́йбери) взяточничество
to convict for ~ (ту конви́кт фор ~) осудить за взятку
~ of an official (~ оф ан оффи́шл) подкуп должностного лица**brigand**
Bridge (бридж) мост
to ~ the gap (ту ~ θи гап) ликвидировать разрыв
Briefing (бри́финг) инструктаж {usu. military}, инструктивное совещание
Brigade (бригэ́йд) бригада
~ leader (~ ли́дэр) бригадир
Brigandage (бри́гандадж) разбой
Bring, to ~ (бринг, ту ~) приносить
Bringing (бри́нгинг) введение
~ a law into effect (~ а лау и́нту иффэ́кт) введение закона в силу
~ of an indictment (~ оф ан инда́йтмэнт) предъявление обвинения
~ to court (~ ту ко́урт) предание суду
Brittle (бриттл) ломкий
Broadcast (бро́дкаст) передача
Broaden, to ~ (бро́дэн, ту ~) расширять

Brochure (брошу́р) брошюра
  promotional ~ (промо́шнал ~)
  рекламная брошюра
Broker (бро́кэр) брокер,
комиссионер, маклер, маклерский
{*adj.*}
  agency of a ~ (эйджэнси оф а ~)
  посредничество маклера
  bill ~ (билл ~) вексельный
  посредник
  charter-~ (ча́ртэр-~) брокер по
  фрахтованию
  charterer's ~ (ча́ртэрэрз ~)
  брокер фрахтователя
  "del credere" ~ (дэл крэдэ́рэ ~)
  брокер делькредере
  discount ~ (ди́скоунт ~)
  занимающийся учётными операциями
  маклер
  freight ~ (фрэйт ~) фрахтовый
  брокер
  grain ~ (грэйн ~) брокер по
  покупкам и продаже зерна
  insurance ~ (иншю́ранс ~)
  страховой брокер, страховой
  маклер
  securities ~ (сэкю́ритиз ~)
  вексельный брокер
  ship ~ (шип ~) корабельный
  маклер
  shipowner's ~ (ши́поунэрз ~)
  брокер судовладельца
  shipping ~ (ши́ппинг ~) маклер по
  фрахтованию судов
  stock ~ (сток ~) биржевой
  брокер, биржевой маклер
  ~ **with a seat on the exchange** (~
  уиθ а сит он θи эксчэ́йндж)
  официальный биржевой маклер
  ~**'s commission** (~'с комми́шн)
  брокераж
Brokerage (бро́кэрадж) брокераж,
брокерский {*adj.*}, брокерское дело,
маклерство
  freight ~ (фрэйт ~) фрахтовая
  комиссия
  note ~ (нот ~) торговля
  векселями
  ~ **fees** (~ физ) вознаграждение
  маклеру
Brothel (бро́θэл) публичный дом
Brother (бро́θэр) брат
Brotherhood (бро́θэрхуд) братство
Brother-in-law (бро́θэр-ин-лау)
деверь {husband's brother}, зять
{sister's husband}, свояк {wife's

sister's husband}, шурин {wife's
brother}
Budget (ба́джэт) бюджет
  advertising ~ (а́двэртайзинг ~)
  бюджет рекламы
  annual ~ (а́ннюал ~) годовой
  бюджет
  balanced ~ (ба́лансд ~)
  сбалансированный бюджет
  capital ~ (ка́питал ~) бюджет
  капиталовложений
  consolidated ~ (консо́лидэйтэд ~)
  сводный бюджет
  current operating ~ (ку́ррэнт
  о́пэрэйтинг ~) текущий бюджет
  draft ~ (драфт ~) проект бюджета
  fixed-revenue ~ (фиксд-рэ́вэну ~)
  жёсткий бюджет
  local ~ (ло́кал) местный бюджет
  low ~ (ло́у ~) небольшой бюджет
  national ~ (на́шэнал ~)
  национальный бюджет
  revenue ~ (рэ́вэну) доходный бюджет
  state ~ (стэйт ~)
  государственный бюджет
  supplementary ~ (сапплэмэ́нтари)
  дополнительный бюджет
  to ~ **for** (ту ~ фор)
  предусматривать в бюджете
  to approve a ~ (ту аппру́в а ~)
  одобрить бюджет
  to cut the ~ (ту кут θи ~)
  сокращать бюджет
  to increase the ~ (ту инкри́с θи
  ~) увеличивать бюджет
  to pass the ~ (ту пасс θи ~)
  утверждать бюджет
  to present a ~ (ту прэзэ́нт а ~)
  представлять бюджетные цены
  to submit a ~ **for deliberation**
  (ту субми́т а ~ фор дилибэрэ́йшн)
  представлять бюджет на
  рассмотрение
  to transfer a figure into the ~
  (ту тра́нсфэр а фи́гюр и́нту θи ~)
  перечислять сумму в бюджет
  unbalanced ~ (анба́лансд ~)
  несбалансированный бюджет
  ~ **cuts** (~ кутс) сокращение
  бюджета
  ~ **contributions** (~ контрибью́шнс)
  взносы в бюджет
  ~ **expenditures** (~ экспэ́ндичюрз)
  расходный бюджет
  ~ **implementation** (~
  имплэмэнтэ́йшн) исполнение
  бюджета

~ **preparation** (~ прэпарэ́йшн) подготовка бюджета
~ **process** (~ про́сэс) составление бюджета
~ **size** (~ сайз) размер бюджета
Budgetary (ба́джэтари) бюджетный
for ~ purposes (фор ~ пу́рпосэз) для учёта в бюджете
Build-up (билд-ап) наращивание
Build, to ~ (билд, ту ~) строить
to ~ up (ту ~ ап) наращивать
Builder (би́лдэр) строитель
home ~ (хом ~) застройщик {one's own house}
Building (би́лдинг) застройка, здание, постройка, сооружение, строение, строительство
administrative ~ (адми́нистрэйтив ~) административное здание
residential ~ (рэзидэ́ншл ~) жилое здание, жилое строение
Bulk (булк) масса, массовый, навалочный, насыпной
in ~ (ин ~) в массе, навалом, насыпью
shipment in ~ (ши́пмэнт ин ~) погрузка без упаковки
to load in ~ (ту лод ин ~) грузить без тары
~ commodities (~ коммо́дитиз) товарная масса
~ shipment (~ ши́пмэнт) перевозка груза насыпью
~ storage (~ сто́рэдж) хранение насыпью
Bulker, grain-~ (бу́лкэр, грэйн-~) землевоз
Bull (бул) бык
~ market (~ ма́ркэт) бойкая торговля
Bulletin (бу́ллэтин) бюллетень
informational ~ (информэ́йшнал ~) информационный бюллетень
price ~ (прайс ~) прейскурантный бюллетень
to publish a ~ (ту па́блиш а ~) издавать бюллетень
trade ~ (трэйд ~) коммерческий бюллетень
Bundle (бу́ндл) тюк
Bunkering (бу́нкэринг) заправка топливом
Bureau (бю́ро) бюро
information ~ (информэ́йшн ~) информационное бюро
marriage ~ (мэ́ррэдж ~) агентство для устройства браков

Burglary (бу́рглари) кража со взломом {breaking and entering}, ограбление
Bureaucracy (бюро́краси) бюрократия
Burlap (бу́рлап) мешковина
Bury, to ~ (бу́ри, ту ~) погребать
Business (би́знэс) бизнес, дело, деловой {adj.}, промысел, служебный
arbitrage ~ (а́рбитраж ~) биржевой арбитраж
big ~ (биг ~) большой бизнес, крупный капитал
branch ~ (бранч ~) отделение фирмы
brokerage ~ (бро́кэрадж ~) маклерское дело
course of ~ (ко́урс оф ~) ход дела
freight forwarding ~ (фрэйт фо́руардинг ~) экспедиторское дело
line of ~ (лайн оф ~) род деятельности
mail order ~ (мэйл о́рдэр ~) посылочная торговля
on ~ (он ~) по делу {for purposes of business}
profitable ~ (про́фитабл ~) выгодное дело, выгодная торговля, прибыльный бизнес, прибыльное дело
publishing ~ (па́блишинг ~) издательское дело
service ~ (сэ́рвис ~) операции по торговле услугами
shady ~ (шэ́йди ~) авантюра
slack ~ (слак ~) вялый бизнес
small ~ (смалл ~) малый бизнес, мелкая фирма
to be away on ~ (ту би ауэ́й он ~) быть в командировке
to be in ~ (ту би ин ~) заниматься торговлей
to conduct ~ (ту конду́кт ~) вести дела, заниматься коммерцией
to direct a ~ (ту дирэ́кт а ~) руководить фирмой
to do ~ (ту ду ~) вести торговлю, делать дело
to establish a ~ (ту эста́блиш а ~) создавать дело
to expand a ~ (ту экспа́нд а ~) расширять дело
to finance a ~ (ту файна́нс а ~) финансировать дело

to **found** a ~ (ту фóунд а ~) учреждать дело
to **have** ~ **with** (ту хэв ~ уиθ) иметь дело с
to **start up** a ~ (ту старт ап а ~) начать дело
to **transact** ~ **through a bank** (ту трансáкт ~ θру а банк) вести дела через банк
to **wind up** a ~ (ту уайнд ап а ~) ликвидировать дело
transportation ~ (транспортэ́йшн ~) транспортное дело
urgent ~ (у́рджэнт ~) неотложное дело
~ **address of a company** (~ аддрэ́с оф а кóмпани) местонахождение фирмы
~ **experience** (~ экспи́риэнс) опыт в делах
~ **planning** (~ плáннинг) планирование выпуска и сбыта продукции
~ **stagnation** (~ стагнэ́йшн) застой в делах
~ **survey** (~ су́рвэй) обзор хозяйственной деятельности
Business Cycle (би́знэс сайкл) конъюнктура
boom in the ~ (бум ин θи ~) высокая конъюнктура
peak in the ~ (пик ин θи ~) высокая конъюнктура
stagnation in the ~ (стагнэ́йшн ин θи ~) вялая конъюнктура
Businessman (би́знэсман) коммерсант
Busline (бу́слайн) автобусная линия
inter-city ~ (и́нтэр-си́ти ~) междугородная автобусная линия
Buy (бай) покупка
to ~ (ту ~) закупать, купить
to ~ **all of** (ту ~ алл оф) скупать
to ~ **out** (ту ~ óут) выкупать
to ~ **up** (ту ~ ап) скупать
Buy-back (бай-бак) компенсационный
Buy-sell (бай-сэл) купли-продажи
~ **agreement** (агри́мэнт) договор купли-продажи
Buyer (бá йэр) заказчик, предприятие-покупатель
commercial ~ (коммэ́ршл ~) брокер по покупкам
Buying (бá йинг) закупка
speculative ~ (спэ́кюлатив ~) спекулятивная закупка
~ **up** (~ ап) скупка

By-laws (бá й-лаус) устав
By-product (бá й-прóдукт) побочный продукт

C

Cable (кэйбл) кабель, канат, телеграмма, трос
dispatch of a ~ (ди́спатч оф а ~) отправка телеграммы
flexible ~ (флэ́ксибл ~) гибкий канат
hoisting ~ (хóйстинг ~) грузоподъёмный канат
official ~ {regulatory instructions} (оффи́шл ~ {рэ́гюлатори инстрá кшнс}) служебная телеграмма
steel ~ (стил ~) стальной канат, стальной трос
to ~ **for** (ту ~ фор) вызывать телеграммой
to **notify by** ~ (ту нóтифай бай ~) уведомлять телеграммой
to **send a** ~ (ту сэнд а ~) высылать телеграмму
urgent ~ (у́рджэнт ~) срочная телеграмма
Calculate, to ~ (кá лкюлэйт, ту ~) исчислять, калькулировать, начислять
Calculation (калкюлэ́йшн) исчисление, калькуляция, начисление, подсчет
annual summary ~ (á ннюал сá ммари ~) сводный годовой расчёт
approximate ~ (аппрóксимат ~) приблизительный расчёт
demurrage ~ (димю́рradж ~) калькуляция демерреджа
final ~ (фá йнал ~) окончательная калькуляция
summary ~ (сá ммари ~) сводный расчёт
~ **of expenses** (~ оф экспэ́нсэз) калькуляция расходов
~ **of income** (~ оф и́нком) исчисление дохода
~ **of interest** (~ оф и́нтэрэст) исчисление процентов
~ **of prices** (~ оф прá йсэз) калькуляция цен
~ **of prime cost** (~ оф прайм кост) калькуляция себестоимости

~ of tax (~ оф такс) исчисление налога
~ of term (~ оф тэрм) исчисление сроков {time}
Calculator (ка́лкюлэйтор) калькулятор, счётная машина
Calendar (ка́лэндар) календарь
Call (кал) востребование, заход {of a vessel at port}, опцион, призыв
  cash ~ on shares (каш ~ он шэйрз) требование уплаты взноса за акции
  courtesy ~ (ку́ртэси ~) визит вежливости
  distress ~ {of a vessel at port} (дистрэ́с ~ {оф а вэ́ссэл ат порт}) вынужденный заход
  margin ~ (ма́рджин ~) требование гарантийного взноса, требование уплаты разницы
  to ~ (ту ~) созывать [perfective: созвать]
  to ~ for (ту ~ фор) вызывать
  to ~ collect (ту ~ колле́кт) звонить по телефону с оплатой абонентом
  to ~ in a loan (ту ~ ин а лон) требовать возврата займа
  to be subject to {cash} **~** (ту би са́бджэкт ту {каш} ~) подлежать возврату по первому требованию
  to pay a ~ (ту пэй а ~) наносить визит
  ~ at port (~ ат порт) остановка в порту
  ~ back (~ бак) возврат
  ~-up point (~-ап пойнт) явочный пункт {for military conscription}
Callable (ка́ллабл) подлежащий взысканию
Calling (ка́ллинг) призвание
  ~ of a meeting (~ оф а ми́тинг) созыв собрания
  ~ to order (~ ту о́рдэр) призвание к порядку
Calm (калм) спокойствие
Calumny (калу́мни) клевета
Campaign (кампэ́йн) кампания
  advertising ~ (а́двэртайзинг ~) рекламная кампания
  broad ~ (брод ~) широкая кампания
  export ~ (э́кспорт ~) кампания по увеличению экспорта
  joint ~ (джойнт ~) совместная кампания

  ongoing ~ (онго́инг ~) текущая кампания
  television ~ (тэлэвижн ~) телевизионная кампания
  to conclude a ~ (ту конклю́д а ~) закончить кампанию
  to conduct a ~ (ту конду́кт а ~) вести кампанию
  to support a ~ (ту суппо́рт а ~) поддерживать кампанию
  to wreck a ~ (ту рэк а ~) сорвать кампанию
  trade press ~ (трэйд прэс ~) торговая кампания в печати
  ~ goal (~ гол) цель кампании
Campaigning (кампэ́йнинг) агитация
  election ~ (иле́кшн ~) выборная агитация
Can (кан) банка
  hermetically-sealed ~ (хэрмэ́тикалли-силд ~) герметическая банка
  swollen ~ (суо́ллэн ~) вздувшаяся банка
  to ~ (ту ~) упаковывать в банку
Canal (кана́л) канал
  to pass through a ~ (ту пасс θру а ~) проходить канал
  ~ toll (~ тол) сбор за проход через канал
Cancelling (ка́нсэллинг) канцелинг
  right to ~ (райт ту ~) право канцелинга
Cancellation (кансэлле́йшн) отмена, расторжение
  ~ of a lease (~ оф а лис) расторжение договора займа
Candidacy (ка́ндидаси) кандидатура
  to declare withdrawal from ~ (ту диклэ́йр уиθдра́уал фром ~) заявить о самоотводе
  withdrawal of ~ (уиθдра́уал оф ~) самоотвод
Candidate (ка́ндидат) кандидат
  political ~ (поли́тикал ~) политический кандидат
  ~ for Master's degree (~ фор ма́стэрз дигри́) аспирант
Canister (ка́нистэр) канистра
Cannery (ка́ннэри) консервный завод, консервная фабрика
Canvas (ка́нвас) холст
  packing ~ (па́ккинг ~) упаковочный холст
  ~ cover (~ ко́вэр) брезент
Capability (кэйпаби́лити) способность

Capable (кэйпабл) способный, распорядительный
Capacious (капэйшос) вместительный
Capacit/y (капа́сити) вместимость, ёмкость, загрузка, мощность, способность

    aggregate ~ (а́ггрэгат ~) суммарная мощность
    annual ~ (а́ннюал ~) годовая мощность
    average ~ (а́вэрэдж ~) средняя мощность
    bale ~ (бэйл ~) киповая грузовместимость
    bunker ~ (бу́нкэр ~) вместимость бункера
    cargo ~ (ка́рго ~) грузовая вместимость
    commissioning of new ~/ies (комми́шнинг оф нью ~из) ввод в действие новых мощностей
    container ~ is ... cu.m. (контэ́йнэр ~ из ... кю́бик ми́тирз) контейнер ёмкостью в ...куб.м.
    continuous ~ (конти́нюос ~) длительная мощность
    crane load-lift ~ (крэйн лод-лифт ~) грузоподъёмность крана
    cubic ~ (кю́бик ~) объёмная вместимость
    deadweight ~ (дэ́дуэйт ~) полная грузоподъёмность судна
    design ~ (диза́йн ~) проектная мощность
    fresh ~ (фрэш ~) новая мощность
    full ~ (фул ~) полная загрузка, полная мощность, полная сила
    full freight ~ (фул фрэйт ~) полная грузовместимость
    general legal ~ (джэ́нэрал ли́гал ~) общая дееспособность
    grain freight ~ (грэйн фрэйт ~) грузовместимость судна для насыпного груза
    guaranteed ~ (гяранти́д ~) гарантированная мощность
    guaranteed deadweight ~ (гяранти́д дэ́дуэйт ~) гарантированная грузоподъёмность
    guaranteed freight ~ (гяранти́д фрэйт ~) гарантированная грузовместимость
    high ~ (хай ~) мощный
    hoisting ~ (хо́йстинг ~) грузоподъёмность подъёмного механизма

    idle ~ (айдл ~) неиспользованная мощность
    in the ~ of (ин θи ~ оф) в качестве
    installed ~ (инста́лд ~) установленная мощность
    legal ~ (ли́гал ~) дееспособность, правоспособность, юридическая способность
    legal ~ of foreigners (ли́гал ~ оф фо́рэнэрз) правоспособность иностранцев
    legal ~ of the parties (ли́гал ~ оф θи па́ртиз) дееспособность сторон
    limited legal ~ (ли́митэд ли́гал ~) ограниченная дееспособность
    load ~ (лод ~) загрузочная мощность
    load-lift ~ (лод-лифт ~) грузоподъёмность
    low ~ (ло́у ~) малоёмкий
    manufacturing ~ (манюфа́кчуринг ~) производственная мощность
    margin of reserve ~ (ма́рджин оф риса́рв ~) резерв установленной мощности
    maximum ~ (ма́ксимум ~) максимальная мощность
    maximum freight ~ (ма́ксимум фрэйт ~) максимальная грузовместимость
    measures of ~ (мэ́жюрз оф ~) меры ёмкости
    net ~ (нэт ~) чистая вместимость
    net freight ~ (нэт фрэйт ~) чистая грузовместимость
    operation at full ~ (опэрэ́йшн ат фул ~) работа на полную мощность
    operational ~/ies (опэрэ́йшнал ~из) действующие мощности
    payload ~ (пэ́йлод ~) полезная грузоподъёмность
    rated ~ (рэ́йтэд ~) расчётная мощность
    reduction in ~ (риду́кшн ин ~) снижение мощностей
    renovation of productive ~/ies (рэнове́йшн оф прода́ктив ~из) обновление производственных мощностей
    required ~ (рикуа́йрд ~) потребная мощность
    reserve ~ (рисэ́рв ~) резервная мощность

restriction of legal ~
(ристрйкшн оф лйгал ~)
ограничение дееспособности
ship ~ (шип ~) вместимость судна
spare ~ (спэйр ~) запасная
мощность
specific ~ (спэсйфик ~) удельная
мощность
storage ~ (стóрадж ~) ёмкость
для хранения
store ~ (стор ~) складская
ёмкость
surplus ~ (сýрплус ~) избыточная
мощность
tank ~ (танк ~) ёмкость цистерны
to commission ~/ies (ту коммйшн
~из) вводить мощности в действие
to reach projected ~ (ту рич
проджэ́ктэд ~) достигать
проектной мощности
total ~ (тóтал ~) общая мощность
traffic ~ (трáффик ~)
потребительская способность
transport ~ (трáнспорт ~)
транспортная ёмкость
warehousing ~ (уэ́рхоузинг ~)
вместимость складских помещений
~ of a ship's hold (~ оф а шипс
холд) вместимость трюма
~ of ship's tank (~ оф шипс
танк) ёмкость для перевоза
жидких грузов на корабле
~ of a train car (~ оф а трэйн
кар) вместимость вагона
~ for labor (~ фор лэ́йбор)
способность к труду
~ plan (~ план) план вместимости
~ per unit (~ пэр ю́нит) мощность
на производственную единицу
~ rate (~ рэйт) коэффициент
мощности
~ to devise (~ ту дивáйз)
способность завещать {property
by will}
~ to enter into an agreement (~
ту э́нтэр йнту ан агрймэнт)
способность вступать в договор
~ to testify (~ ту тэ́стифай)
способность дать показание
Capital (кáпитал) капитал {assets,
etc.}, столица {city}
accumulated ~ (аккю́мюлэйтэд ~)
накопленный капитал
actual ~ (áкчуал ~)
действительный капитал,
фактический капитал

advanced ~ (адвáнсд ~)
авансированный капитал
aggregate ~ (áггрэгат ~)
совокупный капитал
allocation of ~ (алокэ́йшн оф ~)
размещение капитала
available ~ (авáйлабл ~)
свободный капитал
bank ~ (банк ~) банковский
капитал
blocked ~ (блокд ~)
блокированный капитал
borrowed ~ (бóрроуд ~) ссудный
капитал
charter ~ (чáртэр ~) уставный
капитал, уставный фонд
commercial ~ (коммэ́ршл ~)
торговый капитал
commodity ~ (коммóдити ~)
товарный капитал
constant ~ (кóнстант ~)
постоянный капитал
contribution to charter ~
(контрибю́шн ту чáртэр ~) вклад в
уставный фонд
debt ~ (дэт ~) привлечённый
капитал
demand for ~ (димáнд фор ~)
спрос на капитал
depreciation of ~ (диприши́эйшн
оф ~) обесценение капитала
disposable ~ (диспóзабл ~)
денежный капитал
employed ~ (эмплóйд ~)
используемый капитал
export of ~(э́кспорт оф) вывоз
капитала
fixed ~ (фиксд ~) основной
капитал
foreign ~ (фóрэн ~) иностранный
капитал
freezing of ~ (фрйзинг оф ~)
замораживание капитала
frozen ~ (фрóзэн ~) замороженные
фонды
gross working ~ (грос уóркинг ~)
валовой оборотный капитал
idle ~ (айдл ~) мёртвый капитал
industrial ~ (индýстриал ~)
промышленный капитал
inflow of ~ (йнфлоу оф ~) приток
капитала
initial ~ (инйшл ~)
первоначальный капитал
international ~ (интэрнáшэнал ~)
международный капитал

invested ~ (инвэ́стэд ~)
инвестированный капитал
liquid ~ (ли́куид ~) ликвидный
капитал
loan ~ (лон ~) заёмный капитал
long-term ~ (лонг-тэрм ~)
долгосрочный капитал
monopoly ~ (моно́поли ~)
монополистический капитал
private ~ (пра́йват ~) частный
капитал
productive ~ (прода́ктив ~)
производительный капитал
real ~ (рил ~) реальный капитал
registered ~ (рэ́джистэрд ~)
зарегистрированный капитал
release of ~ (рили́с оф ~)
высвобождение капитала
reserve ~ (рисэ́рв ~) запасный
капитал
share in ~ (шэйр ин ~) доля в
капитале
short-term ~ (шорт-тэрм ~)
краткосрочный капитал
state ~ (стэйт ~)
государственный капитал
stated ~ (стэ́йтэд ~) объявленный
капитал
surplus ~ (су́рплус ~) избыточный
капитал
tax on ~ (такс он ~) налог на
капитал
to attract ~ (ту аттра́кт ~)
привлекать капитал
to invest ~ in ... (ту инвэ́ст ~
ин ...) вкладывать капитал в ...
to provide ~ (ту прова́йд ~)
предоставлять капитал
to raise ~ (ту рэйз ~) добывать
капитал
to withdraw ~ (ту уиθдра́у ~)
изымать капитал
transfer of ~ abroad (тра́нсфэр
оф ~ абро́д) перевод капитала за
границу
unblocking of ~ (анбло́кинг оф ~)
разблокирование капитала
unproductive ~ (анпрода́ктив ~)
непроизводительный капитал
variable ~ (ва́риабл ~)
переменный капитал
working ~ (уо́ркинг ~) оборотный
капитал, оборотные средства
~ appropriations (~
аппроприэ́йшнс) ассигнования на
капиталовложение

~ budget (~ ба́джэт) бюджет
капиталовложений
~ expenditures (~ экспэ́ндичюрз)
затраты капитала
~ flight (~ флайт) бегство
капиталов
~ investment (~ инвэ́стмэнт)
вложение капитала,
капиталовложение
~ market (~ ма́ркэт) рынок
капитала
~ movement (~ му́вмэнт) движение
капитала
~ outflow (~ о́утфлоу) отток
капитала
~ shortage (~ шо́ртадж) нехватка
капитала
Capitalism (ка́питализм) капитализм
Capitalist (ка́питалист) капиталист,
капиталистический {adj.}
Capitalized (ка́питалайзд)
капитализированный
Caprice (капри́с) административный
произвол
administrative ~ (адми́нистрэйтив
~) административный произвол
Captain (ка́птэн) капитан ~'s
капитанский
~'s notice (~'с но́тис) нотис
капитана
Captive (ка́птив) пленный
Captivity (капти́вити) плен
Capture (ка́пчур) захват
to ~ (ту ~) совершить захват
~ of a market (~ оф а ма́ркэт)
захват рынка
~ of a ship (~ оф а шип) захват
корабля
Car (кар) вагон {railway}, {see
also automobile}
automobile ~ (аутомоби́л ~)
моторный вагон
availability of ~s (авайлаби́лити
оф ~с) наличие вагонов
baggage ~ (ба́ггадж ~) багажный
вагон
ballast ~ (ба́лласт ~) балластный
вагон
box ~ (бокс ~) грузовой вагон,
крытый вагон
capacity of ~ (капа́сити оф ~)
вместимость вагона
closed ~ (клозд ~) закрытый
вагон
compartment ~ (компа́ртмэнт ~)
купированный вагон

composite ~ (компо́зит ~) вагон смешанного класса

consolidated ~ (консо́лидэйтэд ~) прямой сборный вагон

delivery by ~ (дэли́вэри бай ~) поставка в вагоне

empty ~ (э́мпти ~) порожний вагон

flatbed ~ (фла́тбэд ~) вагон-платформа

freight ~ (фрэйт ~) товарный вагон

high capacity ~ (хай капа́сити ~) большегрузный вагон

light ~ (лайт ~) облегчённый вагон

load onto ~ (лод о́нту ~) грузить в вагон

loading into a ~ (ло́динг и́нту а ~) погрузка в вагон

merchandise ~ (мэ́рчандайс ~) сборный вагон

passenger ~ (па́ссэнджэр ~) пассажирский вагон

postal ~ (по́стал ~) почтовый вагон

railroad ~ (рэ́йлрод ~) железнодорожный вагон

refrigerated ~ (рифри́джэрэйтэд ~) рефрижераторный вагон

refrigerator ~ (рифри́джэрэйтор ~) вагон-холодильник

reloading into a ~ (рило́динг и́нту а ~) перегрузка в вагон

repair ~ (рипэ́йр ~) вагон-мастерская

scale ~ (скэйл ~) вагон-весы

self-propelled ~ (сэлф пропэ́лд ~) автономный вагон

side dump ~ (сайд думп ~) вагон с боковой разгрузкой

sleeper ~ (сли́пэр ~) спальный вагон

tanker ~ (та́нкэр ~) вагон-цистерна

through ~ (θру ~) вагон прямого сообщения

tipping ~ (ти́ппинг ~) саморазгружающий вагон

to load a ~ (ту лод а ~) загружать вагон

trailer ~ (трэ́йлэр ~) прицепной вагон

under-loaded ~ (а́ндэр-ло́дэд ~) недогруженный вагон

under-loading of a ~ (а́ндэр-лдинг оф а ~) недогрузка вагона

ventilated box ~ (вэнтиле́йтэд бокс ~) вентилируемый крытый вагон

"hard" ~ carriage (хард ~ ка́рриадж) жёсткий вагон

Card (кард) карточка

address ~ (аддрэ́с ~) адресная карточка

calling ~ (ка́ллинг ~) визитная карточка

credit ~ (крэ́дит ~) кредитная карточка

identification ~ (айдэнтификэ́йшн ~) идентификационная карточка

index ~ file (и́ндэкс ~ файл) картотека

library ~ (ла́йбрари ~) абонемент библиотеки

party membership ~ (па́рти мэ́мбэршип ~) партбилет

registration ~ (рэджистрэ́йшн ~) регистрационная карточка

report ~ (рипо́рт ~) отчётный бланк

union ~ (ю́нион ~) профбилет

use ~ (юс ~) абонемент

work ~ (уо́рк ~) рабочий наряд

Care (кэйр) забота, помощь

free medical ~ (фри мэ́дикал ~) бесплатная медицинская помощь

home health ~ (хом хэлθ ~) патронаж

medical ~ (мэ́дикал ~) медицинская помощь

Careful (кэ́йрфул) тщательный

Carefully (кэ́йрфулли) тщательно

to ~ examine (ту ~ экза́мин) тщательно проверять

to ~ inspect (ту ~ инспэ́кт) тщательно осматривать

Careless (кэ́йрлэс) небрежный, халатный

Carelessness небрежность, халатность

Cargo (ка́рго) груз, карго

acceptance of ~ (аксэ́птанс оф ~) приём груза

additional ~ (адди́шнал ~) добавочный груз

arrival of ~ (арра́йвал оф ~) прибытие груза

arrived by ship ~ (арра́йвд бай шип ~) прибывший на судне груз

bagged ~ (багд ~) груз в мешках

baled ~ (бэйлд ~) груз в кипах

battening of ~ (ба́ттэнинг оф ~) закрепление груза

booking of ~ (бу́кинг оф ~) букировка груза
boxed ~ (боксд ~) ящичный груз
bulk ~ (булк ~) груз без упаковки, навалочный груз
bulk-break ~ (булк-брэйк ~) сыпучий груз
bulky ~ (бу́лки ~) громоздкий груз
certificate of origin of ~ (сэрти́фикэт оф о́риджин оф ~) свидетельство о происхождении груза
clearance of ~ through customs (кли́ранс оф ~ θру ка́стомз) получение груза из таможни
commercial ~ (комме́ршл ~) коммерческий груз
complete ~ (компли́т ~) полный груз
condition of ~ (конди́шн оф ~) состояние груза
confiscation of ~ (конфиске́йшн оф ~) конфискация груза
congestion of ~ (конджэ́стён оф ~) скопление грузов
containerized ~ (контэ́йнэрайзд ~) груз контейнеризованный
crated ~ (крэ́йтэд ~) груз в обрешётке
damage to ~ (да́мадж ту ~) порча груза
damaged ~ (да́маджд ~) повреждённый груз
dangerous ~ (дэ́йнджэрос ~) опасный груз
delayed ~ (дилэ́йд ~) просроченный груз
delivered ~ (дэли́вэрд ~) доставленный груз, поставленный груз
delivery of ~ (дэли́вэри оф ~) выдача груза, доставка груза, подвозка груза
delivery of ~ for shipment (дэлӣвэри оф ~ фор ши́пмэнт) предъявление груза к перевозке
depreciation of ~ (дипришиэ́йшн оф ~) обесценение груза
detention of ~ (дитэ́ншн оф ~) задержание груза
direct ~ (дирэ́кт ~) адресованный груз
disinfection of ~ (дисинфэ́кшн оф ~) дезинфекция груза
dissipation of ~ (диссипэ́йшн оф ~) утруска груза

distress ~ (дистрэ́с ~) груз судна, терпящего бедствие
dry ~ (драй ~) сухой груз
drying of ~ (дра́йинг оф ~) усушка груза {shrinkage}
duty-free ~ (дю́ти-фри ~) не облагаемый пошлиной груз
explosive ~ (эксплóсив ~) взрывчатый груз
fragile ~ (фра́джайл ~) бьющийся груз
general ~ (джэ́нэрал ~) генеральный груз, сборный груз
heavyweight ~ (хэ́виуэйт ~) тяжеловесный груз
highly-inflammable ~ (ха́йли-инфла́ммабл ~) легковоспламеняющийся груз
hoisting of ~ (хо́йстинг оф ~) подъём груза
hooking of ~ (ху́кинг оф ~) закрючивание груза
inspection of ~ (инспэ́кшн оф ~) досмотр груза
insured ~ (иншу́рд ~) застрахованный груз
jettisoned ~ (джэ́ттисонд ~) выброшенный за борт груз
legal ~ (ли́гал ~) дозволенный груз
lien on ~ (лин он ~) залоговое право на груз
light-weight ~ (лайт-уэйт ~) лёгкий груз
liquid ~ (ли́куид ~) жидкий груз
loading of ~ (ло́динг оф ~) погрузка груза
loose ~ (лус ~) груз россыпью, незакреплённый груз
loss of ~ (лос оф ~) гибель груза, потеря места груза, утрата груза
lost ~ (лост ~) погибший груз
marine ~ (мари́н ~) морской груз
marking of ~ (ма́ркинг оф ~) маркировка груза
misdelivery of ~ (мисдэли́вэри оф ~) неправильная сдача груза
misdirected ~ (мисдирэ́ктэд ~) засланный груз
missing ~ (ми́ссинг ~) недостающий груз
mixed ~ (миксд ~) разнородный груз, смешанный груз
non-delivery of ~ (нон-дэли́вэри оф ~) недоставка груза

optional ~ (óпшнал ~) опционный груз

original ~ (ориджинал ~) первоначальный груз

outbound ~ (óутбоунд ~) экспортный груз

overall dimensions of ~ (овэрáл димэ́ншнз оф ~) габарит груза

oversized ~ (óвэрсайзд ~) негабаритный груз

owner of the ~ (óунэр оф θи ~) владелец груза

packaged ~ (пáкэджд ~) груз в упаковке, тарный груз, упакованный груз

packeted ~ (пáкэтэд ~) груз в пакетах

packing of ~ (пáккинг оф ~) упаковка груза

palletization of ~ (паллэтизэ́йшн оф ~) укладка груза на паллеты

palletized ~ (пáллэтайзд ~) груз на паллетах, пакетизированный груз

perishable ~ (пэ́ришабл ~) скоропортящийся груз

portion of ~ (поршн оф ~) часть груза

preservation of ~ (прэзэрвэ́йшн оф ~) сохранение груза

readiness of ~ (рэ́динэсс оф ~) готовность груза

received ~ (рисивд ~) полученный груз

replacement of ~ (риплэ́йсмэнт оф ~) замена груза

return ~ (ритýрн ~) обратный груз

return of ~ (ритýрн оф ~) возврат груза

right to ~ (райт ту ~) право на груз

safety of ~ (сэ́йфти оф ~) сохранность груза

salvage of ~ (сáлвэдж оф ~) спасение груза

salvaged ~ (сáлвэджд ~) спасённый груз

securing of ~ (сэкю́ринг оф ~) крепление груза

seizure of ~ (си́жюр оф ~) арест на груз

separation of ~ (сэпарэ́йшн оф ~) сепарация груза

short delivery of ~ (шорт дэли́вэри оф ~) недостача груза

short-landed ~ (шорт-лáндэд ~) невыгруженный груз

spoiled ~ (спойлд ~) испорченный груз

spontaneous combustion of ~ (спонтэ́йниос комбýстён оф ~) самовозгорание груза

stacked ~ (стакд ~) штабелированный груз

storage of ~ (стóрадж оф ~) хранение груза

stowage of ~ (стóуадж оф ~) размещение груза

stower of ~ (стóуэр оф ~) укладчик груза

stranded ~ (стрáндэд ~) выброшенный на берег груз

strewing of ~ (стрýинг оф ~) раструска груза

supplementary ~ (сапплэмэ́нтари ~) догрузка

tally of ~ (тáлли оф ~) подсчёт мест груза

to accept ~ for shipping (ту аксэ́пт ~ фор ши́ппинг) принимать груз к перевозке

to cause damage to ~ (ту кауз дáмадж ту ~) наносить ущерб грузу

to deliver ~ (ту дэли́вэр ~) доставлять груз, выдавать груз

to deliver ~ at port (ту дэли́вэр ~ ат порт) сдавать груз в порту

to deliver ~ to ship (ту дэли́вэр ~ ту шип) доставлять груз к судну

to detail ~ (ту ди́тэйл ~) задерживать груз

to discharge ~ (ту ди́счардж ~) разгружать груз

to handle ~ (ту хандл ~) производить транспортную обработку груза

to inspect ~ (ту инспэ́кт ~) осматривать груз

to jettison ~ (ту джэ́ттисон ~) выбрасывать груз

to land ~ from a ship (ту ланд ~ фром а шип) снять груз с судна

to misdirect ~ (ту мисдирэ́кт ~) засылать груз

to pack ~ (ту пак ~) упаковывать груз

to pick up ~ (ту пик ап ~) вывозить груз

to receive ~ (ту риси́в ~) получать груз

to release ~ from the warehouse
(ту рили́с ~ фром θи уэ́рхаус)
выдавать груз со склада
to return ~ (ту риту́рн ~)
возвращать груз
to route ~ (ту ро́ут ~)
направлять грузы
to safeguard ~ (ту сэ́йфгард ~)
защищать груз, предохранять груз
to salvage ~ (ту са́лвадж ~)
спасать груз
to secure ~ (ту сэкю́р ~) крепить
груз
to separate ~ (ту сэ́парат ~)
проводить сепарацию груза
to sling ~ (ту слинг ~)
зацеплять груз стропом
to sort out ~ (ту сорт о́ут ~)
рассортировывать грузы
to stack ~ (ту стак ~)
штабелировать груз
to store ~ (ту стор ~) хранить
груз
to stow ~ (ту сто́у ~) укладывать
груз
to stow ~ on board ship (ту сто́у
~ он борд шип) размещать груз на
судне
to take ~ on ship's tackle (ту
тэйк ~ он шипс такл) принимать
груз на строп· судна
to take delivery of ~ (ту тэйк
дэли́вэри оф ~) принимать
поставку груза
to take in ~ (ту тэйк ин ~)
брать груз
to transfer ~ (ту тра́нсфэр ~)
передавать груз, перемещать груз
to unload ~ (ту анло́д ~)
выгружать груз
to warehouse ~ (ту уэ́рхаус ~)
размещать груз на складе
to weigh ~ (ту уэй ~) взвешивать
груз
total ~ (то́тал ~) весь груз,
габарит груза
transfer of ~ to warehouse
(тра́нсфэр оф ~ ту уэ́рхаус) сдача
груза на склад
transfer to ownership of ~
(тра́нсфэр ту о́унэршип оф ~)
передача права на груз
transit ~ (тра́нзит ~) транзитный
груз
transportable ~ (транспо́ртабл ~)
годный к транспортировке груз

transsship ~ (трансши́п ~)
осуществлять перевалку груза
truck freight ~ (трак фрэйт ~)
автотранспортный груз
uninsured ~ (аниншу́рд ~)
незастрахованный груз
unclaimed ~ (анклэ́ймд ~)
невостребованный груз
undeclared ~ (андиклэ́йрд ~)
незаявленный груз
undelivered (андэли́вэрд)
непоставленный груз
under deck ~ (а́ндэр дэк ~)
трюмный товар
undocumented ~ (андо́кюмэнтэд ~)
бездокументный груз
uniform ~ (ю́ниформ ~) однородный
груз
unloading of ~ (анло́динг оф ~)
выгрузка груза, разгрузка груза
unsealed ~ (анси́лд ~)
незапечатанный груз
unsecured ~ (ансэкю́рд ~)
незатаренный груз
valuable ~ (ва́люабл ~) ценный
груз
voluminous ~ (волю́минос ~)
объёмный груз
warehoused ~ (уэ́рхаусд ~)
складной груз
weight of ~ (уэйт оф ~) вес
груза
wet ~ (уэт ~) подмоченный груз
{water-damaged}
wrongfully declared ~ (ро́нгфулли
диклэ́йрд ~) груз, неправильно
указанный в таможенной
декларации
~ accepted in apparent good
order and condition (~ аксэ́птэд
ин аппа́рэнт гуд о́рдэр энд
конди́шн) принятый в хорошем
состоянии груз
~ afloat (~ афло́т) груз на плаву
~ available for pick-up (~
ава́йлабл фор пик-ап) готовый к
вывозу груз
~ by post (~ бай пост) почтовый
груз
~ consignee (~ консайни́)
получатель груза
~ handling (~ ха́ндлинг)
обращение с грузом
~ has sunk (~ хаз сунк) груз
затонул
~ held below-deck (~ хэлд било́у-
дэк) трюмный груз

~ **in boxes** (~ ин бо́ксэз) груз в коробках
~ **indicated in the bill of lading** (~ индике́йтэд ин θи бил оф лэ́йдинг) груз, поименованный в коносаменте
~ **in parcels** (~ ин па́рсэлс) штучный груз
~ **in sacks** (~ ин сакс) мешковый груз
~ **measurements** (~ мэ́жюрмэнтс) размер груза
~-**owner** (~-о́унэр) грузовладелец
~ **pick-up** (~ пик-ап) вывоз груза
~ **placed in storage** (~ плэ́йсд ин сто́радж) сданный на хранение груз
~ **properties** (~ про́пэртиз) свойства груза
~ **received at warehouse** (~ риси́вд ат уэ́рхаус) принятый на склад груз
~ **received for shipment** (~ риси́вд фор ши́пмэнт) принятый для отправки на судно груз
~ **short against bill of lading** (~ шорт аге́нст бил оф лэ́йдинг) груз, частично недопоставленный по сравнению с коносаментом
~ **stevedoring** (~ сти́вэдоринг) обработка груза
~ **stockpiling** (~ сто́кпайлинг) накопление грузов в порту
~ **tracer** (~ трэ́йсэр) запрос о местонахождении груза
~ **turnover** (~ ту́рновэр) оборот грузов
~ **undeclared to customs** (~ андикле́йрд ту ка́стомз) необъявленный груз
~ **within size range** (~ уиθи́н сайз рэйндж) габаритный груз
Carload (ка́рлод) повагонный груз
by the (~ бай θи ~) вагонами
Carriage (ка́ррадж) завоз, перевозка, провоз, транспортирование, транспортировка
free ~ (фри ~) бесплатный провоз
road ~ (род ~) автоперевозки
~ **by truck** (~ бай трак) автомобильная перевозка
Carrier (ка́рриэр) перевозчик
bulk ~ (булк ~) насыпное судно
common ~ (ко́ммон ~) генеральный перевозчик

common air ~ (ко́ммон эйр ~) линия воздушного транспорта общего пользования
lighter ~ (ла́йтэр ~) лихтеровоз
ore bulk ~ (ор булк ~) танкер-рудовоз
rail ~ (рэйл ~) железнодорожная транспортная фирма
~ **freight** (~ фрэйт) фрахтовщик
Carry, to ~ (кэ́рри, ту ~) транспортировать
to ~ **out** (ту ~ о́ут) провожать, совершать
Carryover (кэ́рриовэр) перенос, репорт
Carrying (кэ́рриинг) проведение, провоз
~ **capacity** (~ капа́сити) провозоспособность {railroad}
~ **out an analysis** (~ о́ут ан ана́лисис) проведение анализа
~ **out investigation** (~ о́ут инвэстиге́йшн) проведение следствия
Cartel (карте́л) картель, картельный {adj.}
association of ~**s** (ассоси́эйшн оф ~с) карательное объединение
export ~ (э́кспорт ~) экспортный картель
sales ~ (сэйлз ~) сбытовой картель
Cartelization (картэлизэ́йшн) картелизация
Cartelize, to ~ (карте́лайз, ту ~) картелировать
Carton (ка́ртон) коробка
collapsible ~ (колла́псибл ~) складная коробка
per ~ (пэр ~) за коробку
standard ~ (ста́ндард ~) стандартная коробка
Case (кэйс) дело {matter}, коробка, место, случай, ящик, ящичный {adj.}
arbitration ~ (арбитрэ́йшн ~) арбитражное дело
collapsible ~ (колла́псибл ~) разборный ящик
contents of a ~ (ко́нтэнтс оф а ~) содержимое ящика
damaged ~ (да́маджд ~) повреждённое место, повреждённый ящик
disposable ~ (диспо́забл ~) ящик одноразового пользования
export ~ (э́кспорт ~) экспортный ящик

fees in a ~ (физ ин а ~) сборы
по делу
folding ~ (фóлдинг ~) складной
ящик
multi-use ~ (мýлти-юс ~)
многооборотный ящик
outcome of a ~ (óутком оф а ~)
исход дела
oversized ~ (óвэрсайзд ~)
негабаритный ящик
packing ~ (пáккинг ~)
упаковочный ящик
panel ~ (пáнэл ~) щитовой ящик
set of ~s (сэт оф ~с) комплект
из нескольких ящиков
skeleton ~ (скéлэтон ~)
решётчатый ящик
timber ~ (тúмбэр ~) тёсовый ящик
to carry in ~s (ту кéрри ин ~с)
перевозить в ящиках
to drop a ~ (ту дроп а ~)
прекращать дело в суде
to hear a ~ (ту хир а ~) слушать
дело
to lose a ~ (ту луз а ~)
проиграть дело
to mark a ~ (ту марк а ~)
маркировать ящик
to nail down a ~ (ту нэйл дóун а
~) забивать ящик
to plead a ~ (ту плид а ~) вести
дело
to refer a ~ to arbitration (ту
рифéр а ~ ту арбитрэйшн)
направлять дело в арбитраж
to sort ~s (ту сорт ~с)
сортировать ящики
to win a ~ (ту уин а ~)
выигрывать дело
watertight ~ (уáтэртайт ~)
водонепроницаемый ящик
weak ~ (уик ~) непрочный ящик
weight of a ~ (уэйт оф а ~) вес
ящика
wooden ~ (уýдэн ~) деревянная
коробка
~s are damaged (~с ар дáмаджд)
ящики повреждены
~ dimensions (~ димэ́ншнз)
габариты ящика
~ is stained by seawater (~ из
стэйнд бай сиуáтэр) ящик имеет
пятна от морской воды
~ of blatant violation (~ оф
блéйтант вайолéйшн) дело о явном
нарушении

~ shows signs of leakage (~ шóуз
сайнс оф лúкадж) ящик имеет
следы течи
~ size (~ сайз) размер ящика
Cased (кэйсд) в ящиках
~ goods (~ гудз) товар в ящиках
Cash (каш) кассовый {adj.},
наличность, наличные деньги
for ~ (фор ~) за наличные
net ~ terms (нэт ~ тэрмз) платёж
наличными без скидки
out of ~ (óут оф ~) без наличных
денег
payable in ~ (пэ́йабл ин ~)
подлежащий оплате наличными
payment by ~ (пэ́ймэнт бай ~) за
наличный расчёт
reserve ~ (рисéрв ~) резервная
наличность
spare ~ (спэ́йр ~) свободная
наличность
to ~ (ту ~) инкассировать {e.g.
draft}
to ~ a check (ту ~ а чэк)
получать деньги по чеку
to check the ~ balance (ту чэк
θи ~ бáланс) проверять кассовую
наличность
to convert into ~ (ту конвéрт
úнту ~) переводить в наличные
to pay ~ (ту пэй ~) платить
наличными
to pay net ~ (ту пэй нэт ~)
платить наличными без скидки
to make a ~ audit (ту мэйк а ~
áудит) проводить ревизию кассы
~ account (~ аккóунт) счёт кассы
~ advance (~ адвáнс) аванс
наличными
~ availability (~ авайлабúлити)
наличие денег
~ balance (~ бáланс) кассовая
наличность, остаток кассы
~ bonus allowance (~ бóнус
аллóуанс) дополнительная выплата
наличными
~ call (~ калл) требование
наличных денег
~ deposit (~ дипóзит) взнос
наличными деньгами
~-in-hand (~-ин-ханд) денежная
наличность
~ mobilization (~ мобилизéйшн)
мобилизация наличности
~ payment (~ пэ́ймэнт) выдача
денег наличными, наличный расчёт

~ price (~ прайс) цена за наличные деньги, цена при уплате наличными, цена при условии оплаты наличными
~ shortage (~ шо́ртадж) недостаток денег
~ terms (~ тэрмз) платёж наличными
~ turnover (~ ту́рновэр) оборот наличных денег
~ withdrawal from an account (~ уиθдра́уал фром ан акка́унт) снятие денег со счёта

Cashier (каши́р) кассир, кассовый {adj.}
~'s desk (~'с дэск) касса

Cashing (ка́шинг) инкассо

Cask (каск) бочка, деревянный барабан

Cassation (кассэ́йшн) кассация

Casual (ка́жюал) случайный

Casualty (ка́жюалти) аварийное происшествие

Casus (ка́сус) повод
~ belli (~ бэ́лли) повод к войне

Catalog (ка́талог) каталог, перечень
company ~ (ко́мпани ~) фирменный каталог
complete ~ (компли́т ~) полный каталог
comprehensive ~ (комприхэ́нсив ~) детальный каталог
exhibition ~ (экзиби́шн ~) выставочный каталог
general ~ (джэ́нэрал ~) общий каталог
illustrated ~ (и́ллустрэйтэд ~) иллюстрированный каталог
latest ~ (лэ́йтэст ~) последний каталог
parts ~ (партс ~) каталог запчастей
publisher of a ~ (па́блишэр оф а ~) издатель каталога
standard ~ (ста́ндард ~) типовой каталог
to compile a ~ (ту компа́йл а ~) составлять каталог
to distribute ~s (ту дистри́бют ~с) раздавать каталоги
to include in a ~ (ту инклю́д ин а ~) вносить в каталог
to issue a ~ (ту и́шю а ~) выпускать каталог
to provide ~s (ту прова́йд ~с) предоставить каталоги

typical ~ (ти́пикал ~) типичный каталог

Catastrophe (ката́строфи) катастрофа

Category (ка́тэгори) категория, разряд
wage ~ (уэ́йдж ~) тарифный разряд

Causality (кауза́лити) причинность

Cause (кауз) повод, причина
good ~ (гуд ~) уважительная причина
to ~ (ту ~) наносить
without ~ (уиθо́ут ~) без повода
~ of action (~ оф акшн) предмет иска

Caution (каушн) предупреждение
to ~ (ту ~) предупреждать

Cede, to (сид, ту ~) переуступать

Censure (сэ́ншор) порицание
public ~ (па́блик ~) общественное порицание
to ~ (ту ~) порицать

Census (сэ́нсус) перепись
special ~ (спэшл ~) специальная перепись
~ of the population (~ оф θи попюлэ́йшн) перепись населения

Cent (сэнт) цент {U.S. coin}
per ~ (пэр ~) процент, на сотню

Center (сэ́нтэр) центр
business ~ (би́знэс ~) деловой центр
commercial ~ (комме́ршл ~) коммерческий центр
computer ~ (компью́тэр ~) вычислительный центр
coordination ~ (координэ́йшн ~) координационный центр
cultural ~ (ку́лчурал ~) культурный центр
data processing ~ (да́та про́сэсинг ~) информационно-вычислительный центр
financial ~ (файна́ншл ~) финансовый центр
in the ~ (ин θи ~) в центре
industrial ~ (инду́стриал ~) промышленный центр
information ~ (информэ́йшн ~) информационный центр
professional training ~ (профэ́шнал трэ́йнинг ~) центр по профессиональной подготовке
research ~ (ри́сэрч ~) научно-исследовательский центр
scientific and technical ~ (сайэнти́фик энд тэ́кникал ~) научно-технический центр

service ~ (сэ́рвис ~) база для оказания услуг, бюро услуг
shopping ~ (шо́ппинг ~) торговый центр
social activism ~ (сошл а́ктивисм ~) агитпункт
technical ~ (тэ́кникал ~) технический центр
technological ~ (тэкноло́джикал ~) технологический центр
to be in the ~ **of attention** (ту би ин θи ~ оф аттэ́ншн) быть в центре внимания
training ~ (трэ́йнинг ~) учебный комбинат, центр обучения
World Trade ~ (уо́рлд трэйд ~) центр международной торговли
Central (сэ́нтрал) центральный
~ **location** (~ локэ́йшн) место в центре
Centralized (сэ́нтралайзд) централизованный
Ceremon/y (сэ́рэмони) обрядность
master of ~**/ies** (ма́стэр оф ~из) распорядитель
Certificate (сэрти́фикэт) абонемент, акт, аттестат, грамота, расписка, свидетельство, сертификат, справка, удостоверение
birth ~ (бэрθ ~) акт рождения, метрическое свидетельство
currency ~ (ку́ррэнси ~) валютный сертификат
customs ~ (ка́стомз ~) таможенное свидетельство
death ~ (дэθ ~) акт о гибели, акт смерти
export ~ (э́кспорт ~) экспортный сертификат
inspection ~ (инспэ́кшн ~) акт осмотра на месте
marriage ~ (мэ́ррэдж ~) акт регистрации брака, брачное свидетельство
medical ~ (мэ́дикал ~) медицинское свидетельство, медицинский сертификат
medical death ~ (мэ́дикал дэθ ~) врачебное свидетельство о смерти
mortgage ~ (мо́ргэдж ~) залоговое свидетельство, залоговый сертификат
notarial ~ (нотэ́йриал ~) нотариальное свидетельство
profit-sharing ~ (про́фит-шэ́йринг ~) пользовательная акция

protest ~ (про́тэст ~) документ об опротестовании векселя
quarantine ~ (куа́рантин ~) карантинное разрешение, карантинное свидетельство
school-leaving ~ (скул-ли́винг ~) аттестат зрелости
temporary customs ~ (тэ́мпорари ка́стомз ~) таможенное свидетельство о временном беспошлинном ввозе
warehouse ~ (уэ́рхаус ~) складочное свидетельство
~ **of authorship** (~ оф а́уθоршип) авторское свидетельство
~ **of deposit** (~ оф дипо́зит) вкладной билет, вкладной сертификат
~ **of pledge** (~ оф плэдж) залоговый сертификат
~ **of indebtedness** (~ оф индэ́тэднэс) долговое свидетельство
~ **of notary** (~ оф но́тари) нотариальный акт
~ **of origin** (~ оф о́риджин) сертификат о происхождении
~ **of payment** (~ оф пэ́ймэнт) платёжный сертификат
~ **of pilotage** (~ оф па́йлотадж) лоцманское свидетельство
~ **of seaworthiness** (~ оф си́уорθинэс) сертификат о мореходности
Certification (сэртифике́йшн) акт свидетельствования {e.g. signature}, выдача удостоверения, легализация
consular ~ (ко́нсюлар ~) консульская легализация
Certified (сэ́ртифайд) заверенный
~ **account** (~ акко́унт) заверенная выписка
~ **in writing** (~ ин ра́йтинг) по письменному удостоверению
Certify, to ~ (сэ́ртифай, ту ~) выдавать удостоверение, заверять, засвидетельствовать, удостоверять
Cessation (сэссэ́йшн) прекращение
~ **clause** (~ клауз) оговорка о прекращении ответственности фрахтователя
Cession (сэшн) переуступка, цессия
deed of ~ (дид оф ~) акт об уступке
~ **of a patent** (~ оф а па́тэнт) уступки патента

~ of rights (~ оф райтс)
переуступка прав
Chain (чэйн) цепной
Chair (чэйр) кресло, стул
to ~ (ту ~) председательствовать
Chairman (чэйрман) председатель,
председательствующий {adj.}
    honorable ~ (онорабл ~) почётный
    председатель
    permanent ~ (пэрманэнт ~)
    постоянный председатель
    ~ pro tem (~ про тэм) временный
    председатель
Chairmanship (чэйрманшип)
председательство
Chairperson (чэйрпэрсон)
председательствующий, председатель
Challenge (чаллэндж) отвод
    to ~ (ту ~) отводить
    [perfective: отвести] {e.g.
    juror}
    to ~ an arbitrator (ту ~ ан
    арбитрэйтор) отвод арбитра
Chamber (чэймбэр) камера, палата
    cold storage ~ (колд сторадж ~)
    рефрижераторная камера
    constitutional ~ (конститушнал
    ~) конституционная палата
    cooling ~ (кулинг ~) холодильная
    камера
    judicial ~ (джюдишл ~) судебная
    палата
    legislative ~ (лэджислэйтив ~)
    законодательная палата
    lower ~ (лоуэр ~) нижняя палата
    upper ~ (аппэр ~) верхняя палата
    international ~ of Commerce
    (интэрнэшнал ~ оф коммэрс)
    международная торговая палата
    ~ of Commerce and Industry (~ оф
    коммэрс энд индустри) торгово-
    промышленная палата
    ~ of Commerce (~ оф коммэрс)
    торговая палата
Chance (чанс) случай
Chandler (чандлэр) москательщик
    ship ~ (шип ~) шипчандлер
Change (чэйндж) замена, перемена,
разменный {adj.}
    loose ~ (лус ~) разменные монеты
    small ~ (смал ~) мелкие деньги,
    разменная монета
    to ~ (ту ~) менять, переменять,
    сменять [perfective: сменить]
    ~ for the worse (~ фор θи уорс)
    изменение к худшему

~ in amendment to sentencing (~
ин амэндмэнт ту сэнтэнсинг)
изменение приговора
~ in exchange rate (~ ин
эксчэйндж рэйт) изменение курса
~ in inventories (~ ин
инвэнториз) изменение запасов
~ in price (~ ин прайс)
изменение цены
~ in status (~ ин статус)
изменение статуса
~ of address (~ оф аддрэс)
изменение адреса, перемена
адреса
~ of cabinet (~ оф кабинэт)
смена кабинета
~ of citizenship (~ оф
ситизэншип) изменение
гражданства, перемена
гражданства
~ of government (~ оф
говэрнмэнт) смена правительства
~ of nationality (~ оф
нашэналити) перемена подданства
~ of occupation (~ оф оккюпэйшн)
перемена занятия
~ of owner (~ оф оунэр) смена
владельца
~ of regime (~ оф рэжим)
перемена режима, смена режима
~ of residence (~ оф рэзидэнс)
перемена места жительства
~ of sovereignty (~ оф совэрнти)
перемена суверенитета
~ of venue (~ оф вэню) передача
юрисдикции
Changeable (чэйнджабл) неустойчивый
Changing (чэйнджинг) смена
Channel (чаннэл) канал, русло
    ship ~ (шип ~) судоходный канал
    banking ~ (банкинг ~) банковские
    каналы
    to determine ~ of distribution
    (ту дитэрмин ~ оф дистрибюшн)
    определять каналы сбыта
    trade ~ (трэйд ~) торговые
    каналы
    unofficial ~ (аноффишл ~)
    неофициальные каналы
Character (карактэр) природа,
характер
    jurisprudential ~
    (джуриспрудэншл ~) юридическая
    природа
    legal ~ (лигал ~) правовая
    природа

normative ~ (нóрматив ~)
нормативная природа
Characteristics (карактэрúстикс)
характеристика
    detailed ~ (дúтэйлд ~) подробная
характеристика
    operational ~ (опэрэ́йшнал ~)
эксплуатационная характеристика
    qualitative ~ (куáлитэйтив ~)
качественная характеристика
    technical ~ (тэ́кникал ~)
техническая характеристика
Charge (чардж) взимание,
начисление, сбор
    additional ~ (аддúшнал ~)
дополнительная плата
    advertising ~ (áдвэртайзинг ~)
цена на рекламу
    customs ~s (кáстомз ~с)
таможенные расходы
    depreciation ~s (диприши́эйшн ~с)
амортизационные начисления
    fixed ~s (фиксд ~с) постоянные
расходы
    extra freight ~s (э́кстра фрэйт
~с) дополнительная уплата фрахта
    freight forwarding ~ (фрэйт
фóруардинг ~) плата за
экспедиторские услуги,
экспедиционный сбор
    generally accepted ~s
(джэ́нэралли аксэ́птэд ~с)
общепринятые начисления
    insurance ~s (иншю́ранс ~с)
страховые расходы
    interest ~s (úнтэрэст ~с)
расходы по уплате процентов
    local ~ (лóкал ~) местный сбор
    postal ~ (пóстал ~) почтовый
сбор
    redraft ~s (ридрáфт ~с) расходы
по обратному переводу векселя
    to ~ (ту ~) начислять, поручать
    to be in ~ (ту би ин ~)
руководить
    to file criminal ~s (ту файл
крúминал ~с) возбудить уголовное
преследование
Charge d'affaires (чарж э́ дафэ́йрз)
поверенный, поверенный в делах
    ~ **pro tempore** (~ про тэмпóрэ)
временный поверенный в делах
Charging (чáрджинг) взимание,
занесение
    ~ **of royalties** (~ оф рóйялтиз)
взимание роялти

    ~ **to an account** (~ ту ан
аккóунт) занесение на счёт
Chart (чарт) схема
    progress ~ (прóгрэс ~) график
выполнения работ
    time ~ (тайм ~) временная
диаграмма
Charter (чáртэр) устав, уставной
{adj.}, фрахтовый {adj.}, чартер
    bank ~ (банк ~) банковский
чартер
    bare-boat ~ (бэйр-бот ~) договор
о фрахтовании судна без экипажа,
фрахтование судна без экипажа,
чартер бэрбоут, чартер
фрахтование судна без экипажа
    berth ~ (бэрθ ~) линейный чартер
    berthing ~ (бэ́рθинг ~)
причальный чартер
    broad ~ (брод ~) широкий чартер
    cancellation of a ~ (кансэллэ́йшн
оф а ~) аннулирование чартера
    clean ~ (клин ~) чистый чартер
    coal ~ (кол ~) угольный чартер
    consecutive voyage ~ (консэ́кютив
вóйадж ~) фрахтование на
последовательные рейсы
    daily hire ~ (дэ́йли хайр ~)
чартер с посуточной оплатой
    dry cargo ~ (драй кáрго ~)
сухогрузный чартер
    general ~ (джэ́нэрал ~)
генеральный чартер
    grain ~ (грэйн ~) зерновой
чартер, хлебный чартер
    liability on a ~ (лайабúлити он
а ~) ответственность по чартеру
    long-term ~ (лонг-тэрм ~)
долгосрочный чартер
    lumpsum ~ (лáмпсум ~) чартер
лумпсум
    marine ~ (марúн ~) морской
чартер
    open ~ (óпэн ~) открытый чартер
    port ~ (порт ~) портовой чартер
    pro forma ~ (про фóрма ~)
проформа чартера
    river ~ (рúвэр ~) речной чартер
    round trip ~ (рóунд трип ~)
чартер фрахтования судна на рейс
в оба конца
    single voyage ~ (сингл вóйадж ~)
рейсовой чартер
    special ~ (спэшл ~) специальный
чартер
    standard ~ (стáндард ~) типовой
чартер

terms and conditions of a ~
(тэрмз энд конди́шнс оф а ~)
условия чартера
timber ~ (ти́мбэр ~) лесной
чартер
time ~ (тайм ~) договор о
фрахтовании судна на время,
чартер на срок
to ~ (ту ~) нанимать, фрахтовать
to ~ a vessel (ту ~ а вэ́ссэл)
брать внаём судно по чартеру,
брать судно в чартер, сдавать
судно в наём по чартеру
to ~ freight (ту ~ фрэ́йт)
зафрахтовать
to cancel a ~ (ту ка́нсэл а ~)
аннулировать чартер, расторгать
чартер
to hold a ~ (ту холд а ~)
владеть чартером
to sign a ~ (ту сайн а ~)
подписывать чартер
~ hire (~ хайр) плата за фрахт
по чартеру
~ of a joint venture (~ оф а
джойнт вэ́нчур) устав совместного
предприятия
~ of a joint stock company (~ оф
а джойнт сток ко́мпани) устав
акционерного общества
~ party (~ па́рти) чартер-партия
Charterer (ча́ртэрэр) фрахтователь,
наниматель судна
as ordered by the ~ (аз о́рдэрд
бай θи ~) согласно распоряжению
фрахтователей
at ~s' option (ат ~с опшн) по
выбору фрахтователей
~'s agent (~с э́йджэнт) агент
фрахтователя
~'s broker (~с бро́кэр) брокер
фрахтователя
~ pays duties (~ пэ́йс дю́тиз)
пошлины подлежат оплате
фрахтователем
Chartering (ча́ртэринг) фрахтование
round trip ~ (ро́унд трип ~)
фрахтование на круговой рейс
time ~ (тайм ~) фрахтование в
тайм-чартер
to perform vessel ~ (ту пэрфо́рм
вэ́ссэл ~) производить
фрахтование судов
voyage ~ (во́йадж ~) рейсовое
фрахтование

~ at necessary tonnage (~ ат
нэ́сэсари то́ннадж) фрахтование
судна необходимого тоннажа
Chattels (ша́ттэлз) движимая
собственность
distraint of ~ (дистрэ́йнт оф ~)
опись движимых имуществ
Cheap (чип) дешёвый, скупой
{parsimonious}
Cheaper (чи́пэр) дешевле
to make ~ (ту мэйк ~) удешевлять
Cheat (чит) жулик, обманщик
to ~ (ту ~) жульничать,
обманывать
Check (чэк) контроль, осмотр, чек,
чековый {adj.}
allonge on a ~ (алло́ндж он а ~)
аллонж к чеку
altered ~ (а́лтэрд ~)
переделанный чек
automatic ~ (аутома́тик ~)
автоматический контроль
bad ~ (бад ~) фиктивный чек
banker's ~ (ба́нкэрз ~) чек,
выписанный банком на другой банк
bearer ~ (бэ́йрэр ~)
предъявительский чек
blank ~ (бланк ~) бланковый чек,
незаполненный чек
cancelled ~ (ка́нсэлд ~)
недействительный чек, погашенный
чек
cashier's ~ (каши́рз ~)
банковский чек
certified ~ (сэ́ртифайд ~)
удостоверенный чек
clearance of ~s (кли́ранс оф ~с)
зачёт чеков
clearinghouse ~ (кли́рингхаус ~)
расчётный чек, чек по
клиринговым расчётам
confirmed ~ (конфи́рмд ~)
подтверждённый банком чек
crossed ~ (кросд ~)
кроссированный чек
currency ~ (ку́ррэнси ~) валютный
чек
dishonored ~ (дисо́норд ~) не
принятый к оплате банком чек
drawer of a ~ (дра́уэр оф а ~)
чекодатель
endorsement on a ~ (эндо́рсмэнт
он а ~) индоссамент на чеке
foreign ~ (фо́рэн ~) иностранный
чек
forged ~ (форджд ~) поддельный
чек

forgery of a ~ (фóрджэри оф а ~) подделка чека

holder of a ~ (хóлдэр оф а ~) чекодержатель

multiple payment ~ (мýлтипл пэ́ймэнт ~) чек, выписанный в оплату по нескольким сделкам

negotiation of a ~ (нэгошиэ́йшн оф а ~) акцепт чека, выплата по чеку, передача чека

non-negotiable ~ (нон-нэгóшабл ~) непередаваемый чек, чек без права передачи

NSF ~ (эн-эс-эф ~) непокрытый чек {insufficient funds}

open ~ (óпэн ~) некроссированный чек, открытый чек

order ~ (óрдэр ~) ордерный чек

outstanding ~ (оутстáндинг ~) неоплаченный чек

paid ~ (пэйд ~) оплаченный чек

payment by ~ (пэ́ймэнт бай ~) оплата чеком, платёж чеком

personal ~ (пэ́рсонал ~) чек, выданный отдельным лицом

postdated ~ (постдэ́йтэд ~) датированный более поздним числом чек

protested ~ (протэ́стэд ~) опротестованный чек

redemption ~ (ридэ́мпшн ~) возвратный чек

refusal to pay a ~ (рифю́зал ту пэй а ~) отказ в оплате чека

returned {"bounced"} **~** (ритýрнд {бóунсд} ~) возвращённый чек

settlement of a ~ (сэ́тлмэнт оф а ~) оплата чека

single multi-payment ~ (сингл мýлти-пэ́ймэнт ~) единый чек на производство нескольких платежей

stale ~ (стэйл ~) просроченный чек

stopped payment ~ (стопд пэ́ймэнт ~) чек, по которому приостановлен платёж

to cancel a ~ (ту кáнсэл а ~) отменять чек

to cash a ~ (ту каш а ~) получать деньги по чеку

to draw a ~ against the bank (ту дрáу а ~ агэ́нст θи банк) трассировать чек на банк

to forge a ~ (ту фордж а ~) подделывать чек

to forward a ~ to the bank (ту фóруард а ~ ту θи банк) посылать чек в банк

to exchange ~s (ту эксчэ́йндж ~с) обменивать чеки

to honor a ~ (ту óнор а ~) уплачивать по чеку

to make out a ~ (ту мэйк óут а ~) выдавать чек, выставлять чек

to make out a ~ in favor of (ту мэйк óут а ~ ин фэ́йвор оф) выписывать чек в пользу

to negotiate a ~ (ту нэгóшиэйт а ~) выплачивать по чеку, передавать чек, разменивать чек

to pay by ~ (ту пэй бай ~) платить чеком, уплачивать чеком

to pay on a ~ (ту пэй он а ~) погашать чек

to present a ~ for payment (ту прэзэ́нт а ~ фор пэ́ймэнт) представлять чек к оплате

to refuse to honor a ~ (ту рифю́з ту óнор а ~) отказываться от уплаты чека

to remit a ~ (ту римúт а ~) пересылать чек

to remit money by ~ (ту римúт мóни бай ~) пересылать деньги чеком

to sign a ~ (ту сайн а ~) подписывать чек

to stop payment on a ~ (ту стоп пэ́ймэнт он а ~) прекратить платёж по чеку

to ~ (ту ~) контролировать

transfer by ~ (трáнсфэр бай ~) перевод чеком

traveler's ~ (трáвэлэрз ~) дорожный чек, туристский чек

~ counterfoil (~ кóунтэрфойл) корешок чека

~ drawn on a bank (~ дрáун он а банк) чек, выписанный на банк

~ endorsement (~ эндóрсмэнт) передаточная надпись на чеке

~ form (~ форм) бланк чека

~ in settlement (~ ин сэ́тлмэнт) чек в погашение

~ in the amount of ... (~ ин θи амóунт оф ...) чек на сумму

~ made out to bearer (~ мэйд óут ту бэ́йрэр) чек на предъявителя

~ number (~ нýмбэр) номер чека

~ on account (~ он аккóунт) чек в счёт суммы

~ **payable to ...** (~ пэ́йабл ту ...) именной чек
~ **payable to bearer** (~ пэ́йабл ту бэ́йрэр) чек, выписанный на предъявителя
~ **rate** (~ рэйт) курс чеков
Checkbook (чэ́кбук) чековая книжка
Checker (чэ́кэр) тальман
shore ~ (шор ~) береговой тальман
Checklist (чэ́клист) контрольный перечень, контрольный список
Checkmark (чэ́кмарк) контрольная отметка
Checkup (чэ́кап) проверка
routine ~ (рути́н ~) плановая проверка
Chief (чиф) начальник, руководитель
~ **of an enterprise** (~ оф ан э́нтэрпрайз) руководитель предприятия
Child (чайлд) ребёнок ~**ren** дети
abandoned ~ (аба́ндонд ~) покинутый ребёнок
abandonment of a ~ (аба́ндонмэнт оф а ~) подкидывание ребёнка
acknowledged ~ (акно́лэджд ~) признанный ребёнок
acknowledged illegitimate ~ (акно́лэджд иллэджи́тэмат ~) признанный незаконный ребёнок
adopted ~ (адо́птэд ~) приёмный ребёнок, приёмыш
birth ~ (бэрθ ~) кровный ребёнок {non-adopted}
illegitimate ~ (иллэджи́тэмат ~) незаконный ребёнок
legitimate ~ (лэджи́тимат ~) законный ребёнок
legitimized ~ (лэджи́тимайзд ~) узаконенный ребёнок
one's own ~ (уа́нз о́ун ~) родной ребёнок {by birth}
switching ~ {at the hospital} (суи́тчинг ~ {ат θи хо́спитал}) подмен ребёнка
to legitimize a ~ **born out of wedlock** (ту лэджи́тимайз а ~ борн о́ут оф уэ́длок) узаконить внебрачного ребёнка
~ **born out of wedlock** (~ борн о́ут оф уэ́длок) внебрачный ребёнок
Choice (чойс) выбор
absence of ~ (а́бсэнс оф ~) отсутствие выбора
at ~ (ат ~) на выбор

buyer's ~ (ба́йэрз ~) выбор покупателя
by ~ (бай ~) на выбор
consumer ~ (консу́мэр ~) потребительский выбор
free ~ (фри ~) свободный выбор
optimal ~ (о́птимал ~) оптимальный выбор
poor ~ (пур ~) бедный выбор
preliminary ~ (прили́минэри ~) предварительный выбор
principle of ~ (при́нсипл оф ~) принцип выбора
random ~ (ра́ндом ~) случайный выбор
supplier's ~ (сапла́йэрз ~) выбор поставщика
to leave it to ~ (ту лив ит ту ~) предоставлять выбор
to make a ~ (ту мэйк а ~) делать выбор
to make a preliminary ~ (ту мэйк а прили́минэри ~) делать предварительный выбор
to not have a ~ (ту нот хэв а ~) не иметь выбора
wrong ~ (ронг ~) ошибочный выбор
~ **from among samples** (~ фром амо́нг самплз) выбор по образцам
~ **of an agent** (~ оф ан э́йджэнт) выбор агента
~ **of assets** (~ оф а́ссэтс) выбор активов
~ **of samples** (~ оф самплз) выбор образцов
Cipher (са́йфэр) шифр
in ~ (ин ~) шифр ом
Circle (сиркл) круг ~**s** круги
business ~**s** (би́знэс ~с) деловые круги
commercial ~**s** (комме́ршл ~с) коммерческие круги
financial ~**s** (файна́ншл ~с) финансовые круги
official ~**s** (оффи́шл ~с) официальные круги
vicious ~ (ви́шос ~) порочный круг
Circular (си́ркюлар) циркуляр, циркулярный {adj.}
ministry ~ (ми́нистри ~) циркулярное письмо министра
Circulate, To ~ (си́ркюлэйт, ту ~) распространять
Circulating (си́ркюлэйтинг) оборотный

Circulation (сиркюлэ́йшн) оборот, обращение, тираж, циркуляция
   franchise ~ (фра́нчайз ~) договорный тираж
   internal ~ (инта́рнал ~) внутреннее обращение
   large ~ (лардж ~) большой тираж
   mass ~ (мас ~) массовый тираж
   monetary ~ (мо́нэтари ~) денежное обращение
   parallel ~ (па́ралэл ~) параллельное обращение
   projected ~ (проджэ́ктэд ~) предполагаемый тираж
   to be in ~ (ту би ин ~) находиться в обращении
   to issue into ~ (ту и́шю и́нту ~) выпустить в обращение
   to release into ~ (ту рили́с и́нту ~) пускать в оборот
   to withdraw from ~ (ту уиθдра́у фром ~) изымать из оборота, изъять из обращения
   ~ of bank notes (~ оф банк нотс) банкнотное обращение
   ~ of bills (~ оф биллс) вексельное обращение
   ~ of commodities (~ оф комми́дитиз) товарное обращение
   ~ of goods (~ оф гудз) обращение товаров
   ~ of money (~ оф мо́ни) циркуляция денег
   ~ of paper money (~ оф пэ́йпэр мо́ни) бумажно-денежное обращение

Circumstance (сэ́ркамстансэз) обстоятельство **~s** обстоятельство
   extenuating ~s (экстэ́нюэйтинг ~с) смягчающее обстоятельство
   factual ~s (фа́кчуал ~с) фактическое обстоятельство
   mitigating ~s (ми́тигэйтинг ~с) оправдывающее обстоятельство
   random ~s (ра́ндом ~с) случайное обстоятельство
   unforeseen ~s (анфорси́н ~с) непредвиденное обстоятельство

Circumvention (сиркамвэ́ншн) обход
Cistern (си́стэрн) цистерна
Citizen (си́тизэн) гражданин {male}, гражданка {female}
   fellow ~ (фэ́лло ~) согражданин
Citizenship (си́тизэншип) гражданство, подданство
   to obtain ~ (ту обтэ́йн ~) преобретать подданство

Claim (клэйм) востребование, иск, претензионное требование, претензия, притязание, требование
   certificate of damage ~ (сэрти́фикэт оф да́мадж ~) рекламационный акт
   counter ~ (ко́унтэр ~) встречная претензия, встречное требование
   dead freight ~ (дэд фрэйт ~) требование уплаты мёртвого фрахта
   direct ~ (дирэ́кт ~) прямой иск
   financial ~ (файна́ншл ~) финансовая претензия
   freight (фрэйт) требование о возмещении убытков грузоотправителя
   grounds for a ~ (гро́ундз фор а ~) обоснование претензионного требования
   indirect ~ (индайрэ́кт ~) непрямой иск
   insurance ~ (иншю́ранс ~) страховой акт
   legal ~ (ли́гал ~) правопритязание
   monetary ~ (мо́нэтари ~) денежная претензия, денежное требование
   patent ~ (па́тэнт ~) патентная заявка
   preferential ~ (прэфэрэ́ншл ~) преимущественное требование
   salvage ~ (са́лвэдж ~) требование уплаты возмещения за спасение
   statutory ~ (ста́тютори ~) законное притязание
   subrogated ~ (су́брогэйтэд ~) иск в силу суброгации
   substantiation of a ~ (субстаншиэ́йшн оф а ~) обоснование претензии
   supplementary ~ (сапплэмэ́нтари ~) дополнительное притязание, дополнительное требование
   to ~ (ту ~) заявлять [perfective: заявить], требоват
   to abandon a ~ (ту аба́ндон а ~) отказаться от иска
   to acknowledge a ~ (ту акно́лэдж а ~) признать иск
   to dismiss a ~ (ту дисми́с а ~) отказать в иске
   to make an insurance ~ (ту мэйк ан иншю́ранс ~) требовать выплат страхового возмещения
   to press a ~ (ту прэс а ~) настаивать на требованиях

to reject a ~ (ту риджэ́кт а ~) отклонить иск
~ against insurance (~ агэ́нст иншю́ранс) страховой акт
~ against a mortgage (~ агэ́нст а мо́ргэдж) иск на ипотеку
~ for back wages (~ фор бак уэ́йджэз) иск об уплате заработной платы
~ for maintenance payments (~ фор мэ́йнтэнанс пэ́ймэнтс) иск о взыскании алиментов
~ for restitution (~ фор рэституˊшн) иск о реституции
~ of cargo (~ оф ка́рго) востребование груза
~ of ownership (~ оф о́унэршип) имущественный иск, притязание собственности
~ of unjust enrichment (~ оф анджа́ст энри́чмэнт) иск к истребованию неосновательного обогащения
~ to property (~ ту про́пэрти) взыскание на имущество
Clash (клаш) столкновение
border ~ (бо́рдэр ~) пограничное столкновение
~ of interests (~ оф и́нтэрэстс) столкновение интересов
Class (класс) класс, классный {adj.}, сорт
first ~ (фэрст ~) первый класс
second ~ (сэ́конд ~) второй класс
~ of goods (~ оф гудз) класс товара
~ of a vessel (~ оф а вэ́ссэл) класс судна
Classed (класд) классифицированный
Classification (классифика́йшн) классификация, номенклатура
customs ~ (ка́стомз ~) таможенная классификация
freight ~ (фрэйт ~) классификация грузов
international commodity ~ (интэрна́шэнал комму́дити ~) международная товарная номенклатура
official ~ (оффи́шл ~) официальная классификация
service ~ (сэ́рвис ~) классификация услуг
temporary ~ (тэ́мпорари ~) временная классификация

~ of commodities (~ оф комму́дитиз) товарная номенклатура
Classifying (кла́ссифайинг) сортировка
Classify, to ~ (кла́ссифай, ту ~) классифицировать, сортировать
Clause (клауз) оговорка, отметка, пункт, статья
arbitration ~ (арбитрэ́йшн ~) арбитражная оговорка
assignment ~ (асса́йнмэнт ~) условия о переуступке
compulsory arbitration ~ (компу́лсори арбитрэ́йшн ~) оговорка об обязательном арбитраже
continuation ~ (континюˊйшн ~) оговорка о пролонгации, условия продления чартера {charter}
exchange ~ (эксчэ́йндж ~) валютная оговорка
exchange rate ~ (эксчэ́йндж рэйт ~) курсовая оговорка
extension ~ (экстэ́ншн ~) условия о продлении срока
force majeure ~ (форс мажюˊр ~) оговорка о форс-мажоре
freight ~ (фрэйт ~) условия о размере и порядке уплаты фрахта
gold ~ (голд ~) золотая оговорка
guarantee ~ (гяранти́ ~) пункт договора о гарантиях
Jacob's ~ (джэ́йкобз ~) оговорка язона
lien ~ (лин ~) оговорка о праве удержания
monopoly ~ (моно́поли ~) монопольная оговорка
monopoly rights ~ (моно́поли райтс ~) пункт договора о монопольном праве
most favored nation ~ (мост фэ́йворд нэ́йшн ~) акт особого благоприятствования, оговорка о наибольшем благоприятствовании
optional ~ (о́пшнал ~) факультативная оговорка
reciprocity ~ (рэсипро́сити ~) оговорка о взаимности
sanity ~ (са́нити ~) оговорка о компетенции
superimposed ~ (супэримпо́зд ~) дополнительная оговорка
territory ~ (тэ́рритори ~) территориальная оговорка

transit ~ (тра́нзит ~) транзитная
оговорка
transport ~ (тра́нспорт ~)
условия перевозки
Clean (клин) чистый
Clear (клир) ясный
to ~ (ту ~) выручать
to ~ **a vessel** {through customs}
(ту ~ а вэ́ссэл {θру ка́стомз})
кларировать
to make ~ (ту мэйк ~) явствовать
Clearance (кли́ранс) допуст,
очистка, урегулирование
customs ~ **bill** (ка́стомз ~ бил)
квитанция таможни об уплате
пошлины
~ **of accounts** (~ оф акко́унтс)
урегулирование расчётов
Clearing (кли́ринг) клиринг,
клиринговый {adj.} ~**s** расчёты по
клирингу
bank ~ (банк ~) банковский
клиринг
bilateral ~ (байла́тэрал ~)
двухсторонний клиринг
compulsory ~ (компу́лсори ~)
принудительный клиринг
currency ~ (ку́ррэнси ~) валютный
клиринг
currency ~ **system** (ку́ррэнси ~
си́стэм) система клиринга
multilateral ~ (мултила́тэрал ~)
многосторонний клиринг
unilateral ~ (юнила́тэрал ~)
односторонний клиринг
~ **account** (~ акко́унт) счёт по
клирингу
~ **agreement** (~ агри́мэнт)
соглашение о клиринге
~ **balance** (~ ба́ланс) сальдо
клиринга
~ **bank** (~ банк) клиринг-банк
~ **debt** (~ дэт) задолженность по
клирингу
~ **house** (~ хаус) ликвидационная
касса
~ **house bank** (~ хаус банк)
клиринговый банк
~ **payment** (~ пэ́ймэнт) платёж по
клирингу
~ **point** (~ пойнт) таможенный
пункт
Clemency (кле́мэнси) милосердие,
помилование
grant of ~ (грант оф ~) акт о
помиловании

Clergyman (кле́рджиман)
священнослужитель
Clerical (кле́рикал) канцелярский
Clerk (клэрк) служащий
head ~ (хэд ~) заведующий
канцелярией
ledger ~ (ле́джэр ~) счетовод
sales ~ (сэйлз ~) торговый
служащий
Client (кла́йэнт) клиент, комитент,
подзащитный
major ~ (мэ́йджор ~) крупный
клиент
potential ~**s** (поте́ншл ~с)
возможные клиенты
solid ~ (со́лид ~) солидный
клиент
primary ~**s** (пра́ймари ~с)
основные клиенты
Clientele (клайэнтэ́л) клиентура
Climate (кла́ймат) климат
business ~ (би́знэс ~) деловой
климат
hot ~ (хот ~) жаркий климат
international ~ (интэрна́шэнал ~)
международный климат
severe ~ (сэви́р ~) суровый
климат
Clinic (кли́ник) клиника
legal ~ (ли́гал ~) юридическая
консультация
Clip (клип) клип
Cloakroom (кло́крум) камера хранения
багажа
Close, to ~ (клоз, ту ~) закрывать
[**perfective:** закрыть]
Closed (клозд) закрытый
Closing (кло́зинг) закрытие
Closure (кло́жюр) закрытие
Club (клаб) клуб, общество
hunting ~ (ха́нтинг ~) охотничье
общество
Co-author (ко-а́уθор) соавтор
Co-authorship (ко-а́уθоршип)
соавторство
Co-belligerent (ко-бэлли́джэрэнт)
совоющий
Co-defendant (ко-дифэ́ндант)
сообщаемый {in criminal
proceedings}
Co-founder (ко-фо́ундэр)
сооснователь
Co-guardian (ко-га́рдиан) соопекун
Co-heir (ко-эйр) сонаследник
Co-owner (ко-о́унэр) совладелец
Co-ownership (ко-о́унэршип)
совладение, сособственность

Co-proprietor (ко-пропра́йэтор) сособственник
Co-trustee (ко-трасти́) соопекун
Coal (кол) уголь
~ ship (~ шип) углевоз
Coarse (корс) грубый, необработанный
Coastal (ко́стал) каботажный
Coasting (ко́стинг) каботажный
~ trade (~ трэйд) каботаж
Code (код) индекс, код, кодекс, свод, шифр
anti-dumping ~ (а́нти-да́мпинг ~) антидемпинговый кодекс
building ~ (би́лдинг ~) строительные нормы
civil ~ (си́вил ~) гражданский кодекс
enciphered ~ (энса́йфэрд ~) шифрованный код
international ~ (интэрна́шэнал ~) международный код
key to a ~ (ки ту а ~) ключ к шифру
machine ~ (маши́н ~) шифр единицы оборудования
postal ~ (по́стал ~) почтовый код
project ~ (про́джэкт ~) код проекта
vendor ~ (вэ́ндор ~) код подрядчика
zip ~ (зип ~) почтовый код
~ of laws (~ оф лаус) свод законов
~ of international law (~ оф интэрна́шэнал лау) кодекс международного права
Codify, to ~ (ко́дифай, ту ~) кодировать
Coefficient (коэффи́шэнт) коэффициент
input ~ (и́нпут ~) коэффициент затрат
weight ~ (уэйт ~) весовой коэффициент
~ of loading (~ оф ло́динг) коэффициент загрузки
~ of performance (~ оф пэрфо́рманс) коэффициент полезного действия
~ of productivity (~ оф продукти́вити) коэффициент продуктивности
Coerce, to ~ (коэ́рс, ту ~) принуждать
Coercion (коэ́ржн) принуждение

collective ~ (колле́ктив ~) коллективное принуждение
direct ~ (дире́кт ~) прямое принуждение
economic ~ (эконо́мик ~) экономическое принуждение
individual ~ (индиви́дюал ~) индивидуальное принуждение
moral ~ (мо́рал ~) моральное принуждение
physical ~ (фи́зикал ~) физическое принуждение
psychological ~ (сайколо́джикал ~) психическое принуждение
Coercive (коэ́рсив) принудительный
Coexist, to ~ (коэкзи́ст, ту ~) сожительствовать
Coexistence (коэкзи́стэнс) сожительство, сосуществование
peaceful ~ (пи́сфул ~) мирное сожительство, мирное сосуществование
Cohabit, to ~ (коха́бит, ту ~) сожительствовать
Cohabitation (кохабитэ́йшн) сожительство
extramarital ~ (экстрама́ритал ~) внебрачное сожительство
Cohesion (кохи́жн) сплочённость
Coin (койн) монета ~s металлические деньги
changing of ~s (чэ́йнджинг оф ~с) размен монет
gold ~s (голд ~с) золотые монеты
silver ~ (си́лвэр ~) серебряная монета
~s of large denominations (~с оф лардж диномине́йшнс) монеты крупного достоинства
~s of small denominations (~с оф смал диномине́йшнс) монеты мелкого достоинства
~s of various denominations (~с оф ва́риос диноминэ́йшнс) монеты разного достоинства
Collaboration (коллаборэ́йшн) кооперация, сотрудничество
fruitful ~ (фру́тфул ~) плодотворная кооперация
inter-firm ~ (и́нтэр-фирм ~) межфирменная кооперация
Collapse (колла́пс) крах, распад
economic ~ (эконо́мик ~) экономическая разруха
financial ~ (файна́ншл ~) финансовый крах

~ **of credit system** (~ оф крэ́дит си́стэм) крах кредитной системы
~ **of currency** (~ оф ку́ррэнси) крах валюты
Collateral (колла́тэрал) двойное обеспечение, обеспечение, побочный {adj.}
   additional ~ (адди́шнал ~) дополнительное обеспечение
   as ~ (аз ~) в качестве обеспечения
   commercial ~ (комме́ршл ~) коммерческое обеспечение
   on (он ~) под двойное обеспечение
   substitution of ~ (субститу́шн оф ~) замена обеспечения
   to serve as ~ (ту сэрв аз ~) служить обеспечением
   ~ **for a loan** (~ фор а лон) обеспечение займа
Colleague (ко́ллиг) коллега
Collect, to ~ (колле́кт, ту ~) инкассировать, отбирать [perfective: отобрать]
   ~ **letter** (~ ле́ттэр) письмо с доплатой
Collection (колле́кшн) взимание платы, взыскание, инкассация, инкассо, коллекция, набор, получение, сбор, сборник, свод, собрание
   debt ~ (дэт ~) взыскание долгов
   documentary ~ (докюме́нтари ~) документарное инкассо
   tax ~ (такс ~) взыскание налогов

   ~ **charge** (~ чардж) вознаграждение за инкассо
   ~ **of a bill** (~ оф а бил) взыскание денег по векселю
   ~ **of a fine** (~ оф а файн) взыскание штрафа
   ~ **of interest** (~ оф и́нтэрэст) взимание процентов
   ~ **of a payment** (~ оф а пэ́ймэнт) инкассовая операция
   ~ **of samples** (~ оф самплз) коллекция образцов
Collective (колле́ктив) коллектив {collective body}, коллективный {adj.}
   labor ~ (лэ́йбор ~) трудовой коллектив {employees of an enterprise}

production ~ {work force} (прода́кшн ~ {уо́рк форс}) производственный коллектив
Collectively (колле́ктивли) солидарно
Collector (колле́ктор) инкассатор, сборщик
   tax ~ (такс ~) налогов инкассатор, сборщик налогов
   ~ **of duties** (~ оф дю́тиз) сборщик пошлин
Collegium (коли́гиум) коллегия
   member of the ~ (мэ́мбэр оф θи ~) член коллегии
   ~ **of Advocates** (~ оф а́двокатс) коллегия адвокатов
Collision (колли́жн) столкновение
   accidental ~ (аксидэ́нтал ~) случайное столкновение
Colonization (колонизэ́йшн) заселение
Color (ко́лор) цвет
   deviation in ~ (дивиэ́йшн ин ~) отклонение в цвете
   in ~ (ин ~) в цвете
   primary ~ (пра́ймари ~) основной цвет
Column (ко́лум) колонка
Combination (комбинэ́йшн) комбинация, комбинированный {adj.}, сочетание
   possible ~ (по́ссибл ~) возможная комбинация
Combine (ко́мбайн) комбинат {amalgamated industrial concern}
   industrial ~s (инду́стриал ~с) промышленный комбинат
   production ~s (прода́кшн ~с) производственные комбинаты
Combine, to ~ (комба́йн, ту ~) совмещать [perfective: совместить]
Combine-harvester (ко́мбайн-ха́рвэстэр) комбайн
Combined (комба́йнд) совместный
Combustibles (комбу́стиблз) горючие материалы
Comfortable (ко́мфортабл) удобный
Command (комма́нд) господство, приказание
   to ~ (ту ~) повелеть, приказывать, распоряжаться
Commentary (ко́ммэнтари) истолкование
Commentator (ко́ммэнтэйтор) публицист
Commerce (ко́ммэрс) коммерция, торговля

maritime ~ (мáритайм ~) морская торговля
~ treaty (~ трúти) договор о торговле
Commercial (коммэ́ршл) коммерческий, торговый
~ paper (~ пэ́йпэр) коммерческие бумаги
Commercialization (коммэршлизэ́йшн) коммерциализация
Commissar (кóммиссар) комиссар
Commission (коммúшн)
вознаграждение, комиссионное вознаграждение, комиссионное поручение, комиссионные {fees}, комиссионный {adj.}, комиссионный процент, комиссионный сбор, комиссия, полномочие, поручение
acceptance ~ (аксэ́птанс ~) акцептная комиссия
agent's ~ (э́йджэнтс ~) агентское вознаграждение
amount of ~ (амóунт оф ~) размер вознаграждения, сумма вознаграждения
broker's ~ (брóкэрз ~) брокерское вознаграждение
del credere ~ (дэл крэдэ́рэ ~) вознаграждение за делькредере
economic ~ (эконóмик ~) экономическая комиссия
expert ~ (э́кспэрт ~) экспертная комиссия
fixed ~ (фиксд ~) твёрдая комиссия
government ~ (гóвэрнмэнт ~) правительственная комиссия
maritime arbitration ~ (мáритайм арбитрэ́йшн ~) морская арбитражная комиссия
maximum ~ (мáксимум ~) максимальное вознаграждение
measure of a ~ (мэ́жюр оф а ~) размер комиссионных
minimum ~ (мúнимум ~) минимальное вознаграждение
net ~ (нэт ~) чистое вознаграждение
on a ~ basis (он а ~ бэ́йсис) на базе комиссионного вознаграждения
percentage ~ (пэрсэ́нтадж ~) процентная комиссия
percentage rate of ~ (пэрсэ́нтадж рэйт оф ~) процент комиссионных
rate of ~ (рэйт оф ~) ставка комиссии

reinsurance ~ (рэиншю́ранс ~) перестраховочные комиссионные
sales ~ (сэйлз ~) комиссионные за продажу
to ~ (ту ~) назначать, поручать
to calculate ~ (ту кáлкюлэйт ~) исчислять вознаграждение
to charge ..% ~ (ту чардж ..% ~) взимать ..% комиссионных
to pay a ~ (ту пэй а ~) платить комиссионные
to receive a ~ (ту рисúв а ~) получать комиссионные
to take goods on ~ (ту тэйк гудз он ~) брать товар на комиссию
~ for acceptance (~ фор аксэ́птанс) комиссия за акцепт
~ for letter of credit (~ фор лэ́ттэр оф крэ́дит) комиссия за аккредитив
~ on advice (~ он адвáйс) комиссия за авизо
~ rate (~ рэйт) ставка вознаграждения
~ scale (~ скэйл) шкала комиссионного вознаграждения
Commissioner (коммúшнэр) комиссар
customs ~s (кáстомз ~с) комиссары таможенного комитета
Commissioning (коммúшнинг) введение в эксплуатацию, ввод
~ ahead of schedule (~ ахэ́д оф скэ́джюл) досрочный ввод
~ of an enterprise (~ оф ан э́нтэрпрайз) ввод в действие предприятия
~ of a factory (~ оф а фáктори) ввод в эксплуатацию завода
~ period (~ пúриод) срок ввода в действие
Commit, to ~ (коммúт, ту ~) обязывать, совершать
to ~ an offense (ту ~ ан оффэ́нс) провиниться
Commitment (коммúтмэнт) обязательство
original ~ (орúджинал ~) первоначальное обязательство
prior ~ (прáйор ~) первоочередное обязательство
monetary ~s (мóнэтари ~с) денежные обязательства
Committee (коммúтти) комиссия, комитет
advisory ~ (адвáйзори ~) консультативный комитет

audit ~ (а́удит ~) ревизионная комиссия

banking ~ (ба́нкинг ~) банковская комиссия

budget ~ (ба́джэт ~) бюджетная комиссия

certifying ~ (сэ́ртифайинг ~) аттестационная комиссия

consultative ~ (ко́нсултэйтив ~) консультативная комиссия

coordinating ~ (коо́рдинэйтинг ~) координационная комиссия, координационный комитет

drafting ~ (дра́фтинг ~) редакционный комитет

evaluating ~ (ива́люэйтинг ~) оценочная комиссия

executive ~ (экзэ́кютив ~) исполком {исполнительный комитет}

financial ~ (файна́ншл ~) финансовый комитет

intergovernmental ~ (интэрговэрнмэ́нтал ~) межправительственный комитет

interim ~ (и́нтэрим ~) временная комиссия, временный комитет

joint ~ (джойнт ~) смешанная комиссия

liquidation ~ (ликуидэ́йшн ~) ликвидационная комиссия

management ~ (ма́наджмэнт ~) управленческий комитет

member of a ~ (мэ́мбэр оф а ~) член комиссии

operating ~ (о́пэрэйтинг ~) операционная комиссия

organizing ~ (о́рганайзинг ~) организационный комитет

oversight ~ (о́вэрсайт ~) контрольная комиссия

planning ~ (пла́ннинг ~) плановая комиссия

preparatory ~ (прэ́паратори ~) подготовительный комитет

purchasing ~ (пу́рчасинг ~) закупочная комиссия

sectoral ~ (сэкто́рал ~) отраслевая комиссия

standing ~ (ста́ндинг ~) постоянная комиссия, постоянный комитет

state ~ (стэйт ~) государственная комиссия

steering ~ (сти́ринг ~) руководящий комитет

stock exchange ~ (сток эксчэ́йндж ~) биржевой комитет

tender ~ (тэ́ндэр ~) тендерный комитет

to form a ~ (ту форм а ~) создавать комиссию

trade ~ (трэйд ~) торговая комиссия

trilateral ~ (трайла́тэрал ~) трёхсторонняя комиссия

unified ~ (ю́нифайд ~) объединённая комиссия

working ~ (уо́ркинг ~) рабочий комитет

Commodit/y (коммо́дити) предмет, продукт, товар, товарный {adj.}

agrarian ~ (агра́риан ~) аграрный продукт

agricultural ~/ies (агрику́лчурал ~из) сельскохозяйственные товары

agricultural ~/ies market (агрику́лчурал ~из ма́ркэт) биржа сельскохозяйственных товаров

barter of ~/ies (ба́ртэр оф ~из) обмен товаров

bulk ~/ies (булк ~из) массовые товары

category of ~/ies (ка́тэгори оф ~из) категория товаров

gross ~ turnover (грос ~ ту́рновэр) валовой товарооборот

market ~/ies (ма́ркэт ~из) биржевые товары

non-dutiable ~/ies (нон-ду́тиабл ~из) беспошлинные товары

physical ~ (фи́зикал ~) реальный товар

quotation on the ~/ies spot market (куотэ́йшн он θи ~из спот ма́ркэт) котировка товара с немедленной сдачей и оплатой

rare ~ (рэйр ~) редкий товар

scarce ~ (скэйрс ~) дефицитный товар

staple ~/ies (стэйпл ~из) основные товары

to barter ~/ies (ту ба́ртэр ~из) обмениваться товарами

to deal in ~/ies (ту дил ин ~из) торговать товаром

trade in strategic ~/ies on the COCOM list (трэйд ин стра́тиджик ~из он θи ко́ком лист) торговля "стратегическими" товарами по спискам КОКОМ

unit of ~ (ю́нит оф ~) единица товара

~ **circulation** (~ сиркюлэ́йшн)
обращение товара
~ **exchange** (~ эксчэ́йндж)
товарообмен
~ **market** (~ ма́ркэт) рынок
товаров
~ **producer** (~ продю́сэр)
товаропроизводитель
~ **turnover** (~ ту́рновэр)
товарооборот
Common (ко́ммон) внешний, единый,
обыкновенный, общий
Commonwealth (ко́ммонуэл θ)
содружество
British ~ **of Nations** (бри́тиш ~
оф нэ́йшнз) британское
содружество наций
~ **of Independent States** {CIS} (~
оф индипэ́ндэнт стэ́йтс {си-ай-
эс}) Содружество Независимых
Государств {СНГ}
Commotion (коммо́шн) смятение
Commune (ко́ммюн) община
peasant ~ (пэ́зант ~)
крестьянская община
religious ~ (рили́джос ~)
религиозная община
Communicate, to ~ (коммю́никэйт, ту
~) сообщать [perfective: сообщи́ть]
Communication (коммюникэ́йшн)
контакт, связь, сообщение
external ~**s** (экстэ́рнал ~с)
внешние контакты
internal ~**s** (интэ́рнал ~с)
внутренние контакты
Communiqué (коммюника́) коммюнике
joint ~ (джойнт ~) совместное
коммюнике
to issue a ~ (ту и́шю а ~)
опубликовать коммюнике
Community (каммю́нити)
общественность, община, общность,
сообщество
Atlantic ~ (атла́нтик ~)
атлантическое сообщество
European Economic ~ (юропи́ан
эконо́мик ~) Европейское
Экономическое Сообщество
international ~ (интэрна́шэнал ~)
международная общность,
международное сообщество
legal ~ (ли́гал ~) законная
общность
marital ~ (ма́ритал ~)
супружеская общность
specialized ~ (спэ́шлайзд ~)
специализированное сообщество

urban ~ (у́рбан ~) городская
община
~ **of nations** (~ оф нэ́йшнз)
сообщество наций
Company (ко́мпани) компания,
общество, фирма
affiliate of a ~ (аффи́лиат оф а
~) филиал компании
aviation ~ (эйвиэ́йшн ~)
авиакомпания
bankrupt ~ (ба́нкрупт ~)
обанкротившаяся фирма
bogus ~ (бо́гус ~) фиктивная
компания
branch office of a ~ (бранч
о́ффис оф а ~) филиал фирмы
civil engineering ~ (си́вил
инджэни́ринг ~) строительная
фирма
civil law limited ~ (си́вил ла́у
ли́митэд ~) акционерное
командитное общество {e.g.
French Societe Anonyme en
Commandite}
competitive ~ (компэ́титив ~)
конкурентная компания
construction ~ (констру́кшн ~)
строительная компания
controlling ~ (контро́ллинг ~)
контролирующее общество
cooperative ~ (коо́пэратив ~)
кооперативная фирма
designing ~ (диза́йнинг ~)
компания-проектировщик
direct marketing ~ (дирэ́кт
ма́ркэтинг ~) сбытовая фирма
distribution ~ (дистрибю́шн ~)
распределительная компания
finance ~ (фа́йнанс ~) финансовая
компания, финансовое общество
foreign ~ (фо́рэн ~) иностранная
компания, иностранная фирма
foreign trade ~ (фо́рэн трэйд ~)
внешнеторговая фирма
freight forwarding ~ (фрэйт
фо́руардинг ~) транспортно-
экспедиционная фирма
general director of a ~
(джэ́нэрал дирэ́ктор оф а ~)
генеральный директор фирмы
head of a ~ (хэд оф а ~) глава
фирмы
holding ~ (хо́лдинг ~) компания-
держатель, контролирующая
компания, холдинговая компания
incorporated ~ (инко́рпорэйтэд ~)
объединённая компания

industrial ~ (инду́стриал ~) промышленная компания, промышленная фирма
insurance ~ (иншю́ранс ~) страховая компания, страховое общество, страховая фирма, страховое учреждение
international ~ (интэрна́шэнал ~) международная компания
investment ~ (инвэ́стмэнт ~) инвестиционная компания
joint stock ~ (джойнт сток ~) акционерная компания, акционерное общество
leading ~ (ли́динг ~) ведущая компания
leasing ~ (ли́синг ~) арендная фирма, лизинговая компания, лизинговая фирма
limited liability ~ (ли́митэд лайаби́лити ~) акционерное общество с ограниченной ответственностью, компания с ограниченной ответственностью
liquidation of a ~ (ликуидэ́йшн оф а ~) ликвидация компании
local ~ (ло́кал ~) местная фирма
mail order ~ (мэйл о́рдэр ~) посылочная компания
major ~ (мэ́йджор ~) крупная компания
manufacturing ~ (манюфа́кчуринг ~) производственная фирма
merger of ~/ies (мэ́рджэр оф ~из) слияние компаний
mixed ~ (миксд ~) смешанная компания
mixed joint stock ~ (миксд джойнт сток ~) смешанное общество
mixed trading ~ (миксд трэ́йдинг ~) смешанная торговая фирма
monopolistic ~ (монополи́стик ~) монополистическая компания
national ~ (на́шэнал ~) национальная фирма
nationalized ~ (на́шэналайзд ~) национализированная компания
oil ~ (ойл ~) нефтяная компания
operations of a ~ (опэрэ́йшнс оф а ~) деятельность фирмы
overseas ~ (овэрси́з ~) заокеанская компания
parent ~ (па́рэнт ~) материнская компания
principal ~/ies (при́нсипал ~из) крупнейшие компании

private ~ (пра́йват ~) частная компания, частная фирма
purchasing ~ (пу́рчасинг ~) фирма-покупатель
railway ~ (рэ́йлуэй ~) железнодорожная компания
reputation of a ~ (рэпютэ́йшн оф а ~) репутация фирмы
salvage ~ (са́лвэдж ~) спасательное общество
separate ~ (сэ́парат ~) отдельная компания
shipping ~ (ши́пинг ~) судоходная компания
solvent ~ (со́лвэнт ~) платежеспособная фирма
specialized ~ (спэ́шлайзд ~) специализированная компания
state ~ with limited liability (стэйт ~ уиθ ли́митэд лайаби́лити) государственная компания с ограниченной ответственностью
state ~ (стэйт ~) государственная компания
state-owned ~ (стэйт-о́унэд ~) государственная фирма
steamship ~ (сти́мшип ~) пароходное общество
stevedoring ~ (сти́вэдоринг ~) стивидорная компания, стивидорная фирма
structure of a ~ (стру́кшр оф а ~) структура фирмы
subsidiary ~ (субси́диари ~) дочерняя компания, дочернее общество, дочерняя фирма
to change the name of a ~ (ту чэйндж θи нэйм оф а ~) переименовывать фирму
to file suit against a ~ (ту файл сут агэ́нст а ~) возбуждать иск против фирмы
to form a ~ (ту форм а ~) создавать компанию
to found a ~ (ту фо́унд а ~) основывать фирму
to place an order with a ~ (ту плэйс ан о́рдэр уиθ а ~) размещать заказ у фирмы
to register a ~ (ту рэ́джистэр а ~) регистрировать фирму
to liquidate a ~ (ту ли́куидэйт ~) ликвидировать компанию
tour ~ (тур ~) турагентская фирма
trading ~ (трэ́йдинг ~) торговая компания, торговое общество

transport ~ (тра́нспорт ~) транспортная фирма
universal ~ (юнивэ́рсал ~) универсальная фирма
unlimited liability ~ (анли́митэд лайаби́лити ~) акционерное общество с неограниченной ответственностью, компания с неограниченной ответственностью
~ name (~ нэйм) название фирмы
~-lessor (~-лэссо́р) фирма-арендодатель
~ with a good reputation (~ уиθ а гуд рэпюте́йшн) фирма с хорошей репутацией
Comparability (компараби́лити) сопоставимость
Comparable (компэ́йрабл) сопоставимый
Comparison (компэ́йрисон) сопоставление, сравнение
~ of prices (~ оф пра́йсэз) сопоставление цен
Compatibility (компатиби́лити) совместимость
Compatible (компа́тибл) совместимый
Compatriot (компэ́йтриот) соотечественник
Compel, to ~ (компэ́л, ту ~) принуждать
Compensate, to ~ (ко́мпэнсэйт, ту ~) возмещать, компенсировать, платить возмещение
refusal to ~ (рифью́зал ту ~) отказ от возмещения
Compensation (компэнсэ́йшн) возмещение убытков, компенсация
adequate ~ (а́дэкуэт ~) достаточная компенсация
as ~ (аз ~) в качестве компенсации
claim form for ~ (клэйм форм фор ~) ходатайство о возмещении убытков
demand for ~ (дима́нд фор ~) требование о возмещении убытков
full ~ (фул ~) полная компенсация
in ~ of (ин ~ оф) в компенсацию
in ~ of damages (ин ~ оф да́мэджэз) в порядке возмещения убытков
inadequate ~ (ина́дэкуэт ~) недостаточная компенсация
means of ~ (минз оф ~) способ вознаграждения

measure of ~ (мэ́жюр оф ~) размер компенсации
monetary ~ (мо́нэтари ~) денежная компенсация
nonrecurring ~ (нонрику́рринг ~) однократное возмещение
payment of ~ (пэ́ймэнт оф ~) выплата возмещения
right to ~ (райт ту ~) право на возмещение
right to ~ for general average losses (райт ту ~ фор джэ́нэрал а́вэрэдж ло́ссэз) право на возмещение убытков по общей аварии
statutory ~ (ста́тютори ~) законная компенсация
to demand ~ for losses (ту дима́нд ~ фор ло́ссэз) требовать возмещения убытков
to give ~ (ту гив ~) давать компенсацию
to insist on ~ (ту инси́ст он ~) настаивать на возмещении
to pay ~ (ту пэй ~) платить компенсацию
to offer ~ (ту о́ффэр ~) предлагать возмещение
to receive ~ for expenditures (ту риси́в ~ фор экспэ́ндичюрз) получать возмещение расходов
to receive ~ for payments (ту риси́в ~ фор пэ́ймэнтс) получать возмещение платежей
to receive ~ from ... (ту риси́в ~ фром ...) получать возмещение от
~ clause (~ клауз) оговорка о возмещении
~ for damages (~ фор да́мэджэз) возмещение убытков
~ for losses (~ фор ло́ссэз) покрытие убытков
~ for shortage (~ фор шо́ртадж) возмещение недостачи
~ in kind (~ ин кайнд) вознаграждение натурой
Compensatory (компэ́нсатори) компенсационный
Compete, to ~ (компи́т, ту ~) конкурировать
covenant not to ~ (ко́вэнант нот ту ~) обязательство не конкурировать
Competence (ко́мпэтэнс) компетенция, правомочие {legal}

to be outside the ~ of (ту би óутсайд θи ~ оф) выходить за пределы компетенции
within the ~ of (уиθи́н θи ~ оф) в пределах компетенции
Competent (ко́мпэтэнт) дееспособный, компетентный, полноправный, правомочный
Competing (компи́тинг) конкурирующий
Competition (компэти́шн) конкуренция, конкурс, соискание, соревнование
  active ~ (а́ктив ~) активная конкуренция
  cutthroat ~ (ку́тθрот ~) ожесточённая конкуренция
  direct ~ (дирэ́кт ~) прямая конкуренция
  electoral campaign ~ (элэ́кторал кампэ́йн ~) предвыборное соревнование
  fair ~ (фэ́йр ~) честная конкуренция
  free ~ (фри ~) свободная конкуренция
  global ~ (гло́бал ~) глобальная конкуренция
  increase in ~ (инкри́с ин ~) обострение конкуренции
  indirect ~ (индайрэ́кт ~) косвенная конкуренция
  intersectoral ~ (интэрсэкто́рал ~) внутриотраслевая конкуренция, межотраслевая конкуренция
  keen ~ (кин ~) острая конкуренция
  latent ~ (лэ́йтэнт ~) скрытая конкуренция
  market ~ (ма́ркэт ~) рыночная конкуренция
  predatory ~ (прэ́датори ~) хищническая конкуренция
  price ~ (прайс ~) ценовая конкуренция
  pure ~ (пюр ~) чистая конкуренция
  restraint of ~ (ристрэ́йнт оф ~) ограничение конкуренции
  ruinous ~ (ру́инос ~) разрушительная конкуренция
  spirited ~ (спи́ритэд ~) оживлённая конкуренция
  stiff ~ (стиф ~) жестокая конкуренция
  to eliminate existing ~ (ту или́минэйт экзи́стинг ~) ликвидировать существующую конкуренцию
  to withstand ~ (ту уиθста́нд ~) выдерживать конкуренцию
  unfair ~ (анфэ́йр ~) недобросовестная конкуренция
  unlimited ~ (анли́митэд ~) неограниченная конкуренция
  without ~ (уиθо́ут ~) безконкурентный
Competitive (компэ́титив) конкурентный, конкурентоспособный {goods, etc.}
  ~ mechanism (~ мэ́канизм) механизм конкуренции
  ~ position (~ пози́шн) конкурентоспособность
  ~ pressure (~ прэ́шюр) давление конкуренции
Competitiveness (компэ́титивнэс) конкурентоспособность
  indicator of ~ (и́ндикэйтор оф ~) показатель конкурентоспособности
  to increase ~ (ту инкри́с ~) повышать конкурентоспособность
Competitor (компэ́титор) конкурент
  main ~ (мэйн ~) основной конкурент
  potential ~ (потэ́ншл ~) потенциальный конкуренты
  foreign ~s (фо́рэн ~с) иностранные конкуренты
  local ~s (ло́кал ~с) местные конкуренты
  major ~s (мэ́йджор ~с) важнейшие конкуренты
  to forestall the market entry of ~s (ту форста́л θи ма́ркэт э́нтри оф ~с) воспрепятствовать проникновению конкурентов
Compiler (компа́йлэр) составитель
Complain, to ~ (комплэ́йн, ту ~) жаловаться
Complainant (комплэ́йнант) податель жалобы
Complaint (комплэ́йнт) жалоба
  cause for ~ (ка́уз фор ~) основание для жалобы
  immaterial ~ (иммати́риал ~) несущественная жалоба
  nature of the ~ (нэ́йчэр оф θи ~) суть жалобы
  numerous ~s (ну́мэрос ~с) многочисленные жалобы
  outstanding ~ (оутста́ндинг ~) неразрешённая жалоба

to **examine an applicant's** ~ (ту экза́мин ан а́пликантс ~) рассматривать жалобу заявителя
to **have a** ~ **about something** (ту хэв а ~ або́ут со́мθинг) иметь жалобу на что-л.
to **have a** ~ **against somebody** (ту хэв а ~ агэ́нст со́мбоди) иметь жалобу на кого-л.
to **lodge a** ~ (ту лодж а ~) обжаловать, обращаться с жалобой, подавать жалобу
to **make** ~**s** (ту мэйк ~с) жаловаться
to **receive** ~**s** (ту риси́в ~с) получать жалобы
written ~ (ри́ттэн ~) письменная жалоба
Complete (компли́т) комплектный
to ~ (ту ~) комплектовать, завершать, укомплектовывать
~ **immunity from punishment** (~ имми́юнити фром пу́нишмэнт) полное освобождение от наказания
~ **with** ... (~ уиθ ...) в комплекте ...
Completed (компли́тэд) заполненный, совершённый
not ~ (нот ~) незаполненный
Completeness (компли́тнэс) комплектность
Completion (компли́шн) завершение, комплектование, окончание
satisfactory ~ (сатисфа́ктори ~) удовлетворительное завершение
successful ~ (суксэ́сфул ~) успешное завершение
~ **of construction** (~ оф констру́кшн) завершение монтажа
~ **of construction supervision** (~ оф констру́кшн супэрви́жн) завершение шефмонтажа
~ **of a course** (~ оф а корс) завершение курса
~ **of delivery** (~ оф дэли́вэри) завершение поставки
~ **of equipment** (~ оф икуи́пмэнт) комплектование оборудования
~ **of negotiations** (~ оф нэгоши́эйшнс) завершение переговоров
~ **of an order** (~ оф ан о́рдэр) завершение выполнения заказа
~ **of purchases** (~ оф пу́рчасс) завершение закупок
~ **of a voyage** (~ оф а во́йадж) завершение рейса

~ **of work** (~ оф уо́рк) завершение работ
~ **of work within the contract period** (~ оф уо́рк уиθи́н θи ко́нтракт пи́риод) завершение работ в установленные сроки
Complex (ко́мплэкс) комплекс, комплексный {adj.}, сложный {adj.}
agro-industrial ~ (а́гро-инду́стриал ~) агро-промышленный комплекс
exhibition ~ (экзиби́шн ~) выставочный комплекс
ferry ~ (фэ́рри ~) паромный комплекс
foreign economic ~ (фо́рэн эконо́мик ~) внешнеэкономический комплекс
hotel ~ (хотэ́л ~) гостиничный комплекс
industrial ~ (инду́стриал ~) промышленный комплекс
manufacturing ~ (манюфа́кчуринг ~) производственный комплекс
petro-chemical ~ (пэ́тро-кэ́микал ~) нефтехимический комплекс
port ~ (порт ~) портовый комплекс
Compliance (компла́йанс) соблюдение
Complicated (ко́мпликэйтэд) сложный
Complicity (компли́сити) соучастие
Comply, to ~ (компла́й, ту ~) следовать
Component (компо́нэнт) деталь, компонент, составная часть
accessory ~**s** (аксэ́ссори ~с) комплектующие детали
finished ~ (фи́нишд ~) готовая деталь
high-quality ~**s** (хай-куа́лити ~с) высококачественные компоненты
principle ~ (при́нсипл ~) основная деталь
separate ~**s** (сэ́парат ~с) отдельные компоненты
specific ~**s** (спэси́фик ~с) специфические компоненты
Composition (компози́шн) сложение, состав, строение
narrow ~ **of a committee** (на́рро ~ оф а комми́тти) узкий состав комитета
narrow ~ **of a council** (на́рро ~ оф а ко́унсил) узкий состав совета
total ~ (то́тал ~) общий состав

~ **of management** (~ оф ма́наджмэнт) состав правления
~ **of population** (~ оф попюлэ́йшн) состав населения
Comprehensive (комприхэ́нсив) комплексный
Compress, to ~ (ко́мпрэс, ту ~) сжигать
Compromise (ко́мпромайз) компромисс, компромиссный {*adj.*}
   to make a ~ (ту мэйк а ~) пойти на компромисс
   to reach a ~ (ту рич а ~) достигать компромисса
Compromiser (ко́мпромайзэр) примиренец {*usu. pejorative*}
Comptroller (комптро́лэр) бухгалтер-контролёр, контролёр, ревизор
   plant ~ (плант ~) заводской контролёр
   ~ **general** (~ джэ́нэрал) генеральный контролёр
Compulsion (компу́лшн) принуждение
   administrative ~ (адми́нистрэйтив ~) административное принуждение
   governmental ~ (гowэрнмэ́нтал ~) государственное принуждение
Compulsorily (компу́лсорили) принудительным порядком
Compulsory (компу́лсори) обязательный, принудительный
Computation (компютэ́йшн) начисление
Compute, to ~ (компю́т, ту ~) начислять
Computer (компю́тэр) вычислительная машина, компьютер
   analog ~ (а́налог ~) аналоговая вычислительная машина
   digital ~ (ди́джитал ~) цифровая вычислительная машина
Conceal, to ~ (конси́л, ту ~) скрывать
Concealed (конси́лд) скрытый
Concealment (конси́лмэнт) скрытие, сокрытие
   ~ **of profits** (~ оф про́фитс) сокрытие прибыли
Conceit (конси́т) самонадеянность
   criminal ~ (кри́минал ~) преступная самонадеянность
Concentrate, to ~ (ко́нсэнтрэйт, ту ~) концентрировать
Concentration (консэнтрэ́йшн) концентрация, осредоточение
   market ~ (ма́ркэт ~) рыночная концентрация

permitted ~ (пэрми́ттэд ~) допустимая концентрация
   ~ **camp** (~ камп) концлагерь
   ~ **of capital** (~ оф ка́питал) концентрация капитала
   ~ **of forces** (~ оф фо́рсэз) сосредоточение сил
   ~ **of material resources** (~ оф мати́риал рисо́рсэз) концентрация материальных ресурсов
Concept (ко́нсэпт) концепция
   legal ~ (ли́гал ~) юридическое понятие
   proprietary ~ **of a firm** (пропра́йэтари ~ оф а фирм) концепция, принадлежащая фирме
   proven ~ (про́вэн ~) доказанная концепция
Concern (консэ́рн) концерн
   banking ~ (ба́нкинг ~) банковский концерн
   industrial ~ (инду́стриал ~) промышленный концерн
   international ~ (интэрна́шэнал ~) международный концерн
   major ~ (мэ́йджор ~) крупный концерн
   multinational ~ (мултина́шэнал ~) многонациональный концерн
Concession (консэ́шн) концессия, уступка
   forced ~ (форсд ~) вынужденная уступка
   foreign ~ (фо́рэн ~) иностранная концессия
   maximum ~ (ма́ксимум ~) максимальная уступка
   mutual ~s (мю́чуал ~с) взаимные уступки
   non-tariff ~s (нон-та́риф ~с) нетарифные уступки
   numerous ~s (ну́мэрос ~с) многочисленные льготы
   special ~s (спэшл ~с) специальные уступки
   tariff ~s (та́риф ~с) тарифные уступки
   tax ~s (такс ~с) налоговые уступки
   to grant a ~ (ту грант а ~) предоставлять концессию
   to make ~s (ту мэйк ~с) делать уступки
   to receive a ~ (ту риси́в а ~) получать концессию
   to renew a ~ (ту риню́ а ~) возобновлять концессию

to seek ~s (ту сик ~с)
добиваться уступок
Concessionaire (консэшнэ́йр)
концессионер, концессионное
предприятие, концессионный {adj.}
Conciliatory (консилиатори)
примирительный
Conclude, to ~ (конклю́д, ту ~)
выводить, заключать
to ~ a contract (ту ~ а
ко́нтракт) заключать договор
Concluding (конклю́динг) итоговый
Conclusion (конклю́жн) вывод ,
заключение
baseless ~ (бэ́йслэс ~)
необоснованный вывод
beneficial ~ (бэнэфи́шл ~)
благоприятное заключение
false ~ (фалс ~) ложный вывод
final ~ (фа́йнал ~) окончательный
вывод
hasty ~ (хэ́йсти ~) поспешный
вывод
incorrect ~ (инкорр́экт ~)
неправильный вывод
practical ~ (пра́ктикал ~)
организационный вывод
preliminary ~ (прили́минэри ~)
предварительное заключение
satisfactory ~ (сатисфа́ктори ~)
удовлетворительный вывод
to arrive at a ~ (ту арра́йв ат а
~) прийти к выводу
to come to a ~ (ту ком ту а ~)
делать вывод
to jump to a ~ (ту джумп ту а ~)
поспешить с выводом
unfavorable ~ (анфэ́йворабл ~)
неблагоприятное заключение
well-founded ~ (уэл-фо́ундэд ~)
обоснованный вывод
~ of an agreement (~ оф ан
агри́мэнт) заключение соглашения
~ of a contract (~ оф а
ко́нтракт) заключение договора,
заключение контракта
~ of a deal (~ оф а дил)
заключение сделки
~ of an expert (~ оф ан э́кспэрт)
заключение эксперта
~ of a peace treaty (~ оф а пис
три́ти) заключение мирного
договора
~ of a treaty (~ оф а три́ти)
заключение договора
Concordance (конко́рданс)
согласование

~ of the text of an agreement (~
оф θи тэкст оф ан агри́мэнт)
согласование текста договора
Condemn, to ~ (кондэ́м, ту ~)
осуждать, приговорить
Condemnation (кондэмнэ́йшн)
принудительное отчуждение
Condescension (кондэсэ́ншн)
снисходительность
Condition (конди́шн) вид, положение,
состояние, условие ~s обстановка,
режим, условия
abnormal ~s (абно́рмал ~с)
ненормальные условия
actual ~s (а́кчуал ~с) реальные
условия, фактическая обстановка
additional ~ (адди́шнал ~)
дополнительное условие
"against all risks" ~ (агэ́нст ал
рикс ~) условия "от всех
рисков"
appropriate ~s (аппро́приат ~с)
подходящие условия
as per ~s (аз пэр ~с) согласно
условиям
atmospheric ~s (атмосфи́рик ~с)
атмосферные условия
auction sale ~s (аукшн сэйл ~с)
условия продажи с аукциона
automatic ~s (аутома́тик ~с)
условия, действующие
автоматически
basic insurance ~s (бэ́йсик
иншю́ранс ~с) основные условия
страхования
best ~s (бэст ~с) наилучшие
условия
business ~s (би́знэс ~с) деловая
конъюнктура
climactic ~s (клайма́ктик ~с)
климатические условия
commodity market ~s (коммо́дити
ма́ркэт ~с) товарная конъюнктура
competitive ~s (компэ́титив ~с)
равноправные условия
critical ~s (кри́тикал ~с)
критические условия
design ~s (диза́йн ~с) проектные
условия
doubtful ~ (до́убтфул ~)
финансовое состояние
economic ~s (эконо́мик ~с)
экономические условия
emergency ~s (эм́эрджэнси ~с)
аварийные условия
established ~s (эста́блишд ~с)
установленные условия

exacting ~s (экза́ктинг ~с) обременительные условия
favorable ~s (фэ́йворабл ~с) благоприятная конъюнктура
financial ~s (файна́ншл ~с) финансовые условия
general terms and ~s of the contract (джэ́нэрал тэрмз энд ~с оф θи ко́нтракт) общие условия контракта
general terms and ~s (джэ́нэрал тэрмз энд ~с) общие условия
housing ~s (хо́узинг ~с) жилищные условия
if present ~s continue ... (иф прэ́ззэнт ~с конти́ню ...) если эти условия всё ещё будут существовать
illegal ~ (илли́гал ~) нелегальное положение
in humid ~s (ин хю́мид ~с) во влажных условиях
in a non-marketable ~ (ин а нон-ма́ркэтабл ~) в нетоварном виде
in marketable ~ (ин ма́ркэтабл ~) в товарном виде
inappropriate ~s (инаппро́приат ~с) неподходящие условия
indispensable ~ (индиспэ́нсабл ~) непременное условие
inflationary ~s (инфлэ́йшнари ~с) инфляционная конъюнктура
labor ~s (лэ́йбор ~с) условия труда
lease ~s (лис ~с) условия сдачи в аренду
loan with certain ~s (лон уиθ сэ́ртэн ~с) заём с определёнными условиями
local ~s (ло́кал ~с) местные условия
macroeconomic ~s (макроэконо́мик ~с) общехозяйственная конъюнктура
market ~s (ма́ркэт ~с) условия рынка
marketable ~ (ма́ркэтабл ~) товарный вид
meteorological ~s (митиороло́джикал ~с) метеорологические условия
model ~s (мо́дэл ~с) типовые условия
mutually agreeable ~s (мю́чуалли агри́абл ~с) взаимоприемлемые условия

non-fulfillment of ~s (нон-фулфи́лмэнт оф ~с) невыполнение условий
non-observance of ~s (нон-обзэ́рванс оф) несоблюдение условий
normal ~s (но́рмал ~с) нормальные условия
normal working ~s (но́рмал уо́ркинг ~с) нормальные условия работы
obligatory ~s of a contract (обли́гатори ~с оф а ко́нтракт) обязательные условия договора
obligatory ~s (обли́гатори ~с) обязательные условия
on ~ (он ~) при условии
on the following ~s (он θи фо́ллоинг ~с) на следующих условиях
operating ~ (о́пэрэйтинг ~) экономическое состояние
operating ~s (о́пэрэйтинг ~с) эксплуатационные условия
other ~s (о́θэр ~с) другие условия
particular ~s (парти́кюлар ~с) частные условия
possible ~s (по́ссибл ~с) возможные условия
practical ~s (пра́ктикал ~с) практические условия
present ~s (прэ́ззэнт ~с) условия, действующие в настоящее время
prevailing ~s (привэ́йлинг ~с) общепринятые условия, преобладающие условия
production ~s (прода́кшн ~с) производственные условия
service ~s (сэ́рвис ~с) условия обслуживания
social ~s (сошл ~с) социально-бытовые условия
special ~s (спэшл ~с) специальные условия
storage ~s (сто́радж ~с) условия хранения
strict ~s (стрикт ~с) строгие условия
stringent technical ~s (стри́нджэнт тэ́кникал ~с) жёсткие технические условия
subject to ~s of ... (са́бджэкт ту ~с оф ...) на условиях ...
subject to observance of the following ~s (са́бджэкт ту обсэ́рванс оф θи фо́ллоинг ~с) при соблюдении следующих условий

subsequent ~s (сáбсикуэнт ~c)
последующие условия
technical ~s (тэ́кникал ~c)
технические условия
technological ~s (тэкноло́джикал
~c) технологические условия
test ~s (тэст ~c) условия
испытаний
to accept ~s (ту аксэ́пт ~c)
принимать условия
to adapt to local ~s (ту адáпт
ту ло́кал ~c) приспосабливать к
местным условиям
to be bound by ~s (ту би бóунд
бай ~c) быть связанным условиями
to be in accordance with ~s (ту
би ин акко́рданс уиθ ~c)
соответствовать условиям
to be subject to a ~ (ту би
сáбджэкт ту а ~) быть
ограниченным условием
to ease ~s (ту из ~c) облегчать
условия
to encounter ~s (ту энко́унтэр
~c) столкнуться с условием
to impose ~s (ту импо́з ~c)
ставить условия
to improve ~s (ту импру́в ~c)
улучшать условия
to include ~s (ту инклю́д ~c)
включать условия
to include additional ~s (ту
инклю́д адди́шнал ~c) включать
условия дополнительно
to meet ~s (ту мит ~c) отвечать
условиям
to present ~s (ту прэзэ́нт ~c)
выставлять условия
to provide ~s (ту провáйд ~c)
создавать условия
to provide working ~s (ту
провáйд уо́ркинг ~c) создавать
условия для работы
to satisfy ~s (ту сáтисфай ~c)
удовлетворять условиям
to stipulate ~s (ту сти́пюлэйт
~c) обусловливать условия
to store goods under proper ~s
(ту стор гудз áндэр про́пэр ~c)
хранить товар в подходящих
условиях
to study economic ~s (ту сту́ди
эконо́мик ~c) изучать
экономические условия
to violate ~s (ту вáйолэйт ~c)
нарушать условия

traffic ~s (трáффик ~c) условия
движения
travel ~s (трáвэл ~c) условия
поездки
under ~s (áндэр ~c) в условиях
under ~s of production (áндэр ~c
оф продáкшн) в производственных
условиях
under actual ~s (áндэр áкчуал
~c) в реальных условиях
under any ~s (áндэр áни ~c) на
любых условиях
under certain ~s (áндэр сэ́ртэн
~c) при определённых условиях
under no ~s whatsoever (áндэр но
~c уатсоэ́вэр) ни при каких
условиях
under working ~s (áндэр уо́ркинг
~c) в рабочих условиях
unfavorable ~s (анфэ́йворабл ~c)
неблагоприятные условия
unfavorable weather ~s
(анфэ́йворабл уэ́θэр ~c)
неблагоприятные погодные условия
unhealthy working ~s (анхэлθи
уо́ркинг ~c) вредные условия
работы
upon the sole ~ (упо́н θи сол ~)
при одном условии
violation of ~s (вайолэ́йшн оф
~c) нарушение условий
~s for construction (~c фор
констру́кшн) условия монтажа
~s of economic management (~c оф
эконо́мик мáнаджмэнт) условия
хозяйствования
~ of the market (~ оф θи мáркэт)
конъюнктура рынка, положение на
рынке
~s of regional markets (~c оф
ри́джонал мáркэтс) конъюнктура
региональных рынков
~s of work (~c оф уо́рк) условия
работы
Conditional (конди́шнал) условный
Conduct (ко́ндукт) поведение
good ~ (гуд ~) хорошее поведение
to ~ (ту ~) провожать
unbecoming ~ (анбико́минг ~)
недостойное поведение
Conducting (конду́ктинг) проведение
Confer, to ~ (конфэ́р, ту ~)
присваивать [perfective: присвоить]
Conference (ко́нфэрэнс) заседание,
конференциальный {adj.},
конференция, совещание, съезд

journal of a ~ (джу́рнал оф а ~)
бюллетень конференции
ministerial ~ (министи́риал ~)
совещание министров
national ~ (на́шэнал ~)
национальный съезд
pre-election ~ (при-иле́кшн ~)
предвыборное совещание
preliminary ~ (прили́минэри ~)
предварительная конференция,
предварительное совещание
~ **of heads of state** (~ оф хэдз
оф стэйт) совещание глав
государств
~ **of the G-7** (~ оф θи джи-се́вэн)
совещание глав правительств
Семерки
Conferment (конфе́рмэнт) присвоение
~ **of authorship** (~ оф а́уθоршип)
присвоение авторства
Confession (конфе́шн) признание
written ~ (ри́ттэн ~) акт
содержащий признание
Confidence (ко́нфидэнс) доверие
abuse of ~ (абю́с оф ~)
злоупотребление доверием
breach of ~ (брич оф ~)
нарушение оказанного доверия
complete ~ (компли́т ~) полное
доверие
loss of ~ (лос оф ~) утрата
доверия
mutual ~ (мю́чуал ~) взаимное
доверие
to enjoy ~ (ту энджо́й ~)
пользоваться доверием
to gain ~ (ту гэйн ~) входить в
доверие
to justify ~ (ту джа́стифай ~)
оправдывать доверие
to win ~ (ту уин ~) завоёвывать
доверие
Confidential (конфиде́ншл)
конфиденциальный
to consider ~ (ту конси́дэр ~)
считать конфиденциальным
Confidentiality (конфидэншиа́лити)
конфиденциальность
guarantee of ~ (гяранти́ оф ~)
обеспечение конфиденциальности
to keep ~ (ту кип ~) соблюдать
конфиденциальность
~ **of deposits** (~ оф дипо́зитс)
тайна вкладов
Configuration (конфигюре́йшн)
конфигурация

distinct ~ (дисти́нкт ~)
различительная форма {as of a
logo}
Confine (ко́нфайн) предел
to ~ (ту конфа́йн) заточить
Confinement (конфа́йнмэнт)
заключение, заточение
solitary ~ (со́литари ~)
одиночное заключение
Confirmation (конфирмэ́йшн) акт о
подтверждении, подтверждение
~ **of a letter of credit** (~ оф а
ле́ттэр оф кре́дит) аккредитивное
подтверждение
~ **of an order** (~ оф ан о́рдэр)
подтверждение заказа
Confiscate, to ~ (ко́нфискэйт, ту ~)
конфисковать
Confiscation (конфиске́йшн) изъятие,
конфискация
~ **of cargo** (~ оф ка́рго) арест на
груз
~ **of passport** (~ оф па́сспорт)
изъятие паспорта
~ **of property** (~ оф про́пэрти)
изъятие имуществ
Conflict (ко́нфликт) конфликт,
столкновение
military ~ (ми́литари ~) военное
столкновение
to avoid ~s (ту аво́йд ~с)
избегать конфликтов
~ **of interests** (~ оф и́нтэрэстс)
конфликт интересов
Conflicting (конфли́ктинг)
конфликтующий, противоречивый
Conform, to ~ (конфо́рм, ту ~)
соответствовать
Conformance (конфо́рманс)
соответствие
full ~ (фул ~) полное
соответствие
Conformity (конфо́рмити) соблюдение,
соответствие
legal ~ (ли́гал ~) закономерность
~ **with a condition** (~ уиθ а
конди́шн) соблюдение условия
Confrontation (конфронтэ́йшн) очная
ставка {of witness, etc.},
сопротивление
Confuse, to ~ (конфю́з, ту ~)
смешивать [perfective: смешать]
Confusion (конфю́жн) смешение,
смятение
Congress (ко́нгрэс) конгресс, съезд
constituent ~ (консти́тюэнт ~)
учредительный съезд

extraordinary ~ (экстраóрдинари ~) внеочередной съезд
international ~ (интэрнáшэнал ~) международный конгресс
scientific ~ (сайэнти́фик ~) научный конгресс
to hold a ~ (ту холд а ~) проводить конгресс
world ~ (уóрлд ~) всемирный конгресс
~ of the Communist Party (~ оф θи ко́ммюнист па́рти) съезд компартии
Conjugal (ко́нджюгал) брачный
Conjunction (конджю́нкшн) соединение
Connect, to ~ with {e.g. by telephone} (коннэ́кт, ту ~ уиθ) связывать [perfective: связать]
Connection (коннэ́кшн) связь
Connivance (конна́йванс) попустительство
Conquer, to ~ (ко́нкуэр, ту ~) завоевать
Conqueror (ко́нкуэрор) завоеватель
Conquest (ко́нкуэст) завоевание
territorial ~ (тэррито́риал ~) территориальное завоевание
the Norman ~ (θи но́рман ~) завоевание Англии Норманнами {historical}
Conscription (конскри́пшн) призыв
military ~ (ми́литари ~) воинская повинность
~ into the army (~ и́нту θи а́рми) призыв в армию
Consecutive (консэ́кютив) последовательный
Consent (консэ́нт) согласие
common ~ (ко́ммон ~) общее согласие
direct ~ (дирэ́кт ~) прямое согласие
mutual ~ (мю́чуал ~) взаимное согласие
oral ~ (о́рал ~) устное согласие
reciprocal ~ (риси́прокал ~) обоюдное согласие
tacit ~ (та́сит ~) молчаливое согласие
to ~ to (ту ~ ту) соглашаться [perfective: согласиться]
verbal ~ (вэ́рбал ~) словесное согласие
voluntary ~ (во́лунтэри ~) добровольное согласие
written ~ (ри́ттэн ~) письменное согласие

Consequence (ко́нсэкуэнс) последствие, следствие
Conservation (консэрвэ́йшн) сохранение
Conservative (консэ́рватив) консервативный
Consider, to ~ (конси́дэр, ту ~) обсуждать, рассматривать [perfective: рассмотреть]
to ~ a complaint (ту ~ а компла́йнт) рассмотрение жалобы
Considerable (конси́дэрабл) значительный
Consideration (консидэрэ́йшн) вознаграждение, встречное исполнение, встречное удовлетворение, обсуждение, рассмотрение, удовлетворение
executory ~ (экзэ́кютори ~) встречное будущее удовлетворение
favorable ~ (фэ́йворабл ~) встречное благоприятное удовлетворение
insufficient ~ (инсуффи́шиэнт ~) встречное недостаточное удовлетворение
judicial ~ (джюди́шл ~) судебное рассмотрение
monetary ~ (мо́нэтари ~) встречное денежное удовлетворение
past ~ (паст ~) встречное предшествовавшее удовлетворение
substantive ~ of a case (су́бстантив ~ оф а кэйс) рассмотрение дела по существу
sufficient ~ (суффи́шиэнт ~) встречное достаточное удовлетворение
valid ~ (ва́лид ~) встречное действительное удовлетворение
valuable ~ (ва́люабл ~) встречное надлежащее удовлетворение
~ for licensing (~ фор ла́йсэнсинг) вознаграждение за выдачу лицензии
~ in general assembly (~ ин джэ́нэрал ассэ́мбли) обсуждение на общем собрании
~ in plenary assembly (~ ин плэ́нари ассэ́мбли) обсуждение на пленарном собрании
~ of an application (~ оф ан аппликэ́йшн) рассмотрение заявки
~ of a bill {in parliament, etc.} (~ оф а бил) обсуждение законопроекта

~ **of a case** (~ оф а кэйс)
рассмотрение дела
Consignee (консáйни́) адресат,
грузополучатель, консигнатор,
получатель, товарополучатель {of
goods}
Consignment (консáйнмэнт)
консигнация, консигнационный
{adj.}, партия, посылка
contract of ~ (кóнтракт оф ~)
договор консигнации
international ~ note
(интэрнáшэнал ~ нот)
международная накладная
non-returnable ~ (нон-ритýрнабл
~) безвозвратная консигнация
returnable ~ (ритýрнабл ~)
возвратная консигнация
term of ~ (тэрм оф ~) срок
консигнации
terms of ~ (тэрмз оф ~) условия
консигнации
to be on ~ (ту би он ~)
находиться на консигнации
to forward on ~ (ту фóруард он
~) отправлять на консигнацию
~ of valuables (~ оф вáлюаблс)
ценная посылка
~ note (~ нот) грузовая
накладная
Consignor (консайнóр) адресант,
грузоотправитель, консигнант,
отправитель
Consolidate, to ~ (консóлидэйт, ту
~) закреплять [**perfective:**
закрепить], консолидировать
Consolidated (консóлидэйтэд)
объединённый
Consolidation (консолидэ́йшн)
консолидация
Consortium (консóршиум) консорциум
to join a ~ (ту джойн а ~)
вступать в консорциум
to withdraw from a ~ (ту уиθдрáу
фром а ~) выходить из
консорциума
~ of banks (~ оф банкс)
банковский консорциум
Constitution (конститýшн)
конституция, состав
physical ~ (фи́зикал ~) сложение
Constructed (констрýктэд)
конструктивный
Construction (констрýкшн)
конструкция, строительство
stand ~ (стáнд ~) монтаж стенда

~ advisor (~ адвáйзор)
консультант по монтажу
~ bank (~ банк) стройбанк
~ schedule (~ скэ́джюл) график
проведения шефмонтажа
Consul (кóнсул) консул
~ General (~ джэ́нэрал)
генеральный консул
Consult, to ~ (консýлт, ту ~)
консультироваться, совещаться
Consultant (консýлтант)
консультант, консультационный
{adj.}, эксперт
chief ~ (чиф ~) главный
консультант
paid ~ (пэйд ~) платный
консультант
scientific ~ (сайэнти́фик ~)
научный консультант
technical ~ (тэ́кникал ~)
технический консультант
Consultation (консултэ́йшн)
консультация
legal ~ bureau (ли́гал ~ бю́ро)
юридическая консультация
technical ~ (тэ́кникал ~)
техническая консультация
Consultative (кóнсултэйтив)
консультативный, совещательный
Consume, to ~ (консýм, ту ~)
израсходовать, потреблять,
расходовать
Consumer (консýмэр) потребитель
domestic ~ (домэ́стик ~)
внутренний потребитель
retail ~ (ри́тэйл ~) розничный
потребитель
wholesale ~ (хóлсэйл ~) оптовый
потребитель
~ demand (~ димáнд) спрос на
товары массового потребления
Consummation (консуммэ́йшн)
заключение
~ of a marriage (~ оф а мэ́ррэдж)
заключение брака
Consumption (консýмпшн) потребление
average ~ (áвэрэдж ~) среднее
потребление
domestic ~ (домэ́стик ~)
внутреннее потребление
energy ~ (э́нэрджи ~)
энергоёмкость
final ~ (фáйнал ~) конечное
потребление
government ~ (гóвэрнмэнт ~)
государственное потребление

household ~ (ха́усхолд ~) домашнее потребление
individual ~ (индиви́дюал ~) индивидуальное потребление
mass ~ (мас ~) массовое потребление
metal ~ (мэ́тал ~) металлоёмкость
per capita ~ (пэр ка́пита ~) потребление на душу населения
personal ~ (пэ́рсонал ~) личное потребление
power ~ (по́уэр ~) потребляемая мощность
private ~ (пра́йват ~) частное потребление
productive ~ (прода́ктив ~) производственное потребление
total ~ (то́тал ~) общее потребление
Contact (ко́нтакт) контакт, общение
business ~s (би́знэс ~с) деловые контакты
close ~ (клос ~) тесный контакт
direct ~s (дирэ́кт ~с) непосредственные контакты
further ~s (фу́рθэр ~с) дальнейшие контакты
indirect ~s (индайрэ́кт ~с) косвенные контакты
initial ~s (ини́шл ~с) начальные контакты
personal ~s (пэ́рсонал ~с) личные контакты
to be in ~ (ту би ин ~) быть в контакте
to be in constant ~ (ту би ин ко́нстант ~) быть в постоянном контакте
to develop personal ~s (ту дивэ́лоп пэ́рсонал ~с) наладить личные контакты
to maintain ~ (ту мэйнтэ́йн ~) поддерживать контакт
to make ~ (ту мэйк ~) вступить в контакт
trade ~s (трэйд ~с) торговые контакты
unofficial ~s (аноффи́шл ~с) неофициальные контакты
Container (контэ́йнэр) контейнер, контейнерный {adj.}, тара, упаковка
aerosol ~ (э́йросол ~) аэрозольная упаковка
arctic ~ (а́рктик ~) арктическая тара

cardboard ~ (ка́рдборд ~) картонная тара, картонная упаковка
cargo ~ (ка́рго ~) грузовой контейнер
closed ~ (клозд ~) закрытая тара
demurrage of a ~ (димю́рradж оф а ~) простой контейнера
disposable ~ (диспо́забл ~) разовая тара
empty ~ (э́мпти ~) пустой контейнер, порожняя тара
fully-loaded ~ (фулли-ло́дэд ~) полногрузный контейнер
handling of ~s (ха́ндлинг оф ~с) обработка контейнеров
heavy tonnage ~ (хэ́ви то́ннадж ~) крупнотоннажный контейнер
high capacity ~ (хай капа́сити ~) большегрузный контейнер
large dimensioned ~ (лардж димэ́ншнд ~) крупногабаритная тара
marked ~ (маркд ~) маркированная тара
moisture-proof ~ (мо́йстюр-пруф ~) влагонепроницаемый контейнер
open ~ (о́пэн ~) открытая тара
packing ~ (па́ккинг ~) тара для упаковки
polyethylene ~ (полиэ́θилин ~) полиэтиленовая тара
polymer ~ (по́лимэр ~) полимерная тара
railway ~ (рэ́йлуэй ~) железнодорожный контейнер
refrigerated ~ (рифри́джэрэйтэд ~) контейнер-холодильник, охлаждаемый контейнер, рефрижераторный контейнер
reinforced ~ (риинфо́рсэд ~) усиленный контейнер
returnable ~ (риту́рнабл ~) инвентарная тара
reusable ~ (рию́забл ~) возвратная тара
sealed ~ (силд ~) опечатанный контейнер
strong ~ (стронг ~) прочная тара
suitable ~ (су́табл ~) пригодная тара
tank ~ (танк ~) контейнер-цистерна
to load a ~ (ту лод а ~) заполнять контейнер
to pick up a ~ (ту пик ап а ~) вывозить контейнер

to **unload** a ~ (ту анло́д а ~)
разгружать контейнер
to **unpack** a ~ (ту ана́к а ~)
распаковать контейнер
transit ~ (тра́нзит ~) транзитный
контейнер
universal ~ (юнивэ́рсал ~)
универсальный контейнер
unrefrigerated ~
(анрифри́джэрэйтэд ~)
неохлаждаемый контейнер
X-foot ~ (икс-фут ~) х-футовый
контейнер {where x denotes
footage, e.g. 20, 40}
~ **dimensions** (~ димэ́ншнз)
габариты тары
~ **leasing** (~ ли́синг) прокат
контейнеров
~ **trailer** (~ трэ́йлэр) контейнер-
прицеп
Containerization (контэйнэризэ́йшн)
контейнеризация
Containerized (контэ́йнэрайзд)
контейнеризованный
~ **vessel** (~ вэ́ссэл)
контейнеровоз
Contango (конта́нго) контанго
{futures exchange}, репорт
Contemplate, to ~ (ко́нтэмплэйт, ту
~) замышлять, предполагать
Content (ко́нтэнт) довольный {adj.},
содержание
gold ~ (голд ~) золотое
содержание
metal ~ **of a coin** (мэ́тал ~ оф а
койн) металлическое содержание
монеты
moisture ~ (мо́йстюр ~)
содержание влаги
specific metal ~ (спэси́фик мэ́тал
~) удельная металлоёмкость
table of ~s (тэ́йбл оф ~с)
оглавление
~ **of impurities** (~ оф импю́ритиз)
содержание примесей {of metals}
Contention (контэ́ншн) оспаривание
Contest (ко́нтэст) конкурс,
оспаривание
international ~ (интэрна́шэнал ~)
международный конкурс
to ~ (ту ~) оспаривать
to participate in a ~ (ту
парти́сипэйт ин а ~) участвовать
в конкурсе
~ **of right** (~ оф ра́йт)
оспаривание права

Contestant (контэ́стант) сторона в
споре
Contiguous (конти́гюос) смежный
Continental (контина́нтал)
континентальный
Contingent (конти́нджэнт)
контингент, непредвиденный {adj.}
individual ~s (индиви́дюал ~с)
индивидуальные контингенты
Continuance (конти́нюанс) отложение
~ **of a case** (~ оф а кэйс)
отложение дела
Continuation (континю́эйшн)
продолжение
~ **of the warranty period** (~ оф
θи уа́рранти пи́риод)
продолжительность гарантийного
срока
Continue, to ~ (конти́ню, ту ~)
откладывать [**perfective**: отложить]
Contraband (ко́нтрабанд)
контрабанда, контрабандный {adj.},
контрабандный товар
seizure of ~ (си́жюр оф ~)
изъятие контрабанды
Contract (ко́нтракт) договор,
договорный акт, контракт,
контрактный {adj.}, соглашение
acceptable ~ (аксэ́птабл ~)
приемлемый контракт
actual requirements of ~ (а́кчуал
рикуа́йрмэнтс оф ~) требования
договора
amendment to a ~ (амэ́ндмэнт ту а
~) поправка к контракту
amount of ~ (амо́унт оф ~) сумма
договора
annex to a ~ (а́ннэкс ту а ~)
приложение к контракту
annual ~s (а́ннюал ~с) ежегодные
контракты
annulment of a ~ (анну́лмэнт оф а
~) аннулирование контракта
appendix to a ~ (аппэ́ндикс ту а
~) дополнение к контракту
appropriate ~ (аппро́приат ~)
соответствующий контракт
article of a ~ (а́ртикл оф а ~)
статья контракта
as per the ~ (аз пэр θи ~)
согласно контракту
bound by ~ (бо́унд бай ~)
обязанный по контракту
bounds of a ~ (бо́ундс оф а ~)
пределы контракта
breach of a ~ (брич оф а ~)
нарушение контракта

buy-sell ~ (бай-сэл ~) контракт купли-продажи
charter-party ~ (ча́ртэр-па́рти ~) контракт на фрахтования судна
claim under a ~ (клэйм а́ндэр а ~) претензия по контракту
classified ~ (кла́ссифайд ~) засекреченный контракт
clause in a ~ (клауз ин а ~) оговорка в контракте
commercial ~ (комме́ршл ~) торговый контракт
commodity ~ (коммо́дити ~) контракт на товар
conditions of a ~ (конди́шнс оф а ~) условия контракта
details of a ~ (ди́тэйлз оф а ~) детали контракта
draft ~ (драфт ~) проект контракта
effective date of a ~ (иффэ́ктив дэйт оф а ~) дата вступления контракта в силу
essence of a ~ (э́ссэнс оф а ~) сущность контракта
exclusive ~ (эксклю́сив ~) исключающий контракт
executed ~ (э́ксэкютэд ~) заключённый контракт
fixed term ~ (фиксд тэрм ~) срочный контракт
form ~ (форм ~) типовой контракт
form of a ~ (форм оф а ~) образец контракта, форма контракта
formal ~ (фо́рмал ~) оформленный контракт
freight ~ (фрэйт ~) фрахтовый контракт
futures ~ (фю́чэрс ~) фьючерсный контракт
future ~s (фю́чэр ~с) будущие контракты
general conditions of a ~ (джэ́нэрал конди́шнс оф а ~) общие условия контракта
global ~ (гло́бал ~) глобальный контракт
government ~ (го́вэрнмэнт ~) правительственный контракт
in accordance with a ~ (ин акко́рданс уиθ а ~) в соответствии с контрактом
in performance of a ~ (ин пэрфо́рманс оф а ~) в исполнение контракта

incentive ~ (инсэ́нтив ~) поощрительный контракт
item of a ~ (а́йтэм оф а ~) пункт контракта
large ~ (лардж ~) большой контракт
long-term ~ (лонг-тэрм ~) долгосрочный контракт
modification to a ~ (модифике́йшн ту а ~) изменение к контракту
mutually profitable ~ (мю́чуалли про́фитабл ~) взаимовыгодный контракт
official ~ (оффи́шл ~) официальный контракт
open-ended ~ (о́пэн-э́ндэд ~) открытый контракт
operating ~ (о́пэрэйтинг ~) действующий контракт
original ~ (ори́джинал ~) первоначальный контракт
original of a ~ (ори́джинал оф а ~) оригинал контракта
outstanding ~ (оутста́ндинг ~) невыполненный контракт
paragraph of a ~ (па́раграф оф а ~) параграф контракта
performance of a ~ (пэрфо́рманс оф а ~) выполнение контракта, исполнение контракта
previous ~ (при́виос ~) предшествующий контракт
prime ~ (прайм ~) основной контракт
privately executed ~ (пра́йватли э́ксэкютэд ~) акт составленный домашним порядком {without witnesses or seal}
production sharing ~ (прода́кшн шэ́йринг ~) контракт "продакшн шеринг"
profitable ~ (про́фитабл ~) выгодный контракт
proposed ~ (пропо́зд ~) предлагаемый контракт
repudiation of a ~ (рэпюдиэ́йшн оф а ~) расторжение контракта
sales ~ (сэйлз ~) контракт на продажу
semi-turn-key ~ (сэ́ми-турн-ки ~) контракт "полу-под-ключ"
service ~ (сэ́рвис ~) контракт на обслуживание
short-term ~ (шорт-тэрм ~) краткосрочный контракт

signature date of a ~ (сигначэр дэйт оф а ~) дата подписания контракта
signing of a ~ (сайнинг оф а ~) подписание контракта
solid ~ (солид ~) солидный контракт {substantial}
spot ~ (спот ~) договор на реальный товар, контракт на реальный товар
stamp tax on a ~ (стамп такс он а ~) гербовой сбор с контракта
standardized ~ (стандардайзд ~) типовой контракт
subject of a ~ (сабджэкт оф а ~) предмет контракта
technical services ~ (тэкникал сэрвисэз ~) контракт на техническое обслуживание
termination of a ~ (тэрминэйшн оф а ~) аннулирование контракта
text of a ~ (тэкст оф а ~) текст контракта
to ~ (ту ~) контрактовать
to accept a ~ (ту аксэпт а ~) принимать контракт
to agree upon a ~ (ту агри апон а ~) соглашаться на контракт
to annul a ~ (ту аннул а ~) аннулировать контракт
to be awarded a ~ (ту би ауардэд а ~) получать контракт
to be in conflict with a ~ (ту би ин конфликт уиθ а ~) противоречить контракту
to breach a ~ (ту брич а ~) нарушать контракт
to bring a ~ into effect (ту бринг а ~ инту иффэкт) вводить контракт в силу
to conclude a ~ (ту конклюд а ~) заключать контракт
to confirm a ~ (ту конфирм а ~) подтверждать контракт
to conform to the terms of a ~ (ту конформ ту θи тэрмз оф а ~) отвечать условиям контракта
to consider a ~ (ту консидэр а ~) рассматривать контракт
to deliver under a ~ (ту дэливэр андэр а ~) поставлять по контракт
to draw up a ~ (ту драу ап а ~) составлять контракт
to execute a ~ (ту эксэкют а ~) оформлять контракт

to finance a ~ (ту файнанс а ~) финансировать контракт
to initial a ~ (ту инишл а ~) парафировать контракт
to make corrections to a ~ (ту мэйк коррэкшнз ту а ~) вносить поправки в контракт
to make modification to a ~ (ту мэйк модификэйшн ту а ~) вносить изменения в контракт
to negotiate a ~ (ту нэгошиэйт а ~) обсуждать контракт
to observe the terms of a ~ (ту обзэрв θи тэрмз оф а ~) соблюдать условия контракта
to perform under a ~ (ту пэрформ андэр а ~) выполнять контракт
to prepare a ~ (ту припэйр а ~) подготовить контракт
to renew a ~ (ту риню а ~) возобновлять контракт
to repudiate a ~ (ту рипюдиэйт а ~) расторгать контракт
to repudiate a ~ in toto (ту рипюдиэйт а ~ ин тото) расторгать контракт полностью
to rescind a ~ (ту рисинд а ~) кассировать контракт
to revise a ~ (ту ривайз а ~) пересматривать контракт
to sign a ~ (ту сайн а ~) подписывать контракт
to submit a ~ for consideration (ту субмит а ~ фор консидэрэйшн) представлять контракт на рассмотрение
to suspend a ~ (ту саспэнд а ~) прекращать действие контракта
total ~ value (тотал ~ валю) общая стоимость контракта
turn-key construction ~ (турн-ки конструкшн ~) контракт на строительство "под ключ"
under the conditions contemplated in a ~ (андэр θи кондишнс контэмплэйтэд ин а ~) на условиях, предусмотренных в контракте
under the conditions of a ~ (андэр θи кондишнс оф а ~) по условиям контракта
valid ~ (валид ~) действительный контракт
verbal ~ (вэрбал ~) словесный контракт
void ~ (войд ~) недействительный контракт

voidable ~ (во́йдабл ~) оспоримый контракт
work on a ~ basis (уо́рк он а ~ бэ́йсис) работа по трудовому договору
~ award (~ ауа́рд) выдача заказа
~ correspondence (~ коррэспо́ндэнс) переписка по контракту
~ currency (~ ку́ррэнси) валюта контракта
~ dispute (~ диспю́т) спор по контракту
~ interpretation (~ интэрпрэтэ́йшн) толкование контракта
~ obligations (~ облигэ́йшнз) обязательства по контракту
~ payments (~ пэ́ймэнтс) выплаты по контракту
~ price (~ прайс) цена по контракту
Contracting (ко́нтрактинг) контрактующий {party}
Contraction (контра́кшн) сокращение
~ of credit (~ оф крэ́дит) сокращение кредита
~ of paper money in circulation (~ оф пэ́йпэр мо́ни ин сиркюлэ́йшн) сокращение бумажных денег в обращении
~ of staff (~ оф стаф) сокращение штатов
Contractor (ко́нтрактор) подрядчик, подрядная фирма, фирма-исполнитель
engineering ~ (инджэни́ринг ~) фирма-подрядчик
~'s fee (~з фи) вознаграждение подрядчику
~'s organization (~з организэ́йшн) подрядная организация
Contractual (контра́кчуал) по договору
on a ~ basis (он а ~ бэ́йсис) на базе контракта
within ~ limits (уиθи́н ~ ли́митс) в пределах контракта
~ delivery (~ дэли́вэри) поставка по контракту
~ understanding (~ андэрста́ндинг) договорённость по контракту
Contradict, to ~ (контради́кт, ту ~) противоречить
Contradiction (контради́кшн) противоречивость, противоречие

statutory ~ (ста́тютори ~) противоречие в законах
Contradictorily (контради́кторили) противоречиво
Contradictory (контради́ктори) противоречивый
Contrary (ко́нтрари) в нарушении
to instructions (ту инстра́кшнс) в нарушении инструкций
Contribute (контри́бют) вкласть, вложить
to ~ to (ту ~ ту) вносить долю, содействовать
Contribution (контрибю́шн) взнос, вклад, долевой взнос, доля, доля участия
additional ~ (адди́шнал ~) дополнительный вклад
budget ~s (ба́джэт ~с) взносы в бюджет
charitable ~ (ча́ритабл ~) благотворительный вклад
counterpart ~ (ко́унтэрпарт ~) параллельный взнос
dollar denominated ~s (доллар диноминэ́йтэд ~с) долларовые вклады
founding ~ (фо́ундинг ~) взнос в уставный фонд
general average ~ (джэ́нэрал а́вэрэдж ~) долевой взнос по общей аварии
important ~ (импо́ртант ~) важный вклад
in ~ to the general average (ин ~ ту θи джэ́нэрал а́вэрэдж ~) в порядке возмещения расходов по общей аварии
lumpsum ~ (ла́мпсум ~) единовременный взнос
major ~ (мэ́йджор ~) крупный вклад
mandatory ~ (ма́ндатори ~) обязательный взнос
material ~ (мати́риал ~) натурально-вещественный вклад
monetary and material ~s (мо́нэтари энд мати́риал ~с) денежные и материальные взнос /ы

proportional ~ (пропо́ршнал ~) пропорциональный взнос
share of ~ (шэйр оф ~) паевой взнос
significant ~ (сигни́фикант ~) значительный вклад

to **make** a ~ (ту мэйк а ~) делать
взнос, делать вклад, производить
взнос
to **recall** a ~ (ту ри́калл а ~)
отзывать вклад
valuation of ~s (валюэ́йшн оф ~с)
оценка вкладов
voluntary ~ (во́лунтэри ~)
добровольный взнос, добровольный
вклад
~ **to the charter fund** (~ ту θи
ча́ртэр фунд) взнос в уставный
фонд
Contrivance (контра́йванс)
приспособление
Control (контро́л) контроль,
контрольный {*adj.*}, регулирование
   accounting ~ (акко́унтинг ~)
   бухгалтерский контроль
   administrative ~ (адми́нистрэйтив
   ~) административный контроль
   banking ~ (ба́нкинг ~) контроль
   над банковской деятельностью
   border ~ (бо́рдэр ~) пограничный
   контроль, пограничный режим
   budget ~ (ба́джэт ~) бюджетное
   регулирование
   commercial fishing ~ (комме́ршл
   фи́шинг ~) регулирование
   рыболовства
   consumer credit ~ (консу́мэр
   крэ́дит ~) контроль над
   потребительским кредитом
   counting ~ (ко́унтинг ~) счётный
   контроль
   credit ~ (крэ́дит ~) кредитный
   контроль, кредитное
   регулирование
   currency exchange ~ (ку́ррэнси
   эксчэ́йндж ~) валютное
   регулирование
   current ~ (ку́ррэнт ~) текущий
   контроль
   customs ~ (ка́стомз ~) таможенный
   контроль
   direct ~ (дирэ́кт ~)
   непосредственный контроль,
   прямой контроль
   environmental ~ (энвайронмэ́нтал
   ~) контроль над загрязнением
   окружающей среды
   export ~ (э́кспорт ~) экспортный
   контроль
   financial ~ (файна́ншл ~)
   финансовый контроль
   fiscal ~ (фи́скал ~) фискальный
   режим

   foreign exchange ~ (фо́рэн
   эксчэ́йндж ~) валютный контроль
   full ~ (фул ~) полный контроль
   health ~s (хэлθ ~с) санитарный
   режим
   immigration ~ (иммигрэ́йшн ~)
   иммиграционный режим
   internal ~ (интэ́рнал ~)
   внутренний контроль
   lack of ~ (лак оф ~) отсутствие
   контроля
   monetary ~ (мо́нэтари ~) денежное
   регулирование
   operational ~ (опэрэ́йшнал ~)
   оперативный контроль
   outside ~ (о́утсайд ~) внешний
   контроль
   passport ~ (па́сспорт ~)
   паспортный контроль
   periodic ~ (пирио́дик ~)
   периодический контроль
   personal ~ (пэ́рсонал ~) личный
   контроль
   popular ~ (по́пюлар ~) народный
   контроль
   price ~ (прайс ~) контроль цен
   price ~s (прайс ~с)
   регулирование цен
   quality ~ (куа́лити ~) контроль
   качества продукции
   quality ~ **method** (куа́лити ~
   мэ́θод) метод контроля качества
   quality ~ **schedule** (куа́лити ~
   скэ́джюл) таблица контроля
   качества
   random ~ (ра́ндом ~) выборочный
   контроль
   reasonable ~ (ри́зонабл ~)
   разумный контроль
   regular ~ (рэ́гюлар ~) регулярный
   контроль
   rent ~ (рэнт ~) регулирование
   квартирной платы
   sequential ~ (сикуэ́ншл ~)
   последовательный контроль
   social ~ (сошл ~) общественный
   контроль
   special ~ (спэшл ~) специальный
   контроль
   standard ~ (ста́ндард ~)
   нормальный контроль
   state ~ (стэйт ~)
   государственный контроль
   strict ~ (стрикт ~) жёсткий
   контроль, строгий контроль
   technical ~ (тэ́кникал ~)
   технический контроль

to ~ (ту ~) регулировать
to **assure** ~ (ту ашу́р ~)
обеспечить контроль
to **establish** ~ (ту эста́блиш ~)
устанавливать контроль
to **exercise** ~ (ту э́ксэрсайз ~)
осуществлять контроль
to **maintain** ~ (ту мэйнтэ́йн ~)
сохранять контроль
to **place under** ~ (ту плэйс а́ндэр
~) передавать под контроль,
ставить под контроль
to **re-establish** ~ (ту ри-
эста́блиш ~) восстанавливать
контроль
to **remove** ~ (ту риму́в ~)
отменять контроль
to **retain** ~ (ту ритэ́йн ~)
сохранять контроль
to **strengthen** ~ (ту стрэ́нгθэн ~)
усиливать контроль
uniform ~ (ю́ниформ ~)
единообразный контроль
uninterrupted ~ (анинтэрру́птэд
~) непрерывный контроль
wage and price ~ (уэ́йдж энд
прайс ~) контроль над ценами и
заработной платой
workers' ~ (уо́ркэрз ~) рабочий
контроль
~ **authority** (~ аθо́рити) орган
контроля
~ **of exchange** (~ оф эксчэ́йндж)
регулирование валюты
Controller (контро́ллэр)
бухгалтер-аналитик
Controversial (контрове́рсиал)
спорный
Controversy (ко́нтроверси) спор
constitutional ~ (конститу́шнал
~) конституционный спор
legal ~ (ли́гал ~) правовой спор
Contumely (конту́мэли) оскорбление
словом
Convene, to ~ (конви́н, ту ~)
собирать [**perfective:** собрать],
созывать [**perfective:** созвать]
Convenient (конви́ниэнт) удобный
Convention (конвэ́ншн) конвенция,
конвенционный {*adj.*}, соглашение
consular ~ (ко́нсюлар ~)
консульская конвенция
customs ~ (ка́стомз ~) таможенная
конвенция, таможенное соглашение
international ~ (интэрна́шэнал ~)
международная конвенция

to conclude a ~ (ту конклю́д а ~)
заключать конвенцию
to ratify a ~ (ту ра́тифай а ~)
ратифицировать конвенцию
to sign a ~ (ту сайн а ~)
подписывать конвенцию
Conventional (конвэ́ншнал)
конвенционный, нормальный, обычный
Conversation (конэрсэ́йшн) разговор
Conversion (конвэ́ржн) акт
незаконного присвоения
{misappropriation}, конверсия,
обмен, перерасчёт
applicable ~ (аппли́кабл ~)
соответствующий обмен
gold ~ (голд ~) обмен золота
~ **of currency** (~ оф ку́ррэнси)
обмен валюты
~ **of a loan** (~ оф а лон)
конверсия займа
~ **of securities** (~ оф сэкю́ритиз)
реализация ценных бумаг
Convert, to ~ (конвэ́рт, ту ~)
конвертировать, обменивать
Convertibility (конвэртиби́лити)
конвертируемость, обратимость
free ~ (фри ~) свободная
обратимость
limited ~ (ли́митэд ~)
ограниченная обратимость
of limited ~ (оф ли́митэд ~)
ограниченно обратимый
partial ~ (паршл ~) частичная
обратимость
~ **of currency** (~ оф ку́ррэнси)
конвертируемость валюты
Convertible (конвэ́ртибл)
конвертируемый, обмениваемый,
обратимый
freely ~ (фри́ли ~) свободно
конвертируемый, свободно
обратимый
Conveyance (конвэ́йянс) доставка,
купчая, передаточный акт, передача,
передвижение, провоз, транспорт
air ~ (эйр ~) воздушное
передвижение
deed of ~ (дид оф ~) акт о
передаче правового титула
means of ~ (минз оф ~) транспорт
~ **by inheritance** (~ бай
инхэ́ританс) передача по
наследству
Convict (ко́нвикт) заключённый,
осуждённый
to ~ (ту ~) осуждать
Convicted (конви́ктэд) осуждённый

Conviction (конви́кшн) осуждение, судимость ~s судимость
    criminal ~ (кри́минал ~) уголовное решение
    to expunge a ~ (ту экспу́ндж а ~) снять судимость
    ~ by the criminal court (~ бай θи кри́минал ко́урт) осуждение уголовным судом
    ~ by default (~ бай дифа́лт) заочное осуждение
Convocation (конвокэ́йшн) Созыв
Convoke, to ~ (конво́к, ту ~) созывать [**perfective:** созвать]
Convoy (ко́нвой) конвой
    truck ~ (трак ~) автопоезд
Cooperate, to ~ (коо́пэрэйт, ту ~) взаимодействовать, кооперировать
Cooperation (коопэрэ́йшн) взаимодействие, кооперация, содействие, сотрудничество
    close ~ (клос ~) тесное взаимодействие
    contractual ~ (контра́кчуал ~) сотрудничество на подрядных условиях
    economic ~ (эконо́мик ~) хозяйственное взаимодействие, экономическое сотрудничество
    financial ~ (файна́ншл ~) финансовое сотрудничество
    foreign economic ~ (фо́рэн эконо́мик ~) внешнеэкономическое сотрудничество
    integrated ~ (и́нтэгрэйтэд ~) комплексное сотрудничество
    international ~ (интэрна́шэнал ~) международное сотрудничество
    legal ~ (ли́гал ~) правовое сотрудничество
    ~ between nations (~ бету́н нэ́йшнз) взаимодействие между странами
    ~ in the judicial sphere (~ ин θи джуди́шл сфир) сотрудничество в судебной области
Cooperative (коо́пэратив) кооператив, кооперативный {adj.}, кооперированный {adj.}
    agricultural marketing ~ (агрику́лчурал ма́ркэтинг ~) сельскохозяйственная артель
    consumer's ~ (консу́мэрз ~) потребительский кооператив
    consumer ~ society (консу́мэр ~ соса́йэти) потребительская кооперация

    economic ~ (эконо́мик ~) экономическая кооперация
    full-scale ~ (фул-скэйл ~) крупномасштабная кооперация
    international ~ (интэрна́шэнал ~) международная кооперация
    marketing ~ (ма́ркэтинг ~) артель
    participant in a ~ (парти́сипант ин а ~) кооперант
    production ~ (прода́кшн ~) производственный кооператив
Coordinate, to ~ (коо́рдинэйт, ту ~) координировать, согласовать
Coordination (координэ́йшн) координация, координационный {adj.}
    exchange rate ~ (эксчэ́йндж рэйт ~) валютное сотрудничество
    export sales ~ (э́кспорт сэйлз ~) координация запродаж
    lack of ~ (лак оф ~) отсутствие координации, разнобой
    overall ~ (овэра́л ~) общая координация
    preliminary ~ (прили́минэри ~) предварительное согласование
Coordinator (коо́рдинэйтор) координатор
    project ~ (про́джэкт ~) проектный координатор
Cop/y (ко́пи) копия, номер, экземпляр
    advance ~ (адва́нс ~) сигнальный экземпляр
    advertising ~ (а́двэртайзинг ~) рекламный текст
    as per enclosed ~ (аз пэр энкло́зд ~) согласно прилагаемой копии
    attestation of a ~ (аттэстэ́йшн оф а ~) засвидетельствование копии
    attested ~ (атт́э́стэд ~) засвидетельствованная копия
    carbon ~ (ка́рбон ~) копия через копирку
    complimentary ~ (комплимэ́нтари ~) рекламный экземпляр
    control ~ (контро́л ~) контрольный экземпляр
    enclosed ~ (энкло́зд ~) прилагаемая копия
    exact ~ (экза́кт ~) точная копия
    executed ~ (э́ксэкютэд ~) оформленный экземпляр
    fair ~ (фэйр ~) чистовая копия
    first ~ (фэрст ~) первый экземпляр

fresh ~ (фрэш ~) новая копия
fully executed ~/ies (фу́лли
эксэкютэд ~из) полностью
оформленные копии
identical ~ (айдэ́нтикал ~)
тождественный экземпляр
in five ~/ies (ин файв ~из) в
пяти экземплярах
in four ~/ies (ин фо́ур ~из) в
четырёх экземплярах
last ~ (ласт ~) последний
экземпляр
legalized ~ (ли́галайзд ~)
легализованная копия
marked ~ (маркд ~) отмеченный
экземпляр
multiple ~/ies (му́лтипл ~из)
многочисленные копии
negotiable ~ (нэго́шабл ~)
действительный экземпляр
non-negotiable ~ (нон-нэго́шабл
~) недействительный экземпляр
number of ~/ies (ну́мбэр оф ~из)
количество экземпляров
official ~ (оффи́шл ~)
официальная копия
photostatic ~ (фотоста́тик ~)
фотостатическая копия
primary ~ (пра́ймари ~) основной
экземпляр
printed ~ (при́нтэд ~) печатная
копия
red-lined ~ (рэд-лайнд ~)
отмеченная копия
second ~ (сэ́конд ~) второй
экземпляр
set of ~/ies (сэт оф ~из)
комплект экземпляров
single ~ (сингл ~) единственный
экземпляр
to append a ~ (ту аппэ́нд а ~)
приложить копию
to certify a ~ (ту сэ́ртифай а ~)
заверить копию
to make a ~ (ту мэйк а ~) делать
копию
to take a ~ (ту тэйк а ~)
снимать копию
true ~ (тру ~) верная копия
unique ~ (юни́к ~) уникальный
экземпляр
xerox ~ (зи́рокс ~) ксероксная
копия
~ of a bill (~ оф а бил) копия
векселя, экземпляр векселя

~ of a bill of lading (~ оф а
бил оф лэ́йдинг) экземпляр
коносамента
~ of a document (~ оф а
до́кюмэнт) копия документа,
экземпляр документа
~ of an invoice (~ оф ан и́нвойс)
копия счёта-фактуры
~ of a letter (~ оф а лэ́ттэр)
копия письма
~ of minutes of a meeting (~ оф
ми́нутс оф а ми́тинг) копия
протокола собрания
~ of a note (~ оф а нот) копия
векселя
~ of a patent (~ оф а па́тэнт)
копия патента
~ of a shipped bill of lading (~
оф а шиппд бил оф лэ́йдинг)
судовой экземпляр коносамента
Copyright (ко́пирайт) авторское
право
proprietary ~ (пропра́йэтари ~)
имущественные авторские права
Cord (корд) верёвка
packing ~ (па́ккинг ~)
шнуровочная верёвка
pendant ~ (пэ́ндант ~) верёвка
для подвески
Corner (ко́рнэр) угол, уголок
to ~ the market (ту ~ θи ма́ркэт)
скупать
one who ~s the market (уа́н ху ~с
θи ма́ркэт) скупщик
Cornering (ко́рнэринг) скупка
~ the market (~ θи ма́ркэт)
скупка
Corporate (ко́рпорат) корпоративный
~ income tax (~ и́нком такс)
налог с доходов корпораций,
налог с доходов акционерных
компаний
~ seal (~ сил) печать корпорации
~ secretary (~ сэ́крэтари)
секретарь корпорации
~ tax (~ такс) налог на
корпорацию
Corporation (корпорэ́йшн)
корпорация, объединение
board of directors of a ~ (борд
оф дирэ́кторз оф а ~) дирекция
корпорации
charter of a ~ (ча́ртэр оф а ~)
устав корпорации
foreign ~ (фо́рэн ~) иностранная
корпорация

industrial ~ (инду́стриал ~)
промышленная корпорация
multinational ~ (мултина́шэнал ~)
многонациональная корпорация
privately-held ~ (пра́йватли-хэлд
~) частная корпорация
public ~ (па́блик ~)
государственная корпорация
sole ~ (сол ~) единоличная
корпорация
stock ~ (сток ~) акционерская
корпорация
transnational ~ (трансна́шнал ~)
транснациональная корпорация
Corps (кор) корпус
consular ~ (ко́нсюлар ~)
консульская служба
diplomatic ~ (диплома́тик ~)
атташат, дипломатическая служба
Corpus (ко́рпус) объект, состав
~ delicti (~ дэли́ктай) объект
преступления, состав
преступления
Correct (коррэ́кт) правильный
Correcting (коррэ́ктинг)
корректирующий
Correction (коррэ́кшн)
корректировка, поправка
Corrective (коррэ́ктив) корректив
~ amendments (~ амэ́ндмэнтс)
коррективы
Correctly (коррэ́ктли) правильно,
точно
Correctness (коррэ́ктнэс)
правильность, точность
Correlation (коррэлэ́йшн)
соотношение
Correlative (коррэ́латив)
корреляционный
Correspond, to ~ (коррэспо́нд, ту ~)
соответствовать
Correspondence (коррэспо́ндэнс)
корреспонденция, переписка,
соответствие
by ~ (бай ~) заочно, заочный
{course, pleading, etc.}
commercial ~ (коммэ́ршл ~)
коммерческая корреспонденция,
коммерческая переписка
exchange of ~ (эксчэ́йндж оф ~)
обмен корреспонденцией
incoming ~ (и́нкоминг ~) входящая
корреспонденция
official ~ (оффи́шл ~)
официальная переписка
outgoing ~ (оутго́инг ~)
исходящая корреспонденция

postal ~ (по́стал ~) почтовая
корреспонденция
preliminary ~ (прили́минэри ~)
предварительная корреспонденция
to review ~ (ту ривю́ ~)
перлюстировать
Correspondent (коррэспо́ндэнт)
корреспондент, корреспондентский
{adj.}
foreign ~ (фо́рэн ~) иностранный
корреспондент
newspaper ~ (нью́зпэйпэр ~)
корреспондент газеты
Corresponding (коррэспо́ндинг)
ведущий переписку {party to
correspondence}, соответствующий
Corrupt (корру́пт) подкурной,
продажный
to ~ (ту ~) совратить
Corrupter (корру́птэр) совратитель
Corruption (корру́пшн) коррупция
~ of minors (~ оф ма́йнорс)
посягательство на моральное
развитие малолетних
Cosmetics (козмэ́тикс) косметические
товары
Cost (кост) затрата, стоимость
actual ~ (а́кчуал ~)
действительная стоимость,
фактическая стоимость
actual ~s (а́кчуал ~с)
фактические затраты
average ~ (а́вэрэдж ~) средняя
стоимость
book ~ (бук ~) балансовая
стоимость
capital ~s (ка́питал ~с)
капитальные затраты
carriage ~s (ка́рриадж ~с)
транспортные издержки
conditional ~ (конди́шнал ~)
условная стоимость
court ~s (ко́урт ~с) издержки
ведения судебного дела, судебные
расходы
current ~s (ку́ррэнт ~с) текущие
издержки
direct ~s (дирэ́кт ~с) прямые
затраты
distribution ~s (дистрибю́шн ~с)
издержки обращения
estimated ~ (эстиматд ~) сметная
стоимость
export ~s (э́кспорт ~с)
экспортные расходы
final ~ (фа́йнал ~) конечная
стоимость

fixed ~s (фиксд ~с) постоянные издержки

freight forwarding ~s (фрэйт фо́руардинг ~с) экспедиторские расходы

full ~ (фул ~) полная стоимость

initial ~s (ини́шл ~с) начальные затраты

legal ~s and expenses (ли́гал ~с энд экспэ́нсэз) судебные пошлины

net ~ (нэт ~) чистая стоимость

operating ~s (о́пэрэйтинг ~с) эксплуатационные затраты, эксплуатационные расходы

original ~ (ори́джинал ~) первоначальная стоимость

postage ~s (по́стадж ~с) почтовые расходы

prime ~ (прайм ~) цена по себестоимости

probable ~ (про́бабл ~) полагаемая стоимость

productive ~s (прода́ктив ~с) производственные затраты

representation ~s (рэприсэнтэ́йшн ~с) представительские расходы

salvage ~ (са́лвэдж ~) ликвидационная стоимость

seasonal ~s (си́зонал ~с) сезонные затраты

storage ~s (сто́радж ~с) складские расходы

supplementary ~s (сапплэмэ́нтари ~с) добавочные расходы

to recoup ~s (ту рику́ ~с) возместить издержки

total ~s (то́тал ~с) общие издержки

transportation ~s (транспортэ́йшн ~с) транспортные расходы

~ accounting (~ акко́унтинг) хозяйственный расчёт

~s in a legal action (~с ин а ли́гал акшн) расходы по делу

~ of weight (~ оф уэйт) весовая стоимость

~ saving (~ сэ́йвинг) экономичный

Cottage (ко́ттадж) кустарный

~ industry (~ и́ндустри) кустарная промышленность

Council (ко́унсил) совет, совещание

administrative ~ (админи́стрэйтив ~) административный совет

city ~ (си́ти ~) городской совет

consultative ~ (ко́нсултэ́йтив ~) консультативный совет

defense ~ (дифэ́нс ~) совет обороны

European ~ (юропи́ан ~) европейский совет

executive ~ (экзэ́кютив ~) исполнительный совет

family ~ (фа́мили ~) семейный совет

grand ~ (гранд ~) большой совет

Krai ~ (край ~) краевой совет

military ~ (ми́литари ~) военный совет

municipal ~ (мюни́сипал ~) муниципальный совет

national ~ (на́шэнал ~) национальный совет

parliamentary ~ (парламэ́нтари ~) парламентский совет

people's ~ (пиплз ~) народный совет

permanent ~ (пэ́рманэнт ~) постоянный совет

revolutionary ~ (рэволю́шнари ~) революционный совет

sanitary ~ (са́нитари ~) санитарный совет

security ~ (сэкю́рити ~) совет безопасности

social ~ (сошл ~) социальный совет

state ~ (стэйт ~) государственный совет

supervisory ~ (супэрва́йзори ~) наблюдательный совет

workers' ~ (уо́ркэрз ~) рабочий совет

~ of Foreign Ministers (~ оф фо́рэн ми́нистэрс) совет министров иностранных дел

~ of Ministers (~ оф ми́нистэрс) совет министров

~ of People's Commissars (~ оф пиплз ко́ммиссарз) совет народных комиссаров {Soviet historical predecessor to Council of Ministers}

~ of regents (~ оф ри́джэнтс) регентский совет

Councillor (ко́унсилор) советник

city ~ (си́ти ~) городской советник

municipal ~ (мюни́сипал ~) муниципальный советник

state ~ (стэйт ~) государственный советник

Counsel (ко́унэл) совет, юрист

in-house ~ (ин-хаус ~) юрисконсульт
outside ~ (óутсайд ~) внешний юрисконсульт
Counsellor (кóунсэлор) советник
general patent ~ (джэ́нэрал пáтэнт ~) генеральный юрисконсульт по патентам
Count (кóунт) подсчет, пункт иска {of complaint, indictment}
improper vote ~ (импрóпэр вот ~) неправильный подсчет голосов
to ~ (ту ~) насчитывать
vote ~ (вот ~) подсчет голосов
Counter (кóунтэр) встречный, счётчик
to advance a ~ claim (ту адвáнс а ~ клэйм) выдвигать контртребование
to contest a ~ claim (ту контэ́ст а ~ клэйм) оспаривать контртребование
to file a ~ claim (ту файл а ~ клэйм) предъявлять контртребование
to reject a ~ claim (ту риджэ́кт а ~ клэйм) отвергать контртребование
vote ~ (вот ~) счётчик голосов
~ balance (~ бáланс) противовес
~ claim (~ клэйм) контртребование
~ offer (~ óффэр) контрофферта
~ proposal (~ пропóзал) контрпредложение
Counteraction (коунтэрáкшн) противодействие
Counterfeit (кóунтэрфит) подделка
to ~ (ту ~) подделывать
Counterfeiter (кóунтэрфитэр) подделыватель
Counterfeiting (кóунтэрфитинг) изготовление поддельных денег
~ of coins (~ оф койнс) подделка монеты
~ of currency (~ оф кýррэнси) подделка денежных знаков
Counterpart (кóунтэрпарт) контрагент {party}, копия
~ of a contract (~ оф а кóнтракт) копия контракта
Countersign (кóунтэрсайн) пароль
to ~ (ту ~) контрассигновать, скрепить подписью
Countersignatory (коунтэрси́гнатори) контрассигнант

Countersignature (коунтэрси́гначэр) контрассигнация, скрепа
Countersigning (кóунтэрсайнинг) скрепление
Countersuit (кóунтэрсут) встречный иск
notice of ~ (нóтис оф ~) встречное исковое заявление
Country (кýнтри) господство, государство, страна
agrarian ~ (аграриан ~) аграрная страна
agricultural ~ (агрикýлчурал ~) сельскохозяйственная страна
belligerent ~ (бэлли́джэрэнт ~) воюющая страна
conquered ~ (кóнкуэрд ~) побеждённая страна
developing ~ (дивэ́лопинг ~) развивающая страна
distant ~ (ди́стант ~) отдалённая страна
enemy ~ (э́нэми ~) враждебная страна
exporting ~ (э́кспортинг ~) экспортирующая страна
importing ~ (и́мпортинг ~) импортирующая страна
industrialized ~ (индýстриалайзд ~) индустриализованная страна
maritime ~ (мáритайм ~) морская страна
neighboring ~ (нэ́йборинг ~) соседняя страна
neutral ~ (нýтрал ~) нейтральная страна
occupied ~ (óккупайд ~) оккупированная страна
sovereign ~ (сóвэрн ~) суверенная страна
third ~ (θирд ~) третья страна
transit ~ (трáнзит ~) транзитная страна
underdeveloped ~ (андэрдивэ́лопд ~) слаборазвитая страна
Coup d'état (ку дэтá) государственный переворот
Coupon (кýпон) абонементный талон, купон, ордер на покупку, талон
detachable ~ (дитáчабл ~) отрывной талон
to detach a ~ (ту дитáч а ~) отрывать купон, отрывать талоны
Courier (кýриэр) курьер, нарочный
diplomatic ~ (дипломáтик ~) дипломатический курьер
Course (корс) курс, путь, русло

completion of a ~ {training, university} (комплйшн оф а ~) завершение курса
consistent ~ (консйстэнт ~) последовательный курс
deviation of a vessel from ~ (дивиэйшн оф а вэссэл фром ~) отклонение судна от курса
inland water ~ (йнланд уатэр ~) внутренний водный путь
required ~ (рикуайрд ~) обязательный курс
ship's ~ (шипс ~) курс корабля
short ~ {of study} (шорт ~ {оф студи}) сокращённый курс
special ~ {of study} (спэшл ~ {оф студи}) спец- курс
to complete a ~ (ту комплйт а ~) заканчивать курс
to deviate from ~ (ту дйвиэйт фром ~) отклоняться от курса
water ~ (уатэр ~) водный путь
Court (коурт) суд
administrative ~ (админйстрэйтив ~) административный суд
arbitral ~ (арбитрал ~) арбитражный суд
arbitration ~ (арбитрэйшн ~) арбитражная палата
circuit ~ (сйркут ~) окружной суд
civil ~ (сйвил ~) гражданский суд, палата по гражданским делам
commercial ~ (коммэршл ~) коммерческий суд
competent ~ (кóмпэтэнт ~) компетентный суд
constitutional ~ (конститушнал ~) конституционный суд
criminal ~ (крйминал ~) уголовный суд
ecclesiastical ~ (экклизиастикал ~) духовный суд
federal ~ (фэдэрал ~) федеральный суд
federal constitutional ~ (фэдэрал конститушнал ~) федеральный конституционный суд
inferior ~ (инфйриор ~) нижестоящий суд
international ~ (интэрнашэнал ~) международный суд
international arbitration ~ (интэрнашэнал арбитрэйшн ~) международный арбитражный суд
judicial ~ (джюдйшл ~) палата по судебным делам

juvenile ~ (джювэнайл ~) детский суд
krai ~ (край ~) краевой суд
law ~ (лау ~) общий суд
local ~ (лóкал ~) местный суд
maritime ~ (маритайм ~) морской суд
municipal ~ (мюнйсипал ~) городской суд
oblast ~ (óбласт ~) областной суд
okrug ~ (óкруг ~) окружной суд
patent ~ (патэнт ~) патентный суд
people's ~ (пиплз ~) народный суд
permanent ~ of International Justice (пэрманэнт ~ оф интэрнашэнал джастис) постоянная палата международного правосудия
raion ~ (район ~) районный суд
regional ~ (рйджонал ~) областной суд, районный суд
revolutionary ~ (рэволюшнари ~) революционный суд
special ~ (спэшл ~) специальный суд
superior ~ (супйриор ~) вышестоящий суд
supreme ~ (супрйм ~) верховный суд
supreme ~ of an autonomous republic (супрйм ~ оф ан аутóномос рипаблик) верховный суд автономной республики
to apply to ~ (ту апплай ту ~) обратиться в суд
to make an appearance in ~ (ту мэйк ан аппйранс ин ~) явиться в суд
upper ~ (уппэр ~) высший суд
world ~ (уóрлд ~) мировой суд
~ martial (~ маршл) военный суд
~ of appeals (~ оф аппйлс) апелляционный суд, апелляционная палата
~ of cassation (~ оф кассэйшн) кассационный суд
~ of customary law (~ оф кастомари лау) суд обычного права
~ of first instance (~ оф фэрст йнстанс) суд первой инстанции
~ of higher instance (~ оф хайэр йнстанс) суд высшей инстанции
~ of law (~ оф лау) суд

~ of second instance (~ оф сэконд инстанс) суд второй инстанции
Courtage (куртадж) куртаж {brokerage fee}
Courtroom (коуртрум) зал суда
Cousin (коузин) двоюродный брат {male}, двоюродная сестра {female}
Cover (ковэр) конверт, крышка, обёртка
   colorful ~ (колорфул ~) красочная обёртка
   degree of ~ (дигри оф ~) степень обеспечения
   metal ~ (мэтал ~) металлическая крышка
   patent ~ (патэнт ~) патентное обеспечение
   to ~ (ту ~) обеспечивать
   under separate ~ (андэр сэпарат ~) в отдельном конверте, в отдельном пакете, в отдельной упаковке
   under the same ~ (андэр θи сэйм ~) в том же конверте
   waterproof ~ (уатэрпруф ~) водонепроницаемый конверт
   ~ policy (~ полиси) ковернот
Cover note (ковэр нот) ковернот
   to issue a ~ (ту ишю а ~) выписывать ковернот
Coverage (ковэрадж) обеспечение, покрытие
   insurance ~ (иншюранс ~) страховое обеспечение
   ~ of risks (~ оф рискс) покрытие рисков
Covering (ковэринг) покрытие, чехол
   external ~ (экстэрнал ~) внешний чехол
   plastic ~ (пластик ~) плёночный чехол
   tarp ~ (тарп ~) брезентовая упаковка
   ~ of expenditures (~ оф экспэндичюрз) покрытие затрат
   ~ of expenses (~ оф экспэнсэз) покрытие издержек
Crack (крак) трещина
   to ~ (ту ~) трескаться
Craft (крафт) ремесленный, судно
   harbor ~ (харбор ~) плавучее портовое средство
   pilot ~ (пайлот ~) лоцманский бот
   small ~ {marine} (смал ~ {марин}) бот

unmanned ~ (анмаанд ~) бэрбоут
Craftsman (крафтсман) мастер, ремесленник
Craftsmanship (крафтсманшип) мастерство, ремесленничество
Crane (крэйн) кран
   construction ~ (констру́кшн ~) монтажный кран
   container ~ (контэйнэр ~) контейнерный кран
   deck-mounted ~ (дэк-моунтэд ~) палубный кран
   dock ~ (док ~) доковый кран
   floating ~ (флоотинг ~) плавучий кран
   gantry ~ (гантри ~) портальный кран
   hoisting ~ (хойстинг ~) подъёмный кран
   lifting ~ (лифтинг ~) грузоподъёмный кран
   mobile ~ (мобил ~) передвижной кран
   shore ~ (шор ~) береговой кран
   wrecking ~ (рэккинг ~) аварийный кран
Crash (краш) крушение
   stock market ~ (сток маркэт ~) крах фондовой биржи
Crate (крэйт) клеть, решётчатая тара, упаковочная корзинка
   skeleton ~ (скэлэтон ~) решётчатый ящик
   wooden ~ (уудэн ~) деревянная клеть
   ~ costs (~ костс) расходы по упаковке в ящики
Crating (крэйтинг) упаковка в ящики
   cost of ~ (кост оф ~) стоимость упаковки в ящики
Create, to ~ (криэйт, ту ~) создавать
Creation (криэйшн) создание
   ~ of reserves (~ оф рисэрвс) создание резервов
Creator (криэйтор) созидатель
Credentials (крэдэншлз) верительные грамоты, удостоверение
   personal ~ (пэрсонал ~) удостоверение личности
   professional ~ (профэшнал ~) удостоверение для специалистов
   proper ~ (пропэр ~) надлежащее удостоверение личности
   to present ~ (ту прэзэнт ~) представить удостоверение личности

Credibility (крэдибилити) доверие
  to impair ~ (ту импэйр ~)
  поколебать доверие
Credit (крэдит) кредит, кредитный
{*adj.*}, кредитовый {*adj.*}
  abuse of ~ (абюс оф ~)
  злоупотребление кредитом
  acceptance ~ (аксэптанс ~)
  акцептный кредит
  against ~ (агэнст ~) в счёт
  кредита
  allocation of bank ~s (алокэйшн
  оф банк ~с) распределение
  банковских кредитов
  amount of ~ (амоунт оф ~) сумма
  кредита
  back-to-back ~ (бак-ту-бак ~)
  компенсационный кредит
  blocked ~ (блокд ~)
  блокированный кредит
  cash ~ (каш ~) наличный кредит
  cheap ~ {low interest rate} (чип
  ~) дешёвый кредит
  collateral ~ (коллатэрал ~)
  ломбардный кредит
  commercial ~ (коммэршл ~)
  коммерческий кредит
  commodity ~ (коммодити ~)
  подтоварный кредит, товарный
  кредит
  company ~ (компани ~) фирменный
  кредит
  consumer ~ (консумэр ~)
  потребительский кредит
  cost of ~ (кост оф ~) стоимость
  кредита
  currency of ~ (куррэнси оф ~)
  валюта кредита
  current account ~ (куррэнт
  аккоунт ~) контокоррентный
  кредит
  direct ~ (дирэкт ~) прямой
  кредит
  discount ~ (дискоунт ~)
  дисконтный кредит
  exhausted ~ (экзаустэд ~)
  исчерпанный кредит
  expansion of ~ (экспаншн оф ~)
  расширение кредита
  export ~ (экспорт ~) экспортный
  кредит
  extended ~ (экстэндэд ~)
  длительный кредит
  extent of ~ (экстэнт оф ~)
  размер кредита
  foreign ~ (форэн ~) иностранный
  кредит

  foreign exchange ~ (форэн
  эксчэйндж ~) валютный кредит
  foreign trade ~ (форэн трэйд ~)
  внешнеторговый кредит
  frozen ~ (фрозэн ~) замороженный
  кредит
  government ~ (говэрнмэнт ~)
  государственный кредит
  guarantee ~ (гяранти ~)
  гарантийный кредит
  guarantee of ~ (гяранти оф ~)
  гарантия кредита
  initial ~ (инишл ~) начальный
  кредит
  interest-free ~ (интэрэст-фри ~)
  беспроцентный кредит
  interest rates for ~ (интэрэст
  рэйтс фор ~) процентные ставки
  по кредитам
  intermediate term ~ (интэрмидиат
  тэрм ~) среднесрочный кредит
  international ~ (интэрнашэнал ~)
  международный кредит
  interstate ~ (интэрстэйт ~)
  межгосударственный кредит
  investment ~ (инвэстмэнт ~)
  инвестиционный кредит
  issuance of ~ (ишюанс оф ~)
  выдача кредита
  lack of ~ (лак оф ~) недостаток
  кредита
  line of ~ (лайн оф ~) кредитный
  лимит
  long term ~ (лонг тэрм ~)
  долгосрочный кредит
  margin of ~ (марджин оф ~) маржа
  по кредиту
  marginal ~ (марджинал ~)
  предельный кредит
  maximum ~ (максимум ~)
  максимальный кредит
  mercantile ~ (мэркантайл ~)
  торговый кредит
  mixed ~ (миксд ~) смешанный
  кредит
  monetary ~ (монэтари ~) денежный
  кредит
  non-installment ~ (нон-
  инсталлмэнт ~) разовый кредит
  on account of ~ (он аккоунт оф
  ~) за счёт кредита
  on-call ~ (он-калл ~) онкольный
  кредит
  open ~ (опэн ~) открытый кредит
  overdue ~ (овэрду ~)
  просроченный кредит

paper ~ (пэйпэр ~) вексельный кредит

preferential ~ (прэфэрэншл ~) льготный кредит

reciprocal ~ arrangement (рисипрокал ~ аррэйнджмэнт) взаимное кредитование

reciprocal ~ facilities (рисипрокал ~ фасилитиз) взаимный кредит

reimbursement ~ (риимбурсмэнт ~) акцептно-рамбурсный кредит, рамбурсный кредит

repayment of ~ (рипэймэнт оф ~) возмещение кредита, погашение кредита

reserve ~ (рисэрв ~) резервный кредит

revolving ~ (риволвинг ~) автоматически возобновляемый кредит

risk attendant to ~ sales (риск аттэндант ту ~ сэйлз) риск при продаже в кредит

secured ~ (сэкюрд ~) обеспеченный кредит

self-liquidating ~ (сэлф-ликуидэйтинг ~) самоликвидирующийся кредит

short term ~ (шорт тэрм ~) краткосрочный кредит

significant ~ (сигнификант ~) значительный кредит

source of ~ (сорс оф ~) источник кредита

stand-by ~ (станд-бай ~) используемый в случае необходимости

swing ~ (суинг ~) свинговый кредит

term ~ (тэрм ~) срочный кредит

tide ~ (тайд ~) связанный кредит

to allocate ~s (ту алокэйт ~с) распределять кредиты

to block ~ (ту блок ~) блокировать кредиты

to buy on ~ (ту бай он ~) покупать в кредит

to exceed ~ (ту эксид ~) превышать кредит

to extend ~ (ту экстэнд ~) кредитовать

to guarantee ~ (ту гяранти ~) гарантировать кредит

to offer ~ (ту оффэр ~) предлагать кредит

to prolong ~ (ту пролонг ~) пролонгировать кредит

to refuse ~ (ту рифюз ~) отказаться от кредита

to renew ~ (ту риню ~) возобновлять кредит

to repay ~ (ту рипэй ~) погашать кредит

to support with ~ (ту суппорт уиθ ~) поддерживать кредитом

to withdraw ~ (ту уиθдрау ~) закрывать кредит

unlimited ~ (анлимитэд ~) бессрочный кредит {term}, неограниченный кредит {amount}

unsecured ~ (ансэкюрд ~) необеспеченный кредит

volume of ~ (волюм оф ~) объём кредита

withdrawal of ~ (уиθдрауал оф ~) лишение кредита

~ advice (~ адвайс) кредит-авизо

~ and monetary (~ энд монэтари) кредитно-денежный

~ and monetary policy (~ энд монэтари полиси) кредитно-денежная политика

~ application (~ аппликэйшн) заявка на кредит

~ balance (~ баланс) остаток кредита

~ demand (~ диманд) спрос на кредит

~ insurance (~ иншюранс) страхование кредита

~ investigation (~ инвэстигэйшн) обследование кредитоспособности

~ market (~ маркэт) рынок кредита

~ on mortgage (~ он моргэдж) ипотечный кредит

~ payments (~ пэймэнтс) платежи по кредиту

~ purchase (~ пурчас) покупка в кредит

~ rating (~ рэйтинг) оценка кредитоспособности

~ reduction (~ ридукшн) сокращение кредита

~ restriction (~ ристрикшн) ограничение кредита

~ squeeze (~ скуиз) стеснение кредитов

~ term (~ тэрм) срок кредита

~ terms (~ тэрмз) условия кредита

~ **union** (~ юнион) общество
взаимного кредита
Crediting (крэ́дитинг) кредитование
Creditor (крэ́дитор) заимодавец,
заимодатель, кредитор, лицо,
предоставляющее кредит
   general ~ (джэ́нэрал ~)
генеральный кредитор
   joint ~ (джойнт ~) совокупный
кредитор
   mortgage ~ (мо́ргэдж ~) кредитор
по закладной
   ordinary ~ (о́рдинари ~) обычный
кредитор
   preferred ~ (прифэ́рд ~)
привилегированный кредитор
   principal ~ (при́нсипал ~)
главный кредитор
   unsecured ~ (ансэкю́рд ~)
необеспеченный кредитор
   to settle with ~**s** (ту сэтл уиθ
~с) рассчитываться с кредиторами
Creditworthiness (крэ́дитуорθинэс)
кредитоспособность
Creditworthy (крэ́дитуорθи)
кредитоспособный
Crew (кру) бригада, команда,
прислуга, экипаж {vessel}
   emergency ~ (эмэ́рджэнси ~)
аварийная бригада, аварийная
команда
   maintenance ~ (мэ́йнтэнанс ~)
бригада технического
обслуживания
   ship's ~ (шипс ~) судовая
команда
   stevedore ~ (сти́вэдор ~) бригада
грузчиков
   training of a ~ (трэ́йнинг оф а
~) обучение команды
Crime (крайм) преступление
   insignificant ~ (инсигни́фикант
~) малозначительное преступление
   war ~ (уа́р ~) военное
преступление
   ~ **against personal freedom** (~
агэ́нст пэ́рсонал фри́дом)
преступление против личной
свободы
   ~ **against personal property** (~
агэ́нст пэ́рсонал про́пэрти)
преступление против личной
собственности
   ~ **against property** (~ агэ́нст
про́пэрти) преступление против
имущества

~ **of negligence** (~ оф
нэ́глиджэнс) преступление
небрежности
Criminal (кри́минал) преступник,
преступный {adj.}
   career ~ (кари́р ~)
профессиональный преступник
   to press ~ **charges against** (ту
прэс ~ ча́рджэз агэ́нст)
возбуждать уголовное дело
   war ~ (уа́р ~) военный преступник
   ~ **case** (~ кэйс) уголовное дело
   ~ **investigation department** (~
инвэстигэ́йшн дипа́ртмэнт) сыскная
полиция
   ~ **investigation unit** (~
инвэстигэ́йшн юнит) криминальная
полиция
Criminality (кримина́лити)
преступность
   career ~ (кари́р ~)
профессиональная преступность
Crisis (кра́йсис) кризис, перелом
   balance of payments ~ (ба́ланс оф
пэ́ймэнтс ~) кризис платёжного
баланса
   economic ~ (эконо́мик ~)
экономический кризис
   industrial ~ (инду́стриал ~)
промышленный кризис
   international ~ (интэрна́шэнал ~)
международный кризис
   monetary ~ (мо́нэтари ~) валютный
кризис, денежный кризис
   monetary and credit ~ (мо́нэтари
энд крэ́дит ~) денежно-кредитный
кризис
   monetary and financial ~
(мо́нэтари энд файна́ншл ~)
валютно-финансовый кризис
   protracted ~ (протра́ктэд ~)
затяжной кризис
   to avert a ~ (ту авэ́рт а ~)
предотвращать кризис
   world ~ (уо́рлд ~) мировой кризис
Criteri/on (крайти́ри/он) критерий
   applicable ~/**a** (аппли́кабл ~/a)
соответствующие критерии
   basic ~/**a** (бэ́йсик ~/a) основные
критерии
   economic ~ (эконо́мик ~)
экономический критерий
   estimation ~ (эстимэ́йшн ~)
оценочный критерий
   general ~ (джэ́нэрал ~) общий
критерий

quality ~/a (куа́лити ~/a)
критерии качества
rejection ~ (риджэ́кшн ~)
критерий браковки
reliability ~/a (рилайаби́лити
~/a) критерии надёжности
sole ~ (сол ~) единственный
критерий
~ **of patentability** (~ оф
патэнтаби́лити) критерий
патентоспособности
Critical (кри́тикал) критический
to make ~ (ту мэйк ~) вызывать
кризис
Criticism (кри́тисизм) отзыв
Crop (кроп) урожай
record ~ (рэ́корд ~) рекордный
урожай
to sell a standing ~ (ту сэл а
ста́ндинг ~) продавать урожай на
корню
Cross-examine, to ~ (крос-экза́мин,
ту ~) опрашивать
Crossing (кро́ссинг) переход
border ~ (бо́рдэр ~) переход
границы
illegal border ~ (илли́гал бо́рдэр
~) незаконный переход границы
~ **the border** (~ θи бо́рдэр)
переезд границы
Crossroads (кро́ссродз) стык
Crude (круд) необработанный
~ **oil** (~ ойл) нефть
Cruel (кру́эл) жестокий
Cruelty (кру́элти) жестокость
Cruise (круз) поход
Crux (кракс) суть
the ~ **of the matter** (θи ~ оф θи
ма́ттэр) суть дела
Cubic (кю́бик) кубический
total ~ **volume** (то́тал ~ во́люм)
общая кубатура
~ **capacity** (~ капа́сити) кубатура
Cultivate, to ~ (ку́лтивэйт, ту ~)
разрабатывать [**perfective:**
разработать]
Cultivation (культивэ́йшн) разработка
joint ~ **of the land** (джойнт ~ оф
θи ланд) совместная обработка
земли
~ **of the land** (~ оф θи ланд)
обработка земли
Cumulative (кю́мюлатив)
кумулятивный, накапливающийся
Currenc/y (ку́ррэнси) валюта,
валютный {*adj.*}, казначейские
билеты

against other ~/ies (агэ́нст о́θэр
~из) по сравнению с другими
валютами
agreed ~ (агри́д ~) согласованная
валюта
backing of ~ (ба́кинг оф ~)
обеспечение валюты
"basket" of ~/ies (ба́скэт оф
~из) "корзина" валют
blocked ~ (блокд ~)
блокированная валюта
clearing ~ (кли́ринг ~)
клиринговая валюта
collapse of ~ (колла́пс оф ~)
крах валюты
collective ~ (коллэ́ктив ~)
коллективная валюта
common ~ (ко́ммон ~) единая
валюта
controlled ~ (контро́лд ~)
регулируемая валюта
conversion of ~ **at the going
rate** (конвэ́ржн оф ~ ат θи го́инг
рэйт) пересчёт валюты по курсу
conversion of ~ **at parity**
(конвэ́ржн оф ~ ат па́рити)
пересчёт валюты по паритету
convertibility of ~
(конвэртиби́лити оф ~)
конвертируемость валюты,
обратимость валюты
convertible ~ (конвэ́ртибл ~)
конвертируемая валюта, обратимая
валюта
corresponding ~ (коррэспо́ндинг
~) соответствующая валюта
counterfeit ~ (ко́унтэрфит ~)
поддельная валюта, поддельный
денежный знак
credit denominated in foreign ~
(крэ́дит дино́минэйтэд ин фо́рэн ~)
кредит в иностранной валюте
demand for ~ (дима́нд фор ~)
спрос на валюту
depreciated ~ (дипри́шиэйтэд ~)
обесцененная валюта
depreciating ~ (дипри́шиэйтинг ~)
падающая валюта
devalorization of ~
(дивалоризэ́йшн оф ~) понижение
курса валюты
devaluation of ~ (дивалюэ́йшн оф
~) девальвация валюты
devalued ~ (дива́люд ~)
девальвированная валюта
domestic ~ (домэ́стик ~) местная
валюта, отечественная валюта

exchange of ~ (эксчэйндж оф ~) обмен валюты

fluctuating ~ (флу́кчуэйтинг ~) колеблющаяся валюта

foreign ~ (фо́рэн ~) иностранная валюта

free ~ (фри ~) свободно конвертируемая валюта

freely convertible ~ (фри́ли конвэ́ртибл ~) свободная валюта

freely floating ~ (фри́ли фло́тинг ~) свободно плавающая валюта

general asset ~ (джэ́нэрал а́ссэт ~) банкноты, не имеющие специального обеспечения

gold content of ~ (голд ко́нтэнт оф ~) золотое содержание валюты

gold-convertible ~ (голд-конвэ́ртибл ~) валюта, обратимая в золото

hard ~ (хард ~) твёрдая валюта

inconvertible ~ (инконвэ́ртибл ~) неконвертируемая валюта

instability of ~ (инстаби́лити оф ~) неустойчивость валюты

issue of ~ (и́шю оф ~) эмиссия денег

key ~ (ки ~) ключевая валюта

local ~ (ло́кал ~) местные деньги

national ~ (на́шэнал ~) национальная валюта

overvaluation of ~ (овэрвалюэ́йшн оф ~) завышенная оценка валюты

paper ~ (пэ́йпэр ~) бумажная валюта

pegged ~ (пэгд ~) валюта, привязанная к валюте другой страны

price of ~ (прайс оф ~) цена валюты

purchasing power of ~ (пу́рчасинг по́уэр оф ~) покупательная способность валюты

reserve ~ (рисэ́рв ~) резервная валюта

revalued ~ (рива́люд ~) ревальвированная валюта

scarce ~ (скэйрс ~) дефицитная валюта

settlement in foreign ~ (сэ́тлмэнт ин фо́рэн ~) расчёт в иностранной валюте

settlement in national ~ (сэ́тлмэнт ин на́шэнал ~) платёж в национальной валюте

sum of ~ (сум оф ~) сумма валюты

stability of ~ (стаби́лити оф ~) устойчивость валюты

stabilization of ~ (стэйбилизэ́йшн оф ~) стабилизация валюты

stable ~ (стэйбл ~) стабильная валюта, устойчивая валюта

surplus of ~ (су́рплус оф ~) излишки валюты

to appreciate ~ (ту аппри́шиэйт ~) повышать курс валюты

to back ~ (ту бак ~) обеспечивать валюту

to compute in ~ (ту компю́т ин ~) исчислять в валюте

to control ~ (ту контро́л ~) регулировать валюту

to convert ~ (ту конвэ́рт ~) конвертировать в валюту

to convert into another ~ (ту конвэ́рт и́нту ано́θэр ~) переводить в другую валюту

to depreciate ~ (ту дипри́шиэйт ~) обесценивать валюту

to devalue ~ (ту дива́лю ~) девальвировать валюту, девалоризировать валюта

to earn ~ (ту эрн ~) зарабатывать валюту

to exchange ~ (ту эксчэ́йндж ~) обменивать валюту

to express in ~ (ту экспрэ́с ин ~) выражать в валюте

to obtain ~ (ту обтэ́йн ~) приобретать валюту

to pay by ~ (ту пэй бай ~) платить валютой

to revalue ~ (ту рива́лю ~) ревальвироват валюту

to sell for {hard} ~ (ту сэл фор {хард} ~) реализировать на валюту

to transfer ~ from one account into another (ту тра́нсфэр ~ фром уа́н акко́унт и́нту ано́θэр) переводить валюту с одного счёта на другой

to transfer ~ into an account (ту тра́нсфэр ~ и́нту ан акко́унт) зачислять валюту на счёт, переводить валюту на счёт

transfer of ~ (тра́нсфэр оф ~) перевод валюты

unit of ~ (ю́нит оф ~) единица валюты

unstable ~ (анстэ́йбл ~) неустойчивая валюта

value of ~ (вáлю оф ~) стоимость валюты
~ at full value (~ ат фул вáлю) полноценная валюта
~ exchange restrictions (~ эксчэ́йндж ристри́кшнс) ограничения в переводе валюты
~ exchange transactions (~ эксчэ́йндж трансáкшнс) операции в валюте
~ fluctuation (~ флукчуэ́йшн) колебание курса валюты
~ pegged to the dollar (~ пэгд ту θи дóллар) валюта, привязанная к доллару
~ reserves (~ рисэ́рвз) запасы валюты
~ shortage (~ шóртадж) нехватка валюты
~ snake (~ снэйк) валютная "змея"
~ swap (~ суап) обмен валютами
Current (кýррэнт) текущий
~ account (~ аккóунт) контокоррент, контокоррентный {adj.}
Curtail, to ~ (куртэ́йл, ту ~) сокращать
Curve (курв) кривая
demand ~ (димáнд ~) кривая спроса
supply ~ (сапплáй ~) кривая предложения
Cushion (кушн) "подушка", запас, защитный период, излишек фондов
~ bond (~ бонд) облигация с "подушкой", облигация с купоном выше текущих рыночных ставок
Custody (кáстоди) сохранение
in carrier's ~ (ин кáрриэрз ~) на хранении у перевозчика
taking into ~ (тэ́йкинг и́нту ~) заключение под стражу
to take into ~ (ту тэйк и́нту ~) заключать под стражу
~ of children (~ оф чи́лдрэн) попечение о детях
Custom (кáстом) обычай, правило, привычка
legal ~ (ли́гал ~) правовой обычай, правовая привычка
local ~ (лóкал ~) местное обыкновение, местный обычай
~-built (~-билт) несерийный
Customer (кáстомэр) заказчик, клиен, комитент
bank ~ (банк ~) клиент банка

defaulting ~ (дифáлтинг ~) неисправный клиент
small ~ (смал ~) мелкий потребитель
Customs (кáстомз) досмотровый {adj.}, таможенный {adj.}, таможня
goods under ~ seal (гудз áндэр ~ сил) товары, пломбированные таможней
international ~ (интэрнáшэнал ~) международные правила
to bring through ~ (ту бринг θру ~) провозить через таможню
to clear ~ (ту клир ~) проходить через таможню
to present a ~ permit (ту прэзэ́нт а ~ пэ́рмит) предъявлять разрешение таможни
~ agent (~ э́йджэнт) таможенник
~ declaration (~ дэкларэ́йшн) декларация таможни
~ officer (~ óффисэр) сотрудник таможни
~ receipt (~ риси́т) квитанция таможни об уплате пошлины
~ schedule (~ скэ́джюл) таможенный тариф
~ schedule of a foreign government (~ скэ́джюл оф а фóрэн гóвэрнмэнт) таможенный тариф иностранного государства
~ seal (~ сил) печать таможни
~ union (~ ю́нион) таможенный союз
Cut (кут) снижение, сокращение
pay ~ (пэй ~) понижение зарплаты
tax ~ (такс ~) сокращение налога
~ in duties (~ ин дю́тиз) сокращение пошлины
~ in expenses (~ ин экспэ́нсэз) сокращение расходов
~ in wages (~ ин уэ́йджэз) снижение зарплаты
Cutting (кýттинг) экономия
cost ~ drive (кост ~ драйв) режим экономии
~ of expenditures (~ оф экспэ́ндичюрз) экономия в расходах
Cycle (сайкл) цикл
business ~ forecast (би́знэс ~ фóркаст) прогноз конъюнктуры
product life ~ (прóдукт лайф ~) жизненный цикл товара

D

Daily (дэ́йли) ежедневный
~ **output** (~ о́утпут) дневной
выпуск
Damage (да́мадж) авария,
повреждение, порча, ~s убыток
action for ~s (акшн фор ~с) иск
об убытках
actual ~ **caused** (а́кчуал ~ каузд)
нанесённый ущерб
amount of ~s (амо́унт оф ~с)
сумма убытков
anticipatory ~s (анти́сипатори
~с) возмещение будущих убытков
assessment of ~s (ассэ́ссмэнт оф
~с) оценка убытков
award of ~s (ауа́рд оф ~с)
решение суда о возмещении
убытков
"carrier not liable for ~s"
(ка́рриэр нот ла́йабл фор ~с)
"перевозчик не отвечает за
убытки"
cause of ~ (кауз оф ~) причина
ущерба
causes of ~s (ка́узэз оф ~с)
причины возникновения убытков
compensation for ~s (компэнсэ́йшн
фор ~с) возмещение ущерба,
компенсация за убытки,
компенсация за ущерб
crop ~ (кроп ~) потрава
determination of ~s
(дитэрминэ́йшн оф ~с) определение
убытков
extent of ~ (экстэ́нт оф ~)
размер ущерба
fire ~ (фа́йр ~) ущерб от пожара
неприятием товара
further ~ (фу́рθэр ~) дальнейший
ущерб
great ~ (грэйт ~) большой ущерб
in case of ~ (ин кэйс оф ~) в
случае ущерба
indirect ~ (индайрэ́кт ~)
косвенный ущерб
indirect ~s (индайрэ́кт ~с)
косвенные убытки
insignificant ~ (инсигни́фикант
~) незначительное повреждение,
незначительный ущерб
level of ~ (лэ́вэл оф ~) уровень
ущерба
liability for ~s (лайаби́лити фор
~с) ответственность за убытки

liquidated ~s (ли́куидэйтэд ~с)
согласованные и заранее
оценённые убытки
lumpsum ~s (ла́мпсум ~с)
паушальная сумма убытков
major ~ (мэ́йджор ~) крупный
ущерб
marginal ~s (ма́рджинал ~с)
предельные убытки
material ~ (мати́риал ~)
материальный ущерб
measure of ~s (мэ́жюр оф ~с)
размер возмещения убытков
monetary ~ (мо́нэтари ~) денежный
ущерб
nature of the ~ (нэ́йчэр оф θи ~)
характер ущерба
obligation to compensate for ~
(облигэ́йшн ту ко́мпэнсэйт фор ~)
обязательство возместить ущерб
partial ~ (паршл ~) частная
авария, частичное повреждение,
частичный ущерб
payment of ~s (пэ́ймэнт оф ~с)
оплата убытков
possible ~ (по́ссибл ~) возможный
ущерб
property ~ (про́пэрти ~)
повреждение имущества, ущерб
собственности
prospective ~s (проспэ́ктив ~с)
возмещение ожидаемых убытков
recovery of ~s (рико́вэри оф ~с)
взыскание убытков
reduction in ~s (риду́кшн ин ~с)
уменьшение убытков
right to recover ~s (райт ту
рико́вэр ~с) право на взыскание
убытков
significant ~ (сигни́фикант ~)
значительный ущерб
storm ~ (сторм ~) ущерб от
шторма
to assess the ~ (ту ассэ́сс θи ~)
оценивать размер ущерба
to assess money ~s (ту ассэ́сс
мо́ни ~с) определять сумму
денежного возмещения
to avoid ~ (ту аво́йд ~) избегать
неисправности
to award ~s (ту ауа́рд ~с)
присуждать убытки
to be liable for ~ (ту би ла́йабл
фор ~) быть ответственным за
ущерб

to bring an action for ~s (ту бринг ан акшн фор ~с) возбуждать иск об убытках убытки
to cause ~ (ту кауз ~) причинять убытки
to compensate ~s (ту кóмпэнсэйт ~с) компенсировать убытки, компенсировать ущерб
to determine the amount of ~s (ту дитéрмин θи амóунт оф ~с) определять сумму убытков
to hold someone harmless for ~s (ту холд сóмуан хáрмлэс фор ~с) избавлять кого-либо от ответственности за убытки
to hold someone liable for ~s (ту холд сóмуан лáйабл фор ~с) считать кого-л. ответственным за
to indemnify for ~ (ту индéмнифай фор ~) возмещать ущерб
to indemnify someone against property ~ (ту индéмнифай сóмуан агéнст прóпэрти ~) застраховать кого-либо от ущерба имуществу
to inflict ~ (ту инфлúкт ~) наносить ущерб
to pay judgment ~s (ту пэй джáджмэнт ~с) возмещать убытки истцу
to pay liquidated ~s (ту пэй лúкуидэйтэд ~с) платить заранее оценённые и согласованные убытки
to prevent ~ (ту привéнт ~) предотвращать ущерб
to recover ~s (ту рикóвэр ~с) взыскать убытки, получать возмещение убытков
to report ~ (ту рипóрт ~) заявить об ущербе
to suffer ~ (ту сýффэр ~) нести убыток, понести ущерб
to ~ (ту ~) портить
total ~ (тóтал ~) общая авария
waiver of ~s (уэ́йвэр оф ~с) отказ от права на возмещение
waiver of right to ~s (уэ́йвэр оф райт ту ~с) отказ от права на возмещение убытков
water ~ (уáтэр ~) повреждение водой, ущерб, нанесённый водой
~ assessment (~ ассéссмэнт) оценка ущерба
~ caused by ... (~ каузд бай ...) ущерб, вызванный ...
~ claim (~ клэйм) заявление об убытках

~ report (~ рипóрт) заявление об ущербе
~ survey (~ сýрвэй) освидетельствование ущерба
~ to crops (~ ту кропс) повреждение сельскохозяйственных культур
~ to goods (~ ту гудз) порча товара
~ to personal property (~ ту пéрсонал прóпэрти) повреждение личного имущества
Danger (дéйнджэр) опасность
social ~ (сошл ~) общественная опасность
~ in the workplace (~ ин θи уóркплэйс) опасность в предприятиях
Data (дáта) данные
acceptance test ~ (аксéптанс тэст ~) данные приёмно-сдаточных испытаний
according to incomplete ~ (аккóрдинг ту инкомплúт ~) по неполным данным
according to official ~ (аккóрдинг ту оффúшл ~) по официальным данным
according to preliminary ~ (аккóрдинг ту прилúминэри ~) по предварительным данным
additional ~ (аддúшнал ~) дополнительные данные
basic ~ (бéйсик ~) исходные данные
biographical ~ (байогрáфикал ~) анкетные данные
bookkeeping ~ (бýккипинг ~) бухгалтерские данные
comparative ~ (компáратив ~) сравнительные данные
complete ~ (комплúт ~) полные данные
comprehensive ~ (комприхéнсив ~) исчерпывающие данные
correct ~ (коррéкт ~) правильные данные
cumulative ~ (кюмюлатив ~) сводные данные
design ~ (дизáйн ~) проектные данные
economic ~ (эконóмик ~) экономический данные
estimated ~ (éстиматд ~) сметные данные

evaluation of technical ~
(ивалюэйшн оф тэкникал ~) оценка
технических данных
ill-founded ~ (ил-фóундэд ~)
малодостоверные данные
incomplete ~ (инкомплúт ~)
неполные данные
incorrect ~ (инкоррэ́кт ~)
неправильные данные
irrefutable ~ (иррифю́табл ~)
неопровержимые данные
manufacturing ~ (манюфáкчуринг
~) данные изготовления
missing ~ (мúссинг ~)
недостающие данные
necessary ~ (нэ́сэсари ~)
необходимые данные
numerical ~ (нумэ́рикал ~)
цифровые данные
official ~ (оффúшл ~)
официальные данные
operating ~ (óпэрэйтинг ~)
эксплуатационные данные
operational ~ (опэрэ́йшнал ~)
рабочие данные
original ~ (орúджинал ~)
первоначальные данные
predicted ~ (прэдúктэд ~)
прогнозируемые данные
preliminary ~ (прилúминэри ~)
предварительные данные
pricing ~ (прáйсинг ~) данные о
ценах
principle ~ (прúнсипл ~)
основные данные
priority ~ (прайóрити ~)
приоритетные данные
rating ~ (рэ́йтинг ~) расчётные
данные
raw ~ (рáу ~) необработанные
данные
reference ~ (рэ́фэрэнс ~)
справочные данные
sample ~ (сампл ~) выборочные
данные
statistical ~ (статúстикал ~)
статистические данные
submission of ~ (субмúшн оф ~)
представление данных
summarized ~ (сýммарайзд ~)
итоговые данные
systemized ~ (сúстэмайзд ~)
систематизированные данные
tabulation of ~ (табюлэ́йшн оф ~)
расположение данных в виде
таблицы

technical ~ (тэ́кникал ~)
технические данные
to collect ~ (ту коллэ́кт ~)
собирать данные
to examine technical ~ (ту
экзáмин тэкникал ~) изучать
технические данные
to furnish ~ (ту фýрниш ~)
выдавать данные
to include ~ (ту инклю́д ~)
включать данные
to process ~ (ту прóсэс ~)
обрабатывать данные
to update (ту ýпдэйт) обновлять
данные
to verify ~ (ту вэ́рифай ~)
проверять данные
~ analysis (~ анáлисис) анализ
данных
Date (дэйт) дата, срок, число
acceptance ~ (аксэ́птанс ~) дата
акцепта
act ~ (акт ~) дата подписания
контракта
advice ~ of a letter of credit
(адвáйс ~ оф а лэ́ттэр оф крэ́дит)
авизованная дата аккредитива
annulled ~ (аннýлд ~) дата
аннулирования
application ~ (аппликэ́йшн ~)
дата заявки
approximate ~ (аппрóксимат ~)
приблизительная дата
cancellation ~ (кансэллэ́йшн ~)
дата расторжения
convenient ~ (конвúниэнт ~)
удобная дата
delivery ~ (дэлúвэри ~) дата
поставки
departure ~ (дипáрчур ~) день
отправления
designated ~ (дэ́зигнэйтэд ~)
установленная дата
dispatch ~ (дúспатч ~) дата
отправки
effective ~ (иффэ́ктив ~) время
вступления в силу, дата
вступления в силу, момент
вступления в силу
effective ~ of an agreement
(иффэ́ктив ~ оф ан агрúмэнт) дата
вступления в силу соглашения
**effective ~ of an insurance
policy** (иффэ́ктив ~ оф ан
иншю́ранс пóлиси) дата выдачи
полиса

expected ~ (экспэ́ктэд ~) предполагаемая дата

expiration ~ (экспирэ́йшн ~) дата окончания срока, конечный срок

filing ~ (фа́йлинг ~) дата подачи заявки

initial ~ (ини́шл ~) начальная дата

initial ~ of warranty period (ини́шл ~ оф уа́рранти пи́риод) дата начала гарантийного периода

interest ~ (и́нтэрэст ~) срок уплаты процентов

invoice ~ (и́нвойс ~) дата выписки счёта

latest ~ (лэ́йтэст ~) последняя дата

licensing ~ (ла́йсэнсинг ~) дата представления лицензии

loading ~ (ло́динг ~) дата погрузки

mailing ~ (мэ́йлинг ~) дата отправки корреспонденции

maturity ~ (мачу́рити ~) дата наступление срока

offer ~ (о́ффэр ~) дата предложения

payment ~ (пэ́ймэнт ~) дата платежа

possible ~ (по́ссибл ~) возможный срок

priority ~ (прайо́рити ~) приоритетная дата

protocol ~ (про́токол ~) дата подписания протокола

publication ~ (публикэ́йшн ~) дата публикации, дата опубликования

rail ~ (рэйл ~) железнодорожное движение

release ~ (рили́с ~) дата выпуска

sailing ~ (сэ́йлинг ~) дата выхода судна в море

stamped ~ (стампд ~) обозначенная штемпелем дата

start-up ~ (старт-ап ~) дата пуска в эксплуатацию

termination ~ of an act (тэрминэ́йшн ~ оф ан акт) дата прекращения действия контракта

test ~ (тэст ~) дата испытания

to ~ (ту ~) помечать числом, датировать, проставлять дату

to affix a later ~ (ту аффи́кс а лэ́йтэр ~) датировать более поздним числом

to affix an earlier ~ (ту аффи́кс ан э́рлиэр ~) датировать более ранним числом

to back ~ (ту бак ~) датировать задним числом

to fix a ~ (ту фикс а ~) определять дату

to modify a dispatch ~ (ту мо́дифай а ди́спатч ~) изменять дату отгрузки

to notate the ~ (ту но́тэйт θи ~) помечать датой

to propose an alternative ~ (ту пропо́з ан алтэ́рнатив ~) предлагать другую дату

to set the last shipment ~ (ту сэт θи ласт ши́пмэнт ~) определять последнюю дату отгрузки

to show shipping ~s (ту шо́у ши́пинг ~с) указывать даты отгрузки

upon ~ of tender (упо́н ~ оф тэ́ндэр) на день предложения

without a ~ (уиθо́ут а ~) без числа

~ from which period tolls (~ фром уич пи́риод толс) дата, от которой исчисляется срок

~ of acceptance (~ оф аксэ́птанс) дата приёмки, день приёмки, приёмный день

~ of application (~ оф апликэ́йшн) срок заявления

~ of arrival (~ оф арра́йвал) дата прибытия

~ of border crossing (~ оф бо́рдэр кро́ссинг) дата перехода границы

~ of claim (~ оф клэйм) дата претензии

~ of commencement of work (~ оф коммэ́нсмэнт оф уо́рк) дата начала работы

~ of delivery (~ оф дэли́вэри) срок доставки

~ of departure (~ оф дипа́рчур) дата выезда

~ of erection {construction} (~ оф ирэ́кшн {констру́кшн}) дата монтажных работ

~ of filing an action (~ оф фа́йлинг ан акшн) дата) предъявления иска

~ of grant of patent (~ оф грант оф па́тэнт) дата выдачи патента

~ **of issuance** (~ оф и́шюанс) дата выдачи
~ **of issue of a bill** (~ оф и́шю оф а бил) дата выписки векселя
~ **of manufacture** (~ оф манюфа́кчур) дата изготовления
~ **of performance** (~ оф пэрфо́рманс) срок исполнения
~ **of receipt** (~ оф риси́т) дата поступления
~ **of shipment** (~ оф ши́пмэнт) дата отгрузки
~ **of ship readiness** (~ оф шип рэ́динэсс) дата готовности к отгрузке
~-**stamp** (~-стамп) календарный штемпель, штемпель-календарь
Dated (дэ́йтэд) датированный
ante-~ (а́нтэ-~) датированный задним числом
post-~ (пост-~) датированный более поздним числом
Dating (дэ́йтинг) датировка {of document, etc.}
Datum (да́тум) исходный факт
Daughter-in-law (да́утэр-ин-ла́у) сноха {of father}, невестка {wife of one's son}
Day (дэй) день
at the end of the ~ (ат θи энд оф θи ~) в конце дня
calendar ~ (ка́лэндар ~) календарный день
consecutive ~s (консэ́кютив ~с) последовательные дни
cumulative ~s (кю́мюлатив ~с) кумулятивные дни
delay of ... ~s (дилэ́й оф ... ~с) опоздание на ...дней
demurrage ~s (димю́рradж ~с) контрсталийные дни
dispatch ~ (ди́спатч ~) дни диспача
from the ~ of issue (фром θи ~ оф и́шю) со дня выдачи
full ~ (фул ~) полный день
grace period ~s (грэйс пи́риод ~с) льготные дни
lay ~s (лэй ~с) дни погрузки и разгрузки судов, сталийные дни
non-working (нон-уо́ркинг ~) нерабочий день
opening ~ (о́пэнинг ~) день открытия
order of the ~ (о́рдэр оф θи ~) распорядок дня

reversible ~ (ривэ́рсибл ~) реверсивный день
running ~s (ру́ннинг ~с) сплошные дни
sailing ~ (сэ́йлинг ~) день отхода судна
settlement ~ (сэ́тлмэнт ~) день расчёта
short work ~ (шорт уо́рк ~) короткий день
to establish ~ off (ту эста́блиш ~ офф) устанавливать дни отдыха день
to fall on a ~ (ту фал он а ~) приходиться на день
to fix a ~ (ту фикс а ~) назначать день
weather working ~ (уэ́θэр уо́ркинг ~) погожий рабочий день
work ~ (уо́рк ~) рабочий день
~s following acceptance (~с фо́ллоинг аксэ́птанс) через ... дней после акцептования
~ of arrival (~ оф арра́йвал) день прибытия
~ of non-payment (~ оф нон-пэ́ймэнт) день неплатежа
~ of payment (~ оф пэ́ймэнт) день платежа
~ off (~ офф) выходной день
~s on demurrage (~с он димю́рradж) дни демерреджа
~s saved (~с сэйвд) сбережённые дни, сэкономленные дни
~s upon site (~с апо́н сайт) через... дней после предъявления день ...
Deacon (ди́кон) дьякон
Deadline (дэ́длайн) крайний срок
Deadtime (дэ́дтайм) простой
Deadweight (дэ́дуэйт) дедвейт
Deal (дил) сделка, сговор
barter ~ (ба́ртэр ~) бартерная сделка
business ~ (би́знэс ~) коммерческая сделка
cash ~ (каш ~) наличная сделка
fair ~ (фэйр ~) честная сделка
package ~ (па́кэдж ~) аккордный контракт, комплексная сделка
re-export ~ (ри-э́кспорт ~) реэкспортная сделка
secret ~ (си́крэт ~) тайная сделка
sham ~ (шам ~) фиктивная сделка
to ~ in (ту ~ ин) торговать

to ~ with (ту ~ уиθ) иметь дело с

to conclude a ~ (ту конклю́д а ~) заключить сделку

trade ~ (трэйд ~) торговая сделка

wholesale ~ (хо́лсэйл ~) оптовая сделка

Dealer (ди́лэр) дилер, посредник, торговец, торговый агент

authorized ~ (а́уθорайзд ~) уполномоченный посредник

bill ~ (бил ~) вексельный брокер

exchange ~ (эксчэ́йндж ~) биржевой брокер, биржевой дилер, биржевой торговец

gemstone ~ (джэ́мстон ~) торговцы драгоценностями

licensed ~ (ла́йсэнсд ~) дилер с лицензией

second-hand ~ (сэ́конд-ханд ~) дилер по продаже подержанного имущества

securities ~ (сэкю́ритиз ~) инвестиционный банк {institutional}, дилер по операциям с ценными бумагами

~ discount (~ ди́скоунт) скидка дилерам

~-importer (~-и́мпортэр) торговец-импортёр

Dealings (ди́лингз) сношение

business ~ (би́знэс ~) торговые дела

Dear (дир) дорогой

Dearly (ди́рли) дорого

to pay ~ (ту пэй ~) платить дорого

Death (дэθ) смерть

Debate (дибэ́йт) дебата, прение, спор

parliamentary ~ (парламэ́нтари ~) парламентские прения

Debenture (дибэ́нчур) дебентура, облигация

customs ~ (ка́стомз ~) удостоверение таможни на возврат таможенной пошлины

long-term ~ (лонг-тэрм ~) долгосрочная облигация

registered ~ (рэ́джистэрд ~) именная облигация

to issue ~s (ту и́шю ~с) выпускать облигации

to redeem ~s (ту риди́м ~с) погашать облигации

transfer of ~s (тра́нсфэр оф ~с) трансферт облигаций

Debit (дэ́бит) дебет

detailed ~ note (ди́тэйлд ~ нот) подробная дебет-нота

to ~ an amount to an account (ту ~ ан амо́унт ту ан акко́унт) записать сумму в дебет счёта

to ~ {an account} (ту ~ {ан акко́унт}) дебетовать

to charge a ~ (ту чардж а ~) записать в дебет

to recall a ~ (ту рика́л а ~) отзывать дебет-ноту

~ and credit (~ энд крэ́дит) дебет и кредит

~ entry (~ э́нтри) дебетование счёта, занесение в дебет

~ note (~ нот) дебет-нота

~ note for ... (~ нот фор ...) дебет-нота на ...

~ note for services rendered (~ нот фор сэ́рвисэз рэ́ндэрд) дебет-нота за услуги

~ of an account (~ оф ан акко́унт) дебет счёта

Debt (дэт) долг ~s задолженность

accrued ~ (аккру́д ~) накопленный долг

acknowledgement of a ~ (акно́лэджмэнт оф а ~) подтверждение долга

amount of a ~ (амо́унт оф а ~) сумма долга

bad ~ (бад ~) безнадёжный долг, безнадёжная задолженность

bonded ~ (бо́ндэд ~) фундированный долг

collateral for a ~ (колла́тэрал фор а ~) обеспечение долга

consolidated ~ (консо́лидэйтэд ~) консолидированный долг

current ~ (ку́ррэнт ~) текущий долг

discharged ~ (дисча́рджд ~) погашенный долг

doubtful ~ (до́убтфул ~) сомнительный долг

foreign ~ (фо́рэн ~) внешний долг, внешняя задолженность

frozen ~ (фро́зэн ~) замороженный долг

heavy ~ (хэ́ви ~) большой долг

hypothecated ~ (хайпо́θэкэйтэд ~) ипотечная задолженность

international ~ (интэрна́шэнал ~) международная задолженность judgment ~ (джа́джмэнт ~) присуждённый долг

liquid ~ (ли́куид ~) ликвидная задолженность

liquidation of ~s (ликуидэ́йшн оф ~с) ликвидация долгов

long-term ~ (лонг-тэрм ~) долгосрочный долг

money ~ (мо́ни ~) денежный долг

mortgage ~ (мо́ргэдж ~) ипотечная задолженность

national ~ (на́шэнал ~) государственный долг

old ~ (олд ~) старый долг

overall ~ (овэра́л ~) общий долг

overdue ~ (овэрду́ ~) отсроченный долг

paid ~ (пэйд ~) уплаченный долг

past due ~ (паст ду ~) просроченный долг

payment of a ~ (пэ́ймэнт оф а ~) уплата долга

public ~ (па́блик ~) государственная задолженность

remainder of a ~ (римэ́йндэр оф а ~) остаток долга

remission of a ~ (рими́шн оф а ~) освобождение от уплаты долга

repayment of ~ (рипэ́ймэнт оф ~) возврат долга

repudiation of a ~ (рипюдиэ́йшн оф а ~) отказ от уплаты долга

secured ~ (сэкю́рд ~) обеспеченный долг

settlement of a ~ (сэ́тлмэнт оф а ~) выплата долга, оплата долга

settlement of ~s (сэ́тлмэнт оф ~с) урегулирование долгов

short-term ~ (шорт-тэрм ~) краткосрочный долг, краткосрочная задолженность

straight ~ (стрэйт ~) прямой долг

to account as payment of a ~ (ту акко́унт ас пэ́ймэнт оф а ~) зачитывать в уплату долга

to acknowledge a ~ (ту акно́лэдж а ~) признавать долг

to be in ~ (ту би ин ~) быть в долгу

to collect ~s (ту колле́кт ~с) взыскивать долги, инкассировать долги, получать деньги в погашение

to deduct a ~ (ту диду́кт а ~) удерживать долг

to demand payment of a ~ (ту дима́нд пэ́ймэнт оф а ~) требовать уплаты долга

to discharge a ~ (ту ди́счардж а ~) погашать долг

to extend the repayment period of ~s (ту экстэ́нд θи рипэ́ймэнт пи́риод оф ~с) продлевать срок выплаты долгов

to extinguish ~ (ту экcти́нгуиш ~) погасить задолженность

to find oneself in ~ (ту файнд уа́нэлф ин ~) находиться в долгу

to forgive a ~ (ту форги́в а ~) прощать долг

to have ~s (ту хэв ~с) иметь долги

to incur ~s (ту инку́р ~с) влезать в долги

to pay off a ~ (ту пэй офф а ~) уплачивать долг

to pay off ~s (ту пэй офф ~с) расплачиваться с долгами

to repay ~ (ту рипэ́й ~) возмещать долг

to repudiate a ~ (ту рипю́диэйт а ~) отказываться от уплаты долга

to satisfy a ~ (ту са́тисфай а ~) удовлетворять долг

to service a ~ (ту сэ́рвис а ~) покрывать долг

to settle a ~ (ту сэтл а ~) выплачивать долг, оплачивать долг

to write off a ~ (ту райт офф а ~) аннулировать долг, списывать долг

unconsolidated ~ (анконсо́лидэйтэд ~) неконсолидированный долг

undischarged ~ (андисча́рджд ~) непогашенный долг

unpaid ~ (анпэ́йд ~) неуплаченный долг

unrecoverable ~ (анрико́вэрабл ~) безвозвратный долг

unsecured ~ (ансэкю́рд ~) необеспеченная задолженность

~ collection (~ колле́кшн) взыскание долгов

~ on loans (~ он лонс) долги по займам

~ repayment schedule (~ рипэ́ймэнт скэ́джюл) график возмещения долгов

~ service (~ сэ́рвис) покрытие долга

~ **service on bonds** (~ сэ́рвис он бондс) выплата процентов по долговым обязательствам
Debtor (дэ́тор) дебитор, должник, заёмщик
   bill ~ (бил ~) векселеобязанный, должник по векселю
   defaulting ~ (дифа́лтинг ~) должник, нарушивший обязательство
   insolvency of a ~ (инсо́лвэнси оф а ~) несостоятельность должника
   judgment ~ (джа́джмэнт ~) должник по иску
   non-creditworthy ~ (нон-крэ́дитуор θи ~) некредитоспособный должник
   primary ~ (пра́ймари ~) основной должник
   principal ~ (при́нсипал ~) главный должник
Decay (дикэ́й) гниль
   to ~ (ту ~) гнить, портиться
Deceive, to ~ (диси́в, ту ~) обманывать [**perfective:** обмануть]
Deceleration (дисэлэрэ́йшн) замедление
Deception (дисэ́пшн) обман
Deceptive (дисэ́птив) обманный
Decide, to ~ (диса́йд, ту ~) решать [**perfective:** решить]
Deciphering (диса́йфэринг) расшифровка
Decision (диси́жн) выбор решения, определение, постановление, решение
   administrative ~ (адми́нистрэйтив ~) административное решение
   appellate ~ (аппэ́лат ~) решение апелляционного суда
   civil law ~ (си́вил лау ~) гражданско-правовое решение
   compulsory ~ (компу́лсори ~) обязательное решение
   contradictory ~ (контради́ктори ~) противоречивое решение
   declaratory ~ (диклэ́йратори ~) декларативное решение
   final ~ (фа́йнал ~) окончательное решение
   final judicial ~ (фа́йнал джюди́шл ~) окончательное судебное решение
   foreign ~ (фо́рэн ~) иностранное решение
   foreign arbitral ~ (фо́рэн а́рбитрал ~) иностранное арбитражное решение

interim ~ (и́нтэрим ~) временное определение
irrevocable ~ (иррэ́вокабл ~) неотменяемое решение
judicial ~ (джюди́шл ~) судебное определение, судебное решение
justified ~ (джа́стифайд ~) обоснованное решение
leaving a ~ **in force** (ли́винг а ~ ин форс) оставление решения в силе
original ~ (ори́джинал ~) первоначальное решение
preliminary ~ (прили́минэри ~) предварительное решение
preliminary judicial ~ (прили́минэри джюди́шл ~) предварительное судебное решение
principal ~ (при́нсипал ~) принципиальное решение
senate ~ (сэ́нат ~) сенатское решение
to affirm a ~ (ту аффи́рм а ~) подтвердить решение
to annul a ~ (ту анну́л а ~) аннулировать решение
to carry out a ~ (ту кэ́рри о́ут а ~) вынести решение
to leave a ~ **in force** (ту лив а ~ ин форс) оставить решение в силе
to overturn a judicial ~ (ту овэрту́рн а джюди́шл ~) отменить судебное решение
unanimous ~ (юна́нимос ~) единогласное решение
~ **by arbitration** (~ бай арбитрэ́йшн) третейское решение
~ **by a court of final instance** (~ бай а ко́урт оф фа́йнал и́нстанс) решение вынесенное судом последней инстанции
~ **by default** (~ бай дифа́лт) заочное решение
~ **of the court** (~ оф θи ко́урт) постановление суда
~ **of the court of cassation** {civil law} (~ оф θи ко́урт оф кассэ́йшн {си́вил ла́у}) кассационное определение
Deck (дэк) борт, бортовой {adj.}
   ship's ~ (шипс ~) борт
Declarant (дэклэ́йрант) заявитель, податель декларации
   original ~ (ори́джинал ~) первоначальный заявитель

Declaration (дэкларэйшн)
декларация, заявка, заявление,
объявление, объяснение,
провозглашение, совместный акт
   consignor's ~ (консайнорз ~)
   декларация грузоотправителя
   currency ~ (куррэнси ~) валютная
   декларация
   customs ~ (кастомз ~) таможенная
   декларация
   export ~ (экспорт ~) экспортная
   декларация
   false ~ (фалс ~) ложное
   заявление
   master's ~ (мастэрз ~)
   декларация капитана
   official ~ (оффишл ~)
   декларативный акт
   purchase ~ (пурчас ~) декларация
   о закупке
   shipper's ~ (шиппэрз ~)
   декларация грузоотправителя
   tariff ~ (тариф ~) тарифная
   декларация
   to fill out a ~ (ту фил оут а ~)
   заполнять декларацию
   value ~ (валю ~) стоимостные
   данные
   warehousing ~ (уэрхоузинг ~)
   декларация о грузах, подлежащих
   хранению в приписных складах
   ~ form (~ форм) бланк декларации
   ~ of annulment (~ оф аннулмэнт)
   объявление недействительности
   ~ of duty-free goods (~ оф дюти-
   фри гудз) декларация о грузах,
   не облагаемой пошлиной
   ~ of incapacity in a legal
   proceeding (~ оф инкапасити ин а
   лигал просидинг) объявление
   недееспособности в судебном
   порядке
   ~ of independence (~ оф
   индэпэндэнс) декларация
   независимости, провозглашение
   независимости, объявление
   независимости
   ~ of insolvency (~ оф
   инсолвэнси) объявление
   несостоятельности
   ~ of neutrality (~ оф нутралити)
   объявление нейтралитета
   ~ of reservation of right (~ оф
   рэзэрвэйшн оф райт) объявление
   выговора права
   ~ of sovereignty (~ оф совэрнти)
   провозглашение суверенитета

   ~ of war (~ оф уар) объявление
   войны, провозглашение состояния
   войны
Declare, to ~ (диклэйр, ту ~)
декларировать, заявлять
[perfective: заявить], объявлять
[perfective: объявить]
Decline (диклайн) падение,
понижение, снижение, сокращение,
спад
   to ~ (ту ~) отказать, отклонять
   ~ in birth rate (~ ин бэрθ рэйт)
   падение рождаемости
   ~ in the business cycle (~ ин θи
   бизнэс сайкл) спад конъюнктуры
   ~ in imports (~ ин импортс)
   сокращение импорта
   ~ in prices (~ ин прайсэз)
   снижение цен
   ~ in the prime cost (~ ин θи
   прайм кост) снижение
   себестоимости
   ~ in spending power (~ ин
   спэндинг поуэр) падение
   покупательной силы
Decoding (дикодинг) расшифровка
Decrease (дикрис) снижение,
уменьшение
   to ~ (ту ~) понижать, уменьшать
   to ~ by ... (ту ~ бай ...)
   уменьшать на
   to ~ to ... (ту ~ ту ...)
   уменьшать до
   to speculate on a ~ (ту
   спэкюлэйт он а ~) играть на
   понижение
   ~ in arbitration fee (~ ин
   арбитрэйшн фи) уменьшение
   размера арбитражного сбора
   ~ in prices (~ ин прайсэз)
   уменьшение цен
   ~ in production (~ ин продакшн)
   сокращение производства
   ~ in rent (~ ин рэнт) уменьшение
   арендной платы
   ~ in weight (~ ин уэйт)
   уменьшение в весе
Decree (дикри) постановление,
распоряжение, указ
   administrative ~ (администрэйтив
   ~) административный акт,
   административное постановление
   consent ~ (консэнт ~)
   концессионный акт
   court ~ (коурт ~) судебный акт
   executive ~ (экзэкютив ~)
   исполнительное постановление

governmental ~ (говэрнмэ́нтал ~)
правительственный акт
presidential ~ (прэзидэ́ншл ~)
указ президента
to ~ (ту ~) постановлять
~ of amnesty (~ оф а́мнэсти)
постановление об амнистии
Deduct, to ~ (диду́кт, ту ~)
производить вычет, производить
удержание, удерживать
to ~ from (ту ~ фром) вычитать
Deductibility (дидуктиби́лити)
возможность вычета
Deductible (диду́ктибл) подлежащий
вычету
Deducting ... (диду́ктинг ...) за
вычетом
Deduction (диду́кшн) вычет,
отчисление, удержание
amortized ~ (а́мортайзд ~)
амортизационное отчисление
automatic ~ (аутома́тик ~)
автоматический вычет
block ~ (блок ~) единый вычет
compulsory ~ (компу́лсори ~)
принудительный вычет
payment without ~ (пэ́ймэнт
уиθо́ут ~) платёж без вычетов
progressive ~ (прогрэ́ссив ~)
прогрессивное удержание
proportional ~ (пропо́ршнал ~)
пропорционально удержание
tax ~ (такс ~) налоговый вычет
to increase a ~ (ту инкри́с а ~)
увеличивать вычет
unauthorized ~ (ана́уθорайзд ~)
неразрешенный вычет
~ from profits (~ фром про́фитс)
отчисление от прибыли
~ of an amount (~ оф ан амо́унт)
удержание суммы
~ of expenses (~ оф экспэ́нсэз)
вычет расходов
~ of franchise (~ оф фра́нчайз)
удержание франшизы
Deed (дид) запись
gift ~ (гифт ~) дарственная
запись
mortgage ~ (мо́ргэдж ~)
закладная, закладной лист
partition ~ (парти́шн ~)
раздельная запись
title ~ (тайтл ~) документ,
подтверждающий право
собственности документ
~ of incorporation (~ оф
инкорпорэ́йшн) конститутивный акт

~ of protest (~ оф про́тэст) акт
о протесте
~ of sale (~ оф сэйл) акт
продажи
Deep-water (дип-уа́тэр)
глубоководный
Default (дифа́лт) невыполнения
обязательств, неплатёж, неуплата
by ~ (бай ~) заочно, заочный
in case of ~ of payment (ин кэйс
оф ~ оф пэ́ймэнт) в случае
неуплаты, в случае неплатежа
in the event of a ~ (ин θи ивэ́нт
оф а ~) в случае невыполнения
обязательств
judgment by ~ (джа́джмэнт бай ~)
заочный приговор
partial ~ (паршл ~) частичное
невыполнение
~ of appearance {at hearing,
trial} (~ оф аппи́ранс {ат
хи́ринг, тра́йал}) неявка в суд
~ of credit (~ оф крэ́дит)
неуплата задолженности по
кредиту
~ of payment (~ оф пэ́ймэнт)
неплатёж
Defaulter (дифа́лтэр) неплательщик
Defeat (дифи́т) поражениеб разгром
Defect (ди́фэкт) дефект, изъян,
неисправность, порок ~s брак
alleged ~ (аллэ́джид ~)
предполагаемый дефект
basic ~ (бэ́йсик ~) основной
дефект
correction of a ~ (коррэ́кшн оф а
~) исправление дефекта
dangerous ~ (дэ́йнджэрос ~)
опасный дефект
description of ~s (дэскри́пшн оф
~с) описание дефектов
design ~ (диза́йн ~) дефект в
конструкции
incidental ~ (инсидэ́нтал ~)
случайный дефект
inherent ~ (инхэ́рэнт ~)
внутренний дефект
initial ~ (ини́шл ~)
первоначальный дефект
insignificant ~ (инсигни́фикант
~) незначительный дефект
latent ~s (лэ́йтэнт ~с) скрытый
дефект, скрытые недостатки
manufacturing ~s (манюфа́кчуринг
~с) дефект завода-изготовителя,
производственные недостатки

material ~s (матириал ~с) существенные недостатки

minor ~ (майнор ~) второстепенный дефект

minor ~s (майнор ~с) мелкие недостатки

natural ~ (начюрал ~) естественный дефект

nature of a ~ (нэйчэр оф а ~) характер дефекта

non-existent ~ (нон-экзистэнт ~) несущественный дефект

obvious ~ (обвиос ~) явный дефект

packing ~ (паккинг ~) дефект упаковки

production ~ (продакшн ~) дефект производства

reason for a ~ (ризон фор а ~) причина дефекта

serious ~ (сириос ~) значительный дефект, серьёзный дефект

serious ~s (сириос ~с) крупные недостатки

slight ~ (слайт ~) мелкий дефект

stated ~ (стэйтэд ~) заявленный дефект

surface ~ (сурфас ~) поверхностный дефект

to be free of ~s (ту би фри оф ~с) не иметь дефектов

to be liable for a ~ (ту би лайабл фор а ~) быть ответственным за дефект

to conceal a ~ (ту консил а ~) скрывать дефект

to correct a ~ (ту коррэкт а ~) исправлять дефект

to discover a ~ (ту дисковэр а ~) обнаруживать дефект

to eliminate a ~ (ту илиминэйт а ~) устранять дефект

to eliminate a ~ at ... expense (ту илиминэйт а ~ ат ... экспэнс) устранять дефект за счёт

to eliminate a ~ without prejudice to the other side (ту илиминэйт а ~ уиθоут прэджюдис ту θи оθэр сайд) устранять дефект без ущемления прав другой стороны

to eliminate a ~ by agreement of the parties (ту илиминэйт а ~ бай агримэнт оф θи партиз)

устранять дефект по соглашению сторон

to have ~s (ту хэв ~с) иметь дефекты

to remedy ~s (ту рэмэди ~с) исправлять недостатки

undiscovered ~ (андисковэрд ~) необнаруженный дефект

visual ~ (вижуал ~) внешний дефект

~ detection (~ дитэкшн) дефектоскопия

~ in goods (~ ин гудз) дефект товара

~ in quality (~ ин куалити) отклонение в качестве

Defection (дифэкшн) переход
~ to the enemy (~ ту θи энэми) переход на сторону врага

Defective (дифэктив) дефектный, забракованный, неисправный, неполноценный

Defend, to ~ (дифэнд, ту ~) защищать [perfective: защитить]

Defender (дифэндэр) защитник
public ~ (паблик ~) общественный защитник

Defense (дифэнс) защита
counsel for the ~ (коунсэл фор θи ~) защитник

joint ~ (джойнт ~) совместная защита

personal ~ (пэрсонал ~) личная защита

political ~ (политикал ~) политическая защитар

to mount a ~ (ту моунт а ~) защищать [perfective: защитить]

~ attorney (~ аттóрни) защитник

~ in court (~ ин коурт) защита в суде

~ of a dissertation (~ оф а диссэртэйшн) защита диссертации

~ of children (~ оф чилдрэн) защита детей

~ of patent right (~ оф патэнт райт) защита патентного права

~ of territory (~ оф тэрритори) защита территории

Defer, to ~ (дифэр, ту ~) отсрочивать

Deferred (дифэрд) отсроченный

Deficiency (дифишэнси) недостаток, недостаточность, недостача, нехватка

liability for ~ (лайабилити фор ~) ответственность за недостачу

Deficient (дифи́шэнт) недостающий, неполный
Deficit (дэ́фисит) дефицит, дефицитный {adj.}, недочёт
   balance of payments ~ (ба́ланс оф пэ́ймэнтс ~) дефицит платёжного баланса
   balancing of a ~ (ба́лансинг оф а ~) сбалансирование дефицита
   budget ~ (ба́джэт ~) бюджетный дефицит
   cash ~ (каш ~) кассовый дефицит
   chronic ~ (кро́ник ~) хронический дефицит
   current ~ (ку́ррэнт ~) текущий дефицит
   current account ~ (ку́ррэнт акко́унт ~) дефицит текущего счёта
   dollar ~ (до́ллар ~) долларовый дефицит
   existing ~ (экзи́стинг ~) существующий дефицит
   external ~ (эксте́рнал ~) внешний дефицит
   financial ~ (файна́ншл ~) финансовый дефицит
   foreign exchange ~ (фо́рэн эксчэ́йндж ~) дефицит валюты
   foreign trade ~ (фо́рэн трэйд ~) внешнеторговый дефицит
   growth of a ~ (гроθ оф а ~) рост дефицита
   insignificant ~ (инсигни́фикант ~) незначительный дефицит
   monetary ~ (мо́нэтари ~) денежная недостача
   outstanding ~ (оутста́ндинг ~) непокрытый дефицит
   short-term ~ (шорт-тэрм ~) краткосрочный дефицит
   size of a ~ (сайз оф а ~) размер дефицита
   to balance a ~ (ту ба́ланс а ~) сальдировать дефицит
   to cause a ~ (ту кауз а ~) вызывать дефицит
   to compensate for a ~ (ту ко́мпэнсэйт фор а ~) покрывать дефицит
   to have a ~ (ту хэв а ~) иметь дефицит
   to offset a ~ (ту о́ффсэт а ~) компенсировать дефицит
   to reduce a ~ (ту ридю́с а ~) сократить дефицит

   trade ~ (трэйд ~) дефицит внешторгового баланса, дефицит торгового баланса
Defilement (дифа́йлмэнт) осквернение
Definite (дэ́финит) определенный
Definition (дэфини́шн) определение
Defray, to ~ (дифрэ́й, ту ~) оплачивать
Defrayal (дифрэ́йал) покрытие
   ~ of expenses (~ оф экспэ́нсэз) покрытие расходов
Defrayment (дифрэ́ймэнт) покрытие
Degree (дигри́) степень, уровень
   academic ~ (акадэ́мик ~) учёная степень
   doctoral ~ (до́кторал ~) докторская степень
   ~ of development (~ оф дивэ́лопмэнт) уровень развития
   ~ of guilt (~ оф гилт) степень виновности
   ~ of risk (~ оф риск) уровень риска
   ~ of service (~ оф сэ́рвис) уровень обслуживания
Del credere (дэл крэдэ́рэ) делькредере
   to stand ~ (ту станд ~) принять на себя делькредере, ручаться
   ~ agent (~ э́йджэнт) комиссионер, берущий на себя делькредере
   ~ commission (~ комми́шн) комиссия за делькредере
Delay (дилэ́й) задержка, замедление, опоздание, отлагательство, отсрочка, промедление, просрочка
   protracted ~ (протра́ктэд ~) большая задержка
   to ~ (ту ~) задерживать, промедлить
   unexcused ~ (анэкскю́зд ~) неоправданное опоздание
   unjustified ~ (анджа́стифайд ~) неоправданная задержка
   ~ in performance (~ ин пэрфо́рманс) задержка в исполнении
Delegate (дэ́лэгат) делегат
   to elect a ~ (ту илэ́кт а ~) избирать делегатом
   to send in the capacity of a ~ (ту сэнд ин θи капа́сити оф а ~) посылать в качестве делегата
   ~ to a conference (~ ту а ко́нфэрэнс) делегат конференции
Delegation (дэлэгэ́йшн) делегация

foreign ~ (фóрэн ~) иностранная делегация

governmental ~ (говэрнмэ́нтал ~) правительственная делегация

head of a ~ (хэд оф а ~) руководитель делегации

high-level ~ (хай-лэ́вэл ~) делегация руководящих деятелей

large ~ (лардж ~) большая делегация

representative ~ (рэпрэзэ́нтатив ~) представительная делегация

to head a ~ (ту хэд ап а ~) возглавлять делегацию

to receive a ~ (ту риси́в а ~) принимать делегацию

trade ~ (трэйд ~) торговая делегация

~ of authority (~ оф аθóрити) передача полномочий

Deliberate, to ~ (дили́бэрэйт, ту ~) совещаться

Deliberately (дили́бэратли) преднамеренно

Deliberative (дили́бэратив) совещательный

Delicate (дэ́ликат) щекотливый

Delict (дэли́кт) правонарушение, преступление

corpus ~/i (кóрпус ~/ай) состав преступления

Delimit, to ~ (дили́мит, ту ~) размежевать

Delinquency (дэли́нкуэнси) преступность

juvenile ~ (джю́вэнайл ~) детская преступность

Deliver, to ~ (дэли́вэр, ту ~) доставлять, сдавать [perfective: сдать]

Deliverable (дэли́вэрабл) подлежащий доставке

Delivered (дэли́вэрэд) доставляемый

free ~ (фри ~) доставка франко

~ free alongside ship (~ фри алонгса́йд шип) выдача груза у борта судна

~ price (~ прайс) цена с доставкой

Delivery (дэли́вэри) вручение, выдача, доставка, завоз, поставка, разнос, рассылка, рассыльный {adj.}, сдача

advance ~ (адва́нс ~) досрочная доставка

cash on ~ {C.O.D.} (каш он ~ {си-о-ди}) наложенный платёж

certificate of ~ (сэрти́фикэт оф ~) приемо-сдаточный акт

contracted ~s (кóнтрактэд ~с) договорные поставки

fresh ~s (фрэш ~с) новые поставки

collect on ~ {C.O.D.} (коллэ́кт он ~ {си-о-ди}) оплата при доставке

complete ~s (компли́т ~с) комплектная поставка

cost of ~s (кост оф ~с) стоимость доставки

delay in ~s (дилэ́й ин ~с) задержка в доставке

door to door cargo ~s (дур ту дур ка́рго ~с) доставка груза на условиях "от двери до двери"

expedited ~s (э́кспэдайтэд ~с) ускоренная поставка

express ~s (экспрэ́с ~с) быстрая доставка

forward ~s (фóруард ~с) будущая сдача

immediate ~s (имми́диат ~с) немедленная доставка

internal ~s (интэ́рнал ~с) внутренняя поставка

land lease ~s (ланд лис ~с) ленд-лизовская поставка

late ~s (лэйт ~с) запоздавшая доставка, запоздалая сдача

legal ~s (ли́гал ~с) юридическая сдача

means of ~ (минз оф ~) средства доставки

package ~ (па́кэдж ~) комплектная поставка

paid ~ (пэйд ~) оплаченная доставка

partial ~ (паршл ~) частичная сдача

payable on ~ (пэ́йабл он ~) с уплатой при доставке

point of ~ (пойнт оф ~) место доставки

safe ~ (сэйф ~) сохранная доставка

satisfactory ~ (сатисфа́ктори ~) удовлетворительная поставка

short ~ (шорт ~) доставка неполного количества, неполная поставка, неполная сдача, убыль в весе

special ~ (спэшл ~) срочная доставка

speedy ~ (спи́ди ~) быстрая поставка
to delay ~ (ту дилэ́й ~) задерживать доставку
to effect ~ (ту иффэ́кт ~) осуществлять доставку
to make ~ (ту мэйк ~) производить доставку
to pay on ~ (ту пэй он ~) платить при доставке
to postpone ~ (ту постпо́н ~) отсрочивать доставку
to suspend ~ (ту саспэ́нд ~) приостанавливать доставку
trial ~ (тра́йал ~) пробная поставка
~ against a letter of commitment (~ агэ́нст а лэ́ттэр оф комми́тмэнт) выдача против обязательственного письма
~ against acceptance (~ агэ́нст аксэ́птанс) выдача против акцента
~ against trust receipt (~ агэ́нст траст риси́т) выдача против сохранной расписки
~ boy (~ бой) рассыльный
~ charge (~ чардж) плата за доставку
~ costs (~ костс) издержки по доставке
~ for export (~ фор э́кспорт) поставка на экспорт
~ for storage (~ фор сто́радж) сдача на хранение
~ free of charge (~ фри оф чардж) бесплатная поставка
~ in partial consignments (~ ин паршл конса́йнмэнтс) поставка по частичным партиям
~ note (~ нот) транспортный коносамент
~ of cargo (~ оф ка́рго) выдача груза, выдача товара
~ of documents (~ оф до́кюмэнтс) вручение документов
~ of documents against payment (~ оф до́кюмэнтс агэ́нст пэ́ймэнт) выдача против платежа
~ on an ex-plant basis (~ он ан экс-плант бэ́йсис) не включая стоимость доставки
~ order (~ о́рдэр) деливери-ордер {customs}, ордер на выдачу товара
~ period (~ пи́риод) срок доставки

Demand (дима́нд) востребование, истребование, потребление, потребность, спрос, требование
active ~ (а́ктив ~) оживлённый спрос
brisk ~ (бриск ~) живой спрос
consumer ~ (консу́мэр ~) потребительский спрос
domestic ~ (домэ́стик ~) внутренние потребности, внутренний спрос
effective ~ (иффэ́ктив ~) эффективный спрос
elastic ~ (ила́стик ~) эластичный спрос
external ~ (экстэ́рнал ~) внешний спрос
immediate ~ (имми́диат ~) срочный спрос
increasing ~ (инкри́синг ~) растущий спрос
inelastic ~ (инила́стик ~) жёсткий спрос
insistent ~ (инси́стэнт ~) настойчивое требование
just ~ (джаст ~) справедливое требование
loan ~ (лон ~) спрос займы
overall ~ (овэра́л ~) общий спрос
persistent ~ (пэрси́стэнт ~) постоянный спрос
plaintiff's ~ (плэ́йнтифс ~с) требования истца
reasonable ~ (ри́зонабл ~) обоснованное требование
sluggish ~ (слу́ггиш ~) вялый спрос
solvent ~ (со́лвэнт ~) платёжеспособный спрос
supply and ~ (суппла́й энд ~) спрос и предложение {literally: demand and supply}
to ~ (ту ~) истребовать, требовать
to ~ one's money back (ту ~ уа́нз мо́ни бак) истребовать обратно уплаченное
to make ~s (ту мэйк ~с) выдвигать требования
to present a ~ (ту прэзэ́нт а ~) заявлять требование
urgent ~ (у́рджэнт ~) срочное требование
~ for credit (~ фор крэ́дит) спрос на кредит
Demarcate, to ~ (дима́ркэйт, ту ~) разграничивать, размежевать

Demarcation (димаркэ́йшн)
разграничение, размежевание
territorial ~ (тэррито́риал ~)
территориальное разграничение
~ of national boundaries (~ оф
на́шэнал бо́ундариз) национально-
государственное размежевание
Demijohn (дэ́миджон) большая,
оплетённая бутыль
Demise (дима́йз) кончина
~ charter (~ ча́ртэр) димайз-
чартер
Demonstration (дэмонстрэ́йшн)
демонстрационный {adj.},
демонстрация, экспонирование
flight ~ (флайт ~) демонстрация
полёта
practical ~ (пра́ктикал ~)
практическая демонстрация
program of ~s (про́грам оф ~с)
программа демонстрации
public ~ (па́блик ~) публичная
демонстрация
to arrange a ~ (ту аррэ́йндж а ~)
устраивать демонстрацию
~ of an invention (~ оф ан
инвэ́ншн) демонстрация
изобретения
Demonstrator (дэ́монстрэйтор)
манифестант
Demote, to ~ (димо́т, ту ~) понижать
в должности
Demotion (димо́шн) перевод на низшую
должность, понижение в должности
~ to a lower position (~ ту а
ло́уэр пози́шн) смещение на низшую
должность
Demurrage (диму́рradж) взыскание
демерреджа, время простоя,
демерредж, контрсталийный
{adj.},контрсталия, контрсталийные
деньги {payment}, простой
calculation of ~ (калкюлэ́йшн оф
~) калькуляция демерреджа
to charge ~ (ту чардж ~) взимать
демерредж
to pay ~ (ту пэй ~) оплачивать
контрсталию
~ calculation (~ калкюлэ́йшн)
расчёт демерреджа
~ claim (~ клэйм) претензия в
связи с демерреджем
~ payment (~ пэ́ймэнт) оплата
демерреджа
~ rate (~ рэйт) ставка
демерреджа
Den (дэн) притон

gambling ~ (га́мблинг ~) игорный
притон
~ of thieves (~ оф θивз)
воровской притон
Denationalization (динашнализэ́йшн)
денационализация
Denationalize, to ~ (дина́шналайз,
ту ~) денационализировать
Denial (дина́йал) опровержение,
отказ, отклонение, отрицание
Denomination (диномин э́йшн)
деноминация, достоинство {monetary
unit}, купюра
~ of a bank note (~ оф а банк
нот) купюра банкноты
~ of an applicant (~ оф ан
а́пликант) наименование
заявителя
Denounce, to ~ (дино́унс, ту ~)
денонсировать
Density (дэ́нсити) плотность
population ~ (попюлэ́йшн ~)
плотность населения
Denunciation (динунсиэ́йшн) акт о
денонсации, денонсация
Deny, to ~ (дина́й, ту ~) отклонять,
отрицать
Depart, to ~ from (дипа́рт, ту ~
фром) отступать
Department (дипа́ртмэнт) бюро,
ведомство, отдел, служба
advertising ~ (а́двэртайзинг ~)
рекламное бюро
branch ~s (бранч ~с) отраслевые
ведомства
design ~ (диза́йн ~)
конструкторское бюро
financial ~ (файна́ншл ~)
финансовый отдел
housing ~ (хо́узинг ~) жилищный
отдел
public-relations ~ (па́блик-
рилэ́йшнс ~) бюро по связи с
общественностью
service ~ (сэ́рвис ~) бюро
обслуживания
technical ~ (тэ́кникал ~)
техническое бюро
~ of Visas and Registration (~
оф ви́зас энд рэджистрэ́йшн) Отдел
Виз и Регистрации {ОВИР}
Departure (дипа́рчур) выезд, вылет
{by air}, отправление, отступление,
отход
actual ~ (а́кчуал ~) фактический
вылет

date of ~ (дэйт оф ~) дата выезда
day of ~ (дэй оф ~) день выезда
scheduled ~ (скэ́джюлд ~) запланированный вылет
Dependability (дипэндаби́лити) надёжность
Dependable (дипэ́ндабл) надёжный
Dependence (дипэ́ндэнс) зависимость, иждивенчество
  complete ~ (компли́т ~) полная зависимость
  economic ~ (эконо́мик ~) экономическая зависимость
  financial ~ (файна́ншл ~) финансовая зависимость
  increasing ~ (инкри́синг ~) растущая зависимость
  partial ~ (паршл ~) частичная зависимость
  personal ~ (пэ́рсонал ~) личная зависимость
  to reduce ~ (ту ридю́с ~) сокращать зависимость
Dependent (дипэ́ндэнт) зависимый {adj.}, иждивенец {family law}
  to be ~ upon (ту би ~ упо́н) находиться в зависимости от
Deploy, to (дипло́й, ту) развёртывать [perfective: развёрнуть]
  to ~ military (ту ~ ми́литари) расчленять
Deployment (дипло́ймэнт) размещение, расчленение {military}
Deponent (дэпо́нэнт) заявитель
Deportation (дэпорт э́йшн) поселение
Deposit (дипо́зит) взнос, вклад, вкладной {adj.}, депозит, депозитный {adj.}, задаток, залог, месторождение {minerals, etc.}
  acceptance of ~s (аксэ́птанс оф ~с) приём вкладов
  amount of a ~ (амо́унт оф а ~) размер взноса
  balance on ~ (ба́ланс он ~) остаток на вкладе
  bank ~ (банк ~) банковский вклад, банковский депозит
  bank ~ receipt (банк ~ риси́т) квитанция банка о принятии вклада
  call ~ (кал ~) депозит до востребования
  cash ~ (каш ~) взнос наличными деньгами, денежные взнос, денежный вклад, денежный депозит

demand ~ (дима́нд ~) бессрочный вклад, вклад до востребования, бессрочный депозит
depreciation of ~ (диприши э́йшн оф ~) обесценение вкладов
Dollar-denominated ~ (до́ллар-дино́минэйтэд ~) долларовый депозит
escrow ~ (э́скро ~) условный депозит
fixed period ~ (фиксд пи́риод ~) срочный вклад
fixed term ~ (фиксд тэрм ~) вклад на срок
freely transferrable ~s (фри́ли трансфэ́рабл ~с) свободно переводимые депозиты
general average ~ (джэ́нэрал а́вэрэдж ~) взнос по общей аварии
general ~ (джэ́нэрал ~) обычный депозит
government ~ (го́вэрнмэнт ~) правительственный депозит
guaranteed ~ (гяранти́д ~) гарантийный депозит
idle ~ (айдл ~) неиспользуемый депозит
increase of ~s (инкри́с оф ~с) увеличение вкладов
initial ~ (ини́шл ~) первоначальный взнос, первоначальный вклад
interest bearing ~ (и́нтэрэст бэ́ринг ~) процентный вклад
interest on ~s (и́нтэрэст он ~с) проценты по вкладам
interest rate on ~ (и́нтэрэст рэйт он ~) ставка процента по вкладам
long term ~ (лонг тэрм ~) долгосрочный вклад
mineral ~ (ми́нэрал ~) месторождение полезных ископаемых
non-interest bearing ~ (нон-и́нтэрэст бэ́ринг ~) беспроцентный вклад
on call ~ (он кал ~) вклад на текущий счёт
ore ~ (ор ~) месторождение руды
period of ~ (пи́риод оф ~) срок вклада
primary ~ (пра́ймари ~) первичный депозит
privacy of ~s (пра́йваси оф ~с) тайна вкладов

refundable ~ (рифу́ндабл ~) возвратный вклад

reserve ~ (рисэ́рв ~) резервный депозит

rich ~ (рич ~) богатое месторождение

savings ~ (сэ́йвингс ~) сберегательный вклад

secured ~ (сэкю́рд ~) застрахованный депозит

service charge on a demand ~ account (сэ́рвис чардж он а диманд ~ акко́унт) проценты по бессрочному вкладу

short-term ~ (шорт-тэрм ~) краткосрочный вклад, краткосрочный депозит

special ~ (спэшл ~) специальный депозит

specific ~ (спэси́фик ~) специальный вклад

sum of ~ (сум оф ~) сумма вклада

term ~ (тэрм ~) срочный депозит

time ~ (тайм ~) временный счёт

to accept a ~ (ту аксэ́пт а ~) принимать вклад

to accept a ~ at interest (ту аксэ́пт а ~ ат и́нтэрэст) принимать вклад под процент

to close out a ~ (ту клоз о́ут а ~) снять депозит

to have a ~ at the bank (ту хэв а ~ ат θи банк) иметь депозит в банке

to hold a ~ (ту холд а ~) иметь вклад

to have on ~ (ту хэв он ~) иметь на вкладе

to make a ~ (ту мэйк а ~) вносить вклад

to make an initial ~ (ту мэйк ан ини́шл ~) платить первоначальный взнос

to pay a ~ (ту пэй а ~) выплачивать деньги по депозиту

to retain a ~ (ту ритэ́йн а ~) удерживать депозит

to transfer money on ~ (ту тра́нсфэр мо́ни он ~) переводить деньги на депозит

to transfer money from ~ (ту тра́нсфэр мо́ни фром ~) перечислять деньги с депозита

to unblock a ~ (ту анбло́к а ~) разблокировать депозит

to withdraw a ~ (ту уиθдра́у а ~) брать вклад из банка

transfer of money on ~ (тра́нсфэр оф мо́ни он ~) перевод денег на депозит

withdrawal of a ~ (уиθдра́уал оф а ~) изъятие вклад

Withdrawal of ~s (уиθдра́уал оф ~с) изъятие депозитов

~ at long notice (~ ат лонг но́тис) вклад с длительным уведомлением

~ at notice (~ ат но́тис) вклад с уведомлением

~ at short notice (~ ат шорт но́тис) вклад с краткосрочным уведомлением

~ of ...% (~ оф ...%) взнос в...%

~ rate (~ рэйт) ставка по депозитам

~ slip (~ слип) бланк для взноса депозита

Depositary (дипо́зитари) депозитарий

Depositee (дипозити́) залогодержатель

Deposition (дэпози́шн) заявление, показание

perjured ~ (пэ́рджюрд ~) ложное заявление

to take a ~ from a witness (ту тэйк а ~ фром а уи́тнэс) отбирать показание у свидетеля

Depositor (дипо́зитор) вкладчик, владелец вклада, депонент, залогодатель

Depository (дипо́зитори) хранилище

Depot (ди́по) база, депо, склад, хранилище

container ~ (контэ́йнэр ~) контейнерная база

maintenance ~ (мэ́йнтэнанс ~) база технического обслуживания и текущего ремонта

sales ~ (сэйлз ~) сбытовая база

supply ~ (суппла́й ~) торговая база

~ ship (~ шип) плавучая база

Depreciate, to ~ (дипри́шиэйт, ту ~) амортизировать {e.g. equipment}, обесценивать {e.g. government action}, обесцениваться {said of currency, etc.}

Depreciated (дипри́шиэйтэд) обесцененный

Depreciation (диприши́эйшн) амортизация, уменьшение стоимости

annual ~ (а́ннюал ~) ежегодная амортизация

gradual ~ (гра́джюал ~)
постепенная амортизация
stepped-up ~ (стэ́ппэд-ап ~)
ускоренная амортизация
~ **of capital** (~ оф ка́питал)
обесценение капитала
~ **of currency against major**
currencies (~ оф ку́ррэнси агэ́нст
мэ́йджор ку́ррэнсиз) обесценение
валюты по отношению к основным
валютам
~ **of the dollar** (~ оф θи до́ллар)
обесценение доллара
~ **of fixed assets** (~ оф фиксд
а́ссэтс) основных фондов износ
~ **of gold prices** (~ оф голд
пра́йсэз) обесценение золота
Depressed (дипрэ́сд) вялый
~ **economic activity** (~ эконо́мик
акти́вити) вялость хозяйственной
деятельности
Depression (дипрэ́шн) депрессия
{economic and psychological},
застой, кризис
acute ~ (акю́т ~) острый кризис
cyclical ~ (си́кликал ~)
циклический кризис
economic ~ (эконо́мик ~)
хозяйственный застой
Deprive, to ~ (дипра́йв, ту ~)
лишать
Deprivation (дэприве́йшн) лишение
Deputize, to ~ (дэ́пютайз, ту ~)
замещать [**perfective:** заместить]
Deputy (дэ́пюти) заместитель
~ **director** (~ дирэ́ктор)
заместитель директора
~ **minister** (~ ми́нистэр)
заместитель заместителя министра
Dereliction (дэрэли́кшн)
пренебрежение
~ **of duty** (~ оф дю́ти)
ненадлежащее выполнение
обязанностей, пренебрежение
своими обязанностями
Derive, to ~ (дира́йв, ту ~) извлечь
Derrick (дэ́ррик) подъёмные
Descendant (дисэ́ндант) потомок ~s
потомство
Descent (дисэ́нт) происхождение
Describe, to ~ (дискра́йб, ту ~)
описать
Description (дискри́пшн) изложение,
описание
patent ~ (па́тэнт ~) патентное
описание

~ **of an article** (~ оф ан а́ртикл)
наименование изделия
~ **of cargo** (~ оф ка́рго)
наименование груза
~ **of chattels** (~ оф ша́ттэлз)
описание имуществ
~ **of defects** (~ оф ди́фэктс)
описание дефектов
~ **of expenditures** (~ оф
экспэ́ндичюрз) описание растрат
~ **of goods** (~ оф гудз)
наименование товара
~ **of invention** (~ оф инвэ́ншн)
описание изобретения
~ **of real property** (~ оф рил
про́пэрти) описание недвижимых
имуществ
~ **of the subject of a lease** (~
оф θи са́бджэкт оф а лис)
описание предмета найма
Deserter (дизэ́ртэр) перебежчик
Design (диза́йн) дизайн,
конструкторский {adj.},
конструкция, проект
advertising ~ (а́двэртайзинг ~)
дизайн рекламного объявления
custom ~ (ка́стом ~) особая
конструкция
faulty ~ (фа́лти ~) неправильная
конструкция
infringement of ~ (инфринджмэнт
оф ~) нарушение конструкции
modern ~ (мо́дэрн ~) современная
конструкция
of the latest ~ (оф θи лэ́йтэст
~) новейшей конструкции
optimum ~ (о́птимум ~)
оптимальная конструкция
patented ~ (па́тэнтэд ~)
запатентованный дизайн
preliminary ~ (прили́минэри ~)
предварительный проект
protection of registered ~s
(протэ́кшн оф рэ́джистэрд ~с)
защита моделей
reliable ~ (рила́йабл ~) надёжная
конструкция
standard ~ (ста́ндард ~) типовая
конструкция
to ~ (ту ~) конструировать
to apply a ~ (ту аппла́й а ~)
применять конструкцию
to check a ~ (ту чэк а ~)
проверять конструкцию
unique ~ (юни́к ~) уникальная
конструкция

unreliable ~ (анрилáйабл ~)
ненадёжная конструкция
~ **analysis** (~ анáлисис) анализ
конструкции
~ **approval** (~ аппрýвал)
одобрение конструкции
~ **consultant** (~ консýлтант)
консультант по дизайну
~ **improvement** (~ импрýвмэнт)
улучшение дизайна
~ **project leader** (~ прóджэкт
лѝдэр) ведущий конструктор
~ **review** (~ ривю) пересмотр
конструкции
~ **selection** (~ сэлѐкшн) выбор
варианта конструкции
Designate, to ~ (дѐзигнэйт, ту ~)
обозначать, предназначать
Designation (дэсигнѐйшн)
назначение, обозначение
letter ~ (лѐттэр ~) буквенное
обозначение
Designer (дизáйнэр) дизайнер,
конструктор
chief ~ (чиф ~) главный
конструктор
Designing (дизáйнинг)
конструирование, проектирование
Desk (дэск) бюро {department}
information ~ (информѐйшн ~)
справочное бюро
Destabilization (дистэйбилизѐйшн)
дестабилизация
~ **of the economy** (~ оф θи
икóноми) дестабилизация
экономики
Destination (дэстинѐйшн) пункт
назначения
airport of ~ (ѐйрпорт оф ~)
аэродром назначения
export ~ (ѐкспорт ~) место
назначения экспортного груза
final ~ (фáйнал ~) конечное
место назначения, конечный пункт
морского пути {sea-going vessel}
inland ~ (ѝнланд ~) место
назначения
required ~ (рикуáйрд ~)
требуемое место назначения
station of ~ (стѐйшн оф ~)
станция назначения
Destitution (дэститýшн) нищета
Destroy, to ~ (дистрóй, ту ~)
истреблять [**perfective:** истребить],
разгромить
Destroyer (дистрóйэр) истребитель

Destruction (дистрýкшн)
истребление, порча
~ **of property** (~ оф прóпэрти)
порча имущества
Detachment (дитáчмэнт) отряд
Detail (дѝтэйл) деталь
in ~ (ин ~) детально
pricing ~s (прáйсинг ~с) детали
расценки
specific ~s (спэсѝфик ~с)
характерные детали
technical ~s (тѐкникал ~с)
технические детали
to provide ~s (ту провáйд ~с)
представлять детали
Detailed (дѝтэйлд)
детализированный, детальный
Detain, to ~ (дитѐйн, ту ~)
задерживать
Detainee (дитэйнѝ) арестованный
Detect, to ~ (дитѐкт, ту ~)
обнаруживать
Detention (дитѐншн) детеншен {of a
vessel}, задержание, удержание
administrative ~ (адмѝнистрэйтив
~) задержание в административном
порядке
legal ~ (лѝгал ~) законное
задержание
subject to ~ (сáбджэкт ту ~)
подлежащий задержанию
to be subject to ~ (ту би
сáбджэкт ту ~) подлежать
задержанию
temporary ~ (тѐмпорари ~)
временное задержание
~ **beyond laydays** (~ бийóнд
лѐйдэйс) сверхконтрсталийные
деньги
~ **charges** (~ чáрджэз) штраф за
задержку разгрузки
~ **of goods** (~ оф гудз)
задержание товаров
Deterioration (дитириорѐйшн) износ,
старение
Determination (дитэрминѐйшн)
определение
~ **of a border** (~ оф а бóрдэр)
определение границы
~ **of legal competency** (~ оф
лѝгал кóмпэтэнси) определение
компетенций
~ **of violation** (~ оф вайолѐйшн)
определение правонарушения
Determine, to ~ (дитѐрмин, ту ~)
определять

Dethrone, to ~ (диθрóн, ту ~) свергнуть с престола
Dethronement (диθрóнмэнт) свержение с престола
Detour (дúтур) обходной маршрут
Detriment (дэтримэнт) ущерб
   without ~ **to the rights of...** (уиθóут ~ ту θи райтс оф...) без ущерба прав...
Detrimental (дэтримэ́нтал) вредный
   it will be extremely ~, **if ...** (ит уил би экстрúмли ~, иф ...) будет нанесён огромный ущерб, если ...
Devaluation (дивалюэ́йшн) девальвация, обесценение
   currency ~ (кýррэнси ~) девальвация валюты
   extent of ~ (экстэ́нт оф ~) размер девальвации
   impending ~ (импэ́ндинг ~) предстоящая девальвация
   rate of ~ (рэйт оф ~) степень обесценения
   ~ **of currency** (~ оф кýррэнси) обесценение валюты
   ~ **of paper money** (~ оф пэ́йпэр мóни) обесценение бумажных денег
Devalue, to ~ (дивáлю, ту ~) девальвировать, обесценивать {e.g., goverment action}, обесцениваться {said of currency, etc.}, проводить девальвацию
Devalued (дивáлюд) девальвированный
Devastate, to ~ (дэвастэйт, ту ~) разгромить
Devastation (дэвастэ́йшн) разгром
Development (дивэ́лопмэнт) развитие, создание, фактор
   chance ~ (чанс ~) случайный фактор
   commercial ~ (коммэ́ршл ~) коммерческое развитие
   economic ~ (экономик ~) экономическое развитие
   engineering ~ (инджэни́ринг ~) доводка опытного образца
   favorable ~ (фэ́йворабл ~) благоприятный фактор
   market ~ (мáркэт ~) расширение рынка
   natural ~ (нáчюрал ~) естественное развитие
   new ~ (нью ~) новое усовершенствование, новый фактор

   operational ~ (опэрэ́йшнал ~) доводка
   peaceful ~ (пúсфул ~) мирное развитие
   rapid ~ (рáпид ~) бурное развитие
Deviate, to ~ **from** (дúвиэйт, ту ~ фром) отступать
Deviation (дивиэ́йшн) отклонение, отступление
   ~ **from parity** (~ фром пáрити) отклонение от паритета
   ~ **from the rules** (~ фром θи рулз) отступление от правил
   ~ **of prices** (~ оф прáйсэз) отклонение цен
Device (дивáйс) механизм
Devise, to ~ (дивáйз, ту ~) записывать [perfective: записать]
Devolve, to ~ **into smaller units** (дивóлв, ту ~ úнту смáллэр юнитс) разукрупнять
Diagnostic (дайагнóстик) диагностический
Diagram (дáйаграм) диаграмма, схема
   block ~ (блок ~) функциональная диаграмма
Diem (дúэм) день
   payment per ~ (пэ́ймэнт пэр ~) оплата за день
   per ~ **allowance** (пэр ~ аллóуанс) суточные
   per ~ (пэр ~) в день
Difference (дúффэрэнс) различие, разница, разногласие, рознь
   fundamental ~**s** (фундамэ́нтал ~с) основные различия
   ~ **in rates** (~ ин рэйтс) разница в курсах
   ~ **of opinions** (~ оф опúнионс) различие мнений, расхождение во мнениях
Differential (диффэрэ́ншл) дифференциальный
   price ~ (прайс ~) разница в ценах
Differentiate, to ~ (диффэрэ́ншиэйт, ту ~) дифференцировать
Differentiation (диффэрэншиэ́йшн) дифференциация
   legal ~ (лúгал ~) правовое разграничение
   price ~ (прайс ~) дифференциация цен
   wage ~ (уэ́йдж ~) дифференциация заработной платы

Difficult (ди́ффикулт)
затруднительный, трудный, тяжёлый
Difficult/y (ди́ффикулти)
затруднение, трудность
   budgetary ~ (ба́джэтари ~)
бюджетное затруднение
   economic ~/ies (эконо́мик ~из)
экономические трудности
   enormous ~/ies (ино́рмос ~из)
огромные трудности
   financial ~/ies (файна́ншл ~из)
финансовые затруднения,
финансовые трудности
   foreign exchange ~/ies (фо́рэн
эксчэ́йндж ~из) валютные
затруднения
   in view of ~/ies (ин вью оф ~из)
ввиду трудностей
   major ~/ies (мэ́йджор ~из)
большие трудности
   minor ~/ies (ма́йнор ~из)
небольшие трудности
   operational ~/ies (опэрэ́йшнал
~из) эксплуатационные трудности
   persistent ~/ies (пэрси́стэнт
~из) постоянные трудности
   significant ~/ies (сигни́фикант
~из) значительные трудности
   technical ~/ies (тэ́кникал ~из)
технические трудности
   to exaggerate ~/ies (ту
экза́джэрэйт ~из) преувеличивать
трудности
   to experience ~/ies (ту
экспи́риэнс ~из) испытывать
трудности
   to indicate ~/ies (ту и́ндикэйт
~из) указывать на трудности
   to meet with ~/ies (ту мит уиθ
~из) встречаться с трудностями
   to overcome ~/ies (ту овэрко́м
~из) преодолевать трудности
   unforeseen ~/ies (анфорси́н ~из)
непредвиденные трудности
Digit (ди́джит) цифр
   carryover ~ (кэ́рриовэр ~) цифра
переноса
Digital (ди́джитал) цифровой
Dignitary (ди́гнитари) сановник
Dimension (димэ́ншн) габарит, размер
~s габарит, размер
   corresponding ~s (коррэспо́ндинг
~с) соответствующий габарит
   equipment ~s (икуи́пмэнт ~с)
габариты оборудования
   oversized ~s (о́вэрсайзд ~с)
нестандартный габарит

   overall ~s (овэра́л ~с) общий
габарит
   physical ~s (фи́зикал ~с)
физические размеры
   standard ~s (ста́ндард ~с)
стандартный габарит, стандартный
размер
Diplomacy (дипло́маси)
дипломатический порядок
   act of ~ (акт оф ~) акт
дипломатии
Diplomat (ди́пломат) дипломат
   career ~ (кари́р ~)
профессиональный дипломат
   foreign ~ (фо́рэн ~) иностранный
дипломат
   Western ~ (уэ́стэрн ~) западный
дипломат
Direction (дирэ́кшн) распоряжение,
трасса **~s** инструкция
   forward ~ (фо́руард ~)
заблаговременное указание
   improper ~s (импро́пэр ~с)
неправильные указания
   proper ~s (про́пэр ~с) правильные
указания
Directive (дирэ́ктив) директива,
руководящий акт **~s** директивные
документы, директивные указания
   administrative ~ (адми́нистрэйтив
~) акт управления
   to issue ~s (ту и́шю ~с)
устанавливать директивы
Director (дирэ́ктор) директор
   board of ~s (борд оф ~с) совет
директоров
   Deputy ~ (дэ́пюти ~) заместитель
директора
   Deputy general ~ (дэ́пюти
джэ́нэрал ~) заместитель
генерального директора
   executive ~ (экзэ́кютив ~)
директор-распорядитель,
исполнительный директор
   exhibit ~ (экзи́бит ~) директор
выставки
   general ~ (джэ́нэрал ~)
генеральный директор
   managing ~ (ма́наджинг ~)
директор-администратор
   technical ~ (тэ́кникал ~)
технический директор
   ~ of an enterprise (~ оф ан
э́нтэрпрайз) директор предприятия
   ~ of finance (~ оф файна́нс)
финансовый директор

Directorate (дирэ́кторат)
директорат, правление,
управленческий аппарат
    general ~ (джэ́нэрал ~)
    генеральная дирекция
Disability (дисаби́лити)
инвалидность, нетрудоспособность,
потеря трудоспособности
    full ~ (фул ~) полная
    инвалидность
    long-term ~ (лонг-тэрм ~)
    длительная инвалидность
    partial ~ (паршл ~) частичная
    инвалидность, частичная
    нетрудоспособность
    permanent ~ (пэ́рманэнт ~)
    постоянная инвалидность
    temporary ~ (тэ́мпорари ~)
    временная нетрудоспособность
    total ~ (то́тал ~) полная
    нетрудоспособность
Disabled (дисэ́йблд)
нетрудоспособный
    ~ person (~ пэ́рсон) инвалид
    ~ veteran (~ вэ́тэран) военный
    инвалид
    ~ worker (~ уо́ркэр) инвалид
    труда
Disadvantageous (дисадвантэ́йджос)
невыгодный
Disaffirm, to ~ (дисаффи́рм, ту ~)
отменять
Disagio (диса́жио) дизажио
Disagreement (дисагри́мэнт)
разногласие, разнобой
Disappear, to ~ (дисаппи́р, ту ~)
исчезать [**perfective:** исчезнуть]
Disappearance (дисаппи́ранс)
исчезновение
Disarmament (диса́рмамэнт)
разоружение
Disarray (дисаррэ́й) смятение
Disband, to ~ (дисба́нд, ту ~)
распустить
Disbandment (дисба́ндмэнт)
расформирование
Disbursement (дисбу́рсмэнт) выплата
~s издержки, дисбурсментские
расходы
    quarterly ~ (куа́ртэрли ~)
    квартальная выплата
Discard (ди́скард) выбрасывание
    to ~ (ту ~) выбрасывать
Discern, to ~ (дисcэ́рн, ту ~)
различать
Discharge (дисча́рдж) освобождение,
отставка, отстранение, погашение

complete ~ of debt (компли́т ~ оф
дэт) полная уплата долга
completion of ~ (компли́шн оф ~)
окончание выгрузки
forced ~ (форсд ~) вынужденная
выгрузка
free ~ (фри ~) бесплатная
выгрузка, свободно от расходов
по выгрузке
optional ~ (о́пшнал ~) опцион
выгрузки
point of ~ (пойнт оф ~) место
выгрузки
scale of ~ (скэйл оф ~) тарифные
ставки по выгрузке
to ~ (ту ~) отстранять,
разгружать
to complete ~ (ту компли́т ~)
заканчивать выгрузку
to effect ~ (ту иффэ́кт ~)
производить выгрузку
warehouse ~ (уэ́рхаус ~) выгрузка
на склад
~ from work (~ фром уо́рк)
отстранение от работы
~ of duties (~ оф дю́тиз)
выполнение обязательств,
выполнение обязанностей
~ of ship freight to rail (~ оф
шип фрэйт ту рэйл) выгрузка с
судна в ж.-д. вагон
~ procedure {shipping} (~
проси́дюр {ши́ппинг}) порядок
выгрузки
Discharging (дисча́рджинг) выгрузка,
разгрузка
Disciplinary (ди́сиплинари)
дисциплинарный
    ~ measure (~ мэ́жюр)
    дисциплинарная репрессия
Disclaim, to ~ (дисклэ́йм, ту ~)
отрицать
Disclosure (дискло́жюр) обнаружение,
раскрытие
    unauthorized ~ (ана́уθорайзд ~)
    разглашение
Discoloration (дисколорэ́йшн)
изменение цвета
Discontinuance (дисконти́нюанс)
прекращение
    ~ of activity (~ оф акти́вити)
    прекращение действия
Discount (ди́скоунт) дисконт,
дисконтный {*adj.*}, скидка, уступка,
учёт, учётный {*adj.*}
    amount of a ~ (амо́унт оф а ~)
    размер дисконта

bank ~ (банк ~) банковский
дисконт
breakage ~ (брэйкадж ~) скидка
на бой
commercial ~ (коммэршл ~)
коммерческая скидка
customary ~ (кастомари ~)
обычная скидка
dealer ~ (дилэр ~) дилерская
скидка
maximum ~ (максимум ~)
максимальная скидка
percentage of a ~ (пэрсэнтадж оф
а ~) процент дисконта
quantity ~ (куантити ~) скидка
за количество
seasonal ~ (сизонал ~) сезонная
скидка
time ~ {on bill, note} (тайм ~
{он бил, нот}) скидка за
досрочную уплату по векселю
to ~ (ту ~) дисконтировать,
учитывать
to give a ~ (ту гив а ~)
уступать в цене
to obtain a ~ (ту обтэйн а ~)
добиться снижения цены
to take on ~ (ту тэйк он ~)
принимать к учёту
volume ~ (волюм ~) рефакция
~ charges (~ чарджэз) расходы по
учёту
~ house (~ хаус) дисконтёр
~ of bills (~ оф билс) учёт
векселей
~ of drafts (~ оф драфтс) учёт
тратт
~ of notes (~ оф нотс) учёт
векселей
~ period (~ пириод) период учёта
{bill, note}
~ rate (~ рэйт) ставка дисконта
Discountable (дискоунтабл)
пригодный к учёту
to be ~ (ту би ~) быть пригодным
к учёту
Discounting (дискоунтинг)
дисконтирование
~ of a bill (~ оф а бил)
дисконтирование векселя
Discoverer (дисковэрэр) автор
открытия
Discovery (дисковэри) изобретение,
открытие
joint ~ (джойнт ~) совместное
изобретение

Discredit, to ~ (дискрэдит, ту ~)
дискредитировать
Discrepancy (дискрэпанси)
отклонение, несоответствие,
разница, разногласие
Discrepant (дискрэпант)
противоречивый
Discrimination (дискриминэйшн)
дискриминация
credit ~ (крэдит ~) кредитная
дискриминация
economic ~ (экономик ~)
экономическая дискриминация
price ~ (прайс ~) ценовая
дискриминация
to eliminate ~ (ту илиминэйт ~)
ликвидировать дискриминацию
trade ~ (трэйд ~) торговая
дискриминация
Discriminatory (дискриминатори)
дискриминационный
Discuss, to ~ (дискас, ту ~)
обсуждать
Discussion (дискушн) обсуждение ~s
переговоры
preliminary ~ (прилиминэри ~)
предварительное обсуждение
amicable ~s (амикабл ~с)
дружественные переговоры
fruitful ~s (фрутфул ~с)
плодотворные переговоры
preliminary ~s (прилиминэри ~с)
предварительные переговоры
Disembarkation (дисэмбаркэйшн)
высадка
airport of ~ (эйрпорт оф ~)
аэродром выгрузки
Disenfranchisement
(дисэнфранчайзмэнт) поражение в
правах
~ of civil rights (~ оф сивил
райтс) поражение гражданских
прав
Disengagement (дисэнгэйджмэнт)
отрыв
Dishonest (дисонэст) нечестный
Dishonor (дисонор) бесчестье,
позор, протест {note, bill}
notice of ~ of a note (нотис оф
~ оф а нот) векселя
notice of ~ (нотис оф ~) протест
notice of ~ of a bill (нотис оф
~ оф а бил) протест векселя
to ~ (ту ~) опротестовать
Disinflation (дисинфлэйшн) дефляция
Disinflationary (дисинфлэйшнари)
дефляционный

Disintegration (дисинтэгрэ́йшн)
развал, распад
Dismantle, to ~ (дисма́нтл, ту ~)
демонтировать
Dismantling (дисма́нтлинг) демонтаж
~ **of equipment** (~ оф икуи́пмэнт)
демонтаж оборудования
~ **of an exhibition** (~ оф ан
экзиби́шн) демонтаж выставки
~ **exhibition stands** (~ экзиби́шн
стандс) демонтаж стендов
~ **of an installation** (~ оф ан
инсталлэ́йшн) демонтаж установки
~ **period** (~ пи́риод) сроки
демонтажа
Dismember, to ~ (дисмэ́мбэр, ту ~)
расчленять
Dismemberment (дисмэ́мбэрмэнт)
расчленение
Dismiss, to ~ (дисми́с, ту ~)
отстранять, распустить, увольнять
[**perfective:** уволить]
Dismissal (дисми́ссал) освобождение,
отставка, отстранение, роспуск,
смещение, увольнение
~ **from a post** (~ фром а пост)
отстранение от должности
~ **of action** (~ оф акшн) отказ в
иске
~ **of a case** (~ оф а кэйс)
прекращение дела
~ **of suit** (~ оф сут) отказ в
иске
Disparity (диспа́рити)
несоответствие
Dispatch (ди́спатч) диспач {shipping
premium}, отправка, посылка
amount of ~ (амо́унт оф ~) размер
диспача
free ~ (фри ~) бесплатная
пересылка
free of ~ (фри оф ~) свободен от
диспача
payment of ~ (пэ́ймэнт оф ~)
выплата диспача
receipt of ~ (риси́т оф ~)
получение диспача
return ~ (риту́рн ~) обратная
пересылка
to ~ (ту ~) отослать ,
отправлять [**perfective:**
отправить], препровождать
~ **loading only** (~ ло́динг о́нли)
диспач только за досрочную
погрузку
~ **rate** (~ рэйт) ставка диспача

Dispensary (диспэ́нсари)
профилакторий
Displace, to ~ (дисплэ́йс, ту ~)
смещать [**perfective:** сместить]
Displacement (дисплэ́йсмэнт)
водоизмещение {of a vessel},
смещение
full load ~ (фул лод ~)
водоизмещение при полном грузе
standard ~ (ста́ндард ~)
стандартное водоизмещение
tonnage ~ (то́ннадж ~) весовое
водоизмещение
vessel of ... tons ~ (вэ́ссэл оф
... тонз ~) судно водоизмещением
в ...тонн
~ **scale** (~ скэйл) шкала
водоизмещения
~ **tonnage** (~ то́ннадж)
водоизмещение судна
Display (дисплэ́й) выкладка,
дисплей, щит
basic ~ (бэ́йсик ~) основная
демонстрация
computer ~ (компью́тэр ~) дисплей
ЭВМ
instore ~ (и́нстор ~) выкладка в
магазине
on ~ (он ~) экспонируемый
open ~ (о́пэн ~) открытая
выкладка
sample ~ (сампл ~) выставка
образцов, демонстрация образцов
shelf ~ (шэлф ~) выставка на
полках
to ~ (ту ~) выставлять
to put samples on ~ (ту пут
самплз он ~) выставлять
экспонаты
window ~ (уи́ндо ~) выставка в
витрине, экспозиция витрины
~ **of goods** (~ оф гудз) выкладка
товара
~ **of new export items** (~ оф нью
э́кспорт а́йтэмс) выставка новинок
экспорта
~ **section** (~ сэкшн) раздел
выставки
~ **unit** (~ ю́нит) выставочный
экспонат
Dispose, to ~ **of** (диспо́з, ту ~ оф)
распоряжаться
to freely ~ **of** (ту фри́ли ~ оф)
свободно распоряжаться
Disposition (диспози́шн) размещение
расположение, распоряжение

testamentary ~ (тэстамэ́нтари ~)
завещательное распоряжение
~ of cargo (~ оф ка́рго)
расположение груза
~ of documents (~ оф до́кюмэнтс)
назначение документов
Dispossession (диспозэ́шн) лишение
собственности
Disprove, to (диспру́в, ту)
опровергать [perfective:
опровергнуть]
Disputant (диспю́тант) спорящая
сторона
Dispute (диспю́т) конфликт, спор,
спорное дело
administrative ~ (адми́нистрэйтив
~) административный спор
border ~ (бо́рдэр ~) пограничный
спор
civil law ~ (си́вил лау ~)
гражданско-правовой спор
commercial ~ (коммэ́ршл ~)
коммерческий спор
customs ~ (ка́стомз ~) таможенный
спор
housing ~ (хо́узинг ~) жилищный
спор
international ~ (интэрна́шэнал ~)
международный спор
interstate ~ (и́нтэрстэйт ~)
межгосударственный спор
labor ~ (лэ́йбор ~) трудовой
конфликт, трудовой спор
land ~ (ланд ~) земельный спор
monetary ~ (мо́нэтари ~) валютный
спор
property ~ (про́пэрти ~)
имущественный спор
settlement of a ~ (сэ́тлмэнт оф а
~) разрешение конфликта
territorial ~ (тэррито́риал ~)
территориальный спор
to ~ (ту ~) оспаривать
to accept a ~ for arbitration
(ту аксэ́пт а ~ фор арбитрэ́йшн)
принимать дело для решения в
порядке арбитража
to resolve a ~ (ту ризо́лв а ~)
разрешить спор
trade ~ (трэйд ~) торговый спор
Disputed (диспю́тэд) конфликтный,
спорный
Disregard (дисрига́рд) несоблюдение
~ of formalities (~ оф
форма́литиз) нарушение
формальностей

~ of instructions (~ оф
инстра́кшнс) несоблюдение
указаний
~ of rules (~ оф рулз)
несоблюдение правил
Disruption (дисру́пшн) срыв
Dissension (диссэ́ншн) рознь
Dissenter (диссэ́нтэр) раскольник
Dissenting (диссэ́нтинг)
раскольнический
Dissolution (диссолю́шн)
расторжение, роспуск
judicial ~ (джюди́шл ~)
расторжение по суду
~ of an agency (~ оф ан
э́йджэнси) ликвидация агентства
~ of a firm (~ оф а фирм)
ликвидация фирмы
~ of a partnership (~ оф а
па́ртнэршип) ликвидация
товарищества
~ of parliament (~ оф па́рламэнт)
роспуск парламента
Dissolve (дизо́лв) растворять
[perfective: растворить]
to ~ parliament (ту ~ па́рламэнт)
распустить парламент
Distinction (дисти́нкшн) отличие,
различие
Distinguish, to ~ (дисти́нгуиш, ту
~) разграничивать, различать
Distort, to ~ (дисторт, ту ~)
извратить, искажать
Distortion (дисто́ршн) деформация,
извращение, искажение
to avoid ~ (ту аво́йд ~) избегать
деформации
Distrain (дистрэ́йн) описать
to ~ property (ту ~ про́пэрти)
описать имущество
Distraint (дистрэ́йнт) опись
~ of inheritance (~ оф
инхэ́ританс) опись наследства
~ of real property (~ оф рил
про́пэрти) опись недвижимого
имущества
Distribute, to ~ (дистри́бют, ту ~)
распределить, распространять
Distribution (дистрибю́шн) отпуск,
продажа, разнос, распределение,
распространение, рассылка
territorial ~ (тэррито́риал ~)
территориальное распространение
~ center (~ сэ́нтэр) центр
распределения
~ in kind (~ ин кайнд)
распределение в натуре

~ **list** (~ лист) разнарядка
~ **of income** (~ оф и́нком)
распределение доходов
~ **of inheritance** (~ оф
инхэ́ританс) распределение
наследства
~ **of inventory** (~ оф и́нвэнтори)
распределение запасов
Distributor (дистри́бютор)
дистрибьютер, распределитель
Distributorship (дистри́бюторшип)
распределение
    wholesale ~ (хо́лсэйл ~) оптовое
распределение
District (ди́стрикт) округ, окружной
{adj.}
    administrative ~ (адми́нистрэйтив
~) административный округ
    appellate ~ (аппэ́лат ~) округ
апелляционной палаты
    consular ~ (ко́нсюлар ~)
консульский район
    electoral ~ (элэ́кторал ~)
избирательный округ
    industrial ~ (инду́стриал ~)
промышленный район
    judicial ~ (джюди́шл ~) судебный
округ
    military command ~ (ми́литари
комма́нд ~) военный округ
    residential ~s (рэзидэ́ншл ~с)
жилые кварталы
    urban ~ (у́рбан ~) городской
район
Disturbance (дисту́рбанс) волнения,
нарушение
    business ~ (би́знэс ~) нарушение
торговой деятельности
Disturbing (дисту́рбинг) тревожный
{adj.}
    ~ **the peace** (~ θи пис) проступок
против общественного порядка
Divergence (дивэ́рджэнс) расхождение

    statutory ~ (ста́тютори ~)
расхождение в законодательстве
Diversification (дивэрсифика́йшн)
диверсификация
    ~ **of activity** (~ оф акти́вити)
диверсификация деятельности
    ~ **of the economy** (~ оф θи
ико́номи) диверсификация
экономики
    ~ **of export capabilities** (~ оф
э́кспорт кэйпаби́литиз)
диверсификация экспортных
возможностей

    ~ **of exports** (~ оф э́кспортс)
диверсификация экспорта
    ~ **of industrial production** (~ оф
инду́стриал прода́кшн)
диверсификация промышленного
производства
    ~ **of mutual trade** (~ оф мю́чуал
трэйд) взаимного диверсификация
товарооборота
    ~ **of a product** (~ оф а про́дукт)
диверсификация продукта
    ~ **of trade** (~ оф трэйд)
диверсификация торговли
    ~ **plan** (~ план) план
диверсификации
    ~ **program** (~ про́грам) программа
диверсификации
Diversified (дивэ́рсифайд)
многоотраслевой
Diversity (дивэ́рсити) разновидность
Divide, to ~ (дива́йд, ту ~) делить
Dividend (ди́видэнд) дивиденд
    amount of a ~ (амо́унт оф а ~)
размер дивиденда
    annual ~ (а́ннюал ~) годовой
дивиденд
    cash ~ (каш ~) денежный
дивиденд, дивиденд, выплаченный
наличными
    crude ~s (круд ~с) накопленные
дивиденды
    declared ~ (диклэ́йрд ~)
объявленный дивиденд
    deferred ~s (дифэ́рд ~с)
отсроченные дивиденды
    payment of ~s (пэ́ймэнт оф ~с)
выплата дивидендов {по
дивидендам}
    quarterly ~ (куа́ртэрли ~)
квартальный дивиденд
    stock ~ (сток ~) дивиденд,
выплаченный акциями
    to declare ~s (ту диклэ́йр ~с)
объявлять о выплате дивидендов
    to pay out a ~ (ту пэй о́ут а ~)
выплачивать дивиденд
    unclaimed ~ (анклэ́ймд ~)
невостребованный дивиденд
    ~ **on account** (~ он акко́унт)
предварительный дивиденд
    ~s **on investment** (~с он
инвэ́стмэнт) дивиденд ы на
вложенный капитал
    ~ **on shares** {share earnings} (~
он шэйрз {шэйр э́рнингз})
дивиденд по акциям

~ payable (~ пэ́йабл) дивиденд к оплате
~ payment (~ пэ́ймэнт) оплата дивиденда
Divisible (диви́зибл) делимый {*adj.*}, разделимый {*adj.*}
Division (диви́жн) отдел, подразделение, раздел, разделение
  claims adjusters' ~ (клэ́ймс аджа́стэрз ~) бюро диспашёров
  judicial ~ (джюди́шл ~) судебный раздел
  volunteer ~ (волунти́р ~) добровольный раздел
  ~ of labor (~ оф лэ́йбор) разделение труда, распределение труда
Divorce (диво́рс) развод
  to ~ (ту ~) разойтись, разводиться [**perfective:** развестись]
  to file for ~ (ту файл фор ~) предъявить иск о разводе
  ~ by mutual consent (~ бай мю́чуал консэ́нт) развод по взаимному согласию
Divulge, to ~ (диву́лдж, ту ~) разглашать
  to ~ (ту ~) оглашать [**perfective:** огласить]
Dock (док) док, доковый {*adj.*}
  commercial ~ (комме́ршл ~) коммерческий док
  dry-~ (драй-~) сухой док
  floating ~ (фло́тинг ~) плавучий док
  free-~ (фри-~) франко док
  graving ~ (грэ́йвинг ~) ремонтный док
  harbor ~s (ха́рбор ~с) портовые доки
  the ~ (θи ~) скамья подсудимых {courtroom seats for accused}
  to ~ a vessel (ту ~ а вэ́ссэл) вводить судно в док
  to deliver to ~ (ту дэли́вэр ту ~) доставлять в док
  to depart a ~ (ту дипа́рт а ~) выходить из дока
  to dry-~ (ту драй-~) доковать
  to enter a ~ (ту э́нтэр а ~) вводить в док
  to lie in ~ (ту лай ин ~) стоять в доке
  to place a vessel in ~ (ту плэйс а вэ́ссэл ин ~) ставить судно в док

  wet ~ (уэт ~) мокрый док
  ~ pass (~ пасс) разрешение на вывоз со склада {for export}
  ~ rent (~ рэнт) аренда дока
  ~ shed (~ шэд) крытый док
Dockage (до́ккадж) стоянка в доке
  ~ fees (~ физ) плата за стоянку в доке
Docker (до́ккэр) докер
Dockyard (до́кярд) верфь
Document (до́кюмэнт) документ
  acceptance of ~s for collection (аксэ́птанс оф ~с фор колле́кшн) принятие документов на инкассо
  accompanying ~s (акко́мпаниинг ~с) сопровождающие документы
  accounting ~s (акко́унтинг ~с) расчётный документы
  against ~s (агэ́нст ~с) против документов
  against presentation of ~s (агэ́нст прэзэнтэ́йшн оф ~с) против представления документов
  appended ~s (аппэ́ндэд ~с) прилагаемые документы
  application ~ (аппликэ́йшн ~) заявочный документ
  authentic ~ (ауθэ́нтик ~) подлинный документ
  authenticated ~ (ауθэнтикэйтэд ~) удостоверенный акт
  authenticity of ~s (ауθэнти́сити оф ~с) подлинность документов
  bank ~ (банк ~) банковский документ
  basic source ~ (бэ́йсик сорс ~) первичный документ
  bearer ~ (бэ́йрэр ~) документ на предъявителя
  certifying ~ (сэ́ртифайинг ~) удостоверяющий документ
  charter ~ (ча́ртэр ~) конститутивный акт
  clean shipping ~s (клин ши́ппинг ~с) чистые погрузочные документы
  conformity of ~s (конфо́рмити оф ~с) соответствие документов
  concluding ~ (конклю́динг ~) итоговый документ
  constituent ~s (консти́тюэнт ~с) учредительные документы
  contents of a ~ (ко́нтэнтс оф а ~) содержание документа
  copy of a ~ (ко́пи оф а ~) копия документа, экземпляр документа
  customs ~s (ка́стомз ~с) таможенные документы

delivery of ~s (дэли́вэри оф ~с)
вручение документов
distribution of ~s (дистрибю́шн
оф ~с) распространение
документов
draft of ~s (драфт оф ~с) проект
документа
exchange of ~s (эксчэ́йндж оф ~с)
обмен документов
financial ~ (файна́ншл ~)
финансовый документ
forged ~ (форджд ~) поддельный
документ, подложный документ
forgery of ~s (фо́рджэри оф ~с)
подделка документов
form of ~s (форм оф ~с) форма
документов
founding ~ (фо́ундинг ~)
учредительный акт
indicated ~ (и́ндикэйтэд ~)
указанный документ
in and out ~s (ин энд о́ут ~с)
входная и выходная документация
incoming ~s (и́нкоминг ~с)
поступающая документация
to initial a ~ (ту ини́шл а ~)
визировать документ
interdepartmental ~s
(интэрдэпартмэ́нтал ~с)
межведомственные документы
to interpret a ~ (ту интэ́рпрэт а
~) толковать документ
jointly-authored ~ (джо́йнтли-
а́уθорд ~) совместный акт
legal ~ (ли́гал ~) правовой
документ, юридический документ
legal ~s (ли́гал ~с)
нормативно-правовые документы
list of ~s (лист оф ~с) перечень
документов
loan against payment ~s (лон
агэ́нст пэ́ймэнт ~с) ссуда под
платёжные документы
missing ~ (ми́ссинг ~)
недостающий документ
negotiable ~ (нэго́шабл ~)
оборотный документ, передаваемый
денежный документ
normative ~ (но́рматив ~)
нормативный документ
official ~ (оффи́шл ~) грамота,
официальный акт
organizational ~s (организэ́йшнал
~с) уставные документы
original ~s (ори́джинал ~с)
оригиналы документов

patent ~ (па́тэнт ~) патентный
документ
payment against ~s (пэ́ймэнт
агэ́нст ~с) платёж против
документов
payment against delivery of ~s
(пэ́ймэнт агэ́нст дэли́вэри оф ~с)
платёж против представления
документов
payment for ~s (пэ́ймэнт фор ~с)
оплата документов
present ~ (прэ́зэнт ~) данный
документ
primary ~ (пра́ймари ~) основной
документ
priority ~ (прайо́рити ~)
приоритетный документ
receipt of ~s for collection
(риси́т оф ~с фор коллэ́кшн)
получение документов на инкассо
redemption of ~s (ридэ́мпшн оф
~с) выкуп документов
registration of ~s (рэджистрэ́йшн
оф ~с) регистрация документов
release of ~s (рили́с оф ~с)
выдача документа
relevant ~ (рэ́лэвант ~)
соответствующий документ
return of ~s (риту́рн оф ~с)
возврат документов
required ~ (рикуа́йрд ~)
требуемый документ
set of ~s (сэт оф ~с) комплект
документов
shipping ~s (ши́ппинг ~с)
грузовые документы, отгрузочные
документы,
товаросопроводительные документы
signed ~ (сайнд ~) подписанный
документ
source ~ (сорс ~) оправдательный
документ
stipulated ~ (сти́пюлэйтд ~)
обусловленный документ
sufficiency of a ~ (суффи́шэнси
оф а ~) достаточность документа
sufficiency of ~s (суффи́шэнси оф
~с) полнота документов
supporting ~ (суппо́ртинг ~)
подтверждающий документ
technical ~s (тэ́кникал ~с)
технические документы
tender ~s (тэ́ндэр ~с) тендерная
документация
"the ~ bears the stamp" (θи ~
бэйрз θи стамп) на документе
проставлен штемпель

to ~ (ту ~) документировать
to **accept presentation of** ~s (ту аксэ́пт прэзэнтэ́йшн оф ~с) принимать документы
to **append** ~s **to** ... (ту аппэ́нд ~с ту ...) прилагать документы к...
to **attest a** ~ (ту аттэ́ст а ~) заверять документ
to **attest** ~s (ту аттэ́ст ~с) удостоверять документы
to **be inconsistent with** ~s (ту би инконси́стэнт уиθ ~с) противоречить документам
to **deliver** ~s (ту дэли́вэр ~с) препровождать документы
to **deliver** ~s **against a trust receipt** (ту дэли́вэр ~с агэнст а траст риси́т) давать документы против расписки
to **dispose of** ~s (ту диспо́з оф ~с) распоряжаться документами
to **draft a** ~ (ту драфт а ~) составлять документ, составить акт
to **draw up** ~s (ту дра́у ап ~с) оформлять документы
to **duplicate a** ~ (ту ду́пликэйт а ~) размножать **document**
to **endorse a** ~ (ту эндо́рс а ~) расписывать на обороте документа
to **enter in a** ~ (ту э́нтэр ин а ~) вносить в документ
to **examine a** ~ (ту экза́мин а ~) рассматривать документ
to **forward a** ~ (ту фо́руард а ~) посылать документ
to **forward** ~s (ту фо́руард ~с) направлять документы, пересылать документы
to **furnish** ~s (ту фу́рниш ~с) предоставлять документы
to **honor** ~s (ту о́нор ~с) оплачивать документы
to **issue** ~s (ту и́шю ~с) выдавать документы
to **legalize a** ~ (ту ли́галайз а ~) узаконивать документ
to **lend against** ~s (ту лэнд агэнст ~с) выдавать ссуду под залог документов
to **list** ~s (ту лист ~с) перечислять документы
to **prepare a** ~ (ту припэ́йр а ~) подготавливать документ
to **register** ~s (ту рэ́джистэр ~с) регистрировать документ

to **release** ~s (ту рили́с ~с) передавать документы
to **release** ~s **against acceptance** (ту рили́с ~с агэ́нст аксэ́птанс) передавать документы против акцепта
to **release** ~s **against payment** (ту рили́с ~с агэ́нст пэ́ймэнт) передавать документы против платежа
to **require a** ~ (ту рикуа́йр а ~) требовать документ
to **sign a** ~ (ту сайн а ~) подписывать документ
to **submit** ~s (ту субми́т ~с) предъявлять документы
to **transfer** ~s **by endorsement** (ту тра́нсфэр ~с бай эндо́рсмэнт) передавать документы по индоссаменту
to **verify** ~s (ту вэ́рифай ~с) проверять документы
to **witness a** ~ (ту уи́тнэс а ~) засвидетельствовать документ
trade ~ (трэйд ~) товарный документ
transport ~ (тра́нспорт ~) транспортный документ
treaty and legal ~s (три́ти энд ли́гал ~с) договорно-правовые документы
undated ~ (андэ́йтэд ~) бессрочный документ
verification of ~s (вэрифике́йшн оф ~с) проверка документов
warehouse ~ (уэ́рхаус ~) складской документ
working ~s (уо́ркинг ~с) рабочий документ
written ~ (ри́ттэн ~) письменный акт
~s **against acceptance** (~с агэ́нст аксэ́птанс) документы против акцепта
~s **against payment** (~с агэ́нст пэ́ймэнт) документы за наличный расчёт
~s **covering goods** (~с ко́вэринг гудз) документ на отправленный товар
~s **for collection** (~с фор колле́кшн) документы на инкассо
~s **for payment** (~с фор пэ́ймэнт) документы для оплаты
~s **for shipment** (~с фор ши́пмэнт) документы на отгрузку

~s of carriage (~с оф ка́рриадж)
перевозочный документы
~s of title to goods (~с оф
тайтл ту гудз)
товарораспорядительные документы
Documentary (докюме́нтари)
документальный, документарный,
документированный
   ~ **pledge** (~ плэдж) залоговый
документ
Documentation (докюмэнтэ́йшн)
документальное обоснование,
документация
   complete ~ (компли́т ~) полная
документация
   completeness of technical ~
(компли́тнэс оф тэ́кникал ~)
комплектность технической
документации
   correct ~ (коррэ́кт ~) правильная
документация
   customs ~ (ка́стомз ~) таможенная
документация
   design ~ (диза́йн ~) проектная
документация
   elaboration of design ~
(илаборэ́йшн оф диза́йн ~)
разработка проектной
документации
   estimate ~ (э́стимэйт ~) сметная
документация
   exchange of ~ (эксчэ́йндж оф ~)
обмен документацией
   export ~ (э́кспорт ~) экспортные
документы
   final ~ (фа́йнал ~) окончательная
документация
   insurance ~ (иншю́ранс ~)
страховая документация
   patent ~ (па́тэнт ~) патентная
документация
   payment ~ (пэ́ймэнт ~) платёжная
документация
   scope of ~ (скоп оф ~) объём
документации
   shipping ~ (ши́ппинг ~)
товаросопроводительная
документация
   standard technical ~ (ста́ндард
тэ́кникал ~) нормативно-
технические документы
   technical ~ (тэ́кникал ~)
проектно-техническая
документация, техническая
документация
   textual ~ (тэ́ксчуал ~)
письменная документация

to compile ~ (ту компа́йл ~)
оформлять документацию
to complete ~ (ту компли́т ~)
комплектовать документацию
to furnish ~ (ту фу́рниш ~)
предоставлять документацию
to recheck the ~ (ту ричэ́к θи ~)
перепроверять документацию
transfer of technical ~
(тра́нсфэр оф тэ́кникал ~)
передача технической
документации
transport ~ (тра́нспорт ~)
транспортная документация
~ **of title** (~ оф тайтл)
товарораспорядительная
документация
Dollar (до́ллар) доллар
   conversion of ~s **into gold**
(конвэ́ржн оф ~с и́нту голд)
размен долларов на золото
   one ~ (уа́н ~) банкнота в 1
доллар
   payment in ~s (пэ́ймэнт ин ~с)
платёж в долларах
   recalculation of ~s **into**
currency of payment
(рикалкюлэ́йшн оф ~с и́нту
ку́ррэнси оф пэ́ймэнт) пересчёт
долларов в валюту платежа
   sale for ~s (сэйл фор ~с)
продажа на доллары
   to convert ~s **into another**
currency (ту конвэ́рт ~с и́нту
ано́θэр ку́ррэнси) конвертировать
доллары в другую валюту
   to exchange ~s **for gold** (ту
эксчэ́йндж ~с фор голд)
обменивать доллары на золото
   to pay in ~s (ту пэй ин ~с)
платить в долларах
   ~ **amount** (~ амо́унт) сумма в
долларах
   ~ **denominated loan** (~
дино́минэйтэд лон) заём в
долларах
   ~ **earnings** (~ э́рнингс)
поступления долларов
   ~ **equivalent** (~ икуи́валэнт)
эквивалент в долларах
   ~ **exchange rate** (~ эксчэ́йндж
рэйт) курс доллара
   ~ **flow** {from a country} (~ фло́у
{фром а ку́нтри}) утечка долларов
   ~ **shortage** (~ шо́ртадж) нехватка
долларов

Domestic (доме́стик) внутренний, отечественный

Domicile (до́мисайл) домицилий
   commercial ~ (комме́ршл ~) торговый домицилий
   to ~ (ту ~) домицилировать

Domiciled (до́мисайлд) домицилированный

Dominance (до́минанс) господство

Dominant (до́минант) доминирующий

Dominate, to ~ (до́минэйт, ту ~) доминировать

Domination (домине́йшн) доминирование, овладения
   market ~ (ма́ркэт ~) овладения рынка

Donated (до́нэйтэд) одаряемый

Donation (доне́йшн) пожертвование
   to collect ~s (ту колле́кт ~с) собирать пожертвование

Dormitory (до́рмитори) общежитие

Double decker (дабл дэ́ккэр) двухпалубный

Doubt (до́убт) сомнение

Doubtful (до́убтфул) сомнительный

Down (до́ун) внизу
   to write ~ (ту райт ~) списывать частично со счёта {as a debt}

Downtime (до́унтайм) время простоя
   production ~ (прода́кшн ~) перерыв заседания

Downturn (до́унтурн) понижение конъюнктуры, спад

Dowry (до́ури) приданое

Draft (драфт) проект, тратта
   acceptance ~ (аксе́птанс ~) акцептованная тратта
   acceptance of a ~ (аксе́птанс оф а ~) акцепт тратты
   advance against a documentary ~ (адва́нс аге́нст а докюме́нтари ~) аванс против документарной тратты
   amount of a ~ (амо́унт оф а ~) сумма переводного векселя, сумма тратты
   bank ~ (банк ~) трассированный банком на другой банк вексель
   banker's ~ (ба́нкэрз ~) банковская тратта
   clean ~ (клин ~) недокументированная тратта
   collection against a ~ (колле́кшн аге́нст а ~) инкассо тратты
   commercial ~ (комме́ршл ~) коммерческая тратта

   documentary ~ (докюме́нтари ~) документированная тратта
   drawee of a ~ (драуи́ оф а ~) плательщик по тратте
   drawing of a ~ (дра́уинг оф а ~) выписка тратты
   long term ~ (лонг тэрм ~) долгосрочная тратта
   maturity of a ~ (мачу́рити оф а ~) срок платежа по тратте
   payment against ~s (пэ́ймэнт аге́нст ~с) платёж против тратт
   reimbursement ~ (риимбу́рсмэнт ~) рамбурсная тратта
   return ~ (риту́рн ~) обратный переводной вексель
   site ~ (сайт ~) предъявительская тратта
   tenor of a ~ (тэнор оф а ~) срок тратты
   time ~ (тайм ~) срочная тратта
   to ~ (ту ~) оформлять {e.g. a document}
   to collect a ~ (ту колле́кт а ~) инкассировать тратту
   to negotiate a ~ (ту нэго́шиэйт а ~) переуступать тратту
   to pay through a ~ (ту пэй θру а ~) платить траттой
   to present a ~ (ту прэзе́нт а ~) представлять тратту
   to rediscount a ~ (ту риди́скоунт а ~) переучитывать тратту
   unaccepted ~ (анаксе́птэд ~) неакцептованная тратта
   valid ~ (ва́лид ~) действительная тратта
   ~ budget (~ ба́джэт) проект бюджета
   ~ of a law (~ оф а лау) проект закона
   ~ resolution (~ рэзолю́шн) проект резолюции
   ~ treaty (~ три́ти) проект договора

Drafting (дра́фтинг) оформление, составление
   proper ~ of an agreement (про́пэр ~ оф ан агри́мэнт) правильное оформление договора
   ~ of an agreement (~ оф ан агри́мэнт) оформление договора
   ~ of a budget (~ оф а ба́джэт) составление бюджета
   ~ of a deed (~ оф а дид) составление акта

~ of a distraint (~ оф а дистрэ́йнт) составление описи
~ of a document (~ оф а до́кюмэнт) составление акта
~ of a will (~ оф а уил) составление завещания

Draw, to ~ (дра́у, ту ~) выписывать, привлекать [perfective: привлечь]
to ~ a bill of exchange (ту ~ а бил оф эксчэ́йндж) трассировать
to ~ for ... dollars (ту ~ фор ... до́лларс) трассировать на ... долларов
to ~ up (ту ~ ап) выставлять {document}

Draw-down of inventory (дра́у-до́ун оф и́нвэнтори) изъятие из запасов

Drawee (драуи́) векселеполучатель {of a bill}, трассат

Drawer (дра́уэр) векселедатель {of a bill}, лицо, выставившее инкассо {on account}, трассант

Drawing (дра́уинг) рисунок
industrial ~s (инду́стриал ~с) промышленные рисунки
payment by ~ (пэ́ймэнт бай ~) платёж траттами
~ authorization (~ ауθоризэ́йшн) право выписки векселей
~ of samples (~ оф самплз) выбор образцов
~ up (~ ап) выписка
~ up of a balance sheet (~ ап оф а ба́ланс шит) составление баланса
~ up of an order (~ ап оф ан о́рдэр) оформление заказа

Dressing of vessels {admiralty} (дрэ́ссинг оф вэ́ссэлс {а́дмиралти}) расцвечивание флагами

Drive (драйв) кампания
profit maximization ~ (про́фит макимизэ́йшн ~) борьба за максимальные прибыли
quality ~ (куа́лити ~) борьба за высокое качество

Drop (дроп) падение
~ in demand (~ ин дима́нд) сокращение спроса
~ in exchange rate (~ ин эксчэ́йндж рэйт) снижение курса
~ in price (~ ин прайс) удешевление
~ in prices (~ ин пра́йсэз) падение цен
~ in the exchange rate of currency (~ ин θи эксчэ́йндж рэйт

оф ку́ррэнси) падение курса валюты

Dropping (дро́ппинг) снятие
~ of restrictions (~ оф ристри́кшнс) снятие ограничений

Drug (друг) лекарство
illegal ~ (илли́гал ~) наркотик
~ addict (~ а́ддикт) наркоман
~ addiction (~ адди́кшн) наркомания

Drum (друм) барабан
board ~ (борд ~) дощатый барабан
cardboard ~ (ка́рдборд ~) картонный барабан
fiberboard ~ (фа́йбэрборд ~) фибровый барабан
iron ~ (айрн ~) железный барабан
plywood ~ (пла́йуу́д ~) фанерный барабан
steel ~ (стил ~) железная бочка
wooden ~ (уу́дэн ~) деревянный барабан

Dry (драй) сухой
"keep ~" {cargo marking} (кип ~) "Хранить в сухом месте" {надпись}

Dual-purpose (ду́ал-пу́рпос) двухцелевой

Dubious (ду́биос) сомнительный

Due (ду) срочный ~s сбор
ballast ~ (ба́лласт ~) балластный сбор
cargo ~ (ка́рго ~) грузовой сбор
harbor ~ (ха́рбор ~) портовые сборы
import ~ (и́мпорт ~) импортный сбор
in ~ course (ин ~ корс) своевременно
lighthouse ~ (ла́йтхаус ~) маячный сбор
navigation ~ (навигэ́йшн ~) навигационный сбор
ship's ~ (шипс ~) корабельный сбор
to be ~ from (ту би ~ фром) причитаться
tonnage ~ (то́ннадж ~) тоннажный сбор

Duly (ду́ли) надлежащим образом

Dumping (да́мпинг) бросовый вывоз, бросовой экспорт, вывоз товаров по бросовым ценам, демпинг, демпинговый {adj.}
currency ~ (ку́ррэнси ~) валютный демпинг

Dun, to ~ (дан, ту ~) напоминать об уплате долга

Dunnage (дýннадж) подстилочный материал

Dunning (дýннинг) напоминание об уплате долга

    ~ letter (~ лэ́ттэр) письмо с напоминанием

Duplicate (дупликэ́йт) дубликат, копия

    in ~ (ин ~) в двух экземплярах

    ~ of an application (~ оф ан аппликэ́йшн) копия заявки

    ~ of a bill of lading (~ оф а бил оф лэ́йдинг) копия коносамента

    ~ of a receipt (~ оф а рисúт) копия квитанции

Duplication (дупликэ́йшн) снятие копий

    to issue a ~ (ту úшю а ~) выдавать копии

Durability (дурабúлити) носкость

Durable (дýрабл) долговечный, прочный **~s** товары длительного пользования

    consumer ~s (консýмэр ~с) потребительские товары длительного пользования

Duration (дурэ́йшн) длительность, продолжительность, срок

Duress (дурэ́с) давление, нажим, принуждение

    under ~ (áндэр ~) под нажимом, по принуждению

Dust (дуст) пыль

Dust-up (дýст-ап) свалка

Dutiable (дýтиабл) облагаемый, подлежащий обложению

Dut/y (дю́ти) обязанность повинность, пошлина, пошлинный сбор, сбор

    absolute ~ (абсолю́т ~) абсолютная обязанность

    ad valorem ~ (ад валóрэм ~) адвалорная пошлина

    additional ~ (аддúшнал ~) дополнительная пошлина

    annual ~ (áннюал ~) ежегодная пошлина

    anti-dumping ~ (áнти-дáмпинг ~) антидемпинговая пошлина

    compensatory ~ (компэ́нсатори ~) компенсационная пошлина

    compound ~ (кóмпоунд ~) смешанная пошлина

    currency defense ~ (кýррэнси дифэ́нс ~) валютная пошлина

    customs ~ (кáстомз ~) таможенная пошлина, таможенный сбор

    customs export ~ (кáстомз э́кспорт ~) вывозная пошлина

    differential ~ (диффэрэ́ншл ~) дифференциальная пошлина

    every-day ~/ies (э́ври-дэй ~из) повседневные обязанности

    excise ~ (э́ксайз ~) акцизный сбор

    exempted from ~ (экзэ́мптэд фром ~) освобождённый от повинностей

    export ~ (э́кспорт ~) экспортная пошлина

    export customs ~ (э́кспорт кáстомз ~) вывозная таможенная пошлина, экспортная таможенная пошлина

    foreign trade ~ (фóрэн трэйд ~) внешнеторговая пошлина

    hypothecation ~ (хайпоθэкэ́йшн ~) ипотечная пошлина

    import ~ (úмпорт ~) ввозная пошлина, импортная пошлина

    import customs ~ (úмпорт кáстомз ~) ввозная таможенная пошлина, импортная таможенная пошлина

    imposition of a ~ (импозúшн оф а ~) обложение пошлиной

    imposition of customs ~/ies (импозúшн оф кáстомз ~из) таможенное обложение

    internal customs ~ (интэ́рнал кáстомз ~) внутренняя таможенная пошлина

    legal ~ (лúгал ~) правовая обязанность

    levied ~ (лэ́вид ~) взимаемая пошлина

    maximum ~ (мáксимум ~) максимальная пошлина

    military ~ (мúлитари ~) военная обязанность

    minimum ~ (мúнимум ~) минимальная пошлина

    moral ~ (мóрал ~) моральное обязательство

    municipal ~ (мюнúсипал ~) муниципальная пошлина

    natural ~ (нáчюрал ~) натуральная повинность

    official ~ (оффúшл ~) служебная обязанность

    penalty ~ (пэ́налти ~) штрафная пошлина

progressive ~ (прогрэ́ссив ~) прогрессивная пошлина
prohibitive ~ (прохи́битив ~) запретительная пошлина
protectionist ~ (протэ́кшнист ~) протекционистская пошлина
protective ~ (протэ́ктив ~) покровительственная пошлина
revenue ~ (рэ́вэну ~) фискальная пошлина
specific ~ (спэси́фик ~) специфическая пошлина
stamp ~ (стамп ~) гербовый сбор
temporary ~ (тэ́мпорари ~) временная пошлина
to levy an excise ~ (ту лэ́ви ан эксайз ~) обложить акцизом
transit ~ (тра́нзит ~) транзитная пошлина
transit customs ~ (тра́нзит ка́стомз ~) транзитная таможенная пошлина
~ to take on pilotage (~ ту тэйк он па́йлотадж) обязанность брать лоцмана
Duty free (дю́ти фри) беспошлинный
to admit goods ~ (ту адми́т гудз ~) разрешать беспошлинный ввоз товара
~ port (~ порт) порт беспошлинного ввоза и вывоза
Dye (дай) краска

E

Earmark, to ~ (и́рмарк, ту ~) предназначать
Earmarking (и́рмаркинг) предназначение
Earn, to ~ (эрн, ту ~) зарабатывать [**perfective:** заработать]
Earnest (э́рнэст) серьёзный
~ money (~ мо́ни) задаток
Earnings (э́рнингз) доход, заработок, заработная плата, зарплата, поступление
actual ~ (а́кчуал ~) фактический заработок
average ~ (а́вэрэдж ~) средний заработок
business ~ (би́знэс ~) доход от предпринимательства
casual ~ (ка́жюал ~) случайный заработок

currency ~ targets (ку́ррэнси ~ та́ргэтс) задания по валютной выручке
dollar denominated ~ (до́ллар дино́минэйтэд ~) долларовая выручка
export ~ (э́кспорт ~) экспортная выручка, доход от экспорта, экспортный доход
foreign exchange ~ (фо́рэн эксчэ́йндж ~) валютная выручка, валютные поступления
foreign trade ~ (фо́рэн трэйд ~) доход от внешней торговли
gross ~ (грос ~) валовая выручка
imputed ~ (импю́тэд ~) вменённый доход
inflow of ~ (инфло́у оф ~) приток доходов
licensing ~ (ла́йсэнсинг ~) лицензионные поступления
minimum ~ (ми́нимум ~) минимальный заработок
monetary ~ (мо́нэтари ~) денежный заработок
piece work ~ (пис уо́рк ~) сдельный заработок
royalty ~ (ро́йялти ~) доход от роялти
~ of foreign currency (~ оф фо́рэн ку́ррэнси) поступление иностранной валюты
~ rate (~ рэйт) норма выручки
Earth (эрθ) земля
Easement (и́змэнт) сервитут
Easily (и́зили) легко
Easing (и́зинг) ослабление
~ of credit (~ оф крэ́дит) предоставление льгот по кредиту
East (ист) восток
Far ~ (фар ~) дальный восток
Middle ~ (мидл ~) средный восток
Near ~ (нир ~) ближный восток
Economic (эконо́мик) хозяйственный, экономический
national ~ development (на́шэнал ~ дивэ́лопмэнт) развитие народного хозяйства
to insure ~ measures (ту иншу́р ~ мэ́жюрз) гарантировать экономию
~ development (~ дивэ́лопмэнт) развитие экономики
~ efficiency (~ иффи́шэнси) экономичность
~ gain (~ гэйн) хозяйственная выгода

~ **rationalization** (~
рашнализэ́йшн) экономия
Economics (эконо́микс) экономика
Economical (эконо́микал)
экономичный, экономный
Economically (эконо́микалли)
экономично
~ **sound** (~ со́унд) экономически
выгодный
Economist (ико́номист) экономист
head ~ (хэд ~) главный экономист
industrial ~ (инду́стриал ~)
промышленный экономист
senior ~ (си́ниор ~) старший
экономист
Economize, to ~ (ико́номайз, ту ~)
выгадывать [**perfective:** выгадать],
осуществлять экономию, экономить
[**perfective:** сэкономить]
to ~ **on** {something} (ту ~ он
{со́мθинг}) экономить на {чём-
либо}
Economizing (ико́номайзинг)
сбережение
~ **measures** (~ мэ́жюрз) меры
экономии
~ **on material** (~ он мати́риал)
экономия материала
~ **through division of labor** (~
θру дивижн оф лэ́йбор) экономия
от разделения труда
Econom/y (ико́номи) хозяйство,
экономика, экономия ~/**ies**
сбережение, экономики
application to the national ~
(аппликэ́йшн ту θи на́шэнал ~)
внедрение в народное хозяйство
backwards ~ (ба́куардс ~)
отсталая экономика
branches of the ~ (бранчэз оф θи
~) отрасли экономики
centrally planned ~ (сэ́нтралли
пландˍ ~) централизованно-
планируемая экономика
commodity-based ~ (коммо́дити-
бэйсд ~) товарная экономика
competitive ~/**ies** (компэ́титив
~из) конкурирующие экономики
developed ~ (дивэ́лопд ~)
развитая экономика
directed ~ (дайрэ́ктэд ~)
контролируемая экономика
diversification of the ~
(дивэрсификэ́йшн оф θи ~)
диверсификация экономики
diversified ~ (дивэ́рсифайд ~)
многоотраслевая экономика

domestic ~ (домэ́стик ~)
внутренняя экономика
entrepreneurial ~
(энтрэпрэню́риал ~)
предпринимательская экономика
expanding ~ (экспа́ндинг ~)
развивающаяся экономика
forced ~/**ies** (форсд ~из)
вынужденное сбережение
global ~ (гло́бал ~) всемирное
хозяйство, мировая экономика
grain ~ (грэйн ~) зерновое
хозяйство
industrial ~ (инду́стриал ~)
промышленная экономика
market ~ (ма́ркэт ~) рыночное
хозяйство, рыночная экономика
market ~/**ies** (ма́ркэт ~из) страны
с рыночной экономикой
national ~ (на́шэнал ~) народное
хозяйство, национальная
экономика
natural ~ (на́чюрал ~)
натуральное хозяйство
planned ~ (пландˍ ~) плановое
хозяйство, плановая экономика
profitable ~ (про́фитабл ~)
рентабельное хозяйство
recovery of the ~ (рико́вэри оф
θи ~) оздоровление экономики
restructuring of the ~
(ристру́кшринг оф θи ~)
перестройка экономики
revival of the ~ (рива́йвал оф θи
~) оживление экономики
rigid ~ (ри́джид ~) строгая
экономия
self-sufficient ~ (сэлф-
суффи́шиэнт ~) самообеспеченная
экономика
stable ~ (стэ́йбл ~) устойчивая
экономика
stagnant ~ (ста́гнант ~)
застойная экономика
state of the ~ (стэйт оф θи ~)
состояние экономики
strengthening of the ~
(стрэ́нгθэнинг оф θи ~)
укрепление экономики
structure of the ~ (стру́кшр оф
θи ~) структура хозяйства
thriving ~ (θра́йвинг ~)
процветающая экономика
to restructure the ~ (ту
ристру́кшр θи ~) перестраивать
экономику

to **revive the** ~ (ту ривáйв θи ~)
оживлять экономику
unintended ~/**ies** (анинтэ́ндэд
~из) незапланированная экономия
unstable ~ (анстэ́йбл ~)
неустойчивая экономика
urban ~ (у́рбан ~) городское
хозяйство
world ~ (уóрлд ~) мировое
хозяйство
~ **of specialization** (~ оф
спэшлизэ́йшн) экономия
обусловленная специализацией
Edit, to ~ (э́дит, ту ~)
редактировать
Editing (э́дитинг) редакция
Edition (эди́шн) выпуск, издание
single-volume ~ (сингл-вóлюм ~)
однотомник
Editor (э́дитор) редактор
Editor-in-chief (э́дитор-ин-чиф)
главный редактор
Editorial (эдитóриал) редакционный
~ **staff** (~ стаф) редакция
Education (эдюкэ́йшн) образование,
просвещение
compulsory ~ (компу́лсори ~)
обязательное обучение
compulsory general ~ (компу́лсори
джэ́нэрал ~) всеобщее
обязательное образование
general ~ (джэ́нэрал ~) всеобщее
образование
liberal ~ (ли́бэрал ~) светское
образование
public ~ (пáблик ~) народное
образование, народное
просвещение
universal ~ (юнивэ́рсал ~)
всеобщее обучение
universal compulsory ~
(юнивэ́рсал компу́лсори ~)
всеобщее обязательное обучение
Effect (иффэ́кт) действие,
результат, эффект
cumulative ~ (кю́мюлатив ~) общий
эффект
desired ~ (дизáйрд ~)
желательный результат
economic ~ (эконóмик ~)
экономический эффект
ill ~ (ил ~) вредное действие
positive ~ (пóзитив ~)
положительный эффект
price distorting ~ (прайс
дистóртинг ~) эффект искажения
цены

retroactive ~ (рэтроáктив ~)
обратная сила
spillover ~ (спи́лловэр ~)
побочный эффект
technical ~ (тэ́кникал ~)
технический эффект
to ~ (ту ~) вводить
to bring an agreement into ~ (ту
бринг ан агри́мэнт и́нту ~)
вводить в действие соглашение
to bring into ~ (ту бринг и́нту
~) вводить в действие
to carry a law into ~ (ту кэ́рри
а лáу и́нту ~) вводить в действие
закон
to give ~ **to** (ту гив ~ ту)
приводить в действие
to have ~ (ту хэв ~) оказывать
действия
to take ~ (ту тэйк ~) вступать в
действие, вступать в силу
to yield an economic ~ (ту йилд
ан эконóмик ~) обеспечивать
экономический эффект
with retroactive ~ (уиθ
рэтроáктив ~) с обратной силой
~ **of circumstances** (~ оф
си́ркамстансэз) действие
обстоятельств
Effective (иффэ́ктив) эффективный
to be economically ~ (ту би
экономикалли ~) давать
экономический эффект
~ **period** (~ пи́риод) срок
действия
Effectiveness (иффэ́ктивнэс)
эффективность
overall ~ (овэрáл ~) общая
эффективность
~ **ratio** (~ рэ́йшио) коэффициент
эффективности
Efficiency (эффи́шэнси)
квалификация, продуктивность,
эффективность
advertising ~ (áдвэртайзинг ~)
эффективность рекламы
calculation of economic ~
(калкюлэ́йшн оф эконóмик ~)
расчёт экономической
эффективности
commercial ~ (коммэ́ршл ~)
коммерческая эффективность
decline in ~ (диклáйн ин ~)
снижение эффективности
economic ~ (эконóмик ~)
экономическая эффективность

high ~ (хай ~) высокая эффективность
improvement of economic ~ (импрувмэнт оф экономик ~) повышение экономичности
increase in ~ (инкрис ин ~) повышение эффективности
investment ~ (инвэстмэнт ~) эффективность капиталовложения
level of ~ (лэвэл оф ~) уровень эффективности
operating ~ (опэрэйтинг ~) производительность, эксплуатационная эффективность
optimum ~ (оптимум ~) оптимальная эффективность
to determine ~ (ту дитэрмин ~) определять эффективность
~ of exports (~ оф экспортс) эффективность экспорта
~ of information (~ оф информэйшн) эффективность информации
~ of an invention (~ оф ан инвэншн) эффективность изобретения
~ of licensing (~ оф лайсэнсинг) эффективность лицензирования
~ of modification (~ оф модификэйшн) эффективность модификации
~ of patenting (~ оф патэнтинг) эффективность патентования
~ of production (~ оф продакшн) эффективность производства
Efficient (эффишэнт) производительный, распорядительный, рациональный, эффективный
Effort (эффорт) усилие, ~s деятельность
propaganda ~s (пропаганда ~с) пропагандистская деятельность
rationalization ~s (рашнаизэйшн ~с) рационализаторская деятельность
to spare no ~ (ту спэйр но ~) не щадить сил
Elaborate, to ~ (илаборэйт, ту ~) разрабатывать [perfective: разработать], разрабатывать детально, тщательно разрабатывать
Elder (элдэр) староста
Elect, to ~ (илэкт, ту ~) избрать
Election (илэкшн) избрание
municipal ~ (мюнисипал ~) муниципальное избрание
Elector (элэктор) избиратель

Electoral (элэкторал) избирательный
Emancipate, to ~ (имансипэйт, ту ~) освобождать [perfective: освободить]
to ~ {serfs} (ту ~ {сэрфс}) раскрепостить
Emancipation (имансипэйшн) освобождение, раскрепощение
Embankment (эмбанкмэнт) набережная
Embargo (эмбарго) блокада, экономическая блокада, эмбарго
breach of an ~ (брич оф ан ~) прорыв блокады
import ~ (импорт ~) запрет на ввоз
technological ~ (тэкнолоджикал ~) технологическая блокада
to ~ (ту ~) наложить секвестр
to impose an ~ (ту импоз ан ~) наложить эмбарго
to lift an ~ (ту лифт ан ~) снимать эмбарго
trade ~ (трэйд ~) торговая блокада
~ on exports (~ он экспортс) эмбарго на экспорт
~ policy (~ полиси) политика эмбарго
Embarkation (эмбаркэйшн) посадка
Embarrassing (эмбэйррассинг) затруднительный
Embassy (эмбасси) посольство
Embezzle, to ~ (эмбэзл, ту ~) растратить
Embezzlement (эмбэзлмэнт) присвоение чужих денежных средств, хищение
official ~ (оффишл ~) растрата казённых денег
Embezzler (эмбэззлэр) растратчик
Embodiment (эмбодимэнт) воплощение
to be the ~ of (ту бу θи ~ оф) воплощаться
Embody, to ~ (эмбоди, ту ~) воплощать
Emboss, to ~ marking (эмбос, ту ~ маркинг) выбивать маркировку
Emergency (эмэрджэнси) чрезвычайный
Emigration (эмигрэйшн) эмиграция
restrictions on ~ (ристрикшнс он ~) ограничение по эмиграции
Emission (эмишн) выпуск, эмиссия
~ of bank notes (~ оф банк нотс) выпуск банкнот
~ of currency (~ оф куррэнси) эмиссия денег

~ of currency into circulation
(~ оф ку́ррэнси и́нту сиркюлэ́йшн)
выпуск денег в обращение
Emit, to ~ (эми́т, ту ~) выпускать
Emperor (э́мпорэр) император
Emphyteusis (эмфитэ́усис) эмфитевзис
   land lease on the basis of ~
   (ланд лис он θи бэ́йсис оф ~)
   аренда земли на началах
   эмфитевзиса
   lease in ~ (лис ин ~)
   эмфитевтическая аренда
Empire (э́мпайр) империя
   colonial ~ (коло́ниал ~)
   колониальная империя
   economic ~ (эконо́мик ~)
   экономическая империя
Employ, to ~ (эмпло́й, ту ~)
нанимать, применять
Employee (эмплойи́) работник,
служащий, сотрудник
представительства
   bank ~ (банк ~) банковский
   служащий
   qualified ~ (куа́лифайд ~)
   квалифицированный служащий
Employer (эмпло́йэр) наниматель,
работодатель
Employment (эмпло́ймэнт) занятость,
наём, приём, применение
   full ~ (фул ~) полная занятость
   permanent ~ (пэ́рманэнт ~)
   постоянная занятость
   ~ agent (~ э́йджэнт) агент по
   найму
   ~ contract (~ ко́нтракт) договор
   найма
   ~ of the death penalty (~ оф θи
   дэθ пэ́налти) применение смертной
   казни
   ~ of trademark (~ оф трэ́йдмарк)
   применение товарного знака
   ~ of the work force (~ оф θи
   уо́рк форс) применение рабочей
   силы
Empty (э́мпти) без груза
{transport}, пустой
Enact, to ~ (эна́кт, ту ~)
постановлять
Enactment (эна́ктмэнт) постановление
   legal ~ (ли́гал ~) законное
   постановление, законное
   распоряжение
Encashment (энка́шмэнт) наличные
поступления
Enclave (э́нклэйв) анклав

Enclose, to ~ (энкло́з, ту ~)
вкладывать, огородить
Enclosure (энкло́жюр) приложение
Encoded (энко́дэд) шифрованный
Encoding (энко́динг) шифровка
Encouragement (энку́раджмэнт)
поощрение
Encroach, to ~ (энкро́ч, ту ~)
покушаться, посягать
   to ~ upon rights (ту ~ апо́н
   райтс) покушаться на права
Encroachment (энкро́чмэнт)
посягательство
   ~ on sovereignty (~ он со́вэрнти)
   посягательство на суверенитет
   ~ upon rights (~ апо́н райтс)
   посягательство на права
Encumber, to ~ (энку́мбэр, ту ~)
обременять
Encumbered (энка́мбэрд)
обременительный
Encumbrance (энку́мбранс)
обременение
   free from ~s (фри фром ~с)
   свободный от обременений,
   свободный от ипотек
Encyclical, papal ~ (энси́кликал,
пэ́йпал ~) послание папы
End (энд) конец
   "this ~ up" (θис ~ ап) верх
Endorse, to ~ (эндо́рс, ту ~) дать
аваль, делать надпись,
индоссировать
Endorsee эндорси́) жиратб индоссат,
лицо, в чью пользу произведён
трансферт
Endorsement (эндо́рсмэнт) аваль,
жиро, индоссамент, надпись,
передаточная надпись
   blank ~ (бланк ~) бланковый
   индоссамент, бланковая надпись
   partial ~ (паршл ~) частичный
   индоссамент
   special ~ (спэшл ~) именной
   индоссамент
   successive ~s (суксэ́сив ~с)
   последовательные надписи
   ~ by bearer (~ бай бэ́йрэр)
   индоссамент на предъявителя
   ~ for collection (~ фор
   колле́кшн) инкассовый индоссамент
   ~ in full (~ ин фул) именная
   надпись
   ~ of a bill {note} (~ оф а бил
   {нот}) вексельный индоссамент
   ~ of a check (~ оф а чэк)
   чековый индоссамент

~ **without recourse** (~ уивóут рúкорс) безоборотная надпись
Endorser (эндóрсэр) жирант, индоссант
Endure, to ~ (эндýр, ту ~) переживать
Enforce, to ~ demands (энфóрс, ту ~ димáндс) добиваться выполнения требований
Enforced ~ (энфóрсд ~) принудительное взыскание
Enforcement (энфóрсмэнт) осуществление, соблюдение
    for the ~ of (фор θи ~ оф) для придания законной силы
Engagement (энгэ́йджмэнт) обязательство
Engineer (инджинúр) инжинир, конструктор
    chief mechanical ~ (чиф мэкáникал ~) главный механик
    process ~ (прóсэс ~) технолог
    to ~ (ту ~) конструировать
Engineering (инджэнúринг) конструирование, проектирование, техника
    chemical ~ (кэ́микал ~) химическое машиностроение
    civil ~ (сúвил ~) гражданское строительство
    heavy ~ (хэ́ви ~) тяжёлое машиностроение
    heavy ~ plant (хэ́ви ~ плант) завод тяжёлого машиностроения
    industrial ~ (индýстриал ~) промышленное строительство
    mechanical ~ (мэкáникал ~) машиностроение
    plant ~ (плант ~) техника эксплуатации и монтажа оборудования
    power plant ~ (пóуэр плант ~) энергическое машиностроение
    precision ~ (прэсúжн ~) точное машиностроение
    transportation ~ (транспортэ́йшн ~) транспортное машиностроение
    ~ defect (~ дúфэкт) дефект в конструкции
    ~ products (~ прóдуктс) продукция машиностроения
Enjoin, to ~ (энджóйн, ту ~) предписывать
    to ~ (ту ~) приказывать
Enjoy, to ~ (энджóй, ту ~) пользоваться
Enjoyment (энджóймэнт) пользование

Enlightenment (энлáйтэнмэнт) просвещение
Enslave, to ~ (энслэ́йв, ту ~) закабалить, поработить
Enslavement (энслэ́йвмэнт) порабощение
Entailing (энтэ́йлинг) сопряжённый
Entente (антáнт) антанта
    Balkan ~ (бáлкан ~) балканская антанта
Enter, to ~ (э́нтэр, ту ~) вступать
    to ~ into an agreement (ту ~ úнту ан агрúмэнт) вступать в соглашение
Entering (э́нтэринг) занесение
    ~ of a default judgment (~ оф а дифáлт джáджмэнт) отзыв на заочное решение
Enterprise (э́нтэрпрайз) предпринимательство, предприятие
    aerospace ~ (э́йроспэйс ~) авиапредприятие
    agricultural ~ (агрикýлчурал ~) сельскохозяйственное предприятие
    air transport ~ (эйр трáнспорт ~) воздушно-транспортное предприятие
    branch ~ (бранч ~) дочернее предприятие
    business ~ (бúзнэс ~) предпринимательство
    commercial ~ (коммэ́ршл ~) коммерческое предприятие
    competing ~ (компúтинг ~) конкурирующее предприятие
    construction ~ (констрýкшн ~) строительное предприятие
    cooperative ~ (коóпэратив ~) кооперативное предприятие
    cottage ~ (кóттадж ~) кустарническое предприятие
    free ~ (фри ~) свободное предпринимательство
    industrial ~ (индýстриал ~) промышленное предприятие
    medium-sized ~ (мúдиум-сайзд ~) среднее предприятие
    mining ~ (мáйнинг ~) горное предприятие
    mixed ~ (миксд ~) смешанное предприятие
    national ~ (нáшэнал ~) национальное предприятие
    nationalized ~ (нáшэналайзд ~) национализированное предприятие

private ~ (прáйват ~) частное предпринимательство, частное предприятие
retail ~ (рúтэйл ~) розничное предприятие
self-financing ~ (сэлф-фáйнансинг ~) хозрасчётное объединение
self-supporting ~ (сэлф-суппóртинг ~) хозрасчетное предприятие
shipping ~ (шúппинг ~) судоходное предприятие
state ~ (стэйт ~) государственное предприятие
subsidiary ~ (субсúдиари ~) подсобное предприятие
trading ~ (трэ́йдинг ~) торговое предприятие
trading and manufacturing ~ (трэ́йдинг энд манюфáкчуринг ~) торгово-промышленное предприятие
transport ~ (трáнспорт ~) транспортное предприятие
unprofitable ~ (анпрóфитабл ~) нерентабельное предприятие, убыточное предприятие
wholesale ~ (хóлсэйл ~) оптовое предприятие
Enthrall, to ~ (энθрáл, ту ~) поработить {enslave}
Enthrallment (энθрáлмэнт) порабощение
Entitle, to ~ (энтáйтл, ту ~) называть
Entrance (э́нтранс) вступительный {adj.}, вход, въездной {adj.}
Entrapment (энтрáпмэнт) подстрекательство к порочной деятельности
   criminal ~ (крúминал ~) подстрекательство к преступлению
Entrenched (энтрэ́нчэд) закреплённый
   ~ faction (~ факшн) реакция
Entrepreneur (энтрэпрэню́р) предприниматель
   agricultural ~ (агрикý лчурал ~) сельскохозяйственный предприниматель
   private ~ (прáйват ~) частный предприниматель
Entrust, to ~ (энтрýст, ту ~) поручать
Entry (э́нтри) въезд, запись, проводка
   bookkeeping ~ (бýккипинг ~) бухгалтерская запись

credit ~ (крэ́дит ~) кредитовая запись, кредитовая проводка
debit ~ (дэ́бит ~) дебетовая запись, дебетовая проводка
duty-free ~ (дю́ти-фри ~) беспошлинный пропуск
right of ~ entrance (райт оф ~ э́нтранс) въезд
to ban ~ (ту бан ~) запрещать въезд
to permit ~ (ту пэ́рмит ~) разрешать въезд
to permit ~ to the construction site (ту пэ́рмит ~ ту θи констрýкшн сайт) разрешать въезд на территорию стройплощадки
to record an ~ (ту рэ́корд ан ~) произвести запись
~ of arbitral judgment (~ оф áрбитрал джáджмэнт) третейская запись
~ of payments received (~ оф пэ́ймэнтс рисúвд) учёт денежных поступлений
~ permit (~ пэ́рмит) разрешение на ввоз, разрешение на въезд
Enumeration (энумэрэ́йшн) перечень, перечисление
   ~ of claims (~ оф клэ́ймс) перечень заявленных претензий
Envelope (э́нвэлоп) конверт, обёртка
   sealed ~ (силд ~) запечатанный конверт
   stamped ~ (стампд ~) конверт с маркой
   to address an ~ (ту аддрэ́с ан ~) надписывать конверт
   to open an ~ (ту óпэн ан ~) вскрывать конверт
   to seal an ~ (ту сил ан ~) запечатывать конверт
   waterproof ~ (уáтэрпруф ~) водонепроницаемый конверт
Environment (энвáйронмэнт) обстановка
Environmental (энвайронмэ́нтал) окружающий
   ~ analysis (~ анáлисис) анализ условий окружающей среды
Envoy (э́нвой) посланник
   diplomatic ~ (дипломáтик ~) дипломатический посланник
   peace ~ (пис ~) парламентёр
   special ~ (спэшл ~) чрезвычайный посланник
Epistle (эпúстл) послание
Equal (úкуал) равный, ровня

~ rights (~ райтс) равенство
прав, равноправие
Equality (икуа́лити) равенство
~ before the law (~ бифо́р θи
лау) равенство перед законом
~ in economic relations (~ ин
экономик рилэ́йшнз) равноправие в
экономических отношениях
Equalization (икуализэ́йшн)
уравнивание
Equalize, to ~ (и́куалайз, ту ~)
уравнивать
Equate, to ~ (икуэ́йт, ту ~)
приравнивать
Equilibrium (икуили́бриум)
равновесие
  demographic ~ (дэмогра́фик ~)
  демографическое равновесие
  market ~ (ма́ркэт ~) конъюнктура
  рынка
  monetary ~ (мо́нэтари ~) денежное
  равновесие
Equip, to ~ (икуи́п, ту ~)
оборудовать
Equipment (икуи́пмэнт) оборудование,
снаряжение, техника
  acceptance of delivery of ~
  (аксэ́птанс оф дэли́вэри оф ~)
  приёмка оборудования
  accessory ~ (аксэ́ссори ~)
  вспомогательное оборудование
  adjustment of ~ (аджа́стмэнт оф
  ~) наладка оборудования
  agricultural ~ (агрику́лчурал ~)
  сельскохозяйственное
  оборудование
  American-made ~ (амэ́рикан-мэйд
  ~) оборудование американского
  производства
  ancillary ~ (а́нсиллари ~)
  комплектующее оборудование
  applicable ~ (аппли́кабл ~)
  соответствующее оборудование
  assembly line ~ (ассэ́мбли лайн
  ~) оборудование на линии сборки
  assembly of ~ (ассэ́мбли оф ~)
  сборка оборудования
  automatic ~ (аутома́тик ~)
  автоматическое оборудование
  auto repair ~ (а́уто рипэ́йр ~)
  гаражно-ремонтное оборудование
  availability of ~ (авайлаби́лити
  оф ~) наличие оборудования
  breakdown of ~ (брэ́йкдоун оф ~)
  поломка оборудования

cargo handling ~ (ка́рго ха́ндлинг
~) погрузочно-разгрузочное
оборудование
commercial ~ (коммэ́ршл ~)
коммерческое оборудование
competitive ~ (компэ́титив ~)
конкурентоспособное оборудование
complete outfit of ~ (компли́т
о́утфит оф ~) комплектное
оборудование
complex ~ (ко́мплэкс ~) сложное
оборудование
construction ~ (констру́кшн ~)
строительное оборудование
consumer of ~ (консу́мэр оф ~)
потребитель оборудования
container ~ (контэ́йнэр ~)
контейнерное оборудование
contract ~ (ко́нтракт ~)
оборудование по контракту
damaged ~ (да́маджд ~)
повреждённое оборудование
defective ~ (дифэ́ктив ~)
дефектное оборудование
delayed ~ (дилэ́йд ~) задержанное
оборудование
delivered ~ (дэли́вэрд ~)
поставляемое оборудование
delivery of ~ (дэли́вэри оф ~)
доставка оборудования
demand for ~ (дима́нд фор ~)
спрос на оборудование
demonstration of ~ (дэмонстрэ́йшн
оф ~) показ оборудования
depreciation of ~ (диприши́эйшн
оф ~) амортизация оборудования
development of new ~
(дивэ́лопмэнт оф нью ~)
разработка нового оборудования
dimensions of ~ (димэ́ншнз оф ~)
габариты оборудования, размеры
оборудования
disassembled ~ (дисассэ́мблд ~)
разобранное оборудование
disassembly of ~ (дисассэ́мбли оф
~) разборка оборудования
dismantling of ~ (дисма́нтлинг оф
~) демонтаж оборудования
display ~ (дисплэ́й ~)
оборудование для выкладки и
экспонирования товара
displayed ~ (дисплэ́йд ~)
экспонируемое оборудование
dollars worth of ~ (до́лларс уо́рθ
оф ~) оборудование стоимостью
... долларов

domestically produced ~
(домэ́стикалли продю́сд ~)
оборудование отечественного
производства
durable ~ (ду́рабл ~) капитальное
оборудование, оборудование
длительного пользования
electrical ~ (элэ́ктрикал ~)
электротехническое оборудование
emergency ~ (эмэ́рджэнси ~)
аварийное оборудование
erection ~ (ирэ́кшн ~) монтажное
оборудование
exportation of ~ (э́кспортэ́йшн оф
~) вывоз оборудования
fire fighting ~ (фа́йр фа́йтинг ~)
противопожарное оборудование
first-class ~ (фэ́рст-класс ~)
первоклассное оборудование
food processing ~ (фуд про́сэсинг
~) оборудование для обработки
пищевых продуктов **heavy ~**
{weight} тяжеловесное
оборудование
high-quality ~ (хай-куа́лити ~)
высококачественное оборудование
high-tech ~ (хай-тэк ~)
наукоёмкое оборудование
highly productive ~ (ха́йли
прода́ктив ~)
высокопроизводительное
оборудование
idle ~ (айдл ~) бездействующее
оборудование
import of ~ (и́мпорт оф ~) ввоз
оборудования
imported ~ (импо́ртэд ~)
импортное оборудование
incomplete set of ~ (инкомпли́т
сэт оф ~) некомплектное
оборудование
individual units of ~
(индиви́дюал ю́нитс оф ~)
отдельное оборудование
industrial ~ (инду́стриал ~)
промышленное оборудование
inspection of ~ (инспэ́кшн оф ~)
осмотр оборудования
installation of ~ (инсталэ́йшн оф
~) монтаж оборудования
installed ~ (инста́лд ~)
установленное оборудование
introduction of ~ {into
operation} (интрода́кшн оф ~
{и́нту опэрэ́йшн}) ввод
оборудования в эксплуатацию

large-scale specialized ~
(лардж-скэйл спэ́шлайзд ~)
крупное оборудование
специального назначения
machining ~ (маши́нинг ~)
машинное оборудование
maintenance of ~ (мэ́йнтэнанс оф
~) уход за оборудованием
manufacturing ~ (манюфа́кчуринг
~) производственное оборудование
material handling ~ (мати́риал
ха́ндлинг ~) погрузочно-
разгрузочные механизмы
metallurgical ~ (мэталлю́рджикал
~) металлургическое оборудование
mining ~ (ма́йнинг ~)
горношахтное оборудование,
шахтное оборудование
miscellaneous ~ (мисэлэ́йниос ~)
разрозненное оборудование
missing ~ (ми́ссинг ~)
недопоставленное оборудование,
недостающее оборудование
modern ~ (мо́дэрн ~) современное
оборудование
modified ~ (мо́дифайд ~)
модифицированное оборудование
next generation ~ (нэкст
джэнэрэ́йшн ~) оборудование новых
поколений
non-standard ~ (нон-ста́ндард ~)
нестандартное оборудование
obsolete ~ (обсоли́т ~)
устаревшее оборудование
office ~ (о́ффис ~) конторское
оборудование
operation of ~ (опэрэ́йшн оф ~)
эксплуатация оборудования
order for ~ (о́рдэр фор ~) заказ
на оборудование
ordered ~ (о́рдэрд ~) заказанное
оборудование
outfit of ~ (о́утфит оф ~)
комплекс оборудования
oversized ~ (о́вэрсайзд ~)
крупногабаритное оборудование,
негабаритное оборудование
packing ~ (па́ккинг ~)
упаковочное оборудование
patented ~ (па́тэнтэд ~)
патентованное оборудование
plant ~ (плант ~) заводское
оборудование
power plant ~ (по́уэр плант ~)
энергетическое оборудование
preservation of ~ (прэзэрвэ́йшн
оф ~) консервация оборудования

primary ~ (пра́ймари ~) основное оборудование

process control ~ (про́сэс контро́л ~) оборудование для управления производственных процессов

production of ~ (прода́кшн оф ~) выпуск оборудования

productivity of ~ (продукти́вити оф ~) производительность оборудования

quality of ~ (куа́лити оф ~) качество оборудования

rapidly-wearing ~ (ра́пидли-уэ́йринг ~) быстроизнашивающееся оборудование

re-export of ~ (ри-э́кспорт оф ~) реэкспорт оборудования

renovation of ~ (рэнове́йшн оф ~) реновация оборудования

rental ~ (рэ́нтал ~) сдаваемое в аренду оборудование

repair of ~ (рипэ́йр оф ~) ремонт оборудования

replaceable ~ (риплэ́йсабл ~) заменяемое оборудование

replacement of ~ (риплэ́йсмэнт оф ~) замена оборудования

reserve ~ (рисэ́рв ~) резервное оборудование

return of ~ (риту́рн оф ~) возврат оборудования

revenue ~ (рэ́вэну ~) коммерчески эксплуатируемое оборудование

road building ~ (род би́лдинг ~) дорожно-строительное оборудование

sale of ~ (сэйл оф ~) реализация оборудования

secondary ~ (сэ́кондари ~) подержанное оборудование

semi-automatic ~ (сэ́ми-аутома́тик ~) полуавтоматическое оборудование

serial ~ (си́риал ~) серийное оборудование

serial production ~ (си́риал прода́кшн ~) оборудование серийного производства

service of ~ (сэ́рвис оф ~) обслуживание оборудования

servicing ~ (сэ́рвисинг ~) подсобное оборудование

shop ~ (шоп ~) торговое оборудование

short-shipped ~ (шорт-шиппд ~) недопоставленное оборудование

spare ~ (спэйр ~) запасное оборудование

specialized ~ (спэ́шлайзд ~) специализированное оборудование

specifications of ~ (спэсификэ́йшнс оф ~) спецификация на оборудование

standard ~ (ста́ндард ~) стандартное оборудование

stock of ~ (сток оф ~) запас оборудования

storage ~ (сто́радж ~) складское оборудование

storage of ~ (сто́радж оф ~) складирование оборудования, хранение оборудования

suitable ~ (су́табл ~) соответствующее оборудование

supplier of ~ (сапла́йэр оф ~) поставщик оборудования

technical characteristics of ~ (тэ́кникал карактэри́стикс оф ~) техническая характеристика оборудования

test ~ (тэст ~) испытательное оборудование

to check ~ (ту чэк ~) проверять оборудование

to design ~ (ту диза́йн ~) проектировать оборудование

to improve ~ (ту импру́в ~) улучшать оборудование

to install ~ (ту инста́л ~) монтировать оборудование, устанавливать оборудование

to manufacture ~ (ту манюфа́кчур ~) производить оборудование

to obtain ~ (ту обтэ́йн ~) приобретать оборудование

to reject defective ~ (ту риджэ́кт дифэ́ктив ~) отказаться от дефектного оборудования

to rent ~ {as lessor} (ту рэнт ~ {аз лэссо́р}) сдавать в аренду оборудование

to secure ~ (ту сэкю́р ~) обеспечивать оборудование

to submit ~ for inspection (ту субми́т ~ фор инспэ́кшн) предъявлять оборудование для осмотра

type of ~ (та́йп оф ~) тип оборудования

unique ~ (юни́к ~) уникальное оборудование

unit of ~ (ю́нит оф ~) единица оборудования

units of ~ (юнитс оф ~) узлы оборудования
used ~ (юзд ~) бывшее в эксплуатации оборудование
user of ~ (юзэр оф ~) пользователь оборудования
wear and tear of ~ (уэйр энд тэйр оф ~) износ оборудования
weighing ~ (уэйинг ~) оборудование для взвешивания
working ~ (уоркинг ~) действующее оборудование, оборудование в действии
worn out ~ (уорн оут ~) изношенное оборудование
~ downtime (~ доунтайм) простой оборудования
~ list (~ лист) перечень оборудования
~ rental (~ рэнтал) аренда оборудования
Equipping (икуиппинг) оснащение
Equitable (экуитабл) справедливый
Equity (экуити) доля, капитал, справедливость
shareholder ~ (шэйрхолдэр ~) акционерный капитал
Erect, to ~ (ирэкт, ту ~) монтировать
Erection (ирэкшн) монтажа, монтажный {adj.}
commencement of ~ (коммэнсмэнт оф ~) начало монтажа
completion of ~ (комплишн оф ~) завершение монтажа, окончание монтажа
cost of ~ (кост оф ~) стоимость монтажа
exclusive of ~ (эксклюсив оф ~) исключая монтаж
expenditures on ~ (экспэндичюрз он ~) расходы по монтажу
general conditions of ~ (джэнэрал кондишнс оф ~) общие условия монтажа
in the course of ~ (ин θи корс оф ~) в процессе монтажа
overall (овэрал) полный монтаж
proper ~ (пропэр ~) правильный монтаж
rapid ~ (рапид ~) быстрый монтаж

timely ~ (таймли ~) своевременный монтаж
~ personnel (~ пэрсоннэл) персонал, занимающийся монтажом

~ specialist (~ спэшлист) специалист по монтажу
~ work (~ уорк) работы по монтажу
Errand (эрранд) поручение
Erratum (эрратум) опечатка {e.g. book, inventory list}
Error (эррор) ошибка
clerical ~ (клэрикал ~) канцелярская ошибка
factual ~ (факчуал ~) фактическая ошибка
judicial ~ (джюдишл ~) судебная ошибка
jurisprudential ~ (джуриспрудэншл ~) юридическая ошибка
legal ~ (лигал ~) правовая ошибка
navigational ~ (навигэйшнал ~) навигационная ошибка
to make an ~ (ту мэйк ан ~) допускать ошибку
Escalation (эскалэйшн) шкала, шкала надбавок и скидок, эскалация
price ~ (прайс ~) эскалация цен
price ~ formula (прайс ~ формула) формула эскалации цен
to be subject to ~ (ту би сабджэкт ту ~) подлежать увеличению, подлежать эскалации
Escape (эскэйп) побег
Escheatment (эщитмэнт) переход наследства к государству
Essence (эссэнс) существо, сущность
Essential (эссэншл) необходимый
Establish, to ~ (эстаблиш, ту ~) учреждать
Establishment (эстаблишмэнт) учреждение
research ~ (рисэрч ~) научно-исследовательское учреждение
Estate (эстэйт) имение {landed property}, сословие
housing ~ {public} (хоузинг ~ {паблик}) посёлок
real ~ (рил ~) недвижимое имущество
Estimate (эстимат) оценка, смета
additional budgetary ~ (аддишнал баджэтари ~) дополнительная бюджетная смета
annual ~ (аннюал ~) годовая оценка
approximate ~ (аппроксимат ~) приблизительная оценка, приблизительная смета

budgetary ~ (бáджэтари ~)
бюджетная смета
design ~s (дизáйн ~с)
проектно-сметная документация
low ~ (лóу ~) заниженная оценка
preliminary ~ (прилúминэри ~)
предварительная смета
sample ~ (сампл ~) выборочная
оценка
statistical ~ (статúстикал ~)
статистическая оценка
to ~ (ту ~) оценивать
to approve an ~ (ту аппрýв ан ~)
одобрить смету
~ of expenditures (~ оф
экспэ́ндичюрз) расходная смета
~ of expenses (~ оф экспэ́нсэз)
смета расходов
~ of income (~ оф úнком) смета
доходов
~ of outlays (~ оф óутлэйз)
смета затрат
Estimation (эстимэ́йшн) калькуляция,
оценка
~ of risk (~ оф риск) оценка
риска
Eurocheques (ю́рочэкс) еврочеки
Eurocredit (ю́рокрэ́дит) еврокредит
Eurocurrency (ю́рокýррэнси)
евровалюта, евровалютный {adj.}
Eurodollars (ю́родóлларс)
евродоллары
Euromarket (ю́ромáркэт) еврорынок
Evaluate, to ~ (ивáлюэйт, ту ~)
оценивать
Evaluation (ивалюэ́йшн) оценка
customs ~ (кáстомз ~) таможенная
оценка
inventory ~ (úнвэнтори ~)
инвентарная оценка
~ of evidence (~ оф э́видэнс)
оценка доказательств
Evasion (ивэ́йжн) обход
~ of the law (~ оф θи лау) обход
закона
tax ~ (такс ~) обход налоговых
законов, уклонение от уплаты
налогов
Event (ивэ́нт) мероприятие,
происшествие, случай
annual ~ (áннюал ~) ежегодное
мероприятие
calendar of ~s (кáлэндар оф ~с)
календарь мероприятий
important ~ (импóртант ~) важное
мероприятие

in the ~ of ... (ин θи ~ оф ...)
в случае ...
sequence of ~s (сúкуэнс оф ~с)
последовательность мероприятий
Eviction (ивúкшн) расквартирование
order of ~ (óрдэр оф ~) ордер на
расквартирование
Evidence (э́видэнс) доказательство,
показание, свидетельство
convincing ~ (конвúнсинг ~)
убедительное доказательство
documentary ~ (докюмэ́нтари ~)
документальное доказательство
false ~ (фалс ~) ложное
показание
irrefutable ~ (иррифю́табл ~)
неоспоримое доказательство
material ~ (матúриал ~)
вещественное доказательство
medical ~ (мэ́дикал ~)
медицинское показание
oral ~ (óрал ~) устное показание
to present ~ (ту прэзэ́нт ~)
представлять доказательства
to give ~ (ту гив ~) дать
показание, свидетельствовать
verification of ~ (вэрификэ́йшн
оф ~) проверка доказательства
written ~ (рúттэн ~) письменное
доказательство, письменное
показание
~ of witnesses (~ оф уúтнэсэз)
свидетельское показание по
судебным делам
Ex- (экс-) франко {freight term}
Exactly (экзáктли) точно
~ to measurement (~ ту
мэ́жюрмэнт) точно по размеру
Exactness (экзáктнэс) точность
Examination (экзаминэ́йшн) досмотр,
опрос {cross or direct}, опросный
{adj.}, осмотр, проверка,
разбирательство, рассмотрение,
экспертиза
administrative ~ (админúстрэйтив
~) административная проверка
arbitration ~ (арбитрэ́йшн ~)
третейское разбирательство
certificate of expert's ~
(сэртúфикэт оф э́кспэртс ~) акт
экспертизы
control ~ (контрóл ~)
контрольная экспертиза
expert ~ clause (э́кспэрт ~
клауз) пункт решения экспертизы
field ~ (филд ~) выездная
проверка

final ~ (фа́йнал ~)
заключительная экспертиза,
окончательная экспертиза
follow-up ~ (фо́лло-ап ~)
повторная экспертиза
formal ~ (фо́рмал ~) формальная
экспертиза
independent ~ (индипэ́ндэнт ~)
независимая экспертиза
judicial ~ (джюди́шл ~) судебный
осмотр
objective ~ (обджэ́ктив ~)
объективная экспертиза
painstaking ~ (пэ́йнстэйкинг ~)
тщательная экспертиза
patent ~ (па́тэнт ~) патентная
экспертиза
patentability ~ (патэнтаби́лити
~) экспертиза на
патентоспособность
postponed ~ (постпо́нд ~)
отсроченная экспертиза
preliminary ~ (прили́минэри ~)
предварительное рассмотрение,
предварительная экспертиза
quarantine and sanitary ~
(куа́рантин энд са́нитари ~)
санитарно-карантинный досмотр
special ~ (спэшл ~) специальная
экспертиза
state ~ (стэйт ~)
государственная экспертиза
technical ~ (тэ́кникал ~)
техническая экспертиза
to resume ~ (ту ризу́м ~)
возобновлять экспертизу
to schedule an ~ (ту скэ́джюл ан
~) назначать экспертизу
to stop an ~ (ту стоп ан ~)
прекращать экспертизу
to withhold an ~ (ту уиθхо́лд ан
~) приостанавливать экспертизу
urgent ~ (у́рджэнт ~) срочная
экспертиза
~ department (~ дипа́ртмэнт)
отдел экспертизы
~ in situ (~ ин са́йту) осмотр
места происшествия, осмотр на
месте
~ of an application (~ оф ан
аппликэ́йшн) экспертиза заявки
~ of a ship (~ оф а шип) досмотр
судна
~ of substantive evidence (~ оф
су́бстантив э́видэнс) осмотр
вещественных доказательств

~ results (~ ризу́лтс) результаты
экспертизы
Examine, to ~ (экза́мин, ту ~)
осматривать [perfective:
осмотреть], подвергать экспертизе,
проверять, рассматривать
[perfective: рассмотреть]
Examiner (экза́минэр) эксперт
assistant ~ (асси́стант ~)
помощник эксперта
patent ~ (па́тэнт ~) эксперт
патентного ведомства
trademark ~ (трэ́йдмарк ~)
эксперт по товарным знакам
~'s objections (~с обджэ́кшнс)
возражения эксперта
~'s statement (~с стэ́йтмэнт) акт
экспертизы
Examiner-in-chief (экза́минр-ин-чиф)
главный эксперт
Exceed, to ~ (экски́д, ту ~)
превышать
Exceeding (экски́динг) превышение
~ demand (~ дима́нд) превышение
спроса
~ limits of necessary defense (~
ли́митс оф нэ́сэсари дифэ́нс)
превышение пределов необходимой
обороны
~ one's authority (~ уа́нз
аθо́рити) превышение власти
~ one's commission (~ уа́нз
комми́шн) превышение полномочий
~ the balance of payments (~ θи
ба́ланс оф пэ́ймэнтс) превышение
платёжного баланса
~ the budget (~ θи ба́джэт)
превышение бюджета
~ the limits of self-defense (~
θи ли́митс оф сэлф-дифэ́нс)
превышение пределов самозащиты
~ the offer (~ θи о́ффэр)
превышение предложения
Exception (эксэ́пшн) исключение
Excerpt (э́ксэрпт) выписка, выписка
из документа, извлечение, отрывок
data ~s (да́та ~с) извлечение
данных
Excess (эксэ́с) избыток, избыточный
{adj.}, излишек, превышение
~ earnings (~ э́рнингз) излишек
доходов
~ moisture (~ мо́йстюр) избыток
влаги
~ money supply {in circulation}
(~ мо́ни суппла́й {ин сиркюлэ́йшн})
излишек денег в обращении

~ **profit** (~ прóфит) сверхприбыль
~ **weight** (~ уэйт) излишек в весе
Excessive (эксэ́сив) чрезмерный
~ **force** (~ форс) перевес сил
Exchange (эксчэ́йндж) биржа, биржевой {*adj.*}, обмен, обменный {*adj.*}, размен

agreement of ~ (агри́мэнт оф ~) договор об обмене
allocation of foreign ~ (алокэ́йшн оф фóрэн ~) распределение валюты
ban on foreign ~ **export** (бан он фóрэн ~ э́кспорт) запрещение вывоза иностранной валюты
bilateral ~ (байлáтэрал ~) двухсторонний обмен
by way of ~ (бай уэй оф ~) в порядке обмена
calculation of ~ **rate** (калкюлэ́йшн оф ~ рэйт) вычисление курса валюты
clearinghouse ~ (кли́рингхаус ~) обмен на основе взаимных расчётов
commercial ~ (коммэ́ршл ~) возмездный обмен
commodity ~ (коммóдити ~) товарная биржа
cotton ~ (кóттон ~) хлопковая биржа
currency ~ (кýррэнси ~) валютная биржа
currency-free ~ (кýррэнси-фри ~) безвалютный обмен
direct barter ~ (дирэ́кт бáртэр ~) непосредственный обмен
equivalent ~ (икуи́валэнт ~) эквивалентный обмен
expansion of ~ (экспáншн оф ~) расширение обмена
foreign ~ (фóрэн ~) валютный баланс
foreign ~ **deficit** (фóрэн ~ дэ́фисит) дефицит валюты
foreign ~ **earnings** (фóрэн ~ э́рнингз) поступления валюты
foreign trade ~ (фóрэн трэйд ~) внешнеторговый обмен
grain ~ (грэйн ~) хлебная биржа
in ~ **for** ... (ин ~ фор ...) в обмен на
informal ~ (инфóрмал ~) неофициальная биржа
international commodities ~ (интэрнэ́шнал коммóдитиз ~) международная товарная биржа

listed on the ~ (ли́стэд он θи ~) котируемый на рынке
lumber ~ (лýмбэр ~) лесная биржа
medium of ~ (ми́диум оф ~) средство обмена
metals ~ (мэ́талз ~) биржа металлов
non-equivalent ~ (нон-икуи́валэнт ~) неэквивалентный обмен
on the ~ (он θи ~) на бирже
parity of ~ (пáрити оф ~) паритет валюты
quoted on the ~ (куóтэд он θи ~) котирующийся на бирже
reciprocal ~ (риси́прокал ~) взаимный обмен
recognized ~ (рэ́когнайзд ~) официальная биржа
securities ~ (сэкю́ритиз ~) биржа ценных бумаг
shipping ~ (ши́ппинг ~) фрахтовая биржа
short-term ~ **rate** (шорт-тэрм ~ рэйт) краткосрочный курс векселя
specialized ~ (спэ́шлайзд ~) специализированная биржа
stock ~ **list** (сток ~ лист) бюллетень курса ценных бумаг на бирже
technological ~ (тэкнолóджикал ~) технологический обмен
terms of ~ (тэрмз оф ~) условия обмена
to ~ (ту ~) менять, обменивать, разменивать [**perfective:** разменять]
to carry out an ~ (ту кэ́рри óут ан ~) производить обмен
to promote ~ (ту промóт ~) поощрять обмен
to surrender for ~ (ту суррэ́ндэр фор ~) сдавать для обмена
trade ~ (трэйд ~) торговый обмен
transaction in foreign ~ (трансáкшн ин фóрэн ~) сделка в валюте
wool ~ (уýл ~) биржа по шерсти
~ **as per endorsement** (~ ас пэр эндóрсмэнт) обмен по курсу, указанному на обороте векселя, курс векселя, указанный на обороте {on bill, note}
~ **at par** (~ ат пар) обмен по паритету, паритетный курс
~ **at the rate of** ... (~ ат θи рэйт оф ...) обмен по курсу ...

~ **bank** (~ банк) банк по обмену валюты
~ **business** (~ бизнэс) операции с валютой
~ **control** (~ контрол) управление обменом
~ **dealer** (~ дилэр) биржевик
~ **in kind** (~ ин кайнд) натуральный обмен
~ **losses** (~ лоссэз) потери на разнице курсов валют
~ **of delegations** (~ оф дэлэгэйшнс) обмен делегациями
~ **of experts** (~ оф экспэртс) обмен специалистами
~ **of information** (~ оф информэйшн) обмен информацией
~ **of know-how** (~ оф ноу-хау) обмен ноу-хау
~ **of knowledge** (~ оф нолэдж) обмен знаниями
~ **of money** (~ оф мони) размен денег
~ **of opinions** (~ оф опинионс) обмен мнениями
~ **of patents** (~ оф патэнтс) обмен патентами
~ **of services** (~ оф сэрвисэз) обмен услугами
~ **of shares** {stock} (~ оф шэйрз {сток}) обмен акций
~ **of trade data** (~ оф трэйд дата) обмен торговыми данными
~ **rate** (~ рэйт) курс валюты {currency}, курс векселя {notes}
~ **system** (~ систэм) система обмена
Exchangeability (эксчэйнджабилити) обратимость
Exchangeable (эксчэйнджабл) годный для обмена, обратимый, товарообменный
Excise (эксайз) акциз
universal ~ (юнивэрсал ~) универсальный акциз
Exclude, to ~ (эксклэд, ту ~) исключать
Exclusive (эксклюсив) исключительный
Exclusively (эксклюсивли) исключительно
Exclusivity (эксклюсивити) исключительность
~ **of verdict and sentencing** (~ оф вэрдикт энд сэнтэнсинг) исключительность решения и приговора

Excuse (экскюс) извинение, оправдание
to ~ (ту ~) оправдать
Execute, to ~ (эксэкют, ту ~) выполнять {carry out}, заключать {e.g. contract}, расстрелять {by firing squad}
Executed (эксэкютэд) выполненный, оформленный
duly ~ (дули ~) выполненный должным образом
Execution (эксэкюшн) выполнение, оформление, проведение, расстрел {by firing squad}
delay an ~ (дилэй ан ~) задержка в выполнении
during the ~ **of the work** (дуринг θи ~ оф θи уорк) во время выполнения работ
painstaking ~ (пэйнстакинг ~) тщательное выполнение
period of ~ (пириод оф ~) срок выполнения
proper ~ (пропэр ~) должное выполнение
successful ~ (суксэсфул ~) успешное выполнение
technical ~ (тэкникал ~) техническое выполнение
time of ~ (тайм оф ~) время выполнения
timely ~ (таймли ~) своевременное выполнение
to be delayed in an ~ (ту би дилэйд ин ан ~) задержаться в выполнении
to proceed with an ~ **of an order** (ту просид уиθ ан ~ оф ан ордэр) приступать к выполнению заказа
~ **of a contract** (~ оф а контракт) выполнение договора
~ **of a special order** (~ оф а спэшл ордэр) выполнение по особому заказу
~ **of an order** (~ оф ан ордэр) выполнение поручения
~ **of formalities** (~ оф формалитиз) выполнение формальностей
~ **of instructions** (~ оф инстракшнс) выполнение инструкций, выполнение указаний
~ **of a patent** (~ оф а патэнт) оформление патента
Executor (экзэкютор) опекун, попечитель

~ **of a will** (~ оф а уил) опекун
назначенный в завещании
~ **of an inheritance** (~ оф ан
инхэ́ританс) над наследством
Exempt (экзэ́мпт) освобождённый
to ~ (ту ~) освобождать
[**perfective**: освободить]
totally ~ (то́талли ~)
освобождённый полностью
~ **from military service** (~ фром
ми́литари сэ́рвис) освобождённый
от военной службы
Exemption (экзэ́мпшн) льгота,
освобождение
partial ~ **from payment of tax**
(паршл ~ фром пэ́ймэнт оф такс)
частичное освобождение от уплаты
налога
~ **from duties** (~ фром дю́тиз)
освобождение от пошлин
tax ~**s** (такс ~с) налоговые
льготы
Exhaustive (экза́устив)
исчерпывающий
~ **list** (~ лист) исчерпывающий
перечень
Exhibit (экзи́бит) образец, экспонат
application for ~ **space**
(аппликэ́йшн фор ~ спэйс) заявка
на место на выставке
collective ~ (коллэ́ктив ~)
коллективная экспозиция
competitive ~ (компэ́титив ~)
конкурентоспособный экспонат
demonstration of ~**s**
(дэмонстрэ́йшн оф ~с)
демонстрация экспонатов
evidentiary ~ (эвидэ́ншиэри ~)
объект доказательства
layout of ~**s** (лэ́йоут оф ~с)
расположение экспонатов
major ~ (мэ́йджор ~) главный
экспонат
open display of ~**s** (о́пэн дисплэ́й
оф ~с) открытый показ экспонатов
preparation of ~**s** (прэпарэ́йшн оф
~с) подготовка экспонатов
range of ~**s** (рэйндж оф ~с)
ассортимент экспонатов
recommended ~ (рэкоммэ́ндэд ~)
рекомендуемый экспонат
sales ~ (сэйлз ~) выставка-
продажа
selection of ~**s** (сэлэ́кшн оф ~с)
отбор экспонатов

to ~ **at a display** (ту ~ ат а
дисплэ́й) экспонировать на
выставке
to arrange ~**s** (ту аррэ́йндж ~с)
размещать экспонаты
to present ~**s** (ту прэзэ́нт ~с)
представлять экспонаты
to put ~**s on display** (ту пут ~с
он дисплэ́й) выставлять экспонаты
на выставке
working ~ (уо́ркинг ~)
действующий экспонат
Exhibiting (экзи́битинг)
экспонирование
Exhibition (экзиби́шн) выставка,
выставочный {*adj.*}
advertising ~ (а́двэртайзинг ~)
рекламная выставка
agricultural ~ (агрику́лчурал ~)
сельскохозяйственная выставка
annual ~ (а́ннюал ~) ежегодная
выставка
application to participate in an
~ (аппликэ́йшн ту парти́сипэйт ин
ан ~) заявка на участие в to
выставке
ceremonial opening of an ~
(сэрэмо́ниал о́пэнинг оф ан ~)
торжественное открытие выставки
collective ~ (коллэ́ктив ~)
изменять расположение товаров на
выставке
consumer goods ~ (консу́мэр гудз
~) выставка товаров широкого
потребления
delivery free ~ (дэли́вэри фри ~)
франко выставка
design of an ~ (диза́йн оф ан ~)
оформление выставки
dismantling of an ~ (дисма́нтлинг
оф ан ~) демонтаж выставки
exchange of ~**s** (эксчэ́йндж оф ~с)
обмен выставками
for ~ **purposes** (фор ~ пу́рпосэз)
для выставки
for the duration of an ~ (фор θи
дурэ́йшн оф ан ~) на время работы
выставки
foreign ~ (фо́рэн ~) заграничная
выставка
goods ~ (гудз ~) товарная
выставка
hardware ~ (ха́рдуэйр ~) выставка
технических средств и
оборудования
industrial ~ (инду́стриал ~)
промышленная выставка

installation of an ~ (инсталэйшн
оф ан ~) монтаж выставки
international ~ (интэрнáшэнал ~)
международная выставка
joint ~ (джойнт ~) совместная
выставка
jubilee ~ (джюбили́ ~) юбилейная
выставка
local ~ (ло́кал ~) местная
выставка
major ~ (мэ́йджор ~) крупная
выставка
multilateral ~ (мултилáтэрал ~)
выставка на многосторонней
основе
national ~ (нáшэнал ~)
национальная выставка
open air ~ (о́пэн эйр ~) выставка
на открытом воздухе
opening address at an ~ (о́пэнинг
аддрэ́с ат ан ~) речь на открытии
выставки
opening ceremony of an ~
(о́пэнинг сэ́рэмони оф ан ~)
церемония открытия выставки
operation of an ~ (опэрэ́йшн оф
ан ~) работа выставки
opportunity to participate in an
~ (оппортю́нити ту партúсипэйт ин
ан ~) возможность участия в
выставке
outdoor ~ grounds (о́утдор ~
гро́ундз) территория выставки под
открытым небом
participating nation at an ~
(партúсипэйтинг нэйшн ат ан ~)
страна-участник выставки
permanent ~ (пэ́рманэнт ~)
постоянная выставка
premises of an ~ (прэ́мисэз оф ан
~) помещение выставки
rearrange the ~ display
(риаррэ́йндж θи ~ дисплэ́й)
коллективная выставка
rent of ~ site (рэнт оф ~ сайт)
аренда помещения для выставки
selection of exhibits for an ~
(сэлэ́кшн оф экзúбитс фор ан ~)
отбор экспонатов для выставки
specialized ~ (спэ́шлайзд ~)
специализированная выставка
specialized trade ~ (спэ́шлайзд
трэйд ~) отраслевая выставка
sponsor of an ~ (спо́нсор оф ан
~) организатор выставки
technical ~ (тэ́кникал ~)
техническая выставка

terms of participation in an ~
(тэрмз оф партисипэ́йшн ин ан ~)
условия участия в выставке
to advertise goods at an ~ (ту
áдвэртайз гудз ат ан ~)
рекламировать товары на выставке
to allocate a site at an ~ (ту
áлокэйт а сайт ат ан ~) выделять
место на выставке
to assess an ~ (ту ассэ́сс ан ~)
давать оценку выставке
to demonstrate at an ~ (ту
дэ́монстрэйт ат ан ~)
демонстрировать на выставке
to draw up an ~ schedule (ту
дрáу ап ан ~ скэ́джул) составлять
график работы выставки
to dress an ~ (ту дрэс ан ~)
оформлять выставку
to finance an ~ (ту файнáнс ан
~) финансировать на выставке
to hold an ~ (ту холд ан ~)
проводить выставку
to open an ~ (ту о́пэн ан ~)
открывать выставку
to organize an ~ (ту о́рганайз а
~) устраивать выставку
to participate in an ~ (ту
партúсипэйт ин ан ~) участвоват
в выставке
to plan an ~ (ту план ан ~)
планировать выставку
to postpone the opening of an ~
(ту постпо́н θи о́пэнинг оф ан ~)
откладывать открытие выставки
to refill the display at an ~
(ту рúфил θи дисплэ́й ат ан ~)
пополнять выставку товарами
to sponsor an ~ (ту спо́нсор ан
~) организовывать выставку
to tour an ~ (ту тур ан ~)
осматривать выставку
to visit an ~ (ту вúзит ан ~)
посещать выставку
tour of an ~ (тур оф ан ~)
осмотр выставки
trade and industrial ~ (трэйд
энд индýстриал ~) торгово-
промышленная выставка
traveling ~ (трáвэлинг ~)
передвижная выставка
universal ~ (юнивэ́рсал ~)
универсальная выставка
upcoming ~ (апко́минг ~)
предстоящая выставка

~ **administration** (~ администрэ́йшн) администрация выставки
~ **booth** (~ буθ) стенд на выставке
~ **grounds** (~ гро́ундз) площадь выставки, территория выставки
~ **guide** (~ гайд) путеводитель по выставке
~ **manager** (~ ма́наджэр) директор выставки
~ **of achievements of science and technology** (~ оф ачи́вмэнтс оф са́йэнс энд тэкно́лоджи) выставка достижений науки и техники
~ **operating hours** (~ о́пэрэйтинг бурз) часы работы выставки
~ **organizer** (~ о́рганайзэр) устроитель выставки
~ **participant** (~ парти́сипант) участник выставки
~ **period** (~ пи́риод) время проведения выставки, продолжительность проведения выставки, срок проведения выставки
~ **program** (~ про́грам) программа выставки
~ **site** (~ сайт) место проведения выставки
~ **space** (~ спэйс) место на выставке
~ **visitor** (~ ви́зитор) посетитель выставки
~ **worker** (~ уо́ркэр) сотрудник выставки
Exhibitioner (экзиби́шнэр) участник выставки
Exhibitor (экзи́битор) экспонент
collective ~ (колле́ктив ~) коллективный экспонент
domestic ~ (доме́стик ~) отечественный экспонент
first-time ~ (фэрст-тайм ~) экспонент, выставляющий в первый раз
foreign ~ (фо́рэн ~) заграничный экспонент
individual ~ (индиви́дюал ~) индивидуальный экспонент
main ~ (мэйн ~) основной экспонент
major ~ (мэ́йджор ~) главный экспонент
overseas ~ (овэрси́з ~) зарубежный экспонент

permanent ~ (пэ́рманэнт ~) постоянный участник, постоянный экспонент
registration of ~**s** (рэджистрэ́йшн оф ~с) оформление участия в выставке
~ **at a fair** (~ ат а фэйр) участник ярмарки
Exigency (э́кзиджэнси) острая необходимость
Exile (э́кзайл) изгнание, изгнанник {person}, ссылка, ссыльный {adj.}
administrative ~ (адми́нистрэйтив ~) административная ссылка, административно-ссыльный {person}
life ~ (лайф ~) пожизненное изгнание
political ~ (поли́тикал ~) политический ссыльный
state of ~ (стэйт оф ~) отбывание ссылки
to ~ (ту ~) изгнать, сослать
Exit (э́кзит) вывоз, выезд, выездной {adj.}
point of ~ (пойнт оф ~) пункт вывоза
to ~ (ту ~) расстаться
~ **permit** (~ пэ́рмит) разрешение на выезд
Exorbitant (экзо́рбитант) чрезмерный
Expand, to ~ (экспа́нд, ту) расширять
Expanse (экспа́нс) пространство
Expansion (экспа́ншн) расширение, рост, увеличение, экспансия
credit ~ (крэ́дит ~) кредитная экспансия
economic ~ (эконо́мик ~) экономическая экспансия
foreign trade ~ (фо́рэн трэйд ~) внешнеторговая экспансия
rapid ~ (ра́пид ~) быстрое расширение
~ **of credit** (~ оф крэ́дит) расширение кредита
~ **of demand** (~ оф дима́нд) расширение спроса
~ **of an enterprise** (~ оф ан э́нтэрпрайз) расширение предприятия
~ **of exhibit space** (~ оф экзи́бит спэйс) увеличение выставочной площади
~ **of exports** (~ оф э́кспортс) расширение экспорта

~ of output (~ оф óутпут)
увеличение производства
~ of production (~ оф продáкшн)
расширение производства
~ of production operations (~ оф
продýкшн опэрэ́йшнс) расширение
масштаба производственной
деятельности
~ of rights (~ оф райтс)
расширение прав

Expediency (экспúдиэнси)
целесообразность
economic and technological ~
(эконóмик энд тэкнолóджикал ~)
экономическая и технологическая
целесообразность
~ of a project (~ оф а прóджэкт)
обоснование проекта

Expend, to ~ (экспэ́нд, ту ~)
израсходовать, расходовать, тратить

Expenditure (экспэ́ндичур) расход,
расходование, трата ~s издержки
actual ~s (áкчуал ~с)
фактические расходы
amortized ~s (áмортайзд ~с)
амортизационные расходы
budgeted ~s (бáджэтэд ~с)
бюджетные расходы
capital ~ (кáпитал ~) затрата
капитала, расходование
капиталовложения
concrete ~ (конкрúт ~)
конкретные затраты
current ~ (кýррэнт ~) текущие
расходы
depreciated ~s (дипрúшиэйтэд ~с)
амортизационные расходы
dollar denominated ~s (дóллар
динóминэйтэд ~с) долларовые
расходы
extraordinary ~s (экстраóрдинари
~с) чрезвычайные расходы
extrabudgetary ~s
(экстрабáджэтари ~с)
внебюджетные расходы
foreign exchange ~ (фóрэн
эксчэ́йндж ~) расход иностранной
валюты
gross ~s (грос ~с) затраты
брутто
material ~s (матúриал ~с)
материальные затраты,
материальные расходы
military ~s (мúлитари ~с)
военные издержки, военные
расходы
net ~s (нэт ~с) затраты нетто

non-productive ~s (нон-продýктив
~с) непроизводительные затраты,
непроизводственные расходы
non-recurrent ~ (нон-рикýррэнт
~) разовый расход
private ~s (прáйват ~с) частные
расходы
public ~s (пáблик ~с)
государственные расходы
social ~s (сошл ~с) социальные
расходы
unforeseen ~ (анфорсúн ~)
непредвиденные расходы
wasteful ~ (уэ́йстфул ~)
непроизводительная трата

Expense (экспэ́нс) затрата, расход,
трата денег
additional ~s (аддúшнал ~с)
дополнительные затраты
administrative ~s
(адмúнистрэйтив ~с)
административные расходы
clerical ~s (клэ́рикал ~с)
канцелярские расходы
current ~s (кýррэнт ~с) текущие
затраты
fixed ~s (фиксд ~с) неизменные
расходы
incidental ~ (инсидэ́нтал ~)
побочный расход
indirect ~s (индайрэ́кт ~с)
косвенные затраты, косвенные
расходы
intangible ~s (интáнджибл ~с)
неосязаемые затраты
labor ~s (лэ́йбор ~с) трудовые
затраты
legal ~s (лúгал ~с) судебные
издержки
legal costs and ~s (лúгал костс
энд ~с) судебные пошлины
necessary ~ (нэ́сэсари ~)
необходимый расход
necessary ~s (нэ́сэсари ~с)
необходимые издержки
obligatory ~ (облúгатори ~)
обязательный расход
office ~s (óффис ~с)
канцелярские расходы
ordinary ~s (óрдинари ~с)
обыкновенные расходы
storage ~s (стóрадж ~с) издержки
по хранению
to cover ~s (ту кóвэр ~с)
покрыть расходы
traveling ~s (трáвэлинг ~с)
дорожные расходы,

командировочные, подъёмные
деньги, путевые издержки
usual ~s (ю́жюал ~с) обычные
издержки
variable ~s (ва́риабл ~с)
переменные издержки
xpensive (экспэ́нсив) дорогой
  to turn out to be ~ (ту турн о́ут
  ту би ~) обходиться дорого
xpensively (экспэ́нсивли) дорого
xperience (экспи́риэнс) мастерство,
пыт
  ~ in business (~ ин би́знэс)
  опытный в делах
xperiment (экспэ́римэнт) опыт
xperimental (экспэримэ́нтал)
робный
xpert (э́кспэрт) мастер, референт,
пециалист, эксперт, экспертный
adj.}
  commercial ~ (коммэ́ршл ~)
  коммерческий эксперт
  commission of ~s (комми́шн оф ~с)
  комиссия экспертов
  commodities ~ (коммо́дитиз ~)
  товаровед
  design ~ (диза́йн ~) эксперт по
  промышленным образцам
  economic ~ (эконо́мик ~) эксперт
  по экономическим вопросам
  multilingual ~ (мултили́нгюал ~)
  эксперт, владеющий несколькими
  языками
  panel of ~s (па́нэл оф ~с) группа
  экспертов
  resident ~ (рэ́зидэнт ~)
  постоянный эксперт
  technical ~ (тэ́кникал ~)
  технический эксперт
  to appoint an ~ (ту аппо́йнт ан
  ~) назначать эксперта
  to request an ~ examination (ту
  рикуэ́ст ан ~ экзаминэ́йшн)
  затребовать экспертизу
  to send ~s (ту сэнд ~с) посылать
  экспертов
  trade ~ (трэйд ~) торговый
  эксперт
  trade-fair ~ (трэйд-фэйр ~)
  специалист по ярмаркам
  traffic ~ {freight} (тра́ффик ~
  {фрэйт}) эксперт по перевозкам
  грузов
  transportation ~ (транспортэ́йшн
  ~) транспортный эксперт
  ~ findings (~ фа́йндингс)
  заключение экспертизы
  ~'s decision (~с диси́жн) решение
  экспертизы
  ~'s findings (~с фа́йндингс)
  показания эксперта
  ~'s report (~'с рипо́рт)
  заключение эксперта
Expertise (экспэрти́з) экспертиза
  to require technical ~ (ту
  рикуа́йр тэ́кникал ~) нуждаться в
  технической экспертизе
Expiration (экспирэ́йшн) истечение
  ~ of concession (~ оф консэ́шн)
  истечение срока концессии
  ~ of lease (~ оф лис) истечение
  срока договора найма
  ~ of statute of limitations (~
  оф ста́тют оф лимитэ́йшнс)
  истечение давности
  **~ of statute of limitations on
  criminal prosecution** (~ оф ста́тют
  оф лимитэ́йшнс он кри́минал
  просэкю́шн) истечение давности
  уголовного преследования
  ~ of term (~ оф тэрм) истечение
  срока
  ~ period (~ пи́риод) предельный
  срок действия
Expire, to ~ (экспа́йр, ту ~) истечь
Explanation (экспланэ́йшн)
объяснение, разъяснение
Explanatory (экспла́натори)
пояснительный
Exploit, to ~ (экспло́йт, ту ~)
эксплуатировать
Export (э́кспорт) экспорт,
экспортный {*adj.*}
  agricultural ~s (агрику́лчурал
  ~с) вывоз продукции сельского
  хозяйств
  articles of ~ (а́ртиклс оф ~)
  предметы экспорта
  ban on ~s (бан он ~с) запрет на
  экспорт
  ban on ~ of foreign exchange
  (бан он ~ оф фо́рэн эксчэ́йндж)
  запрет на вывоз валюты
  cargo available for ~ (ка́рго
  ава́йлабл фор ~) груз готов к
  вывозу
  composition of ~s (компози́шн оф
  ~с) структура экспорта
  decline in ~s (дикла́йн ин ~с)
  падение экспорта
  demand for ~s (дима́нд фор ~с)
  спрос на экспорт
  development of ~s (дивэ́лопмэнт
  оф ~с) развитие экспорта

580

direct ~s (дирэ́кт ~с) прямой экспорт
diversification of ~s (дивэрсификэ́йшн оф ~с) диверсификация экспорта
duty-free ~ (дю́ти-фри ~) беспошлинный вывоз
embargo on ~s (эмба́рго он ~с) эмбарго на экспорт
financing of ~s (фа́йнансинг оф ~с) финансирование экспорта
food ~s (фуд ~с) вывоз продовольствия
high technology ~s (хай тэкно́лоджи ~с) экспорт наукоёмкой продукции
imports and ~s (и́мпортс энд ~с) ввоз и вывоз
increase in ~ surplus (инкри́с ин ~ су́рплус) превышение вывоза над ввозом
increasing ~s (инкри́синг ~с) растущий экспорт
indirect ~s (индайрэ́кт ~с) косвенный экспорт
items of ~ (а́йтэмз оф ~) статьи экспорта
invisible ~s (инви́зибл ~с) невидимый экспорт
marginally profitable ~s (ма́рджиналли про́фитабл ~с) малоприбыльный экспорт
non-agricultural ~s (нон-агрику́лчурал ~с) несельскохозяйственный экспорт
proceeds from ~s (про́сидз фром ~с) поступление от экспорта
production for ~ (прода́кшн фор ~) производство на экспорт
quality of ~s (куа́лити оф ~с) качество экспорта
rationalization of ~ (рашнализэ́йшн оф ~) рационализация экспорта
restriction of ~s (ристри́кшн оф ~с) ужесточение экспорта
to reduce ~s (ту риду́с ~с) сокращать вывоз, сокращать экспорт
to restrict ~s (ту ристри́кт ~с) ограничивать экспорт
share of ~s (шэйр оф ~с) доля экспорта
significant ~ (сигни́фикант ~) значительный экспорт
temporary ~ (тэ́мпорари ~) временный вывоз

to ~ (ту ~) вывозить, экспортировать
to arrange for ~ permit (ту аррэ́йндж фор ~ пэ́рмит) оформля́ вывоз
to ban ~s (ту бан ~с) запрещать вывоз
to be available for ~ (ту би ава́йлабл фор ~) иметь в наличи для экспорта
to be packed for ~ (ту би пакд фор ~) быть упакованным для экспорта
to expand ~s (ту экспа́нд ~с) расширять экспорт
to finance ~s (ту файна́нс ~с) финансировать экспорт
to increase ~s (ту инкри́с ~с) наращивать экспорт, увеличивать вывоз
to increase the volume of ~s (инкри́с θи во́люм оф ~с) увеличивать объём экспорта
to obtain an ~ license (ту обтэ́йн ан ~ ла́йсэнз) получать разрешение на вывоз
total ~s (то́тал ~с) общий экспорт
traditional ~s (тради́шнал ~с) традиционный экспорт
traditional ~ goods (тради́шнал гудз) товары традиционного экспорта
unpaid ~s (анпэ́йд ~с) неоплаченный экспорт
value of ~s (ва́лю оф ~с) стоимость экспорта
volume of ~s (во́люм оф ~с) объ вывоза
world-wide ~s (уо́рлд-уайд ~с) экспорт по всему миру
~ application (~ аппликэ́йшн) заявка экспорт
~ articles (~ а́ртиклс) предмет вывоза
~ ban (~ бан) запрет на вывоз
~ barriers (~ бэ́йрриэрз) затруднение вывоза
~ control (~ контро́л) контроль за экспортом
~ credits (~ крэ́дитс) кредитование экспорта
~ licensing procedures (~ ла́йсэнсинг проси́дюрс) порядок выдачи экспортных лицензий
~ matters (~ ма́ттэрс) вопросы экспорта

~ of agricultural goods (~ оф агрикýлчурал гудз) экспорт продукции сельского хозяйства
~ of capital (~ оф кáпитал) вывоз капитала
~ of foodstuffs (~ оф фýдстуфс) экспорт продовольствия
~ of gold (~ оф голд) вывоз золота
~ of goods and services (~ оф гудз энд сэ́рвисэз) экспорт товаров и услуг
~ of intellectual property (~ оф интэллэ́кшуал прóпэрти) экспорт результатов творческой деятельности
~ of R&D intensive products (~ оф ар энд ди интэ́нсив прóдуктс) экспорт научно-технических результатов
~ of services (~ оф сэ́рвисэз) экспорт услуг
~ of technology (~ оф тэкнóлоджи) экспорт технологии
~ opportunity (~ оппортю́нити) возможность экспорта
~ plan (~ план) план вывоза
~ promotion (~ промóшн) содействие экспорту
~ restrictions (~ ристри́кшнз) ограничение вывоза, ограничение экспорта
~ sale (~ сэйл) продажа на экспорт
~ stimulation (~ стимулэ́йшн) стимулирование экспорта
~ surplus (~ сýрплус) превышение экспорта над импортом
~ transaction (~ трансáкшн) сделка на экспорт
~ turnover (~ тýрновэр) оборот по экспорту
~ volume (~ вóлюм) объём экспорта
~-import (~-и́мпорт) экспортно-импортный

Exportation (э́кспортэ́йшн) вывоз, экспорт
country of ~ (кýнтри оф ~) страна экспорта
duty-free ~ (дю́ти-фри ~) беспошлинный экспорт
technical ~ (тэ́кникал ~) технический экспорт
~ of goods (~ оф гудз) вывоз товаров

~ of machinery and equipment (~ оф маши́нэри энд икуи́пмэнт) экспорт машин и оборудования
Exporter (э́кспортэр) экспортёр
exclusive ~ (эксклю́сив ~) исключительный экспортёр
sole ~ (сол ~) единственный экспортёр
~ of foodstuffs (~ оф фýдстуфс) экспортёр продовольственных товаров
~ of industrial goods (~ оф инду́стриал гудз) экспортёр промышленных товаров
~ of raw materials (~ оф рáу мати́риалс) экспортёр сырьевых товаров
Exposed (экспóзд) без упаковки
~ to ... (~ ту ...) подверженный действию
Exposition (экспози́шн) экспозиция
graphic ~ (грáфик ~) графическая экспозиция
joint ~ (джойнт ~) совместная экспозиция
national ~ (нáшэнал ~) национальная экспозиция
preparation of an ~ (прэпарэ́йшн оф ан ~) подготовка экспозиции
section of an ~ (сэкшн оф ан ~) раздел экспозиции
to hold an ~ (ту холд ан ~) устраивать экспозицию
to organize an ~ (ту óрганайз ан ~) организовать экспозицию
to review a ~ (ту ривю́ а ~) осматривать экспозицию
traditional ~ (тради́шнал ~) традиционная экспозиция
Expound, to ~ (экспóунд, ту ~) истолковывать [perfective: истолковать]
Express (экспрэ́с) чёткий, экспресс
~ service (~ сэ́рвис) экспресс-служба
Expression (экспрэ́шн) выражение
Expressly (экспрэ́сли) чётко
~ indicated (~ и́ндикэйтэд) точно указанный
Extend, to ~ (экстэ́нд, ту ~) продлевать действие, пролонгировать {contract, etc.} расширять, удлинять
to ~ a patent (ту ~ а пáтэнт) продлевать действие патента
Extension (экстэ́ншн) отсрочка, пристройка, продление, продление

срока действия, пролонгация {of
contract, etc.}, расширение
   automatic ~ (аутома́тик ~)
автоматическое продление
   tacit ~ (та́сит ~) молчаливое
продление
   ~ of deadline (~ оф дэ́длайн)
рассрочка исполнения
   ~ of a quota (~ оф а куо́та)
увеличение квоты
   ~ of the statute of limitations
(~ оф θи ста́тют оф лимитэ́йшнс)
продление срока давности
   ~ of the term of an agreement (~
оф θи тэрм оф ан агри́мэнт)
продление срока действия
договора
   ~ of the term of a treaty (~ оф
θи тэрм оф а три́ти) продление
срока действия договора
   ~ of time limit (~ оф тайм
ли́мит) продление срока
   ~ of validity (~ оф ва́лидити)
продление срока действия
Extensive (экстэ́нсив) экстенсивный
Extent (экстэ́нт) объём, размер,
степень
   vast ~ (васт ~) громадный размер
   ~ of a claim (~ оф а клэйм)
размер иска
   ~ of credit (~ оф крэ́дит) размер
кредита
   ~ of insurance coverage (~ оф
иншю́ранс ко́вэрадж) размер
страховки
   ~ of loss (~ оф лос) размер
ущерба
   ~ of operations (~ оф опэрэ́йшнс)
размер операции
   ~ of security for a claim (~ оф
сэкю́рити фор а клэйм) размер
обеспечения претензии
Exterminate, to ~ (экстэ́рминэйт, ту
~) истреблять [perfective:
истребить]
External (экстэ́рнал) внешний
Extinction (экстИ́нкшн)
недействительность
   notice of legal ~ (но́тис оф
ли́гал ~) объявление о
недействительности
Extinguishment (экстИ́нгуишмэнт)
погашение
   ~ of a deed (~ оф а дид)
погашение записи

   ~ of a prescriptive easement (~
оф а прискри́птив и́змэнт)
прекращение давности
Extortion (эксто́ршн)
вымогательство, поборы
Extortionist (эксто́ршнист) бандит-
вымогатель
Extra (э́кстра) добавочный
   at ~ cost (ат ~ кост) за особую
доплату
   without ~ charge (уиθо́ут ~
чардж) без дополнительной
доплаты
   ~-capacity (~-капа́сити)
большегрузный {vessel, etc.}
   ~ weight cargo (~ уэйт ка́рго)
тяжеловес
Extracontractual
(экстраконтра́кчуал) внедоговорный
Extract (э́кстракт) выписка
   to ~ (ту ~) извлечь
   ~ from a contract (~ фром а
ко́нтракт) из контракта
   ~ from a decision (~ фром а
дисИ́жн) выписка из решения
   ~ from a protocol (~ фром а
про́токол) выписка из протокола
   ~ from a statement of account
фром а стэ́йтмэнт оф акко́унт)
выписка из счёта
Extraction (экстра́кшн) добыча
{mining}, происхождение {ancestry}
Extraordinary (экстрао́рдинари)
чрезвычайный

F

Fabrication (фабрикэ́йшн) измышлен
   libelous ~ (ла́йбэлос ~)
клеветническое измышление
Face {of medal, plaque} (фэйс {оф
мэ́дал, плак}) аверс
   to ~ (ту ~) стоять перед лицом
   ~ value (~ ва́лю) номинал
Facility (фасИ́лити) средство ~/ie
оборудование
   additional shipping ~/ies
(аддИ́шнал ши́ппинг ~из)
дополнительный тоннаж
   airport ~/ies (э́йрпорт ~из)
оборудование аэропорта
   design ~ (диза́йн ~) проектно-
конструкторская база
   exhibition ~ (экзибИ́шн ~)
выставочная база

handling ~/ies {cargo} (хáндлинг ~из {кáрго}) перевалочные средства
industrial storage ~/ies (индýстриал стóрадж ~из) заводская база
lending ~ (лéндинг ~) кредит
maintenance ~ (мэ́йнтэнанс ~) ремонтное оборудование
minimum ~/ies (мúнимум ~из) минимальные услуги
pilot production ~ (пáйлот продáкшн ~) опытный завод
port ~/ies (порт ~из) портовое оборудование
production ~ (продáкшн ~) производственная база
production/technical ~ (продáкшн/тэ́кникал ~) производственно-техническая база
refrigeration ~/ies (рифриджэрэ́йшн ~из) холодильное оборудование
repair ~ (рипэ́йр ~) ремонтная база
service ~/ies (сэ́рвис ~из) встроенное оборудование
terminal ~/ies (тэ́рминал ~из) оборудование терминала
to expand production ~/ies (ту экспáнд продáкшн ~из) укреплять производственную базу
to furnish necessary ~/ies (ту фýрниш нэ́сэсари ~из) предоставлять необходимые условия
transport ~/ies (трáнспорт ~из) транспортное хозяйство
Facsimile (факсúмили) телефакс, факсимиле {of signature}
via ~ (вúа ~) по телефаксу
Fact (факт) факт
as a matter of ~ (аз а мáттэр оф ~) в действительности
established ~ (эстáблишд ~) достоверный факт, установленный факт
grave ~ (грэйв ~) веский факт
ill-grounded ~ (ил-грóундэд ~) малодостоверный факт
in accordance with the ~s (ин аккóрданс уиθ θи ~с) в соответствии с фактами
irrefutable ~ (иррифю́табл ~) неопровержимый факт
relevant ~ (рэ́лэвант ~) соответствующий факт

separate ~ (сэ́парат ~) отдельный факт
the above ~ (θи абóв ~) вышеупомянутый факт
the ~, pertaining to this matter (θи ~, пэртэ́йнинг ту θис мáттэр) факт, имеющий отношение к данному вопросу
the ~ remains (θи ~ римэ́йнс) остаётся фактом
the ~s show that (θи ~с шóу θат) факты говорят о том, что
to be faced with the ~ (ту би фэйсд уиθ θи ~) стоять перед фактом
to correspond to the ~s (ту коррэспóнд ту θи ~с) соответствовать действительности
to distort the ~s (ту дистóрт θи ~с) искажать факты
to elicit ~s (ту илúсит ~с) выявить факты
to face ~s (ту фэйс ~с) сталкиваться с реальными фактами
~-finding mission (~-фáйндинг мишн) ознакомительный визит
Factor (фáктор) коэффициент, момент, фактор {agent}
accountable ~ (аккóунтабл ~) учитываемый фактор
cost ~ (кост ~) фактор стоимости
critical ~ (крúтикал ~) критический момент
decisive ~ (дисáйсив ~) решающий фактор
economic ~ (эконóмик ~) экономический фактор
external ~ (экстэ́рнал ~) внешний фактор
human ~ (хю́ман ~) человеческий фактор
important ~ (импóртант ~) важный момент, важный фактор
long-term ~ (лонг-тэрм ~) фактор долговременного действия
loss ~ (лос ~) коэффициент потерь
market ~ (мáркэт ~) фактор сбыта
output ~ (óутпут ~) коэффициент выработки, коэффициент отдачи
permanent ~ (пэ́рманэнт ~) постоянно действующий фактор
secondary ~ (сэ́кондари ~) второстепенный фактор
short-term ~ (шорт-тэрм ~) фактор кратковременного действия

the **above** ~ (θи або́в ~)
вышеназванный фактор
the **principal** ~ (θи при́нсипал ~)
основной фактор
time ~ (тайм ~) фактор времени
Factoring (фа́кторинг) факторинг
Factory (фа́ктори) завод, фабрика,
фабричный {adj.}
  aircraft ~ (э́йркрафт ~)
  авиационный завод
  automated ~ (а́утомэйтэд ~) завод
  с автоматическим управлением
  automobile ~ (аутомоби́л ~)
  автомобильный завод
  central ~ (сэ́нтрал ~)
  центральный завод
  construction of a ~ (констру́кшн
  оф а ~) строительство завода
  experimental ~ (экспэримэ́нтал ~)
  экспериментальный завод
  heavy equipment ~ (хэ́ви
  икуи́пмэнт ~) завод тяжёлого
  машиностроения
  modern ~ (мо́дэрн ~) современный
  завод
  mounted at the ~ (мо́унтэд ат θи
  ~) смонтированный на заводе
  operating ~ (о́пэрэйтинг ~)
  действующий завод
  overhaul ~ (о́вэрхаул ~)
  ремонтный завод
  representative ~ (рэпрэзэ́нтатив
  ~) типовой завод
  to expand a ~ (ту экспа́нд а ~)
  расширять завод
  to manage a ~ (ту ма́надж а ~)
  руководить заводом, управлять
  фабрикой
  to outfit a ~ (ту о́утфит а ~)
  сооружать завод
  to reconstruct a ~ (ту
  риконстру́кт а ~)
  реконструировать завод
  to visit a ~ (ту ви́зит а ~)
  посещать завод
  truck ~ (трак ~) завод грузовых
  машин
  ~ **engineer** (~ инджини́р) инженер
  завода
  ~ **for the production of**
  something (~ фор θи прода́кшн оф
  со́мθинг) завод для производства
  чего-либо
  ~ **inspection** (~ инспэ́кшн)
  посещение завода
  ~ **installation** (~ инстала́йшн)
  монтаж завода

  ~ **owner** (~ о́унэр) владелец
  завода
  ~ **start-up** (~ старт-ап) пуск
  завода
Faculty (фа́култи) кафедра
Fail, to ~ (фэйл, ту ~) выбывать из
строя, провалить
  to ~ **to detect** (ту ~ ту дитэ́кт)
  не обнаруживать
  without ~ (уиθо́ут ~) в
  обязательном порядке
Failure (фэ́йлюр) неудача, провал
  bank ~ (банк ~)
  неплатёжеспособность банка
  ~ **to appear** (~ ту аппи́р) неявка
  ~ **to deliver goods** (~ ту дэли́вэр
  гудз) несдача товара
  ~ **to deliver** (~ ту дэли́вэр)
  несдача
  ~ **to follow procedure** (~ ту
  фо́лло проси́дюр) несоблюдение
  порядка
  ~ **to honor a bill** (~ ту о́нор а
  бил) неоплата векселя
  ~ **to meet the term date** (~ ту
  мит θи тэрм дэйт) несоблюдение
  срока
  ~ **to take measures** (~ ту тэйк
  мэ́жюрз) непринятие мер
Fair (фэйр) объективный {adj.},
правомерный {adj.}, справедливый
{adj.}, сходный {adj.}, ярмарка,
ярмарочный {adj.}
  annual ~ (а́ннюал ~) ежегодная
  ярмарка
  application to participate in a
  ~ (аппликэ́йшн ту парти́сипэйт ин
  а ~) заявка на участие в ярмарке
  area of a ~ (э́йриа оф а ~)
  площадь ярмарки
  at a ~ (ат а ~) на ярмарке
  autumn ~ (а́утум ~) осенняя
  ярмарка
  commercial center of a ~
  (коммэ́ршл сэ́нтэр оф а ~)
  коммерческий центр ярмарки
  entrance pass to a ~ (э́нтранс
  пасс ту а ~) пропуск на ярмарку
  exposition of a ~ (экспози́шн оф
  а ~) экспозиция ярмарки
  general plan of a ~ (джэ́нэрал
  план оф а ~) общий план ярмарки
  horizontal ~ (хоризо́нтал ~)
  горизонтальная выставка
  international ~ (интэрна́шэнал ~)
  международная ярмарка

jubilee ~ (джюбили́ ~) юбилейная ярмарка
organizers of a ~ (о́рганайзрс оф а ~) организаторы ярмарки
plan of participation in ~s (план оф партисипэ́йшн ин ~с) план участия в ярмарках
participants in a ~ (парти́сипантс ин а ~) участники ярмарки
regional ~ (ри́джонал ~) региональная ярмарка
sample ~ (сампл ~) ярмарка образцов
section of a ~ (сэкшн оф а ~) раздел ярмарки
specialized ~ (спэ́шлайзд ~) специализированная ярмарка
specialized trade ~ (спэ́шлайзд трэйд ~) отраслевая ярмарка
spring ~ (спринг ~) весенняя ярмарка
technical ~ (тэ́кникал ~) техническая ярмарка
to arrange a ~ (ту аррэ́йндж а ~) устраивать ярмарку
to hold a ~ (ту холд а ~) проводить ярмарку
to open a ~ (ту о́пэн а ~) открывать ярмарку
to participate in a ~ (ту парти́сипэйт ин а ~) принимать участие в ярмарке
tour of a ~ (тур оф а ~) осмотр ярмарки
trade ~ (трэйд ~) выставка-ярмарка, торговая ярмарка
traditional ~ (тради́шнал ~) традиционная ярмарка
upcoming ~ (апко́минг ~) предстоящая ярмарка
wholesale ~ (хо́лсэйл ~) оптовая ярмарка
world's ~ (уо́рлдз ~) всемирная выставка, всемирная ярмарка
~ administration (~ администрэ́йшн) администрация ярмарки
~ grounds (~ гро́ундз) территория ярмарки
Fairness (фэ́йрнэс) справедливость
Fait accompli (фэйт аккомпли́) совершившийся факт
to confront with a ~ (ту конфро́нт уиθ а ~) поставить перед совершившимся фактом
Faith (фэйθ) вера, доверие

bad ~ (бад ~) недобросовестность
good ~ (гуд ~) добросовестность
in bad ~ (ин бад ~) недобросовестный
to shake ~ in (ту шэйк ~ ин) подрывать доверие к
Fall (фал) падение, понижение
~ in demand (~ ин дима́нд) понижение спроса
~ in the exchange rate (~ ин θи эксчэ́йндж рэйт) понижение курса
~ in the interest rate on a loan (~ ин θи и́нтэрэст рэйт он а лон) понижение ссудного процента
~ of a government (~ оф а го́вэрнмэнт) распад государства
False (фалс) ложный, обманчивый, фиктивный
Family (фа́мили) род, семейство, семья
adopted ~ (адо́птэд ~) приёмная семья
birth ~ (бэрθ ~) родная семья
large ~ (лардж ~) многодетная семья
legal ~ (ли́гал ~) законная семья
Famine (фа́мин) голод
Farm (фарм) ферма, хозяйство, хутор
collective ~ (коллэ́ктив ~) колхоз
experimental ~ (экспэримэ́нтал ~) опытное хозяйство
multiple production ~ (му́лтипл прода́кшн ~) многоотраслевое хозяйство
state ~ (стэйт ~) совхоз
to ~ (ту ~) заниматься сельским хозяйством
Farmer (фа́рмэр) колхозник {on collective farm}, фермер
Farmhand (фа́рмханд) сельскохозяйственный рабочий
Farming (фа́рминг) ведение сельского хозяйства, земледелие
tenant ~ (тэ́нант ~) продовольственная аренда земли
Fashion (фашн) мода
in the latest ~ (ин θи лэ́йтэст ~) по последней моде
to be in ~ (ту би ин ~) быть в моде
to set the ~ (ту сэт θи ~) ввести в моду
Fashionable (фа́шэнабл) модный
to become ~ (ту бико́м ~) входить в моду

Fast-selling (фаст-сэ́ллинг)
быстрореализуемый
Fasten, to (фа́ссэн, ту ~)
крепить, обвязывать
    to ~ horizontally (ту ~
хоризо́нталли) обвязывать
горизонтально
    to ~ vertically (ту ~
вэ́ртикалли) обвязывать
вертикально
Fastening (фа́ссэнинг) крепление,
закрепление
Father (фа́θэр) отец
    adoptive ~ (адо́птив ~) приёмный
отец
    birth ~ (бирθ ~) родной отец
Father-in-law (фа́θэр-ин-лау) свёкор
{father of husband}, тесть {father
of wife}
Fatherland (фа́θэрланд) отечество
Fault (фалт) неисправность,
провинность
    to locate a ~ (ту ло́кэйт а ~)
отыскивать неисправность
Favor (фэ́йвор) льгота, любезность,
одолжение
    to ~ (ту ~) благоприятствовать
    to do official ~s (ту ду оффи́шл
~с) протежировать
Favorable (фэ́йворабл) льготный
    to be ~ (ту би ~)
благоприятствовать
Favored (фэ́йворд)
благоприятствованный
    most ~ nation clause (мост ~
нэ́йшн клауз) оговорка о
наибольшем благоприятствовании
    most ~ nation {mfn} **status** (мост
~ нэ́йшн {эм-эф-эн} ста́тус) режим
наибольшего благоприятствования
    most ~ nation {mfn} **tariff
treatment** (мост ~ нэ́йшн {эм-эф-
эн} та́риф три́тмэнт) тариф на
основе наибольшего
благоприятствования
Favorite (фэ́йворит) избранник
Fax (факс) телефакс
Fear (фир) страх
Feasibility (физиби́лити)
осуществимость
    ~ study of a project (~ сту́ди оф
а про́джэкт) расчёт технико-
экономического обоснования
    to submit a ~ report (ту субми́т
а ~ рипо́рт) представлять
технико-экономическое
обоснование

Feature (фи́чур) признак
    identifying ~ (айдэ́нтифайинг ~)
идентификационный признак
Federal (фэ́дэрал) федеральный
Federated (фэ́дэрэйтэд) федеративный
Fee (фи) гонорар, отчисление
    admission ~ (адми́шн ~)
вступительный взнос
    agent's ~ (э́йджэнтс ~) гонорар
агента
    annual ~ (а́ннюал ~) годовой
взнос, годовой сбор
    arbitration ~ (арбитрэ́йшн ~)
арбитражный взнос, арбитражный
сбор
    arbitrator's ~ (а́рбитрэйторз ~)
гонорар арбитра
    at a nominal ~ (ат а но́минал ~)
с номинальным вознаграждением
    attorney's ~s (атто́рниз ~с)
адвокатские расходы
    auditor's ~ (а́удиторз ~) гонорар
ревизора
    average adjustor ~ (а́вэрэдж
аджа́стор ~) вознаграждение
диспашеру
    brokerage ~ (бро́кэрадж ~)
брокерская комиссия
    certification ~ (сэртифике́йшн ~)
пошлина на удостоверение акта
    commission ~s (комми́шн ~с)
комиссионные издержки
    consular ~ (ко́нсюлар ~)
консульский сбор
    conveyance ~s (конвэ́йянс ~с)
пошлина на переход имущества
    customs ~ (ка́стомз ~) плата за
таможенные услуги
    consultant's ~s (консу́лтантс ~с)
вознаграждение за
консультационные услуги
    established ~ (эста́блишд ~)
установленный сбор
    fixed ~ (фиксд ~) неизменное
вознаграждение
    health ~ (хэлθ ~) санитарный
сбор
    hunting license ~ (ха́нтинг
ла́йсэнз ~) пошлина на право
охоты
    incentive ~ (инсэ́нтив ~)
поощрительное вознаграждение
    inspection ~ (инспэ́кшн ~)
инспекционный сбор
    insurance ~ (иншю́ранс ~)
страховой сбор

license ~ (ла́йсэнз ~) лицензионный сбор
membership ~ (мэ́мбэршип ~) членский взнос
minimal ~ (ми́нимал ~) минимальный сбор
mortgage ~ (мо́ргэдж ~) ипотечный сбор
one-time ~ (уа́н-тайм ~) разовый сбор
patent ~ (па́тэнт ~) патентная пошлина, патентный сбор
patent registration ~ (па́тэнт рэджистрэ́йшн ~) взнос при заявлении патента взнос
pick-up ~s (пик-ап ~с) плата за вывоз
professional ~ (профэ́шнал ~) профессиональный сбор
registration ~ (рэджистрэ́йшн ~) регистрационный взнос, регистрационная пошлина, регистрационный сбор
renewal ~ (рини́ал ~) возобновительная пошлина
sanitation ~ (санитэ́йшн ~) санитарный сбор
subscription ~ (субскри́пшн ~) абонементная плата
to deduct bank ~s from money transfer (ту диду́кт банк ~с фром мо́ни тра́нсфэр) вычесть банковские комиссионные из денежного перевода
to negotiate payment of ~s (ту нэго́шиэйт пэ́ймэнт оф ~с) договариваться об оплате гонорара
to pay a ~ (ту пэй а ~) платить взнос
use card ~ (юс кард ~) абонементная плата
user ~s (ю́зэр ~с) издержки использования
warehouse ~ (уэ́рхаус ~) складской сбор
weighing ~ (уэ́йинг ~) весовой сбор
eebleminded (фи́блмайндэд) шабоумный
eigned (фэ́йнд) мнимый
elon (фэ́лон) уголовный преступник
ence (фэнс) изгородь, скупщик
  to ~ (ту ~) огородить
  ~ of stolen goods (~ оф сто́лэн гудз) скупщик краденого
ertility (фэрти́лити) рождаемость

Fiduciary (фидю́шиари) доверенное лицо
Field (филд) арена, месторождение, область
  coal ~ (кол ~) месторождение угля
  gas ~ (гас ~) месторождение газа
  oil ~ (ойл ~) месторождение нефти
  ~ audit (~ а́удит) ревизия на месте
  ~ change orders (~ чэйндж о́рдэрс) доработка
  ~ of knowledge (~ оф но́лэдж) область знаний
  ~ of law (~ оф ла́у) отрасль права
  ~ service (~ сэ́рвис) обслуживание на месте
Fighter (фа́йтэр) истребитель {jet}
Figure (фи́гюр) цифра
  above-mentioned ~s (або́в-мэншнд ~с) вышеуказанные цифры
  actual ~ (а́кчуал ~) действительная цифра
  adjusted ~s (аджа́стэд ~с) цифры с поправкой на сезонные колебания
  amount in ~s (амо́унт ин ~с) сумма цифрами
  census ~s (сэ́нсус ~с) статистика населения
  firm ~ (фирм ~) твёрдая сумма
  gross ~s (грос ~с) валовые цифры
  ill-founded ~s (ил-фо́ундэд ~с) малодостоверные цифры
  industrial ~s (инду́стриал ~с) статистика промышленности
  in ~s (ин ~с) в цифровом выражении, цифрами
  in round ~s (ин ро́унд ~с) в круглых цифрах
  labor productivity ~s (лэ́йбор продукти́вити ~с) показатель производительности труда
  overall ~s (овэра́л ~с) общие данные
  preliminary ~ (прили́минэри ~) предварительная цифра
  productivity ~s (продукти́вити ~с) показатель производительности
  round ~ (ро́унд ~) округлённое число
  target ~ (та́ргэт ~) намеченная величина, намеченная цифра

to establish the actual ~ (ту эста́блиш θи а́кчуал ~) установить фактическую цифру
to give an exact ~ (ту гив ан экза́кт ~) дать точную цифру
to submit ~s (ту субми́т ~с) представлять цифры
trade ~s (трэйд ~с) статистика торговли
unconvincing ~s (анконви́нсинг ~с) малоубедительные цифры
wage ~s (уэ́йдж ~с) статистика заработной платы
File (файл) досье
application ~ (аппликэ́йшн ~) заявочное досье, комплект материалов заявки
to consult one's ~s (ту консу́лт уа́нз ~с) справиться по картотеке
to open a ~ (ту о́пэн а ~) составлять досье
Filer (фа́йлэр) податель
Filing (фа́йлинг) подача
~ of a complaint (~ оф а комплэ́йнт) подача жалобы
~ of a counter suit (~ оф а ко́унтэр сут) предъявление встречного иска
~ of an action (~ оф ан акшн) подача искового заявления
~ of an application (~ оф ан аппликэ́йшн) подача заявки
~ of a patent application (~ оф а па́тэнт аппликэ́йшн) подача заявки на патент
~ of a suit (~ оф а сут) предъявление иска
Fill, to ~ (фил, ту ~) наливать, наполнять, насыпать
to ~ in bags (ту ~ ин багз) насыпать в мешки
Fill out, to ~ (фил о́ут, ту ~) заполнять
Filling (фи́ллинг) насыпка
Film (филм) кинофильм
advertising ~ (а́двэртайзинг ~) рекламный кинофильм
~ clips (~ клипс) киноматериалы
Final (фа́йнал) итоговый, конечный, окончательный
~ payment (~ пэ́ймэнт) окончательный расчёт
Finalization (файнализэ́йшн) доработка
Finalize, to ~ (фа́йналайз, ту ~) завершать
Finance (фина́нс) финанс ~s финансы

Minister of ~ (ми́нистэр оф ~) министр финансов
Ministry of ~ (ми́нистри оф ~) министерство финансов
public ~ (па́блик ~) государственные финансы
sales ~ company (сэйлз ~ ко́мпани) компания по финансированию продаж в рассрочку
to ~ (ту ~) финансировать
~ and credit (~ энд крэ́дит) финансово-кредитный
~ and economic (~ энд эконо́мик) финансово-хозяйственный
~-and-accounts department (~-энд-акко́унтс дипа́ртмэнт) отдел финансов и отчётности
Financial (файна́ншл) финансовый
~ authorization (~ ауθориз́эйшн) разрешение на финансирование
Financier (файнанси́р) финансист
Financing (фа́йнансинг) финансирование, финансирующий {adj.}
amount of ~ (амо́унт оф ~) объём финансирования
back-to-back ~ (бак-ту-бак ~) взаимное финансирование
bank ~ (банк ~) банковское финансирование
budgetary ~ (ба́джэтари ~) бюджетное финансирование
compensatory ~ (компэ́нсатори ~) компенсационное финансирование
co-sponsored ~ (ко-спо́нсорд ~) совместное финансирование
credit ~ (крэ́дит ~) кредитное финансирование
domestic ~ (домэ́стик ~) внутренние финансирование
equity {stock} ~ (э́куити {сток} ~) финансирование с помощью выпуска акций
export ~ (э́кспорт ~) финансирование экспорта
foreign ~ (фо́рэн ~) внешнее финансирование
forms and methods of ~ (формс энд мэ́θодс оф ~) формы и методы финансирования
import ~ (и́мпорт ~) финансирование импорта
international ~ (интэрна́шэнал ~ международное финансирование
irrevocable ~ (иррэ́вокабл ~) безвозвратное финансирование

long-term ~ (лонг-тэрм ~)
долгосрочное финансирование
medium-term ~ (ми́диум-тэрм ~)
среднесрочное финансирование
mixed ~ (миксд ~) смешанное
финансирование
participation in ~ (партисипэ́йшн
ин ~) долевое финансирование
plan of ~ (план оф ~) план
финансирования
public ~ (па́блик ~)
государственное финансирование
secondary ~ (сэ́кондари ~)
вторичное финансирование
short-term ~ (шорт-тэрм ~)
краткосрочное финансирование
supplementary ~ (сапплэмэ́нтари
~) дополнительное финансирование
sources of ~ (сорсэз оф ~)
источники финансирования
terms of ~ (тэрмз оф ~) условия
финансирования
to arrange for ~ (ту аррэ́йндж
фор ~) договориться о
финансировании
to guarantee ~ (ту гяранти́ ~)
гарантировать финансирование
to provide ~ **for a contract** (ту
прова́йд ~ фор а ко́нтракт)
обеспечивать финансирование
контракта
trade ~ (трэйд ~) финансирование
торговли
~ **funds** (~ фандз) фонды
финансирования
~ **of appropriations** (~ оф
аппроприэ́йшнс) финансирование
ассигнований
Find (файнд) находка
to ~ (ту ~) найти
to ~ **not guilty** (ту ~ нот ги́лти)
не признавать виновным
Findings (фа́йндингс) выводы
комиссии, полученные данные,
экспертиза
Fine (файн) штраф, штрафная пошлина
imposition of a ~ (импози́шн оф а
~) наложение взыскания,
обложение штрафом
money ~ (мо́ни ~) денежный штраф
to ~ (ту ~) оштрафовать,
штрафовать
to accept a ~ (ту аксэ́пт а ~)
признавать штраф
to impose a ~ (ту импо́з а ~)
наложить взыскание, подвергать
штрафу

to incur a ~ (ту инку́р а ~)
подвергаться штрафу
to pay a ~ (ту пэй а ~) платить
штраф
Fined (файнд) оштрафованный
Fingerprint (фи́нгэрпринт) отпечаток
пальца
Finishing (фи́нишинг) обработка
~ **touch** (~ туч) доделка
Fire (фа́йр) огонь
to ~ (ту ~) расстрелять
{weapon}, увольнять [perfective:
уволить] {dismiss}
Firing (фа́йринг) увольнение
Firm (фирм) фирма, фирменный {adj.}
brokerage ~ (бро́кэрадж ~)
брокерская
business brokering ~ (би́знэс
бро́кэринг ~) посредническая
фирма
capital of a ~ (ка́питал оф а ~)
капитал фирмы
capitalist ~ (ка́питалист ~)
капиталистическая фирма
contracting ~ (ко́нтрактинг ~)
фирма-участница договора
co-owner of a ~ (ко-о́унэр оф а
~) совладелец фирмы
division of a ~ (диви́жн оф а ~)
отдел фирмы
engineering ~ (инджэни́ринг ~)
инжиниринговая фирма
engineering consulting ~
(инджэни́ринг консу́лтинг ~)
инженерно-консультационная фирма
entrant ~ (э́нтрант ~) начинающая
фирма
financial ~ (файна́ншл ~)
финансовая фирма
industrial sector ~ (инду́стриал
сэ́ктор ~) отраслевая
производственная фирма
joint ~**s** (джойнт ~с) совместные
фирмы
law ~ **with a patent practice**
(ла́у ~ уиθ а па́тэнт пра́ктис)
патентная фирма
leading ~ (ли́динг ~) ведущая
фирма
liquidation of a ~ (ликуидэ́йшн
оф а ~) ликвидация фирмы
major ~ (мэ́йджор ~) крупная
фирма
marketing ~ (ма́ркэтинг ~)
маркетинговая фирма
medium-sized ~ (ми́диум-сайзд ~)
средняя фирма

participating ~ (парти́сипэйтинг ~) фирма-участница
president of a ~ (прэ́зидэнт оф а ~) президент фирмы
representative of a ~ (рэпрэзэ́нтатив оф а ~) представитель фирмы
retail ~ (ри́тэйл ~) розничная фирма
rival ~s (ра́йвал ~с) конкурирующие фирмы
senior partner of a ~ (си́ниор па́рнтэр оф а ~) глава фирмы
shipping ~ (ши́ппинг ~) судоходная фирма
solid ~ (со́лид ~) солидная фирма

specialized ~ (спэ́шлайзд ~) специализированная фирма
status of a ~ (ста́тус оф а ~) статус фирмы
to do business with a ~ (ту ду би́знэс уиθ а ~) сотрудничать с фирмой
to register a ~ (ту рэ́джистэр а ~) регистрировать фирму
to represent a ~ (ту рэпрэзэ́нт а ~) представлять фирму
venture capital ~ (вэ́нчур ка́питал ~) венчурная фирма
Fisher/y (фи́шэри) рыболовство
coastal ~/ies (ко́стал ~из) прибрежный рыбный промысел
Fishing (фи́шинг) рыболовство
coastal ~ trade (ко́стал ~ трэйд) береговое рыболовство
~ industry (~ и́ндустри) рыболовство
Fit (фит) годный
to deem ~ (ту дим ~) считать годным
~ for... (~ фор...) годный для
~ for grain transport (~ фор грэйн тра́нспорт) годный для перевозки зерна
Fitness (фи́тнэс) пригодность к работе
Fitting (фи́ттинг) надлежащий
Five-year plan (файв-е́ар план) пятилетка
Fix, to ~ (фикс, ту ~) определять, фиксировать
Fixation (фиксэ́йшн) фиксация
Fixed (фиксд) определенный, фиксированный

~-rate payments (~-рэйт пэ́ймэнтс) плата по таксе {government}
Fixing (фи́ксинг) фиксация
price ~ (прайс ~) фиксация цен
~ letter (~ лэ́ттэр) письмо, подтверждающее фрахтование
Fixture (фи́ксчур) закрепление
Flag (флаг) флаг
raising of the ~ (рэ́йсинг оф θи ~) поднятие флага
Flagging (фла́ггинг) поднятие флага
Flammable (фла́ммабл) горючий
Flask (фласк) бутыль
Flaw (флау) изъян, порок
to detect quality ~s (ту дитэ́кт куа́лити ~с) обнаруживать брак
Fleet (флит) флот, флотский {adj.}
air ~ (эйр ~) воздушный флот
dry cargo ~ (драй ка́рго ~) сухогрузный флот
fishing ~ (фи́шинг ~) рыболовный флот
inactive ~ (ина́ктив ~) прикольный флот
inland water ~ (и́нланд уа́тэр ~) речной флот
marine ~ (мари́н ~) морской флот
merchant marine ~ (мэ́рчант мари́н ~) торговый флот
ocean-going ~ (ошн-го́инг ~) океанский флот
oil tanker ~ (ойл та́нкэр ~) нефтеналивной танкерный флот
tanker ~ (та́нкэр ~) наливной флот, танкерный флот
Flexibility (флэксиби́лити) гибкость
Flexible (флэ́ксибл) гибкий
Flexitainer (флэ́кситэйнэр) эластичный контейнер
Flight (флайт) перелёт, полёт
capital ~ (ка́питал ~) иммиграция капитала
international ~ (интэрна́шэнал ~) международный полёт
nonstop ~ (нонсто́п ~) беспосадочный полёт
transit ~ (тра́нзит ~) транзитный полёт
Float, to ~ (фло́т, ту ~) переплавить, плавать, размещать
Floating (фло́тинг) размещение
~ of a loan (~ оф а лон) размещение займа
Floor (флор) минимальный уровень, пол

residential ~ space (рэзидэншл ~ спэйс) жилая площадь
Flotsam (флótсам) плавающий груз
Flourish (флýриш) росчерк
  to ~ (ту ~) процветать
Flow (флóу) поток, приток
  cash ~ (каш ~) поток наличности
  credit ~ (крэдит ~) кредитные потоки
  monetary ~s (мóнэтари ~с) денежные потоки
Fluctuate, to ~ (флýкчуэйт, ту ~) быть неустойчивым, колебаться
Fluctuating (флýкчуэйтинг) колеблющийся, меняющийся
Fluctuation (флукчуэ́йшн) колебание
  adjusted for seasonal ~s (аджáстэд фор сúзонал ~с) с поправкой на сезонные колебания
  constant ~s (кóнстант ~с) постоянные колебания
  currency ~s (кýррэнси ~с) валютные колебания
  cyclical ~s (сúкликал ~с) циклические колебания
  excessive ~s (эксэ́сив ~с) чрезмерные колебания
  exchange rate ~ **band** (эксчэ́йндж рэйт ~ банд) размах колебаний валютного курса
  irregular ~s (иррэ́гюлар ~с) нерегулярные колебания
  local ~s (лóкал ~с) местные колебания
  major ~s (мэ́йджор ~с) большие колебания
  market ~s (мáркэт ~с) колебание конъюнктуры, колебания цен на рынке, конъюнктурные колебания, неустойчивость рынков
  periodical ~s (пэриóдикал ~с) периодические колебания
  seasonal ~s (сúзонал ~с) сезонные колебания
  short-term ~s (шорт-тэрм ~с) кратковременные колебания
  sustained ~s (сустэ́йнд ~с) устойчивые колебания
  temporary ~s (тэ́мпорари ~с) временные колебания
  ~s **in costs** (~с ин костс) колебания стоимости
  ~s **in supply and demand** (~с ин супплáй энд димáнд) колебания спроса и предложения

~ **of the exchange rate** (~ оф θи эксчэ́йндж рэйт) неустойчивость курса валюты
Fluid (флýид) жидкий
F.O.B. (эф-о-би) франко борт
  air-freight (эйр-фрэйт) франко борт самолёта
  delivery ~ (дэлúвэри ~) поставка на условиях ФОБ
  ~ **airplane** (~ эйрплэйн) франко борт самолёта
  ~ **alongside** (~ алонгсáйд) франко вдоль борта судна
  ~ **truck** (~ трак) франко борт грузового автомобиля
Fodder (фóддэр) корм, кормовой {adj.}
Follow, to ~ (фóлло, ту ~) следовать
Foodstuffs (фýдстуфс) продовольственные товары, продовольствие
Force (форс) сила
  agricultural labor ~ (агрикýлчурал лэ́йбор ~) сельскохозяйственная рабочая сила
  armed ~s (áрмэд ~эз) вооружённые силы
  compulsory ~ (компýлсори ~) обязательная сила
  international ~s (интэрнáшэнал ~с) международные силы
  labor ~ (лэ́йбор ~) рабочая сила
  legal ~ (лúгал ~) законная сила
  occupying ~ (óккупайинг ~) оккупант, оккупационные силы
  qualified work ~ (куáлифайд уóрк ~) квалифицированная рабочая сила
  relative ~ (рэ́латив ~) относительная сила
  to come into ~ (ту ком úнту ~) войти в силу
  to remain in ~ (ту римэ́йн ин ~) оставаться в силе
  use of ~ (юс оф ~) акт насилия
  ~ **of a judicial decision** (~ оф а джюдúшл дисúжн) сила судебного решения
  ~ **of law** (~ оф лáу) сила закона
  police ~s (полúс ~с) полицейские силы
  productive ~s (продáктив ~с) производительные силы
Force Majeure (форс мажю́р) непреодолимая сила

conditions of ~ (кондишнс оф ~)
форсмажорное обстоятельство
Forecast (форкаст) прогноз на
ближайшее будущее
Foreclosure (форклоҗюр) лишение
права выкупа закладной
   ~ **upon a mortgage** (~ апон а
   моргэдж) ипотечный иск
Forefather (форфаθэр) предок ~s
предки
Foreign (форэн) внешний,
зарубежный, иностранный
   ~ **economic** (~ экономик)
   внешнеэкономический
   ~ **exchange** {currency} (~
   эксчэйндж {куррэнси}) инвалюта,
   иностранная валюта}
   ~ **trade** (~ трэйд) внешнеторговый
Foreigner (форэнэр) иностранец
Foreman (форман) мастер
   maintenance ~ (мэйнтэнанс ~)
   мастер по текущему ремонту
   senior ~ (синиор ~) старший
   мастер
   shift ~ (шифт ~) сменный мастер
   ~ **of the jury** (~ оф θи джури)
   старшина присяжных заседателей
Forensic (форэнсик)
судебномедицинский
Forestry (форэстри) лесное
хозяйство
Forfeited (форфэтэд) конфискованный
Forfeiture (форфэчур) конфискация
   to be subject to ~ (ту би
   сабджэкт ту ~) подлежать
   конфискации
Forge (фордж) кузница {shop}
   to ~ (ту ~) подделывать
Forged (форджд) поддельный
Forger (форджэр) подделыватель
Forgery (форджэри) подделка, подлог
   ~ **of documents** (~ оф докюмэнтс)
   подделка документов
   ~ **of a trademark** (~ оф а
   трэйдмарк) подделка товарного
   знака
Forgiveness (форгивнэс) прощение
   ~ **of a debt** (~ оф а дэт)
   прощение долга
Forklift (форклифт) тележка
   "Lift here with ~**"** {marking on
   crate} (лифт хир уиθ ~) "Место
   Подъёма Тележкой" {надпись}
Form (форм) анкета, бланк, форма
   application ~ (аппликэйшн ~)
   анкета
   bank ~ (банк ~) банковский бланк

blank {clean} ~ (бланк {клин} ~)
чистый бланк
cable ~ (кэйбл ~) бланк
телеграммы
check ~ (чэк ~) бланк чека
company ~ (компани ~) фирменный
бланк
declaration ~ (дэкларэйшн ~)
бланк декларации
draft ~ (драфт ~) вексельный
бланк
in good order and proper ~ (ин
гуд ордэр энд пропэр ~) в
полном порядке и должной форме
order ~ (ордэр ~) бланк заказа
pre-registration ~ (при-
рэджистрэйшн ~) бланк
предварительной регистрации
printed ~ (принтэд ~) печатная
форма, типографский бланк
printed order ~ (принтэд ордэр
~) печатный бланк
product registration ~ (продукт
рэджистрэйшн ~) бланк для
регистрации покупки
receipt ~ (рисит ~) форма
квитанции, форма расписки
sample ~ (сампл ~) образец
бланка
standard application ~ (стандард
аппликэйшн ~) анкета
установленного образца
standard form ~ (стандард форм
~) форма контракта
standard contract ~ (стандард
контракт ~) бланк контракта
standard document ~ (стандард
докюмэнт ~) бланк документа
subrogation ~ (суброгэйшн ~)
акт о суброгации
to ~ (ту ~) образовать
to complete a ~ (ту комплит а ~
заполнять бланк
~ **letter** (~ лэттэр) бланк письм
~ **of bill of lading** (~ оф бил о
лэйдинг) форма коносамента
~ **of documents** (~ оф докюмэнтс)
форма документов
Formal (формал) оформленный
Formality (формалити) обрядность,
процедура ~/**ies** обрядности
   administrative ~ (администрэйти
   ~) административная процедура
   customs ~/**ies** (кастомз ~из)
   таможенные обрядности
Formation (формэйшн) образование

act of ~ (акт оф ~) акт о
создании
methods of price ~ (мэθодс оф
прайс ~) методика
ценообразования
organizational ~s (организэйшнал
~с) организационные формы
price ~ (прайс ~)
ценообразование
principles of price ~ (принсиплс
оф прайс ~) принципы
ценообразования
~ of capital (~ оф капитал)
образование капитала
~ of government {in
parliamentary system} (~ оф
говэрнмэнт {ин парламэнтари
систэм}) образование государства
~ of stocks (~ оф стокс)
образование запасов
Forsake, to ~ (форсэйк, ту ~)
покидать
Fortuitous (фортуитос) случайный
Forward (форуард) вперёд, передний
balance brought ~ (баланс брот
~) сальдо с переноса
to ~ (ту ~) направлять,
пересылать
to carry ~ (ту кэрри ~)
переносить
Forwarded (форуардэд) направленный
Forwarder (форуардэр) отправитель
freight ~ (фрэйт ~) экспедитор
freight ~s certificate of
receipt (фрэйт ~с сэртификэт оф
рисит) расписка экспедитора
general freight ~ (джэнэрал
фрэйт ~) генеральный экспедитор
order to the freight ~ (ордэр ту
θи фрэйт ~) поручение
экспедитору
to act in the capacity of
freight ~ (ту акт ин θи капасити
оф фрэйт ~) выступать в качестве
экспедитора
to be designated as freight ~
(ту би дэзигнэйтэд ас фрэйт ~)
быть назначенным экспедитором
Forwarding (форуардинг) отправка,
транспортно-экспедиторский {adj.},
экспедиторский {adj.}
~ free of charge (~ фри оф
чардж) безвозмездная посылка
Found (фоунд) найдённый
to ~ (ту ~) основывать,
создавать, учреждать

Foundation (фоундэйшн) основа,
основание, учреждение
legal ~ (лигал ~) правовая
основа
Founder (фоундэр) основатель,
учредитель
Foundry (фоундри) литейный завод
Fraction (фракшн) часть
~ of a transferrable letter of
credit (~ оф а трансфэрабл
лэттэр оф крэдит) часть
переводного аккредитива
Fragile (фраджайл) бьющийся,
ломкий, непрочный
highly ~ (хайли ~)
легкоповреждаемый
Framework (фрэймуорк) конструкция
supporting ~ (суппортинг ~)
опорная конструкция
Fraud (фрауд) мошенническая
проделка, мошенник {person}, обман,
обманщик {person}
by ~ (бай ~) обманным путём
electoral ~ (элэкторал ~)
подделка избирательного
документа
Free (фри) безвозмездно,
безвозмездный, бесплатный,
свободный
duty-~ (дюти-~) беспошлинный
fault-~ (фалт-~) бездефектный
interest-~ (интэрэст-~)
беспроцентный
to ~ (ту ~) освобождать
[perfective: освободить]
to supply ~ of charge (ту
супплай ~ оф чардж) поставлять
бесплатно
trouble-~ (трабл-~)
безаварийный
~ for import (~ фор импорт)
свободно для ввоза
~ in (~ ин) фри-ин
~ in and stowed (~ ин энд стоуд)
фри-ин со штивкой
~ in and trimmed (~ ин энд
тримд) фри-ин с размещением
~ of charge (~ оф чардж)
бесплатно
~ on rail (~ он рэйл) франко
вагон
~ on rail price (~ он рэйл
прайс) цена франко вагон
~ out (~ оут) выгрузка из трюма
за счёт фрахтователя
Freedom (фридом) свобода

basic ~ (бэ́йсик ~) основная
свобода
religious ~ (рили́джос ~)
религиозная свобода
trade union ~ (трэйд ю́нион ~)
профсоюзная свобода
~ of action (~ оф акшн) свобода
действия
~ of assembly (~ оф ассэ́мбли)
свобода собраний
~ of capital movement (~ оф
ка́питал му́вмэнт) свобода
движения капиталов
~ of conscience (~ оф ко́ншэнс)
свобода совести
~ of movement (~ оф му́вмэнт)
свобода движения
~ of movement of labor (~ оф
му́вмэнт оф лэ́йбор) свобода
движения рабочей силы
~ of religion (~ оф рили́джон)
свобода религии
~ of speech (~ оф спич) свобода
слова
Freely (фри́ли) свободно
~ convertible (~ конвэ́ртибл)
свободно-конвертируемый
Freeze (фриз) замораживание
price ~ (прайс ~) замораживание
цен
Freight (фрэ́йт) грузовой {adj.},
фрахт, фрахтовый {adj.}
ad valorem ~ (ад вало́рэм ~)
фрахт "ад валорем"
agreed ~ (агри́д ~) обусловленный
фрахт
air ~ (эйр ~) воздушный груз
amount of ~ (амо́унт оф ~) размер
фрахта
base ~ (бэйс ~) базисный фрахт
calculation of ~ (калкюлэ́йшн оф
~) расчёт фрахта
charter ~ (ча́ртэр ~) фрахт по
чартеру
collection of ~ (колле́кшн оф ~)
взыскание фрахта, оплата фрахта
commercial ~ (комме́ршл ~)
торговый груз
contract ~ (ко́нтракт ~)
контрактный груз
dead ~ (дэд ~) мёртвый фрахт
distance ~ (ди́станс ~)
дистанционный фрахт
double ~ (дабл ~) двойной фрахт
in-transit ~ (ин-тра́нзит ~)
фрахт за транзитный провоз
грузов

inland river ~ (и́нланд ри́вэр ~)
речной фрахт
long-distance ~ (лонг-ди́станс ~)
груз перевозимый на дальние
расстояния
lumpsum ~ (ла́мпсум ~) аккордный
фрахт
ocean-going ~ (ошн-го́инг ~)
морской фрахт
outbound ~ (о́утбоунд ~)
экспортный фрахт
outgoing ~ (оутго́инг ~) фрахт в
один конец
return ~ (риту́рн ~) обратный
фрахт
surcharge on ~ (су́рчардж он ~)
надбавка к фрахту
terms of ~ (тэрмз оф ~) условия
фрахта
through ~ (θру ~) сквозной фрахт
to increase ~ (ту инкри́с ~)
повышать фрахт
to pay ~ (ту пэй ~) уплатить
фрахт
to receive ~ (ту риси́в ~)
получить фрахт
tramp ~ (трамп ~) трамповый
фрахт
transport of ~ (тра́нспорт оф ~)
транспортировка грузов
truck ~ (трак ~) груз
перевозимый автотранспортом
way ~ (уэй ~) попутный груз
~ ad valorem (~ ад вало́рэм)
фрахт, исчисляемый со стоимости
груза
~ advance (~ адва́нс) аванс
фрахта
~ and demurrage (~ энд
димю́рradж) фрахт и плата за
простой судна
~ both ways (~ боθ уэйс) фрахт в
оба конца
~ capacity (~ капа́сити)
грузовместимость
~ commission (~ комми́шн)
комиссия с фрахта
~ contract (~ ко́нтракт) договор
о фрахтовании судна
~ earnings (~ э́рнингз)
поступления от фрахта
~ forward (~ фо́руард) фрахт,
уплачиваемый в порту выгрузки
~ forwarder (~ фо́руардэр)
экспедитор груза
~ forwarding (~ фо́руардинг)
экспедирование грузов

~ **is prepayable** (~ из припэ́йабл) фрахт оплачивается предварительно
~ **paid to ...** (~ пэйд ту ...) фрахт оплачен до
~ **payable at destination** (~ пэ́йабл ат дэстинэ́йшн) фрахт, уплачиваемый в месте назначения
~ **rebate** (~ ри́бэйт) скидка с фрахта
~ **revenues** (~ рэ́вэнус) доходы от фрахта
~ **tax** (~ такс) налог на фрахт
~ **traffic expert** (~ тра́ффик э́кспэрт) эксперт по перевозке грузов
Freightage (фрэ́йтадж) стоимость фрахтования
Freighter (фрэ́йтэр) грузовое судно
Freightline (фрэ́йтлайн) грузовая линия
overland ~ (о́вэрланд ~) грузовая судоходная линия
Frequent (фри́куэнт) многочисленный
Friend (фрэнд) друг
Friendly (фрэ́ндли) дружественный
Fringe (фриндж) кайма, край
benefits (бэ́нэфитс) дополнительные выплаты
From alongside (фром алонгса́йд) от борта
Front (фронт) передняя сторона, фронт {military}
~ **line** (~ лайн) прифронтовой
Frontier (фронти́р) граница
Frost (фрост) мороз
~ **resistant** (~ ризи́стант) морозостойкий
Frozen (фро́зэн) блокированный
Fruit (фрут) плод
forbidden ~ (форби́ддэн ~) запретный плод
Fruitful (фру́тфул) плодоносный
Fuel (фюл) топливо
liquid ~ (ли́куид ~) жидкое топливо
solid ~ (со́лид ~) твёрдое топливо
Fulfill, to ~ (фулфи́л, ту ~) выполнять, исполнить обязанность
to ~ **contractual obligations** (ту ~ контра́кчуал облигэ́йшнз) завершать выполнение контракта
Fulfilled (фулфи́лд) выполненный
Fulfillment (фулфи́лмэнт) выполнение, исполнение, совершение

to cooperate in the ~ **of a plan** (ту коо́пэрэйт ин thи ~ оф а план) сотрудничать в выполнении плана
to delay ~ (ту дилэ́й ~) задерживать выполнение
to ensure the ~ (ту эншю́р thи ~) обеспечивать выполнение
to interfere with the ~ **of a program** (ту интэрфи́р уиthhи ~ оф а про́грам) смешать выполнению программы
to take on for ~ (ту тэйк он фор ~) принимать к выполнению
~ **of contractual obligations** (~ оф контра́кчуал облигэ́йшнз) выполнение договорных обязательств
~ **of an order** (~ оф ан о́рдэр) выполнение заказа
~ **of a plan** (~ оф а план) завершение плана
~ **of a plan ahead of schedule** (~ оф а план ахэ́д оф скэ́джюл) досрочное выполнение плана
Full (фул) полный
~ **reach and burden** (~ рич энд бу́рдэн) полная грузовместимость и грузоподъёмность
Full-service (фул-сэ́рвис) полный цикл услуг
Fullness (фу́ллнэс) полнота
Fully-loaded (фу́лли-ло́дэд) с полным грузом
Function, to ~ (функшн, ту ~) функционировать
Functionary (фу́нкшнари) аппаратчик
Fund (фунд) резерв, фонд
accumulation ~ (кюмюлэ́йшн ~) фонд накопления
amortization ~ (амортизэ́йшн ~) амортизационный фонд
bank's ~**s** (банкс ~с) банковские фонды
basic ~ (бэ́йсик ~) базовый фонд
bonus ~ (бо́нус ~) фонд премирования
borrowed ~**s** (бо́рроуд ~с) заёмные средства
budgetary ~**s** (ба́джэтари ~с) бюджетные средства
capital investment ~ (ка́питал инвэ́стмэнт ~) фонд капитальных вложений
cash ~ (каш ~) денежный фонд
cash ~**s** (каш ~с) наличный капитал

consolidated ~ (консо́лидэйтэд ~) консолидированный фонд
consumption ~ (консу́мпшн ~) фонд потребления
contingency ~ (конти́нджэнси ~) чрезвычайный фонд
contingency ~s (конти́нджэнси ~с) средство на непредвиденные расходы
economic stimulus ~ (эконо́мик сти́мюлус ~) фонд экономического стимулирования
expansion ~ (экспа́ншн ~) фонд развития производства
fixed ~s (фиксд ~с) основные фонды
foreign ~s (фо́рэн ~с) иностранные фонды
foreign exchange ~s (фо́рэн эксчэ́йндж ~с) валютные средства
formation of ~s (форме́йшн оф ~с) формирование фондов
frozen ~s (фро́зэн ~с) замороженные средства
government ~s (го́вэрнмэнт ~с) правительственные фонды
incentive ~ (инсэ́нтив ~) фонд материального поощрения
indemnification ~ (индэмнифике́йшн ~) компенсационный фонд
indivisible ~s (индиви́зибл ~с) неделимые фонды
insurance ~ (иншю́ранс ~) страховой фонд
internal ~s (интэ́рнал ~с) собственные средства
investment ~s (инвэ́стмэнт ~с) инвестиционные фонды
liquid ~s (ли́куид ~с) ликвидный резерв, ликвидные фонды
notice of incoming ~s (но́тис оф и́нкоминг ~с) инкассовое авизо
on account of lack of ~s (он акко́унт оф лак оф ~с) за неимением денег
pension ~ (пэншн ~) пенсионный фонд
pool of ~s (пул оф ~с) общий фонд
public ~s (па́блик ~с) государственные средства, общественные фонды
redemption ~ (риэ́мпшн ~) фонд погашения
relief ~ (рили́ф ~) фонд помощи

reserve ~ (рисэ́рв ~) резервный капитал, резервный фонд
revolving ~ (риво́лвинг ~) автоматически возобновляемый фонд
share of the charter ~ (шэйр оф θи ча́ртэр ~) доля в основном фонде
sinking ~ (си́нкинг ~) выкупной фонд, резерв на погашение задолженности
standby ~s (ста́ндбай ~с) резервные средства
supplementary ~s (сапплэмэ́нтари ~с) дополнительные фонды
to invest ~s (ту инвэ́ст ~с) инвестировать фонды
to raise ~s (ту рэйз ~с) привлекать фонды
to release ~s (ту рили́с ~с) высвобождать деньги
to set aside ~s (ту сэт асайд ~с) создавать фонды
Funding (фу́ндинг) финансирование
state ~ (стэйт ~) государственное фондирование
to cut off ~ (ту кут офф ~) прекратить финансирование
Furlough (фу́рло) отпуск
soldier on ~ (со́лджэр он ~) отпускник
Furnish, to ~ (фу́рниш, ту ~) снабжать [**perfective:** снабдить]
to ~ personnel (ту ~ пэрсонне́л) укомплектовывать личным составом
Furnished (фу́рнищд) доставляемый
Further (фу́рθэр) дальше
~ to the letter (~ ту θи лэ́ттэр) в дополнение к письму
Futures (фю́чэрс) фьючерский
~ market (~ ма́ркэт) фьючерский рынок

G

G-7, the ~ (джи-сэ́вэн, θи ~) Семерка
Gain (гэйн) выручка, прирост
to ~ (ту ~) выгадывать, выигрывать, выручать
total ~ (то́тал ~) общий доход
~s from economies of scale (~с фром ико́номиз оф скэйл) выгоды связанные с массовым производством {production}

Gamble (гамбл) авантюра, игра
   to ~ (гамбл, ту ~) играть,
   спекулировать
Gambler (ѓамблэр) игрок
Game (гэйм) игра
   ~ of chance (~ оф чанс) азартная
   игра
Gang (гэнг) бригада, сборище
Gangster (ѓангстэр) бандит
Gap (гап) разница, разрыв
   inflationary ~ (инфлэ́йшнари ~)
   инфляционный разрыв
Gates (гэйтс) ворота
   town ~ (тóун ~) застава
Gather, to ~ (гá θ эр, ту ~) снимать
[perfective: снять], собирать
[perfective: собрать]
Gathering (гá θ эринг) слёт, снятие,
собрание
   customary ~ (кýстомари ~)
   обыкновенное собрание
Gauge (гэйдж) лекало, шаблон,
эталон
   equipment ~ (икуйпмэнт ~)
   габарит погрузки
Gear (гир) зубчатая передача,
механизм
   hoisting ~ (хóйстинг ~)
   подъёмное оборудование
   hoisting and conveying ~
   (хóйстинг энд конвэ́йинг ~)
   подъёмно-транспортное
   оборудование
General (джэ́нэрал) генерал,
генеральный {adj.}, общий {adj.}
Generosity (джэнэрóсити) щедрость
Generous (джэ́нэрос) щедрый
Genre (джа́нрэ) род
Gift (гифт) подарок
   given as a ~ (гúвэн аз а ~)
   одаряемый
Gifted (гúфтэд) одарённый,
способный
Gigolo (джúголо) альфонс
Give, to ~ (гив, ту ~) выдавать,
сдавать [perfective: сдать]
   on a "~ and take" basis (он а ~
   энд тэйк бэ́йсис) на давальческой
   основе
   to ~ oneself up (ту ~ уáнсэлф
   ап)
   "~ and take" (~ энд тэйк)
   давальческий
Glitch (глитч) заминка
Global (глóбал) глобальный
Glut (глут) перенасыщение

~ of the market (~ оф θ и мáркэт)
пресыщенность рынка
Go, to ~ (го, ту ~) идти, ехать
   to ~ on (ту ~ он) происходить
Gold (голд) золото
   fine ~ (файн ~) высокопробное
   золото
   low-grade ~ (лóу-грэйд ~)
   низкопробное золото
   monetary ~ (мóнэтари ~)
   монетарное золото
   ~ in coins (~ ин койнз) золото в
   монетах
   ~ in ingots (~ ин йнготс) золото
   в слитках
   ~ in nuggets (~ ин нýггэтс)
   золото в самородках
Good (гуд) изделие ~s товар,
товарный {adj.}
   acceptable ~s (аксэ́птабл ~с)
   приемлемый товар
   acceptance of ~s (аксэ́птанс оф
   ~с) приёмка товара
   analogous ~s (анáлогос ~с)
   родственные грузы
   assortment of ~s (ассóртмэнт оф
   ~с) ассортимент товара
   auction ~s (аукшн ~с) аукционный
   товар
   baled ~s (бэйлд ~с) товар в
   тюках
   batch of ~s (батч оф ~с) партия
   товара
   bill of ~s (бил оф ~с)
   номенклатура товаров
   bonded ~s (бóндэд ~с) бондовый
   товар
   brand name ~s (бранд нэйм ~с)
   фирменный товар
   bulky ~s (бýлки ~с) громоздкие
   товары
   clearance of ~s through customs
   (клúранс оф ~с θ ру кáстомз)
   пропуск товара через таможню
   competitive ~s (компэ́титив ~с)
   конкурентоспособные товары
   consignment ~s (консáйнмэнт ~с)
   консигнационный товар
   consumer ~s (консýмэр ~с)
   потребительские товары
   cost of ~s (кост оф ~с)
   стоимость товара
   cost of ~s delivered CIF (кост
   оф ~с дэлúвэрд си-ай-эф)
   стоимость товара на условиях СИФ

cost of ~s delivered FOB (кост
оф ~с дэли́вэрд эф-о-би́)
стоимость товара на условиях ФОБ
cost of ~s on the domestic
market (кост оф ~с он θи
доме́стик ма́ркэт) стоимость
товара на внутреннем рынке
critical ~s (кри́тикал ~с)
дефицитный товар
damaged ~s (да́маджд ~с)
поврежденный товар
defect in ~s (ди́фэкт ин ~с)
порок в товаре
defective ~s (дифэ́ктив ~с)
бракованный товар, дефектный
товар
delayed ~s (дилэ́йд ~с)
задержанный товар
delivery of ~s (дэли́вэри оф ~с)
доставка товара, сдача товара
description of ~s (дискри́пшн оф
~с) описание товара
display of ~s (дисплэ́й оф ~с)
выкладка товаров
display of ~s in a store window
(дисплэ́й оф ~с ин а стор уи́ндо)
выкладка товаров в витрине
dry ~s (драй ~с) сухой товар
export ~s (э́кспорт ~с)
экспортный товар
failure to deliver ~s for
shipment (фэ́йлюр ту дэли́вэр ~с
фор ши́пмэнт) непредъявление
груза к перевозке
fast selling ~s (фаст сэ́ллинг
~с) быстро продающийся товар
finished ~ (фи́нишд ~) готовое
изделие
sample ~ (сампл ~) образец
товара
first class ~s (фэрст класс ~с)
первоклассные товары
flammable ~s (фла́ммабл ~с)
огнеопасный груз, огнеопасный
товар
great diversity of ~s (грэйт
диве́рсити оф ~с) большое
разнообразие товаров
haberdashery ~s (ха́бэрдашэри ~с)
галантерейные товары
hazardous ~s (ха́зардос ~с)
опасный товар
high quality ~s (хай куа́лити ~с)
доброкачественный товар
highly marketable ~s (ха́йли
ма́ркэтабл ~с) быстро реализуемый
товар

household ~s (ха́усхолд ~с)
хозяйственные товары
import ~s (и́мпорт ~с) импортные
товары
import of ~s (и́мпорт оф ~с)
импорт товаров
imported ~s (импо́ртэд ~с)
импортный груз
incoming ~s (и́нкоминг ~с)
поступающий товар
index of ~s (и́ндэкс оф ~с)
список товаров
index of non-dutiable ~s (и́ндэкс
оф нон-ду́тиабл ~с) список
товаров, не облагаемых пошлиной
insufficient stock of ~s
(инсуффи́шэнт сток оф ~с)
недостаточный запас товаров
insured ~s (иншу́рд ~с)
застрахованные товары
investment ~s (инве́стмэнт ~с)
инвестиционный товар
kind of ~s (кайнд оф ~с) вид
товара
labor-intensive ~s (лэ́йбор-
интэ́нсив ~с) трудоёмкий товар
life cycle of ~s (лайф са́йкл оф
~с) жизненный цикл товара
liquid ~s (ли́куид ~с) жидкий
товар
livestock ~s (ла́йвсток ~с)
животноводческие товары
loose ~s (лус ~с) бестарный
товар
low cost ~s (ло́у кост ~с)
малоценный товар
low quality ~s (ло́у куа́лити ~с)
низкосортный товар
marked down ~s (маркд до́ун ~с)
уценённый товар
merchantable ~s (мэ́рчантабл ~с)
реализуемый товар
nature of ~s (нэ́йчэр оф ~с) вид
товара, характер товара
noncomestible ~ (нонкоме́стибл ~)
непродовольственные товары
non-competitive ~s (нон-
компэ́титив ~с)
неконкурентоспособные товары
non-hazardous ~s (нон-ха́зардос
~с) неопасный товар
non-traditional ~s (нон-
тради́шнал ~с) нетрадиционные
товары
order for ~s (о́рдэр фор ~с)
заказ на товар

ordered ~s (о́рдэрд ~с) заказной товар
ordering of ~s (о́рдэринг оф ~с) выписка товаров
origin of ~s (о́риджин оф ~с) происхождение товара
owner of ~s (о́унэр оф ~с) владелец товара
ownership of ~s (о́унэршип оф ~с) собственность на товар
packaged ~s (па́кэджд ~с) упакованные товары
parcel ~s (па́рсэл ~с) парцелльный груз
past due ~s (паст ду ~с) просроченный товар
patented ~s (па́тэнтэд ~с) патентованные товары
pledge on ~s (плэдж он ~с) закладная на товар
pledged ~s (плэджд ~с) заложенный товар
poor quality ~s (пур куа́лити ~с) недоброкачественный товар
popular ~s (по́пюлар ~с) ходкий товар
pre-packaged ~s (при-па́кэджд ~с) расфасованный товар
price reduction of ~s (прайс риду́кшн оф ~с) уценка товара
proprietor of ~s (пропра́йэтор оф ~с) собственник товара
protection of ~s (протэ́кшн оф ~с) защита товара
purchase of ~s (пу́рчас оф ~с) закупка товара
quality of ~s (куа́лити оф ~с) качество товара
quantity of ~s (куа́нтити оф ~с) количество товара
re-exported ~s (ри-э́кспортэд ~с) реэкспортные товары
readiness advice on ~s (рэ́динэс адва́йс он ~с) извещение о готовности товара к осмотру
refrigerated ~s (рифри́джэрэйтэд ~с) замороженный товар, рефрижера) торный груз
rejected ~s (риджэ́ктэд ~с) забракованный товар
rejection of ~s (риджэ́кшн оф ~с) браковка товара, отказ от товара
retail ~s (ри́тэйл ~с) розничные товары
sale of ~s (сэйл оф ~с) реализация товара, сбыт товаров

salvage ~s (са́лвэдж ~с) спасённый товар
second rate ~s (сэ́конд рэйт ~с) второсортные товары
seized ~s (сизд ~с) на который наложен арест груз
seizure of ~s (си́жюр оф ~с) арест на товары
selected ~s (сэлэ́ктэд ~с) отборный товар
semi-finished ~s (сэ́ми-фи́нишд ~с) незавершённое производство
short-delivered ~s (шорт-дэли́вэрд ~с) недопоставленный товар
similar ~s (си́милар ~с) сходные товары
slow selling ~s (сло́у сэ́ллинг ~с) труднореализуемый товар
smuggled ~s (смаглд ~с) контрабандный товар
sold ~s (солд ~с) проданный товар, реализованный товар
sophisticated ~s (софи́стикэйтэд ~с) сложный товар
specification of ~s (спэсификэ́йшн оф ~с) спецификация товара
spoiled ~s (спойлд ~с) испорченный товар
sporting ~s (спо́ртинг ~с) спортивные товары
stale ~s (стэйл ~с) залежалый товар
standard batch of ~s (ста́ндард батч оф ~с) стандартная партия товара
standardized ~s (ста́ндардайзд ~с) стандартизованный товар
strategic ~s (стра́тиджик ~с) стратегические товары
subject ~s (са́бджэкт ~с) данный товар
substitutable ~s (субститу́табл ~с) взаимозаменяемые товары
supplier of ~s (сапла́йэр оф ~с) поставщик товаров
surplus ~s (су́рплус ~с) излишки товара
timber and paper ~s (ти́мбэр энд пэ́йпэр ~с) лесобумажные товары
to "rummage" ~s (ту ру́ммадж ~с) перекладывать грузы
to claim ~s (ту клэйм ~с) востребовать груз

to **clear** ~**s through customs** (ту клир ~с θру ка́стомз) очистить грузы через таможню

to **number** ~**s** (ту ну́мбэр ~с) занумеровывать груз

to **palletize** ~**s** (ту па́ллэтайз ~с) перевозить грузы на поддонах

to **collect** ~**s** (ту колле́кт ~с) забирать товар

to **declare** ~**s** {to customs} (ту дикле́йр ~с {ту ка́стомз}) декларировать товар

to **deliver** ~**s FOB** (ту дэли́вэр ~с эф-о-би) доставлять товар на условиях ФОБ

to **deliver** ~**s CIF** (ту дэли́вэр ~с си-ай-эф) доставлять товар на условиях СИФ

to **dump** ~**s on the market** (ту дамп ~с он θи ма́ркэт) выбрасывать товары на рынок

to **import** ~**s** (ту и́мпорт ~с) импортировать товар

to **insure** ~**s** (ту иншу́р ~с) страховать товар

to **introduce** ~**s to market** (ту интроду́с ~с ту ма́ркэт) внедрять товары на рынок

to **keep** ~**s in a warehouse** (ту кип ~с ин а уэ́рхаус) держать товар на складе

to **pledge** ~**s** (ту плэдж ~с) закладывать товар

to **provide** ~**s** (ту прова́йд ~с) обеспечивать товарами

to **redeem pledged** ~**s** (ту риди́м плэджд ~с) выкупать заложенный товар

to **reject** ~**s** (ту риджэ́кт ~с) браковать товар, отказываться от товара

to **replace defective** ~**s** (ту рипле́йс дифэ́ктив ~с) заменять дефектный товар

to **report damage to** ~**s** (ту рипо́рт да́мадж ту ~с) заявлять о повреждении товара

to **sell** {realize} ~**s** (ту сэл {ри́лайз} ~с) реализовывать товар

to **send** ~**s** (ту сэнд ~с) посылать товар

to **send** ~**s on approval** (ту сэнд ~с он аппру́вал) посылать товар на одобрение

to **send** ~**s on consignment** (ту сэнд ~с он конса́йнмэнт) посылать товар на консигнацию

to **take** ~**s on a trial basis** (ту тэйк ~с он а тра́йал бэ́йсис) апробировать товар

to **test** ~**s** (ту тэст ~с) испытывать товар

to **trace** ~**s** (ту трэйс ~с) следить за движением товара

to **unload** ~**s** (ту анло́д ~с) выгружать товар, отгружать товар

to **unload** ~**s on the dock** (ту анло́д ~с он θи док) выгружать товар на причал

to **value** ~**s** (ту ва́лю ~с) оценивать товар

to **warehouse** ~**s** (ту уэ́рхаус ~с) складировать товар

top quality ~**s** (топ куа́лити ~с) товар высшей марки

total cost of ~**s** (то́тал кост оф ~с) общая стоимость товара

transshipment of ~**s** (трансши́пмэнт оф ~с) перевалка товара

type of ~**s** (тайп оф ~с) тип товара

unclaimed ~**s** (анкле́ймд ~с) неистребованный товар

undamaged ~**s** (анда́маджд ~с) неповреждённый товар

unmerchantable ~**s** (анмэ́рчантабл ~с) невыгодный товар

unordered ~**s** (ано́рдэрд ~с) незаказанный товар

unpacked ~**s** {for shipment} (анпа́кд ~с {фор ши́пмэнт}) незатаренный товар

unsalable ~**s** (ансэ́йлабл ~с) неходовой товар

unsold ~**s** (ансо́лд ~с) непроданный товар

warehoused ~**s** (уэ́рхаусд ~с) складированный товар

wrapped ~**s** (рапд ~с) товар в упаковке

~**s in barrels** (~с ин ба́ррэлс) бочковый груз

~**s in bulk** (~с ин булк) бестарный груз

~**s loaded in bulk** (~с ло́дэд ин булк) погруженный навалом груз

~**s in** {very} **short supply** (~с ин {вэ́ри} шорт суппла́й) остродефицитные товары

~**s listed hereinbelow** (~с ли́стэд хиринбило́у) перечисленные ниже товары

~s of every sort and kind (~с оф эвэри сорт энд кайнд) любые товары

Government (гóвэрнмэнт) государство, правительство

actual ~ (áкчуал ~) фактическое правительство

coalition ~ (коалúшн ~) коалиционное правительство

constitutional ~ (конститýшнал ~) конституционное правительство

de facto ~ (ди фáкто ~) правительство де-факто

de jure ~ (ди джýрэ ~) правительство де-юре

democratic ~ (дэмокрáтик ~) демократическое правительство

depositary ~ {to a convention} (дипóзитари ~ {ту а конвэ́ншн}) правительство депозитарий

dictatorial ~ (диктатóриал ~) диктаторское правительство

federal ~ (фэ́дэрал ~) федеральное правительство

hostile ~ (хóстайл ~) враждебное правительство

interim ~ (úнтэрим ~) временное правительство

labor ~ (лэ́йбор ~) лейбористское правительство

legal ~ (лúгал ~) законное правительство

liberal ~ (лúбэрал ~) либеральное правительство

nonsignatory ~ (нонсúгнатори ~) неподписавшееся правительство

parliamentary ~ (парламэ́нтари ~) парламентское правительство

provincial ~ (провúншал ~) провинциальное правительство

puppet ~ (пýппэт ~) марионеточное правительство

revolutionary ~ (рэволю́шнари ~) революционное правительство

signatory ~ (сúгнатори ~) подписавшееся правительство

stable ~ (стэ́йбл ~) стабильное правительство

to constitute a ~ (ту кóнститют а ~) составить правительство

to form a ~ (ту форм а ~) сформировать правительство

to overthrow the ~ (ту овэрθрó θи ~) свергнуть правительство

totalitarian ~ (тоталитэ́йриан ~) тоталитарное правительство

transitional ~ (транзúшнал ~) переходное правительство

~ in exile (~ ин экзáйл) правительство в изгнании

~ of national unity (~ оф нáшэнал ю́нити) правительство национального единства

~ of social salvation (~ оф сошл салвэ́йшн) правительство общественного спасения

Governmental (говэрнмэ́нтал) государственный, правительственный

Grade (грэйд) качество, сорт, ступень

to ~ (ту ~) сортировать

Grading (грэ́йдинг) сортировка

Gradual (грáджюал) последовательный

Graft (графт) подкуп

Grant (грант) безвозмездная субсидия, выдача, стипендия

application for ~ of patent (апплике́йшн фор ~ оф пáтэнт) ходатайство о выдаче патента

application for a ~ (апплике́йшн фор а ~) заявка на выдачу

government ~ (гóвэрнмэнт ~) государственная стипендия

~ of funds (~ оф фандз) ассигновка

~ of trademark registration (~ оф трэ́йдмарк рэджистрэ́йшн) выдача документа о регистрации товарного знака

to ~ (ту ~) выдавать, предоставлять

Granting (грáнтинг) предоставление

~ a concession (~ а консэ́шн) предоставление концессии

~ a discount (~ а дúскоунт) предоставление скидки

~ independence (~ индэпэ́ндэнс) предоставление независимости

~ a license (~ а лáйсэнз) предоставление лицензии

~ a loan (~ а лон) предоставление займа

~ of asylum (~ оф асáйлум) предоставление убежища

~ of citizenship (~ оф сúтизэншип) предоставление гражданства, приём в гражданство

~ of a loan (~ оф а лон) выдача ссуды

~ priority (~ прайóрити) предоставление приоритета

Grantor (грантóр) лицо, передающее право на имущество

Gratis (гра́тис) безвозмездно
to transfer ~ (ту тра́нсфэр ~)
передавать безвозмездно
Gratuitous (грату́итос) бесплатный
Groceries (гро́сэриз) бакалейные
товары
Grosh (грош) грош {former Russian
monetary unit of small value}
Gross (грос) брутто, валовой, масса
actual ~ weight (а́кчуал ~ уэ́йт)
фактический вес брутто
in ~ (ин ~) оптом
~ **for net** (~ фор нэт) брутто за
нетто
~ **freight** (~ фрэйт) брутто фрахт
~ **mass** (~ мас) масса брутто
~ **operating income** (~ о́пэрэйтинг
и́нком) валовая от продажи
выручка
~ **premium** (~ при́миум) брутто-
ставка
~ **register tonnage** (~ рэ́джистэр
то́ннадж) брутто регистровый
тоннаж
~ **ton** (~ тон) брутто тонна
~ **tonnage** (~ то́ннадж) брутто
тоннаж
~ **weight** (~ уэ́йт) вес брутто
Ground (гро́унд) земля, почва ~s
обоснование, основание, повод
legal ~s (ли́гал ~с) юридическое
обоснование
statutory ~s (ста́тютори ~с)
законное основание
without any ~s (уиθо́ут а́ни ~с)
без всяких оснований
~s **for a decision** (~с фор а
диси́жн) обоснование решения
~s **for divorce** (~с фор диво́рс)
решающий повод к разводу
~ **tenant** (~ тэ́нант)
землепользователь
Groundless (гро́ундлэс)
несостоятельный
Groundlessness (гро́ундлэснэс)
несостоятельность
Growth (гроθ) прирост, рост
explosive population ~
(эксплóсив попюлэ́йшн ~) бурный
рост численности населения
population ~ (попюлэ́йшн ~) рост
населения
significant ~ (сигни́фикант ~)
значительный рост
~ **in employment** (~ ин
эмплóймэнт) рост занятости

Guarantee (гяранти́) гарантия,
обеспечение, подтверждение, порука,
поручительство
additional ~ (адди́шнал ~)
добавочная гарантия
bank ~ (банк ~) банковская
гарантия
collective ~ (колле́ктив ~)
круговая порука
conditional ~ (конди́шнал ~)
условная гарантия
contractual ~s (контра́кчуал ~с)
договорные гарантии
credit ~ (крэ́дит ~) гарантия
кредита
export ~ (э́кспорт ~) вывозная
гарантия
export credit ~ (э́кспорт крэ́дит
~) гарантия экспортных кредитов
export risk ~ (э́кспорт риск ~)
гарантия экспортного риска
extension of the term of the ~
(экстэ́ншн оф θи тэрм оф θи ~)
продление срока гарантии
general ~ (дже́нэрал ~) общая
гарантия
granting of a ~ (гра́нтинг оф а
~) предоставление гарантии
insurance ~ (иншю́ранс ~)
страховая гарантия
irrevocable ~ (иррэ́вокабл ~)
безотзывная гарантия
issuance of a ~ (и́шюанс оф а ~)
выдача гарантии
legal ~s (ли́гал ~с) правовые
гарантии
loan against a ~ (лон аге́нст а
~) ссуда под гарантию
long-term ~ (лонг-тэрм ~)
долгосрочная гарантия
money-back ~ (мо́ни-бак ~)
гарантия возврата платы за товар
oral ~ (о́рал ~) устная гарантия
payment ~ (пэ́ймэнт ~) гарантия
оплаты
performance ~ (пэрфо́рманс ~)
гарантия основных показателей
production ~ (прода́кшн ~)
производственная гарантия
property ~ (про́пэрти ~)
имущественная гарантия
quality ~ (куа́лити ~) гарантия
качества
reliable ~ (рила́йабл ~) надёжная
гарантия
revocable ~ (рэ́вокабл ~)
отзывная гарантия

specific ~ (спэси́фик ~)
специальная гарантия
to ~ (ту ~) гарантировать
возмещение, давать гарантию,
ручаться
to ~ against loss (ту ~ агэ́нст
лос) гарантировать возмещение
убытков
to annul a ~ (ту анну́л а ~)
аннулировать гарантию
to be covered by ~ (ту би ко́вэрд
бай ~) входить в гарантию
to conform with the ~ provisions
(ту конфо́рм уиθ θи ~ прови́жнз)
соответствовать условиям
гарантии
to extend the term of the ~ (ту
экстэ́нд θи тэрм оф θи ~)
продлевать срок гарантии
to have a ~ (ту хэв а ~) иметь
гарантию
to issue a ~ (ту и́шю а ~)
оформлять гарантию
to obtain a ~ (ту обтэ́йн а ~)
получать гарантию
unconditional ~ (анконди́шнал ~)
безусловная гарантия
underwriter's ~ (у́ндэррайтэрз ~)
гарантия страховщика
vendor's ~ (вэ́ндорз ~) гарантия
продавца
written ~ (ри́ттэн ~) письменная
гарантия
~ against losses (~ агэ́нст
ло́ссэз) гарантия от убытков
~ applied to (~ аппла́йд ту)
гарантия, распространяющая на
~ clause (~ клауз) пункт
договора о гарантиях
~ expiration date (~ экспирэ́йшн
дэйт) дата окончания срока
гарантии
~ of creditworthiness (~ оф
крэ́дитуорθинэс) гарантия
кредитоспособности
~ period (~ пи́риод) срок
гарантии
~ terms (~ тэрмз) условия
гарантии
~ valid until... (~ ва́лид
унти́л...) гарантия
действительная до...
Guaranteed (гярянти́д) гарантийный,
гарантированный, гарантируемый
Guarantor (гяранто́р) ведомство-
гарант, гарант, лицо, дающее
гарантию, поручитель

as ~ (аз ~) в качестве гарантии
primary ~ (пра́ймари ~) главный
поручитель
~ for debts (~ фор дэтс)
поручитель по долгам
~ of a bill (~ оф а бил) гарант
по векселю
Guard (гард) охрана
border ~ (бо́рдэр ~) пограничная
охрана, пограничник
coast ~ (кост ~) береговая
охрана
national ~ (на́шэнал ~) народное
ополчение
Guardian (га́рдиан) опекун,
попечитель
Guardianship (га́рдианшип) опека,
опекунство, попечительство
Guidance (га́йданс) руководство
Guide (гайд) справочный {adj.}
Guidebook (га́йдбук) справочник
Guideline (га́йдлайн) установка ~s
директива, руководящие документы,
руководящие указания, установки
administrative ~s
(адми́нистрэйтив ~с)
административная директива
trade policy ~ (трэйд по́лиси ~)
внешнеторговые директивы
Guilty (ги́лти) виноватый, повинный
not ~ (нот ~) невиновный
Gulf (гулф) залив
Gun (ган) пистолет, пушка, ружьё
Gunfire (га́нфайр) орудийный огонь
exchange of ~ (эксчэ́йндж оф ~)
перестрелка

Н

Habit (ха́бит) обыкновение
Hail (хэйл) окрик
Hall (хал) зал
conference ~ (ко́нфэрэнс ~)
конференц-зал
town ~ (то́ун ~) ратуша {in
Belarus, Poland}
union ~ (ю́нион ~) профсоюзная
палата
Halt (халт) приостановка
to ~ (ту ~) приостановить
Hand (ханд) рука ~s рабочие руки
{figuratively, workers}
cash on ~ (каш он ~) деньги в
кассе

Handbill (хэ́ндбилл) листовка ~s листовки
   publicly distributed ~s (па́бликли дистри́бютэд ~с) листовки, раздаваемые на улице
Handbook (хэ́ндбук) указатель
Handicraft (хэ́ндикрафт) кустарный
Handing in (хэ́ндинг ин) вручение
Handle (хандл) ручка
   to ~ (ту ~) перемещать, упаковывать
   "~ with care" (~ уиθ кэйр) "Ломкое"
Handling (хэ́ндлинг) обращение, перемещение
   rough ~ (руф ~) грубое обращение
Hangar (хэ́нгар) ангар
Hanged (хангд) повешенный {person}
Hanging (хэ́нгинг) повешение
Hangman (хэ́нгман) палач
Harbor (ха́рбор) гавань
   to put in at a ~ (ту пут ин ат а ~) входить в гавань
Hard (хард) трудный
Harm (харм) вреда
   bodily ~ (бо́дили ~) телесное повреждение
   irreparable ~ (иррэ́парабл ~) непоправимый ущерб
   serious bodily ~ (си́риос бо́дили ~) тяжкое телесное повреждение
   to ~ (ту ~) повреждать
   to inflict ~ (ту инфли́кт ~) причинять убытки
Harvest (ха́рвэст) урожай
   size of the ~ (сайз оф θи ~) размер урожая
   to ~ (ту ~) снимать [**perfective:** снять], убирать урожай
Harvesting (ха́рвэстинг) уборка урожая
   ~ **expenses** (~ экспэ́нсэз) расходы, связанные с уборкой урожая
Hatch (хатч) люк {vessel}, люковый {adj.}
   cargo ~ (ка́рго ~) грузовой люк
   main ~ (мэйн ~) главный люк
   to batten the ~ (ту баттэ́н θи ~) задраивать люк
   to open the ~ **for loading** (ту о́пэн θи ~ фор ло́динг) открывать люк перед разгрузкой
   to unload a ~ (ту анло́д а ~) разгружать люк
   ~ **cover** (~ ко́вэр) крышка люка

   ~ **cover of the hold** (~ ко́вэр оф θи холд) крышка трюма
Haul (хаул) транзит
   back ~ (бак ~) обратный транзит
   to ~ (ту ~) перевозить, транспортировать
Haulage (ха́уладж) транспортировка
   freight ~ (фрэйт ~) грузовая перевозка
   marine ~ (мари́н ~) буксировка
Haunt (ха́унт) притон
Haven (хэ́йвэн) гавань
   tax ~ (такс ~) налоговая гавань, налоговое убежище
Hazard (ха́зард) риск
Head (хэд) глава, начальник {position}, голова {of body} ~s аверс {of coin}
   ~ **clerk** (~ клэрк) заведующий канцелярией
   ~ **of livestock** {number} (~ оф ла́йвсток) поголовье скота
   ~ **of the marketing department** (~ оф θи ма́ркэтинг дипа́ртмэнт) управляющий отделом маркетинга
Hearing (хи́ринг) процесс, разбор дела, слушание дела, суд, судебное заседание
   administrative ~ (адми́нистрэйтив ~) административный процесс
   civil ~ (си́вил ~) гражданское судебное заседание
   closed judicial ~ (клозд джюди́шл ~) закрытое судебное заседание
   evidentiary ~ (эвидэ́ншиэри ~) расследование доказательства
   open ~ (о́пэн ~) открытый процесс
   open public ~ (о́пэн па́блик ~) открытое судебное заседание
   public ~ (па́блик ~) публичное заседание
   ~ **on a case** (~ он а кэйс) слушание дела
Hearth (харθ) очаг
   ~ **and home** (~ энд хом) домашний очаг
Heavily-loaded (хэ́вили-ло́дэд) с большим грузом
Heavy (хэ́ви) тяжёлый
   ~ **weight** (~ уэ́йт) тяжеловесный
Heavy-duty (хэ́ви-дю́ти) большая мощность, мощный
Hedge (хэдж) хеджирование
   buying ~ (ба́йинг ~) хеджирование покупкой
   selling ~ (сэ́ллинг ~) хеджирование продажей

Hedging (хэ́джинг) хеджирование
Help (хэлп) помощь, содействие
  gratuitous ~ (грату́итос ~)
безвозмездная помощь
  to ~ (ту ~) содействовать
Hemp (хэмп) пеньковая верёвка
Hereditary (хэрэ́дитари)
потомственный
Hermetically (хэрмэ́тикалли)
герметичный {sealed}
Hide (хайд) кожа, шкура
  to ~ (ту ~) скрывать
Hierarchy (ха́йэрарки) иерархия
  to establish a ~ (ту эста́блиш а
~) установить иерархию
High (хай) высокий
  ~ **price allowance** (~ прайс
аллóуанс) надбавка на
дороговизну
  ~ **prices** (~ пра́йсэз) дороговизна
  ~ **quality** (~ куа́лити)
высококачественный
  ~ **technology** (~ тэкно́лоджи)
высокотехнологический
  ~ **tide** (~ тайд) высокая вода
High-end (хай-энд) модный
High-grade (хай-грэйд)
высокосортный
High-priced (хай-прайсд)
дорогостоящий
Higher-ranking (ха́йэр-ра́нкинг)
старший по званию
Highly (ха́йли) высоко
  ~ **profitable** (~ про́фитабл)
высокорентабельный
  ~ **qualified** (~ куа́лифайд)
высококвалифицированный
  ~ **remunerative** (~ римю́нэратив)
высокодоходный
  ~ **specialized** (~ спэ́шлайзд)
высокоспециализированный
Hijack, to ~ (ха́йджак, ту ~)
похищать
Hijacking (ха́йджакинг) похищение
Hinder, to ~ (хи́ндэр, ту ~)
препятствовать
Hindrance (хи́ндранс) помеха,
препятствие
Hire (хайр) наём, прокат
  for ~ (фор ~) напрокат
  to ~ (ту ~) брать внаём, внаймы,
брать напрокат, нанимать
  to ~ **for contracting work** (ту ~
фор ко́нтрактинг уо́рк) подрядить
  to ~ **out** (ту ~ о́ут) сдавать
напрокат, сдавать внаём, внаймы

  work for ~ (уо́рк фор ~) работа
по найму
Hired (хайрд) прокатный
  ~ **transportation** (~
транспорте́йшн) перевозки по
найму
Hiring (ха́йринг) хайринг
  ~ **of personnel** (~ оф пэрсонне́л)
наём персонала
  ~ **of work force** (~ оф уо́рк форс)
наём рабочей силы
  ~ **out** (~ о́ут) сдача, сдача в
наём
  ~ **to a job** (~ ту а джоб) приём
на работу
History (хи́стори) история
Hoarding (хо́рдинг) чрезмерное
накопление
Hoist (хойст) подъёмный механизм
Hoisting (хо́йстинг) грузоподъёмный
Hold (холд) трюм {of a vessel},
трюмный {adj.}
  aft ~ (афт ~) задний трюм
  ample ~ (ампл ~) вместительный
трюм
  capacity of the ~ (капа́сити оф
θи ~) вместимость трюма
  main ~ (мэйн ~) главный трюм
  to ~ (ту ~) держать, занимать
[perfective: занять], обладать
  to ~ **a charter-party** (ту ~ а
ча́ртэр-па́рти) быть владельцем
чартер-партии
  to trim to ~ (ту трим ту ~)
размещать груз в трюме
  trimming of the ~ (три́мминг оф
θи ~) размещение груза в трюме
Holder (хо́лдэр) векселедержатель
{of a bill}, владелец, держатель,
обладатель
  account ~ (акко́унт ~) владелец
банковского счёта, держатель
счёта
  bona fide ~ (бо́на фа́йди ~)
добросовестный держатель
  bond ~ (бонд ~) держатель
облигаций
  certificate ~ (сэрти́фикэт ~)
лицо, имеющее сертификат
  copyright ~ (ко́пирайт ~)
обладатель авторского права
  debenture ~ (дэбэ́нтчур ~)
владелец долгового
обязательства, держатель
облигаций
  fund ~ (фунд ~) владелец
фондовых ценностей

patent ~ (па́тэнт ~) владелец патента

patent ~ and lessor (па́тэнт ~ энд лэссо́р) владелец патентов, продающий лицензии на них

policy ~ (по́лиси ~) держатель страхового полиса

previous ~ (при́виос ~) предыдущий держатель

registered trademark ~ (рэ́джистэрд трэ́йдмарк ~) владелец регистрации товарного знака

subsequent ~ (са́бсикуэнт ~) последующий владелец, последующий держатель

trademark ~ (трэ́йдмарк ~) владелец товарного знака

~ in due course (~ ин ду корс) законной владелец, законный держатель

~ in good faith (~ ин гуд фэйθ) добросовестный владелец

~ of a bill {note} (~ оф а билл {нот}) держатель векселя

~ of a bill of lading (~ оф а билл оф лэ́йдинг) держатель коносамента

~ of a draft {bill of exchange} (~ оф а драфт {билл оф эксчэ́йндж}) держатель тратты

~ of a letter of credit (~ оф а лэ́ттэр оф крэ́дит) держатель аккредитива

~ of a license (~ оф а ла́йсэнз) владелец лицензии, держатель лицензии

~ of a pledge (~ оф а плэдж) держатель залога

~ of documents (~ оф до́кюмэнтс) держатель документов

~ of securities (~ оф сэкю́ритиз) владелец ценных бумаг

Holding (хо́лдинг) владение **~s** авуары

bank ~s (банк ~с) банковские авуары

dollar ~s (до́ллар ~с) долларовая наличность

foreign exchange ~s (фо́рэн эксчэ́йндж ~с) инвалютная наличность

patent ~s (па́тэнт ~с) патентный фонд

~ back (~ бак) выдержка {e.g. goods from market during glut}

Holiday (хо́лидэй) праздничный день

Homeland (хо́мланд) отечество, родина

Honest (о́нэст) честный

Honorable (о́норабл) почётный

Honorarium (онора́риум) гонорар

Honorary (о́норари) почётный

Hook (хук) крюк

load ~ (лод ~) грузовой крюк

Hooky (ху́ки) прогул

Horde (хорд) орда

Golden ~ (го́лдэн ~) золотая орда

Horizontal (горизо́нтал) горизонтальный

Horsepower (хо́рспо́уэр) лошадиная сила

~ per unit of weight (~ пэр ю́нит оф уэ́йт) мощность на единицу веса

Hostage (хо́стадж) заложник

~ taking (~ тэ́йкинг) заложничество

Hour (о́ур) час

actual ~s worked (а́кчуал ~с уо́ркд) фактически проработанные часы

after banking ~s (а́фтэр ба́нкинг ~с) вне рабочих часов банка

cumulative ~s (кю́мюлатив ~с) накопившиеся часы

idle ~s (айдл ~с) часы простоя

non-working ~s (нон-уо́ркинг ~с) нерабочие часы

off ~s (офф ~с) свободные часы

office ~s (о́ффис ~с) присутственные часы, рабочее время, служебные часы

overtime ~s (о́вэртайм ~с) сверхурочные часы

worked ~s (уо́ркд ~с) проработанные часы

working ~s of the bank (уо́ркинг ~с оф θи банк) рабочие часы банка

~s of operation (~с оф опэрэ́йшн) рабочее время

~s worked (~с уо́ркд) наработанные часы

House (хаус) дом, палата, фирма

brokerage ~ (бро́кэрадж ~) агентская фирма

clearing ~ (кли́ринг ~) расчётна палата

mail order ~ (мэйл о́рдэр ~) посылочная фирма

packing ~ (па́кинг ~) упаковочна фирма

publishing ~ (па́блишинг ~) издательство

trading ~ (трэ́йдинг ~) торговый дом, торговая фирма

~ of Deputies (~ оф дэ́пютиз) палата депутатов

~ of Lords (~ оф лордз) палата лордов

Housewares (ха́усуэрз) предметы обычной домашней обстановки и обихода

Housing (хо́узинг) жилое помещение

basic ~ (бэ́йсик ~) основное жилое помещение

furnished ~ (фу́рнишд ~) меблированное помещение

private ~ (пра́йват ~) частное помещение

provision of ~ (прови́жн оф ~) обеспечение жильём

unfurnished ~ (анфу́рнишд ~) помещение без мебели

Humid (хю́мид) влажный

Humidity (хюми́дити) влажность

maximum ~ (ма́ксимум ~) максимальная влажность

relative ~ (рэ́латив ~) относительная влажность

~ control (~ контро́л) контроль за влажностью

Hunting (ха́нтинг) охота

Hush-hush (хаш-хаш) засекреченный

Hypothecation (хайпоθэкэ́йшн) залог

I

Ice (айс) лёд

Ice-free (а́йс-фри́) незамерзающий

Identification (айдэнтификэ́йшн) идентификация, опознание, признак

false ~ (фалс ~) ложное опознание

for purposes of ~ (фор пу́рпосэз оф ~) с целью удостоверения личности

legal ~ (ли́гал ~) судебная идентификация

~ card (~ кард) удостоверение личности

Identity (айдэ́нтити) идентичность

Identify, to ~ (айдэнтифай, ту ~) опознать, отождествлять

Idle (айдл) неиспользованный, неиспользуемый

Illegal (илли́гал) незаконный, нелегальный, противозаконный, противоправный

Illegality (иллига́лити) незаконность, противозаконность

Illumination (иллюминэ́йшн) освещение

Image (и́мадж) имидж

Imbalance (имба́ланс) дисбаланс, нарушение равновесия, несбалансированность

foreign trade ~ (фо́рэн трэйд ~) дисбаланс во внешней торговле

Imbalanced (имба́лансд) несбалансированный

Imitation (имитэ́йшн) подражание

Immediate (имми́диат) немедленный, срочный

Immemorial (иммэмо́риал) исконный

Immigrant (и́ммигрант) иммигрант

Immigrate, to ~ (и́ммигрэйт, ту ~) иммигрировать

Immigration (иммигрэ́йшн) иммиграция

Immoveable (имму́вабл) недвижимый

Immunity (имми́нити) иммунитет, льгота

absolute ~ (абсолю́т ~) абсолютный иммунитет

consular ~ (ко́нсюлар ~) консульский иммунитет

diplomatic ~ (диплома́тик ~) дипломатический иммунитет

financial ~ (файна́ншл ~) финансовый иммунитет

fiscal ~ (фи́скал ~) фискальный иммунитет

functional ~ (фу́нкшнал ~) функциональный иммунитет

jurisdictional ~ (джюрисди́кшнал ~) юрисдикционный иммунитет

legal ~ (ли́гал ~) судебный иммунитет

partial ~ from punishment (паршл ~ фром пу́нишмэнт) частичное освобождение от наказания

parliamentary ~ (парламэ́нтари ~) парламентский иммунитет

personal ~ (пэ́рсонал ~) личный иммунитет

sovereign ~ (со́вэрн ~) иммунитет суверена

tax ~ (такс ~) налоговый иммунитет

~ from arrest (~ фром аррэ́ст) иммунитет от наложения ареста

~ **from confiscation** (~ фром конфискэйшн) иммунитет от конфискаций

~ **from requisitioning** (~ фром рэкуизишнинг) иммунитет от реквизиций

~ **from search** (~ фром сэрч) иммунитет от обыска

~ **from suit** (~ фром сут) иммунитет от исков

Impartial (импа́ршл) объективный

Imparting (импа́ртинг) придание

Impede, to ~ (импи́д, ту ~) препятствовать

Impediment (импэ́димэнт) препятствие

Imperative (импэ́ратив) императивный

Imperfection (импэрфэ́кшн) неполнота

Imperialism (импи́риализм) империализм

Imperialist (импи́риалист) империалист, империалистический {adj.}

Implement (и́мплэмэнт) инструмент, инвентарь, прибор

agricultural ~s (агрику́лчурал ~с) сельскохозяйственный инвентарь

to ~ (ту ~) воплощать, выполнять, осуществлять [perfective: осуществить], реализовывать

Implementation (имплэмэнтэ́йшн) введение, внедрение, выполнение, осуществление, реализация

commercial ~ (комме́ршл ~) промышленное внедрение

efficient ~ (эффи́шэнт ~) эффективное выполнение

period for ~ (пи́риод фор ~) период внедрения

prompt ~ (промпт ~) немедленное осуществление

~ **efforts** (~ э́ффортс) усилия по внедрению

~ **of an agreement** (~ оф ан агри́мэнт) выполнение соглашения

~ **of a contract** (~ оф а ко́нтракт) выполнение контракта

~ **of a plan** (~ оф а план) выполнение плана

Implication (импликэ́йшн) последствие

legal ~s (ли́гал ~с) правовые последствия

Implicit (импли́сит) неявный

Implied (импла́йд) подразумеваемый

Import (и́мпорт) ввозной {adj.}, импорт

easing of ~ **quotas** (и́зинг оф ~ куо́таз) облегчение ввоза

exclusive ~ (эксклю́сив ~) исключительный импортёр

indirect ~ (индайрэ́кт ~) косвенный импорт

invisible ~ (инви́зибл ~) невидимый импорт

to ~ (ту импо́рт) ввозить, импортировать {меняется ударинее}

to obtain ~ **clearance** (ту обтэ́йн ~ кли́ранс) оформлять ввоз товара в порт

valuation of ~s (валюэ́йшн оф ~с) стоимость ввоза

~s **and exports** (~с энд э́кспортс) ввоз и вывоз

~ **items** (~ а́йтэмс) предметы ввоза

~ **permit into port** (~ пэ́рмит и́нту порт) разрешение на ввоз в порт

~ **surplus** (~ су́рплус) превышение ввоза над вывозом

Importation (импортэ́йшн) ввоз

additional ~ (адди́шнал ~) дополнительный ввоз

articles of ~ (а́ртиклз оф ~) статьи ввоза

conditional duty-free ~ (конди́шнал дю́ти-фри ~) условно беспошлинный ввоз

duty-free ~ (дю́ти-фри ~) беспошлинный ввоз

to ban ~ (ту бан ~) запрещать ввоз

total ~ (то́тал ~) общий ввоз

Importer (и́мпортэр) импортёр

Importune, to ~ (импорту́н, ту ~) домогаться

Importunity (импорту́нити) домогательство

Impose, to ~ (импо́з, ту ~) взимать, накладывать, налагать, облагать

to ~ **restrictions** (ту ~ ристри́кшнз) накладывать ограничения

Imposition (импози́шн) введение, обложение, наложение

~ **of a duty** (~ оф а дю́ти) введение пошлины

~ **of duties** (~ оф дю́тиз) взыскание пошлин

~ **of fees** (~ оф физ) взимание сборов
~ **of a fine** (~ оф а файн) взыскание пени, наложение штрафа
~ **of import duties** (~ оф ймпорт дютиз) введение импортной пошлины
~ **of import quotas** (~ оф ймпорт куотас) контингентирование ввоза
~ **of quotas** (~ оф куотас) введение квот
~ **of sentencing** (~ оф сэнтэнсинг) исполнение приговора
~ **of a tax** (~ оф а такс) введение налога

Impossibility (импоссибйлити) невозможность, невыполнимость {of performance}

Impossible (импосибл) невозможный, невыполнимый

Imposting (импостинг) взимание
~ **of duties** (~ оф дютиз) взимание пошлин

Impracticable (импрактикабл) невыполнимый, неподходящий

Impress (ймпрэс) отпечаток, оттиск, штемпель
to ~ (ту ~) произвести хорошее впечатление {create an opinion}, штемпелевать {stamp}
~ **of a seal** {of a company} (~ оф а сил {оф а компани}) оттиск печати

Impression (импрэшн) впечатление

Imprint (ймпринт) отпечаток

Imprison, to ~ (импризон, ту ~) заключать

Imprisonment (импризонмэнт) заключение
false ~ (фалс ~) незаконное заключение, необоснованное заточение, посягательство на свободу
life ~ (лайф ~) пожизненное заключение

Improve, to ~ (импрув, ту ~) рационализировать, улучшать
to tend to ~ (ту тэнд ту ~) иметь тенденцию к улучшению

Improvement (импрувмэнт) оздоровление, повышение, подъём, улучшение, усовершенствование
design ~ (дизайн ~) улучшение конструкции
numerous ~s (нумэрос ~с) многочисленные усовершенствования

patent on an ~ (патэнт он ан ~) патент на усовершенствование
patentable ~ (патэнтабл ~) патентоспособное усовершенствование
patented ~ (патэнтэд ~) запатентованное усовершенствование
potential ~ (потэншл ~) возможное усовершенствование, потенциальное улучшение
quality ~ (куалити ~) улучшение качества
rapid ~s (рапид ~с) быстрые улучшения
technical ~ (тэкникал ~) техническое усовершенствование
technological ~ (тэкнолоджикал ~) технологическое усовершенствование
to bring about an ~ (ту бринг абоут ан ~) приводить к улучшению
to demonstrate an ~ (ту дэмонстрэйт ан ~) показывать усовершенствование
to develop an ~ (ту дивэлоп ан ~) разработать усовершенствование
to incorporate ~s (ту инкорпорэйт ~с) внедрять усовершенствование
to make an ~ (ту мэйк ан ~) сделать усовершенствование
to seek ~s (ту сик ~с) добиваться улучшения
~ **of business conditions** (~ оф бйзнэс кондйшнс) улучшение деловой конъюнктуры
~ **of business** (~ оф бйзнэс) улучшение деловой активности
~ **of containerization** (~ оф контэйнэризэйшн) усовершенствования контейнерной службы
~ **of schedule** (~ оф скэджюл) улучшение графика
~ **of working conditions** (~ оф уоркинг кондйшнс) улучшение условий труда

Impudence (ймпюдэнс) наглость
Impudent (ймпюдэнт) наглый
Impure (импюр) нечистый
Inability (инабйлити) неспособность
Inaccessible (инаксэссибл) недоступный
Inactive (инактив) неактивный

Inadequacy (инэ́дэкуэси) недостаточность, отклонение
Inadequate (инэ́дэкуэт) недостаточный, неудовлетворительный
    ~ demand (~ димэ́нд) недостаточность спроса
    ~ maintenance and repair (~ мэ́йнтэнанс энд рипэ́йр) недостаточность обслуживания и ремонта
Inadmissible (инадми́ссибл) неприемлемый
Inalienable (инэ́йлиэнабл) неотъемлемый
Inapplicable (инаппли́кабл) неподходящий
Incalculable (инка́лкюлабл) неисчислимый
Incapacitated (инкапа́ситэйтэд) нетрудоспособный
Incapacity (инкапа́сити) неспособность,
Incarcerate, to ~ (инка́рсэрэйт, ту ~) заключать в тюрьму
Incarceration (инкарсэрэ́йшн) тюремное заключение
    civil ~ (си́вил ~) гражданский плен
    ~ in prison (~ ин при́зон) заключение в тюрьме
Incendiary (инсэ́ндиари) поджигатель
Incentive (инсэ́нтив) заинтересованность, побудительный фактор, стимул
    additional ~ (адди́шнал ~) стимулирующая надбавка
Incident (и́нсидэнт) инцидент, происшествие
    diplomatic ~ (дипломэ́тик ~) дипломатический инцидент
    frontier ~ (фронти́р ~) пограничный инцидент
Incidental (инсидэ́нтал) случайный
Income (и́нком) доход
    accrued ~ (аккру́д ~) начисленный доход
    accumulated ~ (акки́мюлэйтэд ~) накопленный доход
    actual ~ (а́кчуал ~) фактический доход
    after tax ~ (а́фтэр такс ~) доход, остающийся после уплаты налогов доход
    annual ~ (а́ннюал ~) годовой доход
    average ~ (а́вэрэдж ~) средний доход

    average annual ~ (а́вэрэдж а́ннюал ~) среднегодовой доход
    cash ~ (каш ~) денежный доход
    concealment of ~ (конси́лмэнт оф ~) сокрытие доходов
    corporate ~ tax (ко́рпорат ~ такс) налог с доходов акционерных компаний
    current ~ (ку́ррэнт ~) текущий доход
    deferred ~ (дифэ́рд ~) доход будущих лет
    distribution of ~ (дистрибю́шн оф ~) распределение доходов
    earned ~ (эрнд ~) трудовой доход
    expected ~ (экспэ́ктэд ~) ожидаемый доход
    fixed ~ (фиксд ~) постоянный доход, твёрдый доход
    gross ~ (грос ~) валовой доход, общий размер доходов
    gross national ~ (грос на́шэнал ~) валовой национальный доход
    growth of ~ (гроθ оф ~) рост дохода
    increment of national ~ (и́нкрэмэнт оф на́шэнал ~) прирост национального дохода
    interest ~ (и́нтэрэст ~) процентный доход
    invisible {trade} ~ (инви́зибл {трэйд} ~) доход от невидимых статей экспорта и импорта
    large ~ (лардж ~) высокий доход
    level of ~ (лэ́вэл оф ~) размер дохода
    marginal ~ (ма́рджинал ~) маржинальный доход
    national ~ (на́шэнал ~) национальный доход
    net ~ (нэт ~) чистый доход
    operating ~ (о́пэрэйтинг ~) доход от операций
    per capita ~ (пэр ка́пита ~) доход на душу населения
    primary ~ (пра́ймари ~) первичный доход
    regular ~ (рэ́гюлар ~) регулярный доход
    rental ~ (рэ́нтал ~) рентный доход
    sources of ~ (со́рсэз оф ~) источники дохода
    supplementary ~ (сапплэмэ́нтари ~) дополнительный доход
    taxable ~ (та́ксабл ~) облагаемый налогами доход

to derive an ~ (ту дира́йв ан ~) извлекать доход
to ensure an ~ (ту эншу́р ан ~) обеспечивать доход
to guarantee an ~ (ту гяранти́ ан ~) гарантировать доход
total ~ (то́тал ~) общая сумма дохода
trade ~ (трэйд ~) торговый доход
trading ~ (трэ́йдинг ~) доход от коммерческой деятельности
understatement of ~ (у́ндэрстэйтмэнт оф ~) занижение доходов
unearned ~ (анэ́рнд ~) непроизводственный доход, нетрудовой доход
~ adjustment (~ аджа́стмэнт) регулирование доходов
~ deduction (~ диду́кшн) вычет из облагаемого дохода
~ level (~ лэ́вэл) уровень дохода
~ of an enterprise (~ оф ан энтэрпра́йз) доход предприятия
Incoming (и́нкоминг) поступающий
~ orders (~ о́рдэрс) поступление заказов
Incompetent (инко́мпэтэнт) невменяемый {insanity, minority, etc.}
Incomplete (инкомпли́т) незавершённый, некомплектный, неполный
Incompletely (инкомпли́тли) неполностью
Incompleteness (инкомпли́тнэс) неполнота
Inconvenience (инконви́ниэнс) неудобство
Inconvenient (инконви́ниэнт) неудобный
Inconvertibility (инконвэртиби́лити) необратимость
Inconvertible (инконвэ́ртибл) неконвертируемый, необратимый
Incorporate, to (инко́рпорэйт, ту) включать в состав, объединяться
Increase (инкри́с) наращивание, повышение, приплод, приращение, прирост, рост, увеличение
artificial ~ (артифи́шл ~) искуственное повышение
artificial ~ in the exchange rate (артифи́шл ~ ин θи эксчэ́йндж рэйт) искуственное повышение курса

inflationary ~ (инфлэ́йшнари ~) инфляционное повышение
limited ~ (ли́митэд ~) ограниченное увеличение
one-time ~ (уа́н-тайм ~) разовое увеличение
overall ~ (овэра́л ~) общее увеличение
overall percentage ~ (овэра́л пэрсэ́нтадж ~) общее увеличение в процентном выражении
pension ~ (пэншн ~) повышение размера пенсии
permitted ~ (пэрми́ттэд ~) допустимое увеличение
price ~ (прайс ~) повышение цен
price ~s (прайс ~с) вздорожание
probable ~ (про́бабл ~) вероятное увеличение
rate ~ (рэйт ~) повышение ставки
sharp ~ (шарп ~) резкое увеличение
significant ~ (сигни́фикант ~) значительное увеличение
to ~ (ту ~) набавлять, наращивать, повышать, увеличивать
to ~ in price (ту ~ ин прайс) вздорожать, дорожать
to absorb a price ~ (ту абсо́рб а прайс ~) покрыть увеличение цены
to project an ~ (ту продже́кт ан ~) планировать увеличение
to speculate on price ~s (ту спэ́кюлэйт он прайс ~с) играть на повышение
wage ~ (уэ́йдж ~) рост заработной платы
~ in the bank rate (~ ин θи банк рэйт) повышение ставки банковского учёта
~ in buying power (~ ин ба́йинг по́уэр) повышение покупательной силы
~ in capital investments (~ ин ка́питал инвэ́стмэнтс) увеличение капиталовложений
~ in consumer demand (~ ин консу́мэр дима́нд) рост потребительского спроса
~ in convertible currency receipts (~ ин конвэ́ртибл ку́ррэнси риси́тс) увеличение поступлений валюты
~ in customs duty (~ ин ка́стомз дю́ти) повышение таможенных пошлин

~ **in deliveries** (~ ин дэлúвэриз)
увеличение поставок
~ **in demand** (~ ин димáнд)
повышение спроса, рост спроса
~ **in duties** (~ ин дьютиз)
повышение пошлин
~ **in equipment productivity** (~
ин икуúпмэнт продуктúвити)
увеличение производительности
оборудования
~ **in imports** (~ ин úмпортс)
увеличение импорта
~ **in income** (~ ин úнком)
увеличение доходов
~ **in incomes** (~ ин úнкомс)
повышение доходов
~ **in labor productivity** (~ ин
лэйбор продуктúвити) рост
производительности труда,
увеличение производительности
труда
~ **in manpower** (~ ин мáнпоуэр)
увеличение численного состава
~ **in production** (~ ин продáкшн)
рост производства
~ **in production capacity** (~ ин
продáкшн капáсити) наращивание
производственных мощностей
~ **in productivity** (~ ин
продуктúвити) повышение
производительности, рост
производительности, увеличение
производительности
~ **in profitability** (~ ин
профитабúлити) повышение
рентабельности
~ **in purchasing power** (~ ин
пúрчасинг пóуэр) рост
покупательной способности
~ **in the rate of production** (~
ин θи рэйт оф продúкшн)
наращивание темпа производства
~ **in risk** (~ ин риск) повышение
риска
~ **in sales** (~ ин сэйлз)
увеличение сбыта
~ **in share of inheritance** (~ ин
шэйр оф инхэ́ританс) приращение
наследственной доли
~ **in tariff** (~ ин тáриф)
повышение тарифа
~ **in taxes** (~ ин тáксэз)
увеличение налогов
~ **in the technical level of
production** (~ ин θи тэ́кникал
лэ́вэл оф продáкшн) улучшение
технического уровня продукции

~ **in trade volume** (~ ин трэйд
вóлюм) увеличение объёма
торговли
~ **in turnover** (~ ин тúрновэр)
рост суммы оборота
~ **of deposits** (~ оф дипóзитс)
увеличение вкладов
~ **of prices over cost** (~ оф
прáйсэз óвэр кост) подъём цен
выше стоимости
~ **to ...** (~ ту ...) увеличение
до ...
Increased (инкрúсд) возросший
~ **bid** (~ бид) увеличение
надбавки к цене {auction}
Increment (úнкрэмэнт) приращение
Incur, to ~ (инкúр, ту ~) нести
[imperfective: носить]
Indebtedness (индэ́тэднэс)
задолженность
current ~ (кúррэнт ~) текущая
задолженность
loan ~ (лон ~) ссудная
задолженность
long-term ~ (лонг-тэрм ~)
долгосрочная задолженность
Indelible (индэ́либл) несмываемый
Indemnify, to ~ (индэ́мнифай, ту ~)
гарантировать от убытков,
застраховать, компенсировать
Indemnity (индэ́мнити) гарантия от
убытков, индемнитет
accrued ~ (аккрúд ~) наросшая
компенсация
insurance ~ (иншю́ранс ~)
страховое возмещение, страховая
компенсация
~ **limit** (~ лúмит) предел
возмещения
Independence (индэпэ́ндэнс)
независимость, самостоятельность
economic ~ (эконóмик ~)
хозяйственная самостоятельность
legal ~ (лúгал ~) юридическая
самостоятельность
legislative ~ (лэ́джислэйтив ~)
законодательная
самостоятельность
Independent (индипэ́ндэнт)
независимый, самостоятельный
Index (úндэкс) индекс, показатель,
указатель
alphabetical ~ (алфабэ́тикал ~)
алфавитный указатель
average annual ~ (áвэрэдж áннюэ
~) средний годовой показатель

business ~ (бизнэс ~) индекс бизнеса

classified ~ (кла́ссифайд ~) систематический указатель

consolidated ~ (консо́лидэйтэд ~) сводный указатель

industrial ~ (инду́стриал ~) производственный показатель

industrial production ~ (инду́стриал прода́кшн ~) индекс промышленного производства

money market ~ (мо́ни ма́ркэт ~) индекс денежного рынка

overall ~ (овэра́л ~) общий индекс

patent ~ (па́тэнт ~) патентный указатель

price ~ (прайс ~) индекс цен, указатель цен

production ~ (прода́кшн ~) индекс продукции

productivity ~ (продукти́вити ~) индекс производительности

quality ~ (куа́лити ~) качественный показатель, показатель качества

quantitative ~ (куа́нтитатив ~) количественный показатель

reliability ~ (рилайаби́лити ~) коэффициент надёжности

retail price ~ (ри́тэйл прайс ~) индекс розничных цен

revised ~ (рива́йзд ~) пересмотренный показатель

to ~ (ту ~) заносить в указатель

to compile an ~ (ту компа́йл ан ~) снабжать указателем

value ~ (ва́лю ~) индекс стоимости

wage ~ (уэ́йдж ~) индекс зарплаты

weighted average ~ (уэ́йтэд а́вэрэдж ~) средневзвешенный показатель

wholesale price ~ (хо́лсэйл прайс ~) индекс оптовых цен

~ base point (~ бэйс пойнт) основной показатель

~ of applicants (~ оф а́ппликантс) указатель заявителей

~ of applications (~ оф аппликэ́йшнс) указатель заявок

~ of a book (~ оф а бук) предметный указатель

~ of gross production (~ оф грос прода́кшн) показатель валовой продукции

~ of licenses (~ оф ла́йсэнзс) указатель лицензий

~ of per capita income (~ оф пэр ка́пита и́нком) индекс доходов населения

~ of population density (~ оф попюлэ́йшн дэ́нсити) показатель плотности населения

~ of profitability (~ оф профитаби́лити) показатель рентабельности

~ of trademarks (~ оф трэ́йдмаркс) указатель товарных знаков

Indicate, to ~ (и́ндикэйт, ту ~) указывать

Indicated (и́ндикэйтэд) указанный

as ~ hereinbelow (аз ~ хиринбило́) как указано ниже

Indication (индикэ́йшн) показание, указание

time ~ (тайм ~) указание срока

with the ~ (уиθ θи ~) с указанием

~ of origin (~ оф о́риджин) указание происхождения

~ of quantity (~ оф куа́нтити) указание количества

~ of requirements (~ оф рикуа́йрмэнтс) указание потребностей

~ of the value (~ оф θи ва́лю) указание стоимости

Indicator (и́ндикатор) показатель

economic ~ (эконо́мик ~) экономический показатель

final ~ (фа́йнал ~) окончательный показатель

financial ~ (файна́ншл ~) финансовый показатель

industrial ~ (инду́стриал ~) производственный показатель

misleading ~ (мисли́динг ~) ложное показание

momentary ~ (мо́мэнтари ~) моментный показатель

preliminary ~ (прили́минэри ~) предварительный показатель

~ of efficiency (~ оф эффи́шэнси) показатель эффективности

~ of industrial activity (~ оф инду́стриал акти́вити) показатель промышленной деятельности

Indictment (инда́йтмэнт) обвинительный акт

Individual (индиви́дюал)
индивидуальный {adj.}, личность
{person}
   ~ good (~ гуд) единица товара
Individuality (индивидюа́лити)
индивидуальность
Indivisible (индиви́зибл) единый,
неделимый
Indorsement (индо́рсмэнт) надпись
   general ~ (джэ́нэрал ~) бланковая
надпись
   to make a general ~ (ту мэйк а
джэ́нэрал ~) делать бланковую
надпись
Indulgence (инду́лджэнс)
снисходительность
Industrialist (инду́стриалист)
промышленник
Industrialization
(индустриализэ́йшн) индустриализация
Industrialize, to ~ (инду́стриалайз,
ту ~) индустриализировать
Industry (и́ндустри) индустрия,
промышленность, хозяйство
   agricultural machinery ~
(агрику́лчурал маши́нэри ~)
сельскохозяйственное
машиностроение
   aircraft ~ (э́йркрафт ~)
авиационная промышленность
   atomic ~ (ато́мик ~) атомная
промышленность
   automobile ~ (аутомоби́л ~)
автомобильная промышленность
   chemical ~ (кэ́микал ~)
химическая промышленность
   construction ~ (констру́кшн ~)
строительная индустрия,
строительная промышленность
   cooperative ~ (коо́пэратив ~)
кооперативная промышленность
   cottage ~ (ко́ттадж ~) кустарное
производство, кустарный
промысел, кустарная
промышленность
   dairy ~ (дэ́йри ~) молочная
промышленность
   defense ~ (дифэ́нс ~) оборонная
промышленность
   electronic ~ (элэктро́ник ~)
электронная промышленность
   export ~ (э́кспорт ~) экспортная
промышленность
   extractive ~ (экстра́ктив ~)
добывающая промышленность
   fish ~ (фиш ~) рыбное хозяйство

   food processing ~ (фуд про́сэсинг
~) пищевая промышленность
   footwear ~ (фу́туэйр ~) обувная
промышленность
   gold mining ~ (голд ма́йнинг ~)
золото-добывающая промышленность
   heavy ~ (хэ́ви ~) тяжёлая
индустрия, тяжёлая
промышленность
   light ~ (лайт ~) легкая
промышленность
   local ~ (ло́кал ~) местная
промышленность
   machine building ~ (маши́н
би́лдинг ~) машиностроительная
промышленность
   major ~ (мэ́йджор ~) крупная
промышленность
   metal processing ~ (мэ́тал
про́сэсинг ~)
металлообрабатывающая
промышленность
   metallurgical ~ (мэталлу́рджикал
~) металлургическая
промышленность
   mining ~ (ма́йнинг ~) горная
промышленность
   mining extraction ~ (ма́йнинг
экстра́кшн ~) горнодобывающая
промышленность
   motion picture ~ (мошн пи́кчур ~)
кинематографическая
промышленность
   munitions ~ (мюни́шнз ~) военная
промышленность
   nationalized ~ (на́шэналайзд ~)
национализированная
промышленность
   natural gas ~ (на́чюрал гас ~)
газовая промышленность
   nuclear energy ~ (ну́клиар
э́нэрджи ~) ядерная
промышленность
   petrochemical ~ (пэтрокэ́микал ~)
петрохимическая промышленность
   petroleum ~ (пэтро́лиум ~)
нефтяной промысел, нефтяная
промышленность
   pharmaceutical ~ (фармасу́тикал
~) фармацевтическая
промышленность
   plastic ~ (пла́стик ~)
пластмассовая промышленность
   power ~ (по́уэр ~) энергетическая
промышленность
   private ~ (пра́йват ~) частная
промышленность

processing ~ (прóсэсинг ~)
обрабатывающая промышленность
road-transport {trucking} ~
(род-трáнспорт {трýккинг} ~)
автохозяйство
shipbuilding ~ (шѝпбилдинг ~)
судостроительная промышленность
state-owned ~ (стэйт-óунд ~)
государственная промышленность
textile ~ (тэ́кстайл ~)
текстильная промышленность
timber ~ (тѝмбэр ~) лесная
промышленность
tourism ~ (тýризм ~)
туристическая индустрия
wood products ~ (уýд прóдуктс ~)
деревообрабатывающая
промышленность
neffective (иниффэ́ктив)
эффективный
nefficiency (иниффѝшэнси)
эффективность
economic ~ (экономик ~)
неэкономичность
nequality (иникуáлити)
равенство, различие
nequitable (инэ́куитабл)
равноправный
nexpensive (инэкспэ́нсив) дешёвый,
дорогой
nexperienced (инэкспѝриэнсд)
лоопытный
nfant (ѝнфант) ребёнок
nfeasible (инфѝзибл) невыполнимый
nfectious (инфэ́кшос) инфекционный
nference (ѝнфэрэнс) довод,
аключение
unfounded ~ (анфóундэд ~)
необоснованное заключение
nferior (инфѝриор) неполноценный
~ **quality** (~ куáлити)
низкокачественный
nflammable (инфлáммабл)
оспламеняющийся
highly ~ (хáйли ~)
легковоспламеняющийся
nflate, to ~ (инфлэ́йт, ту ~)
звинчивать
to ~ **prices** (ту ~ прáйсэз)
взвинчивать цены
to ~ **rates of shares** (ту ~ рэ́йтс
оф шэ́йрз) взвинчивать курсы
акций
nflation (инфлэ́йшн) инфляция
budgetary ~ (бáджэтари ~)
бюджетная инфляция

credit ~ (крэ́дит ~) кредитная
инфляция
illegal price ~ (иллѝгал прайс
~) незаконное повышение цен
monetary ~ (мóнэтари ~) денежная
инфляция
uncontrolled ~ (анконтрóлд ~)
неконтролируемая инфляция
Inflict, to ~ (инфлѝкт, ту ~)
налагать, наносить
Inflicting (инфлѝктинг) нанесение
Inflow (ѝнфлоу) наплыв,
поступление, приток
capital ~ (кáпитал ~) приток
капиталов
~ **of applications** (~ оф
апплике́йшнс) поступление заявок
~ **of capital** (~ оф кáпитал)
прилив капитала
~ **of orders** (~ оф óрдэрс) наплыв
заказов
Infomercial (ѝнфомэршл) рекламное
шоу
Inform, to ~ (инфóрм, ту ~)
информировать, оповещать,
осведомлять, сообщать [**perfective:**
сообщить], уведомлять
Information (информэ́йшн)
информация, сведение, сообщение,
справка
additional ~ (аддѝшнал ~)
дополнительное сведение
patent ~ (пáтэнт ~) патентная
информация
reliable ~ (рилáйабл ~) надёжное
сведение
secret ~ (сѝкрэт ~) секретная
информация
service ~ (сэ́рвис ~) служебная
справка
Informational (информэ́йшнал)
справочный
Informed (инфóрмд) осведомлённый
to be ~ **from first-hand sources**
(ту би ~ фром фэрст-ханд сóрсэз)
осведомляться по первоисточникам
Infringe, to ~ (инфрѝндж, ту ~)
нарушать, посягать
Infringement (инфрѝнджмэнт)
нарушение, посягательство,
правонарушение
cause of ~ (кауз оф ~) причина
нарушения
copyright ~ (кóпирайт ~)
нарушение авторского права
criminal ~ (крѝминал ~)
преступное посягательство

gross ~ (грос ~) грубое
нарушение
international ~ (интэрна́шэнал ~)
международное правонарушение
to discontinue ~ (ту дисконти́ню
~) прекратить нарушение
to settle an ~ (ту сэтл ан ~)
урегулировать нарушение
~ of liberty (~ оф ли́бэрти)
посягательство на свободу
~ of a patent (~ оф а па́тэнт)
нарушение патента
~ of property (~ оф про́пэрти)
посягательство на собственность
~ of a right (~ оф а райт)
нарушение права
~ of a trade mark (~ оф а трэйд
марк) нарушение товарного знака
Infringer (инфри́нджэр) нарушитель
patent ~ (па́тэнт ~) нарушитель
патентов
to prosecute the ~ (ту про́сэкют
θи ~) преследовать нарушителя
Ingot (и́нгот) слиток
gold ~ (голд ~) золота в слитках
Inherit (инхэ́рит, ту ~) наследовать
to ~ jointly (ту ~ джойнтли)
сонаследовать
Inheritance (инхэ́ританс) наследство
Initial (ини́шл) начальный ~s параф
to ~ (ту ~) парафировать {e.g.
agreement, treaty}
Initialing (ини́шлинг) парафирование
~ of an agreement (~ оф ан
агри́мэнт) парафирование договора
Initially (ини́шлли) в начальной
стадии
Initiate, to ~ (ини́шиэйт, ту ~)
возбуждать
to ~ proceedings (ту ~
проси́дингс) возбуждать дело
Initiative (ини́шиатив) инициатива,
почин
budget ~ (ба́джэт ~) бюджетная
инициатива
grass roots ~ (грас рутс ~)
народная инициатива
legislative ~ (лэ́джислэйтив ~)
законодательная инициатива
on one's own ~ (он уа́нз о́ун ~)
по своей инициативе, по своему
почину
parliamentary ~ (парламэ́нтари ~)
инициатива парламента
Initiator (ини́шиэйтор)
основоположник

Injunction (инджо́нкшн) предписание
приказание, судебный запрет
Injure, to ~ (и́нджур, ту ~)
повреждать, поранить, ранить
Injury (и́нджури) повреждение,
подрыв, ранение
physical ~ (фи́зикал ~)
физическое повреждение
Inland (и́нланд) сухопутный
~ waters (~ уа́тэрс) внутренние
воды
In-law (ин-ла́у) свойственник
{relation by marriage}
Innocence (и́нносэнс) невинность
outraged ~ (о́утрэйджд ~)
оскорблённая невинность
Innovation (иннов́эйшн) новшество
exportable ~s (э́кспортабл ~с)
экспортные новинки
technological ~s (тэкноло́джикал
~с) технологические новинки
product ~ (про́дукт ~) новинка
technical ~ (тэ́кникал ~)
техническое новшество
to patent an ~ (ту па́тэнт ан ~)
запатентовать новинку
Innumerable (инну́мэрабл)
неисчислимый
Inquest (и́нкуэст) судебное
следствие
board of ~ (борд оф ~) орган
дознания
oral ~ (о́рал ~) устное следстви
Inquire, to ~ (инкуа́йр, ту ~)
запрашивать [perfective: запросить
Inquiry (и́нкуайри) запрос,
расследование, розыск
official ~ (оффи́шл ~)
официальный запрос
preliminary ~ (прили́минэри ~)
предварительное расследование
preliminary substantive ~
(прили́минэри су́бстантив ~)
предварительное расследование п
существу
to hold an ~ (ту холд ан ~)
произвести расследование,
расследовать
Inquisition (инкуизи́шн)
инквизиционный процесс
Insane (инсэ́йн) сумасшедший
Insanity (инса́нити) сумасшествие
temporary ~ (тэ́мпорари ~) аффек
Inscription (инскри́пшн) надпись
~ on a bag (~ он а баг)
маркировка мешка
Insecure (инсэкю́р) ненадёжный

Insecurity (инсэкью́рити)
ненадёжность
Inseparable (инсэ́парабл)
неотделимый
Insert (и́нсэрт) вкладыш
    mailing ~ (мэ́йлинг ~) вкладыш в
    конверте
Insertion (инсэ́ршн) вставка в текст
Insolence (и́нсолэнс) наглость
insolent (и́нсолэнт) наглый
Insolvency (инсо́лвэнси)
неплатёжеспособность,
несостоятельность
    ~ of a debtor (~ оф а дэ́тор)
    несостоятельность должника
Insolvent (инсо́лвэнт)
некредитоспособный,
неплатёжеспособный, несостоятельный
    to become ~ (ту бико́м ~) стать
    несостоятельным
    ~ party (~ па́рти) банкрот
Inspect, to ~ (инспэ́кт, ту ~)
досматривать, осматривать
[**perfective:** осмотреть]
Inspection (инспэ́кшн) досмотр,
надзор, осмотр
    building ~ (би́лдинг ~)
    строительный надзор
    certificate of ~ (сэрти́фикэт оф
    ~) акт контроля, акт о проверке
    customs ~ (ка́стомз ~) таможенный
    досмотр, таможенный осмотр
    field ~ (филд ~)
    эксплуатационный контроль
    final ~ (фа́йнал ~) окончательная
    проверка
    health ~ (хэлθ ~) санитарный
    осмотр
    sanitary ~ (са́нитари ~)
    санитарный надзор
    technical ~ (тэ́кникал ~)
    технический надзор
    to be exempt from ~ (ту би
    экзэ́мпт фром ~) освобождать от
    досмотра
    to carry out an ~ (ту кэ́рри о́ут
    ан ~) проводить досмотр
    to pass through customs ~ (ту
    пасс θру ка́стомз ~) проводить
    таможенный досмотр
    ~ method (~ мэ́θод) метод
    контроля
    ~ of baggage (~ оф ба́ггадж)
    досмотр багажа
    ~ of cargo (~ оф ка́рго) досмотр
    грузов

    ~ of goods (~ оф гудз) осмотр
    товаров
    ~ of property (~ оф про́пэрти)
    досмотр имущества
Inspector (инспэ́ктор) инспектор
    chief ~ (чиф ~) генеральный
    инспектор
    customs ~ (ка́стомз ~)
    досмотрщик, таможенный
    инспектор, таможенный контролёр
    insurance claims ~ (иншю́ранс
    клэ́ймс ~) страховой инспектор
    tax ~ (такс ~) налоговой
    инспектор
Instability (инстаби́лити)
нестабильность, неустойчивость
    economic ~ (эконо́мик ~)
    экономическая нестабильность
    price ~ (прайс ~) неустойчивость
    цен
    ~ of the monetary system (~ оф
    θи мо́нэтари си́стэм)
    неустойчивость валютной системы
Install, to ~ (инста́л, ту ~)
монтировать
Installation (инсталлэ́йшн) монтаж,
общие условия монтажа, установка
    cost of ~ (кост оф ~) стоимость
    монтажа
    defense ~ (дифэ́нс ~) сооружение
    delay in ~ (дилэ́й ин ~) задержка
    монтажа
    during ~ (ду́ринг ~) во время
    монтажа
    equipment ~ (икуи́пмэнт ~) монтаж
    оборудования
    factory ~s (фа́ктори ~с) цеховое
    оборудование
    fixed ~s (фиксд ~с) стационарное
    оборудование
    floating ~s (фло́тинг ~с)
    плавучее портовое оборудование
    plant ~ (плант ~) монтаж завода
    prior to ~ (пра́йор ту ~) до
    начала монтажа
    shore ~s (шор ~с) береговое
    портовое оборудование
Installer (инста́ллэр) монтажник
Installment (инста́лмэнт) взнос,
часть
    advance ~ (адва́нс ~) авансовый
    взнос
    annual ~ (а́ннюал ~) ежегодный
    взнос
    by equal ~s (бай и́куал ~с)
    равными взносами

618

by monthly ~s (бай мо́нθли ~с)
ежемесячными взносами
by weekly ~s (бай уи́кли ~с)
еженедельными взносами
delivery in ~s (дэли́вэри ин ~с)
сдача по частям
equal ~s (и́куал ~с) равные
взносы
exemption from ~ payments
(экзэ́мпшн фром ~ пэ́ймэнтс)
освобождение от уплаты взносов
initial ~ (ини́шл ~)
первоначальный взнос
last ~ (ласт ~) последний взнос
minimum ~ (ми́нимум ~)
минимальный взнос
monthly ~ (мо́нθли ~) ежемесячный
взнос
next ~ (нэкст ~) очередной взнос
overdue ~ (овэрду́ ~)
просроченный взнос
payment by ~s (пэ́ймэнт бай ~с)
платёж частями
quarterly ~ (куа́ртэрли ~)
квартальный взнос
semi-annual ~ (сэ́ми-а́ннюал ~)
полугодовой взнос
subsequent ~ (са́бсикуэнт ~)
последующий взнос
to be payable in annual ~s (ту
би пэ́йабл ин а́ннюал ~с)
подлежать оплате ежегодными
взносами
to pay by ~ (ту пэй бай ~)
выплачивать взносами, платить в
рассрочку
weekly ~ (уи́кли ~) еженедельный
взнос
~ against debt (~ агэ́нст дэт)
взнос в счёт погашения долга
~ of ... {amount} (~ оф ...
{амо́унт}) взнос в размере ...
~ plan (~ план) рассрочка
~ premium (~ при́миум) очередной
страховой взнос
Instance (и́нстанс) инстанция
court of first ~ (ко́урт оф фэрст
~) суд первой инстанция
first ~ (фэрст ~) первая
инстанция
Instigate, to ~ (и́нстигэйт, ту ~)
подстрекать
Instigation (инстигэ́йшн)
подстрекательство
~ to war (~ ту уа́р)
подстрекательство к войне

Instigator (и́нстигэйтор)
подстрекатель , провокатор
Institute (и́нститут) институт
financial ~ (файна́ншл ~)
финансовый институт
international ~ (интэрна́шэнал ~)
международный институт
International ~ for the
Unification of Private Law
(интэрна́шэнал ~ фор θи
юнификэ́йшн оф пра́йват лау)
международный институт по
унификации частного права
International Patent ~
(интэрнэ́шнал па́тэнт ~)
международный патентный институт
legal ~ (ли́гал ~) правовой
институт
scientific research ~
(сайэнти́фик ри́сэрч ~) научно-
исследовательский институт
Scientific Research ~ for the
Study of Criminal Behavior
(сайэнти́фик ри́сэрч ~ фор θи
сту́ди оф кри́минал бихэ́йвёр)
научно-исследовательский
институт криминалистики
~ of Comparative Law (~ оф
компа́ратив ла́у) институт
сравнительного права
~ of Financial Law (~ оф
файна́ншл ла́у) финансово-правовой
институт
~ of International Law (~ оф
интэрна́шэнал ла́у) институт
международного права
Institution (институ́шн) институт,
учреждение
banking ~ (ба́нкинг ~) банковский
институт
credit ~ (крэ́дит ~) кредитная
организация
credit and financial ~ (крэ́дит
энд файна́ншл ~) кредитно-
финансовое учреждение
financial ~ (файна́ншл ~)
финансовое объединение,
финансовое учреждение
government ~ (го́вэрнмэнт ~)
государственное учреждение
issuing ~ (и́шюинг ~) эмиссионный
институт
legal ~s (ли́гал ~с) правовые
учреждения
lending ~ (лэ́ндинг ~) кредитное
учреждение

permanent arbitral ~ (пэрманэнт
а́рбитрал ~) перманентный
арбитраж
scientific ~ (сайэнти́фик ~)
научное учреждение
standing arbitral ~ (ста́ндинг
а́рбитрал ~) постоянно
действующий арбитраж
Instruct, to ~ (инстру́кт, ту ~)
поручать
to ~ the bank (ту ~ θи банк)
давать указания банку
Instruction (инстра́кшн) обучение,
поручение, распоряжение ~s
инструкция, указание
applicant's ~s (а́пликантс ~с)
указания заявителя
as per ~s (аз пэр ~с) согласно
указанию
assembly ~s (ассэ́мбли ~с)
указания о порядке сборки
banker's ~s (ба́нкэрз ~с)
банковское поручение
contrary ~s (ко́нтрари ~с)
противоположные указания
detailed ~s (ди́тэйлд ~с)
подробные указания
diplomatic ~s (диплома́тик ~с)
дипломатическое поручение
free ~ (фри ~) бесплатное
обучение
further ~s (фу́рθэр ~с)
дополнительные указания
general ~s (джэ́нэрал ~с) общие
указания
governmental ~ (говэрнмэ́нтал ~)
правительственное распоряжение
in accordance with ~s (ин
акко́рданс уиθ ~с) в соответствии
с указаниями
marking ~s (ма́ркинг ~с) указания
относительно маркировки
normative ~ (но́рматив ~)
нормативное предписание
non-observance of ~s (нон-
обсэ́рванс оф ~с) несоблюдение
указаний
notwithstanding ~s
(нотуиθста́ндинг ~с) независимо
от указаний
operating ~s (о́пэрэйтинг ~с)
указания по эксплуатации
oral ~s (о́рал ~с) устные
указания
packed and marked as per ~s
(пакд энд маркд ас пэр ~с) в

упаковке и с маркировкой
согласно указаниям
pending further ~s (пэ́ндинг
фу́рθэр ~с) в ожидании дальнейших
указаний
technical ~s (тэ́кникал ~с)
технические указания
to await further ~s (ту ауэ́йт
фу́рθэр ~с) ожидать указаний
to comply with ~s (ту компла́й
уиθ ~с) выполнять указания
to follow ~s (ту фо́лло ~с)
следовать директивам, следовать
указаниям
to give ~s (ту гив ~с) давать
указания
to give written ~s (ту гив
ри́ттэн ~с) давать письменные
указания
to perform per ~s (ту пэрфо́рм
пэр ~с) делать по указанию
to transmit ~s (ту трансми́т ~с)
передавать указания
under the ~s of ... (а́ндэр θи ~с
оф ...) на основании указаний
work ~s (уо́рк ~с) указания по
выполнению работы
written ~s (ри́ттэн ~с)
письменное указание
~ for carrying out the work (~
фор кэ́рриинг о́ут θи уо́рк)
указания по выполнению работ
~ from a ministry (~ фром а
ми́нистри) инструкция
министерства
~ to advise (~ ту адва́йз)
распоряжение об авизовании
~ to deliver (~ ту дэли́вэр)
распоряжение о доставке
Instrument (и́нструмэнт) акт,
инструмент, орудие, прибор
contractual ~ (контра́кчуал ~)
договорный акт
credit ~ (крэ́дит ~) кредитный
документ , кредитное орудие
international ~ (интэрна́шэнал ~)
международный акт
mortgage ~ (мо́ргэдж ~) акт об
установлении ипотеки
order ~ (о́рдэр ~) ордерный
документ
~ of payment (~ оф пэ́ймэнт)
орудие платежа
Insufficient (инсуффи́шэнт)
недостаточный
Insulation (инсюлэ́йшн) изоляция
{technical}

Insult (инсулт) оскорбление
 to ~ (ту ~) оскорблять
 [perfective: оскорбить]
Insulted (инсултэд) оскорблённый
Insulting (инсултинг)
оскорбительный
Insurable (иншурабл) страхуемый
Insurance (иншоранс) страхование
 aviation ~ (эйвиэйшн ~)
 воздушное страхование
 casualty ~ (кажюалти ~)
 страхование от аварий
 exchange risk ~ (эксчэйндж риск
 ~) страхование валютных рисков
 group ~ (груп ~) групповое
 страхование
 joint ~ (джойнт ~) совместное
 страхование
 life ~ (лайф ~) пожизненное
 страхование
 mandatory ~ (мандатори ~)
 обязательное страхование
 maritime ~ (маритайм ~) морское
 страхование
 mutual ~ (мючуал ~) взаимное
 страхование
 personal ~ (пэрсонал ~) личное
 страхование
 private ~ (прайват ~) частное
 страхование
 property ~ (пропэрти ~)
 имущественное страхование
 state ~ (стэйт ~)
 государственное страхование
 supplementary ~ (сапплэмэнтари
 ~) дополнительное страхование
 ~ claim (~ клэйм) заявление о
 выплате страхового возмещения
 ~ coverage (~ ковэрадж)
 страховка
Insure, to ~ (иншур, ту ~)
застраховать, страховать
Insured (иншурд) застрахованное
лицо {person}
Insurer (иншурэр) страховщик
Insurgent (инсурджэнт) повстанец
{person}, повстанческий {adj.}
Intact (интакт) неповреждённый
Integral (интэграл) неотъемлемый
Integration (интэгрэйшн) интеграция
 economic ~ (экономик ~)
 экономическая интеграция
 European ~ (юропиан ~)
 европейская интеграция
 political ~ (политикал ~)
 политическая интеграция
Integrity (интэгрити) целостность

Intellectual (интэллэкчуал)
интеллигент {person},
интеллектуальный {adj.}
 export and import of ~ property
 (экспорт энд импорт оф ~
 пропэрти) экспорт и импорт
 результатов творческой
 деятельности
Intelligence (интэллиджэнс)
интеллект, разведка {gathering
information}
 ~ officer (~ оффисэр) разведчик
Intend, to ~ (интэнд, ту ~)
предполагать
Intense (интэнс) напряжённый
Intensity (интэнсити) напряжённость
Intent (интэнт) намерение,
предположение
 legislative ~ (лэджислэйтив ~)
 законодательное предположение
 letter of ~ (лэттэр оф ~)
 меморандум о намерении,
 соглашение о намерениях
 protocol of ~ (протокол оф ~)
 протокол о намерениях
Intention (интэншн) намерение,
предположение
Interbank (интэрбанк) межбанковский
Inter-city (интэр-сити)
междугородный
Inter-corporation (интэр-
корпорэйшн) межфирменный
Interdepartmental
(интэрдэпартмэнтал) межцеховой
Inter-firm (интэр-фирм)
межфирменный
Intergovernmental
(интэргэвэрнмэнтал)
межправительственный
Intersectoral (интэрсэкторал)
межотраслевой
Interact, to ~ (интэракт, ту ~)
взаимодействовать
Interaction (интэракшн)
взаимодействие
 investment ~ (инвэстмэнт ~)
 инвестиционное взаимодействие
 ~ of supply and demand (~ оф
 суппла́й энд диманд)
 взаимодействие спроса и
 предложения
Intercede, to ~ (интэрсид, ту ~)
просить
Interchangeability
(интэрчэйнджабилити)
взаимозаменяемость, сменяемость

Interchangeable (интэрчэ́йнджабл)
взаимозаменяемый, сменяемый
Intercourse (и́нтэркорс) общение,
сношение
    sexual ~ (сэ́кшуал ~) половое
    сношение
Interdependence (интэрдипэ́ндэнс)
взаимная зависимость
Interest (и́нтэрэст)
заинтересованность, интерес,
процент
    accumulating ~ (аккю́мюлэйтинг ~)
    наросшие проценты
    bank ~ (банк ~) банковский
    процент
    collective ~**s** (колле́ктив ~с)
    коллективные интересы
    common ~ (ко́ммон ~) общие
    интересы
    community of ~**s** (коммю́нити оф
    ~с) общность интересов
    compound ~ (ко́мпоунд ~)
    анатоцизм, сложные проценты
    consignor's ~**s** (конса́йнорз ~с)
    интересы грузоотправителя
    contractual ~ (контра́кчуал ~)
    договорные проценты
    contrary to public ~ (ко́нтрари
    ту па́блик ~) противоречащий
    публичному интересу
    current ~ (ку́ррэнт ~) текущие
    проценты
    double ~ (дабл ~) анатоцизм
    financial ~ (файна́ншл ~)
    финансовый интерес
    future ~ {estate} (фю́чэр ~
    {эсте́йт}) будущее имущество
    legal ~ (ли́гал ~) законный
    интерес
    monopoly ~**s** (моно́поли ~с)
    монополистические круги
    mortgage ~ (мо́ргэдж ~) ипотечные
    проценты
    permissible ~ (пэрми́сибл ~)
    узаконенные проценты
    personal ~ (пэ́рсонал ~) личная
    заинтересованность
    private ~ (пра́йват ~) частный
    интерес
    property ~**s** (про́пэрти ~с)
    имущественные интересы
    public ~ (па́блик ~) общественный
    интерес, публичный интерес
    short-term ~ (шорт-тэрм ~) доход
    от краткосрочных вложений
    simple ~ (симпл ~) простые
    проценты

    to defend one's ~ (ту дифэ́нд
    уа́нз ~) защищать интерес
    usurious ~ (юсу́риос ~)
    ростовщические проценты
    vital ~ (ва́йтал ~) жизненные
    интересы
    ~ **payment on a loan** (~ пэ́ймэнт
    он а лон) уплата процентов по
    займу
    ~ **rate increase** (~ рэйт инкри́с)
    увеличение процентов
Interested (и́нтэрэстэд)
заинтересованный
Interim (и́нтэрим) временный {adj.},
промежуточный {adj.}, промежуток
Interior (инти́риор) внутренний
Intermediary (интэрми́диари)
посредник
    financial ~ (файна́ншл ~)
    финансовый посредник
Intermediate (интэрми́диат)
промежуточный
Intern (и́нтэрн) стажёр
    to ~ (ту ~) интернировать {as in
    a camp}
International (интэрна́шэнал)
международный
Internationalism (интэрна́шэнализм)
интернационализм
Internationalist (интэрна́шэналист)
интернациональный
Internationalization
(интэрашнализэ́йшн)
интернационализация
Internationalize, to ~
(интэрна́шналайз, ту ~)
интернационализировать
Internee (интэрни́) интернированный
    civilian ~ (сиви́лян ~)
    гражданский интернированный
    political ~ (поли́тикал ~)
    политический интернированный
Internship (и́нтэрншип) стажировка
Internuncio (интэрну́нсио)
интернунций
    Papal ~ (пэ́йпал ~) папский
    интернунций
Interpellant (интэрпэ́ллант)
интерпеллянт
Interpellation (интэрпэлла́йшн)
интерпелляция {question in
Parliament}
Interpret, to ~ (интэ́рпрэт, ту ~)
истолковывать [perfective:
истолковать]

Interpretation (интэрпрэтэ́йшн) интерпретация, истолкование, разъяснение
    limited ~ (ли́митэд ~) ограничительное истолкование
    ~ of the Supreme Court (~ оф θи супри́м ко́урт) разъяснение верховного суда
Interrogate, to ~ (интэ́ррогэйт, ту ~) опрашивать
Interrogation (интэррогэ́йшн) опрос, опросный {adj.}
Interrogatory (интэрро́гатори) опросный лист
Interruption (интэрру́пшн) перерыв
    ~ in prescription period (~ ин прэскри́пшн пи́риод) перерыв течения давности
    ~ in the period of the running of the statute of limitations (~ ин θи пи́риод оф θи ру́ннинг оф θи ста́тют оф лимитэ́йшнз) перерыв течения давности
    ~ of work (~ оф уо́рк) перерыв в работе
Intersection (и́нтэрсэкшн) пересечение
    ~ of borders (~ оф бо́рдэрс) пересечение границы
Interstate (и́нтэрстэйт) межгосударственный
Interval (и́нтэрвал) промежуток
    ~ in the proceedings (~ ин θи проси́дингз) перерыв прений
Intervene, to ~ (интэрви́н, ту ~) интервенировать
Intervention (интэрвэ́ншн) вмешательство, интервенция
    act of ~ (акт оф ~) акт вмешательства
    collective ~ (колле́ктив ~) коллективная интервенция
    currency ~ (ку́ррэнси ~) валютная интервенция
    diplomatic ~ (дипломати́к ~) дипломатическая интервенция
    economic ~ (эконо́мик ~) экономическая интервенция
    joint ~ (джойнт ~) совместная интервенция
    legal ~ (ли́гал ~) юридическая интервенция
    military ~ (ми́литари ~) военная интервенция
Interventionist (интэрвэ́ншнист) интервент, интервенционистский {adj.}

Intoxicating (инто́ксикэйтинг) одурманивающий {as of a narcotic}
Intoxication (интоксикэ́йшн) опьянение
    public ~ (па́блик ~) появление в пьяном виде
Intra-factory (и́нтра-фа́ктори) внутризаводской
Intrasectoral (и́нтрасэкто́рал) внутриотраслевой
Intrigues (и́нтригз) интрига, махинация, происки
Introduce, to ~ (интродю́с, ту ~) вводить, внедрять
Introduction (интрода́кшн) внедрение, вступительный раздел {e.g. to book}
    product ~ (про́дукт ~) внедрение продукции
    ~ market ~ (~ ма́ркэт ~) выпуск товара на рынок
    ~ of equipment (~ оф икуи́пмэнт) внедрение машин
    ~ of new product types (~ оф нью про́дукт тайпс) внедрение новых видов продукции
    ~ of new technology (~ оф нью тэкно́лоджи) внедрение новой техники и технологии
    ~ of progressive industrial processes (~ оф прогре́ссив инду́стриал про́сэсэз) внедрение прогрессивных технологий
    ~ of standards (~ оф ста́ндардс) внедрение нормативов
    ~ of technology (~ оф тэкно́лоджи) внедрение технологии
    ~ of testimony (~ оф тэ́стимони) получение показания
    ~ phase (~ фэйз) этап внедрения
Introductory (интроду́ктори) вступительный
Invader (инвэ́йдэр) захватчик, оккупант
Invalid ({1} инва́лид или {2} и́нвалид) {1} недействительный, без силы {2} инвалид
Invalidity (инвали́дити) недействительность
    ~ of a certificate of authorship (~ оф а сэрти́фикэт оф а́уθоршип) недействительность авторского свидетельства
    ~ of a patent (~ оф а па́тэнт) недействительность патента

~ **of a trade mark** (~ оф а трэйд марк) недействительность товарного знака
Invent, to ~ (инвэ́нт, ту ~) изобрести
Invention (инвэ́ншн) изобретение
   additional ~ (адди́шнал ~) дополнительное изобретение
   foreign ~ (фо́рэн ~) иностранное изобретение
   in-house ~ (ин-хаус ~) изобретение, сделанное на предприятии
   industrial ~ (инду́стриал ~) промышленное изобретение
   joint ~ (джойнт ~) совместное изобретение
   patentable ~ (па́тэнтабл ~) патентоспособное изобретение
   patented ~ (па́тэнтэд ~) запатентованное изобретение
Inventiveness (инвэ́нтивнэс) изобретательство
Inventor (инвэ́нтор) автор изобретения, изобретатель
   first and genuine ~ (фэрст энд джэ́нюайн ~) действительный и первый изобретатель
Inventory (и́нвэнтори) опись, перепись, роспись
   agricultural ~ (агрику́лчурал ~) сельскохозяйственная перепись
   industrial ~ (инду́стриал ~) промышленная перепись
   partial ~ (паршл ~) частичная перепись
   statistical ~ (стати́стикал ~) статистическая перепись
   taking ~ (тэ́йкинг ~) инвентаризация
   to ~ (ту ~) описать, составить опись
   to take ~ (ту тэйк ~) инвентаризировать, производить перепись
Invest, to ~ (инвэ́ст, ту ~) вкладывать, инвестировать
Investigate, to ~ (инвэ́стигэйт, ту ~) обследовать, расследовать
Investigation (инвэстигэ́йшн) изыскание, обследование, разбирательство, следствие
   budget ~ (ба́джэт ~) бюджетное обследование
   criminal ~ (кри́минал ~) уголовный розыск

   preliminary ~ (прили́минэри ~) предварительное следствие
   to call off an ~ (ту кал офф ан ~) прекратить следствие
   to carry out an ~ (ту кэ́рри о́ут ан ~) производить следствие
   under ~ (а́ндэр ~) подследственный
~ **act** (~ акт) акт обследования
Investigator (инвэ́стигэйтор) следователь
   judicial ~ (джюди́шл ~) судебный следователь
Investing (инвэ́стинг) инвестирование
Investment (инвэ́стмэнт) вложение ~s инвестиции
   capital ~s (ка́питал ~с) капитальные вложения
   domestic ~s (домэ́стик ~с) внутренние капиталовложения
   foreign ~s (фо́рэн ~с) заграничные капиталовложения, иностранные инвестиции
   gross ~s (грос ~с) валовые капиталовложения
   joint capital ~s (джойнт ка́питал ~с) совместные капиталовложения
   low-yield ~s (ло́у-йилд ~с) малоприбыльные капиталовложения
   major ~s (мэ́йджор ~с) крупные капиталовложения
   monetary ~ (мо́нэтари ~) взнос денежных средств
   net ~s (нэт ~с) чистые инвестиции
   original ~s (ори́джинал ~с) первоначальные капиталовложения
   planned ~s (планд ~с) плановые капиталовложения
   portfolio ~s (портфо́лио ~с) портфельные инвестиции
   profitability of ~s (профитаби́лити оф ~с) рентабельность вложений
   public ~s (па́блик ~с) государственные капиталовложения
   secure ~s (сэкю́р ~с) надёжные капиталовложения
   to curtail ~s (ту куртэ́йл ~с) сокращать капиталовложения
   to increase capital ~s (ту инкри́с ка́питал ~с) увеличивать капиталовложения
~ **abroad** (~ абро́д) инвестиции за границей

624

~ **incentives** (~ инсэ́нтивс)
стимулы для капиталовложений
~ **of capital** (~ оф ка́питал)
вклад капитала
~ **opportunities** (~ оппортю́нитиз)
возможности для капиталовложений
~ **plan** (~ план) план
капиталовложений
Investor (инвэ́стор) инвеститор
foreign ~ (фо́рэн ~) иностранный
вкладчик
major ~ (мэ́йджор ~) крупный
вкладчик
Invisible (инви́зибл) невидимый
Invitation (инвитэ́йшн)
пригласительный билет, приглашение
Invoice (и́нвойс) счёт, фактура
certified ~ (сэ́ртифайд ~)
заверенная фактура
commercial ~ (комме́ршл ~)
коммерческая фактура, счёт-
фактура
consular ~ (ко́нсюлар ~)
консульская фактура
final ~ (фа́йнал ~) окончательная
фактура
original of the ~ (ори́джинал оф
θи ~) оригинал фактуры
preliminary ~ (прили́минэри ~)
предварительная фактура
pro forma ~ (про фо́рма ~)
ориентировочная фактура
shipper's ~ (ши́ппэрз ~) счёт
грузоотправителя
specimen ~ (спэ́симэн ~)
примерная фактура
to append a copy of an ~ (ту
аппэ́нд а ко́пи оф ан ~) прилагать
копию фактуры
to fraudulently alter an ~ (ту
фра́удюлэнтли а́лтэр ан ~)
переделывать фактуру
to include in an ~ (ту инклю́д ин
ан ~) включать в фактуру
to issue an ~ (ту и́шю ан ~)
выписывать фактуру
to reduce the ~ **amount** (ту ридю́с
θи ~ амо́унт) уменьшать сумму
фактуры
~ **amount** (~ амо́унт) сумма
фактуры
~ **copy** (~ ко́пи) копия фактуры
~ **date** (~ дэйт) дата фактуры
~ **for ...** (~ фор ...) фактура на
~ **specification** (~ спэсифике́йшн)
фактура-спецификация

~~-**license** (~~-ла́йсэнз) фактура-
лицензия
Invoiced (и́нвойсд) фактурный
Invoicing (и́нвойсинг) выписка
счёта, фактурирование
Involuntary (инво́лунтари)
непроизвольный
Involve, to ~ (инво́лв, ту ~)
связывать [**perfective:** связать]
Irregular (ирре́гюлар) нерегулярный
Irremovable (иррэмо́вабл)
неустранимый
Irresponsible (ирриспо́нсибл)
неответственный
legally ~ (ли́галли ~)
невменяемый {insanity, minority,
etc.}
Irrevocable (иррэ́вокабл)
безотзывный
Isolation (айсоле́йшн) изоляция
{political}, обособленность
economic ~ (эконо́мик ~)
хозяйственная изоляция
Isolationism (айсоле́йшнизм)
изоляционизм
Isolationist (айсоле́йшнист)
изоляционист, изоляционистический
{adj.}
Issuance (и́шюанс) выдача,
оформление
contest the ~ **of a patent**
(конте́ст θи ~ оф а па́тэнт)
оспаривать выдачу патента
date of ~ (дэйт оф ~) дата
выдачи
month of ~ (монθ оф ~) месяц
выдачи
patent ~ **fee** (па́тэнт ~ фи)
пошлина за выдачу патента
patent ~ **rules** (па́тэнт ~ рулз)
правила выдачи патентов
place of ~ (плэйс оф ~) место
выдачи
to delay ~ (ту диле́й ~)
задерживать выдачу
~ **of a bill** (~ оф а бил) выдача
векселя
~ **of a credit** (~ оф а крэ́дит)
выдача кредита
~ **of a document** (~ оф а
до́кюмэнт) выдача документа
~ **of a draft** {note} (~ оф а
драфт {нот}) выписка тратты
~ **of a guarantee** (~ оф а
гяранти́) выдача гарантии

~ of a letter of credit (~ оф а
лэ́ттэр оф крэ́дит) выдача
аккредитива
~ of a patent (~ оф а па́тэнт)
выдача патента
~ of a visa (~ оф а ви́за) выдача
визы
~ of a waybill (~ оф а уэ́йбил)
выдача транспортной накладной
~ of shares (~ оф шэйрз) выпуск
акций
~ of stock (~ оф сток) выдача
акций
Issue (и́шю) вопрос, выпуск, номер
{periodical}, приплод {livestock},
проблема, эмиссия {bonds, etc.}
consideration of an ~
(консидэрэ́йшн оф ан ~)
рассмотрение вопроса
controversial ~ (контрове́рсиал
~) спорный пункт
date of ~ (дэйт оф ~) дата
выпуска
internal ~ (инте́рнал ~)
внутренний выпуск
legal ~ (ли́гал ~) правовая
проблема
place of ~ (плэйс оф ~) место
выпуска
rate of ~ (рэйт оф ~) курс
выпуска
to consider an ~ (ту конси́дэр ан
~) рассматривать вопрос
to plan a special ~ (ту план а
спэшл ~) планировать специальный
выпуск
to ~ a receipt (ту ~ а риси́т)
выдать расписку
unresolved ~ (анризо́лвд ~)
неразрешенный вопрос
~ date of an invoice (~ дэйт оф
ан и́нвойс) дата выписки счёта
~ of an author's certificate (~
оф ан а́уθорз сэрти́фикэт) выдача
авторского свидетельства
~ of bank notes (~ оф банк нотс)
эмиссия банкнот
~ of certification (~ оф
сэртификэ́йшн) выдача
свидетельства
~ of debentures (~ оф дибэ́нчурс)
выпуск облигаций
~ of a loan (~ оф а лон) выпуск
займа
~ of a receipt (~ оф а риси́т)
выдача расписки

~ of securities (~ оф сэкю́ритиз)
эмиссия ценных бумаг
~ under consideration (~ а́ндэр
консидэрэ́йшн) рассматриваемый
Issuing (и́шюинг) эмиссионный
~ an invoice (~ ан и́нвойс)
выдача накладной
Item (а́йтэм) предмет, пункт, пункт
договора, статья, штука
balance sheet ~ (ба́ланс шит ~)
статья баланса
contraband ~ (ко́нтрабанд ~)
контрабандный предмет
exhibited ~ (экзи́битэд ~)
экспонируемый предмет
fragile ~ (фра́джайл ~) хрупкий
предмет
luxury ~ (лу́кшури ~) предмет
роскоши
requisitioned ~ (рэкуизи́шнд ~)
реквизированный предмет
~s of consumption (~с оф
консу́мпшн) предметы потребления
~ of contraband (~ оф
ко́нтрабанд) предмет контрабанды
~ of export (~ оф э́кспорт)
статья экспорта
~ of income (~ оф и́нком)
доходная статья
Itinerary (айти́нэрари) маршрут

J

Jacket (джа́кэт) обёртка {of book,
etc.}
Jar (джар) банка
sealed ~ (силд ~) запечатанная
банка
to preserve in a ~ (ту присе́рв
ин а ~) упаковывать в банку
Jenny (джэ́нни) подъёмные
Jettison (джэ́тисон) выбрасывание
~ of cargo (~ оф ка́рго)
выбрасывание груза за борт
Job (джоб) задание, рабочее место,
работа
additional ~ (адди́шнал ~)
дополнительная работа
rush ~ (раш ~) срочная работа
slipshod ~ (сли́пшод ~) халтура
temporary ~ (тэ́мпорари ~)
временная работа
Jobber (джо́ббэр) биржевой
спекулянт, комиссионер, спекулянт
Jobbing (джо́ббинг) спекуляция

stock ~ (сток ~) биржевая
спекуляция, игра на бирже
Join, to ~ (джойн, ту ~) вступать,
вступать в члены {organization,
etc.}, присоединять, присоединяться
Joinder (джо́йндэр) присоединение
~ to a suit (~ ту а сут)
присоединение к иску
Joining (джо́йнинг) соединение
Joint (джойнт) единый, совместный,
смешанный
~ liability (~ лайаби́лити)
солидарность
Jointly (джо́йнтли) солидарно
Journal (джу́рнал) ведомость,
журнал, регистр
cash ~ (каш ~) кассовый журнал
medical ~ (мэ́дикал ~)
медицинский журнал
purchase ~ (пу́рчас ~) журнал
учёта закупок
sanitary ~ (са́нитари ~)
санитарный журнал
technical ~ (тэ́кникал ~)
технический журнал
Journalize, to ~ (джу́рналайз, ту ~)
записывать в журнал учёта
Journey (джу́рни) поездка, проезд,
путешествие
Judge (джадж) судья
competent ~ (ко́мпэтэнт ~)
компетентный судья
federal ~ (фэ́дэрал ~)
федеральный судья
local ~ (ло́кал ~) местный судья
to ~ (ту ~) судить
Judgment (джа́джмэнт) присуждение,
суждение
money ~ (мо́ни ~) присуждение к
уплате денежной суммы
to be subject to a ~ (ту би
са́бджэкт ту а ~) подлежать
взысканию
~ by default (~ бай дифа́лт)
заочный приговор
~ for the plaintiff (~ фор θи
плэ́йнтиф) удовлетворение иска
~ of the court (~ оф θи ко́урт)
судебный приговор
Judicial (джюди́шл) судебный
Junction (джункшн) стык
railway ~ (рэ́йлуэй ~) узловая
станция
Juncture (джу́нкчур) конъюнктура
Juridical (джюри́дикал) юридический
~ person (~ пэ́рсон) юридическое
лицо

Juridically (джюри́дикалли)
юридически
Jurisdiction (джюрисди́кшн)
компетенция {subject matter},
подсудность , правило о
подсудности, юрисдикция
advisory ~ (адва́йзори ~)
консультативная юрисдикция
alternative ~ (алтэ́рнатив ~)
альтернативная подсудность
civil ~ (си́вил ~) гражданская
подсудность, гражданская
юрисдикция
consular ~ (ко́нсюлар ~)
консульская юрисдикция
criminal ~ (кри́минал ~)
уголовная подсудность
exclusive ~ (эксклю́сив ~)
исключительная подсудность,
исключительная юрисдикция
foreign ~ (фо́рэн ~) иностранная
юрисдикция
general ~ (джэ́нэрал ~) общая
подсудность, общая юрисдикция
mandatory ~ (ма́ндатори ~)
обязательная подсудность
national ~ (на́шэнал ~)
национальная юрисдикция
state ~ (стэ́йт ~)
государственная юрисдикция
subject matter ~ (са́бджэкт
ма́ттэр ~) предметная подсудность
territorial ~ (тэррито́риал ~)
территориальная подсудность
to come under the ~ of (ту ком
а́ндэр θи ~ оф) входить в
компетенцию
to fall within the ~ (ту фалл
уиθи́н θи ~) подпадать под
юрисдикцию
within the ~ (уиθи́н θи ~)
подведомственный
within the ~ of (уиθи́н θи ~ оф)
подсудный
~ over a case (~ о́вэр а кэйс)
подсудность дела
~ over subject matter (~ о́вэр
са́бджэкт ма́ттэр) подсудность по
предмету
Jurisprudence (джюриспру́дэнс)
юридические науки, юриспруденция
Jurist (джу́рист) правовед
Juror (джу́рор) присяжный заседатель
Juryman (джу́риман) присяжный
заседатель

Just (джаст) правомерный, справедливый
Justice (джа́стис) правосудие, верховный судья {person}, справедливость, юстиция
    administration of criminal ~ (администрэ́йшн оф кри́минал ~) правосудие по уголовным делам
    criminal ~ (кри́минал ~) уголовное правосудие
    international ~ (интэрна́шэнал ~) международное правосудие
    rough ~ (руф ~) расправа
    social ~ (сошл ~) социальная справедливость
    Ministry of ~ (ми́нистри оф ~) министерство юстиции
    ~ of the peace (~ оф θи пис) мировой судья
Justification (джастифике́йшн) обоснование, обоснованность
    economic ~ (эконо́мик ~) экономическое обоснование
    in ~ of (ин ~ оф) в обоснование
    technical ~ (тэ́кникал ~) техническое обоснование
Justified (джа́стифайд) обоснованный
Justify, to ~ (джа́стифай, ту ~) обосновывать

К

Keep, to ~ (кип, ту ~) содержать, сохранять [perfective: сохранить]
Key (ки) ключ, ключевой {adj.}
    ~ position (~ пози́шн) ключевая позиция
    ~ to a code (~ ту а код) ключ к шифру
Kidnap, to ~ (ки́днап, ту ~) похищать
Kidnapping (ки́днаппинг) похищение
    ~ of a child (~ оф а чайлд) похищение ребёнка
Kind (кайнд) вид, род, сорт
    compensation in ~ (компэнсэ́йшн ин ~) возмещение в натуре
    in ~ (ин ~) в вещественном виде, в натуральном выражении, в натуральном виде
    payment in ~ (пэ́ймэнт ин ~) оплата натурой
    remuneration in ~ (римюнэрэ́йшн ин ~) вознаграждение натурой
    tax in ~ (такс ин ~) продналог

Kindling (ки́ндлинг) разжигание
Kinship (ки́ншип) родство
    illegitimate ~ (иллэджи́тэмат ~) внебрачное родство
Kit (кит) комплект, набор
    tool ~ (тул ~) комплект инструментов, набор инструментов
Know-how (но́у-ха́у) ноу-хау, опыт
    disclosed ~ (дискло́зд ~) разглашённое ноу-хау
    exchange of ~ (эксчэ́йндж оф ~) обмен ноу-хау
    general ~ (джэ́нэрал ~) общее ноу-хау
    licensed ~ (ла́йсэнсд ~) ноу-хау по лицензии
    licensor's ~ (лайсэнсо́рз ~) ноу-хау лицензиара
    manufacturing ~ (манюфа́кшуринг ~) ноу-хау на изготовление
    operational ~ (опэрэ́йшнал ~) производственный опыт
    owner of ~ (о́унэр оф ~) владелец ноу-хау
    patented ~ (па́тэнтэд ~) патентованное ноу-хау
    protection of ~ (протэ́кшн оф ~) охрана ноу-хау
    technical ~ (тэ́кникал ~) техническое ноу-хау
    to furnish ~ (ту фу́рниш ~) выдавать ноу-хау
    to supply ~ (ту суппла́й ~) предоставлять ноу-хау
    to surrender ~ (ту суррэ́ндэр ~) отказываться от ноу-хау
    to use ~ (ту юз ~) использовать ноу-хау
    transfer of ~ (тра́нсфэр оф ~) передача ноу-хау
    undisclosed ~ (андискло́зд ~) неразглашённое ноу-хау
    unpatented ~ (анпа́тэнтэд ~) незапатентованное ноу-хау
    ~ package (~ па́кэдж) комплекс ноу-хау
    ~ transfer agreement (~ тра́нсфэр агри́мэнт) договор на передачу ноу-хау
Knowledge (но́лэдж) знание, сведение
    public ~ (па́блик ~) общеизвестность
Known (но́ун) известный
    well ~ (уэл ~) общеизвестный

L

Label (лэ́йбэл) бирка, этикетка, ярлык

  back ~ (бак ~) этикетка на задней части упаковки

  brand ~ (бранд ~) клеймо

  cargo ~ (ка́рго ~) этикетка груза

  coded ~ (ко́дэд ~) этикетка с артикулом

  descriptive ~ (дискри́птив ~) описательная этикетка

  detailed ~ (ди́тэйлд ~) подробная этикетка

  enclosed ~ (энкло́зд ~) прилагаемая этикетка

  package ~ (па́кэдж ~) этикетка места

  paper ~ (пэ́йпэр ~) бумажная наклейка, бумажная этикетка

  private ~ (пра́йват ~) марка торгового посредника {distributor's brand}

  recipe ~ (рэ́сипи ~) этикетка, содержащая рецепт для приготовления продуктов

  "red" ~ (рэд ~) этикетка "красная" {denotes dangerous cargo}

  to affix a ~ (ту аффи́кс а ~) прикреплять наклейку

  to apply a ~ (ту аппла́й а ~) прикреплять этикетку

  to attach a ~ (ту атта́ч а ~) прикреплять бирку, наклеивать этикетку

  with ~s (уиθ ~с) с этикетками

  without ~s (уиθо́ут ~с) без этикеток

Labeling (лэ́йбэлинг) маркировка

Labor (лэ́йбор) труд

  division of ~ (диви́жн оф ~) разделение труда

  efficient ~ (эффи́шэнт ~) производительный труд

  highly skilled ~ (ха́йли скилд ~) высококвалифицированный труд

  individual ~ (индиви́дюал ~) индивидуальная трудовая деятельность

  in-factory division of ~ (ин-фа́ктори диви́жн оф ~) внутризаводское разделение труда

  manual ~ (ма́нюал ~) ручной труд

  non-productive ~ (нон-прода́ктив ~) непроизводительный труд

  productive ~ (прода́ктив ~) продуктивный труд

  productivity of ~ (продукти́вити оф ~) производительность труда

  remuneration of ~ (римюнирэ́йшн оф ~) оплата труда

  setting of ~ **quotas** (сэ́ттинг оф ~ куо́тас) нормирование труда

  skilled ~ (скилд ~) квалифицированный труд

  ~ **content** (~ ко́нтэнт) трудоёмкость

  ~ **intensive** (~ интэ́нсив) трудоёмкий

Laboratory (ла́боратори) лаборатория, лабораторный {adj.}

  joint ~ (джойнт ~) совместная лаборатория

  research ~ (ри́сэрч ~) исследовательская лаборатория

  specially equipped ~ (спэшлли икуи́пд ~) специально оборудованная лаборатория

Laborer (лэ́йборэр) рабочий

  auxiliary ~ (аукзи́лиэри ~) вспомогательный рабочий

  casual ~ (ка́жюал ~) временный рабочий

  day ~ (дэй ~) подённый рабочий

  hired ~ (ха́йрд ~) наёмный рабочий

  seasonal ~ (си́зонал ~) сезонный рабочий

  unskilled ~ (ански́лд ~) неквалифицированный рабочий

Laborious (лабо́риос) труднодоступный

Lack (лак) голод, недостаток, недостача, неимение, нехватка, отсутствие

  for ~ **of ...** (фор ~ оф ...) за недостатком ...

  to ~ **for** (ту ~ фор) испытывать недостаток

  ~ **of agreement** (~ оф агри́мэнт) отсутствие согласия

  ~ **of authority** (~ оф аθо́рити) отсутствие правомочий

  ~ **of evidence** (~ оф э́видэнс) отсутствие доказательства

  ~ **of** {foreign} **exchange** (~ оф {фо́рэн} эксчэ́йндж) нехватка валюты

  ~ **of jobs** (~ оф джобс) недостаток вакансий

~ **of previous convictions** (~ оф
при́виос конви́кшнс) отсутствие
судимости
~ **of quorum** (~ оф куо́рум)
отсутствие кворума
~ **of raw materials** (~ оф ра́у
мати́риалс) нехватка сырья
Lacking (ла́ккинг) отсутствующий
to be ~ (ту би ~) отсутствовать
Land (ланд) земля, земельный
{*adj.*}, поземельный {*adj.*}
arable ~ (э́йрабл ~) пахотная
земля
border ~ (бо́рдэр ~) пограничная
земля
cultivated ~ (ку́лтивэйтэд ~)
возделанная земля
fallow ~ (фалло́у ~) залежная
земля
individual ~ **tenure** (индиви́дюал
~ тэ́нюр) единоличное
землепользование
leased ~ (лисд ~) арендованная
земля
occupied ~ (о́ккюпайд ~) занятая
земля
state ~**s** (стэ́йт ~с) казённая
земля
urban ~ (у́рбан ~) городская
земля
~ **owner** (~ о́унэр) землевладелец
~ **ownership** (~ о́унэршип)
землевладение
~ **tax** (~ такс) поземельный налог
~ **surveyor** (~ су́рвэйор) землемер
~ **tenure** (~ тэ́нюр)
землепользование
~ **tenure regulation** (~ тэню́р
рэгюлэ́йшн) землеустройство
Landed (ла́ндэд) на берег
~ **price** (~ прайс) цена с
выгрузкой на берег
~ **terms** (~ тэрмз) на условиях с
выгрузкой на берег
Landing (ла́ндинг) посадка
forced ~ (форсд ~) вынужденная
посадка
to pay ~ **charges** (ту пэй ~
ча́рджэз) платить расходы по
выгрузке
unforeseen ~ (анфорси́н ~)
непредвиденная посадка
~ **charges** (~ ча́рджэз) лэндинг
Language (ла́нгюадж) язык, языковой
{*adj.*}
~ **barrier** (~ бэ́йриэр) языковой
барьер

Lapse (лапс) прекращение
~ **of a patent** (~ оф а па́тэнт)
прекращение патента
Larceny (ла́рсэни) кража
Large (лардж) большой, крупный
Large-format (лардж-фо́рмат)
крупноформатный
Large-scale (лардж-скэйл)
крупномасштабный
Lash, to (лаш, ту ~) крепить
верёвками, обвязывать
to ~ together (ту ~ тогэ́θэр)
связывать верёвкой
Lashing (ла́шинг) верёвка
cargo ~ (ка́рго ~) верёвка для
крепления груза
to secure the ~**s** (ту сэкю́р θи
~с) крепить верёвкой
Latent (лэ́йтэнт) скрытый
Lateral (ла́тэрал) горизонтальный
Launching (ла́унчинг) выпуск
~ **of a new product** (~ оф а нью
про́дукт) выпуск нового продукта
Lavish, to (ла́виш, ту) расточать
to ~ praise upon (ту ~ прэйз
упо́н) расточать похвалы
Law (ла́у) закон, правило, право
administrative ~ (адми́нистрэйтив
~) административное право
admiralty ~ (а́дмиралти ~)
морское право
applicable ~ (аппли́кабл ~)
применимое право
banking ~ (ба́нкинг ~) банковский
закон
canon ~ (ка́нон ~) каноническое
право
civil ~ (си́вил ~) гражданское
право
codified ~ (ко́дифайд ~)
кодифицированное право
commercial ~ (комме́ршл ~)
коммерческое право
common ~ (ко́ммон ~) общее право
comparative ~ (компа́ратив ~)
сравнительное право
constitutional ~ (конститу́шнал
~) конституционный закон,
конституционное право
criminal ~ (кри́минал ~)
уголовное право
customary ~ (ка́стомари ~)
обычный закон, обычное право
customs ~ (ка́стомз ~) таможенный
закон
discriminatory ~ (дискри́минатори
~) дискриминационный закон

dry ~ (драй ~) сухой закон
ecclesiastical ~ (экклизиáстикал
~) церковное право
economic ~ (эконóмик ~)
экономический закон
emergency ~ (эмэ́рджэнси ~)
чрезвычайный закон
existing ~ (экзи́стинг ~)
существующий закон
family ~ (фáмили ~) семейное
право
federal ~ (фэ́дэрал ~)
федеральный закон
fiscal ~ (фи́скал ~) фискальный
закон
formal ~ (фóрмал ~) формальный
закон, формальное право
Grisham's ~ (гри́шамз ~) закон
грешема
intergovernmental ~
(интэрговэрнмэ́нтал ~)
внутригосударственное право
intergovernmental ~ and order
(интэрговэрнмэ́нтал ~ энд óрдэр)
внутригосударственный
правопорядок
intragovernmental ~
(и́нтрагвэрнмэ́нтал ~)
внутригосударственный закон
international ~ (интэрнáшэнал ~)
международное право
international ~ and order
(интэрнáшэнал ~ энд óрдэр)
международный правопорядок
international administrative ~
(интэрнáшэнал адми́нистрэйтив ~)
международное административное
право
international admiralty ~
(интэрнáшэнал áдмиралти ~)
международное морское право
international civil ~
(интэрнáшэнал си́вил ~)
международное гражданское право
international criminal ~
(интэрнáшэнал кри́минал ~)
международное уголовное право
international customary ~
(интэрнáшэнал кáстомари ~)
международное обычное право
international ~ of outer space
(интэрнáшэнал ~ оф óутэр спэйс)
международное космическое право
international positive ~
(интэрнáшэнал пóзитив ~)
международное позитивное право

international private ~
(интэрнáшэнал прáйват ~)
международное частное право
international public ~
(интэрнáшэнал пáблик ~)
международное публичное право
international trade ~
(интэрнáшэнал трэйд ~)
международное торговое право
iron ~ (айрн ~) железный закон
Islamic ~ (ислáмик ~)
мусульманское право
labor ~ (лэ́йбор ~) трудовой
закон, трудовое право
local ~ (лóкал ~) местное право
military ~ (ми́литари ~) военное
право
military criminal ~ (ми́литари
кри́минал ~) военное уголовное
право
model ~ (мóдэл ~) типовой закон
municipal ~ (мюни́сипал ~)
муниципальный закон
Murphy's ~ (мýрфиз ~) закон
подлости
national ~ (нáшэнал ~)
национальный закон, национальное
право
natural ~ (нáчюрал ~)
естественное право
organic ~ (оргáник ~)
органический закон
patent ~ (пáтэнт ~) патентный
закон
penal ~ (пи́нал ~) карательное
право
positive ~ (пóзитив ~)
позитивное право
private ~ (прáйват ~) частное
право
private admiralty ~ (прáйват
áдмиралти ~) частное морское
право
procedural ~ (проси́дюрал ~)
процессуальное право
proposed ~ (пропóзд ~)
законопредложение
public ~ (пáблик ~)
государственное право, публичное
право
race ~ (рэйс ~) расовый закон
Roman ~ (рóман ~) римское право
science of ~ (сáйэнс оф ~)
правоведение
societal ~ (сосáйэтал ~)
общественный закон

~ **of previous convictions** (~ оф привиос конвикшнс) отсутствие судимости
~ **of quorum** (~ оф куорум) отсутствие кворума
~ **of raw materials** (~ оф рау матириалс) нехватка сырья
Lacking (лаккинг) отсутствующий
to be ~ (ту би ~) отсутствовать
Land (ланд) земля, земельный {adj.}, поземельный {adj.}
arable ~ (эйрабл ~) пахотная земля
border ~ (бордэр ~) пограничная земля
cultivated ~ (култивэйтэд ~) возделанная земля
fallow ~ (фаллоу ~) залежная земля
individual ~ **tenure** (индивидюал ~ тэнюр) единоличное землепользование
leased ~ (лисд ~) арендованная земля
occupied ~ (оккюпайд ~) занятая земля
state ~**s** (стэйт ~с) казённая земля
urban ~ (урбан ~) городская земля
~ **owner** (~ оунэр) землевладелец
~ **ownership** (~ оунэршип) землевладение
~ **tax** (~ такс) поземельный налог
~ **surveyor** (~ сурвэйор) землемер
~ **tenure** (~ тэнюр) землепользование
~ **tenure regulation** (~ тэнюр рэгюлэйшн) землеустройство
Landed (ландэд) на берег
~ **price** (~ прайс) цена с выгрузкой на берег
~ **terms** (~ тэрмз) на условиях с выгрузкой на берег
Landing (ландинг) посадка
forced ~ (форсд ~) вынужденная посадка
to pay ~ **charges** (ту пэй ~ чарджэз) платить расходы по выгрузке
unforeseen ~ (анфорсин ~) непредвиденная посадка
~ **charges** (~ чарджэз) лэндинг
Language (лангюадж) язык, языковой {adj.}
~ **barrier** (~ бэйриэр) языковой барьер

Lapse (лапс) прекращение
~ **of a patent** (~ оф а патэнт) прекращение патента
Larceny (ларсэни) кража
Large (лардж) большой, крупный
Large-format (лардж-формат) крупноформатный
Large-scale (лардж-скэйл) крупномасштабный
Lash, to ~ (лаш, ту ~) крепить верёвками, обвязывать
to ~ **together** (ту ~ тогэθэр) связывать верёвкой
Lashing (лашинг) верёвка
cargo ~ (карго ~) верёвка для крепления груза
to secure the ~**s** (ту сэкюр θи ~с) крепить верёвкой
Latent (лэйтэнт) скрытый
Lateral (латэрал) горизонтальный
Launching (лаунчинг) выпуск
~ **of a new product** (~ оф а нью продукт) выпуск нового продукта
Lavish, to (лавиш, ту) расточать
to ~ **praise upon** (ту ~ прэйз упон) расточать похвалы
Law (лау) закон, правило, право
administrative ~ (администрэйтив ~) административное право
admiralty ~ (адмиралти ~) морское право
applicable ~ (алпликабл ~) применимое право
banking ~ (банкинг ~) банковский закон
canon ~ (канон ~) каноническое право
civil ~ (сивил ~) гражданское право
codified ~ (кодифайд ~) кодифицированное право
commercial ~ (коммэршл ~) коммерческое право
common ~ (коммон ~) общее право
comparative ~ (компаратив ~) сравнительное право
constitutional ~ (конститушнал ~) конституционный закон, конституционное право
criminal ~ (криминал ~) уголовное право
customary ~ (кастомари ~) обычный закон, обычное право
customs ~ (кастомз ~) таможенный закон
discriminatory ~ (дискриминатори ~) дискриминационный закон

dry ~ (драй ~) сухой закон
ecclesiastical ~ (экклизиастикал
~) церковное право
economic ~ (экономик ~)
экономический закон
emergency ~ (эмэрджэнси ~)
чрезвычайный закон
existing ~ (экзистинг ~)
существующий закон
family ~ (фамили ~) семейное
право
federal ~ (фэдэрал ~)
федеральный закон
fiscal ~ (фискал ~) фискальный
закон
formal ~ (формал ~) формальный
закон, формальное право
Grisham's ~ (гришамз ~) закон
грешема
intergovernmental ~
(интэрговэрнмэнтал ~)
внутригосударственное право
intergovernmental ~ and order
(интэрговэрнмэнтал ~ энд ордэр)
внутригосударственный
правопорядок
intragovernmental ~
(интраговэрнмэнтал ~)
внутригосударственный закон
international ~ (интэрнашэнал ~)
международное право
international ~ and order
(интэрнашэнал ~ энд ордэр)
международный правопорядок
international administrative ~
(интэрнашэнал администрэйтив ~)
международное административное
право
international admiralty ~
(интэрнашэнал адмиралти ~)
международное морское право
international civil ~
(интэрнашэнал сивил ~)
международное гражданское право
international criminal ~
(интэрнашэнал криминал ~)
международное уголовное право
international customary ~
(интэрнашэнал кастомари ~)
международное обычное право
international ~ of outer space
(интэрнашэнал ~ оф оутэр спэйс)
международное космическое право
international positive ~
(интэрнашэнал позитив ~)
международное позитивное право

international private ~
(интэрнашэнал прайват ~)
международное частное право
international public ~
(интэрнашэнал паблик ~)
международное публичное право
international trade ~
(интэрнашэнал трэйд ~)
международное торговое право
iron ~ (айрн ~) железный закон
Islamic ~ (исламик ~)
мусульманское право
labor ~ (лэйбор ~) трудовой
закон, трудовое право
local ~ (локал ~) местное право
military ~ (милитари ~) военное
право
military criminal ~ (милитари
криминал ~) военное уголовное
право
model ~ (модэл ~) типовой закон
municipal ~ (мюнисипал ~)
муниципальный закон
Murphy's ~ (мурфиз ~) закон
подлости
national ~ (нашэнал ~)
национальный закон, национальное
право
natural ~ (начюрал ~)
естественное право
organic ~ (органик ~)
органический закон
patent ~ (патэнт ~) патентный
закон
penal ~ (пинал ~) карательное
право
positive ~ (позитив ~)
позитивное право
private ~ (прайват ~) частное
право
private admiralty ~ (прайват
адмиралти ~) частное морское
право
procedural ~ (просидюрал ~)
процессуальное право
proposed ~ (пропозд ~)
законопредложение
public ~ (паблик ~)
государственное право, публичное
право
race ~ (рэйс ~) расовый закон
Roman ~ (роман ~) римское право
science of ~ (сайэнс оф ~)
правоведение
societal ~ (сосайэтал ~)
общественный закон

Soviet ~ (со́виэт ~) советское право

special ~ (спэшл ~) специальный закон

study of comparative ~ (сту́ди оф компа́ратив ~) сравнительное правоведение

supranational ~ (супрана́шэнал ~) наднациональное право

tariff ~ (та́риф ~) тарифный закон

tax ~ (такс ~) налоговый закон , налоговое право

temporary ~ (тэ́мпорари ~) временный закон

"thieves in the ~" (θивз ин θи ~) воры в законе {organized criminal groupings in the former USSR}

to administer the ~ (ту адми́нистэр θи ~) отправлять правосудие

to evade a ~ (ту ивэ́йд а ~) обойти закон

trade ~ (трэйд ~) торговое право

unwritten ~ (анри́ттэн ~) неписаное право

written ~ (ри́ттэн ~) письменный закон , писанное право

~ and order (~ энд о́рдэр) правопорядок

~ department {law school} (~ дипа́ртмэнт {ла́у скул}) юридический факультет {abbrev.: юрфак}

~ of arbitration (~ оф арбитрэ́йшн) арбитражное право

~ of bills of exchange (~ оф билс оф эксчэ́йндж) вексельное право

~ of civil procedure (~ оф си́вил проси́дюр) гражданское процессуальное право

~ of contracts (~ оф ко́нтрактс) договорное право

~ of estates (~ оф эстэ́йтс) вещное право

~ of evidence (~ оф э́видэнс) доказательственное право

~ of general application (~ оф джэ́нэрал аппликэ́йшн) общий закон

~ of guardianship (~ оф га́рдианшип) опекунское право

~ in force (~ ин форс) действующее право

~ of obligations (~ оф облигэ́йшнз) обязательственное право

~ of outer space (~ оф о́утэр спэйс) космическое право

~ of property (~ оф про́пэрти) имущественное право

~ of real property (~ оф рил про́пэрти) недвижимое имущественное право

~ of subterranean resources (~ оф субтэррэ́йниан рисо́рсэз) горное право

~-abiding person (~-аба́йдинг пэ́рсон) законник

Lawful (ла́уфул) правовой

Lawlessness (ла́улэснэс) незаконность

Lawsuit (ла́усут) исковая претензия

Lawyer (ла́уер) адвокат, законник {colloquial}, юрист

Lay (лэй) класть, положить
to ~ a claim to (ту ~ а клэйм ту) притязать

Layday (лэ́йдэй) контрсталийный {adj.}, контрсталия ~s сталийное время, стояночное время

Layout (лэ́йоут) макет
floor plan ~ (флор план ~) макет экспозиции

Laytime (лэ́йтайм) время стоянки
allowed (алло́уд ~) разрешённое время стоянки судна

L/C (эл-си) аккредитив

Leader (ли́дэр) руководитель
brigade ~ (бригэ́йд ~) бригадир

Leadership (ли́дэршип) руководство

Leading (ли́динг) руководящий

Leaflet (лифлэ́т) листовка
distribution of ~s (дистрибю́шн оф ~с) распространение листовок
to distribute ~s (ту дистри́бют ~с) распространять листовки

League (лиг) лига, союз
Communist Youth ~ {Komsomol} (ко́ммунист юθ ~ {ко́мсомол}) коммунистический союз молодежи {комсомол}

Lease (лис) аренда, наём
agricultural ~ (агрику́лчурал ~) сельскохозяйственная аренда
for ~ (фор ~) внаём, внаймы
gratuitous ~ (грату́итос ~) бесплатная аренда
ground ~ (гро́унд ~) земельная рента

income ~ (и́нком ~) рентная аренда {income property}
international ~ (интэрна́шэнал ~) международная аренда
kiosk ~ (ки́оск ~) аренда киоска
land ~ (ланд ~) аренда земли
long-term ~ (лонг-тэрм ~) долгосрочная аренда
perpetual ~ (пэрпэ́тчуал ~) бессрочная аренда
short-term ~ (шорт-тэрм ~) краткосрочная аренда
to ~ (ту ~) брать внаём, внаймы, взять в аренду {as lessee}
to ~ (ту ~) арендовать, отдать в аренду, сдать в аренду, сдавать внаём, внаймы {as lessor}
to ~ a vessel under a charter party (ту ~ а вэ́ссэл а́ндэр а ча́ртэр па́рти) сдавать внаём, внаймы судно по чартеру {as lessor}
to give up for ~ (ту гив ап фор ~) уступить в аренду
to offer for ~ (ту о́ффэр фор ~) предоставить в аренду
unlimited term ~ (анли́митэд тэрм ~) неограниченная сроком аренда
~ conditions (~ конди́шнс) условия найма в аренду
~ of agricultural land (~ оф агрику́лчурал ланд) аренда сельскохозяйственных земель
~ of space (~ оф спэйс) аренда площади
Leaseholding (лисхо́лдинг) владение на основе аренды
Leasing (ли́синг) лизинг, лизинговый {adj.}, сдача
Leave (лив) отпуск
additional ~ (адди́шнал ~) дополнительный отпуск
annual ~ (а́ннюал ~) ежегодный отпуск
maternity ~ (матэ́рнити ~) отпуск по беременности, отпуск по беременности и родам
post-maternity ~ (пост-матэ́рнити ~) послеродовой отпуск
pre-maternity ~ (при-матэ́рнити ~) дородовой отпуск
sick ~ (сик ~) отпуск по болезни
to ~ (ту ~) расстаться
worker on ~ (уо́ркэр он ~) отпускник
Ledger (лэ́джэр) бухгалтерская книга

Legal (ли́гал) законный, легальный, правовой, судебный, юридический
by ~ means (бай ~ минз) правовым средством
from a ~ standpoint (фром а ~ ста́ндпойнт) с юридической точки зрения
~ advice (~ адва́йс) консультация юриста
~ advisor (~ адва́йзор) юрисконсульт
~ clinic (~ кли́ник) юридическая консультация
~ relations (~ рилэ́йшнс) правоотношения
~ sciences (~ са́йэнсэз) юридические науки
Legality (лига́лити) законность
international ~ (интэрна́шэнал ~) международная законность
socialist ~ (со́шлист ~) социалистическая законность
Legalization (лигализэ́йшн) легализация, правовое оформление
Legalize, to ~ (ли́галайз, ту ~) оформлять
Legalized (ли́галайзд) легализованный
Legally (ли́галли) законно, юридически
Legation (лэгэ́йшн) миссия
Legislate, to ~ (лэ́джислэйт, ту ~) законодательствовать
Legislation (лэджислэ́йшн) законодательство
agrarian ~ (агра́риан ~) аграрное законодательство
anti-dumping ~ (а́нти-да́мпинг ~) законодательство против демпинга
anti-trust ~ (а́нти-траст ~) антимонопольное законодательство
arbitration ~ (арбитрэ́йшн ~) арбитражное законодательство
banking ~ (ба́нкинг ~) банковское законодательство
budgetary ~ (ба́джэтари ~) бюджетное законодательство
civil ~ (си́вил ~) гражданское законодательство
civil aviation ~ (си́вил эйвиэ́йшн ~) воздушное законодательство
civil procedure ~ (си́вил проси́дюр ~) гражданское процессуальное законодательство
collective farm ~ (коллэ́ктив фарм ~) колхозное законодательство

colonial ~ (колóниал ~) колониальное законодательство
commercial ~ (коммэ́ршл ~) торговое законодательство
constitutional ~ (конститу́шнал ~) конституционное законодательство
credit ~ (крэ́дит ~) кредитное законодательство
currency exchange ~ (ку́ррэнси эксчэ́йндж ~) валютное законодательство
customs ~ (ка́стомз ~) таможенное законодательство
domestic ~ (домэ́стик ~) отечественное законодательство
economic ~ (эконóмик ~) экономическое законодательство
emergency ~ (эмэ́рджэнси ~) чрезвычайное законодательство
family ~ (фа́мили ~) семейное законодательство
federal ~ (фэ́дэрал ~) федеральное законодательство
financial ~ (файна́ншл ~) финансовое законодательство
fiscal ~ (фи́скал ~) фискальное законодательство
foreign ~ (фóрэн ~) иностранное законодательство
health ~ (хэл θ ~) санитарное законодательство
housing ~ (хóузинг ~) жилищное законодательство
immigration ~ (иммигрэ́йшн ~) иммиграционное законодательство
in force (ин форс) действующее законодательство
insurance ~ (иншю́ранс ~) страховое законодательство
internal ~ (интэ́рнал ~) внутреннее законодательство
international ~ (интэрна́шэнал ~) международное законодательство
labor ~ (лэ́йбор ~) трудовое законодательство
land ~ (ланд ~) земельное законодательство
local ~ (лóкал ~) местное законодательство
marital ~ (ма́ритал ~) брачное законодательство
maritime ~ (ма́ритайм ~) морское законодательство
military ~ (ми́литари ~) военное законодательство

mining ~ (ма́йнинг ~) горное законодательство
national ~ (на́шэнал ~) национальное законодательство
parallel ~ (па́ралэл ~) параллельное законодательство
patent ~ (па́тэнт ~) патентное законодательство
penal ~ (пи́нал ~) уголовное законодательство
postal ~ (пóстал ~) почтовое законодательство
procedural ~ (проси́дюрал ~) процессуальное законодательство
racist ~ (рэ́йсист ~) расистское законодательство
rent-control ~ (рэнт-контрóл ~) законодательство о квартирной плате
riparian ~ (райпэ́йриан ~) водное законодательство
rural ~ (ру́рал ~) сельское законодательство
tax ~ (такс ~) налоговое законодательство
timber ~ (ти́мбэр ~) лесное законодательство
Legislative (лэ́джислэйтив) законодательный
Legislator (лэ́джислэйтор) законодатель
Legitimate (лэджи́тимат) законный, обоснованный
  ~ **child** (~ чайлд) законнорождённый
Leisure (лэ́жюр) досуг, отдых
  at your ~ (ат юр ~) на досуге
Lend, to ~ (лэнд, ту ~) давать в долг, давать взаймы, давать в кредит, одалживать [perfective: одолжить], ссужать [perfective: ссудить]
Lender (лэ́ндэр) заимодавец, заимодатель, кредитор
  private ~ (пра́йват ~) частный кредитор
Lending (лэ́ндинг) кредит, кредитование, ссудный {adj.}
  foreign exchange ~ (фóрэн эксчэ́йндж ~) валютное кредитование
  targeted ~ (та́ргэтэд ~) целевое кредитование
Length (лэнг θ) длина {dimension}, продолжительность {duration}
  overall ~ (овэра́л ~) габаритная длина

Lessee (лэсси́) арендатор, съёмщик
  primary ~ (пра́ймари ~) основной
  съёмщик
Lessor (лэссо́р) арендодатель
Let, to ~ (лэт, ту ~) сдавать в
наём
Letter (лэ́ттэр) письмо
  anonymous ~ (ано́нимос ~)
  анонимное письмо
  cash ~ (каш ~) кассовое письмо
  cover ~ (ко́вэр ~)
  сопроводительное письмо
  dunning ~ (ду́ннинг ~) письмо с
  требованием уплаты долга
  express ~ (экспрэ́с ~) срочное
  письмо
  official ~ (оффи́шл ~) служебное
  письмо
  registered ~ (рэ́джистэрд ~)
  заказное письмо
  registered ~ **with declared value**
  (рэ́джистэрд ~ уиθ дикла́йрд ва́лю)
  ценное письмо
  registered ~ **with return**
  notification (рэ́джистэрд ~ уиθ
  риту́рн нотифика́йшн) заказное
  письмо с обратной распиской
  threatening ~ (θрэ́тэнинг ~)
  угрожающее письмо
  ~**-head** (~-хэд) бланк для письма
  со штампом фирмы
  ~ **of consular credentials** (~ оф
  ко́нсюлар крэдэ́ншлз) письмо о
  назначении консула
  ~**s of exchange** (~с оф эксчэ́йндж)
  обменные письма
  ~ **of hypothecation** (~ оф
  хайпоθэкэ́йшн) залоговое
  свидетельство
Letter of credit (лэ́ттэр оф крэ́дит)
аккредитив, аккредитивное письмо
  back-to-back ~ (бак-ту-бак ~ оф
  крэ́дит) компенсационный
  аккредитив
  bank ~ (банк ~ оф крэ́дит)
  банковский аккредитив
  blank ~ (бланк ~ оф крэ́дит)
  бланковый аккредитив
  circular ~ (си́ркюлар ~ оф
  крэ́дит) циркулярный аккредитив
  clean ~ (клин ~ оф крэ́дит)
  чистый аккредитив
  commercial ~ (комме́ршл ~ оф
  крэ́дит) товарный аккредитив
  confirmed ~ (конфи́рмд ~ оф
  крэ́дит) подтверждённый
  аккредитив

  divisible ~ (диви́зибл ~ оф
  крэ́дит) делимый аккредитив
  documentary ~ (докюмэ́нтари ~ оф
  крэ́дит) документарный аккредитив
  export ~ (э́кспорт ~ оф крэ́дит)
  экспортный аккредитив
  installment ~ (инста́лмэнт ~ оф
  крэ́дит) аккредитив с платежом в
  рассрочку
  irrevocable ~ (иррэ́вокабл ~ оф
  крэ́дит) безотзывный аккредитив
  long term ~ (лонг тэрм ~ оф
  крэ́дит) долгосрочный аккредитив
  non-transferable ~ (нон-
  трансфэ́рабл ~ оф крэ́дит)
  непереводный аккредитив
  registered ~ (рэ́джистэрд ~ оф
  крэ́дит) именной аккредитив
  revolving ~ (риво́лвинг ~ оф
  крэ́дит) автоматически
  возобновляемый аккредитив,
  револьверный аккредитив
  traveler's ~ (тра́вэлэрз ~ оф
  крэ́дит) путевой аккредитив
  unconfirmed ~ (анконфи́рмд ~ оф
  крэ́дит) неподтверждённый
  аккредитив
  ~ **payable in freely convertible**
  currency (~ оф крэ́дит пэ́йабл ин
  фри́ли конвэ́ртибл ку́ррэнси)
  аккредитив с платежом в свободно
  конвертируемой валюте
  ~ **valid for ...** (~ оф крэ́дит
  ва́лид фор ...) аккредитив сроком
  действия на ...
Letting (лэ́ттинг) отдача, сдача в
наём
  ~ **for rent** (~ фор рэнт) отдача в
  наём
Level (лэ́вэл) ступень, уровень
  at a high ~ (ат а хай ~) на
  высоком уровне
  at any ~ (ат а́ни ~) на любом
  уровне
  at the ~ **of world standards** (ат
  θи ~ оф уо́рлд ста́ндардс) на
  уровне мировых стандартов
  at the ministerial ~ (ат θи
  министэ́риал ~) на уровне
  министров
  at the required ~ (ат θи
  рику́айрд ~) на должном уровне
  at the same ~ (ат θи сэйм ~) на
  одном уровне
  average ~ (а́вэрэдж ~) средний
  уровень

first-class ~ (фэрст-класс ~) первоклассный уровень
funding ~ (фу́ндинг ~) размер ассигнований
growth in wage ~s (гроθ ин уэйдж ~с) рост уровня заработной платы
high ~ negotiations (хай ~ нэгошиэ́йшнс) переговоры на высшем уровне
income ~ (и́нком ~) уровень дохода
minimum ~ (ми́нимум ~) минимальный уровень
peak ~ (пик ~) высший уровень
preferential ~ (прэфэрэ́ншл ~) льготный уровень
professional ~ (профэ́шнал ~) профессиональный уровень
sales ~ (сэйлз ~) уровень запродаж
scientific and technological ~ (сайэнти́фик энд тэкноло́джикал ~) научно-технический уровень
stable ~ (стэ́йбл ~) устойчивый уровень
to be at the ~ of ... (ту би ат θи ~ оф ...) стоять на уровне ...
to be on the ~ of world standards (ту би он θи ~ оф уо́рлд ста́ндардс) быть на уровне мировых стандартов
to guarantee a high ~ of service (ту гяранти́ а хай ~ оф сэ́рвис) гарантировать высокий уровень обслуживания
wage ~ (уэ́йдж ~) уровень зарплаты
~ of achievements (~ оф ачи́вмэнтс) уровень достижений
~ of best world standards (~ оф бэст уо́рлд ста́ндардс) уровень лучших мировых образцов
~ of business activity (~ оф би́знэс акти́вити) уровень деловой активности
~ of economic activity (~ оф эконо́мик акти́вити) уровень экономической активности
~ of economic development (~ оф эконо́мик дивэ́лопмэнт) уровень экономического развития
~ of education and experience (~ оф эдюкэ́йшн энд экспи́риэнс) уровень образования и опыта
~ of engineering (~ оф инджэни́ринг) технический уровень

~ of income (~ оф и́нком) размер дохода
~ of prices (~ оф пра́йсэз) уровень цен
~ of production (~ оф прода́кшн) уровень производства
~ of profitability (~ оф профитаби́лити) уровень рентабельности
~ of rates (~ оф рэйтс) уровень ставок
~ of rental payment (~ оф рэ́нтал пэ́ймэнт) уровень арендной платы
~ of sales (~ оф сэйлз) уровень сбыта
Leveling off (лэ́вэлинг офф) выравнивание
~ of conditions (~ оф конди́шнс) уравнивание условий
Lever (лэ́вэр) рычаг
control ~ (контро́л ~) рычаг управления
~ of economic control (~ оф эконо́мик контро́л) экономический рычаг
Levy (лэ́ви) взимание, обложение
tax ~ (такс ~) налоговый сбор
to ~ (ту ~) взимать, облагать
~ of taxes (~ оф та́ксэз) взимание налогов
Liabilit/y (лайаби́лити) долг, задолженность, обязанность, обязательство, ответственность за ущерб, пассив
accrued ~/ies (аккру́д ~из) срочные обязательства
civil ~ (си́вил ~) гражданская ответственность
collective ~ (коллэ́ктив ~) коллективная ответственность
contingent ~ (конти́нджэнт ~) условный долг, условное обязательство, условная ответственность
contractual ~ (контра́кчуал ~) договорная ответственность
criminal ~ (кри́минал ~) уголовная ответственность
deferred ~/ies (дифэ́рд ~из) отсроченные обязательства
deposit ~ (дипо́зит ~) обязательство по депозиту
future ~ (фю́чэр ~) будущее обязательство
gross ~/ies (грос ~из) общая сумма пассива

increased ~ (инкри́сд ~)
повышенная ответственность
joint ~ (джойнт ~) взаимная
ответственность, совместное
обязательство, солидарная
ответственность
judicial ~ (джюди́шл ~) судебная
ответственность
limitation of ~ (лимитэ́йшн оф ~)
ограничение ответственности
limited ~ (ли́митэд ~)
ограниченная ответственность
material ~ (мати́риал ~)
материальная ответственность
maximum ~ (ма́ксимум ~)
максимальная ответственность
non-contractual ~ (нон-
контра́кчуал ~) внедоговорная
ответственность
outstanding ~/ies (оутста́ндинг
~из) непокрытые обязательства
primary ~ (пра́ймари ~) основная
ответственность
sight ~ (сайт ~) бессрочное
обязательство
solo ~ (со́ло ~) индивидуальная
ответственность
tax ~ (такс ~) налоговое
обязательство, налоговая
ответственность
to be subject to judicial ~ (ту
би са́бджэкт ту джюди́шл ~)
подлежать судебной
ответственности
to exclude ~ (ту эксли́од)
исключить ответственность
to incur ~ (ту инку́р ~) нести
ответственность
tort ~ (торт ~) деликтная
ответственность
uncovered ~/ies (анко́вэрд ~из)
открытые обязательства
unlimited ~ (анли́митэд ~)
неограниченная ответственность
~ for breach (~ фор брич)
ответственность за нарушение
~ for debts (~ фор дэтс)
долговая ответственность
~ for infringement (~ фор
инфри́нджмэнт) ответственность за
нарушение
~ on balance sheet (~ он ба́ланс
шит) статья пассива
~ under warranty (~ а́ндэр
уа́рранти) гарантийная
ответственность
Liable (ла́йабл) ответственный

Liaison (лиэ́йзон) атташе
press ~ (прэс ~) атташе печати
Liberal (ли́бэрал) либеральный
{adj.}
Liberalization (либэрализэ́йшн)
либерализация
economic ~ (эконо́мик ~)
либерализация экономики
import ~ (и́мпорт ~)
либерализация импорта
trade ~ (трэйд ~) либерализация
торговли
~ of trade (~ оф трэйд)
либерализация
внешнеэкономических связей
Liberation (либэрэ́йшн) освобождение
Liberty (ли́бэрти) свобода
at ~ (ат ~) поднадзорная свобода
personal ~ (пэ́рсонал ~) личная
свобода
to set at ~ (ту сэт ат ~)
освобождать на волю
LIBOR {London InterBank Offering
Rate} (ла́йбор {ло́ндон интэрба́нк
о́ффэринг рэйт}) либор {Лондонская
межбанковская ставка}
License (ла́йсэнз) лицензионный
{adj.}, лицензия, разрешение
active ~ (а́ктив ~) активная
лицензия, продаваемая лицензия
annulment of a ~ (анну́лмэнт оф а
~) аннулирование лицензии
application for a ~ (апплике́йшн
фор а ~) заявка на лицензию
assignable ~ (асса́йнабл ~)
лицензия с правом передачи
blanket ~ (бла́нкэт ~) общая
лицензия
compulsory ~ (компу́лсори ~)
принудительная лицензия
concession of a (консэ́шн оф а)
предоставление лицензии
contractual ~ (контра́кчуал ~)
договорная лицензия
copy of a ~ (ко́пи оф а ~)
дубликат лицензии
cross ~ (крос ~) перекрёстная
лицензия
customs ~ (ка́стомз ~) таможенная
лицензия
denial of a ~ (дина́йал оф а ~)
отказ в предоставлении лицензии
driver's ~ (дра́йвэрз ~) право
водителя
equipment ~ (икуи́пмэнт ~)
лицензия на оборудование

exclusive ~ (эксклю́сив ~)
исключительная лицензия, полная
лицензия
export (э́кспорт) лицензия на
вывоз, экспортная лицензия
export of ~s (э́кспорт оф ~с)
экспорт лицензий
feedback ~ (фи́дбак ~) обратная
лицензия
free ~ (фри ~) свободная
лицензия
general ~ (джэ́нэрал ~)
генеральная лицензия
geographically limited ~
(джиогра́фикалли ли́митэд ~)
лицензия действующая на
определённой территории
global ~ (гло́бал ~) глобальная
лицензия
grant of a ~ (грант оф а ~)
выдача лицензии
hunting ~ (ха́нтинг ~) разрешение
на право охоты
import ~ (и́мпорт ~) импортная
лицензия, лицензия на ввоз
indivisible ~ (индиви́зибл ~)
неделимая лицензия
industrial process ~ (инду́стриал
про́сэс ~) лицензия на право
использования технологического
процесса
know-how ~ (но́у-ха́у ~) лицензия
на ноу-хау
label ~ (лэ́йбэл ~) лицензия на
этикетку
legal ~ (ли́гал ~) юридическое
лицензия
limited ~ (ли́митэд ~)
ограниченная лицензия
manufacture under ~ (манюфа́кчур
андэр ~) изготовление по
лицензии
manufacturing ~ (манюфа́кчуринг
~) лицензия на право
производства
non-exclusive ~ (нон-эксклю́сив
~) неисключительная лицензия
non-patent ~ (нон-па́тэнт ~)
беспатентная лицензия
non-transferrable ~ (нон-
трансфэ́рабл ~) не подлежащая
передаче лицензии
open general ~ (о́пэн джэ́нэрал ~)
открытая общая лицензия
operating ~ (о́пэрэйтинг ~)
лицензия на использование,
лицензия на эксплуатацию

owner of a ~ (о́унэр оф а ~)
владелец лицензии
package ~ (па́кэдж ~) комплексная
лицензия
passive ~ (па́ссив ~) пассивная
лицензия
process ~ (про́сэс ~) лицензия на
процесс
production under ~ (прода́кшн
а́ндэр ~) выпуск продукции по
лицензии
purchase of a ~ (пу́рчас оф а ~)
закупка лицензии
recipient of a ~ (риси́пиэнт оф а
~) получатель лицензии
reciprocal ~ (риси́прокал ~)
взаимная лицензия
registration of a ~
(рэджистрэ́йшн оф а ~)
регистрация лицензии
retroactive ~ (рэтроа́ктив ~)
ретроактивная лицензия
revocation of a ~ (рэвокэ́йшн оф
а ~) аннулирование лицензии
royalty-bearing ~ (ро́йялти-
бэ́ринг ~) предусматривающая
уплату роялти лицензия
royalty-free ~ (ро́йялти-фри ~)
лицензия без уплаты роялти
sales ~ (сэйлз ~) лицензия на
сбыт
scope of a ~ (скоп оф а ~) объём
лицензии
simple ~ (симпл ~) простая
лицензия
special import ~ (спэшл и́мпорт
~) импортная, специальная
лицензия
subject matter of a ~ (са́бджэкт
ма́ттэр оф а ~) предмет лицензии
subsidized ~ (су́бсидайзд ~)
субсидируемое лицензия
tenure of a ~ (тэ́нюр оф а ~)
срок владения лицензией
term of ~ validity (тэрм оф ~
вали́дити) срок действия лицензии
termination of a ~ (тэрмина́йшн
оф а ~) прекращение действия
лицензии
to ~ (ту ~) лицензировать
to ~ a production process (ту ~
а прода́кшн про́сэс) предоставлять
лицензию на производство
to ~ technology (ту ~
тэкно́лоджи) предоставлять
лицензию на технологию

to **annul** a ~ (ту аннýл а ~)
аннулировать лицензию
to **extend** a ~ (ту экстэнд а ~)
продлевать лицензию
to **grant** a ~ (ту грант а ~)
выдавать лицензию, предоставлять
лицензию
to **have** a ~ (ту хэв а ~) иметь
лицензию
to **hold** a ~ **invalid** (ту холд а ~
инвáлид) признавать лицензию
недействительной
to **obtain** a ~ (ту обтэйн а ~)
приобретать лицензию
to **produce under** ~ (ту продю́с
áндэр ~) производить по лицензии
to **receive** a ~ (ту рисúв а ~)
получать лицензию
to **revoke** a ~ (ту ривóк а ~)
отзывать лицензию
to **sell** a ~ (ту сэл а ~)
продавать лицензию
trade in ~s (трэйд ин ~с)
торговля лицензиями
trademark ~ (трэ́йдмарк ~)
лицензия на товарный знак
transshipment ~ (транссши́пмэнт ~)
лицензия на перегрузку товара
transferrable ~ (трансфэ́рабл ~)
лицензия с правом переуступки
unconditional ~ (анконди́шнал ~)
безусловная лицензия
under ~ (áндэр ~) по лицензии
valid ~ (вáлид ~) действительная
лицензия
validity of a ~ (вали́дити оф а
~) действительность лицензии
voluntary ~ (вóлунтэри ~)
добровольная лицензия
~ **department** (~ дипáртмэнт)
отдел лицензий
~ **fee** (~ фи) плата за лицензию
~ **for foreign patent filing** (~
фор фóрэн пáтэнт фáйлинг)
лицензия на зарубежное
патентование
~ **for a patent** (~ фор а пáтэнт)
лицензия на патент
~ **for the use of an invention** (~
фор θи юс оф ан инвэ́ншн)
лицензия на использование
изобретения
~ **holder** (~ хóлдэр) держатель
лицензии
~ **of fishing rights** (~ оф фи́шинг
райтс) аренда рыбной ловли

~ **on a foreign invention** (~ он а
фóрэн инвэ́ншн) лицензия на
изобретение
~ **project** (~ прóджэкт) проект
лицензирования
~ **under patent** (~ áндэр пáтэнт)
патентная лицензия
~ **without right of transfer** (~
уиθóут райт оф трáнсфэр)
лицензия без права передачи
Licensed (лáйсэнсд) лицензированный
~ **dealer** (~ ди́лэр) дилер с
лицензией
~ **personnel** (~ пэрсоннэ́л)
персонал лицензиата
~ **product** (~ прóдукт) продукция
по лицензии
Licensee (лайсэнси́) владелец
лицензии, лицензиат
exclusive ~ (эксклю́сив ~)
лицензиат исключительной
лицензии
non-exclusive ~ (нон-эксклю́сив
~) лицензиат неисключительной
лицензии
prospective ~ (проспэ́ктив ~)
будущий лицензиат
~'**s obligations** (~с облигэ́йшнз)
обязательства лицензиата
~'**s operations** (~с опэрэ́йшнз)
деятельность лицензиата
Licensing (лáйсэнсинг)
лицензирование
compulsory ~ (компу́лсори ~)
принудительное лицензирование
compulsory ~ **legislation**
(компу́лсори ~ лэджислэ́йшн)
законодательство о
принудительном лицензировании
contractual ~ (контрáкчуал ~)
договорное лицензирование
cross ~ (крос ~) перекрёстное
лицензирование
date of ~ (дэйт оф ~) дата
предоставления лицензии
domestic ~ (домэ́стик ~)
отечественное лицензирование
effectiveness of ~ (иффэ́ктивнэс
оф ~) эффективность
лицензирования
mutual ~ (мю́чуал ~) взаимное
лицензирование
overseas ~ (овэрси́з ~)
зарубежное лицензирование
package ~ (пáкэдж ~) пакетное
лицензирование

scope of ~ (скоп оф ~) объём лицензирования
to suspend ~ (ту саспэнд ~) приостанавливать лицензирование
~ arrangements (~ аррэйнджмэнтс) меры по лицензированию
~ fee (~ фи) лицензионное вознаграждение
~ of an industrial design (~ оф ан индустриал дизайн) лицензирование промышленного образца
~ of a patent (~ оф а патэнт) лицензирование патента
~ of a trademark (~ оф а трэйдмарк) лицензирование товарного знака
~ of game {hunting} **rights** (~ оф гэйм {хантинг} райтс) аренда охоты
~ of know-how (~ оф ноу-хау) лицензирование ноу-хау
~ of products (~ оф продуктс) выдача лицензии на товар
~ program (~ програм) программа лицензирования
~ of technological information (~ оф тэкнолоджикал информэйшн) лицензирование технологической информации
Licensor (лайсэнсор) лицензиар
~'s amenability (~з амэнабилити) ответственность лицензиара {to suit}
~'s ownership right (~з оунэршип райт) право собственности лицензиара
Licentiousness (лайсэншоснэс) самоволие
Lid (лид) крышка
plastic ~ (пластик ~) пластмассовая крышка
Lien (лин) задержание, залоговое право, право удержания
Life (лайф) долговечность, жизнь
rated ~ (рэйтэд ~) номинальная долговечность
shelf ~ (шэлф ~) длительность хранения, долговечность при хранении
working ~ (уоркинг ~) длительность эксплуатации
~ imprisonment (~ импризонмэнт) пожизненное заключение
Lifestyle (лайфстайл) образ жизни
settled ~ (сэтлд ~) оседлость
Lifetime (лайфтайм) пожизненный

~ annuity (~ аннюити) пожизненная рента
Lift (лифт) подъём
Lifting (лифтинг) грузоподъёмный {adj.}, подъёмные {adj.}, снятие
~ of immunity (~ оф иммюнити) снятие иммунитета
Light (лайт) лёгкий {of weight}, легковесный {of weight}, светлый
~ duty (~ дюти) малая нагрузка
Lighter (лайтэр) лихтер, лихтерный {adj.}
in a ~ (ин а ~) на лихтере
to ~ (ту ~) выгружать на лихтер
to deliver by ~ (ту дэливэр бай ~) доставлять на лихтере
to place a ~ (ту плэйс а ~) подавать лихтер
Lighterage (лайтэрадж) лихтерный сбор {fee}, лихтеровка, плата за пользование лихтером, расходы по лихтеровке
to pay ~ (ту пэй ~) оплачивать лихтер
Lighting (лайтинг) освещение
Lightly (лайтли) легко
Limit (лимит) лимит, лимитный {adj.}, предел, предельная норма, предельный {adj.}
credit ~ (крэдит ~) предел кредита
lower ~ (лоуэр ~) минимальный размер, нижний предел
maximum ~ (максимум ~) максимальный предел
minimal ~ (минимал ~) минимальный предел
speed ~ (спид ~) ограничение скорости
territorial ~ (тэрриториал ~) предел территории, территориальный предел
to ~ (ту ~) лимитировать, ограничивать
to exceed the ~ (ту экскид θи ~) превышать лимит
to fix a ~ (ту фикс а ~) устанавливать лимит
upper ~ (уппэр ~) максимальный размер
weight ~ (уэйт ~) предел веса
~ of competence (~ оф компэтэнс) предел правомочия
~ of liability (~ оф лайабилити) предел ответственности

~ **of territorial waters** (~ оф
тэррито́риал уа́тэрс) предел
территориальных вод
Limitation (лимитэ́йшн) ограничени,
рестрикция
   abbreviated statute of ~s
(аббри́виэйтэд ста́тют оф ~с)
сокращённый срок давности
   arms ~ (армз ~) ограничение
вооружений
   statute of ~s (ста́тют оф ~с)
закон об исковой давности
   term of ~ (тэрм оф ~) срок
давности
   territorial ~ (тэррито́риал ~)
территориальное ограничение
   ~ **of jurisdiction** (~ оф
джюрисди́кшн) ограничение
юрисдикции
   ~ **of legal claims** (~ оф ли́гал
клэймс) исковая давность
   ~ **of sovereignty** (~ оф со́вэрнти)
ограничение суверенитета
Limited (ли́митэд) лимитируемый,
ограниченный
Limiting (ли́митинг) ограничивающий,
ограничительный
Linchpin (ли́нчпин) рычаг
Line (лайн) лимит, линейный {adj.},
линия, поток
   assembly ~ (ассэ́мбли ~) линия
сборки
   bus ~ (бус ~) автобусная линия
   conference ~ (ко́нфэрэнс ~)
конференциальная линия
   container ~ (контэ́йнэр ~)
контейнерная линия
   experimental ~ (экспэримэ́нтал ~)
опытная линия, экспериментальная
линия
   express ~ (экспрэ́с ~) линия
скорых перевозок
   joint ~ (джойнт ~) смешанная
линия
   principal ~ (при́нсипал ~)
магистральная линия
   production ~ (прода́кшн ~)
поточная линия
   railway ~ (рэ́йлуэй ~)
железнодорожная линия
   rapidly readjustable production
~ (ра́пидли риаджа́стабл прода́кшн
~) быстроперелаживаемая
поточная линия
   shipping ~ (ши́ппинг ~) линия
между портами, судоходная линия

   steamship ~ (сти́мшип ~)
пароходная линия
   telephone ~ (тэ́лэфон ~)
телефонная линия
   world-wide container ~ (уо́рлд-
уайд контэ́йнэр ~) кругосветная
контейнерная линия
Linear (ли́ниар) линейный
Liner (ла́йнэр) лайнер
   passenger ~ (па́ссэнджэр ~)
пассажирское судно
Lining (ла́йнинг) прокладка
Link (линк) звено, связь
   causal ~ (ка́узал ~) казуальная
связь
Linkage (ли́нкадж) общение, связь
   economic ~ (эконо́мик ~)
экономическое общение
Liquid (ли́куид) быстрореализуемый,
жидкий, ликвидный {fiscal}
   international ~ assets
(интэрна́шэнал ~ а́ссэтс)
международные ликвиды
   ~ **foreign exchange assets** (~
фо́рэн эксчэ́йндж а́ссэтс) валютные
ликвиды
Liquidate, to ~ (ли́куидэйт, ту ~)
ликвидировать, погашать
Liquidated (ли́куидэйтэд)
ликвидированный
   to deduct ~ damages (ту диду́кт ~
да́мэджэз) вычитать неустойку
   ~ **damages clause** (~ да́мэджэз
клауз) оговорка о возмещении
Liquidation (ликуидэ́йшн)
ликвидационный {adj.}, ликвидация
   actual ~ (а́кчуал ~) фактическая
ликвидация
   company in the course of ~
(ко́мпани ин θи корс оф ~)
общество в ходе ликвидации
   complete ~ (компли́т ~) полная
ликвидация
   compulsory ~ (компу́лсори ~)
принудительная ликвидация
{court-ordered}
   forced ~ (форсд ~) вынужденная
ликвидация
   inventory ~ (и́нвэнтори ~)
ликвидация запасов
   partial ~ (паршл ~) частичная
ликвидация
   voluntary ~ (во́лунтэри ~)
добровольная ликвидация
   ~ **of a debt** (~ оф а дэт) выплата
долга

~ of a joint venture (~ оф а джойнт вэнчур) ликвидация совместного предприятия
~ of a loan (~ оф а лон) выплата займа

Liquidity (ликуйдити) ликвидность, обеспеченность платёжными средствами

degree of ~ (дигри оф ~) степень ликвидности
excess ~ (эксэс ~) избыточная ликвидность
international ~ (интэрнашэнал ~) международная ликвидность
limited ~ (лимитэд ~) ограниченная ликвидность
official ~ (оффишл ~) официальная ликвидность
on a net ~ basis (он а нэт ~ бэйсис) на базе ликвидности
overall ~ (овэрал ~) общая ликвидность
~ of assets (~ оф ассэтс) ликвидность активов
~ ratio (~ рэйшио) коэффициент ликвидности

List (лист) ведомость, лист, опись, перечень, реестр, роспись, список

banned-book ~ (банд-бук ~) индекс запрещённых книг
black ~ (блак ~) чёрный список
delivery ~ (дэливэри ~) комплектовочная ведомость
duplicate packing ~ (дупликат паккинг ~) упаковочный в двух экземплярах
export ~ (экспорт ~) экспортный список
inventory ~ (инвэнтори ~) инвентарная опись
jury ~ (джури ~) список присяжных заседателей
mailing ~ (мэйлинг ~) рассылочная ведомость, список адресатов
optional parts ~ (опшнал партс ~) ведомость запасных частей за отдельную плату
packing ~ (паккинг ~) комплектация, упаковочный лист
parts ~ (партс ~) ведомость запасных частей
personnel ~ (пэрсоннэл ~) персональный список
priority ~ (прайорити ~) порядок очерёдности

reference ~ (рэфэрэнс ~) справочный список
stock exchange rate ~ (сток эксчэйндж рэйт ~) курсовая таблица
tally ~ (талли ~) список товаров
to draw up a ~ (ту драу ап а ~) составлять ведомость
transmission ~ (трансмишн ~) передаточная ведомость
verification ~ (вэрификэйшн ~) проверочная ведомость
waiting ~ (уэйтинг ~) список населения
~ of attendees (~ оф аттэндис) список присутствующих
~ of demands (~ оф димандс) список требований
~ of questions (~ оф куэстёнс) перечень вопросов

Literacy (литэраси) грамотность
Litigation (литигэйшн) судебный процесс, тяжба

to be in ~ with (ту би ин ~ уиθ) судиться

Live (лайв) живой

to ~ (ту ~) проживать

Livestock (лайвсток) живой инвентарь, скот

Load (лод) нагрузка

additional ~ (аддишнал ~) добавочная нагрузка
average ~ (авэрэдж ~) средняя нагрузка
deck ~ (дэк ~) палубный груз
design ~ (дизайн ~) расчётная нагрузка
fixed ~ (фиксд ~) постоянная нагрузка
full ~ (фул ~) полная нагрузка
maximum ~ (максимум ~) наибольшая нагрузка
minimum ~ (минимум ~) минимальная нагрузка
over ~ (овэр ~) чрезмерная нагрузка
permissible ~ (пэрмисибл ~) допускаемая нагрузка
permissible {safe} ~ (пэрмисибл {сэйф} ~) безопасная нагрузка
prescribed ~ (прискрайбд ~) нормативная нагрузка
rated ~ (рэйтд ~) номинальная нагрузка
service ~ (сэрвис ~) полезная нагрузка, полезный вес

shipment ~ volume (шѝпмэнт ~ вóлюм) объём груза
temporary ~ (тэ́мпорари ~) временная нагрузка
test ~ (тэст ~) пробная нагрузка
to ~ (ту ~) грузить, нагружать, погружать
to endure a ~ (ту эндю́р а ~) выдерживать нагрузку
trial ~ (тра́йал ~) испытательная нагрузка
under ~ (а́ндэр ~) под нагрузкой
work ~ (уо́рк ~) рабочая нагрузка
Load-lifter (лод-лѝфтэр) грузоподъёмник
Loading (ло́динг) загрузка
to complete ~ of cargo (ту компли́т ~ оф ка́рго) догружать
Loan (лон) заём, ссуда, ссудный {adj.}
agricultural ~ (агрику́лчурал ~) сельскохозяйственная ссуда
as a ~ (аз а ~) взаймы
bad ~ (бад ~) просроченная ссуда
bank ~ (банк ~) банковский заём, банковская ссуда
cash ~ (каш ~) денежный заём
commercial ~ (комме́ршл ~) коммерческая ссуда
consolidated ~ (консо́лидэйтэд ~) консолидированный заём
consumer ~ (консу́мэр ~) потребительская ссуда
demand ~ (дима́нд ~) возвратная ссуда
easy ~ (и́зи ~) льготная ссуда
fixed date ~ (фиксд дэйт ~) срочная ссуда
forced ~ (форсд ~) принудительный заём
funded ~ (фу́ндэд ~) облигационный заём
guaranteed ~ (гяранти́д ~) гарантированный заём
industrial ~ (инду́стриал ~) промышленная ссуда
interest-bearing ~ (и́нтэрэст-бэ́ринг ~) процентный заём
interest-free ~ (и́нтэрэст-фри ~) беспроцентная ссуда
international ~ (интэрна́шэнал ~) международный заём
long-term ~ (лонг-тэрм ~) долгосрочный заём, долгосрочная ссуда
low-interest ~ (ло́у-и́нтэрэст ~) льготный заём

money ~ (мо́ни ~) денежная ссуда
mortgage ~ (мо́ргэдж ~) ипотечный заём
past-due ~ (паст-ду ~) просроченный заём
private ~ (пра́йват ~) частный заём
profitable ~ (про́фитабл ~) рентный заём
public ~ (па́блик ~) государственный заём
redeemable ~ (ридѝмабл ~) выкупная ссуда
short-term ~ (шорт-тэрм ~) краткосрочный заём, краткосрочная ссуда
to cover a ~ (ту ко́вэр а ~) покрыть заём
to guarantee a ~ (ту гяранти́ а ~) гарантировать заём
to negotiate a ~ (ту нэго́шиэйт а ~) заключить заём
to remit a ~ (ту рими́т а ~) переводить долг
~ against commodities (~ агэ́нст коммо́дитиз) ссуда под залог товаров
~ against a pledge (~ агэ́нст а плэдж) заём под залог
~ against securities (~ агэ́нст сэкю́ритиз) ссуда под залог ценных бумаг
~ against security (~ агэ́нст сэкю́рити) ссуда под залог
~ charge (~ чардж) плата за кредит
~ of money (~ оф мо́ни) ссуда денег
~ on easy terms (~ он и́зи тэрмз) льготная ссуда
~ secured by mortgage (~ сэкю́рд бай мо́ргэдж) заём обеспеченный ипотекой
Local (ло́кал) локальный, местный
Location (локэ́йшн) местонахождение, местоположение, помещение, расположение
entry ~ (э́нтри ~) место ввоза {cargo}
pick-up ~ (пик-ап ~) место вывоза
~ of a stand (~ оф а станд) местоположение стенда
Lock-out (лок-о́ут) локаут
to declare a ~ (ту диклэ́йр а ~) объявить локаут
Loco (ло́ко) локо

~ **price** (~ прайс) цена локо
Lodge (лодж) ложа, сторожка
   to ~ (ту ~) помещать
   to ~ a complaint (ту ~ а комплэйнт) обращаться с жалобой
Log (лог) журнал
   entries in the ship's ~ (энтриз ин θи шипс ~) выписки из судового журнала
   operation ~ (опэрэйшн ~) данные о работе
   operations ~ (опэрэйшнс ~) журнал учёта работ
   ship's ~ (шипс ~) судовой журнал

   to ~ (ту ~) заносить в журнал
   to keep a ~ (ту кип а ~) вести журнал
   ~ **sheet** (~ шит) монтажный журнал
Logo (лого) знак, лого
   state ~ (стэйт ~) казначейский знак
Long-term (лонг-тэрм) долгосрочный
Longevity (лонжэвити) долговечность
   design ~ (дизайн ~) расчётная долговечность
   guaranteed ~ (гярантид ~) гарантированная долговечность
   operating ~ (опэрэйтинг ~) эксплуатационная долговечность
Loose (лус) навалом
   ~ **cargo** (~ карго) незатаренный груз
   ~ **freight** (~ фрэйт) навалочный фрахт
Loro (лоро) лоро
   ~ **account** (~ аккоунт) счёт лоро
Lose, to ~ (луз, ту ~) проиграть, терять [**perfective:** потерять]
Loser (лузэр) казанская сирота
Loss (лос) гибель, потеря, проигрыш, убыль, убыток, ущерб
   absolute total ~ (абсолют тотал ~) абсолютная гибель
   accidental ~ (аксидэнтал ~) случайный убыток
   actual ~ (акчуал ~) фактическая гибель
   actual ~es (акчуал ~эз) реальные убытки, фактические убытки
   actual total ~ (акчуал тотал ~) действительная полная гибель
   anticipated ~ (антисипэйтэд ~) предполагаемый убыток
   average ~es (авэрэдж ~эз) аварийные убытки

   breakage ~ (брэйкадж ~) убыток, причинённый поломкой
   by way of ~es (бай уэй оф ~эз) в порядке возмещения убытков
   casualty ~es (кажюалти ~эз) потеря причиненная стихийными бедствиями
   compensated ~ (компэнсэйтэд ~) возмещённый убыток
   consolidated profit and ~ statement (консолидэйтэд профит энд ~ стэйтмэнт) сводный счёт прибылей и убытков
   constructive total ~ (конструктив тотал ~) конструктивная полная гибель
   estimated ~es (эстиматд ~эз) оценённые убытки
   eventual ~es (эвэнчуал ~эз) возможные убытки
   excessive ~es (эксэсив ~эз) чрезмерные убытки
   financial ~ (файнаншл ~) финансовый убыток
   general average ~es (джэнэрал авэрэдж ~эз) убытки от общей аварии
   guarantee against ~es (гяранти агэнст ~эз) гарантия от убытков
   heavy ~es (хэви ~эз) большие убытки
   indemnified ~ (индэмнифайд ~) страховой убыток
   insignificant ~ (инсигнификант ~) незначительный ущерб
   insignificant ~es (инсигнификант ~эз) незначительные потери
   interest on ~es (интэрэст он ~эз) проценты по погашению убытков
   major ~es (мэйджор ~эз) крупные убытки
   minimal ~ (минимал ~) минимальный ущерб
   monetary ~ (монэтари ~) денежный убыток, денежный ущерб
   natural ~ (начюрал ~) естественная убыль
   net ~ (нэт ~) чистый убыток
   operating ~es (опэрэйтинг ~эз) убытки при эксплуатации
   partial ~ (паршл ~) частичная гибель, частичный убыток
   particular average ~es (партикюлар авэрэдж ~эз) убытки от частной аварии

production ~ value (прода́кшн ~ ва́лю) стоимость убытков, возникших в производстве
profit and ~ statement (про́фит энд ~ стэ́йтмэнт) счёт прибылей и убытков
property ~ (про́пэрти ~) материальный убыток
recoverable ~es (рико́вэрабл ~эз) возместимые потери
salvage ~ (са́лвэдж ~) убыток при реализации спасённого имущества
significant ~ (сигни́фикант ~) значительный ущерб
significant ~es (сигни́фикант ~эз) значительные убытки
single ~es (сингл ~эз) единичные убытки
to adjust ~es (ту аджа́ст ~эз) уточнять убытки
to adjust general average ~es (ту аджа́ст джэ́нэрал а́вэрэдж ~эз) оценивать убытки по общей аварии
to avert ~es предотвращать убытки
to avoid ~es (ту аво́йд ~эз) избежать убытков
to compensate for ~es (ту ко́мпэнсэйт фор ~эз) возмещать убытки
to cover ~es (ту ко́вэр ~эз) покрывать убытки
to demand compensation for ~es (ту дима́нд компэнсэ́йшн фор ~эз) требовать возмещения убытков
to entail ~es (ту энтэ́йл ~эз) повлечь убытки
to include ~ or damage (ту инклю́д ~ ор да́мадж) включать убытки или ущерб
to incur ~es (ту инку́р ~эз) нести убытки
to incur significant ~es (ту инку́р сигни́фикант ~эз) нести значительные убытки
to inflict a ~ (ту инфли́кт а ~) наносить ущерб
to minimize ~ (ту ми́нимайз ~) сокращать убытки до минимума
to operate at a ~ (ту о́пэрэйт ат а ~) работать с убытком
to sell at a ~ (ту сэл ат а ~) продавать с убытком
to show ~es (ту шо́у ~эз) показывать убытки
to suffer ~ (ту су́ффэр ~) понести ущерб

to sustain ~es (ту сустэ́йн ~эз) приносить убытки, терпеть убытки
total ~ (то́тал ~) полная гибель
total ~es (то́тал ~эз) общая сумма убытков
~ analysis (~ ана́лисис) анализ убытков
~ by reason of jettison (~ бай ри́зон оф джэ́ттисон) ущерб от выбрасывания груза за борт
~ due to non-fulfillment of obligations (~ ду ту нон-фулфи́лмэнт оф облигэ́йшнз) ущерб вследствие неисполнения обязательств
~ during discharge (~ ду́ринг ди́счардж) убыток при разгрузке
~ of cargo (~ оф ка́рго) гибель груза
~ of citizenship (~ оф си́тизэншип) потеря гражданства
~ of goods {spoilage or theft} (~ оф гудз {спо́йладж ор θэфт}) гибель товара
~ of profit (~ оф про́фит) ущерб в виде упущенной выгоды
~ of property (~ оф про́пэрти) гибель имущества
~ of right (~ оф райт) потеря права
~ of sovereignty (~ оф со́вэрнти) потеря суверенитета
~ of weight during ocean shipment (~ оф уэйт ду́ринг ошн ши́пмэнт) убыль веса во время морской перевозки
~ on loans (~ он лонс) убытки по займам
~es suffered in connection with ... (~эз су́фэрд ин коннэ́кшн уиθ ...) убытки, понесённые в связи с ...
~ to be compensated (~ ту би ко́мпэнсэйтэд) возмещаемый убыток
Lost (лост) потерянный, упущенный
~ opportunity (~ оппорту́нити) упущенная выгода
Lot (лот) парк, партия, часть
automobile ~ (аутомоби́л ~) автомобильный парк
delivery in ~s (дэли́вэри ин ~с) поставка по частям
taxi ~ (та́кси ~) автопарк
to be drawn as ~s (ту би дра́ун аз ~с) выйти в тираж
Lottery (ло́ттэри) лотерея
Low (ло́у) низкий

~ **grade** (~ грэйд) низкосортный
Lower (ло́уэр) нижний
  to ~ (ту ~) понижать
Lowering (ло́уэринг) понижение
  ~ **of customs barriers** (~ оф ка́стомз ба́рриэрз) снижение таможенных барьеров
  ~ **of duties** (~ оф дю́тиз) понижение пошлин
Luggage (лу́ггадж) багаж
  ~ **tag** (~ таг) этикетка багажа
Lumpsum (ла́мпсум) единовременный
  ~ **charter** (~ ча́ртэр) лумпсум-чартер
  ~ **freight** (~ фрэйт) лумпсум-фрахт
Lynch, to ~ (линч, ту ~) линчевать
Lynching (ли́нчинг) самосуд
  ~ **party** (~ па́рти) самосуд

M

Machiavellian (макиэвэ́ллиан) махиевеллевский
Machination (машинэ́йшн) интрига, махинация **~s** происки
Machine (маши́н) машина, машинный {adj.}
  advantages of a ~ (адва́нтэджэз оф а ~) преимущества машины
  communist party ~ (ко́ммюнист па́рти ~) партийный аппарат
  damaged ~ (да́маджд ~) повреждённая машина
  design of a ~ (диза́йн оф а ~) конструкция машины
  idle ~ (айдл ~) бездействующая машина
  idle time of a ~ (айдл тайм оф а ~) простой машины
  introduction of a ~ (интрода́кшн оф а ~) пуск машины
  modern ~ (мо́дэрн ~) современная машина
  operating conditions of a ~ (о́пэрэйтинг конди́шнс оф а ~) рабочий режим машины
  operation of a ~ (опэрэ́йшн оф а ~) работа машины
  outdated ~ (оутдэ́йтэд ~) устаревшая машина
  packing ~ (па́ккинг ~) машина для расфасовки и упаковки

per unit metal content of a ~ (пэр ю́нит мэ́тал ко́нтэнт оф а ~) металлоёмкость машины
productivity of a ~ (продукти́вити оф а ~) производительность машины
reliability of a ~ (рилайаби́лити оф а ~) надёжность работы машины
rental ~s (рэ́нтал ~с) арендуемые машины
service life of a ~ (сэ́рвис лайф оф а ~) длительность эксплуатации машины, срок службы машины
simple ~ (симпл ~) простая машина
sound ~ (со́унд ~) исправная машина
standard ~ capacity (ста́ндард ~ капа́сити) норма выработки машины
tabulating ~ (та́бюлэйтинг ~) счётно-аналитическая машина
to observe a ~ in operation (ту обзэ́рв а ~ ин опэрэ́йшн) наблюдать за работой машины
to operate a ~ (ту о́пэрэйт а ~) управлять машиной
to quote a price on a ~ (ту куо́т а прайс он а ~) назначить цену за машину
to redesign a ~ (ту ридиза́йн а ~) переделывать конструкцию машины
to service a ~ (ту сэ́рвис а ~) обслуживать машину
working ~ (уо́ркинг ~) действующая машина
workmanship of a ~ (уо́ркманшип оф а ~) отделка машины
~ **building** (~ би́лдинг) машиностроительный
~ **certificate** (~ сэрти́фикэт) паспорт машины
~ **components** (~ компо́нэнтс) детали машин машина
~ **maintenance** (~ мэ́йнтэнанс) обслуживание машин
Machinery (маши́нэри) техника
  range of ~ (рэ́йндж оф ~) ассортимент машин
  textile ~ (тэ́кстайл ~) текстильное оборудование
  ~ **of state** (~ оф стэйт) государственный аппарат
Machining (маши́нинг) обработка
Magazine (магази́н) журнал

business ~ (би́знэс ~)
коммерческий журнал
illustrated ~ (иллюстрэ́йтэд ~)
иллюстрированный журнал
informational ~ (информэ́йшнал ~)
информационный журнал
trade ~ (трэйд ~) журнал по
торговле
Magistrate (ма́джистрэйт) судья
canton ~ (ка́нтон ~) кантональный
судья
police ~ (поли́с ~) полицейский
судья
Magnitude (ма́гнитуд) масштаб
~ **of inflation** (~ оф инфлэ́йшн)
масштаб инфляции
Maid (мэйд) прислуга
Mail (мэйл) почта, почтовый {adj.}
registered ~ (рэ́джистэрд ~)
заказная корреспонденция,
заказное отправление, заказная
почта
surface ~ (су́рфас ~) обычная
почта
to ~ (ту ~) отправить по почте
unregistered ~ (анрэ́джистэрд ~)
простая почта
Mailer (мэ́йлэр) рассылка
advertising ~ (а́двэртайзинг ~)
рассылка рекламных материалов
one-time advertising ~ (уа́н-тайм
а́двэртайзинг ~) разовая рассылка
рекламных материалов
Mailing (мэ́йлинг) отправление,
почтовое отправление
Maintain, to ~ (мэйнтэ́йн, ту ~)
содержать
Maintenance (мэ́йнтэнанс) график
текущего ремонта, иждивение,
обеспечение, поддержание,
содержание, эксплуатация
factory ~ (фа́ктори ~)
эксплуатация завода
regular ~ (рэ́гюлар ~) текущий
ремонт
routine ~ (рути́н ~) профилактика
~ **of equipment** (~ оф икуи́пмэнт)
техническое содержание
~ **of order** (~ оф о́рдэр)
поддержание порядка
~ **of peace** (~ оф пис)
поддержание мира
~ **of price levels** (~ оф прайс
лэ́вэлс) поддержание цен
~ **of public order** (~ оф па́блик
о́рдэр) поддержание публичного
порядка

Major (мэ́йджор) крупный
Majority (маджо́рити) большая часть,
большинтство, возмужалость,
зрелость, совершеннолетие
certification of ~ (сэртифика́йшн
оф ~) аттестат зрелости
general civil ~ (джэ́нэрал си́вил
~) общегражданское
совершеннолетие
legal ~ (ли́гал ~) юридическое
совершеннолетие
marital ~ (ма́ритал ~) брачное
совершеннолетие
Make (мэйк) марка товара, модель
to ~ (ту ~) делать [**perfective:**
сделать], производить
to ~ **out** (ту ~ о́ут) выписывать
{draft, check}
to ~ **part of** (ту ~ парт оф)
включать в состав
to ~ **up** (ту ~ ап) образовать
various ~**s and models** (ва́риос ~с
энд мо́дэлс) различные модели
Maker (мэ́йкэр) производитель
~ **of a bill** (~ оф а бил)
трассант
Makeup (мэ́йкап) состав
Making out (мэ́йкинг о́ут) выписка
~ **a receipt** (~ а риси́т) выписка
квитанция
Malfeasance (малфи́занс)
преступление по службе
Malfunction (малфу́нкшн)
неисправность
Malicious (мали́шэс) злостный
Malingerer (мали́нгэрэр) симулянт
Malingering (ма́лингэринг) симуляция
Man-day (ман-дэй) человекодень
Man-hour (ман-о́ур) человеко-час
Man-month (ман-мон θ) человек-месяц
Man-week (ман-уик) человек-неделя
Manage, to ~ (ма́надж, ту ~)
распорядиться, руководить
Management (ма́наджмэнт)
директорский {adj.}, дирекция,
правление, регулирование,
руководство, управленческий {adj.}
central ~ (сэ́нтрал ~)
центральное правление
company ~ (ко́мпани ~)
руководство фирмы
competent ~ (ко́мпэтэнт ~)
квалифицированное руководство
economic ~ (эконо́мик ~)
хозяйствование

methods of economic ~ (мэ́θодс оф эконо́мик ~) методы хозяйствования

middle ~ (мидл ~) средний руководящий персонал

plant ~ (плант ~) руководство завода

technical ~ (тэ́кникал ~) техническая дирекция

top ~ (топ ~) высшее руководство

Manager (ма́наджэр) администратор, директор, заведующий, менеджер, распорядитель, руководитель, управляющий

advertising department ~ (а́двэртайзинг дипа́ртмэнт ~) заведующий отделом рекламы

assistant ~ (асси́стант ~) заместитель заведующего, помощник управляющего

association (ассосиэ́йшн) администратор товарищества

branch ~ (бранч ~) заведующий отделением

credit ~ (крэ́дит ~) распорядитель кредитов, управляющий отделом кредитования

dock ~ (док ~) заведующий доком

employment ~ (эмпло́ймэнт ~) заведующий отделом найма

export ~ (э́кспорт ~) заведующий отделом экспорта, управляющий по экспорту

general ~ (джэ́нэрал ~) главный управляющий

general sales ~ (джэ́нэрал сэйлз ~) генеральный директор по сбыту

group ~ (груп ~) управляющий группой

import ~ (и́мпорт ~) управляющий по импорту

pavilion ~ (пави́льон ~) директор павильона

personnel ~ (пэрсонне́л ~) управляющий по кадрам

plant ~ (плант ~) директор завода, управляющий заводом

production ~ (прода́кшн ~) управляющий производством

property ~ (про́пэрти ~) управляющий недвижимостью

sales ~ (сэйлз ~) заведующий отделом сбыта, коммерческий директор

statistics ~ (стати́стикс ~) заведующий отделом статистической информации

subcontracts department ~ (су́бконтрактс дипа́ртмэнт ~) заведующий отделом субподрядов

supply ~ (суппла́й ~) директор по снабжению

traffic ~ (тра́ффик ~) заведующий транспортным отделом

~ of business development (~ оф би́знэс дивэ́лопмэнт) управляющий отделом развития торговли

~ of sales department (~ оф сэйлз дипа́ртмэнт) управляющий отделом сбыта

Managing (ма́наджинг) руководящий

~ director (~ дирэ́ктор) управляющий

Manifest (ма́нифэст) манифест

cargo ~ (ка́рго ~) грузовой манифест, декларация

certified ~ (сэ́ртифайд ~) заверенный консулом манифест

passenger ~ (па́ссэнджэр ~) список пассажиров

ship's ~ (шипс ~) декларация судового груза, судовой манифест

Manner (ма́ннэр) способ

in the established ~ (ин θи эста́блишд ~) в установленном порядке

~ of payment (~ оф пэ́ймэнт) способ платежа

Manning (ма́ннинг) комплектование рабочей силой

Manpower (ма́нпоуэр) кадры

~ shortage (~ шо́ртадж) нехватка кадров

Manual (ма́нюал) инструкция

classification ~ (классифике́йшн ~) указатель классов

~ of methods (~ оф мэ́θодс) указатель методов

Manufacture, to ~ (манюфа́кчур, ту ~) выпускать, производить

Manufacturer (манюфа́кчурэр) изготовитель, производитель, фирма-изготовитель

Manufacturing (манюфа́кчуринг) производство

commercial ~ (коммэ́ршл ~) выпуск продукции на рынок

March (марч) поход

Margin (ма́рджин) маржа, наценка, предел, разница

bank ~ (банк ~) банковская маржа

budget ~ (ба́джэт ~) бюджетная наценка

credit ~ (крэ́дит ~) маржа по кредиту

insurance ~ (иншю́ранс ~) страховая наценка

profit ~ (про́фит ~) размер прибыли

thin ~ (θин ~) недостаточная маржа

trade ~ (трэйд ~) торговая наценка

usual ~ (ю́жюал ~) обычная маржа

wide ~ (уайд ~) большая маржа

~ business (~ би́знэс) сделки с маржей

~ credit (~ крэ́дит) кредит по операциям с маржей

~ requirement (~ рикуа́йрмэнт) предписываемая законом маржа

Marijuana (мариуа́на) марихуана

Marine (мари́н) морской, пехотинец {soldier} ~s пехота {armed force}

Marital (мэ́йритал) брачный

Maritime (ма́ритайм) морской

Mark (марк) заметка, знак, отметка, примета

distinguishing ~ (дисти́нгуишинг ~) отличительный знак

honorable ~ of distinction (о́норабл ~ оф дисти́нкшн) почётный знак отличия

identification ~ (айдэнтификэ́йшн ~) опознавательный знак, опознавательное клеймо

leading ~s (ли́динг ~с) основная маркировка

prohibited ~ (прохи́битэд ~) запрещённый знак

shipping ~ (ши́ппинг ~) отметка грузоотправителя

shipping ~s (ши́ппинг ~с) грузовая маркировка, отгрузочная маркировка

signature ~ (си́гначэр ~) знак-подпись {e.g. x mark by illiterate}

to ~ (ту ~) маркировать, наносить марку, обозначать, отмечать [perfective: отметить], ставить маркировку, ставить метку

to ~ by paint (ту ~ бай пэйнт) наносить маркировку краской

to ~ in indelible paint (ту ~ ин индэ́либл пэйнт) наносить маркировку несмываемой краской

to ~ in weatherproof paint (ту ~ ин уэ́θэрпруф пэйнт) наносить

маркировку погодоустойчивой краской

to ~ in water insoluble paint (ту ~ ин уа́тэр инсо́любл пэйнт) наносить маркировку водостойкой краской

~ of distinction (~ оф дисти́нкшн) отличительная марка

Mark-up (ма́рк-ап) надбавка к цене, наценка, повышение

price plus ~ (прайс плюс ~) цена с надбавкой

retail ~ (ри́тэйл ~) розничная наценка

Marked (маркд) марочный, обозначенный

as ~ on the blueprint (аз ~ он θи блю́принт) как обозначено на чертеже

not ~ (нот ~) без маркировки

to be ~ (ту би ~) иметь маркировку

Marker (ма́ркэр) знак, маркировщик {person}, метка

border ~ (бо́рдэр ~) пограничный знак

Market (ма́ркэт) базар, биржа, рыночный

acceptance ~ (аксэ́птанс ~) акцептный рынок

agricultural ~ (агрику́лчурал ~) сельскохозяйственный рынок

arms ~ (армз ~) рынок вооружений

bill note ~ (бил нот ~) вексельный рынок

black ~ (блак ~) чёрный рынок

broad ~ (брод ~) оживлённый рынок

buyer's ~ (ба́йэрз ~) конъюнктура рынка, выгодная для покупателя

capital ~ (ка́питал ~) рынок капитала

capital lending ~ (ка́питал лэ́ндинг ~) рынок ссудных капиталов

capitalist ~ (ка́питалист ~) капиталистический рынок

closed ~ (клозд ~) замкнутый рынок

closing ~ prices (кло́синг ~ пра́йсэз) цены при закрытии биржи

commodities ~ (коммо́дитиз ~) товарный рынок

common ~ (ко́ммон ~) общий рынок

competitive ~ (компэ́титив ~)
конкурирующий рынок
controlled ~ (контро́лд ~)
контролируемый рынок
currency ~ (ку́ррэнси ~) валютный
рынок
discount ~ (ди́скоунт ~) учётный
рынок
domestic ~ (домэ́стик ~)
внутренний рынок
export ~ (э́кспорт ~) экспортный
рынок
external ~ (экстэ́рнал ~) внешний
рынок
foreign ~ (фо́рэн ~) заграничный
рынок, иностранный рынок
free ~ (фри ~) свободный рынок
free currency ~ (фри ку́ррэнси ~)
свободный валютный рынок
global ~ (гло́бал ~) мировой
рынок
glutted ~ (глу́ттэд ~)
пересыщенный рынок
grain ~ (грэ́йн ~) зерновая биржа
gray ~ (грэ́й ~) полулегальный
рынок
import ~ (и́мпорт ~) импортный
рынок
integrated ~ (и́нтэгрэйтэд ~)
интегрированный рынок
international ~ (интэрна́шэнал ~)
международный рынок
international currency ~
(интэрна́шэнал ку́ррэнси ~)
международный валютный рынок
labor ~ (лэ́йбор ~) рынок рабочей
силы
license ~ (ла́йсэнз ~) рынок
лицензий
local ~ (ло́кал ~) местный рынок
money ~ (мо́ни ~) денежный рынок
national ~ (на́шэнал ~)
национальный рынок
official ~ (оффи́шл ~)
официальный рынок
open ~ (о́пэн ~) открытый рынок
opening ~ prices (о́пэнинг ~
пра́йсэз) цены при открытии биржи
organized ~ (о́рганайзд ~)
организованный рынок
overseas ~ (овэрси́з ~)
зарубежный рынок
preferential ~ (прэфэрэ́ншл ~)
преференциальный рынок
produce ~ (проду́с ~) биржа
сельскохозяйственных товаров

protected ~ (протэ́ктэд ~)
защищённый рынок
regional ~ (ри́джонал ~)
региональный рынок
regulated ~ (рэ́гюлэйтэд ~)
регулируемый рынок
securities ~ (сэкю́ритиз ~) рынок
ценных бумаг
seller's ~ (сэ́ллэрз ~)
конъюнктура рынка, выгодная для
продавца
stagnant ~ (ста́гнант ~) вялый
рынок
stock ~ (сток ~) биржевой рынок,
фондовая биржа
street-~ (стрит-~) неофициальная
биржа
to ~ (ту ~) сбыть
to glut the ~ (ту глут θи ~)
переполнить рынок
to introduce into the ~ (ту
интродю́с и́нту θи ~) выпустить на
рынок
to play the ~ (ту плэй θи ~)
играть на бирже
tonnage ~ (то́ннадж ~) фрахтовый
рынок
traditional ~ (тради́шнал ~)
традиционный рынок
unofficial ~ (аноффи́шл ~)
неофициальный рынок
~ share price (~ шэйр прайс)
биржевой курс
Marketable (ма́ркэтабл)
легкореализуемый
Marketeer (маркэти́р) делец
  black ~ (блак ~) делец чёрного
рынка
Marketing (ма́ркэтинг) маркетинг,
продажа, торговля
  trade and ~ (трэйд энд ~)
торгово-сбытовая деятельность
  ~ campaign (~ кампэ́йн) кампания
по продвижению товара на рынок
Marking (ма́ркинг) маркировка,
нанесение маркировки
  clear ~ (клир ~) чёткая
маркировка
  container ~ (контэ́йнэр ~)
маркировка контейнера
  distinct ~ (дисти́нкт ~)
отчётливая маркировка
  duplicate ~ (ду́пликат ~) двойная
маркировка
  export ~ (э́кспорт ~) экспортная
маркировка

exterior ~ (экстириор ~) внешняя маркировка
faded ~ (фэйдэд ~) выцветшая маркировка
incorrect ~ (инкоррэкт ~) неправильная маркировка
indistinct ~ (индистинкт ~) неясная маркировка
insufficient ~ (инсуффишэнт ~) недостаточная маркировка
packaging ~ (паккаджинг ~) маркировка тары
price ~ (прайс ~) маркировка цен
proper ~ (пропэр ~) правильная маркировка
special ~ (спэшл ~) специальная маркировка
stained ~ (стэйнд ~) запачканная маркировка
sufficiency of ~ (суффишэнси оф ~) достаточность маркировки
to emboss ~ on a metal plate (ту эмбос ~ он а мэтал плэйт) выбивать маркировку на металлической пластине
transport ~ (транспорт ~) транспортная маркировка
visible ~ (визибл ~) видимая маркировка
~ in ... (~ ин ...) маркировка делается на ... языке {language}
~ of cases (~ оф кэйсэз) маркировка ящиков
~ of goods (~ оф гудз) маркировка товара
~ of packages (~ оф пакэджэз) маркировка товарных мест
~ of packing container (~ оф паккинг контэйнэр) маркировка упаковки

Marriage (мэррэдж) брак, женитьба {said of husband}, замужество {said of wife}, свадьба {ceremony}, супружество
annulment of ~ (аннулмэнт оф ~) аннулирование брака

Martial (маршл) военный
~ law (~ лау) военное положение

Mass (мас) масса, массовый {adj.}
bulk ~ (булк ~) общая масса
gross ~ (грос ~) масса брутто
net ~ (нэт ~) масса нетто
package ~ (пакэдж ~) масса грузового места
standard ~ (стандард ~) стандартная масса

unit of ~ (юнит оф ~) единица массы
~ of profit (~ оф профит) масс прибыли

Massacre (массакр) кровавая расправа

Master (мастэр) капитан {of vessel}, хозяин {of household, etc.}
~'s капитанский
~ of Arts (~ оф артс) Магистр исскуств
~'s declaration (~с дэкларэйшн декларация капитана

Mastery (мастэри) освоение {of a process, etc.}

Match (матч) ровня

Mate (мэйт) помощник капитана {on vessel}, супруг {husband}, супруг {wife}
first ~ (фэрст ~) старший помощник капитана
second ~ (сэконд ~) второй помощник капитана

Material (матириал) материал, материальный {adj.}
advertising ~ (адвэртайзинг ~) рекламный материал
amount of required ~ (амоунт о рикуайрд ~) затрата материала
analogous ~ (аналогос ~) аналогичный материал
application ~s (аппликэйшн ~с) заявочные материалы
artificial ~s (артифишл ~с) искусственные материалы
auxiliary ~s (аукзилиэри ~с) вспомогательные материалы
available ~s (авайлабл ~с) наличные материалы
basic ~ (бэйсик ~) основной материал
bulky ~ (булки ~) массивный материал
cheaper ~ (чипэр ~) более дешёвый материал
classified ~ (классифайд ~) классифицированный материал
commercial ~ (коммэршл ~) коммерческий материал
competitive ~ (компэтитив ~) конкурентный материал
consumable ~s (консумабл ~с) потребляемые материалы, расходуемые материалы

construction ~s (констру́кшн ~с)
конструкционные материалы,
строительный материал

consumption of ~ (консу́мпшн оф
~) расход материала

copyrighted ~ (ко́пирайтэд ~)
охраняемый авторским правом

cost of ~s (кост оф ~с)
стоимость материалов

defective ~ (дифэ́ктив ~)
дефектный материал

demonstration ~ (дэмонстрэ́йшн ~)
демонстрационный материал

description of ~ (дэскри́пшн оф
~) описание материала

descriptive ~ (дэскри́птив ~)
наглядный материал

display ~s (дисплэ́й ~с)
художественно-оформительские
материалы

documentary ~ (докюмэ́нтари ~)
документальный материал

educational ~ (эдюкэ́йшнал ~)
учебный материал

enclosed ~ (энкло́зд ~)
прилагаемый материал

exhibition ~ (экзиби́шн ~)
выставочный материал

expendable ~ (экспэ́ндабл ~)
расходный материал

finishing ~ (фи́нишинг ~)
отделочный материал

first-class ~ (фэрст-класс ~)
первоклассный материал

high quality ~ (хай куа́лити ~)
высококачественный материал

illustrated ~ (и́ллюстрэйтэд ~)
иллюстрированный материал

informational ~ (информэ́йшнал ~)
информационный материал

kind of packing ~ (кайнд оф
па́ккинг ~) вид упаковочного
материала

lack of ~s (лак оф ~с)
недостаток материалов

list of ~s (лист оф ~с) перечень
материалов

lower grade ~ (ло́уэр грэйд ~)
низкосортный материал

market for raw ~s (ма́ркэт фор
ра́у ~с) рынок сырьевых товаров

missing ~ (ми́ссинг ~)
недостающий материал

necessary ~ (нэ́сэсари ~)
необходимый материал

nonstandard ~ (нонста́ндард ~)
нестандартный материал

operational ~s (опэрэ́йшнал ~с)
эксплуатационные материалы

printed ~ (при́нтэд ~) печатный
материал

printing of ~s (при́нтинг оф ~с)
печатание материалов

poor quality ~ (пур куа́лити ~)
недоброкачественный материал

protective ~ (протэ́ктив ~)
защитный материал

purchased ~s (пу́рчасд ~с)
закупленные материалы

raw ~s (ра́у ~с) сырьевые
материалы, сырьевой товар

raw ~ intensive (ра́у ~ интэ́нсив)
материалоёмкий

reduction in ~ input ratio
(риду́кшн ин ~ и́нпут рэ́йшио)
снижать материалоёмкость
поризводства

reduction of ~ inputs (риду́кшн
оф ~ и́нпутс) снижение
материалоёмкости

scarce ~ (скэ́йрс ~) дефицитный
материал

schedule of ~s (скэ́джул оф ~с)
ведомость материалов

sealing ~ (си́линг ~)
прокладочный материал

selection of ~ (сэлэ́кшн оф ~)
подбор материала

source ~ (сорс ~) исходный
материал

standard ~ (ста́ндард ~)
стандартный материал

strategic ~ (страти́джик ~)
стратегический материал

sturdy ~ (сту́рди ~) прочный
материал

submitted ~ (субми́ттэд ~)
представленный материал

substandard ~ (субста́ндард ~)
некондиционный материал

suitable ~ (су́табл ~) подходящий
материал

supplementary ~ (сапплэмэ́нтари
~) дополнительный материал

tare ~s (тэйр ~с) тарный
материал

testing of ~s (тэ́стинг оф ~с)
испытание материалов

textual ~ (тэ́ксчуал ~) текстовой
материал

to forward ~ (ту фо́руард ~)
направлять материал

to process ~ (ту про́сэс ~)
обрабатывать материал

to **procure** ~ (ту прокю́р ~)
приобретать материалы
to **reject** ~ (ту риджэ́кт ~)
браковать материалы
to **select** ~ (ту сэлэ́кт ~)
подбирать материал
unfit ~ (анфи́т ~) непригодный
материал
unused ~ (аню́зд ~)
неиспользованный материал
used ~ (юзд ~) использованный
материал
waterproof ~ (уа́тэрпруф ~)
водонепроницаемый материал
working ~ (уо́ркинг ~) рабочий
материал
wrapping ~ (ра́ппинг ~)
обёрточный материал
written ~ (ри́ттэн ~) письменный
материал
~ **and technical** (~ энд тэ́кникал)
материально-технический
~ **input** (~ и́нпут)
материалоёмкость
~ **usage** (~ ю́садж) употребление
материала
Matriculation (матрикюлэ́йшн)
посещаемость
~ **at university level** (~ ат
юнивэ́рсити лэ́вэл) посещаемость
учебных заведений
Matter (ма́ттэр) вещество, вопрос
{issue}
business ~ (би́знэс ~) деловой
вопрос
decision on a ~ (диси́жн он а ~)
решение по вопросу
delicate ~ (дэ́ликат ~)
щекотливое дело
disputed ~ (диспю́тэд ~)
конфликтное дело
grey ~ (грэй ~) серое вещество
outside ~**s** (о́утсайд ~с)
посторонние дела
to **clarify the** ~ (ту кла́рифай θи
~) внести ясность в вопрос
to **decide in a disputed** ~ (ту
диса́йд ин а диспю́тэд ~)
принимать решение по делу
to **investigate a** ~ (ту
инвэ́стигэйт а ~) рассматривать
дело
to **make a decision on a** ~ (ту
мэйк а диси́жн он а ~) решать
вопрос
to **put** ~**s to rights** (ту пут ~с
ту райтс) урегулировать дело

to **take a** ~ **to court** (ту тэйк а
~ ту ко́урт) передавать дело в
суд
urgent ~ (у́рджэнт ~) срочное
дело
~ **of common knowledge** (~ оф
ко́ммон но́лэдж) общеизвестный
факт
~ **of great significance** (~ оф
грэйт сигни́фиканс) дело большой
важности
~ **of mutual interest** (~ оф
мю́чуал и́нтэрэст) представляющий
взаимный интерес вопрос
~ **of principle** (~ оф при́нсипл)
принципиальный вопрос
Mature (мачу́р) готовый, зрелый,
взрослый
to ~ (ту ~) выдерживать,
наступать {of a bill, draft}
Maturity (мачу́рити) возмужалость,
готовность, зрелость, срок
~ **of bill** (~ оф бил) срок
векселя
Maximum (ма́ксимум) максимальный
Means (минз) способ, средство
by ~ **of** (бай ~ оф) путём
by legal ~ (бай ли́гал ~) в
судебном порядке
conventional ~ (конвэ́ншнал ~)
обычные средства
diplomatic ~ (диплома́тик ~)
дипломатический путь,
дипломатические средства
modern ~ (мо́дэрн ~) современные
средства
peaceful ~ (пи́сфул ~) мирные
средства
~ **of defense** (~ оф дифэ́нс)
средство защиты
~ **of payment** (~ оф пэ́ймэнт)
способ оплаты
~ **of payment in kind** (~ оф
пэ́ймэнт ин кайнд) способ оплаты
натурой
~ **of production** (~ оф прода́кшн)
средство производства
~ **of transport** (~ оф тра́нспорт)
вид транспорта
Measure (мэ́жюр) мера, мерка {size},
мероприятие
anti-inflationary ~**s** (а́нти-
инфлэ́йшнари ~с) антиинфляционные
меры
appropriate ~**s** (аппро́приат ~с)
соответствующее мероприятие,
соответствующие меры

cargo salvage ~s (ка́рго са́лвэдж ~с) мероприятия по спасению груза

compulsory ~s (компу́лсори ~с) принудительные меры

corrective ~s (корре́ктив ~с) корректировочные

counter-~s (ко́унтэр-~с) контрмеры, ответные мер

devaluation ~s (дивалю́йшн ~с) мероприятия по девальвации

discriminatory trade and economic ~s (дискри́минатори трэйд анд эконо́мик ~с) дискриминационные торгово-экономические меры

dry ~s (драй ~с) меры сыпучих тел

economic policy ~s (эконо́мик по́лиси ~с) мероприятия экономической политики

effective ~s (иффэ́ктив ~с) действенные меры, эффективные меры

emergency ~s (эмэ́рджэнси ~с) экстренные меры

extraordinary ~s (экстрао́рдинари ~с) чрезвычайные меры

extreme ~s (экстри́м ~с) крайние меры

follow-up ~s (фо́лло-ап ~с) последующие мероприятия

further ~s (фу́рθэр ~с) дополнительные меры

immediate ~s (имми́диат ~с) немедленные меры

ineffective ~s (иниффэ́ктив ~с) неэффективные меры

legislative ~s (лэ́джислэйтив ~с) законодательные меры

metric ~s (мэ́трик ~с) метрические меры

mutually acceptable ~s (мю́чуалли аксэ́птабл ~с) взаимоприемлемые меры

package of ~s (па́кэдж оф ~с) комплекс мероприятий, пакет мероприятий

practical ~s (пра́ктикал ~с) практические меры

precautionary ~s (прика́ушнари ~с) предохранительные меры

preliminary ~s (прили́минэри ~с) предварительные меры

preparatory ~s (прэ́паратори ~с) подготовительные меры

preventative ~s (приве́нтатив ~с) предупредительные меры

prompt ~s (промпт ~с) срочные меры

proper ~s (про́пэр ~с) надлежащие меры

protectionist ~s (проте́кшнист ~с) протекционистские меры

restorative ~s (ристо́ратив ~с) меры по исправлению

restrictive ~s (ристри́ктив ~с) ограничительные меры {rationing}

security ~s (сэкю́рити ~с) меры безопасности

similar ~s (си́милар ~с) подобные меры

sufficient ~s (суффи́шэнт ~с) достаточные меры

temporary ~s (тэ́мпорари ~с) временные меры

timely ~s (та́ймли ~с) своевременные меры меры

to ~ (ту ~) мерить

to put ~s into effect (ту пут ~с инту иффэ́кт) осуществлять мероприятия

to take ~s (ту тэйк ~с) принимать меры

to use as a ~ (ту юз ас а ~) использовать в качестве меры

unit of ~ (ю́нит оф ~) единицы меры

urgent ~s (у́рджэнт ~с) безотлагательные меры

useful ~ (ю́сфул ~) полезное мероприятие

~ for export restraint (~ фор э́кспорт ристрэ́йнт) меры по сдерживанию экспорта

~ for import restraint (~ фор и́мпорт ристрэ́йнт) меры по сдерживанию импорта

~ for labor protection (~ фор лэ́йбор проте́кшн) меры по охране труда

~ of area (~ оф э́йриа) меры площади

~ of capacity (~ оф капа́сити) меры веса

~ of efficiency (~ оф иффи́шэнси) меры эффективности

~ of length (~ оф лэнгθ) меры длины

~ of liquid (~ оф ли́куид) меры жидкости

~ of precision (~ оф прэси́жн) меры точности

~ of reliability (~ оф рилайабйлити) меры надёжности
~ of value (~ оф вáлю) мера стоимости
~ of volume (~ оф вóлюм) меры ёмкости, меры объёма
Measurement (мэжюрмэнт) размер, измерение, обмер **~s** измерительные нормативы
    test ~s (тэст ~с) контрольное измерение
    total ~s (тóтал ~с) общий размер
Measuring (мэжюринг) мерительный
Mechanic (мэкáник) механик, техник
    maintenance ~ (мэйнтэнанс ~) механик по оборудованию
Mechanical (мэкáникал) механический
Mechanism (мэканизм) механизм
    competitive ~ (компэтитив ~) механизм конкуренции
    credit ~ (крэдит ~) механизм выдачи кредита
    currency ~ (кýррэнси ~) денежно-валютный механизм
    currency allocation ~ (кýррэнси алокэйшн ~) механизм валютных отчислений
    economic ~ (эконóмик ~) хозяйственный механизм
    exchange rate ~ (эксчэйндж рэйт ~) механизм валютных курсов
    market ~ (мáркэт ~) рыночный механизм
    money transfer ~ (мóни трáнсфэр ~) механизм перечисления денежных средств
    organizational ~ (организэйшнал ~) организационный механизм
    price ~ (прайс ~) механизм цен
    unloading ~ (анлóдинг ~) разгрузочный механизм
Mechanization (мэканизэйшн) механизация
    comprehensive ~ (комприхэнсив ~) комплексная механизация
    full ~ (фул ~) полная механизация
    rational ~ (рáшнал ~) рациональная механизация
    ~ of agriculture (~ оф áгрикулчур) механизация сельского хозяйства
    ~ of labor-intensive processes (~ оф лэйбор-интэнсив прóсэсэз) механизация трудоёмких процессов
    ~ of production (~ оф продáкшн) механизация производства

Mechanized (мэканайзд) механизированный
Mediate, to ~ (мúдиэйт, ту ~) посредничать
Mediation (мидиэйшн) посредничество, посредство
Medium (мúдиум) средство
Meet, to ~ (мит, ту ~) заседать
Meeting (мúтинг) встреча, заседание, собраниеб совещание
    closed ~ (клозд ~) закрытое совещание
    emergency ~ (эмэрджэнси ~) чрезвычайное заседание, чрезвычайное собрание
    emergency general ~ (эмэрджэнси джэнэрал ~) чрезвычайное общее собрание
    extraordinary ~ (экстраóрдинари ~) внеочередное собрание
    founder's ~ (фóундэрз ~) учредительское собрание {e.g. of new company}
    general ~ (джэнэрал ~) общее собрание
    official ~ (оффúшл ~) официальное заседание
    shareholders' ~ (шэйрхолдэрз ~) собрание акционеров
    ~ a deficit (~ а дэфисит) покрытие дефицита
    ~ demand (~ димáнд) удовлетворение спроса
    ~ of mutual trade commitments (~ оф мючуал трэйд коммúтмэнтс) выполнение обязательств по взаимным поставкам
Member (мэмбэр) член, членский {adj.}
    board ~ (борд ~) член правления
    collegium ~ (коллúгиум ~) член коллегии
    crew ~ (кру ~) член экипажа
    full-fledged ~ (фул-флэджд ~) полноправный член
    non-voting ~ (нон-вóтинг ~) член без права голоса
    permanent ~ (пэрманэнт ~) постоянный член
    ~ of congress (~ оф кóнгрэс) член конгресса
    ~ of parliament (~ оф пáрламэнт) член парламента
Membership (мэмбэршип) членство, членский {adj.}
Memorandum (мэморáндум) меморандум, памятная записка

deal ~ (дил ~) деловая записка
insurance ~ (иншю́ранс ~)
меморандум страховой
~ of understanding (~ оф
андэрста́ндинг) меморандум о
соглашении
Mercantile (мэ́ркантайл) торговый
Mercenary (мэ́рсэнари) продажная
душа, продажный {adj.}
Merchandise (мэ́рчандайс) товар
Merchandising (мэ́рчандайзинг)
распространение
Merchant (мэ́рчант) коммерсант,
купец, торговец
    export ~s (э́кспорт ~с)
    экспортная фирма
    import ~s (и́мпорт ~с) импортная
    фирма
    wholesale ~s (хо́лсэйл ~с)
    оптовая фирма
Mercy (мэ́рси) пощада
Merge, to ~ (мэрдж, ту ~) сливаться
Merger (мэ́рджэр) новация
{novation}, слияние
    ~ of enterprises (~ оф
    э́нтэрпрайзс) слияние предприятий
    ~ of separate uses in land (~ оф
    сэ́парат ю́сэз ин ланд) слияние
    отдельных землепользований
Merit (мэ́рит) качество
Message (мэ́сэдж) послание,
сообщение
    advertising ~ (а́двэртайзинг ~)
    рекламное обращение
    encoded ~ (энко́дэд ~)
    шифрованное сообщение
Messenger (мэ́сэнджэр) нарочный,
посланец, связной
Metallurgical (мэталю́ржикал)
металлургический
Metallurgy (мэ́таллюржи) металлургия
    ferrous ~ (фэ́ррос ~) чёрная
    металлургия
    non-ferrous ~ (нон-фэ́ррос ~)
    цветная металлургия
Meteorological (митиороло́джикал)
метеорологический
Method (мэ́θод) метод, порядок,
способ, форма
    accounting ~s (акко́унтинг ~с)
    методы бухгалтерского учёта
    approved ~ (аппру́вд ~)
    одобренный метод
    batch ~ of production (батч ~ оф
    прода́кшн) метод изготовления
    продукции партиями
    cost ~ (кост ~) метод оценки

cost-saving ~ (кост-сэ́йвинг ~)
метод снижение расходов
costing ~ (ко́стинг ~) метод
калькуляции
design ~ (диза́йн ~) метод
расчёта, метод проектирования
direct export ~ (дирэ́кт э́кспорт
~) метод прямого экспорта
direct import ~ (дирэ́кт и́мпорт
~) метод прямого импорта
economical ~ (эконо́микал ~)
экономичный метод
effective ~ (иффэ́ктив ~)
эффективный метод
forecasting ~s (фо́ркастинг ~с)
методы прогнозирования
general ~ (джэ́нэрал ~) общий
метод
generalized ~ (джэ́нэралайзд ~)
обобщённый метод
genetic engineering ~s (джэнэ́тик
инджэни́ринг ~с) методы генной
инженерии
indirect export ~ (индайрэ́кт
э́кспорт ~) метод косвенного
экспорта
indirect import ~ (индайрэ́кт
и́мпорт ~) метод косвенного
импорта
industrial ~ (инду́стриал ~)
индустриальный метод
inspection ~s (инспэ́кшн ~с)
методы проверки
mass distribution ~s (мас
дистрибю́шн ~с) методы массового
сбыта
modern distribution ~s (мо́дэрн
дистрибю́шн ~с) современные
методы сбыта,
normative ~s (но́рматив ~с)
нормативные методы
operating ~ (о́пэрэйтинг ~) метод
работы, метод эксплуатации
patented ~ (па́тэнтэд ~)
запатентованный способ
practical ~s (пра́ктикал ~с)
практические методы
pricing ~ (пра́йсинг ~) метод
калькуляции цен
printing ~ (при́нтинг ~) метод
печати
production ~s (прода́кшн ~с)
метод производства
quality assessment ~ (куа́лити
ассэ́ссмэнт ~) метод определения
качества

quality control ~ (куа́лити контро́л ~) метод контроля качества продукции
rapid ~ (ра́пид ~) скоростной метод
reliable ~ (рила́йабл ~) надёжный метод
sampling ~ (са́мплинг ~) метод отбора проб
satisfactory ~ (сатисфа́ктори ~) удовлетворительный метод
scientific ~ (сайэнти́фик ~) научный метод
special ~ (спэшл ~) особый метод
standard ~ (ста́ндард ~) стандартный метод
straight flow ~ (стрэйт фло́у ~) поточный метод
to employ a ~ (ту эмпло́й а ~) использовать метод
to follow a ~ (ту фо́лло а ~) придерживать метода
traditional ~ (тради́шнал ~) традиционный метод
training ~s (трэ́йнинг ~с) методы обучения
usual ~ (ю́жюал ~) обычный метод, обычный способ
~ of calculation (~ оф калкюлэ́йшн) метод подсчёта
~ of collaboration (~ оф колаборэ́йшн) метод сотрудничества
~ of comparison (~ оф компа́рисон) метод сравнения
~ of delivery (~ оф дэли́вэри) метод поставки
~ of distribution (~ оф дистрибю́шн) метод распределения
~s of management (~с оф ма́наджмэнт) методы управления
~ of payment (~ оф пэ́ймэнт) метод платежа, форма платежа, форма расчёта
~ of planning (~ оф пла́ннинг) метод планирования
~ of processing (~ оф про́сэсинг) способ обработки
~ of production (~ оф прода́кшн) метод изготовления
Metric (мэ́трик) метрический
~ area (~ э́йриа) метраж
MFN (эм-эф-эн) нация наибольшего благоприятствования
to grant ~ treatment (ту грант ~ три́тмэнт) предоставлять режим наибольшего благоприятствования

Middleman (ми́длман) комиссионер, посредник
Midwife (ми́дуайф) акушерка
Migrant (ма́йгрант) переселенец
Militia (мили́ша) ополчение, орган милиции {police}
Mill (мил) завод
cotton spinning ~ (ко́ттон спи́ннинг ~) хлопкопрядильная фабрика
dressing ~ (дрэ́ссинг ~) обогатительная фабрика
ex ~ contract provision (экс ~ ко́нтракт прови́жн) с завода
ex ~ (экс ~) франко завод
ex seller's ~ (экс сэ́ллэрз ~) франко завод продавца
ex seller's ~ contract provision (экс сэ́ллэрз ~ ко́нтракт прови́жн) с завода продавца
iron and steel ~ (айрн энд стил ~) металлургический завод
paper ~ (пэ́йпэр ~) бумажная фабрика
silk ~ (силк ~) шелкопрядильная фабрика
spinning ~ (спи́ннинг ~) прядильная фабрика
textile ~ (тэ́кстайл ~) текстильная фабрика
weaving ~ (уи́винг ~) ткацкая фабрика
Millhand (ми́лханд) фабричный рабочий
Mind (майнд) разум, ум
to ~ (ту ~) прислушиваться
with this possibility in ~ ... (уиθ θис поссиби́лити ин ~ ...) с учётом этой возможности
Mine (майн) шахта
~ working (~ уо́ркинг) разработка
Miner (ма́йнэр) шахтёр
Mineral (ми́нэрал) ископаемое
Minimal (ми́нимал) минимальный
Minimum (ми́нимум) минимальный
Mining (ма́йнинг) горный промысел, горная разработка
Minister (ми́нистэр) министр
assistant to a ~ (асси́стант ту а ~) помощник министра
deputy ~ (дэ́пюти ~) заместитель министра
prime ~ (прайм ~) премьер-министр
Ministry (ми́нистри) министерство
sectoral ~ (сэкто́рал ~) отраслевое министерство

~ **of finance** (~ оф файна́нс) министерство финансов
~ **of foreign affairs** (~ оф фо́рэн аффэ́йрс) министерство иностранных дел
~ **of health** (~ оф хэлθ) министерство здравоохранения
~ **of inland water transport** (~ оф и́нланд уа́тэр тра́нспорт) министерство речного флота
~ **of justice** (~ оф джа́стис) министерство юстиции
~ **of the merchant marine** (~ оф θи мэ́рчант мари́н) министерство морского флота
Mint (минт) монетный двор, мята {plant}
Minting of coins (ми́нтинг оф койнс) изготовление монеты
Minute (ми́нут) минута ~**s** протокол {of a meeting, etc.}
~ **of a meeting** (~ оф а ми́тинг) протокол собрания
~ **of proceedings** (~ оф проси́дингс) протокол заседания
Misadventure (мисадвэ́нтюр) несчастный случай
homicide by ~ (хо́мисайд бай ~) случайное убийство
Misappropriate, to ~ (мисаппро́приэйт, ту ~) присваивать [perfective: присвоить], расхищать
Misappropriation (мисаппроприэ́йшн) незаконное присвоение, расхищение
Miscegenation (миссэджэнэ́йшн) кровосмешение
product of ~ (про́дукт оф ~) происхождение от кровосмешения
Misconstrue, to ~ (мисконстру́, ту ~) извратить
Misdemeanor (ми́сдиминор) проступок
anti-social ~ (а́нти-сошл ~) антиобщественный проступок
Miserly (ма́йзэрли) скупой
Mishandling (мисха́ндлинг) дурное обращение
Misinterpretation (мисинтэрпрэтэ́йшн) извращение
Misprint (ми́спринт) опечатка {e.g. book, inventory list}
Missing (ми́ссинг) недостающий, отсутствующий
Mission (мишн) миссия
trade ~ (трэйд ~) торговая миссия
Mistake (мистэ́йк) ошибка
Mistaken (мистэ́йкэн) ошибочный

Mistress (ми́стрэс) сожительница {lover}, хозяйка {of household, etc.}
Misunderstanding (мисандэрста́ндинг) недоразумение
Misuse (мисю́з) неправильная эксплуатация
~ **of credit** (~ оф крэ́дит) злоупотребление кредита
~ **of force** (~ оф форс) злоупотребление силой
Mitigating (ми́тигэйтинг) смягчающий
Mitigation (митигэ́йшн) смягчение
Mix, to ~ (микс, ту ~) смешивать [perfective: смешать]
Mixed (миксд) смешанный
Mixture (ми́ксчур) смешение
Mob (моб) сборище
~ **justice** (~ джа́стис) самосуд
Mobile (мо́бил) передвижной
Mobilization (мобилизэ́йшн) мобилизация
industrial ~ (инду́стриал ~) мобилизация промышленности
~ **of cash** (~ оф каш) мобилизация наличности
~ **of financial resources** (~ оф файна́ншл рисо́рсэз) мобилизация финансовых средств
~ **of resources** (~ оф рисо́рсэз) мобилизация ресурсов
Mock-up (мок-ап) макет
engineering ~ (инджэни́ринг ~) технологический макет
Mode (мод) способ
~ **of application** (~ оф аппликэ́йшн) способ применения
~ **of conveyance** (~ оф конвэ́йянс) вид транспортировки, способ перевозки
~ **of reimbursement** (~ оф риимбу́рсмэнт) метод возмещения
~ **of transport** (~ оф тра́нспорт) вид транспорта
Model (мо́дэл) макет, марка товара, модель, образец, типовой {adj.}
approved ~ (аппру́вд ~) одобренная марка
competing ~ (компи́тинг ~) конкурирующая модель
cut-away ~ (кут-ауэ́й ~) модель в разрезе
economic growth ~ (эконо́мик гроθ ~) модель экономического роста
financial ~ (файна́ншл ~) финансовая модель

industrial ~ (индустриал ~)
промышленный образец
life-size ~ (лайф-сайз ~) макет
в натуральную величину
new ~ (нью ~) новая модель
obsolete ~ (обсолит ~)
устаревшая модель
previous ~ (привиос ~)
предыдущая модель
production ~ (продакшн ~)
серийная модель
recent ~ (рисэнт ~) современная
модель
reduced ~ (ридюсд ~) упрощённая
модель
reduced scale ~ (ридюсд скэйл ~)
модель в уменьшенном размере
registered ~ (рэджистэрд ~)
зарегистрированная модель
selected ~ (сэлэктэд ~)
отобранная модель
to test a ~ (ту тэст а ~)
испытывать модель
various makes and ~s (вариос
мэйкс энд ~с) различные модели
working ~ (уоркинг ~)
действующий макет, действующая
модель, рабочая модель
~ name (~ нэйм) название модели
~ of a freighter (~ оф а
фрэйтэр) марка грузового судна
Moderate (модэрат) умеренный
Modernization (модэрнизэйшн)
модернизация, обновление
fundamental ~ (фундамэнтал ~)
коренная модернизация
technical ~ (тэкникал ~)
техническое обновление
~ of the economy (~ оф θи
икономи) модернизация экономики
Modernize, to ~ (модэрнайз, ту ~)
модернизировать, обновлять
Modernized (модэрнайзд) обновлённый
Modification (модификэйшн)
модификация, поправка
patentable ~ (патэнтабл ~)
запатентованная модификация
Modified (модифайд)
модифицированный
Modify, to ~ (модифай, ту ~)
изменить, модифицировать
Moist (мойст) влажный
Moisture (мойстюр) влажность
excess ~ (эксэс ~) повышенная
влажность
timber ~ content (тимбэр ~
контэнт) влажность древесины

to damage by excess ~ (ту дамадж
бай эксэс ~) повреждать
повышенной влажностью
~ allowance (~ аллоуанс) скидка
за влажность
~ certificate (~ сэртификэт)
сертификат о влажности
~ clause (~ клауз) оговорка о
влажности
Moment (момэнт) момент
crucial ~ (крушл ~) критический
момент
Monetary (монэтари) валютный,
валютно-финансовый, денежный,
монетарный, монетный
~ movement (~ мувмэнт) движение
денег
Money (мони) деньги, денежный
{adj.}, денежный знак
balance {remainder} of ~ (баланс
{римэйндэр} оф ~) остаток денег
changing ~ (чэйнджинг ~) размен
денег
cheap ~ (чип ~) дешёвые деньги
circulation of ~ (сиркюлэйшн оф
~) обращение денег
circulation of paper ~
(сиркюлэйшн оф пэйпэр ~)
обращение бумажных денег
counterfeit ~ (коунтэрфит ~)
фальшивые деньги
debt ~ (дэт ~) кредитные деньги
depreciation of ~ (дипришиэйшн
оф ~) обесценение денег
emission of paper ~ (эмишн оф
пэйпэр ~) выпуск бумажных денег
expenditure of ~ (экспэндичур оф
~) расходование денег
expensive ~ (экспэнсив ~)
дорогие деньги
"hot" ~ (хот ~) "горячие" деньги
inconvertibility of paper ~
(инконвэртибилити оф пэйпэр ~)
необратимость бумажных денег
irredeemable ~ (иррэдимабл ~)
неразменные деньги
lot ~ (лот ~) вознаграждение
аукционисту {auction}
paper ~ (пэйпэр ~) банкноты,
бумажные деньги
prize ~ (прайз ~) призовые
деньги
purchase ~ (пурчас ~) деньги на
покупку
purchasing power of ~ (пурчасинг
поуэр оф ~) покупательная сила
денег

659

real ~ (рил ~) реальные деньги
release of holdback ~ (рилйс оф хо́лдбак ~) разблокирование удержанных денег
remittance of ~ (римйттанс оф ~) перевод денег
smart ~ (смарт ~) отступные деньги {buy-out money}
tight ~ (тайт ~) денежный голод
to allocate ~ (ту а́локэйт ~) ассигновать деньги
to be short of ~ (ту би шорт оф ~) испытывать недостаток в деньгах
to borrow ~ (ту бо́рро ~) занимать деньги
to borrow ~ against an insurance policy (ту бо́рро ~ агэ́нст ан иншю́ранс по́лиси) занимать деньги под страховой полис
to borrow ~ at zero interest (ту бо́рро ~ ат зйро йнтэрэст) занимать деньги без процентов
to borrow ~ under mortgage (ту бо́рро ~ а́ндэр мо́ргэдж) занимать деньги под закладную
to borrow ~ up to a specified amount (ту бо́рро ~ ап ту а спэ́сифайд амо́унт) занимать деньги до определённой суммы
to change ~ (ту чэйндж ~) менять деньги
to deposit ~ at a specified interest rate (ту дипо́зит ~ ат а спэ́сифайд йнтэрэст рэйт) вкладывать деньги из определённого процента
to deposit ~ in a bank (ту дипо́зит ~ ин а банк) вкладывать деньги в банк, класть деньги в банк
to draw ~ from a bank (ту дра́у ~ фром а банк) получать деньги в банке
to earn ~ (ту эрн ~) зарабатывать деньги
to expend ~ (ту экспэ́нд ~) расходовать деньги
to hoard ~ (ту хорд ~) копить деньги
to issue ~ (ту йшю ~) выпускать деньги
to keep ~ in a bank (ту кип ~ ин а банк) держать деньги в банке, хранить деньги в банке

to lend ~ at interest (ту лэнд ~ ат йнтэрэст) ссужать деньги под проценты
to pay in ~ (ту пэй ин ~) вносить деньги
to place ~ in a bank (ту плэйс ~ ин а банк) вносить деньги в банк
to place ~ in escrow (ту плэйс ~ ин э́скро) вносить деньги на условный счёт
to place ~ on account (ту плэйс ~ он акко́унт) вносить деньги на счёт
to place ~ on deposit (ту плэйс ~ он дипо́зит) вносить деньги в депозит
to provide with ~ (ту прова́йд уиθ ~) предоставлять деньги
to raise ~ (ту рэйз ~) доставать деньги
to receive ~ on deposit (ту рисйв ~ он дипо́зит) принимать деньги на вклад
to refund ~ (ту рйфунд ~) возмещать деньги
to reimburse ~ (ту риимбу́рс ~) возмещать израсходованные деньги
to remit ~ (ту римйт ~) переводить деньги
to remove ~ from circulation (ту риму́в ~ фром сиркюлэ́йшн) изымать деньги из обращения
to repay borrowed ~ (ту рипэ́й бо́рроуд ~) возвращать деньги, взятые взаймы
to reserve ~ (ту рисэ́рв ~) резервировать деньги
to save ~ (ту сэйв ~) экономить деньги
to send ~ by postal money order (ту сэнд ~ бай по́стал мо́ни о́рдэр) переводить деньги по почте
to spend ~ (ту спэнд ~) тратить деньги
to transfer ~ (ту тра́нсфэр ~) пересылать деньги
to wire ~ (ту уайр ~) переводить деньги по телеграфу
to withdraw ~ from an account (ту уиθдра́у ~ фром ан акко́унт) снимать деньги со счёта
token ~ (то́кэн ~) символические деньги
transfer of ~ in check form (тра́нсфэр оф ~ ин чэк форм) пересылка денег в форме чека

unexpended ~ (анэкспэ́ндэд ~)
неизрасходованные деньги
universal ~ (юнивэ́рсал ~)
всемирные деньги
waste of ~ (уэ́йст оф ~)
непроизводительная трата денег
withdrawal of ~ from circulation
(уиθдра́уал оф ~ фром сиркюлэ́йшн)
изъятие денег из обращения
world ~ (уо́рлд ~) мировые деньги
~ damages (~ да́мэджэз) денежное
возмещение
~-grubber (~-гру́ббэр) стяжатель
~ in circulation (~ ин
сиркюлэ́йшн) деньги в обращение
~ loan (~ лон) заём денег
~ substitute (~ су́бститут)
заменитель денег
~ supply (~ суппла́й) запас денег
Monitor (мо́нитор) слухач, староста,
экран {computer screen}
to ~ (ту ~) контролировать
Monitored (мо́ниторд) контролируемый
Monitoring (мо́ниторинг) контроль,
контролирование, контролирующий
detailed ~ (ди́тэйлд ~) подробный
контроль
process ~ (про́сэс ~)
контролирование процесса
Monometalism (мономэ́тализм)
монометаллизм
Monometallic (мономэта́ллик)
монометаллический
Monopolization (монополизэ́йшн)
монополизация
Monopolize, to ~ (моно́полайз, ту ~)
монополизировать
Monopoly (моно́поли)
монополистическое объединение,
монополия, монопольный {adj.}
accidental ~ (аксидэ́нтал ~)
случайная монополия
all-encompassing ~ (ал-
энко́мпассинг ~) всеобъемлющая
монополия
bank ~ (банк ~) банковская
монополия
bilateral ~ (байла́тэрал ~)
двухсторонняя монополия
commercial ~ (комме́ршл ~)
торговая монополия
complete ~ (компли́т ~) полная
монополия
export ~ (э́кспорт ~) экспортная
монополия
financial ~ (файна́ншл ~)
финансовая монополия

fiscal ~ (фи́скал ~) фискальная
монополия
foreign exchange ~ (фо́рэн
эксчэ́йндж ~) валютная монополия
group ~ (груп ~) групповая
монополия
industrial ~ (инду́стриал ~)
промышленная монополия
international ~ (интэрна́шэнал ~)
международная монополия
merger of ~s (мэ́рджэр оф ~c)
слияние монополий
multinational ~ (мултина́шэнал ~)
транснациональная монополия
patent ~ (па́тэнт ~) патентная
монополия
private ~ (пра́йват ~) частная
монополия
state ~ (стэйт ~)
государственная монополия
temporary ~ (тэ́мпорари ~)
временная монополия
~ power (~ по́уэр) власть
монополий
Monthly (мо́нθли) ежемесячный,
месячный
Monument (мо́нюмэнт) памятник
historical ~ (хисто́рикал ~)
исторический памятник
~ of Antiquity (~ оф анти́куити)
памятник старины
Moonlight, to ~ (му́нлайт, ту ~)
халтурить
Moonlighting (му́нлайтинг) халтура
Moonshine (му́ншайн) самогон
{illegal spirits}
Moonshiner (му́ншайнэр) самогонщик
{maker of illegal spirits}
Moor, to ~ (мур, ту ~) стоять,
швартоваться
Moorage (му́радж) место причала,
стоянка в порту
Mooring (му́ринг) стоянка, швартовка
~ prohibited (~ прохи́битэд)
стоянка запрещена
Moratorium (мората́риум) мораторий
extension of a ~ (экстэ́ншн оф а
~) продление моратория
imposition of a ~ (импози́шн оф а
~) установление моратория
to declare a ~ (ту дикла́йр а ~)
объявить мораторий
to impose a ~ (ту импо́з а ~)
вводить мораторий на
Mortality (морта́лити) смертность
infant ~ (и́нфант ~) детская
смертность

Mortgage (мóргэдж) залог, залоговый {adj.}, ипотека, ипотечный {adj.}, обременение ипотекой
    encumbered with a ~ (энкáмбэрд уиθ а ~) обременённый ипотекой ипотека
    first ~ (фэрст ~) первая ипотека
    higher in priority (хáйэр ин прайóрити) ипотека выше по рангу
    lower in priority (лóуэр ин прайóрити) ипотека ниже по рангу
    maritime ~ (мáритайм ~) ипотека морского судна, морская ипотека
    privileged ~ (прúвилэджд ~) привилегированная ипотека
    release of real property from a ~ (рилúс оф рил прóпэрти фром а ~) очистка недвижимости от ипотеки
    security by ~ (сэкю́рити бай ~) обеспечение с помощью закладной
    to ~ (ту ~) закладывать [perfective: заложить], установить ипотеку
    ~ of an air vessel (~ оф ан эйр вэ́ссэл) ипотека воздушного судна
    ~ of land (~ оф ланд) ипотека земельного участка
    ~ of real property (~ оф рил прóпэрти) залог недвижимого имущества
    ~-deed (~-дид) залоговое свидетельство
Mortgagee (моргэджú) залогодержатель, закладодержатель
Mortgaging (мóргэджинг) отдача под опеку
Mortgagor (моргэджóр) должник по закладной, закладчик, залогодатель
Most (мост) наибольший
    at ~ (ат ~) максимально
Mother-in-law (мóθэр-ин-лау) свекровь {mother of husband}
Motion Picture (мошн пúкшр) кинофильм
    ~ equipment (~ икуúпмэнт) кинооборудование
Motive (мóтив) побуждение, мотив
Motor (мóтор) двигатель, мотор
Motorboat (мóторбот) моторное судно
Mount, to ~ (мóунт, ту ~) монтировать
Mounter (мóунтэр) монтажник
Mounting (мóунтинг) монтаж
Move, to ~ (мув, ту ~) перемещать
Movement (мýвмэнт) движение

    free ~ (фри ~) свободное передвижение
    labor ~ (лэ́йбор ~) профсоюзное движение
    monetary ~ (мóнэтари ~) движение денег
    ~ of funds (~ оф фандз) движение фондов
    capital ~s (кáпитал ~с) передвижение капиталов
    credit ~s (крэ́дит ~с) передвижение кредита
    price ~s (прайс ~с) движение цен
    troop ~s (труп ~с) передвижение войск
Movie (мýви) кинофильм
    ~ equipment (~ икуúпмэнт) киноаппаратура
    ~ film (~ филм) кинолента
    ~ projector (~ проджэ́ктор) киноустановка
    ~ theater (~ θúатэр) кинозал
Moving (мýвинг) перемещение
Multicurrency (мултикýррэнси) мультивалютный
Multilateral (мултилáтэрал) многосторонний
Multilinear (мултилúниар) многоколонный
Multiple (мýлтипл) множественный, сложный
Multitude (мýлтитуд) множество
Munitions (мюнúшнс) военные припасы
Mutual (мю́чуал) обоюдный
    ~ advantage (~ адвáнтэдж) взаимная выгода
    ~ interest (~ úнтэрэст) взаимная заинтересованность
Mutuality (мючуáлити) обоюдность
Mutually (мю́чуалли) взаимно
    ~ acceptable (~ аксэ́птабл) взаимоприемлемый
    ~ agreed (~ агрúд) взаимосогласованный
    ~ provided (~ провáйдэд) взаимопоставляемый

N

Nail (нэйл) гвозд
    to ~ (ту ~) крепить гвоздями
Name (нэйм) название, наименование
    brand ~ (бранд ~) название марки
    conditional ~ (кондúшнал ~) условное наименование

first ~ (фэрст ~) имя
last ~ (ласт ~) фамилия
manufacturer's ~ (манюфа́кчурэрз ~) наименование завода-изготовителя
ship's ~ (шипс ~) название судна, наименование судна
to ~ (ту ~) именовать, называть
to change the ~ (ту чэйндж θи ~) изменить название
trade ~ (трэйд ~) торговое наименование, торговое название товара
~ of a beneficiary (~ оф а бэнэфи́шиари) наименование бенефициара
~ of a firm (~ оф а фирм) фирменное наименование
~ of an invention (~ оф ан инвэ́ншн) название изобретения
National (на́шэнэл) государственный, национальный, подданный {person}
foreign ~ (фо́рэн ~) иностранный подданный
Nationality (нашэна́лити) национальная принадлежность, подданство
mark of ~ (марк оф ~) обозначение страны
Nationalization (нашинализэ́йшн) национализация, огосударствление
act of ~ (акт оф ~) акт о национализации {of property}
Nationalize, to ~ (на́шэналайз, ту ~) национализировать, огосударствлять
Nationwide (нэ́йшнуайд) общегосударственный
Native (нэ́йтив) абориген {person}, родной {adj.}
Natural (на́чюрал) натуральный
Naturalization (начюрализэ́йшн) принятие в гражданство
act of ~ (акт оф ~) акт натурализации
decree of ~ (дикри́ оф ~) акт о натурализации
Nature (нэ́йчэр) природа
~ of goods (~ оф гудз) вид товара
Naval (нэ́йвал) флотский
Navigable (на́вигабл) судоходный
Navigating (на́вигэйтинг) навигационный
Navigation (навигэ́йшн) навигация, мореплавание, плавание, судоходство

air ~ (эйр ~) воздушная навигация
closed to ~ (клозд ту ~) закрытый для навигации
coastal ~ (ко́стал ~) каботажное плавание
inland ~ (и́нланд ~) внутреннее плавание
marine ~ (мари́н ~) морская навигация
open for ~ (о́пэн фор ~) открытый для навигации
safety of ~ (сэ́йфти оф ~) безопасность мореплавания
~ officer (~ о́ффисэр) штурман
Necessary (нэ́сэсари) необходимый
Necessit/y (нэсэ́сити) необходимость, нужда
basic ~/ies (бэ́йсик ~из) предметы первой необходимости
paramount ~ (парамо́унт ~) крайняя необходимость
pressing ~ (прэ́ссинг ~) настоятельная необходимость
Need (нид) потребность
future ~s (фю́чэр ~с) будущие потребности
Negligence (нэ́глиджэнс) небрежность, пренебрежение
~ clause (~ клауз) оговорка о возмещении убытков, причинённых небрежностью
Negligent (нэ́глиджэнт) небрежный
~ behavior (~ бихэ́йвиор) пренебрежение
Negotiable (нэго́шабл) оборотный
Negotiate, to ~ (нэго́шиэйт, ту ~) договариваться, негоциировать
Negotiation (нэгоши́эйшн) дисконтирование {e.g. draft}, негоциация ~s переговоры
bilateral ~s (байла́тэрал ~с) двухсторонние переговоры
collective ~s (коллэ́ктив ~с) коллективные переговоры
commercial ~s (коммэ́ршл ~с) коммерческие переговоры
diplomatic ~s (диплома́тик ~с) дипломатические переговоры
direct ~s (дирэ́кт ~с) непосредственные переговоры
financial ~s (файна́ншл ~с) финансовые переговоры
initiation of ~s (инишиэ́йшн оф ~с) открытие переговоров

intergovernmental ~s
(интэрговэрнмэ́нтал ~с)
межправительственные переговоры
multilateral ~s (мултила́тэрал
~с) многосторонние переговоры
preliminary peace ~s
(прили́минэри пис ~с)
предварительные переговоры о
мире
to conduct ~s (ту конду́кт ~с)
вести переговоры
to effect a ~ (ту иффэ́кт а ~)
производить негоциацию
trade ~s (трэйд ~с) торговые
переговоры
~ **against documents** (~ агэ́нст
до́кюмэнтс) негоциация против
документов
~s **for peace** (~с фор пис)
переговоры о мире
~ **of a bill** (~ оф а бил) выплата
по векселю
~ **of a check** (~ оф а чэк)
выплата по чеку
~ **of drafts** (~ оф драфтс)
негоциация тратт
~ **of a check** (~ оф а чэк)
передача чека
Negotiator (нэго́шиэйтор) негоциант
Nephew (нэ́фю) племянник
Net (нэт) без вычетов, нетто,
чистый
actual ~ **weight** (а́кчуал ~ уэйт)
реальный вес нетто
gross for ~ (грос фор ~) брутто
за нетто
legal ~ **weight** (ли́гал ~ уэйт)
легальный вес нетто
on a ~ **basis** (он а ~ бэ́йсис) на
основе нетто
to ~ (ту ~) выручать
~ **amount** (~ амо́унт) сумма нетто
~ **exporter of a commodity** (~
э́кспортэр оф а коммо́дити)
нетто-экспортёр товара
~ **mass** (~ мас) масса нетто
~ **of depreciation** (~ оф
дипришиэ́йшн) за вычетом
амортизации
~ **price** (~ прайс) цена нетто
~ **proceeds** (~ про́сидс) выручка
нетто
~ **registered ton** (~ рэ́джистэрд
тон) нетто-регистровая тонна
~ **weight** (~ уэйт) вес нетто
Network (нэ́туорк) сеть

commercial ~ (комме́ршл ~)
торговая сеть
communications ~ (коммюникэ́йшнс
~) сеть связи
dealership ~ (ди́лэршип ~)
дилерская сеть
distribution ~ (дистрибью́шн ~)
распределительная сеть
railway ~ (рэ́йлуэй ~)
железнодорожная сеть
~ **of trade relations** (~ оф трэйд
рилэ́йшнс) сеть торговли
Neutral (ну́трал) нейтральный
News (ньюз) новости
flash (флаш) экстренное
сообщение
Newsletter (нью́злэттэр) бюллетень
monthly ~ (мо́нθли ~) ежемесячный
бюллетень
Newsprint (нью́зпринт) газетная
бумага
Nickname (ни́кнэйм) прозвище
Niece (нис) племянница
Nomenclature (но́мэнклэйчур)
номенклатура
equipment ~ (икуи́пмэнт ~)
номенклатура оборудования
expansion of the ~ **of goods**
(экспа́ншн оф θи ~ оф гудз)
расширение номенклатуры товаров
uniform ~ (ю́ниформ ~) единая
номенклатура
Nominal (но́минал) именной,
нарицательный, номинальный
~ **roll** (~ рол) именной список
Nominate, to ~ (но́минэйт, ту ~)
назначать
to ~ **an arbitrator** (ту ~ ан
а́рбитрэйтор) производить
назначение арбитра
Nomination (номинэ́йшн) назначение
refusal to accept ~ (рифю́зал ту
аксэ́пт ~) самоотвод
Nominee (номини́) назначенное лицо
Non-acceptance (нон-аксэ́птанс)
неакцепт, непринятие
risk of ~ (риск оф ~) риск
непринятия
~ **of goods** (~ оф гудз)
непринятие товара
Non-assembled (нон-ассэ́мблд) в
разобранном виде
Non-cartelized (нон-ка́ртэлайзд)
некартелированный
Non-cash (нон-каш) безналичный
{transaction}

Non-commercial (нон-коммэ́ршл) неторговый

Non-competition (нон-компэти́шн) неконкурентность
    clause (клауз) оговорка о неконкурентности

Non-competitive (нон-компэ́титив) безконкурентный, неконкурентный

Non-competitiveness (нон-компэ́титивнэс) неконкурентность

Non-compliance (нон-компла́йанс) несоблюдение

Non-compulsory (нон-компу́лсори) необязательный

Non-conference (нон-ко́нфэрэнс) некартельный

Non-conforming (нон-конфо́рминг) бракованный {e.g. goods}

Non-cumulative (нон-кю́мюлатив) некумулятивный

Non-delivery (нон-дэли́вэри) недоставка

Non-discriminatory (нон-дискри́минатори) недискриминационный

Non-durable (нон-ду́рабл) недлительный

Non-dutiable (нон-ду́тиабл) не подлежащий обложению

Non-essentials (нон-эссэ́ншлз) второстепенные товары

Non-exclusive (нон-экскл́юсив) неисключительный

Non-frost resistant (нон-фрост ризи́стант) неморозостойкий

Non-fulfillment (нон-фулфи́лмэнт) невыполнение, неисполнение
    ~ of an order (~ оф ан о́рдэр) невыполнение заказа

Non-liquid (нон-ли́куид) неликвидный {not readily cashed}

Non-liquidity (нон-ликуи́дити) отсутствие наличности

Non-negotiable (нон-нэго́шабл) без права передачи, непередаваемый

Non-observance (нон-обзэ́рванс) несоблюдение
    ~ of a schedule (~ оф а скэ́джюл) несоблюдение графика
    ~ of formalities (~ оф форма́литиз) несоблюдение формальностей
    ~ of the terms of agreement (~ оф θи тэрмз оф агри́мэнт) несоблюдение условий договора
    ~ of the terms of a contract (~ оф θи тэрмз оф а ко́нтракт) несоблюдение условий контракта

Non-payment (нон-пэ́ймэнт) неоплата
    advice of ~ (адва́йс оф ~) авизо о неплатеже

Non-performance (нон-пэрфо́рманс) неисполнение, невыполнение
    penalty for ~ of a contract (пэ́налти фор ~ оф а ко́нтракт) штраф за невыполнение договора
    sanctions for ~ (санкшнс фор ~) санкции за неисполнение
    ~ of a contract (~ оф а ко́нтракт) невыполнение контракта, невыполнение договора

Non-perishable (нон-пэ́ришабл) непортящийся

Non-productive (нон-прода́ктив) непроизводительный

Nonprofit (нонпро́фит) бесприбыльный, некоммерческий

Non-sectoral (нон-сэкто́рал) неотраслевой

Non-tariff (нон-та́риф) нетарифный

Non-taxable (нон-та́ксабл) не подлежащий обложению, необлагаемый

Non-transferrable (нон-трансфэ́рабл) без права передачи

Non-urgent (нон-у́рджэнт) несрочный

Non-waterproof (нон-уа́тэрпруф) водопроницаемый

Non-working (нон-уо́ркинг) нерабочий

Nonpayment (нонпэ́ймэнт) неуплата
    as a result of ~ (аз а ризу́лт оф ~) в результате неуплаты
    due to ~ (ду ту ~) ввиду неуплаты
    ~ of taxes (~ оф та́ксэз) неуплата налогов

Norm (норм) норма, норматив
    economic ~s (эконо́мик ~с) экономические нормативы
    introduction of ~s (интрода́кшн оф ~с) введение норм
    legal ~s (ли́гал ~с) правовые нормы
    new ~s (нью ~с) новые нормы
    present ~s (прэ́зэнт ~с) действующие нормы
    stability of ~s (стаби́лити оф ~с) стабильность нормативов
    to apply ~s (ту аппла́й ~с) применять нормы
    to prescribe ~s (ту прискра́йб ~с) указывать нормы
    to revise ~s (ту рива́йз ~с) пересматривать нормы
    to set ~s (ту сэт ~с) нормировать

Normal (нóрмал) нормальный
Normalization (нормализэ́йшн)
нормализация, оздоровление
    ~ of international relations (~
    оф интэрнáшэнал рилэ́йшнс)
    нормализация международных
    отношений
Normalized (нóрмалайзд)
нормированный
Normative (нóрматив) нормативный
Nostro (нóстро) ностро
    ~ account (~ аккóунт) счёт
    ностро
    ~ overdraft (~ óвэрдрафт)
    овердрафт ностро
Notarial (нотэ́йриал) нотариальный
Notarially (нотэ́йриалли)
нотариально
Notarization (нотаризэ́йшн)
нотариальный акт
Notarize, to ~ (нóтарайз, ту ~)
засвидетельствовать нотариально
Notary (нóтари) нотариус
    ~ public (~ пáблик) нотариус
    to submit a complaint to the ~'s
    office (ту субмúт а комплэ́йнт ту
    θи ~з óффис) заявить протест
    нотариусу
Notation (нотэ́йшн) обозначение,
отметка
    system of ~ (сúстэм оф ~)
    система обозначений
Note (нот) билет, записка, нота
    accompanying ~ (аккóмпаниинг ~)
    сопроводительная накладная
    air consignment ~ (эйр
    консáйнмэнт ~) грузовая
    воздушная квитанция
    backing of bank ~s (бáкинг оф
    банк ~с) обеспечение банкнот
    bank ~ (банк ~) банковский билет
    bearer ~ (бэ́йрэр ~) вексель на
    предъявителя
    consignment ~ (консáйнмэнт ~)
    грузовая квитанция , накладная
    на груз {way-bill},
    товаросопроводительная накладная
    contract ~ (кóнтракт ~)
    договорная запись
    demand ~ (димáнд ~)
    предъявительский вексель
    export ~ (экспорт ~) бланк учёта
    экспортных операций
    extended ~ (экстэ́ндэд ~)
    пролонгированный вексель
    gold ~ (голд ~) погашенный
    золотом вексель

    interest bearing ~ (úнтэрэст
    бэ́ринг ~) процентный вексель
    joint ~ (джойнт ~) простой
    вексель, с двумя или более
    подписями
    maturity term of a ~ (мачýрити
    тэрм оф а ~) срок векселя
    non-interest bearing ~ (нон-
    úнтэрэст бэ́ринг ~) беспроцентный
    вексель
    one pound ~ (уáн пóунд ~)
    банкнота в 1 фунт стерлингов
    promissory ~ (прóмиссори ~)
    долговое обязательство, простой
    вексель
    single-name ~ (сингл-нэйм ~)
    соло-вексель
    short-term ~ (шорт-тэрм ~)
    простой, краткосрочный вексель
    sight ~ (сайт ~) срочный по
    предъявлении вексель
    term ~ (тэрм) вексель на срок
    to ~ (ту ~) отмечать
    [perfective: отметить]
    to collect a ~ (ту коллэ́кт а ~)
    получать деньги по векселю
    to draw a ~ for (ту дрáу а ~
    фор) выписывать вексель сроком
    на
    to pay by ~s (ту пэй бай ~с)
    платить векселями
    transfer ~ (трáнсфэр ~)
    переводной вексель
    treasury ~s (трэ́жюри ~с)
    казначейские билеты
    ~ payable (~ пэ́йабл) вексель к
    оплате
    ~s receivable (~с рисúвабл)
    векселя к получению
Notice (нóтис) авизо, заметка,
заявление, извещение, нотис,
объявление, уведомление
    advance ~ (адвáнс ~)
    заблаговременное уведомление,
    предварительное заявление
    auction ~ (аукшн ~) уведомление
    об аукционе
    by written ~ (бай рúттэн ~)
    посредством письменного
    уведомления
    cancellation ~ (кансэллэ́йшн ~)
    уведомление об отмене
    captain's ~ (кáптэнз ~) нотис
    капитана
    death ~ (дэθ ~) извещение о
    смерти, объявление смерти

due ~ (ду ~) надлежащее уведомление
immediate ~ (иммúдиат ~) срочное уведомление
official ~ (оффúшл ~) официальное заявление
one week's ~ (уáн уикс ~) уведомление за одну неделю
patent ~ (пáтэнт ~) патентная маркировка
preliminary ~ (прилúминэри ~) предварительное извещение, предварительный нотис, предварительное уведомление
statutory ~ (стáтютори ~) предписанное законом уведомление
subject to timely ~ (сáбджэкт ту тáймли ~) при условии немедленного уведомления
timely ~ (тáймли ~) своевременное уведомление
to accept a ~ (ту аксэ́пт а ~) принять нотис
to file a ~ (ту файл а ~) регистрировать уведомление
to forward a ~ (ту фóруард а ~) послать нотис
to give ~ (ту гив ~) подать нотис
to give formal ~ (ту гив фóрмал ~) официально уведомлять
to give prior ~ (ту гив прáйор ~) предварительно уведомлять
to receive ~ (ту рисúв ~) получать уведомление
written ~ (рúттэн ~) письменное извещение
~ by cable (~ бай кэйбл) уведомление по телеграфу
~ by mail (~ бай мэйл) уведомление по почте
~ by telex (~ бай тэ́лэкс) уведомление по телексу
~ of appropriation (~ оф аппроприэ́йшн) извещение о выделении товара для исполнения договора
~ of arrival (~ оф аррáйвал) уведомление о прибытии
~ of claim (~ оф клэйм) заявление о возмещении убытка, уведомление о предъявлении претензии
~ of claim against insurance (~ оф клэйм агэ́нст иншюранс) заявления о выплате страхового озмещения

~ of expiration (~ оф экспирэ́йшн) уведомление об истечении срока
~ of legal action (~ оф лúгал акшн) уведомление об иске
~ of opening of a letter of credit (~ оф óпэнинг оф а лэ́ттэр оф крэ́дит) авизо об открытии ккредитива
~ of receipt (~ оф рисúт) извещение о получении
Notification (нотификэ́йшн) извещение, нотификация, оповещение, осведомление, повестка, уведомление
act of ~ (акт оф ~) акт уведомления
bank ~ (банк ~) банковское уведомление
consider this letter to be official ~ ... (консúдэр θис лэ́ттэр ту би оффúшл ~ ...) считайте это письмо официальным уведомлением ...
loading ~ (лóдинг ~) уведомление о погрузке
official ~ (оффúшл ~) официальное уведомление
telephonic ~ (тэлэфóник ~) уведомление по телефону
to provide written ~ (ту провáйд рúттэн ~) представлять письменное уведомление
to send ~ (ту сэнд ~) посылать уведомление
upon ~ (упóн ~) по уведомлении
within a reasonable period from ~ (уиθúн а рúзонабл пúриод фром ~) с заблаговременным уведомлением
written ~ (рúттэн ~) письменное заявление, письменное уведомление
~ of a letter of credit (~ оф а лэ́ттэр оф крэ́дит) уведомление об аккредитиве
Notify, to ~ (нóтифай, ту ~) оповещать, уведомлять
Notorious (нотóриос) пресловутый
Novation (новэ́йшн) новация
~ of an agreement (~ оф ан агрúмэнт) новация договора
Novelt/y (нóвэлти) новизна, новинка
demonstrating ~/ies (дэ́монстрэйтинг ~из) экспонирование новинок
exhibition of ~/ies (экзибúшн оф ~из) выставка новинок

patented ~ (па́тэнтэд ~) патентоспособная новизна
Null (нул) недействительный
  to declare ~ and void (ту дикле́йр ~ энд войд) признать недействительным
  ~ and void (~ энд войд) недействительный
Nullification (нуллифике́йшн) канцеллинг, признание недействительности
  ~ of registration (~ оф рэджистре́йшн) признание недействительности регистрации
Nullify, to ~ (ну́ллифай, ту ~) признавать недействительным
Nullity (ну́ллити) недействительность
  ~ of a contract (~ оф а ко́нтракт) недействительность договора
  ~ of a treaty (~ оф а три́ти) недействительность договора
Number (ну́мбэр) количество, номер, цифра, число
  actual ~ (а́кчуал ~) фактическая численность
  approximate ~ (аппро́ксимат ~) приблизительная цифра
  batch ~ (батч ~) серийный номер
  code ~ (код ~) кодовой номер
  consecutive ~ (консе́кютив ~) номер по порядку
  contract ~ (ко́нтракт ~) номер контракта
  even ~ (и́вэн ~) чётное число
  final ~ (фа́йнал ~) конечная цифра
  fixed ~ (фиксд ~) постоянное число
  flight ~ (флайт ~) номер рейса
  fractional ~ (фра́кшнал ~) дробное число
  inventory ~ (и́нвэнтори ~) инвентарный номер
  item ~ in a catalog (а́йтэм ~ ин а ка́талог) код товара в каталоге
  key ~ (ки ~) номер по телеграфному коду
  letter of credit ~ (ле́ттэр оф кре́дит ~) номер аккредитива
  lot ~ (лот ~) номер партии
  maximum ~ (ма́ксимум ~) максимальное число
  minimal ~ (ми́нимал ~) минимальное число

  odd ~ (од ~) нечётное число, нечет
  order ~ (о́рдэр ~) номер заказа
  ordinal ~ (о́рдинал ~) порядковый номер, порядковое число
  patent ~ (па́тэнт ~) номер патента
  record ~ (ре́корд ~) рекордное число
  reference ~ (ре́фэрэнс ~) номер для ссылок
  registration ~ (рэджистре́йшн ~) регистрационный номер
  sequence of ~s (си́куэнс оф ~с) последовательность номеров
  serial ~ (си́риал ~) заводской номер
  stock ~ (сток ~) номенклатурный номер
  telephone ~ (те́лэфон ~) номер телефона
  to ~ (ту ~) нумеровать
  to delete a ~ (ту дили́т а ~) вычеркнуть цифру
  total ~ (то́тал ~) общая численность
  voyage ~ (во́йадж ~) номер рейса
  ~ of cases (~ оф кэ́йсэз) число мест {freight}
  ~ of units/parcels (~ оф ю́нитс/па́рсэлс) количество мест груза
Numbering (ну́мбэринг) нумерация
  consecutive ~ (консе́кютив ~) последовательная нумерация
  comparable ~ (ко́мпарабл ~) сравнительные цифры
  round ~ (роунд ~) круглые цифры
  target ~ (та́ргэт ~) контрольные цифры
Numeral (нюмэрал) цифра
Numerical (нуме́рикал) цифровой
Numerous (ну́мэрос) многократный, многочисленный
Nuptial (ну́пшл) брачный

O

Oath (оθ) присяга
  judicial ~ (джюди́шл ~) судебная присяга
  to administer an ~ (ту адми́нистэр ан ~) привести к присяге

to take an ~ (ту тэйк ан ~)
принести присягу, присягать
under ~ (áндэр ~) под присягой
~ of loyalty (~ оф лóйялти)
присяга на верность
Object (óбджэкт) объект
Objection (обджэ́кшн) протест
~ by the prosecution (~ бай θи
просэкью́шн) протест прокурора
Objective (обджэ́ктив) объективный
Oblast (óбласт) область {Russian
geographical and admin. subdivi-
sion}
Obligation (облигэ́йшн) обязанность,
обязательство, повинность
bearer ~ (бэ́йрэр ~)
обязательство на предъявителя
charter ~s (чáртэр ~с) уставная
обязанность
contractual ~ (контрáкчуал ~)
договорное обязательство
direct ~ (дирэ́кт ~) прямое
обязательство
financial ~ (файнáншл ~)
финансовое обязательство
international ~s (интэрнáшэнал
~с) международные обязательства
international legal ~s
(интэрнáшэнал лúгал ~с)
международное правовое
обязательство
legal ~ (лúгал ~) правовое
обязательство, юридическая
обязанность
long-term ~ (лонг-тэ́рм ~)
долгосрочное обязательство
maintenance ~ (мэ́йнтэнанс ~)
алиментное обязательство,
алиментная обязанность {e.g.
alimony}
monetary ~ (мóнэтари ~) денежная
повинность
mortgage ~ (мóргэдж ~) ипотечное
обязательство
multilateral ~ (мултилáтэрал ~)
многостороннее обязательство
mutual ~s (мью́чуал ~с) взаимные
обязательства
pecuniary ~ (пэкью́ниари ~)
денежное обязательство
personal ~ (пэ́рсонал ~) личная
повинность
short-term ~ (шорт-тэ́рм ~)
краткосрочное обязательство
statutory ~ (стáтютори ~)
законное обязательство

supplementary ~ (сапплэмэ́нтари
~) придаточное обязательство
to release from an ~ (ту рилúс
фром ан ~) освободить от
обязательства
to undertake an ~ (ту андэртэ́йк
ан ~) принять обязанность на
себя
warranty ~ (уáрранти ~)
гарантийное обязательство
~ to compensate loss (~ ту
кóмпэнсэйт лос) обязательство
возмещения убытка
~ under warranty (~ áндэр
уáрранти) обязательство по
гарантии
Obligatory (облúгатори)
обязательный
Oblige, to ~ (облáйдж, ту ~)
обязывать
Observance (обсэ́рванс) соблюдение
to insist on the ~ of conditions
(ту инсúст он θи ~ оф кондúшнс)
настаивать на выполнении условий
~ of a right (~ оф а райт)
соблюдение права
~ of formalities (~ оф
формáлитиз) соблюдение
формальностей
Observation (обсэрвэ́йшн) замечание,
наблюдение
Obsolescence (обсолэ́сэнс)
устаревание
planned ~ (планд ~) моральный
износ
Obstacle (óбстакл) помеха,
препятствие
forbidding ~ (форбúддинг ~)
запретительное препятствие
Obstruction (обстрý́кшн) обструкция
~ in parliament (~ ин пáрламэнт)
обструкция в парламенте
Obtain, to ~ (обтэ́йн, ту ~)
приобретать
Obtained (обтэ́йнд) достигнутый
Obverse (óбвэрс) лицевой {of a
coin, etc.}
Occupation (оккюпэ́йшн) занятие,
оккупация {military}
paid ~ (пэйд ~) оплачиваемое
занятие
primary ~ (прáймари ~) главное
занятие
Occupy, to ~ (óккюпай, ту ~)
занимать [perfective: занять],
оккупировать {militarily}

Occur, to ~ (оккýр, ту ~)
происходить
Occurrence (оккýррэнс)
происхождение, явление
Oceanliner (óшнлáйнэр) лайнер
Odd (од) нечётный, странный
Off (офф) вне, дальный, незанятый
    to take ~ (ту тэйк ~) вылетать
    {by air}
Off-the-floor sale (офф-θи-флор
сэйл) продажа экспонатов со стенда
Offend, to ~ (оффэ́нд, ту ~)
оскорблять [perfective: оскорбить]
Offended (оффэ́ндэд) оскорблённый
Offender (оффэ́ндэр) нарушитель,
оскорбитель, правонарушитель
    juvenile ~ (джю́вэнайл ~)
    несовершеннолетний
    правонарушитель
    mentally incompetent ~ (мэ́нталли
    инкóмпэтэнт ~) невменяемый
    правонарушитель
Offense (оффэ́нс) оскорбление,
правонарушение, провинность
    civil ~ (си́вил ~) гражданское
    правонарушение
    continuing ~ (конти́нюинг ~)
    продолжаемое преступление
    criminal ~ (кри́минал ~)
    уголовное преступление
    electoral ~ (элэ́кторал ~)
    преступление против
    избирательной системы
    felony ~ (фэ́лони ~) преступление
    first ~ (фэрст ~) первое
    преступление
    material ~ (мати́риал ~)
    материальное преступление
    repeated ~ (рипи́тэд ~) повторное
    преступление
    serious ~ (си́риос ~) тяжкое
    оскорбление, тяжкое преступление
    sexual ~ (сэ́кшуал ~) половое
    преступление
    to commit an ~ (ту комми́т ан ~)
    совершить правонарушение
    ~ against minors (~ агэ́нст
    мáйнорс) правонарушение на
    несовершеннолетних
    ~ against public morals (~
    агэ́нст пáблик мóралс)
    преступление против общественной
    нравственности
    ~ characterized by the use of
    violence (~ кáрактэрайзд бай θи
    юс оф вáйолэнс) преступление

характеризующееся применением
насилия
    ~ committed in a state of
    intoxication (~ комми́ттэд ин а
    стэ́йт оф интоксикэ́йшн)
    преступление совершённое в
    состоянии опьянения
Offensive (оффэ́нсив) наступление,
противный {adj.}
    to go on the ~ (ту го он θи ~)
    перейти в наступление
Offer (óффэр) оферта, предложение
    aggregate ~ (áггрэгат ~)
    совокупное предложение
    conditional ~ (конди́шнал ~)
    условное предложение
    to ~ (ту ~) выдавать, предлагать

    to reject an ~ (ту риджэ́кт ан ~)
    отклонить предложение
    ~ of credit (~ оф крэ́дит)
    предложение кредита
    ~ of employment (~ оф
    эмплóймэнт) приглашение на
    работу
    ~ to contract (~ ту кóнтракт)
    предложение вступить в договор
Offeree (оффэри́) офертант
Offeror (оффэрóр) оферент
Office (óффис) канцелярия, контора,
конторский {adj.}, отделение
    administrative ~ (адми́нистрэйтив
    ~) административное учреждение
    audit ~ (áудит ~) ревизионная
    контора
    corporate registry ~ (кóрпорат
    рэ́джистри ~) бюро регистрации
    акционерных компаний
    customs ~ (кáстомз ~) таможенное
    ведомство
    design ~ (дизáйн ~) проектная
    контора
    exchange ~ (эксчэ́йндж ~)
    разменная контора
    executive ~ (экзэ́кютив ~)
    аппарат управления
    export ~ (э́кспорт ~) экспортная
    контора
    freight ~ (фрэ́йт ~) грузовая
    контора, фрахтовая контора
    governmental ~ (говэрнмэ́нтал ~)
    правительственные учреждения
    head ~ (хэд ~) главная контора
    import ~ (и́мпорт ~) импортная
    контора
    insurance ~ (иншю́ранс ~)
    страховая контора

notary ~ (нóтари ~) нотариальная контора
passport and visa ~ (пáсспорт энд вѝса ~) бюро по выдаче паспортов и виз
patent ~ (пáтэнт ~) патентное бюро
post ~ (пост ~) почтовое отделение
press-release ~ (прэс-рѝлис ~) бюро объявлений
prosecutor's ~ (прóсэкютэрз ~) прокурорский аппарат, прокурорский орган
registered ~ (рэ́джистэрд ~) зарегистрированная контора
registration ~ (рэджистрэ́йшн ~) регистрационное бюро
rental ~ (рэ́нтал ~) бюро проката
sales ~ (сэйлз ~) торговое отделение, учреждение по продаже
social insurance ~ (сошл иншю́ранс ~) страховая касса {in Russia}
technical inspection ~ (тэ́кникал инспэ́кшн ~) бюро технического надзора
ticket ~ (тѝкэт ~) билетная касса
to assume ~ (ту ассу́м ~) вступить в должность
to nominate to an ~ (ту нóминэйт ту ан ~) выдвигать на должность
to open an ~ (ту óпэн ан ~) открыть контору
trade fair ~ (трэйд фэйр ~) дирекция ярмарки
~ hours (~ оурз) часы работы учреждения
~ manager (~ мáнаджэр) директор конторы
Officer (óффисэр) офицер
police ~ (полѝс ~) офицер полиции
Official (оффѝшл) официальный {adj.}, служебный {adj.}, должностное лицо {person}
Officially (оффѝшлли) официально
Offloading (óффлодинг) выгрузка, разгрузка
to ~ (ту ~) разгружать
to arrange for ~ (ту аррэ́йндж фор ~) организовывать выгрузку
to delay ~ (ту дилэ́й ~) задерживать выгрузку
~ standards (~ стáндардз) нормы выгрузки

Offset (óффсэт) зачёт
as an ~ against (аз ан ~ агэ́нст) в виде вознаграждения
contractual ~ (контрáкчуал ~) договорный зачёт
judicial ~ (джюдѝшл ~) судебный зачёт
Often (óфтэн) неоднократно
Oil (ойл) нефть
bunker ~ (бу́нкэр ~) бункерное топливо
to lay an ~ pipeline (ту лэй ан ~ пáйплайн) прокладывать нефтепровод
~ cargo (~ кáрго) нефтегруз
~ carrier (~ кáрриэр) нефтевоз
~ pipeline (~ пáйплайн) нефтепровод
~ reservoir (~ рэ́зэрвуар) нефтехранилище
Okrug (óкруг) округ {territorial division of the Russian Federation}
Oligarchy (óлигарки) олигархия
Omen (óмэн) примета
bad ~ (бад ~) дурная примета
good ~ (гуд ~) хорошая примета
On-call (он-кал) онкольный
Onset (óнсэт) наступление
Onstream (онстрѝм) в строй
to go ~ (ту го ~) вступать в строй
Open (óпэн) открытый, явный
to ~ (ту ~) вскрывать
"~ for signing" (~ фор сáйнинг) «открыто для подписания» {of a convention, etc.}
Opening (óпэнинг) открытие
~ of an account (~ оф ан аккóунт) открытие счёта
~ of a conference (~ оф а кóнфэрэнс) открытие конференции
~ of a letter of credit (~ оф а лэ́ттэр оф крэ́дит) открытие аккредитива
~ of a line of credit (~ оф а лайн оф крэ́дит) открытие кредита
~ of a market (~ оф а мáркэт) открытие рынка
~ of a store (~ оф а стор) открытие магазина
Openly (óпэнли) открыто, публично
Operate, to ~ (óпэрэйт, ту ~) работать, эксплуатировать
Operating (óпэрэйтинг) действующий
under ~ conditions (áндэр ~ кондѝшнс) в условиях эксплуатации

~ **conditions** (~ конди́шнс) условия эксплуатации
~ **manual** (~ ма́нюал) руководство по эксплуатации
~ **period** (~ пи́риод) время эксплуатации
~ **process** (~ про́сэс) процесс эксплуатации
~ **right** (~ райт) право на эксплуатацию
~ **techniques** (~ тэхни́кс) техника эксплуатации
Operation (опэрэ́йшн) операция, работа, эксплуатация
commercial ~ (комме́ршл ~) коммерческая операция, промышленная эксплуатация
company ~ (ко́мпани ~) деятельность компании
designed for ~ (диза́йнд фор ~) предназначенный для эксплуатации
export/import ~ (э́кспорт/и́мпорт ~) экспортно-импортная операция
forward ~ (фо́руард ~) операция на срок
guaranteed ~ (гяранти́д ~) гарантийная эксплуатация
hedging ~ (хэ́джинг ~) операция хеджирования
insurance ~ (иншю́ранс ~) страховая операция
international ~ (интэрна́шэнал ~) эксплуатация международной линии
lending ~ (лэ́ндинг ~) кредитная операция
licensee's ~s (лайсэнси́с ~с) деятельность лицензиата
licensor's ~s (лайсэнсо́рс ~с) деятельность лицензиара
loan ~ (лон ~) ссудная операция
method of ~ (мэ́θод оф ~) метод эксплуатации
military ~s (ми́литари ~с) военные операции
normal ~ (но́рмал ~) нормальная эксплуатация
period of ~ (пи́риод оф ~) период эксплуатации
purchasing ~ (пу́рчасинг ~) операция по закупке
putting into ~ (пу́ттинг и́нту ~) ввод в эксплуатацию
reliable ~ (рила́йабл ~) надёжный в эксплуатации
retirement from ~ (рита́йрмэнт фром ~) вывод из эксплуатации

routine ~ (рути́н ~) обычная работа
salvage ~s (са́лвэдж ~с) спасательные работы
to bring into ~ (ту бринг и́нту ~) вводить в эксплуатацию
to come into ~ (ту ком и́нту ~) вступать в строй
to go into ~ (ту го и́нту ~) вступать в эксплуатацию
to put into ~ (ту пут и́нту ~) сдать в эксплуатацию
trade ~ (трэйд ~) торговая операция
trouble-free ~ (трабл-фри ~) бесперебойная эксплуатация
turn-key ~ (турн-ки ~) операция «под ключ»
unfit for further ~ (анфи́т фор фу́рθэр ~) непригодный к дальнейшей эксплуатации
unreliable ~ (анрила́йабл ~) ненадёжный в эксплуатации
~ **report** (~ рипо́рт) отчёт об эксплуатации
Operative (о́пэратив) делец
Operator (о́пэрэйтор) делец, механик
exchange ~ (эксчэ́йндж ~) биржевой делец
groupage ~ (гру́падж ~) экспедитор по сборным отправкам
Opinion (опи́нион) мнение, суждение {legal}
Opponent (оппо́нэнт) оппонент, противник
~ **in a dispute** (~ ин а диспю́т) противник в споре
Opportunism (оппорту́низм) оппортунизм
Opportunist (оппорту́нист) оппортунист
Opportunistic (оппортуни́стик) оппортунистический
Opportunity (оппорту́нити) благоприятный случай, возможность, случай
Oppose, to ~ (оппо́з, ту ~) сопротивляться
Opposition (оппози́шн) оппозиция {political}, оппозиционный {adj.}, противодействие
Oppress, to ~ (оппрэ́с, ту ~) притеснять
Opt, to ~ **for** (опт, ту ~ фор) оптировать
Option (опшн) выбор, опцион, оптация {e.g. of dual citizenship}

at the ~ of ... (ат θи ~ оф ...)
по выбору
available at ~ (ава́йлабл ат ~)
поставляемый по выбору заказчика
option, right of ~ право выбора
future ~ (фю́чэр ~) будущий выбор
seller's ~ (сэ́ллэрз ~) выбор
продавца
to have an ~ (ту хэв ан ~) иметь
право выбора
to have an ~ on goods (ту хэв ан
~ он гудз) иметь право выбора
товара
to provide ~s (ту прова́йд ~с)
предоставлять право выбора
Oral (о́рал) словесный
Orator (о́рэйтор) оратор
Order (о́рдэр) заказ, истребование,
наряд, орден {award, group}, ордер,
поручение, порядок, предписание,
приказ, распорядок, регламент,
спокойствие, строй
additional ~s (адди́шнал ~с)
дополнительный регламент
agrarian ~ (агра́риан ~) аграрный
строй
alphabetical ~ (алфабэ́тикал ~)
алфавитный порядок
by ~ of ... (бай ~ оф ...) по
указанию
cancellation of an ~
(кансэллэ́йшн оф ан ~)
аннулирование заказа
cash ~ (каш ~) кассовый ордер
consular ~s (ко́нсюлар ~с)
консульский регламент
court ~ (ко́урт ~) предписание
суда
direct ~ (дирэ́кт ~) прямое
предписание
economic ~ (эконо́мик ~)
экономический порядок,
экономический строй
executive ~ (экзэ́кютив ~)
исполнительный акт,
исполнительный приказ,
исполнительный регламент
heavy ~ (хэ́ви ~) большой заказ
in good ~ and proper form (ин
гуд ~ анд про́пэр форм) в полном
порядке и должной форме
law and ~ (ла́у энд ~)
правопорядок
legal ~ (ли́гал ~) правовой
порядок, юридический порядок
legislative ~ (лэ́джислэйтив ~)
законодательный порядок

money ~ (мо́ни ~) денежное
поручение
new international economic ~
(нью интэрна́шэнал эконо́мик ~)
новый международный
экономический порядок
on his ~ (он хиз ~) по его
приказу
out of ~ (о́ут оф ~) неисправный,
в неисправности
payment ~ (пэ́ймэнт ~) обменный
ордер, платёжное поручение
postal ~ (по́стал ~) почтовое
поручение
postal money ~ (по́стал мо́ни ~)
денежный почтовый перевод
public ~ (па́блик ~) общественное
спокойствие, публичный порядок
religious ~ (рили́джос ~)
религиозный орден
repeat ~ (ри́пит ~) повторный
заказ
reverse ~ (ривэ́рс ~) обратный
порядок
social ~ (сошл ~) строй,
общественный порядок
standing ~s (ста́ндинг ~с)
регламент
standing ~ to the bank (ста́ндинг
~ ту θи банк) постоянное
распоряжение банку
state ~ (стэйт ~) госзаказ,
государственный заказ
strict ~ (стрикт ~) строгий
порядок
to ~ (ту ~) заказывать
[perfective: заказать],
предписывать, приказывать,
распоряжаться
to fill an ~ (ту фил ан ~)
выполнить заказ
to issue an ~ to confiscate (ту
и́шю ан ~ ту ко́нфискэйт) издать
приказ о конфискации
to call to ~ (ту кал ту ~)
призвать к порядку
transfer ~ (тра́нсфэр ~)
переводное поручение
trial ~ (тра́йал ~) пробный заказ
violating public ~ (ва́йолэйтинг
па́блик ~) противоречащий
публичному порядку
warehouseman's ~ (уэ́рхаусманз ~)
разрешение таможни на выдаче
груза со склада
work ~ (уо́рк ~) наряд на работу

working ~ (уо́ркинг ~) судоходное состояние
written ~ (ри́ттэн ~) письменный приказ
~ of appeal (~ оф аппи́л) порядок обжалования
~ of distribution (~ оф дистрибью́шн) порядок распределения
~ of Jesus {Jesuits} (~ оф джи́сус {джэ́зуитс}) иезуитский орден
~ of Lenin (~ оф лэ́нин) орден Ленина {Soviet award}
~ of Malta (~ оф ма́лта) мальтийский орден
~ of payment (~ оф пэ́ймэнт) порядок уплаты
~ of preference (~ оф прэ́фэрэнс) порядок предпочтения
~ of priority (~ оф прайо́рити) порядок приоритета
~ of seniority (~ оф синёрити) порядок старшинства
~ of the court (~ оф θи ко́урт) приказ суда
~ of the day (~ оф θи дэй) распорядок дня, приказ по войскам {military}
Orderly (о́рдэрли) ординарец {person}, закономерный {adj.}
Ordnance (о́рднанс) орудие
Organ (о́рган) орган {of government, etc.}
autonomous ~ (аутоно́мос ~) автономный орган
executive ~ (экзэ́кютив ~) исполнительный аппарат
purchasing ~ (пу́рчасинг ~) закупочный орган
Organism (о́рганизм) организм
Organization (организэ́йшн) организация
administrative ~ (адми́нистрэйтив ~) административная организация
arbitral ~ (а́рбитрал ~) арбитражная организация
autonomous ~ (аутоно́мос ~) автономная организация
charitable ~ (ча́ритабл ~) благотворительное общество
consumer ~ (консу́мэр ~) потребительское общество
cooperative ~ (коо́пэратив ~) кооперативная организация
criminal ~ (кри́минал ~) преступная организация

economic ~ (эконо́мик ~) хозяйственная организация, экономическая организация
financial ~ (файна́ншл ~) финансовая организация
Food and Agricultural ~ of the United Nations {FAO} (фуд энд агрику́лчурал ~ оф θи юна́йтэд нэйшнз {эф-эй-о}) продовольственная и сельскохозяйственная организация объединенных наций {ФАО}
foreign trade ~ (фо́рэн трэйд ~) внешнеторговая организация
industrial ~ (инду́стриал ~) промышленная организация
inspection ~ (инспэ́кшн ~) инспекционная организация
International Civil Aviation ~ (интэрна́шэнал си́вил эйви́эйшн ~) организация международной гражданской авиации
judicial ~ (джюди́шл ~) судебная организация
labor ~ (лэ́йбор ~) профсоюзная организация
legal ~ (ли́гал ~) правовая организация
mass ~ (мас ~) массовая организация
North Atlantic Treaty ~ {NATO} (норθ атла́нтик три́ти ~ {нэ́йто}) организация северо-атлантического договора
nonprofit ~ (нонпро́фит ~) некоммерческая организация
official ~ (оффи́шл ~) официальная организация
party ~ (па́рти ~) партийная организация
permanent ~ (пэ́рманэнт ~) постоянная организация
professional ~ (профэ́шнал ~) профессиональная организация
regional ~ (ри́джонал ~) региональная организация
Southeast Asian Treaty ~ {SEATO} (со́уθист э́йжан три́ти ~ {си́то}) организация договора юго-восточной Азии {СЕАТО}
self-financing ~ (сэлф-фа́йнансинг ~) хозрасчётная организация
subversive ~ (субвэ́рсив ~) подрывная организация
trade ~ (трэйд ~) торговая организация

United Nations ~ {UN} (юнáйтэд нэйшнз ~ {ю-эн}) организация объединённых наций {ООН}
voluntary ~ (вóлунтэри ~) добровольное общество
World Health ~ {WHO} (уóрлд хэл θ ~ {дáблю-эч-о}) всемирная организация Здравоохранения
~ of African Unity {OAU} (~ оф áфрикан юнити {о-эй-ю}) организация Африканского Единства
~ of American States {OAS} (~ оф амэрикан стэйтс {о-эй-эс}) организация Американских Государств {ОАГ}
~ of Economic Cooperation and Development {OECD} (~ оф экономик коопэрэйшн анд дивэлопмэнт {о-и-си-ди}) организация экономического сотрудничества и развития

Organize, to ~ (óрганайз, ту ~) налаживать
Organizer (óрганайзэр) устроитель
Organ (óрган) орган
bureaucratic ~s (бюрокрáтик ~с) аппарат
Orient (óриэнт) восток
to ~ (ту ~) ориентировать
Orientation (ориэнтэйшн) ориентация
Origin (óриджин) происхождение, род

airport of ~ (эйрпорт оф ~) аэродром отправления
certificate of ~ (сэртификэт оф ~) свидетельство о происхождении

place of ~ (плэйс оф ~) место происхождения
~ of a product (~ оф а прóдукт) происхождение изделия
Original (ориджинал) оригинал, оригинальный {adj.}, подлинник {of a document}
~ copy of a decision (~ кóпи оф а дисижн) подлинник решения
~ deed (~ дид) первоначальная запись
Originate, to ~ (óриджинэйт, ту ~) создавать
Orphan (óрфан) сирота
Orphanhood (óрфанхуд) сиротство
Out-of-season (óут-оф-сизон) несезонный
Outcome (óутком) последствие, результат

legal ~ (лигал ~) законное последствие
Outfit (óутфит) снаряжение
Outfitting (óутфиттинг) оснащение
Outlay (óутлэй) затрата, расход **~s** издержки
additional ~ (аддишнал ~) дополнительные издержки
net ~ (нэт ~) чистые издержки
production ~ (продáкшн ~) издержки производства
total ~ (тóтал ~) общие расходы
Outlet (óутлэт) отделение
Communist Party propaganda ~ (кóммюнист пáрти пропагáнда ~) агитпункт
sales ~s (сэйлз ~с) торговая сеть
Outlook (óутлук) перспектива
economic ~ (экономик ~) будущая экономическая конъюнктура
economic development ~ (экономик дивэлопмэнт ~) перспектива развития экономики
market ~ (мáркэт ~) перспектива рынка
Outnumber, to ~ (оутнýмбэр, ту ~) превосходить числом
Outpace, to ~ (óутпэйс, ту ~) обгонять
Outpost (óутпост) аванпост **~s** сторожевое охранение
Output (óутпут) выпуск, мощность, продукция
agricultural ~ (агрикýлчурал ~) сельскохозяйственная продукция
annual ~ (áннюал ~) годовая мощность
daily ~ (дэйли ~) суточный выпуск
decline in ~ (диклáйн ин ~) снижение мощностей
export ~ (экспорт ~) экспортная продукция
gross ~ (грос ~) валовая продукция
industrial ~ (индýстриал ~) промышленная продукция
net ~ (нэт ~) чистая продукция
nominal ~ (нóминал ~) номинальная мощность
recorded ~ (рэкóрдэд ~) учитываемый выпуск продукции
to decrease ~ (ту дикрис ~) сокращать выпуск

to guarantee the ~ (ту гяранти́ θи ~) гарантировать выпуск продукции
to increase ~ (ту инкри́с ~) увеличивать выпуск
to limit ~ (ту ли́мит ~) ограничивать выпуск продукции
~ of by-products (~ оф бай-про́дуктс) выпуск побочной продукции
~ of commodities (~ оф коммо́дитиз) товарная продукция
~ of production exceeding the target (~ оф прода́кшн экси́динг θи та́ргэт) сверхплановой выпуск продукции
~ program (~ про́грам) план выпуска продукции
"Outsider" (оутса́йдэр) аутсайдер {on Board of Directors, etc.}
Outstanding (оутста́ндинг) невзысканный, невыполненный, нереализованный {unsold}, неуплаченный
~ interest (~ и́нтэрэст) процент к уплате
Over (о́вэр) над, слишком
~ height cargo (~ хайт ка́рго) негабарит по высоте
~ width cargo (~ уид θ ка́рго) негабарит по ширине
Overall (овэра́л) общий
Overboard (о́вэрборд) за бортом
to jettison ~ (ту джэ́ттисон ~) выбрасывать за борт
Overcharge (овэрча́рдж) завышенная цена
to ~ (ту ~) завышать цену, назначать завышенную цену
Overcome, to ~ (о́вэрком, ту ~) обгонять
Overdraft (о́вэрдрафт) овердрафт
account ~ (акко́унт ~) задолженность банку
credit ~ (крэ́дит ~) превышение кредитного лимита
~ of bank credit (~ оф банк крэ́дит) превышение банковского кредита
Overdraw, to ~ an account (овэрдра́у, ту ~ ан акко́унт) выписывать чек сверх остатка на текущем счету, допускать овердрафт
Overestimate, to ~ (овэрэ́стимэйт, ту ~) переоценивать

Overfulfill, to ~ (овэрфулфи́л, ту ~) перевыполнять [perfective: перевыполнить]
Overfulfillment (овэрфулфи́лмэнт) перевыполнение
Overhaul (о́вэрхаул) восстановительный ремонт
complete ~ (компли́т ~) коренное обновление
Overhead (о́вэрхэд) накладные расходы
allocation of ~ (алокэ́йшн оф ~) распределение накладных расходов
plant ~ (плант ~) общезаводские накладные расходы
production ~ (прода́кшн ~) производственные накладные расходы
~ expenses (~ экспэ́нсэз) накладные {расходы}
Overheating (овэрхи́тинг) перенапряжение
~ of the market (~ оф θи ма́ркэт) перенапряжение конъюнктуры
Overinvoicing (овэри́нвойсинг) по завышенным ценам
Overload, to ~ (о́вэрлод, ту ~) нагружать чрезмерно, перегружать
Overloading (овэрло́динг) перегрузка
Overpay, to ~ (овэрпэ́й, ту ~) переплатить
Overpopulation (овэрпопюлэ́йшн) перенаселение
agrarian ~ (агра́риан ~) аграрное перенаселение
Overproduction (овэрпроду́кшн) перепроизводство
~ of commodities (~ оф коммо́дитиз) перепроизводство товара
Overrun (о́вэррун) перерасход
budget ~ (ба́джэт ~) перевыполнение бюджета
cost ~ (кост ~) перерасход
term ~ (тэрм ~) просрочка
Overside (о́вэрсайд) бортовой, через борт
Oversight (о́вэрсайт) надзор
administrative ~ (адми́нистрэйтив ~) административный надзор
Oversize (о́вэрсайз) негабаритный
~ cargo (~ ка́рго) негабарит
Oversized (о́вэрсайзд) крупногабаритный
Overstock (овэрсто́к) затоваривание
Overt (овэ́рт) явный
Overthrow (овэр θ ро́) свержение

to ~ (ту ~) свергнуть
~ of the government (~ оф θи
гóвэрнмэнт) свержение
правительства
~ of the regime (~ оф θи рэжи́м)
свержение режима
Overtime (óвэртайм) сверхурочный
~ payments (~ пэ́ймэнтс) доплата
за сверхурочную работу
~ rate (~ рэйт) размер выплаты
за сверхурочную работу
~ work (~ уóрк) переработка
Overturn, to ~ (овэрту́рн, ту ~)
отвергать
~ of a sentence (~ оф а сэ́нтэнс)
отмена приговора
Overvaluation (овэрвалюэ́йшн)
завышенная оценка, переоценка
Overvalue, to ~ (овэрва́лю, ту ~)
переоценивать
Overweight (óвэруэйт) перевес
Owing (óуинг) задолженный
to be ~ (ту би ~) причитаться
Own (óун) собственный
to ~ (ту ~) владеть
Owner (óунэр) владелец,
собственник, хозяин {male}, хозяйка
{female}
at ~'s risk (ат ~с риск) на риск
владельца
cargo ~ (ка́рго ~) владелец груза
co-~ (ко-~) совместный владелец
commodity ~ (коммóдити ~)
владелец товара
copyright ~ (кóпирайт ~)
владелец авторского права
exhibition ~ (экзиби́шн ~)
владелец стенда
factory ~ (фа́ктори ~) владелец
завода
patent ~'s charge (па́тэнт ~с
чардж) поручение владельца
патента
private ~ (пра́йват ~) частный
владелец
property ~ (прóпэрти ~) владелец
собственности
ship ~ (шип ~) владелец судна,
судовладельческая фирма
tug ~ (туг ~) владелец судна,
буксирного
~ of know-how (~ оф нóу-ха́у)
владелец ноу-хау
~ of real estate (~ оф рил
эстэ́йт) владелец недвижимости
~'s right (~с райт) право
владельца

Ownership (óунэршип) собственность
commercial ~ (коммэ́ршл ~)
коммерческая собственность
common ~ (кóммон ~) общественная
собственность
communal ~ of chattels (коммю́нал
~ оф ша́ттэлз) общность движимых
имуществ
communal ~ of property (коммю́нал
~ оф прóпэрти) общность
имущества
community of ~ (каммю́нити оф ~)
общность владения
exclusive ~ (эксклю́сив ~)
исключительная собственность
individual ~ (индиви́дюал ~)
индивидуальная собственность
joint ~ (джойнт ~) совместная
собственность
legal title of ~ (ли́гал тайтл оф
~) право на имущество
mutual ~ (мю́чуал ~) нейтральная
собственность
state ~ (стэйт ~)
государственная собственность
~ right (~ райт) право владения

P

Pace (пэйс) темп, шаг
at a rapid ~ (ат а ра́пид ~) в
ускоренном темпе
to pick up the ~ (ту пик ап θи
~) ускорять темп
to slow the ~ (ту слоу θи ~)
замедлять темп
~ of development (~ оф
дивэ́лопмэнт) темп развития
~ of growth (~ оф грoθ) темп
роста
~ of work (~ оф уóрк) темп
работы
Pacification (пасификэ́йшн)
усмирение
Pacifism (па́сифизм) пацифизм
Pack, to ~ (пак, ту ~) осуществлять
упаковку, упаковывать
to ~ in the proper manner (ту ~
ин θи прóпэр ма́ннэр) упаковывать
должным образом
to ~ securely (ту ~ сэкю́рли)
упаковывать прочно
to hand ~ (ту ханд ~)
упаковывать вручную

to machine ~ (ту маши́н ~) упаковывать машинным способом
unit ~ (ю́нит ~) индивидуальная тара

ackage (па́кэдж) комплекс, место, акет, пачка
contents of a ~ (ко́нтэнтс оф а ~) содержание места
equipment ~ (икуи́пмэнт ~) комплекс оборудования
insert in a ~ (и́нсэрт ин а ~) вкладыш в упаковку
know-how ~ (но́у-ха́у ~) комплекс ноу-хау
licensing ~ (ла́йсэнсинг ~) пакет услуг, предоставляемых по лицензии
lost ~ (лост ~) потерянное место
number of ~s (ну́мбэр оф ~с) количество мест, число мест груза
oversized ~ (о́вэрсайзд ~) место большого размера
single ~ (сингл ~) отдельное место
unwieldy ~ (ануи́лди ~) громоздкая посылка
~ dimensions (~ диме́ншнз) размеры места, размеры упаковки
~ number (~ ну́мбэр) номер места
~ of services (~ оф сэ́рвисэз) комплекс услуг
~ unit weight (~ ю́нит уэйт) вес грузового места

ackaged (па́кэджд) в упаковке
in final ~ form (ин фа́йнал ~ форм) в окончательной упаковке

ackaging (па́каджинг) упаковка
airfreight ~ (э́йрфрэйт ~) упаковка, предназначенная для воздушной транспортировки
airtight ~ (э́йртайт ~) воздухонепроницаемая упаковка
appropriate ~ (аппро́приат ~) соответствующая упаковка
bad ~ (бад ~) плохая упаковка
damaged ~ (да́маджд ~) повреждённая упаковка
effective ~ (иффэ́ктив ~) эффективная упаковка
export ~ (э́кспорт ~) экспортная упаковка
external ~ (экстэ́рнал ~) наружная упаковка
factory ~ (фа́ктори ~) заводская упаковка, фабричная упаковка

feasible ~ (фи́зибл ~) целесообразная упаковка
frame ~ (фрэйм ~) упаковка в обрешётке
in the process of ~ (ин θи про́сэс оф ~) в процессе упаковки
inappropriate ~ (инаппро́приат ~) несоответствующая упаковка
intact ~ (инта́кт ~) целая упаковка
ordinary ~ (о́рдинари ~) обыкновенная упаковка
price includes ~ (прайс инклю́дс ~) цена, включая упаковку
proper ~ (про́пэр ~) надлежащая упаковка
protective ~ (протэ́ктив ~) защитная упаковка
returnable ~ (риту́рнабл ~) многоразовая упаковка
satisfactory ~ (сатисфа́ктори ~) удовлетворительная упаковка
seaworthy ~ (си́уорθи ~) упаковка, пригодная для морской перевозки
special ~ (спэшл ~) специальная упаковка
standard ~ (ста́ндард ~) стандартная упаковка
strength of ~ (стрэнгθ оф ~) прочность упаковки
sturdy ~ (сту́рди ~) жёсткая упаковка
supplier's ~ (сапла́йэрз ~) упаковка поставщика
timely ~ (та́ймли ~) своевременная упаковка
to commence ~ (ту коммэ́нс ~) начинать упаковку
to examine ~ (ту экза́мин ~) проверять упаковку
to secure the necessary ~ (ту сэкю́р θи нэ́сэсари ~) обеспечивать должную упаковку
total ~ (то́тал ~) общая упаковка
uncrated ~ (анкрэ́йтэд ~) упаковка без ящиков
undamaged ~ (анда́маджд ~) упаковка без повреждений
waterproof ~ (уа́тэрпруф ~) водонепроницаемая упаковка
~ department (~ дипа́ртмэнт) отдел фасовки и упаковки
~ for tropical conditions (~ фор тро́пикал конди́шнс) тропическая упаковка

~ **in cartons** (~ ин ка́ртонс)
упаковка в коробки
~ **method** (~ мэ́θод) способ
упаковки
~ **recommendations** (~
рэкоммэндэ́йшнс) рекомендации по
упаковке
~ **requirements** (~ рикуа́йрмэнтс)
требования к упаковке
~ **technique** (~ тэкни́к) метод
упаковки
~ **with instructions included** (~
уиθ инстра́кшнс инклю́дэд)
упаковка с инструкциями
~ **with rope handles** (~ уиθ роп
хандлз) упаковка с верёвочными
ручками
Packed (пакд) упакованный
vacuum ~ (ва́кюм ~) вакуумная
упаковка
~ **measurements** (~ мэ́жюрмэнтс)
размеры в упаковке
Packet (па́кэт) пакет
Packing (па́ккинг) затаривание
груза, прокладка, упаковочный
{*adj.*}
adequacy of ~ (а́дэкуэси оф ~)
правильность упаковки
adequate ~ (а́дэкуэт ~)
достаточная упаковка
canvas ~ (ка́нвас ~) парусиновая
упаковка
container ~ (контэ́йнэр ~)
контейнерная упаковка
cost of ~ (кост оф ~) стоимость
упаковки
defective ~ (дифэ́ктив ~)
дефектная упаковка
during ~ (ду́ринг ~) во время
упаковки
export ~ **charge** (э́кспорт ~
чардж) плата за экспортную
упаковку
export ~ **services** (э́кспорт ~
сэ́рвисэз) услуги по упаковке
товара на экспорт
freight ~ (фрэйт ~) транспортная
упаковка
good quality ~ (гуд куа́лити ~)
доброкачественная упаковка
hermetically sealed ~
(хэрмэ́тикалли силд ~)
герметичная упаковка
import ~ (и́мпорт ~) импортная
упаковка
insufficient ~ (инсуффи́шэнт ~)
недостаточная упаковка

kind of ~ (кайнд оф ~) вид
упаковки
maritime ~ (ма́ритайм ~) морская
упаковка
negligent ~ (нэ́глиджэнт ~)
небрежная упаковка
new type of ~ (нью тайп оф ~)
новый вид упаковки
non-standard ~ (нон-ста́ндард ~)
нестандартная упаковка
nonreturnable ~ (нонриту́рнабл ~
безвозвратная упаковка
oversized ~ (о́вэрсайзд ~)
громоздкая упаковка,
негабаритная упаковка
poor quality ~ (пур куа́лити ~)
недоброкачественная упаковка
removal of ~ (риму́вал оф ~)
вывоз упаковки
sample ~ (сампл ~) образец
упаковки
soft ~ (софт ~) мягкая упаковка
standard export ~ (ста́ндард
э́кспорт ~) обычная экспортная
упаковка
strong ~ (стронг ~) прочная
упаковка
suitable ~ (су́табл ~) годная
упаковка, подходящая упаковка
tight ~ (тайт ~) плотная
упаковка
to complete ~ (ту компли́т ~)
завершать упаковка
to determine the sufficiency of
~ (ту дитэ́рмин θи суффи́шэнси оф
~) определять достаточность
упаковки
to handle ~ (ту хандл ~)
производить упаковку
to include ~ (ту инклю́д ~)
включать упаковку
to pay for ~ (ту пэй фор ~)
платить за упаковку
to proceed with ~ (ту проси́д уи
~) приступать к упаковке
to secure timely ~ (ту сэкю́р
та́ймли ~) обеспечивать
своевременную упаковку
to send in ~ (ту сэнд ин ~)
посылать в упаковке
to ship ~ **goods** (ту шип ~ гудз)
отгружать товар в упаковке
torn ~ (торн ~) разорванная
упаковка
undamaged ~ (анда́маджд ~)
неповреждённая упаковка

unfit ~ (анфи́т ~) непригодная упаковка
unnecessary ~ (анне́сэсари ~) ненужная упаковка
unsatisfactory ~ (ансатисфа́ктори ~) неудовлетворительная упаковка
unsuitable ~ (ансу́табл ~) неподходящая упаковка
wooden ~ (уу́дэн ~) деревянная упаковка
wrapping (ра́ппинг) обёрточный
~ contract (~ ко́нтракт) контракт на упаковку товара
~ equipment (~ икуи́пмэнт) оборудование для упаковки
~ expenses (~ экспэ́нсэз) расходы по упаковке
~ extra (~ э́кстра) упаковка за счёт покупателя
~ extra at cost (~ э́кстра ат кост) упаковка по себестоимости за счёт покупателя
~ facilities (~ фаси́литиз) средства упаковки
~ in bags (~ ин багз) упаковка в мешки
~ instructions (~ инстра́кшнс) правила упаковки
~ not included (~ нот инклю́дэд) цена без упаковки {in cost}
~ per contract (~ пэр ко́нтракт) упаковка по контракту
~ services (~ сэ́рвисэз) услуги по упаковке
~ standards (~ ста́ндардз) стандарты упаковки
~ suitable for ... (~ су́табл фор ...) упаковка, пригодная для
~ tape (~ тэйп) лента, используемая при упаковке
"~ wet" (~ уэт) "подмоченная упаковка" {marking on cargo}
~ will be charged extra (~ уил би чарджд э́кстра) за упаковку будет начислена отдельная плата
Pact (пакт) пакт
aggressive ~ (аггрэ́сив ~) агрессивный пакт
Balkan ~ (ба́лкан ~) балканский пакт
federal ~ (фэ́дэрал ~) федеральный пакт
international ~ (интэрна́шэнал ~) международный пакт
military ~ (ми́литари ~) военный пакт

mutual aid ~ (мю́чуал эйд ~) пакт о взаимной помощи
mutual assistance ~ (мю́чуал асси́станс ~) договор о взаимопомощи
mutual defense ~ (мю́чуал дифэ́нс ~) пакт о совместной обороне
neutrality ~ (нутра́лити ~) пакт о нейтралитете
North Atlantic ~ (нор θ атла́нтик ~) северо-атлантический пакт
organizational ~ (организэ́йшнал ~) организационный пакт
Peace ~ (пис ~) пакт мира
Quadrilateral ~ (куадрила́тэрал ~) четырёхсторонний пакт
Rhine ~ (рэйн ~) рейнский пакт
security ~ (сэкю́рити ~) пакт о безопасности
Trilateral ~ (трайла́тэрал ~) трёхсторонний пакт
~ of League of Nations (~ оф лиг оф нэ́йшнз) пакт лиги наций
Page (пэйдж) лист, страница
supplementary ~ (сапплэмэ́нтари ~) вкладной лист
title ~ (тайтл ~) заглавный лист, титульный лист
Paid (пэйд) оплаченный
Paint (пэйнт) краска
indelible ~ (индэ́либл ~) несмываемая краска
quick-drying ~ (куик-дра́йинг ~) быстровысыхающая краска
rust-proof ~ (руст-пруф ~) антикоррозионная краска
waterproof ~ (уа́тэрпруф ~) водостойкая краска
Pale (пэйл) бледный
~ of Settlement (~ оф сэ́тлмэнт) черта оседлости {historical}
Pallet (па́ллэт) лоток, ящик-лоток
Palletization (паллэтизэ́йшн) укладка на паллеты
of cargo (оф ка́рго) укладка груза на паллеты
Pamphlet (па́мфлэт) буклет
illustrated ~ (и́ллустрэйтэд ~) иллюстрированный буклет
Panamerican (панамэ́рикан) панамериканский
Panamericanism (панамэ́риканизм) панамериканизм
Panderer (па́ндэрэр) альфонс, сводник
Pandering (па́ндэринг) сводничество
Panel (па́нэл) коллегия

arbitration ~ (арбитрэ́йшн ~)
арбитражная комиссия
Panhandle, to ~ (па́нхандл, ту ~)
попрошайничать
Panhandling (па́нхандлинг)
попрошайничество
Paper (пэ́йпэр) бумага, вексель,
документ, лист, тратта
   acceptance of commercial ~
   (аксэ́птанс оф комме́ршл ~) акцепт
   коммерческих документов
   commercial ~ (комме́ршл ~)
   торговая тратта
   commodity ~ (коммо́дити ~)
   подтоварный вексель
   fine bank ~ (файн банк ~)
   первоклассный банковский вексель
   first class ~ (фэрст класс ~)
   первоклассный вексель
   piece of ~ (пис оф ~) лист
   purchased ~ (пу́рчасд ~)
   купленный вексель
   ship's ~**s** (шипс ~с) судовые
   документы
   stamped ~ (стампд ~) гербовая
   бумага
   three month's ~ (θри монθс ~)
   трёхмесячный вексель
   trade ~ (трэйд ~) торговый
   вексель
   two name ~ (ту нэйм ~) вексель с
   двумя подписями
   watermark ~ (уа́тэрмарк ~)
   гербовая бумага
   waterproof ~ (уа́тэрпруф ~)
   водонепроницаемая бумага
   ~ **currency** (~ ку́ррэнси) бумажный
   денежный знак
Paperclip (пэ́йпэрклип) скрепка
Par (пар) номинал
   above ~ (або́в ~) выше номинала
   at ~ (ат ~) альпари, по
   номиналу, по номинальному курсу,
   по паритету, по нарицательной
   цене
   below ~ (било́у ~) ниже номинала
   no ~ **value** (но ~ ва́лю) без
   нарицательной цены
   to buy at below ~ (ту бай ат
   било́у ~) покупать по цене ниже
   нарицательной
   to sell above ~ (ту сэл або́в ~)
   продавать по цене выше номинала
   to sell below ~ (ту сэл било́у ~)
   продавать ниже номинальной цены
   to sell over ~ (ту сэл о́вэр ~)
   продавать выше номинальной цены

Paragraph (па́раграф) абзац,
параграф, статья
Parameter (пара́мэтэр) показатель
   cost ~ (кост ~) стоимостный
   показатель
   overall cost ~ (овэра́л кост ~)
   общий стоимостный показатель
   ~ **of cost** (~ оф кост) показатель
   стоимости
Paramilitary (парами́литари)
полувоенный
Parcel (па́рсэл) единица груза,
пакет, пачка, посылка
   airmail ~ (э́йрмэйл ~)
   авиапочтовая посылка
   contents of a ~ (ко́нтэнтс оф а
   ~) содержание груза
   express ~ (экспрэ́с ~) срочная
   посылка
   fragile ~ (фра́джайл ~) хрупкая
   посылка
   postal ~ (по́стал ~) почтовая
   посылка
   postal ~ **with declared value**
   (по́стал ~ уиθ дикле́йрд ва́лю)
   почтовая посылка с объявленной
   ценностью
Pardon (па́рдон) извинение,
прощение, помилование
   appeal for a ~ (аппи́л фор а ~)
   просьба о помиловании
   legal ~ (ли́гал ~) закономерное
   прощение
   to ~ (ту ~) помиловать
Parent (па́рэнт) родитель
   adoptive ~**s** (адо́птив ~с)
   приёмные родители
   birth ~**s** (бэрθ ~с) кровные
   родители
Parentage (па́рэнтэдж) происхождение
Parity (па́рити) паритет, паритетный
{adj.}, равенство, соотношение
   dollar ~ (до́ллар ~) паритет с
   долларом
   Exchange rate ~ (эксчэ́йндж рэйт
   ~) валютный паритет
   gold ~ (голд ~) золотой паритет
   mint ~ (минт ~) монетный паритет
   official ~ (оффи́шл ~)
   официальный паритет
   on a basis of ~ (он а бэ́йсис оф
   ~) на паритетных началах
   ~ **of currencies** (~ оф ку́ррэнсиз)
   соотношение валют
   ~ **of prices** (~ оф пра́йсэз)
   соотношение цен
Park (парк) заповедник, парк

Parking space (па́ркинг спэйс)
стоянка
Parliament (па́рламэнт) парламент
  European ~ (юропи́ан ~)
  европейская парламентская
  ассамблея, европейский парламент
  to dissolve ~ (ту дизо́лв ~)
  распустить парламент
Parliamentarian (парламэнтэ́йриан)
парламентарий
Parliamentarianism
(парламэнтэ́йрианизм) парламентаризм
Parliamentary (парламэ́нтари)
парламентский
Parricide (пэ́ррисайд) отцеубийство
{crime}, отцеубийца {person}
Part (парт) деталь, часть
  auxiliary ~ (аукзи́лиэри ~)
  вспомогательная деталь
  central ~ (сэ́нтрал ~) суть
  damaged ~ (да́маджд ~)
  повреждённая деталь
  defective ~s (дифэ́ктив ~с)
  дефектные части
  essential ~ (эссэ́ншл ~) суть
  expendable ~s (экспэ́ндабл ~с)
  расходуемые детали
  important ~ (импо́ртант ~) важная
  деталь, важная часть
  individual ~ (индиви́дюал ~)
  отдельная деталь
  in ~s (ин ~с) по частям
  integral ~ (и́нтэграл ~)
  неотъемлемая часть
  interchangeable ~s
  (интэрчэ́йнджабл ~с)
  взаимозаменяемые детали
  machine ~s (маши́н ~с) детали к
  машине
  missing ~ (ми́ссинг ~)
  недостающая деталь
  non-essential ~s (нон-эссэ́ншл
  ~с) второстепенные детали
  principal ~ (при́нсипал ~)
  основная часть
  rapidly wearing ~ (ра́пидли
  уэ́йринг ~) быстроизнашивающаяся
  деталь, быстроизнашивающиеся
  части
  rejected ~ (риджэ́ктэд ~)
  бракованная деталь
  repair ~ (рипэ́йр ~) ремонтная
  деталь
  replacement ~ (риплэ́йсмэнт ~)
  сменная деталь, сменная часть
  spare ~ (спэйр ~) запчасть,
  запасная деталь

  spare ~s (спэйр ~с) запасные
  части
  standard ~ (ста́ндард ~)
  стандартная деталь
  substantial ~ (сабста́ншл ~)
  значительная часть
  the greater ~ (θи грэ́йтэр ~)
  большая часть
  the lesser ~ (θи лэ́ссэр ~)
  меньшая часть
  to ~ (ту ~) расстаться
  to replace ~s (ту риплэ́йс ~с)
  заменять детали
  to stock ~s (ту сток ~с) иметь
  деталь на складе
  updated ~ (у́пдэйтэд ~)
  улучшенная деталь
  ~ load consignment (~ лод
  конса́йнмэнт) частично
  отгруженная партия товара
  ~ number (~ ну́мбэр) номер детали
  ~ to a machine (~ ту а маши́н)
  деталь машины
  ~-time (~-тайм) неполный день
  ~-time employees (~-тайм
  эмплойи́с) частично занятые
  служащие
Partial (паршл) пристрастный
{favoring}, частичный
Partiality (паршиа́лити) пристрастие

Partially (па́ршиалли) частично
  to ~ modify (ту ~ мо́дифай)
  изменять частично
  to ~ perform obligations (ту ~
  пэрфо́рм облигэ́йшнз) выполнять
  обязательства частично
  to ~ satisfy (ту ~ са́тисфай)
  удовлетворять частично
  ~ owned by (~ о́унд бай) частично
  принадлежащий
  ~ paid shares (~ пэйд шэйрз)
  частично оплаченные акции
Participant (парти́сипант)
соучастник, участник
  listed ~s (ли́стэд ~с) список
  участников
  major ~ (мэ́йджор ~) основной
  участник
  potential ~ (потэ́ншл ~)
  потенциальный участник
  prospective ~s (проспэ́ктив ~с)
  предполагаемые участники
  registration of ~s (рэджистрэ́йшн
  оф ~с) регистрация участников
  to ~ (ту ~) принимать участие

to actively ~ (ту áктивли ~)
принимать активное участие
Participating (партúсипэйтинг)
участвующий
   ~ **bond** (~ бонд) облигации на
участие в прибылях компании
Participation (партисипэ́йшн)
долевой {adj.}, соучастие, участие
   alternating ~ (áлтэрнэйтинг ~)
поочерёдное участие
   application for ~ (апплике́йшн
фор ~) заявка на участие
   collective ~ (колле́ктив ~)
коллективное участие
   direct ~ (дире́кт ~)
непосредственное участие
   financial ~ (файна́ншл ~)
финансовое участие
   joint ~ (джойнт ~) совместное
участие
   large-scale ~ (лардж-скэйл ~)
крупное участие
   official governmental ~ (оффи́шл
говэрнмэ́нтал ~) официальное
участие на правительственном
уровне
   scale of ~ (скэйл оф ~) масштаб
участия
   to apply for ~ (ту аппла́й фор ~)
давать заявку на участие
   to confirm ~ (ту конфи́рм ~)
подтверждать участие
   to designate people to ~ (ту
дэ́зигнэйт пипл ту ~) назначать
людей для участия
   to justify ~ (ту джа́стифай ~)
обосновать участие
   total ~ (то́тал ~) общее число
участников
   with the ~ **of foreign firms** (уиθ
θи ~ оф фо́рэн фирмс) с участием
иностранных фирм
   ~ **expenses** (~ экспэ́нсэз) расходы
по участию
Particularism (парти́кюляризм)
партикуляризм
Partisan (па́ртизан) партизан
Partition (парти́шн) разъединение
   uncontested ~ (анконтэ́стэд ~)
раздел в бесспорном порядке
   writ of ~ (рит оф ~) акт раздела

   ~ **in kind** (~ ин кайнд)
натуральный раздел
   ~ **of property** (~ оф про́пэрти)
раздел имущества

Partitioning (парти́шнинг)
разъединение
   ~ **of properties** (~ оф про́пэртиз)
разъединение имуществ
Partner (па́ртнэр) партнёр,
компаньон, совладелец, участник
   foreign ~ (фо́рэн ~) иностранный
компаньон
   junior ~ (джу́ниор ~) младший
компаньон
   managing ~ (ма́наджинг ~) главный
компаньон
   senior ~ (си́ниор ~) старший
компаньон
   silent ~ (са́йлэнт ~) компаньон,
не принимающий активного участия
в ведении дела
Partnership (па́ртнэршип) общество,
товарищество
   general ~ (джэ́нэрал ~) полное
товарищество
   Limited {liability} ~ (ли́митэд
{лайаби́лити} ~) товарищество с
ограниченной ответственностью
   to enter into a ~ (ту э́нтэр и́нту
а ~) вступать в товарищество
   to withdraw from a ~ (ту уиθдра́у
фром а ~) выходить из
товарищества
   ~ **arrangement** (~ аррэ́йнджмэнт)
договорённость об участии
   ~ **en commandite** (~ эн коммандú́т)
коммандитное товарищество {civil
law form of limited partnership}
Part/y (па́рти) лицо, партия,
сторона, участник
   absent ~ (а́бсэнт ~)
отсутствующая сторона
   adverse ~ (а́двэрс ~) противная
сторона
   appropriate ~ (аппро́приат ~)
соответствующее лицо
   authorized ~ (а́уθорайзд ~)
уполномоченное лица
   Bolshevik ~ (бо́лшэвик ~)
большевистская партия
   Christian Democrat ~ (кри́стиан
дэ́мократ ~) христианско-
демократическая партия
   Coalition ~ (коали́шн ~)
коалиционная партия
   Communist ~ (ко́ммюнист ~)
коммунистическая партия
   Conservative ~ (консэ́рватив ~)
консервативная партия
   contracting ~ (ко́нтрактинг ~)
участник договора

Democratic ~ (дэмокра́тик ~) демократическая партия
disputing ~ (диспу́тинг ~) спорящая сторона
equal ~/ies (и́куал ~из) равноправные участники
guilty ~ (ги́лти ~) виновная сторона
injured ~ (и́нджюрд ~) потерпевшая сторона
innocent ~ (и́нносэнт ~) невиновная сторона
interested ~ (и́нтэрэстэд ~) заинтересованное лицо, заинтересованная сторона
Labor ~ (лэ́йбор ~) лейбористская партия
liable ~ (ла́йабл ~) ответственное лицо, ответственная сторона
Liberal ~ (ли́бэрал ~) либеральная партия
Liberal-Democratic ~ (ли́бэрал-дэмокра́тик ~) либерально-демократическая партия
negotiating ~ (нэго́шиэйтинг ~) участник переговоров
opposing ~ (оппо́зинг ~) возражающая сторона
opposition ~ (оппози́шн ~) оппозиционная партия
Peasant ~ (пэ́зант ~) крестьянская партия {rural party}
People's ~ (пиплз ~) народная партия
political ~ (поли́тикал ~) политическая партия
Progressive ~ (прогрэ́ссив ~) прогрессивная партия
Radical ~ (ра́дикал ~) радикальная партия
Radical Democratic ~ (ра́дикал дэмокра́тик ~) радикально-демократическая партия
responsible ~ (риспо́нсибл ~) виновник
Revolutionary ~ (рэволю́шнари ~) революционная партия
ruling ~ (ру́линг ~) правящая партия
Social Democratic ~ (сошл дэмокра́тик ~) социал-демократическая партия
Socialist ~ (со́шлист ~) социалистическая партия

third ~ (θирд ~) третье лицо, третья сторона
to exclude from the ~ (ту эксклю́д фром θи ~) исключить из партии
unified ~ (ю́нифайд ~) единая партия
Unified Socialist ~ (ю́нифайд со́шлист ~) объединённая социалистическая партия
via third ~ (ви́а θирд ~) через третье лицо
Worker's ~ (уо́ркэрз ~) рабочая партия
working ~ (уо́ркинг ~) рабочая комиссия
~ boosterism (~ бу́стэризм) партийность {usu. Communist}
~ committee (~ комми́тти) партком {abbrev.}
~ conference (~ ко́нфэрэнс) партконференция {abbrev.}
~ congress (~ ко́нгрэс) партсъезд
~ organization (~ организэ́йшн) парторганизация {abbrev.}
~ organizer (~ о́рганайзэр) парторг {abbrev.}
~ reading room (~ ри́динг рум) парткабинет
~ to a joint venture (~ ту а джойнт вэ́нчур) участник в совместных предприятиях
~ to an agreement (~ ту ан агри́мэнт) участник договора
~/ies to an agreement (~из ту ан агри́мэнт) участники соглашения
~ to the proceedings (~ ту θи проси́дингз) сторона в суде
Pass (пасс) пропуск, путёвка, талон
boarding ~ (бо́рдинг ~) посадочный талон
permanent ~ (пэ́рманэнт ~) постоянный пропуск
to obtain a ~ (ту обтэ́йн а ~) абонировать
train ~ (трэйн ~) проездной абонемент
~-holder (~-хо́лдэр) абонент
Passage (па́ссадж) отрывок, проезд, проход
peaceful ~ (пи́сфул ~) мирный проход
Passbook, bank ~ (па́ссбук, банк ~) расчётная банковская книжка
Passenger (па́сэнджэр) пассажир
~ turnover (~ ту́рновэр) пассажирооборот

Passion (пашн) страсть
  fit of ~ (фит оф ~) аффект
Passport (пáсспорт) паспорт
  diplomatic ~ (дипломáтик ~)
  дипломатический паспорт
  foreign ~ (фóрэн ~) иностранный
  паспорт
  foreign travel ~ (фóрэн трáвэл
  ~) заграничный паспорт {under
  Soviets}
  government ~ (гóвэрнмэнт ~)
  государственный паспорт
  Nansen ~ (нáнсэн ~) нансеновский
  паспорт
  to issue a ~ (ту úшю а ~) выдать
  паспорт
  valid ~ (вáлид ~) действительный
  паспорт
Password (пáссуорд) пароль
Pasture (пáсчур) пастбище
  common ~ (кóммон ~) общее
  пастбище
Patent (пáтэнт) патент, патентный
{adj.}, явный {adj., e.g. not
latent}
  additional ~ (аддúшнал ~)
  дополнительный патент
  artisan's ~ (áртизанз ~) патент
  на право самостоятельно
  заниматься ремеслом
  consular ~ (кóнсюлар ~)
  консульский патент
  domestic ~ (домэ́стик ~)
  отечественный патент
  exclusive ~ (эксклю́сив ~)
  исключительный патент
  foreign ~ (фóрэн ~) иностранный
  патент
  industrial ~ (индýстриал ~)
  промышленный патент
  international ~ (интэрнáшэнал ~)
  международный патент
  invalidated ~ (инвáлидэйтэд ~)
  патент признанный
  недействительным
  inventor's ~ (инвэ́нторз ~)
  патентное право на изобретение
  issued ~ (úшюд ~) выданный
  патент
  reinstated ~ (риинстэ́йтэд ~)
  возобновляемый патент
  revocation of a ~ (рэвокэ́йшн оф
  а ~) аннулирование патента
  ship ~ (шип ~) судовой патент
  to ~ (ту ~) запатентовать,
  патентовать

  to assign a ~ (ту ассáйн а ~)
  отчудить патент
  to invalidate a ~ (ту инвáлидэйт
  а ~) признать патент
  недействительным
  ~ agent (~ э́йджэнт) патентный
  поверенный
  ~ holder (~ хóлдэр)
  патентовладелец,
  патентообладатель
Patentability (патэнтабúлити)
патентоспособность
Patentable (пáтэнтабл)
патентоспособный
Patented (пáтэнтэд)
запатентованный, патентованный
Patenting (пáтэнтинг) патентование
  foreign ~ (фóрэн ~) заграничное
  патентование
Paternity (патэ́рнити) отцовство
  contest of ~ (кóнтэст оф ~)
  оспаривание отцовства
  illegitimate ~ (иллэджúтэмат ~)
  незаконное отцовство
  legitimate ~ (лэджúтимат ~)
  законное отцовство
  ~ out of wedlock (~ óут оф
  уэ́длок) внебрачное отцовство
Path (паθ) тропинка, путь
  constitutional ~ (конститýшнал
  ~) конституционный путь
  the shortest ~ (θи шóртэст ~)
  кратчайший маршрут
Patriotic (патриóтик)
отечественныйff
Patron (пэ́йтрон) покровитель
Patronize, to ~ (пэ́йтронайз, ту ~)
покровительствовать
Pattern (пáттэрн) модель, образец,
образчик
  sample ~ (сампл ~) образец
  модели
Pause (пауз) перерыв
Pawn (паун) пешка {chess, also
figuratively}
  to ~ (ту ~) закладывать
  [perfective: заложить]
  ~ shop (~ шоп) ломбард
Pawning (пáунинг) заклад
Pay (пэй) заработок, оклад, плата
  actual ~ (áкчуал ~) фактический
  оклад
  average hourly ~ (áвэрэдж óурли
  ~) средний часовой заработок
  average ~ (áвэрэдж ~) средняя
  плата

back ~ (бак ~) задержанная
зарплата
base ~ (бэйс ~) базовая плата
basic ~ (бэ́йсик ~) основной
заработок, основной оклад
equal ~ (и́куал ~) равная оплата
труда
guaranteed ~ (гяранти́д ~)
гарантированная оплата
high ~ (хай ~) высокая оплата
hourly ~ (о́урли ~) почасовая
плата, часовой заработок
incentive ~ (инсэ́нтив ~)
поощрительная оплата
piece-work ~ (пис-уо́рк ~)
сдельная оплата
take-home ~ (тэйк-хом ~)
реальная зарплата
to ~ (ту ~) заплатить,
оплачивать, платить
to ~ cash (ту ~ каш) заплатить
наличными
to ~ down (ту ~ до́ун) погашать
to ~ in full (ту ~ ин фул)
выплачивать сполна {полностью}
to ~ in cash (ту ~ ин каш)
платить наличными
to ~ on a piece-work basis (ту ~
он а пис-уо́рк бэ́йсис) платить по
сдельно
to ~ out on a monthly basis (ту
~ о́ут он а мо́нθли бэ́йсис)
выплачивать ежемесячно
weekly ~ (уи́кли ~) недельный
заработок
Payable (пэ́йабл) оплачиваемый
accounts ~ (акко́унтс ~)
кредиторская задолженность
to be ~ (ту би ~) подлежать
выплате
Payee (пэйи́) лицо, получающее
платёж
~ of a check (~ оф а чэк)
предъявитель чека, получатель
чека
Payer (пэ́йэр) плательщик
slow ~ (слоу ~) неаккуратный
плательщик
Payload (пэ́йлод) коммерческая
нагрузка
Paymaster (пэ́ймастэр) кассир
Payment (пэ́ймэнт) выплата, оплата,
отдача, плата, платёж, уплата
additional ~ (адди́шнал ~)
дополнительная выплата,
дополнительная оплата,
дополнительный платёж

advance ~ (адва́нс ~) авансовый
платёж
annual ~ (а́ннюал ~) годовой
платёж
annuity ~ (анню́ити ~)
уплачиваемый периодически взнос
average ~ (а́вэрэдж ~) аварийный,
страховой взнос
bonus ~ (бо́нус ~) премиальная
оплата
cash ~ (каш ~) денежная выплата,
денежная оплата
cash ~s in advance (каш ~с ин
адва́нс) выплата авансовых
платежей наличными
certificate of ~ (сэрти́фикэт оф
~) денежный аттестат
check in ~ (чэк ин ~) чек в
уплату
collecting ~ by proxy
(колле́ктинг ~ бай про́кси)
выплата по доверенности
commission ~ (комми́шн ~) выплата
комиссионного вознаграждения
compensatory ~ (компэ́нсатори ~)
компенсационная выплата
deferred ~ (дифэ́рд ~)
отсроченный платёж
demand for ~ (дима́нд фор ~)
требование уплаты
direct ~ (дирэ́кт ~) прямой взнос
financial ~ (файна́ншл ~)
финансовый расчёт
freight ~ (фрэйт ~) уплата
фрахта
guaranteed ~ (гяранти́д ~)
гарантийная выплата
have a right to ~ of interest
(хэв а райт ту ~ оф и́нтэрэст)
иметь право на выплату процентов
immediate ~ (имми́диат ~)
немедленная уплата
incentive ~ (инсэ́нтив ~)
премиальная выплата
incoming ~s (и́нкоминг ~с)
поступления денег
interest ~ (и́нтэрэст ~) выплата
процентов, уплата процентов
lapsed ~ (ла́псд ~) рассроченный
платёж
lumpsum ~ (ла́мпсум ~) аккордная
плата, единовременная выплата,
единовременный платёж,
паушальный взнос
maintenance ~s (мэ́йнтэнанс ~с)
алименты

minimal ~ (ми́нимал ~)
минимальная плата
money ~ (мо́ни ~) денежный платёж
monthly ~ (мо́нθли ~) ежемесячная
оплата, ежемесячный платёж,
ежемесячная уплата
nominal ~ (но́минал ~)
номинальная плата
non-commercial ~ (нон-комме́ршл
~) неторговый платёж
notice of ~ (но́тис оф ~) авизо о
платеже
on-time ~ (он-тайм ~) досрочный
платёж
overtime ~ (о́вэртайм ~) выплата
за сверхурочную работу
partial ~ (паршл ~) частичный
взнос, частичный платёж,
частичная уплата
past-due ~ (паст-ду ~)
просроченный платёж
patent licensing ~s (па́тэнт
ла́йсэнсинг ~с) выплаты по
патентной лицензии
payroll ~s (пэ́йрол ~с) выплата
жалования
periodic ~ (пирио́дик ~)
периодический платёж
preliminary ~ (прили́минэри ~)
предварительный платёж
prompt ~ (промпт ~) немедленная
оплата, своевременная уплата
quarterly ~ (куа́ртэрли ~)
квартальный платёж
rental ~ (рэ́нтал ~) арендная
плата, арендный платёж
same day ~ arrangement (сэйм дэй
~ арре́йнджмэнт) договорённость о
выплате денег в день
предъявления счёта
security for ~ (сэкю́рити фор ~)
обеспечение уплаты
subsidy ~ (су́бсиди ~) выплата
субсидии
support ~ (суппо́рт ~) алиментный
платёж
support ~s (суппо́рт ~с) алименты
на содержание
timely ~ (та́ймли ~) срочный
платёж
to advance money in ~ (ту адва́нс
мо́ни ин ~) авансировать деньги
на уплату
to affect ~ (ту аффэ́кт ~)
совершить платёж

to approve ~ (ту аппру́в ~)
разрешать выплату, утверждать
выплату
to defer ~ (ту дифэ́р ~)
отсрочить платёж
to effect ~ (ту иффэ́кт ~)
производить выплату
to exempt from ~ (ту экзэ́мпт
фром ~) освобождать от уплаты
to insist on immediate ~ (ту
инси́ст он имми́диат ~) настаивать
на немедленной уплате
to refuse ~ (ту рифю́з ~)
отказываться от уплаты
to stop ~ (ту стоп ~)
приостановить платёж
~ against statement (~ агэ́нст
стэ́йтмэнт) платёж против выписки
счёта
~ ahead of schedule (~ ахэ́д оф
скэ́джюл) досрочная оплата
~ by check (~ бай чэк) платёж
чеком
~ by installments (~ бай
инста́ллмэнтс) выплата частями
~ by letter of credit (~ бай
лэ́ттэр оф крэ́дит) выплата с
аккредитива
~ exceeding the amount of the
debt (~ экси́динг θи амо́унт оф θи
дэт) платёж превышающий
действительную сумму долга
~s for credits (~с фор крэ́дитс)
выплаты по кредитам
~ for screening (~ фор скри́нинг)
платёж за прокат фильмов
~ in advance (~ ин адва́нс)
выплата авансом
~ in anticipation (~ ин
антисипэ́йшн) уплата раньше
сроков
~ in cash (~ ин каш) платёж за
наличный расчёт, уплата
наличными
~ in dollars (~ ин до́лларс)
выплата в долларах
~ in foreign exchange (~ ин
фо́рэн эксчэ́йндж) платёж в
инвалюте
~ in full (~ ин фул) полная
уплата
~ in gold (~ ин голд) уплата
золотом
~ in kind (~ ин кайнд) плата
натурой, натуральная оплата,
уплата натурой

~ **in installments** (~ ин
инста́ллмэнтс) выплата в
рассрочку
~ **into the budget** (~ и́нту θи
ба́джэт) платёж в бюджет
~ **of an advance** (~ оф ан адва́нс)
выдача аванса
~ **of an amount** (~ оф ан амо́унт)
уплата суммы, выплата суммы
~ **of the arbitration fee** (~ оф
θи арбитрэ́йшн фи) уплата
арбитражного сбора
~ **of a commission** (~ оф а
комми́шн) уплата комиссии
~ **of compensation** (~ оф
компэнсэ́йшн) выплата возмещения,
уплата вознаграждения
~ **of debt** (~ оф дэт) уплата
долга
~ **of a deposit** (~ оф а дипо́зит)
выплата по депозиту
~ **of dividends** (~ оф ди́видэндс)
выплата дивидендов
~ **of duty** (~ оф дю́ти) уплата
пошлины
~ **of a fee** (~ оф а фи) уплата
сбора
~ **of full freight** (~ оф фул
фрэйт) полная уплата фрахта
~ **of initial deposit** (~ оф ини́шл
дипо́зит) уплата первоначального
взноса
~ **of the initial fee** (~ оф θи
ини́шл фи) уплата первоначального
взноса
~ **of insurance indemnity** (~ оф
иншю́ранс индэ́мнити) выплата
страхового возмещения
~ **of an insurance premium** (~ оф
ан иншю́ранс при́миум) выплата
страховой премии
~ **of insurance premiums** (~ оф
иншю́ранс при́миумс) уплата
страховых взносов
~ **of interest on deposit** (~ оф
и́нтэрэст он дипо́зит) уплата
процентов по вкладу
~ **of monetary damages** (~ оф
мо́нэтари да́мэджэз) уплата
денежного возмещения
~ **of profits** (~ оф про́фитс)
выплата прибыли
~ **of principal and interest** (~
оф при́нсипал анд и́нтэрэст)
уплата капитала и процентов

~ **of remuneration** (~ оф
римюнэрэ́йшн) уплата
вознаграждения
~ **of retention money** (~ оф
ритэ́ншн мо́ни) выплата
гарантийной суммы
~ **of royalty** (~ оф ро́йялти)
выплата роялти
~ **of seniority benefits** (~ оф
синёрити бэ́нэфитс) выплата
вознаграждения за выслугу лет
~ **of a service commission** (~ оф
а сэ́рвис комми́шн) уплата
комиссии за услуги
~ **of social security benefits** (~
оф сошл сэкю́рити бэ́нэфитс)
выплаты по социальному
обеспечению
~ **of taxes** (~ оф та́ксэз) уплата
налогов
~ **on account** (~ он акко́унт)
предварительный взнос
~ **on delivery** (~ он дэли́вэри)
уплата при поставке
~ **under subrogation** (~ а́ндэр
суброгэ́йшн) платёж с суброгацией
~ **time** (~ тайм) время выплаты
Payout (пэ́йоут) выплата
~ **order** (~ о́рдэр) приказ о
выплате денег
~ **period** (~ пи́риод) период
выплаты
Payroll (пэ́йрол) платёжная
ведомость, расчётный лист
to meet ~ (ту мит ~) оплачивать
платёжную ведомость
to put on the ~ (ту пут он θи ~)
включать в платёжную ведомость
Paysheet (пэ́йшит) расчётная
ведомость
Peace (пис) мир
Peaceful (пи́сфул) мирный
for ~ **purposes** (фор ~ пу́рпосэз)
в мирных целях
Peak (пик) пик
Peasant (пэ́зант) крестянин
~ **of modest earnings** (~ оф
мо́дэст э́рнингз) середняк
Pecuniary (пэкю́ниари) денежный
~ **reward** (~ риуа́рд) денежное
вознаграждение
Peddler (пэ́ддлэр) коробейник,
разносчик
Peg, to ~ **the market** (пэг, ту ~ θи
ма́ркэт) поддерживать курс
искусственно, поддерживать цены на
одном уровне

Penal (пи́нал) штрафной
Penalize, to ~ (пи́налайз, ту ~)
оштрафовать, штрафовать
Penalized (пи́налайзд) оштрафованный
Penalty (пэ́налти) взыскание,
неустойка обложение штрафом, пеня,
штраф
    alternative ~ (алтэ́рнатив ~)
альтернативная неустойка
    amount of ~ (амо́унт оф ~) сумма
штрафа
    contractual ~ (контра́кчуал ~)
договорная неустойка, договорный
штраф
    conventional ~ (конвэ́ншнал ~)
обычный штраф
    customs ~ (ка́стомз ~) таможенный
штраф
    demurrage ~ (диму́ррадж ~) штраф
за простой
    exclusive ~ (эксклю́сив ~)
исключительная неустойка
    heavy ~ (хэ́ви ~) большая
неустойка
    imposition of a ~ (импози́шн оф а
~) наложение взыскания,
наложение штрафа
    size of ~ (сайз оф ~) размер
штрафа
    subject to ~ (са́бджэкт ту ~)
подлежащий штрафу
    tax ~ (такс ~) налоговая санкция
    to apply the ~ clause (ту аппла́й
θи ~ клауз) применять пункт о
штрафах
    to calculate a ~ (ту ка́лкюлэйт а
~) начислять штраф
    to calculate a ~ on the cost of
... (ту ка́лкюлэйт а ~ он θи кост
оф ...) исчислять штраф со
стоимости
    to enforce a ~ (ту энфо́рс а ~)
взыскивать штраф
    to impose a ~ (ту импо́з а ~)
наложить взыскание, налагать
штраф
    to incur a ~ (ту инку́р а ~)
подвергнуть взысканию
    to recover or exact a ~ (ту
рико́вэр ор экза́кт а ~)
производить взыскание
    to renounce a ~ (ту рино́унс а ~)
отказываться от оплаты штрафа
    ~ clause (~ клауз) пункт о
штрафах
    ~ for delay (~ фор дилэ́й) штраф
за задержку

    ~ for late delivery (~ фор лэйт
дэли́вэри) штраф за задержку
поставки
    ~ for late payment (~ фор лэйт
пэ́ймэнт) штраф за просрочку
платежа
    ~ in kind (~ ин кайнд) пеня
натурой
    ~ relief (~ рили́ф) освобождение
от уплаты штрафа
Penetration (пэнэтрэ́йшн)
проникновение
    economic ~ (эконо́мик ~)
экономическое проникновение
    ~ of new markets (~ оф нью
ма́ркэтс) открытие новых рынков
Penitentiary (пэнитэ́ншиари)
пенитенциарный
Pension (пэншн) пенсия
    civil ~ (си́вил ~) гражданская
пенсия
    disabled worker ~ (дисэ́йблд
уо́ркэр ~) пенсия по
нетрудоспособности
    lifetime ~ (ла́йфтайм ~)
пожизненная пенсия
    lifetime ~ for disability
(ла́йфтайм ~ фор дисаби́лити)
пожизненная пенсия по
инвалидности
    military ~ (ми́литари ~) военная
пенсия
    retirement ~ (рита́йрмэнт ~)
пенсия при выходе в отставку
    service ~ (сэ́рвис ~) пенсия за
выслугу лет
    state ~ (стэйт ~)
государственная пенсия
    to issue a ~ (ту и́шю а ~) выдать
пенсию
    to retire on ~ (ту рита́йр он ~)
уйти на пенсию
    widow's ~ (уи́доз ~) пенсия
вдовам
Pensioner (пэ́ншнэр) пенсионер
    disabled ~ (дисэ́йблд ~)
пенсионер по инвалидности
    disabled veteran ~ (дисэ́йблд
вэ́тэран ~) пенсионер-инвалид
войны
    old age ~ (олд эйдж ~) пенсионер
по старости
Percentage (пэрсэ́нтадж) процент
Perestroika (пиристро́йка)
перестройка
Perfection (пэрфэ́кшн)
усовершенствование

Perform (пэрфо́рм) выполнять
failure to ~ an agreement
(фэ́йлюр ту ~ ан агри́мэнт)
невыполнение договора
to ~ a duty (ту ~ а дю́ти)
исполнить обязанность
Performance (пэрфо́рманс)
выполнение, исполнение
compulsory ~ (компу́лсори ~)
принудительное исполнение
during ~ of a contract (дю́ринг ~
оф а ко́нтракт) по ходу
выполнения контракта
faithful ~ (фэ́йθфул ~) честное
выполнение
high quality ~ (хай куа́лити ~)
высококачественное выполнение
operating ~ (о́пэрэйтинг ~)
оперативная деятельность
part ~ (парт ~) частичное
выполнение
partial ~ (паршл ~) частичное
исполнение
preliminary ~ (прили́минэри ~)
предварительное исполнение
sound ~ (со́унд ~)
доброкачественное выполнение
timely ~ (та́ймли ~)
своевременное выполнение
обязательств {of a contract}
to delay ~ (ту дилэ́й ~)
приостановить исполнение
to guarantee ~ (ту гяранти́ ~)
гарантировать выполнение
voluntary ~ (во́лунтэри ~)
исполнение добровольное
исполнение
~ in kind (~ ин кайнд)
исполнение в натуре
~ of a contract (~ оф а
ко́нтракт) завершение контракта
~ of work (~ оф уо́рк) выполнение
работ
~ up to standards (~ ап ту
ста́ндардз) выполнение норм
выработки
Peril (пэ́рил) риск
Period (пи́риод) время, период, срок
berthing ~ (бэ́рθинг ~) время
стоянки у причала
budget ~ (ба́джэт ~) бюджетный
период
calendar ~ (ка́лэндар ~)
календарный период
contingent ~ (конти́нджэнт ~)
условленный срок

contractual ~ (контра́кчуал ~)
договорный срок
credit ~ (крэ́дит ~) кредитный
срок
demurrage ~ (диму́ррадж ~)
контрсталийное время
depreciation ~ (диприши́эйшн ~)
срок амортизации
established ~ (эста́блишд ~)
установленный срок
exhibition ~ (экзиби́шн ~) время
проведения выставки
grace ~ (грэ́йс ~) льготный
период, льготный срок
legal ~ (ли́гал ~) юридический
срок
licensing ~ (ла́йсэнсинг ~) время
действия лицензии
operating ~ (о́пэрэйтинг ~) время
эксплуатации
permissible unloading ~
(пэрми́ссибл анло́динг ~) дни на
разгрузку
probationary ~ (пробэ́йшнари ~)
испытательный стаж
reasonable ~ of time (ри́зонабл ~
оф тайм) справедливый срок
reporting ~ (рипо́ртинг ~)
отчётный период
test ~ (тэст ~) испытательный
срок
transition ~ (транси́шн ~)
переходный период
transport ~ (тра́нспорт ~) время
транспортировки
warranty ~ (уа́рранти ~)
гарантируемый срок
~ of effect (~ оф иффэ́кт) срок
действия
~ of validity (~ оф вали́дити)
срок действия
Periodic (пирио́дик) регулярный
Periodical (пэрио́дикал) журнал,
периодический журнал
monthly ~ basis (мо́нθли ~
бэ́йсис) помесячная периодичность
specialized ~ (спэ́шлайзд ~)
специализированный журнал
~ basis of deliveries (~ бэ́йсис
оф дэли́вэриз) периодичность
поставок
Perishable (пэ́ришабл) портящийся
highly ~ (ха́йли ~)
легкопортящийся
Perjury (пэ́рджури) ложная присяга
Permissible (пэрми́ссибл)
дозволенный

Permission (пэрми́шн) разрешение
   overflight ~ (о́вэрфлайт ~)
разрешение на полёт над
   preliminary ~ (прили́минэри ~)
предварительное разрешение
   standing ~ (ста́ндинг ~)
постоянное разрешение
   visiting ~ (ви́зитинг ~)
разрешение на свидание с
заключённым {with convict}
   written ~ (ри́ттэн ~) письменное
разрешение
Permissiveness (пэрми́сивнэс)
попустительство
Permit (пэ́рмит) пропуск
   export ~ (э́кспорт ~) экспортное
разрешение
   foreign exchange ~ (фо́рэн
эксчэ́йндж ~) валютное разрешение
   prospecting ~ (про́спэктинг ~)
разрешение на разведку
месторождений
   residence ~ (рэ́зидэнс ~)
прописка
   single entry ~ (сингл э́нтри ~)
разовое разрешение
   to ~ (ту ~) допускать,
пропустить, разрешать
[perfective: разрешить]
   temporary ~ (тэ́мпорари ~)
временное разрешение
   to ~ for transport (ту ~ фор
тра́нспорт) допускать к перевозке
   work ~ (уо́рк ~) разрешение на
право работы
Perpetrate, to ~ (пэ́рпэтрэйт, ту ~)
совершать
Perpetration (пэрпэтрэ́йшн)
совершение
   ~ of a crime (~ оф а крайм)
совершение преступления
Perpetuity (пэрпэтю́ити) бессрочное
владение
Person (пэ́рсон) лицо
   authorized ~ (а́уθорайзд ~) лицо,
наделённое правами
   average ~ (а́вэрэдж ~) середняк
   juridical ~ (джюри́дикал ~)
юридическое лицо {legal entity}
   natural ~ (на́чюрал ~) физическое
лицо {individual}
   private ~ (пра́йват ~) частное
лицо
   stateless ~ (стэ́йтлэс ~) апатрид
Persona non grata (пэрсо́на нон
гра́та) персона нон грата

Personal (пэ́рсонал) лицевой,
личный, собственный
Personality (пэрсона́лити) личность
Personnel (пэрсоннэ́л) кадры, личный
состав, персонал, штат
   administrative ~ (адми́нистрэйтив
~) административный персонал,
административный состав
   ancillary ~ (а́нсиллари ~)
подсобный персонал
   auxiliary court ~ (аукзи́лиэри
ко́урт ~) вспомогательный
судебный персонал
   civil service ~ (си́вил сэ́рвис ~)
гражданский персонал
   consular ~ (ко́нсюлар ~)
консульский персонал
   diplomatic ~ (диплома́тик ~)
дипломатический персонал,
дипломатический состав
   executive ~ (экзэ́кютив ~)
исполнительный персонал
   highly qualified ~ (ха́йли
куа́лифайд ~)
высококвалифицированные кадры
   management ~ (ма́наджмэнт ~)
руководящие кадры,
управленческий персонал
   managerial ~ (манаджи́риал ~)
руководящий состав
   military ~ (ми́литари ~) военный
персонал
   paramilitary ~ (парами́литари ~)
полувоенный персонал
   production ~ (прода́кшн ~)
производственный персонал,
производственный штат
   professional ~ (профэ́шнал ~)
профессиональные кадры
   qualified ~ (куа́лифайд ~)
квалифицированные кадры
   scientific ~ (сайэнти́фик ~)
научные кадры
   scientific and technical ~
(сайэнти́фик энд тэ́кникал ~)
научно-технические кадры
   support ~ (суппо́рт ~)
вспомогательный персонал
   technical ~ (тэ́кникал ~) штат
технических сотрудников
   to provide ~ (ту прова́йд ~)
обеспечивать кадрами
   to reduce ~ (ту ридю́с ~)
сокращать штат
   to retain ~ (ту ритэ́йн ~)
сохранять кадры

to select ~ (ту сэлэ́кт ~) подбирать кадры
to staff up with qualified ~ (ту стаф ап уиθ куа́лифайд ~) укреплять квалифицированными кадрами
~ department (~ дипа́ртмэнт) отдел кадров
~ director (~ дирэ́ктор) управляющий по кадрам
~ records (~ рэ́кордз) учёт кадров
~ recruitment (~ рикру́йтмэнт) набор кадров
Perspective (пэрспэ́ктив) перспектива
Perversion (пэрвэ́ржн) извращение, искажение
Pervert (пэ́рвэрт) совратитель
to ~ (ту ~) искажать, совратить
Petition (пэти́шн) петиция, ходатайство
to ~ (ту ~) обращаться с ходатайством
to grant a ~ (ту грант а ~) удовлетворять ходатайство
to make a ~ (ту мэйк а ~) подавать ходатайство
to obtain by formal ~ (ту обтэ́йн бай фо́рмал ~) исходатайствовать
to receive a ~ (ту риси́в а ~) принимать ходатайство
~ for postponement (~ фор постпо́нмэнт) ходатайство об отсрочке
~ for review (~ фор ривю́) ходатайство о пересмотре решения
Petitioner (пэти́шнэр) петиционер, проситель
Petrodollars (пэ́тродо́лларз) нефтедоллары
Petroleum (пэтро́лиум) нефть
refining (рифа́йнинг) нефтепереработка
Phase (фэйз) полоса, ступень, стадия
preliminary investigation ~ (прили́минэри инвэстигэ́йшн ~) стадия предварительного следствия
procedural ~ (проси́дюрал ~) процессуальная стадия
production ~ (прода́кшн ~) стадия производства
~ of development (~ оф дивэ́лопмэнт) ступень развития
~ of a plan (~ оф а план) этап выполнения плана
Phenomenon (фэно́мэнон) явление
Pick-up and Delivery (пик-ап энд дэли́вэри) вывоз и доставка грузов
cargo ~ services (ка́рго ~ сэ́рвисэз) услуги по вывозу груза
pier ~ (пир ~) вывоз с пирса
rates include ~ (рэйтс инклю́д ~) цена включает вывоз
~ location (~ локэ́йшн) место вывоза
Piece (пис) штука, штучный {adj.}
~-work (~-уо́рк) сдельщина
~-worker (~-уо́ркэр) сдельщик
Pile (пайл) кипа
Pilferage (пи́лфэрадж) хищение
to insure goods against ~ (ту иншу́р гудз агэ́нст ~) страховать товар против хищения
Pillage (пи́лладж) разграбление
Pilot (па́йлот) лоцман, лоцманский {adj.}, пилот
coasting ~ (ко́стинг ~) прибрежный лоцман
marine ~ (мари́н ~) морской лоцман
river ~ (ри́вэр ~) речной лоцман
senior ~ (си́ниор ~) старший лоцман
to apply to the ~ (ту аппла́й ту θи ~) вызывать лоцмана
to assign a ~ (ту асса́йн а ~) направлять лоцмана
to ~ (ту ~) пилотировать
to sail without a ~ (ту сэйл уиθо́ут а ~) плавать без лоцмана
to take on a ~ (ту тэйк он а ~) принимать лоцмана
Pilotage (па́йлотадж) вознаграждение за проводку судка, лоцманское дело, лоцманский сбор {dues}, пилотаж, проводка
~ outward (~ о́утуард) вывод судна лоцманов
~ service (~ сэ́рвис) обслуживание лоцманом
Pimp (пимп) альфонс, сводник
Pimping (пи́мпинг) сводничество
Pin (пин) значок
Pipeline (па́йплайн) трубопровод
gas ~ (гас ~) газопровод
to lay a gas ~ (ту лэй а гас ~) прокладывать газопровод
Piracy (па́йраси) морской разбой, пиратство

act of ~ (акт оф ~) акт
пиратства
Pirate (пайрат) пират, разбойник
copyright ~ (копирайт ~)
нарушитель авторского права
Piratical (пайратикал) разбойничий
Placard (плакард) афиша, место,
плакат
appropriate ~ (аппроприат ~)
подходящее место
berthing ~ (бёрθинг ~) место
швартовки
dry ~ (драй ~) сухое место
first ~ (фэрст ~) первенство
inconvenient ~ (инконвиниэнт ~)
неудобное место
in the indicated ~ (ин θи
индикэйтэд ~) в указанном месте
in one ~ (ин уан ~) в одном
месте
siting ~ (сайтинг ~) место
стоянки
to ~ (ту ~) размещать
~ of acceptance (~ оф аксэптанс)
место приёмки
~ of concluding contract (~ оф
конклюдинг контракт) место
заключения контракта
~ of delivery (~ оф дэливэри)
место поставки
~ of fabrication (~ оф
фабрикэйшн) место изготовления
~ of origin (~ оф ориджин) место
происхождения
~ of payment (~ оф пэймэнт)
место платежа
~ of performance (~ оф
пэрформанс) место деятельности
~ of presentation (~ оф
прэзэнтэйшн) место предъявления
~ of protest (~ оф протэст)
место опротестования
~ of registration (~ оф
рэджистрэйшн) место регистрации
~ of residence (~ оф рэзидэнс)
место жительства, место
пребывания
Placement (плэйсмэнт) вложение
~ of forces (~ оф форсэз)
расстановка сил
~ of government debt (~ оф
говэрнмэнт дэт) размещение
государственного долга
~ of orders (~ оф ордэрс)
размещение заказов
~ of shares (~ оф шэйрз)
размещение акции

Plagiarism (плэйгяризм) плагиат
Plagiarist (плэйгярист) плагиатор
Plagiarizer (плэйгярайзэр)
нарушитель авторского права
Plaintiff (плэйнтиф) истец
civil ~ (сивил ~) гражданский
истец
original ~ (ориджинал ~)
первоначальный истец
primary ~ (праймари ~) основной
истец
Plan (план) план, проект, схема
advertising ~ (адвэртайзинг ~)
план рекламных мероприятий
budget ~ (баджэт ~) бюджетное
планирование
budgeted ~ (баджэтэд ~)
бюджетный план
centralized ~ (сэнтралайзд ~)
централизованное планирование
counter ~ (коунтэр ~) встречный
план
economic ~ (экономик ~)
экономический план,
экономическое планирование
financial ~ (файнаншл ~)
финансовый план, финансовый
проект
five-year ~ (файв-еар ~)
пятилетка, пятилетний план
forward ~ (форуард ~)
перспективный план
industrial and financial ~
(индустриал энд файнаншл ~)
промфинплан {abbrev.}
investment ~ (инвэстмэнт ~) план
капиталовложений
land survey ~ (ланд сурвэй ~)
план кадастра
long-term ~ (лонг-тэрм ~)
долгосрочный план
master ~ (мастэр ~) генеральный
план
original ~ (ориджинал ~)
первоначальный проект
procurement ~ (прокурмэнт ~)
план закупок
production ~ (продакшн ~)
производственный план
seven-year ~ (сэвэн-еар ~)
семилетний план
to ~ (ту ~) замышлять
to propose a payment ~ (ту
пропоз а пэймэнт ~) предлагать
график платежей

~ **of industrialization** (~ оф индустриализэйшн) план индустриализации

~ **of modernization** (~ оф модэрнизэйшн) план модернизации

Planned (планд) планируемый, плановый

Planning (плэннинг) планирование

Plant (плант) завод, оборудование, фабрика, фабричный {adj.}

chemical ~ (кэмикал ~) химический завод

copper smelting ~ (коппэр смэлтинг ~) медеплавильный завод

dairy processing ~ (дэйри просэсинг ~) молочный завод

engineering ~ (инджэниринг ~) машиностроительный завод

individual ~s (индивидуал ~с) отдельные заводы

licensee's ~ (лайсэнсиз ~) завод лицензиата

machine tool ~ (машин тул ~) станкостроительный завод

major ~ (мэйджор ~) крупный завод

manufacturer's ~ (манюфакчурэрз ~) завод изготовителя

mechanical ~ (мэканикал ~) механический завод

operation of a ~ (опэрэйшн оф а ~) эксплуатация завода

petrochemical ~ (пэтрокэмикал ~) нефтехимический завод

petroleum processing ~ (пэтролиум просэсинг ~) нефтеперерабатывающий завод

pilot ~ (пайлот ~) опытная фабрика

subcontractor's ~ (субконтрактэрз ~) субподрядчика завод

the ~ **goes on stream** (θи ~ гоз он стрим) завод начинает выпуск продукции

the ~ **is operating** (θи ~ из опэрэйтинг) завод работает

the ~ **is operating at full capacity** (θи ~ из опэрэйтинг ат фул капасити) завод работает на полную мощность

to close down a ~ (ту клоз доун а ~) закрывать завод

to commission a ~ (ту коммишн а ~) вводить завод в строй

to commit to a ~ (ту коммит ту а ~) поручать выполнение плана

~ **capacity** (~ капасити) мощность завода, производственные мощности завода

~ **layout** (~ лэйоут) планировка завода

~ **manager** (~ манаджэр) директор завода, директор фабрики

~ **safety rules** (~ сэйфти рулз) заводские правила техники безопасности

~ **site** (~ сайт) местонахождения завода, площадка завода

Plastic (пластик) пластмассовый

~ **money** (~ мони) пластмассовые деньги {credit cards}

Plate (плэйт) лист, полоса, тарелка

tin ~ (тин ~) металлический ярлык

Platform (платформ) платформа

campaign ~ (кампэйн ~) избирательная платформа

Play, to ~ (плэй, ту ~) играть

Plea (пли) судебное заявление

to hold a ~ (ту холд а ~) разбирать дело

~ **of not guilty** (~ оф нот гилти) судебное заявление о невинности

Plead, to ~ (плид, ту ~) признавать

to ~ **guilty** (ту ~ гилти) сознаваться

to ~ **nolo contendere** (ту ~ ноло контэндэрэ) признать иск

to ~ **not guilty** (ту ~ нот гилти) отрицать виновность, признавать себя не виновным

Pleadings (плидингз) судебные прения, судоговорение

Plebiscite (плэбисайт) плебисцит

Pledge (плэдж) заклад, закладная, залог, залоговый {adj.}, заложенный объект, ипотека, ипотечный {adj.}

junior ~ (джюниор ~) ипотека ниже по рангу

senior ~ (синиор ~) ипотека выше по рангу

secured ~ (сэкюрд ~) обеспеченный залог

to ~ (ту ~) отдать в залог

to give money against a ~ (ту гив мони агэнст а ~) дать деньги под залог

to put up a ~ (ту пут ап а ~) внести залог

unredeemed ~ (анридимд ~) невыкупленный залог

~ **of chattels** (~ оф шаттэлз) залог движимости

~ **of semi-finished goods** (~ оф
сэ́ми-фи́нишд гудз) залог товаров
в переработке
Pledgee (плэджи́) залогодержатель
Pledging (плэ́джинг) отдача в залог
Plenary (плэ́нари) неограниченный,
пленарный
~ **session** (~ сэшн) пленум
~ **session of all chambers** (~
сэшн оф алл че́ймбэрз) пленум
всех палат
~ **session of the Supreme Court**
(~ сэшн оф θи супри́м ко́урт)
пленум верховного суда
Plenipotentiary (плэнипоте́ншиари)
полномочный
~ **ambassador** (~ амба́ссадор)
полномочный представитель
{abbreviated as: полпред}
Plentitude (плэ́нтитюд) полнота
Plenum (плэ́нум) пленум
Plot (плот) сговор
Plunder (пла́ндэр) разграбление,
хищение
to ~ (ту ~) расхищать
Plunderer (пла́ндэрэр) расхититель
Plundering (пла́ндэринг) расхищение
Plural (плу́рал) множественный
~ **vote** (~ вот) плюральный вотум
Pluralism (плю́рализм) плюрализм
~ **of officership** (~ оф
о́ффисэршип) совместительство
{e.g. holding multiple offices}
Poaching (по́чинг) незаконная охота
Pogrom (по́гром) погром
organizer of a ~ (о́рганайзэр оф
а ~) погромщик
Point (пойнт) пункт
air transfer ~ (эйр тра́нсфэр ~)
аэродром пересадки
command ~ (комма́нд ~) командный
пункт
discharge ~ (дисча́рдж ~) место
выгрузки
discharging ~ (дисча́рджинг ~)
место разгрузки
lashing ~ (ла́шинг ~) место
крепления верёвкой
lifting ~ (ли́фтинг ~) место
крепления стропов
shipping ~ (ши́ппинг ~) место
отгрузки
transhipment ~ (трансши́пмэнт ~)
место перевалки груза
turning ~ (ту́рнинг ~) перелом
~ **of arrival** (~ оф арра́йвал)
место прибытия

~ **of contention** (~ оф конте́ншн)
предмет разногласия
~ **of delivery** (~ оф дэли́вэри)
место доставки, место сдачи
~ **of entry** (~ оф э́нтри) входной
пункт, пункт ввоза
~ **of exit** (~ оф э́ксит) выходной
пункт
~ **of shipment** (~ оф ши́пмэнт)
место отправления
Poison (по́йзон) отрава, яд
to ~ (ту ~) отравлять
Poisoning (по́йзонинг) отравление
Pole (пол) столб
Polemicist (поле́мисист) полемист
Polemicize, to ~ (поле́мисайз, ту ~)
полемизировать
Polemics (поле́микс) полемика
Police (поли́с) орган милиции,
полиция, полицейский
government ~ (го́вэрнмэнт ~)
государственная полиция
local ~ (ло́кал ~) местная
полиция
maritime ~ (ма́ритайм ~) морская
полиция
metropolitan ~ (мэтропо́литан ~)
городская полиция
military ~ (ми́литари ~) военная
полиция
railroad ~ (рэ́йлрод ~)
железнодорожная полиция
Policy (по́лиси) полис, политика
agrarian ~ (агра́риан ~) аграрная
политика
anti-cyclical ~ (а́нти-си́кликал
~) противоциклическая политика
cancellation of an insurance ~
(кансэлле́йшн оф ан иншю́ранс ~)
расторжение договора страхования
credit ~ (крэ́дит ~) кредитная
политика
customs ~ (ка́стомз ~) таможенная
политика
customs/tariff ~ (ка́стомз/та́риф
~) таможенно-тарифная политика
deflationary ~ (дифлэ́йшнари ~)
дефляционная политика
demographic ~ (дэмогра́фик ~)
демографическая политика
discount ~ (ди́скоунт ~)
дисконтная политика
discriminatory ~ (дискри́минатори
~) дискриминационная политика
domestic ~ (доме́стик ~)
внутренняя политика

economic ~ (эконо́мик ~)
экономический курс,
экономическая политика
employment ~ (эмпло́ймэнт ~)
политика в области занятости
energy ~ (э́нэрджи ~) политика в
области энергетики
expansionist ~ (экспа́ншнист ~)
экспанционистская политика
financial ~ (файна́ншл ~)
финансовая политика
foreign ~ (фо́рэн ~) внешняя
политика
foreign exchange ~ (фо́рэн
эксчэ́йндж ~) девизная политика
general ~ (дже́нэрал ~) общая
политика
good neighbor ~ (гуд нэ́йбор ~)
политика добрососедских
отношений
government ~ (го́вэрнмэнт ~)
правительственная политика
group ~ (груп ~) групповой полис
immigration ~ (иммигрэ́йшн ~)
иммиграционная политика
insurance ~ (иншю́ранс ~)
страховой полис
international monetary ~
(интэрна́шэнал мо́нэтари ~)
валютная политика
investment ~ (инвэ́стмэнт ~)
инвестиционная политика
land ~ (ланд ~) земельная
политика
monetary ~ (мо́нэтари ~) денежная
политика
non-alignment ~ (нон-ала́йнмэнт
~) политика неприсоединения к
блокам
non-interference ~ (нон-
интэрфи́рэнс ~) политика
невмешательства
nuclear ~ (ну́клиар ~) ядерная
open cover ~ (о́пэн ко́вэр ~)
открытый полис
protectionist ~ (протэ́кшнист ~)
протекционистская политика
racist ~ (рэ́йсист ~) расистская
политика
social ~ (сошл ~) социальная
политика
tariff ~ (та́риф ~) тарифная
политика
tax ~ (такс ~) налоговая
политика
tight credit ~ (тайт крэ́дит ~)
политика сокращения кредита

tough ~ (туф ~) жёсткий курс
trade ~ (трэйд ~) внешнеторговая
политика, торговая политика
unified agricultural ~ (ю́нифайд
агрику́лчурал ~) единая
сельскохозяйственная политика
wage ~ (уэ́йдж ~) политика
заработной платы
worldwide ~ (уо́рлдуайд ~)
мировая политика
~ from position of strength (~
фром пози́шн оф стрэнг θ) политика
с позиции силы
~ of annexation (~ оф
аннэксэ́йшн) политика аннексий
~ of capital investments (~ оф
ка́питал инвэ́стмэнтс) политика
капитальных вложений
~ of discrimination (~ оф
дискриминэ́йшн) политика
дискриминации
~ of full employment (~ оф фул
эмпло́ймэнт) политика полной
занятости
~ of intervention (~ оф
интэрвэ́ншн) политика интервенции
~ of neutrality (~ оф нутра́лити)
нейтралистская политика
~ of racism (~ оф рэ́йсизм)
политика расизма
~ on bearer (~ он бэ́йрэр) полис
на предъявителя
Politburo (поли́тбюро) политбюро
Political (поли́тикал) политический
~ economy (~ ико́номи)
политэкономия
~ emigrant (~ э́мигрант)
политэмигрант
Politician (полити́шн) политик
Politics (по́литикс) политика
Poll (пол) голосование
to ~ (ту ~) собирать
[perfective: собрать]
Pollution (поллю́шн) загрязнение
~ of the environment (~ оф θи
энва́йронмэнт) загрязнение
окружающей среды
Polygamy (поли́гами) полигамия
Ponzi (по́нзи) Понзи {известный
итальянский мошенник}
~ investment (~ инвэ́стмэнт)
пирамида
Pool (пул) объединённый фонд
to ~ (ту ~) объединять
dollar ~ (до́ллар ~) объединённый
долларовый фонд
Poor (пур) бедный

~ **selling** (~ сэ́ллинг)
труднореализуемый
Popular (по́пюлар) народный,
популярный
~ **favorite** (~ фэ́йворит) народа
избранник
Pornographic (порногра́фик)
порнографический
~ **matter** (~ ма́ттэр)
порнографическое издание
Port (порт) порт
blockaded ~ (блокэ́йдэд ~)
блокированный порт
commercial ~ (комме́ршл ~)
коммерческий порт
customs ~ (ка́стомз ~) таможенный
порт
final ~ (фа́йнал ~) порт
окончательного назначения
fishing ~ (фи́шинг ~) рыбный порт
FOB ~ (эф-о-би́ ~) франко гавань
free ~ (фри ~) вольная гавань,
порто-франко, свободный порт
home ~ (хом ~) порт приписки
intermediate ~ (интэрми́диат ~)
попутный порт
loading ~ (ло́динг ~) порт
погрузки
naval ~ (нэ́йвал ~) военный порт
neutral ~ (ну́трал ~) нейтральный
порт
open ~ (о́пэн ~) открытый порт
original ~ **of destination**
(ори́джинал ~ оф дэстинэ́йшн) порт
первоначального назначения
river ~ (ри́вэр ~) речной порт
trading ~ (трэ́йдинг ~) торговый
порт
~ **of arrival** (~ оф арра́йвал)
порт прибытия
~ **of call** (~ оф кал) порт захода
~ **of departure** (~ оф дипа́рчур)
порт отправления
~ **of destination** (~ оф
дэстинэ́йшн) порт назначения
~ **of discharge** (~ оф ди́счардж)
порт выгрузки
~ **of refuge** (~ оф рэ́фюдж) порт-
убежище
~ **of registry** (~ оф рэ́джистри)
порт приписки, порт регистрации
Portable (по́ртабл) передвижной
~ **movie projector** (~ му́ви
проджэ́ктор) передвижная
киноустановка
Portfolio (портфо́лио) портфель

bank ~ (банк ~) банковский
портфель
business ~ (би́знэс ~) деловой
портфель
insurance ~ (иншю́ранс ~)
страховой портфель
ministerial ~ (министи́риал ~)
министерский портфель
~ **of bills** (~ оф билс)
вексельный портфель
~ **of securities** (~ оф сэкю́ритиз)
портфель ценных бумаг
~ **of stock** (~ оф сток) портфель
акций
Portion (поршн) доля, часть
Portofranco (по́ртофра́нко) порто-
франко
Position (пози́шн) довод, должность
{job}, местоположение, позиция,
рабочее место {job}, состояние
competitive ~ (компэ́титив ~)
конкурентная позиция
dominating ~ (до́минэйтинг ~)
доминирующее положение
exceptional ~ (эксэ́пшнал ~)
исключительное положение
foreign exchange ~ (фо́рэн
эксчэ́йндж ~) валютное положение
leading ~ (ли́динг ~) руководящий
пост
market ~ (ма́ркэт ~) позиция на
рынке
monetary ~ (мо́нэтари ~) денежное
положение
monopoly ~ (моно́поли ~)
монопольная позиция
preferential ~ (прэфэрэ́ншл ~)
предпочтительное местоположение
privileged ~ (при́вилэджд ~)
привилегированная позиция
temporary ~ (тэ́мпорари ~)
временная должность
to take somebody on in a ~ (ту
тэйк со́мбоди он ин а ~)
зачислять кого-л. на должность
~ **of an order** (~ оф ан о́рдэр)
ход выполнения заказа
Possess, to ~ (позэ́с, ту ~)
владеть, обладать
to ~ **jointly** (ту ~ джойнтли)
владеть совместно
Possession (позэ́шн) собственность
foreign ~s (фо́рэн ~с)
иностранные владения
taking ~ (тэ́йкинг ~) вступление
во владение

to assume ~ (ту ассю́м ~)
вступать во владение
to be in ~ (ту би ин ~)
находиться во владении
to give ~ over to (ту гив ~ о́вэр
ту) передавать во владение
to obtain ~ (ту обтэ́йн ~)
получать во владение
to pass into ~ (ту пасс и́нту ~)
переходить во владение
Possessor (позэ́сор) обладатель
Post (пост) должность {job}, пост,
почта, столб
book-rate ~ (бук-рэ́йт ~)
бандероль, почтовая бандероль
border ~ (бо́рдэр ~) пограничный
пост, пограничный пункт,
пограничный столб {marker}
consular ~ (ко́нсюлар ~)
консульский пост
customs ~ (ка́стомз ~) таможенный
пост, таможенный пункт
diplomatic ~ (диплома́тик ~)
дипломатический пост
director's ~ (дирэ́кторз ~)
директорский пост
government ~ (го́вэрнмэнт ~)
государственный пост
international ~ (интэрна́шэнал ~)
международное почтовое
отправление
non-registered parcel ~ (нон-
рэ́джистэрд па́рсэл ~) простая
бандероль
parcel ~ (па́рсэл ~) бандероль
registered parcel ~ (рэ́джистэрд
па́рсэл ~) заказная бандероль
to occupy a ~ (ту о́ккюпай а ~)
занимать должность
to send by book-rate ~ (ту сэнд
бай бук-рэйт ~) посылать
бандеролью
vacant ~ (вэ́йкант ~) вакантный
пост
~ office (~ о́ффис) почта
~-dated (~-дэ́йтэд) помеченный
более поздним числом
Postal (по́стал) почтовый
~ payment (~ пэ́ймэнт) почтовый
расчёт
Postcard (по́сткард) почтовая
карточка
Poste restante (пост рэста́нтэ) до
востребования
Poster (по́стэр) афиша, плакат
wall ~ (уал ~) настенное
объявление

Posterity (постэ́рити) потомство
Postmark (по́стмарк) дата почтового
штемпеля, почтовый знак, почтовый
штемпель
~ date (~ дэйт) дата почтового
штемпеля
Postpone, to ~ (постпо́н, ту ~)
откладывать [perfective: отложить],
отсрочивать, переносить
Postponed (постпо́нд) отсроченный
Postponement (постпо́нмэнт)
отсрочка, перенос
Potential (потэ́ншл) потенциал
economic ~ (эконо́мик ~)
экономический потенциал
industrial ~ (инду́стриал ~)
промышленный потенциал
military ~ (ми́литари ~) военный
потенциал
Potentiality (потэншиа́лити)
потенция
economic ~ (эконо́мик ~)
экономическая потенция
Pouch (по́уч) внутренняя почта,
мешок
diplomatic ~ (диплома́тик ~)
дипломатическая почта
Pound (по́унд) фунт
account denominated in ~s
sterling (акко́унт дино́минэйтэд
ин ~с стэ́рлинг) счёт в фунтах
стерлингов
credit denominated in ~s
sterling (крэ́дит дино́минэйтэд ин
~с стэ́рлинг) кредит в фунтах
стерлингов
demand for ~s sterling (дима́нд
фор ~с стэ́рлинг) спрос на фунты
стерлингов
devaluation of the ~ sterling
(дивалюэ́йшн оф θи ~ стэ́рлинг)
девальвация фунта стерлингов
in ~s sterling (ин ~с стэ́рлинг)
в фунтах стерлингов
loan denominated in ~s sterling
(лон дино́минэйтэд ин ~с
стэ́рлинг) заём в фунтах
стерлингов
parity of the ~ sterling (па́рити
оф θи ~ стэ́рлинг) паритет фунта
стерлингов
payment in ~s sterling (пэ́ймэнт
ин ~с стэ́рлинг) платёж в фунтах
стерлингов
to change a ~ note (ту чэйндж а
~ нот) разменять фунты

to **exchange** ~**s for dollars** (ту
эксчэйндж ~с фор до́лларс)
обменивать фунты на доллары
~ **sterling** (~ стэ́рлинг) фунт
стерлингов
Pour, to ~ (поур, ту ~) наливать
Power (по́уэр) власть, мощность,
сила
   absolute ~ (абсолю́т ~) полнота
власти
   active ~ (а́ктив ~) активная
мощность
   actual ~ (а́кчуал ~) фактическая
мощность
   actual purchasing ~ (а́кчуал
пу́рчасинг ~) реальная
покупательная способность
   arbitrary exercise of ~
(а́рбитрари э́ксэрсайз оф ~)
произвольный акт власти
   centralized ~ (сэ́нтралайзд ~)
централизованная власть
   economic ~ (эконо́мик ~)
экономическая
   effective ~ (иффэ́ктив ~)
эффективная мощность
   emergency ~s (эмэ́рджэнси ~с)
чрезвычайные полномочия
   engine ~ (э́нджин ~) двигателя
мощность
   executive ~ (экзэ́кютив ~)
исполнительная сила
   general ~ of attorney (джэ́нэрал
~ оф атто́рни) общая доверенность
   high ~ (хай ~) большая мощность
   legislative ~ (лэ́джислэйтив ~)
законодательная власть
   low ~ (ло́у ~) малая мощность
   monopoly ~ (моно́поли ~)
монопольная власть
   operating ~ (о́пэрэйтинг ~)
рабочая мощность
   purchasing ~ (пу́рчасинг ~)
покупательная сила,
покупательная способность
   service ~ (сэ́рвис ~)
эксплуатационная мощность
   starting ~ (ста́ртинг ~) пусковая
мощность
   to annul a ~ of attorney (ту
анну́л а ~ оф атто́рни)
аннулировать доверенность
   to be within one's ~ (ту би
уиθи́н уа́нз ~) быть в своей
власти
   to exercise ~ (ту э́ксэрсайз ~)
осуществлять власть

   **to exercise monopoly ~ in the
market** (ту э́ксэрсайз моно́поли ~
ин θи ма́ркэт) осуществлять
монопольную власть на рынке
   to grant a ~ of attorney (ту
грант а ~ оф атто́рни) выдавать
доверенность
   to have a ~ of attorney (ту хэв
а ~ оф атто́рни) иметь
доверенность
   to have ~ over (ту хэв ~ о́вэр)
иметь власть над
   to present a ~ of attorney (ту
прэзэ́нт а ~ оф атто́рни)
предъявлять доверенность
   to revoke a ~ of attorney (ту
риво́к а ~ оф атто́рни) отменять
доверенность
   to transfer ~ of attorney (ту
тра́нсфэр ~ оф атто́рни)
передоверять [**perfective:**
передоверить]
   useful ~ (ю́сфул ~) полезная
мощность
   **within the limits of
discretionary ~** (уиθи́н θи ли́митс
оф дискрэ́шнари ~) в пределах
предоставленной власти еренность
   ~ of attorney (~ оф атто́рни)
доверенность
   ~ of attorney valid for ... days
(~ оф атто́рни ва́лид фор ...
дэйс) доверенность действительна
на ...дней
   special ~s (спэшл ~с) особые
полномочия
Powerful (по́уэрфул) мощный
Practice (пра́ктис) практика,
привычка
   administrative ~ (адми́нистрэйтив
~) административная практика
   arbitration ~ (арбитрэ́йшн ~)
арбитражная практика
   banking ~ (ба́нкинг ~) банковская
практика
   commercial ~ (коммэ́ршл ~)
коммерческая практика
   consular ~ (ко́нсюлар ~)
консульская практика
   diplomatic ~ (дипломати́к ~)
дипломатическая практика
   discriminatory ~ (дискри́минатори
~) дискриминационная практика
   in ~ (ин ~) на деле
   international ~ (интэрна́шэнал ~)
международная практика

international legal ~
(интэрнашэнал лигал ~)
международная судебная практика
jurisprudential ~
(джуриспрудэншл ~) юридическая
практика
legislative ~ (лэджислэйтив ~)
законодательная практика
notarial ~ (нотэйриал ~)
нотариальная практика
prohibited ~ (прохибитэд ~)
запрещенная практика
regular ~ (рэгюлар ~) обычный
порядок
trade ~ (трэйд ~) торговая
практика
~ of law (~ оф лау) адвокатская
практика, практика адвокатуры
Prank (пранк) проделка
Pre-condition (при-кондишн)
предварительное условие
Pre-date, to ~ (при-дэйт, ту ~)
антидатировать
Pre-pack, to ~ (при-пак, ту ~)
фасовать
Pre-packing (при-паккинг) фасовка
Prepaid (припэйд) заранее уплачено
"freight ~" stamp (фрэйт ~
стамп) отметка об уплате фрахта
Pre-registration (при-рэджистрэйшн)
предварительная регистрация
Pre-tax (при-такс) до удержания
налогов
Preamble (приамбл) преамбула
Precaution (прикаушн)
предостережение ~s защитные меры
safety ~s (сэйфти ~с) меры
предосторожности
to ~ against (ту ~ агэнст)
предостерегать
Precedence (прэсэдэнс)
первоочерёдность
~ of delivery (~ оф дэливэри)
первоочерёдность поставки
Precedent (прэсэдэнт) прецедент
legal {case} ~ (лигал {кэйс} ~)
судебный прецедент
Precisely (присайзли) точно, в
точности
to determine ~ (ту дитэрмин ~)
точно определять
to identify ~ (ту идэнтифай ~)
точно идентифицировать
Precision (прэсижн) точность
absolute ~ (абсолют ~)
абсолютная точность

estimate of ~ (эстимат оф ~)
оценка точности
high ~ equipment (хай ~
икуйпмэнт) особо точная техника
~ analysis (~ аналисис) анализ
точности
Predecessor (прэдэсэсор)
предшественник
~ in title (~ ин тайтл)
предшественник по праву
Predetermine, to ~ (придитэрмин, ту
~) предопределять, предрешать
Predilection (прэдилэкшн)
пристрастие
Predominance (придоминанс)
преобладание
Predominant (придоминант)
преобладающий
Prefect (прифэкт) префект
Prefecture (прифэкчур) префектура
Prefer, to ~ (прифэр, ту ~)
предпочитать
Preferable (прифэрабл)
предпочтительный
Preference (прэфэрэнс)
преимущество, предпочтение
customs ~s (кастомз ~с)
таможенные преференции
imperial ~s (импириал ~с)
имперские преференции
legal ~ (лигал ~) правовое
преимущество
mutual ~s (мючуал ~с) взаимные
преференции
unilateral ~ (юнилатэрал ~)
односторонняя преференция
Preferential (прэфэрэншл) льготный,
преференциальный
~ customs treatment (~ кастомз
тритмэнт) таможенные льготы
~ tariffs (~ тарифс) тарифные
льготы
~ treatment (~ тритмэнт)
преференция
Prejudice (прэджюдис) нанесение
ущерба, повреждение, предрассудок
to ~ the rights (ту ~ θи райтс)
наносить ущерб правам
without ~ (уиθоут ~) без ущерба
without ~ to the contract
(уиθоут ~ ту θи контракт) без
ущерба для контракта
without ~ to the purchaser's
rights (уиθоут ~ ту θи пурчасэрз
райтс) без ущерба прав
покупателя

without ~ to the insurance
policy (иншӯранс пóлиси) без
ущерба для договора страхования
Prejudicial (прэджюдѝшл) наносящий
ущерб
Preliminary (прилѝминэри)
предварительный
Premeditated (примѐдитэйтэд)
преднамеренный
Premeditation (примэдитѐйшн)
преднамеренность
Premises (прѐмисэз) здание
    industrial ~ (индýстриал ~)
    промышленное здание
    office ~ (óффис ~) здание
    учреждения
Premium (прѝмиум) денежная
надбавка, лаж, надбавка,
премиальное вознаграждение,
премиальная надбавка, премия
    additional ~ (аддѝшнал ~)
    дополнительный взнос
    average ~ (ávэрэдж ~) средний
    страховой взнос
    call ~ (кал ~) предварительная
    премия
    fixed ~ (фиксд ~) страховой
    взнос в постоянном размере взнос
    foreign exchange ~ (фóрэн
    эксчѐйндж ~) валютная скидка
    incentive ~ (инсѐнтив ~)
    поощрительная надбавка
    insurance ~ (иншӯранс ~)
    страховой взнос, страховой
    платёж
    minimum ~ (мѝнимум ~)
    минимальная премия
    overload ~ (óвэрлод ~) надбавка
    за тяжеловесный груз
    receipt for ~ (рисѝт фор ~)
    квитанция за уплату премии
    reinsurance ~ (рэиншӯранс ~)
    перестраховочный платёж
    risk ~ (риск ~) надбавка за
    риск, премия за риск
    share ~ (шэйр ~) эмиссионная
    премия
    single ~ (сингл ~)
    единовременный страховой взнос
    to pay an insurance ~ (ту пэй ан
    иншӯранс ~) платить страховой
    взнос
    to sell at a ~ (ту сэл ат а ~)
    продавать с надбавкой
    ~ **on gold** (~ он голд) лаж на
    золото

    ~ **paid** (~ пэйд) уплаченный
    страховой взнос
Prepackaged (припáкэджд) в
упаковке, в фасовке
    ~ **goods** (~ гудз) товар,
    продающийся в упаковке
Preparation (прэпарѐйшн)
изготовление, подготовка
    budget ~ (бáджэт ~) подготовка
    бюджета
    ~ **of drawings** (~ оф дрáуингс)
    оформление чертежей
Prepare, to ~ (припэйр, ту ~)
собирать [**perfective:** собрать]
Prepayment (припѐймэнт) досрочная
оплата
    ~ **of a debt** (~ оф а дэт)
    досрочное погашение долга
Prerequisite (прирѐкуизит)
предпосылка
    juridical ~ (джюрѝдикал ~)
    юридическая предпосылка
Prerogative (прэрóгатив)
прерогатива
Prescribe, to ~ (прискрáйб, ту ~)
прописать
Prescription (прэскрѝпшн)
приобретательная давность
Presence (прѐзэнс) присутствие
    ~ **of a latent defect** (~ оф а
    лѐйтэнт дѝфэкт) наличие скрытого
    дефекта
Present (прѐзэнт) наличный,
подношение
    to ~ (ту ~) представлять
Presentation (прэзэнтѐйшн)
представление, предъявление
    payable upon ~ (пѐйабл апóн ~)
    оплачиваемый по представлению
    ~ **for acceptance** (~ фор
    аксѐптанс) предъявление для
    акцепта
    ~ **for payment** (~ фор пѐймэнт)
    предъявление на инкассо
    ~ **of a check** (~ оф а чэк)
    предъявление чека
    ~ **of notices** (~ оф нóтисэз)
    вручение нотисов
Presented (прэзѐнтэд)
представленный
Presenter (прэзѐнтэр) докладчик
    ~ **of supplementary report** (~ оф
    сапплэмѐнтари рипóрт)
    содокладчик
Presentment (прэзѐнтмэнт) подача
Preservation (прэзэрвѐйшн)
сохранение

~ **of cultural treasures** (~ оф
ку́лчурал трэ́жюрз) защита
культурных ценностей
~ **of health** (~ оф хэл θ) охрана
здоровья, санитарная защита
Preserve (присэ́рв) заповедник
to ~ (ту ~) сохранять
[**perfective**: сохранить]
Presidency (прэ́зидэнси)
председательство
President (прэ́зидэнт) президент
honorable ~ (о́норабл ~) почётный
президент
~ **of the government** (~ оф θи
го́вэрнмэнт) президент
правительства
~ **of the republic** (~ оф θи
рипа́блик) президент республики
Presidium (прэзи́диум) президиум
honorable ~ (о́норабл ~) почётный
президиум
Press (прэс) печать, пресса
national ~ (на́шэнал ~)
национальная печать
official ~ (оффи́шл ~)
официальная печать
state-owned ~ (стэйт-о́унд ~)
государственная печать
the ~ (θи ~) печать, пресса
~ **agency** (~ э́йджэнси) агенство
печати
~ **center** (~ сэ́нтэр) пресс-
референт
~ **conference** (~ ко́нфэрэнс)
пресс-конференция
Pressing (прэ́ссинг) неотложный
Pressure (прэ́шюр) давление,
напряжение
high ~ (хай ~) высокое
напряжение
inflationary ~ (инфлэ́йшнари ~)
инфляционное давление
inventory ~ (и́нвэнтори ~)
давление товарных запасов
market ~ (ма́ркэт ~)
напряжённость рынка, сжатие
рынка
price ~ (прайс ~) давление цен
to be subjected to ~ (ту би
сабджэ́ктэд ту ~) испытывать
давление
to exert ~ **upon** (ту экзэ́рт ~
упо́н) оказывать давление на
to increase the ~ (ту инкри́с θи
~) усиливать давление
to withstand ~ (ту уиθста́нд ~)
выдерживать давление

under ~ (а́ндэр ~) под давлением
work ~ (уо́рк ~) занятость
~ **of competition** (~ оф
компэти́шн) давление конкуренции
Presume, to ~ (призу́м, ту ~)
презюмировать
Presumption (призу́мпшн)
предположение, презумпция
absolute legal ~ (абсолю́т ли́гал
~) абсолютное законное
предположение
evidentiary ~ (эвидэ́ншиэри ~)
доказательственная презумпция
irrefutable ~ (иррифю́табл ~)
неопровержимая презумпция
legal ~ (ли́гал ~) законное
предположение, законная
презумпция
legal ~ **of guilt** (ли́гал ~ оф
гилт) законное предположение
вины
rebuttable ~ (риба́ттабл ~)
опровержимая презумпция
to establish a ~ (ту эста́блиш а
~) установить презумпцию
Pretense (при́тэнс) притворство
false ~ (фалс ~) мнимое
основание
Prevail (привэ́йл) выигрывать
to ~ **in a dispute** (ту ~ ин а
диспю́т) выигрывать конфликтное
дело
Prevent, to ~ (привэ́нт, ту ~)
предотвратить
Preventative (привэ́нтатив)
предупредительный
Prevention (привэ́ншн) защита,
предотвращение
~ **of accidents** (~ оф а́ксидэнтс)
предотвращение несчастных
случаев
~ **of conflicts** (~ оф ко́нфликтс)
предотвращение конфликтов
~ **of crime** (~ оф крайм)
предотвращение преступлений
~ **of surprise attack** (~ оф
сурпра́йз атта́к) предотвращение
внезапного нападения
Preventive (привэ́нтив)
превентивный, профилактический
Price (прайс) цена
above-mentioned ~ (або́в-мэ́ншнэд
~) вышеуказанная цена
acceptable ~**s** (аксэ́птабл ~с)
приемлемые цены
actual ~ (а́кчуал ~) фактическая
цена

actual transaction ~ (а́кчуал
транса́кшн ~) цена фактической
сделки
addition to the ~ (адди́шн ту θи
~) накидка на цену
additional ~ (адди́шнал ~)
дополнительная цена
affordable ~s (аффо́рдабл ~с)
общедоступные цены
aggregate ~ (а́ггрэгат ~)
итоговая цена
agreed ~ (агри́д ~) согласованная
цена
agreement on a ~ (агри́мэнт он а
~) договорённость о цене
anticipated ~s (анти́сипэйтэд ~с)
ожидаемые цены
approximate ~ (аппро́ксимат ~)
приблизительная цена
approximated ~ (аппро́ксимэйтэд
~) ориентировочная цена
asking ~ (а́скинг ~)
запрашиваемая цена
at the ~ of (ат θи ~ оф) по цене
at the agreed ~ (ат θи агри́д ~)
по согласованной цене
at any ~ (ат а́ни ~) по любой
цене
at a concrete ~ (ат а ко́нкрит ~)
по конкретной цене
at an increased ~ (ат ан инкри́сд
~) по возросшей цене
at the indicated ~ (ат θи
и́ндикэйтэд ~) по указанной цене
at the market ~ (ат θи ма́ркэт ~)
по рыночной цене
at a maximum ~ (ат а ма́ксимум ~)
по максимальной цене
at a minimum ~ (ат а ми́нимум ~)
по минимальной цене
at a reduced ~ (ат а риди́юсд ~)
по сниженной цене
attractive ~ (аттра́ктив ~)
привлекательная цена
average ~ (а́вэрэдж ~) средняя
цена
average market ~ (а́вэрэдж ма́ркэт
~) средняя рыночная цена
base ~ (бэйс ~) базисная цена
base ~ schedule (бэйс ~ ске́джюл)
прейскурант базисных цен
best ~ (бэст ~) лучшая цена
best possible ~ (бэст по́ссибл ~)
наилучшая возможная цена
better ~ (бэ́ттэр ~) наилучшая
цена

blanket ~ (бла́нкэт ~) цена со
всеми надбавками
breakdown ~s (брэ́йкдоун ~с) цена
с разбивкой по позициям
buyer's ~ (ба́йэрз ~) цена
покупателя, цена, выгодная для
покупателей
cash ~ (каш ~) цена за наличные,
цена при уплате наличными
CIF ~ list (си-ай-эф ~ лист)
прейскурант с ценами СИФ
closing ~ (кло́синг ~) цена при
закрытии биржи
commodity ~ (коммо́дити ~) цена
товара, цена на товар
comparable ~s (ко́мпарабл ~с)
сопоставимые цены
comparison of ~s (компэ́йрисон оф
~с) сопоставление цен
competitive ~ (компэ́титив ~)
конкурирующая цена
concrete {solid} ~ (ко́нкрит
{со́лид} ~) конкретная цена
conditional ~ (конди́шнал ~)
условная цена
confirmation of a ~ (конфирмэ́йшн
оф а ~) подтверждение цены
confirmed ~s (конфи́рмд ~с)
подтверждённые цены
constant ~ (ко́нстант ~)
неизменная цена
consumer ~s (консу́мэр ~с) цены
на потребительские товары
cost-related ~s (кост-рилэ́йтэд
~с) переменные цены
contract ~ (ко́нтракт ~)
договорная цена, контрактная
цена, цена по контракту
conventional ~ (конвэ́ншнал ~)
обычная цена
correct ~ (коррэ́кт ~) правильная
цена
corrected ~ (коррэ́ктэд ~)
скорректированная цена
corresponding ~ (коррэспо́ндинг
~) соответствующая цена
cost ~ (кост ~) цена
производства
cost plus ~ (кост плюс ~) цена с
приплатой
current ~ (ку́ррэнт ~) текущая
цена
dealer ~ (ди́лэр ~) дилерская
цена
deduction from ~ (диду́кшн фром
~) вычет из цены, удержание из
цены

delivered ~ (дэли́вэрд ~) цена, включающая расходы по доставке, цена с доставкой
demand ~ (дима́нд ~) цена спроса
desired ~ (диса́йрд ~) желаемая цена
detailed ~s (ди́тэйлд ~с) подробная цена
determination of a ~ (дитэрмина́йшн оф а ~) определение цены
deviation of ~s from value (дивиа́йшн оф ~с фром ва́лю) отклонения цен от стоимости
difference in ~s (ди́ффэрэнс ин ~с) разница в ценах
discount ~ (ди́скоунт ~) цена со скидкой
domestic market ~ (доме́стик ма́ркэт ~) цена внутреннего рынка
drop in securities ~s (дроп ин сэкю́ритиз ~с) падение курса ценных бумаг
dual ~ (ду́ал ~) двойная цена
dumping ~ (да́мпинг ~) бросовая цена, демпинговая цена
duty-paid ~ (дю́ти-пэйд ~) цена, включающая пошлину
end-user ~ (энд-ю́зэр ~) цена, предоставляемая конечному потребителю
equilibrium ~ (икуили́бриум ~) сбалансированная цена, конъюнктурная цена
equivalent ~ (икуи́валэнт ~) эквивалентная цена
error in a ~ (э́ррор ин а ~) ошибка в цене
escalating ~s (э́скалэйтинг ~с) растущие цены
escalation of ~s (эскала́йшн оф ~с) эскалация цен
established ~ (эста́блишд ~) установленная цена
establishment of ~s (эста́блишмэнт оф ~с) установление цен
estimated total ~ (э́стиматэд то́тал ~) предварительная итоговая цена
exact ~ (экза́кт ~) точная цена
exchange ~ (эксчэ́йндж ~) биржевая цена
export ~ (э́кспорт ~) экспортная цена
external ~s (экстэ́рнал ~с) внешнеторговые цены

extra ~ (э́кстра ~) особая цена
factory ~ (фа́ктори ~) фабричная цена
fair ~ (фэйр ~) подходящая цена, сходная цена
falling ~s (фа́ллинг ~с) снижающиеся цены
"fancy" ~ (фа́нси ~) дутая цена {pejorative}
final ~ (фа́йнал ~) окончательная цена
firm ~ (фирм ~) твёрдая цена
fixed ~ (фиксд ~) постоянная цена, фиксированная цена
flexible ~ (флэ́ксибл ~) гибкая цена
fluctuating ~ (флу́кчуэйтинг ~) колеблющаяся цена
FOB ~s list (эф-о-би́ ~с лист) прейскурант с ценами ФОБ
free market ~ (фри ма́ркэт ~) цена свободного рынка
full ~ (фул ~) полная цена
global ~ (гло́бал ~) глобальная цена
government-set ~s (го́вэрнмэнт-сэт ~с) государственные цены
gross ~ (грос ~) валовая цена
growth of ~s (гро θ оф ~с) рост цен
guaranteed ~ (гяранти́д ~) гарантированная цена
guideline ~ (га́йдлайн ~) ведущая цена
high ~ (хай ~) высокая цена
highest ~ (ха́йэст ~) высшая цена, самая высокая цена
identical ~ (айдэ́нтикал ~) одинаковая цена
import ~ (и́мпорт ~) импортная цена, цена на импортные товары
in bond ~ (ин бонд ~) цена без включения пошлины
increased ~s (инкри́сд ~с) возросшие цены
indicated ~ (и́ндикэйтэд ~) указанная цена
individual ~ (индиви́дюал ~) отдельная цена
inflated ~s (инфлэ́йтэд ~с) вздутые цены
inflexible ~ (инфлэ́ксибл ~) негибкая цена
instability of ~s (инстаби́лити оф ~с) неустойчивость цен
international ~ (интэрна́шэнал ~) международная цена

invoice ~ (и́нвойс ~) фактурная цена

invoice unit ~ (и́нвойс ю́нит ~) фактурная цена за единицу товара

issue ~ (и́шю ~) выпускная цена

itemized ~ (а́йтэмайзд ~) позиционная цена

landed ~ (ла́ндэд ~) цена с выгрузкой на берег

limit ~ (ли́мит ~) предельная цена

list ~ (лист ~) цена по прейскуранту

local ~ (ло́кал ~) местная цена

local market ~ (ло́кал ма́ркэт ~) цена местного рынка

loco ~ (ло́ко ~) цена локо

low ~ (ло́у ~) низкая цена

lowest ~ (ло́уэст ~) самая низкая цена

lumpsum ~ (ла́мпсум ~) паушальная цена

maladjustment of ~s (маладжа́стмэнт оф ~с) несоответствие в ценах

manufacturer's ~ (манюфа́кчурэрз ~) цена завода-изготовителя

manufacturer's suggested ~ (манюфа́кчурэрз суджэ́стэд ~) цена, предлагаемая изготовителем

marked ~ (маркд ~) обозначенная цена

market ~ (ма́ркэт ~) рыночная цена

market ~ trend (ма́ркэт ~ трэнд) тенденция рыночных цен

maximum ~ (ма́ксимум ~) максимальная цена

method of calculation of ~s (мэ́θод оф калкюлэ́йшн оф ~с) метод калькуляции цен

minimum ~ (ми́нимум ~) минимальная цена

moderate ~ (мо́дэрат ~) доступная цена, невысокая цена, умеренная цена

monopoly ~ (моно́поли ~) монопольная цена

net ~ (нэт ~) цена нетто

new ~s (нью ~с) новые цены

nominal ~ (но́минал ~) нарицательная цена, номинальная цена

normal ~ (но́рмал ~) нормальная цена

offering ~ (о́фферинг ~) предлагаемая цена

official ~ (оффи́шл ~) официальная цена

officially posted ~ (оффи́шлли по́стэд ~) официально объявленная цена

opening ~ (о́пэнинг ~) цена при открытии биржи

original ~s (ори́джинал ~с) первоначальные цены

outside ~ (о́утсайд ~) крайняя цена

packing ~ (па́ккинг ~) цена тары

parity ~ (па́рити ~) паритетная цена

parity of ~s (па́рити оф ~с) соотношение цен

payment of mutually agreed ~s (пэ́ймэнт оф мю́чуалли агри́д ~с) платёж по согласованным ценам

piece ~ (пис ~) штучная цена

posted ~ (по́стэд ~) справочная цена

pre-increase ~ (при-инкри́с ~) цена до повышения

preferential ~ (прэфэрэ́ншл ~) льготная цена

preliminary ~ (прили́минэри ~) предварительная цена

premium ~ (при́миум ~) цена выше номинала

present-day ~ (прэ́ззэнт-дэй ~) цена дня

prevailing ~ (привэ́йлинг ~) преобладающая цена, существующие цены

produce ~s (про́дюс ~с) цена на сельскохозяйственные продукты

producer's ~ (продю́сэрз ~) цена производителя

profitable ~ (про́фитабл ~) выгодная цена

prohibitive ~s (прохи́битив ~с) недоступные цены

published ~ (па́блищд ~) публикуемая цена

purchase ~ (пу́рчас ~) закупочная цена, покупная цена

quarterly ~ review (куа́ртэрли ~ ривю́) ежеквартальный пересмотр цен

quoted ~ (куо́тэд ~) котировальная цена

raw material ~s (ра́у мати́риал ~с) цена на сырьевые товары

real ~ (рил ~) действительная цена

realizable ~ (ри́лайзабл ~) реализационная цена
reasonable ~ (ри́зонабл ~) обоснованная цена, разумная цена
received ~ (риси́вд ~) полученная цена
recommended ~s (рэкомме́ндэд ~с) рекомендуемые цены
redemption ~ (риде́мпшн ~) выкупная цена
reduced ~ (риди́сд ~) сниженная цена
regulated ~s (рэ́гюлэйтэд ~с) регулируемые цены
relative ~ (рэ́латив ~) относительная цена
resale ~ (ри́сэйл ~) цена при перепродаже
reserve ~ (рисе́рв ~) отправная цена, резервируемая цена
restriction of ~s (ристри́кшн оф ~с) ограничение цен
retail ~ (ри́тэйл ~) розничная цена
rounding off of ~s (ро́ундинг офф оф ~с) округление цен
satisfactory ~s (сатисфа́ктори ~с) удовлетворительные цены
sales ~ (сэйлз ~) продажная цена
salvage ~ (са́лвэдж ~) цена спасательных работ
seasonal ~s (си́зонал ~с) сезонные цены
seller's asking ~ (сэ́ллэрз а́скинг ~) цена, требуемая продавцом
sellers' ~ (сэ́ллэрз ~) цена, выгодная для продавцов
selling ~ (сэ́ллинг ~) запродажная цена
set ~ (сэт ~) назначенная цена
settlement ~ (сэ́тлмэнт ~) расчётная цена
share ~ (шэйр ~) курс акций
sliding-scale ~s (сла́йдинг-скэйл ~с) скользящие цены
spot ~ (спот ~) цена при условии немедленной оплаты наличными, цена по кассовым сделкам
spot market ~ (спот ма́ркэт ~) цена с немедленной сдачей
stability of ~s (стаби́лити оф ~с) стабильность цен
stable ~ (стэйбл ~) стабильная цена
standard of ~s (ста́ндард оф ~с) масштаб цен

standard ~ (ста́ндард ~) стандартная цена
standard list ~ (ста́ндард лист ~) прейскурантная цена
starting ~ (ста́ртинг ~) начальная цена
steady ~ (стэ́ди ~) устойчивая цена
stipulated ~ (сти́пюлэйтэд ~) обусловленная цена, условленная цена
subscription ~ (субскри́пшн ~) подписная цена
supply ~ (суппла́й ~) цена поставки
target ~ (та́ргэт ~) плановая цена
tariff ~ (та́риф ~) тарифная цена, цена по тарифу
tender ~ (тэ́ндэр ~) цена, предложенная на торгах, цена при продаже с торгов
terminal ~s (тэ́рминал ~с) цена по срочным сделкам
to accept a ~ (ту аксэ́пт а ~) принимать цену
to agree on ~s (ту агри́ он ~с) согласовать цены
to agree to a ~ (ту агри́ ту а ~) согласиться на цену
to apply ~s to ... (ту аппла́й ~с ту ...) применять цену к
to ask a ~ (ту аск а ~) просить цену
to base a ~ on ... (ту бэйс а ~ он ...) основывать цену на
to bid up a ~ (ту бид ап а ~) набавлять цену {at auction}
to break down a ~ (ту брэйк до́ун а ~) разбивать цену
to buy at the ~ of ... (ту бай ат θи ~ оф ...) покупать по цене
to buy at less than asking ~ (ту бай ат лэс θан а́скинг ~) купить по цене, ниже предложенной
to calculate a ~ (ту ка́лкюлэйт а ~) калькулировать цену
to calculate ~s (ту ка́лкюлэйт ~с) рассчитывать цены
to charge a ~ (ту чардж а ~) взимать цену
to charge an extra ~ (ту чардж ан э́кстра ~) посчитать отдельную цену
to come to an agreement on a ~ (ту ком ту ан агри́мэнт он а ~) договориться о цене

to **compare** ~s (ту компэ́йр ~с) сравнивать цены

to **confirm** a ~ (ту конфи́рм а ~) подтверждать цену

to **correct** ~s (ту корр́экт ~с) корректировать цены

to **cover** a ~ **increase** (ту ко́вэр а ~ инкри́с) покрывать увеличение цены

to **deduct from** a ~ (ту диду́кт фром а ~) вычитать из цены, удерживать из цены

to **depend on** a ~ (ту дипэ́нд он а ~) зависеть от цены

to **determine** a ~ (ту дит́эрмин а ~) определять цену

to **dictate** ~s (ту ди́ктэйт ~с) диктовать цены

to **double the** ~ (ту дабл θи ~) увеличивать цену в 2 раза

to **economize on** ~s (ту ико́номайз он ~с) экономить на ценах

to **effect** ~ **competition** (ту иффэ́кт ~ компэти́шн) создать конкуренцию по ценам

to **effect payment at** a ~ **of** (ту иффэ́кт пэ́ймэнт ат а ~ оф) производить расчёт по цене

to **establish** a ~ (ту эст́аблиш а ~) устанавливать цену

to **exceed** a ~ (ту экси́д а ~) превышать цену

to **exert influence on** ~s (ту экз́эрт и́нфлуэнс он ~с) оказывать влияние на цены

to **finalize** a ~ (ту фа́йналайз а ~) окончательно договориться о цене

to **fix** a ~ (ту фикс а ~) фиксировать цену

to **freeze** ~s (ту фриз ~с) замораживать цены

to **get** a ~ (ту гэт а ~) получать цену

to **give** a **firm** ~ (ту гив а фирм ~) назначать твёрдую цену

to **grant** a **special** ~ (ту грант а спэшл ~) предоставлять особую цену

to **include in** a ~ (ту инкл́юд ин а ~) включать в цену товара

to **increase the** ~ (ту инкри́с θи ~) повышать цену

to **increase** ~s (ту инкри́с ~с) увеличивать цены

to **increase the** ~ **by** ... % (ту инкри́с θи ~ бай ... %) увеличивать цену на ... %

to **indicate** a ~ (ту и́ндикэйт а ~) указывать цену

to **itemize** ~s (ту а́йтэмайз ~с) показывать цену каждой позиции в отдельности

to **justify** ~s (ту джа́стифай ~с) обосновывать цены

to **lower** a ~ (ту ло́уэр а ~) занижать цену

to **lower** ~s (ту ло́уэр ~с) снижать цены

to **maintain** ~s (ту мэйнт́эйн ~с) сохранять цены

to **negotiate** a ~ (ту нэго́шиэйт а ~) договариваться о цене

to **obtain** a **lower** (ту обт́эйн а ло́уэр ~) добиться более высокой цены

to **pay the** ~ (ту пэй θи ~) платить цену

to **prevent** a **decline in** ~s (ту привэ́нт а дикла́йн ин ~с) препятствовать падению цен

to **publish** ~s (ту па́блиш ~с) опубликовывать цены

to **quote** a ~ (ту куо́т а ~) котировать цену

to **raise the** ~ (ту рэйз θи ~) поднимать цену

to **rationalize** ~s (ту ра́шналайз ~с) упорядочить цены

to **realize** a ~ (ту ри́лайз а ~) выручать цену, реализовать цену

to **recalculate** ~s (ту рика́лкюлэйт ~с) пересчитывать цены

to **recover** a ~ (ту рико́вэр а ~) возмещать цену

to **reduce** a ~ (ту ридю́с а ~) уменьшать цену

to **regulate** ~s (ту р́эгюлэйт ~с) регулировать цены

to **review** ~s (ту ривю́ ~с) пересматривать цены

to **revise** ~s **downwards** (ту рива́йс ~с до́унуардз) пересматривать цены в сторону понижения

to **revise** ~s **upwards** (ту рива́йз ~с у́пуардс) пересматривать цены в сторону повышения

to **sell at** a ~ **of** ... (ту сэл ат а ~ оф ...) продавать по цене

to **set a low** ~ (ту сэт а лóу ~)
назначать низкую цену
to **set a** ~ (ту сэт а ~)
назначать цену
to **set a lower** ~ (ту сэт а лóуэр
~) назначать более низкую цену
to **settle a** ~ (ту сэтл а ~)
урегулировать цену
to **sink in** ~ (ту синк ин ~)
падать в цене
to **sink sharply in** ~ (ту синк
шáрпли ин ~) падать резко в цене
to **specify a** ~ (ту спэ́сифай а ~)
уточнять цену
to **stabilize** ~s (ту стэ́йбилайз
~с) стабилизировать цены
to **supply goods at ...** ~s (ту
суппла́й гудз ат ... ~с)
поставлять товар по ценам
to **support** ~s (ту суппóрт ~с)
поддерживать цены
to **sustain a** ~ (ту сустэ́йн а ~)
удерживать цену
to **triple the** ~ (ту трипл θи ~)
увеличивать цену в 3 раза
to **undercut** ~s (ту андэркýт ~с)
сбивать цены
to **verify** ~s (ту вэ́рифай ~с)
проверять цены
today's ~ (тудэ́йз ~) сегодняшняя
цена
total ~ (тóтал ~) общая цена
trade ~ (трэйд ~) торговая цена
transfer ~s (трáнсфэр ~с)
внутрифирменные цены
typical ~ (тúпикал ~) типичная
цена
uncontrollable ~s (анконтрóллабл
~с) неконтролируемые цены
undercharged ~ (андэрчáрджд ~)
заниженная цена
uniform ~ (ю́ниформ ~) единая
цена
unit ~ (ю́нит ~) единичная
расценка
unrealistic ~s (анрилúстик ~с)
нереальные цены
unstable ~s (анстэ́йбл ~с)
неустойчивые цены
wholesale ~ (хóлсэйл ~) оптовая
цена, цена для оптовых
покупателей
world gross ~ (уóрлд грос ~)
валовая цена на мировом рынке
world market ~ (уóрлд мáркэт ~)
цена мирового рынка
zone ~ (зон ~) зональная цена

~s **adjusted for shipping rates**
(~с аджáстэд фор шúппинг рэйтс)
цена с поправкой на фрахтовые
ставки
~ **adjustment** (~ аджáстмэнт)
изменение цены, поправка в цене
~s **apply to ...** (~с аппла́й ту
...) цены применимы к
~s **are falling** (~с ар фáллинг)
цены падают
~s **are subject to change at any
time** (~с ар сáбджэкт ту чэйндж
ат áни тайм) цены подлежат
изменению в любое время
~s **are subject to change without
warning** (~с ар сáбджэкт ту
чэйндж уиθóут уáрнинг) цены
подлежат изменению без
предупреждения
~s **are up ... %** (~с ар ап ... %)
цены повысились на ... %
~s **are up** (~с ар ап) цены
повысились
~ **at the current exchange rate**
(~ ат θи кýррэнт эксчэ́йндж рэйт)
цена по валютному курсу
~ **behavior** (~ бихэ́йвиор)
движение цен
~ **C&F** (~ си энд эф) цена КАФ
~ **calculation** (~ калкюлэ́йшн)
калькуляция цен
~ **category** (~ кáтэгори)
категория цен
~ **ceiling** (~ сúлинг) лимит цен
~ **chargeable to the buyer** (~
чáрджабл ту θи бáйэр) цена,
относимая за счёт покупателя
~ **competition** (~ компэтúшн)
конкуренция по ценам
~ **computation** (~ компютэ́йшн)
расчёт цен
~ **control** (~ контрóл) контроль
над ценами
~ **differentiation** (~
диффэрэншиэ́йшн) дифференциация
цен
~ **discrepancy** (~ дискрэ́панси)
ножницы цен {price scissors}
~ **divergence** (~ дивэ́рджэнс)
расхождения цен
~ **does not include VAT** (~ дуз
нот инклю́д ват) цены не включают
НДС
~ **escalation** (~ эскалэ́йшн)
скольжение цен
~ **evaluation** (~ ивалюэ́йшн)
оценка цены

~ **ex-barge** (~ экс-бардж) цена с баржи, цена франко-баржа
~ **ex-factory** (~ экс-фа́ктори) цена франко-завод
~ **ex-quay** (~ экс-кэй) цена франко-пристань
~ **ex-ship** (~ экс-шип) цена с судна, цена франко-судно
~ **ex-warehouse** (~ экс-уэ́рхаус) цена со склада, цена франко-склад
~ **excluding packing** (~ эксклю́динг па́ккинг) цена без упаковки
~ **FAS** (~ эф-эй-эс) цена ФАС, цена франко вдоль борта
~ **FAS port of shipment designated by seller** (~ эф-эй-эс порт оф ши́пмэнт дэ́зигнэйтэд бай сэ́ллэр) цена ФАС порт отгрузки, указанный продавцом
~ **fixing** (~ фи́ксинг) фиксация цен
~ **fluctuations** (~ флукчуэ́йшнс) колебания цен
~ **FOB** (~ эф-о-би) цена ФОБ
~ **FOB factory unboxed** (~ эф-о-би фа́ктори анбо́ксд) цена ФОБ без фабричной упаковки
~ **FOB stowed** (~ эф-о-би сто́уд) цена ФОБ со штивкой
~ **FOR** (~ эф-о-ар) цена ФОР, цена франко-вагон
~ **formula** (~ фо́рмюла) формула цены
~ **FOT** (~ эф-о-ти) цена ФОТ
~ **free at border** (~ фри ат бо́рдэр) цена франко граница
~ **freeze** (~ фриз) замораживание цена
~**s have dropped** (~с хэв дропд) цены понизились
~ **in convertible currency** (~ ин конвэ́ртибл ку́ррэнси) цена в валюте
~ **including freight and duty** (~ инклю́динг фрэйт энд дю́ти) цена, включающая фрахт и пошлину
~ **including VAT** (~ инклю́динг ват) цены включают НДС
~ **index** (~ и́ндэкс) индекс цен, указатель цен
~ **indicated in the invoice** (~ и́ндикэйтэд ин θи и́нвойс) цена, указанная в счёте-фактуре
~ **information** (~ информэ́йшн) информация о ценах

~ **is subject to change** (~ из са́бджэкт ту чэйндж) цена подлежит изменению
~ **less discount** (~ лэс ди́скоунт) цена за вычетом скидки
~ **level** (~ лэ́вэл) уровень цен
~ **level adjustment** (~ лэ́вэл аджа́стмэнт) поправка на изменение цены
~ **list** (~ лист) прейскурант, ценник
~ **marking** (~ ма́ркинг) маркировка цен
"~**s may be annulled or changed without warning**" (~с мэй би анну́лд ор чэйнджд уиθо́ут уа́рнинг) цены могут быть аннулированы или изменены без предупреждения
~ **mechanism** (~ мэ́канизм) механизм цен
~ **negotiations** (~ нэгоши́эйшнс) переговоры по ценам
~ **norms** (~ нормз) нормативы цен
~ **of an offer** (~ оф ан о́ффэр) цена предложения
~ **of freight** (~ оф фрэйт) цена фрахта
~ **of the previous transaction** (~ оф θи при́виос транса́кшн) цена предыдущей сделки
~ **on day of shipment** (~ он дэй оф ши́пмэнт) цена на день отгрузки
~ **on the world market** (~ он θи уо́рлд ма́ркэт) цена на мировом рынке
~ **per item** (~ пэр а́йтэм) поштучная цена
~ **per metric ton** (~ пэр мэ́трик тон) цена за метрическую тонну
~ **per piece** (~ пэр пис) цена за штуку
~ **per pound** (~ пэр по́унд) цена за фунт
~ **per set** (~ пэр сэт) цена за комплект
~ **per unit** (~ пэр ю́нит) цена за единицу товара
~ **per weight unit** (~ пэр уэйт ю́нит) цена за весовую единицу
~ **plus mark-up** (~ плюс марк-уп) цена с надбавкой
~ **quoted in an offer** (~ куо́тэд ин ан о́ффэр) цена, указанная в предложении

~ **regulation** (~ рэгюлэ́йшн) регулирование цен
~s **remain stable** (~с римэ́йн стэ́йбл) цены остаются устойчивыми
~s **remain unchanged** (~с римэ́йн анчэ́йнджд) цены остаются без изменений
~s **remain unsettled** (~с римэ́йн ансэ́тлд) цены остаются неустойчивыми
~ **renegotiation** (~ ринэгоши́эйшн) пересмотр цен, совместный пересмотр цен
~ **review** (~ ривю́) обзор цен
~ **revision formula** (~ риви́жн фо́рмюла) формула пересмотра цен
~ **roll back** (~ рол бак) возврат к прежним ценам
~ **savings** (~ сэ́йвингс) экономия на ценах
~ **spiral** (~ спа́йрал) спираль цен
~ **stability** (~ стаби́лити) устойчивость цен
~ **stabilization** (~ стэйбилизэ́йшн) стабилизация цен
~ **structure** (~ стру́кчур) структура цен
~s **subject to confirmation** (~с са́бджэкт ту конфирмэ́йшн) цены подлежат подтверждению
~ **supports** (~ суппо́ртс) поддержание цен
~ **tag** (~ таг) этикетка с ценой
~ **trend** (~ трэнд) тенденция цен
~s **under consideration** (~с а́ндэр консидэрэ́йшн) обсуждаемые цены
~ **valid until** ... (~ ва́лид унти́л ...) цена действительна до
~ **variation clause** (~ вариэ́йшн клауз) пункт об изменении цен
~ **war** (~ уар) война цен
~ **without obligation** (~ уи#о́ут облигэ́йшн) цена без обязательства
Pricing (пра́йсинг) расценка, ценообразование
acceptable ~ (аксэ́птабл ~) приемлемая расценка
competitive ~ (компэ́титив ~) конкурентное ценообразование
cost plus ~ (кост плюс ~) назначение цен с надбавкой
net ~ (нэт ~) назначение цен нетто
progressive ~ (прогрэ́ссив ~) прогрессивная расценка

ramp ~ (рамп ~) непомерная цена
zonal ~ (зо́нал ~) зональное установление цен
~ **data** (~ да́та) данные о ценах
~ **practice** (~ пра́ктис) практика ценообразования
Primacy (пра́ймаси) примат
~ **of domestic law** (~ оф домэ́стик лау) примат внутреннего права
~ **of international law** (~ оф интэрна́шэнал лау) примат международного права
Primage (пра́ймадж) вознаграждение капитану с фрахта, прибавка к фрахту
Prime (прайм) первоклассный, первый
~ **banker's acceptance** (~ ба́нкэрз аксэ́птанс) первоклассный вексель, акцептованный банком
~ **manufacturing** ~ **cost** (~ манюфа́кчуринг ~ кост) фабрично-заводская себестоимость
~ **cost** (~ кост) себестоимость
Principal (при́нсипал) комитент, доверитель, крупный {adj.}, принцип
~s принципиальные положения
basic ~ (бэ́йсик ~) основной принцип
constitutional ~ (конститу́шнал ~) конституционный принцип
general ~s **of law** (джэ́нэрал ~с оф лау) общие принципы права
generally recognized ~s (джэ́нэралли рэ́когнайзд ~с) общепризнанные принцип
national-territorial ~ (на́шэнал-тэррито́риал ~) национально-территориальный принцип
territorial ~ (тэррито́риал ~) территориальный принцип
~ **of mutuality** (~ оф мючуа́лити) принцип взаимности
Print (принт) копия, оттиск
to ~ (ту ~) печатать
~ **of a drawing** (~ оф а дра́уинг) копия чертежа
Printed (при́нтэд) напечатанный
~ **matter** (~ ма́ттэр) печатное издание
Printing (при́нтинг) печать
Priority (прайо́рити) первоочерёдность, порядок срочности, привилегия, приоритет
convention ~ (конвэ́ншн ~) конвенционный приоритет
first ~ (фэрст ~) первая очередь

governmental ~ (говэрнмэ́нтал ~)
государственный приоритет
high ~ (хай ~) высокий приоритет
partial ~ (паршл ~) частичный
приоритет
preferential ~ (прэфэрэ́ншл ~)
льготный приоритет
to claim ~ (ту клэйм ~)
претендовать на приоритет
~ of an invention (~ оф ан
инвэ́ншн) приоритет на
изобретение
~ of authorship (~ оф а́уθоршип)
авторский приоритет
~ of filing (~ оф фа́йлинг)
приоритет подачи заявки
Prisoner (при́зонэр) заключённый
captivity of ~s of war
(капти́вити оф ~с оф уар) военный
плен
political ~ (поли́тикал ~)
политический заключённый
to take ~ (ту тэйк ~) взять в
плен
Privacy (пра́йваси) тайна
Private (пра́йват) закрытый, личный,
частный
Privately-owned (пра́йватли-о́унд)
частновладельческий
Privilege (при́вилэдж) льгота,
преимущество, привилегия
consular ~ (ко́нсюлар ~)
консульская привилегия
diplomatic ~ (диплома́тик ~)
дипломатическая привилегия
royal ~ (ро́йял ~) королевская
привилегия
stop-off ~ (стоп-офф ~) льгота
на остановку в пути следования
transit ~ (тра́нзит ~) транзитная
льгота
to grant ~s (ту грант ~с)
предоставлять льготы
to secure ~s (ту сикю́р ~с)
добиваться льгот
Prize (прайз) приз
Pro rata (про ра́та) пропорционально
~ freight (~ фрэйт)
пропорциональная часть фрахта
Probationer (пробэ́йшнэр) стажёр
Problem (про́блэм) проблема,
трудность
money ~s (мо́ни ~с) денежные
затруднения
payment ~s (пэ́ймэнт ~с)
платёжные трудности

serious ~s (си́риос ~с) серьёзные
трудности
to cause ~s (ту ка́уз ~с)
вызывать трудности
to create ~s (ту криэ́йт ~с)
создавать трудности
Procedural (проси́дюрал)
процессуальный
Procedure (проси́дюр) метод,
методика, порядок, процедура
administrative ~ (адми́нистрэйтив
~) административный порядок
appellate ~ (аппэ́лат ~)
процедура обжалования
arbitral ~ (а́рбитрал ~)
арбитражный порядок
arbitration ~ (арбитрэ́йшн ~)
порядок арбитража
attestation ~ (аттэстэ́йшн ~)
порядок аттестации
clear-cut ~ (клир-кут ~)
определённый метод
constitutional ~ (конститу́шнал
~) конституционный порядок,
конституционная процедура
conventional ~ (конвэ́ншнал ~)
обычная Методика
correct ~ (коррэ́кт ~) правильная
методика
criminal ~ (кри́минал ~)
уголовный порядок
design ~ (диза́йн ~) методика
проектирования
diplomatic ~ (диплома́тик ~)
дипломатический порядок
dispute resolution ~ (диспю́т
рэзолю́шн ~) порядок разрешения
споров
election ~ (илэ́кшн ~) порядок
выборов
electoral ~ (элэ́кторал ~)
процедура выборов
established ~ (эста́блищд ~)
установленный порядок
estimation ~ (эстимэ́йшн ~)
оценка методики
extrajudicial ~ (э́кстраджюди́шл
~) внесудебный порядок
in accordance with the ~ (ин
акко́рданс уиθ θи ~) в
соответствии с порядком
**in accordance with the
established ~** (ин акко́рданс уиθ
θи эста́блищд ~) в установленном
порядке
international legal ~
(интэрна́шэнал ли́гал ~)

международный юридический
порядок
judicial ~ (джюди́шл ~) судебная
процедура
legal ~ (ли́гал ~) законный
порядок
normative ~ (но́рматив ~)
нормативный порядок
notarial ~ (нотэ́йриал ~)
нотариальный порядок
operating ~ (о́пэрэйтинг ~)
методика работы, порядок
эксплуатации
parliamentary ~ (парламэ́нтари ~)
парламентская процедура
patent issuance ~ (па́тэнт и́шюанс
~) порядок выдачи патентов
payment ~ (пэ́ймэнт ~) порядок
платежей
preliminary ~ (прили́минэри ~)
предварительная процедура
proper ~ (про́пэр ~) надлежащая
методика
quality control ~ (куа́лити
контро́л ~) методика контроля
качества
ratification ~ (ратифике́йшн ~)
порядок ратификации
recommended ~ (рэкоммэ́ндэд ~)
рекомендуемая методика
reconciliation ~ (рэконсилие́йшн
~) порядок примирения
revised ~ (рива́йзд ~)
пересмотренная методика
rule of court ~ (рул оф ко́урт ~)
судебное правило
simplified ~ (си́мплифайд ~)
упрощённый порядок
special ~ (спэшл ~) особая
методикаб специальный порядок,
специальная процедура
standard ~ (ста́ндард ~)
стандартная методика
survey ~ (су́рвэй ~) методика
обследования
testing ~ (тэ́стинг ~) методика
испытаний
to adhere to a ~ (ту адхи́р ту а
~) придерживаться методики
to adopt a ~ (ту адо́пт а ~)
принять методику
to review a ~ (ту ривю́ а ~)
пересмотреть метод
voting ~ (во́тинг ~) порядок
голосования

~ for making a claim (~ фор
мэ́йкинг а клэйм) порядок
предъявления претензии
Proceeding (проси́динг)
преследование, прения,
производство, процесс
administrative ~ (адми́нистрэйтив
~) административное
преследование, административное
производство, административное
судопроизводство
adversarial ~s (адвэрсэ́йриал ~с)
спорное производство
appellate ~s (аппэ́лат ~с)
апелляционное производство
arbitral ~s (а́рбитрал ~с)
арбитражный процесс ,
арбитражное разбирательство
arbitration ~s (арбитрэ́йшн ~с)
арбитражное производство
civil ~s (си́вил ~с) гражданское
производство, гражданский
процесс, гражданское
судопроизводство
closed court ~s (клозд ко́урт ~с)
закрытое судебное
разбирательство
court martial ~s (ко́урт маршл
~с) военное производство
criminal ~s (кри́минал ~с)
уголовное судопроизводство,
уголовный процесс
disciplinary ~ (ди́сиплинари ~)
дисциплинарное преследование
divorce ~s (диво́рс ~с)
бракоразводный процесс
international ~s (интэрна́шэнал
~) международный процесс
investigatory ~s (инвэ́стигатори
~) следственное производство
judicial ~ (джюди́шл ~) судебное
производство
legal ~s (ли́гал ~с) судебное
разбирательство, судебный
процесс, судопроизводство
legislative ~ (лэ́джислэйтив ~с)
законодательный процесс
non-adversarial ~s (нон-
адвэрсэ́йриал ~с) бесспорное
производство
oral ~s (о́рал ~с) устное
производство, устное
судопроизводство
public ~s (па́блик ~с) открытое
разбирательство
summary ~s (са́ммари ~с)
суммарное производство

to institute ~s (ту институт ~с) начать производство по делу

to institute criminal ~s (ту институт криминал ~с) привлекать к уголовной ответственности

~s behind closed doors (~с бихайнд клозд дорз) процесс при закрытых дверях

Proceeds (просидс) выручка, вырученная сумма, приход

estimated ~s (эстимэйтэд ~с) предполагаемая выручка

export ~s (экспорт ~с) выручка от экспорта

gross ~s (грос ~с) валовая выручка

net ~s (нэт ~с) чистая выручка

remittance of sale ~s (римиттанс оф сэйл ~с) перевод выручки от продажи

to expend the ~s (ту экспэнд θи ~с) расходовать выручку

to receive the ~s of a sale (ту рисив θи ~с оф а сэйл) получать выручку от продажи

to surrender export ~s (ту суррэндэр экспорт ~с) сдавать выручку от экспорта товаров

~s from contract work (~с фром контракт уорк) выручка по договорным работам

~s of sales (~с оф сэйлз) выручка от продажи {от реализации}

Process (просэс) процесс

budget ~ (баджэт ~) бюджетный процесс

construction ~ (конструкшн ~) методы строительства

manufacturing ~ (манюфакчуринг ~) производственный процесс

patented ~ (патэнтэд ~) запатентованный процесс

technological ~ (тэкнолоджикал ~) технологический метод

Processing (просэсинг) обработка, переработка

secondary ~ (сэкондари ~) вторичная обработка

Proclaim, to ~ (проклэйм, ту ~) объявлять [perfective: объявить], оглашать [perfective: огласить], провозглашать

Proclamation (прокламэйшн) провозглашение

~ of a blockade (~ оф а блокэйд) объявление блокады

Procrastinate, to ~ (прокрастинэйт, ту ~) промедлить

Procrastination (прокрастинэйшн) отлагательство

Procure, to ~ (прокюр, ту ~) приобретать

Procurement (прокюрмэнт) приобретение

state ~ (стэйт ~) заготовительный {adj.}, заготовка

state ~s (стэйт ~с) государственные закупки

~ officer (~ оффисэр) заготовитель

Procurer (прокюрэр) поставщик, сводник {pimp}

Procuring (прокюринг) поставка, сводничество {pimping}

Produce (продюс) продукты

requisitioning of ~ (рэкуизишининг оф ~) продразвёрстка

to ~ (ту ~) выпускать, производить

Produced (продюсд) представленный

Producer (продюсэр) производитель, фирма-производитель

agricultural ~ (агрикулчурал ~) сельскохозяйственный производитель

Product (продукт) изделие, продукт, товар

advertised ~s (адвэртайзд ~с) рекламируемый товар

agricultural ~ (агрикулчурал ~) сельскохозяйственный продукт

chemical ~s (кэмикал ~с) химические товары

competing ~ (компитинг ~) конкурирующий продукт

cotton ~s (коттон ~с) хлопчатобумажные товары

development of new export ~s (дивэлопмэнт оф нью экспорт ~с) освоение новых товаров для экспорта

fashionable ~s (фашнабл ~с) модные товары

final ~ (файнал ~) конечный продукт

finished ~ (финишд ~) готовый продукт

fodder ~s (фоддэр ~с) кормовые продукты

foreign-made ~s (форэн-мэйд ~с) заграничные товары

fur ~s (фур ~с) пушной товар
gross ~ (грос ~) валовой продукт
gross domestic ~ (грос домэстик ~) валовой внутренний продукт
gross national ~ (грос нашэнал ~) валовой национальный продукт
grouping of ~s (групинг оф ~с) группировка товаров
high-quality ~ (хай-куалити ~) высококачественный продукт, доброкачественное изделие
imported ~ (импортэд ~) импортный продукт
industrial ~ (индустриал ~) промышленный продукт
industrial ~s (индустриал ~с) промышленные товары
invoice cost of a ~ (инвойс кост оф а ~) фактурная стоимость товара
manufactured ~ (манюфакчурд ~) промышленное изделие
new ~s (нью ~с) новые товары
patented ~ (патэнтэд ~) патентованное изделие
pharmaceutical ~s (фармасутикал ~с) фармацевтические товары
pre-packaging of food ~s (припакаджинг оф фуд ~с) расфасовка пищевых товаров
promising ~ (промисинг ~) перспективный товар
to advertise ~s (ту адвэртайз ~с) рекламировать товар
to launch a ~ (ту лаунч а ~) начать выпуск продукции
trade name of a ~ (трэйд нэйм оф а ~) торговое название товара
unbreakable ~s (анбрэйкабл ~с) небьющиеся товары
~ brand (~ бранд) марка товара
~ image (~ имадж) имидж товара
Production (продакшн) выпуск продукции, продукция, произведение, производство
aerospace ~ (эйроспэйс ~) авиапромышленность
agricultural ~ (агрикулчурал ~) сельскохозяйственное производство
assembly line ~ (ассэмбли лайн ~) поточное производство
automobile ~ (аутомобил ~) автомобилестроение
batch ~ (батч ~) серийный выпуск, серийное производство

commodity ~ (коммодити ~) товарное производство
curtailed ~ (куртэйлд ~) сокращённое производство
deficit ~ (дэфисит ~) дефицитная продукция
domestic ~ (домэстик ~) внутреннее производство
finished ~ (финишд ~) готовая продукция
imported ~ (импортэд ~) импортная продукция
industrial ~ (индустриал ~) промышленное производство
local ~ (локал ~) местная продукция
mass ~ (мас ~) массовое производство
national ~ (нашэнал ~) национальное производство
potential ~ (потэншл ~) потенциал производства
renovation of ~ (рэновэйшн оф ~) обновление производства
seasonal ~ (сизонал ~) сезонное производство
to coordinate annual ~ (ту координэйт аннюал ~) согласовывать годовой выпуск продукции
to increase manufacturing ~ (ту инкрис манюфакчуринг ~) наращивать выпуск продукции
to organize ~ (ту органайз ~) осваивать выпуск продукции
to speed up ~ (ту спид ап ~) ускорять выпуск
unfinished ~ (анфинишд ~) незавершённое производство
world ~ (уорлд ~) мировое производство
~ of documents (~ оф докюмэнтс) представление документов
~ of high quality goods (~ оф хай куалити гудз) выпуск высококачественных товаров
~ of high quality products (~ оф хай куалити продуктс) выпуск продукции, высококачественная
~ of proof (~ оф пруф) представление доказательств
Productive (продактив) производительный
Productivity (продуктивити) продуктивность, производительность

agricultural ~ (агрику́лчурал ~)
продуктивность сельского
хозяйства
higher ~ (ха́йэр ~) высшая
производительность
industrial ~ (инду́стриал ~)
промышленная производительность
~ of labor (~ оф лэ́йбор)
производительность труда
Profession (профэ́шн) профессия
by ~ (бай ~) по профессии
legal ~ (ли́гал ~) адвокатура
~ association (~ ассоси́эйшн)
сословие
Profit (про́фит) выгода, прибыль
actual ~ (а́кчуал ~) фактическая
прибыль
anticipated ~ (анти́сипэйтэд ~)
вероятная прибыль
balance sheet ~ (ба́ланс шит ~)
балансовая прибыль
distributable ~ (дистри́бютабл ~)
распределяемая прибыль
distributed ~ (дистри́бютэд ~)
распределенная прибыль
entrepreneurial ~
(энтрэпрэнью́риал ~)
предпринимательская прибыль
false ~ (фалс ~) фиктивная
прибыль
for the sake of ~ (фор θи сэйк
оф ~) ради выгоды
gross ~ (грос ~) валовая прибыль
loss of ~ insurance (лос оф ~
иншю́ранс) страхование упущенной
выгоды
monopoly ~ (моно́поли ~)
монопольная прибыль
net ~ (нэт ~) чистая прибыль
net ~ ratio (нэт ~ рэ́йшио)
коэффициент рентабельности
realized ~ (ри́лайзд ~)
реализованная прибыль
repatriation of ~s (рипатри́эйшн
оф ~с) репатриация доходов
speculative ~ (спэ́кюлатив ~)
спекулятивная прибыль
taxable ~ (та́ксабл ~) облагаемая
прибыль
to realize ~ (ту ри́лайз ~)
реализовать прибыль
to repatriate ~s (ту рипа́триэйт
~с) репатриировать доходы
trade ~ (трэйд ~) торговая
прибыль
undistributed ~ (андистри́бютэд
~) нераспределённая прибыль

unexpected ~ (анэкспэ́ктэд ~)
непредвидимая прибыль
usurious ~ (юсу́риос ~)
ростовщическая прибыль
windfall ~ (уи́ндфал ~) случайная
прибыль
Profitability (профитаби́лити)
доходность, прибыльность,
рентабельность
determination of ~ (дитэрмин́эйшн
оф ~) определение экономичности
Profitable (про́фитабл) прибыльный,
рентабельный
insufficiently ~ (инсуффи́шэнтли
~) малорентабельный
marginally ~ (ма́рджиналли ~)
малодоходный, малоприбыльный
to turn out to be ~ (ту турн о́ут
ту би ~) оказаться выгодным
Profitably (про́фитабли) с выгодой
Pro forma (про фо́рма) проформа
Progeny (про́джэни) потомок
Program (про́грам) программа
advertising ~ (а́двэртайзинг ~)
рекламное шоу
capital investment ~ (ка́питал
инвэ́стмэнт ~) программа
капиталовложений
economic ~ (эконо́мик ~)
экономическая программа
expansion ~ (экспа́ншн ~)
программа экспансии
feasible ~ (фи́зибл ~) выполнимая
программа
government ~ (го́вэрнмэнт ~)
правительственная программа
investment ~ (инвэ́стмэнт ~)
программа инвестиций
manufacturing ~ (манюфа́кчуринг
~) производственная программа
~ of duties to be carried out
pursuant to the contract(~ оф
дю́тиз ту би кэ́йррид о́ут пурсу́ант
ту θи ко́нтракт) программа
выполнения работ по контракту
price support ~ (прайс суппо́рт
~) гарантирование цен
promotion ~ (промо́шн ~) план
мероприятий по стимулированию
сбыта
to continue with a ~ (ту конти́ню
уиθ а ~) продолжать выполнение
программы
to launch a ~ (ту лаунч а ~)
приступать к выполнению
программы

to start work in accordance with the ~ (ту старт уóрк ин аккóрданс уиθ θи ~) начинать работы по выполнению программы
Progress (прóгрэс) прогресс, продвижение
   social ~ (сошл ~) социальный прогресс
   ~ **of the construction site** (~ оф θи констрýкшн сайт) ход выполнения работ на строительной площадке
   ~ **of implementation** (~ оф имплэмэнтэ́йшн) ход выполнения
   ~ **of the implementation of an agreement** (~ оф θи имплэмэнтэ́йшн оф ан агри́мэнт) ход выполнения соглашения
   ~ **of implementation of a contract** (~ оф имплэмэнтэ́йшн оф а кóнтракт) ход выполнения контракта
   ~ **of a project** (~ оф а прóджэкт) ход выполнения проекта
   ~ **under a program** (~ áндэр а прóграм) ход выполнения программы
Progressive (прогрэ́ссив) прогрессивный
   ~ **taxation** (~ таксэ́йшн) прогрессия обложения
Prohibit, to ~ (прохи́бит, ту ~) запрещать
Prohibition (прохиби́шн) запрещение, запретительное постановление
   export ~ (э́кспорт ~) запрещение вывоза
   import ~ (и́мпорт ~) запрещение ввоза
Project (прóджэкт) объект, проект, строительство
   major ~ (мэ́йджор ~) крупномасштабный проект
   model ~ (мóдэл ~) типовой проект
Projected (проджэ́ктэд) планируемый
Projection (проджэ́кшн) прогноз на ближайшее будущее, проект
Proletarian (пролэтэ́йриан) пролетарий, пролетарский {adj.}
Proletarianization (пролэтэ́йрианизэ́йшн) пролетаризация
Proletariat (пролэтэ́йриат) пролетариат
   industrial ~ (индý стриал ~) промышленный пролетариат
   rural ~ (рý рал ~) сельский пролетариат

Prolong, to ~ (пролóнг, ту ~) продлевать, удлинять
Prolongation (пролонгэ́йшн) продление
Prolonged (пролóнгд) длительный
Promise (прóмис) обещание, обязательство
   unconditional ~ (анконди́шнал ~) безусловное обязательство {e.g. in contract}
Promising (прóмисинг) многообещающий
Promissory (прóмиссори) долговой
   ~ **note** (~ нот) долговое обязательство, долговая расписка
Promote, to ~ (промóт, ту ~) выдвигать, продвигать
   to ~ **sales** (ту ~ сэйлз) содействовать увеличению запродаж
Promoter (промóтэр) устроитель, лицо, содействующее какому-либо мероприятию
   fair ~ (фэйр ~) устроитель ярмарки
   foreign ~ (фóрэн ~) иностранный устроитель
Promotion (промóшн) поощрение, продвижение, продвижение по службе, реклама, рекламная деятельность
   export ~ (э́кспорт ~) поощрение экспорта
   sales ~ (сэйлз ~) продвижение товара на рынок, кампания по организации и стимулированию сбыта
   sales ~ **agency** (сэйлз ~ э́йджэнси) учреждение, содействующее продаже товара
   ~ **expenses** (~ экспэ́нсэз) расходы по учреждению акционерного общества {of joint stock company}
   ~ **in rank** (~ ин ранк) повышение ранга
Prompt (промпт) немедленный, своевременный, срочный
Promptness (прóмптнэс) срочность
Promulgation (промулгэ́йшн) опубликование
   ~ **of a law** (~ оф а лáу) опубликование закона
   ~ **of a regulation** (~ оф а рэгюлэ́йшн) принятие регламента
Pronouncement (пронóунсмэнт) объявление

~ **of sentence** (~ оф сэ́нтэнс)
объявление приговора
Proof (пруф) доказательство
~ **of damages** (~ оф да́мэджэз)
доказательство ущерба
~ **of interest** (~ оф и́нтэрэст)
доказательство
заинтересованности
~ **of novelty** (~ оф но́вэлти)
доказательство новизны
~ **of quality** (~ оф куа́лити)
доказательство качества
Propaganda (пропага́нда) пропаганда
~ **center** (~ сэ́нтэр) парткабинет
Propagandist (пропага́ндист)
пропагандист
Proper (про́пэр) надлежащий,
правильный
Properly (про́пэрли) надлежащим
образом, правильно
Property (про́пэрти) владение,
имущественные средства, имущество,
собственность
acquired ~ (аккуа́йрд ~)
приобретённое имущество
agricultural ~ (агрику́лчурал ~)
сельскохозяйственное имущество
church ~ (чурч ~) церковные
имущества
collectivized ~ (колле́ктивайзд
~) обобществленное имущество
common ~ (ко́ммон ~) общая
собственность
communal ~ (коммю́нал ~)
имущество общин
community ~ (каммю́нити ~) общее
имущество, общая собственность
супругов, общность имуществ
супругов, супружеская
собственность
cooperative ~ (коо́пэратив ~)
кооперативная собственность
cooperative landed ~ (коо́пэратив
ла́ндэд ~) кооперативная
земельная собственность
copyright ~ (ко́пирайт ~)
авторская собственность
divided ~ (дива́йдэд ~)
раздельное имущество
domestic ~ (доме́стик ~) домашнее
имущество
encumbered ~ (энка́мбэрд ~)
обременённое имущество
exclusive ~ (эксклю́сив ~)
исключительная собственность
family ~ (фа́мили ~) семейное
имущество

inalienable ~ (инэ́йлиэнабл ~)
неотчуждаемое имущество
industrial ~ (инду́стриал ~)
промышленная собственность
inherited ~ (инхэ́ритэд ~)
наследственное имущество
insured ~ (иншу́рд ~)
застрахованное имущество
intellectual ~ (интэлле́кчуал ~)
интеллектуальная собственность
intestate ~ (интэ́стэйт ~)
имущество без наследника
landed ~ (ла́ндэд ~) земельная
собственность
leased ~ (лисд ~) арендованное
имущество
leasehold ~ (ли́схолд ~)
арендованная земельная
собственность
literary ~ (ли́тэрари ~)
литературная собственность
literary and artistic ~
(ли́тэрари энд арти́стик ~)
литературная и художественная
собственность
mortgaged ~ (мо́ргэджд ~)
заложенное имущество
movable ~ (мо́вабл ~) движимое
имущество {chattels}
nationalized ~ (на́шэналайзд ~)
национализированное имущество
partnership ~ (па́ртнэршип ~)
имущество товарищества
personal ~ (пэ́рсонал ~) личное
имущество, личная собственность,
собственное имущество
pledged ~ (плэджд ~) заложенное
имущество
poorly managed ~ (пу́рли ма́наджд
~) бесхозяйственно содержимое
имущество
private ~ (пра́йват ~) частное
имущество, частная собственность
public ~ (па́блик ~) народная
собственность, публичное
имущество
real ~ (рил ~) недвижимая
собственность
sequestered ~ (сэкуэ́стэрд ~)
секвестрированное имущество
state ~ (стэйт ~)
государственное имущество
state-owned ~ (стэйт-о́унд ~)
государственная собственность
tangible ~ (та́нджибл ~) реальная
собственность

to acquire ~ (ту аккуа́йр ~) приобрести в собственность
undivided ~ (андива́йдэд ~) безраздельная собственность
vesting of a ~ interest (вэ́стинг оф а ~ и́нтэрэст) введение во владение
~ encumbered by a mortgage (~ энка́мбэрд бай а мо́ргэдж) имущество, обременённое ипотекой
~ of a commune (~ оф а ко́ммюн) имущество общин
~ of an individual (~ оф ан индиви́дюал) имущество отдельного лица
~ of a legal entity (~ оф а ли́гал э́нтити) имущество юридического лица
Propiska (пропи́ска) прописка {residence permit}
Proportion (пропо́ршн) доля, часть
sizable ~ (са́йзабл ~) значительная доля
small ~ of profits (смал ~ оф про́фитс) небольшая часть прибыли
Proposal (пропо́зал) предложение
compromise ~ (ко́мпромайз ~) компромиссное предложение
concrete ~ (ко́нкрит ~) конкретное предложение
package ~ (па́кэдж ~) комплексное предложение
Propose, to ~ (пропо́з, ту ~) предлагать
Proposition (пропози́шн) предложение
practical ~ (пра́ктикал ~) реальное
Proprietor (пропра́йэтор) владелец, собственник, хозяин {male}, хозяйка {female}
sole ~ (сол ~) единоличный владелец
~ of an enterprise (~ оф ан э́нтэрпрайз) владелец предприятия
Proprietorship (пропра́йэторшип) владение, предпринимательство
sole ~ (сол ~) единоличное владение, единоличное предприятие
Propriety (пропра́йэти) правильность
Prosecute, to ~ (про́сэкют, ту ~) преследовать
to ~ (ту ~) преследовать в судебном порядке
Prosecution (просэкю́шн) преследование, судебное преследование

criminal ~ (кри́минал ~) уголовное преследование
Prosecutor (про́сэкютэр) прокурор
general ~ {attorney general} (джэ́нэрал ~ {атто́рни джэ́нэрал}) генеральный прокурор
office of the ~ (о́ффис оф θи ~) прокуратура
office of the municipal ~ (о́ффис оф θи мюни́сипал ~) городская прокуратура
public ~ (па́блик ~) прокурор
Prospect (про́спэкт) перспектива
economic ~s (эконо́мик ~с) экономические перспективы
market ~s (ма́ркэт ~с) рыночные перспективы
to ~ (ту ~) разведывать [perfective: разведать]
Prospecting (про́спэктинг) разведка
Prospective (проспэ́ктив) перспективный
Prospectus (проспэ́ктус) проспект
Prostitute (про́ститут) проститутка
registered ~ (рэ́джистэрд ~) зарегистрированная проститутка
Prostitution (проститу́шн) проституция
Protect, to ~ (протэ́кт, ту ~) защищать [perfective: защитить], покровительствовать, сберегать
Protection (протэ́кшн) защита, ограждение, охрана
consular ~ (ко́нсюлар ~) консульская защита
copyright ~ (ко́пирайт ~) охрана авторского права
diplomatic ~ (дипло́матик ~) дипломатическая защита
double ~ (дабл ~) двойная охрана
international ~ (интэрна́шэнал ~) международная защита
international legal ~ (интэрна́шэнал ли́гал ~) международно-правовая защита
judicial ~ (джюди́шл ~) судебная защита
legal ~ (ли́гал ~) законная защита, правовая защита, правовая охрана
patent ~ (па́тэнт ~) охрана патента, патентная защита, патентная охрана
special ~ (спэшл ~) специальная защита
temporary ~ (тэ́мпорари ~) временная защита

~ of the border (~ оф θи бо́рдэр) охрана границы
~ of children (~ оф чи́лдрэн) охрана детей
~ of industrial drawings and models (~ оф инду́стриал дра́уингс энд мо́дэлз) охрана промышленных рисунков и моделей
~ of industrial property (~ оф инду́стриал про́пэрти) охрана промышленной собственности
~ of interests (~ оф и́нтэрэстс) защита интересов
~ of an invention (~ оф ан инвэ́ншн) защита изобретения
~ of minorities (~ оф майно́ритиз) защита меньшинств
~ of property (~ оф про́пэрти) защита имущества
~ of rights (~ оф райтс) защита прав, ограждение прав, охрана прав
~ of rights to an invention (~ оф райтс ту ан инвэ́ншн) охрана прав на изобретения
~ of the rights of minors (~ оф θи райтс оф ма́йнорз) охрана прав несовершеннолетних
~ of trademarks (~ оф трэ́йдмаркс) охрана товарных знаков и торговых марок
Protectionism (протэ́кшнизм) протекционизм
Protectionist (протэ́кшнист) протекционист
Protectorate (протэ́кторат) протекторат
colonial ~ (коло́ниал ~) колониальный протекторат
international ~ (интэрна́шэнал ~) международный протекторат
Protégé (про́тэжэй) ставленник
Protest (про́тэст) опротестование, протест
collective ~ (коллэ́ктив ~) коллективный протест
ship's ~ (шипс ~) морской протест об авариях
to ~ (ту ~) опротестовать
~ of a bill (~ оф а бил) опротестование векселя
Protestation (протэстэ́йшн) опротестование
Protocol (про́токол) протокол, протокольный {adj.}
final ~ (фа́йнал ~) итоговый протокол

ship's ~ (шипс ~) морской протокол
supplementary ~ (сапплэмэ́нтари ~) дополнительный протокол
temporary ~ (тэ́мпорари ~) временный протокол
to ~ (ту ~) протоколировать
~ of agreement (~ оф агри́мэнт) протокол соглашения
~ of change order (~ оф чэйндж о́рдэр) протокол о внесении изменений
Prototype (про́тотайп) прототип
Provenance (про́вэнанс) происхождение
Provide, to ~ (ту ~) обеспечивать
to ~ at no cost (прова́йд, ту ~ ат но кост) безвозмездно предоставлять
Provided that ... (прова́йдд θат ...) при условии, что если
Providing (прова́йдинг) предоставление
~ a credit (~ а крэ́дит) предоставление кредита
~ a credit under pledge (~ а крэ́дит а́ндэр плэдж) предоставление кредита под залог
~ a credit under pledge of securities (~ а крэ́дит а́ндэр плэдж оф сэкю́ритиз) предоставление кредита под залог ценных бумаг
~ overdraft facilities (~ о́вэрдрафт фаси́литиз) предоставление овердрафта
Province (про́винс) провинция
"the ~s" (θи ~с) провинция
Provision (прови́жн) обеспечение, оказание, положение, резерв, снабжение, ~s провиант
additional ~s (адди́шнал ~) дополнительное положение
basic ~ of the law (бэ́йсик ~ оф θи ла́у) основное положение права
constitutional ~ (конститу́шнал ~) конституционное положение
contract ~ (ко́нтракт ~) договорное положение
conversion ~ (конвэ́ржн ~) оговорка об обмене акций
fundamental ~s of a contract (фундамэ́нтал ~с оф а ко́нтракт) основные условия договора
in accordance with the ~s (ин акко́рданс уиθ θи ~с) в соответствии с условиями

legislative ~ (лэ́джислэйтив ~)
законодательное положение
material ~ {of a contract}
(мати́риал ~) существенная
оговорка
overall ~s (овэра́л ~с) общие
положения
policy ~s (по́лиси ~с) условия
полиса
printed ~s (при́нтэд ~с)
напечатанные условия
probable ~s (про́бабл ~с)
вероятные условия
special ~ (спэшл ~) специальная
оговорка
standard ~s (ста́ндард ~с)
стандартные условия
to deviate from contractual ~s
(ту ди́виэйт фром контра́кчуал ~с)
отступать от условий контракта
to enjoy warranty ~s (ту энджо́й
уа́рранти ~с) пользоваться
условиями гарантии
to offer warranty ~s (ту о́ффэр
уа́рранти ~с) предоставлять
условия гарантии
to waive ~s (ту уэ́йв ~с)
отказываться от условий
under the ~s of clauses (а́ндэр
θи ~с оф кла́узэз) по условиям
статей
uninterrupted ~ (анинтэрру́птэд
~) бесперебойное
warranty ~s (уа́рранти ~с)
условие гарантии
written ~ (ри́ттэн ~) письменная
оговорка
written ~s (ри́ттэн ~с)
записанные условия
~ of a contract (~ оф а
ко́нтракт) положение контракта,
пункт договора
~s of a contract (~с оф а
ко́нтракт) условия контракта
~ of credit arrangements (~ оф
крэ́дит аррэ́йнджмэнтс) кредитные
вложения
~ of goods (~ оф гудз)
обеспечение товарами
~ of housing (~ оф хо́узинг)
предоставление жилой площади
~ of know-how (~ оф но́у-ха́у)
выдача ноу-хау, предоставление
ноу-хау
~ of services (~ оф сэ́рвисэз)
оказание услуг, предоставление
услуг

~s on a vessel (~с он а вэ́ссэл)
провиант на судне
Provisional (прови́жнал) временный
Proviso (прова́йзо) оговорка,
оговорка к договору, условие
Provocateur, agent ~ (провакату́р,
э́йджэнт ~) провокатор
Provocation (провокэ́йшн) провокация
military ~ (ми́литари ~) военная
провокация
Provoke, to ~ (прово́к, ту ~)
вызывать
to ~ (ту ~) спровоцировать
Proxy (про́кси) доверенное лицо,
доверенность, передача голоса,
полномочие
by ~ (бай ~) по доверенности
to sign by ~ (ту сайн бай ~)
подписывать по доверенности
Pseudonym (су́доним) псевдоним
Public (па́блик) государственный
{adj.}, общественность,
общественный {adj.}, публичный
{adj.}
~ intoxication (~ интоксикэ́йшн)
появление в пьяном виде
~ law (~ ла́у) публичное право
Publication (пабликэ́йшн) выпуск,
издание, оглашение, опубликование,
публикация
daily ~ (дэ́йли ~) дневной выпуск
not for ~ (нот фор ~) не
подлежит оглашению
official ~ (оффи́шл ~)
официальное опубликование,
официальное издание
periodical ~ (пэрио́дикал ~)
периодическое издание
trade ~ (трэйд ~) отраслевая
публикация
weekly ~ (уи́кли ~) еженедельный
выпуск
~ of a court decision (~ оф а
ко́урт диси́жн) оглашение решения
суда
~ of a decision (~ оф а диси́жн)
опубликование решения
~ release (~ рили́с) выпуск из
печати
Publicist (па́блисист) публицист
Publicity (пабли́сити) огласка,
публичность
Publicly (па́бликли) публично
Publish, to ~ (па́блиш, ту ~)
издать, публиковать
Publisher (па́блишэр) издатель

Punctilious (пунктӥлиос)
щепетильный
Punctuality (пункчуа́лити) точность
Punishment (пу́нишмэнт) расправа
    most lenient ~ (мост лӥниэнт ~)
    низший предел наказания
    most severe ~ (мост сэви́р ~)
    высший предел наказания
Punitive (пю́нитив) карательный
    ~ **measure** (~ мэ́жюр) репрессия
Purchase (пу́рчас) купля, покупка,
покупной
    additional ~ (адди́шнал ~)
    дополнительная покупка
    advantageous ~ (адвантэ́йджэс ~)
    преимущественная покупка
    speculative ~ (спэ́кюлатив ~)
    спекулятивная покупка
    to ~ (ту ~) купить
    ~ **and sale** (~ энд сэйл) купля-
    продажа
    ~ **for cash** (~ фор каш) покупка
    за наличный расчёт
    ~ **on credit** (~ он крэ́дит)
    покупка в кредит
    ~ **on the exchange** (~ он θи
    эксчэ́йндж) покупка на бирже
Purchased (пу́рчасд) купленный
Purchaser (пу́рчасэр) покупатель
    bulk ~ (булк ~) крупный
    потребитель
    direct ~ (дайрэ́кт ~)
    непосредственный покупатель
Purchasing (пу́рчасинг) закупка
    ~ **agent** (~ э́йджэнт) закупщик
    ~ **broker** (~ бро́кэр) брокер по
    покупкам
Pure (пюр) чистый
    ~ **interest** (~ и́нтэрэст) нетто-
    процент
Purge (пурдж) очистка
    to carry out a ~ (ту кэ́рри о́ут а
    ~) произвести очистку
Purpose (пу́рпос) намерение
Purposeful (пу́рпосфул) целевой
Pursue, to ~ (пурсу́, ту ~)
провожать
Pursuit (пурсу́т) занятие, погоня
    remunerative ~ (римю́нэратив ~)
    доходное занятие
    temporary ~ (тэ́мпорари ~)
    временное занятие
Put (пут) опцион
Putsch (путч) путч
Pyramid (пи́рамид) пирамида
    ~ **scheme** (~ ским) пирамида

Q

Q.C. (кю-си) {quality control}
контроль качества
    ~ **inspector** (~ инспэ́ктор)
    браковщик
Qualification (куалификэ́йшн)
квалификация, ценз
    age ~ (эйдж ~) возрастной ценз
    educational ~ (эджюкэ́йшнал ~)
    образовательный ценз
    necessary ~ (нэсэса́ри ~)
    необходимая квалификация
    property ~ (про́пэрти ~)
    имущественный ценз
    tax ~ (такс ~) налоговый ценз
Qualified (куа́лифайд)
квалифицированный, ограниченный
    highly-~ expert (ха́йли-~
    э́кспэрт) специалист высокой
    квалификации
Qualify, to ~ (куа́лифай, ту ~)
квалифицировать
Qualifying (куа́лифайинг)
квалификационный
Qualitative (куа́литэйтив)
качественный
Quality (куа́лити) качественный,
качество {*adj.*}
    acceptable ~ (аксэ́птабл ~)
    приемлемое качество
    appropriate ~ (аппро́приат ~)
    надлежащее качество
    average ~ (а́вэрэдж ~) среднее
    качество
    base ~ (бэйс ~) базисное
    качество
    best ~ (бэст ~) лучшее качество
    business ~/**ies** (би́знэс ~из)
    деловые качества
    change in ~ (чэйндж ин ~)
    изменение качества
    cheap ~ (чип ~) дешёвое качество
    commercial ~ (коммэ́ршл ~)
    коммерческое качество
    excellent ~ (э́ксэллэнт ~)
    отличное качество
    expert's ~ **report** (э́кспэртс ~
    рипо́рт) экспертиза по качеству
    export ~ (э́кспорт ~) экспортное
    качество
    first-class ~ (фэрст-класс ~)
    первоклассное качество
    guaranteed ~ (гяранти́д ~)
    гарантированное качество

high ~ (хай ~) высокое качество, доброкачественность, доброкачественный {adj.}

higher ~ (хáйэр ~) высшее качество

inferior ~ (инфúриор ~) недоброкачественность, ненадлежащее качество

low ~ (лóу ~) низкое качество

operational ~ (опэрэ́йшнал ~) эксплуатационные качества

optimal ~ (óптимал ~) оптимальное качество

overall ~ (овэрáл ~) общее качество

poor ~ (пур ~) недоброкачественный

product ~ analysis (прóдукт ~ анáлисис) анализ качества продукции

sample for ~ analysis (сампл фор ~ анáлисис) образец продукта для оценки качества

standard ~ (стáндард ~) нормативное качество

standard of ~ (стáндард оф ~) норма качества

stipulated ~ (стúпюлэйтэд ~) качество, обусловленное договором

technical ~ (тэ́кникал ~) техническое качество

to accept goods on the basis of ~ (ту аксэ́пт гудз он θи бэ́йсис оф ~) принимать товар по качеству

to change the ~ (ту чэйндж θи ~) изменять качество

to engage in ~ control (ту энгэ́йдж ин ~ контрóл) контролировать качество

to evaluate ~ (ту ивáлюэйт ~) оценивать качество

to guarantee high ~ (ту гяранти́ хай ~) гарантировать высокое качество

to provide ~ (ту провáйд ~) обеспечивать качество

to stipulate ~ (ту стипюлэ́йт ~) обусловить качество

tolerance ~ (тóлэранс ~) допустимое качество

unimpeachable ~ (анимпи́чабл ~) безупречное качество

unsatisfactory ~ (ансатисфáктори ~) неудовлетворительное качество

very best ~ (вэ́ри бэст ~) самое лучшее качество

violation of ~ standards (вайолэ́йшн оф ~ стáндардс) нарушение стандарта качества

~ analysis (~ анáлисис) оценка качества

~ certificate (~ сэрти́фикат) свидетельство о качестве

~ check (~ чэк) проверка качества

~ clearance (~ кли́ранс) аттестат качества

~ control (~ контрóл) контроль качества

~ control inspection (~ контрóл инспэ́кшн) инспекция по качеству

~ control table (~ контрóл тэ́йбл) таблица контроля качества

~ guarantee (~ гяранти́) гарантия качества

~ indicator (~ и́ндикэйтор) показатель качества

~ inspection (~ инспэ́кшн) бракераж

~ specification (~ спэсифике́йшн) спецификация качества

Quantitative (куáнтитэйтив) количественный

Quantity (куáнтити) количество, численность, число

annual ~ (áннюал~) ежегодное количество

appreciable ~ (аппри́шабл ~) ощутимое количество

available ~ (авэ́йлабл ~) наличное количество

contracted ~ (кóнтрактэд ~) контрактное количество

in limited ~ (ин ли́митэд ~) в ограниченном количестве

initial ~ (ини́шл ~) начальное количество

innumerable ~ (инню́мэрабл ~) бесчисленное количество

insignificant ~ (инсигни́фикант ~) незначительное количество

insufficient ~ (инсуффи́шэнт ~) недостаточное количество

large ~ (лардж ~) большое количество

limited ~ (ли́митэд ~) ограниченное количество

maximum possible ~ (мáксимум пóссибл ~) максимальное возможное количество

mean ~ (мин ~) средняя величина

ordered ~ (о́рдэрэд ~) заказное
количество
overall ~ (овэра́л ~) общее
количество
record ~ (рэ́корд ~) рекордное
количество
required ~ (рикуа́йрд ~)
необходимое количество
significant ~ (сигни́фикант ~)
значительное количество
small ~ (смал ~) малое
количество
stipulated ~ (сти́пюлэйтэд ~)
обусловленное количество
supplementary ~ (сапплэмэ́нтари
~) добавочное количество
tolerance ~ (то́лэранс ~)
допустимое количество
total ~ (то́тал ~) общее число
unspecified ~ (анспэ́сифайд ~)
неуточнённое количество
~ delivered (~ дили́вэрд)
выгруженное количество
~ discount (~ ди́скоунт) скидка
за количество
Quarantine (куа́рантин) карантин,
карантинный {adj.}
lifting of ~ (ли́фтинг оф ~)
снятие карантина
to introduce a ~ (ту интродю́с эй
~) вводить карантин
to release from ~ (ту рили́с фром
~) выпустить из карантина
to subject to ~ (ту са́бджэкт ту
~) подвергнуть карантину
under ~ (а́ндэр ~) в карантине
~ certificate (~ сэрти́фикат)
свидетельство о снятии карантина
Quarter (куа́ртэр) квартал, монета
25 сентов {США}, ~s круги
current accounting ~ (ку́ррэнт
акко́унтинг ~) текущий квартал
to be several ~s past due (ту би
сэ́вэрал ~с паст ду) задолжать за
несколько кварталов
Quartering (куа́ртэринг) постой
Quarterly (куа́ртэрли)
ежеквартальный, квартальный
Quasi-state (куа́зи-стэйт)
полугосударственный
Quay (кэй) набережная, пристань,
причал
discharging ~ (дисча́рджинг ~)
разгрузочная набережная
free alongside ~ {FAQ} (фри
алонгса́йд ~) франко набережная

~ terms (~ тэрмз) условия
погрузки и выгрузки у стенки
Question (куэ́стён) вопрос, проблема
to raise a ~ (ту рэ́йиз эй ~)
поднимать вопрос
Queue (кю) очередь
Quit-rent (куи́трэнт) оброк
Quota (куо́та) квота, контингент,
норма
abolition of a ~ (аболи́шн оф а
~) отмена квоты, отмена
контингента
differential ~ (диффэрэ́ншл ~)
дифференцированная норма
established ~ (эста́блишд ~)
установленная квота
export ~ (э́кспорт ~) экспортная
квота, экспортные контингенты
foreign exchange ~ (фо́рэн
эксчэ́йндж ~) валютный лимит
global ~ (гло́бал ~) общая квота
immigration ~ (иммигрэ́йшн ~)
иммиграционная квота
import ~ (и́мпорт ~) импортная
квота, ввозные контингенты,
импортные контингенты
International Monetary Fund ~
{IMF} (интэрна́шнл мо́нэтари фунд
~ {ай-эм-эф}) квота в
Международном Валютном Фонде
introduction of ~s (интроду́кшн
оф ~с) введение квот
maximum ~ (ма́ксимум ~)
максимальная квота
minimum ~ (ми́нимум ~)
минимальная квота
quantitative ~ (куа́нтитэйтив ~)
количественная квота
sea freight ~ (си фрэйт ~) квота
морского фрахта
tariff ~ (та́риф ~) тарифная
квота
tax ~ (такс ~) налоговая квота
to fulfill the ~ (ту фу́лфил θи
~) выполнять норму
to impose a system of ~s (ту
импо́з эй си́стэм оф ~с) применять
систему квот
to overfulfill the ~ (ту
о́вэрфулфил θи ~) перевыполнять
норму
~ allocation (~ аллокэ́йшн)
квотирование
~ allocation of foreign exchange
(~ аллокэ́йшн оф фо́рэн эксчэ́йндж)
квотирование иностранной валюты

Quotation (куотэ́йшн) котировка,
назначение, предложение, расчёт
    additional ~ (ади́шнал ~)
    дополнительная котировка
    closing ~ (кло́синг ~) котировка
    при закрытии биржи
    detailed ~ (ди́тэйлд ~) подробная
    котировка
    enclosed ~ (энкло́зд ~)
    приложенная котировка
    exchange ~ (эксчэ́йндж ~)
    биржевая котировка
    exchange rate ~ (эксчэ́йндж рэ́йт
    ~) котировка курсов
    final ~ (фа́йнал ~) окончательная
    котировка
    firm ~ (фирм ~) твёрдая
    котировка
    foreign exchange ~ (фо́рэн
    эксчэ́йндж ~) валютная котировка
    itemized ~ (а́йтэмайзд ~)
    позиционная котировка
    market ~ (ма́ркэт ~) рыночная
    котировка
    nominal ~ (но́минал ~)
    номинальная котировка
    official ~ (оффи́шл ~)
    официальная котировка
    opening ~ (о́пэнинг ~) котировка
    при открытии биржа
    previous ~ (при́виес ~)
    предыдущая котировка
    pro forma ~ (про́ фо́рма ~)
    примерная котировка
    revised ~ (рива́йзд ~)
    пересмотренная котировка
    specimen ~ (спэ́симэн ~)
    ориентировочная котировка
    spot market ~ (спот ма́ркэт ~)
    котировка на товары с
    немедленной сдачей
    starting ~ (ста́ртинг ~)
    начальная котировка
    stock ~ (сток ~) котировка акций
    to consider a ~ (ту конси́дэр а
    ~) рассмотреть котировку
    ~ of prices (~ оф пра́йсэз)
    котировка цен, назначение цен
Quote (куо́т) предложение
    to ~ (ту ~) котировать {price,
    rate}
Quoted (куо́тэд) котировочный
    to be ~ (ту би ~) котироваться
    {on exchange, etc.}
Quoting (куо́тинг) котирование
    ~ of prices (~ оф пра́йсэз)
    котирование цен

R

Racism (рэ́йсизм) расизм
Racist (рэ́йсист) расист {person},
расистский {adj.}
Racketeer (ракэти́р) бандит-
вымогатель, ракэтир
Racketeering (ракэти́ринг)
вымогательство, ракэтирство
Radical (ра́дикал) радикал {person},
радикальный {adj.}
Radicalism (ра́дикализм) радикализм
Radio (рэ́йдио) радио
    ~ advertising (~ а́двэртайзинг)
    радиореклама
Raft (рафт) сплавной плот
    to ~ (ту ~) переплавить
Rail (рэйл) железнодорожный {adj.
of railway}, ограждение {for
protection, etc.}, рельс {of
railway}
    to install guard ~s (ту инста́л
    гард ~з) поставить ограждение
Railroad (рэ́йлрод) железная дорога,
железнодорожный {adj.}
Raion (райо́н) район {admin.
division of Russian Federation}
Raise (рэйз) повышение {gen.},
увеличение зарплаты {in pay}
    annual ~ (а́ннюал ~) ежегодная
    надбавка
    to ~ (ту ~) повышать
    ~ in pay (~ ин пэй) прибавка к
    заработной плате
    ~ in wages (~ ин уэ́йджэз)
    повышение заработной платы
Rally (ра́лли) оживление {e.g. stock
market}, слёт {meeting}
Range (рэ́йндж) ассортимент, выбор,
номенклатура
    broad ~ of goods (брод ~ оф
    гудз) широкий ассортимент
    commercial ~ of goods (комме́ршл
    ~ оф гудз) товарный ассортимент
    expanded ~ (экспа́ндэд ~)
    укрупнённая номенклатура
    expanding ~ (экспа́ндинг ~)
    растущая номенклатура
    fixed ~ (фиксд ~) закреплённая
    номенклатура
    to determine the ~ of goods (ту
    дэтэ́рмин θэ ~ оф гудз)
    определять номенклатуру товаров
    wide ~ (уа́йд ~) широкая
    номенклатура

~ **of goods** (~ оф гудз) выбор
товара
~ **of products** (~ оф про́дуктс)
сортамент
Rank (ранк) звание, разряд, ранг
civil service ~ (си́вил сэ́рвис ~)
служебный ранг
class ~ (класс ~) ранг
military ~ (ми́литэри ~) военное
звание
to demote in ~ (ту димо́т ин ~)
лишить военного звания
Rape (рэйп) изнасилование
to ~ (ту ~) изнасиловать
Rapprochement (раппрошмо́н)
сближение
Rate (рэйт) коэффициент, курс,
норма, ставка, тариф, темп
acceptable ~ of natural loss
(акцэ́птабл ~ оф на́тюрал лосс)
нормы естественной убыли
advertising ~ (а́двэртайзинг ~)
рекламный тариф
allowable ~ of depreciation
(алло́уэбл ~ оф дэприши́йшн)
норма амортизации
at the ~ of ... (ат θи ~ оф ...)
по курсу ...
at the established ~ (ат θи
эста́блишд ~) по установленной
норме
average ~ (а́вэрэдж ~) средняя
норма, средняя ставка
average annual ~ (а́вэрэдж а́ннюэл
~) средняя годовая ставка
baggage ~ (ба́ггэдж ~) багажный
тариф
base ~ (бэйс ~) базисный тариф
basing ~ (бэ́йсинг ~) начальный
тариф
birth ~ (берт ~) статистика
рождаемости
black market ~ (блэк ма́ркэт ~)
курс чёрного рынка
bridge ~ (бридж ~) промежуточный
тариф
capacity ~ (капа́сити ~)
коэффициент мощности
central bank ~ of exchange
(сэ́нтрал банк ~ оф эксчэ́йндж)
центральный курс
change in exchange ~ (чэйндж ин
эксчэ́йндж ~) изменение курса
class ~ (класс ~) классный тариф
closing ~ (кло́синг ~)
заключительный курс

combined ~ (комба́йнд ~)
комбинированный тариф
commission ~ (комми́шн ~)
комиссионная ставка
compulsory exchange ~
(компу́лсори ~) обязательный курс
conditional ~ (конди́шнал ~)
условный курс
conversion ~ (конвэ́ржн ~)
обменный курс
cross ~**s** (кросс ~с)
перекрещивающиеся курсы
currency exchange ~ (ку́ррэнси
эксчэ́йндж ~) валютный курс
current ~ (ку́ррэнт ~)
действующий тариф
daily ~ (дэ́йли ~) дневная норма
discount ~ (ди́скоунт ~) ставка
по учёту тратты, учётная ставка,
учётный курс
domestic ~ {of exchange on two
tier system} (доме́стик ~ {оф
эксчэ́йндж он ту тир си́стэм})
внутренний курс
dual ~ (ду́ал ~) двойная ставка
estimated ~**s** (э́стимэйтд ~с)
подсчитанные нормы
**exchange ~ as of the day of
actual payment** (эксчэ́йндж ~ ас
оф θи дэй оф а́кчуал пэ́ймэнт)
курс дня фактического платежа
exchange ~ mechanism (эксчэ́йндж
~ ме́ханизм) механизм валютных
курсов
exchange ~ of the day (эксчэ́йндж
~ оф θи дэй) курс дня
exchange ~ of the dollar
(эксчэ́йндж ~ оф θи до́ллар) курс
доллара
fall in the exchange ~ (фалл ин
θи эксчэ́йндж ~) падение курса
favorable ~ of exchange
(фэ́йворабл ~ оф эксчэ́йндж)
благоприятный курс
first ~ (фэрст ~) первого
разряда
fixed ~ (фиксд ~) твердая
ставка, фиксированный курс
flat ~ (флат ~) аккордная ставка
floating ~ (фло́тинг ~) плавающая
ставка
fluctuating exchange ~
(флу́ктуэйтинг эксчэ́йндж ~)
колеблющийся курс
**fluctuation in the currency
exchange** ~ (флуктуэ́йшн ин θи

кýрренси эксчэ́йндж ~) колебание курса валюты

fluctuation in the exchange ~ against the ruble (флуктуэ́йшн ин θи кýрренси эксчэ́йндж ~ аге́нст θи рубл) колебание курсов валют к рублю

free exchange ~ (фри эксчэ́йндж ~) свободный курс

freight ~ (фрэ́йт ~) грузовой тариф, фрахтовая ставка

full value ~ (фулл ва́лю ~) полноценный курс

going ~ (го́инг ~) действующая ставка, существующий курс

government-fixed ~ (го́вэрнмэнт-фи́ксд ~) такса

group ~ (груп ~) групповой тариф

growth of the exchange ~ (гро́ут оф θи эксчэ́йндж ~) рост курса

high ~ (хай ~) высокий курс

hourly ~ (а́урли ~) норма почасовая

increased ~ (инкри́сд ~) повышенная ставка

interest ~ (и́нтэрэст ~) процентная ставка

international ~ (интэрнэ́шнал ~) международный тариф

liner ~s (ла́йнэр ~с) линейный тариф

mail transfer ~ (мэйл тра́нсфэр ~) курс почтовых переводов

marginal ~ (ма́рджинал ~) предельная ставка

marine transport ~ (мари́н тра́нспорт ~) морской тариф

market ~ (ма́ркэт ~) рыночный курс

market interest ~ (ма́ркэт и́нтэрэст ~) уровень процента на денежном рынке

maximum ~ (ма́ксимум ~) максимальный курс

mean ~ of exchange (мин ~ оф эксчэ́йндж) средний курс

minimum ~ (ми́нимум ~) минимальная ставка, минимальный курс

monetary exchange ~ (мо́нэтэри эксчэ́йндж ~) денежный курс

mortality ~ (морта́лити ~) статистика смертности

net ~ {tariff} (нэт ~ {тэ́риф}) тарифная ставка с учётом скидок

nominal exchange ~ (но́минал эксчэ́йндж ~) номинальный курс

official exchange ~ (оффи́шал эксчэ́йндж ~) официальный курс

one-time ~ (уа́н-тайм ~) одноразовый тариф

open ~ (о́пэн ~) открытая ставка

pegged ~ (пэгд ~) привязанный курс

per diem ~ (пэр ди́эм ~) дневная ставка

piece ~ (пис ~) сдельная расценка

postal ~ (по́стал ~) почтовая ставка

posted ~ (по́стэд ~) справочный курс

preferential ~ (прэфэрэ́ншл ~) льготная ставка, преференциальная ставка

preferential discount ~ (прэфэрэ́ншл ди́скоунт ~) размер преференциальных скидок

premium ~ (при́миум ~) премиальная ставка

prime ~ (пра́йм ~) базисная ставка

profit ~ (про́фит ~) норма прибыли

profitability ~s (профитаби́лити ~с) нормативы рентабельности

progressive ~ (прогрэ́ссив ~) прогрессивная ставка

proportional ~ (пропо́ршнал ~) пропорциональный тариф

quotation of exchange ~s (куотэ́йшн оф эксчэ́йндж ~с) котировка курсов

reciprocal ~ (рисэ́прикал ~) взаимный курс

regressive ~ (ригрэ́ссив ~) регрессивная ставка

regulation of the currency exchange ~ (рэгюлэ́йшн оф θи кýррэнси эксчэ́йндж ~) урегулирование валютного курса

second ~ (сэ́конд ~) второго разряда

securities ~ (сэкю́ритиз ~) курс ценных бумаг

settlement ~ (сэ́ттлмэнт ~) расчётный курс

slowing the ~s of growth (сло́уинг θи ~с оф гро́ут) замедление темпов роста

slowing the ~s of development (сло́уинг θи ~с оф дэвэ́лопмэнт) замедление темпов развития spot ~ (спот ~) курс по сделкам "спот"

stabilization of exchange ~s (стэйбилизэ́йшн оф эксчэ́йндж ~с) стабилизация курса валюты

stable exchange ~ (стэйбл эксчэ́йндж ~) устойчивый курс

standard ~ (ста́ндард ~) основной тариф, стандартный курс

supplementary ~ (сапплэмэ́нтари ~) дополнительный курс

tax ~ (такс ~) налоговая ставка

the ~ of inflation (θи ~ оф инфлэ́йшн) темп инфляции

third ~ (тирд ~) третьего разряда

through ~ (тру ~) сквозной тариф

to ~ (ту ~) тарифицировать

to artificially support the exchange ~ (ту артифи́шалли суппо́рт θи эксчэ́йндж ~) поддерживать курс искусственно

to exchange at the official ~ (ту эксчэ́йндж ат θи оффи́шл ~) обменивать по официальному курсу

total ~ (то́тал ~) общий коэффициент

trade at the going ~ (трэйд ат θи го́инг ~) обмен по курсу

traffic ~ (тра́ффик ~) транспортный тариф

two tier exchange ~ (ту тир эксчэ́йндж ~) двойной курс

uniform ~ (ю́ниформ ~) единая ставка

unitary ~ (ю́нитари ~) единый курс

varying ~ (ва́ринг ~) меняющийся курс

wage ~ (уэ́йдж ~) расценка

~ change (~ чэйндж) изменение ставки

~ of conversion (~ оф конвэ́ржн) перерасчётный курс

~ of freight (~ оф фрэйт) размер фрахта

~ of issue (~ оф и́шю) курс выпуска, эмиссионный курс

~ of markdown (~ оф ма́ркдаун) величина скидки

~ of option (~ оф о́пшн) размер премии

~ of premium (~ оф при́миум) размер премии

~ of turnover (~ оф ту́рновэр) скорость оборота

~ schedule (~ скэ́дюл) прейскурант тарифов

Ratification (ратификэ́йшн) ратификация

certificate of ~ (сэрти́фикэт оф ~) акт ратификации

subject to ~ (са́бджэкт ту ~) подлежит ратификации

Ratified (ра́тифайд) ратифицированный

Ratify, to ~ (ра́тифай, ту ~) ратифицировать

Rating (рэ́йтинг) классификация

credit ~ (крэ́дит ~) оценка кредитоспособности

vessel ~ system (вэ́ссэл ~ си́стэм) классификация судов

Ratio (рэ́йшио) коэффициент, соотношение

design ~ (диза́йн ~) расчётный коэффициент

earnings ~ (э́рнингз ~) коэффициент доходности

gross profit ~ (гросс про́фит ~) коэффициент валовой прибыли

liquidity ~ (ликуи́дити ~) коэффициент ликвидности

net profit ~ (нэт про́фит ~) коэффициент рентабельности

reserve ~ (ризэ́рв ~) резервная норма

return ~ (риту́рн ~) коэффициент окупаемости

utilization ~ (ютилизэ́йшн ~) коэффициент использования

~ of supply and demand (~ оф суппла́й энд дима́нд) соотношение спроса и предложения

Ration (рэ́йшн) паёк {share}, рацион {e.g. food}

food ~ (фуд ~) продовольственная развёрстка

~s (~с) продовольствие

Rational (ра́шнал) рациональный

Rationalization (рашнализэ́йшн) рационализация

economic ~ of inventories (эконо́мик ~ оф и́нвэнториз) экономия в результате сокращения объёма запасов

~ of labor (~ оф лэ́йбор) рационализация методов работы, рационализация труда

Rationalize, to ~ (ра́шнализ, ту ~) рационализировать

Raw (ра́у) необработанный

~ material (~ мати́риал) сырьё

Re-arm, to ~ (ри-арм, ту ~)
перевооружить
Re-discount (ридискоунт) редисконт
Re-equip, to ~ (ри-икуип, ту ~)
обновить оборудование
    to ~ a department (ту ~ a
дэпáртмэнт) обновить
оборудование цеха
Re-export (ри-экспорт) реэкспорт
    restriction of ~ (ристрикшн оф
~) ограничение реэкспорта
Re-import (ри-импорт) реимпорт
    to ~ (ту ~) вновь импортировать
Reaction (риакшн) реакция
Reactionary (риакшнэри) реакционер,
реакционный {adj.}
Readily (рэдили) легко, с
готовностью
    to ~ find a market (ту ~ файнд a
мáркэт) легко находить сбыт
    to sell ~ (ту сэлл ~) легко
продаваться
Readiness (рэдинэсс) готовность
    certificate of ~ (сэртификэт оф
~) сертификат о готовности
    notice of ~ (нóтис оф ~)
извещение о готовности
    notice of ~ of vessel for
unloading (нóтис оф ~ фор
анлóдинг) извещение о готовности
судна к выгрузке
    ~ for acceptance (~ фор
аксэптанс) готовность к приёмке
    ~ of goods (~ оф гудз)
готовность товара к отгрузке
Readjustment (риаджýстмэнт)
перестройка
Ready (рэди) готов(а), наличный
    ~ money (~ мóни) наличные
Real estate (рил эстэйт)
недвижимость
    owner of ~ (óунэр оф ~) владелец
недвижимости
    ~ market (~ мáркэт) рынок
недвижимости
    ~ mortgage (~ мóргэдж) закладная
под недвижимость
    ~ tax (~ такс) налог на
недвижимость
Reality (риáлити) действительность,
реальность
    objective ~ (обджэктив ~)
объективная действительность
Realization (риализэйшн)
осуществление

Realize, to ~ (риалайз, ту ~)
обращать, осуществлять [perfective:
осуществить]
Realized (риалайзд) реализованный
Realm (рэлм) сфера
Rearrangement (риаррáнджмэнт)
перестановка
Reason (ризон) основание
{justification}, причина {cause},
разум {mental capacity}
Reasonable (ризонэбл) разумный,
сходный, умеренный
Reasonably (ризонэбли) достаточно,
разумно, умеренно
    ~ beneficial (~ бэнэфишл)
достаточно выгодный
Reballotting (рибáллотинг)
перебаллотировка
Rebate (рибэйт) возврат, уступка
    ~ of amount overpaid (~ оф
амóунт овэрпэйд) возврат
переплаты
    ~ of interest (~ оф интэрэст)
вычет процентов
Rebellion (рэбэлен) бунт, поворот,
революция
    agrarian ~ (аграриан) аграрная
революция
Rebuff (рибýф) отпор
Rebuild, to ~ (рибилд, ту ~)
восстанавливать
Rebuilding (рибилдинг)
восстановление
Recalculation (рикалкюлэйшн)
перерасчёт, пересчёт
    ~ into gold (~ инто голд)
пересчёт в золоте
    ~ of foreign exchange (~ оф
фóрэн эксчэйндж) пересчёт валют
Recall (рикал) отзыв
    to ~ {a representative} (ту ~ {a
рэпризэнтатив}) отзывать
[perfective: отозвать]
    ~ of diplomatic personnel (~ оф
дипломáтик пэрсонэл) отзыв
{дипломатического персонала}
Recantation (рикантэйшн) отречение
    ~ of testimony (~ оф тэстимони)
снятие показаний
Receipt (рисит) акт сдачи,
квитанция, получение, приём,
приемо-сдаточный акт, расписка ~s
выручка, приход
    airmail ~ (эйрмэйл ~) квитанция
авиапочтового отправления
    annual ~s (áннюал ~с) годовая
выручка

bailee ~ (бэйли́ ~) сохранная
расписка
budget ~s (бу́джэт ~с) бюджетные
доходы, бюджетные поступления
cash ~s (каш ~с) кассовые
поступления
contract ~s (ко́нтракт ~с)
выручка за работы, выполненные
по контракту
daily ~s (дэ́йли ~с) дневная
выручка, суточная выручка
deposit ~ (дипо́зит ~) вкладное
свидетельство, депозитная
квитанция
dock ~ (док ~) расписка о
принятии груза для отправки
filing ~ (фа́йлинг ~) квитанция о
принятии заявки
foreign exchange ~s (фо́рэн
эксчэ́йндж ~с) приход иностранной
валюты
insurance premium ~ (иншю́ранс
при́миум ~) квитанция об уплате
страхового взноса
interim ~ (и́нтэрим ~) временная
квитанция
net ~s (нэт ~с) выручка нетто
non-cash ~s (нон-каш ~с)
безденежные поступления
official ~ (оффи́шл ~)
официальная расписка
operating ~s (о́пэрэйтинг ~с)
текущие поступления
parcel post ~ (па́рсэл пост ~)
квитанция на почтовую посылку
postal ~ (по́стал ~) почтовая
квитанция
railway ~ (рэ́йлуэй ~)
железнодорожная квитанция
safe deposit ~ (сэйф дипо́зит ~)
сохранная квитанция
standardized ~ (ста́ндардайзд ~)
бланк квитанции
subscription ~ (субскри́пшн ~)
квитанция о подписке
to convert ~s to rubles (ту
конвэ́рт ~с ту рублз)
пересчитывать выручку в рубли
to issue a ~ (ту и́шю а ~)
выдавать квитанцию
to submit a ~ (ту субми́т а ~)
представлять квитанцию
total ~s (то́тал ~с) общая
выручка
trade ~s (трэйд ~с) торговая
выручка

warehouse ~ (уэ́йрхаус ~)
складская квитанция
~s from trade (~с фром трэйд)
выручка от торговли
~ of a complaint (~ оф а
компле́йнт) поступление жалобы
~ of a letter (~ оф а лэ́ттэр)
получение письма
Receivable (риси́вабл) 1. получаемый
2. **~s** (~с) оборот по счетам,
поступления, причитающиеся суммы
accounts ~ (акко́унтс ~)
дебиторская задолженность
incoming ~s (и́нкоминг ~с)
денежные поступления
Receive, to ~ (риси́в, ту ~)
получать
~d in full (~д ин фулл) сполна
получил
Receiving (риси́винг) получение
~ country (~ ко́унтри) страна
назначения
~ of stolen goods (~ оф сто́лэн
гудз) сокрытие краденого
Reception (рисэ́пшн) приём
Recession (рисэ́шн) застой, спад
Recidivist (риси́дивист) рецидивист
Recipient (риси́пиэнт) получатель
grant ~ (грант ~) субсидируемое
лицо
Reciprocal (риси́прокал) взаимный,
обоюдный
~ agreement (~ агри́мэнт)
соглашение на основе взаимности
~ trade (~ трэйд) торговля на
основе взаимности
~ treaty (~ три́ти) договор на
основе взаимности
Reciprocally (риси́прокалли) взаимно
Reciprocity (рэсипро́сити)
взаимность, обоюдность
Reckon, to ~ (рэ́кон, ту ~)
зачитывать [perfective: зачесть]
Recognition (рэкогни́шн) признание
collective ~ (коллэ́ктив ~)
коллективное признание
de facto ~ (ди фа́кто ~)
признание де-факто
de jure ~ (ди джю́рэ ~) признание
де-юре
diplomatic ~ (диплома́тик ~)
дипломатическое признание
international ~ (интэрнэ́шнал ~)
международное признание
international legal ~
(интэрнэ́шнал ли́гал ~)
международное правовое признание

legal ~ (лńгал ~) правовое признание
official ~ (оффńшл ~) акт признания
preliminary ~ (прилńминэри ~) предварительное признание
revocation of consular ~ (рэвокэ́йшн оф ко́нсюлар ~) аннулирование экзекватуры
unilateral ~ (юнила́тэрал ~) одностороннее признание
~ by the court (~ бай θи ко́урт) судебное признание
~ of authorship (~ оф а́уторшип) признание на авторство
~ of border (~ оф бо́рдэр) признание границы
~ of independence (~ оф индэпэ́ндэнс) признание независимости
~ of lawful rights (~ оф ла́уфул райтс) признание законных прав
~ of legal precedents (~ оф лńгал прэ́сэдэнтс) признание судебных решений
~ of sovereignty (~ оф со́вэрнти) признание суверенитета
Recognizance (рико́гнизанс) обязательство, данное в суде
to release on one's own ~ (ту рилńс он уо́нз оун ~) освободить под честное слово
Recognize, to ~ (рэ́когнайз, ту ~) признавать
~d (~д) признан, явный
~d benefit (~д бэ́нэфит) явная выгода
Recommendation (рэкоммэндэ́йшн) отзыв, рекомендация
to give a good ~ (ту гив а гуд ~) дать хороший отзыв
Recompense (рэ́компэнс) возмещение ущерба, компенсация
in ~ for (ин ~ фор) в возмещение
Reconcilable (рэконса́йлабл) примиримый
Reconcile (рэ́консайл) **to ~** (ту ~) примирять
Reconciliation (рэконсилиэ́йшн) примирение
Reconditioning (рикондńшнинг) восстановление, ремонт
~ of parts (~ оф партз) восстановление деталей
Reconnaissance (рэко́нэсэнс) разведка

Reconnoitre, to ~ (рэконно́йтр, ту ~) разведывать [**perfective:** разведать]
Reconsideration (риконсидэрэ́йшн) пересмотр
~ of a decision (~ оф а дисńжн) пересмотр решения
~ of a sentence (~ оф ф сэ́нтэнс) пересмотр приговора
Reconstruct, to ~ (риконстра́кт, ту ~) восстанавливать
Reconstruction (риконстракшн) восстановление, перестройка, реконструкция
~ of industry (~ оф ńндустри) восстановление промышленности
Reconversion (риконвэ́ржн) реконверсия
Record (рэ́кокд) запись, протокол ~s (~с) учётно-регистрационная документация
administrative ~ (адмńнистрэйтив ~) административный протокол
accounts and ~s (акко́унтс энд ~с) расчётный документы
demand ~s (дима́нд ~с) учёт спроса
examination ~ (эксаминэ́йшн ~) протокол допроса
performance ~ (пэрфо́рманс ~) производственный учёт
personnel ~s (пэрсоннэ́л ~с) учёт кадров
public ~ (па́блик ~) публичный реестр
repair ~ (рипэ́йр ~) ремонтажная ведомость, данные о ремонте
service ~ (сэ́рвис ~) послужной список
to ~ (ту рэко́рд) протоколировать
to keep ~s (ту кип ~с) вести учёт
to note in the ~ (ту нот ин θи ~) приобращать к делу
to put on ~ (ту пут он ~) зафиксировать
work ~s (уэрк ~с) учёт работы
~ of a judicial hearing (~ оф а джюдńшл хńринг) протокол судебного заседания
Record-keeping (рэ́корд-кńпинг) ведение учёта
Recorder (рико́рдэр) регистратор
Recoup (рику́) **to ~** (ту ~) вычитать
Recourse (рńкорс) оборот, обращение, регресс, регрессное требование

final ~ (фа́йнал ~) последняя инстанция
legal ~ (ли́гал ~) судебная инстанция
right of ~ (райт оф ~) право оборота, право регресса
with ~ (уиθ ~) с оборотом, с регрессом
without ~ (уиθо́ут ~) без оборота
without ~ to drawer (уиθо́ут ~ ту дра́уэр) без оборота на трассанта
~ to force (~ ту форс) обращение к силе
~ to the court (~ ту θи ко́урт) обращение в суд
~ to war (~ ту уа́р) обращение к войне
Recover, to ~ (рико́вэр, ту ~) возмещать по суду {legal damages}, инкассировать
to ~ one's expenses (ту ~ уа́нз экспэ́нсэз) выручать затраченное
Recovery (рико́вэри) возмещение, оживление, оздоровление, подъём, исцеление
amount of ~ (амо́унт оф ~) размер взыскания
business ~ (би́знес ~) восстановление торговли, подъём конъюнктуры
cost ~ (кост ~) взыскание издержек
cyclical ~ (си́кликал ~) циклический подъём
economic ~ (эконо́мик ~) оздоровление экономии, экономическое восстановление, экономическое оживление
full ~ (фулл ~) полное возмещение
industrial ~ (инда́стриал ~) промышленный подъём
liable for ~ (ла́йабл фор ~) подлежащий возмещению
partial ~ (па́ршл ~) частичное возмещение
sum of ~ (сум оф ~) сумма взыскания
to proceed against for ~ (ту проси́д аге́нст фор ~) подать к взысканию на
~ for breakage (~ фор брэ́йкэдж) возмещение за поломку
~ for losses (~ фор ло́ссэз) возмещение потерь

~ for vessel detention (~ фор вэ́ссэл дитэ́ншн) возмещение за задержку судна сверх срока
~ in kind (~ ин кайнд) возмещение в натуре
~ of a sum (~ оф а сум) взыскание суммы
~ of damages (~ оф да́маджэз) взыскание неустойки
~ of {legal} damages (~ оф {ли́гал} да́маджэз) взыскание убытков
~ of money (~ оф мо́ни) взыскание денег
~ of money invested (~ оф мо́ни инвэ́стэд) возврат инвестированных денег
~ of the business cycle (~ оф θи би́знэсс сайкл) оживление конъюнктуры
Recruit, to ~ (рикру́т, ту ~) привлекать [**perfective:** привлечь], рекрутировать
Recruiting (рикру́тинг) привлечение
~ office (~ о́ффис) явочный участок
Recruitment (рикру́тмэнт) набор штата
Red-handed {in expression} (рэд-ха́ндэд) поличное {выражение}
to catch ~ (ту кэтч ~) поймать с поличным
Redeem, to ~ (рэди́м, ту ~) выкупать
Redeemability (риди́мабилити) возможность выкупа
Redeemable (риди́мабл) обмениваемый
Redelivery (ридэли́вэри) возврат зафрахтованного судна
Redemption (ридэ́мпшн) возврат, выкуп, погашение
prior ~ (пра́йор ~) досрочный выкуп
right of ~ (райт оф ~) право выкупа
~ notice (~ но́тис) объявление о выкупе
~ of documents (~ оф до́кюмэнтз) выкуп документов
~ of mortgage (~ оф мо́ргэдж) выкуп закладной
~ of shares (~ оф шэрз) выкуп акций
~ period (~ пи́риод) срок возврата денег
~ of a bond (~ оф а бонд) погашение облигации

~ **of a loan** (~ оф а лон) уплата займа

Redesign (ридизáйн) изменение в конструкции

Rediscount (ридúскоунт) переучёт
~ **of a bill** (~ оф а бил) переучёт векселя

Redistribution (ридистрбю́шн) передел, перераспределение
~ **of income** (~ оф úнком) перераспределение доходов
~ **of territory** (~ оф тэ́рритори) перераспределение территории

Redraft (рúдрафт) встречная тратта

Reduce, to ~ (ридýс, ту ~) сокращать, уменьшать
to ~ **by ... times** (ту ~ бай ... таймз) уменьшать в ... раз
to ~ **by a quarter** (ту ~ бай а куáртэр) уменьшать вчетверо

Reduction (ридакшн) снижение, сокращение, уменьшение
arms ~ (армз ~) сокращение вооружений
freight ~ (фрэйт ~) фрахтовая льгота
~ **in cost** (~ ин кост) снижение стоимости
~ **in expenses** (~ ин экспэ́нсэз) уменьшение расходов
~ **in outlays** (~ ин óутлэй) снижение затрат
~ **in rank** {military} (~ ин рэнк {мúлитэри}) снижение в воинском звании
~ **in revenue** (~ ин рэ́вэню) сокращение доходов
~ **of a deficit** (~ оф а дэ́фисит) сокращение дефицита
~ **of allocations** (~ оф аллокэ́йшнз) сокращение ассигнований
~ **of customs barriers** (~ оф кáстамз бáрриерз) сокращение таможенных барьеров
~ **of customs tariff** (~ оф кáстамз тэ́риф) сокращение таможенного тарифа
~ **of duties** (~ оф дýтиз) снижение пошлин
~ **of share capital** (~ оф шэр кэ́питал) уменьшение акционерного капитала
~ **of tariff** (~ оф тáриф) снижение тарифа
~ **of taxes** (~ оф тáксэз) снижение налогов

Redundancy (ридýнданси) избыточность, излишек
~ **in manpower** (~ ин мáнпоуэр) избыток рабочей силы

Reeducation (риэдюкэ́йшн) перевоспитание

Reelect, to ~ (риэлэ́кт, ту ~) переизбирать

Reelection (риэлэ́кшн) перевыборы, переизбрание

Reencumbrance (риэнкýмбранс) перезаклад

Reexamination (риэкзаминэ́йшн) пересмотр

Reexchange (риэксчэ́йндж)
~ **amount** (~ амóунт) сумма обратного переводного векселя

Reexport (риэ́кспорт) реэкспорт
to ~ (ту ~) реэкспортировать

Refer (рифэ́р) **to** ~ (ту ~) **to** отсылать

Referee (рэфэрú) судья; ~s {sports} судейский аппарат
arbitral ~ (áрбиртал ~) третейский судья

Reference (рэ́фэрэнс) отзыв, справка, {adj.} справочный, ссылка
work ~ (уэ́рк ~) справка с места работы
~ **book** (~ бук) справочник

Referendum (рэфэрэ́ндум) референдум
mandatory ~ (мáндатори ~) обязательный референдум
optional ~ (óпшнал ~) факультативный референдум

Refinery (рифáйнэри) очистительный завод
oil ~ (ойл ~) нефтеочистительный завод

Reflagging (рифлáггинг) перевод судна под другой флаг

Reform (рифóрм) преобразование, реформа
administrative ~ (адмúнистрэйтив ~) административная реформа
agrarian ~ (аграрúян ~) аграрное преобразование, аграрная реформа
bank ~ (банк ~) банковская реформа
credit ~ (крэ́дит ~) кредитная реформа
currency ~ (кýрренси ~) валютная реформа
economic ~ (экономúк ~) экономическое преобразование
electoral ~ (элэ́кторал ~) избирательная реформа

financial ~ (файна́ншл ~)
финансовая реформа
judicial ~ (джюди́шл ~) судебная
реформа
land ~ (ланд ~) земельное
преобразование, земельная
реформа
parliamentary ~ (парламэ́нтэри ~)
парламентская реформа
social ~ (со́шл ~) социальная
реформа
tax ~ (такс ~) налоговая реформа
to ~ (ту ~) преобразовывать
Reformer (рифо́рмэр)
преобразователь, реформистский
{adj.}
Reformism (рифо́рмизм) реформизм
Reformist (рифо́рмист) реформист,
реформистский {adj.}
Reforwarding (рифо́руардинг)
переотправка {freight}
Refresher (рифрэ́шр) дополнительный
{adj.}
~ course (~ ко́урс)
переподготовка
Refund (ри́фунд) возврат,
cash ~ (каш ~) денежная
компенсация
delay in ~ (дилэ́й ин ~) задержка
в возврате
demand for ~ (дима́нд фор ~)
требование о возврате
premium ~ (при́миум ~)
возвращённый страховой взнос
subject to ~ (су́бджэкт ту ~)
подлежащий возврату
tax ~ (такс ~) возврат налога
~ of a deposit (~ оф ф дипо́сит)
возврат из депозита
~ of customs duties (~ оф
ка́стомз дю́тиз) возврат пошлины
~ of purchase price (~ оф пу́рчас
прайс) возврат уплаченной цены
Refundable (рифу́ндабл) подлежащий
возврату
to be ~ (ту би ~) подлежать
возврату
~ deposit (~ дипо́сит)
возмещаемый взнос
Refusal (рифю́зал) отказ
direct ~ (дайрэ́кт ~) прямой
отказ
~ to give evidence (~ ту гив
э́виденс) отказ от дачи показаний
~ to pay (~ ту пэй) отказ
платить

~ to perform (~ ту пэрфо́рм)
отказ от выполнения
Refuse, to ~ (рифю́з, ту ~)
отказать, отклонять
Refutation (рэфютэ́йшн) опровержение
Refute, to ~ (рифю́т, ту ~)
опровергать [perfective:
опровергнуть]
~d (~эд) опровержимый
Regency (ри́джэнси) регентство
Regent (ри́джэнт) регент
Regime (режи́м) рижим, строй
currency control ~ (ку́рренси
контро́л ~) валютный режим
customs ~ (ка́стомз ~) таможенный
режим
discriminatory {trade} ~
(дискри́минатори {трэйд} ~)
дискриминационный режим
fascist ~ (фа́шист ~) фашистский
режим
governmental ~ (говэрнмэ́нтал ~)
государственный строй
legal ~ (ли́гал ~) правовой режим
licensing ~ (ла́йсэнсинг ~)
лицензионный режим
political ~ (поли́тикал ~)
политический режим
tax ~ (такс ~) налоговый режим
totalitarian ~ (тоталитэ́риян ~)
тоталитарный режим
transitional ~ (транзи́шнал ~)
переходный режим
Region (ри́джон) район
autonomous ~ (ауто́номус ~)
автономный район
Regional (ри́джонал) зональный
~ executive committee (~
эксэ́кютив комми́тти) райисполком
{abbrev.}
Register (рэ́джистэр) ведомость,
регистр, реестр
business names ~ (би́знэсс нэ́ймз
~) реестр наименований фирм
cash ~ (каш ~) касса
check ~ (чэк ~) расходная книга
civil ~ (си́вил ~) гражданский
регистр
copyright ~ (ко́пирайт ~) реестр
авторских прав
patent ~ (па́тэнт ~) патентный
реестр
principle ~ (при́нсипал ~)
основной реестр
to ~ (ту ~) взять на учёт,
записывать [perfective:
записать], зарегистрировать,

оформлять, прописать,
регистрировать
to keep a ~ (ту кип а ~) вести
журнал
trade ~ (трэйд ~) торговый
реестр
transaction ~ (трансакшн ~)
регистр оборотов
with enclosed ~ (уйт энклóзд ~)
с приложением ведомости
~ of companies (~ оф кóмпаниз)
регистр акционерных компаний
~ of construction projects (~ оф
констракшн прóджэктз) ведомость
монтажных работ
Registered (рэ́джистэрд) именной
to be ~ (ту би ~) становиться на
учёт
Registrar (рэ́джистрар) регистратор,
регистрационное бюро
~ of companies (~ оф кóмпаниз)
бюро регистрации акционерных
компаний
Registration (рэджистрэ́йшн)
оформление, прикрепление,
регистрация, учёт, учётный {*adj.*}
compulsory ~ (компýлсори ~)
обязательная регистрация
international ~ (интэрнэ́шнал ~)
международная регистрация
land ~ (ланд ~) земельная
регистрация
legal ~ (лѝгал ~) правовое
оформление
legal ~ of a vessel (лѝгал ~ оф
а вэ́ссэл) правовая регистрация
судна
notarial ~ (нотáриал ~)
нотариальная регистрация
official ~ (оффѝшл ~)
официальная регистрация
to nullify ~ (ту нýллифай ~)
признать регистрацию
недействительной
trade ~ (трэйд ~) торговая
регистрация
~ of birth (~ оф бирт) запись о
рождении
~ of criminal offenders (~ оф
крѝминал оффэ́ндэрз) уголовная
регистрация
~ of mortgage (~ оф мóргадж)
запись ипотеки
~ of privilege (~ оф прѝвилэдж)
запись привилегии

~ of renewal of mortgage (~ оф
рѝнюал оф мóргадж) запись
возобновления ипотеки
~ of vital statistics (~ оф
вáйтал статѝстикс) метрическая
запись
Registry (рэ́джистри) регистратура
state ~ of civil aircraft (стэйт
~ оф сѝвил э́йркрафт)
государственный реестр
гражданских воздушных судов
~ of death certificate (~ оф дэθ
сэртѝфикат) запись акта о смерти
Regroup (ригрýп) **to ~** (ту ~)
перегруппировать
Regrouping (ригрýпинг)
перегруппировка
Regular (рэ́гюлар) закономерный,
нормальный, правильный, регулярный
Regularity (рэгюлэ́рити)
закономерность, правильность
Regularly (рэ́гюларли) правильно,
регулярно
Regulate, to ~ (рэ́гюлэйт, ту ~)
регламентировать, регулировать
Regulated (рэ́гюлэйтд) регулируемый
~ monopoly (~ монóполи)
регулируемая монополия
Regulation (рэгюлэ́йшн) подзаконный
акт, правило, распоряжение,
регламентация, регламентный {*adj.*}
регулирование **~s** инструкция,
регламент
administrative ~ (админѝстрэйтив
~) административное распоряжение
administrative ~s
(админѝстрэйтив ~с)
административный регламент
air force ~ (эйр форс ~) военно-
воздушное постановление
air traffic ~s (эйр трáффик ~с)
правила передвижения в воздухе
basic ~ (бэ́йсик ~) основное
постановление
civil law ~ (сѝвил лау ~)
гражданско-правовое
регулирование
commercial ~ (коммэ́ршл ~)
коммерческое регулирование
compulsory ~ (компýлсори ~)
обязательное постановление
control ~s (контрóл ~с) правила
контроля
customs ~ (кáстомз ~) таможенное
постановление

economic ~ (эконо́мик ~)
экономическое, экономическое
регулирование
employment ~s (эмпло́ймэнт ~с)
положение в отношении занятости
financial ~ (файна́ншл ~)
финансовое постановление,
финансовое правило
fiscal ~ (фи́скал ~) налоговое
регулирование
fishing ~s (фи́шинг ~с) правила
рыбной ловли
foreign exchange ~ (фо́рэн
эксчэ́йндж ~) валютное правило
health ~s (хэлт ~с) санитарный
регламент
hunting ~s (ху́нтинг~с) правила
охоты
immigration ~ (иммигрэ́йшн ~)
иммиграционные правила
internal ~s (интэ́рнал ~с)
правила внутреннего распорядка
international flight ~s
(интэрнэ́шнал флайт ~с) правила
международных полётов
international postal ~
(интэрнэ́шнал по́стал ~)
международное почтовое правило
jurisprudential ~
(джюриспрудэ́ншл ~) юридическое
регулирование
legal ~ (ли́гал ~) правовое
регулирование
market ~ (ма́ркэт ~)
регулирование рынка
market ~s (ма́ркэт ~с) рыночные
правила
marking ~s (ма́ркинг ~с) правила
маркировки
military ~ (ми́литэри ~) военное
постановление
naval ~ (нэ́йвал ~) военно-
морское постановление
official ~s (оффи́шл ~с)
служебный регламент
operating ~ (о́пэрэйтинг ~)
правило эксплуатации
port authority ~s (порт аθо́рити
~с) портовые правила
postal ~s (по́стал ~с) почтовые
правила
preliminary ~ (прили́минари ~)
предварительное распоряжение
procedural ~ (проси́дюрал ~)
процедурное постановление
public ~ (пу́блик ~)
государственное регулирование

quarantine ~ (куа́рантин ~)
карантинное правило
safety ~s (сэ́йфти ~с) правила
безопасности
safety equipment ~ (сэ́йфти
икуи́пмэнт ~) правило техники
безопасности
service ~s (сэ́рвис ~с) служебная
инструкция
shipping ~s (ши́ппинг ~с) правила
судоходства
tariff ~ (та́рифф ~) тарифное
постановление
traffic ~ (тра́ффик ~)
регулирование автодвижения
voting ~s (во́тинг ~с) правила
голосования
~s for resident foreigners (~с
фор рэ́зидэнт фо́рэнэрс) правила
проживания иностранцев
~ of elections (~ оф элэ́кшнз)
положение о выборах
~ of finances (~ оф фина́нсэз)
правило о финансах
~ of personnel (~ оф пэрсоннэ́л)
правило о личном составе
~ of priority (~ оф прайо́рити)
правило о приоритете
~ of the air waves {radio} (~ оф
θи эйр уэ́йвз {рэ́йдио})
регулирование радиосношения
~ of transportation (~ оф
транспортэ́йшн) правило перевозки
Regulatory (рэ́гюлатори) нормативный
Rehabilitate, to ~ (рихаби́литэйт,
ту ~) реабилитировать
Rehabilitation (рихаби́литэйшн)
реабилитация
Reimburse, to ~ (риэмбу́рс, ту ~)
возмещать, компенсировать,
предоставлять возмещение
Reimbursement (риэмбу́рсмэнт)
возмещение, отдача, рамбурс
direct ~ of expenses (дайрэ́кт ~
оф экспэ́нсэз) прямое возмещение
затрат
method of ~ (мэ́тод оф ~) способ
возмещения
warranty ~ (уа́рранти ~) возврат
гарантийной суммы
~ for outlays (~ фор о́утлэйз)
возмещение расходов
~ of charges (~ оф ча́рджэз)
возврат сборов
~ of expenditures (~ оф
экспэ́ндитюрз) возмещение
ассигнований

~ **of expenses** (~ оф экспэ́нсэз)
возмещение затрат
Reimport (рии́мпорт) реимпорт
to ~ (ту ~) реимпортировать
Reinsurance (рииншю́ранс)
перестрахование
    marine ~ (мари́н ~) морское
    перестрахование
    personal ~ (пэ́рсонал ~) личное
    перестрахование
    voluntary ~ (во́лунтэри ~)
    добровольное перестрахование
Reinsure, to ~ (рииншю́р, ту ~)
перестраховать
Reinsurer (рииншю́рэр)
перестраховщик
Reinvestment (риинвэ́стмэнт)
реинвестиция
Reject (ри́джэкт, риджэ́кт) брак,
отвергать
    production ~ (продакшн ри́джэкт)
    производственный брак
    to ~ (ту риджэ́кт) браковать,
    выбраковывать, отвергать,
    отводить [**perfective:** отвести]
    {e.g. arbitrator}, отклонять,
    провалить
    ~ **rate** (ри́джэкт рэйт) процент
    брака
Rejection (риджэ́кшн) браковка,
выбрасывание, отвод
    implicit ~ (импли́сит ~)
    молчаливый отказ
    public ~ (па́блик ~) публичный
    отказ
    total ~ (то́тал ~) общий отказ
    ~ **criterion** (~ крайти́рион)
    критерий браковка
    ~ **of a patent application** (~ оф
    а па́тэнт апплике́йшн) отказ в
    выдаче патента
    ~ **of a petition** (~ оф а пэти́шн)
    отклонение ходатайства
    ~ **of an offer** (~ оф ан о́ффэр)
    отклонение предложения
    ~ **of application** (~ оф ан
    апплике́йшн) отклонение заявки
Rejoinder (риджо́йндр) реплика
Rejuvenation (риджювэнэ́йшн)
омоложение
    demographic ~ (дэмогра́фик ~)
    демографическое омоложение
    ~ **of the population** (~ оф θи
    попюле́йшн) омоложение населения
Relation (риле́йшн) отношение, связь
~**s** (~с) общение, сношение

    border ~**s** (бо́рдэр ~с)
    пограничные сношения
    business ~**s** (би́знэс ~с) деловые
    отношения
    consular ~**s** (ко́нсюлар ~с)
    консульские отношения
    contractual ~ (контра́кшуал ~)
    договорное отношение
    contractual ~**s** (контра́кшуал ~с)
    договорные взаимоотношения
    currency ~**s** (ку́рренси ~с)
    валютные отношения
    diplomatic ~**s** (диплома́тик ~с)
    дипломатические отношения,
    дипломатические сношения
    economic ~**s** (эконо́мик ~с)
    экономические отношение
    family ~**s** (фа́мили ~с)
    родственные отношения
    financial ~**s** (файна́ншл ~с)
    финансовые отношения
    foreign trade ~**s** (фо́рэн трэйд
    ~с) внешнеторговые отношения
    foreign ~**s** (фо́рэн ~с) внешние
    сношения
    good neighborly ~**s** (гуд нэ́йборли
    ~с) добрососедские отношения
    intergovernmental ~**s**
    (интэрговэрнмэ́нтл ~с)
    межгосударственное общение
    international ~**s** (интэрнэ́шнл ~с)
    международное общение,
    международные отношения,
    международные сношения
    interstate ~**s** (интэрстэ́йт ~с)
    межгосударственные
    взаимоотношения
    legal ~ (ли́гал ~) правовое
    отношение
    legal ~**s** (ли́гал ~с) юридические
    взаимоотношения
    long-term ~**s** (лонг-тэ́рм ~с)
    длительные отношения
    marital ~ (ма́ритал ~) брачная
    связь
    member ~**s** (мэ́мбэр ~с) членские
    отношения
    mutual ~**s** (мю́тюал ~с)
    взаимоотношения
    peaceful ~**s** (пи́сфул ~с) мирные
    отношения
    postal ~**s** (по́стал ~с) почтовые
    сношения
    productive ~**s** (проду́ктив ~с)
    полезные взаимоотношения
    property ~**s** (про́пэрти ~с)
    имущественный отношение

self-supporting ~s (сэлф-суппо́ртинг ~с) хозрасчётные отношения
trade ~s (трэйд ~с) торговые взаимоотношения, торговые сношения
~s between the parties (~с биту́ин θи па́ртиз) взаимоотношения сторон
Relationship (риле́йшншип) отношение, родство
blood ~ (блад ~) кровное родство
in-law ~ (ин-лау ~) свойство
legal ~ (ли́гал ~) законное родство, правовая связь
working ~ (уэ́ркинг ~) сотрудничество
Relative (рэ́латив) родственник, относительный {adj.}, соответствующий {adj.}
blood ~ (блад ~) кровный родственник
Relativity (рэлати́вити) относительность
Release (рили́с) освобождение
early ~ (э́рли ~) досрочное освобождение
freight ~ (фрэйт ~) разрешение на выдачу груза
press ~ (прэсс ~) разрешённая публикация
to ~ (ту ~) освобождать [perfective: освободить], отпускать [perfective: отпустить]
to ~ from an obligation (ту ~ фром эн облиге́йшн) освобождать от обязанности
to ~ from confinement (ту ~ фром конфа́йнмэнт) отпускать на волю
to obtain customs ~ (ту обтэ́йн ка́стомс ~) получать разрешение на ввоз
to ~ a blocked account (ту ~ а блокд акко́унт) разблокировать
warehouse ~ (уэ́рхаус ~) разрешение на выдачу товара со склада
~ for sale (~ фор сэйл) выпуск в продажу
~ for shipment (~ фор ши́пмэнт) разрешение на вывоз
~ of blocked account (~ оф блокд акко́унт) разблокирование
~ of defendant on bail (~ оф дифэ́ндант он бэ́йл) передача подсудимого на поруки

Relevant (рэ́лэвант) относящийся к делу
Reliability (рилайаби́лити) надёжность
assurance of ~ (ашю́ранс оф ~) обеспечение надёжности
design ~ (диза́йн оф ~) расчётная надёжность
measures of ~ (мэ́жюрз оф ~) меры надёжности
operating ~ (о́пэрэйтинг ~) эксплуатационная надёжность
variations in ~ (вариэ́йшнз ин ~) изменение надёжности
~ analysis (~ ана́лисис) анализ надёжности
Reliable (рила́йабл) надёжный
Relief (рили́ф) пособие
Religion (рили́джин) религия
state ~ (стэ́йт ~) государственная религия
Reload, to ~ (рило́д, ту ~) перегружать
Rem (рэм) предмет {латинское слово}
action in ~ against vessel and cargo (акшн ин ~ агэ́нст вэ́ссэл энд ка́рго) наложение запрещения на судно и груз {буквально: "иск на предмет против судно и груз"}
Remainder (римэ́йндр) остаток
~ of stock (~ оф сток) остаток запасов
~ of sum (~ оф сум) остаток суммы
Remark (рима́рк) замечание {noun}, замечать [perfective: заметить] {adj.}
Remedial (рими́диал) исправляющий
~ work (~ уэрк) работа по возмещению убытков, работа по возмещению ущерба
Remilitarization (римилитаризэ́йшн) ремилитаризация
Reminder (рима́йндэр) напоминание
numerous ~ (ню́мэрос ~с) многократные напоминания
official ~ (офи́шл ~) официальное напоминание
second ~ (сэ́конд ~) повторное напоминание
~ of payment due (~ оф пэ́ймэнт дю) напоминание о платеже
Remit, to ~ (рими́т, ту ~) отослать, перечислять
Remittance (рими́ттанс) перечисление, пересылка, ремитирование

certificate of ~ (сэртификат оф
~) акт сдачи
foreign ~ (фóрэн ~) перевод за
границу
international ~ (интэрнэ́шнл ~)
международный платёж
Remitter (римúттэр) ремитент
Removal (римýвал) вывод, вывоз,
смещение, снятие
judicial ~ of an injunction
(джюдишл ~ оф эн инджю́нкшн)
судебное снятие запрета
~ expenses (~ экспэ́нсэз) расходы
по вывозу
~ from service (~ фром сэ́рвис)
вывод из эксплуатации
~ from jurisdiction (~ фром
джюрисдúкшн) изъятие из
юрисдикции
~ of a blockade (~ оф а блокэ́йд)
снятие блокады
~ of empties (~ оф э́мптиз) вывоз
тары
~ of exhibits (~ оф экзúбитс)
вывоз экспонатов
~ of a mortgage (~ оф а мóргэдж)
снятие записи ипотеки
~ of packing (~ оф пáкинг) вывоз
упаковки
~ time срок (~ тайм) вывоза
Remove, to ~ (римýв, ту ~)
выводить, вывозить, смещать
[perfective: сместить], снимать
[perfective: снять]
to ~ from the ship's hold
выгружать из трюма
Remuneration (римюнэрэ́йшн) оплата,
плата
amount of ~ (амóунт оф ~) размер
вознаграждения
appropriate ~ (апрóприет ~)
соответствующее вознаграждение
expected ~ (экспэ́ктэд ~)
ожидаемое вознаграждение
gross ~ (гросс ~) вознаграждение
брутто
lumpsum (лýмпсум) ~ (лмп сум ~)
единовременное вознаграждение
material (матúриал) ~ (матúриал
~) материальное вознаграждение
maximum ~ (мáксимум ~)
максимальное вознаграждение
monthly rate of ~ (мóнθли рэйт
оф ~) месячное вознаграждение
right to receive ~ (рáйт ту
рисúв ~) право на {получение}
вознаграждение/я

to have the right to ~ (ту хэв
θи райт ту ~) иметь право на
вознаграждение
to pay ~ (ту пэй ~) выплачивать
вознаграждение
to reduce ~ (ту ридю́с ~)
сокращать вознаграждение
to refuse ~ (ту рифю́з ~)
отказывать в вознаграждении
to specify ~ (ту спэ́сифай ~)
уточнять вознаграждение
Renaming (ринэ́йминг) переименование
Rendering (рэ́ндэринг) оказание
~ of services (~ оф сэ́рвисэз)
Rendezvous (рандэвý) явка
Renew, to ~ (риню́, ту ~)
возобновлять, продлевать
option to ~ (óпшн ту ~) право на
возобновление
to fully ~ (ту фýлли ~)
возобновлять полностью
Renewal (риню́ал) возобновление,
продление
~ of an agreement (~ оф эн
агрúмэнт) возобновление
соглашения, возобновление
договора
~ of application (~ оф
аппликэ́йшн) восстановление
заявки
~ of a contract (~ оф а
кóнтракт) возобновление
контракта, перезаключение
договора
~ of documents (~ оф дóкюмэнтз)
обмен документов
~ of a lease (~ оф а лис)
возобновление аренды
~ of a letter of credit (~ оф а
лэ́ттэр оф крэ́дит) возобновление
аккредитива
~ of an insurance policy (~ оф
ан иншю́ранс пóлиси)
возобновление страхового полиса
~ period (~ пэ́риод) период, на
который возобновляется соглашение
Renounce, to ~ (ринóунс, ту ~)
отказать, отрекаться [perfective:
отречься]
Renovate, to ~ (рэ́новэйт, ту ~)
восстанавливать, обновлять
Renovated (рэ́новэйтэд) обновлённый
Renovation (рэновэ́йшн) обновление
plant ~ (плант ~) модернизация
завода

Rent (рэнт) аренда, доход с недвижимости, прокат, рента
absolute ~ (абсолю́т ~) абсолютная рента
apartment ~ (апа́ртмэнт ~) квартирная плата
capitalized ~ (ка́питалайзд ~) капитализированная рента
differential ~ (диффэрэ́ншл ~) дифференциальная рента
for ~ (фор ~) напрокат
money ~ (мо́ни ~) денежная рента
monopoly ~ (моно́поли ~) монопольная рента
pure ~ (пюр ~) чистая рента
supplemental ~ (саппламэ́нтал ~) добавочная рента
to ~ (ту ~) нанимать
to ~ an apartment (ту ~ ан апа́ртмэнт) брать квартиру внаём
~ in kind (~ ин кайнд) натуральная рента
Rentable (рэ́нтабл) могущий быть сданным внаём
Rental (рэ́нтал) наёмный, прокатный
video ~ (ви́дио ~) платёж за прокат фильмов
~ fee (~ фи) взимание аренды
Rentier (рэнтие́р) рантье
life ~ (лайф ~) пожизненный рантье
Renunciation (ринунсиэ́йшн) отказ, отречение
~ of a given right (~ оф а ги́вэн райт) отречение от данного права
Reorganization (риорганизэ́йшн) перестройка, преобразование, реорганизация
~ of the government (~ оф θи го́вэрнмэнт) реорганизация правительства
~ of society (~ оф соса́йэти) преобразование общества
Reorganize, to ~ (рио́рганайз, ту ~) преобразовывать, реорганизовать
Repackaging (рипа́каджинг) перетарка
Repair (рипэ́йр) ремонт
minor ~ (ма́йнор ~) мелкий ремонт
Repairman (рипэ́йрман) монтёр
Reparation (рэпарэ́йшн) репарация
Repartition (рипарти́шн) передел
Repatriate (рипа́триэйт) репатриант {person}
to ~ (ту ~) репатриировать
Repatriation (рипатриэ́йшн) репатриация

~ of capital (~ оф ка́питал) репатриация капитала
Repay, to ~ (рипэ́й, ту ~) выкупать, выплачивать
to ~ in rubles (ту ~ ин ру́блз) выплачивать в рублях
Repayment (рипэ́ймэнт) возмещение, погашение, уплата
debt ~ (дэт ~) погашение задолженности
debt ~ schedule (дэт ~ скэ́дюл) график возмещения долгов
final ~ of a debt (фа́йнал ~ оф а дэт) окончательная уплата долга
loan ~ (лон ~) возврат займа
timeliness of ~ of a credit (та́ймлинэсс оф ~ оф а крэ́дит) своевременность возмещения кредита
~ of an amount (~ оф ан амо́унт) возмещение суммы
~ of a credit (~ оф а крэ́дит) возмещение кредита, возврат кредита
~ of a debt (~ оф а дэт) возмещение долга, возврат долга
~ of a loan (~оф а лон) погашение ссуды
~ of obligations (~ оф облигэ́йшнз) погашение обязательств
~ of principle on a loan (~ оф при́нсипал он а лон) выплата основной суммы займа
~ of a sum (~ оф а сум) возврат суммы
~ on credit (~ он крэ́дит) погашение кредита
Repeal (рипи́л) отмена
~ of a law (~ оф а ла́у) отмена закона
~ of a mandate (~ оф а ма́ндэйт) отмена мандата
Repeated (рипи́тэд) многократный
~ offense (~ оффэ́нс) рецидив
~ sampling (~ са́мплинг) повторный выбор
Repeatedly (рипи́тэдли) неоднократно
Repentance (рипэ́нтанс) раскаяние
heartfelt ~ (ха́ртфэлт ~) чистосердечное раскаяние
Repetition (рэпити́шн) повторение
Replace (риплэ́йс) to ~ (ту ~) заменять [**perfective:** заменить], сменять [**perfective:** сменить]
Replaceable (риплэ́йсабл) заменимый

Replacement (риплэ́йсмэнт) замена,
смена **~s** (~с) замененные товары
    warranty ~ (уáрранти ~) замена
по гарантии
    ~ of arbitrator (~ оф
áрбитрэйтор) замена арбитра
    ~ of capital (~оф кáпитал)
возмещение капитала
    ~ of value (~ оф вáлю)
возмещение стоимости
Replenishment (риплэ́нишмэнт)
возобновление, восстановление
    ~ of inventories (~ оф
йнвэнториз) восстановление
уровня запасов
    ~ of stocks (~ оф стакс)
возобновление запасов
Reply (риплáй) ответ
    to ~ (ту ~) отвечать
Report (рипóрт) бюллетень, протокол
    accident ~ (áксидэнт ~) акт об
аварии
    annual ~ (áннюал ~) ежегодный
бюллетень
    court-ordered medical ~ (кóурт-
óрдэрд мэ́дикал ~) судебно-
медицинский акт
    customs inspector's ~ (кáстомз
инспэ́кторз ~) акт таможенного
досмотра
    damage ~ (дáмадж ~) дефектная
ведомость
    economic ~ (экономик ~)
экономический бюллетень
    exchange-rate ~ (эксчэ́йндж-рэйт
~) бюллетень курса валюты
    expense ~ (экспэ́нс ~) расходный
документ
    final ~ (фáйнал ~) итоговая
ведомость
    financial performance ~
(файнáншл ~) отчётный баланс
    inquest ~ (йнкуэст ~) акт
обследовании
    inspection test and repair ~
(инспэ́кшн тэст энд рипэ́йр ~)
ведомость осмотра проверок и
ремонта
    medical ~ (мэ́дикал ~)
медицинский акт
    official ~ (оффúшл ~)
официальное сообщение
    outturn ~ (óуттýрн ~) ведомость
выгруженного товара
    patent ~ (пáтэнт ~) патентный
бюллетень

    personnel ~ (пэрсоннэ́л ~)
характеристика
    preliminary investigation ~
(прилúминэри инвэстигэ́йшн ~) акт
расследования
    securities exchange ~ (сэкю́ритиз
эксчэ́йндж ~) бюллетень курса
ценных бумаг на бирже
    stock status ~ (сток стáтус ~)
ведомость наличия на складе
    stockmarket ~ (стóкмáркэт ~)
биржевой бюллетень
    surveyor's ~ (сýрвэйорз ~) акт
сюрвейера
    to ~ (ту ~) сообщать
[**perfective:** сообщúть], явиться
{show up}
    to ~ for duty (ту ~ фор дю́ти)
явиться на службу
    to draw up a ~ (ту дрáу ап а ~)
составить протокол
    trade ~ (трэйд ~) торговый
бюллетень
Repossession (рипозэ́шн)
восстановление во владении
Representation (рэпризэнтэ́йшн)
представительство
    consular ~ (кóнсюлар ~)
консульское представительство
    contractual ~ (контрáкшуал ~)
договорное представительство
    diplomatic ~ (дипломáтик ~)
дипломатическое
представительство
    exclusive ~ (эксклю́сив ~)
исключительное представительство
    foreign ~ (фóрэн ~) заграничное
представительство
    international ~ (интэрнэ́шнал ~)
международное представительство
    legal ~ (лúгал ~) законное
представительство
    permanent ~ (пэ́рманэнт ~)
постоянное представительство
    permanent diplomatic ~
(пэ́рманэнт дипломáтик ~)
постоянное дипломатическое
представительство
    proportional ~ (пропóршнал ~)
пропорциональное
представительство
    temporary ~ (тэ́мпорари ~)
временное представительство
Representative (пэприсэ́нтатив)
представитель, представительный
{adj.}

accredited ~ (аккрэ́дитэд ~) аккредитованный представитель
consular ~ (ко́нсюлар ~) консульский представитель
contractual ~ (контра́ктшуал ~) договорный представитель
diplomatic ~ (диплома́тик ~) дипломатический представитель
exclusive ~ (эксклю́сив ~) исключительный представитель
juridical ~ (джюри́дикал ~) юридический представитель
legal ~ (ли́гал ~) законный представитель
official ~ (оффи́шл ~) официальное лицо
people's ~ (пи́плз ~) народный представитель
permanent ~ (пэ́рманэнт ~) постоянный представитель
special ~ (спэ́шл ~) специальный представитель
trade ~ (трэйд ~) торговый атташе, торговый представитель
~ office (~ о́ффис) представительство
Repression (рипрэ́шн) подавление
Reprimand (рэ́прима́нд) замечание, порицание
Reprint (ри́принт) перепечатка
Reprisal (рипра́йзал) репрессалии
act of ~ (акт оф ~) акт репрессалии
Reprivatization (рипрайватизэ́йшн) реприватизация
Reprivatize, to ~ (рипра́йватайз, ту ~) проводить денационализацию, реприватизировать
Republic (рипу́блик) республика
autonomous ~ (ауто́номус ~) автономная республика
Federal ~ of Germany {FRG} (фэ́дэрал ~ оф джэ́рмани {эф-ар-джи}) Федеративная Республика Германии {ФРГ}
federal ~ (фэ́дэрал ~) федеративная республика
people's ~ (пиплз ~) народная республика
presidential ~ (прэзидэ́ншл ~) президентская республика
unitary ~ (ю́нитари ~) унитарная республика
United Arab ~ (ю́найтэд а́раб ~) объединённая арабская республика
Republican (рипу́бликан) республиканский {adj., also historically of Soviet republics},

республиканец {member of a republican party}
Repudiate, to ~ (рипю́диэйт, ту ~) отказать
Repudiation (рипюдиэ́йшн) денонсация
unilateral ~ (юнила́тэрал ~) односторонняя денонсация
~ of an agreement (~ оф ан агри́мэнт) денонсация договора
~ of debts (~ оф дэтс) отказ от долгов
~ of inheritance (~ оф инхэ́ританс) отказ от наследства
Repulse (рипу́лс) отпор
to ~ (ту ~) дать отпор
Reputation (рэпютэ́йшн) репутация
Requalification (рикуалификэ́йшн) переквалификация
Request (рикуэ́ст) запрос, просьба, требование, ходатайство
informal ~ (инфо́рмал ~) неформальная просьба
official ~ (оффи́шл ~) почтительная просьба
payment ~ (пэ́ймэнт ~) платёжное требование
preliminary ~ (прили́минари ~) предварительная просьба
to ~ (ту ~) затребовать
to grant a ~ (ту грант а ~) удовлетворить просьбу
urgent ~ (у́рджэнт ~) настоятельное требование
written ~ (ри́ттэн ~) письменная просьба
~ for examination (~ фор экзаминэ́йшн) ходатайство о проведении экспертизы
Require, to ~ (рикуа́йр, ту ~) затребовать, требовать
Requirement (рикуа́йрмэнт) потребность, требование **~s** (~с) запрос
common ~ (ко́ммон ~) обычное требование
end ~ (энд ~) окончательное требование
exact ~s (экза́кт ~с) точные требования
fulfillment of ~s (фулфи́лмэнт оф ~с) выполнение требований
general ~s (джэ́нэрал ~с) общие требования
general operating ~s (джэ́нэрал о́пэрэйтинг ~с) общие эксплуатационные требования

mandatory ~ (мáндатори ~)
обязательное требование
market ~s (мáркэт ~с)
потребности рынка
one-time ~ (уáн-тайм ~) разовая
потребность
operating ~s (óпэрэйтинг ~с)
эксплуатационные требования
quantitative ~s (куáнтитэйтив
~с) количественные требования
space ~s (спэйс ~с) потребности
в площади
specific ~ (спэсúфик ~)
специальное требование
strict ~ (стрикт ~) строгое
требование
technical ~s (тэ́кникал ~с)
технические требования
to design to the ~s of ... (ту
дизáйн ту θи ~с оф ...)
проектировать с учётом
требований ...
to have specific ~s (ту хэв
спэсúфик ~с) иметь особые
требования
violation of ~s (вайолэ́йшн оф
~с) нарушение требований
Requisites (рэ́куизитс) реквизиты
Requisition (рэкуизúшн) бланк
заявки, постановление реквизиции,
реквизиция
to ~ (ту ~) реквизировать
~ of supplies (~ оф суппláйз)
требование на материалы
Resale (рúсэйл) перепродажа
Rescaling (рискэ́йлинг) изменение
масштаба
Rescind, to ~ (рисúнд, ту ~)
аннулировать договор {agreement,
act, or treaty}, кассировать,
расторгать [perfective:
расторгнуть]
to ~ a contract (ту ~ а
кóнтракт) расторгать договор
Rescission (рисúжн) расторжение
~ of a contract (~ оф а
кóнтракт) расторжение договора
Research (рисэ́рч) изыскание,
изучение
market ~ (мáркэт ~) изучение
рынка
Resell (рисэ́лл) **to ~** (ту ~)
перепродавать
Reseller (рисэ́ллэр) перепродавец
Reservation (рэсэрвэ́йшн)
бронирование, заказ, оговорка,
отметка

general ~ (джэ́нэрал ~) общая
оговорка
with ~ (уит ~) с оговоркой
without ~ (уитóут ~) без
оговорок
~ in bill of lading (~ ин билл
оф лэ́йдинг) отметка в
коносаменте
~ upon ratification (~упóн
ратификэ́йшн) оговорка при
ратификации {convention}
Reserve (ризэ́рв) запас, условность,
фонд **~s** (~) резерв
allocations to the monetary ~
(аллокэ́йшнз ту θи мóнэтари ~)
отчисления в валютный фонд
cash ~ (каш ~) кассовый резерв
currency ~s (кýррэнси ~)
валютные резервы, фонд валютных
отчислений
current ~s (кýррэнт ~) текущие
резервы
financial ~ (файнáншл ~)
финансовый резерв
free ~ (фри ~) свободный резерв
general ~ (джэ́нэрал ~) общий
резерв
gold ~s (голд ~с) золотой запас,
золотые резервы
hidden ~s (хúддэн ~с) скрытые
резервы
material ~ (матúриал ~)
материальные резервы
monetary ~ (мóнэтари ~) валютный
фонд, денежный запас, денежные
резервы
to ~ (ту ~) бронировать,
заказывать [perfective:
заказать], оставлять
[perfective: оставить]
to ~ the right (ту ~ θи райт)
оставлять за собой право
productive ~ (продýктив ~)
производственные запасы,
производственные резервы
strategic metal ~ (стратúджик
мэ́тал ~) металлический запас
world ~ (уóрлд ~) мировые запасы
Reservoir (рэ́зэрвуар) хранилище
Resettle, to ~ (рисэ́ттл, ту ~)
переселяться
Resettlement (рисэ́ттлмэнт)
переселение, поселение в новое
помещение
compulsory ~ (компýлсори ~)
принудительное переселение

internal ~ (интэ́рнал ~)
внутреннее переселение
Reside, to ~ (риза́йд, ту ~)
проживать
Residence (рэ́зидэнс) пребывание,
резиденция
   consular ~ (ко́нсюлар ~)
   консульское помещение
   permanent ~ (пэ́рманэнт ~)
   постоянное пребывание
   temporary ~ (тэ́мпорари ~)
   временная резиденция
Resident (рэ́зидэнт) резидент {in-
country intelligence officer}
Residual (рэзи́дюал) остаток
Resign, to ~ (риза́йн, ту ~) выйти в
отставку
Resignation (рэзигнэ́йшн) отставка
   to **submit one's ~** (ту субми́т
   уанз ~) подать в отставку
   ~ of a post (~ оф а пост)
   отречение от должности
Resist, to ~ (рizи́ст, ту ~)
сопротивляться
Resistance (ризи́станс)
сопротивление
   passive ~ (па́ссив ~) пассивное
   сопротивление
Resolution (рэзолю́шн) заключение,
постановление, резолюция
   charter ~ (ча́ртэр ~) уставное
   постановление
   confirming ~ (конфи́рминг ~)
   подтвердительная резолюция
   constitutional ~ (конститу́шнал
   ~) конституционное постановление
   dispute ~ (диспю́т ~)
   урегулирование спора
   final ~ (фа́йнал ~) окончательная
   резолюция
   general ~ (джэ́нэрал ~) общее
   постановление
   joint ~ (джойнт ~) совместная
   резолюция
   legislative ~ (лэ́джислэйтив ~)
   законодательное постановление
   motivated ~ (мо́тивэйтэд ~)
   мотивированное постановление
   political ~ (поли́тикал ~)
   политическое постановление
   special ~ (спэшл ~) специальное
   постановление
   ~ of confidence (~ оф ко́нфидэнс)
   резолюция доверия
   ~ of no confidence (~ оф но-
   ко́нфидэнс) резолюция недоверия

Resolve, to ~ (ризо́лв, ту ~)
постановлять, решать [**perfective:**
решить]
Resources (рисо́урсэз) ресурсы
   available ~ (авэ́йлабл ~)
   свободные денежные средства
   cash ~ (каш ~) наличные средства
   credit ~ (крэ́дит ~) кредитные
   ресурсы, кредитные фонды
   economic ~ (эконо́мик ~)
   экономические ресурсы
   exhaustible ~ (экза́устибл ~)
   истощимые ресурсы
   financial ~ (файна́ншл ~)
   финансовые ресурсы, финансовые
   средства
   liquid ~ (ли́куид ~) ликвидные
   средства
   material ~ (мати́риал ~)
   материальные ресурсы
   monetary ~ (мо́нэтари ~) денежные
   ресурсы, денежные средства
   natural ~ (на́тюрал ~) природные
   ресурсы
   private monetary ~ (пра́йват
   мо́нэтари ~) частные денежные
   средства
   productive ~ (проду́ктив ~)
   производственные ресурсы
Respective (риспэ́ктив)
соответствующий
Respondent (риспо́ндэнт) ответчик
{in judicial proceeding}
Responsibility (риспонсиби́лити)
ответственность
   additional ~ (адди́шнал ~)
   дополнительная ответственность
   administrative ~ (администрэ́йтив
   ~) административная
   ответственность
   civic ~ (си́вик ~) гражданское
   обязательство
   direct ~ (дайрэ́кт ~)
   непосредственная ответственность
   full ~ (фул ~) полная
   ответственность
   individual ~ (индиви́дюал ~)
   индивидуальная ответственность
   joint ~ (джойнт ~) совместная
   ответственность
   moral ~ (мо́рал ~) моральная
   ответственность
   official ~ (оффи́шл ~) служебная
   ответственность
   personal ~ (пэ́рсонал ~) личная
   ответственность, персональная
   ответственность

primary ~ (праймари ~) основная
обязанность
professional ~ (профэшнал ~)
профессиональная обязанность,
профессиональная ответственность
Responsible (риспóнсибл)
ответственный
Restitution (рэститýшн) реституция
~ in kind (~ ин кайнд)
реституция в натуре
Restocking (ристóкинг)
восстановление уровня запасов {of
inventories}
Restoration (рэсторэйшн)
восстановление, реставрация
~ of a lapsed patent (~ оф а
лáпсэд пáтэнт) восстановление
патента, срок действия которого
истёк
~ of rights (~ оф райтс)
восстановление в правах
Restore, to ~ (ристóр, ту ~)
реставрировать
Restraint (ристрэйнт) замораживание
import ~ (импорт ~) ограничение
импорта
moral ~ (мóрал ~) нравственное
обуздание
~ of exports (~ оф э́кспортз)
ограничение экспорта
~ of liberty (~ оф либэрти)
ограничение свободы
~ of personal liberty (~ оф
пэрсонал либэрти) ограничение
личной свободы
~ of property (~ оф прóпэрти)
замораживание собственности
Restrict (ристрикт) to ~ (ту ~)
ограничивать
Restricted (ристриктэд)
ограниченный
Restriction (ристрикшн)
ограничение, рестрикция
customs ~ (кýстомз ~) таможенное
ограничение
license ~ (лáйсэнс ~)
ограничение лицензии
monetary exchange ~s (мóнэтари
эксчэ́йндж ~с) ограничение обмена
денег
qualitative ~ (куáлитэйтив ~)
качественное ограничение
quantitative ~ (куáнтитэйтив ~)
количественное ограничение
quantitative ~s (куáнтитэйтив
~с) контингентирование {trade}

traffic ~ (трáффик ~)
ограничение движения
Result (ризýлт) результат, эффект
end ~ (энд ~) конечный результат
test ~s (тэст ~с) данные
испытаний
~s of elections (~с оф илэ́кшнз)
результаты выборов
Resume, to ~ (ризýм, ту ~)
возобновлять
Resumé (рэ́зюмэй) резюме
firm ~ (фирм ~) фирменный буклет
Resumption (ризýмпшн) возобновление
~ of activity (~ оф активити)
возобновление деятельности
~ of cooperation (~оф
коопэрэйшн) возобновление
сотрудничества
~ of deliveries (~ оф диливэриз)
возобновление поставок
~ of legal action (~ оф лигал
акшн) возобновление иска
~ of negotiations (~ оф
нэгошиэйшнз) возобновление
переговоров
~ of operations (~ оф опэрэйшнз)
возобновление деятельности
Retail (ритэйл) розница, розничный
{adj.}
at ~ (ат ~) в розницу
members only ~ establishment
(мэ́мбэрз óнли ~ эстáблишмэнт)
закрытый распределитель
to sell at ~ (ту сэлл ат ~)
продать в розницу
Retain, to ~ (ритэйн, ту ~)
удерживать
Retaliate, to ~ (ритáлиэйт, ту ~)
применять репрессалии
Retaliation (риталиэйшн)
репрессалии
Retaliatory (ритáлиатори)
карательный
Retinue (рэ́тиню) свита
Retire, to ~ (ритáйр, ту ~) выйти в
отставку
Retired (ритáйрд) отставной
Retirement (ритáйрмэнт) выкуп,
отставка
~ of bonds (~ оф бондз) выкуп
облигаций
~ of equipment (~ оф экуипмэнт)
ликвидация оборудования
Retool, to ~ (ритýл, ту ~)
перевооружить
Retort (ритóрт) отпор, реплика
Retortion (ритóршн) реторсия

Return (риту́рн) возврат,
возвращение, доход
   field warranty ~ (филд уа́рранти
~) рекламационный возврат
используемого изделия
   gross ~s (гросс ~с) валовые
поступления
   marginal ~ (ма́рджинал ~)
предельный доход
   partial ~ (паршл ~) частичный
возврат
   poor ~ (пур ~) низкий доход
   right of ~ (райт оф ~) право
возврата
   sale or ~ (сэйл ор ~) продажа
или возврат
   subsequent ~ (су́бсэкуэнт ~)
последующий возврат
   tax ~ (такс ~) налоговая
декларация
   to ~ (ту ~) возвращать, отсылать
   to arrange for a ~ (ту аррэ́йндж
фор а ~) организовывать возврат
   to demand the ~ of a sum (ту
дима́нд θи ~ оф а сум) требовать
возврата суммы
   to increase ~s on capital (ту
йнкрис ~с он ка́питал)
увеличивать фондоотдачу
   ~s in rubles (~с ин рублз)
выручка в рублях
   ~ of an advance (~ оф ан адва́нс)
возврат аванса
   ~ of cargo (~ оф ка́рго) возврат
груза
   ~ of a commission (~ оф а
комми́шн) возврат выплаченного
вознаграждения
   ~ of a delivery (~ оф а
дэли́вэри) возврат поставки
   ~ of documents (~ оф до́кюмэнтс)
возврат документов
   ~ of goods (~ оф гудз) возврат
товара, рекламация {e.g.
damaged}
   ~ of an insurance premium (~ оф
ан иншю́ранс при́миум) возврат
страхового взноса
   ~ of overpaid amount (~ оф
о́вэрпэйд амо́унт) возврат суммы,
ошибочно переплаченной
   ~ of a pledge (~ оф а плэдж)
возврат обеспечения
   ~ of rejected goods (~ оф
риджэ́ктэд гудз) возврат
бракованного товара

   ~ of unduly collected taxes (~
оф ундю́ли колле́ктэд та́ксэз)
возврат налогов, взысканных по
ошибке
   ~ on investment (~ он
инве́стмэнт) доход от
капиталовложений
Returnable (риту́рнабл) возвратный
Revalorization (ривалоризэ́йшн)
ревалоризация
   ~ of currency (~ оф ку́ррэнси)
ревалоризация валюты
Revaluation (ривалюэ́йшн)
переоценка, ревальвация
Reveal, to ~ (риви́л, ту ~)
вскрывать
Revenue (ре́вэню) доход, поступление
   annual ~ (а́ннюал ~) ежегодный
доход
   freight ~s (фрэйт ~с) доход от
фрахта
   public ~s (пу́блик ~с)
государственные доходы
   sales ~ (сэйлз ~) доход от
запродаж
   tax ~ (такс ~) доход от налогов
   to receive ~ (ту риси́в ~)
получать доход
   ~ account (~ акко́унт) счёт
доходов
Reversal (риве́рсал) кассация,
отмена, поворот
   ~ of a judgment (~ оф а
джу́джмэнт) кассация судебного
решения
   ~ of a sentence (~ оф а се́нтэнс)
отмена решения
Reverse (риве́рс) оборотный {adj.},
реверс {e.g. of a coin}
   on the ~ (он θи ~) на обороте
{side of document, etc.}
   "please see ~" (плиз си ~)
"смотри на обороте"
   to ~ (ту ~) кассировать
   to ~ a judgment (ту ~ а
джу́джмэнт) кассировать решение
суда
   **to endorse on the ~ of a
document** (ту эндо́рс он θи ~ оф а
до́кюмэнт) расписываться на
обороте документа
Review (ривю́) обзор, пересмотр,
рецензия
   budget ~ (бу́джэт ~) бюджетный
обзор
   economic ~ (эконо́мик ~)
экономический обзор

foreign market ~ (фо́рэн ма́ркэт ~) обзор иностранных рынков
official ~ (оффи́шл ~) акт по пересмотру
periodical ~ (пэрио́дикал ~) периодический обзор
price ~ (прайс ~) обзор цен
to ~ (ту ~) делать обзор
Reviewer (ривью́эр) рецензент, референт
Revision (риви́жн) изменение, переработка, ревизия
~ of a constitution (~ оф а конститу́шн) пересмотр конституции
~ of a contract (~ оф а ко́нтракт) пересмотр договора
Revisionism (риви́жнизм) ревизионизм
Revisionist (риви́жнист) ревизионист, ревизионистский {adj.}
Revivor (рива́йвор) возобновление дела
Revocable (рэ́вокабл) отзывной
Revocation (рэвокэ́йшн) отмена
~ of export privileges (~ оф э́кспорт при́вэлэджэз) лишение экспортных привилегий
~ of a gift (~ оф а гифт) отмена дарения
~ of immunity (~ оф имму́нити) отмена иммунитета
~ of power of attorney (~ оф по́уэр оф атто́рни) отмена доверенности
~ of a will (~ оф а уи́л) отмена завещания
Revoke, to ~ (риво́к, ту ~) лишать, отменять [**perfective:** отмени́ть]
empowered to ~ (эмпо́уэрд ту ~) аннулирующий
Revolt (риво́лт) переворот
palace ~ (па́лас ~) дворцовый переворот
Revolution (рэволу́шн) переворот, революция
bourgeois ~ (буржуа́ ~) буржуазная революция
demographic ~ (дэмогра́фик ~) демографическая революция
industrial ~ (инду́стриал ~) промышленная переворот, промышленный революция
October ~ (окто́бэр ~) октябрьская революция
political ~ (поли́тикал ~) политический переворот

Revolutionary (рэволю́шнэри) революционер {person}, революционный {adj.}
Reweigh, to ~ (риуэ́й, ту ~) вторично взвешивать
Rial {Middle Eastern currency} (риа́л) риал {валюта Среднего Востока}
Ribbon (ри́ббон) лента
paper ~ (пэ́йрэр ~) бумажная лента
Rifleman (ра́йфлман) стрелок
Rigging (ри́ггинг) оснащение
~ of a vessel (~ оф а вэ́ссэл) оснащение судна
Right (райт) правая {e.g. right-hand side} право {entitlement}
absolute ~ (абсолу́т ~) абсолютное право
acquired ~ (акуа́йрд ~) благоприобретенное право, приобретенное право
affirmative ~ (аффи́рматив ~) положительное право
anchorage ~ (а́нкорэдж ~) право стоянки на якоре
autonomous ~ (ауто́номус ~) автономное право
basic ~s and obligations of citizens (бэ́йсик ~с энд облигэ́йшнз оф си́тизенс) основные права обязанности граждан
by ~s (бай ~с) по праву
charter ~ (ча́ртэр ~) уставное право
civil ~s (си́вил ~с) гражданские права
civil and political ~s (си́вил энд поли́тикал ~с) гражданские и политические права
collective ~ (колле́ктив ~) коллективное право
conditional ~ (конди́шнал ~) условное право
confirmation of ~ (конфирмэ́йшн оф ~) акт подтверждающий право
conjugal ~ (ко́нджугал ~) брачное право
contradictory ~ (контради́ктори ~) противоречащее право
cultural ~s (ку́лчурал ~с) культурные права
diplomatic ~ (дипломати́к ~) дипломатическое право
divine ~ (дива́йн ~) божественное право

eternal ~ (итэ́рнал ~) вечное
право
exclusive ~ (эксклю́сив ~)
исключительное право
exclusive ~s (эксклю́сив ~с)
исключительные права
exclusive ~ to sell (эксклю́сив
~с ту сэлл) исключительное право
продажи
exclusive ~ to manufacture
(эксклю́сив ~с ту манюфа́ктюр)
исключительное право
производства
exclusive ~ to operate
(эксклю́сив ~ ту о́пэрэйт)
исключительное право на
эксплуатацию
exclusive publication ~
(эксклю́сив публикэ́йшн ~)
исключительное право на издание
extreme ~ (экстри́м ~) крайняя
правая
fishing ~ (фи́шинг ~) рыболовное
право
flagging ~ (фла́ггинг ~) право на
вывешивание флага
fundamental ~ (фундамэ́нтал ~)
основное право
grazing ~ (грэ́йзинг ~) право
выпаса скота
having a ~ (ха́винг а ~) имеющий
право
having full ~s (ха́винг фулл ~с)
полноправный
human ~s (хю́ман ~с) человеческие
права
inalienable ~ (инэ́йлиэнабл ~)
неотчуждаемое право,
неотъемлемое право
incorporeal ~ (инкорпо́риал ~)
бестелесное право
intergovernmental ~
(интэрговэрнмэ́нтал ~)
межгосударственное право
inventor's ~ (инвэ́нторс ~)
изобретательское право
juridical ~s (джури́дикал ~с)
юридические права
legal ~ (ли́гал ~) законное право
legal ~s (ли́гал ~с) законные
права
material ~ (мати́риал ~)
материальное право
monopoly ~ (моно́поли ~)
монопольное право

monopoly ~ to issue (моно́поли ~
ту и́шю) монопольное эмиссионное
право
parental ~s (парэ́нтал ~с)
родительские права
pasturage ~ (па́стюрадж ~) право
пастбища
patent ~ (па́тэнт ~) патентное
право
patent ~s (па́тэнт ~с) права из
патента
political ~s (поли́тикал ~с)
политические права
preferential ~ (прэфэрэ́ншл ~)
преимущественное право
prescriptive ~ (прискри́птив ~)
право денонсации
property ~ (про́пэрти ~)
имущественное право
property ~s (про́пэрти ~с)
имущественные права
qualified voting ~ (куа́лифайд
во́тинг ~) цензовое избирательное
право
receiving citizenship ~s
(риси́винг си́тизэншип ~с)
получивший права гражданства
restriction of ~s (ристри́кшн оф
~с) ограничение прав
territorial ~ (тэррито́риал ~)
территориальное право
to affect sovereign ~s (ту
аффэ́кт со́вэрэн ~с) осуществлять
суверенные права
to encroach on a ~ (ту энкро́ч
апо́н а ~) ущемить право
to have a ~ (ту хав а ~) иметь
право
to have the ~ (ту хав θи ~)
обладать правом
to insist on one's ~s (ту инси́ст
апо́н уо́нз ~с) отстаивать свои
права
to waive one's ~s (ту уэ́йв уо́нз
~с) отказаться от своих прав
unlimited ~ (унли́митэд ~)
бессрочное право
veto ~ (ви́то ~) право на вето
~s and interests (~с энд
и́нтэрестс) права и интересы
~ of access (~ оф а́ксесс) право
доступа
~ of appeal (~ оф аппи́л) право
кассационного опротестования
~ of citizenship (~ оф
си́тизэншип) право гражданства

~ of entry (~ оф энтри) право на въезд

~ of first refusal (~ оф фэрст рифюзал) право первого выбора

~s of man (~с оф ман) права человека

~ of rescission (~ оф рисижн) право расторжения

~ of rescission of contract (~ оф рисижн оф контракт) право на расторжение договора

~ of self-defense (~ оф сэлф-дифэнс) право на самооборону

~ of self-determination (~ оф сэлф-дитэрминэйшн) право на самоопределение

~ of seniority (~ оф синёрити) право старшинства

~ on schedule (~ он скэдюл) точно по графику

~s passing by inheritance (~с пассинг бай инхэританс) права перешедшие по наследству

~ to an attorney (~ ту ан атторни) право на судебную защиту

~ to be elected (~ ту би элэктд) право быть избранным

~ to be heard in court (~ ту би хэрд ин коурт) право быть выслушанным в суде

~ to compensation of harm (~ ту компэнсэйшн оф харм) право на возмещение вреда

~ to compensation of losses (~ ту компэнсэйшн оф лоссэз) право на возмещение убытков

~ to compensation (~ ту компэнсэйшн) право на возмещение

~ to devise by will (~ ту дивэйз бай уил) право завещать

~ to dividend (~ ту дивидэнд) право на дивиденд

~ to object (~ ту обджэкт) право на возражение

~ to restitution (~ ту рэститушн) право на реституцию

~ to strike (~ ту страйк) право на забастовку

~ to vote (ту вот) право голоса

Right-of-way (райт-оф-уэй) право на проход

Rightful (райтфул) законный

Rigid (риджид) жёсткий

Rigidity (риджидити) жёсткость

Rise (райз) рост

~ in export prices (~ ин экспорт прайсэс) удорожание экспорта

~ in price (~ ин прайс) удорожание

Risk (риск) риск, страх, рисковый {adj.}

accepted ~ (аксэптд ~) принятый риск

assigned ~ (ассайнд ~) установленный уровень риска

at one's own ~ (ат уанз оун ~) на свой страх и риск

commercial ~ (коммэршл ~) коммерческий риск

conditional ~ (кондишнал ~) условный риск

currency ~ (куррэнси ~) валютный риск

insurance ~ (иншюранс ~) страховой риск

insured ~ (иншюрд ~) застрахованный риск

maritime ~ (мэритайм ~) морской риск

professional ~ (профэшнал ~) профессиональный риск

special ~ (спэшл ~) особый риск

uninsurable ~ (униншюрабл ~) нестрахуемый риск

~ of loss (~ оф лосс) риск потери

~ of war (~ оф уар) военный риск

Risky (риски) рисковый

Rite (райт) обрядность

Rival (райвал) соперник

Rivalry (райвалри) соперничество

Riverboat (ривэрбоут) речное судно

Road (род) путь, дорожный {adj.}

Road-building (род-билдинг) дорожно-строительный {adj.}

Rob (роб) to ~ (ту ~) ограбить

Robber (роббэр) разбойник, разбойничий {adj.}

Robbery (роббэри) грабёж, ограбление, разбой

act of ~ (акт оф ~) акт грабежа

Roll (ролл) реестр, список лиц {list of persons}

electoral ~ (элэкторал ~) список избирателей

party membership ~ (парти мэмбршип ~) партийный список

Roll-back (ролл-бак) отмена {закона, и.т.д.}

~ of a tax (~ оф а такс) отмена налога

Room (рум) комната

reception ~ (рисэ́пшн ~)
приёмочная контора
Rope (роп) верёвка, канат,
пеньковая верёвка, трос
   load ~ (лод ~) грузовой канат
   wire ~ (уа́йр ~) проволочный
   канат, проволочный трос
Rostrum (ро́струм) кафедра
Rotation (ротэ́йшн)
последовательность
Roundtable (ра́ундтэбл) круглый стол
Route (рут) маршрут, трасса,
маршрутный {*adj.*}
   air ~ (эйр ~) воздушная трасса
   by the cheapest ~ (бай θи чи́пэст
   ~) по самому дешёвому маршруту
   by the fastest ~ (бай θи фа́стэст
   ~) по самому быстрому маршруту
   by the usual ~ (бай θи ю́жюал ~)
   обычным маршрутом
   deviation from the ~ (дивиэ́йшнс
   фром θи ~) отклонение от
   маршрута
   direct ~ (дайрэ́кт ~) прямой
   маршрут
   extended ~ (экстэ́ндэд ~)
   протяжённый маршрут
   land ~ (ланд ~) наземный путь
   optimal ~ (а́птимал ~)
   оптимальный маршрут
   overland ~ (о́вэрланд ~)
   судоходный путь
   regular ~ (рэ́гюлар ~) регулярный
   маршрут
   river ~ (ри́вэр ~) речной маршрут
   scheduled air ~ (скэ́дюлд эйр ~)
   линия воздушного транспорта
   sea ~ (си ~) морской путь
   the arterial ~ (θи арти́риал ~)
   магистральный маршрут
   through ~ (тру ~) сквозной
   маршрут
   to ~ (ту ~) направлять,
   устанавливать маршрут
   trade ~ (трэйд ~) торговый
   маршрут
   transit ~ (трэ́нсит) транзитная
   линия
Routine (рути́н) плановый {*adj.*},
распорядок {дня}, регламентный
{*adj.*}, текущий {*adj.*}, шаблонный
   implemented ~ (и́мплэмэнтд ~)
   заведённый порядок
   internal ~ (интэ́рнал ~)
   внутренний распорядок

Royalty (ро́йялти) авторские
{author's ~s}, вознаграждение,
гонорар, роялти
   author's ~ (а́уторз ~) авторское
   вознаграждение
   graduated scale ~ (грэ́дюэйтд
   скэ́йл ~) ступенчатое роялти
   non-recurring ~ (нон-рэку́рринг
   ~) лицензионное, разовое
   вознаграждение
   running ~ (ра́ннинг ~)
   лицензионное, текущее
   вознаграждение
   ~ **obligations** (~ облигэ́йшнз)
   обязательства по выплате роялти
Ruble (рубл) рубль {Russian
currency} рублёвый {*adj.*}
Ruin (ру́ин) разруха
Rule (рул) норма, правило
   administrative ~ (адми́нистэйтив
   ~) административное правило
   conflict ~ (ко́нфликт ~)
   коллизионная норма
   customs ~ (ка́стомз ~) таможенное
   правило
   domestic ~s (домэ́стик ~с)
   внутренние правила
   fire safety ~s (файр сэ́йфти ~с)
   противопожарные правила
   firm ~ (фирм ~) жёсткое правило
   fiscal ~s (фи́скал ~с) фискальные
   правила
   ground ~ (гро́унд ~) основное
   правило
   house ~s (ха́ус ~с) правила
   внутреннего распорядка
   internal ~s (интэ́рнал ~с)
   внутренний регламент
   jurisdiction ~ (джурисди́кшн ~)
   правило о подведомственности
   navigational ~s (навигэ́йшнал ~с)
   навигационные правила
   payment ~ (пэ́ймэнт ~) правило
   оплаты
   plant ~s (плант ~с) заводской
   регламент
   procedural ~ (проси́дюрал ~)
   процессуальное правило
   special ~ (спэ́шл ~) специальное
   правило
   substantive ~ (су́бстантив ~)
   правило относящееся к существу
   to violate the ~s **of**
   international law (ту ва́йолэйт
   θи ~с оф и́нтэрнашнал ла́у)
   нарушать нормы международного
   права норма

work ~s правила о работе
~ of cognizance (~ оф кóгнизанс)
правило о подсудности
~s of competition (~с оф
компэтишн) правила конкуренции
~s of international law (~с оф
интэрнашнал лáу) нормы
международного права
~ of public order (~с оф пáблик
óрдэр) правило публичного
порядка
Ruling (рýлинг) постановление
court ~ (кóурт ~) судебное
постановление
customs ~ (кáстомз ~) таможенное
постановление
tariff ~ (тáриф ~) тарифное
постановление
tax ~s (тэкс ~) налоговые
правила
Run (ран) пробег, тираж
empty ~ (эмпти ~) порожний
пробег
press ~ (прэсс ~) тираж печатных
изданий
to ~ (ту ~) эксплуатировать
to ~ in (ту ~ ин) обкатывать
trial ~ (трайл ~) проба, пробное
обследование
Rung (рунг) ступень
Running (рáннинг) обкатка, пробег,
эксплуатация
~ aground (~ агрóунд) посадка на
мель
Running-in (рáннинг-ин) обкатка
non-load ~ (нон-лод ~) обкатка
без нагрузки
~ of units (~ оф юнитс) обкатка
агрегатов
~ period (~ пúриод) период
обкатки
Rupee (рýпи) рупия {currency of
certain Asian nations}
Rupture (рáпчэр) разрыв
Rush (раш) спешка
~ hour (~ áур) час пик

S

Sabotage (сáботаж) диверсия,
саботаж
to ~ (ту ~) саботировать
Saboteur (саботýр) саботажник
Sack (сак) куль, мешок

sad ~ (сад ~) казанская сирота
{colloquial}
to fill ~s (ту фил ~с)
расфасовывать в мешки
Sacrafice (сáкрафайс) жертва
to ~ (ту ~) жертвовать
Sad (сад) грустный {adj.}
~ sack (~ сак) казанская сирота
{colloquial}
Safe (сэйф) безопасный {adj.}, сейф
{to store valuables}
Safeguarding (сэйфгардинг)
охранение
Safety (сэйфти) безопасность,
сохранность
fire ~ (файр ~) пожарная
безопасность
navigational ~ (навигэйшнал ~)
безопасность мореплавания
personnel ~ (пэрсоннэл ~)
безопасность персонала
plant ~ (плант ~)
технологическая безопасность
to insure ~ (ту иншýр ~)
обеспечивать безопасность
to observe ~ rules (ту обзэрв ~
рулз) соблюдать правила техники
безопасности
violation of ~ regulations
(вайолэйшн оф ~ рэгюлэйшнс)
нарушение правил техники
безопасности
~ instructions (~ инстрáкшнс)
инструкции по технике
безопасности
~ regulations (~ рэгюлэйшнс)
техника безопасности
~ rules (~ рулз) техника
безопасности
~ standards (~ стáндардс) нормы
техники безопасности
Sail, to ~ (сэйл, ту ~) плавать
Sailing (сэйлинг) отправление,
отход, парусный спорт
Sailor (сэйлор) матрос
Salary (сáлари) должностной оклад,
зарплата
average ~ (áвэрэдж ~) средняя
зарплата
monthly ~ (мóнθли ~) месячный
оклад
Sale (сэйл) продажа, распродажа,
реализация, сбыт ~s сбытовой {adj.}
bulk ~ (булк ~) массовая
продажа, массовый сбыт
co-op ~ (ко-оп ~) кооперативная
продажа

conditional ~ (конди́шнал ~)
условная продажа
credit ~ (крэ́дит ~) продажа в
кредит
delayed ~ (дилэ́йд ~) отложенная
продажа
direct ~ (дирэ́кт ~) прямой сбыт,
публичная продажа
discount ~ (ди́скоунт ~)
дисконтная продажа
exclusive ~ (эксклю́сив ~)
исключительная продажа
fire ~ (файр ~) срочная
распродажа
first ~ of the day (фэрст ~ оф
θи дэй) почин
for ~ (фор ~) продажный
forced ~ (форсд ~)
принудительная продажа с
публичных торгов
foreclosure ~ (форкло́зюр ~)
реализация заложенного имущества
intermediate ~ (интэрми́диат ~)
посредническая продажа
panic ~ (па́ник ~) срочная
распродажа
retail ~ (ри́тэйл ~) розничная
продажа
secret ~ (си́крэт ~) тайная
продажа
sham ~ (шам ~) фиктивная продажа
speculative ~ (спэ́кюлатив ~)
спекулятивная продажа
street ~ (стрит ~) уличная
продажа
to go on ~ (ту го он ~) вступить
в продажу
~ at auction (~ ат аукшн)
аукционная продажа
~ at discount prices (~ ат
ди́скоунт пра́йсэз) распродажа по
пониженным ценам
~ by commission (~ бай комми́шн)
комиссионная продажа
~ of chattels (~ оф ша́ттэлз)
продажа движимых имуществ
~ of contraband (~ оф
ко́нтрабанд) контрабандный сбыт
~ of goods (~ оф гудз)
реализация товара
~ of a license (~ оф а ла́йсэнз)
продажа лицензии
~ of plots of land (~ оф плотс
оф ланд) распродажа земельных
участков
Saleable (сэ́йлабл) ходкий

~ products (~ про́дуктс) ходкая
продукция
Salesman (сэ́йлзман) продавец
traveling ~ (тра́вэлинг ~)
разъездной агент, разъездной
торговец
Salvage (са́лвэдж) спасение
maritime ~ (ма́ритайм ~) спасение
на море
~ money (~ мо́ни) вознаграждение
за спасение
~ on cargo (~ он ка́рго)
вознаграждение за спасение груза

~ on ship (~ он шип)
вознаграждение за спасение судна
Sample (сампл) выборочный {adj.},
образец, проба, экспонат
free ~ (фри ~) бесплатный
образец
selection of ~s (сэлэ́кшн оф ~с)
подбор экспонатов
to remove a ~ (ту риму́в а ~)
отбирать экспонат
to show ~s (ту шо́у ~с)
демонстрировать экспонаты
~ of goods (~ оф гудз) образец
товаров, образчик товаров
Sampling (са́мплинг) выборочный
{adj.}
Sanction (санкшн) санкция ~s
репрессалии
administrative ~ (адми́нистрэйтив
~) административная санкция
civil ~ (си́вил ~) гражданская
санкция
collective ~ (коллэ́ктив ~)
коллективная санкция
contractual ~ (контра́кчуал ~)
договорная санкция
credit ~ (крэ́дит ~) кредитная
санкция
criminal ~ (кри́минал ~)
уголовная санкция
diplomatic ~ (диплома́тик ~)
дипломатическая санкция
economic ~ (эконо́мик ~)
экономическая санкция
financial ~ (файна́ншл ~)
финансовая санкция
fiscal ~ (фи́скал ~) фискальная
санкция
military ~ (ми́литари ~) военная
санкция
moral ~ (мо́рал ~) моральная
санкция

oppressive ~ (оппрэ́сив ~) репрессивная санкция
parliamentary ~ (парламэ́нтари ~) парламентская санкция
penalty ~ (пэ́налти ~) штрафная санкция
to ~ (ту ~) санкционировать
to apply a ~ (ту апплáй а ~) применить санкцию
trade ~ (трэйд ~) торговая санкция
~ of the law (~ оф θи лау) санкция закона
~ quality (~ куáлити) разрешённое к выпуску количество
Sanctuary (сáнкчуари) убежище
Satisfaction (сатисфáкшн) удовлетворение
in ~ (ин ~) в удовлетворение
in full and final ~ (ин фул энд фáйнал ~) в полное и окончательное удовлетворение
to complete ~ (ту комплúт ~) к полному удовлетворению
to give ~ (ту гив ~) дать удовлетворение
to meet with ~ (ту мит уиθ ~) находить удовлетворение
to mutual ~ (ту мю́чуал ~) к взаимному удовлетворению
to perform to someone's ~ (ту пэрфóрм ту сýмоунз ~) делать к чьему-либо удовлетворению
to the ~ of all concerned (ту θи ~ оф ал консэ́рнд) к удовлетворении всех сторон
~ of a claim (~ оф а клэйм) удовлетворение претензии
~ of a creditor (~ оф а крэ́дитор) удовлетворение кредитора
~ of demands (~ оф димáндс) удовлетворение требований
~ of a request (~ оф а рикуэ́ст) удовлетворение просьбы
~ of requirements (~ оф рикуáйрмэнтс) удовлетворение потребностей
Satisfactory (сатисфáктори) удовлетворительный
Satisfied (сáтисфайд) удовлетворённый
to be fully ~ (ту би фýлли ~) получить полное удовлетворение
Saturation (сачюрэ́йшн) насыщение
demand ~ (димáнд ~) насыщение спроса

market ~ (мáркэт ~) насыщение рынка
Save, to ~ (сэйв, ту ~) сберегать, сэкономить
Saving (сэ́йвинг) сбережение, экономия **~s** сберегательный {adj.}
annual ~s (áннюал ~с) годовая экономия
cost ~s (кост ~с) экономия на издержках
foreign exchange ~s (фóрэн эксчэ́йндж ~с) валютная экономия
gross ~s (грос ~с) валовое сбережение
maximum ~ (мáксимум ~) максимальная экономия
money ~ (мóни ~) денежное сбережение
net ~s (нэт ~с) чистые сбережения
personal ~s (пэ́рсонал ~с) личные сбережения
price ~s (прайс ~с) экономия на ценах
significant ~ (сигнúфикант ~) значительная экономия
space ~s (спэйс ~с) экономия места
time ~s (тайм ~с) экономия времени
to achieve ~s (ту ачúв ~с) добиться экономии средств
to achieve ~s on ... (ту ачúв ~с он ...) получить экономию на
~s account pass book (~с аккóунт пас бук) сберегательная книжка, сберкнижка {abbrev.}
~s bank (~с банк) сберкасса
~s deposit (~с дипóзит) вклад в сберегательную кассу
~ of financial resources (~ оф фáйнэшл рисóрсэз) экономия финансовых ресурсов
~s on sales costs (~с он сэйлз костс) экономия на торговых издержках
Sawmill (сáумил) лесопильный завод
Scale (скэйл) масштаб, сетка, шкала **~s** весы {measuring}
automatic ~s (аутомáтик ~с) весы-автомат
bagging ~s (бáггинг ~с) весы для автоматической упаковки в мешки
commission ~ (коммúшн ~) шкала комиссионного вознаграждения
deadweight ~ (дэ́дуэйт ~) грузовая шкала

discharge ~ (ди́счардж ~) шкала выгрузки
displacement ~ (дисплэ́йсмэнт ~) шкала водоизмещения
economically justified ~ (эконо́микалли джа́стифайд ~) экономически эффективный масштаб
electronic ~s (электро́ник ~с) электронные весы
global ~ (гло́бал ~) глобальный масштаб
hopper ~s (хо́ппэр ~с) бункерные весы
increased ~ (инкри́сд ~) увеличенный масштаб
internal ~ (инте́рнал ~) внутренняя шкала
large ~ (лардж ~) большой масштаб, масштабный {adj.}
major ~ (мэ́йджор ~) крупный масштаб
metric ~ (мэ́трик ~) масштаб в метрах
official ~ (оффи́шл ~) официальная шкала
on a broad ~ (он а брод ~) в широком масштабе
on an enlarged ~ (он ан энла́ржд ~) в увеличенном масштабе
on an industrial ~ (он ан инду́стриал ~) в промышленных масштабах
on an international ~ (он ан интэрна́шэнал ~) в международном масштабе
on a large ~ (он а лардж ~) в большом масштабе
on a limited ~ (он а ли́митэд ~) в ограниченных масштабах
on a market-wide ~ (он а ма́ркэт-уайд ~) в масштабах всего рынка
on a reduced ~ (он а ридю́сд ~) в уменьшенном масштабе
on a significant ~ (он а сигни́фикант ~) в значительном масштабе
on a smaller ~ (он а сма́ллэр ~) в меньшем масштабе
on a world ~ (он а у́орлд ~) в мировом масштабе
pay ~ (пэй ~) шкала оплаты
precision ~s (приси́жн ~с) точные весы
production ~ operation (прода́кшн ~ опэрэ́йшн) операция производственного масштаба

rate ~ (рэйт ~) тарифное расписание
reduced ~ (ридю́сд ~) уменьшенный масштаб
reduced ~ model (ридю́сд ~ мо́дэл) модель в уменьшенном масштабе
salary ~ (са́лари ~) оклад
sliding ~ (сла́йдинг ~) скользящая шкала
small-~ (смал-~) мелкомасштабный
standard ~ (ста́ндард ~) нормальный масштаб
tariff ~ (та́риф ~) тарифная сетка
testing ~s (тэ́стинг ~с) испытательные весы
time ~ (тайм ~) масштаб времени
tonnage ~ (то́ннадж ~) шкала вместимости
wage ~ (уэ́йдж ~) шкала заработной платы
wage rate ~ (уэ́йдж рэйт ~) тарифная сетка заработной платы
~ of charges (~ оф ча́рджэз) шкала расходов
~ of discounts (~ оф ди́скоунтс) шкала скидок
~ of fees (~ оф физ) шкала сборов
~ of operations (~ оф опэрэ́йшнз) масштаб операций
~s pan (~с пан) чашка весов
~s test (~с тэст) проверка весов
Scam (скам) жульничество, обман
Scarcity (скэ́йрсити) нехватка
Schadenfreude (ша́дэнфройдэ) злодаство {joy over others' misfortunes}
Schedule (скэ́джюл) график, опись, программа, расписание, табель, таблица
adjustment of ~ (аджа́стмэнт оф ~) корректировка графика
advertising ~ (а́двэртайзинг ~) план рекламной кампании
budget ~ (ба́джэт ~) бюджетная роспись
busy ~ (би́зи ~) плотный график
comprehensive ~ (комприхэ́нсив ~) сводный график
conformance with the ~ (конфо́рманс уиθ θи ~) соответствие графику
construction ~ (констру́кшн ~) график строительных работ, график монтажа

daily work ~ (дэ́йли уо́рк ~) график рабочего дня

debt repayment ~ (дэт рипэ́ймэнт ~) график возмещения долгов

delivery ~ (дэли́вэри ~) график поставок

detailed ~ (ди́тэйлд ~) детальный график

disruption of ~ (дисру́пшн оф ~) нарушение графика

exhibition ~ (экзиби́шн ~) график выставок

feasible ~ (фи́зибл ~) осуществимый график

final ~ (фа́йнал ~) окончательный график

firm ~ (фирм ~) твёрдый график

income ~ (и́нком ~) доходное расписание

linear ~ (ли́ниар ~) линейный график

master ~ (ма́стэр ~) контрольный график, основной график

meeting ~ (ми́тинг ~) выполнение графика

non-observance of ~ (нон-обзэ́рванс оф ~) несоблюдение графика

off ~ (офф ~) в соответствии с графиком

operating ~ (о́пэрэйтинг ~) график работ

payment ~ (пэ́ймэнт ~) график платежей

personnel ~ (пэрсоннэл ~) штатное расписание

preliminary ~ (прили́минэри ~) предварительный график

price ~ (прайс ~) тарифная сетка цен

production ~ (прода́кшн ~) производственный график

project ~ (про́джэкт ~) график проектных работ

revised ~ (рива́йзд ~) пересмотренный график

right on ~ (райт он ~) точно по графику

shipment ~ (ши́пмэнт ~) график отгрузок

supporting ~ (суппо́ртинг ~) вспомогательная ведомость, дополнительная ведомость

tariff ~ (та́риф ~) таможенная справка

tight ~ (тайт ~) напряжённый график

to adhere to ~ (ту адхи́р ту ~) придерживать графика

to approve a ~ (ту аппру́в а ~) утверждать график

to be ahead of ~ (ту би ахэ́д оф ~) опережать график

to be behind ~ (ту би биха́йнд ~) отставать от графика

to break ~ (ту брэйк ~) нарушать график

to coordinate the ~ (ту коо́рдинэйт θи ~) согласовывать график

to draw up a ~ (ту дра́у ап а ~) составлять график

to finalize the ~ (ту фа́йналайз θи ~) согласовать график

to meet the delivery ~ (ту мит θи дэли́вэри ~) выполнять график поставок

to operate on the ~ (ту о́пэрэйт он θи ~) выдерживать график

to revise the delivery ~ (ту рива́йз θи дэли́вэри ~) пересматривать график поставок

~ of deliveries (~ оф дэли́вэриз) программа поставки

~ of earnings (~ оф э́рнингз) роспись доходов

~ of expenses (~ оф экспэ́нсэз) роспись расходов

~ of services (~ оф сэ́рвисэз) график услуг

Schematic (скэма́тик) схема

Scheme (ским) замысел, порядок, проект

government ~ (го́вэрнмэнт ~) правительственный проект

Scene (син) арена, место действия, сцена

Schism (скизм) раскол

Schismatic (скизма́тик) раскольник, раскольнический {adj.}

Scientific (сайэнти́фик) научный

Scope (скоп) масштаб, объём

~ of expenditures (~ оф экспэ́ндичюрз) объём расходов

~ of participation (~ оф партисипэ́йшн) масштаб участия

~ of a project (~ оф а про́джэкт) масштаб проекта

~ of work (~ оф уо́рк) масштаб работ

Scoundrel (ско́ундрэл) злодей

Screw (скру) винт

to ~ (ту ~) крепить винтами

Scrivener (скри́вэнэр) стряпчий

Scrupulous (скру́пюлос) щепетильный
Scrutinize, to ~ (скру́тинайз, ту ~)
тщательно рассматривать
Scrutiny (скру́тини) рассмотрение
~ **of the budget** (~ оф θи ба́джэт)
рассмотрение бюджета
Scuffle (скафл) свалка
Sea (си) море
   access to the ~ (а́ксэс ту θи ~)
выход в море
   at ~ (ат ~) в море
   closed ~ (клозд ~) закрытое море
   free ~ (фри ~) свободное море
   heavy ~ (хэ́ви ~) бурное море
   inland ~ (и́нланд ~) внутреннее
море
   open ~ (о́пэн ~) открытое море
   shallow ~ (ша́лло ~) мелководное
море
   to have no access to the ~ (ту
хэв но а́ксэс ту θи ~) не иметь
выхода в море
   ~ damage (~ да́мадж) повреждение
на море
   ~ passage (~ па́ссадж) переход
морем
   ~ voyage (~ во́йядж) путешествие
по морю
Sea-borne (си-борн) перевозимый
морем
Seagoing (си́гоинг) мореходный
Seal (сил) печать, пломба, штемпель
   broken ~ (бро́кэн ~) сорванная
пломба
   customs ~ (ка́стомз ~) таможенное
запломбирование, таможенная
пломба
   official ~ (оффи́шл ~) пломба
   to ~ (ту ~) запечатывать
[perfective: запечатать],
запломбировать, поставить
печать, проставлять штемпель
   to ~ up (ту ~ ап) опечатать
   translator's ~ (тра́нзлэйторз ~)
штемпель переводчика
   ~ of the consignor (~ оф θи
консайно́р) пломба отправителя
Sealed (силд) упакованный
Sealing (си́линг) запломбирование
Seaman (си́ман) матрос
Seaport (си́порт) морской порт
Search (сэрч) обыск, поиск, розыск
   computer ~ (компю́тэр ~)
автоматизированный поиск
   personal ~ (пэ́рсонал ~) личный
обыск
   to ~ (ту ~) обыскивать

   to conduct a ~ (ту конду́кт а ~)
производить обыск
   ~ of a house (~ оф а хаус) обыск
на дому
   ~ of personal effects (~ оф
пэ́рсонал иффэ́ктс) обыск личных
вещей
Season (си́зон) сезон
   off ~ (офф ~) мёртвый сезон
Seat (сит) место
   to reserve ~s (ту рисэ́рв ~с)
бронирование места
Seaworthiness (си́уорθинэс)
мореходность, мореходное состояние,
пригодность к мореплаванию
   absolute ~ (абсолю́т ~)
абсолютная мореходность
   certificate of ~ (сэрти́фикэт оф
~) сертификат о мореходности
   ~ of a vessel (~ оф а вэ́ссэл)
мореходность судна
Seaworthy (си́уорθи) пригодный к
мореплаванию
Secondary (сэ́кондари)
второстепенный
   to be of ~ importance (ту би оф
~ импо́ртанс) иметь
второстепенное значение
Seconding (сэ́кондинг) поддержка
Secret (си́крэт) засекреченный
{adj.}, секрет, тайна
   commercial ~ (коммэ́ршл ~)
коммерческая тайна
   professional ~ (профэ́шнал ~)
профессиональный секрет
   trade ~ (трэйд ~) промышленный
секрет
   ~ police (~ поли́с) тайная
полиция
Secretariat (сэкрэта́риат)
секретариат
   general ~ (джэ́нэрал ~)
генеральный секретариат
Secretary (сэ́крэтари) секретарь,
составитель протокола {compiler of
minutes}
   administrative ~ (адми́нистрэйтив
~) административный секретарь
   executive ~ (экзэ́кютив ~)
исполнительный секретарь
   first ~ (фэрст ~) первый
секретарь
   general ~ (джэ́нэрал ~)
генеральный секретарь
   parliamentary ~ (парламэ́нтари ~)
парламентский секретарь

permanent ~ (пэ́рманэнт ~)
постоянный секретарь
senior ~ (си́ниор ~) старший
секретарь
state ~ (стэйт ~)
государственный секретарь
~ of the Treasury (~ оф θи
трэ́жюри) секретарь казначейства
~ of the World Court (~ оф θи
уо́рлд ко́урт) секретарь мирового
судьи
Section (сэкшн) круг, отдел,
раздел, секция
administrative ~ (адми́нистрэйтив
~) административная секция
broad ~s (брод ~с) широкие круги
consular ~ (ко́нсюлар ~)
консульский отдел
financial ~ (файна́ншл ~)
финансовый раздел
legal ~ (ли́гал ~) юридическая
секция
Sector (сэ́ктор) отрасль, сектор
agricultural ~ (агрику́лчурал ~)
сельскохозяйственный сектор
economic ~ (эконо́мик ~)
экономический сектор
industrial ~ (инду́стриал ~)
промышленный сектор
key ~ (ки ~) ключевой сектор
nationalized ~ (на́шэналайзд ~)
национализированный сектор
private ~ (пра́йват ~) частный
сектор экономики
productive ~ (прода́ктив ~)
производственный сектор
state ~ (стэйт ~)
государственный сектор
state-owned ~ (стэйт-о́унд ~)
государственный сектор экономики
Secularization (сэкюляризэ́йшн)
секуляризация
Secularize, to ~ (сэ́кюларайз, ту ~)
секуляризировать
Secure (сэкю́р) безопасный
to ~ (ту ~) закреплять
[perfective: закрепить],
обвязывать, обеспечивать
Secured (сэкю́рд) обеспеченный
Securit/y (сэкю́рити) безопасность,
залог, имущественное
поручительство, обеспеченность
~/ies (~из) валютные ценности,
ценные бумаги
against ~ (агэ́нст ~) под
обеспечение

call on ~ (кал он ~) требование
обеспечения
cash ~ (каш ~) денежное
обеспечение
collateral ~ (колла́тэрал ~)
имущественное обеспечение
currency ~ (ку́ррэнси ~) валютное
обеспечение
financial ~ (файна́ншл ~)
финансовое обеспечение
foreign ~/ies (фо́рэн ~из)
иностранные ценные бумаги
high-grade ~ (хай-грэйд ~)
первоклассное обеспечение
job ~ (джоб ~) обеспеченность
работой
material ~ (мати́риал ~)
материальная обеспеченность
perfected ~ interest (пэрфэ́ктэд
~ и́нтэрэст) ипотека занесенная в
реестр
personal ~ (пэ́рсонал ~) личная
гарантия, личное поручительство
pledged ~ (плэджд ~) залоговое
обеспечение
property ~ (про́пэрти ~)
вещественное обеспечение
readily marketable ~/ies (рэ́дили
ма́ркэтабл ~из) легкореализуемые
ценные бумаги
registered ~/ies (рэ́джистэрд
~из) именные ценные бумаги
return of ~ (риту́рн оф ~)
возврат обеспечения
sufficient ~ (суффи́шэнт ~)
достаточное обеспечение
tangible ~ (та́нджибл ~)
материальное обеспечение
to deposit as ~ (ту дипо́зит ас
~) депонировать в качестве
обеспечения
to lend against ~ (ту лэнд
агэ́нст ~) одолжить под залог
to provide ~ (ту прова́йд ~)
предоставить обеспечение
to put up ~ (ту пут ап ~) внести
залог
to stand ~ (ту станд ~) ручаться
to stand as ~ for ... (ту станд
аз ~ фор ...) поручиться за ...
to take as ~ (ту тэйк аз ~)
взять в залог
~ for a claim (~ фор а клэйм)
обеспечение иска
**~ in the form of a bank
guarantee** (~ ин θи форм оф а

банк гяранти́) обеспечение в
форме банковской гарантии
~ **measures** (~ ме́жюрз) меры для
обеспечения безопасности
~ **of payment** (~ оф пэ́ймэнт)
гарантия платежа
Seduce, to ~ (сэду́с, ту ~)
соблазнить
Seducer (сэду́сэр) соблазнитель
See, to (си, ту) видеть
to ~ **to** (ту ~ ту) распорядиться
Seek, to ~ (сик, ту ~) искать
Seize, to ~ (сиз, ту ~) отбирать
[**perfective:** отобра́ть], совершить
захват
Seized (сизд) конфискованный
Seizure (си́жюр) арест, захват,
изъятие
maritime ~ (ма́ритайм ~) арест
судна
tax ~ (такс ~) налоговое изъятие
~ **note** (~ нот) акт о конфискации
груза таможней
~ **of goods** (~ оф гудз) наложение
ареста на товары
~ **of power** (~ оф по́уэр) захват
власти
~ **of property** (~ оф про́пэрти)
наложение ареста на имущество
~ **of a vessel** (~ оф а вэ́ссэл)
захват судна
Selection (сэлэ́кшн) ассортимент,
выбор
design ~ (диза́йн ~) выбор
проектного решения
varied ~ (вэ́йрид ~)
разнообразный выбор
wide ~ (уайд ~) широкий выбор
~ **from a range of goods** (~ фром
а рэ́йндж оф гудз) выбор по
ассортименту
~ **of a trademark** (~ оф а
трэ́йдмарк) выбор знака
Self-defense (сэлф-дифэ́нс)
самооборона {as a legal defense to
a charge of murder, etc.},
самозащита {e.g. martial arts}
legal ~ (ли́гал ~) законная
самооборона
Self-determination (сэлф-
дитэрминэ́йшн) самоопределение
Self-financing (сэлф-фа́йнансинг)
самофинансирование
Self-government (сэлф-го́вэрнмэнт)
самоуправление
Self-help (сэлф-хэлп) самовольный
захват {repossession}, самопомощь

Self-management (сэлф-ма́наджмэнт)
самоуправление
workers' ~ (уо́ркэрз ~) рабочее
самоуправление
Self-sufficiency (сэлф-суффи́шэнси)
хозрасчёт
to transition to complete ~ (ту
транзи́шн ту компли́т ~)
переходить на полный хозрасчёт
transition of enterprise to ~
(транзи́шн оф э́нтэрпрайз ту ~)
переход предприятия на хозрасчёт
Self-sustaining (сэлф-сустэ́йнинг)
хозрасчётный
Sell, to ~ (сэл, ту ~) запродать
{wholesale}, реализовывать, сбыть
Sell-out (сэл-о́ут) распродажа
Selling (сэ́ллинг) продажа
distress ~ (дистрэ́с ~)
вынужденная продажа
secondary ~ (сэ́кондари ~)
вторичная продажа
Semi-colonial (сэми-коло́ниал)
полуколониальный
Semi-official (сэ́ми-оффи́шл)
официозный, полуофициальный
~ **organ** (~ о́рган) официоз {of
the press}
Semi-processed (сэ́ми-про́сэсд)
полуфабричный
~ **goods** (~ гудз) полуфабрикаты
Semi-wholesale (сэ́ми-хо́лсэйл)
полуоптовая продажа
Senate (сэ́нат) сенат, сенатский
{adj.}
Senator (сэ́натор) сенатор
Send, to ~ (сэнд, ту ~) пересылать,
послать
to ~ **back** (ту ~ бак) послать
обратно
Senior (си́ниор) староста {of a
group}, старший {adj.}
~ **representative** (~
рэпрэзэ́нтатив) старшина
Seniority (синёрити) старшинство
by ~ (бай ~) по старшинству
Sentence (сэ́нтэнс) осуждение,
приговор
criminal ~ (кри́минал ~)
уголовный приговор
death ~ (дэθ ~) присуждение к
смерти, смертный приговор
suspended ~ (саспэ́ндэд ~)
условное осуждение, условный
приговор
to ~ (ту ~) осуждать,
приговорить

to **carry out** a ~ (ту кэ́рри о́ут а ~) приводить приговор в исполнение
to **confirm** a ~ (ту конфи́рм а ~) оставлять приговор
to **pass** ~ (ту пасс ~) вынести приговор
to **reverse** a ~ (ту риве́рс а ~) отменять приговор
to **reverse** a ~ **on appeal** (ту риве́рс а ~ он аппи́л) отменять приговор в аппеляционной инстанции
Sentencing (сэ́нтэнсинг) постановление приговора
Separate (сэ́парат) раздельный
Separate, to ~ (сэ́парат, ту ~) разъединить
Separation (сэпаре́йшн) разлука {e.g. of spouses}, разъединение
　　trial ~ (тра́йал ~) пробная разлука
　　~ **of powers** (~ оф по́уэрз) разделение властей
Separatism (сэ́паратизм) сепаратизм
Separatist (сэ́паратист) сепаратист, сепаратистский {adj.}
Sequence (си́куэнс) очередность
Sequestrate, to ~ (сэкуэ́стрэйт, ту ~) наложить секвестр
Sequestration (сэкуэстре́йшн) наложение ареста на имущество, передача в секвестр, секвестр
　　judicial ~ (джюди́шл ~) судебный секвестр
Servant (сэ́рвант) прислуга, слуга
　　civil ~ (си́вил ~) государственный служащий
Serve, to ~ (сэрв, ту ~) служить
Service (сэ́рвис) линия {transport}, обслуживание, служба, услуга, эксплуатация
　　additional ~s (адди́шнал ~с) дополнительные услуги
　　agency ~s (э́йджэнси ~с) услуги агентства
　　agent's ~s (э́йджэнтс ~с) услуги агента
　　airmail ~ (э́йрмэйл ~) авиапочтовая служба
　　at your ~ (ат ёр ~) к Вашим услугам
　　auditing ~s (а́удитинг ~с) аудиторские услуги
　　automated ~ (а́утомэйтэд ~) автоматическая линия

　　auxiliary ~s (аукзи́лиэри ~с) вспомогательная служба
　　banking ~s (ба́нкинг ~с) банковские услуги
　　chartering ~s (ча́ртэринг ~с) услуги по фрахтованию
　　civil ~ (си́вил ~) государственная служба
　　cleaning ~s (кли́нинг ~с) услуги по уборке
　　coastline ~ (ко́стлайн ~) береговая линия
　　commercial ~s (комме́ршл ~с) коммерческие услуги
　　commission for ~ (комми́шн фор ~) комиссия за услуги
　　communal ~s (комм́юнал ~с) коммунальные службы
　　competitive ~ (компе́титив ~) конкурентные услуги
　　comprehensive ~ (комприхэ́нсив ~) комплексные услуги
　　construction engineering ~s (констру́кшн инджэни́ринг ~с) инженерно-строительные услуги
　　consulting ~s (консу́лтинг ~с) консультационные услуги
　　cost of ~s (кост оф ~с) стоимость услуг
　　design ~s (диза́йн ~с) конструкторские услуги
　　domestic ~ (доме́стик ~) внутренняя служба
　　engineering ~s (инджэни́ринг ~с) инжиниринговые услуги
　　expert ~s (э́кспэрт ~с) экспертные услуги
　　export of ~s (э́кспорт оф ~с) экспорт услуг
　　financial ~s (файна́ншл ~с) финансовые услуги
　　fit for military ~ (фит фор ми́литари ~) годный к военной службе
　　foreign trade ~s (фо́рэн трэйд ~с) внешнеторговые услуги
　　free ~s (фри ~с) бесплатные услуги
　　friendly ~ (фрэ́ндли ~) дружеская услуга
　　harbor ~s (ха́рбор ~с) портовые услуги
　　health ~s (хэлθ ~с) обслуживания здравоохранения, санитарная служба
　　immigration ~ (иммигре́йшн ~) иммиграционная служба

758

import of ~s (импорт оф ~с)
импорт услуг
industrial ~s (индустриал ~с)
производственно-технические
услуги
insurance ~s (иншюранс ~с)
услуги по страхованию
insurance and loading ~
{shipping} (иншюранс энд лодинг
~ {шиппинг}) агентирование
intelligence ~ (интэллиджэнс ~)
разведочная служба
intermediary ~s (интэрмидиари
~с) посреднические услуги
"invisible" ~s (инвизибл ~с)
"невидимые" услуги
judicial ~ (джюдишл ~) судебная
служба
legal ~ (лигал ~) юридическая
служба
length of ~ (лэнгθ оф ~) стаж
low density transport ~ (лоу
дэнсити транспорт ~)
малозагруженная транспортная
линия
management ~s (манаджмэнт ~с)
управленческие услуги
market for ~s (маркэт фор ~с)
рынок услуг
marketing ~s (маркэтинг ~с)
маркетинговые услуги
maximum volume of ~s (максимум
волюм оф ~с) максимальный объём
услуг
military ~ (милитари ~) военная
служба, военный стаж
nature of ~s (нэйчэр оф ~с)
характер услуг
overseas ~ (овэрсиз ~) внешняя
служба
package of ~s (пакэдж оф ~с)
комплекс услуг, пакет услуг
paid ~s (пэйд ~с) платные услуги
payment for ~s (пэймэнт фор ~с)
оплата услуг
personnel ~s (пэрсоннэл ~с)
услуги персонала
pilotage ~ (пайлотадж ~)
лоцманская служба
polite ~ (полайт ~) вежливое
обслуживание
pre-sales ~s (при-сэйлз ~с)
услуги по организации продажи
private transport ~ (прайват
транспорт ~) частная
транспортная линия

professional ~s (профэшнал ~с)
профессиональные услуги
public ~ (паблик ~) публичная
служба
public ~s (паблик ~с) публичные
службы
railway ~ (рэйлуэй ~)
железнодорожное сообщение
range of ~s (рэйндж оф ~с)
ассортимент услуг
reciprocal ~s (рисипрокал ~с)
взаимные услуги
record of ~ (рэкорд оф ~) стаж
работы
regular ~ (рэгюлар ~) регулярная
линия
regular air ~ (рэгюлар эйр ~)
регулярная линия воздушного
транспорта
rendering of ~s (рэндэринг оф
~с) оказание услуг
sanitary ~s (санитари ~с)
санитарная служба
scope of ~s (скоп оф ~с) объём
услуг
secret ~ (сикрэт ~) агентура
shuttle ~ (шаттл ~) транспортная
линия с челночным движением
social ~ (сошл ~) социальная
служба
support ~s (суппорт ~с) услуги
по поддержанию
technical ~s (тэкникал ~с)
технические услуги
technological ~s (тэкнолоджикал
~с) технологические услуги
thoroughness of ~s (θоронэс оф
~с) полнота услуг
to ~ equipment (ту ~ икуипмэнт)
обслуживать оборудование
to be in ~ (ту би ин ~)
находиться в эксплуатации
to bid a ~ package (ту бид а ~
пакэдж) предлагать пакет услуг
to employ the ~s of ... (ту
эмплой θи ~с оф ...)
воспользоваться услугами ...
to maintain regular ~ (ту
мэйнтэйн рэгюлар ~) поддерживать
регулярное движение
to put into ~ (ту пут инту ~)
вводить в строй
to require ~s (ту рикуайр ~с)
прибегать к услугам
to take out of ~ (ту тэйк оут оф
~) выводить из эксплуатации

to utilize ~s (ту ютилайз ~с)
пользоваться услугами
tourist ~s (турист ~с)
туристические услуги
trade of ~s (трэйд оф ~с)
торговля услугами
training ~s (трэйнинг ~с) услуги
по обучению
transport ~ (транспорт ~)
транспортная линия
transportation ~s (транспортэйшн
~с) транспортные услуги, услуги
по перевозке
unfit for military ~ (анфит фор
милитари ~) не пригодный к
военной службе
unscheduled ~ (анскэджюлд ~)
нерегулярная транспортная линия
use of ~s (юс оф ~с) потребление
услуг
voluntary ~ (волунтэри ~)
добровольная служба
~ abroad (~ аброд) заграничная
служба
~s agreement (~с агримэнт)
договор о предоставлении услуг
~ center (~ сэнтэр) бюро услуг
~ experience (~ экспириэнс) опыт
эксплуатации
~ life (~ лайф) период действия
~ record (~ рэкорд) стаж
~ regulations (~ рэгюлэйшнс)
правила эксплуатации
~s sector (~с сэктор) сфера
услуг
Serviceable (сэрвисабл) годный к
эксплуатации
Servitude (сэрвитуд) сервитут
continuity of a ~ (континюити оф
а ~) преемственность сервитута
Session (сэшн) заседание, сессия
budgetary ~ (баджэтари ~)
бюджетная сессия
closed ~ (клозд ~) закрытое
заседание
closed ~ of court (клозд ~ оф
корт) закрытое заседание суда
closing ~ (клосинг ~)
заключительное заседание
emergency ~ (эмэрджэнси ~)
чрезвычайная сессия
extraordinary ~ (экстраординари
~) внеочередная сессия
joint ~ (джойнт ~) совместное
заседание
plenary ~ (плэнари ~) пленарное
заседание

public ~ (паблик ~) открытое
заседание
regular ~ (рэгюлар ~) очередное
заседание, очередная сессия
~ of criminal court (~ оф
криминал корт) уголовное
судебное заседание
~ of parliament (~ оф парламэнт)
сессия парламента
Set (сэт) комплект, набор
complete ~ (комплит ~) полный
комплект, полный набор
complete ~ of bills of lading
(комплит ~ оф билс оф лэйдинг)
полный комплект коносаментов
duplicate ~ (дупликат ~) двойной
комплект
individual ~ (индивидюал ~)
индивидуальный комплект
price per ~ (прайс пэр ~) цена
за комплект
standby ~ (стандбай ~) резервный
комплект
to ~ off against (ту ~ офф
агэнст) противопоставить
to make a ~ (ту мэйк а ~)
комплектовать
to provide a complete ~ (ту
провайд а комплит ~)
предоставлять полный комплект
to provide as a ~ (ту провайд ас
а ~) поставлять в комплекте
~ of documents (~ оф докюмэнтс)
комплект документов
~ of equipment (~ оф икуипмэнт)
комплект оборудования
~ of instruments (~ оф
инструмэнтс) комплект приборов
~ of packing lists (~ оф паккинг
листс) комплект упаковочных
листов
~ of samples (~ оф самплз)
комплект образцов
~ of spare parts (~ оф спэйр
партс) комплект запчастей
Set-up (сэт-ап) установка
Setting against (сэттинг офф
агэнст) противопоставление
Settle, to ~ (сэтл, ту ~)
оплачивать, разрешать [perfective:
разрешить], решать [perfective:
решить], урегулировать
to ~ accounts (ту ~ аккоунтс)
расплачиваться
to ~ by means of negotiation (ту
~ бай минз оф нэгошиэйшн)
урегулировать путём переговоров

to refuse to ~ (ту рифю́з ту ~) отказываться от удовлетворения
Settled (сэтлд) урегулированный
Settlement (сэ́тлмэнт) заселение, оседлость, платёж, поселение, разрешение, расчёт безналичный расчёт, решение, селение, уплата, урегулирование

amicable ~ (а́микабл ~) дружественное урегулирование, мирное решение

amicable ~ of a claim (а́микабл ~ оф а клэйм) мирное урегулирование претензии

clearinghouse ~ (кли́рингхаус ~) клиринговый расчёт

compromise ~ (ко́мпромайз ~) компромиссное решение, компромиссное урегулирование

currency ~ (ку́ррэнси ~) валютный расчёт

early ~ (э́рли ~) досрочная уплата

equitable ~ (э́куитабл ~) равномерное погашение

final ~ (фа́йнал ~) окончательный расчёт, окончательное урегулирование

general ~ (дже́нэрал ~) общее решение

insufficient ~ (инсуффи́шэнт ~) недостаточное погашение

interbank ~ (интэрба́нк ~) межбанковский расчёт

international ~ (интэрна́шэнал ~) международный расчёт

judicial ~ (джюди́шл ~) судебное разрешение, судебное урегулирование

motivated ~ (мо́тивэйтэд ~) мотивированное решение

national arbitral ~ (на́шэнал а́рбитрал ~) национальное арбитражное решение

partial ~ (паршл ~) частичное удовлетворение, частичное урегулирование

to achieve an amicable ~ (ту ачи́в ан а́микабл ~) достигать мирного урегулирования

to motivate a ~ (ту мо́тивэйт а ~) мотивировать решение

to negotiate a ~ (ту нэго́шиэйт а ~) вести переговоры об урегулировании

urban ~ (у́рбан ~) городское поселение

~ negotiations (~ нэгошиэ́йшнс) переговоры по урегулированию

~ of a claim (~ оф а клэйм) урегулирование претензии

~ of debts (~ оф дэтс) ликвидация долгов, урегулирование долгов

~ of a dispute (~ оф а диспю́т) разрешение спора

~ of losses (~ оф ло́ссэз) ликвидация убытков

~ on an exchange (~ он ан эксчэ́йндж) ликвидация сделок
Settler (сэ́тлэр) переселенец

convict ~ {exile} (ко́нвикт ~ {э́кзайл}) ссыльнопоселенец
Settling (сэ́ттлинг) погашение
Settlor (сэ́ттлор) доверитель
Setup (сэ́тап) наладка

manual ~ (ма́нюал ~) ручная наладка

supervision of ~ (супэрви́жн оф ~) руководство наладкой

to ~ (ту ~) налаживать

to provide ~ (ту прова́йд ~) проводить наладку
Sever, to (сэ́вэр, ту) разорвать

to ~ diplomatic relations (ту ~ дипло́матик рилэ́йшнс) разорвать дипломатические сношения
Severance (сэ́вэранс) разрыв

~ of diplomatic relations (~ оф дипло́матик рилэ́йшнс) разрыв дипломатических сношений

~ of economic ties (~ оф эконо́мик тайз) разрыв экономических связей
Sewage (су́адж) сточные воды
Shadowing (ша́доинг) слежка {closely following}
Sham (шам) мнимый
Share (шэйр) акция, долевой, доля, доля участия, пай, фондовый

a ~ of ... % (эй ~ оф ... %) на долю приходится ... %

agreed ~ (агри́д ~) оговорённая доля

bearer ~ (бэ́йрэр ~) акция на предъявителя

bearer ~s (бэ́йрэр ~с) предъявительские акции

competition for market ~ (компэти́шн фор ма́ркэт ~) борьба за рынки

cooperative ~ (коо́пэратив ~) кооперативный пай

deposited ~s (дипо́зитэд ~с)
депонированные акции
equal ~ (и́куал ~) равная доля
founder's ~s (фо́ундэрз ~с)
учредительские акции
founding ~ (фо́ундинг ~)
учредительный пай
gratuity ~ (грату́ити ~)
бесплатная акция
in equal ~s (ин и́куал ~с)
равными долями
individual ~ (индиви́дюал ~)
долевое участие
investment ~ (инвэ́стмэнт ~)
инвестиционная акция
market ~ (ма́ркэт ~) часть рынка
maximum ~ (ма́ксимум ~)
максимальная доля
minimum ~ (ми́нимум ~)
минимальная доля
multiple voting ~ (му́лтипл
во́тинг ~) многоголосная акция
nominal ~ (но́минал ~) именная
акция
plural voting ~ (плю́рал во́тинг
~) плюральная акция
pro rata ~ (про ра́та ~)
пропорциональная доля
respective ~ (риспэ́ктив ~)
соответствующая доля
small ~ (смал ~) малая доля
subscription ~ (субскри́пшн ~)
подписанная акция
sufficient ~ (суффи́шэнт ~)
достаточная доля
to establish ~ (ту эста́блиш ~)
определять долю
to go by ~s (ту го бай ~с)
входить в долю
to offer a ~ in (ту о́ффэр а ~
ин) предлагать участие
"vincular" ~ (ви́нкюлар ~)
винкулированная акция
~ in capital (~ ин ка́питал) доля
в капитале
~ in the form of commodities (~
ин θи форм оф коммо́дитиз) вклад
в товарной форме
~ of capital contribution (~ оф
ка́питал контрибю́шн) доля участия
в акционерном капитале
~ of charter fund (~ оф ча́ртэр
фунд) доля в уставном фонде
~ of commission (~ оф комми́шн)
комиссионная доля
~ of common stock (~ оф ко́ммон
сток) обыкновенная акция

~ of a company (~ оф а ко́мпани)
доля в акционерной компании
~ of deliveries (~ оф дэли́вэриз)
доля в поставках
~ of general average
contribution {for lost cargo} (~
оф джэ́нэрал а́вэрэдж контрибю́шн
{фор лост ка́рго}) доля,
причитающаяся по общей аварии
~ of a joint stock company (~ оф
а джойнт сток ко́мпани) пай
акционерного общества
~ of a partnership (~ оф а
па́ртнэршип) пай товарищества
~ of preferred stock (~ оф
прифэ́рд сток) привилегированная
акция
~ of profits (~ оф про́фитс) доля
прибыли, часть прибыли
~ of services (~ оф сэ́рвисэз)
доля услуг
~ of the world market (~ оф θи
уо́рлд ма́ркэт) доля мирового
рынка
~ paid in full (~ пэйд ин фул)
акция покрытая деньгами
~ "vinculum juris" (~ ви́нкюлум
джу́рис) винкулированная акция
Sharecropper (шэ́йркроппэр)
издольщик
Sharecropping (шэ́йркро́ппинг)
издольщина, половничество
Shareholder (шэ́йрхолдэр) акционер,
владелец акций, держатель акций
common ~ (ко́ммон ~) владелец
акций, обыкновенных
registered ~ (рэ́джистэрд ~)
владелец акций, именных
Shareholdings (шэ́йрхолдингс)
владение акциями
Sharing (шэ́йринг) разделение
cost ~ (кост ~) распределение
затрат
profit ~ (про́фит ~)
распределение выгод
~ of currency risks (~ оф
ку́ррэнси рискс) распределение
валютный рисков
~ of experience (~ оф
экспи́риэнс) обмен опытом
~ of losses (~ оф ло́ссэз)
распределение убытков
~ of risks (~ оф рискс)
распределение рисков
Sheet (шит) лист, список
balance ~ (ба́ланс ~) отчётная
ведомость

cargo ~ (ка́рго ~) грузовая ведомость
cost ~ (кост ~) ведомость издержек, калькуляционная ведомость, калькуляционный лист
fact ~ (факт ~) фактические данные
inventory ~ (и́нвэнтори ~) инвентарная ведомость
tally ~ (та́лли ~) тальманский лист
time ~ (тайм ~) ведомость учёта времени, затраченного на погрузку и выгрузку судна {shipping}, ({ши́ппинг},) табель учёта отработанных часов
work (уо́рк) рабочий лист
wrapper ~ (ра́ппэр ~) обёрточный лист
Sheeting (ши́тинг) чехол
polyethylene ~ (полиэ́θэлин ~) полиэтиленовый чехол
Shield (шилд) щит
Shift (шифт) бригада, смена
day ~ (дэй ~) дневная смена
night ~ (найт ~) ночная смена
to ~ (ту ~) переменять, передвигать
Shifting (ши́фтинг) перестановка
~ of risk (~ оф риск) переход риска
~ of the burden of proof (~ оф θи бу́рдэн оф пруф) переложение бремени доказания
Ship (шип) корабль, судно
dry cargo ~ (драй ка́рго ~) сухогрузное судно
mail ~ (мэ́йл ~) почтовый пароход
sister ~ (си́стэр ~) однотипное судно
to ~ (ту ~) отгружать, отправлять [**perfective:** отправить], транспортировать
to ~ by water (ту ~ бай уа́тэр) перевозить по воде
to ~ by rail (ту ~ бай рэйл) перевозить железнодорожным транспортом
~ owner (~ о́унэр) судовладелец
~ with ... tons burden (~ уиθ ... тонз бу́рдэн) судно грузоподъёмностью в ... тонн
Shipbroker (ши́пбро́кэр) судовой брокер
Shipbuilding (ши́пбилдинг) судостроение, судостроительный {adj.}

Shipload (ши́плод) корабельный груз
Shipment (ши́пмэнт) отгрузка, отправка, перевозка, погрузка, поставка
conventional ~ (конвэ́ншнал ~) конвенциональный груз
priority ~ (прайо́рити ~) срочный груз
rail ~ (рэйл ~) железнодорожный груз
short ~ (шорт ~) часть груза, не принятая на судно
single ~ (сингл ~) разовая поставка
water-borne ~ (уа́тэр-борн ~) водная перевозка
Shipper (ши́ппэр) грузоотправитель, отправитель, товароотправитель
Shipping (ши́ппинг) мореплавание, плавание, судоходство
coastal ~ (ко́стал ~) каботажное судоходство
container ~ (контэ́йнэр ~) контейнерная транспортировка
inland ~ (и́нланд ~) речное судоходство
internal ~ (интэ́рнал ~) внутреннее судоходство
international ~ (интэрна́шэнал ~) международное судоходство, международное торговое мореплавание
merchant ~ (мэ́рчант ~) торговое судоходство
ocean ~ (о́шн ~) морское судоходство, океанское плавание
seagoing ~ (си́гоинг ~) морская транспортировка
to provide ~ (ту прова́йд ~) обеспечивать транспортировкой
tramp ~ (трамп ~) трамповое судоходство
~ rates (~ рэйтс) ставки фрахта
Shipwreck (ши́прэк) гибель корабля, крушение судна
Shipyard (ши́пярд) судоверфь, судостроительный завод
Shop (шоп) лавка, магазин, мастерская
specialty ~ (спэ́шлти ~) специализированный магазин
to keep ~ (ту кип ~) держать магазин
Shopkeeper (шо́пкипэр) владелец магазина

Short (шорт) короткий {not tall},
недостающий {lacking},
непродолжительный {period of time}
   ~ delivered (~ дэли́вэрд)
   недопоставленный
   ~ payment (~ пэ́ймэнт) недоплата
   ~ received (~ риси́вд)
   недополученный
   ~ shipment (~ ши́пмэнт) недогруз
   ~ shrift (~ шрифт) короткая
   расправа
   ~ weight (~ уэ́йт) недовес
Shortage (шо́ртадж) голод, дефицит,
недостаток, недостача, недочёт,
нехватка
   actual ~ (а́кчуал ~) фактическая
   недостача
   acute ~ (акю́т ~) острый голод,
   острая нехватка
   claim for ~ of goods (клэйм фор
   ~ оф гудз) претензия по
   недостаче товара
   currency ~ (ку́ррэнси ~) валютный
   голод
   declared ~ (диклэ́йрд ~)
   заявленная недостача
   labor ~ (лэ́йбор ~) дефицит
   рабочей силы
   major ~ (мэ́йджор ~) крупная
   недостача
   manpower ~ (ма́нпоуэр ~) нехватка
   рабочей силы
   personnel ~ (пэрсоннэ́л ~)
   нехватка кадров
   supply ~ (суппла́й ~)
   недостаточность снабжения
   temporary ~ (тэ́мпорари ~)
   временная нехватка
   to compensate for ~ (ту
   ко́мпэнсэйт фор ~) возместить
   недостачу
   to cover a ~ (ту ко́вэр а ~)
   покрывать недостачу
   ~ in weight (~ ин уэ́йт)
   недостача в весе
   ~ of goods (~ оф гудз) дефицит
   товаров
   ~ report (~ рипо́рт) акт о
   недостаче
Shot (шот) стрелок
Shout (шо́ут) окрик
Showroom (шо́урум) демзал
   to open a ~ (ту о́пэн а ~)
   открывать демзал
Shrinkage (шри́нкадж) обесценение
Shut, to ~ (шут, ту ~) закрывать
[perfective: закрыть]

Sick (сик) больной
   ~ pay (~ пэй) пособие по болезни
Side (сайд) сторона
   obverse ~ (о́бвэрс ~) лицевая
   сторона {coin}
   reverse ~ (ривэ́рс ~) оборотная
   сторона {coin}
Siege (сидж) осада
Sight (сайт) предъявление
   payable on ~ (пэ́йабл он ~)
   оплачиваемый по предъявлению
Sign (сайн) знак, метка, признак,
примета
   border ~ (бо́рдэр ~) граничный
   знак
   official ~ (оффи́шл ~)
   официальный знак
   official ~ of guarantee (оффи́шл
   ~ оф гяранти́) официальный знак
   гарантии
   to ~ (ту ~) подписывать
   to ~ a receipt (ту ~ а риси́т)
   расписаться в получении
   to ~ for (ту ~ фор) расписаться
   to ~ for a registered letter (ту
   ~ фор а рэ́джистэрд лэ́ттэр)
   расписаться в получении
   заказного письма
Signal (си́гнал) сигнал
   distress ~ (дистрэ́с ~) сигнал
   бедствия
Signatory (си́гнатори) подписавшее
лицо, подписавшаяся сторона
   authorized ~ (а́уθорайзд ~) лицо,
   имеющее право подписи
Signature (си́гначэр) подпись
   attested ~ (аттэ́стэд ~)
   заверенная подпись
   one's own ~ (уа́нз о́ун ~)
   собственноручная подпись
   personal ~ (пэ́рсонал ~) личная
   подпись
   second ~ (сэ́конд ~) вторая
   подпись
   to authenticate a ~ (ту
   ауθэ́нтикэйт а ~) удостоверять
   подпись
Significance (сигни́фиканс)
значительность
   real ~ (рил ~) сущность
Significant (сигни́фикант)
значительный
Signing (са́йнинг) подписание
   ~ of a contract (~ оф а
   ко́нтракт) подписание договора
Silver (си́лвэр) серебро

~ **in a coin** (~ ин а койн)
серебро в монете
Simple (симпл) простой
Simulation (симюлэйшн) симуляция
Single (сингл) однократный {one time}
Sinking (синкинг) понижение
Sister (систэр) сестра
    illegitimate ~ (иллэджитэмат ~)
    внебрачная сестра
Sister-in-law (систэр-ин-лау)
золовка {husband's sister},
свояченица {wife's sister}
Sit, to ~ (сит, ту ~) заседать
Site (сайт) место, местонахождение
    advertising ~ (адвэртайзинг ~)
    место для установки рекламного
    щита или панели
    at installation ~ (ат
    инсталлэйшн ~) на месте монтажа
    building ~ (билдинг ~) место для
    строительства, постройка,
    строительный объект
    installation ~ (инсталлэйшн ~)
    место монтажа, место установки
    job ~ (джоб ~) место работы
    on ~ (он ~) на месте
    on-~ workers (он-~ уоркэрз)
    рабочие на местах
    outdoor advertising ~ (оутдор
    адвэртайзинг ~) местонахождение
    средства наружной рекламы
    permanent exhibition ~
    (пэрманэнт экзибишн ~) место
    постоянной выставки
    plant ~ (плант ~)
    местонахождение завода
    test ~ (тэст ~) место испытаний
    warehousing ~ (уэрхоузинг ~)
    место складирования
    ~ **adjustment** (~ аджастмэнт)
    регулировка на месте
Situation (сичуэйшн) обстановка,
ситуация
    actual ~ (акчуал ~) фактическое
    положение
    awkward ~ (аукуард ~) неловкое
    положение
    deterioration of the economic ~
    (дитириорэйшн оф θи экономик ~)
    ухудшение конъюнктуры
    economic ~ (экономик ~)
    хозяйственная обстановка,
    экономическое положение
    general economic ~ (джэнэрал
    экономик ~) общее экономическое
    положение

improvement of the economic ~
(иммпрувмэнт оф θи экономик ~)
улучшение конъюнктуры
international ~ (интэрнашэнал ~)
международная обстановка
material ~ (матириал ~)
имущественное положение
peaceful ~ (писфул ~) мирное
положение
personal ~ (пэрсонал ~) личное
положение
unavoidable ~ (анавойдабл ~)
непреодолимый случай
unforeseen ~ (анфорсин ~)
непредвиденный случай
~ **of force majeure** (~ оф форс
мажор) непреодолимый случай
Size (сайз) величина, размер
    actual ~ (акчуал ~) натуральная
    величина
    case ~ (кэйс ~) габарит ящика
    container ~ (контэйнэр ~)
    габарит тары
    increased ~ (инкрисд ~)
    повышенный размер
    maximum ~ (максимум ~)
    максимальный размер
    middle ~ (мидл) средней величины
    minimum ~ (минимум ~)
    минимальный размер
    nominal ~ (номинал ~)
    номинальный размер
    to ~ (ту ~) сортировать
    to ~ **up** (ту ~ ап) определять
    величину
    ~ **of depreciation** (~ оф
    дипришиэйшн) размер амортизации
    ~ **of the market** (~ оф θи маркэт)
    объём рынка
    ~ **of penalty** (~ оф пэналти)
    размер штрафа
    ~ **of pension** (~ оф пэншн) размер
    пенсии
    ~ **of staff** (~ оф стаф) размер
    персонала
Sizing (сайзинг) сортировка
Skids (скидз) салазки
    on ~ (он ~) на салазках
Skill (скил) квалификация,
мастерство
    great professional ~ (грэйт
    профэшнал ~) высокое
    профессиональное
    high professional ~ (хай
    профэшнал ~) высокая
    профессиональная квалификация

operating ~s (о́пэрэйтинг ~с) рабочее мастерство
professional ~ (профэ́шнал ~) производственная квалификация
technical ~ (тэ́кникал ~) техническое мастерство
to improve ~s (ту импру́в ~с) повышать квалификацию
to acquire professional ~ (ту акку́айр профэ́шнал ~) получать производственную квалификацию
Skilled (скилд) квалифицированный
Skirmish (ски́рмиш) стычка
Skyscraper (ска́йскрэйпэр) небоскрёб
Slander (сла́ндэр) клевета, оговор
to ~ (ту ~) клеветать
Slate (слэйт) сланец {material}, список {list}
~ of candidates (~ оф ка́ндидэйтс) список кандидатов
Slave (слэйв) раб
Slaveholder (слэ́йвхолдэр) рабовладелец, рабовладельческий {adj.}
Slaveholding (слэ́йвхолдинг) рабовладельческий {adj.}
Slavery (слэ́йвэри) рабство
Sliding (сла́йдинг) скользящий
~-scale (~-скэйл) скользящий
Sling (слинг) верёвка для подъёма груза
Slip (слип) билет, бланк
deposit ~ (дипо́зит ~) бланк для взноса депозита, бланк для вклада, вкладной билет
duplicate deposit ~ (ду́пликат дипо́зит ~) дубликат бланка о взносе депозита
tonnage ~ (то́ннадж ~) мерительное свидетельство {of a vessel}
Slipshod (сли́пшод) халатный
Sluggishness (слу́ггишнэс) вялость
Slump (слумп) спад конъюнктуры
Smuggled (смаглд) контрабандный
~ food stocks (~ фуд стокс) контрабандные съестные припасы
Smuggling (сма́глинг) контрабанда
to be engaged in ~ (ту би энгэ́йджд ин ~) заниматься контрабандой
Soaked (сокд) промокнули водой
to become ~ (ту бико́м ~) мокнуть
Sobriquet (со́брикэт) прозвище
Social (сошл) общественный

~ insurance benefits (~ иншу́ранс бэ́нэфитс) выплаты по социальному страхованию
Socialism (со́шлисм) социализм
state ~ (стэйт ~) государственный социализм
Socialist (со́шлист) социалист {person}, социалистический {adj.}
Socialization (сошлизэ́йшн) социализация
Society (соса́йэти) общество
classless ~ (кла́слэс ~) бесклассовое общество
comparative law ~ (компэ́йратив лау ~) общество сравнительного права
cooperative ~ (коо́пэратив ~) кооперативное объединение, кооперативное общество, кооперативное товарищество
mutual aid ~ (мю́чуал эйд ~) общество взаимопомощи
secret ~ (си́крэт ~) тайное общество
Soft (софт) мягкий, необратимый
Software (со́фтуэйр) программное обеспечение
Soil (сойл) земля, почва
Soiling (со́йлинг) загрязнение
Sol (сол) соль {Peruvian currency}
Sold (солд) реализованный
to be ~ out (ту би ~ о́ут) разойтись
Solicit, to ~ (соли́сит, ту ~) домогаться
Solicitation (солиситэ́йшн) домогательство
Solicitor (соли́ситор) адвокат {British}, поверенный
Solidarity (солида́рити) солидарность
Solidary (со́лидари) солидарный {civil law obligation}
Solution (солю́шн) разрешение, решение
possible ~ (по́ссибл ~) возможное решение
Solvency (со́лвэнси) бонитет, кредитоспособность, платежеспособность
guarantee of ~ (гяранти́ оф ~) гарантия кредитоспособности
~ of a consignee (~ оф а консайни́) платёжеспособность грузополучателя
Solvent (со́лвэнт) кредитоспособный, платежеспособный

Son (сон) сын
  adopted ~ (адо́птэд ~) приёмный
  сын
Son-in-law (сон-ин-лау) зять
Sophisticated (софи́стикэйтэд)
сложный
  ~ equipment (~ икуи́пмэнт)
  сложная техника
Sort (сорт) вид, качество, класс,
разряд, сорт
Sorting (со́ртинг) бракераж
Sound (со́унд) звук, пролив
{geographical}, устойчивый {adj.}
Soundness (со́унднэс)
обоснованность, устойчивость
Source (сорс) источник
  independent ~ of income
  (индипэ́ндэнт ~ оф и́нком)
  самостоятельный источник дохода
  jurisprudential ~s
  (джуриспрудэ́ншл ~с) юридические
  источники
  raw input ~ (рау и́нпут ~)
  сырьевая база {materials}
  reliable ~ (рила́йабл ~) верный
  источник
  ~ of accumulation (~ оф
  аккюмюлэ́йшн) источник накопления
  ~ of credit (~ оф крэ́дит)
  источник кредита
  ~ of energy (~ оф э́нэрджи)
  источник энергии
  ~ of evidence (~ оф э́видэнс)
  источник доказательства
  ~ of financing (~ оф фа́йнансинг)
  источник финансирования
  ~ of income (~ оф и́нком)
  источник дохода
Sovereign (со́вэрн) суверен
Sovereignty (со́вэрнти)
полновластие, суверенитет
  domestic ~ (домэ́стик ~)
  внутренний суверенитет
  full ~ (фул ~) полный
  суверенитет
  legal ~ (ли́гал ~) правовой
  суверенитет
  limited ~ (ли́митэд ~)
  ограниченный суверенитет
  military ~ (ми́литари ~) военный
  суверенитет
  territorial ~ (тэррито́риал ~)
  территориальный суверенитет
  ~ in foreign affairs (~ ин фо́рэн
  аффэ́йрс) внешний суверенитет
Soviet (со́виэт) совет {council},
советский {adj.}

  People's ~ (пиплз ~) народный
  совет
  Supreme ~ (супри́м ~) верховный
  совет {historical}
Sovnarkom (со́внарком) совнарком
Sow, to ~ (со, ту ~) засевать
[perfective: засеять]
Space (спэйс) космос, место,
площадь, пространство
  advertising ~ (а́двэртайзинг ~)
  место для публикации рекламы
  air ~ (эйр ~) воздушное
  пространство
  blank ~ (бланк ~) свободное
  место
  cargo ~ (ка́рго ~) грузовое
  место, место для погрузки
  cost of ~ (кост оф ~) стоимость
  места
  designated ~ (дэ́зигнэйтэд ~)
  указанное место
  exhibit ~ (экси́бит ~) место для
  экспонатов
  exhibition ~ (экзиби́шн ~) место
  на выставке
  forbidden air ~ (форби́ддэн эйр
  ~) запретное воздушное
  пространство
  freight ~ (фрэйт ~)
  грузовместимость судна
  narrow ~ (на́рро ~) узкое место
  purchase of advertising ~
  (пу́рчас оф а́двэртайзинг ~)
  покупка рекламного места
  rental ~ (рэ́нтал ~) арендованная
  зона
  sales floor ~ (сэйлз флор ~)
  торговая площадь
  savings of ~ (сэ́йвингс оф ~)
  экономия места
  storage ~ (сто́радж ~) место для
  хранения
  to arrange shipping ~ (ту
  аррэ́йндж ши́пинг ~) обеспечить
  место
  to receive cargo ~ (ту риси́в
  ка́рго ~) получить место на судне
  to rent ~ (ту рэнт ~) арендовать
  место {as lessee}, сдавать место
  в аренду {as lessor}
  to save ~ (ту сэйв ~) экономить
  место
  warehouse ~ (уэ́рхаус ~) складное
  помещение
  working ~ (уо́ркинг ~) робочая
  площадь

~ **on vessel** (~ он вэ́ссэл) место на судне
Spare (спэйр) запасной
   to ~ (ту ~) щадить
   to ~ no effort (ту ~ но э́ффорт) не щадить сил
Special (спэшл) специальный
Specialist (спэ́шлист) специалист, эксперт
   to consult a ~ (ту консу́лт а ~) консультироваться с экспертом
Specialization (спэшлизэ́йшн) специализация
   ~ **of product line** (~ оф про́дукт лайн) специализация производства
Specific (спэси́фик) специальный
Specification (спэсификэ́йшн) норматив, спецификация
   contract ~s (ко́нтракт ~с) технические условия договора, технические условия контракта
   job ~s (джоб ~с) квалификационные требования
   order ~s (о́рдэр ~с) условия заказа
   performance ~s (пэрфо́рманс ~с) рабочие технические условия
   process ~s (про́сэс ~с) технические условия производственного процесса
   safety ~s (сэ́йфти ~с) технические условия для обеспечения безопасности
   temporary ~s (тэ́мпорари ~с) временные технические условия
   to be contrary to ~s (ту би ко́нтрари ту ~с) противоречить условиям спецификации
   to examine technical ~s (ту экза́мин тэ́кникал ~с) изучать технические условия
   ~ **of taxes and fees** (~ оф та́ксэз энд физ) перечень налогов и сборов
Specified (спэ́сифайд) указанный
   packed and marked as ~ (пакд энд ма́ркэд аз ~) в упаковке и с маркировкой согласно указаниям
   unless otherwise ~ (анлэ́с о́θэруиз ~) при отсутствии иных указаний
Specify, to ~ (спэ́сифай, ту ~) указывать
Specimen (спэ́симэн) образчик, экземпляр
Speculate, to ~ (спэ́кюлэйт, ту ~) спекулировать

   to ~ on a downturn (ту ~ он а до́унтурн) спекулировать на понижение
   to ~ on an upturn (ту ~ он ан у́птурн) спекулировать на повышение
Speculation (спэкюлэ́йшн) спекуляция
   commodity ~ (коммо́дити ~) товарная спекуляция
   currency ~ (ку́ррэнси ~) валютная спекуляция
   monetary ~ (мо́нэтари ~) денежная спекуляция
   successful ~ (суксэ́сфул ~) удачная спекуляция
   unsuccessful ~ (ансуксэ́сфул ~) неудачная спекуляция
   ~ **on the margin** (~ он θи ма́рджин) игра на разнице
Speculative (спэ́кюлатив) спекулятивный
Speculator (спэ́кюлэйтор) спекулянт
Speech (спич) прения, речь
   free ~ (фри ~) свобода слова
   royal ~ (ро́йял ~) тронная речь
Speed (спид) скорость, темп
   air ~ (эйр ~) скорость полёта
   loaded ~ (ло́дэд ~) грузовая скорость
   slow ~ (слоу ~) малая скорость
Spend, to ~ (спэнд, ту ~) тратить
Spending (спэ́ндинг) трата
Spendthrift (спэ́ндθрифт) расточитель, расточительный {*adj.*}
Sphere (сфир) область, сфера
   ~ **of activity** (~ оф акти́вити) область деятельности, отрасль деятельности
   ~ **of application** (~ оф алликэ́йшн) область применения
   ~ **of cooperation** (~ оф коопэрэ́йшн) область сотрудничества
   ~ **of industry** (~ оф и́ндустри) отрасль промышленности
   ~ **of influence** (~ оф и́нфлуэнс) сфера влияния
   ~ **of interests** (~ оф и́нтэрэстс) сфера интересов
   ~ **of production** (~ оф прода́кшн) отрасль производства
Split (сплит) раздел, раскол
Spoil, to ~ (спойл, ту ~) портить, распустить
Spoilage (спо́йладж) брак, гниль, порча
   ~ **rate** (~ рэйт) допуск брака

Sponsor (спóнсор) гарант, финансирующее лицо

    joint ~ (джойнт ~) совместный гарант

Sponsorship (спóнсоршип) гарантирование

Spot market transaction (спот мáркэт трансáкшн) сделка на наличный товар

Spouse (спóус) супруг {husband}, супруга {wife}

    divorced ~ (дивóрсд ~) разведённый супруг {husband}, разведённая супруга {wife}

Spread (спрэд) разница

    exchange rate ~ (эксчэйндж рэйт ~) разница в валютах

    to ~ (ту ~) распространять

    ~ sheet (~ шит) разработочная таблица

Squander, to ~ (скуáндэр, ту ~) разбазарить, расточать, растратить

Squandering (скуáндэринг) разбазаривание, расточительство, растрата

Square (скуэйр) квадрат, квадратный {adj.}, площадь

Squeeze (скуиз) рестрикция

    credit ~ (крэдит ~) кредитная рестрикция

Stability (стабúлити) стабильность, устойчивость

    exchange rate ~ (эксчэйндж рэйт ~) устойчивость курса валюты

    market ~ (мáркэт ~) стабильность рынка

    price ~ (прайс ~) стабильность цен, устойчивость цен

    ~ of employment (~ оф эмплóймэнт) стабильность занятости

    ~ of exchange rate (~ оф эксчэйндж рэйт) стабильность курса

    ~ of personnel (~ оф пэрсоннэл) стабильность кадров

Stabilization (стэйбилизэйшн) стабилизация

    economic ~ (экономик ~) экономическая стабилизация

    ~ of exchange rates (~ оф эксчэйндж рэйтс) стабилизация валютных курсов

    ~ of prices (~ оф прáйсэз) стабилизация цен

Stabilize, to ~ (стэйбилайз, ту ~) стабилизировать

Stabilized (стэйбилайзд) стабилизированный

Stabilizing (стэйбилайзинг) стабилизирующий

    ~ influence (~ úнфлуэнс) стабилизирующее влияние

Stack (стак) кипа, штабель

    to ~ (ту ~) укладывать, штабелировать

    to ~ up (ту ~ ап) укладывать в штабеля

Stacking (стáккинг) укладка, укладка пиломатериалов на прокладки

    upside down ~ (úпсайд дóун ~) укладка вверх дном

Staff (стаф) кадры, персонал, состав, штат, штатный {adj.}

    basic ~ (бэйсик ~) основной штат

    clerical ~ (клэрикал ~) канцелярский персонал

    domestic ~ (домэстик ~) обслуживающий домашний персонал

    experienced ~ (экспúриэнсэд ~) опытные кадры

    highly qualified ~ (хáйли куáлифайд ~) высококвалифицированный штат

    judicial ~ (джюдúшл ~) судейский аппарат

    key ~ (ки ~) основной состав

    office ~ (óффис ~) служебный персонал

    permanent ~ (пэрманэнт ~) постоянный штат

    regular ~ (рэгюлар ~) штатный персонал

    special ~ (спэшл ~) специальный персонал

    to add to the ~ (ту ад ту θи ~) зачислять в штат

    to be on the ~ (ту би он θи ~) быть в штате

    ~ overage (~ óвэрадж) раздутый штат

Staffing (стáффинг) комплектование рабочей силой

    regular ~ (рэгюлар ~) штатная численность

Stage (стэйдж) стадия, уровень, этап, шаг

    final ~ (фáйнал ~) конечная стадия

    ~ of prefabrication (~ оф прифабрикэйшн) уровень комплектности

Stagnation (стагнэйшн) вялость, застойная конъюнктура, спад market ~ (ма́ркэт ~) вялость рынка

~ of trade (~ оф трэйд) застой торговли

Stale (стэйл) лежалый

Stalinism (ста́линисм) сталинизм

Stamp (стамп) марка {postage}, оттиск, печать, штамп, штемпель

acceptance ~ (аксэ́птанс ~) приёмочное клеймо

bank ~ (банк ~) штемпель банка

brand ~ (бранд ~) клеймо

business ~ (би́знэс ~) штемпель фирмы

control ~ (контро́л ~) контрольный штемпель

customs ~ (ка́стомз ~) печать таможни

date ~ by border station (дэйт ~ бай бо́рдэр стэйшн) дата штемпеля пограничной станции

guarantee ~ (гяранти́ ~) гарантийная марка, гарантийный штамп

mill ~ (мил ~) фабричное клеймо

official ~ (оффи́шл ~) гербовая печать

personal ~ (пэ́рсонал ~) личное клеймо

revenue ~ (рэ́вэну ~) гербовая марка

to ~ (ту ~) клеймить, поставить печать, проставлять штемпель, ставить клеймо, штамповать

to ~ with a seal (ту ~ уиθ а сил) скреплять печатью

to affix a ~ (ту аффи́кс а ~) наклеить марку, ставить штамп

to certify by ~ (ту сэ́ртифай бай ~) заверять штампом

weight ~ (уэйт ~) штемпель о весе

Stamped (стампд) гербовый

Stand (станд) стенд {for products}

display ~ (дисплэ́й ~) выставочная витрина

to ~ (ту ~) стоять

Standard (ста́ндард) норма, норматив, проба, стандарт, типовой {adj.}, уровень

above ~ (або́в ~) выше нормы

below ~ (било́у ~) ниже нормы

departure from accepted ~s (дипа́рчур фром аксэ́птэд ~с) отклонение от нормы

design ~ (диза́йн ~) уровень проектирования

engineering ~s (инджэни́ринг ~с) технические нормы

generally accepted ~ (джэ́нэралли аксэ́птэд ~) общепринятая норма

gold ~ (голд ~) золотая база, золотой стандарт

gold bullion ~ (голд бу́ллён ~) золото-слитковый стандарт

gold coin ~ (голд койн ~) золото-монетный стандарт

growth in the ~ of living (гроθ ин θи ~ оф ли́винг) рост уровня жизни

in conformance with ~ (ин конфо́рманс уиθ ~) в соответствии с нормой

increase in ~ of living (инкри́с ин ~ оф ли́винг) повышение уровня жизни

industry ~s (и́ндустри ~с) отраслевые нормы

international ~s (интэрна́шэнал ~с) международные аналоги

international sanitary ~s (интэрна́шэнал са́нитари ~с) международные санитарные правила

low ~ (ло́у ~) низкая норма

minimum ~s (ми́нимум ~с) минимальные нормы

monetary ~ (мо́нэтари ~) монетный стандарт

paper ~ (пэ́йпэр ~) бумажный стандарт

plant ~s (плант ~с) заводские нормы

present ~s (прэ́зэнт ~с) действующие нормы

productivity ~s (продукти́вити ~с) нормы производительности

progressive ~s (прогрэ́ссив ~с) прогрессивные нормативы

sanitary ~s (са́нитари ~с) сантехническая норма, санитарные правила

sanitary hygiene ~s (са́нитари ха́йджин ~с) санитарно-гигиенические требования

state ~ (стэйт ~) государственный стандарт

tight ~s (тайт ~с) жёсткие нормы

time ~ (тайм ~) норма времени

to apply ~s (ту аппла́й ~с) применять нормы

to conform with ~s (ту конфо́рм уиθ ~с) соответствовать нормам

to establish ~s (ту эста́блиш ~с) нормировать, устанавливать нормы

to fall within the ~s (ту фал
уиθи́н θи ~с) совпадать с нормами
to review ~s (ту ривю́ ~с)
пересматривать нормы
to revise ~s (ту рива́йз ~с)
пересматривать нормативы
top world ~ (топ уо́рлд ~)
наивысший мировой уровень
~s for duty-free import (~с фор
дю́ти-фри и́мпорт) норма на
беспошлинный ввоз
~ of design (~ оф диза́йн)
уровень оформления
~ of examination (~ оф
экзамина́йшн) уровень экспертизы
~ of living (~ оф ли́винг)
уровень жизни
~ of patentability (~ оф
па́тэнтаби́лити) уровень
патентоспособности
~ of quality (~ оф куа́лити)
стандарт качества
Standardization (стандардиза́йшн)
нормирование, стандартизация
~ department (~ дипа́ртмэнт)
отдел нормирования
Standardize, to ~ (ста́ндардайз, ту
~) стандартизировать
Standing (ста́ндинг)
правоспособность, репутация
administrative ~ (адми́нистрэйтив
~) административная
правоспособность
commercial ~ (комме́ршл ~)
коммерческая репутация
contractual ~ (контра́кчуал ~)
договорная правоспособность
legal ~ (ли́гал ~) правовое
положение
legal ~ of foreigners (ли́гал ~
оф фо́рэнэрс) правовое положение
иностранцев
~ to prosecute and defend (~ ту
про́сэкют энд дифэ́нд)
правоспособность искать и
отвечать на суде
~ to sue (~ ту су)
правоспособность искать на суде
Staple (стэйпл) основной продукт ~s
товары первой необходимости
Start-up (старт-ап) пуск в
эксплуатацию
factory ~ (фа́ктори ~) пуск
завода в эксплуатацию
to meet ~ date (ту мит ~ дэйт)
пускать в эксплуатацию
назначенный срок

~ date (~ дэйт) дата пуска в
эксплуатацию
~ program (~ про́грам) программа
ввода в эксплуатацию
State (стэйт) государственный
{adj.}, государство, состояние,
штат {e.g. of USA}
intact ~ (инта́кт ~) сохранность
~ of emergency (~ оф имэ́рджэнси)
чрезвычайное положение
~ of the market (~ оф θи ма́ркэт)
конъюнктура
Statement (стэ́йтмэнт) акт,
ведомость, протокол, смета
annual ~ (а́ннюал ~) годовая
смета
annual budgetary ~ (а́ннюал
ба́джэтари ~) годовая бюджетная
смета
bank financial ~ (банк файна́ншл
~) банковский баланс
budgetary financial ~ (ба́джэтари
файна́ншл ~) бюджетный баланс
capital and credit ~ (ка́питал
энд крэ́дит ~) баланс движения
капиталов и кредитов
condensed financial ~ (кондэ́нсд
файна́ншл ~) сжатый баланс
consolidated ~ (консо́лидэйтэд ~)
сводная ведомость
detailed financial ~ (ди́тэйлд
файна́ншл ~) подробный баланс
diplomatic ~ (дипломáтик ~)
дипломатическое заявление
financial ~ (файна́ншл ~)
бухгалтерский баланс
formal ~ (фо́рмал ~) формальное
заявление
general ~ (джэ́нэрал ~)
генеральный акт
general average ~ (джэ́нэрал
а́вэрэдж ~) аварийный акт
joint ~ (джойнт ~) совместное
заявление
liquidation financial ~
(ликуидэ́йшн файна́ншл ~)
ликвидационный баланс
oral ~ (о́рал ~) устное заявление
preliminary ~ (прили́минэри ~)
предварительное заявление
pursuant to the enclosed ~
(пурсу́ант ту θи энкло́зд ~)
согласно прилагаемой ведомости
reconciliation ~ (риконсилиэ́йшн
~) бланк для сверки депозитного
счёта {bank statement}

salvage ~ (сáлвэдж ~) распределение вознаграждения за спасение
to make a ~ (ту мэйк а ~) сделать заявление
to produce a financial ~ (ту продю́с а файнáншл ~) предоставлять баланс
to verify a ~ (ту вэ́рифай а ~) уточнять ведомость
~ of accounts (~ оф аккóунтс) документы финансовый отчётности
~ of deposit (~ оф дипóзит) выписка о состоянии депозитов
Station (стэйшн) станция
air loading ~ (эйр лóдинг ~) аэродром погрузки
air transshipment ~ (эйр транссши́пмэнт ~) аэродром перегрузки
border ~ (бóрдэр ~) пограничная станция
central ~ (сэ́нтрал ~) центральная станция
customs ~ (кáстомз ~) таможенная станция
gas ~ (гас ~) автозаправочная станция
railway ~ (рэ́йлуэй ~) железнодорожная станция
repair ~ (рипэ́йр ~) ремонтная мастерская
sanitary-health ~ (сáнитари-хэл θ ~) санитарная станция
service ~ (сэ́рвис ~) станция техобслуживания
way ~ (уэй ~) промежуточная станция
Statistic (стати́стик) статистика ~s статистика, статистики
agricultural ~s (агрику́лчурал ~с) сельскохозяйственная статистика
crime ~s (крайм ~с) статистика преступности
customs ~s (кáстомз ~с) таможенная статистика
demographic ~s (дэмогрáфик ~с) демографическая статистика
foreign trade turnover ~s (фóрэн трэйд ту́рновэр ~с) статистика внешнеторгового оборота
judicial ~s (джюди́шл ~с) судебная статистика
transportation ~s (транспортэ́йшн ~с) транспортная статистика

Status (стáтус) положение, состояние, статус
civil ~ (си́вил ~) гражданское состояние
colonial ~ (колóниал ~) колониальный статус
consultative ~ (кóнсултэйтив ~) консультативный статус
cultural ~ (ку́лчурал ~) культурный статус
diplomatic ~ (дипломáтик ~) дипломатический статус
financial ~ (файнáншл ~) финансовое положение
international ~ (интэрнáшэнал ~) международный статус
legal ~ (ли́гал ~) правовое состояние, правовой статус, юридическое положение
marital ~ (мáритал ~) семейное положение
political ~ (поли́тикал ~) политический статус
privileged ~ (при́вилэжд ~) преимущественное положение, привилегированный статус
social ~ (сошл ~) социальный статус
Status quo (стáтус куó) статус-кво
territorial ~ (тэрритóриал ~) территориальный статус-кво
Statute (стáтют) акт, закон, законоположение, положение закона
antitrust ~ (антитрáст ~) антимонопольный закон
applicable ~ (аппли́кабл ~) применимый закон
arbitration ~ (арбитрэ́йшн ~) арбитражный закон
civil ~ (си́вил ~) гражданский закон
colonial ~ (колóниал ~) колониальный закон
domestic ~ (домэ́стик ~) внутренний закон, отечественный закон
draft ~ (драфт ~) законопроект
electoral ~ (элэ́кторал ~) избирательный закон
fundamental ~ (фундамэ́нтал ~) основной закон
government ~ (гóвэрнмэнт ~) государственный закон
immigration ~ (иммигрэ́йшн ~) иммиграционный закон
land ~ (ланд ~) земельный закон
local ~ (лóкал ~) местный закон

minimum wage ~ (ми́нимум уэ́йдж ~) закон заработной платы
mining ~ (ма́йнинг ~) горный закон
penal ~ (пи́нал ~) уголовный закон
permitted by ~ (пэрми́ттэд бай ~) дозволенный законом
procedural ~ (проси́дюрал ~) процессуальный закон
proscriptive ~ (проскри́птив ~) запретительный закон
racist ~ (рэ́сист ~) расистский закон
repealed ~ (рипи́лд ~) отменяемый закон
territorial ~ (тэррито́риал ~) территориальный закон
to adopt a ~ (ту адо́пт а ~) принять закон
to apply a ~ (ту аппла́й а ~) применить закон
to publish a ~ (ту па́блиш а ~) издать закон
to repeal a ~ (ту рипи́л а ~) отменить закон
to violate a ~ (ту ва́йолэйт а ~) нарушить закон
~ in force (~ ин форс) действующий закон
~ on social welfare (~ он сошл уэ́лфэйр) положение о социальном обеспечении
Stay (стэй) пребывание
length of ~ (лэнг θ оф ~) продолжительность визита
to ~ (ту ~) стоять
Steal, to ~ (стил, ту ~) похищать
Steamer (сти́мэр) пароход
cargo ~ (ка́рго ~) грузовой пароход
Steamship (сти́мшип) пароход
passenger ~ (па́ссэнджэр ~) пассажирский пароход
propaganda ~ (пропага́нда ~) агитпароход
~ line (~ лайн) пароходство
Stencil (стэ́нсил) трафарет
to ~ (ту ~) наносить маркировку по трафарету
Step (стэп) мероприятие, шаг
Stepchild (стэ́пчайлд) пасынок
Stepfather (стэ́пфа θ эр) отчим
Sterling (стэ́рлинг) фунт стерлинг
~ draft bill (~ драфт бил) тратта с платежом в фунтах стерлингов

~ rate (~ рэйт) курс в фунтах стерлингов
Stevedore (сти́вэдор) стивидор
Stevedoring (сти́вэдоринг) погрузка и выгрузка
~ operations (~ опэрэ́йшнс) операция по укладке, работы по погрузке и выгрузке
Stick, to ~ (стик, ту ~) наклеивать {with adhesive}
Stick-on (стик-он) наклейка {label}
Stimulus (сти́мюлус) стимул
Stipend (ста́йпэнд) стипендия
government ~ (го́вэрнмэнт ~) государственная стипендия
Stipulate, to ~ (сти́пюлэйт, ту ~) оговорить, ставить условием
Stipulation (стипюлэ́йшн) обусловленность, оговорка
mutual ~s (мю́чуал ~с) взаимная обусловленность
Stock (сток) акция, запас, инвентарь, резерв, состав, фондовый {adj.} **~s** фонд
basic ~ (бэ́йсик ~) базовый
buffer ~ (бу́ффэр ~) буферный запас
dead ~ (дэд ~) затоваривание
rolling ~ (ро́ллинг ~) подвижной
taking ~ (тэ́йкинг ~) инвентаризация
to take ~ of (ту тэйк ~ оф) проводить учёт
~ turnover (~ ту́рновэр) оборот акций {shares}
Stock-in-trade (сток-ин-трэйд) запасы товаров, товарная наличность, торговый инвентарь
Stock-jobbing (сток-джо́ббинг) ажиотаж
Stockbroker (сто́кброкэр) брокер фондовой биржи
Stockholder (сто́кхолдэр) пайщик
Stockpile (сто́кпайл) запас
national ~ (на́шэнал ~) государственный запас
to ~ (ту ~) делать запас, накапливать
Stockpiling (сто́кпайлинг) заготовка, накопление {товарных запасов}
Stop (стоп) прекращение, стоп
to ~ (ту ~) прекратить
~ payment order (~ пэ́ймэнт о́рдэр) прекращение выдачи наличных денег

Stoppage (стóппадж) прекращение, приостановка, срыв
  work ~ (уóрк ~) приостановка работы, срыв работы

Storage (стóрадж) складирование, хранение, хранилище
  adequate ~ (áдэкуэт ~) соответствующее хранение
  bulk ~ (булк ~) хранение навалом
  carryover ~ (кэрриовэр ~) хранение с переходящим остатком
  cold ~ (колд ~) хранение в холодильнике
  cost of ~ (кост оф ~) стоимость хранения
  document ~ (дóкюмэнт ~) хранение дел
  improper ~ (импрóпэр ~) неправильное хранение
  inadequate ~ (инáдэкуэт ~) несоответствующее хранение
  indoor ~ (индóр ~) закрытое хранение
  limited ~ (лúмитэд ~) ограниченное хранение
  long-term ~ (лонг-тэрм ~) длительное {долгосрочное} хранение
  mode of ~ (мод оф ~) способ хранения
  negligent ~ (нэглиджэнт ~) небрежное хранение
  normal ~ (нóрмал ~) нормальное хранение
  outside ~ (óутсайд ~) открытое хранение {под открытым небом}
  pending-repair ~ (пэндинг-рипэйр ~) хранение ремонтного фонда
  period of ~ (пúриод оф ~) срок хранения
  shelf ~ (шэлф ~) хранение готовой продукции
  short-term ~ (шорт-тэрм ~) кратковременное хранение
  small-lot ~ (смал-лот ~) хранение продукции малыми партиями
  standby ~ (стáндбай ~) резервное хранение
  temporary ~ (тэмпорари ~) временное хранение
  terminal ~ (тэрминал ~) хранение у терминала
  to accept for ~ (ту аксэпт фор ~) принимать на хранение
  to provide ~ (ту провáйд ~) обеспечивать хранение

  to turn in for ~ (ту турн ин фор ~) сдавать на хранение
  ~ agreement (~ агрúмэнт) договор хранения
  ~ at a customs warehouse (~ ат а кáстомз уэрхаус) хранение на таможенном складе
  ~ conditions (~ кондúшнс) условия хранения
  ~ expenses (~ экспэнсэз) расходы по хранению
  ~ facilities (~ фасúлитиз) складское хозяйство
  ~ in bags (~ ин багз) хранение в мешках
  ~ inspection (~ инспэкшн) проверка хранения
  ~ of cargo (~ оф кáрго) хранение груза
  ~ of goods (~ оф гудз) хранение продукции
  ~ of spare parts (~ оф спэйр партс) хранение запчастей
  ~ operations (~ опэрэйшнс) операция хранения
  ~ quality (~ куáлити) качество хранения
  ~ regulations (~ рэгюлэйшнс) правила хранения
  ~ space (~ спэйс) место для хранения
  ~ system (~ сúстэм) система хранения
  ~ temperature (~ тэмпэрачур) температура хранения

Store (стор) магазин **~s** припасы
  chain ~ (чэйн ~) фирменный магазин
  customs ~ (кáстомз ~) таможенный склад
  department ~ (дипáртмэнт ~) универсальный магазин
  retail ~ (рúтэйл ~) розничный магазин
  self-service ~ (сэлф-сэрвис ~) магазин самообслуживания
  ~ hours (~ óурз) часы торговли магазинов
  ~ locations (~ локэйшнс) размещение магазинов
  ~ owner (~ óунэр) владелец магазина

Stored (сторд) складированный
Storehouse (стóрхаус) склад
Storm (сторм) шторм
  strong ~ (стронг ~) сильный шторм

Story (стóри) история, рассказ, сказка
Stow (стóу) укладка, штивка
  bottom ~ (бóттом ~) укладка внизу
  loose ~ (лус ~) свободная укладка
  tight ~ (тайт ~) плотная укладка
  to ~ (ту ~) обеспечивать укладку, производить штивку, размещать, укладывать
  top ~ (топ ~) укладка сверху
Stowage (стóуадж) расходы по укладке {fee}, складочное место, штивка
  improper ~ (импрóпэр ~) неправильная штивка
  negligent ~ (нэ́глиджэнт ~) небрежная укладка, небрежная штивка
  price FOB with ~ (прайс эф-о-би уиθ ~) цена ФОБ со штивкой
  refrigerated ~ (рифри́джэрэйтэд ~) укладка в рефрижераторном помещении
  special ~ (спэшл ~) специальная штивка
  ~ **certificate** (~ сэрти́фикэт) свидетельство о штивке
  ~ **cost** (~ кост) стоимость штивки
  ~ **in crates** (~ ин крэйтс) укладка в ящики
  ~ **plan** (~ план) каргоплан
  ~ **requirements** (~ рикуáйрмэнтс) требования по укладке
Stowed (стóуд) со штивкой
  FOB ~ (эф-о-би ~) ФОБ включая штивку
  free in and ~ (фри ин энд ~) фри ин со штивкой
Stowing (стóуинг) укладка
  multi-level ~ (мýлти-лэ́вэл ~) многоярусная укладка ящиков
  to complete ~ (ту компли́т ~) завершить укладку
Strain (стрэйн) напряжение
Strait (стрэйт) пролив
Strap (страп) лямка
  to ~ (ту ~) крепить лямкой
Strapping (стрáппинг) крепление лямкой
Straw (стрáу) солома
  ~ **man** (~ ман) подставное лицо
Stream (стрим) поток
  to come on ~ (ту ком он ~) вступать в действие

Streetwalker (стри́туалкэр) продажная женщина
Strength (стрэнгθ) сила
Stress (стрэс) напряжение
  to withstand ~ (ту уиθстáнд ~) выдержать напряжение
Strict (стрикт) жёсткий
Strictness (стри́ктнэс) жёсткость
Strike (страйк) забастовка, стачка
  economic ~ (эконóмик ~) экономическая забастовка
  general ~ (джэ́нэрал ~) всеобщая забастовка
  longshoremen's ~ (лонгшóрмэнз ~) забастовка портовых рабочих
  nationwide ~ (нэ́йшнуайд ~) общенациональная забастовка
  political ~ (поли́тикал ~) политическая стачка
  protracted ~ (протрáктэд ~) длительная забастовка
  short-term ~ (шорт-тэрм ~) кратковременная забастовка
  to call a ~ (ту кал а ~) объявлять забастовку
  to call off a ~ (ту кал офф а ~) прекращать забастовку
  wildcat ~ (уáйлдкат ~) дикая стачка
  ~ **clause** (~ клауз) оговорка о забастовке
  ~ **insurance** (~ иншóранс) страхование от забастовок
Striker (стрáйкэр) стачечник
Striking (стрáйкинг) исключение
  ~ **from the register** (~ фром θи рэ́джистэр) исключение из реестра {company, etc.}
String (стринг) верёвка
  to pull ~**s for** (ту пул ~с фор) протежировать
Stroke (строк) росчерк, удар, штрих
  with a single ~ **of the pen** (уиθ а сингл ~ оф θи пэн) одним росчерком пера
Strongbox (стрóнгбокс) прочный ящик
Structure (стрýкшр) сооружение, строение, структура
  business ~ (би́знэс ~) хозяйственное строение
  commercial ~ (коммэ́ршл ~) коммерческая структура
  economic ~ (эконóмик ~) экономическая структура
  financial ~ (файнáншл ~) финансовая структура

legal ~ (ли́гал ~) правовая структура
~ of the legal system (~ оф θи ли́гал си́стэм) юридическая структура
Struggle (страгл) борьба
competitive ~ (компэ́титив ~) конкурентная борьба
Student (сту́дэнт) студент
graduate ~ (гра́джюат ~) аспирант
graduate ~s (гра́джюат ~с) аспирантура {collective}
Study (ста́ди) изучение
feasibility ~ (физиби́лити ~) изучение возможностей выполнения, технико-экономическое обоснование, экспертиза на осуществимость
post-graduate ~ (пост-гра́джюат ~) аспирантура
Stupefying (сту́пэфайинг) одурманивающий {as of a narcotic}
Style (стайл) мода
to go out of ~ (ту го о́ут оф ~) выйти из моды
Subcharter (субча́ртэр) договор субфрахтования
Subcommittee (су́бкоммитти) подкомитет
Subcontract (су́бконтракт) договор с субподрядчиком, субподряд
Subcontracting (су́бконтрактинг) выдача субподряда
Subcontractor (су́бконтрактор) субподрядная фирма, субподрядчик
Subdivision (су́бдивижн) подотдел, подразделение
territorial ~ (тэррито́риал ~) территориальное подразделение
Subgroup (су́бгруп) подгруппа
Subject (са́бджэкт) субъект
civil law ~ (си́вил лау ~) субъект гражданского права
contractual ~ (контра́кчуал ~) договорный объект, договорный субъект
hypothecated ~ matter (хайпо́θэкэйтэд ~ ма́ттэр) предмет ипотеки
legal ~ (ли́гал ~) законный предмет
patented ~ (па́тэнтэд ~) запатентованный предмет
to buy ~ to inspection and approval (ту бай ~ ту инспэ́кшн энд аппру́вал) покупать с

условием предварительного осмотра и одобрения
to be ~ to arrest (ту би ~ ту аррэ́ст) подвергаться аресту
~ of international agreement (~ оф интэрна́шэнал агри́мэнт) объект международного договора
~ of a patent (~ оф а па́тэнт) предмет патента
~ of taxation (~ оф таксэ́йшн) объект обложения
~ to (~ ту) в зависимости от, подлежащий
~ to alterations (~ ту алтэрэ́йшнс) при условии изменений
~ to approval (~ ту аппру́вал) при условии одобрения
~ to availability (~ ту авайлаби́лити) при условии наличия
~ to the jurisdiction (~ ту θи джюрисди́кшн) подчинение юрисдикции
~ to prompt notice (~ ту промпт но́тис) при условии немедленного уведомления
~ to proper delivery (~ ту про́пэр дэли́вэри) при условии правильной поставки
~ to termination (~ ту тэрминэ́йшн) при условии окончания
Subjection (субджэ́кшн) привлечение
~ to civil liability (~ ту си́вил лайаби́лити) привлечение к гражданской ответственности
~ to disciplinary action (~ ту ди́сиплинари акшн) привлечение к дисциплинарной ответственности
~ to liability (~ ту лайаби́лити) привлечение к ответственности
Subject matter (са́бджэкт ма́ттэр) предмет
~ of a contract (~ оф а ко́нтракт) предмет договора
~ of a dispute (~ оф а диспю́т) предмет спора
Subjugate, to ~ (су́бджюгэйт, ту ~) покорять
Subjugation (субджюгэ́йшн) покорение
Sublease (су́блис) субаренда
Sublet, to ~ (су́блэт, ту ~) сдавать в поднаём
Subletting (су́блэттинг) сдача в поднаём
Sublicense (су́блайсэнс) сублицензия

Submerge, to ~ (субмэ́рдж, ту ~)
погружать
Submission (субми́шн) подача,
представление, предъявление
   ~ of a cassation (~ оф а
кассэ́йшн) подача кассационной
жалобы
   ~ of a demand (~ оф а дима́нд)
предъявление требования
   ~ of a matter to a court (~ оф а
ма́ттэр ту а ко́урт) передача дела
в суд
   ~ to arbitration (~ ту
арбитрэ́йшн) передача на арбитраж
Submit, to ~ (субми́т, ту ~)
представлять
Submitted (субми́ттэд)
представленный
Subordinate (субо́рдинэйт)
подчинённый
   to ~ (ту ~) подчинять
   to be ~ to (ту би ~ ту)
подчиниться
Subordination (субординэ́йшн)
подчинённость, подчинение
   legal ~ (ли́гал ~) юридическое
подчинение
Subpoena (супи́на) вызов в суд,
повестка о вызове в суд, привод
   to ~ (ту ~) вызвать в суд
Subrogation (суброгэ́йшн) суброгация
   ~ clause (~ клауз) оговорка
суброгации
Subscribe, to ~ (субскра́йб, ту ~)
абонировать
Subscriber (субскра́йбэр) абонент,
подписчик
   bond ~ (бонд ~) подписчик на
облигации
   ~ to shares (~ ту шэйрз)
подписчик на акции
Subscription (субскри́пшн)
абонемент, подписка
   direct ~ from the publisher
(дирэ́кт ~ фром θи па́блишэр)
непосредственная подписка у
издателя
   mail ~ (мэйл ~) подписка по
почте
   public ~ (па́блик ~) публичная
подписка
   to cover a ~ (ту ко́вэр а ~)
покрывать подпиской
   ~ for securities (~ фор
сэкю́ритиз) подписка на ценные
бумаги

   ~ for shares (~ фор шэйрз)
подписка на акции
Subsidiary (субси́диари) дочерний
{*adj.*}, дочерняя компания
Subsidize, to ~ (су́бсидайз, ту ~)
давать дотацию, субсидировать
Subsidizing (су́бсидайзинг)
субсидирование
Subsidy (су́бсиди) дотация, субсидия
   budgetary ~ (ба́джэтари ~)
бюджетная дотация
   direct ~ (дирэ́кт ~) прямая
субсидия
   economic ~ (эконо́мик ~)
экономическая субсидия
   export ~ (э́кспорт ~) субвенция
при вывозе
   federal ~ (фэ́дэрал ~)
федеральная субсидия
   indirect ~ (индайрэ́кт ~)
косвенная субсидия
   military ~ (ми́литари ~) военная
субсидия
   state ~ (стэйт ~)
государственная субсидия,
субвенция от государства
   to provide a ~ (ту прова́йд а ~)
предоставить субсидию
Substance (су́бстанс) вещество,
существо
Substandard (субста́ндард)
некачественный, нестандартный
Substantial (сабста́ншл) крупный
Substantiate, to ~ (субста́ншиэйт,
ту ~) обосновывать
Substantiated (субста́ншиэйтэд)
обоснованный
Substantiation (субстанши́эйшн)
обоснование
   scientific ~ (сайэнти́фик ~)
научное обоснование
Substantive (су́бстантив)
существенный
   ~ review (~ ривю́) пересмотр по
существу
Substitute (су́бститут) заменитель,
суррогат
   monetary ~ (мо́нэтари ~) денежный
суррогат
   to ~ (ту ~) заменять
[*perfective*: заменить], замещать
[*perfective*: заместить]
Substitution (субститу́шн) замена,
замещение, субститут
   ~ of collateral (~ оф
колла́тэрал) замена обеспечения

Sub-tenant (суб-тэ́нант)
субарендатор
Suburb (су́бурб) пригород
Subvention (субвэ́ншн) субвенция
   export ~ (э́кспорт ~) субвенция
   при вывозе
   state ~ (стэйт ~) субвенция от
   государства
Subversion (сабвэ́ржн) диверсия
Succession (суксэ́шн) очередность,
последовательность,
преемственность, преемство
Successive (суксэ́сив)
последовательный
Successor (суксэ́сор) преемник
   legal ~ (ли́гал ~) законный
   преемник
   ~ in a matter (~ ин а ма́ттэр)
   правопреемник в деле
Sue, to (су, ту ~) искать в суд,
предъявить претензию
Sufficiency (суффи́шэнси)
достаточность, полнота
   ~ of documents (~ оф до́кюмэнтс)
   полнота документов
   ~ of marking (~ оф ма́ркинг)
   достаточность маркировки
   ~ of packing (~ оф па́ккинг)
   достаточность упаковки
Sufficient (суффи́шэнт) достаточный
Suffrage (су́ффрадж) избирательное
право
   direct ~ (дирэ́кт ~) прямое
   избирательное право
   limitation of ~ (лимитэ́йшн оф ~)
   ограничение прав в выборах
   universal ~ (юнивэ́рсал ~)
   всеобщее избирательное право
   women's ~ (уи́мэнз ~)
   избирательное право женщин
Suggest, to ~ (саджэ́ст, ту ~)
предлагать
Suggestion (саджэ́стён) предложение
Suicide (су́исайд) самоубийство,
самоубийца {person committing}
   to commit ~ (ту комми́т ~)
   покончить жизнь самоубийством
Suit (сут) иск
   civil ~ (си́вил ~) гражданский
   иск
   counter-~ (ко́унтэр-~) встречный
   иск
   notice of ~ (но́тис оф ~) исковое
   заявление
   original ~ (ори́джинал ~)
   основной иск

paternity ~ (патэ́рнити ~) иск об
оспаривании отцовства
to file ~ (ту файл ~) возбудить
иск, предъявить иск, предъявить
претензию
to drop a ~ (ту дроп а ~) изъять
из суда
~ for compensation of damages (~
фор компэнсэ́йшн оф да́мэджэз)
претензия на возмещение убытков
~ for divorce (~ фор диво́рс) иск
о разводе иск
~ for infringement of a patent
(~ фор инфри́нджмэнт оф а па́тэнт)
иск о нарушении патента
Suitability (сутаби́лити)
пригодность к работе
Suitable (су́табл) применимый,
соответствующий
Sum (сум) сумма
   advance ~ (адва́нс ~) авансовая
   сумма
   aggregate ~ (а́ггрэгат ~) общая
   сумма
   amortized ~ (а́мортайзд ~)
   амортизационная сумма
   claimed ~ (клэймд ~) исковая
   сумма
   gross ~ (грос ~) валовая сумма
   guaranteed ~ (гяранти́д ~)
   гарантийная сумма
   insured ~ (иншу́рд ~) страховая
   сумма
   large ~ (лардж ~) большая сумма
   licensing ~ (ла́йсэнсинг ~)
   лицензионная сумма
   maximum ~ (ма́ксимум ~)
   максимальная сумма
   minimum ~ (ми́нимум ~)
   минимальная сумма
   monetary ~ (мо́нэтари ~) денежная
   сумма
   net ~ (нэт ~) чистая сумма
   nominal ~ (но́минал ~)
   номинальная сумма
   pledged ~ (плэджд ~) залоговая
   сумма
   principal ~ (при́нсипал ~)
   капитальная сумма долга
   redemption ~ (ридэ́мпшн ~)
   выкупная сумма
   share ~ (шэйр ~) паевая сумма
   substantial ~ (сабста́ншл ~)
   крупная сумма
   trivial ~ (три́виал ~) ничтожная
   сумма

~ in controversy (~ ин
ко́нтровэрси) спорная сумма
~ of indemnity (~ оф индэ́мнити)
отступная сумма
Summary (са́ммари) сводка
Summon, to ~ (су́ммон, ту ~)
вызывать
Summons (су́ммонз) вызов в суд,
судебная повестка
to ~ (ту ~) вызвать в суд
~ of the electors (~ оф θи
эле́кторз) созыв избирателей
Superannuation (супэранню́йшн)
давность
Superscribe, to ~ (су́пэрскрайб, ту
~) надписывать
Superstition (супэрсти́шн) суеверие
Supervise, to ~ (су́пэрвайз, ту ~)
осуществлять надзор, руководить
to ~ a construction contract (ту
~ а констру́кшн ко́нтракт)
осуществлять шефмонтаж
Supervised (су́пэрвайзд)
контролируемый
Supervision (супэрви́жн) контроль,
наблюдение, надзор
competent contract ~ (ко́мпэтэнт
ко́нтракт ~) компетентный
шефмонтаж
complete contract ~ (компли́т
ко́нтракт ~) полный шефмонтаж
constant ~ (ко́нстант ~)
постоянный контроль
contract ~ (ко́нтракт ~)
шефмонтаж
performance of contract ~
(пэрфо́рманс оф ко́нтракт ~)
проведение шефмонтажа
state ~ (стэйт ~)
государственный надзор
to provide contract ~ (ту
прова́йд ко́нтракт ~) обеспечивать
шефмонтаж
Supervisor (су́пэрвайзор)
руководитель
construction ~ (констру́кшн ~)
шефмонтёр
senior construction ~ (си́ниор
констру́кшн ~) старший шефмонтёр
to employ the services of a ~
(ту эмпло́й θи сэ́рвисэс оф а ~)
пользоваться услугами шефмонтёра
Supervisory (супэрва́йзори)
контролирующий
appropriate ~ personnel
(аппро́приат ~ пэрсоннэл)
соответствующий шефперсонал

seller's ~ personnel (сэ́ллэрз ~
пэрсоннэ́л) шефперсонал продавца
~ personnel (~ пэрсоннэ́л)
шефперсонал
Supplement (су́пплэмэнт) дополнение,
дополнительный акт
to publish a ~ (ту па́блиш а ~)
издавать дополнение
Supplemental (супплэмэ́нтал)
добавочный
Supplementary (сапплэмэ́нтари)
дополнительный
Supplier (сапла́йэр) компания-
поставщик, поставщик, предприятие-
поставщик, фирма-поставщик
principal ~ (при́нсипал ~)
главный поставщик
wholesale ~ (хо́лсэйл ~) оптовый
поставщик
Supply (сапла́й) запас, поставка,
снабжение, ~/ies припасы
money ~ (мо́ни ~) денежная масса
to ~ (ту ~) поставлять, снабжать
[perfective: снабдить]
~ of goods (~ оф гудз)
предложение товаров
~ of labor (~ оф лэ́йбор)
предложение труда
~ on the market (~ он θи ма́ркэт)
предложение на рынке, снабжение
рынка
Support (суппо́рт) гарантирование,
поддержка
diplomatic ~ (диплома́тик ~)
дипломатическая поддержка
financial ~ (файна́ншл ~)
финансовая поддержка
to ~ (ту ~) содерживать
Supporter (суппо́ртэр) сторонник
Supranational (супрана́шнал)
сверхнациональный
Surcharge (су́рчардж) дополнительная
надбавка, дополнительный сбор,
надбавка, штраф
imposition of a ~ (импози́шн оф а
~) наложение штрафа
includes a ~ of ... % (инклю́дс а
~ оф ... %) включать надбавку в
размере ...%
seasonal ~ (си́зонал ~) сезонная
надбавка
to add a ~ to the price (ту ад а
~ ту θи прайс) делать надбавку к
цене
to pay a ~ (ту пэй а ~) платить
надбавку

Surety (шю́рэти) аваль, гарант, поручитель, поручительство, ручательство
    as ~ for (аз ~ фор) в качестве гарантии, в качестве поручителя
    joint ~ (джойнт ~) совместная гарантия, совместный гарант, совместный поручитель, совместное поручительство
    one who makes a ~ (уа́н ху мэйкс а ~) авалист
    to provide a ~ (ту прова́йд а ~) дать аваль
    ~ for a bill of exchange (~ фор а бил оф эксчэ́йндж) аваль векселя, вексельное поручительство
    ~ on a bill (~ он а бил) вексельный поручитель
Surplus (су́рплус) избыток, избыточный {*adj.*}, излишек, перевес
    agricultural ~/es (агрику́лчурал ~эз) сельскохозяйственные излишки
    capital ~ (ка́питал ~) избыток капитала
    economic ~ (эконо́мик ~) перевес экономический
    export ~/es (э́кспорт ~эз) экспортные излишки
    import ~/es (и́мпорт ~эз) импортные излишки
Surrender (суррэ́ндэр) капитуляция, отдача, представление
    to ~ (ту ~) сдавать [**perfective:** сдать]
Surveillance (сурвэ́йлланс) надзор
    under ~ (а́ндэр ~) под опекой, поднадзорная свобода, поднадзорный {*adj.*}
Survey (сурвэ́й) обзор
    business ~ (би́знэс ~) обзор хозяйственной деятельности
    exhaustive ~ (экза́устив ~) исчерпывающий обзор
    land ~ (ланд ~) кадастр
    scope of ~ (скоп оф ~) рамки обзора
    statistical ~ (стати́стикал ~) статистический обзор
Surveyor (сурвэ́йор) инспектор
    insurance ~ (иншю́ранс ~) аварийный комиссар
    plant ~ (плант ~) фабричный инспектор
    ~ of the port (~ оф θи порт) портовой инспектор

Survivor (сурва́йвор) потерпевший
Suspect (су́спэкт) арестованный
Suspect, to ~ (суспэ́кт, ту ~) заподозрить, подозревать
Suspend, to ~ (саспэ́нд, ту ~) откладывать [**perfective:** отложить], приостановить
    to ~ a sentence (ту ~ а сэ́нтэнс) приостановить исполнение приговора
Suspension (суспэ́ншн) временное прекращение, приостановка
    ~ of military activities (~ оф ми́литари акти́витиз) приостановка военных действий
    ~ of payments (~ оф пэ́ймэнтс) приостановка платежей
Suspicion (суспи́шн) подозрение
    inciting ~ (инса́йтинг ~) возбуждающий подозрение
Sustain, to ~ (сустэ́йн, ту ~) выдерживать
Suzerainty (су́зэрэнти) сюзеренитет
Swear, to ~ (суэйр, ту ~) присягать
Swindle (суиндл) жульничество, мошенническая проделка
    to ~ (ту ~) жульничать
Swindler (суи́ндлэр) жулик, обманщик
Swing (суинг) колебание
    sharp ~ (шарп ~) резкое колебание
Switching (суи́тчинг) подмен
    ~ children {at the hospital} (~ чи́лдрэн {ат θи хо́спитал}) подмен ребёнка
Sworn (суо́рн) присяжный
    ~ testimony (~ тэ́стимони) показание под присягой
Symbol (си́мбол) знак, индекс, обозначение
    notational ~ (нотэ́йшал ~) обозначение на схеме
    well-known ~ (уэл-ноун ~) общеизвестный знак
Syndicalism (си́ндикализм) синдикализм
Syndicalist (си́ндикалист) синдикалист, синдикалистский {*adj.*}
Syndicate (си́ндикат) консорциум, синдикат
    banking ~ (ба́нкинг ~) консорциум банков
    industrial ~ (инду́стриал ~) промышленный синдикат
    international ~ (интэрна́шэнал ~) международный консорциум

labor ~ (лэ́йбор ~) рабочий синдикат
to ~ (ту ~) синдицировать
System (си́стэм) система, строй
banking ~ (ба́нкинг ~) банковская система
bicameral ~ (байка́мэрал ~) двухпалатная система
budget ~ (ба́джэт ~) бюджетная система
constitutional ~ (конститу́шнал ~) конституционная система
court ~ (ко́урт ~) аппарат суда
credit ~ (крэ́дит ~) кредитная система
currency ~ (ку́ррэнси ~) валютная система
economic ~ (эконо́мик ~) экономическая система
electoral ~ (элэ́кторал ~) избирательная система
financial ~ (файна́ншл ~) финансовая система
judicial ~ (джюди́шл ~) судебная система
legal ~ (ли́гал ~) правовая система
metric ~ (мэ́трик ~) метрическая система
monetary ~ (мо́нэтари ~) денежная система
multilateral ~ **of payments** (мултила́тэрал ~ оф пэ́ймэнтс) многосторонняя система платежей
parliamentary ~ (парламэ́нтари ~) парламентарная система
passport ~ (па́сспорт ~) паспортная система
penal ~ (пи́нал ~) пенитенциарная система
political ~ (поли́тикал ~) политический строй
preferential ~ (прэфэрэ́ншл ~) преференциальная система
proportional ~ **of voting** (пропо́ршнал ~ оф во́тинг) пропорциональная система выборов
proportional electoral ~ (пропо́ршнал элэ́кторал ~) пропорциональная избирательная система
tax ~ (такс ~) налоговая система
two-party ~ (ту-па́рти ~) двухпартийная
unicameral ~ (юника́мэрал ~) однопалатная система

~ **of production** (~ оф прода́кшн) производственная структура

T

Table (тэйбл) реестр, стол, табель, таблица
abridged ~ (абри́джд ~) сокращённая таблица
comparative ~ (компа́ратив ~) сравнительная таблица
computational ~ (компютэ́йшнал ~) расчётная таблица
individual ~ (индиви́дюал ~) детализированная таблица
reference ~ (рэ́фэрэнс ~) справочная таблица
single tabulation ~ (сингл табюлэ́йшн ~) однотипная таблица
summary ~ (са́ммари ~) сводная таблица
tariff rate ~ (та́риф рэйт ~) таблица тарифных ставок
tax ~ (такс ~) налоговая таблица
time ~ (тайм ~) расписание
to compile a ~ (ту компа́йл а ~) составлять таблицу
Tabulate, to ~ (та́бюлэйт, ту ~) представлять цифры в виде таблицы, вносить в таблицу
Tag (таг) бирка, метка, этикетка, ярлык
goods tear-away ~ (гудз тэр-ауэ́й ~) товарный ярлык
inventory ~ (и́нвэнтори ~) инвентарный ярлык
luggage ~ (лу́ггадж ~) багажная бирка
metal ~ (мэ́тал ~) металлическая бирка
paper ~ (пэ́йпэр ~) бумажная бирка, бумажный ярлык
plastic ~ (пла́стик ~) пластмассовый ярлык
price ~ (прайс ~) бирка с указанием цены, этикетка с ценой, ярлык с указанием цены
special ~ (спэшл ~) специальная бирка
tear-away ~ (тэр-ауэ́й ~) отрывной ярлык
to attach a ~ (ту атта́ч а ~) наклеивать ярлык
Take, to ~ (тэйк, ту ~) снимать
[perfective: снять]

to ~ **an oath** (ту ~ ан оθ)
принимать присягу
to ~ **something on trial** (ту ~
сóмθинг он трáйал) опробовать
Taking (тэ́йкинг) снятие
~ **of an oath** (~ оф ан оθ)
получение присяги
Talented (тáлэнтэд) одарённый
Talks (талкс) переговоры
armistice ~ (áрмистис ~)
переговоры о перемирии
economic ~ (экономик ~)
экономические переговоры
peace ~ (пис ~) мирные
переговоры
secret ~ (сикрэт ~) секретные
переговоры
Tally (тáлли) отметка, сверка,
тальманский {*adj.*}
ship's outturn ~ (шипс óуттурн
~) счёт выгруженного веса
to ~ (ту ~) учитывать
~ **of cargo** (~ оф кáрго) подсчёт
количества мест груза
~ **sheet** (~ шит) перечень товаров
Tallyman (тáллиман) отметчик при
погрузке и выгрузке, тальман
Tank (танк) бак, ёмкость, танк
{*military*}, цистерна
ex-~ (экс-~) франко-цистерна
in ~s (ин ~с) наливом, в
цистернах
to pour into a ~ (ту пор инту а
~) наливать в бак
to store in a ~ (ту стор ин а ~)
хранить в бак, хранить в
цистерне
to transport by ~ **cars** (ту
трáнспорт бай ~ карз) перевозить
в цистернах
~ **capacity** (~ капáсити) ёмкость
цистерны
~ **car** (~ кар) железнодорожная
цистерна
Tankage (тáнкадж) наполнение
резервуара
Tanker (тáнкэр) танкер
bunkering ~ (бýнкэринг ~)
танкер-бункеровщик
major ~ (мэ́йджор ~)
крупнотоннажный танкер
motorized ~ (мóторайзд ~)
наливной теплоход
oil ~ (ойл ~) нефтеналивное
судно, нефтяной танкер
refueling ~ (рифю́линг ~) танкер-
заправщик

to load a ~ (ту лод а ~)
загружать танкер
Tape (тэйп) лента
adhesive ~ (адхи́зив ~) клейкая
лента
magnetic ~ (магнэ́тик ~)
магнитная лента
packing ~ (пáккинг ~)
упаковочная лента
Tardiness (тáрдинэс) опоздание
Tare (тэйр) вес тары, тара
actual ~ (áкчуал ~)
действительный вес тары
actual ~ **weight** (áкчуал ~ уэ́йт)
действительный вес тары
average ~ (áвэрэдж ~) средний
вес тары
customary ~ (кáстомари ~) вес
тары установленный обычаем,
обычный вес тары
damaged ~ (дáмаджд ~)
повреждённая тара
defects in ~ (дифэ́ктс ин ~)
дефекты тары
empty ~ (эмпти ~) порожный вес
estimated ~ (эстиматд ~)
предполагаемый вес тары
invoice ~ (инвойс ~) фактурный
вес тары
invoice ~ **weight** (инвойс ~ уэ́йт)
вес упаковки, указанный в счёте
reusable ~ (рию́забл ~)
многооборотная тара
sack ~ (сак ~) мешкотара
super ~ (сýпэр ~) вес тары
превышающий нормальный
to ~ (ту ~) делать скидку на
тару
warehousing of ~ (уэ́рхоузинг оф
~) хранение тары на складе
~ **allowance** (~ аллóуанс) скидка
с веса на тару
~ **weight** (~ уэ́йт) вес тары, вес
упаковки
Target (тáргэт) норма
above ~ (абóв ~) выше нормы
financial ~ (файнáншл ~)
плановая цифра
high ~ (хай ~) высокая норма
initial ~s (инишл ~с) плановые
данные
introduction of ~s (интродáкшн
оф ~с) введение норм
plan ~ (план ~) плановое задание
production ~ (продáкшн ~)
производственное задание

Tariff (та́риф) тариф, тарифный {adj.}

agency ~ (э́йджэнси ~) агентский тариф

autonomous ~ (ауто́номос ~) автономный тариф

basic ~ (бэ́йсик ~) жёсткий тариф

blanket ~ (бла́нкэт ~) единый тариф

conference ~ (ко́нфэрэнс ~) конференциальный тариф

convention ~ (конвэ́ншн ~) конвенционный тариф

conventional ~ (конвэ́ншнал ~) договорные пошлины

discrepancy between ~ **rates** (дискрэ́панси битуи́н ~ рэйтс) расхождение между тарифами

discriminatory ~ (дискри́минатори ~) дискриминационный тариф

export ~ (э́кспорт ~) экспортный тариф

flat rate ~ (флат рэйт ~) тариф аккордных ставок

flexible ~ **rate** (флэ́ксибл ~ рэйт) гибкий тариф

general ~ (джэ́нэрал ~) общий тариф

government ~ (го́вэрнмэнт ~) государственный тариф

high ~ (хай ~) высокий тариф

import ~ (и́мпорт ~) импортный тариф

in accordance with railway ~ (ин акко́рданс уиθ рэ́йлуэй ~) в соответствии с железнодорожным тарифом

increase in ~**s** (инкри́с ин ~с) повышение тарифов

load ~ (лод ~) низкий тариф

local ~ (ло́кал ~) местный тариф

maximum ~ (ма́ксимум ~) максимальный тариф

minimum ~ (ми́нимум ~) минимальный тариф

multilinear ~ (мултили́ниар ~) сложный тариф

multiple ~ **system** (му́лтипл ~ си́стэм) система множественных тарифов

postal ~ (по́стал ~) почтовый тариф

preferential ~ (прэфэрэ́ншл ~) льготный тариф

prohibitive ~ (прохи́битив ~) запретительный тариф

protectionist ~ (протэ́кшнист ~) протекционистский тариф

protective ~ (протэ́ктив ~) покровительственный тариф

railway ~ (рэ́йлуэй ~) железнодорожный тариф

reduction in ~**s** (риду́кшн ин ~с) снижение тарифов

retaliatory ~ (рита́лиатори ~) карательный тариф

sliding scale ~ (сла́йдинг скэйл ~) дифференциальный тариф

special ~ (спэшл ~) особый тариф

straight line ~ (стрэйт лайн ~) простой тариф

to adjust a ~ (ту аджа́ст а ~) изменять тариф

to apply a ~ (ту аппла́й а ~) применять тариф к

to increase a ~ (ту инкри́с а ~) поднимать тариф

to set a ~ **upon** (ту сэт а ~ упо́н) тарифицировать

transit ~ (тра́нзит ~) транзитный тариф

unified ~ (ю́нифайд ~) унифицированный тариф

zone ~ (зон ~) зональный тариф

~ **for tare carriage** (~ фор тэйр ка́ррадж) тарный тариф

~ **rates** (~ рэйтс) ставки тарифов

~ **rating** (~ рэ́йтинг) тарификация

Taring (тэ́йринг) определения веса тары

~ **regulations** (~ рэгюлэ́йшнс) правила определения веса тары

Tarp[aulin] (та́рпалин) брезентовый чехол, брезент

to cover with a ~ (ту ко́вэр уиθ а ~) покрывать брезентом

Task (таск) задание

Taste (тэйст) вкус

to ~ (ту ~) дегустировать

Tasting (тэ́йстинг) дегустация

free sample ~ (фри сампл ~) бесплатная дегустация

Tax (такс) налог, налоговый {adj.}

ad valorem ~ (ад вало́рэм ~) адвалорный налог

after ~ (а́фтэр ~) за вычетом налога

before ~ (бифо́р ~) до вычета налога

capital ~ (ка́питал ~) налог на капитал

collection of ~**es** (коллэ́кшн оф ~эз) сбор налогов

corporate income ~ (кóрпорат
йнком ~) налог с доходов
акционерных компаний
delinquent ~ (дилйнкуэнт ~)
неуплаченный налог
direct ~ (дирэ́кт ~) прямой налог
discriminatory ~ (дискрйминатори
~) дискриминационный налог
equalization ~ (икуализэ́йшн ~)
уравнительный налог
estate ~ (эстэ́йт ~) пошлина на
наследственное имущество
exempt from ~es (экзэ́мпт фром
~эз) свободный от уплаты налогов
federal ~ (фэ́дэрал ~)
федеральный налог
government ~ (гóвэрнмэнт ~)
государственный налог
heavy ~ (хэ́ви ~) большой налог
high ~ (хай ~) высокий налог
import ~ (импорт ~) ввозной
сбор, налог на импорт
imposition of a ~ (импозйшн оф а
~) введение налога
income ~ (йнком ~) подоходный
налог
indirect ~ (индайрэ́кт ~)
косвенный налог
inheritance ~ (инхэ́ританс ~)
наследственный сбор, пошлина на
наследование
inheritance transfer ~
(инхэ́ританс трáнсфэр ~) сбор с
перехода имуществ по наследству
land ~ (ланд ~) земельный налог,
land ~ (ланд ~) поземельный сбор
local ~ (лóкал ~) местный налог
lumpsum ~ (лáмпсум ~) аккордный
налог
non-payment of a ~ (нон-пэ́ймэнт
оф а ~) неуплата налога
one-sided ~ (уáн-сáйдэд ~)
односторонний налог
onerous ~ (óнэрос ~) непомерный
налог
proceeds from ~es (прóсидз фром
~эз) поступления от налогов
progressive ~ (прогрэ́ссив ~)
прогрессивный налог
property ~ (прóпэрти ~)
поимущественный налог
proportional ~ (пропóршнал ~)
пропорциональный налог
reduction in ~es (ридýкшн ин
~эз) сокращение налогов

reserve for income ~ (рисэ́рв фор
йнком ~) резерв по уплате
подоходного налога
royalty ~ (рóйялти ~) налог с
роялти
single stage ~ (сингл стэйдж ~)
одноступенчатый налог
specific ~ (спэсйфик ~)
специфический налог
stamp ~ (стамп ~) гербовая
пошлина
to ~ (ту ~) облагать
to be exempt from the payment of
~es (ту би экзэ́мпт фром θи
пэ́ймэнт оф ~эз) быть
освобождённым от уплаты налогов
to collect ~ (ту коллэ́кт ~)
собирать налоги
to evade ~es (ту ивэ́йд ~эз)
уклоняться от уплаты налогов
to exempt from ~es (ту экзэ́мпт
фром ~эз) освобождать от налогов
to increase ~es (ту инкрйс ~эз)
повышать налоги
to levy a ~ (ту лэ́ви а ~)
взимать налог
to pay ~es (ту пэй ~эз)
выплачивать налоги, платить
налоги
to subject to a ~ (ту сáбджект
ту а ~) облагать налогом
to withhold ~es (ту уиθхóлд ~эз)
удерживать налоги
trade licensing ~ (трэйд
лáйсэнсинг ~) промысловый налог
turnover ~ (тýрновэр ~) налог на
оборот, налог с оборота
unitary ~ (юнитари ~) единый
налог
~ abatement (~ абэ́йтмэнт) скидка
с налога
~ deferment (~ дифэ́рмэнт)
отсрочка налога
~ exemption (~ экзэ́мпшн)
освобождение от налогов
~ in kind (~ ин кайнд)
натуральный налог
~ on personal property (~ он
пэ́рсонал прóпэрти) налог на
личное имущество
~ on real property (~ он рйл
прóпэрти) налог на недвижимость
~ on wages (~ он уэ́йджэз) налог
на зарплату
~ preferences (~ прэ́фэрэнсэз)
льготы на налог
~ rate (~ рэйт) ставка налога

~ **refund** (~ ри́фунд) возврат налога
~ **revenue** (~ рэ́вэну) доход от налогов
~ **revenues** (~ рэ́вэнуз) налоговые поступления
~ **schedule** (~ скэ́джюл) шкала налогов
~ **surcharge** (~ су́рчардж) дополнительный налог
~ **withholding** (~ уи θ хо́лдинг) удержание налогов
Taxable (та́ксабл) облагаемый, подлежащий обложению
Taxation (таксэ́йшн) налогообложение, обложение, обложение налогом
  double ~ (дубл ~) двойное налогообложение
  heavy ~ (хэ́ви ~) тяжёлое налогообложение
  preferential ~ (прэфэрэ́ншл ~) льготное налогообложение
  progressive ~ (прогрэ́ссив ~) прогрессивное обложение налогом, прогрессивное налогообложение
  proportional ~ (пропо́ршнал ~) пропорциональное налогообложение
  system of ~ (си́стэм оф ~) система налогов, система налогообложения
  to be subject to ~ (ту би са́бджэкт ту ~) подлежать обложению налогом
Taxi (та́кси) такси
  ~ **stand** (~ станд) стоянка такси
Taxpayer (та́кспэйэр) налогоплательщик
Team (тим) бригада, команда
  management ~ (ма́наджмэнт ~) управленческая команда
  negotiating ~ (нэго́шиэйтинг ~) прибывшая для проведения переговоров делегация
  repair ~ (рипэ́йр ~) ремонтная бригада
Tear (тэйр) разрыв, убыль
  normal wear and ~ (но́рмал уэйр энд ~) нормальная убыль и нормальный износ
  to ~ **apart** (ту ~ апа́рт) разорвать
Technical (тэ́кникал) технический
  ~ **and economic** (~ энд эконо́мик) технико-экономический
  ~ **excellence** (~ э́ксэлэнс) превосходство в технике

~ **maintenance station** (~ мэ́йнтэнанс стэ́йшн) базы техобслуживания
~ **maintenance** (~ мэ́йнтэнанс) техобслуживание
Technically (тэ́кникалли) технически
  ~ **acceptable** (~ аксэ́птабл) технически приемлемый
  ~ **correct** (~ коррэ́кт) технически правильный
  ~ **feasible** (~ фи́зибл) технически возможный
  ~ **optimal solution** (~ о́птимал солюшн) технически оптимальное решение
Technician (тэкни́шн) техник
Technique (тэкни́к) метод выполнения работ
  production ~ (прода́кшн ~) способ изготовления
  testing ~ (тэ́стинг ~) метод испытаний, метод проведения испытаний
  to master a ~ (ту ма́стэр а ~) осваивать метод
Technological (тэкноло́джикал) технологический
  ~ **achievements** (~ ачи́вмэнтс) достижения техники
Technology (тэкно́лоджи) техника, технология
  advanced ~ (адва́нсд ~) передовая техника, передовая технология
  application of ~ (аппликэ́йшн оф ~) применение технологии
  basic ~ (бэ́йсик ~) базовая технология
  capital intensive ~ (ка́питал интэ́нсив ~) капиталоёмкая технология
  communications ~ (коммюникэ́йшнс ~) техника связи
  energy-saving ~ (э́нэрджи-сэ́йвинг ~) энергосберегающая технология
  export of ~ (э́кспорт оф ~) экспорт технологии
  field of ~ (филд оф ~) область техники
  general ~ (джэ́нэрал ~) общая технология
  high ~ (хай ~) наукоёмкая технология, наукоёмкий
  introduction of new ~ (интрода́кшн оф нью ~) внедрение новой технологии

labor-intensive ~ (лэ́йбор-интэ́нсив ~) трудоёмкая технология
labor-saving ~ (лэ́йбор-сэ́йвинг ~) трудосберегающая технология
leak of ~ (лик оф ~) утечка технологии
low waste ~ (ло́у уэ́йст ~) безотходная технология
monopoly on ~ (моно́поли он ~) монополия на технологию
new ~ (нью ~) новая технология
next generation ~ (нэкст джэнэрэ́йшн ~) техника новых поколений
package ~ (па́кэдж ~) комплексная технология
performance of ~ (пэрфо́рманс оф ~) характеристика технологии
recently developed ~ (ри́сэнтли дивэ́лопд ~) недавно разработанная технология
resource-conserving ~ (ри́сорс-консэ́рвинг ~) ресурсосберегающая технология
suitable ~ (су́табл ~) подходящая технология
superior ~ (супи́риор ~) превосходная технология
to apply modern ~ (ту аппла́й мо́дэрн ~) привлекать современную технологию
to approve ~ (ту аппру́в ~) одобрять технологию
to develop ~ (ту дивэ́лоп ~) развивать технологию
to evaluate ~ (ту ива́люэйт ~) оценивать технологию
to make ~ **accessible** (ту мэйк ~ аксэ́ссибл) делать технологию доступной
to master ~ (ту ма́стэр ~) владеть технологией
to obtain ~ (ту обтэ́йн ~) приобретать технологию
to update ~ (ту у́пдэйт ~) обновлять технологию
~ **assessment** (~ ассэ́ссмэнт) оценка техники
~ **transfer** (~ тра́нсфэр) передача технологии
Telecommunications (тэлэкоммюникэ́йшнс) связь
~ **worker** (~ уо́ркэр) связист
Telegram (тэ́лэграм) телеграмма
encoded ~ (энко́дэд ~) шифрованная телеграмма

express ~ (экспрэ́с ~) телеграмма-молния
ordinary ~ (о́рдинари ~) обычная телеграмма
to notify by ~ (ту но́тифай бай ~) уведомлять телеграммой
to send a ~ (ту сэнд а ~) высылать телеграмму
~ **form** (~ форм) бланк телеграммы
Telegraph (тэ́лэграф) телеграф
to ~ (ту ~) телеграфировать
Telegraphic (тэлэгра́фик) телеграфный
Telephone (тэ́лэфон) телефон, телефонный {adj.}
by ~ (бай ~) по телефону
notice by ~ (но́тис бай ~) уведомление по телефону
~ **inquiry** (~ и́нкуири) запрос по телефону
~ **message** (~ мэ́ссадж) телефонограмма
~ **number** (~ ну́мбэр) номер телефона
Teletype (тэ́лэтайп) телетайп, телетайпный {adj.}
Telex (тэ́лэкс) телекс, телексный {adj.}
official ~ (оффи́шл ~) служебный телекс
reply to a ~ (рипла́й ту а ~) ответ на телекс
to confirm a ~ (ту конфи́рм а ~) подтверждать телекс
to send a ~ (ту сэнд а ~) направлять телекс
urgent ~ (у́рджэнт ~) срочный телекс
Teller (тэ́ллэр) счётчик
bank ~ (банк ~) счётчик в банке
Template (тэ́мплэйт) трафарет, шаблон
Tempo (тэ́мпо) темп
Temporal (тэ́мпорал) светский
Temporary (тэ́мпорари) временный
Tenancy (тэ́нанси) владение на основе аренды, владение недвижимость
joint ~ (джойнт ~) совместное владение
~ **in common** (~ ин ко́ммон) долевое владение
Tenant (тэ́нант) владелец недвижимости, съёмщик
Tendenc/y (тэ́ндэнси) тенденция
basic ~ (бэ́йсик ~) основная тенденция

prevailing ~ (привэ́йлинг ~) преобладающая тенденция
protectionist ~/ies (протэ́кшнист ~из) протекционистские тенденции
to exhibit a ~ (ту экзи́бит а ~) проявлять тенденцию
Tender (тэ́ндэр) заявка, полный тендер, тендер, условия предложения ~s торги
  international ~s (интэрна́шэнал ~с) международные тендеры, международные торги
  invitation of ~s (инвитэ́йшн оф ~с) объявление торгов
  isolated ~s (а́йсолэйтэд ~с) изолированные тендеры
  legal ~ (ли́гал ~) законный тендер
  notice of ~s (но́тис оф ~с) извещение о торгах
  to forward a ~ (ту фо́руард а ~) направлять тендер
  to win ~s (ту уин ~с) выигрывать торги
  ~ conditions (~ конди́шнс) условия тендера
  ~ for competitive bids (~ фор компэ́титив бидз) предложение конкуренции
  ~ number (~ ну́мбэр) номер тендера
Tension (тэ́ншн) напряжение, напряжённость
  relaxation of ~ (рилаксэ́йшн оф ~) ослабление напряжённости
  to reduce ~ (ту риду́с ~) ослабить напряжение
Tenure (тэ́нюр) владение недвижимость, срок владения
  ~ of office (~ оф о́ффис) заместительство
Term (тэрм) сессия, срок, термин, условие
  acceptable ~s (аксэ́птабл ~с) приемлемые условия
  advantageous ~s (адвантэ́йджэс ~с) преимущественные условия
  agreed ~s and conditions (агри́д ~с энд конди́шнс) согласованные условия
  alternative ~s of payment (алтэ́рнатив ~с оф пэ́ймэнт) иные условия платежа
  annual ~ (а́ннюал ~) годовая сессия
  attractive ~s (аттра́ктив ~с) привлекательные условия

barter ~s (ба́ртэр ~с) условия мены
basic ~s of delivery (бэ́йсик ~с оф дэли́вэри) базисные условия поставки
berth ~s (бэрθ ~с) линейные условия, причальные условия
charter-party ~s (ча́ртэр-па́рти ~с) условия чартера
collection ~s (коллэ́кшн ~с) условия инкассо
commercial ~s (коммэ́ршл ~с) коммерческие условия
contemplated ~s and conditions (ко́нтэмплэйтэд ~с энд конди́шнс) предусмотренные условия
credit ~s (крэ́дит ~с) методы финансирования, условия кредита
deferred ~s of payment (дифэ́рд ~с оф пэ́ймэнт) отсроченные условия платежа
definite ~ (дэ́финит ~) определённый срок
delivery ~s (дэли́вэри ~с) условия поставки
designated ~ (дэ́зигнэйтэд ~) назначенный срок
draft ~s (драфт ~с) условия о производстве платежа векселем {траттой}
equal ~s (и́куал ~с) равные условия
favorable ~s (фэ́йворабл ~с) благоприятные условия
general ~s and conditions (джэ́нэрал ~с энд конди́шнс) общие правила
import payment ~s (и́мпорт пэ́ймэнт ~с) условия платежа за импорт товара
in ~s of value (ин ~с оф ва́лю) в стоимостном выражении
in real ~s (ин ри́л ~с) в реальном выражении
indefinite ~ (индэ́финит ~) неопределённый срок
inequitable ~s (инэ́куитабл ~с) неравноправные условия
initial ~ (ини́шл ~) начальный срок
lease ~s (лис ~с) условия аренды
mutually profitable ~s (мю́чуалли про́фитабл ~с) взаимовыгодные условия
non-observance of ~s (нон-обзэ́рванс оф ~с) несоблюдение условий

on credit ~s (он крэ́дит ~с) на условиях кредита

on equal ~s (он и́куал ~с) на равных началах

on general contract ~s (он джэ́нэрал ко́нтракт ~с) на условиях генерального подряда

on other similar ~s (он о́θэр си́милар ~с) на прочих равных условиях

on preferential ~s (он прэфэрэ́ншл ~с) на льготных условиях

on profitable ~s (он про́фитабл ~с) на выгодных условиях

on usual ~s (он ю́жуал ~с) на обычных условиях

original ~s of a contract (ори́джинал ~с оф а ко́нтракт) первоначальные условия контракта

payment ~s (пэ́ймэнт ~с) условия платежа

preferential ~s (прэфэрэ́ншл ~с) льготные условия

profitable ~s (про́фитабл ~с) выгодные условия

proposed ~s (пропо́зд ~с) предложенные условия

purchase ~s (пу́рчас ~с) условия покупки

sales ~s (сэ́йлз ~с) условия продажи

scientific ~s (сайэнти́фик ~с) научные термины

settlement ~s (сэ́тлмэнт ~с) условия расчёта

shipment ~s (ши́пмэнт ~с) условия отгрузки

short ~ (шорт ~) краткосрочный

similar ~s (си́милар ~с) аналогичные условия

special ~s of payment (спэшл ~с оф пэ́ймэнт) специальные условия платежа

subject to the ~s and conditions (са́бджэкт ту θи ~с энд конди́шнс) в зависимости от условий

to act in accordance with the ~s and conditions (ту акт ин акко́рданс уиθ θи ~с энд конди́шнс) contract действовать в соответствии с условиями контракта

to agree to acceptable ~s (ту агри́ ту аксэ́птабл ~с) договориться о приемлемых условиях

to comply with ~s and conditions (ту компла́й уиθ ~с энд конди́шнс) соблюдать условия

to define ~s (ту дифа́йн ~с) определять условия

to discuss ~s and conditions (ту диска́с ~с энд конди́шнс) обсуждать условия

to entail amendment of the ~s and conditions (ту энтэ́йл амэ́ндмэнт оф θи ~с энд конди́шнс) вызывать изменения условий соглашения

to fall outside the ~s of the contract (ту фал о́утсайд θи ~с оф θи ко́нтракт) выходить за пределы условий контракта

to fulfill the ~s and conditions of a contract (ту фулфи́л θи ~с энд конди́шнс оф а ко́нтракт) выполнять условия контракта

to grant ~s and conditions (ту грант ~с энд конди́шнс) предоставлять условия

to honor the ~s of credit (ту о́нор θи ~с оф крэ́дит) выполнять условия кредита

to honor the payment ~s (ту о́нор θи пэ́ймэнт ~с) выполнять условия платежа

to incorporate ~s in the letter of credit (ту инко́рпорэйт ~с ин θи лэ́ттэр оф крэ́дит) включать в условия аккредитива

to maintain ~s (ту мэйнтэ́йн ~с) придерживаться условий

to meet the ~s (ту мит θи ~с) выполнять условия

to negotiate ~s (ту нэго́шиэйт ~с) договариваться об условиях

to offer the most favorable ~s (ту о́ффэр θи мост фэ́йворабл ~с) предоставлять самые благоприятные условия

to outline ~s and conditions (ту о́утлайн ~с энд конди́шнс) намечать условия

to pay on credit ~s (ту пэй он крэ́дит ~с) платить на условиях кредита

to phrase the ~s and conditions of a contract (ту фрэйз θи ~с энд конди́шнс оф а ко́нтракт) формулировать условия контракта

to quote ~s (ту куо́т ~с) назначать условия

to reject the ~s and conditions of a contract (ту риджэ́кт θи ~с энд конди́шнс оф а ко́нтракт) отвергать условия контракта

to review ~s and conditions (ту ривю́ ~с энд конди́шнс) рассматривать условия

to revise ~s and conditions (ту рива́йз ~с энд конди́шнс) пересматривать условия

to set out ~s and conditions (ту сэт о́ут ~с энд конди́шнс) выдвигать условия

to stipulate ~s and conditions (ту сти́пюлэйт ~с энд конди́шнс) предусматривать условия

to study the ~s (ту сту́ди θи ~с) изучать условия

to violate ~s (ту ва́йолэйт ~с) нарушать условия

to violate the ~s of a contract (ту ва́йолэйт θи ~с оф а ко́нтракт) нарушать условия контракта

unacceptable ~s (анаксэ́птабл ~с) неприемлемые условия

under similar ~s (а́ндэр си́милар ~с) с аналогичными условиями

under the ~s stipulated in the contract (а́ндэр θи ~с сти́пюлэйтд ин θи ко́нтракт) на условиях, предусмотренных в контракте

under the ~s and conditions of a contract (а́ндэр θи ~с энд конди́шнс оф а ко́нтракт) по условиям контракта

under the mutually agreed ~s (а́ндэр θи мю́чуалли агри́д ~с) на взаимосогласованных условиях

uniform ~s (ю́ниформ ~с) единые условия

unless otherwise provided by the ~s of the letter of ~ (унлэ́с о́θэруайз прова́йдэд бай θи ~с оф θи лэ́ттэр оф крэ́дит) credit если условия аккредитива не предписывают иного

usual ~s (ю́жуал ~с) обычные условия

usual ~s of payment (ю́жуал ~с оф пэ́ймэнт) обычные условия платежа

~s and conditions of an auction (~с энд конди́шнс оф ан аукшн) условия аукциона

~s and conditions of a bid (~с энд конди́шнс оф а бид) условия предложения

~s and conditions of a buy-sell contract (~с энд конди́шнс оф а бай-сэл ко́нтракт) условия купли-продажи

~s and conditions of consignment (~с энд конди́шнс оф конса́йнмэнт) условия консигнации

~s and conditions of a contract (~с энд конди́шнс оф а ко́нтракт) условия договора

~s and conditions of a financing package (~с энд конди́шнс оф а фа́йнансинг па́кэдж) условия предоставления финансовых услуг

~s and conditions of a licensing agreement (~с энд конди́шнс оф а ла́йсэнсинг агри́мэнт) условия лицензионного договора

~s and conditions of a treaty (~с энд конди́шнс оф а три́ти) условия договора

~ has expired (~ хаз экспа́йрд) срок действия истёк

~s of acceptance (~с оф аксэ́птанс) условия приёмки

~ of amortization (~ оф амортизэ́йшн) срок амортизации

~s of annulment (~с оф анну́лмэнт) условия аннулирования

~s of art (~с оф арт) торговые термины

~s of an average bond (~с оф ан а́вэрэдж бонд) условия аварийного бонда

~s of a bill of lading (~с оф а бил оф лэ́йдинг) условия коносамента

~s of a commercial transaction (~с оф а комме́ршл транса́кшн) условия коммерческой сделки

~ of contract (~ оф ко́нтракт) срок договора

~s of conveyance (~с оф конвэ́йанс) условия транспортировки

~s of cooperation (~с оф коопэрэ́йшн) условия сотрудничества

~s of a deal (~с оф а дил) условия сделки

~s of debenture (~с оф дибэ́нчур) условия долгового обязательства

~s of financing (~с оф фа́йнансинг) условия финансирования

~s of freight (~с оф фрэ́йт) условия фрахта

~ of lease (~ оф лис) срок аренды

~s of a letter of credit (~с оф а лэттэр оф крэдит) условия аккредитива

~ of prescription (~ оф прэскрипшн) срок давности

~s of trade (~с оф трэйд) условия торговли

Terminal (тэрминал) терминал

container ~ (контэйнэр ~) контейнерный терминал

freight liner ~ (фрэйт лайнэр ~) терминал для грузовых судов

marine ~ (марин ~) морской терминал

Termination (тэрминэйшн) окончание, прекращение

~ of an act (~ оф ан акт) прекращение действия договора

~ of a commission (~ оф а коммишн) прекращение поручения

~ of a contract (~ оф а контракт) прекращение договора

~ of a force majeure situation (~ оф а форс мажур ситюэйшн) окончание форс-мажорной ситуации

~ of a license (~ оф а лайсэнз) прекращение действия лицензии

~ of a patent grant (~ оф а патэнт грант) прекращение действия патента

~ of a power of attorney (~ оф а поуэр оф атторни) прекращение доверенности

Terminology (тэрминолоджи) терминология

legal ~ (лигал ~) юридическая терминология

scientific ~ (сайэнтифик ~) научная терминология

Territorial (тэрриториал) территориальный

Territory (тэрритори) зона, территория

agreed ~ (агрид ~) согласованная территория

customs ~ (кастомз ~) таможенная территория

disputed ~ (диспютэд ~) спорная зона

eastern ~ (истэрн ~) восточная зона

exclusive ~ (эксклюсив ~) исключительная территория

licensed ~ (лайсэнсд ~) лицензированная территория

neutral ~ (нутрал ~) нейтральная зона

occupied ~ (оккюпайд ~) оккупированная зона

quarantined ~ (куарантинд ~) карантинизированная зона

sales ~ (сэйлз ~) сбытовая территория

~ under jurisdiction (~ андэр джюрисдикшн) зона юрисдикции

Test (тэст) измерение, испытание, контроль, проверка, тест, экзамен

load ~ (лод ~) испытание под нагрузкой

to ~ (ту ~) пробовать, проводить тест

to carry out a ~ **run of units** (ту кэрри оут а ~ ран оф юнитс) производить контрольную обкатку агрегатов

to put to the ~ (ту пут ту θи ~) подвергать тесту

to stand the ~ (ту станд θи ~) выдерживать тест

~ certification (~ сэртификэйшн) акт испытаний

Tested (тэстэд) проверенный

to be laboratory ~ (ту би лаборатори ~) пройти испытания в лабораторных условиях

Testify, to ~ (тэстифай, ту ~) свидетельствовать

Testimonial (тэстимониал) аттестат

Testimony (тэстимони) показание, свидетельство

preliminary ~ (прилиминэри ~) предварительное свидетельство

~ of the defendant (~ оф θи дифэндант) показание обвиняемого

~ of witnesses (~ оф уитнэсэз) показание свидетелей

Testing (тэстинг) измерение, испытание

completion of ~ (комплишн оф ~) окончание испытаний

Text (тэкст) текст

agreed ~ (агрид ~) согласованный текст

alteration of a ~ (алтэрэйшн оф а ~) исправление текста

altered ~ (алтэрд ~) исправленный текст

authentic ~ (ауθэнтик ~) подлинный текст

full ~ (фул ~) полный текст

original ~ (ориджинал ~) первоначальный текст

supplement to a ~ (сáпплэмэнт ту а ~) дополнение к тексту
to approve a ~ (ту аппрýв а ~) одобрять текст
to print a ~ (ту принт а ~) печатать текст
~ of a contract (~ оф а кóнтракт) текст контракта
~ of a telex (~ оф а тэ́лэкс) текст телекса
Textiles (тэ́кстайлз) текстильные товары
Theft (θэфт) кража, похищение
~ of government property (~ оф гóвэрнмэнт прóпэрти) похищение государственного имущества
Thei/f (θиф) вор, разбойник **~/ves** (θивз) воры, разбойники
den of ~/ves (дэн оф θивз) воровской притон, разбойничий притон
Thing (θинг) вещь
Third (θирд) третий
~ bill of exchange (~ билл оф эксчэ́йндж) терция
Thorough (θу́ро) тщательный
Thoroughfare (θу́рофэйр) проезд
Thoroughly (θу́роли) тщательно
to ~ investigate (ту ~ инвэ́стигэйт) тщательно исследовать
Thrifty (θри́фти) экономный
Throne (θрон) престол
Heavenly ~ (хэ́вэнли ~) престол святейший
heir to the ~ (эйр ту θи ~) престолонаследник
succession to the ~ (суксэ́шн ту θи ~) престолонаследие
to abdicate the ~ (ту áбдикэйт θи ~) отречься от престола
to mount the ~ (ту мóунт θи ~) вступить на престол
Through (θру) транзитный
Ticket (ти́ккэт) билет
airline ~ (эйрлайн ~) билет на самолёте
baggage claim ~ (бáггадж клэйм ~) багажная квитанция
broker's ~ {auction} (брóкэрз ~ {аукшн}) аукционный меморандум
pawn ~ (пáун ~) закладочное свидетельство, залоговая квитанция, ломбардная расписка
railway ~ (рэ́йлуэй ~) железнодорожный билет

return ~ (риту́рн ~) обратный билет
Tie (тай) галстук {clothing}, связь {connection}
Tight (тайт) напряжённый
~ credit (~ крэ́дит) нехватка кредита
~ money (~ мóни) нехватка денег
Till (тил) касса
~ balance (~ бáланс) кассовая наличность
Tilt, to ~ (тилт, ту ~) кантовать
Timber (ти́мбэр) лесоматериал
floating ~ (флóтинг ~) сплав
Time (тайм) время, срок
at the appointed ~ (ат θи аппóйнтэд ~) в назначенное время
changeover ~ (чэ́йнджовэр ~) время перехода к выпуску новой продукции {production}
construction ~ (констру́кшн ~) график хода строительства
detention ~ (дитэ́ншн ~) сверхпростойное {сверхсталийное} время, сверхурочное время
effective ~ (иффэ́ктив ~) фактическое время
estimated ~ (э́стиматд ~) расчётное время
expected ~ of arrival {ETA} (экспэ́ктэд ~ оф аррáйвал {и-ти-эй}) предполагаемая дата прибытия
loading ~ (лóдинг ~) время погрузочное
local ~ (лóкал ~) местное время
onloading ~ (онлóдинг) время продолжительности погрузки
processing ~ (прóсэсинг ~) длительность обработки
running ~ (рáннинг ~) длительность работы
serving ~ (сэ́рвинг ~) отбывание {e.g. in prison}
set up ~ (сэт ап ~) установочное время
standard base ~ (стáндард бэйс ~) норма времени
to lose ~ (ту луз ~) терять время
to save ~ (ту сэйв ~) экономить время
to take up ~ (ту тэйк ап ~) занимать время
turnaround ~ {maritime} (ту́рнараунд ~ {мáритайм}) время оборота судна в порту

~ **bill** (~ бил) дата-вексель
~ **note** (~ нот) дата-вексель
~ **of arrival** (~ оф аррáйвал) время прибытия
~ **of delivery** (~ оф дэлúвэри) время доставке
~ **of departure** (~ оф дипáрчур) время отправления
~ **of execution** (~ оф экзэкю́шн) время выполнения
~ **savings** (~ сэ́йвингз) экономия времени
Time-charter (тайм-чáртэр) тайм-чартер
Time-charterer (тайм-чáртэрэр) фрахтователь по тайм-чартеру
~'**s liability** (~'с лайабúлити) ответственность фрахтователя по тайм-чартеру
Time-line (тайм-лайн) линейный график
Timely (тáймли) своевременный
Timesheet (тáймшит) табель
daily ~ (дэ́йли ~) ежедневная ведомость
monthly ~ (мóнθли ~) ежемесячная ведомость, текущий табель {for factory workers}
to fill out daily ~**s** (ту фил óут дэ́йли ~с) выписывать ведомость ежедневного учёта времени, составлять ежедневные временные графики
Timetable (тáймтэйбл) график, расписание
ship ~ (шип ~) расписание движения судов
to establish a production ~ (ту эстáблиш а продáкшн ~) устанавливать график работ
train ~ (трэйн ~) расписание движения поездов
Tip, to ~ (тип, ту ~) кантовать
"**do not** ~" (ду нот ~) "не кантовать"
Title (тайтл) звание, название, титул {ownership}, титульный {adj.}
abstract of ~ (áбстракт оф ~) справка о титуле, выписка из реестра
conveyance of legal ~ (конвэ́йанс оф лúгал ~) передача правового титула
document of ~ {shipped goods} (дóкюмэнт оф ~ {шиппд гудз}) товарораспорядительный документ
good ~ (гуд ~) законный титул

honorary ~ (óнорари ~) почётное звание
legal ~ (лúгал ~) правовой титул, юридическое звание
to show good ~ (ту шóу гуд ~) показать законный титул
voidable ~ (вóйдабл ~) оспоримый титул
~ **of an invention** (~ оф ан инвэ́ншн) наименование изобретения
~ **to chattels** (~ ту шáтэлз) титул на движимое имущество
~ **to real property** (~ ту рúл прóпэрти) титул на недвижимое имущество
Token (тóкэн) знак, примета
Tolerable (тóлэрабл) допустимый
Tolerance (тóлэранс) снисходительность
to adhere to specified ~**s** (ту адхúр ту спэ́сифайд ~с) выдерживать допуски
wear ~ (уэйр ~) допуск на износ
zero-defect ~ (зúро-дúфэкт ~) бездефектность
Toll (тол) дорожный налог, пошлина
railway ~ (рэ́йлуэй ~) железнодорожный сбор
road ~ (род ~) дорожная пошлина, дорожный сбор
Ton (тон) тонна
~ **burden** (~ бýрдэн) тонна вместимости
Tonnage (тóннадж) тоннаж
cargo ~ (кáрго ~) грузовой тоннаж
chartered ~ (чáртэрд ~) зафрахтованный тоннаж
compensated ~ (кóмпэнсэйтэд ~) компенсированный тоннаж
gross ~ (грос ~) валовая вместимость, валовой тоннаж
idle ~ (айдл ~) бездействующий тоннаж
inland ~ (úнланд ~) речной тоннаж
liner ~ (лáйнэр ~) линейный тоннаж
low ~ (лóу ~) малотоннажный
maritime ~ (мáритайм ~) морской тоннаж
maximum ~ (мáксимум ~) максимальный тоннаж
registered ~ (рэ́джистэрд ~) регистровая вместимость

significant ~ (сигни́фикант ~) значительный тоннаж
stipulated ~ (сти́пюлэйтэд ~) обусловленный тоннаж
tanker ~ (та́нкэр ~) наливной тоннаж
to book ~ (ту бук ~) буксировать тоннаж
to register ~ (ту ре́джистэр ~) регистрировать вместимость
total ~ (то́тал ~) общий тоннаж
tramp ~ (трамп ~) трамповый тоннаж
~ **demand** (~ дима́нд) спрос на тоннаж
~ **of a ship** (~ оф а шип) грузоподъёмность судна
~ **scale** (~ скэйл) шкала вместимости
Tool (тул) инструмент, орудие, прибор
~ **kit** (~ кит) комплект инструментов
Toolmaker (ту́лмэйкэр) машиностроитель
Top (топ) верх
Topic (то́пик) тема
delicate ~ (де́ликат ~) щекотливая тема
Tort (торт) деликт
Torture (то́рчэр) истязание
interrogation under ~ (интэрроге́йшн а́ндэр ~) допрос с пристрастием
to ~ (ту ~) истязать
Total (то́тал) итог {sum}, общий
grand ~ (гранд ~) общий итог
to ~ (ту ~) насчитывать
~ **operating hours** (~ о́пэрэйтинг о́урз) учёт количества отработанных часов
Totality (тота́лити) совокупность
Toughness (ту́фнэс) вязкость
Tourism (ту́рисм) туризм
development of ~ (диве́лопмэнт оф ~) развитие туризма
foreign ~ (фо́рэн ~) иностранный туризм
international ~ (интэрна́шэнал ~) международный туризм
Tourist (ту́рист) туристический
Tow, to ~ (то́у, ту ~) буксировать
Towing (то́уинг) буксирный {adj.}, буксировка, обслуживание буксирами
marine ~ (мари́н ~) морская буксировка
Track (трак) путь

Tractor-trailer (тра́ктор-трэ́йлэр) грузовик с прицепом
Trade (трэйд) промысел, ремесленный {adj.}, товарный {adj.}, торговля, торговый {adj.}
annual ~ (а́ннюал ~) годовая торговля
barter ~ (ба́ртэр ~) бартерная торговля
bilateral ~ (байла́тэрал ~) двусторонняя торговля, двухсторонний торговый обмен
brisk ~ (бриск ~) оживлённая торговля
cash ~ (каш ~) торговля за наличные
coasting ~ (ко́стинг ~) каботажная торговля
counter ~ (ко́унтэр ~) встречная торговля
diplomatic ~ (дипло́матик ~) дипломатическая торговля
direct transit ~ (дире́кт тра́нзит ~) прямая транзитная торговля
diversification of ~ (дивэрсифике́йшн оф ~) диверсификация торговли
domestic ~ (доме́стик ~) внутренняя торговля
duty-free ~ (дю́ти-фри ~) беспошлинная торговля
expansion of ~ (экспа́ншн оф ~) развёртывание торговли
export ~ (э́кспорт ~) экспортная торговля
field of ~ (филд оф ~) отрасль торговли
foreign ~ (фо́рэн ~) внешняя торговля
free ~ (фри ~) свободная торговля
illicit ~ (илли́сит ~) контрабандная торговля
indirect transit ~ (индайре́кт тра́нзит ~) косвенная транзитная торговля
intermediary ~ (интэрми́диари ~) посредническая торговля
interregional ~ (интэрри́джёнал ~) межрегиональная торговля
interstate ~ (интэрстэ́йт ~) межгосударственная торговля
"invisible ~" (инви́зибл ~) "невидимая" торговля
lawful ~ (ла́уфул ~) законная торговля

licensed ~ (лайсэнсд ~) лицензионная торговля
multilateral ~ (мултилátэрал ~) многосторонняя
national ~ (нáшэнал ~) национальная торговля
preferential ~ (прэфэрэ́ншл ~) преференциальная торговля
private ~ (прáйват ~) частная торговля
receipts from ~ (риси́тс фром ~) выручка от торговли
regional ~ (ри́джонал ~) региональная торговля
retail ~ (ри́тэйл ~) розничная торговля
seasonal ~ (си́зонал ~) сезонная торговля
significant ~ (сигни́фикант ~) значительная торговля
slow ~ (слоу ~) вялый бизнес
stagnant ~ (стáгнант ~) вялая торговля
stagnation in ~ (стагнэ́йшн ин ~) застой в торговле
to ~ (ту ~) вести торговлю, торговать
to encourage ~ (ту энкýрадж ~) поощрять торговлю
to impede the development of ~ (ту импи́д θи дивэ́лопмэнт оф ~) препятствовать развитию торговли
unlawful ~ (анлáуфул ~) незаконная торговля
"visible ~" (ви́зибл ~) видимая торговля
volume of ~ (вóлюм оф ~) объём торговли
wholesale ~ (хóлсэйл ~) оптовая продажа, оптовая торговля
world ~ (уóрлд ~) мировая торговля
~ acceptance (~ аксэ́птанс) акцептованный торговый вексель
~ days (~ дэйз) дни работы ярмарки, отведённые для бизнесменов
~ expansion policy (~ экспáншн пóлиси) политика расширения торговли
~ imbalance (~ имбáланс) дисбаланс торговли
~ liberalization (~ либэрализэ́йшн) либерализация торговли
~ mission (~ мишн) торгпредство

~ prospects (~ прóспэктс) перспективы торговли
~ recovery (~ рикóвэри) оживление торговли
~ representative (~ рэпрэзэ́нтатив) торгпред
~ restriction (~ ристри́кшн) ограничение торговли
~ show (~ шóу) ярмарка-выставка
Trademark (трэ́йдмарк) товарный знак, товарная марка
annulment of a ~ (аннýлмэнт оф a ~) аннулирование знака
manufacturer's ~ (манюфáкчурэрз ~) заводская марка, заводское клеймо, фабричная марка
registered ~ (рэ́джистэрд ~) зарегистрированный товарный знак, официально зарегистрированная марка
to bear a ~ (ту бэйр a ~) носить фабричную марку
~ designations (~ дэсигнэ́йшнс) условные обозначения марок
Trader (трэ́йдр) купец
currency ~ (кýррэнси ~) камбист
independent ~ (индипэ́ндэнт ~) индивидуальный торговец
market ~ (мáркэт ~) рыночный торговец
small ~ (смал ~) мелкий торговец
wholesale ~ (хóлсэйл ~) оптовый торговец
Tradesman (трэ́йдсман) торговец
retail ~ (ри́тэйл ~) розничный торговец
Trading (трэ́йдинг) коммерция
commodities ~ (коммóдитиз ~) товарный арбитраж
currency ~ (кýррэнси ~) валютный арбитраж
exchange ~ (эксчэ́йндж ~) биржевая торговля
metals ~ (мэ́талс ~) торговля металлами
state ~ (стэ́йт ~) государственная торговля
~ obstacles (~ óбстаклз) помехи в торговле
Tradition (тради́шн) традиция
Traffic (трáффик) движение, сообщение, торговля, транзит
air ~ (эйр ~) воздушное движение, воздушное сообщение
freight ~ (фрэ́йт ~) грузоперевозка, грузовое движение

goods ~ (гудз ~) товарное движение
overland ~ (о́вэрланд ~) сухопутное сообщение
overseas ~ (овэрси́з ~) морское сообщение
passenger ~ (па́ссэнджэр ~) пассажирское движение
river ~ (ри́вэр ~) речное сообщение
shipping ~ (ши́ппинг ~) пароходное сообщение
short-haul ~ (шорт-хаул ~) местное сообщение
to stop ~ (ту стоп ~) прекратить движение
~ **conditions** (~ конди́шнс) условия движения
~ **in transit** (~ ин тра́нзит) транзитное движение
Trailer (трэ́йлэр) кинореклама {motion picture}, трайлер
cargo-~ (ка́рго-~) карго-трайлер
piggy-back ~ (пи́гги-бак ~) контрейлер, контрейлерный {adj.}
Train (трэйн) поезд
hospital ~ (хо́спитал ~) санитарный поезд
Training (трэ́йнинг) обучение, подготовка, стажировка
in-plant ~ (ин-плант ~) обучать специалистов в заводских условиях
management ~ (ма́наджмэнт ~) обучение руководящих кадров, подготовка кадров
military ~ (ми́литари ~) военное обучение
on the job ~ (он θи джоб ~) обучение на заводе, обучение по месту работы
personnel ~ (пэрсонн́эл ~) подготовка кадров
Traitor (трэ́йтор) изменник, предатель
Tramp (трамп) трамповый {adj.: vessel}
~ **steamer** (~ сти́мэр) трамп
Tranquility (транку́илити) спокойствие
Trans-Atlantic (транс-атла́нтик) трансатлантический
Transaction (транса́кшн) дело, операция, сделка, трансакция
bad faith ~ (бад фэйθ ~) недобросовестная сделка

bank ~ (банк ~) банковская сделка, банковская операция, банковская трансакция
barter-exchange ~ (ба́ртэр-эксчэ́йндж ~) меновая сделка
bilateral ~ (байла́тэрал ~) двухсторонняя сделка
business ~ (би́знэс ~) деловая операция
buy-back ~ (бай-бак ~) компенсационная сделка
buy-sell ~ (бай-сэл ~) сделка купли-продажи
cash ~ (каш ~) кассовая сделка
clearinghouse ~ (кли́рингхаус ~) клиринговая операция
commodity swapping ~ (комм́одити суа́ппинг ~) товарообменная сделка
consignment ~ (конса́йнмэнт ~) комиссионная операция
credit ~ (крэ́дит ~) кредитная сделка
currency exchange ~ (ку́ррэнси эксчэ́йндж ~) валютная трансакция
discount ~ (ди́скоунт ~) учётная операция, учётная сделка
discount lending ~ (ди́скоунт лэ́ндинг ~) учётно-ссудная операция
exchange ~ (эксчэ́йндж ~) биржевая операция {stock exchange}, валютная операция {currency}
fictitious ~ (фикти́шос ~) фиктивная сделка
financial ~ (файна́ншл ~) финансовая операция, финансовая сделка, финансовая трансакция
foreign trade ~ (фо́рэн трэйд ~) внешнеторговая сделка
forward ~ (фо́руард ~) биржевая сделка на срок
forward currency ~ (фо́руард ку́ррэнси ~) срочная сделка с иностранными валютами
futures ~ (фю́чэрз ~) операция на срок, срочная сделка
hedge ~ (хэдж ~) хеджевая сделка
interbank ~ (интэрба́нк ~) межбанковская операция
international buy-sell ~ (интэрна́шэнал бай-сэл ~) международная сделка купли-продажи
issuing ~ (и́шюинг ~) эмиссионная операция

middleman ~ (мидлман ~) посредническая сделка
monetary ~s (монэтари ~с) денежные операции
money-losing ~ (мони-лозинг ~) убыточная сделка
non-cash ~ (нон-каш ~) безналичный расчёт
payment ~ (пэймэнт ~) расчёт
profitable ~ (профитабл ~) прибыльная сделка, рентабельная операция
single ~ (сингл ~) разовая сделка
speculative ~ (спэкюлатив ~) спекулятивная операция, спекулятивная сделка
spot market ~ (спот маркэт ~) кассовая сделка

Transcontinental (трансконтинэнтал) трансконтинентальный
Transfer (трансфэр) акт перенесения, перевалка, перевод, передача, пересылка, трансферт, трансфертный {adj.}, цессия
assignment ~ {work} (ассайнмэнт ~ {уорк}) перевод на другую работу
bank ~ (банк ~) банковский перевод, банковский трансферт
bank ~ of sums from one account to another (банк ~ оф сумз фром уан аккоунт ту аноθэр) банковское перечисление сумм со счёта на счёт
certificate of ~ (сэртификэт оф ~) передаточный акт
compulsory ~ (компулсори ~) передача по принуждению, принудительный перевод
credit ~ (крэдит ~) кредитный трансферт
deed of ~ (дид оф ~) трансферт
inter-vivos ~ (интэр-вайвос ~) передача между живыми, переход между живыми
international ~ (интэрнашэнал ~) международный перевод
money ~ (мони ~) денежный перевод
postal ~ (постал ~) почтовое перечисление
savings ~ (сэйвингс ~) сберегательный перевод
testamentary ~ (тэстамэнтари ~) передача путём завещания

to ~ (ту ~) записывать [**perfective**: записать] {e.g. property}, переводить [**perfective**: перевести], передавать, переносить [**perfective**: перенести], перечислять
to ~ a case (ту ~ а кэйс) перепоручить дело
wire ~ (уайр ~) телеграфный перевод
~ by inheritance (~ бай инхэританс) переход по наследству
~ of capital (~ оф капитал) перевод капитала
~ of capital abroad (~ оф капитал аброд) перевод капиталов за границу
~ of foreign exchange (~ оф форэн эксчэйндж) перевод иностранной валюты
~ of funds (~ оф фандз) перевод фондов
~ of an invention (~ оф ан инвэншн) передача изобретения
~ of a license (~ оф а лайсэнз) передача лицензии
~ of a portfolio (~ оф а портфолио) передача портфеля
~ of property (~ оф пропэрти) передача имуществ, переход имущества
~ of property by inheritance (~ оф пропэрти бай инхэританс) переход имущества по наследству
~ of rights (~ оф райтс) переход прав
~ of sovereignty (~ оф совэрнти) передача суверенитета, переход суверенитета
~ of sums (~ оф сумз) перечисление сумм
~ of territory (~ оф тэрритори) передача территории
~ through a bank (~ θру а банк) перевод через банк
~ to an account (~ ту ан аккоунт) перечисление на счёт

Transferee (трансфэри) лицо, в чью пользу произведён трансферт {on bill, note}, переводополучатель, получатель по трансферту
Transferor (трансфэрор) индоссант, переводоотправитель
Transit (транзит) транзит, транзитный {adj.}

in ~ (ин ~) транзитом
~ visa (~ ви́са) виза для
транзита
Transition (транзи́шн) переход
Translate, to ~ (тра́нслэйт, ту ~)
переводить [**perfective:** перевести]
Translation (транслэ́йшн) перевод
  written ~ (ри́ттэн ~) письменный
  перевод
Translator (тра́нслэйтор) переводчик
  court ~ (ко́урт ~) судебный
  переводчик
Transport (тра́нспорт) перемещение,
транспорт, транспортировка
  air ~ (эйр ~) авиационный
  транспорт, воздушная перевозка,
  воздушный транспорт
  air ~ of freight (эйр ~ оф
  фрэйт) воздушная перевозка груза
  air ~ of passengers (эйр ~ оф
  па́ссэнджэрз) воздушная перевозка
  пассажиров
  airmail ~ (э́йрмэйл ~) воздушная
  перевозка почты
  automobile ~ (аутомоби́л ~)
  автотранспорт, автомобильный
  транспорт
  civil ~ (си́вил ~) гражданский
  транспорт
  coasting-trade ~ (ко́стинг-трэйд
  ~) каботажная перевозка
  commercial ~ (комме́ршл ~)
  коммерческая перевозка
  direct ~ (дире́кт ~) прямая
  перевозка
  freight ~ (фрэйт ~) грузовой
  транспорт
  highway ~ (ха́йуэй ~) шоссейная
  перевозка
  inland ~ (и́нланд ~) внутренний
  транспорт
  inland water ~ (и́нланд уа́тэр ~)
  внутренний водный транспорт
  international ~ (интэрна́шэнал ~)
  международная перевозка
  international air ~
  (интэрна́шэнал эйр ~)
  международная воздушная
  перевозка
  mail ~ (мэйл ~) почтовая
  перевозка
  marine ~ (мари́н ~) морская
  перевозка, морской транспорт
  military ~ (ми́литари ~) военная
  перевозка
  mixed ~ (миксд ~) смешанная
  перевозка

  mode of ~ (мод оф ~) вид
  транспорта
  passenger ~ (па́ссэнджэр ~)
  пассажирская перевозка,
  пассажирский транспорт,
  перевозка пассажиров
  public ~ (па́блик ~) общественный
  транспорт
  rail ~ (рэйл ~) железнодорожная
  перевозка, железнодорожный
  транспорт, речная перевозка,
  речной провоз, речной транспорт
  road ~ (род ~) автоперевозки,
  дорожный транспорт
  to ~ (ту ~) перевозить,
  перемещать, транспортировать
  urban ~ (у́рбан ~) городской
  транспорт
  water ~ (уа́тэр ~) водный
  транспорт
  ~ by barge (~ бай бардж)
  перевозка на барже
  ~ by trucks (~ бай тракс)
  перевозка на грузовиках
  ~ of P.O.W.s (~ оф пи-о-да́бл-ю́з)
  перевозка военнопленных
  ~ on deck (~ он дэк) перевозка
  на палубе
Transportation (транспорта́йшн)
провоз, транспортное сообщение,
транспортный {adj.}
  convenient ~ (конви́ниэнт ~)
  удобное сообщение
  free ~ (фри ~) безвозмездная
  перевозка
  ~ in direct railroad-truck link
  (~ ин дире́кт рэ́йлрод-трак линк)
  перевозка в прямом
  железнодорожно-дорожно-
  автомобильном сообщении
  ~ system (~ си́стэм) система
  транспорта
Transporting (транспо́ртинг)
транспортирование
Transshipment (трансши́пмэнт)
перегрузка
Transshipping (трансши́ппинг)
перевалка
Travel (тра́вэл) путешествие
  business ~ (би́знэс ~)
  командирование
  field ~ by experts (филд ~ бай
  э́кспэртс) командирование
  специалистов
  international ~ (интэрна́шэнал ~)
  международное путешествие

Traveling (трáвэлинг) передвижной {adj.}, разъездной {adj.}
  ~ expenses (~ экспэ́нсэз) командировочные, разъездные деньги
Treachery (трэ́чэри) предательство
Treason (трúзон) измена
  high ~ (хай ~) государственная измена
Treasure (трэ́жюр) сокровище
Treasurer (трэ́жюрэр) казначей, кассир
  assistant ~ (ассúстант ~) помощник казначея
  deputy ~ (дэ́пюти ~) заместитель казначея
  ~/bookkeeper (~/бýккипэр) казначей-бухгалтер
  ~ of a corporation (~ оф а корпорэ́йшн) казначей корпорации
Treasury (трэ́жюри) казна, казначейство
Treatment (трúтмэнт) обращение, режим
  favorable ~ (фэ́йворабл ~) благоприятный режим
  most favored nation ~ (мост фэ́йворд нэйшн ~) режим наиболее благоприятствуемой нации
  national ~ (нáшэнал ~) национальный режим
  preferential ~ (прэфэрэ́ншл ~) благоприятствование, льготный режим
  tax ~ (такс ~) налоговый режим
Treaty (трúти) договор
  bilateral ~ (байлáтэрал ~) двусторонний договор
  denunciation of a ~ (динунсиэ́йшн оф а ~) денонсация договора
  economic ~ (экономúк ~) хозяйственный договор
  equitable ~ (э́куитабл ~) равноправный договор
  multilateral ~ (мултилáтэрал ~) многосторонний договор
  patent cooperation ~ (пáтэнт коопэрэ́йшн ~) договор о патентном сотрудничестве
  to accede to a ~ (ту аксúд ту а ~) присоединяться к договору
  to denounce a ~ (ту динóунс а ~) денонсировать договор
  to renounce a ~ (ту ринóунс а ~) отказываться от договора
  to withdraw from a ~ (ту уиθдрáу фром а ~) выходить из договора

  ~ of unlimited duration (~ оф анлúмитэд дюрэ́йшн) бессрочный договор
  ~ on commerce (~ он кóммэрс) договор о торговле
  ~ on cooperation (~ он коопэрэ́йшн) договор о сотрудничестве
Trend (трэнд) тенденция
  definitive ~ (дэфúнитив ~) определённая тенденция
  downward ~ (дóунуард ~) понижательная тенденция
  economic ~ (экономúк ~) развитие конъюнктуры
  general ~ (джэ́нэрал ~) общая тенденция
  long term ~ (лонг тэрм ~) долговременная тенденция
  market ~ (мáркэт ~) рыночная тенденция
  market ~ analysis (мáркэт ~ анáлисис) анализ тенденций рынка
  price ~ (прайс ~) направление движения цен, тенденция цен
  short-term ~ (шорт-тэрм ~) кратковременная тенденция
  upward ~ (áпуард ~) движение вверх, повышательная тенденция
  ~ analysis (~ анáлисис) анализ тенденций
Trial (трáйал) пробный {adj.}, процесс, суд
  jury ~ (джюри ~) суд присяжных
  speedy ~ (спúди ~) быстрый суд
  to bring to ~ (ту бринг ту ~) привлекать к суду
  ~ by combat (~ бай кóмбат) суд Божий
Tribunal (трибю́нал) суд
  arbitration ~ (арбитрэ́йшн ~) арбитраж, третейский суд
  consular ~ (кóнсюлар ~) консульский суд
Tribute (трúбют) дань {payment to conqueror}, подношение
Trick (трик) проделка
  To ~ (ту ~) обмануть
Trim, to ~ (трим, ту ~) размещать
Trimming (трúмминг) тримминг {of vessel}, укладка {of cargo}
Trip (трип) поездка, рейс
  business ~ (бúзнэс ~) командировка, служебная поездка
  business ~ abroad (бúзнэс ~ абрóд) зарубежная командировка

extended business ~ (экстэ́ндэд би́знэс ~) длительная командировка
official business ~ (оффи́шл би́знэс ~) служебная командировка

one-way ~ (уа́н-уэй ~) рейс , в один конец
return ~ (риту́рн ~) обратный провоз
round ~ (роунд ~) круговой рейс
short-term business ~ (шорт-тэрм би́знэс ~) краткосрочная командировка
to send on a business ~ (ту сэнд он а би́знэс ~) командировать
Triplicate, in ~ (три́пликат, ин ~) в трёх экземплярах
to enclose documents in ~ (ту энкло́з до́кюмэнтс ин ~) приложить документы в трёх экземплярах
to issue a bill in ~ (ту и́шю а бил ин ~) выставлять трату в трёх экземплярах
Tropical (тро́пикал) тропический
Trouble (трабл) трудность
to bear ~ (ту бэйр ~) выносить трудности
to withstand ~ (ту уи́θста́нд ~) выдерживать трудности
Troubleshooter (тра́блшутэр) аварийный монтёр
Troubleshooting (тра́блшутинг) нахождение неисправностей
Trousseau (труссо́) приданое
Truancy (тру́анси) прогул
Truck (трак) грузовой автомобиль, грузовая машина, грузовик
closed ~ (клозд ~) крытый грузовик
FOB ~ (эф-о-би ~) франко грузовик
heavy-duty ~ (хэ́ви-дю́ти ~) тяжёлый грузовик
light-duty ~ (лайт-дю́ти ~) грузовик малой грузоподъёмности
shipment by ~ pre-paid (ши́пмэнт бай ~ при-пэйд) за перевозку на грузовике уплачено
to load onto a ~ (ту лод и́нту а ~) грузить на грузовик
to ship by ~s (ту ши́п бай ~с) перевозить на грузовиках
to transfer to ~ (ту тра́нсфэр ту ~) перегружать на грузовик
to unload a ~ (ту анло́д а ~) разгружать грузовик

Trunk (трунк) ящик
overseas ~ (овэрси́з ~) ящик для морской перевозки
Trust (траст) доверие, трест {socialized group of enterprises}
breach of ~ (брич оф ~) злоупотребление доверием
to lose ~ (ту луз ~) потерять доверие
Trustee (трусти́) опекун, попечитель
statutory ~ (ста́тютори ~) законный опекун
Trusteeship (трусти́шип) опека, попечительство
administrative ~ (адми́нистрэйтив ~) административная опека
international ~ (интэрна́шэнал ~) международная опека
statutory ~ (ста́тютори ~) законная опека
to be under ~ (ту би а́ндэр ~) находиться под опекой
Truth (тру θ) истина, правда
Try, to ~ (трай, ту ~) пробовать, судить
to ~ behind closed doors (ту ~ биха́йнд клозд дорс) судить при закрытых дверях
Tsar (цар) царь
Tsarism (ца́ризм) царизм
Tug, to ~ (туг, ту ~) буксировать
Tug-boat (туг-бот) буксир, буксирное судно
port ~ (порт ~) портовый буксир
~ contract (~ ко́нтракт) договор морской буксировки
~ service (~ сэ́рвис) обслуживание буксирами
Tuggage (ту́ггадж) буксирный {adj.}, буксировка
marine ~ (мари́н ~) морская буксировка
Turn (турн) очередь
to ~ to (ту ~ ту) обращать
to ~ oneself in {to the authorities} (ту ~ уа́нсэлф ин {ту θи ауθо́ритиз}) явиться с повинной
to ~ over (ту ~ о́вэр) перегружать {cargo}, перепоручить
Turn-key (турн-ки) "под ключ"
~ contract (~ ко́нтракт) контракт "под ключ"
~ project (~ про́джэкт) проект "под ключ"

Turnover (ту́рновэр)
оборачиваемость, оборот
   annual ~ (а́ннюал ~) годовой
оборот
   capital ~ (ка́питал ~)
оборачиваемость капитала, оборот
капитала
   cash ~ (каш ~) оборот наличных
денег
   daily ~ (дэ́йли ~) дневной оборот
   domestic ~ (домэ́стик ~) оборот
внутри страны
   export ~ (э́кспорт ~) оборот по
экспорту
   fluctuations in ~ (флукчуэ́йшнс
ин ~) колебание оборота
   freight ~ (фрэ́йт ~) грузооборот,
оборот грузов
   import ~ (и́мпорт ~) оборот по
импорту
   merchandise ~ (мэ́рчандайс ~)
товарный оборот
   minimum ~ (ми́нимум ~)
минимальный оборот
   money ~ (мо́ни ~) денежный оборот
   overall ~ (овэра́л ~) общий
оборот
   plant ~ (плант ~)
оборачиваемость основного
капитала
   rate of ~ (рэ́йт оф ~) скорость
оборота
   rate of stock ~ {goods} (рэ́йт оф
сток ~ {гудз}) скорость оборота
товарных запасов
   sales ~ (сэ́йлз ~) оборот по
продажам
   volume of ~ (во́люм оф ~) размер
оборота
   wholesale ~ (хо́лсэйл ~) оптовый
оборот
   work-in-process ~ (уо́рк-ин-
про́сэс ~) оборачиваемость
незавершённого производства
   ~ of deposits (~ оф дипо́зитс)
оборачиваемость депозитов
   ~ of finished goods (~ оф фи́нишд
гудз) оборачиваемость готовой
продукции
   ~ of stock (~ оф сток)
оборачиваемость товарных запасов
   ~ of working capital (~ оф
уо́ркинг ка́питал) оборачиваемость
оборотных средств
Twine (туа́йн) шпагат
   binder ~ (ба́йндэр ~) увязочный
шпагат

Two-fold (ту-фолд) двойной
Type (тайп) род, сорт
   to ~ (ту ~) писать на машинке
Typewriter (та́йпрайтэр) пишущая
машинка
Typewritten (та́йприттэн)
напечатанный

U

Ultimate (а́лтимат) конечный
Umpire (у́мпайр) суперарбитр
{arbitration}
   third party ~ (θирд па́рти ~)
третий арбитр
Unacceptable (анаксэ́птабл)
неприемлемый
Unaccepted (анаксэ́птэд)
неакцептованный, непринятий
Unaccomplished (анакко́мплишд)
незавершённый
Unacknowledged (анакно́лэджд)
неподтверждённый
Unaddressed (анаддрэ́сд)
неадресованный
Unanimity (юнани́мити) единодушие
Unanimous (юна́нимос) единодушный
Unbreakable (анбрэ́йкабл) небьющийся
Uncalled (анка́ллд) невостребованный
{pursuant to a cash call, etc.}
Uncertainty (ансэ́ртанти) сомнение
Uncertified (ансэ́ртифайд)
незаверенный
Unclean (анкли́н) нечистый
Uncompensated (анко́мпэнсэйтэд) без
обязательства возмещения ущерба,
безвозмездный, некомпенсированный
Unconditional (анконди́шнал)
безоговорочный, безусловный
Unconfirmed (анконфи́рмд)
неподтверждённый
Uncontemplated (анко́нтэмплэйтэд)
непредусмотренный
Uncontrolled (анконтро́ллэд)
неконтролируемый
Uncover, to ~ (анко́вэр, ту ~)
обнаруживать
Uncovered (анко́вэрд) без упаковки,
непокрытый
   to ship ~ (ту шип ~) перевозить
без упаковки
Undamaged (анда́маджэд)
неповреждённый
Undeclared (андикла́рд)
незадекларированный, необъявленный

Undelivered (андэли́вэрд)
недоставленный
Underdeveloped (андэрдивэ́лопд)
слаборазвитый
   ~ nation (~ нэ́йшн) слаборазвитая
   страна
Underestimate (а́ндэрэ́стимэйт)
недооценка
   to ~ (ту ~) недооценивать
Undergraduate (а́ндэргра́джюат)
абитуриент
Underground (а́ндэргроунд) подполье,
подпольный
Underload (андэрло́д) недогрузка
   to ~ (ту ~) недогружать
Underloading (андэрло́динг) недогруз
   ~ of a vessel (~ оф а вэ́ссэл)
   недогруз судна
Undermining (а́ндэрмайнинг) подрыв
   ~ the credit system (~ θи крэ́дит
   си́стэм) подрыв кредитной системы
   ~ the economy (~ θи эко́номи)
   подрыв экономики
   ~ of discipline (~ оф ди́сиплин)
   подрыв дисциплины
Underpay, to ~ (андэрпэ́й, ту ~)
недоплачивать
Understanding (андэрста́ндинг)
договорённость, понятие, соглашение
   mutual ~ (мю́чуал ~) взаимная
   договорённость
   private ~ (пра́йват ~) частная
   договорённость, частное
   соглашение
   pursuant to our ~ (пурсу́ант ту
   о́ур ~) согласно нашей
   договорённости
   to come to an ~ (ту ком ту ан ~)
   достичь договорённости
   to reach an ~ in writing (ту рич
   ан ~ ин ра́йтинг) оформить
   договорённость письменно
Undervaluation (андэрвалю́йшн)
недооценка
Undervalue, to ~ (андэрва́лю, ту ~)
недооценивать
Underwriter (а́ндэрра́йтэр)
страховщик
   marine ~ (мари́н ~) морской
   страховщик
Undischarged (андисча́ржд)
неразгруженный {freight}
Undocumented (андо́кюмэнтэд)
недокументированный
Uneconomical (анэконо́микал)
неэкономичный
Unemployed (анэмпло́йд) безработный

Unemployment (анэмпло́ймэнт)
безработица
Unendorsed (анэндо́рсд)
неиндоссированный
Unequal (ани́куал) неравноправный,
неравный
UNESCO (юнэ́ско) ЮНЕСКО {организация
по вопросам образования и культуры}
Unexecuted (анэ́ксэкютэд)
невыполненный, неисполненный,
неоформленный
Unfinished (анфи́нишд) незаконченный
Unfit (анфи́т) негодный,
неподходящий, непригодный
   ~ for intended use (~ фор
   интэ́ндэд юс) негодный к
   употреблению
Unfitness (анфи́тнэс) негодность,
непригодность
Unforeseen (анфорси́н)
непредвиденный
Unfreeze, to ~ (анфри́з, ту ~)
размораживать {e.g. assets}
Unfulfilled (анфулфи́лд)
невыполненный
Ungraded (ангрэ́йдэд)
несортированный
Unguaranteed (ангяранти́д)
негарантированный
Unification (юнифик5́йшн) унификация
   ~ of documents (~ оф до́кюмэнтс)
   унификация документов
Unilateral (юнила́терал)
односторонний
Unincorporated (анинко́рпорэйтэд)
некорпоративный
Uninsured (аниншу́рд)
незастрахованный
Union (ю́нион) объединение, союз
   administrative ~ (адми́нистрэйтив
   ~) административный союз
   atlantic ~ (атла́нтик ~)
   атлантический союз
   currency ~ (ку́ррэнси ~) валютный
   союз
   customs ~ (ка́стомз ~) таможенный
   союз
   interparliamentary ~
   (интэрпарламэ́нтари ~)
   межпарламентский союз
   labor ~ (лэ́йбор ~) профсоюзный
   орган, профессиональный союз
   {профсоюз}, профсоюзный {adj.}
   marital ~ (мэ́ритал ~) брачный
   союз
   monetary ~ (мо́нэтэри ~) монетный
   союз

privileged ~ (привилэжд ~)
привилегированный союзник
Soviet ~ (со́виэт ~) Советский
Союз
~ **of industrialists** (~ оф
инду́стриалистс) союз
предпринимателей
~ **of Soviet Socialist Republics**
{USSR} (~ оф со́виэт со́шалист
рипа́бликс {ю-эс-эс-ар}) Союз
Советских Социалистических
Республик {СССР}
Unique (юни́к) уникальный
Unit (ю́нит) единица, штука
basic monetary ~ (бэ́йсик
мо́нэтари ~) основная денежная
единица
contract ~ **of measurement**
(ко́нтракт ~ оф мэ́жюрмэнт)
контрактная единица измерения
conventional ~ (конвэ́ншнал ~)
условная единица
currency ~ (ку́ррэнси ~) валютная
единица
European Currency ~ {ECU}
(юропи́ан ку́ррэнси ~ {э́кю})
европейская валютная единица
international ~**s** (интэрна́шэнал
~с) международные единицы
metric ~**s** (мэ́трик ~с)
метрические единицы
monetary ~ (мо́нэтари ~) денежная
единица
payment ~ (пэ́ймэнт ~) расчётная
единица
per ~ (пэр ~) на единицу
separate ~ (сэ́парат ~) отдельная
единица
transport ~ (тра́нспорт ~)
транспортная единица
~ **cost** (~ кост) себестоимость
единицы продукции
~ **of equipment** (~ оф икуи́пмэнт)
единица оборудования
~ **of measurement** (~ оф
мэ́жюрмэнт) единица измерения
~ **of production** (~ оф прода́кшн)
единица продукции
~ **of production costs** (~ оф
прода́кшн костс) единица издержек
производства
~ **of time** (~ оф тайм) единица
времени
~ **of value** (~ оф ва́лю) единица
стоимости
~ **of weight** (~ оф уэ́йт) единица
веса

~ **price goods** (~ прайс гудз)
цена за единицу товара
Unite, to ~ (юна́йт, ту ~)
объединяться
United (юна́йтэд) соединённый
~ **Kingdom** (~ ки́нгдом)
Соединённое Королевство
~ **States of America** (~ стэ́йтс оф
амэ́рика) Соединённые Штаты
Америки
Unity (ю́нити) сплочённость
Universal (юнивэ́рсал) универсальный
Unjustified (анджа́стифайд)
неоправданный
Unlawful (анла́уфул) незаконный
Unlicensed (анла́йсэнсд)
безлицензионный, нелицензированный
Unlikely (анла́йкли) маловероятный
Unlimited (анли́митэд) бессрочный
{period of time}, нелимитируемый
Unload, to ~ (анло́д, ту ~)
выгружать
Unloading (анло́динг) выгрузка
queue for ~ (кю фор ~) очередь
на выгрузку
Unmarketable (анма́ркэтабл) неходкий
~ **products** (~ про́дуктс)
неликвиды
Unmerchantable (анмэ́рчантабл)
непригодный
Unnavigable (анна́вигабл)
несудоходный
Unnumbered (анна́мбэрд)
ненумерованный
Unobtainable (анобтэ́йнабл)
недоступный
Unofficial (аноффи́шл) неофициальный
Unorganized (ано́рганайзд)
неорганизованный
Unoriginal (анори́джинал) шаблонный
Unoriginality (анориджина́лити)
шаблонность
Unpacked (анпа́кд) незапакованный,
неупакованный
Unpaid (анпэ́йд) неоплаченный,
непогашенный, неуплаченный
~ **capital** (~ ка́питал)
недоплаченная часть акционерного
капитала
Unpatentable (анпа́тэнтабл)
непатентоспособный
Unpatented (анпа́тэнтэд)
беспатентный, незапатентованный
Unpre-packed (анпри-па́кд)
нерасфасованный
Unprofitability (анпрофитаби́лити)
нерентабельность

Unprofitable (анпрóфитабл) бесприбыльный, невыгодный, неприбыльный, нерентабельный
Unprotested (анпротэ́стэд) неопротестованный {e.g. bill or note}
Unprovided for (анпровáйдэд фор) непредусмотренный
Unquoted (анкуóтэд) некотирующийся
Unrated (анрэ́йтэд) нетаксированный
Unredeemed (анридúмд) невыкупленный
Unreliability (анрилайабúлити) ненадёжность
Unreliable (анрилáйабл) ненадёжный
Unremunerative (анримю́нэратив) неприбыльный, нерентабельный
Unrestricted (анристрúктэд) неограниченный
Unsaleable (ансэ́йлабл) непродаваемый, неходкий
Unsatisfactory (ансатисфáктори) неудовлетворительный
Unseal, to ~ (ансúл, ту ~) вскрывать
Unsealed (ансúлд) незапечатанный
Unseasonable (ансúзонабл) несезонный
Unsecured (ансэкю́рд) без обеспечения, необеспеченный, непокрытый
Unsettled (ансэ́тлд) непогашенный, неурегулированный
Unshipped (аншúпд) неотправленный
Unsold (ансóлд) непроданный
Unsorted (ансóртэд) несортированный
Unspent (анспэ́нт) неизрасходованный
Unstable (анстэ́йбл) нестабильный, неустойчивый
Unsuitable (ансу́табл) негодный, непригодный
Unused (аню́зд) неиспользованный
Unvalued (анвáлюд) неоценённый, нетаксированный
Upkeep (áпкип) ремонт, содержание
Upper (áппэр) верхний
Upside down (áпсайд дóун) вверх дном
   ~ stacking (~ стáккинг) укладка вверх дном
Upsurge (áпсурдж) подъём, рост
   ~ in prices (~ ин прáйсэз) рост цен
Upswing (áпсуинг) подъём
   economic ~ (экономик ~) экономический подъём
   ~ in production (~ ин продáкшн) подъём производства

   ~ in productivity (~ ин продуктúвити) подъём производительности
Urgency (у́рджэнси) безотлагательность, срочность
Urgent (у́рджэнт) безотлагательный, неотложный, срочный, экстренный
Usage (ю́садж) обыкновение, обычай
   banking ~ (бáнкинг ~) банковский обычай
   commercial ~ (коммэ́ршл ~) торговое обыкновение, торговый обычай
   constitutional ~ (конститу́шнал ~) конституционный обычай
   diplomatic ~ (дипломáтик ~) дипломатический обычай
   international ~ (интэрнáшэнал ~) международный обычай
   international law ~ (интэрнáшэнал лау ~) международно- правовой обычай
   maritime ~ (мáритайм ~) морской обычай
Use (юс) полезность, польза, пользование, потребление, применение
   end ~ (энд ~) конечное применение
   illegal ~ (иллúгал ~) противоправное применение
   illegal ~ of trademark (иллúгал ~ оф трэ́йдмарк) незаконное применение товарного знака
   marginal ~ (мáрджинал ~) предельная полезность
   of little ~ (аф литл ~) малопригодный
   ready for ~ (рэ́ди фор ~) готовый к эксплуатации
   to ~ (ту ~) пользоваться, потреблять
   ~ of force (~ оф форс) применение силы
User (ю́зэр) потребитель
   end ~ (энд ~) конечный потребитель
   marginal ~ (мáрджинал ~) предельный потребитель
Usufruct (ю́суфрукт) плод, узуфрукт
Usurer (ю́сэрэр) ростовщик
Usurious (юсу́риос) ростовщический
Usurpation (юсурпэ́йшн) захват
Usury (ю́сури) анатоцизм, ростовщичество
Utility (ютúлити) полезность

Utilization (ютилизэ́йшн)
привлечение, эксплуатация

V

Vacation (вэйкэ́йшн) аннулирование,
отпуск
    paid ~ (пэйд ~) оплачиваемый
    отпуск
    ~ of a decision (~ оф а диси́жн)
    аннулирование решения
Vacuum-packed (ва́кюм-пакд) упаковка
вакуумная
Valid (ва́лид) годный, действующий,
действительный
    legally ~ (ли́галли ~) юридически
    действительный
    ~ for... (~ фор...) годный для
Validate, to ~ (ва́лидэйт, ту ~)
признавать действительным,
ратифицировать
Validity (вали́дити) действие,
действительность, обоснованность,
сила
    statistical ~ (стати́стикал ~)
    статистическое обоснование
    to acknowledge the ~ of a
    license (ту акно́лэдж θи ~ оф а
    ла́йсэнз) признавать
    действительность лицензии
    to acknowledge the ~ of a patent
    (ту акно́лэдж θи ~ оф а па́тэнт)
    признавать действительность
    патента
    to acknowledge the ~ of rights
    (ту акно́лэдж θи ~ оф райтс)
    признавать действительность прав
    to contest the ~ (ту контэ́ст θи
    ~) оспаривать действительность
    to verify the ~ of a patent (ту
    вэ́рифай θи ~ оф а па́тэнт)
    проверять действительность
    патента
    ~ of a document (~ оф а
    до́кюмэнт) действительность
    документа
    ~ of a letter of credit (~ оф а
    лэ́ттэр оф крэ́дит) действие
    аккредитива
    ~ of a license (~ оф а ла́йсэнз)
    действительность лицензии
    ~ of an offer (~ оф ан о́ффэр)
    действительность предложения

    ~ of a patent (~ оф а па́тэнт)
    действительность патента,
    действие патента
    ~ of rights (~ оф райтс)
    действительность прав
    ~ of a trademark (~ оф а
    трэ́йдмарк) действительность
    товарного знака
Valorization (валоризэ́йшн)
валоризация
Valuable (ва́люабл) ценный **~s**
ценности
    mortgaged ~s (мо́ргэджд ~с)
    заложенные ценности
    to deposit ~s in a bank (ту
    дипо́зит ~с ин а банк)
    депонировать ценности в банке
Valuation (валюэ́йшн) расценка
Value (ва́лю) стоимость, ценность
    actual ~ (а́кчуал ~) реальная
    стоимость
    aggregate ~ (а́ггрэгат ~) общая
    стоимость
    assessed ~ (ассэ́ссд ~) оценочная
    стоимость
    at ~ (ат ~) по цене дня
    barter ~ (ба́ртэр ~) меновая
    стоимость
    capitalized ~ (ка́питалайзд ~)
    капитализированная стоимость
    cash ~ (каш ~) денежная
    стоимость
    commercial ~ (коммэ́ршл ~)
    коммерческая стоимость
    declared ~ (диклэ́йрд ~)
    заявленная стоимость,
    объявленная стоимость
    domestic ~ (домэ́стик ~)
    внутренняя стоимость
    exchange ~ (эксчэ́йндж ~) меновая
    стоимость
    gross ~ (грос ~) валовая
    стоимость
    higher ~ (ха́йэр ~) наёмная
    стоимость
    liquidation ~ (ликуидэ́йшн ~)
    ликвидационная стоимость
    market ~ (ма́ркэт ~) курсовая
    стоимость, рыночная стоимость
    material ~ (мати́риал ~)
    материальная ценность
    nominal ~ (но́минал ~)
    нарицательная стоимость
    objective ~ (обджэ́ктив ~)
    объективная стоимость
    of little ~ (оф литл ~)
    малоценный

purchase ~ (пу́рчас ~) покупная стоимость
real ~ (ри́ал ~) реальная ценность
reappraisal of ~s (риаппрэ́йзал оф ~с) переоценка ценностей
rental ~ (рэ́нтал ~) арендная стоимость
sale ~ (сэйл ~) запродажная стоимость
subjective ~ (сабджэ́ктив ~) субъективная стоимость
surplus ~ (су́рплас ~) прибавочная стоимость
to have great ~ (ту хэв грэйт ~) иметь большую ценность
to have little ~ (ту хэв литл ~) иметь малую ценность
to have no ~ (ту хэв но ~) не иметь никакой ценности, не представлять никакой ценности
unit ~ (ю́нит ~) единичная стоимость
unit of ~ (ю́нит оф ~) единица ценности
use ~ (юс ~) потребительная стоимость
Valueless (ва́люлэс) не имеющий ценности
Van (ван) автофургон
Vandalism (ва́ндалисм) вандализм
act of ~ (акт оф ~) акт вандализма
Vanguard (ва́нгард) передовой отряд
Variability (вариаби́лити) неустойчивость
Variable (ва́риабл) колеблющийся, неустойчивый
Variation (вариэ́йшн) колебание
cost ~ (кост ~) изменение стоимости
minor ~s (ма́йнор ~с) небольшие колебания
~ in prices (~ ин пра́йсэз) колебание цен
Variety (вара́йэти) ассортимент, разновидность
Vary, to ~ (вари, ту ~) колебаться
Varying (ва́риинг) меняющийся
Vat (ват) бак
to pour into a ~ (ту по́ур и́нту а ~) наливать в бак
to store in a ~ (ту стор ин а ~) хранить в бак
Vector (вэ́ктор) вектор
Venal (ви́нал) продажный

Venality (вина́лити) коррупция, продажность
Vendor (вэ́ндор) продавец, торговец
Venture (вэ́нчэр) предприятие
joint ~ (джойнт ~) совместное предприятие
Venue (вэ́ню) место дела, юрисдикция
arbitration ~ (арбитрэ́йшн ~) место арбитража
Verbal (вэ́рбал) словесный
Verdict (вэ́рдикт) приговор
public ~ (па́блик ~) общественный приговор
unjust ~ (анджу́ст ~) неправосудный приговор
Verification (вэрификэ́йшн) контроль, проверка
total ~ (то́тал ~) сплошной контроль
Verify, to ~ (вэ́рифай, ту ~) проверять
Version (вэржн) вариант
production ~ (прода́кшн ~) серийный вариант
Vessel (вэ́ссэл) судно
cargo ~ (ка́рго ~) грузовое судно
cargo tramp ~ (ка́рго трамп ~) трамповое судно
Coast Guard ~ (кост гард ~) таможенное судно
coasting ~ (ко́стинг ~) каботажное судно
container ~ (контэ́йнэр ~) контейнерное судно
government ~ (го́вэрнмэнт ~) государственное судно
harbor ~ (ха́рбор ~) портовое судно
hospital ~ (хо́спитал ~) госпитальное судно
incoming ~ (и́нкоминг ~) прибывающее судно
merchant ~ (мэ́рчант ~) торговое судно
motorized ~ (мо́торайзд ~) теплоход
naval ~ (нэ́йвал ~) военно-морское судно
pirate ~ (па́йрат ~) пиратское судно
registered ~ (рэ́джистэрд ~) зарегистрированное судно
salvage ~ (са́лвэдж ~) спасательное судно
seagoing ~ (си́гоинг ~) морское судно

sound ~ (со́унд ~) неповреждённое судно

timber-hauling ~ (ти́мбэр-ха́улинг ~) лесовоз

to arrest a ~ (ту аррэ́ст а ~) арестовать судно

Vest, to ~ (вэст, ту ~) вводить во владение {e.g. an interest}

to ~ someone with authority (ту ~ со́муан уиθ ауθо́рити) облекать кого-то полномочиями

Vesting (вэ́стинг) введение во владение

Veterinary (вэ́тэринари) ветеринарный

Veto (ви́то) вето

right of ~ (райт оф ~) право вето

to ~ (ту ~) налагать вето

Viability (вайаби́лити) осуществимость

economic ~ (эконо́мик ~) доходность

Vice (вайс) вице {part of title}, порок {bad habit}

~-consul (~-ко́нсул) вице-консул

Vicious (ви́шос) порочный

~ circle (~ сиркл) порочный круг

Victim (ви́ктим) пострадавший, потерпевший

~ of harm (~ оф харм) потерпевший вреда

Victory (ви́ктори) победа

election ~ (элэ́кшн ~) победа на выборах

Victuals (ви́кчуалз) провиант

Video (ви́дио) клип {advertisement, music}

Vigilant (ви́джилант) недремлющий

"the law favors the ~" (θи лау фэ́йворз θи ~) «Право благоприятствует недремлющим»

Villain (ви́ллэн) злодей

Violate, to ~ (ва́йолэйт, ту ~) нарушать

Violation (вайолэ́йшн) нарушение, несоблюдение

currency ~s (ку́ррэнси ~с) валютные нарушения

fine for ~ (файн фор ~) штраф за нарушение

gross ~ (грос ~) грубое нарушение

investigation of a ~ (инвэстигэ́йшн оф а ~) рассмотрение дела о нарушении

sanctions for ~ (са́нкшнс фор ~) санкции за нарушение

to avoid ~s (ту аво́йд ~с) избегать нарушений

to impose a penalty for a ~ (ту импо́с а пэ́налти фор а ~) наложить штраф за нарушение

~ of conditions (~ оф конди́шнс) нарушение условий

~ of exclusivity (~ оф эксклюси́вити) нарушение исключительности

~ of a law (~ оф а лау) нарушение закона

~ of safety regulations (~ оф сэ́йфти рэгюлэ́йшнс) нарушение правил по технике безопасности

Violator (ва́йолэйтор) нарушитель

Violence (ва́йолэнс) насилие

act of ~ (акт оф ~) акт насилия

VIP (ви-ай-пи) важное лицо

Visa (ви́са) виза

business ~ (би́знэс ~) виза для деловой поездки, деловая виза

confirmation of a ~ (конфирмэ́йшн оф а ~) подтверждение визы

consular ~ (ко́нсюлар ~) консульская виза

date of a ~ (дэйт оф а ~) дата визы

entry ~ (э́нтри ~) въездная виза

exempt ~ (экзэ́мпт ~) привилегированная виза

exit ~ (э́кзит ~) выездная виза

export ~ (э́кспорт ~) вывозная виза

extension of a ~ (экстэ́ншн оф а ~) продление визы

import ~ (и́мпорт ~) ввозная виза

issuance of a ~ (и́шюанс оф а ~) выдача визы

multiple entry ~ (му́лтипл э́нтри ~) многократная виза

ordinary ~ (о́рдинари ~) обыкновенная виза

permanent ~ (пэ́рманэнт ~) постоянная виза

receipt of a ~ (риси́т оф а ~) получение визы

refusal of a ~ (рифю́сал оф а ~) отказ в визе

to apply for a ~ (ту аппла́й фор а ~) запрашивать визу {обращаться визой}

to extend a ~ (ту экстэ́нд а ~) продлевать визу

to **issue a** ~ (ту и́шю а ~) визировать, выдавать визу
to **receive a** ~ (ту риси́в а ~) получать визу
to **refuse to grant a** ~ (ту рифю́с ту грант а ~) отказать в выдаче визы
to **support a** ~ **application** (ту суппо́рт а ~ аппликэ́йшн) поддерживать просьбу о предоставлении визы, поддерживать визу
tourist ~ (ту́рист ~) туристическая виза
transit ~ (тра́нзит ~) транзитная виза
valid term of a ~ (ва́лид тэрм оф а ~) срок действия визы
~ **application** (~ аппликэ́йшн) заявление на выдачу визы {() обращение за визой}
~ **department** (~ дипа́ртмэнт) отдел виз виза
~-**invitation** (~-инвитэ́йшн) виза-приглашение
Viscosity (виско́сити) вязкость
Vise, to ~ (визэ́й, ту ~) проставлять визу в паспорте
to **have one's passport** ~**d** (ту хэв уа́нз па́сспорт ~д) получать визу на паспорт
Visit (ви́зит) визит, посещение
aim of a ~ (эйм оф а ~) цель визита
an annual ~ (ан а́ннюал ~) ежегодной визит
business ~ (би́знэс ~) деловой визит
conclusion of a ~ (конклю́жн оф а ~) завершение визита
construction site ~ (констру́кшн сайт ~) визит на место строительства
extended ~ (экстэ́ндэд ~) длительной визит
follow-up ~ (фо́ллоуап ~) последующий визит
friendly ~ (фрэ́ндли ~) дружеской визит
itinerary for a ~ (айти́нэрари фор а ~) программа визита
official ~ (оффи́шл ~) официальный визит
opportunity for a ~ (оппорту́нити фор а ~) возможность визита
outcome of a ~ (о́утком оф а ~) результаты визита

period of a ~ (пи́риод оф а ~) срок визита
planned ~ (планд ~) запланированной визит
postponement of a ~ (постпо́нмэнт оф а ~) отсрочка визита
private ~ (пра́йват ~) частный визит
proposed ~ (пропо́зд ~) планируемый визит, предложенный визит
regular ~ (рэ́гюлар ~) очередной визит
regular ~**s** (рэ́гюлар ~с) регулярные визиты
return ~ (ритурн ~) ответный визит
short ~ (шорт ~) короткий визит
time of a ~ (тайм оф а ~) время визита
to ~ (ту ~) посещать
to **arrange a** ~ (ту аррэ́йндж а ~) договорить о визите
to **arrive on a** ~ (ту арра́йв он а ~) прибывать с визитом
to **cancel a** ~ (ту ка́нсэл а ~) отменять визит
to **coordinate** ~**s** (ту ко́ординэйт ~с) координировать визиты
to **expedite a** ~ (ту э́кспэдайт а ~) ускорять визит
to **plan a** ~ (ту план а ~) запланировать визит
to **prepare an itinerary for a** ~ (ту припэ́йр ан айти́нэрари фор а ~) подготовить программу визита
to **put off a** ~ (ту пут офф а ~) откладывать визит
to **return a** ~ (ту ритурн а ~) наносить ответный визит
unsuccessful ~ (ансуксэ́сфул ~) неудачный визит
until the next ~ (анти́л θи нэкст ~) до следующего визита
upcoming ~ (апко́минг ~) предстоящий визит
~ **for purposes of inspection** (~ фор пу́рпосэз оф инспэ́кшн) инспекционный визит
~ **to establish contacts** (~ ту эста́блиш ко́нтактс) визит для установления контактов
Vneshekonom Bank (внэ́шэконом банк) Внешэкономбанк {Russian foreign trade bank}
Vocation (вокэ́йшн) призвание
Void (войд) недействительный

null and ~ (нул энд ~) недействительный
to declare null and ~ (ту диклэйр нул энд ~) признать недействительным
Volume (вóлюм) ёмкость, объём
foreign trade ~ (фóрэн трэйд ~) объём внешней торговли
market ~ (мáркэт ~) ёмкость рынка
trade ~ (трэйд ~) торговый оборот
~ of demand (~ оф димáнд) объём потребления
~ of expenses (~ оф экспэ́нсэз) размер расходов
~ of exports (~ оф э́кспортс) объём экспорта
~ of gross output (~ оф грос óутпут) объём валовой продукции
~ of investment (~ оф инвэ́стмэнт) объём капитальных вложений
~ of production (~ оф продáкшн) объём производства
~ of turnover (~ оф тýрновэр) объём оборота
~ on the exchange (~ он θи эксчэ́йндж) объём рынка
~ production (~ продáкшн) производство большого масштаба
Voluntary (вóлунтэри) добровольный, общественный
Vote (вот) голос
to ~ (ту ~) проголосовать
Voter (вóтэр) избиратель
Vacancy (вэ́йканси) отсутствие, путёвка {in resort, tourist group}
Voucher (вóучэр) ордер, ваучер
expenditure ~ (экспэ́ндичэр ~) расходный ордер
Voyage (вóйядж) плавание, путешествие, рейс
maiden ~ (мэ́йдэн ~) первое плавание

W

Wage (уэ́йдж) заработная плата **~s** зарплата
average ~s (áвэрэдж ~с) средняя зарплата
average hourly ~ (áвэрэдж óурли ~) средняя почасовая плата
day ~s (дэй ~с) подённая оплата труда

fair ~ (фэйр ~) справедливая плата
fixed ~ (фиксд ~) твёрдая зарплата
guaranteed annual ~ (гярантúд áннюал ~) гарантированная годовая зарплата
guaranteed minimum ~ (гярантúд мúнимум ~) гарантированный минимальный размер заработной платы
hourly ~ (óурли ~) почасовой оклад, почасовая оплата
minimum ~ (мúнимум ~) минимальный размер заработной платы
monthly ~s (мóнθли ~с) ежемесячная зарплата
nominal ~s (нóминал ~с) номинальная зарплата
time ~s (тайм ~с) повременная оплата труда
weekly ~s (уúкли ~с) понедельная оплата
~ freeze (~ фриз) замораживание заработной платы
Wager (уэ́йгэр) заклад
to ~ (ту)
Waive, to (уэйв, ту) отказываться
to ~ obligations (ту ~ облигэ́йшнз) отказываться от выполнения обязательства
Waiver (уэ́йвэр) отказ
~ of rights (~ оф райтс) отказ от прав
~ of right to appeal (~ оф райт ту аппúл) отказ от права обжалования
Wall (уалл) стена
border ~ (бóрдэр ~) разграничивающая стена
common ~ (кóммон ~) общая стена
Want (уант) недостаток, неимение, нужда
for ~ of ... (фор ~ оф ...) за неимением ...
to ~ (ту ~) хотеть
Wanton (уáнтон) порочный
War (уар) война
brewing of a ~ (брýинг оф а ~) разжигание войны
credit ~ (крэ́дит ~) кредитная война
currency ~ (кýррэнси ~) валютная война
economic ~ (эконóмик ~) экономическая война

monetary and financial ~
(мо́нэтари энд файна́ншл ~)
валютно-финансовая война
price ~ (прайс ~) война цен
tariff ~ (та́риф ~) таможенная
{тарифная} война
to drag into ~ (ту драг и́нту ~)
втянуть в войну
to start a ~ (ту старт а ~)
начать в войну
to wage ~ (ту уэ́йдж ~) вести
войну
trade ~ (трэйд ~) торговая война
Ward (уард) опекаемый, питомец
~ of the state (~ оф θи стэйт)
питомец нации
Wardship (уа́рдшип) опека,
попечительство
under ~ (а́ндэр ~) подопечный
Warehouse (уэ́рхаус) амбар, склад
bonded ~ (бо́ндэд ~) бондовый
склад
consignee's ~ (консайни́з ~)
склад грузополучателя
customs ~ (ка́стомз ~) таможенная
база
private ~ (пра́йват ~) частный
склад
station ~ (стэйшн ~) товарный
склад
wholesale ~ (хо́лсэйл ~)
складская база
Warehouseman (уэ́рхаусман) владелец
склада, управляющий складом
Warehousing (уэ́рхоузинг)
складирование, складское хранение
~ of tare (~ оф тэйр) хранение
тары на складе
Wares (уэрз) товар
to profitably demonstrate ~ (ту
про́фитабли дэмонстрэйт ~)
выгодно демонстрировать товар
Warn, to ~ (уарн, ту ~)
предупреждать
to ~ against (ту ~ агэ́нст)
предостерегать
Warning (уа́рнинг) предупреждение
to be let off with a ~ (ту би
лэт офф уиθ а ~) получить
выговор с предупреждением
to provide advance ~ (ту прова́йд
адва́нс ~) посылать уведомление
заблаговременно
Warrant (уа́ррант) варрант,
доверенность, купон, наряд, ордер,
полномочие, расписка

customs ~ (ка́стомз ~) таможенный
варрант
dock ~ (док ~) доковый варрант
expiration of ~ (экспирэ́йшн оф
~) истечение срока гарантии
freight ~ (фрэйт ~)
товаросопроводительная квитанция
interest ~ (и́нтэрэст ~)
процентный купон
search ~ (сэрч ~) ордер на
обыск, ордер на право обыска
special ~ (спэшл ~) специальное
полномочие
term of a ~ (тэрм оф а ~) срок
действия доверенность
to ~ (ту ~) гарантировать,
оправдать, ручаться
to draw up a ~ (ту дра́у ап а ~)
оформлять доверенность
to pay ~ credit (ту пэй ~
крэ́дит) оплачивать варрант
to redeem a ~ (ту риди́м а ~)
получать деньги по купону
warehouse ~ (уэ́рхаус ~)
складской варрант
wharfingers ~ (уа́рфингэрс ~)
складской варрант, выданный
товарной пристанью
~ for receipt (~ фор риси́т)
доверенность на получение
~ in the name of ... (~ ин θи
нэйм оф ...) доверенность на имя
Warrantor (уарранто́р) поручитель
Warranty (уа́рранти) гарантийный
{adj.}, гарантия, поручительство,
ручательство
basic ~ (бэ́йсик ~) основная
гарантия
breach of ~ (брич оф ~)
нарушение гарантии
covered by ~ (ко́вэрд бай ~)
гарантируемый
expiration of ~ (экспирэ́йшн оф
~) окончание срока гарантии
implied ~ (импла́йд ~)
подразумеваемая гарантия
liability under the ~
(лайаби́лити а́ндэр θи ~)
ответственность по гарантии
oral ~ (о́рал ~) устная гарантия
short-term ~ (шорт-тэрм ~)
краткосрочная гарантия
standard ~ (ста́ндард ~) гарантия
стандартная
to be covered by ~ (ту би ко́вэрд
бай ~) покрываться гарантией

to make a ~ (ту мэйк а ~) давать гарантию
under the ~ (а́ндэр θи ~) по гарантии
upon expiration of the ~ (апо́н экспирэ́йшн оф θи ~) по истечении срока гарантии
vendor's maintenance ~ (вэ́ндорз мэ́йнтэнанс ~) гарантия продавца о техническом обслуживании
~ clause (~ клауз) пункт договора о гарантиях
~ of fitness (~ оф фи́тнэс) гарантия годности товара
~ of merchantability (~ оф мэрчантаби́лити) гарантия пригодности для торговли
~ provisions (~ прови́жнз) условия гарантии
Waste (уэ́йст) потеря, расточительство, убыток
to ~ (ту ~) расточать, растратить, тратить напрасно
Wasteful (уэ́йстфул) расточительный
~ spending (~ спэ́ндинг) растрата
Watchman (уа́тчман) сторож
night ~ (найт ~) ночной сторож
Water (уа́тэр) вода
boundary ~s (бо́ундари ~с) пограничные воды
coastal ~s (ко́стал ~с) прибрежные воды
deep ~ (дип ~) полная вода
exposure to ~ (экспо́жюр ту ~) подмочка водой
impermeable to ~ (импэ́рмиабл ту ~) непроницаемый для воды
industrial waste ~ (инду́стриал уэ́йст ~) сточные, промышленные воды
ingress of sea ~ (и́нгрэс оф си ~) проникновение морской воды
neutral ~s (ну́трал ~с) нейтральные воды
open ~ (о́пэн ~) открытая вода
port ~s (порт ~с) портовые воды
sea ~ (си ~) морская вода
territorial ~s (тэррито́риал ~с) территориальные вода
via ~ (ви́а ~) по воде
~ repellent (~ рипэ́ллэнт) водоотталкивающий
~ resistant (~ ризи́стант) влагостойкий, водостойкий
~ supply (~ саппла́й) запас воды, снабжение водой

Water-cooled (уа́тэр-кулд) охлаждаемый водой
Water-damage (уа́тэр-да́мадж) повреждение водой
Water-logged (уа́тэр-ло́гд) пропитавшийся водой
Watermark (уа́тэрмарк) водяной знак
Watermarked (уа́тэрмаркд) гербовый
Waterproof (уа́тэрпруф) водонепроницаемый
Watertight (уа́тэртайт) водоупорный
Way (уэй) проход, путь, способ
only ~ (о́нли ~) единственный способ
Way Bill (уэй билл) накладная, транспортная накладная
against a ~ (агэ́нст а ~) по накладной
air ~ (эйр ~) авиагрузовая накладная
counterfoil ~ (ко́унтфрфойл ~) корешок накладной
drawing up of a ~ (дра́уинг ап оф а ~) оформление накладной
railroad ~ (рэ́йлрод ~) железнодорожная накладная
road ~ (род ~) автонакладная
to present a ~ (ту прэзэ́нт а ~) представить накладную
to submit a ~ (ту сабми́т а ~) предъявлять накладную
~ copy (~ ко́пи) копия накладной
~ duplicate (~ ду́пликат) дубликат транспортной накладной
Weapons (уэ́понз) оружие
banned ~ (банд ~) запрещённое оружие
Wear (уэр) износ
normal ~ and tear (но́рмал ~ энд тэр) нормальная убыль и нормальный износ
Wedding (уэ́ддинг) свадьба
Weigh, to ~ (уэ́й, ту ~) взвешивать, определять вес, производить взвешивание
to ~ again (ту ~ агэ́н) заново взвешивать
to ~ empty (ту ~ э́мпти) в пустом виде взвешивать
to ~ test (ту тэст ~) производить контрольное взвешивание
Weighage (уэ́йадж) плата за взвешивание
Weighbridge (уэ́йбридж) мостовые весы

~ **charges** (~ чáрджэз) плата за
взвешивание на мостовых весах
Weigher (уэ́йэр) весовщик
official ~ (оффи́шл ~)
официальный весовщик
sworn ~ (суóрн ~) присяжный
весовщик
Weighing (уэ́йинг) взвешивание,
завес, определение веса
control ~ (контрóл ~)
контрольный завес
net ~ (нэт ~) определение веса
нетто
test ~ (тэст ~) контрольное
взвешивание
~ **device** (~ дивáйс) прибор для
взвешивания
~ **equipment** (~ икуи́пмэнт)
оборудование для взвешивания
Weight (уэ́йт) вес, весовой {adj.}
actual ~ (áкчуал ~) фактический
вес
actual gross ~ (áкчуал грос ~)
фактический вес брутто
actual net ~ (áкчуал нэт ~)
реальный вес нетто
allowable ~ (аллóуабл ~)
допустимый вес
approximate ~ (аппрóксимат ~)
ориентировочный вес,
приблизительный вес
average ~ (áвэрэдж ~) средний
вес
baggage ~ (бáггадж ~) вес багажа
bill of lading ~ (билл оф
лэ́йдинг ~) коносаментный вес
bulk ~ (балк ~) насыпной вес
calculated ~ (кáлкюлэйтэд ~)
расчётный вес
cargo ~ (кáрго ~) вес груза
case ~ (кэйс ~) вес ящика
certificate of ~ (сэрти́фикэт оф
~) сертификат веса
chargeable ~ (чáрджабл ~) вес,
подлежащий оплате
check ~ (чэк ~) контрольный вес
dead ~ (дэд ~) убойный вес
decrease in ~ (ди́крис ин ~)
уменьшение в весе
discrepancy in ~ (дискрэ́панси ин
~) несоответствие по весу
dry ~ (драй ~) вес в сухом
состоянии, сухой вес
estimated ~ (э́стиматэд ~)
оценочный вес

excess ~ (эксэ́с ~) избыточный
вес, излишек веса, превышение
веса
gross ~ (грос ~) вес брутто,
общий вес
gross ~ **for net** (грос ~ фор нэт)
вес брутто за нетто
increase in ~ (инкри́с ин ~)
увеличение веса
indication of ~ (индикэ́йшн оф ~)
отметка о весе
intake ~ (и́нтэйк ~) принятый
груз
invoice ~ (и́нвойс ~) фактурный
вес
landed ~ (лáндэд ~) вес при
выгрузке, доставленный вес
legal net ~ (ли́гал нэт ~)
легальный вес нетто
live ~ (лайв ~) живой вес
marketable ~ (мáркэтабл ~)
продажный вес
maximum ~ (мáксимум ~)
максимальный вес
maximum ~ **limit** (мáксимум ~
ли́мит) предельный вес
net ~ (нэт ~) вес нетто, чистый
вес
non-standard ~ (нон-стáндард ~)
нестандартный вес {short
weighted}
on a dry ~ **basis** (он а драй ~
бэ́йсис) на основе сухого веса
on a purchased ~ **basis** (он а
пу́рчасд ~ бэ́йсис) на основе
купленного веса
package ~ (пáкэдж ~) вес
грузового места
packed ~ (пакд ~) вес с
упаковкой
pre-shipment ~ (при-ши́пмэнт ~)
вес до отгрузки
sale by ~ (сэйл бай ~) продажа
на
shipped ~ (шиппд ~) вес при
погрузке, отгруженный вес
short ~ (шорт ~) недостача в
весе, потеря веса
sole ~ (сол ~) собственный вес
specific ~ (спэси́фик ~) удельный
вес
specified ~ (спэ́сифайд ~)
заданный вес
standard ~ (стáндард ~)
нормальный вес, стандартный вес
starting ~ (стáртинг ~)
первоначальный вес

tariff ~ (та́риф ~) тарифный вес
to adjust the ~ (ту аджа́ст θи ~)
корректировать вес
to check the ~ (ту чэк θи ~)
проверять вес
to declare the ~ (ту дикле́йр θи
~) заявлять вес
to distribute the ~ (ту
дистри́бют θи ~) распределять вес
to purchase by ~ (ту пу́рчас бай
~) покупать по весу
to sell by ~ (ту сэл бай ~)
продавать на вес
under ~ (а́ндэр ~) недостающий
вес
unit ~ (ю́нит ~) вес единицы
одного изделия
unit of ~ (ю́нит оф ~) единица
веса
volume ~ (во́люм ~) объёмный вес
wet ~ (уэт ~) вес во влажном
состоянии
~ allowance (~ алло́уанс) допуск
по весу
~ checking (~ чэ́ккинг) проверка
веса
~ in running order (~ ин ра́ннинг
о́рдэр) эксплуатационный вес
~ limit (~ ли́мит) ограничение
веса, предел веса
~ note (~ нот) справка о
взвешивании
~ of goods (~ оф гудз) вес
товара
~ of packing (~ оф па́кинг) вес
упаковки
~ sheet (~ шит) весовая
ведомость
~ stamp (~ стамп) штемпель о
весе
~ to be shipped (~ ту би шиппд)
отгрузочный вес
Welfare (уэ́лфэйр) благосостояние,
обеспечение
social ~ (со́шл ~) социальное
обеспечение
Well-founded (уэл-фо́ундэд)
основанный на фактах
Wet (уэт) мокрый
Wharf (уарф) пристань, причал
Wharfage (уа́рфадж) хранение грузов
на пристани
Wharfinger (уа́рфингэр) владелец
товарной пристани
Wholesale (хо́лсэйл) оптовый
by ~ (бай ~) оптом
Wholesaler (хо́лсэйлр) оптовик

Wholesaling (хо́лсэйлинг) оптовый
сбыт
Width (уид θ) ширина
Will (уил) воля
free ~ (фри ~) автономия воли
Willful (уи́лфул) злостный
Win (уин) победа
to ~ (ту ~) выигрывать
Winch (уинч) грузоподъёмные машины
Winding up (уа́йндинг ап)
добровольная ликвидация
~ of a company (~ оф а ко́мпани)
ликвидация компании
Window (уи́ндо) витрина, окно
~ display (~ дисплэ́й) экспозиция
витрины
~ dressing (~ дрэ́ссинг)
оформление витрины
shop ~ (шоп ~) витрина
to set up a shop ~ (ту сэт ап а
шоп ~) оформлять витрину
Wire (уайр) проволовка, телеграмма
to ~ (ту ~) телеграфировать
to ~ for (ту ~ фор) вызывать
телеграммой
Withdraw, to ~ (уиθдра́у, ту ~)
изымать, изъять, отказаться от
участия, снимать [perfective:
снять]
to ~ from an account (ту ~ фром
ан акко́унт) брать деньги со
счёта
to ~ from a project (ту ~ фром а
про́джэкт) выйти из участия в
работе над проектом
Withdrawal (уиθдра́уал) изъятие,
отзыв, списание
to make a ~ from the bank (ту
мэйк а ~ фром θи банк) брать
деньги из банка
~ from an account (~ фром ан
акко́унт) списание со счёта
~ of credit (~ оф крэ́дит)
лишение кредита, отзыв кредита
~ of a deposit (~ оф а дипо́зит)
изъятие вклада
~ of an exhibitor (~ оф ан
экзи́битор) отказ экспонента от
участия
~ of money from circulation (~
оф мо́ни фром сиркюлэ́йшн) изъятие
денег из обращения
Withholding (уиθхо́лдинг) вычет,
удержание
tax ~ (такс ~) удержание налогов
~ from payments (~ фром
пэ́ймэнтс) удержание из платежей

~ **from wages** (~ фром уэйджэз)
вычет из зарплаты
~ **of rent** (~ оф рэнт)
прекращение аренды
Without (уиθóут) без
~ **losses** (~ лóссэз) безубыточный
Witness (уи́тнэс) свидетель
accused ~ (аккю́зд ~) обвиняемый
свидетель
eye-~ (эй-~) свидетель-очевидец
official ~ (оффи́шл ~) понятой
~ **for the defense** (~ фор θи
дифэ́нс) свидетель защиты
~ **for the prosecution** (~ фор θи
просэкью́шн) свидетель обвинения
Woodcutting (уу́дкаттинг) порубка
illegal ~ (илли́гал ~) незаконная
порубка
unlicensed ~ (анла́йсэнсд ~)
безбилетная порубка
Word (уорд) слово
on one's ~ (он уа́нз ~) честное
слово
to give one's ~ (ту гив уа́нз ~)
дать свое слово
~ **in conclusion** (~ ин конклю́шн)
заключительное слово
~ **of honor** (~ оф óнор) слово
чести
Work (уóрк) произведение, работа ~**s**
промысел
anonymous ~ (анóнимос ~)
анонимное произведение
anonymously released ~
(анóнимосли рили́сд ~)
произведение выпущенное анонимно
assembly line ~ (ассэ́мбли лайн
~) поточная работа
clerical ~ (клэ́рикал ~)
канцелярская работа
completed ~ (компли́тэд ~)
завершённая работа
creative ~ (криэ́йтив ~)
произведение
labor-intensive ~ (лэ́йбор-
интэ́нсив ~) трудоёмкая работа
literary and artistic ~**s**
(ли́тэрари энд арти́стик ~с)
литературные и художественные
произведения
night ~ (найт ~) ночная работа
original ~ (ори́джинал ~)
оригинальное произведение
overtime ~ (óвэртайм ~)
сверхурочная работа
piece ~ (пис ~) аккордная
работа, сдельная работа

plagiarized ~ (плэ́йгярайзд ~)
подделанное произведение
posthumous ~ (пóстхюмос ~)
посмертное произведение
preparatory ~ (прэ́паратори ~)
подготовительная работа
regular ~ (рэ́гюлар ~) постоянная
работа
seasonal ~ (си́зонал ~) отхожий
промысел, сезонная работа
shift ~ (шифт ~) сменная работа
testing ~ (тэ́стинг ~)
проверочная работа
to ~ (ту ~) работать,
разрабатывать **[perfective:**
разработать] {in a mine}
to ~ **for hire** (ту ~ фор хайр)
работать по найму
to ~ **for wages** (ту ~ фор
уэйджэз) работать по найму
to ~ **in a slipshod manner** (ту ~
ин а сли́пшод ма́ннэр) халтурить
to get to ~ (ту гэт ту ~)
приступать к делу
unpublished ~ (анпу́блишд ~)
неизданное произведение
~ **capacity** (~ капа́сити)
трудоспособность
~ **released under pseudonym** (~
рили́сд а́ндэр сýдоним)
произведение выпущенное под
псевдонимом
~ **supervision** (~ супэрви́жн)
надзор за выполнением
Worker (уóркэр) рабочий, сотрудник
agricultural ~ (агрикýлчурал ~)
сельскохозяйственный рабочий
bench ~ (бэнч ~) рабочий от
станка
clerical ~ (клэ́рикал ~)
канцелярский служащий
domestic ~ (домэ́стик ~) домашний
работник
exemplary production ~
(экзэ́мплари продáкшн ~)
передовик производства
{communist term}
factory ~ (фáктори ~) заводской
рабочий
industrial ~ (индýстриал ~)
промышленный рабочий
municipal ~ (мюни́сипал ~)
муниципальный служащий
office ~ (óффис ~) работник
postal ~ (пóстал ~) почтовый
служащий
salaried ~ (сáларид ~) окладчик

skilled ~ (скилд ~)
квалифицированный рабочий,
компетентный работник
temporary ~ (тэмпорари ~)
временный работник
~ safety (~ сэйфти) охрана труда
Worker's (уоркэрз) рабочий
Working (уоркинг) рабочий
end of ~ life (энд оф ~ лайф)
окончание трудовой жизни
maximum daily ~ hours (максимум
дэйли ~ оурз) максимальная
продолжительность рабочего
времени
~ conditions (~ кондишнс)
условия труда
~ off (~ офф) отработка {a debt}
Workmanship (уоркманшип)
ремесленничество
Worksheet (уоркшит) рабочая
ведомость
Workshop (уоркшоп) мастерская
World (уорлд) мир, мировой {adj.}
business ~ (бизнэс ~) деловой
мир
trading ~ (трэйдинг ~) торговый
мир
Worldly (уорлдли) светский
Worldwide (уорлдуайд) мировой
Worry (уорри) беда, забота, тревога
to ~ (ту ~) переживать
Wound (уунд) рана
to ~ (ту ~) поранить, ранить
Wrap, to ~ (рап, ту ~) завёртывать,
упаковывать
to ~ up (ту ~ ап) обёртывать
Wrapped (рапд) упакованный
Wrapping (раппинг) покрытие,
упаковка
bright ~ (брайт ~) яркая обёртка
gift ~ (гифт ~) подарочная
упаковка
inner ~ (иннэр ~) внутренняя
упаковка
polyethylene ~ (полиэθэлин ~)
упаковка в полиэтиленовую плёнку
Wreck (рэк) крушение
Wrecked (рэкд) затонувший,
to be ~ (ту би ~) потерпеть
крушение
Writ (рит) акт, запрет, ордер,
повестка о вызове в суд, судебный
документ, судебный приказ
~ of arrest (~ оф аррэст)
распоряжение о наложении ареста
~ of execution (~ оф экзэкюшн)
исполнительный лист

~ of seizure of cargo (~ оф
сижюр оф карго) акт о
конфискации груза
Write-off (райт-офф) безнадёжная
задолженность
to ~ (ту ~) снимать с учёта
Writing off (райтинг офф) списание
~ an account (~ ан аккаунт)
списание со счёта
~ of debts (~ оф дэтс) списание
долгов

X

X (экс) икс {unknown}
Xerox (зирокс) ксерокс
Xenophobe (зинофоб) ксенофоб
Xenophobia (зинофобия) ксенофобия
Xenophobic (зинофобик) отличающийся
ксенофобией

Y

Yard (ярд) двор
lumber ~ (лумбэр ~) биржа
лесоматериалов
timber ~ (тимбэр ~) лесной склад
Year (еар) год
accounting ~ (аккаунтинг ~)
отчётный год
base ~ (бэйс ~) базисный год
budget ~ (баджэт ~) бюджетный
год
calendar ~ (калэндар ~)
календарный год
completion of operational ~
(комплишн оф опэрэйшнал ~)
окончание операционного года
contract ~ (контракт ~)
договорный год
current ~ (куррэнт ~) текущий
год
financial ~ (файнаншл ~)
финансовый год
fiscal ~ (фискал ~) балансовый
год, финансовый год
many ~s (мэни ~с) многолетний
production ~ (продакшн ~)
производственный год,
хозяйственный год
~ made (~ мэйд) год изготовления
~ published (~ паблищд) год
издания

Yield (йилд) добыча, доход, урожай
  annual ~ (а́ннюал) годовой доход
  average ~ (а́вэрэдж ~) средний
  урожай
  capital investment ~ (ка́питал
  инве́стмэнт ~) фондоотдача
  dividend ~ (ди́видэнд ~) доход на
  акцию
  effective ~ (эффэ́ктив ~)
  реальный доход
  gross ~ (гросс ~) валовой урожай

  to ~ (ту ~) приносить доход
  to ~ a good return (ту ~ а гуд
  риту́рн) приносить хороший доход
  to ~ interest (ту ~ и́нтэрэст)
  приносить процентный доход
  to ~ poorly (ту ~ пу́рли)
  приносить малый доход

Z

Zemstvo (зэ́мства) земство
{*historical*}
Zloty (зуа́ти) злотый {Polish
currency}
Zonal (зо́нал) поясной
Zone (зон) зона, зональный {*adj.*},
полоса, пояс
  air defense ~ (эйр дифэ́нс ~)
  воздушная оборонительная
  опознавательная зона
  blockaded ~ (блокэ́йдэд ~)
  запретная зона
  border ~ (бо́рдэр ~) пограничный
  район
  closed fisheries ~ (клозд
  фи́шэриз ~) закрытая рыболовная
  зона
  coastal ~ (ко́стал ~) прибрежная
  зона
  coastal maritime ~ (ко́стал
  ма́ритайм ~) прибрежная морская
  зона
  currency ~ (ку́ррэнси ~) валютная
  зона, валютный район
  customs ~ (ка́стомз ~) таможенный
  район, таможенная зона
  defense ~ (дифэ́нс ~)
  оборонительная зона
  demilitarized ~ (дими́литарайзд
  ~) демилитаризованная зона
  dollar ~ (до́ллар ~) долларовая
  зона

  duty-free ~ (дю́ти-фри ~)
  беспошлинная зона
  fishery ~ (фи́шэри ~) рыболовная
  зона, рыболовный район
  forbidden ~ (форби́ддэн ~)
  запретная полоса, запретный
  район
  forbidden border ~ (форби́ддэн
  бо́рдэр ~) запретная пограничная
  полоса
  forbidden frontier ~ (форби́ддэн
  фронти́р ~) запретная пограничная
  зона
  free ~ (фри ~) свободная зона
  free economic ~ (фри эконо́мик ~)
  свободная экономическая зона
  free trade ~ (фри трэйд ~) зона
  свободной торговли
  frontier ~ (фронти́р ~)
  пограничная зона
  frontier customs ~ (фронти́р
  ка́стомз ~) пограничная
  таможенная зона
  immigration ~ (иммигрэ́йшн ~)
  иммиграционная зона
  maritime ~ (ма́ритайм ~) морская
  зона, морской пояс
  neutralized ~ (ню́тралайзд ~)
  нейтрализованная зона
  security ~ (сэкю́рити ~) зона
  безопасности
  special maritime ~ (спэшл
  ма́ритайм ~) специальная морская
  зона
  sterling ~ (стэ́рлинг ~)
  стерлинговая зона
  tax ~ (такс ~) налоговая зона
  "thieves in the ~" (θивз ин θи
  ~) воры в зоне {members of
  criminal organization in camps}
  ~ of neutrality (~ оф нутра́лити)
  зона нейтралитета

NOTES

NOTES

NOTES

NOTES

NOTES

Related Dictionaries from Hippocrene . . .

UKRAINIAN PHRASEBOOK AND DICTIONARY
Olesj Benyuch and Raisa I. Galushko
This invaluable guide to the Ukrainian language, including a 3,000 word mini-dictionary, provides situational phrases and vocabulary that's the most up-to-date available.
More than simply a dictionary, the book offers advice for ordering meals, making long-distance calls, shopping procedures, and countless tips to greatly enhance your visit to the new republic of Ukraine. Accompanying audio cassettes designed to increase vocabulary and pronunciation are also available.
255 pages   5 1/2 x 8 1/2 $11.95 paper   ISBN 0-7818-0188-5
Accompanying Cassettes: $12.95 set of two   ISBN 0-7818-0191-5

MASTERING RUSSIAN
Erica Haber
This imaginative course, designed for both individual and classroom use, assumes no previous knowledge of the language. The unique combination of practical exercises and step-by-step grammar emphasizes a functional approach to new scripts and their vocabularies. Everyday situations and local customs are explored variously through dialogues, drawings and photos. Cassettes are available to accompany the lessons.
278 pages $14.95 paper   0-7818-0270-9

Mastering Russian Audio Cassettes
Set of two: $12.95   0-7818-0271-9
Mastering Russian Book and Cassettes Set
Set of cassettes & book: $27.90   0-7818-0272-5

ENGLISH-RUSSIAN COMPREHENSIVE DICTIONARY
Oleg Benyukh
With over 50,000 entries compiled by a consortium of linguists, scholars, and lexicography experts in modern-day Russia, this dictionary is the ultimate reference tool for students, scholars, business persons, and anyone requiring in-depth coverage of English-Russian vocabulary and pronunciation.
800 pages   8 1/2 x 11 $60.00 cloth   ISBN 0-7818-0353-5

(ALL PRICES SUBJECT TO CHANGE.)
TO PURCHASE HIPPOCRENE BOOKS CONTACT YOUR LOCAL BOOKSTORE, OR WRITE TO: HIPPOCRENE BOOKS, 171 MADISON AVENUE, NEW YORK, NY 10016. PLEASE ENCLOSE CHECK OR MONEY ORDER, ADDING $5.00 SHIPPING (UPS) FOR THE FIRST BOOK AND $.50 FOR EACH ADDITIONAL BOOK.

NOTES

Related Dictionaries
from Hippocrene . . .

UKRAINIAN PHRASEBOOK AND DICTIONARY
Olesj Benyuch and Raisa I. Galushko
This invaluable guide to the Ukrainian language, including a 3,000 word mini-dictionary, provides situational phrases and vocabulary that's the most up-to-date available.
More than simply a dictionary, the book offers advice for ordering meals, making long-distance calls, shopping procedures, and countless tips to greatly enhance your visit to the new republic of Ukraine. Accompanying audio cassettes designed to increase vocabulary and pronunciation are also available.
255 pages   5 1/2 x 8 1/2 $11.95 paper   ISBN 0-7818-0188-5
Accompanying Cassettes: $12.95 set of two   ISBN 0-7818-0191-5

MASTERING RUSSIAN
Erica Haber
This imaginative course, designed for both individual and classroom use, assumes no previous knowledge of the language. The unique combination of practical exercises and step-by-step grammar emphasizes a functional approach to new scripts and their vocabularies. Everyday situations and local customs are explored variously through dialogues, drawings and photos. Cassettes are available to accompany the lessons.
278 pages $14.95 paper   0-7818-0270-9

Mastering Russian Audio Cassettes
Set of two: $12.95   0-7818-0271-9
Mastering Russian Book and Cassettes Set
Set of cassettes & book: $27.90   0-7818-0272-5

ENGLISH-RUSSIAN COMPREHENSIVE DICTIONARY
Oleg Benyukh
With over 50,000 entries compiled by a consortium of linguists, scholars, and lexicography experts in modern-day Russia, this dictionary is the ultimate reference tool for students, scholars, business persons, and anyone requiring in-depth coverage of English-Russian vocabulary and pronunciation.
800 pages   8 1/2 x 11 $60.00 cloth   ISBN 0-7818-0353-5

(ALL PRICES SUBJECT TO CHANGE.)
TO PURCHASE HIPPOCRENE BOOKS CONTACT YOUR LOCAL BOOKSTORE, OR WRITE TO: HIPPOCRENE BOOKS, 171 MADISON AVENUE, NEW YORK, NY 10016. PLEASE ENCLOSE CHECK OR MONEY ORDER, ADDING $5.00 SHIPPING (UPS) FOR THE FIRST BOOK AND $.50 FOR EACH ADDITIONAL BOOK.

MORE SLAVIC AND BALTIC LANGUAGE DICTIONARIES FROM HIPPOCRENE

Bulgarian-English/English-Bulgarian Practical Dictionary
0331   ISBN 0-87052-145-4 $11.95 pb

Byelorussian-English/English-Byelorussian Concise Dictionary
1050   ISBN 0-87052-114-4 $9.95 pb

Czech-English/English-Czech Concise Dictionary
0276   ISBN 0-87052-981-1 $11.95 pb

Estonian-English/English-Estonian Concise Dictionary
1010   ISBN 0-87052-081-4 $11.95 pb

Latvian-English/English-Latvian Dictionary
0194   ISBN 0-7818-0059-5 $16.95 pb

Lithuanian-English/English-Lithuanian Concise Dictionary
0489   ISBN 0-7818-0151-6 $14.95 pb

Russian-English/English-Russian Standard Dictionary
0440   ISBN 0-7818-0083-8 $16.95 pb

English-Russian Standard Dictionary
1025   ISBN 0-87052-100-4 $11.95 pb

Russian-English Standard Dictionary
0578   ISBN 0-87052-964-1 $11.95 pb

Russian-English/English-Russian Concise Dictionary
0262   ISBN 0-7818-0132-X $11.95 pb

Slovak-English/English-Slovak Concise Dictionary
1052   ISBN 0-87052-115-2 $8.95 pb

Ukrainian-English/English Ukrainian Practical Dictionary
1055   ISBN 0-87052-116-0 $11.95 pb

Ukrainian-English/English-Ukrainian Standard Dictionary
0006   ISBN 0-7818-0189-3 $24.95 pb